$$\frac{249}{8^{13}}$$

well researched ①
well written —
but rather more
detail than most
people will be.
interested in

DARWIN

Also by Adrian Desmond

THE HOT-BLOODED DINOSAURS
THE APE'S REFLEXION
ARCHETYPES AND ANCESTORS
THE POLITICS OF EVOLUTION

Also by James Moore

THE POST-DARWINIAN CONTROVERSIES
RELIGION IN VICTORIAN BRITAIN (editor)
HISTORY, HUMANITY AND EVOLUTION (editor)

DARWIN

ADRIAN DESMOND & JAMES MOORE

WARNER BOOKS

A Time Warner Company

First published in Great Britain by Michael Joseph Ltd.

Warner Books Edition
Copyright © 1991 by Adrian Desmond and James Moore
All rights reserved.

Warner Books, Inc, 1271 Avenue of the Americas, New York, NY 10020

A Time Warner Company

Printed in the United States of America
First Warner Books Printing: July 1992

Library of Congress Cataloging in Publication Data
Desmond, Adrian J., 1947–
    Darwin / Adrian Desmond and James Moore.
       p.   cm.
    "First published in Great Britain 1991 by Penguin Books Ltd"—T.p.
verso.
    Includes bibliographical references (p.   ) and index.
    ISBN 0-446-51589-2
    1. Darwin, Charles, 1809–1882.   2. Naturalists—England—
Biography.   I. Moore, James R. (James Richard), 1947–
II. Title.
QH31.D2D47   1992
575'.0092—dc20
    [B]   91-50412
                                                              CIP

Contents

v

Contents

Illustrations

Illustrations

Illustrations

Acknowledgements

WE ARE ESPECIALLY grateful to friends and colleagues who interrupted busy lives to help us meet our deadlines: to Fred Burkhardt, Nellie Flexner, Elisabeth Leedham-Green, David Kohn, Mike Petty, Jim and Anne Secord, and Steven Shapin for reading draft chapters; to Alison Winter for listening to extracts; to John Thackray, Jim Secord, and David Stanbury for providing information; to Fiona Erskine, Marsha Richmond, and Godfrey Waller for supplying manuscript material (and the late Dov Ospovat for a transcription of Darwin's notes on his 1856 meeting with Huxley, Hooker, and Wollaston); to Richard Milner for sharing his unpublished research on Darwin and Wallace; to Stephen Pocock, Anne Secord, and the Darwin letters project team at Cambridge University Library for supplying advance proofs of volumes of the Darwin correspondence; to Peter Gautrey and Simon Schaffer for assisting with transcriptions and a translation; to Jane Clark, Tony Coulson, Kirsteen Mitcalfe, Solene Morris, and Mike Petty for supplying illustrations; and to the Revd Geoffrey Evans for a tour of Shrewsbury and the High Street Unitarian Church.

Personal debts can never be adequately acknowledged. John and Ellen Greene gave unstinting support in more ways than one; their detailed commentary on the manuscript was a labour of love. Ralph Colp, Jr, was a constant inspiration and resource for his insight into the details of Darwin's private life; we thank him heartily for sharing Darwin's health diary, reading our chapters, and discussing them on a transatlantic phone. Nick Furbank and Dick Aulie also perused our pages and gave expert advice.

Gordon Moore and Robert Tollemache kept half the project going when all else seemed to fail. Similar timely help came from Simon

Acknowledgements

Schaffer and Anita Herle, Alison Winter, Iwan Morus, and Nigel Leask. Gill Knott and Marcus offered escapes to Ilkley and other regions, while Chris and Barrie Vincent at the White Hart kept a snuggery nearer home. Jessica Drader and Harry Flexner Desmond will now see more of their dads. We thank them most of all, for their patience and love.

We would like to thank George Pember Darwin who graciously consented to our publishing extracts of Darwin's letters and manuscripts. We are indebted to the Syndics of Cambridge University Library for allowing us to quote from unpublished material held in the Darwin Archive and in other collections. And we express our gratitude to the Syndics of Cambridge University Press, whose magnificent *Correspondence of Charles Darwin* provides such a rich source of material.

For allowing us to study, and in instances quote from, manuscript material, we also wish to thank the following institutions and individuals: American Philosophical Society Library; Avon County library, Bath Central library for the Leonard Jenyns correspondence; British Museum (Natural History) for the Richard Owen papers; British Library, Department of Manuscripts; Charles Darwin Museum, Down House, by courtesy of the Royal College of Surgeons of England; Christ's College Library, Cambridge, for the Darwin-Fox letters; County of Hereford and Worcester Record Office; Dr Williams's Library, London; Edinburgh University Library; Ernst-Haeckel Haus, Friedrich-Schiller-Universität, Jena; General Register Office, London; Harvard University Library for the University Archives; Imperial College of Science and Technology, London, for the Huxley Papers, Ramsay Papers, and College Archives; R. G. Jenyns, Bottisham Hall, Bottisham, Cambridgeshire, for the Leonard Jenyns papers; Keele University Library for the Wedgwood-Mosley Collection by courtesy of the Wedgwood Museum Trustees, Barlaston, Stoke-on-Trent, Staffordshire; Kent County Archives Office for the Downe parish papers; Public Record Office, Kew and Quality Court, London; Royal Botanic Gardens, Kew; Royal Institution, London, for the Tyndall Papers; University College London Library for the Brougham Papers and Society for the Diffusion of Useful Knowledge correspondence; University of British Columbia Library, Vancouver; Wellcome Institute for the History of Medicine Library, London; and the Zoological Society of London Library.

What a book a Devil's Chaplain might
write on the clumsy, wasteful, blundering
low & horridly cruel works of nature!

Charles Darwin in 1856, about to
start the *Origin of Species*

A Devil's Chaplain?

It is 1839. England is tumbling towards anarchy, with countrywide unrest and riots. The gutter presses are fizzing, fire-bombs flying. The shout on the streets is for revolution. Red evolutionists – visionaries who see life marching inexorably upward, powered from below – denounce the props of an old static society: priestly privilege, wage exploitation, and the workhouses. A million socialists are castigating marriage, capitalism, and the fat, corrupt Established Church. Radical Christians join them, hymn-singing Dissenters who condemn the 'fornicating' Church as a 'harlot,' in bed with the State.

Even science must be purged: for the gutter atheists, material atoms are all that exist, and like the 'social atoms' – people – they are self-organizing. Spirits and souls are a delusion, part of the gentry's cruel deceit to subjugate working people. The science of life – biology – lies ruined, prostituted, turned into a Creationist citadel by the clergy. Britain now stands teetering on the brink of collapse – or so it seems to the gentry, who close ranks to protect their privileges.

At this moment, how could an ambitious thirty-year-old gentleman open a secret notebook and, with a devil-may-care sweep, suggest that headless hermaphrodite molluscs were the ancestors of mankind? A squire's son, moreover, Cambridge-trained and once destined for the cloth. A man whose whole family hated the 'fierce & licentious' radical hooligans.

The gentleman was Charles Darwin: well heeled, imperturbably Whig, a privately financed world traveller who had spent five years aboard HMS *Beagle* as a dining companion to the aristocratic captain. He had a private fortune in prospect and a reputation as an up-and-coming geologist. He also had an enduring wish to escape

xvii

'abominable murky' London, to live in a rustic parish like his clerical friends, so vilified by the mob.

Clergymen from molluscs! How had he arrived at such damning beliefs?

And this was not the worst part. He embraced a terrifying materialism. Only months before he had concluded in his covert notebooks that the human mind, morality, and even belief in God were artefacts of the brain: 'love of the deity [is the] effect of organization, oh you Materialist!' he upbraided himself. Working through the implications gave him migraines, left him writhing on his sick bed, fearing persecution. Wasn't it treachery? Didn't it threaten the last scientific safeguards of the old social order? Weren't these incendiary beliefs perfect weapons for the loutish hordes, already at the gates? He peered into the future. The 'whole fabric totters & falls,' he prophesied of the unreformed Creationist cosmos.

Tormented, he finally fled London's 'dirt, noise vice & misery' to lead a clergyman's life in rural Kent. He sought sanctuary, emulating the man most 'respectable and happy,' the country curate. Idyllic and isolated it might have been, living in an old parsonage, but a third of his working life was spent doubled up, trembling, vomiting, and dowsing himself in icy water. He sat on his theory of evolution for twenty years, scarcely mooting his innermost thoughts about 'monkey-men' and apes evolving morality, castigating himself as a 'Devil's Chaplain.' Even in 1859 he had to be prodded into publishing the *Origin of Species*, and then he let it go with barely a hint about human origins.

The full enigma of Darwin's life has never been grasped. Indeed, previous biographies have been curiously bloodless affairs.[1] They have broken little new ground and made no contact with the inflammatory issues and events of his day.

Our *Darwin* sets out to be different – to pose the awkward questions, to probe interests and motivations, to portray the scientific expert as a product of his time; to depict a man grappling with immensities in a society undergoing reform.

When Darwin did come out of his closet and bare his soul to a friend, he used a telling expression. He said it was 'like confessing a murder.' Nothing captures better the idea of evolution as a social crime in early Victorian Britain. Anglicans damned it as false, foul, French, atheistic, materialistic, and immoral. It was dangerous knowledge, and tempting. Darwin had known this for years, hence his ruminations were confined to secret notebooks. He cut himself off, ducked parties and declined engagements; he even installed a mirror outside his study window to spy on visitors as they came up his drive. Day after day, week after week, his stomach plagued him, and for years after reaching his rural retreat he refused to sleep anywhere else, unless it was a safe house, a close relative's home. This was a worried man.

How then did such a wealthy Whig gentleman break the impasse and make evolution acceptable? How did he present it as underpinning middle-class values? Did he ever resolve the antitheses? – failed ordinand and pillar of the parish, reformer of nature and friend of the unreformed clergy, upright citizen who wrote of 'monkey-men.' Understand Darwin's scientific status, his social obligations, his Dissenting heritage, the political context, and the contradictions start to resolve themselves.

In building this new picture of Darwin, we have exploited a spate of new material. Darwin was a hoarder; he destroyed precious little. Notebooks, old manuscripts, torn-out pages, annotated offprints, and letters were all salted away. Gradually these sources have been tapped by a generation of transcribers.[2] But only in the last few years has the trickle of published material turned into a torrent.

Since 1985 alone a staggering amount has come out, capped by the meticulously edited *Correspondence of Charles Darwin* (which has reached volume seven by 1991). The Victorian *Life and Letters*, censored, shorn, and stitched, is covered in dusty cobwebs. It served a purpose a century ago in securing Darwin's immortality. But today's needs are different. We want to know about his personality, his business acumen, his domestic life, and his science. We want to understand how his theories and strategies were embedded in a reforming Whig society.

A second injection for the so-called 'Darwin Industry' came with the definitive 750-page transcription of *Charles Darwin's Notebooks* in 1987. Painstaking research by an international team, hacking through the intractable jungle of Darwin's illegible and cryptic script, has revealed unimaginable treasures. We now know more about the piecemeal, day-by-day development of Darwin's evolutionary views than about any other scientific theory in history. But then we need to; no other has been so shattering.

We also have a *Calendar* (1985) of the fourteen thousand known letters to and from him. At a stroke the biographer is faced by a fivefold increase in correspondence. The harvest is enormously rich. It gives insights into how he sealed and severed friendships, cajoled and equivocated, courted champions, dispensed patronage, and winkled out scientific tidbits. It opens up a new world, showing us his social circle – his neighbours, house-guests, extended family, and colleagues.[3]

In the last few years, too, historians have revolutionized our understanding of Darwin's dogged, jogging path to the theory of natural selection – the central plank of biology today. The path was riddled with dead-ends and littered with half truths. We see his persistence, like a terrier shaking a rat, teasing at the evolutionary mechanism from every side, trying for any new angle. We can trace the political roots of his key ideas, following his reading on population, the poor laws, and charity.[4] But we cannot stop at mere reading of books. We have to see him as part of an active Whig circle, in an age when the Whig government was building the workhouses and the poor were burning them down. Appreciate Darwin's attitude to the workhouse culture, and his science acquires a deeper political meaning.

So far this wider context has been largely ignored. The textual analysts and historians of disembodied ideas – of intellectual ghosts – have carried the day. Social historians have consistently failed to follow up, to re-locate Darwin in his age.[5] As a result we have lost sight of the larger world that made Darwin's evolution possible.

Any new biography must take account of the recent upheaval in the history of science, and its new emphasis on the cultural conditioning of knowledge. Gone is the day when Darwin could be depicted as a seer, a genius out of time. Ours is a defiantly social portrait. We make contact with the public events and institutions of Victorian England, with reform bills, poor law riots, learned societies, industrial innovation, radical medicine, Church debates – and, not least, with the new views of creation among reforming naturalists, and the old practices of museum keepers. We see Darwin on the streets, sitting in with apes at the zoo, picking up pigeon lore in gin palaces, conniving with his heterodox dining circle, living a squire's life, investing in factories, worrying about religion and confronting death. Viewed in this light, his fears and foibles become intelligible and his evolutionary achievements make sense.[6]

Irony and ambiguity shrouded Darwin as no other eminent Victorian. He hunted with the clergy and ran with the radical hounds; he was a paternalist full of *noblesse oblige*, sensitive, mollycoddled, cut off from wage-labour and competition, who unleashed a bloody struggle for existence; a hard-core scientist addicted to quackery, who strapped 'electric chains' to his stomach and settled for weeks at fashionable hydropathic spas; a man of clockwork routine, his days alike as 'two peas,' who infused natural history with contingency and chance.

What of Darwin's own latter-day prejudices? He thought blacks inferior but was sickened by slavery; he subordinated women but was totally dependent on his redoubtable wife. How did his views on sex, race, and empire reflect the late-Victorian ethos? Was he still remaking the world in the image of his times in the *Descent of Man* (1871)? Did he see society, like nature, progress by culling its unfit members? 'Social Darwinism' is often taken to be something extraneous, an ugly concretion added to the pure Darwinian corpus after the event, tarnishing Darwin's image. But his notebooks make plain that competition, free trade, imperialism, racial extermination, and sexual inequality were written into the equation from the start – 'Darwinism' was always intended to explain human society.

And how did grave Victorians observe the observer? – this man who, Ruskin rudely noted, felt 'a deep and tender interest about the brightly coloured hinder half of certain monkeys.' The butt of jokes, yes. The godsend to cartoonists, of course. Yet his science became a pillar of late-Victorian liberalism. How else to explain the earl and two dukes, representing Gladstone's government, acting as pallbearers in his Westminster Abbey funeral? How, indeed, to explain the body ending up there at all? Or *The Times*'s comment that 'the Abbey needed it more than it needed the Abbey'?

Beetle-browed, scowling physiognomy: everyone knows the image – it is one of the totems of the twentieth century. To some he was the founder of a new biology, to one outraged Welshman just 'an old Ape with a hairy face.' But for everyone his gentleness was overwhelming. Leslie Stephen felt that there was 'something almost pathetic in his simplicity and friendliness.'[7] Darwin is arguably the best known scientist in history. More than any modern thinker – even Freud or Marx – this affable old-world naturalist from the minor Shropshire gentry has transformed the way we see ourselves on the planet.

The time is ripe for a richer portrait of a troubled man at a turning point of history.

1809–1831

1

Catching a Falling Christian

CHARLES DARWIN'S grandfather Erasmus had a lacerating wit and a loathing of meddling gods. Scurrility and whimsy wrapped themselves up in his rotund frame, and no one was spared. He could roast a goose-brained king, or kick the crutch from a friend's faith. 'A featherbed to catch a falling Christian' he called the Unitarian beliefs of Charles's other grandfather, the pottery patriarch Josiah Wedgwood.[1]

Josiah had dropped so much supernatural paraphernalia that he had lost sight of the Christian heights. Fall any further and he would land with an atheistic bump. Josiah's was Christianity stripped naked: the Trinity had been discarded, along with Jesus's divinity.

The featherbed had broken Josiah's fall; but there was no such soft landing for Erasmus. 'Horrid wretches' like him had already crashed resoundingly to earth.[2] What need of Christianity when men can sup 'the milk of science'? Did not the priestess of Nature explain all things? – even Creation itself?

> Nurs'd by warm sun-beams in primeval caves
> Organic Life began beneath the waves . . .
> Hence without parent by spontaneous birth
> Rise the first specks of animated earth.[3]

There spoke Erasmus, a hard-headed freethinker, like so many in the sun-lit years of the Enlightenment. He adored in the Temple of Nature; for him Reason was divine, and Progress its prophet. The two grandfathers agreed on much, but on religion they parted company, bequeathing a mixture of freethought and radical Christianity to their grandchildren.

*

Charles Darwin mused on this twin inheritance in 1879 as he put the finishing touches to a sketch of old Erasmus's life. He had just turned seventy himself and felt as though he were already communing 'with the dead.' It was time to take stock of his life. How much of Erasmus's make-up had he inherited, and how much was he passing on? There was Josiah's blood in him too, and his wife Emma was a Wedgwood. So what future for their offspring if traits run in families?[4] Which grandfather would they take after?

Dr Erasmus Darwin was a giant, a brilliant *bon viveur* whose shadow stretched across the generations. Blasted by smallpox, crippled and corpulent, he was a renowned physician with a fatal attraction for women. He sired a dozen children by a pair of wives and two more by a governess. He prescribed sex for hypochondria and composed lush erotic verse. With his close friend Josiah Wedgwood, he helped to foment England's industrial revolution in the eighteenth century. He rhapsodized about England's great inventors – Matthew Boulton and James Watt – dreamt up mechanical marvels of his own, and maintained a deep commitment to evolution.[5]

Charles caught glimpses of himself here. Erasmus admitted the natural ascent of life and the kinship of all creatures; he 'abhorred slavery,' 'admired philanthropy,' and 'insisted on humanity to the lower animals.' He believed in a distant Deity – a 'Potent-power, all-great, all-good' - and prayed, 'Teach me, Creation, teach me how / T'adore the vast Unknown.' Yet 'he was unorthodox,' and for this he was 'grossly calumniated.' No sooner had he died in 1802 than he was attacked for doubting the Bible. A story was even started that he had called for Jesus on his deathbed. 'Such was the state of Christian feeling in this country at the beginning of the present century,' Charles wryly closed; 'we may at least hope that nothing of the kind now prevails.'

He sent the biography in proof to his daughter Henrietta. She had long hovered at his elbow, an able critic, fussy about the family reputation – the in-house editor to touch up his lack-lustre prose. She was her mother's watchdog, eight years married but still wedded to Emma's welfare. They saw eye-to-eye on most things, and Henrietta had a nose for trouble. She sniffed through the proofs. Unitarianism a 'featherbed' – old Josiah and her mother 'falling Christians'! Was this how Emma was to be portrayed for her Wedgwood faith? And as for advertising Erasmus's debauchery, let alone his religious infidelity! It was permissible a hundred years ago, perhaps, but unbecoming a Darwin now. Alluding to his foibles was sheer folly; it could cost the family dear. The proofs needed pruning, not polishing.

Wielding a bright red pencil, Henrietta pitched in. The sex was cut back. Too much talk of illegitimacy, too much 'wine, women, [and] warmth.' A quotation from Erasmus with 'damned' in it was lopped, and his lines about the 'vast Unknown' sounded awfully agnostic. The paragraph on his unorthodoxy was plucked altogether. It reflected ill on Christianity and was too obviously written by the 'calumniated' author of the *Origin of Species*. The deathbed story had to go. Henrietta slashed scarlet down the page, marking the spots where her father should cut and chop.

She returned the proofs, and her father resigned himself to the changes. The biography now contained more than family history; it held hard evidence of heredity. The assertions and deletions spoke for the two sides of the family. Henrietta was like her mother and old Josiah after all. A hundred years of Unitarian piety had marked the Wedgwood mind.[6] The censor had her way. The world could wait another century to read about the family forces that had shaped Charles's destiny.

These forces were generated in the age of iron and steam. The blasts of Coalbrookdale and the wheeze and snort of Boulton engines echoed across the English Midlands in the mid-eighteenth century. New money was to be made, new families were on the rise. These calliper-carrying industrialists had faith in a progressive nature, a democracy of intellect, and technological salvation. They were marginal men, but on the make; *arrivistes*-merchants, standing outside the old, complacent squirearchy.

Typical was Charles's maternal grandfather, Josiah Wedgwood, who built his pottery business at Burslem, near Stoke-on-Trent. From the 1760s, he was one of the technocrats inside Birmingham's élite industrial circle, the 'Lunar Society' – so called because its members, the 'Lunaticks,' met on moonlit nights, when they could see to stumble home afterwards. Birmingham was the centre of the new industrial culture. The Lunar mechanics introduced new technology, a chemical industry, and a factory mentality. Boulton and Watt were turning out steam engines, and employing a thousand men at their Soho works in Birmingham. Here they sold 'what all the world desires to have – POWER.' Other Lunar craftsmen specialized in clocks and precision instruments. Wedgwood perfected factory organization on the Soho model. In his ceramics sheds he regimented the workforce and created a division of labour, making 'such *machines* of the Men as cannot err.' His factory's name, 'Etruria' (after the Etruscan painting techniques on his ceramics), was coined by his 'favorite Asculapius,' the physician to the group, Charles's paternal grandfather Erasmus Darwin.

Erasmus was a poetic, inventive physician, a mechanic himself who tinkered with 'the animal machine.' His lucrative practice was in the town of Lichfield, fifteen miles north of Birmingham. Lichfield's other literary son, Dr Johnson, defended the locals as 'the most sober, decent people in England, the genteelest in proportion to their wealth.' He could not say the same of Erasmus; their mutual loathing was apparent, and the stammering Darwin dodged Dr Johnson's stiletto wit and 'stentor lungs.' Erasmus's diagnostic skills were extraordinary and in demand far outside Lichfield's sober circle. He designed a carriage that could steer at speed without overturning and travelled 10,000 miles a year to minister to the new Midlands élite. He was a polymathic 'Lunatick,' a doctor suffering from an 'Infection of Steam Enginry,' a poet with an eye to industry. He designed a horizontal windmill for grinding pigments at Wedgwood's works, and even a speaking-machine 'capable of pronouncing the Lord's Prayer, the Creed and Ten Commandments in the Vulgar Tongue,' for which Boulton promised to pay £1000.[7]

Not that these men of 'mechanical Fame' put much store in orthodoxy. Most were self-made Dissenters, outsiders in a world where political and educational opportunities were reserved for members of the Anglican Church. They belonged to a chapel counter-culture, thriving in the growing industrial towns. Erasmus's freethinking apart, their intellectual avant-garde were Unitarians, like Josiah.[8] When Joseph Priestley came to Birmingham in 1780 to serve as minister of the New Meeting House, the Lunar Society acquired a powerful ally in the leading Unitarian philosopher, chemist, and theologian of the day.

Priestley studied airs and gases, and arguably discovered oxygen (and ammonia, carbon monoxide, sulphur dioxide . . . the list goes on). His researches intrigued Erasmus, who soon had people breathing '6 gallons of pure oxygene a day' from balloon-like bladders to cure their lung diseases. Wedgwood thought Priestley a genius. Josiah supplied the minister with lab-ware, subsidized his experiments, and followed up with industrial trials. Priestley's works provided clues about clays and colours, which Josiah used to improve the pottery's output. The Wedgwood firm even honoured their preacher by casting a medallion with his bust in bas-relief.[9]

Priestley's theology was probably even more influential, for it shaped the outlook of three generations of intermarried Darwins and Wedgwoods. He aimed to restore Christianity to its pristine purity

8

and make it a religion of universal happiness in this life and the next. Anglicans found this dangerous, with God ordaining happiness for everyone impartially, without regard for rank or ritual. It was damnable too. For Priestley immortal souls do not exist any more than immaterial 'spirits' in chemistry. Nor were miracles and mysteries like the Trinity and the Incarnation part of his Christianity. God's benevolence is expressed in a wholly material world, where the laws of nature hold sway and everything has a physical cause. Human flesh is resurrected in the next life, as Jesus's was, according to some unknown physical law.

This was a robust, hopeful faith, reflecting the self-confidence of the new industrial élite. As in some self-correcting engine, pleasure and pain operate almost mechanically on people to improve them. Those who abide by Christian principles will live this life happily. In the next, any remaining defective parts will be repaired, and everyone will be restored to a perfect existence. Wedgwood remained Priestley's disciple and appointed a Unitarian minister to teach in his school at Etruria. Erasmus's young son Robert (Charles's father) was educated here, as were the 'Wedgwoodikins' – as Erasmus called them – Jos Jr and Susannah (Charles's mother).

Not all Unitarians went so far as to deny a soul. On the other hand freethinkers like Erasmus went much further, discarding the Bible and Jesus as well – and claiming that 'no particular providence is necessary to roll this Planet round the Sun.'[10] But all shared an optimistic egalitarianism in the long eighteenth-century summer before the French Revolution of 1789.

Erasmus's wife drank gin and died inebriate, leaving him with five children. A decade's philandering followed, and then, at forty-nine, Erasmus found himself fat, lame, and in love – to which end he dedicated his devastating pen:

> Ah, who unmoved that radiant brow descrys,
> Sweet pouting lips, and blue voluptuous eyes?

This was to a beautiful married patient, herself unconventional and the illegitimate daughter of an earl. When her rich husband died in 1780, the widowed Erasmus married her, moved in, and shifted his operations to her country mansion outside Derby. They pooled their eight offspring, who lived amid the trappings of wealth (Erasmus commanded ten guineas a day – four months' wages for a farm hand). Included among the growing brood were his two bastards and her late husband's one. Such open profligacy was a sign that a

9

fashionable libertinism affected the best families. But then polite society seemed to be cemented by its adulteries and ménages, and Dr Johnson advised sensible wives to turn a blind eye to philandering husbands.[11] This wasn't what Priestley meant by the pleasure-and-pain principle, but sin and sex were peeling apart, and Erasmus prescribed the latter to cure the guilt of the former.

In 1783 his son Robert made room for the first of seven more babies when he left for Edinburgh University. Robert was reluctant to take up medicine at first, and Edinburgh had melancholy associations. His eldest brother, Charles, had died delirious and paralysed as a student there five years earlier, having infected his finger dissecting a child's brain. But after the death, Erasmus's medical hopes had transferred to Robert, and the Doctor had to be obeyed.

Erasmus himself was not above pulling strings. Robert switched to the University of Leiden and received his MD in only two years, for a thesis partly written by Erasmus, or based on his work. Erasmus settled his twenty-year-old son into a practice in the quaint old market town of Shrewsbury. It was an ideal spot, the resort of Shropshire's leading families who came for the 'balls, suppers,' and 'oyster-feasts.' It was only a day's journey from Birmingham and Etruria, yet far enough from the family home to ensure his independence. Erasmus's contacts brought Robert a steady stream of patients, while the Lunaticks inducted him into London's élite scientific club, the Royal Society, in the hope that it would give him a philosophical bent. Robert not only had his father's money; he had his shrewdness and sympathy, and an uncanny ability to win patients' confidence. Business was brisk, and the Darwin name acted as a beacon.[12]

The hysterical aftermath to the French Revolution threatened to dim that beacon. Erasmus was a democrat, who cheered the 'success of the French against a confederacy of kings' – indeed, who thought 'a goose may govern a kingdom' as well as any 'idiot . . . in his royal senses.' In Britain a period of unprecedented repression set in: radical Dissenters were attacked for believing in the '*wrongs* of Providence, and *rights* of Man.' The Lunaticks' republicanism was ridiculed, their egalitarian religion denounced. Erasmus had put out feelers for the post of Poet Laureate, but what chance now? The Lord Chamberlain seemed curiously indisposed to offer a royal reward to this supporter of the American and French Revolutions – this poet of love and machines who spreads 'the happy contagion of Liberty.'

Erasmus was versifying about the new French liberties and finishing his medico-evolutionary book *Zoonomia* when Priestley fell into the 'sacrilegious hands of the savages of Birmingham.' His chapel and house were gutted by a mob crying 'No philosophers – Church and King for ever.' The riots of 1791 spelled the end of the Lunar Society. Priestley was offered asylum at Etruria but eventually fled to America. Darwin's erotic botany was denounced as titillating trash; his 'atheism' lambasted as the sort of demoralizing philosophy which had spawned the Terror. This backlash finally put an end to the fashionable libertinism of Erasmus's day. It ushered in a period of respectability and evangelical rectitude, which was to mark the younger generations of Darwin-Wedgwoods.

Wedgwood was now in bad health. He saw his second son Tom – a keen chemical (and opium) experimenter – suffer a nervous breakdown. With England and France at war in 1793, he withdrew from the business and made out his will. He placed the factory in the hands of his eldest son, Jos II, now married to a squire's daughter, Bessy Allen.[13]

Marriage for the Darwins, like everything else, was managed by old Erasmus. For Robert he picked that Etruscan beauty of the Lunar circle, Josiah's daughter Susannah. She had been in and out of the Darwins' Derby house since childhood, and had given Erasmus music lessons. Clever and capable, she was her father's favourite. Josiah and Erasmus reached an understanding that Robert would marry her when his means permitted. In the event they wed in April 1796, a year after Josiah's death. Robert was now established, and Susannah's £25,000 inheritance was an acceptable addition to the family fortune.[14]

Robert bought land on the edge of Shrewsbury, on a steep 100-foot bank along the Severn, and built a plain but imposing red-brick residence, The Mount. With five bays adorning the two-and-a-half storeys, and ample lower wings, it emphasized the young doctor's stature. He was a man of substance, in every way: tall, six feet two inches, with a steadily increasing girth. Their first child was a girl, Marianne; two more daughters followed, Caroline in 1800 and Susan in 1803, the year after Erasmus's peaceful death. Then came their first son. Susannah delivered him on 29 December 1804, five years to the day after Robert's elder brother, a rich solicitor with a bank of debts, had drowned himself in the River Derwent.[15] They named the baby after him and his late grandfather – Erasmus.

The second generation Wedgwoods were – like the Darwins – aspiring gentry. Jos was Sheriff of Dorset, and dashed around 'like Royalty,' in a velvet-curtained carriage drawn by four white horses. In the war economy the pottery business had slumped; Jos moved back to Staffordshire to take charge of the firm and, unhappy as a

11

manufacturer, sought a second home in the country, a weekend bolt-hole away from the business grind. Robert Darwin loaned him £30,000 to buy a thousand-acre estate near the Staffordshire village of Maer, an hour's ride from Etruria and thirty miles from Shrewsbury. The manor had a large Elizabethan house, Maer Hall, set in extensive gardens (designed by Capability Brown) on a hill overlooking a lake, and surrounded by woods full of game. Here Jos and Bessy came to live in 1807 with their six children. On 2 May 1808, when Bessy was forty-four, their last baby, Emma, was born. Jos's social elevation was reflected in his choice of schools. He sent the two oldest boys to Eton.[16]

Susannah Darwin was long-suffering as the Doctor's wife, amanuensis, and receptionist. He might have been sympathetic to patients, but he had a brusqueness at home that sat incongruously with his 'high squeaky voice.' Even trifles riled him, and sometimes Susannah caught the brunt of his temper. Since her difficult second pregnancy, her 'old life and spirits' had waned, and she aged quickly. 'Everybody seems young but me,' she once sighed to Jos at The Mount.[17]

Another baby was delivered on 12 February 1809, in her forty-fourth year. They called him Charles Robert Darwin, after the medical men in the family – his father Robert and dead uncle Charles – in the hope of a bright career. Respectable gentry themselves now, ensconced in the imposing Mount, they had the baby baptized at the new St Chad's Anglican Church on 17 November. It was becoming for the Doctor, and prudent. The country was still at war with France and a conspiratorial underground suspected; now was no time to wave the family's liberal flag. Old Erasmus had been pilloried by government-inspired propaganda for his pro-French poetry. The name of Darwin was already associated with subversive atheism.[18] Dr Robert was himself a closet freethinker, so it paid to tread carefully in these conservative years.

But Susannah stood quietly by her heritage. She took the children on Sundays to the Unitarian chapel. Set back from the High Street, it stood on the site of Shrewsbury's first meeting house for Dissenters, which had been razed by an Anglican mob a century before. George Case had been invited to preach here by Susannah and the town's Unitarian leaders, and to augment his pay he ran a day school at his house in Claremont Hill.[19]

Charles's education began at home, with his sister Caroline, in her early teens, taking charge. He competed for her affection with

Catherine, fifteen months younger, and Susannah's last child. Charles was boisterous and mischievous, and one of his earliest memories was of trying to break the windows in a room where he had been locked as a punishment. He was an attention-seeker; he wanted praise, and was often made to feel guilty for it. For her part Caroline was inexperienced and at times heavy-handed, and Charles came to dread facing her, wondering 'What will she blame me for now?'

To be let alone was liberating under Caroline's zealous regime. With the others so much older, Charles learned to amuse himself around The Mount. The Doctor had a splendid library, and a flair for fashionable natural history. The greenhouse, just off the morning-room, was an exotic indoor jungle. His mother kept fancy pigeons, famed for their 'beauty, variety, and tameness,' and the gardens contained fruit trees and rare shrubs. Beyond the north terrace, down a steep wooded incline, was the river. Here Charles sat fishing for hours. He used worms for bait, killing them first in salt water – as his sisters instructed – to spare them the ordeal of being spitted.

He was an inveterate collector and hoarder – shells, postal franks, birds' eggs, and minerals. They were trophies, piled up for praise. He craved it so much – he even started imagining that people admired him, only to feel guilty about it. But then he was guilty anyway. He was stealing to gain attention: at night he made off with the Doctor's peaches and plums, then hid the fruit so that he could 'discover' and report the cache the next day. Or sometimes his booty became a bribe. He offered apples to older boys if they would first marvel at how quickly he could run. Innocent mischief, but it helped him to stand out in a house full of older sisters. 'Inventing deliberate falsehoods' became a regular method of seeking the spotlight.[20]

Susannah sent him to Mr Case's school shortly after his eighth birthday in 1817. Each morning he walked over from The Mount, across the Welsh Bridge and up through narrow winding streets to the three-storey manse overlooking St Chad's churchyard. Many of the boys were older. Charles, reserved and rather chunky, shrank from their ritual wrestling matches and hurried home in the afternoon, dodging the dogs in Barker Street. He would still do anything at school 'for the pure pleasure of exciting attention & surprise,' and his cultivated 'lies . . . gave [him] pleasure, like a tragedy.' He told tall tales about natural history, reported strange birds, and boasted of being able to change the colour of flowers. Once he invented an elaborate story designed to show how fond he was of telling the truth. It was a boy's way of manipulating the world.[21]

13

The shock of Susannah's death in July was traumatic for the family. Its impact on Charles, difficult to assess, was certainly profound. She suffered appallingly with a tumour, and in the last days only Marianne and Caroline – who helped with the nursing – were allowed to see her. On the 15th, when the end came, Charles and the others were sent for. The Doctor showed them the body on the bed, dressed in a black velvet gown. Caroline comforted Charles, and they cried together. But after the funeral on the 20th the children's feelings were bottled up. The older ones could not even mention their mother's name.

When Charles returned to Case's school, his grief manifested itself in peculiar ways. One month after his mother's burial, he watched, transfixed, out of the classroom window, as a horse was led to an open grave in the churchyard. The saddle was empty, with a man's boots and carbine hanging at the side. So soon after his mother's interment, the effect overwhelmed him. The military cortège assembled and the clergyman read the service as the coffin was lowered. Then a cavalryman from the 15th Hussars stepped out, in full regimental attire, and raised his rifle. As the shots echoed across the Severn valley, pent-up emotion surged through the eight-year-old's body. Though in later life he could barely remember his mother, or her death – indeed he would have 'no particularly happy or unhappy recollections of this time' – he never forgot this scene. He remembered the dead soldier.[22]

The Mount became a teenage matriarchy, with Marianne heading up the household, Caroline acting as Catherine's minder, and Susan becoming her father's aide. The triumvirate was not to be trifled with. The sisters were a moral force, the inheritors of Susannah's piety. Charles and brother Erasmus submitted to their discipline, knowing that they could still escape to school.

When the Doctor arrived from his rounds, there was no escape for anyone. His portly presence, like some immense gravitational field, made life whirl about him. It was a vertiginous experience, and nobody felt at ease. With patients he was renowned for gentleness, and his advice always reassured. At home these qualities became less apparent after Susannah's death. His tenderness could still inspire love, but his tactlessness made the children fearful; he grew fastidious and opinionated, overwhelming them with his prodigious memory and his power to read minds, which 'seemed almost supernatural.' He interrogated and pontificated by turns; to be summoned was like being hauled before the Most High – except for the tiny falsetto

14

voice. It was a subtle reminder that this overfed hulk was a mere mortal.[23]

Visitors noted the tension. After Maer's 'careless freedom and absence of restraint,' the young Wedgwoods found The Mount claustrophobic. Everyone had to conform to the Doctor's 'orderly and correct' standards. He was harder on the boys, whose untidiness repulsed him, but the girls suffered too. Elizabeth and Charlotte, in their twenties, were best friends with the Darwin sisters. Bessy Wedgwood had lived in 'nervous dread' of her own table-thumping father, and had brought up her daughters to view men as 'dangerous creatures who must be humoured.' Certainly the precept applied to The Mount. The girls laughed while the Doctor was away, always aware of the sea-change that was in store. 'Sunday we dined at half-past one, drest afterwards, and sat about 3 hours expecting the tide to come in about dark,' Elizabeth reported gloomily on one visit; 'and rather stiff and awful the evening was.'[24]

Overawed, the Darwin boys formed a close alliance. In September 1818, Charles joined thirteen-year-old Eras as a boarder at Shrewsbury School: a minor public school, across the river, opposite the castle ruins. The buildings were centuries old, dating back to Edward VI, with facilities to match – dark, damp dormitories and frigid baths. The brothers endured the hardships, knowing that home comforts were only a sprint away. Although, faced with the Doctor and mothering sisters, they may even have preferred the regime of the Revd Samuel Butler.

Butler had been headmaster for twenty years. Locally, his status rivalled Dr Darwin's; nationally his school was becoming known as a seat of excellence. The reputation had been hard won, for pampered squires' sons were not easy to restrain; one, caught drunk, pulled a knife on him; another carried a loaded pistol; and a whole gang terrorized local farmers, killing their pigs. The Revd Butler cracked the whip, or when appropriate, allowed the boys to settle their differences honourably in fist-fights.[25] He enforced hard-working habits, convinced that disciplined young men were Anglican society's first need.

The classics provided the core curriculum. The ability to read, write, and dissect dead languages was the mark of a gentleman. The more he knew about ancient cultures, the better able he was to command his own. Such was the theory. The practice Charles loathed. Latin and Greek numbed him. Education at Shrewsbury consisted of rote learning and recitation, with verse-making as a creative outlet. On the whole his lessons were 'carefully prepared & correctly said,' but only as a result of hand-me-down schoolboy tricks. He and his friends compiled a 'grand collection of old verses' that could be patched together to meet any contingency of poem writing. True, he enjoyed some of the odes of Horace, when he could recall them, but, like his other lines, most left him within a week. Byron's poetry was more memorable, and Shakespeare's historical plays. Propped up in a window seat, set in the school's thick walls, he pored over them by the hour.[26]

Classmates remembered Charles being 'old for his age,' both 'in manner and in mind.' The Mount had left its solemn mark on him; he was keen to please yet anxious to avoid pain, and reticence masked his frustration. Craving acceptance, he swallowed his anger (as he was always to do) and took after his frail and studious elder brother. Neither liked sports. While Eras burrowed into books and pottered with plants, Charles amassed his collections and went on 'long solitary walks.' Stirred by the Revd C. C. Clarke's *Wonders of the World*, he fantasized about more distant trips, day-dreaming of tropical islands and South American landscapes. It was all a refuge from the stultifying grown-ups.[27]

The ten-year-old was a handful for his mothering sisters. When, in July 1819, they took him to the Welsh coast for three weeks, he was quarrelsome and morose; he 'swore like a trooper' and took off alone, walking the beach, watching the sea-birds, entering another world. There was the excitement of new insects – large mottled sap-suckers and splendid moths. Another collection was started, but then a sister dictated that 'it was not right to kill insects' for this purpose – dead ones would have to do. A year later, freed from his female chaperones, he rode a short distance into Wales with Erasmus. By twelve, he and Eras were galloping all the way to Bangor with their Wedgwood cousins Frank and Hensleigh. Over the Welsh mountains they rode; past rugged peaks with their sombre scenes of primal desolation.

No longer so withdrawn, he was beginning to share his interests. At school he became keen to 'gratify his fellows.' He brought plants for the boys' garden and struggled to explain how his mother used to name them from their blossoms. He looked up to the older boys, Eras's friends, and one, the tall John Price, looked down on him 'in every sense.' Darwin brought 'Old Price' a shell one day to see if he could identify it. A 'dog periwinkle' of course, Price snapped, which left Charles wide-eyed with wonder.[28] Learning names was essential when every genteel drawing-room had its cabinet of curios, and Charles's training began in the playground.

*

The five years between the brothers shrank once Charles reached his teens. Erasmus led the way as always, pulling Charles fast up behind him. Bored with the classical curriculum, Eras took an explosive interest in chemistry, and in 1822 he co-opted Charles as his assistant. A 'Lab' was fitted out in the garden shed, after the Doctor banished them and their noxious gases from the house.

It was an expensive hobby, fit for gentlemen dilettantes in an industrial age. Probably the boys picked it up from the practical Wedgwoods, who understood kiln chemistry and kept recipe books of experiments. Eras and Charles set up a fund for apparatus and fuelled it from the family purse (the 'cow' to be 'milked,' as they called it). Fifty pounds or so – over a year's wage for a servant – went a long way.[29] They bought test tubes from a glass-blower, fetched stop-cocks from London, and equipped benches full of crucibles, retorts, evaporating dishes, and burners. But there was scarcely time to enjoy being together. Eras was seventeen and leaving school, intending to follow the family tradition in medicine. As the experiments began, the Doctor considered the educational choices.

Eras could go to Scotland to receive a liberal, science-based training, perhaps to Edinburgh University, as he himself had. Or he could purchase an expensive apprenticeship for the boy at one of the best London hospitals; £500 would buy him a top spot in the profession.

Or Eras could proceed to Oxford or Cambridge, the only two English universities. If, that is, he did not mind subscribing to the Thirty-nine Articles of the Anglican faith; and the Darwins did not – two generations of wealth had left them cloaked in Anglican respectability. These were Church universities, and members had to toe the doctrinal line. Here Eras would receive an upstanding rather than an outstanding education, starting – as in Shrewsbury School – with a grounding in classics. It was designed to keep the physician on a social par with his gentrified patients. Here the future gentry, doctors, and clergy were to be united – they would close ranks against the vulgar classes and protect the 'precious birthright of an *English gentleman*.' Oxford and Cambridge moulded 'the morals, manners, yea, the whole formation' of a gentleman physician, allying rank and wealth with professional honour.[30]

Cambridge it was, and Eras went up to Christ's College in October 1822. Thereafter father received notes from his 'spendpenny son,' with essential termly bills attached – debts to be cleared, thirteen guineas owed to the wine merchant, '& I shall be much obliged to the D[r] if he will pay it.' Charles's letters were chock-full of chemical tidbits. Sights and smells were quintessential, and Eras described the mineralogy professor, John Stevens Henslow, incinerating arsenic with a blowpipe to release a gastronomic garlic odour. He reported back on students who 'got perfectly tipsy with . . . laughing gas' (something first tried by the Wedgwoods' friend Coleridge twenty years earlier). 'One man said he felt just as if he could fly, & when he was drinking the gas, he began to jump, & twiddle his fingers, & make a kind half laughing & screaming noise.'

'The lab will look very insignificant after all the grand things I see here,' Eras confessed. The boys had money to burn, or rather corrode, and obtained their silver by dissolving up sixpences. It was pure indulgence and burnt a hole in both pockets. Charles planned to visit Eras at Christ's during the summer holidays of 1823, to marvel at the strutting 'Noblemen & such.' Eras, dissipated and broke from his amusements, told him to 'bring up a good supply of money, for by that time I shall not have so much as a brass farthing to buy some broth with when you come starving off yᵉ coach.' During term-time, Charles scurried home at weekends, eager to exchange the classics for Parkes's *Chemical Catechism* or Brande's *Manual of Chemistry*. Inevitably, word spread at school about his smelly shed, and 'Gas' became his nickname. Revd Butler got wind of it too. He embarrassed Charles in front of the boys by calling him a 'poco curante' (a trifler), which sounded dreadful. Classics, not chemistry, moulded the character.[31]

It was a fad, but 'Gas' Darwin enjoyed the hours out in the shed alone, and he always had fond memories of his chemical self-education. By fifteen, he took up a more characteristic pursuit for a son of the Shropshire gentry. He was old enough to carry a gun and hunting became his passion. Blasting at birds was a 'most holy cause,' and since quail were more edible than insects his sisters did not cavil. He felt powerful, armed and tramping through the field. Making gas was nothing to massacring his first snipe, although the thrill was just as physical. It left him trembling so violently that he could barely reload.

Permission was needed to hunt, but the Doctor was hand in glove with the local squires, and Charles had no lack of bushes to beat. The best hunting was at Maer, where the easy-going Wedgwoods turned the shoots into parties, a respite from the autocratic atmosphere of The Mount. Uncle Jos joined in, and there were always cousins Jos III, Harry, Frank, and Hensleigh. They were all in their twenties, and Hensleigh was Eras's age and had been at Cambridge with him. He was the scholar of the family and reminded Uncle Jos of his precocious brother Tom, who had died at thirty-four, a burnt-out opium addict. Charles also took after Tom, who had been similarly obsessed with chemistry; Uncle Jos doted on him and Hensleigh alike. And lanky Charles, unprepossessing but full of promise, was bracing company for his girls.[32]

The four Wedgwood daughters were easy-going. They wore spectacles and came in pairs. Of the older ones, Charlotte was considered eligible, but Elizabeth was dwarfish, with severe spinal curvature. The others, Fanny and Emma, had been inseparable since childhood and were known as the 'Doveleys,' the family pets. Fanny was short, plain, and tidy, Emma quite the opposite. She had thick brown hair, grey eyes, a high forehead, and was as charming as she was chaotic, as messy as a boy. 'Little Miss Slip-Slop,' they called her. The pair had already studied abroad and spent a year at a London school, while at home the older sisters were in charge of their lessons. Emma helped Elizabeth with the village Sunday school and even wrote simple moral tales to aid the instruction. The school was held in the Maer Hall laundry; here the girls gave sixty children their only formal training in the three Rs – reading, writing, and religion.

Religion was a serious matter for the Wedgwoods, but since the 1790s the family had become more conformist. Like so many second- and third-generation Unitarians, cosseted in wealth, secure in business, they were adopting Anglican respectability. Jos was the parish patron, lining up his nephew to take charge as vicar. It made sense for Emma to stay on the safe side and be confirmed as an Anglican. Certainly her mother was for the respectability, or at least for covering her options. It was 'better to conform to the ceremonies' of the Church, she said, 'for one can never be quite sure that in omitting them we are not liable to sin.'

So Emma was duly confirmed at St Peter's Church, Maer. The ceremony took place on 17 September 1824. The partridge season had opened, and a fortnight later Charles drove over with Susan and Catherine to celebrate the rite. Besides the shooting, there was an impromptu family performance of *The Merry Wives of Windsor*, an apt choice for Charles with his Shakespearean tastes, and for the girls. They had 'wicked times,' it was reported: '1st Oct. Revels; 2nd, Revels; 4th, Revels . . . 6th Oct., quiet evening!'[33] One wonders who played Falstaff . . .

No such revels occurred at Shrewsbury. The Doctor was becoming more censorious, and Charles a trial. He was not shining at Dr Butler's school, the whole family knew it. He seemed too ordinary for a Darwin, perhaps even deficient. The spectres of his self-destructive uncles, Tom and Erasmus, hovered about The Mount. And with Eras away, he had become too fond of the gun. Determined to shake Charles to his senses, the Doctor reacted like one of the boys' experiments. Towards the end of the school year he exploded: 'You care for nothing but shooting, dogs, and rat-catching, and you will be a disgrace to yourself and all your family'![34]

The Doctor had a strong purgative, something to cleanse him of this partridge affliction. He took Charles out of school in June 1825, two years early. Give him a career, a direction – the rigours of medicine would do the trick. Charles was to follow in his brother's and father's footsteps to professional respectability.

2

The Northern Athens

WITH A MEDICAL CAREER in mind the sixteen-year-old, qualified only by a squire's confidence and the family's good name, spent the summer of 1825 practising on the sick poor of Shropshire. Sometimes he accompanied the Doctor, administering the medicines. He relished his father's approval and enjoyed the apprenticeship. Within weeks he had a dozen patients of his own – 'chiefly women and children in Shrewsbury.' He recorded symptoms and his father made up the prescriptions. All in all, the Doctor saw distinct prospects in his bedside manner.[1]

The reports from Erasmus at Christ's were less encouraging. Charles heard how his brother was given the filthy jobs, preparing the corpses for dissection and cleaning up the limbs afterwards. Eras was inured to the blood and stench of the anatomy theatre, but he felt Charles becoming queasy even as he talked of his menial work on the cadavers: 'I dont fancy it w^{ld}. have suited your stomack especially before breakfast.'

Erasmus thought it 'ten thousand pities if you do not come to Cambridge.' But to no avail. The Doctor had decided on Edinburgh University for Charles, the 'Northern Athens.' It was more the family tradition. He would be a third-generation Darwin to study medicine here, following his father and grandfather. Family ties with the Edinburgh academics went back a long way. The professor of natural philosophy, John Leslie, 'an enormous mass of flesh and an extremely agreeable man,' had even once tutored the Wedgwood sons at Maer.[2] As a result Charles would leave home with letters that would place him at the best intellectual dinner tables.

Then there were the medical considerations. Edinburgh was better equipped, better staffed, and offered better hospital facilities than the cloistered English universities. It turned out not only better-educated MDs than Oxford and Cambridge, but vastly more of them.[3] Edinburgh had long been a haven for wealthy Dissenters, barred from Oxford and Cambridge by the Thirty-nine Articles. Here they studied a wide array of medical and scientific subjects, including botany, chemistry, and natural history. The students were also exposed to the latest Continental thought, particularly in the thriving extramural schools clustered around the university. Many graduates went to Paris after their final year and returned full of the latest French notions. They kept Edinburgh students briefed on the best, the most heterodox, and the most innovative new sciences, as Charles was to find out.

Fortunately, Erasmus could do his external hospital study at Edinburgh, so plans were laid for him to accompany Charles, to cast a protective coat over his brother's shoulders. Eras came home from Cambridge in July and the two began planning. They would anatomize, collect fossils, and continue their chemical entertainments. Erasmus could not wait. 'It will be very pleasant our being together, we shall be as cozy as possible, & I almost think that when you have arrived at the dignity of a "Varsity" man, that I shall leave of[f] licking you.'

Charles and Eras arrived at Edinburgh late in October. They checked in to the Star Hotel in Princes Street, overlooking the ravine that bisects the city, and began hunting for digs. There was no lack of choice with all the lodging houses packed claustrophobically around the university. But most rooms were dark, dank 'little holes.' They found the exception. At 11 Lothian Street the landlady, Mrs Mackay, specialized in students. She was 'a nice clean old body, and exceedingly civil & attentive.' (A generation of doctors and naturalists had their first taste of Edinburgh hospitality from Mrs Mackay.) It was convenient, the university stood at the end of the street, a few minutes' walk away. She gave the lads two light and airy bedrooms and a sitting-room four flights up for twenty-six shillings a week. They settled in and began to explore.

They walked all over town, lost in admiration. The ravine was astonishing, the city seemed perched on a precipice: 'indeed Bridge Street is the most extraordinary thing I ever saw,' Charles wrote home, 'and when we first looked over the side we could hardly believe our eyes, when, instead of a fine river we saw a stream of people.' They took in everything: the Old Town with its gothic

22

skyline, the business centre, and the bustling university area, teeming with students. 'Auld Reekie' lived up to its name here, with overcrowded tenements and crime. Then there was the classical New Town, now favoured by the merchants and professionals. The boys paced the broad cobbled streets, up and down winding flights of steps, admiring the imposing stone buildings. At the Parliament House they could see the clubbing Tory barristers 'showing their feathers at their more-employed and laborious Whigs, as a race soon to be exterminated.'⁴ The sons of Dr Darwin, Whigs to a tee, appreciated this fine piece of political miscalculation.

Scotch fare had to be tried: fried oysters, stewed herrings, cods' heads stuffed with oatmeal. And shopping in the new market, with its narrow stalls crammed with fresh vegetables. Then it was off to see Weber's *Der Freischütz* or some other terpsichorean delight at the Theatre-Royal by night.

On Sundays they sampled the churches. Edinburgh was the religious capital of Scotland and soot-stained steeples littered the hilly landscape. The mighty edifices were the backbone of the Establishment, their stern preachers appointed by noble patrons and the Crown. This was the Church of Scotland: wealthy, dogmatic, and self-assured. The Kirk's legislative body, the General Assembly, met in Edinburgh amid much pomp. Everyone turned out – Charles and Eras included – to see the black-robed delegates convening to debate the moral health of the nation. The boys' first service, though, came as a bit of a surprise; instead of a two-hour 'soul-cutting discourse,' they were agreeably released after a moderate twenty-minute sermon.

The city was cosmopolitan. One would pass a German physician here, a French nobleman there. The American John James Audubon, dressed like a backwoodsman, was in town in 1826 to sign up subscribers for his *Birds of America*. Rosy-faced women trundled along, leather straps of their baskets over foreheads; their bearded menfolk rude and unkempt. It was a city of wonderful sights and fearful sciences: of socialists experimenting with cooperative living, and phrenological shopkeepers eyeing their customers' heads; of professors debating the earth's origin, and anatomists debunking the creation of life. Visitors could only marvel at the metropolis, basking in the 'brazenfrontedness of her own self-idolatry.'⁵

There were plenty of social contacts for the grandsons of Erasmus Darwin to make. They looked up friends of their father's and dined with professors. Charles kept Susan apprised of the 'Gaieties:'

> We also have been very dissipated. – We dined at D^r. Hawley's
> on Saturday, & had a very pleasant party, after which we
> went to the Theatre . . . D^r. Hawley has procured some
> information about my Fathers questions, & I will write it
> shortly to him. Next Friday we are going to the old D^r.
> Duncan [an octogenarian, but still joint-professor of the
> Theory of Physic], & I hope it will be a pleasanter party than
> the last; which [was] a very specimen of stupidity . . . I have
> been most shockingly idle, actually reading two novels at once.
> [A] good scolding would do me a vast deal of good, & I hope
> you will send one of your most severe one's.

This party-going was diplomatic; the Duncans had long known the Darwins. Charles's uncle and namesake – who died after the dissecting accident – lay interred in Duncan's family vault. The old doctor inevitably had a paternal attitude towards the latest Charles in his class.[6]

Elegant Whig doors were opened to the boys. Perhaps no longer boys: a mocking indignance that the Doctor should *still* be calling Charles one showed his changing persona. Relatives gave him a letter of introduction to the Whig leading-light Leonard Horner, geologist, educationalist, and soon to be Warden of the new London University. Horner took Charles off to the Royal Society of Edinburgh, where they saw Sir Walter Scott, Audubon's 'celestial being,' though a sad one after his shocking bankruptcy. Still, greatness told, and Charles viewed 'the whole scene with some awe and reverence.'[7]

All his life Charles had been cosseted in a world of wealthy Whiggism. Now it was his *entrée* into liberal Edinburgh. He never had to find his political feet. The whole family was committed to the Whigs' manifesto of extended suffrage, open competition, religious emancipation (allowing Dissenters, Jews, and Catholics to hold office), and the abolition of slavery. The Church-and-King Tories governed in 1825, as they had for the best part of fifty years, and Whigs like the Darwin-Wedgwoods detested their opponents' corrupt hold on power. But the family's dyed-in-the-wool Whiggism did not preclude a certain devilment on Charles's part. He delighted in telling Susan that he was taking the scandalous Tory rag *John Bull*. It was pure political titillation: he revelled in its outrageous xenophobic extremism, its scandal-and-scare format. Eras went one better. Not for him *John Bull*; he switched to *The Age* because it was 'ten times the more scurrilous of the two.' 'Do you approve?' he asked Charles impishly.

The girls did not. Charles's good-natured rebellion against his mothering sisters was one thing; posting them his copies of *John Bull* was another. Tory gutter journalism got pretty near the knuckle, no more so than on the subject of slavery, which for the Darwin-Wedgwoods was sacrosanct. Reading this lurid rag, Catherine was appalled that it should make slaves out to be happy and content. Susan wondered why he was not reading a reforming daily: 'I shall be better pleased when I hear you are studying "The Morning Chronicle",' she scolded him.[8]

Then there was student life. This was the usual brew of heavy work and high spirits, and as always the older generation worried. To the devout Scottish mind the students were notorious. Drunkenness and brawling were common. And the teachers who spread scare stories did not help, warning apocalyptically that long hours stretched over corpses were driving these young souls into bars and brothels. Even the theatre was suspect; some thought it sure to arouse the passions already awakened by anatomy. For many, medical schools were no better than charnel houses dealing in stolen flesh, corrupting young minds. Wasn't it true that those who dissected flesh and bone lost their faith in a residual soul? Some teachers hardly set the best example. In London it was nothing to find one dictating notes in his local gin palace or indoctrinating students with political propaganda. London was bad enough; there, students were to riot in the new university. But Erasmus believed that the Scottish students were worse.[9]

Of course things were never as bad as the press made out. Newspapers thrived on public outrage; there was money in drunken students playing high jinks. Prurient readers wanted to be shocked. True, the Darwins' chemical experiments turned into a jape as they got tipsy on laughing gas, and they indulged in the craze for Syrian snuff. But their gambling was hardly new; hot toddies merely kept out the cold, and theatre-going was innocent enough to be the mainstay of letters home.

Actually the boys were diligent at the start. Erasmus had wanted to get to Edinburgh early so 'we can both read like horses.' After they had settled in, this is what they did. They were voracious bookworms, taking more volumes out of the library that first term than anybody else in the university. Other texts Charles bought. Money was no problem, with the Doctor there to pick up the tab, and Charles could always send home for a ten-pound note to tide him over.[10] Anyway, if things became desperate he could sell his insects to buy a botany book, as Erasmus was to do.

The medical school enrolled nine hundred pupils in Charles's year, more than a quarter of them from England. It still offered the best medical education in Britain, although no one was blind to its decline since the halcyon days of the Enlightenment. And most recognized the cause: the Tory Town Council (rather than the university) appointed two thirds of the professors, often from its list of party loyalists, and always with the Kirk's approval. This political influence led to bickering and hardly the best set of teachers.

Some professors even inherited their chairs, treating them as family property. Charles was appalled by the crusty professor of anatomy, Alexander Monro III. He held his father's and grandfather's seat, and it showed. 'Unimpassioned indifference' was how one student described his manner, and his classes later degenerated into riots. Like so many anatomy lecturers fresh from the dissecting theatre, he was bloody and begrimed. 'I dislike him & his Lectures so much that I cannot speak with decency about them,' said Charles, moved to anger. 'He is so dirty in person & actions.'[11]

Monro's soporific talks forced many students over the road to hear Robert Knox's scintillating Continental lectures. The foppish Knox taught in one of the competing private schools in Surgeons' Square. His lectures were not all they came to hear. The flamboyant, one-eyed, gold-vested Knox savaged the city's clergy and elders, to the undoubted delight of his listeners. His slashing satires on religion made him the scourge of the Kirk. But the student response was rapturous. His stiletto wit only served to make Monro appear more of a drudge, and Knox's class numbers shot up. Between 1826 and 1828 – when he was caught unwittingly accepting Burke and Hare's murder victims for dissection – he taught more students than all the other private lecturers put together.[12]

Erasmus enrolled with Knox's chief rival, John Lizars, on the other side of Surgeons' Square. He was 'charming' and certainly more respectable. Charles enrolled with no private teacher. He found surgery stomach-churning, and one can see why. In 1826 Audubon met Knox, 'dressed in an overgown and with bloody fingers,' and was escorted around his dissecting theatre. It was a moment of indescribable horror. The severed limbs and dissected torsos left him gasping. 'The sights were extremely disagreeable, many of them shocking beyond all I ever thought could be. I was glad to leave this charnel house and breathe again the salubrious atmosphere of the streets.' Charles felt the same.[13] Monro had put him off human anatomy for life. As a consequence he was never taught dissection techniques properly, something he was later to regret.

It was not only Monro whom he disliked. Charles complained to Caroline in January 1826 about 'a long stupid lecture from Duncan' on medicines. Dr Andrew Duncan *secundus* was a fellow professor with his father and, in Charles's view, 'so very learned that his wisdom has left no room for his sense.' The lecture could not 'be translated into any word expressive enough of its stupidity.' Unmerited criticism perhaps, for Duncan, well travelled, *au fait* with the best French thought, was reckoned 'a man of most versatile genius.' (He was also the man who isolated the quinine-relative cinchonin from Peruvian bark.) The problem was young Charles. He was simply not ready for the drudgery of medical learning. He persevered on frosty mornings, listening to Duncan's descriptions of medicinal plants; indeed – having paid his half-a-crown experiment money – 'tasting and smelling them' from a smorgasbord spread out at the front of the class. But in the end he just could not reconcile himself to clambering out of bed to spend 'a whole, cold, breakfastless hour on the properties of rhubarb!'[14]

Charles's disenchantment was accelerated by his clinical studies. He walked the wards of the Royal Infirmary, next to the College, but what he saw distressed him. He shared his father's horror of bleeding, but, unlike the Doctor, he never persevered to overcome his squeamishness. His two visits to operating theatres turned his stomach, reinforcing his morbid fear of human blood. Here the cutting was gory and swift; in the days of heroic surgery, before anaesthetic, speed was of the essence to reduce the trauma in the strapped, screaming patient. Dirty hands clasped dirty saws, hacking and cutting quickly, the blood running into buckets of sawdust. The students jostled all around in the tense, steamy atmosphere, straining for a view. During a particularly bad operation on a child, Charles finally fled the room, unable to watch, and determined never again to enter an operating theatre.[15] The vision remained to haunt him for life.

About the only lectures to escape his epithet 'dull' were Professor Thomas Hope's on chemistry. But then Tommy Hope's 'chemical drama' was unabashed entertainment. It was all done 'with great *eclat*,' and as a result it attracted the largest class in the university. (Charles was one of 503 students that year.) Living solely off his fees, Hope had dropped all research and perfected his chemical amusements, using large-scale apparatus visible to everybody. He even started a popular course, which ladies could attend, even if they had to slip in through a back door. This became the talk of the town. 'The Doctor is in absolute extacy [sic] with his audience of veils and feathers,' quipped a commentator. 'I wish some of his experiments would blow him up. Each female student would get a bit of him.' Charles thought differently. He dined with Hope and wrote home, 'I like both him & his lectures *very* much.'¹⁶ As with all the boys, it seems, 'Gas' Darwin, himself a chemical dilettante, relished the distraction from the grim realities of the sickbed. It was about the only saving grace of his first year at Edinburgh.

There were, of course, diversions. He walked along the coastline with Eras, picking up cuttlefish, sea-mice, and sea-slugs. And for a game-shooting squire's son, needing to display trophies, he found other digressions.

'I am going to learn to stuff birds, from a blackamoor,' he informed his sisters. The 'blackamoor' in question was a freed black slave, John Edmonstone, whom the eccentric Catholic 'Squire' and traveller Charles Waterton had brought back from Guiana in South America. John (the 'Edmonstone' was adopted from his master) had been taught taxidermy by the Squire, one of the best stuffers in the country. John had taken lodgings at 37 Lothian Street and set up shop in the Edinburgh Museum, passing on his skill to the students. The lessons were cheap; 'he only charges one guinea, for an hour every day for two months,' Charles reported. His tutor was 'very pleasant and intelligent,' and he frequently sat with him.¹⁷ John, who had travelled with the eccentric Waterton, found a willing listener for his daily stories of the Tropics. Charles learned the tricks of the stuffing trade. More, he heard at first hand of a slave's life and the luxuriance of the South American rain-forest.

This daily escape to torrid places was a far cry from the reality of frosty Edinburgh. It was icy cold and he was miserable. Romantic talk of forests he revelled in; getting up for Duncan's dreary lectures he resented. Susan tried to cheer him up, writing in March: 'For this next month devote y[ou]rself to wisdom & you will be much happier.' But he could see no wisdom in medicine. It probably did not help to receive a stream of girlish gossip on the jollities at home, or tales of the flirtations at Shrewsbury's spring balls.

Caroline, concerned as usual about the hereafter, tried a different message. She exhorted him to read the Bible in order to learn 'what is necessary to feel & do to go to heaven after you die.' 'I suppose,' she added, wanting a stronger commitment, 'you do not feel ready yet to take the sacrament.' A suppliant Charles responded: 'What part of the Bible do you like best? I like the Gospels. Do you know which of them is generally reckoned the best?' They agreed on the Gospel of John, and Caroline lamented, 'I often regret myself that when I was younger & fuller of pursuits & high spirits I was not more religious – but it is difficult to be so habitually.'

Charles began to reflect on a life he had taken for granted. He was starting to appreciate the devotion Susan and Caroline had shown him after his mother's death. Their letters now sparked an emotional response as he tried to put his thoughts into words. 'It makes me feel how very ungrateful I have been to you for all the kindness and trouble you took for me when I was a child,' he conceded to Caroline. 'Indeed I often cannot help wondering at my own blind Ungratefulness.'

His half-heartedness at medical school was apparent to the Doctor. He scolded Charles in March for the desultory manner in which he picked and chose lectures, telling him bluntly: 'If you do not discontinue your present indulgent way, your course of study will be utterly useless.'[18] And he warned him against cutting lectures and coming home early.

Charles finally escaped Edinburgh at the end of term. The summer was infinitely more pleasant, hiking through the Welsh hills with a Shrewsbury School friend. A copy of the Revd Gilbert White's classic *Natural History of Selborne* taught him to treat birds less like moving targets; and he began to observe their habits and habitats, scrawling his observations in a pocket diary. He relived the enchantment of his childhood rambles by the Welsh coast, and wondered to himself 'why every gentleman did not become an ornithologist.' Not that he was entirely converted to such placid avocations. When the season opened on 1 September, he made a good effort at reducing Maer's bird population, and his diary switched from notes on behaviour to a body count – fifty-five partridges, three hares, and a rabbit in the first week.[19]

He did not relish returning to Edinburgh by himself. During the first year Erasmus and Charles had explored and studied together. They were inseparable, whether reading, lecture-going, or sampling the dissipations of Edinburgh nightlife. But Erasmus had finished his year and now enrolled at a London anatomy school, leaving Charles to his own devices.

Pressured by his father, Charles kept reading. He browsed through his grandfather's medical *magnum opus* on the laws of life and health, the *Zoonomia*. The Doctor doted on it, praising the book for its insights into inheritable disease; although the tome dwelt on much more, the connection of mind and body, and the perpetual transformation of life.[20] Charles read sympathetically and was full of admiration – for what he wasn't sure, perhaps because it was written by his grandfather. But it left his view of medicine unchanged.

3

Sea-Mats & Seditious Science

CHARLES WAS BACK IN Edinburgh in November 1826. Away from home and alone, he began drifting, unsure of the future. Hints that his father would leave him comfortably off dampened any remaining determination to make a go of medicine. The professors had seen it all before. Losing their well-to-do students when they came into money was a perennial problem in an age of occupational gentlemen.[1]

The disenchantment showed; he did not even bother to join the library this year. His interest had plainly petered out. With little commitment and a lot of time, he threw himself into the student societies, and here he found excitement in the unlikeliest place.

In these bustling societies the lawyers and doctors-to-be sharpened their wits by debating contemporary topics. The gatherings provided camaraderie, and the debates were often raucous. The Plinian Society's meetings could be electric, while some topics bordered on the indictable. The Plinian had been founded in 1823 by Robert Jameson, the shy, wild-haired Regius Professor of Natural History.[2] Every Tuesday, all types, from sixteen-year-olds to long-standing graduates, streamed into one of the basement rooms to hear the talks. When Darwin joined in 1826 it had been penetrated by radical students – fiery, freethinking democrats who demanded that science be based on physical causes, not supernatural forces. They were challenged by the religiously orthodox, and for many listeners, like Darwin, the ensuing clashes provided that *frisson* missing from mainstream lectures.

Darwin was actually proposed for the Plinian by the militant William Browne (one of its five Presidents – the Plinian was a very democratic affair). Browne was a brilliant 21-year-old demagogue who graduated in 1826 with an interest in madness. He was deeply involved in radical science and anti-clerical politics. He had no time for souls and saints. Radicals like him were intent on reforming a Church-dominated society. The Established Churches of Scotland and England ruled all aspects of life, monopolizing political offices, regulating hospital, university, and legal posts, prescribing the rites surrounding birth, marriage and death, restricting civil liberties, and suppressing other religious groups. They were hated by the radical democrats for their corrupt power, and Browne himself despised 'Priestcraft.' Moreover, he had a unique way of lampooning it. He studied the inmates of Montrose Lunatic Asylum to prove that the fanatics canonized by the Church across the centuries had been madmen. They had over-developed organs of 'Veneration' in the brain. A more enlightened nineteenth century would have locked them away as insane.[3]

The very day Darwin petitioned to join, on 21 November 1826, he heard Browne announce his intention of refuting Charles Bell's pious *Anatomy and Physiology of Expression* (a book, by the self-proclaimed 'captain of anatomists,' that Darwin himself was to target in later years). Bell claimed that the Creator had endowed the human face with unique muscles that allowed man to express his unique emotions, which reflected his unique moral nature. Browne scorned such anatomical chauvinism and, seeing no essential difference between men and animals, issued a flat denial.

The following week Darwin was elected with William Greg, a student his own age. Greg was just as heretical as Browne. He immediately offered to give a talk proving that 'the lower animals possess every faculty & propensity of the human mind.' The son of a mill owner, a Manchester cotton king, Greg had been educated in a Unitarian school. Here he had learned to see nature purely in terms of physical forces. (Unitarians had no truck with orthodox Creationist science, the sort taught in Anglican schools: species were not miraculously created, nor did man stand outside nature.) His masters had even proclaimed the human mind subject to physical law – an idea that Anglicans abhorred, knowing that morality was God's gift, not nature's. Greg read his paper on the animal and human mind.[4] Darwin, with his heritage of Wedgwood Unitarianism, heard it, and probably without surprise. The illicit excitement of these meetings was enormous. Established Church doctrines were being impugned, dissident sciences championed. It must have affected the impressionable seventeen-year-old. He was quick to take an active part. On 5 December, the day Browne tore Bell's book apart, Darwin was elected to the Council.

Darwin's new-found friends were not only involved in politics. Browne and Greg were fierce phrenologists intent on proselytizing the students. Phrenology was a fashionable anti-establishment science among Edinburgh's traders, pressing for more political power. Its advocates argued that each faculty of thought – Love, Morality, Veneration, or whatever – was located in its own 'organ' of the brain, and the size of each organ was reflected in the shape of the head. This is what made phrenology popular. There was no art or mystery. Anyone could look at the bumps on a person's head and see their gifts. Self-help appealed to the mandarins of new wealth confronted by the hauteur of the old; knowing one's true talents made a mockery of patronage and the old-boy network.[5]

Of course, the meetings were not all high-brow heresy and student radicalism; they flew high and low, moving from the cuckoo's habits to the classification of animals, from instinct to the existence of sea-serpents. Many talks concerned local sightings – of whales, algal blooms, and rare plants – which left great scope for audience participation. The young Darwin stood to add his bit on cuckoos and classification, and, all in all, seems to have found the Society a great boon.

He went scouring the Firth of Forth shoreline with his Plinian friends and accompanying the trawlers dredging the ocean bottom. Sometimes they ventured further afield: along the coast of Fifeshire, where they sheltered from storms in the Inchkeith lighthouse, or to the Isle of May out in the estuary.[6] Always, however, Darwin was looking for washed-up sea creatures, especially sponges or stalked, feathery sea-pens and their relatives.

Others shared his fascination. The studious John Coldstream was two years older than Darwin, and equally absorbed by the local corals, sponges, and sea-pens, which he collected and shared. Coldstream had joined the Plinian on its foundation, and he was another of the Presidents who put Darwin up for election. But he was a different cut from Browne and Greg. As a boy in nearby Leith, Coldstream had been intensely evangelical – an earnest Bible-believing proselytizer. He maintained that Britain should be saved through Christian moral regeneration, not Browne's irreligious politics. Coldstream had written for the local Bible Society, and even at Edinburgh Darwin found him 'prim, formal, highly religious and most kind-hearted.'[7]

Of all Darwin's Edinburgh mentors, one stood out: a tall, satirical, sponge expert, Robert Edmond Grant. He became closer to Charles and did more to influence him than anyone else in this period.

Grant was a native of the city, born in fashionable Argyle Square. He was sixteen years older and a doctor of twelve years' standing. But he had forsaken medical practice to study marine life, living on a legacy after his father's death (although the money was running out). He was another Plinian stalwart, and a sad, cynical, and fascinating figure. There was no more passionate Francophile, nor one so committed to a radical overhaul of science and society. Theirs was a decisive meeting. Darwin was coming under the wing of an uncompromising evolutionist.

Nothing was sacred for Grant. As a freethinker, he saw no spiritual power behind nature's throne. The origin and evolution of life were due simply to physical and chemical forces, all obeying natural laws. Like his French heroes, the maligned Jean-Baptiste Lamarck and Etienne Geoffroy St Hilaire – evolutionists both – he believed that a new imaginative vision was needed. But evolution was almost universally condemned by Church and scientific authorities. It was castigated as morally degenerate and subversive. Were men to see themselves as brutes, they would act accordingly. God was the arch-paternalist, working through patrician priests; His beneficence flowed from His Church into society. If nature and culture were *self*-evolving, if the clergy could not point to miraculously created species as a sign of His power operating from above, the Church's legitimacy was undermined. The logic was stark – even if it was rarely spelled out. The day people accepted that nature and society evolved unaided, the Church would crash, the moral fabric of society would be torn apart, and civilized man would return to savagery.

The few evolutionists kept their heads down. They were usually inspired by the revolutionary French, and were often radical democrats wanting to open up society. For them the power for change came from below, in both nature and politics. (Hence their democratic ideals – power came from the people, it was not delegated downwards from wealthy paternalists.) Grant's praise for old Lamarck in France was unbounded. Lamarck was still alive, a blind octogenarian in Paris. In his day he had been an exceptional biologist (he coined the word) – the Kepler of Biology, as a contemporary called him. The professor of 'insects and worms' at the Natural History Museum in Paris, he had revolutionized study of the lower invertebrates. Even the British Museum's collection of shells was arranged according to Lamarck's principles. Yet there was another side to Lamarck's science – his evolution – which met with a hysterical reaction. Execrable, most called it. The Old Etonian keeper rearranging the Museum's shells spat venom at the Frenchman for his evolutionary ideals. He seethed at the 'abominable trash vomited forth by Lamarck and his disciples,' damning these naturalists 'who have rashly, and almost blasphemously, imputed a period of comparative imbecility to Omnipotence.'[8]

So godless evolutionary talk was anathema in conservative Britain. The libertarian freedoms of the eighteenth century were gone, crushed underfoot in the reaction to the French Revolution. In the long Tory-dominated years after the Napoleonic Wars, pedantic specialization and description were safer occupations for a savant. The time was past for blasphemous babblings about a self-evolving nature.

But Grant was no blinkered patriot, and he was never one to kow-tow. A quiet intransigence dominated his career. His cavalier attitude to convention verged on the self-destructive. He continually touched a raw nerve, not only in his scientific views and sham-hating radicalism, but in his lifestyle (tittle-tattle had him a homosexual, though no one is sure).

In a jingoistic age, he was a man of deep European learning. He had travelled widely and was well known in Paris. Like Lamarck, Grant worked on the sponges, fascinated because they were so little understood. The very simplicity of these primitive sea animals, he believed, would enable us to understand their tissues more easily, and thereby to solve some of the knottier problems of the complex higher animals, including man. Grant rejected the wisdom of the Oxford and Cambridge clergy – that the fossil record, with its progression of extinct animals and plants, testified to a series of divine Creations. Rather, the evolution of men and monkeys could be put down to environmental and climatic causes. The naturalist's job was to expose these causes. This irreverent probing of Creation put him out of step with the safe taxonomic preoccupations south of the border.

This was Darwin's walking companion. And a good walking companion, too. Grant had already crossed the Alps seven times on foot, visiting the universities in France, Germany, Italy, and Switzerland. They marched out towards the coast together, umbrellas in hand, rapt in conversation, an inquisitive Darwin learning the questions to ask. Grant was a marvellous raconteur, and their talk would take in exotic sponges, the life in some Hungarian hamlet, or the soprano at the Theatre-Royal. Leaving Edinburgh, they could look back on the city, 'rising in gradual amphitheatre, most sublimely backed by mountainous clouds.'[9] On to Leith, with its iron jetty and new harbour full of Dutch vessels and herring fishermen. They would greet the returning oyster boats. Grant was fascinated by a strange fleshy creature that colonized oyster shells, and which he interpreted as an evolutionary half-way house between sponges and polyps. Darwin struck up friendships with the trawler crews himself and began accompanying them out to sea, examining the catch as it was dredged up.

Through the winter and spring of 1827 he got to know Grant well. Darwin found him stiff and starchy at first, not surprisingly, for Grant was always formally dressed in tail coat and choker. Beneath the exterior, though, he was kind, enthusiastic, and funny, with a lashing wit that left nothing sacrosanct. Not even the Scriptures; and a succession of students, Darwin undoubtedly one, listened guiltily to Grant's jokes about Providence. Grant's austere crust concealed an even greater enthusiasm for microscopic life. Others called it a 'burning zeal' for his precious polyps – and he attacked the subject, like so much else, with selfless energy. He would tell his students of the

> eight or ten hours of a sleety day in February which he had
> spent, cold and hungry, wading in the shallows of the Firth of
> Forth . . . 'I had nothing to eat or drink, I was wet through,
> my hands were half-frozen, and I was chilled to the marrow;
> but, gentlemen, I was amply rewarded: I became the happy
> possessor of no less than three of these beautiful little
> creatures, these Dorises [sea-slugs],' and he held up a phial
> containing three hardly visible little bladder-like animals.[10]

The sacrifice was obviously lost on some students, but not Darwin. He was quickly infected by Grant's enthusiasm for sea-slugs and their like. What he learned from Grant in these months was to shape his own initial approach to evolution ten years later.

Grant took a house on the rocky shore at Prestonpans, ten miles from Edinburgh. Here he spent the chilly winter months scouring the tidal pools for cast-up sponges and stalked sea-pens. The bay, though on the cold, choppy North Sea, had one of the richest marine environments, and he was able to catch and keep alive hundreds of sponges, sea-mats, sea-pens, and dead-men's fingers. He bred them all from eggs, spending weeks poring over the tiny frail organisms, each sea-mat and sea-pen a colony of tiny tentacled polyps. The result was a string of twenty papers in the Edinburgh journals in 1826 and 1827, during Darwin's stay, mostly on sponges, eggs, and larvae. It won him a European reputation. Even the French –. world leaders in these matters – admitted the importance of his sponge papers, and in a show of magnanimity had them translated. Darwin's unofficial tutor was now a world expert on marine invertebrates.

Grant pointed out what to look for, and Darwin filled a notebook in March and April 1827 with observations on the larvae of molluscs and sea-mats, and the stalked sea-pens. He was fascinated. These creatures were very primitive; arguments even flared over whether sponges were animals or plants. With Darwin's help, Grant was showing that they lay close to the root of the animal kingdom, and he believed that they held clues to the common foundations of all life. His talks on the sea-mat *Flustra*, a primitive moss-like animal comprising a colony of tentacle-waving polyps, were illustrated by huge blown-up drawings, making their microscopic structure easier to understand.[11] Darwin, drinking it all in, began to make original observations himself, and the first of these was announced at another of the student bodies – the Wernerian Natural History Society.

The Wernerian was a longer-established society, which met fortnightly in Professor Jameson's room in the university museum. To the newcomer the setting was stark indeed, just two tables, a fireplace, and rows of benches; no adornments, no warmth, nothing but a stuffed swordfish or such on the table. But the thronged meetings gave it instant life: Kirk ministers would discuss Noah's Flood, tyros brought their sea-slugs and octopuses, senior students reported on the marsupials shipped from the new Australian settlements. Here Grant – a council member who had given fifteen talks since 1825 – exhibited live sponges and unravelled their structure. He had shown that the larvae of many sponges and polyps could swim using their surface cilia. Late in 1826 Grant began bringing Darwin to meetings (only MDs could join, the students came as guests). As an old man Darwin could still remember seeing Audubon, with his black flowing locks, exhibit a drawing of a buzzard at the Society and describe his ingenious method of wiring up dead birds for painting. Grant also blew Darwin's trumpet; on 24 March 1827 he announced that Darwin had unravelled the mystery of the black peppercorn-like bodies found inside oyster shells, and thought by fishermen to be seaweed spores. They were the eggs of a skate leech. Grant published an account of the parasite, and congratulated his 'zealous young friend Mr Charles Darwin' for his discovery.[12]

Darwin was now treading in Grant's footsteps. He too observed waving hair-like cilia on the larvae of another species of *Flustra* brought up by the dredge boats. He checked the Paris authorities to see if anyone else had noticed them. Grant, a fluent French speaker and friend of the savants, pushed him deeper into the writings of

Lamarck and his colleagues. French was a bother for Darwin. Susan had insisted he keep up the language. 'I hope,' she badgered him, 'you are reading something more interesting than the *Baroness & Countess*' silly letters' and that 'you like French better than you did.' In truth it remained a chore, but at least Lamarck could not be dismissed as so much French fripperie. Darwin also got hold of Lamarck's *System of Invertebrate Animals* and found the classification charts easier to translate. No, the French had not spotted the cilia. Darwin saw his observation help to confirm Grant's belief that the larvae of all these marine animals were free-swimming.[13]

This was what he said three days later at the Plinian Society, during an eventful meeting on 27 March. He stood to announce his modest discoveries, that the sea-mat's larvae could swim, and that the black specks in old oyster shells were leech eggs. It was his first public presentation, and he proudly responded when asked to lay his specimens before the Society. Grant followed up with an authoritative talk on the strange, amorphous sea-mat.

But what happened next eclipsed all innocent talk of polyps. Browne, the fiery radical, gave such an inflammatory harangue on matter and mind that it sparked a raging debate. He provoked the students by arguing that mind and consciousness are not spiritual entities, separate from the body; they are simple spin-offs from brain activity.[14] Such a notion raised dreadful questions, the sort that terrorized the Kirk's élite: if life was not a supernatural gift, if the mind was not some incorporeal entity, what became of the soul? With no soul, no after-life, no punishment or reward, where was the deterrent against immorality? What would stop the downtrodden masses from rising up to redress their grievances? All Darwin's new-found friends entered the fray.

Someone was so incensed that he struck Browne's proposition from the Minutes. Whoever it was even went back to the previous week's announcement of Browne's paper to cross that out too. Heresy, censorship: the younger students were agog. It was Darwin's first exposure to militant freethought – and to the storm it whipped up.

The reaction was typical. Conservatives across the country were aghast at this sort of godless philosophy. An ageing Coleridge damned it as subversive. He saw it undermine religious authority and encourage political upheaval. The staunch *Quarterly Review* wanted it legally suppressed: such wretched views would 'impair the welfare of society . . . break down the best and holiest sanctions of moral obligation, and . . . give a free rein to the worst passions of the human heart.' In an undemocratic age, with Church and State striving to keep order, the reaction was shrill. Nor was it surprising: the Cato Street conspiracy, a plan to assassinate the Cabinet in 1820 and proclaim a democracy, was still fresh in the authorities' minds.

Vigilant teachers feared that the young bud would be blighted by these poisonous ideas. The future headmaster of Rugby School, Thomas Arnold, knew it to be true; he believed the rumours of medical students degenerating into 'materialist atheists of the greatest personal profligacy.'[15] Here was the teenage Darwin, mixing with just such people. He was watching debates that touched on the most sensitive issues of the day.

Darwin's tiny polyps were important beyond their own sake. They were a central plank in Grant's evolutionary research. Grant rejected the conventional explanation: that animals were Creatively 'designed,' each unique and perfect for its niche. This did not explain why a bird's wing, a man's hand, and a bear's paw have identical bones. Grant believed that the same organs in different animals were homologous; the livers of, say, fish, frogs, and fowl were built of the same parts and conformed to a common blueprint. There was an underlying plan.

The notion that vertebrates displayed a 'unity of plan' was much in vogue in Paris in the early 1820s. But Grant, like his friend Geoffroy (a professor at the Paris Muséum), took it to radical extremes. He argued that *all* animals, from people to polyps, shared similar organs, which differed only in their complexity. This was not immediately apparent; jellyfish did not seem to have nervous systems, nor sponges hearts. Hence his excitement at one Wernerian meeting, when he announced that he had identified the pancreas in molluscs – and he exhibited a pinned-out *Doris* to prove the point.[16] He had found the homology of a mammal's organ in the sea-slugs.

The pay-off was this: with all animals structurally related, they could be threaded into a chain. And this is what gave the lowly beings at the base a fundamental importance. Their tissues were simpler versions of those in man. They could be used to explain human organs – to reveal their primitive origin and primal function.

Grant was even more controversial in giving the animals in this threaded sequence a real blood line. Walking with Darwin, he sang Lamarck's praises. At first Darwin was surprised – after all, the prevailing view was that each species had been directly created. But Grant's provocative ideas were well known. In his talks he had presented the sponge as the 'parent' of higher animals. Nor was he alone; free rein was given to speculation in the Edinburgh Museum. Even dry-as-dust Jameson penned an anonymous paper in 1826 praising 'Mr Lamarck' for explaining how the higher animals had 'evolved' from the 'simplest worms.' (This was the first use of the word 'evolved' in a modern sense.) Grant assumed that, as the primal earth cooled, changing conditions drove life towards higher, hotter-blooded forms. A progressive sequence of fossils stood as proof. He explained it as they strode along, and Darwin listened in 'silent astonishment.'[17]

Grant probably also mentioned his love of old Erasmus's *Zoonomia*. He had cited the book in his doctoral thesis, and admitted that it opened his 'mind to some of "the laws of organic life".' Now, here he was, walking with Erasmus's grandson; the opportunity was surely not lost. With Charles equally fond of the *Zoonomia*, their talk must have turned to those 'perpetual transformations' of nature which had so delighted its author.[18]

Grant went beyond Lamarck on one point: he traced the plant and animal kingdoms back to the simplest algae and polyps and accepted that they were related – that they had a common evolutionary starting point. The similar eggs of these primitive plants and animals were, he believed, analogous to the 'monads,' or elementary living particles. They gave a glimpse of life's basic building blocks. Since these monads could also emerge spontaneously from non-living matter, they held the key to the ultimate laws of life. Here, where the kingdoms converged, was the most fertile ground for the philosophical naturalist.

However unwittingly, Darwin was involved in research that was designed to reveal nature's innermost secrets. He had been offered a Lamarckian solution to one of the most profound problems of biology. Later he was to rejoin the path that Grant had started him on; for the present, he gave no hint that he appreciated its direction. But his teachers had shown him that naturalists *could* attempt to lift 'the veil that hangs over the origin and progress of the organic world.'[19] The trouble was that those tearing aside the veil, men like Knox and Grant, were so savagely anti-Christian. If Darwin knew that transmutation was not forbidden, he could see that it was far from respectable.

Others in Scotland were reinforcing the point, inexorably connecting politics and science. A timber merchant, Patrick Matthew, announced that inherited privilege ran counter to nature's law of progress through competition. An aristocracy was debilitating, it bucked evolution. If society did not change, he warned, Nature would 'avenge' herself; she would plunge the British race into decrepitude, push it into a bywater of history. Commercial struggle in a meritocracy, and that alone, could make the political leaders – degenerate aristocrats had no place in an evolving world.[20] It was a rationale for unfettered capitalism, and Darwin was to take this science to its logical extreme.

But in 1827 it was subversive science. It was what evangelicals had in view when they declared that evolutionists 'become turbulent subjects and bad men.' The false philosophy turns them into flaming democrats and Church-haters. They trust in lowly matter instead of Mind. Without a restraining faith in the soul, they lose their moral moorings and seek political redress in this world rather than the next. And innocent young lives run the risk of being devastated, swept along by the radical tide.

Just how devastated was shown by Coldstream. The Plinian debates on mind and matter threw him into a crisis. Nagging doubts crippled him throughout the 1826-27 session. Shortly after the 27 March meeting he graduated and went to Paris to gain hospital experience, but almost immediately he suffered a mental breakdown. The doctor reported that, although the young man was of 'blameless life,' he was still 'more or less in the dark on the vital question of religion, and was troubled with doubts arising from certain Materialist views.'[21]

But Darwin took all the heretical talk in his stride. Perhaps, coming from a line of freethinking males and Unitarians, he considered it passé. But he did learn one lesson: that passions were aroused by this alternative science. He also saw that it was the firebrands who were exploiting it, subversives intent on undermining Church authority and shifting power to the merchants.

Darwin's Plinian friends spent much of their time in the museum run by Robert Jameson. They probably advised Darwin to sit Jameson's natural history course, which he did. Jameson was famous as a 'Neptunian' geologist: he taught that the rock strata had been precipitated from a universal ocean. Darwin had already heard an opposite view from Professor Hope. Hope told *his* students that the granites had crystallized from a white-hot molten mass. The question – were the rocks solidified crust or muddy sediment – was of long standing. Too long, in fact; it had run its course elsewhere. But Hope and Jameson prolonged the set-piece debate in Edinburgh, to the delight of the students, whose fees provided the inducement. 'It would be a misfortune if we all had the same way of thinking,'

41

Jameson admitted. 'Dr. Hope is decidedly opposed to me, and I am opposed to Dr. Hope, and between us we make the subject interesting.'

Not enough for Darwin, evidently. He liked Hope, liked his style, and took his side, seeing geology in terms of the chemistry of cooling rock. Charles, the chemical dabbler, appreciated this sort of geology and the way it drove what his grandfather called the 'Earth-machine.'[22] Jameson on the other hand bored him. The Regius Professor, seen by some as one of the academic immortals, was dismissed with a yawn.

And yet Jameson's course was immensely popular, and Darwin learned from it. It was popular almost in spite of Jameson, who had all the flair of a master reading a roll call. *Geology* was what the audience came to hear. The subject was in vogue; it was practical and popular with the town's tradesmen, and in Darwin's year 200 attended, from students to city silversmiths and surveyors. The course was as comprehensively assorted as the audience. There was something for the jewellers and farmers as well as the students: mineralogy and meteorology, geology and natural history. Perhaps a little more if one looked; given Jameson's Lamarckian paper, one wonders what Charles made of his closing lectures on the 'Origin of the Species of Animals.'

Jameson met his students three times a week for practicals in the museum. Here he described exhibits, especially the minerals; and Darwin assiduously studied these, scribbling notes in his textbook and checking specimens against those in his own 'Cabinet.' He also learned the sequence of the rock strata, from the Scottish Old Red Sandstone to the Downs Chalk, and how to 'read' them like the pages of a book.[23]

The field trips too were popular, because many of the students were training to become surveyors and civil engineers. Jameson showed them rocks *in situ*, and Darwin heard him on the Salisbury Crags just outside town, ridiculing his rivals. For Jameson these trips were a crucial part of his course. Many of his auditors were young East India Company men, budding military surgeons and engineers. The Army Board recommended his class because it taught recruits leaving for the colonies how to keep records of the flora and fauna. It was designed to prepare the empire's doctor-wallahs for their travels.[24]

There were benefits from attending Jameson's class. His students were given free access to the magnificent museum. Here Darwin spent untold hours browsing, bird-stuffing, and taking notes. The museum was the 'city's pride and the country's boast.' Jameson had built it up, moving the exhibits into extensive new premises in 1820. The collection grew rapidly as ex-students sent exotic species from the colonies, the more so as their packages came in duty free by special concession. By now, too, His Majesty's surveying ships deposited half their natural treasures here (the rest went to the British Museum). As a result still more rooms had to be fitted out in 1826. In Darwin's day it was the fourth largest museum of its kind in Europe. But it was very much Jameson's preserve, and he ran it in a despotic manner. He hid skulls from phrenologists and kept rocks out of the hands of his rivals, causing one of Darwin's friends to dub him the 'absolute Dictator.'[25] Still, there is no denying that Darwin found himself in a rich environment, and he made good use of it.

The image of Darwin dissecting, stuffing, annotating, observing, taking sides, making discoveries, and enthralled by debates shows that his second year was no sterile period. His intellectual training had begun. Britain's best invertebrate zoologist had taught him to study minute detail while asking the larger questions. Darwin had become a geological observer, of the rocks as much as of the rocky debates. Even the medical lectures were formative in unexpected ways. Duncan's, however else they failed, promoted the Swiss botanist Augustin de Candolle's 'natural system' of classification.[26] This was Darwin's introduction to De Candolle, whose emphasis on the 'war' among competing species was to prove useful in later years. Even now, he was challenged to understand why plants and animals are classified the way they are.

Still more burning issues engulfed him: mind and matter, a disquieting Lamarckism, censorship, and authority. These were the issues that inflamed passions, and they revealed science as something more than accurate observation. It was a complex piece of political negotiation.

Of course, he was young, and much of it passed over his head. Moreover, he was actually here to study medicine, which he loathed. He was no nearer finding his professional feet. His mind was just not on a career. His homesickness increased as he thought of the shooting season. He asked Caroline, staying with the Wedgwoods, whether the gamekeeper 'was still Lord paramount' at Maer, and he wanted 'to know how many head of game have been killed.' 'He and Erasmus are quite troublesome in being so fond of letters from home,' Elizabeth Wedgwood confided. His misery with medicine was all too apparent, and in April 1827 he left for good – without a degree.

It was a decisive parting; most of his friends now went their separate ways. Grant accepted the chair of zoology at the new 'godless college,' London University. Browne went off to revolutionary Paris. Coldstream, recovering from his breakdown, at last found 'joy and peace in believing' and set up the Edinburgh Medical Mission Society. And Greg was called away to manage one of his father's mills.[27]

These reforming sons, flexing their professional muscles, had shown Darwin the meaning of intellectual dissidence. Nowhere was the tension between natural and supernatural explanations, capitalism and privilege, more apparent than in these Edinburgh debates. The struggle to redefine man as a material being, and nature as a secular, competitive market place, was a move against the old Kirk authority. For a moment, Darwin had glimpsed the social side to science. Perhaps, even, a new world in the making.

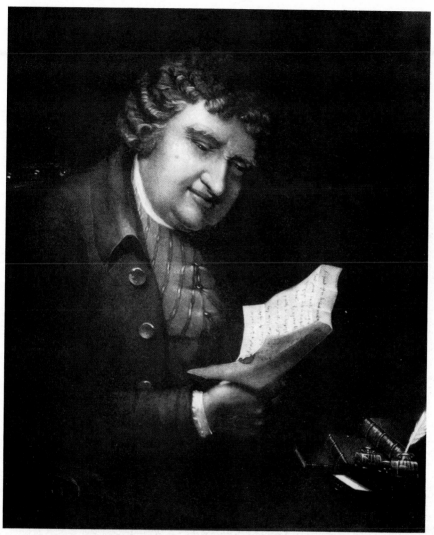

1. Charles's grandfather, Dr Erasmus Darwin of Lichfield, physician, botanist and erotic poet.

2. Dr Robert Darwin, Charles's father: 'the largest man . . . I ever saw'.

3. (*Opposite, above*) The Mount, where Charles grew up, built by Robert Darwin after his marriage in 1796.

4. (*Opposite, below*) To the manor born: Charles and his sister Catherine, the babes of the family.

5. His first school, run by Mr Case, minister of the Unitarian chapel in Shrewsbury. The classroom windows overlooked a graveyard. In August 1817, a month after his mother's death, Charles was traumatized by the sight of a dragoon soldier being buried here.

6. (*Opposite, above*) Shrewsbury School, run by the Revd Samuel Butler. Darwin was a day boy here until the age of sixteen.

7. (*Opposite, below*) Edinburgh University, where Darwin abortively studied medicine.

8. Edinburgh street life, showing a typical lodging house (far left).

9. (*Opposite*) The Plinian Society minutes of 27 March 1827, recording Darwin's short talk before the censored debate on the material basis of mind. The transcription reads:

> Mr. Darwin communicated to the Society two discoveries which he had made –
> 1. That the ova of the Flustra [a 'sea-mat' composed of tentacled hydra-like polyps] possess organs of motion.
> 2. That the small black globular body hitherto mistaken for the young Fucus Lorius [a seaweed], is in reality the ovum of the Pontobdella muricata [a leech that infests skates].
>
> At the request of the Society he promised to draw up an account of the facts and to lay ~~them~~ it, together with specimens, before the Society next evening.
>
> Dr. Grant detailed a number of facts regarding the Natural History of the Flustra.
>
> ~~Mr. Browne then read his paper on organization as connected with Life & Mind – in which he endeavoured to establish the following propositions.~~

[There then follow four propositions, which culminate in the heretical conclusion:]

> ~~And V. That mind as far as one individual sense, & consciousness are concerned, is material.~~
> ~~A discussion ensued between Messrs. Binns, Greg, Dr Grant, Ainsworth, & Browne~~ – after which the Society adjourned.

Mr Darwin communicated to the Society two Discoveries which he had made —

   1. That the ova of the Flustra possess organs of motion.

   2. That the small black globular body hitherto mistaken for the young Fucus Lorius, is in reality the ovum of the Pontobdella muricata.

At the request of the Society he promised to draw up an account of the facts and to lay ~~them~~ it, together with specimens, before the Society next evening.

Dr Grant detailed a number of facts regarding the Natural History of the Flustra.

~~Mr Brown the dead he gave on aggregation as connected with life & mind in which he endeavoured to establish the following propositions.~~

   ~~I. That all vitality in organism~~

   ~~II. That it is the gradually increased perfection in the arrangement of the parts constituting organization,~~

   ~~which is the cause of the animals perceptible in the views of the function & not species difference~~

   ~~III. That life is the effect of the organization inherent in these modes of arranging matter.~~

   ~~IV. That mind is to be distinguished from life, being rather one of the functions or manifestations of quality, by the constitution of which life is constituted in creation individually in which~~

   ~~And V. That mind as far as an individual is concerned is not to be~~

~~A discussion ensued between Professors Brown, Grant, Mr Grant, Ainsworth, & Brown~~ — After which the Society adjourned.

The members present were Messrs

10. The best of rambling companions: Darwin's Edinburgh mentor, the radical Lamarckian Robert E. Grant.

11. Christ's College, Cambridge: the view from Bacon the tobacconist's where Darwin first lodged.

12. (*Inset*) Darwin's second cousin, who started him beetling at Cambridge, Revd William Darwin Fox.

13. (*left*) Darwin's upstairs rooms in Christ's.

14. (*Below*) The Mill Pool, looking downstream towards the colleges. Darwin hired a collector to scour the barge bottoms for beetles.

15. 'Go it Charlie!' Albert Way's sketch of Darwin beetling.

16. Gateway to the Cambridge town jail with the Spinning House for streetwalkers on the right. Darwin lived further up the road.

17. (*Inset*) The terror of wandering women: head of the vice squad, the geologist Revd Adam Sedgwick, in his official robes.

18. Revd Robert Taylor, the 'Devil's Chaplain'. In May 1829 he publicly challenged his old Cambridge teachers to debate the truth of Christianity.

> PEMBROKE LODGE, *May 23*, 1829.
>
> **AGREED** that the Lodging-House Licence of **WILLIAM HADDON SMITH**, of 7. Rose Crescent, in the Parish of St. Michael, be revoked, and that Notice thereof be sent to the Tutors of the several Colleges.
>
> G. AINSLIE, *Vice-Chancellor.*
> H. KIRBY, *Senior Proctor.*
> J. POWER, *Junior Proctor.*

19. The warning to students to steer clear of Smith's lodging house, where Taylor stayed.

20. Inside the Rotunda, headquarters of the street radicals in 1830–31. Taylor preached here until his celebrated imprisonment in the summer before Darwin sailed on the *Beagle*.

H.M.S. BEAGLE

MIDDLE SECTION FORE AND AFT

1832

1. *Mr. Darwin's Seat in Captain's Cabin*
2. *Mr. Darwin's Seat in Poop Cabin with Cot slung behind him*
3. *Mr. Darwin's Chest of Drawers*
4. *Bookcase*
5. *Captain's Skylight*

Azimuth Compass
Gunroom Skylight
Whale boat 2 on Slids
Skids
Midshipmans berths
Gunroom
Gunroom Store room
Slop room
Spirit room
Pump Well
Gangway
Furl amidships with bunks inside
Men's mess tables
Main Hatchway
Main Magazine
Cabooses or Galleys
Cook's room
Sick bay
Lockers
Bits
Fore Hatchway
Sailroom
Chain locker
Coalhole
Forehold
Captain's Cabin
Bread room
Captain's Store room
Magazine

UPPER DECK

1832

1. *Poop Ladders*
2. *Signal Flag Lockers*
3. *After Companion*
4. *Gangways*
5. *Brass nine pounders, Captain's private property*
6. *Six pounders*
7. *Hammock Nettings*
8. *Patent Windlass*

Cat head
Top gallant
Forecastle
Cat head
Fore Mast
Fire hearth
Booms, spare Spars
Clitter Inside Vchl
Booms, spare Spars
Main Mast
Main Hatch
Skids
Main Bits
Gunroom Skylight
Captain's Skylight
Cutter 2nd (Gig)
Captain's Whale Boat
Azimuth Compass
Mizen Mast
Poop Cabin Skylight
Poop Deck
Jigger Mast
Jolly Boat

21. Darwin's home afloat, after a drawing by his former shipmate Philip King.   22. (*Inset*) The botanist Revd John

23. Moritz Rugendas's engraving, 'La forêt du Brésil', fired Darwin to visit the tropics. The real rainforest he found even more luxuriant.

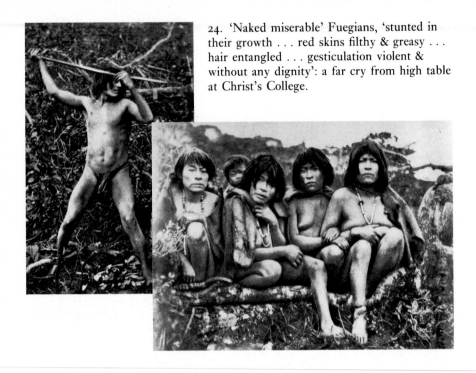

24. 'Naked miserable' Fuegians, 'stunted in their growth . . . red skins filthy & greasy . . . hair entangled . . . gesticulation violent & without any dignity': a far cry from high table at Christ's College.

25. Nature's indiscriminate power: the cathedral at Concepción after the earthquake of 1835, 'the grandest pile of ruins' Darwin had ever seen.

4

Anglican Orders

CHARLES DID NOT GO straight home to Shrewsbury. With spring in the air, he sniffed sweet freedom and set out from Edinburgh to explore. He travelled around Scotland, then on to Belfast and Dublin. In May 1827 he went to see sister Caroline in London. This was his first glimpse of the capital. Cousin Harry Wedgwood, a fresh-faced barrister at the Temple, met him and played the jaded city-dweller to his visiting innocent. Charles enjoyed himself, whatever his reservations about this 'horrid smoky wilderness.'[1] The two of them represented the clans at Dr Henry Holland's 'family' dinner, where their host, a fashionable society physician and distant relative, shocked Charles by calling whales cold-blooded, and everybody else by eating off his knife.

In town Charles plotted an excursion to Paris, his first (and only) trip across the Channel. The Doctor tipped off Jos Wedgwood: 'He has a lark in plan, which is, if you allow him, to join you & cross the sea, that he may have been in France, then return back again.' Uncle Jos was just leaving for Geneva, to fetch his younger daughters Fanny and Emma, who had been staying with their Aunt Jessie – Madame de Sismondi – for eight months. Caroline was to accompany him ('and how agreeable a companion she is'); Charles could travel safely in her company. Permission was granted, and he survived the rainy crossing, just. Even 'though not quite well' he managed to tuck into a hearty dinner of roast beef on board. At Paris the party divided, leaving Charles to fend for himself. With Browne and Coldstream in Paris, perhaps they showed him the *arrondissements* and scientific landmarks – the Natural History Muséum and the Jardin des Plantes. Anyway, a few weeks later Charles was rejoined by Uncle Jos and the girls, Emma looking lovely though 'a little

45

bronzed,' and Fanny only 'one degree nearer prettiness' than before.[2] The trip was over too soon, and by July they were all safely back in England.

He took up where he left off the previous summer, hobnobbing with the Shropshire squires and planning the autumn shoot. His few friends were spread far and wide, but then it was nothing for the gentry to ride a dozen miles to visit one another's homes. Many were old family friends, like the Owens of Woodhouse, a morning's canter from Shrewsbury. William Mostyn Owen, formerly of the Royal Dragoons, was a 'peppery and despotic squire of the old school,' but he had daughters. Sarah and Fanny Owen had been close to the Darwin sisters since childhood, when they took singing lessons together at The Mount. Here was sport of a more genteel sort. Charles had heard at Edinburgh of how 'agreeable' they were, 'full of fun and nonsense.' 'They are very much admired,' Catherine baited him, 'and get plenty of partners at the Balls,' but 'Fanny ... has quite the preference to Sarah ... there is something so very engaging and delightful about her.' Neither of the girls, however, was in love with anything but France, and Charles, fresh from Paris, had stories to tell.[3]

The hunting season opened on 1 September. Squire Owen had a magnificent wooded estate, teeming with game, and Charles's own love was shooting. He paid so many visits to Woodhouse in the next few months that the girls began to see him as a 'shootable' too – eligible and personable, a catch. At times it was difficult to tell who was chasing whom. Sarah at twenty-three was slightly disadvantaged, being five years older than Charles. She also suffered by comparison with her precocious sister. Fanny, just turned twenty, was a natural charmer, dark-eyed and petite, with a rollicking spirit. She endured painting lessons for her father's sake, but preferred to play at billiards with the boys and to ride with the hunt. This sent her hot blood racing – and Charles noticed. He took her in tow and together they galloped off into the forest. Fanny would not hear of standing by while he enjoyed the action, a 'housemaid' to his 'postillion' as she put it in her quaint, coded language. She insisted on shooting too, and he helped her point the gun. The kick was fierce and left her slim shoulder black and blue, as she proved. But she did not wince. She was dreaming about the future, and bigger game.

All grand flirtation, of course – and maybe more. Charles, teased and tantalized by this raven-haired beauty, was infatuated. But he knew that he would have to make something of himself before he could ask the daunting Squire Owen for her hand. He thought of his own uncertain future as he travelled on to Maer, his usual hunting ground. On arrival he found Sir James Mackintosh in residence. The venerable Whig MP, Uncle Jos's brother-in-law, was licking his wounds after failing to get into Canning's Cabinet, and working hard at his *History of England.* Here was a success story for Charles to savour: a man made eminent after scraping through medical studies at Edinburgh only to change his career. Sir James was now the doyen of British political commentators and an expert on economics. He talked Darwin's ear off – about history, moral philosophy, and public affairs. The encounter made a lasting impression on them both. Darwin was awe-struck that anyone so famous should talk shop with him. And even Sir James confided afterwards, 'There is something in that young man that interests me.'[4] A rare compliment, for the only other male inhabitant of Maer Hall he seems to have found agreeable was Charles's cousin Hensleigh Wedgwood, who had taken a shine to one of his daughters.

When it came to a career, Darwin now had little choice. While he was swanning about the country, carefree, his life was being mapped out. The Doctor, disappointed about Edinburgh and his son's disdain for medicine, now laid down the law with his usual heavy-handedness. No more misspent money, no more wasted time: if Charles reckoned he could fall back on his father's wealth, he had better think again. He would have to give an account of himself in a profession before he could have the security of the family purse. The only question was, if not medicine, which? The Darwins had produced lawyers and military men, true, but Charles lacked the self-discipline required of their ranks. There was, however, a safety-net to stop second sons becoming wastrels: the Church of England.

Dr Darwin, a confirmed freethinker, was sensible and shrewd. He had only to look around him, recall the vicarages he had visited, ponder the country parsons he entertained at home. One did not have to be a believer to see that an aimless son with a penchant for field sports would fit in nicely. Was the Church not a haven for dullards and dawdlers, the last resort of spendthrifts? What calling but the highest for those whose sense of calling was nil? And in what other profession were the risks of failure so low and the rewards so high?[5]

The Anglican Church, fat, complacent, and corrupt, lived luxuriously on its tithes and endowments, as it had for a century. Desirable parishes were routinely auctioned to the highest bidder. A fine rural 'living' with a commodious rectory, a few acres to rent or farm, and perhaps a tithe barn to hold the local levy worth hundreds of pounds a year, could easily be bought as an investment by a gentleman of Dr Darwin's means and held for his son. It was inducement enough for a young man to subscribe to almost any creed. When Charles was duly educated and ordained, he would simply step into the job. He would be set up for life. Among the gentry he knew so well, he would enjoy social prominence, a steady income, and eventually a handsome legacy.[6] He could even resume the hunting and hobnobbing that, at the moment, were jeopardizing his career.

There were family precedents besides. Both the Doctor's uncle and his half-brother had been Nottinghamshire rectors, and a couple of years earlier Uncle Jos had installed his own nephew as vicar of Maer.[7] Even now a Darwin cousin, William Darwin Fox, was preparing for the Church at Christ's College, Cambridge. That settled the matter. Charles would keep faith with one family tradition if not another. Send the boy to study with Fox, who would set him an example. Let him be educated for three years as a gentleman, take the Bachelor of Arts degree, and spend another year, if he liked, attending theology lectures to prepare for ordination. He could marry afterwards while apprenticed as a curate, and then be presented to a rural benefice not far from Shrewsbury – the perfect resting-place for a wayward second son.

It sounded like a *fait accompli*, but Charles wanted to think it over. Being a country parson would suit him to a tee, and not just the recreational aspects. It would buy him the time to follow in Grant's footsteps; in a rural parish he could devote himself to the tiniest members of creation. There was, needless to say, the small matter of his faith. He had a niggling doubt about what he actually believed. Edinburgh, after all, had exposed him to every conceivable type of unorthodoxy. But he had learned from his sisters to take religion seriously. And his own father, though not renowned for piety, counselled rectitude in all things, intellectual and moral alike – as did Uncle Jos, whom everyone respected as 'the very type of an upright man.' Anyway, a spell with divinity books would salve his conscience. So between the hunting and flirting, Charles ploughed through Bishop Pearson's elderly *Exposition of the Creed* and a few other turgid tomes.

One was by an up-and-coming Anglican apologist, the Revd John Bird Sumner. His *Evidences of Christianity* had been published only three years before, and its reasoning was overwhelming. Charles pitched into the book with pen poised, following Sumner step by step. This was the best defence of the faith he had ever come across. It stretched into one long argument, and the logic-chopping, massing of evidence, and weighing of probabilities all made sceptics look silly. Deftly, Sumner reduced their unbelief to a dilemma and impaled them on its horns: if Christianity be untrue, then 'either Jesus did not exist, or he actually lived, but was not the Son of God, hence an imposter.' The supposition of non-existence was 'evidently absurd,' Charles jotted, therefore sceptics must hold that Jesus 'deceived himself.' But the Gospels made this highly 'improbable.' They revealed a man whose miracles convinced unbelievers; we have 'no right to deny' the possibility of such events, Charles noted. And Jesus's religion remained 'wonderfully suitable . . . to our ideas of happiness in this & the next world.' Thus scepticism was undermined, Christianity proved. There was 'no other way except by [Jesus's] divinity,' Darwin concluded, 'of explaining the series of evidence & probability.'[8]

Charles found nothing objectionable in Sumner and the other books – nothing he could not say he believed – and in October, accordingly, he was accepted as a 'pensioner' to Christ's College, a full fee-paying undergraduate. Even so, he did not go up to the university that term – Michaelmas in Cambridge. Having examined his conscience, he had some hard swotting to do first.

Cambridge was a long way from Edinburgh. Intellectually it was much closer to Shrewsbury School. The classical learning that the Revd Butler drilled into young heads was *de rigueur* at the great Anglican seminary; yet much of it had gone right through Charles's, and he could scarcely remember the Greek alphabet, let alone parse a verb. The Doctor paid for a private tutor, and soon Charles was puzzling out the optative and wrestling with crasis. It was onerous work, and boring. Twice again he escaped to Woodhouse, but there was only game to stalk, the Owen girls having gone on holiday to Brighton. He dragged himself back to the books. By Christmas he was translating bits of Homer and the New Testament. Erasmus returned from London for the festivities and was revising too. After months at the Great Windmill Street Anatomy School, he was ready to qualify in medicine at Cambridge. So early in the new year, 1828, the brothers set off together once more.[9] Eras would sit the Bachelor of Medicine exam and reward himself with a grand tour of the Continent. But Charles faced four years' further study before taking his reward – a country parish.

The spires of Cambridge stuck out of the flat fenland like stalagmites, encrustments of feudal privilege built up over six centuries. This was low country, God's country. Fourteen parishes, seventeen colleges,

49

sixteen thousand inhabitants – all crammed into little more than a square mile along the banks of the River Cam. The land was rich, like its owners, and the river flushed the soil down among the colleges where the drains spewed out, and the open sewer swilled northwards past Ely Cathedral to empty into the sea. This was a commercial artery, and Cambridge was the furthest navigable point inland. Bargees heaved and cursed their twenty-ton cargoes – coal and corn, oil and butter – dragging them upstream through the sediment and stench, along the 'backs' of the colleges to the Mill Pool, where the line to unload often stretched boisterously beneath the sacred precincts. Collegians objected to the racket, and their own imprecations only added to the din. A half-mile away in the town centre lay the market-place. Supplied by wagon from the Pool and surrounding farms, it offered provisions of all sorts. Prices were high, as they were in the shops and lodging houses packed together in the narrow streets that honeycombed the neighbourhood. The two thousand resident collegians had an appetite to match their collective wealth. And unlike the gownsmen of Edinburgh, they dominated the town.

All were Anglicans of course. They subscribed to the Thirty-nine Articles and accepted Christianity – according to the Church of England – as part and parcel of the law of the land. Cambridge and environs, if not a society of Christians, was at least regarded as a Christian society. Belief and conduct went together like high pheasant and vintage port. The fabric was held together by God himself through his personal agents, the clergy. Virtually all the college heads and most of the professors and Fellows had taken holy orders. About half the undergraduates, like Darwin, were destined for the Church. Many could look forward to a comfortable living with public responsibilities to match. The colleges held the patronage of a third of the parishes in Cambridgeshire, and almost half of the county's magistrates were parish priests. With agrarian disturbances on the rise, as impoverished farm workers fought for fair wages, the university was a cornerstone of law and order.[10]

In the town its influence was greater still. The mayor was obliged to maintain the privileges of the university, which were extensive and resented. Traders could be visited by the university Taxors, who monitored the market and fixed the price of bread. Publicans, landlords, and others with establishments used by undergraduates had licences from the university Vice-Chancellor, and these could be withdrawn if the Proctors reported any irregularities. The Proctors and their 'bulldogs,' burly college servants who backed them up, were the university's own police force. They shared duties with the local constabulary. They maintained 'public morals' – sexual proprieties – and regulated the behaviour of ex-students in town for three years after graduation. The Proctors' powers extended a mile beyond the town in all directions, and included the right to enter any suspect house and apprehend anyone they deemed in breach of regulations.[11]

These regulations were complex, archaic, and generally ignored. Few had read them and fewer worried about them. The situation was ripe for selective enforcement, and the Proctors were not above making examples of students. To stay on the right side of the law, Darwin learned a simpler set of rules from Eras: keep the college curfew, no fisticuffs or duelling, remain sober in public, *never* be seen with girls, and always, always wear a cap and gown.

Nothing was more likely to land an undergraduate in trouble than being out-of-gown. It was practically an admission that he was up to mischief. Why else would anyone wish to appear incognito? The cap and gown told who you were. Gownsmen could be spotted at once among the townsmen, who outnumbered them three to one. And the quality of the gown, its embellishments, and the cap announced your place in the university hierarchy. A Doctor of Divinity looked different from a Doctor of Civil Law; a graduate could be distinguished from an undergraduate. Even an undergraduate's social class was revealed in his dress.[12]

But while every student could be identified, the Proctors wore the same dress as the other Masters of Arts who milled about the town: plain black gowns with full-length, square-cut sleeves. Such camouflage had advantages, Erasmus warned his brother; it made proctorizing more like spying than policing. Anonymity was the privilege of those who enforced the law. And like spies, the Proctors were few in number – just a Senior Proctor, a Junior, and a couple of Proproctors to help them. To be really effective they needed extra eyes and ears, so they relied on tip-offs from students and staff. Once informed, they swung into action. Offenders were arrested, tried, and sentenced by the university's own court, presided over by the Vice-Chancellor.

The Vice-Chancellor had autocratic powers. He was almost invariably a senior clergyman, and sometimes a chaplain-in-ordinary to the King. He sat as solitary judge over town and gown alike. Justice was summary: townspeople could be fined, imprisoned, or 'discommuned' – banned from associating with collegians – which often meant economic ruin. But the nearest to imprisonment a collegian ever came was short-term confinement to college. Even severer penalties left him at large: banishment from town for a number of terms, or – at worst – expulsion from the university.[13]

Still, the pall of repression that hung over Cambridge was punctured from time to time by resentful outbursts. The Darwins reached town just as the reverberations of the latest incident were being felt. On the pretext of celebrating the failure of the Gunpowder Plot – Guy Fawkes's legendary attempt to blow up Parliament in 1605 – a crowd had taken to the streets on 5 November and tried to blow up the police and Proctors by hurling fireworks. At first gownsmen led the way, only to be swamped by locals. The Proctors waded in and arrested the troublemakers. A few students were reprimanded, but seven townsmen were hauled before the Vice-Chancellor and given gaol terms ranging from a month to a year.

The felons were thrown into the Town Gaol in St Andrew's Street, and were being held there the day Darwin reported to Christ's College, two minutes up the road. Next door to the gaol was the university's own penitentiary, the so-called Spinning House, which was even more notorious among the collegians. It was 'chiefly used for the confinement of such lewd women as the Proctors apprehend,' Darwin heard with astonishment, and could accommodate ten of them in squalid nine-by-seven-foot cells. The town-crier had been known to drop in and 'discipline the ladies of pleasure with his whip,' for which he received a fee of one shilling each. It was paid by the Vice-Chancellor, who was also the women's judge and jury. He held court in the Spinning House as often as required, with only the Proctors giving evidence. Convictions were inevitable; sentences could last up to several months, with worse treatment for reoffenders, including a spell on Castle Hill in the County Gaol.[14]

Charles found Christ's College full at the beginning of the new term – Lent (lasting until Easter). So he took lodgings over Bacon the tobacconist's in Sidney Street, a main thoroughfare leading straight up from St Andrew's Street towards the Cam and Castle Hill. Here he was in the thick of things, with the market-place a block away, Holy Trinity Church next door, and his college just across the road. Eras had briefed him well on the local lore and mores.[15] The authorities were despots all right, but he had little to fear so long as he kept in good company. Charles, for his part, could see his social options from the first day he donned cap and gown to explore the town.

On every street corner, in every pub, he saw examples of how young gents went about studying for the BA. The bookshops even sold a ribald guide that caricatured the two approaches: the 'varmint method' and the 'reading method.' The varmint was a man who cut lectures, skipped college chapel (thereby incurring fines), gave late-night feasts, smoked cigars, drove a coach, drank copiously, gambled compulsively, and proved 'a rum one at Barnwell,' home of the 'Cyprian tribes' (the riverside district a mile or so behind Christ's College noted for its young women). He cared only for field sports when sober, caught 'Barnwell ague' one drunken night, got picked up by the Proctors, and was threatened with 'rustication' (banishment). Only in his last term did he realize that he had to *read* for his degree, which he somehow managed to scrape through by 'cramming' for the exam.

The 'reading man' was a model of diligence. He attended lectures, never missed chapel, shunned parties, kept curfew, read twelve hours a day, seldom drank or smoked, never gambled, strove for academic honours and walked off with all the prizes. Though not the cleverest student, he would become a college tutor, then a Fellow, even a leader in the university – and all through his 'desperate perseverance in study.'[16]

Walking around, Charles could see that varmints tended to be well-heeled and upper-class. He could not afford the high life, even if so inclined, though he was a dab hand at having fun. He would happily mix with the reading men instead. Besides, he was under Doctor's orders to behave himself. Then there was his oath of matriculation. This was administered on the cold marble pavement of the Senate House, with the freshmen swearing in groups. Charles marched up one morning in January 1828, stood in a line before the Senior Proctor, and repeated after him in crisp ecclesiastical Latin that he would observe all the statutes and customs, remain unfalteringly attached to the university, and defend it under all circumstances, '*ita me Deus adjuvet et sancta Dei Evangelia*' – 'so help me God and his holy Gospels.'[17]

The Senior Proctor was the Revd Adam Sedgwick, whom Charles would come to know well in future years. Sedgwick had come up the hard way, a poor Yorkshire vicar's son who entered Trinity College as a sizar, took holy orders and gave up marriage to obtain a college Fellowship, became Woodwardian Professor of Geology at the age of thirty-three, and now, ten years later, was head of the vice squad and campus police. It showed what a reading man could achieve. Sedgwick, however, was no plodder, like other reverend professors. He was an established scholar – a Vice-President of the Geological Society of London – and passionately devoted to research on the most ancient and little-known stratified rocks. At the moment he was describing the magnesian limestone of northern England, or would have been but for his pressing proctorial duties. They called for the same fine eye, the same attention to detail as geological fieldwork. As Charles settled in that winter Sedgwick honed his skills razor-sharp on the lower strata of society, scouring the streets of Cambridge rather than the dales of Yorkshire. He was left 'hardly a spare hour' for weeks on end.[18]

Sedgwick penetrated the Cambridge underworld: layer upon layer of laxity, just beneath the surface, with suggestive outcrops everywhere. In the all-male collegiate community who could miss them? Old bachelors and young bucks alike knew where to take their pleasure. The geological Proctor's job was to study the terrain minutely, map it and make it his own. He knew from personal experience that temptation was rife (siring 'bastards' was all too common among students, as court cases showed). His object was to eradicate the cause, flush out those infernal females. The blasted girls flocked to town from across East Anglia and Lincolnshire, endless Janes and Sarahs and Elizas and Mary Anns. They were young, usually in their teens, labourers' daughters and sisters, or sad orphans. All of them were hungry, especially the pregnant ones and the mothers. There were rich pickings in Cambridge: tables to be cleared, laundry to be done, young sirs eager to spend. The temptation was irresistible, though a girl might be forced to live out along 'Maid's Causeway,' past the 'Garden of Eden,' as far as the gas works in Barnwell.

If she dared. No wandering woman was safe with the Revd Sedgwick on the prowl. In the market-place, along the Cam, on the Barnwell footpath that led from the rear of Darwin's college, he was ready to arrest her and swear in court that she had been 'streetwalking.' This January alone Sedgwick committed fifteen girls to the Spinning House, seven of them in one day. It was the more necessary at the start of term. Innocent freshmen like Charles had to be protected, lest they be ruined and the moral fabric of society with them. The ploy seemed to work. For the rest of the year Sedgwick's busy schedule was interrupted by less than two committals a week.[19]

Charles could tell. He wrote to Sarah Owen that he had not set eyes on a girl since leaving home. 'What *can* you mean,' she retorted incredulously; 'have the Doctors, Proctors, Deans &c &c &c neither Wives or Daughters!! or are the Cambridge shootables thought too *dangereux* to be seen by them? pray satisfy my curiosity.' She had missed the point, unfamiliar with the game laws in Cambridge. Here the shootables were never in season; the hunters were always too *dangereuse*. But then Charles himself hardly needed protection; his first thoughts were all of Fanny. She seemed to be slipping away.

Fanny had been shocked to hear from Sarah that he was 'to become a *DD* instead of an *MD*.' You 'never let *me* into the secret,' she protested from Brighton. Charles could feel the chill in her letter. With seaside balls and nightly parties and real shootables galore, she would forget their autumn trysts. The romance was as good as over, even if she flaunted her eligibility – 'the Housemaid . . . is a year *older*,' she reminded him, and ordered 'Burn this'! He wrote back with a heavy heart, supposing that his would be the letter burned. Fanny played for time, and then offered a lame excuse. The gossiping old dears would be aghast at their exchanges – couldn't he just hear them? 'Dear me Ma'am would you believe it Miss "*Fanny Owen corresponds with a young man Ma'am at the University*".' Why, the very thought of such chit-chat 'worked upon my *heated fancy* to such a degree that *after mature deliberation* I thought it best to *remain silent* and if the Postillion should be in a *fury* at *my ingratitude* to explain it all away when we shall meet once more at the Forest.'

Cold comfort this, in the dead of winter, with Easter vacation two months away. Anything could happen before he looked into those dark eyes again. Still, his hopes rekindled, Charles answered warmly. But once more Fanny was coy, sitting on his 'long effusion' until just before term ended. Then off went another of her sparkling newsy notes, with talk of rectory parties and intrigues at the Assizes. In between she beckoned beguilingly: 'I have not yet learn't to play at *Billiards* . . . I have not been riding *near so much* as I *wish* . . . [P]ray tell me . . . when you expect to come home.' She assumed that 'my d^r. Postillion' would soon be paying his 'faithfull Housemaid' a long visit at Woodhouse. But 'for *Heaven's* sake burn this,' she insisted again, fantasizing about the stir her note would make if this time it fell 'into the hands of any of the *young men*.'

The reply came as spring broke. Woodhouse was in flower, the Assizes had begun, and the sisters were planning a trip to Wrexham Fair to shop and gad about – when, that is, Fanny was fully recovered. For she had taken to the upstairs bedrooms – '*Paradise Row*' in her secret coded notes – and had lain sick for days. Charles would be spending the vacation in Cambridge. If only he 'could *chaunce to come by*,' even '*out of the shooting Season*,' he might accompany them to the Fair.[20] But no, it was impossible. Fanny was devastated.

*

That first term above Bacon's shop had been a social whirl. Cambridge, for all its strictness, could be exhilarating. Young men confined at close quarters for months on end made fast friendships and shared new horizons. By Easter 1828 Charles's priorities had changed. Fanny, for all her flirtation, was not so much forgotten as demoted. Nor was it entirely her own fault.

College routine was absorbing enough, with compulsory tutorials and daily chapel. But it was the endless extra-mural activities that made Cambridge unique. Everywhere freshmen like Charles were discovering common interests and combining to indulge them. With their other lusts held in check, they expected meat and drink in pleasurable excess. Dining clubs proliferated and provided their gratification, although the loutish element needed only a bottle. Outdoor sports divided up similarly: there were popular pastimes for reading men and reckless diversions for the varmints. Shooting, steeplechasing, and carriage racing took place far away from town, where they were frowned on. But cricket was all the rage, and rowing on the Cam had just received official sanction with the formation of the University Boat Club (making the cruder water combats between gownsmen and bargees redundant). And, with so much loose money around, betting was ubiquitous; everything had odds, from batsmen bowled out to bottles drunk. Serious gamblers met regularly, playing 'Van John' (Blackjack) until the small hours, or having a flutter on the horses at Newmarket.

Leisure time was not just for games. Everyone joined conversation clubs where the hottest topics were thrashed out in smoke-filled rooms. The Union Debating Society, favoured by aspiring barristers and politicians, was open to anyone who subscribed one gold sovereign a year. It met on Tuesday evenings in the 'low, ill-ventilated, ill-lit, cavernous, tavernous gallery, at the back of the Red Lion Inn' in Petty Cury, a stone's throw from Darwin's digs. Other clubs provided for more genial discussion. The most exclusive, and reputedly most brilliant, was 'The Apostles,' whose twelve members included young Alfred Tennyson. (Erasmus had been a member briefly in 1823.) They gathered on Saturday evenings to wrangle over everything from fornication and the division of labour to the fraught question of whether mankind had 'descended from one stock.' No curriculum dared embrace such issues, and the Apostles, missionaries of romantic enlightenment, condemned the whole unreformed Cambridge system. Tennyson himself, in some bitter undergraduate lines, stigmatized

... your Halls, your ancient Colleges,
Your portals statued with old kings and queens,
Your gardens, myriad-volumed libraries,
Wax-lighted chapels, and rich carven screens,
Your doctors, and your proctors, and your deans,

for hypocrisy and humbug, for reducing Christianity to rote learning, and for failing to meet the moral and intellectual needs of the rising generation.[21]

The Apostles had no monopoly on religious seriousness. The 'Sims,' as their detractors called them, were a pious clique who pestered students like Darwin continually. They followed the Revd Charles Simeon, the evangelical vicar of Holy Trinity Church, who had spent the best part of fifty years convincing the university that saving lost souls did not conflict with its traditions. Simeon held forth to capacity congregations, within earshot of Darwin's bedroom. 'His action is absurd in the extreme,' reported a curious freshman that year. 'He brandishes his spectacles when he talks of the terrible, and smirks and smiles when he offers consolation.' It was unctuousness rather than eloquence that brought Simeon his following, and on Friday evenings he welcomed the Sims to his rooms in King's College, 'smiling and bowing with the accomplished manners of a courtier.' Tea was served, with the young ordinands seated at their master's feet. Many were destined for the livings that the wealthy Simeon and his friends bought as a means of spreading their evangelical message.[22]

Charles was headed for the Church but unconcerned about his soul; the Sims failed to recruit him. Nor did he fall in with the literary set, or the cricketing and boating fraternity. That spring – Easter term – he read Shakespeare with his old friend Jonathan Cameron from Shrewsbury and took in the Fitzwilliam Museum with another schoolmate, Charles Whitley, who showed him the fine engravings. He acquired a taste for music, though he was tone-deaf, and went with Whitley's cousin, John Herbert, to King's College chapel, where he was ecstatic about the anthems.[23] But his real passion, his one serious sport, was the pursuit of beetles. Even chasing Fanny took second place.

He was in good company, with a beetle craze sweeping the nation. City dwellers, shut off from nature by the ugly industrial sprawl, were filling their cabinets with remnants of a lost Arcadia. Their bible was a beautifully written four-volume handbook, *An Introduction to*

Entomology, by the Suffolk rector William Kirby and a Hull business-man, William Spence. The craze spread to pastoral Cambridge too, indeed flourished there. The neighbouring fens teemed with rare species, and the colleges were crawling with trainee clergymen, taught to treasure the infinite diversity of God's creation.[24] And if ever there were an infinity of insects, it was shiny beetles. Many students were bitten by the bug, as species after species turned up new. Beetling was a field sport as much as any other, and one of the chief competitors was William Darwin Fox.

Cousin Fox belonged to the Derbyshire branch of the family – he was Charles's great-uncle's grandson, to be precise. A country gentle-man, like so many student pensioners, he had grown up at Osmaston Hall near Derby, surrounded by hunting parsons and wild life, which he adored. After three years at Cambridge – he had been at Christ's with Erasmus and was the same age – he was well groomed for a rural parish. He had mastered the fens, knew all the authorities on local flora and fauna, and perfected the art of netting beetles. Fox was a storehouse of facts about natural history, as Charles discovered the day they met. When Fox strode up, with his dog 'little Fan' trotting dutifully behind, Charles took to him instantly. Here was someone to look up to – a respectable Grant and Erasmus all in one, a companion and role-model. Soon Charles was sporting a dog of his own, a pint-sized bitch he called Sappho, who followed him around town and slept in his bed at night.[25]

The cousins and their dogs were inseparable during Easter term. They explored along the Cam, rooted through Jesus Ditch, and ransacked Midsummer Common in the quest for beetles. Sometimes Fox's friend Albert Way joined them. Charles clung to Fox's every word. Now was his chance to shine. He already had a head start, having conquered the most esoteric aspects of invertebrate anatomy in Edinburgh. Fox and his friends could be bettered, Charles felt sure, if only he listened attentively and helped himself to their lore. Beetling in Cambridge had become just as competitive as cricket or rowing – but with one difference. It was no team sport. A painstaking observer could win the student accolades. Charles, such a disappoint-ment to his father, became obsessed with the idea.

Nothing was spared in the trophy hunt. He bought a sweeping net and learned how to trap tiny jumping and flying insects. Sheaves of cardboard were festooned with beetles, each pinned in its proper place. He also hired a local to collect the debris from the bottom of barges that brought reeds from the fens, which he sifted through, hunting down his prey. It was not a simple slaughter, for some beetles had unexpected defences. One day, on stripping bark from a dead tree, he pinned down two rare types, one in each hand. Suddenly he saw a third, a new species, too good to lose. His action was that of a trained egg-collector. He popped the right-hand one in his mouth. Unfortunately it was a bombardier beetle, which promptly lived up to its name by squirting a noxious boiling fluid into his throat, momentarily stunning him. He spat the beetle out, losing it on the ground, and in the confusion dropped the others too.[26]

Charles had been well prepared for the ups and downs of small-game hunting on his annual outings at Woodhouse and Maer. Indeed, the chase, the mounting for display, and the ritual bragging among the beetle brotherhood were like the shoot, on a smaller scale. But there was another, technical side. The insects had to be identified, which meant scrutinizing their structure and habits. Manuals had to be consulted and their descriptions compared – Stephens's *Illustrations of British Entomology*, Samouelle's *Entomologist's Useful Compendium*, and the trusty Kirby and Spence. As in Edinburgh, Charles ran into problems of classification, and again he turned to the world leader on invertebrates, Lamarck. Proudly he informed Fox that he had identified a most 'valuable insect' in his collection: it was a rough-bodied, black beetle with red antennae, which the books gave as *Melasis flabellicornis*. With rising excitement, he exclaimed, 'the description & habits in Samouelle & Lamarck *perfectly* agree.'[27] He had caught a German species. At last he was in the running, with a beetle so rare in England that it had been seen only twice before, and never around Cambridge.

When really stuck for a name, Charles had experts he could call on. There was more to the academic side of beetling than books. While other gownsmen drank themselves into a stupor on Friday nights or sipped tea with the Revd Simeon, Fox took Darwin to the home of the Revd John Stevens Henslow for claret and convivial discussions on natural history. Henslow, only thirty-two, had taught Erasmus mineralogy, and Charles knew of his reputation for scientific omnicompetence. Now in his third year as professor of botany, Henslow made his soirées a hive of activity for budding naturalists, a club for young ordinands like Charles whose main interests lay outside the classical curriculum. Occasionally other reverend professors attended – great guns like Sedgwick, or the polymathic William Whewell, the new professor of mineralogy.[28] Clerical tutors such as George Peacock or country parsons such as Leonard Jenyns, Henslow's brother-in-law, would also drop in to mingle with the undergraduates.

No raucous Plinian Society this, torn by infidel ideas, but it was still a thrill to hear the dons 'conversing on all sorts of subjects, with the most varied and brilliant powers.'[29] They could answer Charles's queries, and some, like Jenyns, collected beetles themselves. By term's end Darwin was fired up for natural history as never before. He knew he had found his niche. The Doctor had been right, the Church was the place to be.

5

Paradise & Punishment

HOME FROM CAMBRIDGE for the summer, he kicked his heels, 'dying by inches from not having any body to talk to about insects.' He mooched around, intoning 'I do wish Fox was here.' The beetles had deserted him too, and even his collecting slackened off. A long list of captures from Fox and Way sent a 'pang of jealousy' shooting through him. It was not unlike the chill feeling when he worried about his girlfriend Fanny and her other flames. He fretted, fearing that she was with someone else. There was nothing for it but to find out. Who knew, maybe she had forgiven his absence at Easter? And if not, he might still turn up some beetles in Squire Owen's forest. Anything was better than idling around Shrewsbury with clucking sisters and Erasmus away. So towards the end of June 1828 he trotted off. Yes, Fanny was waiting for him; the 'dutiful Housemaid' was still there, delighted to see her 'd^r. Postillion.' Nothing had changed.

Or almost nothing; they were a year older, and growing up fast. Charles was tall, nearly six feet, and rather 'thick set,' though hardly overweight. He had a new 'varsity' poise about him, yet he was still his 'placid, unpretending, & amiable' self. Not by any stretch handsome, but Fanny found him fun – in fact, he gave her an illicit thrill. She was definitely a young woman now, coming of age and filling out. Charles thought her 'the prettiest, plumpest, Charming personage that Shropshire posseses [sic],' and it showed. He took her hunting again, for beetles. It was strawberry season and Woodhouse was full of beds. Perfect stalking ground: they got down on hands and knees, then lower still, and before long they were stretched out 'full length' beside each other, 'grazing' the luscious fruit, behaving like beasts.[1]

It was almost too much of a good thing, and Charles had to tear himself away. He had an appointment with Cambridge friends at Barmouth on the Welsh coast. Here they planned to read for three months with private tutors. Reading parties were a jolly junket, an excuse for undergraduates to dress as they pleased, stay out late, and let off steam without fear of the Proctors. Charles's own subject was maths, but he wanted to combine both worlds and looked on it as an 'Entomo-Mathematical expedition,' although he hoped 'by the blessings of Providence' that '*the science*' (insects) would not 'drive out of my poor noddle the Mathematics.' It was a tacit admission that his maths was suffering. After two terms of tutoring, he was still baffled by the basics of algebra. The binomial theorem was beyond him, and he could see no reason in irrational numbers.[2] The time should have been used in catching up.

Instead, insects got the upper hand. By the end of July he had all but given up maths. 'I stick fast in the mud at the bottom & there I shall remain in statu quo,' he admitted to Fox, struggling to stay afloat himself while revising for his BA exam. In truth, there were too many diversions along the Cardigan Bay shore. He could not have kept his mind on algebraic abstractions had he wanted to. Most days were spent boating in the estuary, or walking the hills, or flyfishing in nearby lakes. His constant companions were two other hopeful ordinands, Thomas Butler, the son of his old Shrewsbury headmaster, and his musical friend John Herbert, who had taken him to King's College chapel. Both were older, but for the first time Charles was the leader, and he savoured the experience. Climbing 3000 feet to the top of Cader Idris, eight miles away, he perched on a precipice and nonchalantly shot the passing birds, while the others waited below to retrieve the corpses for stuffing. Herbert had the alcohol for killing insects, and Darwin netted untold numbers of beetles and butterflies, showing his friends the tricks of the trade.[3] Dealing with nature, he felt more at ease, more in control.

Beetling was the 'Business,' though Fox left him feeling that he had a lot to learn. Every few weeks the cousins exchanged letters. Darwin bragged about his captures, begged 'instructions about keeping Crysalises' from his 'old master,' and insisted on prompt replies. 'It is quite absurd,' he half apologized, 'how interested I am getting about the science.' Fox invited him to visit Osmaston for the first time after the reading party was over. It was too good an offer to turn down, and Darwin left Wales early, at the end of August, in time for the hunting season. So much for mathematics.

Actually he had been dying to see Fox, and, after killing a 'very contemptable [sic]' seventy-five head of game at Maer in a week, spent the rest of September with him. Osmaston Hall was a perfect menagerie, packed with creatures 'alive & dead.' Darwin was in his element. He fired off instructions to Herbert and Butler to capture certain beetles for his cousin, and promised him some of the stuffed birds. This was competition tempered by gratitude, catches conspicuously given away. But then Fox remained a paragon of generosity, and Darwin really could not thank him enough. 'Formerly I used to have two places, Maer & Woodhouse, about which, like a wheel on a pivot I used to revolve,' he enthused to him. 'Now I am luckier in having a third.'[4]

One of these places remained to be visited, his last port of call before returning to Cambridge. He could hardly wait to reach Woodhouse, with its beds of strawberries and the ones upstairs, as the girls teased, on 'Paradise Row.' It was 'a paradise,' he confided to Fox, 'about which, like any good Mussulman I am always thinking' – full of sensuous pleasures and voluptuous nymphs. Only here, he added, 'the black-eyed Houris . . . do not merely exist in Mahomets noddle, but are real substantial flesh & blood.'

All summer his imagination had run riot. Back in Squire Owen's forest, Fanny was 'as charming as ever.' They galloped through the woods again, played at billiards, and frolicked. It was a week lived to the full. After he left, Fanny chased him with a letter dated 'Paradise Row ½ past 12 – Saturday night.' She laced it with innuendo, complaining in her coquettish way that she now had '*nobody* to *ride with*' or to give her billiard lessons. 'I . . . shall forget all my *fine strokes*,' she purred. But her memories remained fresh. His gifts made sure of that – the books, and the swallow-tail butterfly, which she found so '*werry pecoolier*.' Nor did Charles lack for gratifying thoughts. As he rode back to Cambridge he carried a keepsake of his own, a handsome snuff box for his new habit, compliments of the Squire.[5] The outlook for romance was good.

Christ's College was now his home. It wasn't one of the older colleges, having existed for only three centuries, nor was it among the largest, with only a hundred-odd resident members. It was altogether middle-of-the-road: rather quiet, somewhat given to 'horsiness,' with a fairly high proportion of noblemen to pensioners, which made it a congenial place for men with spending money. The religious atmosphere was self-contented and relaxed, in keeping with tradition. John Milton, the poet, had been a student here; Ralph Cudworth and Henry More, the latitudinarian theologians, Master and Fellow respectively. In the elegant stone-cased front court of the college, on the south side, up G staircase to the first floor, were the rooms traditionally inhabited by the theologian best known to students for his pellucid, passionless prose, the author of their set texts, *The Evidences of Christianity* and *The Principles of Moral and Political Philosophy*, the Revd William Paley.[6] On All Saints' Day 1828, with the arrival of a new tenant in Paley's rooms, the nameplate on the door read 'C. Darwin.'

Charles was three weeks late and wasted no time settling in. He unpacked his brand-new, £20 double-barrelled shotgun – a parting gift requisitioned from his father and sisters – and dozens of boxes of beetles. A veteran Shropshire collector, the Revd Frederick Hope, had looked over the lot before Charles left home and pronounced it the richest annual haul he had seen in years. Charles was longing to tell his cousin, and when they met up at last the talk was all of trophies. This was Fox's last term before sitting the BA examination. He had been dilatory about his studies and now it was a case of cram or fail. The two of them breakfasted together daily and as the weeks passed Darwin saw his cousin grow desperate. Just before Christmas, he found Fox sitting forlornly in his rooms, wind howling at the windows, in 'awe and tribulation about his degree.' He would have to stay in college for the holidays, studying alone, but – generous as ever – he gave Charles an exotic present for the Doctor, a pair of live Death's Head hawk moths that squeaked like mice when stroked.

Charles forgot to say goodbye. Back in Shrewsbury he posted an apology, pitying his cousin's dismal state 'from the bottom of my heart.' Then in the new year he went to Fanny's mansion for a week. There was real shooting this time, and one of the Owen boys was gashed in the eye by a percussion cap. Charles had never been 'half so much frightened' at the sight of blood, even though this was an accident, and not his old bogey, surgery. When he returned home from his kissing and hunting trip he had a worrying lesion of his own, inflamed lips. They became so dreadfully painful that he began taking 'small doses' of arsenic for relief. That month he had planned to visit Edinburgh once more, 'before all my friends entirely leave.' But while Coldstream, now recovered from his breakdown, expected his arrival daily, geeing him along with news that 'the *Plinian* is flourishing most vigorously' under the same mad doctor William Browne, Darwin was laid up for weeks.[7] The trip was lost. Shortly after his twentieth birthday, his mouth finally healed, and he headed off for London, as a way stage back to Cambridge.

Erasmus had just returned to the 'dreary wilderness of houses' after his Continental tour, and Charles wanted to hear all about

Munich, Milan, and Vienna. Even more, as a man obsessed, he wanted to meet the beetle top brass. There was nowhere better. Insects were all the rage in London, where the experts had recently grouped themselves into an informal Entomological Club, breaking away from the crusty Linnean Society's constraints. His Shropshire friend, the Revd Hope, 'the most generous of Entomologists,'provided his *entrée*. Hope, in town that week, knew all the collectors. Darwin spent a day with him and came away clutching 160 new species. Another among the top brass, almost literally, was the Admiralty man James Stephens, whose *Illustrations of British Entomology* proved so useful. He had 'the best collection of British insects in the country' and kept an open house, welcoming fellow addicts. Darwin found him a 'very goodhumoured pleasant little man.' He picked up the tittle-tattle, hearing Stephens and Hope run down the Revd Jenyns, the senior beetle collector in Cambridge, as 'selfish & illiberal' (such was honour among insect men). With experts confiding in him and enriching his collection, Darwin felt his stature rising. He ordered a new £15 drawered cabinet to house his specimens in splendour, as Stephens did. And he boasted that 'only Stephens & Hope' also possessed the rare 'Diaporis Anea' (a round, broad-headed beetle, *Diaperis*), which he had taken in Shropshire over the holiday.

With Erasmus as his guide, Charles launched out and made the rounds of scientific London: 'the Royal Institution, Linnean society, & Zoological gardens, & many other places where Naturalists are gregarious.' Five days of this was the biggest 'dose of "the Science"' yet. Eras knew the tawdry venues too, places where animals were gregarious, like Cross's Menagerie, with its huge mandrill that 'indulged in a pipe & a glass of grog daily at one o'clock.' Already he had seen this massive monkey with a Union-Jack complexion nearly wrench the arm off a man who, supposing with Lamarck that it might be a distant relative, tried to shake its hand. Lamarck's notions of human ancestry were familiar enough to the Darwin brothers, but this was taking credulity too far. They behaved themselves respectfully, and Charles even planned to drop in on his old Lamarckian rambling companion, Robert Grant, now delivering his first course at London University. Then it was straight back to Christ's College and more sacred topics. He boarded the Cambridge coach at the George and Blue Boar in Holborn.

Back in college, the weather was miserable – 'rain, sleet & cold winds, alternating' – and Charles's mood matched. It was such a letdown after Woodhouse and London; so empty, dreary, and sad. Fox had scraped through his exam with an undistinguished pass and left the university. He was casting about for a curacy near Osmaston, though with such little success that a bishop was pulling strings. Darwin felt keenly for his cousin, but even more for himself.[8] He was at a loose end and missed Fox badly.

He was losing direction again, as at Edinburgh. His aimlessness was made worse by seeing his brother gallivanting about on the family fortune. Nor was Fox around to snap him into shape and talk him into holy orders. The first inkling of the problem had come during the reading party the previous summer. In a freewheeling conversation, Darwin had asked Herbert whether he really felt 'inwardly moved by the Holy Spirit' to enter the Church. When the bishop put the question to him in the ordination service, what would he reply? 'No,' answered Herbert; he could not say that he felt moved. Darwin chimed in, 'Neither can I, and therefore I cannot take orders.' He had doubts, as many did, but then he was in Wales, talking off the record. His verdict was rigorous rather than serious. He laughed off their true confessions by baiting Herbert for unbelief, dubbing him 'Cherbury' after Herbert of Cherbury, the father of English Deism.[9]

Come Lent term 1829, Darwin had real qualms. He might not have been moved by the Holy Spirit, but he hadn't been moved by his studies either. He was now a year into his degree, and his tutor warned him that he was ill prepared to attempt even the preliminary exam, the so-called 'Little Go.' He was running into trouble and seemed helpless to make amends. He marvelled at those getting on with their careers, especially Fox; his cousin still had no parish in sight, but at least he was poring over divinity books for his ordination exam. Charles begged him for advice on the subject, desperate for encouragement: 'You need not be afraid of preaching to me prematurely,' he pleaded. He latched on to others. 'Old Price,' the Darwins' Shrewsbury schoolmate, was tutoring in Cambridge and 'reading very hard' for his own ordination. Charles stuck to him so closely that it seemed to Price like 'hero worship.' One day, as they walked to the Cherry Hinton quarries south of town, Price stopped, pointed out some common plants, and proceeded to identify them. Darwin was astounded. 'Price Price,' he exclaimed, 'what w^d. I give to be such a naturalist as you'![10]

Despite this sentiment, a sort of 'scientific seediness' was setting in. Even his enthusiasm for insects was waning. He was 'sadly in want of somebody to entomologize with' and the two locals he employed to catch beetles were letting him down. In fact, one was offering first pick to a fellow collector, Charles ('Beetles') Babington, a future botany professor, who presumably paid more. Charles caught him in the act and had it out, threatening to throw the 'd - - d rascal' down the stairs if ever he came to his rooms again.

Fox's support seemed to be failing too. Charles grew exasperated. Weeks went by without an answer to his letters. 'You idle wretch,' he finally exploded on April Fools' Day, why do you not 'treat me like a gentleman'? 'If you did but know how often I think of you & how often I regret your absence, I am sure I should have heard from you long enough ago.' Charles topped it with more complaints and manipulation. Cambridge was 'rather stupid;' his lips were playing up; there was 'scarcely any one' to walk with but Whitley – and he, Charles jabbed, 'has begun to take your place.' Even the dog had to go. Sappho, the last living reminder of their beetling days together, was given away.[11]

Self-obsessed and self-pitying, Darwin was in the doldrums. Maybe Erasmus had noticed the first signs of it while they were together in London. Maybe he had warned Charles about the dangers of mid-course *ennui* – drifting into shallow company, brushing with the law, wrecking his career, and angering the Doctor. Whatever was said, Charles took it ill, and he fell out with Eras too. Now he could no more summon the courage to write to his 'injured brother' than Fox seemed able to communicate with him. It was a distressing time.

He was lonely but not alone. He laughed and sluiced his sorrows away with a crowd of drinking pals. His angry letter to Fox – soon regretted – was written while under the influence. Nor was this his first such 'debauch.' Herbert and Whitley had been 'giving some very gay parties,' with up to sixty men at each binge. They smoked and joked and gambled, and enjoyed plenty of lubrication. On the mornings after, Darwin sobered up by reading Gibbon's *Decline and Fall of the Roman Empire*, the perfect tonic for an overindulgent ordinand. It became a regular habit. He put in some hard riding too. One night the eastern sky was lit up, and he set out with three others to investigate. The blaze turned out to be eleven miles away, and they 'rode like incarnate devils' there and back. It was two in the morning and pitch black before he crept into college, violating curfew. Rustication, as he knew, was now an ace away.[12]

Others were more openly tempting the police, if not Providence. Events came to a head at the end of term in an ugly street scene, just a few hundred yards from Darwin's college. If he didn't rush from his rooms on hearing the tumult, he soon received firsthand reports.

For months resentment had been building up against the Proctors, the Revds Alexander Wale and Henry Melville. Wale, Sedgwick's successor, was zealous in his job, and Spinning House committals were his *forte*, which no doubt helped charge the air. On the morning of 9 April the storm broke. Students thronged the galleries of the Senate House, where the Proctors were marshalling undergraduates for their exams. They bellowed, 'Groans for Melville,' 'Groans for Wale,' following each with an appropriate noise. Melville cleared the galleries and marched outside with Wale to disperse the crowds, hissing and jeering in the rain. When the students spotted Wale, the real abuse began – 'Burke him!' some cried, and others, 'Stinking fish!' The Proctors retreated inside the Senate House and re-emerged fifteen minutes later only to find a well-armed mob. They bolted down Trinity Street and made for the safety of Wale's college, St John's. The mob gave chase, shouting insults and hurling turnips, dung, and dead rats. At the college gates the students tried to force their way in, but the Proctors escaped. The uproar lasted for two and a half hours.

Darwin, on the students' side, wrote to Fox the next day exulting in the scene. (Wale was Fox's friend, so Charles trod gingerly, but still he could not conceal his sympathies.) The Senior Proctor had been 'most gloriously hissed,' he reported, '& pelted with mud.' He was 'driven so furious' that even his servant 'dared not go near him for an hour.' Little did Darwin realize that revenge was already being wreaked on those, like himself, who abetted Wale's humiliation. Wale and Melville had glimpsed familiar faces in the crowd, and the culprits were summoned before the Vice-Chancellor, who was passing sentence even as Darwin wrote. For being out-of-gown and shouting abuse, four were rusticated and one was fined and admonished publicly before the Senate.[13]

By the next day Darwin and everyone else knew about the sentences. Outraged by what they considered leniency, the Proctors and Proproctors had quit *en masse*. They printed their resignation note and posted it around the colleges. The university had made examples of a few, but the students had won the victory and rid themselves of the hated Proctors. For Darwin's part, he was jolted into reflecting on the consequences of law-breaking. Other events too brought him up with a start. After weeks of abusing Fox for not writing, he opened a note from his cousin, only to learn, to his shame and sorrow, that Fox's sister was dying. And he had been selfishly pestering the man for a supportive letter. He was thrown into a sombre reassessment of his whole conduct.

That same Saturday, 11 April, another moral lesson was being taught, this time to everyone in Cambridge: a young man was being led to his death on Castle Hill. Here, in the County Gaol, men accused of capital offences – some two hundred crimes carried the death penalty in 1829 – awaited trial in the Shire Hall, above the butchers' stalls in the market-place. The guilty had their sentences carried out on Castle Hill as an example to the community. Public hanging was the ultimate deterrent in this world, just as hell-fire was in the next. The fear of the law and the fear of the Lord were all of a piece in Cambridge.

As Darwin shuddered at Fox's news, a noose was tightening. The execution had been well publicized. In an open letter, an evangelical clergyman had invited the whole county to attend and offer prayers 'for the unfortunate Culprit, that repentance and faith and so forgiveness may be granted him.' For 'highway robbery' a few miles west of town, William Osborne was hanged on the gallows.[14]

By now Charles had frittered away his entire allowance, leaving tutors' bills unpaid. Still, he sallied out with Whitley to London for the first part of the Easter break, and presumably made his peace with Eras. On returning to college, he found a grim note from Catherine in Shrewsbury. Fox's sister was dead. Charles sent his cousin a tortuous condolence. Certain that all sympathy would be useless, he set store by Fox's own 'good principles & religion' and pointed him perfunctorily to the Bible's 'pure & holy . . . comfort.' His tone was formal and detached; he was distancing himself from pain. When Fox, his spirits lifted, replied in May with an invitation to visit Osmaston, Charles sent him his itinerary for the coming months. They could not possibly see each other before September, Darwin insisted.

His devil-may-care lifestyle continued, despite recent salutary events:

> I have been in such a perfect & absolute state of idleness,
> that it is enough to paralyze all ones faculties; riding &
> walking in the morning, gambling at Van John to the most
> disgusting extent in the evenings, compose the elegant &
> instructive routine of my life. Lord help me . . .

The 'less that is said about it, the better,' he told Fox. 'What a great deal of advice I should receive were you but here.' Not that he would have paid any attention to Fox's reprimands, being too busy 'riding & Entomologizing.' 'Preaching' about divinity was the last thing he

69

wanted; a parish was the farthest from his mind.[15] The future would take care of itself.

May saw Professor Henslow's first 'public herborizing excursion' of the year, on which students collected plants. The Revd Jenyns addressed the Cambridge Philosophical Society on the divine design of feathers. On Tuesday the 19th a pair of undergraduates ascended in a balloon with the renowned aeronaut Mr Green. Lift-off was at 6.30 a.m. from a yard in Barnwell; scores of students assembled to cheer them on, and the balloon sailed forty miles west, all the way to Castle Ashby in Northamptonshire. Darwin meanwhile was making air raids on insects. With the late spring, the netting competition was fierce. He had locals scouring pond and fen for him again, and his own success with water beetles was spectacular. 'I think I beat Jenyns' on this score, he bragged to Fox on the eve of the balloon ascent.[16]

It was a jolly, good-natured time – the calm shortly to be shattered by an outrage against the staid Anglican order. Easter term was to end in criminal convulsions, as Lent had. Again Darwin was in the thick of things, watching society take revenge. But this time the lesson to be learned was even more memorable.

On Thursday the 21st, the veteran radicals Richard Carlile and the Revd Robert Taylor tramped into Cambridge. They were notorious freethinkers, their reputations preceding them: proselytizers whipping up anti-Christian passions among the rabble. Carlile was a cobbler's son and a former tinplateman by trade. He had made his name as a fiery republican journalist and been given a six-year gaol sentence for blasphemous and seditious libel in the wake of the 1819 Peterloo Massacre (when innocent civilian demonstrators were cut down by cavalry). Taylor, his comrade-in-arms since his release, had himself just served a year for blasphemy. Blasphemy was a social crime because Christianity was part of the law of the land. By loosening the faith of 'illiterate' workers (as the Attorney General confirmed), Carlile and Taylor were lessening their ability 'to bear up against the pressure of misery and misfortune.' These demagogues, spokesmen for the secular working classes, were the bane of respectable society – clerical Cambridge not least.

In town, Taylor took the lead. He was another who had given up medicine for the Church, and he knew the university well, having been at St John's for three years. The Revd Simeon had even gained him his first curacy. But five years after ordination Taylor gave up Christianity, and his evangelical ebullience turned into eccentric anti-clericalism. He set up a Christian Evidence Society and began lecturing in London pubs. Wearing baroque vestments, he lampooned the

70

Anglican liturgy and lashed out at the barbarities of the Establishment and its pagan creed. The law caught up with him; he was gaoled and in his cell wrote *The Diegesis*, a biting attack on Christianity based on comparative mythology.[17]

Now, with his book hot off the press and Carlile by his side, Taylor was courting more trouble with an 'infidel home missionary tour.' That Thursday they sauntered around the colleges and sized up the opposition, bracing themselves in the evening with a hell-fire sermon from the Revd Simeon at Holy Trinity Church ('one of the worst imaginable for the morals of mankind,' they sneered). The next morning they set up their 'Infidel Head-Quarters' just off the market-place, in a lodging above a print shop in Rose Crescent. This was the heart of enemy territory, a stone's throw from the Senate House and two blocks from Christ's College. It was a shop that Darwin knew, having acquired a taste for engravings.[18] The unsuspecting landlord, William Smith, booked his guests in for a fortnight.

Four days of moral mayhem followed. By noon on Friday Taylor and Carlile had sent a printed challenge to the Vice-Chancellor, the leading Doctors of Divinity, the heads of all the colleges, and the Revd Simeon.

CIRCULAR

The Rev. Robert Taylor, A.B., of Carey-street, Lincoln's Inn, and Mr. Richard Carlile, of Fleet-street, London, present their compliments as Infidel missionaries, to (*as it may be*) and most respectfully and earnestly invite discussion on the merits of the Christian religion, which they argumentatively challenge, in the confidence of their competence to prove, that such a person as Jesus Christ, alleged to have been of Nazareth, never existed; and that the Christian religion had no such origin as has been pretended; neither is it in any way beneficial to mankind; but that it is nothing more than an emanation from the ancient Pagan religion. The researches of the Rev. Robert Taylor, on the subject, are embodied in his newly-published work, THE DIEGESIS, in which may be found the routine of their argument.

They also impugn the honesty of a continued preaching, while discussion is challenged on the whole of the merits of the Christian religion.

Here was a calculated attack on the faith 'by law established,' an outrageous ploy to rend the social fabric and raze feudal Cambridge. As a further affront, the missionaries made a mockery of etiquette, adding a postscript: 'At home, for conversation, at any appointed time. 7, Rose Crescent.'[19]

The divines went into a holy huddle late on Friday, plotting their revenge. The infidels meanwhile continued their rakish progress around town. Taylor, immaculately clad in cap and gown, paced through the sacred precincts greeting old friends, searching for freethinkers, and handing out circulars. Collegians might rattle off rote answers to his challenge – they had learned their Anglican apologetics, as Darwin had, from the likes of the Revd Sumner – but none had ever received a challenge personally, from a Cambridge-educated ex-convict, an infidel in academic robes. That fine evening the colleges were eerily silent.[20] The temperature began to rise.

Saturday brought the backlash, though not the kind Taylor and Carlile had expected. A promised article in the morning paper, advertising their mission, failed to appear. Then one of the new Proctors turned up to interrogate the landlord, Mr Smith. Soon after, another came and demanded his lodging-house licence. Smith refused to hand it over and appealed to the Vice-Chancellor, begging 'most deferentially' to know the reason. He had not violated the lodging-house regulations. Indeed, his licence had only been granted its annual renewal the day before. No reply came. Instead, that afternoon a notice was issued by the Vice-Chancellor and Proctors, officially revoking his licence. It was posted in the butteries of all the colleges, a warning to Darwin and his friends lest they fall foul of the law themselves. The lodgings at 7 Rose Crescent were now off bounds.[21]

Taylor and Carlile, infuriated by this 'paltry spite,' struck back. They posted their own notice on Sunday. It went up on the door of the University Library, next to the Senate House, in public view. Written in Latin and Greek, it carried their challenge to the university at large – a university that 'punishes the innocent,' 'crushes the weak,' 'oppresses,' and 'persecutes.' Smith, with a wife and six children, had been deprived of half his livelihood at the stroke of a clerical quill. By the next day everyone was talking about the 'iniquity' of his fate and the brash infidel challenge. It was an object lesson on the perils of religious inadvertence. Even Smith's plea for mercy fell on deaf ears.

But who was to blame? The authorities were not universally adored, yet Taylor himself could still be held responsible for the outrage, and a gang of 'young men' prepared to avenge the hapless landlord. A turncoat clergyman deserved ducking in the Cam for cloaking himself in academic attire and deceiving the tradesman about his true identity. It was dishonourable conduct, unbecoming of a gentleman. Only Proctors went incognito.

On Tuesday, when Taylor and Carlile got wind of the vigilantes, they apologized to Smith, prodded the Vice-Chancellor again to restore his licence, and slipped out of town. Not wholly empty-handed: they had uncovered 'about fifty . . . young collegians, who were somewhat bold in avowing Infidelity among each other' – even an Apostle or two perhaps. But only a handful of the students, the diehards knew, would ever 'break . . . the shackles' of a Cambridge education and become out-and-out unbelievers. And they would have 'a most painful conflict to endure.'[22]

One such was Darwin. In later years he would remember Taylor as 'the Devil's Chaplain,' fearing that he himself might be similarly reviled, an outcast from respectable society, a terror to the innocent, an infidel in disguise. But for now he was safe – and ready to mend his ways.

6

The Man Who Walks With Henslow

THE CHURCH OF ENGLAND was under more serious attack than this. While Darwin had been at Cambridge, Parliament had passed bills allowing Dissenters and Catholics to hold public office for the first time in centuries. The Anglican ascendancy had been snapped, aristocratic nepotism was on the wane, and a vast liberal tide was gathering to break down the ancient walls of privilege. Even in Cambridge, cracks had appeared during Darwin's dissipations. Town and gown fought against the new freedoms, but in June 1829, after a bitter election, the 21-year-old William Cavendish – later the Duke of Devonshire – was returned for the university as Whig MP. At Oxford meanwhile, where Darwin was invited to watch the first annual boat race between the sister universities, the clergy kicked out their Tory member Robert Peel as a traitor for supporting Catholic emancipation. The boat race went easily to Oxford, a token perhaps that reform would remain an uphill struggle.[1]

Back in Shrewsbury for the summer, Charles sobered up. He had heard the warning bells as the university cracked down on moral turpitude and social deviance. He had seen the innocent suffer. Even wide-eyed beetle collectors were reminded of the shaky foundations of their leisured lifestyle. The Revd Taylor reminded the gentry, on their affluent islands, that they risked being engulfed by the ocean of miserable poor. Atheism, republicanism, and revolution swirled together in fierce working-class eddies, eroding the Establishment's defences, threatening its privileges. Freethought, as a political creed, sent a double shudder down the clerical spine. Away from the hurly-burly, Charles had time to ponder it all – more than he wanted, in fact.

He found himself laid up. He had been entomologizing with the

Revd Hope in North Wales in mid-June, when his lips became inflamed again, and he headed for home 'with grief & sorrow' to be tended by the Doctor and his sisters. Hope sent some stunning click beetles to cheer him up – 'bright scarlet' Elaters – but with his own mouth red and sore, it seemed like a bad joke. Charles cried on Fox's shoulder, contrasting his own paltry catches. He felt 'dreadfully stupid' kicking around The Mount, constantly reminded of life's duties. Nor had his tutor's parting advice made him feel any better: the preliminary exam for his degree next year – the 'Little Go' – would be tougher than ever.

Recovery took a fortnight, and Charles emerged a new man. These weeks would be the last of his 'perfectly idle & wandering life,' and he intended to make the most of them, 'taking care to have as little of home & as much of Woodhouse as possible.' Come term-time, all would change. 'I must read for my little Go,' he resolved, for there is 'the very devil to pay amongst all idle men & Entomologists.'[2]

So for the summer Charles cantered around Shropshire and Staffordshire, with a week out for abortive beetling at Barmouth. In Shrewsbury he stood godfather to infant nephews, the younger sons of sister Marianne and Henry Parker. At Maer he stalked insects and shot grouse. And in between, he went back time and again to Woodhouse for the wild life in Squire Owen's forest. Letters from 'la belle Fanny' had thinned out, but still he adored her. They had other ways of communicating, in summers at least. He saw her once more just before the hunting season, after which he hastened to visit Fox.[3]

Months had passed since the cousins last clasped hands. Charles had tidied up Fox's affairs in Cambridge, shipped his belongings back, captured scores of beetles for him, and generally returned many favours. Old failings were forgotten; the future hailed them both. But Fox, preparing for the Church, was clearly lagging in 'the science.' Charles was raring to go, spurred on by seeing his name in print – a capturing credit in an instalment of Stephens's *Illustrations of British Entomology*. Now no one would surpass him, not even Leonard Jenyns in Cambridge. He had Fox down on his knees like a penitent, determined to 'redeem your character in Entomology,' he quipped. They scooped up scores of insects, and Darwin catechized his cousin on the magnificent 'Fungiverous' species.[4] Their roles had reversed. Charles was now in charge.

It was only a short visit, but Charles expected Fox soon in Cambridge, where they would be 'very snug . . . together once more.' He had to hurry back to Shrewsbury to see Erasmus. His brother was giving up medicine. The Doctor considered that his 'delicate frame' could not withstand a career 'involving, if successful, a severe strain upon body & mind,' and so was pensioning him off. Eras was, quite naturally, 'very agreeable' to retirement at the age of twenty-five. He planned to settle in London, with 'an air-cushion in his rooms' to put Charles up overnight. This seemed satisfactory all round, and the brothers celebrated at the Birmingham Music Festival in early October, taking in several concerts and operatic performances by Giuseppe de Begnis and the enchanting young soprano Maria Malibran. Charles lodged near his Wedgwood cousins and 'lived entirely with them.' All told, it was the 'most glorious' cultural experience. And between the arias he managed to acquire fifteen shillings' worth of insects from a buff in town. Finally, he returned to Cambridge, anxious to be back at the beginning of term.[5]

Michaelmas was full of distractions, but Charles's resolve held. He attended tutorials and burrowed into classical texts for his Little Go. It was dry, demeaning work. Erasmus visited for a spell, and their fine arts education continued at the Fitzwilliam Museum. Charles even squeezed in a few days' hunting. But on the last one his horse had 'two such aweful [sic] rolls as nearly knocked my lungs out,' and he called a halt to it. Otherwise he kept upright in all things: he abandoned his old carousing companions and sought out a superior class. From the time of Fox's leaving, he had slighted the clerical naturalists and their genial mentor the Revd Henslow. Although he had signed up for Henslow's botany lectures in the spring, he did not so much as mention the fact to Fox, who had introduced him to the professor. Now everything was different. He became a fixture at Professor Henslow's Friday night parties and moved with a new set.

One was the Revd Jenyns, of ill repute in the beetling fraternity. The Eton-educated son of a parson-magistrate, the squire of Bottisham near Cambridge, he sprang from the old order. His father had set him up in the parish of Swaffham Bulbeck, near the family estate. Here as vicar, Jenyns 'resolved never to have anything to do with' worldly pursuits, unlike his father. Instead he spent his spare time enlarging his boyhood horde of insects. A thirty-year-old bachelor, he was retiring and austere, with a scientific mien to match: methodical in manner, fastidious about facts, and thoroughly orthodox. He kept a 'naturalist's calendar' like his hero, the Revd Gilbert White, and suffered from frequent 'sick headaches,' which further reduced his social profile. Friends pressed him to stand for a 'zoological Professorship,' but to no avail. One Friday night, however, Darwin managed a coup. He persuaded the dour young fogey to drop by

Christ's College and inspect his beetles. Although Jenyns said little about the collection, he was grateful to receive 'a good many insects' from his admirer. Maybe, thought Darwin, the man was not as bad as his 'grim and sarcastic expression' suggested.[6]

That term Fox never visited and Fanny never wrote. Charles bore their neglect with fortitude. He was becoming his own man. Active beetle collectors took precedence for him now, and big brothers. At Christmas he slept on Eras's air-bed for three weeks and did as he pleased. London turned out to be more enjoyable than he had expected, which meant quiet. He raced through Samuel Richardson's blockbuster *Clarissa*, all but finishing the seven-volume saga of ruined courtship. He considered headier matters over dinner with Sir James Mackintosh, who was still struck with him. Mackintosh pitched into phrenology, which Charles had encountered at Edinburgh. He explained that if education can alter the faculties of the brain – the compartments dealing with love, hate, reason and so on – then these faculties are not innate, so the shape of the head cannot reflect them. Charles had to agree. His faint belief in cranial bumps was 'battered down.' He went back to a sounder science, entomology. Hope was in town after Christmas to talk to, and Stephens gave up a couple of evenings to tutor his varsity friend. Darwin was introduced to a young architect, George Waterhouse, a budding collector with some brilliant captures. Waterhouse favoured him with a box of 'most glorious insects.'[7] It would not be forgotten.

Back in Cambridge on New Year's Day, a fortnight before term started, Darwin repaid Jenyns's visit. He rode out to Swaffham Bulbeck and found the vicar comfortable, snug, and smug. Darwin gave him 'an awesome lot of insects,' hoping in return for Jenyns's duplicate specimens from the fens. All he received were a couple of good beetles and '2 or 3 more common ones.' Jenyns lacked Waterhouse's generosity and it rankled. Darwin snidely noted that his own water beetles had astonished Jenyns's 'weak mind,' and he determined to work even harder to outshine him – once he had passed his Little Go.

By now the second-year men were 'all in a dreadful plight, from fear & anxiety,' with only two months left before their ordeal. They had known for almost a year what they would be examined on: prescribed texts in Latin and Greek to translate and construe; portions from the Gospels or the Book of Acts; and ten questions on Paley's *Evidences of Christianity*. They had to acquit themselves in a single day: three hours in the morning on the classics, and three in the afternoon on the New Testament and Paley. This is what now made the Little Go so strict. Candidates would be examined orally, each being called on to speak in turn. It was to be a public performance under pressure, with no scope for prevarication. 'First class' men would gain full credit; those in the 'second class' would have to try again next year.[8]

Charles force-fed himself on the ancient languages, wishing merely to pass. What really whetted his appetite was Paley. His *Evidences* was like Sumner's (which he had read in Shrewsbury), only better. Paley himself, who died in 1805 a rich rector, archdeacon, and Cambridge Doctor of Divinity, was not above suspicion for unorthodoxy, but at least his book remained a touchstone for right belief and conduct.[9] All high-minded Englishmen accepted its premises; every Cambridge ordinand swore by its conclusions. Its cold, clear reasoning proved Christianity, made apologists of young gents, and underpinned the Anglican order.

Paley's 'logic' so delighted Charles that he learnt it by heart. The sheer elegance of the deductions fascinated him: given that God exists, he would obviously reveal himself, and how else but by miracles? Nor can such miracles be dismissed as contrary to experience when there is so much historical evidence. The mere fact that early Christians suffered persecution rather than deny Jesus's miracles makes the New Testament account of the Resurrection compelling. No other miracles have been confirmed in so striking a manner. Therefore the Christian revelation is both true and unique: a 'Jewish peasant' had indeed pointed the way to God.

What difference did it make? By the time Charles finished the *Evidences*, the practical political answer was unforgettable. The Christian revelation, according to Paley, establishes the existence of 'a future state of reward and punishment.' And retribution in the next life is eminently useful for regulating human conduct in this one. Without the threat of eternal torture, men 'want a *motive*' to do their duty, and 'their rules want authority.' Promise them future rewards, on the other hand, and a perennial problem is solved: the unequal and 'promiscuous distribution' of power and wealth. The swilling masses will put up with their hardships and degrading 'stations' once they accept that any injustice will be rectified hereafter. 'This one truth changes the nature of things,' the *Evidences* declared. It 'gives order for confusion: makes the moral world of a piece with the natural.'[10]

To Charles, charmed by the argument, Paley's world was his own. Cambridge conformed to the *Evidences*, worked on the same principles. It was a microcosm where authority was vouchsafed by God, stations in life were assigned, and penalties for misconduct came with sovereign severity, just as rewards for excellence were bountifully bestowed. Here the 'truth of Christianity' depended on facts and he was about to be tested on them. Judgment day for Charles was Wednesday, 24 March 1830, when he entered the exam room. With his future at stake, he felt 'shattered,' tortured by guilty memories of 'idleness.' His inquisitors were strict and asked 'a wonderful number of questions,' but the next day, when the results came out, he let off a whoop: 'I am through my little Go,!!! . . . I am through through through'! Triumphant in his success, he could hardly wait to get back to entomology. 'Heaven protect the beetles & Mr Jenyns'![11]

Fanny was fading from his life. He was sure of it now. After a term's silence, a note from her had finally arrived while he was poring over Paley, but it was maddeningly vague. No reasons, no apology, no encouragement, just a prolix pout. 'Why did you not come home this Xmas?' Fanny demanded. 'I suppose some *dear little Beetles . . .* kept you away.' Her mocking continued. She assumed she would have to catch a strange species herself, 'a **Scrofulum morturorum**' (meaning of course a disease), before he could be 'induced to come down!' This was beyond the pale, coming from someone so devoted to her own hobby, painting, that she couldn't even write a letter! But lest Charles thought she had actually been dying to see him, Fanny resorted to riddles. The holidays had brought 'hard times,' she moaned, leaving her in the red. 'My finances are in a most pitiable state & the *Mortgages* on *my Estate incalculable*.' With creditors pressing, a debtor's prison lay ahead. 'What a **horrid disgusting thing money** is – I hate the name of it – *don't* you,' she ended disingenuously; 'it is fit for *vulgar souls* – not **Beetle** *hunters* – and *Paint brush drivers*!!!'

The message was easy to decode. Charles could read 'love' for 'money' between the lines. The silly girl had overextended her heart. Others had a claim on her affections: suitors ('creditors') besieged her, and wedlock (the 'debtor's prison') loomed. The 'Housemaid' and 'Postillion' were no more, their forest trysts were done. It was just as well that he had not gone home at Christmas. The '*dear little Beetles*' were a safer fancy than a flighty female. At least they were easier to pin down. And with his exam passed, he drowned his sorrow by doing the real thing. The new cabinet he had ordered a year before arrived at last, a 'gay little affair' with shallow drawers for displaying his specimens. He could hardly wait, and spent Easter in college, labelling, mounting, and cataloguing. 'There is not a single inducement for me to leave Cambridge,' he sighed to Fox.[12]

Another reason to stay was Henslow, who had taken a shine to him. Maybe it was the way Darwin 'hung upon' his words each Friday night, or perhaps his constant questioning. Whatever, Henslow was impressed and took him aside. By the end of term they could be seen walking the streets together, deep in conversation. Belatedly, Darwin was discovering how much he had in common with the 'goodnatured & agreeable' professor.[13]

Henslow was the scion of a prosperous professional family. Like Darwin, he had grown up dabbling in chemistry and collecting natural objects. His father had packed him off to Cambridge, emphatic on a church career. But science got in the way. As a student he excelled at maths and studied chemistry and mineralogy, while amassing the obligatory collections of shells and insects. Later he helped Sedgwick, his geological tutor, found the Cambridge Philosophical Society, to fire the undergraduates' interest in natural history. He became professor of mineralogy at the young age of twenty-six and married Jenyns's sister a year later. Only then, to augment his modest £100 annual stipend, did he take holy orders and accept the curacy of Little St Mary's Church, a short stroll from the university's Botanic Garden.

The Garden was where he taught now, and strolled with his pupil. Such were the prerogatives of the new Regius Professor of Botany, by appointment of the Crown. The post had come easily and it doubled his teaching income. His predecessor had held the post for sixty-three years, not lectured for thirty, and ceased even to reside in the university. He had neglected the Garden and left its museum in a mess. Under Henslow all this was changing. Plans were afoot to move the dilapidated garden to a prime site outside town and to set up a proper herbarium. Lectures were delivered each Easter term, accompanied by practical sessions. Here students were given plant specimens, which they 'pulled to pieces for themselves.'[14] On herborizing expeditions – now a local rite of spring – they scoured the countryside, gathering as many species as possible.

Charles first glimpsed the glad life of a clerical don on his walks with Henslow this term. He was 'awe-struck' by his mentor's versatility, just as he had been by Grant's on their seaside rambles near Edinburgh. And as the professor paced the fenland paths, he revealed other talents. Botanizing was not the only rite he attended to. He had proctorial duties as well.

In springtime a young man's fancy was easily distracted. Flowers had their charms but other beauties beckoned, and the lanes around town had many a blossom to catch his roving eye. These were the habitats the botanical proctor patrolled. Henslow had been uprooting and replanting females in the Spinning House since the previous term. In April and May, his months of wild herborizing, he was extra-vigilant, committing eight girls in the Easter break alone. He was the ideal law officer, a man of principle, motivated by 'a vigorous and determined will,' yet above 'any paltry feeling' of spite, and always 'cordial, and unpretending.' Or so said 'the man who walks with Henslow,' as the dons dubbed Charles. 'The more I see him the more I like him,' Darwin enthused. 'I have some thought of reading divinity with him the summer after next.'[15]

For now, though, plants held his fancy. Botanizing turned out to be as much fun as beetling, and even more instructive. He threw himself into Henslow's outings, soon proving his superiority over the common-or-garden students. In mid-May they all piled into stage-coaches, clutching nets and boxes, for the fifteen-mile trip to Gamlingay heath, where wild lilies-of-the-valley grew. As soon as they arrived, Darwin excelled himself. He knew it was the breeding season for toads, and that sharp, intermittent trill meant rare natterjacks. He caught a number and passed them round, prompting Henslow to ask whether Mr Darwin intended to 'make a natter-jack pie.' Later that day, Darwin came up with another surprise, anemones never found locally before.

A week later, the naturalists floated down the Cam, their barge bound for Bottisham and the fens. Out in the wet fenlands the party disembarked and poked around. Some men chased swallow-tail butterflies across the treacherous terrain, much to Henslow's amusement. Darwin searched high and low for new plants. Across a muddy dike he spied an insect-eating bladderwort, on Henslow's most-wanted list. Showing off, he tried to reach it using his vaulting pole (one of his old beetling companions had taught him the trick). Taking a mighty lunge, he propelled himself heavenward – but with insufficient thrust. The pole stuck vertically in the ditch, with Darwin clinging to the top. Sheepishly, he slid into the mire, waded to the specimen, and returned to present it to Henslow. That night, when the party dined at a nearby inn, Darwin's bravado was toast of the term. Their annual herborizing had ended in triumph with almost 300 species bagged.[16]

Henslow's botany lectures went on five days a week. Seventy-eight men attended, including the Revds Whewell and Peacock. Darwin was clearly the 'favourite pupil.' He turned up early for the practicals and arranged baskets of plants and dissecting knives on a side-table, where the students could help themselves. And he constantly quizzed the professor. 'What a fellow that D. is for asking questions,' Henslow exclaimed, conscious that his guidance was paying off.[17]

Darwin's precocity served him well. So did his old Edinburgh interest in primitive plant-like animals, or rather the spontaneous motion of their eggs. Under Henslow he now switched his focus to pollen. One day, watching a geranium pollen grain in alcohol under a microscope, he saw 'three transparent cones' emerge from its side. One burst, spraying 'numberless granules' through the liquid with 'great violence.' Not only primitive eggs, but the matter inside seemed to have a self-activating power. He showed Henslow, only to have it explained quite differently. For Henslow the minute granules were indeed the constituent atoms of pollen – perhaps the ultimate stuff of life – but they had no intrinsic vital power. Life was impressed on matter from without; it was an endowment and ultimately derived its power from God. There were no self-activating atoms of life, whatever more 'speculative' naturalists argued.[18] Darwin had heard otherwise from Grant – that matter moved itself – and paused to reflect. He was learning to bide his time before announcing discoveries.

That summer he was expected at 'sweet-home,' as he called it through clenched teeth. Not having seen the Doctor for eight months, he had to give some account of himself, and he was not looking forward to it. For that matter, he hadn't seen Fox either, so why not have him come to The Mount? Shrewsbury was just a couple of coach rides from Osmaston, a day's travel at most. It would be immensely convenient and might cushion the debriefing. And Charles could show off his collection of minuscule, water-side beetles, the Bembidiidae, of which he now had 208 in his new cabinet, two-thirds of the British species. 'Write soon,' he instructed Fox with a wry smile, and 'be sure do not say no to [the] Shrewsbury scheme else I will never forgive you.'

Fox agreed and Charles took heart. 'The sooner you come the better,' he shot back as he packed his bags. Fox turned up at The Mount, but their reunion was spoiled. They had no time to themselves, no peace and quiet. Charles rehearsed the year's events for the Doctor – his Little Go, natural history, Henslow and divinity – but even his up-beat report did little to pacify the household. Everyone was tense. They worried about him, and the Doctor had not been well. Things eventually blew up into 'a row & confusion' that left Charles longing to escape. When Fox had gone, he went off to join Hope and some friends 'entomologizing' in North Wales.

This summer his lips played along. He spent three weeks in August among the hills, beetling on fine days, trout fishing on rainy ones, and generally becoming 'disgusted with Hopes egotism & stupidity.' As clergymen went, Hope kept a decent cabinet, but he was no field naturalist. Darwin sensed his growing superiority. With Professor Henslow as his model, he was set to become a different sort of priest, unlike Hope or Jenyns, or even Fox. His devotion to natural history would be rounded and complete. Holy orders need not detain him; a country parish might well be opportune. He began to relish the prospect again. From Barmouth he wrote to ask Fox what he was reading for his ordination exam. Then he headed off for Maer where a Wedgwood was the vicar, keen to start the partridge season with a bang and – this year for once – without 'even the least dread of the *Parish*.'[19]

The shooting was poor, but he made up for it by killing beetles and ogling cousin Charlotte, twelve years his senior. He returned home in high spirits on 10 September to be startled by a letter from Fanny. It was written 'by Papa's desire.' The stern Squire had been 'rather expecting' him to 'slay some of his Partridges' as usual; now he wanted to see him for a man-to-man talk, and within a week. Charles half-guessed and, riding over, braced himself for the worst. Sure enough, it was just a formality. He was among the first to know – not surprisingly, given the Squire's soft spot and expectations for Charles. Fanny was to be engaged. Her intended was John Hill, a clergyman, the brother of the local Tory MP. He had been with her at Brighton the winter before last, *that* winter when Charles was cloistered in Cambridge with his suspicions. Everyone called him 'The Hill.'

Three weeks later Charles was back in college. He had grumpily trampled over hill after hill getting there on his huge new horse – '16 hands & one inch' – and 'the poor beast was so tired that he hardly knew whether he stood on his heels or his head.' 'I am positively in love with him,' Charles crooned. 'Beetles, partridges & everything else, are as nothing to me.' Not even Fanny. She had rushed a letter to Shrewsbury before he left, enclosing a portrait of him that she had drawn. She promised *really and truly* to do a better one 'when you *next* honor the Forest with y^r presence.' Wasn't that typical, playing on the emotions? But then, as she admitted, she would never learn to 'write "like a lady".'[20] No, Fanny Owen was history now. Horses were more dependable.

7

Every Man For Himself

IN THE COUNTRY political events were moving fast. England stood aghast as Paris tumbled once more towards revolution. In July 1830, the reactionary French monarch Charles X had abolished the government. Republican workers and students took to the barricades; the stock market collapsed, a *tricolore* flag fluttered atop Notre Dame. Soldiers mutinied; the Louvre was stormed, the Tuileries sacked, and a republic was declared. A week later the King fled to England, arriving as Darwin was beetling in Wales. The middle classes now held sway in France, with Louis Philippe, the 'citizen king,' on the throne.

Priests had lost power too, and Catholicism ceased to be the French state religion. With the Tory government sheltering the deposed monarch at home, Whig reformers made political capital, warning of an English 'July Revolution' if Parliament were not reformed and democracy extended. In the autumn, when Charles was back in college, the Duke of Wellington, the hardline Tory prime minister, dug his heels in and the stock market shuddered. Street radicals bellowed their rage, demanding fair wages, union power, and suffrage – and the ruination of rich English parsons. The republican atheists massed in The Rotunda, a ramshackle building on the south bank of the Thames recently reopened by Richard Carlile.

Here Carlile installed his fellow infidel missionary Robert Taylor, and the apostate priest performed in The Rotunda's auditorium several times a week. Wearing rakish canonicals, he staged infidel melodramas and preached bombastic sermons before artisan audiences. In two outrageous Sunday discourses on 'The Devil!' he pronounced 'God and the Devil . . . to be but one and the self-same

84

being ... Hell and Hell-fire ... are, in the original, nothing more than names and titles of the Supreme God.' For this he was dubbed 'the Devil's Chaplain' – the label that stuck in Darwin's mind for life – and his sermons circulated by the thousand in a disreputable rag, *The Devil's Pulpit*. In November, when Wellington's ministry collapsed, Taylor was in his pulpit railing against the Establishment while above him, on the roof, a tricolour snapped smartly in the breeze.[1]

Anglican priests looked nervously about them. With the growing political uncertainty, many continued to see the Tories as the best defenders of Church and Crown. In Cambridge, once noted for its reformist tendencies, the dons moved decisively to the right. Out-and-out Whigs had to watch their step, even those caught in the feverish preparation for final exams.

By this time Darwin was reading in earnest, 'desperate' about his own ordeal, only two months away. Beetles were dropped and only Friday nights were left free for Henslow's parties. Nothing would induce him to miss them, and he sometimes came early to join the family for dinner. Mrs Henslow struck him as 'devilish odd' (he wasn't to know that she was pregnant for the first time). Henslow he loved. He was 'quite the most perfect man I ever met with.' They had grown steadily closer, and his walking companion was now his private tutor. Henslow's subjects were maths and theology, which was just as well for Darwin. He relished their tutorial hour together as 'the pleasantest in the whole day.'[2]

Word had it that Henslow held 'some curious religious opinions' but Darwin could find no evidence. On the contrary, their discussion of Paley's *Principles of Moral and Political Philosophy* alone must have placed his orthodoxy beyond doubt. The book had to be mastered for the exam, and unlike the *Evidences* – on which there would also be questions – it now served Cambridge more as a foil than an infallible guide. Old and outdated – published in 1785 – it was a worn-out piece of academic furniture, an heirloom to dusty traditionalists, but a piece of dilapidated junk to others. Liberal Apostles and evangelical Sims deplored it; dons like Sedgwick and Whewell wrote it off.[3] It was unspiritual and dangerous, they said.

Even Darwin, none too earnest about religion, would have realized this as he began his political education under Henslow. Paley's ideas belonged to a bygone era when Christianity was the faith of reasonable men, and reasonable men ruled the world. Then the Church sat comfortably, free to contemplate changes it knew would never come about. Paley saw the arguments for democracy but opposed them; he acknowledged that Parliament failed to represent the nation but upheld its gross inequities; he recognized defects in the administration of justice but defended a brutal criminal code. Always, he based his notions of right and wrong on purely natural reasoning, confident that all men could be brought to agree.

Thus, Darwin discovered, Paley saw no supernatural sanction for the sovereign or the State. Simple 'expediency' was his rule. One had a duty to obey the government *only* so long as it 'cannot be resisted or changed without public inconveniency.' Resistance might be justified, Paley allowed in his cosy way, if grievances become so great and the call to redress them so strong that the danger and expense to society is outweighed. And who, he asked calmly, shall make this judgment? 'We answer, "Every man for himself".'

Daring words in 1830. Nor was this Paley's only political heresy. Darwin learned that he saw nothing sacrosanct about an Established Church either. It formed 'no part of Christianity,' he declared in a notorious chapter, but was only a means of instilling the faith. Its authority lay 'in its utility,' as indeed did subscription to 'articles of religion.' The Thirty-nine Articles of the Church of England set up an exclusion zone, keeping hostile parties from ecclesiastical office. Subscribing to them might serve to maintain 'order and tranquillity,' but in stable 1785 they seemed redundant and Paley thought that they should be abolished. Nor did he think that subscription to the Thirty-nine Articles necessitated an 'actual belief of each and every separate proposition contained in them.'[4]

Here Henslow drew the line: he would have none of Paley's doctrinal laxity. Henslow might have been warming to reform, having just switched parties with the Cambridge MP Lord Palmerston, who joined Earl Grey's new Whig administration. But, he solemnly informed Darwin, he cared so much for the Thirty-nine Articles that 'he should be grieved if a single word . . . was altered.'[5] The Establishment had to remain strong, not least because the times were perilous. With Dissenters clamouring for equality and religious liberty, hasty reforms could bring about the disestablishment of the Church, an eventuality Paley did not seriously entertain. Worse, Paley's views played into the hands of the secular radicals, who saw insurrection as now the simplest expediency. 'Every man,' they cried, must decide 'for himself' whether the authorities should be obeyed.

It was a cry heard across England as Darwin attended tutorials, learning to respect authority. Massive campaigns of civil disobedience gave an eloquent answer. Falling wages and starvation were causing rage and frustration among agricultural labourers. From the Home

Counties to the Midlands and East Anglia, they went on the rampage. Landowners and parsons were threatened with a series of demands; their haystacks were torched, barns gutted, and threshing machines smashed. The uprising reached Cambridgeshire in mid-November.

As Darwin pondered Paley, the arson attacks began in outlying villages to the north. By 2 December the incendiaries had reached Coton, two miles west, and wage-riots had broken out in hamlets to the south and east. Magistrates – many of them clergymen – met in the town on Friday the 3rd and drew up plans to defend the colleges. Rumours flew that the labourers of Cherry Hinton, Bottisham, and other villages were planning to march into Cambridge on market day, if their demands were not met. They would sweep in via Barnwell, itself 'full of bad characters of all descriptions,' and take over the market square. The magistrates feared that it would spark a 'general rising of the people,' and only a show of force could stop it. They appealed for special constables, and 800 merchants, curates, dons, and students flocked to the Town Hall to be sworn in.[6]

The weekend went off without violence, and the colleges escaped attack. Deterrence worked. But then Cambridge was well practised in defending the status quo. By now Darwin realized this better than ever, but one petty incident rammed the point home. Sick of studying, he prevailed on Herbert one day to ride into the fens in search of wildlife. That night they returned exhausted, dined in Darwin's rooms, and fell asleep in lounge chairs. Herbert woke at 3 a.m. and panicked. He was in breach of curfew and feared the worst, knowing that the strict rules were never bent. He was right. The Dean of St John's was implacable. Here was Herbert, a hard-working tutor with a half-dozen pupils, never offended before, but still he was confined to college for the rest of term. Herbert's friends were in 'perfect ferment,' and Darwin's 'indignation' at the 'stupid injustice & tyranny' of the Dean 'knew no bounds.'[7]

Darwin stayed in college for the Christmas holidays, cramming – 'far too much plagued to enjoy any thing,' even a visit from Fox. Now he knew the agony his cousin had endured two years before. The final exam – three days of written papers – was scheduled for the third week in January 1831. When the time came Darwin shuffled once more on to the cold marble floor of the Senate House and sat at the appointed desk. He fretted the whole morning over Homer, and all afternoon over Virgil. But it was a mediocre performance. Next day after breakfast he tackled a dozen questions on Paley's *Evidences of Christianity*, and after lunch polished off the *Moral and Political*

Philosophy and questions on Locke's *Essay concerning Human Understanding*. Here he shone. The last day he dreaded – mathematics. He did well on the Euclidean proofs, making up for his wretched arithmetic and algebra. And the questions in physics – on statics, dynamics, and astronomy – turned out to be manageable, just.

By the end of the week, when the results were posted, he was dazed and proud. He ranked tenth in the pass-list of 178. The BA was his at last! He was also exhausted and unaccountably depressed. 'I do not know why the degree should make one so miserable,' he groaned to Fox.[8]

Still, a celebration was called for, even if he had to drag himself to it. Fortunately friends were on hand to help. Herbert and Whitley had taken their degrees already; Cameron from Shrewsbury was just through his exam. These, with Darwin and four others, had already constituted themselves the 'Glutton Club' for the purpose of dining on 'strange flesh.' The Gluttons were not gourmets, but neither were they gluttonous. Their weekly meals in one another's rooms featured some rare morsel obligingly cooked by the college staff: a bird or beast one of them had procured, which was previously 'unknown to human palate.' But the collective appetite for exotica did not last long: it came to grief one night when they tried to eat an 'old brown owl.' The Gluttons – presided over by Darwin – now resorted to more traditional fare, topped off by Van John and port.[9] Darwin began to relax.

They were a chaste bunch, and mostly old friends. Five of the Gluttons were studying for holy orders, including James Heaviside, a tutor at Sidney Sussex College with decorations in maths. Not all future priests were of this calibre. Henry Matthew was an exception. A country rector's son, he had already been thrown out of Oxford, and survived only a year at Trinity College before sidling off to Sidney Sussex, where Heaviside became his tutor and introduced him to Darwin. Matthew was a fop, a rascal, and a genius. He was elected President of the Union Debating Society that year, but he flouted respectability and refused to fit in. The model varmint, he was poised to self-destruct even before the Proctors could catch up with him.

Darwin saw it all at close quarters. Sidney Sussex was practically next door to Christ's, and he often popped over to Matthew's rooms. He was staggered by the way Matthew could reel off literary quotations, and even tempted perhaps to play the libertine himself. Never mind Matthew's chaffing at science, or his belief that Moses was 'a better authority on mundane cosmogony' than a beetle collector.

Even his gin-swilling could be tolerated – or sometimes shared. No, there was something wildly appealing about the man. Darwin felt himself being sucked into the maelstrom.

Then the truth came out. Matthew was married, and that was not the worst of it. The woman was a wench, and he loved another. He had a bastard child besides, and all by the age of twenty-three. He was in deep trouble and disappeared from town, although no one knew where. Then one day, a fortnight after Darwin's exam, a letter arrived from Matthew. He was hiding in a dingy London garret, struggling to make ends meet by selling his love poems to periodicals. His women plagued him with letters, and he had been summoned to appear before a magistrate 'about my bastard, with one sovereign in my pocket to meet Law expences [sic], arrears, and advance for a quarter.' The next stop, clearly, was gaol. Darwin took pity and sent a 'generous remittance' to spare him further punishment.[10]

Darwin's residence requirement kept him in Cambridge until June. The time was ripe to begin grooming himself for a country parish. Fox had passed his ordination exam at last and taken a curacy near Nottingham. Darwin, foreseeing 'the time . . . when I must suffer,' asked him about the state of his nerves, what divinity he had read and how closely. Other fields opened up with the start of the beetling season. Jenyns was the textbook parson-naturalist, and Darwin had learned to read friendship between the grim lines of his face. He rode out to Swaffham Bulbeck from time to time, and together they forayed into the fens, or sacked Squire Jenyns's woods at Bottisham Hall, capturing beetles for their cabinets. Ordination never came up, so intent were they on this clerical pastime.[11]

But in his mind Darwin roamed further afield, guided by Henslow. They saw each other constantly, at botany lectures, Friday soirées, and field trips. The future became more focused. Darwin had a vision of what he might become. More than anyone, Henslow was the kind of man he yearned to be – a clerical naturalist or professor – the sort that even the Doctor might approve of. Indeed, they were half-living together, which showed that Henslow's livelihood suited him well. 'I do not know, whether I love or respect' him more, Darwin confessed helplessly.[12] Who better to steer his career than one so congenial? Henslow would prepare him for ordination, see him into the Church. His advice would be indispensable.

His example would be too. Taking orders had been a leisurely affair for Henslow, something he got around to only after he married and obtained his first chair. Until then he had broadened his horizons through reading and travel, making the most of opportunities that came along. Charles thought this ideal and began to follow suit. With his exam out of the way, and only graduation to attend, he stuck his nose into books and his head into the clouds, daydreaming about how he might spend his time *en route* to a country parish.

Wide reading was vital, his passport to the wider world. He had always been struck by Paley's works. Now he picked up the last of the archdeacon's famous trilogy, the keystone of his entire system, *Natural Theology*. Here was a beautiful evocation of life abounding with goodness and joy: 'it is a happy world' teeming 'with delighted existence,' Paley enthused. 'In a spring noon, or a summer evening, on whichever side I turn my eyes, myriads of happy beings crowd upon my view.' Life was a summer's teatime on the vicarage lawn, with swarming bees and cheerful beetles testifying to God's kindness. It *was* good, life *was* happy, because all beings were adapted to their surroundings. Animals, including humans, are complex mechanisms from the divine workshop, and exquisitely fitted to their places in the world. They are so obviously designed, there has to be a Designer. For Paley such a rational proof of God's existence would make men look for signs of revelation and attend to their civic duties.

This was a different way of viewing the world for Darwin. He had even heard it ridiculed at Edinburgh. Nor did it accord with his grandfather's theory of life. Dead atoms, according to Paley, have no innate intelligence, no inherent vitality, nor does animal matter itself, as Erasmus and Dr Grant had taught. But then Erasmus's theory 'coincides with atheism' because it dispenses with 'an intelligent, designing, mind' which plans and constructs living bodies.[13] God alone creates the world, endows it with life, and keeps everything running smoothly.

Darwin nodded assent. Paley and his grandfather held radically different views, much as Henslow and Grant did. And Paley saw no evidence whatever to justify old Erasmus's science to a Cambridge man. But what sorts of 'evidence,' 'facts,' and 'laws of nature' were acceptable, and how were they established? Darwin swotted up the subject from a new, compact book by the doyen of science, Sir John Herschel, astronomer and physicist, the son of Sir William Herschel (the discoverer of Uranus). This was Sir John's year: he was knighted by the Whigs and his turgidly titled *Preliminary Discourse on the Study of Natural Philosophy* was hot off the press. It ignited Darwin. He glimpsed the limitless scope for scientific explanation and the rapid progress of every branch of knowledge. As Herschel remarked in a passage Darwin scored, 'To what, then, may we not look forward . . . what may we not expect from the exertions of powerful minds,' building on the 'acquired knowledge of past generations'? The sky was the limit. Darwin closed his eyes and exuded a 'burning zeal' for science.[14]

He also borrowed a book that Henslow heartily approved of. Darwin had picked up Alexander von Humboldt's *Personal Narrative* once before, only to put it down. Reading a seven-volume, 3754-page account of a turn-of-the-century trip to South America called for stamina. This time he summoned it up. Henslow had confided his own unfulfilled ambition to globe-trot, to 'explore regions but little known, and enrich science with new species.' For years he had longed to visit Africa, becoming 'depressed and out of spirits' when the prospect receded. Now it was out of the question, and he settled for memories of the Isle of Wight and the Isle of Man instead, where he had geologized after graduation.[15] But nothing need stop Darwin. Maybe his favourite pupil could find a suitable island to explore. He was still young and free, and in the future might regret passing up the chance. He could even take his divinity books along.

This was the incentive Darwin needed. He tore through Humboldt, still aglow from Herschel, and everything fell into place. Tropical scenery had long fascinated him, all those talks with the freed slave in Edinburgh, and the fine travellers' prints in the Fitzwilliam Museum. And Humboldt's account of Tenerife in the Canary Islands, with its lush lowland vegetation and rugged volcanic terrain, was enthralling. Why not go there? And take Henslow too – the Canaries were the next best thing to Africa, right off the coast in fact. What a view of God's world it would open up, not to mention the botanical teasers. Darwin plotted on one of Henslow's outings. He read out long passages from Humboldt to whet the party's appetite. Imagine the new species they would find on Tenerife's 'sandy, dazzling, plains,' and in its 'gloomy silent forest.' They would see 'the Great Dragon tree' and climb to the volcanic peak and . . .

The response was mixed. Only Henslow and three others were interested. But this was enough for Charles. He raced to Shrewsbury at Easter to get his father's view. The expedition would not set out for another year and would last only a month. It would not be cheap, but then Cambridge was not cheap either. The Doctor knew this only too well, as he handed Charles 'a 200£ note' to pay his debts – and with it, permission to cost out the trip. Everything spelled go.[16]

Nothing could stop Charles now, not even a simpering note from Fanny. 'Ashamed of myself for being so troublesome to you,' she asked him to pick up some artists' paint in Shrewsbury with 'half a dozen small brushes' and bring them over to Woodhouse – not forgetting 'a juicy Book of some kind' for her delectation. Charles caved in and made a flying visit. If it was a portrait she wanted, a portrait she could have, but he had other urgent business. Erasmus was waiting for him in London.

The capital was electric when Charles arrived on the weekend of 15 April. Six weeks before, Earl Grey had brought in the great Reform Bill, aiming to redistribute parliamentary seats to London and the industrial towns, and to extend the middle-class vote. The Whigs were now doing their utmost to contain and direct the broad-based reform movement. Carlile had been fined £200 and was serving a two-year sentence for seditious libel (writing in support of the rioting farm workers). *The Times* was full of the story; and Taylor had been nailed only the previous Monday, indicted for blasphemy in two Easter sermons. The Rotunda was on its last legs as a centre for artisan rebellion. But the Reform Bill had equally run into trouble. Its provisions appalled the Tory opposition. They were in full cry, with the outcome in the balance.

During the bill's second reading Darwin and Wedgwood supporters sat on the edges of their seats. Sir James Mackintosh's daughter Fanny (just engaged to Hensleigh Wedgwood) even went down to the House of Commons to hear the results first-hand. It passed by a whisker, only to be mangled by Tory diehards in committee stage. Everyone knew that the bill and Grey's ministry stood or fell together. So Grey left the King to decide. The choice was stark: either dissolve Parliament and cause a General Election, which would bring in enough reformers to carry the bill, or accept the government's resignation, lose the bill, and face a revolution.[17]

It was a cruel, exciting dilemma, and London was on tenterhooks. The tide for change was running high, and a General Election would demolish the Tories. Beneath the pall of smoke and soot, people held their breath.

Charles stayed with Erasmus and was plied with the latest news. Erasmus was a cosmopole, never far from Paris or some other European city, in thought if not in person. He was political and had his ear to the ground, but for all that he failed to impress his younger brother with the gravity of the hour. Charles was in the Canaries in *his* thoughts, and he found his visit to fevered London 'very fatiguing.' 'I expect Erasmus did also,' he observed with unwonted sensitivity. 'I begin to think Natural Hist[ory]: makes people Egotistical.' He was full of the expedition, his 'head . . . running about the Tropics,' his 'enthusiasm so great' he could 'hardly sit still.' There were shipping lines to contact, fares to compare, and a broker to consult. Eras proved useful in his way, advising that Spanish was the language to learn, not Italian. They did take time out for an 'Antient music' concert, but what Charles really liked was the Zoological Gardens in Regent's Park. 'On a hot day when the beasts look happy and the people gay it is most delightful,' he rhapsodized in a Paleyan way. It reminded him of the tropics.

The next weekend, as he prepared to leave, there was no ignoring the crisis. With great qualms William IV had decided to dissolve Parliament. The streets seethed with cheering crowds on Friday the 22nd as the King processed through the capital to Westminster. Cannons thundered, announcing his intention, and the people roared their approval. That night a 'general illumination' lit up the city and reform parties were held across the country. The nation returned from the brink while Charles returned to college. He arrived in plenty of time to sign the Thirty-nine Articles at his degree ceremony on Tuesday.[18]

Cambridge was gripped by election fever. No one could remember a poll held at such short notice, within a fortnight of a dissolution. Two MPs represented the university – the town itself had none. The college Tories put up Wellington's Chancellor of the Exchequer and the brother of Robert Peel as their candidates. Against them stood young Cavendish and Palmerston, the Foreign Secretary. The dons pitched in – Sedgwick, Whewell, and Peacock for the Whigs – and so did many students. Feelings ran high. The Vice-Chancellor banned a Tory election-eve rally at the Red Lion Inn, warning that students who attended would be 'proceeded against' for violating university discipline. Darwin himself went 'gossiping about town,' glad to put in a word for the Whigs (as a lodger, he had no actual voting rights). But he was fired by other things. He was dying to discuss his Tenerife plans with Henslow, grumbling because 'Henslow is Lord Palmerston's right-hand man, and he has no time for walks.' So other friends were bombarded with the 'Canary scheme' instead, and 'most wish me there,' Charles chuckled after both Tories had won, 'I plague them so with talking about tropical scenery.'

By now he was fixing to cast off, mentally at least. He accepted 'a most magnificent . . . present of a Microscope' from his friend Herbert, who could not decide 'whether M^r. Darwin's talents or his sincerity be the more worthy of admiration.' He cold-shouldered Fox, postponing an overdue visit, ostensibly on financial grounds but really because of Henslow's lectures and the 'scheme.' He began 'working like a tiger' on the expedition, especially the Spanish and geology. 'The former I find as intensely stupid,' he declared, 'as the latter most interesting.' Henslow had known that Darwin would need geological skills on any island jaunt. He promised to 'cram me' with the subject, Charles said.[19] But what Henslow apparently had in mind was something simpler: introducing him to the geology professor Adam Sedgwick.

They had met before. Sedgwick, decked in stately robes, had administered his oath of matriculation. They had also seen each other occasionally at Henslow's parties on Friday evenings, and Sedgwick was familiar with Darwin's undergraduate record. Once hell-bent on becoming an 'idle man,' drinking and dabbling in field sports, Darwin was now a novice naturalist with a well-stocked cabinet and a penchant for travel. So Henslow had told Sedgwick. Geological training was what Darwin needed – fast. It would keep up his interest in natural history and prepare him for a trip to Tenerife. Sedgwick agreed, remembering how Henslow himself had responded to his tuition when he was Darwin's age. In fact, their field work together on the Isle of Wight had been a great stimulus to them both; and at the moment Sedgwick needed another such tonic. Exhausted by the general election, he was about to begin a new phase of his stratigraphic studies. A young man's enthusiasm would do him good. Darwin would be welcome to attend his lectures and accompany him on a geological tour in the summer.

Henslow introduced Darwin formally, knowing that a fellow Proctor and clergyman would look after his best interests. Sedgwick was, indeed, among Henslow's oldest and closest friends; they were of one mind on religion, politics, and morals. No better tutor could be found to take a young man into the field, shepherd and guide him on to the paths of truth.

For his part, Darwin was fired up by Sedgwick's lectures that spring. They were incomparably better than Jameson's at Edinburgh, which he had hated. Sedgwick's reminded him of Humboldt, Herschel, and Paley, wrapped into one. They opened up new vistas of God's world, exposed the grandeur of creation. 'What a capital hand is Sedgewick [sic] for drawing large cheques upon the Bank of Time!' Darwin marvelled. And as for space, the professor revealed how much more of the globe remained to be conquered. 'It strikes *me*,' Darwin reflected, 'that all our knowledge about the structure of our Earth is very much like what an old hen w^d know of the hundred-acre field in a corner of which she is scratching.'

Undaunted by his ignorance, Darwin was – as usual – anxious to please and took the initiative. When Sedgwick mentioned a local spring, flowing from a chalk hill, which deposited lime in a delicate tracery on twigs, Darwin rode out, found it, and threw a whole bush in. Later he retrieved it, an extraordinary white-coated spray, so exquisite that Sedgwick exhibited it in class; whereupon others followed suit, and encrusted branches were soon adorning rooms all over the university.[20]

The summer was to see more serious field work. Darwin left Cambridge in June for London, where he bought his first geological instrument, a clinometer, for measuring the angle of inclined rock strata. Back home he put it to use, piling 'all the tables in my bedroom, at every conceivable . . . direction' and then sizing up their angles like 'any Geologist going could do.' He even ventured into the countryside to try his hand at mapping Shropshire. Extrapolating wildly, he felt like the 'old hen' in her field, scratching in a corner, taking it for the whole. This was youthful extravagance, but then hypotheses were cheap, and his were 'such powerful ones,' he laughed to Henslow, 'that I suppose, if they were put into action but for one day, the world would come to an end.'

His mind also took flight, Daedalus-like, in visions of Tenerife. Henslow's own 'Canary ardor' was cooling. After his wife's safe delivery he found himself with new responsibilities. So 'the most likely person . . . to be my companion,' Darwin told Fox, was the last of the original enthusiasts, a college tutor of Henslow's generation, Marmaduke Ramsay. Darwin kept Ramsay informed about his plans, and meanwhile 'read & reread Humboldt.' The 'Great Dragon tree' entranced him, the volcanic hills and tropical forests too.[21] His reveries went on, accompanied by earth-shaking speculations, until 4 August, when they came abruptly to a halt. Sedgwick rattled up to The Mount in his gig, armed to the teeth with tools and climbing gear, ready for the ascent into North Wales.

For the professor it was an expedition long overdue. Wales was becoming an area of enormous geological importance. Sedgwick had run into problems sorting out the oldest rocks of northern England. Strata seemed to be missing, like pages torn out of a book, and he guessed that equivalent ones would turn up in the rugged Welsh mountains. If he could find those ancient fossil-bearing rocks below the Old Red Sandstone, he could put the opening pages back into the geological book, enabling the history of life to be read from scratch. This was territory that Henslow might have helped him map a few years before, and who better now than Henslow's prize student?

That week Sedgwick hammered his way cross country from Cambridge, preparing for the Welsh invasion by chipping at conformable strata *en route*. He arrived in Shrewsbury tired and sore, and the next day drove off with Darwin under menacing skies, heading north into the Vale of Clwyd. On the way a thunderstorm broke and they were drenched. 'As the Prince of the Air would have it, I was almost drowned,' Sedgwick declared, playing up their plight, conscious that the Devil interferes with factual research whenever he can.[22]

And serious geology was what Darwin learned in Sedgwick's on-the-spot tutorials, as well as the skills that books could never impart. The clinometer came in handy, and Sedgwick checked the accuracy of Darwin's measurements. In less than a week he learned how to identify specimens, interpret strata, and generalize from his observations. It was the best crash course in geological practice, and Darwin hardly missed a trick, developing intellectual muscle as he burnt off the flab. Sedgwick sent him off to collect rock samples and check the stratification. When they met up, Darwin reported that he found no Old Red Sandstone in the Vale of Clwyd. This contradicted the national geological map, and Sedgwick's discussions of the implications made him 'exceedingly proud.'

Before they left the hills and headed for the coast, Darwin had fallen for the romance of geology. In limestone caverns above St Asaph, along the River Elwy, the two found mammal bones embedded in mud and easily extracted after the rains. The landowner actually had a rhinoceros tooth from these caves in his collection. Here was startling evidence of a lost fauna, from an age when rhinos wandered the Welsh countryside. It had a tremendous impact. And if such discoveries could be made in Britain, what awaited him abroad?[23]

They made for Bangor on the North Wales coast and there climbed steeply towards Capel Curig, twelve miles inland, searching in vain for fossils. Along the way Darwin heard the Revd Sedgwick swear for the first time. A blunt Yorkshireman, he was sure that the 'd – – d' waiter at their inn the night before had not passed on a sixpence tip to the chambermaid. He whirled the gig around and started back, determined to see justice done. Darwin remonstrated with him, asking on what grounds would he accuse the waiter of theft. Sedgwick had none, except that the waiter was 'an ill-looking fellow.' It rather dented Darwin's faith in the former Proctor as a judge of human character. Cautiously – for he was questioning high authority – he suggested that this was insufficient reason to accuse a man of criminal misconduct. The thought slowly registered, and at last Sedgwick reversed direction again, grumbling and growling.

At Capel Curig Darwin, self-assured as never before, left Sedgwick and struck out on his own. He had a map and compass, and his wits about him. With his new geological skills, this was all he needed. He would show Sedgwick what he could accomplish by himself. His route angled south-west, through 'some strange wild places.' Thirty miles away lay Barmouth and a Cambridge reading party. He followed a straight line through the hills, avoiding the beaten paths unless they went in his direction. He identified the strata along the way, revelling in his freedom, and finished up with a hearty fortnight among Gluttonous old friends.

Partridges were next on his agenda. Not even geology would keep him from shooting his fair share at Uncle Jos's. With only days before the season opened, he was preparing to leave Barmouth when a message came: Ramsay had died. The news took a moment to sink in, and when it did, six months' well-laid plans came crashing down. His travelling companion was lost, leaving the 'Canary scheme' in limbo. Ramsay had been so young, not even forty. Darwin returned to Shrewsbury, pinching himself, unable to 'believe he is no more.' The expedition was up to him now – if he dared attempt it on his own.

Arriving on Monday night, 29 August, he found a fat envelope franked 'London' awaiting him. He opened it perfunctorily, exhausted from his trip, and found letters from Henslow and Peacock.[24] Not more bad news – far from it. Staggered, he read on breathlessly. He was being offered passage on a voyage around the world.

1831–1836

8

My Final Exit

THE HOUR WAS LATE, his body exhausted, but Charles leapt at the offer. Henslow was adamant: 'You are the very man they are in search of.' The Admirals were scouting out someone to accompany Capt. Robert FitzRoy on his two-year survey of coastal South America. FitzRoy, only twenty-six himself, wanted a young companion, a well-bred '*gentleman*' who could relieve the isolation of command, someone to share the captain's table. Better still if he were a naturalist, for there would be unprecedented opportunities. The ship was equipped for 'scientific purposes' and a 'man of zeal & spirit' could do wonders, Henslow enthused. Charles might not be a '*finished* naturalist,' but taking 'plenty of Books' would help, and he was the obvious choice.

So he was. He was well qualified scientifically, and perfectly so socially. Jameson's Edinburgh course, as luck would have it, had catered for colonial travellers. He had learned to identify minerals and disentangle strata, and Sedgwick had fired up his feeling for the subject. Grant had given him the best instruction in Britain on lowly sea life. Darwin had worked his way round Lamarck's systematics and the latest insect identification guides. And what he lacked in experience he made up for in enthusiasm. He could shoot, skin, and stuff, and Henslow had topped his training off with a grounding in botany. He was, as Henslow said, 'amply qualified for collecting, observing, & noting,' and that is what counted.

It was the chance of a lifetime – the Church could wait. The post was at his 'absolute disposal,' according to Peacock's letter, and Peacock spoke for his friend Capt. Francis Beaufort, the Admiralty hydrographer (coastal map-maker) in charge of the voyage. Anyway, the Canaries scheme was in peril, and perhaps it had always been a

101

bit of a bubble. This one was a reality, here and now. The ship was due to sail in a month.[1] He blurted out to his sisters that he would accept. All he had to do was convince his father. Charles forced himself up to bed, dizzy with anticipation.

By the next morning, 30 August 1831, his sisters had briefed the Doctor. His refusal was a cruel blow, and neither Henslow's nor Peacock's endorsement would budge him. It was further evidence of his son's aimless preoccupation with enjoying himself. The voyage would be a useless, dangerous distraction. The unsettling years in the company of sailors would taint Charles and spoil him for the Church. It would ruin his professional chances again. Besides, why was a naturalist being sought with only weeks to spare? Something must be wrong with the vessel, the voyage, or FitzRoy. No, the whole plan looked reckless, and Susan, Caroline, and Catherine agreed.

Charles could ignore the Doctor's views if the Admiralty footed the bill. But he felt 'uncomfortable' at the thought of disobeying his father. With some sadness he declined the offer and went to Maer on the last day of August to vent his frustration on the partridges. He carried a sealed note from the Doctor to Uncle Jos, who was uncomfortable himself, with a 'buffy discharge from the bowels.' It prescribed 'turpentine pills' for his condition and then remarked on Charles's. His proposed 'voyage of discovery' was folly, the Doctor declared, but added, 'if you think differently from me I shall wish him to follow your advice.' This was unexpected, and Charles's hopes revived. Uncle Jos came out in favour of the voyage, followed by Aunt Bessy and the cousins. They were all emphatic, especially Hensleigh: he must go.

His father would listen now – he always trusted Jos's judgment, his industrialist's good sense. A jittery Charles sat up that night drafting a reply with his uncle. It might make the Doctor more uncomfortable than all of them, but he had asked for a second opinion. Far from being too dangerous or expensive, a global voyage could do him the world of good. It would shape his character, argued Jos, and might well ready him for a profession; after all, 'Natural History . . . is very suitable to a Clergyman.' Or considering him as 'a man of enlarged curiosity,' rather than an ordinand, the voyage was a golden opportunity to see 'men and things.' This alone would make it worthwhile. The Admiralty would look after him well, rump candidate or not – but, Jos ended, 'you & Charles . . . must decide.'

For his part, Charles begged 'one favor . . . a decided answer, yes or no,' and retired for a sleepless night. He tossed and turned, his mind 'like a swinging pendulum,' moving back and forth between his indulgent uncle and awesome father. If only they saw him as Henslow did. Early the next day, Thursday 1 September, the reply went off post-haste to Shrewsbury and Charles went hunting. Scarcely had he shot his first bird before Uncle Jos sent word to the field: the issue was so momentous, they should go to The Mount themselves. But it was not necessary. On arriving a few hours later, they found that their message had done the trick. The Doctor had relented. A potter's opinion had swayed him where the professors' had failed, and Charles was now to be entrusted to FitzRoy and the Admiralty. He would receive 'all the assistance in my power,' the Doctor chirped munificently.[2]

A mad scramble ensued. Charles, ecstatic, dashed off a letter of acceptance to Capt. Beaufort, worried that the post might be filled already. Then he threw some clothes in a bag, dozed a few hours, and at three in the morning started on the stage for Cambridge. He hired carriages to whisk him the last fifty miles cross country and reached Henslow by nightfall. The botanist, recovering from Charles's precipitant appearance, briefed him about the offer. True, he was not the first to receive it. The old-boy network had been buzzing for weeks: Jenyns had turned it down on account of his parish duties. Henslow himself had flirted with going, but his wife 'looked so miserable' that he withdrew. Both men then nominated Darwin, neither married nor ordained.

No sooner had Charles begun savouring his 'good fortune' than a courteous message came from FitzRoy. Regrettably, Peacock had misrepresented the offer. The Captain had already promised the place to a friend, but if this fell through Charles would have first claim. FitzRoy hoped no one had been inconvenienced.

Charles was crushed. It had been a 'tremendous, hard week,' an emotional turmoil, and all apparently in vain. He slept fitfully again that night and went to London first thing on Monday. There were contingency plans to make in case the offer was renewed, and an appointment to keep with FitzRoy. But he was no longer sanguine about the voyage. Frankly, he and Henslow had '*entirely* given it up.'[3]

London was in festive mood, with the coronation of William IV, the 'sailor king,' three days off, but Charles was glum. He elbowed his way through the streets to the Admiralty building in Whitehall, and finally met FitzRoy in Beaufort's office. FitzRoy was slight and dark, with fine features and an aristocratic hauteur. He was the grandson of the third Duke of Grafton on his father's side, and of the first

Marquis of Londonderry on his mother's – a direct descendant of Charles II. Crisp and composed, he came to the point at once. His friend had just refused the offer, not five minutes before. Was Mr Darwin still interested?

Was he? Charles felt buffeted, like a weathervane in a cyclone, but he managed a nod. Well and good. FitzRoy proceeded: the voyage would last not two years, but nearly three; it would not necessarily take them around the world. The cabin would be cramped, their dinners plain with 'no wine,' and the costs – up to £500 in all – would not be borne by the Admiralty. Seasickness could be expected, and Darwin would be free to leave for England at any time, or stay behind in 'some healthy, safe & nice country.' If he remained on board, however, he would be closely confined with the Captain for weeks or months on end, so it was imperative that they get along.

The reason for the position was becoming apparent. FitzRoy could not be familiar with his subordinates lest it weaken his command, but shunning all society was risky. Loneliness and isolation could take a terrible toll at sea. The *Beagle*'s former captain Pringle Stokes had shot himself off the South American coast. And FitzRoy feared his own hereditary disposition – in 1822 his uncle, Viscount Castlereagh, had slit his throat in a fit of depression when Home Secretary. So he had decided to take a dining companion. As long as he was a gentleman, mannered and cultivated, even a Whig would do. FitzRoy, the failed Tory candidate for Ipswich in the General Election, knew all about the Darwins' politics. (Being an unbending Tory, he probably also wondered about the grandson of the profligate Erasmus Darwin.) He had a 'horror of . . . having somebody he should not like on board.' Obviously, they had to know each other better, and he advised Charles not to make up his mind 'quite yet.'[4]

Charles stayed close-by. With Erasmus out of town, he took lodgings in Spring Gardens, next to the Admiralty, and splashed out on a guinea seat for the coronation procession. He revelled in the pomp and glitter, though the subdued crowds convinced him that coronations would soon be a thing of the past. For the rest of the week he was at FitzRoy's disposal. They dined together and drove about in his gig, 'ordering things.' The Captain struck him as extravagant, though 'very scientific.' He lavished money on books, barometers, and at least £400 on firearms. Charles figured out that he would need a £5 'telescope, with compass,' and some weapons of his own. He bought a £50 rifle for the wildlife and a pair of 'good pistols' to 'keep the natives . . . quiet.' 'We shall have plenty of fighting with those d – – Cannibals,' he crowed to Whitley. 'It would be something to shoot the King of the Cannibal Islands.'

It was 'capital fun,' and Charles felt as though he himself had just been crowned. He was 'happy as a king,' his 'confidence in Cap. Fitzroy' unbounded. He had taken to him 'at first sight' and begun to trust him almost involuntarily. FitzRoy became his 'beau ideal of a Captain,' and his kindness left Charles feeling as if he had been predestined to make the voyage – though he asked his sisters to refrain from chit-chat until his mind was finally made up. FitzRoy, too, liked what he saw and heard. His fears about Darwin had been unfounded; in the event, manners and breeding transcended party and family.[5]

A few things remained to be settled. Beaufort assured Darwin that he would be free to dispose of any collections he made, provided they went to some 'public body.' And FitzRoy repeated that he could leave the ship, 'as soon & wherever' he liked. He doubted that Darwin actually had the stamina to see the trip through. FitzRoy, addicted to physiognomy, judged a man's character by his face, and Darwin's nose foretold a lack of 'energy and determination.' But there was no shortage of it for the present. He was fired up, hoping that it would it be a circumnavigation. He wanted to go right around the globe, and badgered Beaufort about it without success. Finally FitzRoy promised to whisper the word in the ear of Tory friends. He told Darwin that he had 'interest enough' with people in high places 'to get the ship ordered home by whatever track he likes' – 'particularly if this [Whig] administration is not everlasting.' Charles relayed the story home, joking, 'I shall soon turn Tory!' The circumnavigation was 'all but certain.'[6]

His enthusiasm might have been checked if he had seen the size of the ship. FitzRoy knew his table-guest had no inkling of the 'square inches' he would be allotted. On Sunday the 11th he took Darwin to see her at Devonport – the long way. They left London by steam packet, chugging down the Thames, around the Kent coast into the English Channel, past Spithead and on to the safety of Plymouth Sound. The trip lasted almost three days and gave FitzRoy the chance to judge Darwin's sea legs.

He also briefed him about the Admiralty's assignment. The South American survey had begun five years ago. The continent was an open house for trade, a vast market for manufactured goods and a storehouse of raw materials. Rich Britons and their bankers had invested millions of pounds in the emerging national governments; companies had capitalized to the hilt to exploit its resources. Some of the speculation had proved ill judged, and even now the future was uncertain. That was why the Royal Navy was involved. If merchants were to beat competitors from Spain and the United States, their vessels needed easy access to South American ports. Islands and coastlines had to be mapped, harbours and channels sounded. The initial survey, which ended only a year before, had accomplished much, and FitzRoy himself – in his first command after Stokes's suicide – had served in its latter stages. But the charts needed checking and extending; tides and weather conditions remained to be logged – and FitzRoy would be the first to plot wind forces around the globe using Beaufort's scale. Parts of Patagonia and the Falkland Islands also had to be surveyed, as well as the desolate maze of channels at the continent's southern tip, in Tierra del Fuego.[7] This was his job.

He had come by it rather oddly, though, and Charles heard how. The summer before in Tierra del Fuego, while a party of his men were camping on shore, 'some Fuegians . . . approached with the dexterous cunning peculiar to savages' and stole their boat. His ship gave chase and the culprits' families were 'brought on board as hostages.' Most escaped, a few were released, and one was killed in a scuffle (his body was duly skeletonized 'for further study'). Eventually FitzRoy held two men, a boy, and a girl, none of whom could be put ashore conveniently. So he decided to try an evangelical experiment: he would civilize the savages, teach them 'English . . . the plainer truths of Christianity . . . and the use of common tools,' and then send them back to Tierra del Fuego as missionaries. The four returned with him to England. One died from a smallpox vaccination. The rest – named York Minster, age about 27, Jemmy Button, 15, and the girl Fuegia Basket, 10 – had spent the year with friends of the Church Missionary Society. In June, unable to find a ship to repatriate them, FitzRoy was on the point of sailing for Tierra del Fuego at his own expense when 'a kind uncle' interceded at the Admiralty and landed him the *Beagle* command. The Fuegians, civilized enough to be presented at Court during the summer, were joining his ship with their minder Richard Matthews, a trainee missionary himself.[8] Such was providence. The survey would be completed because the savages had been converted – the Lord was delivering native South America into English hands.

Charles marvelled at the Captain. His manners were impeccable, even towards the 'little Midshipman' he brought along, Musters, who turned out to know Charles's Derbyshire uncle, Sir Francis Darwin. By Tuesday, when the mail-boat put in at Devonport, the two of them were getting on famously. Charles had no misgivings on this account, though he sensed that his 'violent admiration' could not last. Then he saw the ship.

106

The *Beagle* was a ten-gun brig, eleven years old and rotting. It was being completely rebuilt as a three-masted bark in the naval dockyard. FitzRoy was personally supervising the work, and no expense was spared, even if he had to dip into his own pocket. She had a new upper deck with skylights, a reinforced copper bottom, and all up-to-date technologies: a specially designed rudder, a patented galley stove, advanced lightning conductors, and brass cannons instead of iron to avoid interference with the compasses. Charles took it in as he met the officers, an 'active determined set of young fellows.' What made him wince was the *Beagle*'s size – only 90 feet long and 24 feet wide amidships. She had only two cabins, and these were tiny. The poop cabin, behind the wheel, measured 10 feet by 11, and six-foot Charles had to stoop when inside. It held a vast chart table with three small chairs, and the mizzen-mast passed through it. The Captain's cabin was below deck, beneath the wheel, and even smaller. There were luxurious mahogany fitments everywhere, but this was no consolation. Close quarters yes, but Charles had never imagined them *this* close. His spirits sank.

He was soon buoyant again. Just before he left for London on Friday the cabin nameplates were fitted. Mercifully, his went on to the larger poop cabin (although he would also have the run of FitzRoy's cabin, and mess there too). The forward corner portside would be his part, with a few square feet of the chart table as well as a wall full of drawers, opposite the ship's library with its several hundred volumes at the rear. His cabin mate was to be the officer he liked best, John Lort Stokes, the nineteen-year-old Assistant Surveyor. They would both work here, each at his own seat, with the third place reserved for a fourteen-year-old Midshipman, Philip King, whose father had commanded the first survey. Sleeping arrangements would be awkward but adequate. Stokes's bed was in a cubicle outside the door, and King's below-deck. Charles would sling his hammock above the chart table, with his face two feet beneath the skylight.

FitzRoy took pains to make Charles comfortable in his poop cabin 'home.'[9] Charles left Devonport marginally reassured, trying to see the *Beagle* as more cosy than cramped.

Sailing had been postponed a few weeks, with FitzRoy fussing about the refit, but Charles still had to rush. His plans were 'fixed & certain' now. At last he could tell everyone, and bid them farewell. He raced up from Plymouth to London – an astonishing '250 miles in 24 hours' – and from there by night coach to Cambridge, where he talked Henslow's ear off for a couple of days. Henslow agreed to store his collections as they were sent back piecemeal and gave him a parting present, a copy of Humboldt's *Personal Narrative*. He also recommended taking the first volume of Charles Lyell's *Principles of Geology*, just published, but 'on no account' to accept all its views. Then Charles was off again, overnight to Shrewsbury, arriving early on Thursday the 22nd.[10]

The family had been at his beck and call for the last three weeks, collecting his belongings, packing his clothes, and providing bank drafts. This was his last chance to thank them in person, the dear old nay-sayers, and show his love. The Mount had often seemed like a prison but now it wore a different aspect. This great stone pile, built by his father, was home, not FitzRoy's bobbing bark. Security was a family and four solid walls, a refuge from the tempestuous world. Yet he was giving it all up, and with it 'half a chance of life.' They would be years apart; perhaps he would never see his father and sisters again. They meant more than ever to him, and he let them know. The Doctor was now 'much more reconciled' to the voyage, and his blessing made parting easier.

At the weekend Charles went to Woodhouse, only to be unnerved by the news of Fanny's broken engagement. The Revd Hill had jilted her, and she had gone away to do a 'severe Penance' for foolishly falling in love – being '*taken alive*' like some beast, as she put it. Charles scarcely knew whether to feel sorrier for himself or her. As he left, bearing a keepsake pin from Sarah, the Squire and all the family were melancholy too. At Maer the mood was brighter. He rode over and retailed FitzRoy's stories about Patagonian peat bogs and cannibals, and the 'detestable climate.' Charlotte worried that his third year at sea would put paid to 'the country parish & parsonage,' but otherwise the clan preened itself for persuading Dr Darwin and congratulated Charles on his courage.[11]

He returned to The Mount for a few days, and then on Sunday 2 October took his leave. He could hardly bear to embrace his father and sisters for the last time, but to hesitate now would betray them all. Resolve was needed. He had to prove his mettle. He choked back the tears and set his face towards London, Plymouth, and the world.

Back in London he teamed up with FitzRoy's other 'shore-going fellow,' the landscape artist Augustus Earle. Earle too was travelling in a private capacity, taken on by the Captain to provide a painted record of the *Beagle*'s stopover points. He was already well salted, having trained at the Royal Academy and then voyaged round the world, visiting and painting in Europe, North America, Brazil, and Australia. Darwin found him a bit 'eccentric.'

In the capital politics dominated life. The Whigs, swept to power with an increased majority in the General Election, had consolidated their hold on the reform movement. Rioting farm labourers had been hanged or transported; Carlile was appealing in vain against his conviction, and Taylor languished in Horsemonger-lane gaol, a broken man, his protest letters in *The Times* snubbed by the Home Secretary. A new Reform Bill was holding the headlines. It had passed its third reading ten days before and been sent to the House of Lords.

As Darwin began packing in his digs, just off Whitehall, the Lords' debate was heating up half a mile away. Everyone feared the worst. Sure enough, the next Saturday, 8 October, the peers threw out the bill and the country erupted. Gold soared; the stock market plunged. Pro-reform papers reported the death of the bill in black-edged editions. Riots and arson broke out in the major towns. Dukes were manhandled and their mansions attacked; the Tory bishops were jeered for having voted against the bill. In Cambridge Henslow feared being taken for a Tory and having his 'windows smashed.' On the 19th the King tried to calm the country by suspending Parliament, but nothing could stop 70,000 demonstrators marching through the capital, calling for fresh legislation.[12]

Darwin felt the strain. He was 'daily . . . more anxious to be off.' With introductions from Henslow, he darted around seeking specialist advice. The best display of skins and shells was at the zoo's West End museum, a short walk along Piccadilly. This was boom time for the zoo; gate takings had soared at the Regent's Park menagerie, leaving the museum curators £1000 a year to spend on anatomical specimens. Not that they needed it; exotic corpses were flooding in from the naval surveys, like Darwin's. As a result the museum, based in Lord Berkeley's town house in Bruton Street, was already packed. Darwin found it a kleptomaniac's delight, with carcasses everywhere – 600 mammals, 4000 birds, 1000 reptiles and fish, and 30,000 insects greeted him. And to this Capt. King's specimens from the previous *Beagle* survey of Patagonia were still being added.

Here Darwin met the taxidermists whose speciality was preserving, stuffing and storing. Everyone provided pointers: Benjamin Leadbeater, exhibiting cockatoos from Australia, taught him to pack skins in turpentine-soaked boxes. One of the zoo's prime movers, William Yarrell, a fellow sportsman building a fish collection, showed how to seal jars using bladders, tin foil, and varnish. Capt. King explained the use of 'Arsenical soap & preserving powder.' On marine invertebrates, though, Robert Grant was still his chief authority. He gave Darwin a list of pickling tips: crabs and the like to have their abdomens slit and gills flushed out; delicate zoophytes to be killed 'by gradual additions of fresh water,' sea anemones 'by pouring boiling water in their interiors.' Crack open 'spiral shells' to allow the preservatives to reach 'all parts.' An equal mix of water and wine spirits should do, except for crabs, which take their spirits neat.[13] At the British Museum, the top botanist in town, Robert Brown, briefed him. Brown was exceptionally shy, but a brilliant microscopist (he described the cell nucleus and Brownian motion). He advised Darwin on the best microscope to buy, and Darwin promised to pick him some Patagonian orchids.

Darwin was armed with the best advice a naturalist could carry, fully prepared (as Henslow said) for 'collection, observing, & noting.' He was on his way – or should have been.

News came of another delay. The *Beagle* would not be ready to sail until 4 November. By now Charles had assembled all his possessions, but the extra time came in handy with all the packing necessary. Shoes and slippers, breeches and boots, a dozen shirts marked 'DARWIN,' and Sarah Owen's pin – the personal items mounted up fast. His scientific gear, once crated, took on frightful proportions: specimen jars stuffed with chemicals and preservatives, dissecting tools in trays, boxed precision instruments – microscope, clinometer, telescope, compass, rain gauge, barometer – as well as an iron-chain trawling net, spare parts for the guns, his geological hammer, and of course Humboldt, Lyell and other books. 'I have *been as economical as I possibly could*,' he assured FitzRoy, but if 'the worst' came and he exceeded his allotted space, then 'two big cases' had been earmarked to be left behind.

All the crates went off by steamer in a south-westerly gale, and Charles followed on land, arriving in Plymouth late on Monday 24 October.[14] In ten days the *Beagle* would put to sea.

He was exhausted. He hadn't stayed a week in one place since August, or even a dozen days at home. He had travelled 1500 miles, spent his father's money with impunity, rubbed shoulders with naval bigwigs, and felt his life turned upside down. But now the time was near; he was about to take the plunge, leave the old world behind – make 'my final exit.' And what a relief, he wanted it over fast.

FitzRoy fixed him up in quayside lodgings with Stokes and himself, so that the *Beagle*'s intelligentsia could become acquainted. After a riotous dinner below deck in the Gun Room, the officers' mess, Darwin was glad of it. The men were 'rather rough, & their conversation . . . so full of slang & sea phrases' that it was as 'unintelligible as

Hebrew.' Among them was the Surgeon, Robert McCormick, the ship's official naturalist. He was thirty-one, hospital trained, petulant and the product of three voyages. Surgery was a menial grade in the King's navy, and only gentlemen could share the Captain's table (which is why Darwin was along). Darwin got on amicably with McCormick, even if he was 'an ass' and worried more about the *Beagle*'s paintwork than scientific pursuits.[15] There was no escaping science for Charles, or at any rate trigonometry. He began swotting again, wanting to hold his own when the talk turned to navigation. Stokes and FitzRoy primed him as they toured the dockyard, calibrating their instruments.

The gales persisted, and the sailing was postponed again. Saturday, 5 November, Guy Fawkes's Day, was to have been their first full day at sea. But while bishops were burnt in effigy across the country instead of traditional Guys, Charles sat pensively in his room, trying to read. It was a 'wretched, miserable' non-event. He went with Musters to the dockyard chapel on Sunday, took in a concert during the week, and had a geological jaunt or two. None of it cheered him up.

Next weekend, the four Fuegian missionaries arrived, laden with the trappings of civilization. Well-meaning churchgoers had inundated them with 'clothes, tools, crockery-ware, books' – everything necessary for their outpost. Somehow their cargo was stowed in the *Beagle*'s tiny hold, the sailors muttering about the crush and hooting at the toffs who sent complete sets of crockery. The missionaries had a lofty moral purpose, but they were travelling at other people's expense, in more ways than one. Darwin had paid for his passage. And having jettisoned every non-essential, he still wondered how everything of his would fit in. Claustrophobia struck, leaving him in 'continual fear.' 'The absolute want of room,' he glowered, 'is an evil, that nothing can surmount.'[16]

The sailing date kept receding. Now it was put off until early December. Alone many days, with only provisions to buy and the cabin to rearrange, he became despondent. He worried about seasickness and was tortured by thoughts of death. Ramsay's loss haunted him ominously. Then on the 21st a sailor slipped overboard and drowned. If this could happen in port, what were his chances of surviving three years – or four, as FitzRoy now mooted – at sea? Then he noticed his heart palpitating and he developed chest pains. Was it heart disease? He bottled up his fears, said nothing to surgeon McCormick, and put on a brave face in letters home.[17] If his father found out he would stop him going, Uncle Jos or no. Come what may, Charles was resolved to sail.

Through all the 'wearisome anxiety' he thought of family and friends. He was abandoning everyone he loved, and he wondered whether the voyage, if he lived through it, would compensate him for the loss. People wrote, but endearing letters only made him lonelier. Henslow preached a sermon about tolerating the crew's 'coarse or vulgar' behaviour. Fox, whom he had brushed off and had not seen in a year, was gracious, reminding him of the stories that they would swop 'by the fire' one day. Whitley brought back memories of Cambridge camaraderie and 'the simple, the elegant, Glutton club.' Those weekly meals were better by far than FitzRoy's sumptuous 'ships warming' luncheon on the 28th. 'But . . . there is no use thinking about it,' Charles replied mournfully. 'It is all over.' 'Remember me . . . especially to old Matthew if you see him,' and 'God bless you.'

No one touched him like Fanny, who was now pouring her heart out. It was the cruellest irony. They had passed like ships in the night, their lives headed in opposite directions. Back in September, when he was in Devonport with FitzRoy inspecting the *Beagle*, she was in Exeter, only fifty miles away, completing her 'Penance.' Indeed, they were both actually in Plymouth one day, but never met. Afterwards she heard of his plans and sent him a *'leetle* purse' as a memento, but by the time she returned to Woodhouse he was gone. Missing her had put Charles in a 'Blue devilish humour.' He wrote plaintively, hoping that she would not forget him. Her reply, for once it seemed, was candid. She pined for their tender past and longed to see him again, predicting that his return would find her 'in *status quo* at the Forest, only grown **old** & *sedate*.' 'The many happy hours we have had together from the time we were **Housemaid & Postillion** . . . are not to be forgotten,' she vowed, adding provocatively, '& would that there was not to be an end of them!!'

Her last letter came on Saturday 3 December, an apt sequel giving an eager account of Sarah's wedding. But with two days before sailing, Charles determined to 'talk or think' only of the voyage.[18] And Erasmus had just arrived to help concentrate his mind.

There was so much to show Erasmus – the *Beagle* gleaming and shipshape, with its twenty-four chronometers for determining exact longitudes of islands around the globe; FitzRoy's hearty provisions, and not least that miniature, mahogany-lined compartment, his home. Things looked better, seen through Eras's eyes, and that Saturday night Charles braved staying aboard for the first time. He had the 'most ludicrous difficulty' getting into his hammock, attempting it feet first while balanced on the chart table; but after mastering the trick of seat-first entry, all went well. He even slept through a minor storm, so perhaps he would escape seasickness. Erasmus wished everyone *bon voyage* at the evening meal, and saluted his brother goodbye. FitzRoy was ready to leave in the morning.

A southerly gale blew up at midday, mocking the last-minute preparations. It kept up all week. On the morning of the 10th, while Erasmus was on board saying goodbye, the weather finally cleared, and FitzRoy gave the order to hoist sails. The effect was electric – 'Coxswains piping, the manning [of] the yards, the men working at the hawsers to the sound of a fife,' and all with breathtaking 'rapidity & decision.' At nine o'clock the *Beagle* weighed anchor and moved out as far as the breakwater, where Erasmus disembarked to a chorus of fraternal shouts.[19] Then the tiny bark ploughed through the Sound and on to the open sea.

Charles's misery began immediately. Nausea nailed him to the rail, and he spewed his breakfast into the swell. Nothing stayed down all day. In the evening a fierce gale came on from the south-west, and the *Beagle* began pitching 'bows under' into mountainous waves. It was his worst nightmare. All through the watches he swung violently in his cabin, retching helplessly, while in the blackness outside the howling wind, the 'roar of the sea, [and] the hoarse screams of the officers & shouts of the men' reached a crescendo. In the chaos FitzRoy remembered his companion. He staggered in from behind the wheel and made Charles comfortable, adjusting his hammock. The next morning the Captain admitted defeat. He headed the ship back to Plymouth, resolved to await a favourable east wind.

At anchor, the waiting went on and on. The ship was 'full of grumblers & growlers' and Charles became 'as bad as the worst.' On Wednesday the 21st the sun, the sea, and the wind were perfect. FitzRoy made a fresh start – and promptly ran the ship aground. It was low tide, and the *Beagle* could be freed only by everyone running in unison back and forth across the deck, causing the vessel to swing. They reached the Channel in the afternoon and, after a bout of sickness, Charles slept soundly overnight. In the morning he checked a pocket compass and – incredibly – it pointed back towards England. Eleven miles off the Lizard a south-westerly gale had set in. The Captain had turned the ship and was making for Plymouth Sound.[20]

Charles was past wanting anything now except to be under way, once and for all. Christmas left him cold. He went to church that Sunday and heard an old Cambridge friend preach. At four he dined in the Gun Room and thanked the Lord that he shared FitzRoy's table. The officers carried on like varmints, but with the manners of 'freshest freshmen.' Their high spirits came straight out of a bottle, just like the sailors', and without a tincture of the Gluttons' good fellowship. By nightfall no one on board was sober, not even Charles. Needless to say the next day was ideal for sailing, except for 'the drunkedness & absence of nearly the whole crew.' The ship remained in a 'state of anarchy,' with sailors in 'heavy chains' incarcerated below deck, ranting and blubbering by turn. The Captain restored order ruthlessly, and by evening the stragglers on shore had all turned up to face their punishment. Everyone settled down – to wait.

On 27 December the *Beagle*'s seventy-three souls awoke to a crystal sky washed by a light easterly breeze. FitzRoy spoke the word and the ship sprang to life, with officers barking orders and the sailors scrambling over the deck and up the masts, readying the sails. The supernumeraries kept clear, the missionaries below in their private quarter, and Charles in his cabin, scribbling last-minute letters home. At eleven o'clock, as the ship weighed anchor, he joined FitzRoy and Lieutenant Bartholomew Sulivan aboard the local naval commissioner's yacht for a farewell luncheon. While the *Beagle* warped from the shelter of Barnpool and tacked out into the Sound, the party glided on a parallel course, dining elegantly. They rejoined their ship outside the breakwater, and immediately, with every sail unfurled, she scudded slowly out to sea. The 'mutton chops & champagne,' Charles jotted in his diary, 'may I hope excuse the total absence of sentiment which I experienced on leaving England.'[21]

9

A Chaos of Delight

HE WAS SICK AGAIN, dreadfully. It started the second day at sea, while FitzRoy doled out punishments for the Christmas crimes. Four men between them received 134 lashes for insolence, disobedience, and neglect of duty. Darwin cringed as the whip hissed and the felons howled. This brutal justice turned his stomach – or was it the constant pitching and rolling?

Soon enough he knew, for the nausea remained. It went 'far far beyond' anything he had imagined. For ten days nothing stayed down but dry 'biscuit & raisins,' or when that revolted him, hot spiced wine mixed with sago. He nearly fainted from exhaustion when he tried to stand; only a 'horizontal position' brought relief. As the tiny *Beagle* bobbed through heavy seas in the Bay of Biscay he was swinging beneath the poop cabin skylight, tormented by 'dark & gloomy thoughts.' Re-reading Humboldt's 'glowing accounts of tropical scenery' bucked him up a little. And, swaying there at night, it was 'rather amusing' to watch the moon and stars performing 'small revolutions in . . . new apparent orbits.' Otherwise there was nothing but vomiting and regrets. New Year was more a time for recriminations than resolutions. The voyage was a mistake. If only he had heeded the Doctor.[1]

FitzRoy steered past Madeira, but Darwin, sick in his cabin, missed the landfall. As they made for Tenerife the air grew balmy and the swell subsided. Everyone was itching for shore leave, not least Darwin. He began to feel better, and was thrilled when the island's volcanic peak appeared above the clouds. It looked like 'another world,' 'twice as high' as he had ever dreamed. Here was compensation for the agony of seasickness. As the *Beagle* tacked into the sun-baked port of Santa Cruz on 6 January 1832, he could hardly

115

take his eyes off the mountain, so long the 'object of my ambition.' But when the anchor dropped, a boat came alongside with urgent orders. The *Beagle* was to be quarantined for twelve days because of the cholera outbreak in England, an official shouted. No 'personal communication,' no shore going.

All eyes turned to the Captain. Would he wait? The answer came at once. 'Up Jib,' FitzRoy cried, and slowly the *Beagle* moved off into the gathering dusk. Darwin was devastated. The quarantine orders came like a 'death-warrant.' He did not have 'the slightest prospect' of visiting this tropical paradise again. The ship was becalmed a few miles off shore, and he sought solace in the night. It 'does its best to smooth our sorrow,' he confided to his diary, 'the air is still & deliciously warm – the only sounds are the waves rippling on the stern & the sails idly flapping round the masts . . . The sky is so clear & lofty, & stars innumerable shine so bright that like little moons they cast their glitter on the waves.'[2]

Two days later Tenerife disappeared. It was 'like parting from a friend,' Darwin sighed. The *Beagle* tacked south in a fine breeze and it grew hotter by the day. He lay quietly in the cabin, reading the first volume of Lyell's *Principles of Geology*. Or he ventured on to the deck to try a plankton net he had made from coarse cloth. He dropped it overboard from the poop deck and let it drag in the wake. The harvest was huge, with myriad tiny creatures 'most exquisite in their forms & rich colours.' He had never seen the like, not even with Grant. Why 'so much beauty' in the vastness of the ocean, with nobody to admire it? It seemed 'created for such little purpose.'

The weather was excellent, with light winds and puffy clouds in azure skies, and stunning sunsets. St Jago in the Cape Verde Islands, 300 miles off the African coast, was to be their first landing. A wretched place, he had read; it would not give the 'lasting impression of beauty' that he craved from the tropics.

Shrouded in thick haze, St Jago could not be seen distinctly until the *Beagle* was within three miles. It lived up to its reputation – an excrescence of desolate volcanic hills. Still, after the *Beagle* anchored off Porto Praya on the 16th, Darwin was relieved just to be walking on solid ground. He went with FitzRoy to meet the islands' Portuguese governor and the American consul. Then he finally realized his dream – he saw his first tropical vegetation. In a deep valley he came upon a scene reminiscent of Humboldt's descriptions, a lush tangle of fruit trees and palms. He was awestruck and felt like a blind man being given his sight: 'overwhelmed' and unable to 'comprehend it.' St Jago had been redeemed, and Darwin began to relish the weeks ahead on shore.[3]

A Chaos of Delight

While FitzRoy set up an observatory and took measurements, Darwin rushed everywhere – hiking with Musters and McCormick, pony-trekking inland with Rowlett and Bynoe (the Purser and the Assistant Surgeon), or exploring by himself. It was like a Barmouth reading party, but infinitely more exciting. Wild cats bounded past, gaudy kingfishers darted around, and he stumbled on 'the celebrated Baobob trees,' a massive thirty-six feet in girth, but as graffiti covered 'as any one in Kensington Gardens.' He carried weapons of course. 'Very good for black man,' his interpreter nodded, quite nonchalant about murder. But Darwin had never seen anyone 'more intelligent than . . . the Negro or Molatto children,' who '*immediately* perceived' and were 'astonished at the percussion guns.' 'They examine everything with the liveliest attention, & if you let them . . . will pull everything out of your pockets. My silver pencil case was . . . much speculated upon.'

Darwin was in his element. On his Edinburgh walks he had often 'gazed at the little pools of water left by the tide: & from the minute corals . . . pictured to myself those of larger growth.' Now here he was, collecting brilliantly coloured sponges and exquisite tropical corals on the coast. What most enthralled him was the volcanic terrain. Walking alone over sun-scorched plains strewn with 'black & burnt rocks' was ecstasy, his imagination running riot on nature's primeval forces. The barrenness and solitude forced all mortal thoughts from the mind: he was left facing the earth's awesome power.

He spotted something odd – a horizontal white band running through the rocks, about thirty feet above sea-level. It was made of compressed shells and corals, and continued as far as the eye could see. Obviously the whole area had once been under water, but why not now? Darwin, fascinated, took up the challenge.

Sedgwick in North Wales had inducted him into Cambridge-style geology – a science of violent crustal movements, wrenching strata, and mountain thrusts. But how had this seashell band arrived at this height above the ocean? Lyell's *Principles of Geology* could help here, even though Henslow had said to beware. Lyell pictured a world constantly and slowly changing, with the past no more violent than the present – so that today's climates, volcanic activity, and earth movements are all we need to explain the ancient world. Crustal movements balance one another: land rises in one area as it falls in another, not cataclysmically, as Sedgwick thought, but gradually.

Was Lyell right? Thousands of miles from Cambridge, Darwin thought for himself. It was impossible that the sea itself had fallen; a

117

lower Atlantic was unimaginable in St Jago's volcanic lifetime. So had the island risen slowly or abruptly? He inspected the oyster band again. It was practically intact, showing no sign of catastrophic violence. And it varied in height above sea-level along its length, suggesting secondary subsidence in places. St Jago, at least, seemed to prove Lyell's point. Darwin started to view the world as slowly and gradually changing.[4]

With his notepads filling up, Darwin now realized that he could make a serious contribution to geology. He even imagined writing his own book on the subject, based on the countries he would visit. Only occasionally did his thoughts revert to 'England & its politicks;' the promise of tropical vistas had stopped even the sailors talking 'reform.' FitzRoy weighed anchor on 8 February. Darwin again could think of little but South American vegetation. He expected to find it even more luxuriant, though he knew that his first St Jago impressions would 'never be effaced.'[5]

'Squeamish and uncomfortable,' he described himself as the *Beagle* dashed for the Equator. Most days nausea flattened him, and he hated lying about. As he dangled in his cabin, dead animals stared at him, awaiting 'labels and scientific epitaphs.' It grew 'damp & oppressive' inside, and still he could not get up, even to air his sticky limbs. Mercifully, some nights were cool, but by day it was like being 'stewed in . . . warm melted butter.'

FitzRoy stopped for fresh food at St Paul's Rocks, 'the top of a submarine mountain' covered with nesting boobies and noddies. Darwin pulled ashore for the slaughter with Stokes and First Lieutenant John Wickham. The gulls, knowing no predators, seemed almost tame. The men filled their hats with eggs, and then laid about the birds 'like schoolboys,' crushing their skulls with stones. Darwin's geological hammer came in handy; one of the men wielded it so violently that the shaft snapped. They piled up the corpses while the sailors in the boat hooked groupers and other fish, competing for them with the sharks. It led to a glorious glut – everything the *Beagle* needed to celebrate 'crossing the line' on 16 February.

The Equator provided the traditional excuse to let off steam. Discipline was suspended and the ceremonies began that night. FitzRoy, dressed as Father Neptune, summoned each of the novices to the forecastle, where half-naked sailors daubed in paints and dancing like demons waited to perform the initiation. Thirty-two had never crossed, and Darwin was the first to be called. One look at FitzRoy and he ran down the fore hatchway, convinced that the ship had gone mad. But the demons caught and blindfolded him, stood him on a plank, and flipped him into a water-filled sail. Dragging him out, they lathered his 'face & mouth with pitch and paint, & scraped some of it off with a piece of roughened iron hoop,' then tipped him head over heels again into the water. This was light treatment, though unpleasant enough; others fared worse. Eventually the whole ship became 'a shower bath,' with water 'flying about in every direction . . . Not one person, even the Captain, got clear of being wet through.'[6]

So passed 17 February too, in mummery and mayhem. Darwin awoke in the southern hemisphere, marvelling at the heavens. Out on deck he saw the sun to the north, and at night the Southern Cross and Magellan's Cloud. His stomach felt calmer now, aided by the 'variables' – the light equatorial winds. But the temperature was oppressive, and sleeping an ordeal. He took to the chart table finally – anywhere to escape the clinging hammock – but even then his heated mind worked overtime. The coming years with all their risks frightened him. A new world was beckoning, but his heart remained at home. If only he were now looking back safely on the voyage, surrounded by loved ones and friends! The yearning came over him again and again, especially on 'soft & delicious' tropical nights.[7]

A trade wind caught the *Beagle* and blew her steadily to Brazil. She hove to at Bahia (Salvador), anchoring in All Saints Bay amid a forest of large ships, and on 28 February Darwin first set foot on the continent. The old town, with its stinking wharfs and narrow streets, reminded him of student days in Auld Reekie. But here the lofty houses were 'embosomed in a luxuriant wood,' and whitewashed churches and imposing porticos glistened against the verdure. It was the rainy season, and no time better to see the forest.

At last he had his wish. Humboldt's word-pictures came to life, yet even his 'glorious descriptions' did not do justice. Darwin wandered by himself hour after hour, dazed by 'the luxuriance of the vegetation . . . the elegance of the grasses, the novelty of the parasitical plants, the beauty of the flowers.' His mind was 'a chaos of delight.' Pausing in a shady nook, he listened to the droning, croaking, throbbing life. Now, as in ages past, when no human interlopers were around to hear, the forest reverberated to 'a most paradoxical mixture of sound & silence,' like some great cathedral at evensong, with the anthem fading to 'universal stillness.' Adding 'raptures to . . . raptures,' he began collecting: flowers enough 'to make a florist go wild,' and countless beetles. Such 'transports of pleasure' he had never known. And imagine, he said after shooting a huge beautiful lizard, that such delight should be called 'duty'! He had to tell his father, and wrote passionately of his success, sending 'my love to every soul at home, & to the Owens.'"

Back in town it was the carnival season, and he braved the festive streets with Lieutenants Wickham and Sulivan, only to beat a hasty retreat under a barrage of 'wax balls full of water' and the spray of 'large tin squirts.' But there was little to celebrate here. In the merchants' warehouses, he wrote tartly, 'all the labor is done by black men.' They came so cheap that capital investment was nil; only one 'wheel carriage' was to be seen. The blacks carried everything. Still, 'when staggering under their heavy burthens,' they 'beat time & cheer themselves by a rude song.'

It was a sore point, the travails of the black man, and potentially divisive aboard ship, with FitzRoy justifying the Negroes' lot. One day he remarked that slavery was not intolerable, for Brazilians in general treat their black servants well. FitzRoy was widely travelled and Darwin was not, but in his Whig heart Darwin knew wrong from right. Slavery was the one institution that his whole family had inveighed against. It was evil, and Darwin suggested that the only solution was emancipation. FitzRoy boiled over: 'Hot Coffee' the crew called the Captain for his temper, and Darwin was scalded. FitzRoy had heard a slave-owner ask his servants whether they were unhappy or wished to be free. 'No,' they had replied – so shouldn't their wishes be respected? Darwin asked what a slave's answer in his master's presence was worth. At this FitzRoy exploded, declaring that they could not live together any longer; his word had been questioned. And then he stalked out of the cabin.

That was that. To think that Darwin had feared falling overboard when being kicked off was so easy. The news spread, and he was glad for an invitation to mess with the Gun Room officers, who briefed him about FitzRoy's flare-ups. Sure enough, a few hours later the Captain sent an apology and asked him to remain. Capt. Paget of the *Samarang*, a 'real fighting' vessel, was aboard, paying call, and Darwin was invited to eat with them. Now came sweet revenge. Paget had seen as much of the world as FitzRoy. He knew about slavery, and as a guest he could not be gainsaid. All the atrocities he could recall were trotted out over dinner. He too quoted a well-treated slave, who longed 'to see my father & my two sisters once again.' Such, Darwin fumed afterwards, was the anguish of the black men, 'who are ranked by the polished savages in England as hardly their brethren, even in Gods eyes.'⁹

*

FitzRoy put to sea on 18 March after completing a chart of the harbour. The *Beagle* ran south along the Brazilian coast, sounding near the rocky Abrolhos islets and stopping to load up with fresh fowl. Then on towards Rio de Janeiro in a 'rattling breeze,' with April Fool's jokes along the way. At midnight Sulivan burst into the poop cabin, crying, 'Darwin, did you ever see a Grampus'? Darwin bolted from his hammock to catch a glimpse of the dolphin – only to be 'received by a roar of laughter from the whole watch.'

Things were looking up. He saw his first water spout, caught his first shark, and eagerly awaited his first post from home. The mail bag came aboard on 5 April as the *Beagle* slid into Rio harbour, a mere surveying ship, raising and lowering all her canvas with split-second precision before the men-o'-war. Darwin left off helping with the display and rushed below to read his letters. Even the view of Rio, 'gaudy with its towers & Cathedrals,' and guarded by the Sugar Loaf mountain, took second place.

The gossip was overwhelming. Everyone, it seemed, was getting married: Hensleigh to Fanny Mackintosh, his sister Charlotte to a parson liked by the whole family. Charlotte longed to see Charles settled down with a wife 'in your parsonage,' and becoming a 'good active religious clergyman,' like her own Charles Langton. It was the 'happiest life in the world,' she glowed.

Another wedding was announced – Fanny Owen's. Stunned at first, Charles broke down as he read. She had been engaged since the new year, not a month after her last letter. A rich varmint-like character named Biddulph (an aspiring politician, of course) had hovered about her after the Hill affair, taken pity on her distress, and finally proposed. It had happened 'in the course of a secret ride' – shades of housemaid and postillion – and the wedding was in March. Fanny would be 'a *motherly old married woman* when you come back,' sister Catherine said, rubbing it in. Charles, tears streaming, was incoherent. He tried to be philosophical about it, but inside was 'really melting with tenderness,' and he cried 'my dearest Fanny' over and over again to himself. Oh, what a country curate's wife she would have made! – 'by the fates, at this pace I have no chance for the parsonage.'[10]

Overwrought, he plunged headlong into the interior. He teamed up with a rag-bag group of British adventurers from Rio, heading a hundred miles north, where one of them owned an estate. The ride was tortuous, the lodgings *en route* filthy, and the food meagre. Charles fell ill in the blistering heat but pressed on, 'faint & exhausted.' The sights made up for his discomfort: conical ants' nests rising twelve feet from the ground, egrets wading in salt lagoons, vampire bats supping on horses' blood, and a profusion of orchids and cabbage palms.

On arriving at the estate, he saw another 'horrible & flagrant' example of 'miserably overworked' blacks. The owner, his travelling companion, quarrelled with the foreman running the ranch, and threatened to sell the man's favourite mulatto child at a public auction. The dispute escalated, and the owner angrily rounded up all the women and children from thirty slave families, intent on selling them separately from their husbands in Rio. This was despicable. How could a man otherwise so congenial reach such depths of degradation? 'How weak are the arguments of those who maintain that slavery is a tolerable evil!'

The estate had been carved out of virgin jungle, and Charles rambled off into the steamy stillness. He was entranced again – no, profoundly moved. Alone with his gun and notebook, he knew that there was no Fanny awaiting him, no black-haired beauty to share the forest with. Seated on a mossy log, the scene reminded him of her, and his feelings flowed. 'Twiners entwining twiners,' his pencil twitched, 'tresses like hair – beautiful lepidoptera – Silence – hosannah.' It was 'sublime devotion' he felt, love displaced by nature. He felt his soul responding and thought of Nature's God.[11]

The visit lasted only a few days, and Charles headed back to Rio along a 'glaring hot sandy plain' near the coast. The *Beagle* was returning to Bahia to check the longitude, but he decided to wait here for its return. He collected his belongings and on 25 April rowed to Botafogo Bay, a good base from which he could go on collecting. As he came ashore a heavy sea crashed over the boat, knocking him 'head over heels.' When he righted himself, there, to his horror, were all his papers, 'books, instruments & gun cases' floating away in the surf. He caught everything, but the damage was done, and he wasted a whole day drying out and making repairs in a local rented cottage.

The cottage was shared with the ship's artist Augustus Earle, suffering from rheumatism but busy painting the 'beautiful spot,' and one of the civilized savages, 'Miss Fuegia Basket, who daily increases in every direction except height.' The site was idyllic, yet within walking distance of the town, where he could take in the Botanic Garden or find the aqueduct that led to the Corcovado mountain. Twice he climbed this 2000-foot 'Hunchback,' revelling in the scenery, shuddering to think what a 'horrible lovers leap' it would make.[12]

Weeks wore on with no sign of the *Beagle*. But he was absorbed in his work, trapping and shooting one day, preserving the next, with the evenings devoted to correspondence. His longest letter went to Henslow. Charles was bursting with news: geological facts to pique Mr Lyell's interest, reports of marine molluscs, octopuses with their instant colour changes, and his latest exploits around the bay. The forest inland was a veritable 'gold mine.' Here he encountered his first new-world monkey, dead. While hunting with a Portuguese padre, he saw the bearded beast hanging by its prehensile tail in an enormous tree. It had been shot the day before, and was retrieved by simply chopping the tree down. He heard chirping frogs and screaming parrots, saw glow-worms and iridescent hummingbirds, and witnessed lizards fleeing columns of predatory ants.

But what always thrilled him most was the low life. Hacking through the undergrowth, sometimes in torrential rain, he turned up 'gaily-coloured' flatworms under decaying logs. And beetles galore; on 23 June alone he caught sixty-eight species. Most of the tiny ones had never been seen in Europe, and he rallied Henslow, 'tell Entomologists to look out & have their pens ready for describing.' He was 'red-hot with Spiders' too, even finding one minuscule sort that lived on others' webs, feigning death when threatened and falling off. And one nasty parasite he was never to forget: a predatory wasp, which stung caterpillars and stuffed them into its clay cell as food for the larvae.

Geology was exciting, Fox heard, 'like the pleasure of gambling,' for one could set the odds of finding certain rocks before arriving in a locality. 'I can eat Salt Beef & musty biscuits for dinner,' he bragged to Gluttonous Herbert; 'see what a fall man may come to'! The folks in Shrewsbury received an inkling of how he viewed his prospects, now that both Charlotte and Fanny were taken. 'Maer & Woodhouse ... might as well be shut up,' he sighed, still picturing to himself 'a very quiet parsonage ... through a grove of Palms.' At least he would always have natural history. It would offer 'employment & amusement for the rest of my life,' even 'if I gain no other end.'[13]

The *Beagle* finally returned with distressing news. Three of the crew were dead. They had taken ill after a snipe-shooting party, were seized by a violent fever and had died within a week. The last to go was 'poor little Musters,' his first Gun Room friend. Only days before Musters had heard of his mother's death, Charles wrote home, ending on a tasteless pun, 'What numbers snipe-shooting has killed, & how rapidly they drop off.'

They had lost someone else just as precipitately. Robert McCormick, the ship's Surgeon-naturalist, had quit and shipped home, sick of living in a rich landlubber's shadow. He had been put out by the social preference: Darwin was allowed ashore; Darwin collected as he liked; and it was not only the Captain's table that Darwin shared. His gentleman's standing placed him with the cream of colonial society. As Darwin admitted, 'I am [the] only one in the ship who is regularly asked to the Admirals, Chargé d'affaires & other great men' – and this was important in an age when ambassadors took an interest in local geology. It was always Darwin. McCormick's own collecting had gone to pieces. Prickly about his status, he annoyed the Captain, who was glad to see the back of him. His departure suited Darwin too, now ex officio naturalist to the expedition.

Darwin rejoined the 'beautiful' *Beagle*, which had been fitted with a new gun. We are, he joked, ready to take on any 'pirate a float' or 'a thousand savages together.' As he stowed his gear back in 'my own corner,' he even felt part of the Royal Navy. 'The men foreward singing; the centinel [sic] pacing above my head & the little creeking [sic] of the furniture' were reassuring sounds.

On Sunday 1 July he attended a religious service on board the battleship *Warspite* and thrilled when 650 men doffed their hats as the band played 'God Save the King.' 'Seeing, when amongst foreigners, the strength & power of ones own Nation,' he realized, 'gives a feeling of exultation which is not felt at home.' Certainly when among Brazilians, anyway. He loathed these ill-mannered slave-owners. The men were 'ignorant, cowardly, & indolent in the extreme,' and the 'older women' full of 'cunning, sensuality & pride.' The 'monks' were as bad or worse. All degraded themselves by brutalizing the blacks, whom Darwin admired for their courage. He foresaw the day when the slaves would 'assert their own rights & forget to avenge their wrongs.'[14]

The *Beagle* tripped anchor on the 5th. She continued south in winter, along stormy coasts, further towards the treacherous tip of the continent. Everyone shivered in anticipation and grew beards to suit the 'barbarous regions,' even the officers, who began to look aptly patriarchal. The temperature dropped into the fifties a fortnight out, and the skies turned grey, sweeping the deck with squalls. Darwin was nauseous again and found his hammock tiresome. His copy of Milton's *Paradise Lost* afforded some comfort. He carried a pocket edition everywhere, inspired by its vision of a prehistoric world torn by titanic struggle. Nature and art now reached an accord as the ship approached the River Plate. Lightning split the night in a fiendish fireworks display. The *Beagle* lit up, her mast-heads shining with St Elmo's fire, as if painted with phosphorus. At the same time the

OCEAN

Copiapó

Guasco

Coquimbo

Rio Salado

Santa Fé

Rio Paraná

Rio Uruguay

Valparaiso

Mendoza

Santiago

Mercedes

Buenos Aires

Maldonado

Montevideo

River Plate

Concepción

Bahia Blanca

SOUTH

Rio Colorado

Rio Negro

ATLANTIC

Valdivia

Patagones

OCEAN

Island of Chiloé

PACIFIC

Chonos Archipelago

PATAGONIA

Darwin's South America
His main visits to the southern
part of the continent from
26 July 1832 to 6 July 1835

Port Desire

Rio Santa Cruz

FALKLAND ISLANDS

Port Louis

Straits of Magellan

TIERRA DEL FUEGO

Miles

0   100   200   300

Beagle Channel

Cape Horn

0   100 200 300 400 500
Kilometres

ocean was so luminous with micro-organisms that penguins could be 'tracked by . . . their wake.' The sea offered no more 'extraordinary spectacle.'[15]

On the 26th they anchored in the River Plate at Montevideo. Charles was hoping to hear from home but no letters awaited. A political up-date would have been welcome. For weeks speculation had been rife aboard, everyone wondering the fate of the Reform Bill. Was a revolution likely, or had one already occurred? Then came word that the bill was finally passed. Herbert gleefully relayed how Tory lords had defected under pressure, allowing it to scrape through. The two-faced Tories ratting on reform now looked like a dying breed: 'you I think are amongst a Tory Crew; just put one of them in Pickle as by the time you return home, he will be more valuable as a specimen for the Cabinet of the Antiquarians, than your Fungi & Coleoptera . . . If you can get hold of one with [a] Tail, or with ears prolongated, it will be a doubly-interesting specimen.' So, the high Tory FitzRoy growled, the only question left was 'whether there is [to be] a King or a republic.'

Scarcely had Charles begun to think it over than they were caught in their own political upheaval. Montevideo had an unpredictable military government, and Buenos Aires up-river was in a state of permanent revolution. British troops had helped to destabilize the two capitals, having sacked them both twenty-five years before. They had left a bitter legacy, and the Royal Navy still prowled the Plate, protecting the interests of English merchants. To some, the *Beagle* was an intruder. As FitzRoy sailed into Buenos Aires, a shot whistled overhead from a guardship at the port. Furious, the Captain refused to accept the official explanation that it was a quarantine warning. He loaded a broadside and turned the *Beagle* around, informing the guardship as they passed its rotting hulk that next time the greeting would be answered.

More trouble lay back in Montevideo, when the ship returned. The police chief pleaded for help in quelling an insurrection among the local black troops. British residents were at risk, so FitzRoy dispatched fifty-two of the ship's complement, armed to the teeth, to occupy the fort until reinforcements arrived. Darwin accompanied them into the 'dirty town,' pistols in his belt and a cutlass at his side. The black rebels held the ammunition dump and manned cannons in the streets, and they had released and armed prisoners. The *Beagle*'s rag-tag regiment took the fort without incident and, while negotiations went on, grilled 'beefsteaks in the Courtyard.' But Darwin, crushed by a headache, retreated to the ship to watch events unfold.

He was followed by the others, when armed citizens took their place. Within days the shooting started in the town centre. Darwin wondered 'whether Despotism is not better than such uncontrolled anarchy.' Admittedly, he derived 'a great deal of pleasure in the excitement of this sort of work,' but it was not what 'we Philosophers . . . bargain for.'[16]

On 19 August Darwin shipped off his first box of specimens to Henslow, who would store them for his return. The same day the *Beagle* began the first of its charting forays up and down the Patagonian coast. The passage south was rough, but there were compensations. Off Bahia Blanca Darwin witnessed swarms of bristle-jawed worms near the surface. Millions of them, transparent, with hooked claws on their horseshoe-shaped mouths, and all distended with eggs. He had no idea what they were, but he netted huge numbers, driven on by the prospect of examining the spawn. He was back to his first love, kindled by Grant, the sea's tiniest larvae. Using his high-quality microscope, he teased open the eggs; it was precision work, they were minuscule, no bigger than one fiftieth of an inch.[17] But he managed to split them, allowing their 'molecules' to spill out, still suspecting that these were the ultimate particles of life.

He filled reams of zoological notes, with the polyp-bearing creatures dominating his thoughts. There was no blind collecting here; he was following up his Edinburgh interests. He systematically studied reproduction in encrusting sea-mats like *Flustra*. He uprooted a sea-pen *Virgularia* from the mud at Bahia Blanca and wrote page after page on the granular movement inside its stem. This wafting feather-like creature consisted of thousands of feeding polyps all moving together, but with one ovary for the lot, leading him to wonder about the very meaning of individuality.[18]

Bahia Blanca was a remote settlement. Set up as a 'frontier fort' by the government, it stood in a barren expanse of scrubby hills and pampas – 'Devil's Country' to the local Indians. The land was theirs, although seized by the Spanish. Skirmishes were frequent, and a half-caste gaucho cavalry patrolled the region, 'the most savage picturesque group' of men he had ever seen. Only their Indian captives, gnawing the bones of a 'half-roasted horse,' looked more like 'wild beasts.' He heard atrocious stories of the frontier war and its barbarities. 'The Indians torture all their prisoners & the Spaniards shoot theirs.' Even chiefs under a white flag coming to parley were summarily shot. The plains were being ruthlessly cleared, and Darwin found himself fraternizing with murderers.

Englishmen were usually safe, provided they carried guns and local dollars. Darwin had plenty of both and the gauchos were civil. They took him riding, and showed him how to bring down a fleet-footed 'ostrich' (rhea) with their bolas. Then they served roast armadillo and 'ostrich' egg dumplings around an open fire. 'The Armadilloes . . . cooked without their cases, taste & look like duck' and made excellent eating, he decided. Stranger flesh no Glutton ever consumed. He spent September as he would in England, shooting. Deer were common, and he killed three, while an agouti – a twenty-pound chocolate-coloured rodent – furnished 'the very best meat I ever tasted.'[19]

He was in some trepidation whether he would find any good fossils in South America. He learned to his disgust that the French collector Alcide d'Orbigny had been working the area for six months, picking up plum specimens for the Paris Muséum. It was galling; Darwin had paid his own way here, only to find the French government sponsoring their man, allowing him to roam the pampas on a free ticket for six years. It spoke volumes for the serious French attitude towards science. 'I am very selfishly afraid he will get the cream of all the good things,' Darwin reported to Henslow.

His fears were unfounded. On 22 September he was scouring the bay at Punta Alta, ten miles from the *Beagle*. Checking some low cliffs, he spotted the fossilized bones of a colossal extinct mammal. Excitedly, he disinterred teeth and a thigh bone from the quartz and pebble gravel and loaded his pack horses. The Captain was laconic and twitted his companion, smiling 'at the cargoes of apparent rubbish' being carried up the gang plank. It was fine talk with all the Fuegians' clutter in the hold, and Darwin was not to be deterred.

Darwin returned the next day and found a huge skull 'imbedded in a soft rock.' 'It took me nearly three hours to get it out,' and it was dark before he managed to manhandle it on board. The best part of the following day was spent 'packing up the prizes.' He knew little of mammal fossils, such Brobdingnagians least of all. His best guess was that they were 'allied to the Rhinoceros' (which now lives in Africa and Asia). On the 25th he found still more bones. Many were nothing to look at, huge and shattered, and others on the beach had been rolled by the waves. But they were precious. In all England there was only one giant South American fossil – a ground sloth just acquired by the College of Surgeons.

On 8 October he was back, prying out a jawbone. Its one tooth was characteristic, and revealed it to be a megatherium, a huge ground-living relative of the sloth. Near by were six-inch polygonal bony plates, and he mentally amalgamated all the finds to come up with an 'ante-diluvial' armour-coated cow-sized sloth. He wondered how the bones had arrived there, indeed how the embedding gravels had been formed. Perhaps a flood of 'extreme violence' had swept over the pampas, washing bones and pebbles before it? Lyell might not have approved, but then Henslow had warned him off Lyell's gradualist extremism. No matter, finding them was the important part. 'I have been wonderfully lucky,' he wrote home. Some of the mammals were gigantic, and 'many of them are quite new.' Henslow heard that he had fragments of at least six animals – ground sloths, giant armadillo shells, teeth from an enormous rodent, guinea-pig relatives. He crated them ready to ship to Cambridge, 'very curious' to know exactly what he had found.[20]

On 19 October the *Beagle* headed north again, back to Montevideo. She ploughed through luminous seas that reminded him of 'the regions of Chaos & Anarchy' described in *Paradise Lost*. Milton again seemed so apt as they approached the wretched River Plate, for here, with revolutions brewing around, FitzRoy would prepare for their onslaught on that Satanic stronghold, the 'land of fire,' Tierra del Fuego. He had a divine legation to land there, three Fuegians and an Englishman, and this was now the *Beagle*'s first priority. The ship slipped into Montevideo to collect the waiting missionaries and fortify herself for the southerly assault. Darwin readied himself while reading the latest mail.[21]

Cousin Fox relayed the political gossip: the monarchy was intact, although for 'some days we certainly were on the very verge of Revolution.' Still, feelings were running 'very high indeed' with a reformed House of Commons to be elected. Charles's sisters filled in the family news. Hensleigh's father-in-law, Sir James Mackintosh, was dead. Even sadder for Charles, they told of Fanny Owen – her sumptuous wedding, her '*canvassing* Denbighshire with Mr Biddulph' (who was standing for the Whigs), and her vanquished '*housemaid* spirits.' This was not what he wanted to hear. But at least the family loved his diary, which he was sending in instalments, and everyone had great expectations. Susan, echoing the Doctor, thrilled at the thought of 'the quiet Parsonage' where he would eventually settle. Catherine chimed in, baiting him with a prospective bride – Fanny Wedgwood – Charlotte and Emma's sister. A 'nice little invaluable Wife she would be,' and 'an excellent Clerg[y]man's' choice.

Erasmus, ensconced in London with a 'lab in my lodgings,' poured acid on the scheme. He was horrified to hear 'that you still look forward to the horrid little parsonage in the desert.' He wanted his brother set up in town 'near the British Museum or some other learned place.' 'My only chance,' Eras admitted, 'is the Established Church being abolished, & in some places they are beginning to demand pledges to that effect.' With bishop-baiting radicals demanding disestablishment, talk of a church career could be academic.

Eras's letter continued with screeds on politics, talk of the ballot, abolition of tithes, removal of newspaper taxes (originally brought in to cripple the radical press), and the National Political Union refusing toasts to the King. But Eras wondered if his brother was listening: 'I have written you all this politics tho' I suppose you are too far from England to care much about it. Politics wont travel.'[22]

Charles didn't know what to think. Home was constantly on his mind, especially on 'calm, delightful' days, but his old world seemed to be crumbling. Cholera, like reform, had swept across the country, even reaching Shrewsbury. Cambridge friends were acquiring their fellowships, professorships, and parishes. And he was so far away. 'Poor dear old England,' he sighed to Fox. 'I hope my wanderings will not unfit me for a quiet life & that in some future day, I may be fortunate enough to be qualified to become, like you a country Clergyman ... But the Captain says if I indulge in such visions, as green fields & nice little wives &c &c, I shall certainly make a bolt. So ... I must remain contented with sandy plains & great Megatheriums.'

He did, but only just. With the southern regions to explore, he was anxious to push on. The 'detestable' Plate depressed him. 'I would much sooner live in a coal-barge in the Cam,' he moaned to his father and sisters. Fortunately, 'a very nice gentlemanlike person,' Robert Hamond, had recently joined the *Beagle* as a Midshipman. Here was someone to pass the time with, and together he and Darwin planned their final flings ashore. At Buenos Aires the ship anchored, unmolested this time. The gents sallied into town and rode about the muddy chequerboard streets, sizing up the *señoritas*. 'Watching ... these angels gliding' by, they despaired of 'foolish English women.' Even from behind, feasting on 'their charming backs,' Darwin could not help imagining 'how beautiful' they must be.[23]

He also shopped – cigars and scissors, notebooks and pens – saw a dentist, took in a play, and still longed to be off. Each day's delay meant one less during the short summer in the south, where the winds turned vicious in winter. On Sunday 4 November he took in 'several of the Churches.' 'Idolatry' it might be, but he had to 'respect the fervor which appears to reign during the Catholic service as compared with the Protestant.' And all the more impressive for the 'equality of ... ranks' evident during worship. Before departing, he and Hamond sought to make their own peace with God. Hamond, a relative of Musters, knew as well as Darwin what perils lay ahead, and they asked the naval chaplain to give them Holy Communion. He refused a private sacrament, suggesting that, if they were sincere, they should come back with other shipmates.[24] Darwin and Hamond rejoined the *Beagle*, thrown back on FitzRoy's seamanship and other means of grace.

A treat arrived in the post at Montevideo, the second volume of Lyell's *Principles*. It was curiously different from the first. Where that had delved into the gradual changes in past landscapes, this asked whether animals and plants had been modified to match. Was there a natural mechanism for slowly transforming them to keep pace? No, was the short answer. Darwin had received a book-long refutation of Lamarck. He mulled over Lyell's view that each species of animal or plant was adapted to its birth-spot – its 'centre of creation.' Any change, any environmental stress would exterminate it, not transform it. (Darwin could appreciate this, having seen the Megatherium tombs.) Species are continually turning over; as old ones die naturally, new ones are born mysteriously.

It was a sprightly, brilliantly written book, a lawyer's book, piled with clever arguments against the idea that life had evolved and could be represented as a family tree. Can all animals trace their ancestry back to a single stem? Lyell answered no, appalled at the thought of a chimpanzee in the family, of an ape aspiring to 'the attributes and dignity of man.' He went further, arguing that the history of life on earth had been completely misunderstood. The sequence of fossils from ancient times showed no overall progress towards humanity, he argued, idiosyncratically.[25] He knew that with no progress there could be no transmutation. But Lyell had at least posed the question of how species die and are reborn, and in a more genealogical way than Darwin had ever encountered. It was food for thought.

At Montevideo Darwin did more than nose through Lyell's new book. He attended the 'grand ball' at the theatre to 'celebrate the reestablishment of the President,' and returned the next night for Rossini's *Cenerentola*. He worked hard too: two large casks of fossil bones and a small one with skins, beetles, and pickled fish went off to Henslow on the 24th, two days before they sailed. Slumped in the poop cabin, tired out, he wondered how much more he could take. 'One year is nearly completed & the second will be so before we even leave the East coast of S[outh] America. – And then our voyage may be said really to have commenced.'[26] He was desperate to press on, to reach Tierra del Fuego, and then to set off around the world.

10

Troubled Spirits from Another World

SAVAGES HE HAD EXPECTED. They were to be one of the highlights of the voyage – wild primitives, people from another age, the objects of FitzRoy's mission. But the shock of the first encounter still left him reeling.

Three weeks out of Montevideo he saw them. The air had 'the bracing *feel* of an English winter' as the *Beagle* braved the squalls and sailed into Good Success Bay, near the southern tip of Tierra del Fuego. Yet there they were, 'perched on a wild peak overhanging the sea' – naked. Raw 'untamed' Fuegians, yelling hoarsely and flailing their arms, showing their 'dirty copper' complexion beneath the scanty animal skins slung over their shoulders.

Never in his wildest imagination had he thought that the three native missionaries aboard – York Minster, Jemmy Button, and Fuegia Basket – had been like this. On 18 December 1832 he rowed ashore to meet the savages with FitzRoy and a well-armed guard. The young men were nearly his own height and powerfully built, with long black hair, painted faces, and startled expressions. Timid at first, and terrified of the guns, they jabbered and gesticulated. Then, warming to a gift of red cloth, they engaged the officers in a ludicrous charade, pulling 'hideous grimaces' at one another, back-slapping merrily, and dancing around the beach. It was 'without exception the most curious & interesting spectacle' that Darwin had ever seen, and he drew conclusions swiftly. These 'wretched looking beings' had no proper clothes, no fit language, and no decent homes or property, barring bows and arrows. 'How entire the difference between savage & civilized man is. – It is greater than between a wild & [a] domesticated animal ... I believe if the world was searched, no lower grade of man could be found.'[1]

Were they even men? Their dress recalled the 'Devils on the Stage' in the opera *Der Freischütz* that he had seen at Edinburgh. Their gestures made them seem like 'the troubled spirits of another world.' He almost begrudged them the status of 'fellow-creature.' 'A wild man is a miserable animal,' he shook his head solemnly. Yet what of York and Jemmy, who – though from different tribes – also came ashore with their missionary-minder Richard Matthews? Hadn't they been civilized? Didn't their year in England show their kinship – and point up man's enormous 'power of improvement'? Dressed sensibly for an English winter, they stood apart on the beach, mocking the wild men. When the oldest Fuegian came up to York and harangued him for growing a beard, York burst into 'an immoderate fit of laughter.' Surely here was proof of the plasticity of human nature.

With everyone back on board, young Matthews remarked glibly that the savages 'were no worse than he had supposed them to be.' This was sheer sang-froid coming from one who was about to be left among them for years. And what was this callow chap's scope for comparison? Darwin remembered Cambridge – Sedgwick's and Henslow's soirées and the great guns at high table. Did these lofty moralists come from such stock too? Did Shakespeare and Newton? As he surveyed the district he was in a sombre mood. Climbing into the mountains, he collected alpine plants and insects amid 'universal signs of violence.' The 'decaying & fallen trees' harked back to the tropical forest, but here, he sensed, 'in this still solitude, death instead of life is the predominant spirit.' It was a curious Christmas vigil, held at the end of the world: he was pondering a grim outlook for man. Days later, as the *Beagle* rounded the mariner's graveyard at Cape Horn, heading for York Minster's country in the west, nature played an awful counterpoint, with 'black clouds . . . rolling across the sky' and hailstones lashing the sea.

On 24 December FitzRoy ran in to Wigwam Cove on Hermit Island, further south and facing the Antarctic. All duty was suspended, and the hills resounded as the sailors shot fresh game for their feast. On the 'gala day' the grog came out while Darwin set off with Sulivan and Hamond to climb the island's principal mountain. It was an easy ascent, and along the way they added to the din, 'screaming to find out echos, Sulivan amusing himself by rolling . . . huge stones' down the precipice, and 'I,' Darwin jotted in his diary, 'impetuously hammering . . . the rocks.' The Fuegians were watching, it transpired. 'They must have thought us the powers of darkness,' he laughed, for fear 'kept them concealed.'[2]

This was his last laugh for weeks. The weather worsened. Putting to sea during a lull on New Year's Eve turned out to be a mistake. The wind veered southwesterly with a vengeance, and the *Beagle* had to fight her way along the rugged underbelly of the continent, league by agonizing league. For Darwin it was hell. Constantly retching at the rail, with the temperature in the forties and the deck awash, he knew that his 'spirits, temper, & stomach' could not 'hold out much longer.' On Saturday 12 January 1833 the gale turned into a fearsome storm. Blinded by the spray, the Captain lost track of the ship's position. He confessed that he had never seen conditions so bad.

At noon on Sunday the storm was at its height. Three gigantic rollers bore down on the *Beagle*. She 'met and rose over the first unharmed but ... her way was checked; the second deadened her way completely, throwing her off the wind; and the third great sea, taking her right a-beam, turned her so far over, that all the lee bulwark ... was two or three feet under water.' The whale-boat broke loose and had to be cut free; the sea poured into the poop cabin and below deck. Everything was in chaos. Then slowly, 'like a cask,' she righted herself, and with the ports 'knocked open,' the water drained away. Another such wave and the bark would have lived up to her class's reputation and become a 'coffin.' But the worst was over, and FitzRoy took shelter behind False Cape Horn, where Darwin checked the damage. His 'drying paper & plants' were ruined by the salt water. Terrified by the gales, he prayed 'May Providence keep the Beagle out of them.'[3]

Yet this was God's odyssey – his protection could be assumed. The Captain now decided to set up his mission station among Jemmy's people, as York 'from his free choice' had agreed to live there. (So Darwin said. FitzRoy noted the 'attentions' that York was paying to 'his intended wife, Fuegia,' which 'afforded much amusement.') A large party, Darwin among them, set off in a flotilla of small boats from the ship, following the Beagle Channel – discovered on the last voyage – to Ponsonby Sound, and Jemmy's home in Woollya cove. On 23 January they beached the boats and unloaded the 'wine glasses, butter-bolts, tea-trays, soup turins [sic], mahogany dressing case, fine white linen ... & an endless variety of similar things,' all of which to Darwin showed 'culpable folly.' Huts were built and gardens planted, with scores of inscrutable Fuegians looking on.

Matthews, piously resolved, bade his shipmates farewell, knowing that the Captain would pay him a final visit after the party explored further west.

The scenery was spectacular. They proceeded along the Beagle Channel, tracking a granite ridge of mountains, the backbone of Tierra del Fuego. To Darwin its horizontal tree-line looked like the 'high-water mark' on a beach, and he gloried in the 'mantle of perpetual snow.' The steep slopes plummeted straight down to the channel, where vast 'beryl blue' glaciers fed the waves with icebergs. One of the glaciers nearly marooned them. While dining on shore half a mile away, they heard a 'thundering crash' as a huge mass of ice fell from its face. The impact sent 'great rolling waves' racing towards their flotilla. Darwin was quick to act. He and others seized the boats, hauling them to safety just as the first breaker crashed down. FitzRoy was so impressed that, the next day, he named an expanse of water 'Darwin Sound.' But Darwin had acted less out of bravado than fear. Without the boats, he reflected, 'how dangerous would our lot have been, surrounded ... by hostile Savages & deprived of ... provisions.'⁴

Some Fuegians were indeed hostile. With courage 'like that of a wild beast,' they menaced the party's overnight camp, and armed guards were posted. Charles, keeping watch, shivered at his vulnerability in this land. 'The quiet of the night is only interrupted by the heavy breathing of the men & the cry of the night birds. – the occasional distant bark of a dog reminds one that the Fuegians may be prowling, close to the tents, ready for a fatal rush.' Everyone believed that they were among cannibals. Jemmy, when asked about the practice, had given the expected answer, stating tongue-in-cheek that 'in winter they sometimes eat the women.' No one questioned his authority, and the party dreaded what they might find back at 'the Settlement.' Returning along the Channel after nine days, they found that Matthews and the rest had suffered from little more than bullying and systematic looting. All their possessions had been divided indiscriminately among the Fuegians. Here was further evidence of co-operative savagery, Darwin surmised. 'The perfect equality of all the inhabitants will for many years prevent their civilization.' Until 'some chief' rises who 'by his power' can heap up possessions for himself, 'there must be an end to all hopes of bettering their condition.'

Given the mayhem, Matthews conceded defeat and rejoined his shipmates, leaving eleven-year-old Fuegia with York, and a disconsolate Jemmy, to the mercies of their countrymen. York would try to live 'like an Englishman,' Darwin believed, but none would be happy. 'They have far too much sense not to see the vast superiority of civilized over uncivilized habits.' Their only hope lay in the gardens that he had helped plant. Tilling the soil would teach them discipline and improve their diet. Eventually the example of their prosperity might alter the habits of many 'savage inhabitants,' and the whole Fuegian coast would welcome English sailors.[5]

With the added ballast of Darwin's granite and slate samples, the *Beagle* steered for the Falkland Islands, or the Malvinas, as they were called in Buenos Aires. He expected to be the guest of Argentine colonists, who had been settling them for years. But on 1 March, when the ship anchored at Port Louis, the most eastern point in the archipelago, he saw a Union Jack flying. British warships had taken the islands for the Crown in January, forcing out the Argentine army. All South America was 'in a ferment' about the British action, Darwin heard. 'By the aweful [sic] language of Buenos Ayres one would suppose this great republic meant to declare war against England!' It seemed ludicrous, the more so because only one English-man actually lived on the islands, a storekeeper named Dickson who kept the flag. But Darwin saw their strategic importance for east-west trade, and this, as FitzRoy explained, was why he intended to make an accurate survey.[6]

While the measurements went on, Darwin wandered about the country, 'breaking rocks, shooting snipes, & picking up the few living' creatures he could find on East Falkland. The region was desolate, and the weather 'cold & boisterous,' but by way of compensation he stumbled on 'most primitive looking' sandstones. He knew that Sedgwick was preoccupied with the oldest fossil-bearing rocks like these. Sure enough, they contained lamp-shells, bivalve molluscs, like the rocks in Wales. At a stroke of his geological hammer, the 'whole aspect' of the Falklands changed. Here was a fine chance to compare ancient faunas from two corners of the world. And not only fossil faunas; he was taking more interest in the spread of living animals and plants. He had never spent so long on a small offshore island, and made a memo to observe 'differences of species & proportionate Numbers,' and to relate them to their habitats.[7]

He kept returning to his first love, the tiny marine creatures, intrigued by the granules spewed from their disrupted eggs, convinced he was looking at the ultimate atoms of life. On the Falklands he collected some of 'that ambiguous tribe,' the encrusting algae: primi-

136

tive, stony, branching tufts. So primitive, in fact, that even the kingdom they belonged to was debated: Grant called them plants, Lamarck animals. Darwin kept dissecting, trying to determine which. He also studied their egg-matter, like Henslow thinking it inert and acted on by some external 'creative power.'[8] Eventually he came to the conclusion that these incrustations must be strange primitive plants.

FitzRoy meanwhile had dipped into his pocket again. He bought a schooner from a swashbuckling sealer and cannibalized a wreck to refit her. It was without Admiralty approval, but it allowed him to double his charting efforts. The two ships put to sea in early April heading north, back up the Patagonian coast to the mouth of the Rio Negro, 170 miles from Bahia Blanca. For months Darwin had been keen to go ashore here, where the 'interior country is *totally* unknown.' Gliding along in 'celestial' weather, he eyed the cliffs longingly. They looked like 'an El Dorado to a Geologist.' But the Captain's plans kept changing, and at the last minute the wind, 'that omnipotent & overbearing master,' put paid to the visit. The *Beagle* tailed her sister ship all the way back to the loathsome River Plate, where she anchored at Montevideo. Nothing much had happened here during that period, 'with the exception of a few revolutions,' Darwin noted as he collected five months' post.

The schooner had to be fitted with a new copper bottom to protect it from boring worms. The work was being done at Maldonado, sixty miles away at the mouth of the estuary, and would last several months. When FitzRoy went to check the progress, Darwin accompanied him and took lodgings. The town was barren, and the hilly countryside teemed with horses, cattle, and bandits. His Spanish was bad, but he managed to find a pair of guides to show him the hinterland, and on 9 May they galloped off in 'high spirits,' rattling with 'pistols & sabres.'[9]

They spent days riding through 'endless green hills' littered with cactus and stony outcrops. He was struck by the rhea flocks, commenting on the impressive sight of thirty birds passing over the crest of a hill. They nested together, according to the gauchos. Many females lay at the same spot (Darwin himself had counted twenty-seven eggs in a clutch) and one male incubates and protects the brood. At night Darwin stayed at 'drinking shops,' where moustachioed gauchos with 'daggers at their waist' and 'great spurs clanking on their heels' stood around, swilling spirits and smoking cigars. Some evenings he had a taste of home. In Uruguayan cattle country hospitality was never refused, and though even rich landowners lived on mud floors they offered plentiful food. He repaid his hosts with gadgetry. His pocket compass was much admired for its 'powers' of showing direction, and he amazed them by striking matches with his teeth. After the antics, the men lit cigars, and 'with a little impromptu singing accompanied by the Guitar,' a pleasant day came to an end.

Two weeks later Darwin was back in Maldonado, having covered over 200 miles. The whole area was inundated, with swampy plains and swollen rivers. No one could remember electric storms of such ferocity. The power of the bolts was evident in the dunes outside town. He picked up smooth, glassy tubes, some extending five feet into the sand, where the lightning shafts had fused the grains into glass. Turning to the wildlife, he found that flashing a coin in town worked wonders, bringing every boy with a stray creature to his door. The carcasses piled up – rats, mice, snakes – and skinning them was messy nauseous work, especially the deer, which gave off an 'overpoweringly strong and offensive odour.'[10]

He took 'almost every bird in this neighbourhood,' eighty species in all, killing a dozen new ones a week – owls, cuckoos, flycatchers, mockingbirds, shrikes, and strange scissor-birds, which skim the water with their lower bill trailing for fish. He slit open stomachs, picking through the half-digested contents, and noted habits, song, and nest sites. It was too much work for one person and was made easier by the help of a sixteen-year-old sailor. Syms Covington was the *Beagle*'s fiddler and odd-job man, and no jobs came odder than Mr Darwin's. In no time he learned to shoot and skin birds. The arrangement had FitzRoy's blessing, but with the schooner almost ready and the *Beagle* about to sail, Darwin wanted to make it permanent. Having a full-time servant would enable him to step up his capture rate. He offered to take Covington on at his own expense. FitzRoy agreed, and let the boy go cheaply to Darwin, £30 a year.[11]

He and the Captain were getting on fine. Or at least FitzRoy regarded the 'Philosopher' – his new nickname – as 'a very superior young man,' with the right mix of 'necessary qualities which makes him feel at home, and happy, and makes everyone his friend.'

Darwin did not always feel as contented as his dining companion made out. In early July, pitching at anchor outside Montevideo, he was dying to 'double the Horn' and head off around the world for England. At times like this only crab larvae and the 'old bones' kept him from bolting back across the Atlantic.

Letters from home enticed him still more. The news was old of course – three months at least, but no less bracing for a reformer confined with an arch-Tory. In the December General Election Uncle Jos had stood for the Whigs in the new borough of Stoke-on-Trent and been returned with a handsome majority. Unfortunately the 'March of liberal opinion' was becoming a charge, and the whole family began to quail. Radicals were streaming into the Commons, shouting their demands for democracy and disestablishment. Jos couldn't bear them. Susan reported that they were becoming 'so fierce & licentious . . . that Papa gets more & more of a Tory every day.' Charles revelled in the political gossip, and, expecting an end to 'that monstrous stain on our boasted liberty, Colonial Slavery,' cheered 'Hurrah for the honest Whigs'! 'Thank God the cold-hearted Tories . . . have for the present run their race.'[12]

The post-bag held other surprises. The Wedgwood newly-weds were having babies, and the latest, born to Hensleigh and Fanny, had apparently forestalled a scandal. In London Erasmus had been seeing rather a lot of his cousin's wife. It was an open secret, the whole family knew. Fanny seems 'quite as much married to him as to Hensleigh,' wrote sister Catherine, 'and Papa continually prophecies a fine paragraph in the Paper about them.' But the baby put an end to Ras's 'junkitting [sic] at her house,' at least temporarily, and the family were spared from coping with dishonour.

Central to all the letters, however, was the story of Fanny Wedgwood's death. The cousin Charles had been matched with had died the previous August. Charles's sisters and cousin Charlotte relayed the whole distressing story. It was all over in a week: the fever with 'vomitings & pain,' followed by a few days' comfort, then a sudden relapse and within hours, the end. She was only twenty-six. Maer was melancholy as never before. Just two of his cousins remained there: Elizabeth the eldest, hunchbacked and only four feet tall, who was resigned to spinsterhood; and Emma, the youngest, who had been closest to Fanny and felt the loss acutely. It was expected that Charles would too. He had never been taken with Fanny – she was short and plain – but as a parson's wife, said his sisters, she would have been ideal. Everyone feared that marriage and the Church would now pass from his mind.[13]

Charles, bobbing in the Plate, never mentioned Fanny's death. He stonewalled his sisters in reply, asking for books, boots, lenses, tape measures, and more matches to astound the natives. He boasted of his hard work, adding that natural history would remain his 'favourite pursuit' for many years to come: 'doing what *little* one can to encrease [sic] the general stock of knowledge is as respectable an object of life, as one can in any likelihood pursue.' Not that he lacked a 'delightful vision' to match his sisters' happy 'day dream' of his future. He still yearned for a 'dear little lady' to take care of him and his house. But he did not confide it to his sisters, whose nannying made him uneasy. Only Fox found out his real feelings, when Charles admitted that 'so much time spent wandering' was indeed 'a serious evil.' 'I often conjecture, what will become of me; my wishes certainly would make me a country clergyman.'

One letter was left to write, to Henslow. Charles saved it until last, not having heard whether his collections had arrived safely. He sent Henslow the next consignment with trepidation: four barrels of corpses, skins, pickled fish, beetles in pill-boxes, and rocks – half his summer's haul. Henslow also received the future itinerary. Charles was itching to leave 'this stupid, unpicturesque side' of the continent and reach Valparaiso in Chile, where he could 'cross & recross the grand chain of the Andes.' Once past Tierra del Fuego finally it would 'all be Holidays.' The very thought of 'fine Coralls [sic], the warm glowing weather, [and] the blue sky of the Tropics' made him 'wild with delight.' So too did the prospect of Henslow's first letter, should it ever arrive.

FitzRoy renamed his schooner *Adventure*, and on the evening of 24 July the sister ships sailed south at last for the Rio Negro. 'The whole sky was brilliant with lightning; it was a wild looking night to go to sea, but time is too precious to lose even a bad portion of it.'[14]

After a tedious passage in adverse winds they arrived at the mouth of the river. Darwin rode upstream to the town of Patagones, where he decided to proceed overland and meet the *Beagle* back at Bahia Blanca. This was 'Devil's Country' again, full of salt lakes and sandstone and marauding Indians. Geologically it was as intriguing as it was politically dangerous. He paid £20 for a 'trusty' guide and they set off with a British trader and a band of gauchos to see General Juan Manuel de Rosas, whose army had been sent from Buenos Aires with orders to 'exterminate the Indians.' His permission was needed to pass north.

On 13 August they reached Rosas' camp on the Rio Colorado. The 'villainous Banditti-like army' and their 600 Indian allies presented the most extraordinary mix of races that Darwin had ever seen. But the most striking character of all was the General. He was 'a perfect gaucho,' with a gaudy shawl about his waist, 'fringed drawers' beneath, and a poncho. His horsemanship was as legendary as his 'despotic powers.' From keeping 300,000 head of cattle on his ranches, he knew all about rounding up and slaughtering. Darwin shook a hand soaked in blood. Rosas was grave, and the interview went off 'without a smile.' He granted Darwin a passport and even put government horses at his disposal to whisk the 'Naturalista' across the pampas.

These flat, grassy plains were the home of Indians, anteaters, and armadillos. And another, rarer creature, Darwin heard. The gauchos repeatedly mentioned a bird called 'Avestruz Petise,' a rhea – but smaller and darker than the common form, with feathered legs and blue-tinged eggs.[15] Few had seen one, but the nests had been found, and everyone confirmed that it was more plentiful further south.

Darwin was becoming quite a gaucho himself. The rough-riding suited him perfectly. At night, crouched around a fire, eating roasted game, he jotted down notes and relaxed. 'I . . . drink my Mattee & smoke my cigar, & then lie down & sleep as comfortably with the Heavens for a Canopy as in a feather bed.' Well armed, with fresh horses and ruthless companions, he had little to fear from the hostiles. Indeed, he was beginning to appreciate the 'great benefits' of General Rosas's 'war of extermination.' For landowners it promised a bonanza. 'It will . . . throw open four or 500 miles in length of fine country for the produce of cattle.'

Back at Bahia Blanca Darwin kicked around for a few days waiting for the *Beagle*. Then he bought a 'fine powerful young horse' for less than five pounds and rode back to the cliffs at Punta Alta. His luck was still holding. This time he took 'nearly an entire skeleton' from its rocky tomb: a bizarre horse-sized mammal with an enormous pelvis and a small, long face like an anteater's. This was a real prize because it had remained undisturbed, in its original place (rather than in pieces on the beach). Page after page of his notepad was filled up as he thought on the implications. It had lived before the sea shells, found in the layer above; and everything pointed to a gradual deposition of sediments and then uplift of the strata. But how old were all these megatheriums? What did the country look like in their day? And why had they all died out? He dreamed himself back to an archaic world, where bull-sized sloths roamed unimaginable plains.

The spot was secluded and the quietness 'almost sublime,' but he was living under no illusions. It was still an infernal land, where saline lakes encrusted with snow-white saltpetre baked in the blazing sun. Its conquerors were much the same. Beneath a fair veneer of civility, the gauchos were butchers. Back at the fort, he heard the latest about the General's war.

Everyone believed that it was 'the justest war' because it was being waged 'against Barbarians.' No tactic was too extreme. Prisoners were taken and treated like animals – corralled into a 'Christian's zoo,' Darwin seethed. The Indian women 'who appear above twenty years old, are massacred in cold blood,' he was informed. The younger ones too, if ugly. Tactfully he complained 'that this appeared rather inhuman,' only to be told by a soldier that 'they breed so.' Genocide was not the way God intended population growth to be checked. 'Who would believe in this age in a Christian, civilized country that such atrocities were committed?' The butchery might benefit the economy, but it would corrupt the people. 'The country will be in the hands of white Gaucho savages instead of copper-coloured Indians. The former being a little superior in civilization, as they are inferior in every moral virtue.'[16]

When the *Beagle* arrived, Covington fetched the bones from Punta Alta while Darwin made arrangements to travel 400 miles overland to Buenos Aires, where he would meet with the ship again. On 8 September he set off with his guide, heading north along the line of fortified 'postas,' left by Rosas in conquered territory. Kill or die was the unwritten law of this godforsaken plain. There was '*nothing* to eat' but what could be caught – rheas, deer, armadillos – and the vultures circled ominously overhead. Like a gaucho Darwin survived for days on nothing but meat, and enjoyed it – even 'one of the very favourite dishes of the country,' foetal puma. Still, on reaching Buenos Aires two weeks later, he was grateful to live with an English merchant's family, sip a cup of tea, and enjoy 'all the comforts' of home.

The *Beagle* was back surveying in the Plate. Darwin sent Covington out to shoot and skin birds while he stayed just long enough to stock up on sugar, snuff, cigars, gunpowder, and shot. Then he continued another 150 miles up-country to hunt for more bones. He found only one 'enormous gnawing' tooth and a few huge 'Mastodon' bones along the Rio Parana. But these were 'so completely decayed & soft' that they fell apart in his hands, and he pushed on to the 'straggling town' of Santa Fé, where he collapsed with a fever in the first week of October. Two days on his back convinced him to cut his ride short. He remembered Musters, who had died of fever within a week. Given the choice of deathbeds, Darwin preferred one in Buenos Aires; he dragged himself down to the Parana and booked passage on a pocket-sized sloop. The trip down river was tortuous, with gales and voracious mosquitoes. Darwin languished in bed, cursing, unable even to sit up in his tiny cabin. His fever left and, fed up with the boat, he paddled the rest of the way to the capital in a canoe. A local revolution had broken out. He found the Spanish military in Buenos Aires blockaded by 'a furious cut-throat set of rebels' loyal to General Rosas. Darwin shuttled back and forth between the armies, and eventually obtained leave to enter the city on foot after he mentioned the General's former 'civility.' He bribed a man to smuggle in Covington, who had 'nearly lost his life in a quicksand & my gun completely.' Together they darted about the city for ten days, dodging the 'lawless soldiery' while arranging for their possessions to be shipped out. There was one true 'Gentleman in Buenos Ayres, the English Minister,' who came to their aid. FitzRoy in Montevideo had sent a message that he was preparing to sail. On 2 November they squeezed on to a packet crowded with refugees and fled for Montevideo as the musket volleys started. The 'utter profligacy' of dictatorship dominated Darwin's thoughts as he picked his way through sick women and children on the deck. He wished the revolutionaries 'would, like Kilkenny Cats, fight till nothing but the tails' were left.[17]

At Montevideo Darwin rushed aboard the *Beagle*, raring to go, thinking of 'the blue skys & the Bananas of the Tropics.' But no. FitzRoy was delayed by his chartwork. And the sister ship had yet to be provisioned for the treacherous passage around the Horn. He made the best of the time. He had letters to read and answer – the last, he feared, for many months. The news was all titillation and tut-tuts. Eras, still carrying on with Hensleigh's wife, was being paired off with Emma Wedgwood to avert 'an *action* in the Papers.' Fanny Biddulph, miserably married to a 'desperately selfish' ogre, had begun asking 'prettily & coquettishly' about her 'old Postillion.' And his sisters – imagine it – were 'afraid when ever we read of your enjoying yourself.'

Darwin busied himself packing two boxes and a cask, containing 'nearly 200 skins of birds & animals,' a collection of mice, a jar of fish, a case of insects, a box of stones, and 'a bundle of seeds, which,' he told Henslow, 'I send as a most humble apology for my idleness in Botany.' His fossil bones and rocks went separately to Plymouth in an immense box. Again he despatched everything with a heavy heart. Still no letter had come. For all he knew his caskets were in Davy Jones's locker. Or if not, perhaps Sedgwick and the rest were laughing at them – he had no idea. He was anxious for his collections to be applauded, desperate to find out 'whether I am going the right road.'[18]

By now the fossils meant everything to him, the romance of calling up ancient life. Nothing touched the raw excitement of the cliff face: 'the pleasure of the first days partridge shooting ... cannot be compared to finding a fine group of fossil bones, which tell their story of former times with almost a living tongue.' He decided to make a 400-mile round journey to Mercedes near the Rio Uruguay, where he had missed some curious rock formations after falling ill. Like all the 'galloping' trips since Punta Alta, it had one main object: to examine the sediments entombing the sloths – to understand the megatheriums' world and its end. He rode from ranch to ranch until he reached the picturesque megatherium country. He stayed at an estate belonging to a Mr Keen (presumably an Englishman) on 22 November. His host knew of a farm with 'giant's bones' simply lying in the yard and, four days later, they rode over. For eighteen pence Darwin came away with the best part of a perfect skull, 2 feet 4 inches long with strange curved teeth.[19] Despite the weight, he carried his one-and-sixpenny prize in triumph the 120 miles back to Montevideo.

In town, Darwin packed up and 'prepared to leave for ever.' It was an unsentimental farewell. The people of the Plate depressed him, and he had been among them too long. Robbery was rife, murder condoned, and justice at a premium. 'Every *public officer* is to be bribed,' and there were no 'Gentlemen par excellence.' Their absence was vexing, and on 5 December he was relieved to be back in FitzRoy's company as the *Beagle* made ready to sail. The artist Earle's health had 'so entirely broken up' that he quit the ship, and the Captain introduced his replacement, Conrad Martens, endorsing him in typical FitzRoy fashion, quirkily: 'By my faith in Bumpology, I am sure you will like him.' With twelve months' stores on board and the *Adventure* under the command of Mr Wickham, they were 'now on the road (though not the shortest) to England.'[20] Darwin was counting the days.

FitzRoy weighed anchor at four the next morning, and for seventeen days the sister ships sailed down the Patagonian coast. On 23 December they put in at Port Desire for the holiday, 600 miles north of Cape Horn. Darwin 'by great good luck' shot a llama-like guanaco, which fully dressed weighed 170 pounds, and a hearty Christmas dinner was had by all. Martens went one better and shot a small rhea, and it was only after the bird had been cooked and consumed that Darwin, suddenly and embarrassingly, recalled the gaucho story of the rare 'petise.' His first sight of the new bird, and he had eaten it unknowingly! Fortunately 'the Head neck legs, one wing' and larger feathers could be rescued, and they were promptly preserved and packed in the hold.

The 'stillness & desolation' here gave him inexplicable pleasure. Walking for miles on the faceless plain, he took a score of new birds. And in the shore cliffs he found 'the same great oyster bed' – just above sea level – that occurred the length of the continent, showing the recent upheaval of the land. But there were no fossils to exhume. He was already thinking of himself as a 'fossil Resurrectionist,' somewhat more respectable than the Burke and Hare variety, and when the *Beagle* dropped anchor at Port St Julian in January 1834 – 110 miles further south – he searched again. It was a wasteland, devoid of fresh water, and the only large mammal – the guanaco – could drink from the salt-lakes. Again, in the cliffs on the harbour's edge he found bits of spine and a complete hind leg of 'some large animal, I fancy a Mastodon.' 'This is interesting,' he mused; these great beasts clearly ranged far down into cold latitudes, and evidently a number of them 'were fellow brethren in the ancient plains.'[21] The old question popped up: what was the mastodon's world like, and was it as waterless and windswept as the one he tramped over?

Beating against strong westerly gales, the *Beagle* entered the Straits of Magellan on 26 January and proceeded to St Gregory's Bay, where members of a semi-civilized tribe of Patagonian 'giants' – over six feet tall – were entertained on board. 'They behaved quite like gentlemen,' despite their red-painted faces, guanaco hides, and streaming hair, and they 'used a knife & fork & helped themselves with a spoon,' Darwin noted, impressed. These Indians had long traded with the sealers, and they spoke smatterings of English and Spanish. They were 'excellent practical naturalists,' and Darwin had 'the greatest faith in their observations.' He quizzed one half-breed born in the northern provinces about the 'petise' rhea, and heard that it was the *only* rhea this far south. The two species met around the Rio Negro; otherwise the common rhea kept to the north, the 'petise' to the south. It confirmed that he had a new species with a distinct range.

Civilized savages showed how improvable humans were. Red-dyed Indians with real table manners were proof that the chasm between the brutal races and refined Englishmen could be bridged. But would the effect last – would these tame Indians turn wild again? The answer lay further south. He was curious about the fate of Jemmy, York, and Fuegia.

The ship pressed on to Tierra, anchoring at Port Famine in

'piercingly cold' gusty rain. Here hundreds of Spanish colonists had starved in the sixteenth century, and the *Beagle*'s Capt. Stokes had taken his life in 1826. On 6 February Darwin left the ship, compass in hand, to ascend 2600-foot Mount Tarn. As before, his mood matched the terrain. 'In the deep ravines the death-like scene of desolation exceeds all description,' he shuddered in the chill. 'Great mouldering trunks' lay strewn about, and 'everything was dripping with water.' 'Even the very Fungi could not flourish.' At the summit he found 'shells in the rocks' and a 'true Tierra del Fuego view:' 'irregular chains of hills, mottled with patches of snow; deep yellowish-green valleys; & arms of the sea running in all directions.' In the distance, ninety miles away, the highest peak in the south, awesome Mount Sarmiento, stood cloaked in perpetual snow.

FitzRoy threaded the ship back through the maze of waterways, past Spermaceti whales jumping out of the water. He completed his survey of the north-east region, and on 24 February anchored under Wollaston Island, just above the Horn.[22] This was Fuegian country, and everyone mingled with the inhabitants for ten days. As in his first shattering encounter with these 'troubled spirits,' Darwin was left reeling, asking questions, hard insistent ones.

What was he to make of these wretched people? Had they lived here in their present state 'since the creation'? If not, why did they leave 'the fine regions of the North' – the tropics – 'to enter upon one of the most inhospitable countries in the world'? Why did they remain naked? – he saw one pregnant woman 'absolutely so,' with the rain 'dripping from her body.' Why were they unkempt, 'their red skins filthy & greasy, their hair entangled, their voices discordant, their gesticulation violent & without any dignity'? Lyell in his *Principles of Geology* worried about Lamarck's chimpanzee ancestry crushing man's 'belief in the high genealogy of his species.' But how high the genealogy here – among aboriginals scarcely better than brutes? Where was the dignity for humans who slept uncovered 'on the wet ground . . . coiled up like animals'? Or who were locked in perpetual warfare over 'the means of subsistence'? He found these 'unbroken savages' detestable, 'more amusing than any Monkeys' but less able to enjoy their existence in this forlorn country. Yet he was helplessly intrigued. He had to find an explanation – 'Whence have these people come?'[23]

Nothing had intrigued him more, or appalled him more: 'one can hardly make oneself believe that they are fellow creatures placed in the same world.' Like animals, they were bereft of the higher pleasures:

They cannot know the feeling of having a home – & still less that of domestic affection . . . What is there for imagination to paint, for reason to compare, for judgement to decide upon. – to knock a limpet from the rock does not even require cunning, that lowest power of the mind. Their skill, like the instinct of animals is not improved by experience; the canoe, their most ingenious work, poor as it may be, we know has remained the same for the last 300 years.

'Although essentially the same creature,' Darwin conceded, remembering the civilized Jemmy and his friends, 'how little must the mind of one of these beings resemble that of an educated man.'

It all seemed to fly in Lyell's face – Lyell, who damned talk of monkeys and savages and philosophers linked in an evolutionary train. Lyell would have no smooth mental scale 'from "apes with foreheads villa[i]nous low,"' through savages to sherry-sipping Anglo-Saxons. Human beings might be diverse, but they showed only a 'slight deviation from a common standard.' Here spoke a man who had never seen savages; this was comforting armchair philosophy. Darwin was facing the most degraded natives, and being forced to recognize a world of difference – a world of improvement – 'between the faculties of a Fuegian savage & a Sir Isaac Newton.'

Yet for all their defects, the Fuegians were not dying out, so they must possess 'a sufficient share of happiness (whatever its kind may be) to render life worth having.' In fact, their miserable minds and manners seemed suited to their despicable environment. Nature, 'by making habit omnipotent,' had strangely 'fitted the Fuegian to the climate & productions of his country.'[24] The question was, did Jemmy's table manners mean that savages could be successfully civilized in only a few years? Could his old habits be broken so easily?

As Darwin pondered, the *Beagle* sailed fifty miles north, entering Ponsonby Sound to pay a final call on Jemmy. The mountains ahead were magnificent. Snow-clad and gilded in the rosy morning light, their 'broken & sharp peaks' presented 'a feast to the mind.' FitzRoy, marking the Philosopher's twenty-fifth birthday, had named the highest one Mount Darwin. They anchored near Woollya cove, where the missionaries had been left a year before. The huts were deserted, the gardens trampled and overgrown. In the distance canoes approached, a couple of the occupants anxiously scrubbing their faces. One looked familiar; it was Jemmy. But Darwin had never seen 'so complete & grievous a change.' It was 'painful to behold

147

him; thin, pale, & without a remnant of clothes, excepting a bit of blanket round his waist: his hair, hanging over his shoulders; & so ashamed of himself, he turned his back to the ship' as the canoe came alongside. Then he looked up and raised his hand, 'as a sailor touches his hat.' A pathetic salute. FitzRoy was overwhelmed. They bundled him on board and clothed him immediately in preparation for dinner at the Captain's table. He used his cutlery properly, and, speaking 'as much English as ever,' told Darwin and FitzRoy of his companions' villainy. York Minster had persuaded him to come back to his own country with Fuegia. There one night, while he slept, the pair had absconded with all his possessions, leaving him as FitzRoy had first found him, naked.

Outside in a canoe 'a young, & for a Fuegian ... beautiful Squaw,' was crying implacably. She was pregnant, and said to be Jemmy's wife; only his reappearance on deck soothed her. The next day after breakfast Jemmy bade them goodbye. No, he had 'not the least wish to return to England.' He was 'happy and contented,' he declared, with 'plenty fruits,' 'plenty birdies,' 'ten guanaco in snow time,' and 'too much fish.' From his abundance he left gifts – a pair of 'beautiful otter skins,' arrows for the Captain, and 'two spearheads expressly for Mr Darwin.' He had made them himself. The ship got under way while he was still on board, sending his squaw into another fit of tears. Quickly he entered the canoe and dried them.

Everyone was 'sorry to shake hands with poor Jemmy for the last time,' Darwin recorded. 'I hope & have little doubt that he will be as happy as if he had never left his country; which is much more than I formerly thought.' Jemmy's habits were ingrained, it was now obvious. For untold generations his people had adapted to this wilderness, and no civilizing influence could erase his deep-seated instincts. Human differences were more profound than Lyell knew.

As his ancestors had done for centuries in this 'land of fire,' Jemmy lit 'a farewell signal ... as the ship stood out of Ponsonby Sound, on her course to East Falkland Island.'[25]

11

Shaken Foundations

THE *BEAGLE* ARRIVED at Port Louis, East Falkland, on 10 March 1834 – with perfect timing. An uprising had occurred. Gauchos and Indians had butchered British nationals, including the Union Jack keeper. 'Cold-blooded murder, robbery, plunder, suffering,' the atrocities were endless. The navy had sent in four armed sailors under a lieutenant, and they had flushed the rebels from the countryside, gaoling them ready for trial. But the 'principal murderer,' Antonio Rivero, was still at large. He was holding out on an islet in Berkeley Sound, swearing revenge, and the lieutenant, who now acted as Governor, asked FitzRoy to take him. And so the *Beagle*'s marines captured the 'villain,' clapping him in irons in the ship's hold.

Darwin viewed the whole episode with disdain. No one on East Falkland, 'this little miserable seat of discord,' deserved any praise. Of course the Buenos Aires government would call it 'a just revolt,' and talk of 'their poor subjects groaning under the tyranny of England.' For England's part, the navy's paltry police-action was unworthy of the Crown. 'Here we, dog-in the manger fashion seize an island & leave to protect it a Union jack; the possessor has been of course murdered: we now send a Lieutenant, with four sailors, without authority or instructions,' and 'the murderers have all been taken. – their [sic] being now as many prisoners as inhabitants.' What a short-sighted attitude to an island that 'must some day become a very important halting place in the most turbulent sea in the world.' Indeed, England's expanding trade only made her colonial half-heartedness seem more contemptible. 'How different from old Spain.' The Admiralty should have followed the *conquistadores*' example and turned East Falkland into a fortress.[1]

The ship that had landed the lieutenant also left the mail. Charles forgot the politics and savoured the gossip. Fanny was still asking about him; cousin Charlotte was happily ensconced in a parsonage; Erasmus was surrounded by 'all his favourites' – Hensleigh's wife and baby, and Emma Wedgwood. Talk of the parsonage continued, but Charles did not share Caroline's fear that 'the quiet clerical life you used to say you would return to' was irretrievably lost.

At last, too, he saw a letter with Henslow's handwriting, and this contained the best news. His collections were getting through safely. The plants were welcome, and the fossil megatheriums fabulously prized, revealing features never seen before. With typical diffidence, Darwin told Fox that he was 'only a sort of Jackall, a lions provider,' but the lions were roaring their approval. His megatheriums had been displayed before the cream of British science, at the Cambridge meeting of the British Association for the Advancement of Science. Your 'name is likely to be immortalized,' his beetling friend Frederick Hope said, and 'Darwin' was the word on everybody's lips. Send more bones, Henslow urged – 'every scrap of Megatherium skull you can set your eyes upon. – & *all* fossils.' Stick with the expedition; don't jump ship. 'I suspect you will always find something to keep up your courage.'[2]

Darwin was overjoyed. Nothing in two years had bucked him up so. He knew that his time had not been wasted, that all the galloping, hammering, and crating had been worthwhile. He felt proud. He had proved himself as a field naturalist and won the approval of those he respected. For the next three weeks he carried on like a man possessed. The weather was appalling, but it didn't matter. All around the island he made the rocks ring – some 'as big as Churches' – tussled with jackass penguins, and collected fragments of 'curious little Corallines.' He kept a handful of seeds too, a token of gratitude that he slipped in with a long excited letter back to his mentor.

He no longer saw himself as a random collector, a 'lions provider.' He was becoming a theorizer in his own right – a philosophical lion who could chew over old bones and explain them himself. He took fright at Henslow's talk of cleaning the megatheriums. Darwin feared that his identification numbers would be scrubbed off, making it impossible to relate the fossils to the embedding rocks. Both were needed to understand the megatheriums' world.

Their rock matrix told so much. Some fossil sloths were entombed with modern shells and agouti remains, suggesting that the bones were less ancient than he had thought. The shellfish and agoutis had obviously lived through the period of the Megatheriums' decline, making it impossible that a catastrophe had ravaged the land. The giant sloths must have died out naturally. Darwin's great diorama of the continent was changing: at the back, the coast of South America was rising out of the Atlantic – slowly, in phases, leaving a series of step-like plateaux. In the foreground, the 'ancient plains' were dominated by megatheriums and mastodons, thriving in a world no more cataclysmic than his own.[3]

Having reassured Henslow that he would 'stick to the voyage,' even if they did 'return a fine set of white-haired old gentlemen,' Darwin left the Falklands as he had arrived, on a grim note. On Sunday 6 April, while the *Beagle* was preparing for sea, a drowned English sailor was found on the beach in Berkeley Sound. FitzRoy buried him the next morning. They weighed anchor in the afternoon and tacked westward, with Rivero still chained in the hold, destined for a military court and execution. The ship headed for the Rio Santa Cruz in southern Patagonia, where the Captain planned to lead a party to the unexplored headwaters. If this 'glorious scheme' succeeded, Darwin would catch his first sight of the grandest mountain chain in the world, the Andes.[4]

The *Beagle* reached the mouth of the Santa Cruz on the 13th, and three days later the expedition set off. FitzRoy, Darwin, Stokes, Bynoe (the surgeon), and a few Gun Room men, supported by eighteen sailors and marines, were in the party. They took three whaleboats, tied together and dragged upstream by the men in teams, working hour-and-a-half shifts. It was strenuous work, pulling against water often running at seven knots; everyone took his turn, officers and ratings alike. When they weren't straining, Darwin and Stokes or Bynoe scouted ahead, walking on the embankments, rifles at the ready, always on the lookout for Indians and pumas. Neither was ever far away, as the tracks proved.[5]

They covered fifteen or twenty miles a day along the snaking stream, and were 100 miles west of the Santa Cruz estuary within a fortnight. At intervals between chasing guanacos and shooting condors, Darwin was puzzling out the geology. The river valley, five to ten miles wide, was bounded by walls over three hundred feet high. These led up to 'perfectly horizontal plains' on either side. The shells and shingle there showed that these plateaux had once been under water. It was while inspecting one with FitzRoy that Darwin plucked up courage to moot his hypothesis: that the terrace – indeed the whole Andes – had been raised slowly from the ocean bottom.

FitzRoy knew that this fitted with the latest Lyellian gradualist thought. He had been brought up with the biblical interpretation of the earth's crust – taught that the sea had risen violently a few thousand years ago at the time of Noah's flood, drowned the South American continent, and left the terraces and valleys much as they now appeared on receding. But he had not taken this 'scriptural geology' very seriously, and Darwin in his winsome way was talking him out of it. The Captain shook his head as he looked around, admitting that these raised plains 'could never have been effected by a forty days' flood.'[6]

Further on the plains were capped by a field of lava and the river entered a wild volcanic glen. Ahead lay a heavy bank of clouds, and on the 29th Darwin and Stokes climbed the cliffs to get a better view. Nine hundred feet above the river, they bellowed out their discovery: through 'the dusky envelope of clouds,' they could just make out the snowy summits of the Andes. The party, though footsore and weary, pressed on for a few days until provisions ran low. Thirty miles from the mountains, awestruck by the spectacle, they had to turn back. No matter, Darwin knew that he would reach the Andes from the other side within a year. As they raced downstream, he could think only of 'standing . . . on one of their pinnacles & looking down on the plains below.'

On 12 May the *Beagle* set sail from the eastern shores of South America for the last time. Lashed by sleet and hail, she pitched headlong into mountainous seas as FitzRoy made for the Straits of Magellan. The temperature dropped, and looking up from his hammock, where he lay 'sick & miserable' as usual, Darwin watched an inch of ice form on the skylight. Outside the Straits the *Adventure* joined them from the Falklands, bringing the mail, and the ships scudded down the famous waterway to Port Famine in ever shorter days. It was in the twenties now and snowing. How odd to receive a parcel that had been posted before Christmas. Still, it made June a festive season even at the bottom of the world, and Darwin tore into it like a child. With 'no roaring fire,' and a snow-covered upper deck, he cherished every reminder of home.[7]

There were letters and gifts galore. His sisters bubbled as usual, enjoying his diary immensely, but longing for him to be 'quite settled,' even if it meant aborting the voyage. Fanny echoed them pertly, her note a part of the orchestrated campaign. She looked forward to visiting him and his '*little Wife* in the *little Parsonage*!!' A browbeaten invalid with a six-month-old daughter, she was under the Doctor, and the Darwin sisters had clearly recruited her to their cause. Charles, feeling henpecked, put the subject 10,000 miles out of mind. Fanny's experience of marriage did not commend the institution any more than her urging enhanced the Church.

More to the point were the gifts – a purse, a chain for his pencil case, hiking boots, and a handful of books. He scanned the reading matter, always glad of additions to the ship's library. Caroline, worried by his close escapes, had sent *Scriptural Revelations concerning a Future State*, as 'we often used to find we liked the same kind' of literature. And all his sisters recommended *Poor Laws and Paupers Illustrated*, which came in several pamphlet-sized parts. Its author was 'a great Lion in London,' a fiercely independent lady, Harriet Martineau. She was the darling of the Whigs, a one-woman advertising agency, whose soap-opera novellas popularized and explained the reforms. 'Erasmus knows her & is a very great admirer & every body reads her little books & if you have a dull hour you can, and then throw them overboard, that they may not take up your precious room.'[8]

Ironic, really – here he was, in a desolate settlement called, of all things, Port Famine, distributing booklets to the men advocating sexual restraint as a way of escaping starvation. Actually they went down well. Everybody talked about her 'politico-economical tales,' homely yarns of indigence, passion, delayed marriages, and heroic prudence rescuing couples from penury and the poor house. On the ship, as in London, they were devoured as avidly as Walter Scott's novels.

Back in Britain they were doing more to pave the way for the new Poor Law than all the government propaganda. The ministers knew it; the Lord Chancellor Henry Brougham had actually commissioned them to ease in the unpopular law, feeding Martineau secret commission reports as source material. Her edifying homilies spread the word of the Revd Thomas Malthus, an economist for the East India Company. The core of his theory was bleak: as population rises faster than food supply, struggle and starvation must inevitably result. Public charities – the old poor relief – only aggravated the problem; hand-outs made paupers comfortable and encouraged them to breed. More mouths, more poor, more demands for welfare – it was a vicious circle.[9]

By now welfare was out of control and the population exploding. The 1831 census showed an unbelievable twenty-four million people in Britain, a doubling in thirty years. In bad winters one in ten was on hand-outs. Enough was enough for middle-class ratepayers; heroic surgery was needed to cut out this 'gangrene of the state,' as Martineau called it. Why should they support the work-shy? Why should they subsidize 'marriage between pauper boys and girls' and the birth of still more destitute children?

Drastic measures were sanctioned by the Poor Law Amendment Bill, just becoming law as Darwin's shipmates read the booklets. It ended relief for all but the most destitute, those so ill or old that they would enter the abominable workhouses to receive food or money. Since their prison regimes were designed to discourage entry – wives were torn from husbands to prevent breeding – few were expected to apply for relief and a vast saving was guaranteed. Martineau argued that this would benefit the paupers themselves, by making them self-reliant. But really by forcing them to compete for jobs, the Whigs were decreasing labour costs and increasing profits. By heeding the Revd Malthus, they will do 'more for the country than all the Administrations since the Revolution,' one pundit cheered. The new Poor Law will 'immortalize them.'[10]

What the *Beagle*'s shiftless seamen made of Martineau may be surmised. Charles's sisters saw the Poor Law as the 'great topic of interest,' and the Doctor argued its merits with local Tories. But Charles was too distant and kept his own counsel, although no one was to have a more crucial influence on his science than Malthus.

He was in another world, lost in wonder at the 'rugged snowy crags, blue glaciers, [and] rainbows' as FitzRoy steered from Port Famine, under the face of Mount Sarmiento, and into the Cockburn Channel. At the base of vast vertical cliffs in a tiny cove Charles saw a deserted wigwam, a reminder that man sometimes wandered this wilderness. 'Imagination,' he noted sombrely, 'could scarcely paint a scene' where humans seem 'to have less . . . authority.' The elemental forces prevail. In this desolation the 'wider power[s] of nature despise control,' as if to say 'We are the sovereign.' Here mankind 'does not look like the Lord of all.'[11]

After sailing dangerously in circles for fourteen hours in pitch darkness, the *Beagle* emerged from the Cockburn Channel on 10 June. At long last they had reached the west coast. Setting 'every inch of canvas,' she battled out into the long swell of the Pacific, the *Adventure* alongside. Here the rugged granite coast, pounded by roaring breakers, was enough to give landsmen nightmares about 'peril & shipwreck.' Howling northerly gales intensified the effect, whipping up angry seas. These were not the only sirens of death. As FitzRoy struggled at the helm, the oldest officer lay fighting for his life below-deck. Rowlett, thirty-eight, the Purser, had been Darwin's friend since trekking together on St Jago; on the 27th they watched him succumb to 'a complication of diseases.' The next day, as the ship approached San Carlos on the island of Chiloé, 1000 miles above the Horn, FitzRoy read the funeral service on the quarter-deck and Rowlett's remains were committed to the deep. To Darwin, safely through the storms, 'the splash of the waters over the body of an old ship-mate' was 'an aweful & solemn sound.'

Chiloé was drenched. Only 'an amphibious animal could tolerate the climate,' Darwin moaned as he poked around. He was heartened by the 'Tropical scenery' – the best since Brazil – and the evidence of volcanic activity and recent uplift. The birds were interesting too, inviting comparison with those in Tierra del Fuego. But most curious of all was a story he heard. A whaler's surgeon told him that the lice infesting the Sandwich Islanders died in a few days if they transferred to Englishmen. How strange: what did this say about the human races? He began working through the implications in his notes: 'Man springing from one stock' - that was his axiom. From this it followed that all the human types were *varieties,* so were their parasites closely related too? If he could prove, this, it would be a blow to the apologists of slavery, who made the blacks a separate species. Here was a line to follow up with the experts back in London.

Two weeks in the rain here and the *Beagle* moved on, 600 miles further up the coast, against an 'anything but "Pacific" Ocean.' FitzRoy planned to sit out the stormy months in central Chile while the sister-ships were refitted. On 23 July they anchored in the crowded harbour of Valparaiso, backed by steep hills with 'glimpses of the Andes' to the north. The climate here was 'quite delicious,' 'the sky so clear & blue, the air so dry & the sun so bright,' that 'all nature seemed sparkling with life.'[12]

Darwin went into town – 'a sort of London or Paris' where one was 'obliged to shave & dress decently' – and lodged with Richard Corfield, an old classmate from Shrewsbury School, now a merchant. Corfield had a fine suburban house close to open country, and Darwin rambled out to survey the scene. The hills abounded with gorgeous flowers and scrubby aromatic bushes. He found beds of modern shells at 1300 feet but, oddly enough, few insects, birds, or mammals. Perhaps none had 'been created since this country was raised from the sea.'

In the distance the Andes beckoned, or rather the foothills, which were safer to climb in winter. To take a closer look, he bought 'a small troop of horses' to use in rotation, and set off on 14 August. The landscape was like Tierra del Fuego's. No doubt these plains too had been a sea-bottom, with the distant hills marking the shoreline.

Higher up, some 4000 feet, he looked down on the 'patchwork . . . Paradise' of the valley below. At this altitude the laval rocks had been 'frizzled melted and bedevilled in every possible fashion,' and not so long ago. Volcanoes had spewed them up, and earthquakes still shook and shattered them; here man was a puny being, and Darwin hurried past massive overhangs waiting to crash down. It was impossible not to marvel at 'the wonderful force which has upheaved these mountains, & even more so the countless ages' that it took 'to have broken through, removed & levelled whole masses of them.'[13]

Darwin reached Santiago on the 27th and spent a week naturalizing by day and dining with merchants at night. Corfield was also there 'to admire the beauties of nature, in the form of Signoritas,' and they teamed up for the return trip to Valparaiso. At a wealthy hacienda *en route* Darwin obliged the 'pretty Signoritas' with stories of his travels. But the air chilled when he mentioned his sermon-sampling in Buenos Aires. Being Catholics, the ladies

> turned up their charming eyes in pious horror at my having
> entered a Church to look about me; they asked . . . why I did
> not become a Christian, "for our religion is certain"; I assured
> them I was a sort of Christian; they would not hear of it . . .
> "Do not your padres, your very bishops marry" – The
> absurdity of a Bishop having a wife particularly struck them,
> [and] they scarcely knew whether to be most amused or
> horrified at such an atrocity.

It was enough to remind him of home – of sisters, parsonages, and wives. A Catholic 'sort of Christian' he could never be, but what about his own Church?

He did not know. Months had passed since he last conjured up visions of 'retirement, green cottages, & white petticoats.' The voyage had worn on, and now he felt 'like a ruined man, who does not see or care how to extricate himself.' All he knew was that geology held 'a never failing interest.' It was of course religious in its way, giving him 'the same grand ideas' about the earth that 'Astronomy does for the universe.' The Revd Sedgwick had taught him as much, but now, surrounded by 'sublime masses of snow,' he felt in his heart that it was true.

They rode on through breathtaking scenery, still making for Valparaiso. At an American gold mine Darwin watched pale young men carrying 200 pounds of stone up a laddered 450-foot shaft. They were 'allowed only beans & bread,' the proprietor explained as the guests sipped local wine. A few hours later Darwin fell ill, and although a few days' rest seemed to cure him, once in the saddle again his stomach erupted, his appetite vanished, and he became fevered. It was that sour wine, he felt sure. By 21 September he could scarcely mount his horse. Rest-stops became more frequent, although nothing could prevent him from chipping fossil barnacles from beds along the plain – the proof positive of its marine origin. A further week of suffering and he was back in Valparaiso, a shambling wreck. He went to bed and stayed there a month.[14]

Bynoe, the Surgeon, brought medications and startling news from the *Beagle*: FitzRoy had suffered a breakdown. He was a brittle perfectionist and the obsessive chartwork had rattled him. Refitting the *Adventure* had proved too expensive and the Admiralty Lords had reprimanded him for buying her. Under a great strain, he had sold the ship – and snapped. First, he decided to return to that 'confounded country' Tierra del Fuego to check his measurements, risking a mass desertion by the crew, Darwin with them. Then, depressed and doubting his sanity, he had resigned his command. He feared his uncle's fate and remembered Stokes's suicide. Wickham was now in charge, with instructions to finish surveying the west coast and then return directly to England.

The news sent Darwin into a spin. The circumnavigation was lost, no Pacific, no Indian Ocean; his mind 'a swinging pendulum' again, downcast and homesick by turns, the gloom of a lost world brightened by the prospect of an early family reunion. Bewildered, he spent a night agonizing: should he cut and run? No, his 'geological castles in the air' came first. He would not sacrifice these for all the parsonages and petticoats in England. He decided to travel alone through Chile and Peru, cross the Andes to Buenos Aires, and sail from there for home. A fine fifteen months it would be.

FitzRoy was swinging as wildly. After some arm-twisting from the officers, he changed tack, withdrew his resignation, and announced that they would cross the Pacific after all. There was no turning back; he would hoist sails as soon as the Philosopher regained his feet. Word reached Corfield's, providing the tonic Darwin needed. 'What a revolution . . . five minutes . . . effected in all my feelings,' he exulted to his family. The *Beagle* would stay in coastal waters for several months; then 'crossing the Pacific & from Sydney home' would be a breeze. The world lay before him again.

Fired up, on 7 November he finished a long letter to Henslow, his 'father' and 'pro-proctor' in natural history, detailing his discoveries. By now Henslow's scientific son understood the Patagonian geology.

He was knowledgeable enough to query Lamarck's classification of corals; he had puzzled at the formation of the Andes, written '600 small quarto pages' of notes, and shipped two more boxes of specimens. Better was to come, for in three days he was leaving for the Chonos archipelago, where they could 'steer by the light of a Volcano.' The future looked so bright that Darwin did not know 'which part of the voyage, now offers the most attractions.'[15]

The island of Chiloé was the gateway to the archipelago. After a fair passage south, the *Beagle* arrived at San Carlos harbour on the 21st. FitzRoy took the *Beagle* off surveying, leaving Sulivan in charge of the ship's yawl and whaleboat with orders to chart the east coast of Chiloé to its southern extremity. Darwin of course went with Sulivan for the 100-mile ride. Two days out and he saw three great volcanoes billowing smoke. And, ten days later, his first petrified tree, a beautiful fossil in yellow sandstone, its trunk 'thicker than my body' and its veins transparent quartz.

Rendezvousing with the *Beagle*, they sailed along Chiloé's 'lofty weather-beaten' south coast and then tracked down to the Chonos archipelago. Christmas Day was depressing; the wind was fierce and the sodden deserted islands reminded everyone of the Horn. Not quite deserted – on the 28th they spotted a sailor wildly waving his shirt on a point of land, and a boat was sent out, with Darwin in it. They encountered five American castaways. 'I never saw such anxiety . . . in mens faces,' he wrote. The wretches had deserted a Massachusetts whaler 'without knowing which way to go or where they were.' Their boat had been smashed, and for over a year they had survived on seal flesh, shellfish, and hope. In all that time they had seen sails only once, and were 'nearly jumping into the water' as the boat picked them up.[16]

FitzRoy surveyed the islands, finishing up in Low's Harbour at the northern end of the archipelago. For a week the crew stocked up on game, oysters, and potatoes. After wild people, FitzRoy thought wild potatoes were the highlight of the trip, and Darwin collected seeds for Henslow. He also set his traps and caught a 'singular little mouse.' It was common on some islands, the natives said, but absent on others, leading him to wonder why colonization was such a serendipitous affair. He also picked up dozens of conches on the beach, each '*completely* drilled' with cavities. The shells were riddled with minuscule parasites. Under the microscope, they appeared as boring barnacles, no bigger than pins' heads. These were surely the smallest, oddest barnacles in the world, and he took hundreds away to study.

The *Beagle* was back at Chiloé on 15 January 1835, anchored at San Carlos, where they were to rest up for three weeks. At about midnight on the 19th, the sentry reported 'something like a large star' slowly increasing on the horizon. By 3 a.m. Darwin and the officers were on deck, taking turns with an eye-glass: seventy miles away, volcanic Mount Osorno was putting on a spectacular show. It was one 'great red glare,' an explosion of rocks, with lava spewing down its slopes. The whole molten mass glowed so brightly that the sky was lit up and the sea reflected the display. It died down, a minor eruption, and by morning, Darwin noted, 'the Volcano seemed to have regained its composure.'[17]

While FitzRoy checked his bearings, Darwin hired a guide and spent a week criss-crossing Chiloé with Midshipman King. The weather was fine, and the beetles abundant. The settlements were surrounded by orchards. Apple trees were everywhere, along the roadsides, in the towns, he had never seen so many. At the end they climbed a hill to see the volcanoes once more and alighted on yet another bed of shells, 350 feet above the sea.[18] The west coast of the continent, no less than the east, had risen out of the ocean recently, and in the same stop-go manner.

On 5 February the *Beagle* headed north finally, and Darwin settled in to his cramped cabin to write his notes. He returned to the vexed question of the megatheriums and their demise. Lyell was right about the 'gradual birth and death of species,' Darwin jotted. After the deaths, 'successive births must repeople the globe,' replenishing species to keep the harmony established by the 'Author of Nature.'

He harked back to the 'Mastodon' found at Port St Julian. No flooding or catastrophe could have killed it; at least the rocks showed no evidence. Moreover, it was buried in a gully, in the sort of loam that overlay the shelly gravel on the plateau above. This could mean only that the animal had lived *after* these shells. And since similar shellfish thrive in the ocean today, the climate could not have changed much. Nor could the vegetation; these gravels were too poor to support anything more than scrub. At a stroke Darwin had thrown out the two commonest explanations of extinction: a catastrophic flood, or a change in climate. He still believed in Lyell's Creator but had broken with his climatic theory; he was branching out on his own.[19]

Lyell spoke of the 'succession of deaths' as part of 'the ordinary course of nature.' But what could cause a whole species to die like a single individual? Why had all the megatheriums perished?

For a novel answer Darwin now crossed over to his other interest:

the vital force in living matter. But he took a new angle. Common apples were the key – to be more exact the ubiquitous Chiloé apple trees. Even as he wrote, the *Beagle* was putting into the port of Valdivia, 150 miles up the coast, a ramshackle settlement 'completely hidden in a wood of Apple trees.' The 'streets are merely paths in an orchard,' he observed on disembarking. 'I never saw this fruit in such abundance.' He now realized what made these trees so fertile:

> the inhabitants possess a marvellously short method of making an orchard. At the lower part of almost every branch, small, conical, brown, wrinkled points project; these are always ready to change into roots, as may sometimes be seen, where any mud had been accidentally splashed against the tree.

Cuttings would root immediately, and the inhabitants were taking advantage of the fact. Whole orchards sprang from one tree. The cuttings themselves grew so rampantly in this climate that in eighteen months cuttings from cuttings could be taken.

It set him thinking about what a cutting actually was. Were all the cuttings from one tree *part* of that parent? Were they the severed pieces of one individual? If so, they should share its life span. As Darwin put it, 'all these thousand trees are subject to the duration of life which one bud contained.'[20] They would be bound by one life force, enormously extended by cutting, but still limited, or so he believed. And once it was expended, all the offshoots would die simultaneously. Darwin now took a giant leap and suggested an analogy with species. Perhaps all the megatheriums shared one life-force; perhaps sexually reproduced animals are like 'cuttings' from an original stock. Is that why all the ground sloths vanished together?

In Valdivia he nosed around, eager for excitement. The Captain threw a party on board. A boatload of blushing *señoritas* was engaged for the event and, alas, 'bad weather compelled them to stay all night.' It was a 'sore plague' to everyone, Darwin quipped. Otherwise his hours were idled away, wandering through the forest.

On 20 February he lay resting on its floor at ten o'clock in the morning when the earth moved, sending his mind into a slow-motion swirl. He had felt a tremor once before, while convalescing at Corfield's, but nothing like this. It started suddenly, became violent, and seemed to go on forever. He tried to stand but sank to his knees, dizzy and distraught. In a split second, the one abiding security of life – the firm ground – disappeared. 'The world, the very emblem of all that is solid,' he gasped, shuddered beneath our feet 'like a crust over a fluid.' The quake lasted only two minutes but encompassed an eternity; all moorings were lost, leaving him philosophically giddy for weeks. He raced into town and was greeted by ..1e sight of wooden houses askew and 'horror pictured in the faces of all the inhabitants.' To have '*seen* as well as felt an earthquake' was an awesome experience, and he dreaded to think of the destruction in the great city of Concepción, 200 miles north.[21]

The *Beagle* stood out to sea and sailed up the coast. The shoals were treacherous and she lost two anchors, the sixth and seventh of the voyage, before gaining the harbour at Concepción. The devastation was staggering. 'The whole coast was strewed over with timber & furniture as if a thousand great ships had been wrecked.' Huge slabs of rock had been thrown up on to the beach, and the town itself looked like an ancient ruin. Houses and schools were heaps of rubble and the great cathedral lay half-razed, its four-foot-thick walls tottering on battered foundations. The quake was Chile's 'worst ever,' he heard. It gave no notice and struck with ferocity. Shock after shock hit the city, 'rumbling ... like distant thunder' and darkening the sky with a dense cloud of dust. Fires broke out everywhere. People ran screaming from their homes. Then a twenty-foot tidal wave swept across the land, carrying a schooner into the town. Scores were drowned or crushed, and even now, two weeks later, untold numbers lay buried in the rubble. Looters prowled the streets, mixing 'religion in their depradations ... At each little trembling of the ground, with one hand they beat their breasts & cried out "Miserecordia," [sic] & with the other continued to filch from the ruins.'

The carnage was inconceivable, and Darwin's thoughts turned to home. What if an earthquake struck England, with its 'lofty houses, thickly packed cities, the great manufactories, the beautiful private & public buildings?' What 'a horrible destruction there would be of human life.' The country would 'become bankrupt; all papers, accounts, [and] records ... would be lost ... Government could not collect the taxes.' It was a terrifying prospect – a revolution like no other, the violent overthrow of all that he held dear. And still worse, no one could predict when a quake might strike. 'Who can say how soon such will happen?'

Emotionally drained, Darwin began to think coolly. He found fresh mussel beds lying above high tide, the shellfish all dead – the land had risen, and by a few feet! What had he been mooting all along, but the continent's emergence from the sea? And now to have *experienced* it! Lyell had shown the same for Naples Bay, where a submerged Roman temple had been hoisted out of the water by an earthquake. It was the final confirmation that mountains are not thrown up in one colossal upheaval. Lyell was right: they grow barely perceptibly, the product of thousands of tiny rises like this over the aeons. Time, unimaginable time, that was the key; given it, anything could be achieved. Darwin now understood. He plotted the quake's epicentre and pinned down its cause to incipient volcanic action. Hot springs and 'bubbles of gas & discoloured water' percolating into the sea proved beyond doubt that 'the earth is a mere crust over a fluid melted mass of rock.'

Earthquakes and volcanoes had revealed Nature's awesome power, its driving force. But where did man – puny man – fit into her picture? It was 'bitter & humiliating' to contemplate his vulnerability, 'skating over very thin ice,' a crustal sheet, above a fiery furnace. Yet accept it he must.[22]

12

Colonial Life

THEY WEREN'T TO BE white-haired gents on their return to England. As the *Beagle* sailed into Valparaiso to fetch new anchors, FitzRoy announced that they would be home in eighteen months. At last Darwin could see the journey's 'definite & certain end.'

On 12 March 1835 he moved back into Corfield's villa, preparing for the Andes expedition that he had dreamt of for two years. While the ship finished charting, he would cross the mountains. But even while packing his 'horse cloths stirrups pistols & spurs,' he was thinking of home, planning 'the very coaches by which I shall . . . reach Shrewsbury in the shortest time.' He fired off a new set of expectant letters. Oh to be 'living quietly in Cambridge' again, he sighed to Henslow at the end of a report proving 'that both sides of the Andes have risen in the recent period.' Fox – and his new wife – received an even more wistful note. 'You a married clergyman, ave maria, how strange it sounds to my ears.' Would they have anything but memories in common by the time Darwin arrived home? He could no longer see what the future in England held. 'What I shall ultimately do with myself – Quien Sabe?' – Who knows? 'But it is very un-Sailor-like to think of the Future.'[1]

With winter approaching, his mountain trek would have to be quick. He made his way to Santiago, and from there on the 18th began the long ascent to the Portillo Pass with ten mules, a mare, two guides, and 'a good deal of food, in case of being snowed up.' With a 'strong passport from the President' of Chile, they slipped through the frontier customs, and on the 21st Darwin perched on the continental divide, panting. At 13,000 feet, the wind was 'violent and very cold,' and his head and chest felt tight. Then he looked behind him.

The atmosphere so resplendently clear, the sky an intense blue, the profound valleys, the wild broken forms, the heaps of ruins piled up during the lapse of ages, the bright colored rocks, contrasted with the quiet mountains of Snow, together produced a scene I never could have imagined . . . I felt glad I was by myself, it was like watching a thunderstorm, or hearing in the full Orchestra a Chorus of the Messiah.

Welling up with emotion, he was in 'another world.' Yet even here, in this barren wasteland with 'neither plant nor bird,' he found fossil shells in the rocks.

This was the first of the two main ridges in the Andes. The party traversed the central tract, gazing on 22,000-foot snow-covered Mount Tupungato. They plodded on through icy clouds to the Portillo, a 'narrow cleft' in the second ridge, from where the descent was short and steep. While they camped that night, sheltering from the bitter frost beneath great shattered rocks, the clouds cleared. The effect was 'quite magical.' A full moon bathed the mountains, and stiletto stars pricked the dry still air. Static electricity completed the illumination. Every 'hair on a dogs back crackled' and Darwin's flannel waistcoat glowed when rubbed, 'as if washed with Phosphorus.' Ahead lay the pampas, which he had longed to see from such a height. But come morning the view was disappointing; it was flat and featureless, broken only by rivers running 'like silver threads' before the rising sun.[2]

They reached Mendoza on the 28th after crossing more pebbly plateaux and fighting through a swarm of locusts. ('The noise of their approach was that of a strong breeze passing through the rigging of a Ship.') Giant Vinchuca bugs plagued them; it was 'horribly disgusting' to wake at night and feel them, 'an inch long . . . black and soft,' crawling over 'your person – gorged with your blood.' After resting a day in the 'forlorn & stupid' town, they turned north-west to re-cross the Andes through the Uspallata Pass. At 7000 feet Darwin came upon a striking grove of fossilized trees. 'I confess I was at first so much astonished that I could scarcely believe the plainest evidence of it' – a petrified forest, fifty fossilized trunks in a sandstone escarpment, 'snow white columns Like Lots wife,' perfectly crystallized. Even the impressions of bark were visible and the growth rings could be counted. The sandstone sediments told the full story. This 'cluster of fine trees had once waved their branches on the shores of the Atlantic, when that ocean (now driven back 700 miles) approached the base of the Andes.'[3] The land sank, drowning the luxuriant tropical forest, burying it in sand and silt thousands of feet thick. These sediments compressed into rock, crystallizing the wood, and lava overflowed it. Then slowly, inexorably, the continent began its rise out of the sea, until this eerie grove came to stand high in the freezing mountains.

He was now literally building 'geological castles in the air.' In the rarefied atmosphere, amid the towering crags and jagged ravines, he put together a theory to explain the Andes. Their granite core had been heaved up piecemeal along a north-south line, 'overturning in the most extraordinary manner the overlying strata.' These tree-entombing sandstones had been 'tossed about like the crust of a broken pie.' Powerful forces – acting with slow-motion primal violence, as it must seem to humans – had tilted and smashed the overlying rocks, leaving the trees at an angle. The sight left him gasping: 'I cannot imagine any part of the world presenting a more extraordinary scene of the breaking up of the crust of the globe.'[4]

At night he 'could hardly sleep,' for thinking of crustal oscillation and heaving continents. On 4 April, as the mule train snaked through the most treacherous passes, he was almost blasé, yet one slip would have pitched him headlong into the abyss, joining 'Las Animas' – The Souls – after whom one of the gaps was named. Beyond, the Uspallata snowstorms were overdue, but Darwin went on enjoying 'the brightest fortune' and awe-inspiring scenery, 'a fine Chaos of huge mountains divided by profound ravines.' The team descended along the valley of the Rio Aconcagua, arriving in Santiago on the 10th. A week later he was safely back in Valparaiso with 'half a mule's load' of specimens.

He packed them in two crates, which would be the last shipment to reach home before he did, and wrote Henslow an account of the expedition. This letter had top priority. 'Absurd & incredible' his discoveries seemed, still he sketched them breathlessly, with broad geological brush-strokes, painting images of fossil shells and trees that testified to the recent stuttering uplift of the continent. It was a daring performance for a novice naturalist. But he was keen for credit, eager to be thought objective and unbiased, swearing that 'no previously formed conjecture warped my judgement.'

He was equally anxious to impress his father and sisters. He boasted that his findings, if accepted, would be crucial to 'the theory of the formation of the world.' He wanted another sort of credit from the Doctor too. For the second time in six months he had 'drawn a bill for £100,' and assumed that his extravagance would be condemned. It was a 'black & dismal' subject, 'that horrid phantom money.' All his budgets had been broken. He piled up excuses like so many hypotheses, but then confessed his openness to temptation: geological field trips were as irresistible as they were expensive. Crossing the Andes alone had cost £60, and given the chance he would no doubt 'spend money in the very moon.'[5]

The extra money was of course for the next expedition. While the *Beagle* charted north towards the Peruvian capital, Lima, Darwin followed on land, starting on 27 April with four horses, two mules, and a guide. They took the road to Coquimbo, through parched valleys and over barren mountains. Prospectors roamed these hills, searching for copper and gold. Fabulous fortunes had been made and wasted; even some English workmen 'who came out as Mechanicks' had made 'some thousand pounds' and bought their own mine. Darwin visited the diggings and saw once more the dreadful labour involved.

At Coquimbo the *Beagle* was being refitted for the long haul home. After touring the countryside he washed his clothes, picked up *Paradise Lost* from the poop cabin, and set out on 1 June for Copiapó, 200 miles north, where he would rejoin the ship. This leg of the expedition was a trial for man and beast alike. Water and firewood were scarce, and the vegetation grew scantier. In the Guasco valley they had a few days' respite, but from there to Copiapó was unremitting desert. But for the joys of hammering, it would have been 'down right Martyrdom.'

He was suffering for his geology and loving it. And as if to test his pain threshold, he took one last expensive risk. Arriving in Copiapó on the 23rd, he hired a guide and eight mules for a week in the wintry Andes. Here he checked his ideas about elevation, deducing from the Indian ruins that the climate must have been more hospitable in the past. The mountains proved 'very tame,' but the night wind was ferocious. It froze the water and penetrated their clothing. 'I suffered much . . . so that I could not sleep, & in the morning rose with my body quite dull & benumbed.'[6] For once he was relieved to see the ship.

The refurbished *Beagle* cast off on 6 July, for the long northern run up the coast. A week later they reached Iquique, but the town was in tumult, reflecting the 'Anarchy' of Peruvian politics, with churches looted and foreigners blamed. The jittery inhabitants had even caught and tortured some Englishmen before the authorities could restore a semblance of order. It was a foretaste of what they would find in Lima, 700 miles further north. No sooner had the ship docked in Lima harbour on the 19th than the crew was briefed: four armed factions were vying for power, and the President was 'shooting & murdering any one who disobeys his orders.' He had even been known to unfurl a black flag with a 'death's head' during Mass, and had decreed that 'all property should be at the disposal of the state.' Here too it was open season on foreigners. Three, including the British consul, had just been assaulted by renegade soldiers, stripped naked 'excepting their drawers' and robbed blind. This was an act of 'warm Patriotism.' The thugs had 'waved the Peruvian banner & intermingled crys of "Viva la Patria"; "give me your jacket". "Libertad Libertad" . . . "Off with youʳ trowsers"'!

A young English gentleman had to tread carefully. Darwin entered the city safely but could not stray beyond its bounds. He noted the 'remarkably mongrel population,' the numbers of churches among the 'heaps of filth,' and the 'wretched state of decay.' There was faded grandeur, but only one thing turned his head. He 'could not keep [his] eyes' off the *tapadas* – the elegant ladies. Their dress and manners brought out the sailor in him. He felt as though he had fallen amongst 'nice round mermaids.'

> The . . . elastic gown fits the figure closely & obliges the
> ladies to walk with small steps which they do very elegantly
> & display very white silk stockings & very pretty feet. – They
> wear a black silk veil, which is fixed round the waist behind,
> is brought over the head, & held by the hands before the
> face, allowing only one eye to remain uncovered. – But then
> that one eye is so black & brilliant & has such powers of
> motion & expression, that its effect is very powerful.

These alluring creatures were more 'worth looking at than all the churches & buildings in Lima.'[7]

Through July and August the country lurched from crisis to crisis; the main road from the port to town became impassable, 'infested with gangs of mounted robbers.' The *Beagle* was Darwin's only haven. But time was hanging heavy, and FitzRoy, having found some 'old charts & Papers' to study, showed no sign of putting to sea. It was yet another 'grievous' delay, even though the Captain vowed to set off around the world soon enough.

Confined to the poop cabin, Darwin put the time to use, writing up notes. Whiling away the warm days, he continued to build his geological edifice. If the continent were rising, presumably the Pacific floor was sinking. This would fit with Lyell's theory of an oscillating

167

crust, and Darwin now considered himself Mr Lyell's 'zealous disciple.' But how to prove it? The evidence, he guessed, lay in the palm-fringed coral islets dotting the Pacific. Are they sinking? Part of FitzRoy's Admiralty brief was to take soundings around these islands to determine if the coral rings really sat on 'the summits of extinct volcanoes.' Travellers knew that coral polyps required warmth, light, and shallows, and many assumed that they encrusted *rising* volcanic rims. Even Lyell did. But what if Lyell was wrong on this point?

Darwin had questioned his master before – good disciples do – and now he suspected the whole theory was topsy-turvy. It seemed more likely that the reefs encircled mountain tops which were *vanishing*. As the land sank, the coral accumulated, rising to compensate, keeping itself at the optimum depth.[8] He had an answer for the Sea Lords before he ever saw a coral island. Nothing remained but to find one and confirm it.

He fired off letters: Henslow heard about Chilean geology, and the family about his first week's appointments on arriving home. 'In truth,' he alerted them, 'I shall have a great deal to do, for a long time after we return.' Fox, his father-confessor, heard more. Fox had written extolling marriage, talking of his 'dear little wife' and child on the way. He implored Charles for a letter, a frank note about his thoughts, and it struck a responsive chord. Charles compared the happy couple beside the parsonage hearth with himself, stuck in a cramped cabin in a stinking port. He opened his heart:

> This voyage is terribly long. – I do so earnestly desire to
> return, yet I dare hardly look forward to the future, for I do
> not know what will become of me. – Your situation is above
> envy; I do not venture even to frame such happy visions. To a
> person fit to take the office, the life of a Clergyman is a type
> of all that is respectable & happy: & if he is a Naturalist &
> has the "Diamond Beetle", ave Maria; I do not know what to
> say. – You tempt me by talking of your fireside, whereas it is
> a sort of scene I never ought to think about.

He envied curate-naturalists their lives, and their wives. An 'English lady' was someone 'very angelic & good,' a type he had 'almost forgotten' about. The women here 'wear Caps & petticoats & a very few have pretty faces & then all is said.' But Darwin was trying to forget the beauty he saw in town as the *Beagle* prepared for the lonely Pacific passage. His first love, geology, would meet his emotional needs.

Anyway, to think of firesides and female company was folly.

They were about to set off at last around the world – across the Pacific to Australia, then atoll-hopping across the Indian Ocean to South Africa. And he was looking forward to the next stop, 'the Galapagos, with more interest than any other part of the voyage.'⁹

He was almost nostalgic as the ship prepared to leave South America finally. So much had he seen in three and a half years: earthquakes, volcanic eruptions, gigantic fossils, savages. He bade goodbye to the Andes, and to shipmates remaining in their graves. But there were always new faces – and not only human ones. A forecastle sailor, J. Davis, brought on board a coati mundi, a South American racoon-relative with a long flexible snout, which joined the crew for the rest of the voyage.¹⁰

A week out of Lima and the *Beagle* was 600 miles away, approaching the Galapagos Islands. It was 15 September when they first sighted the closest island, Chatham. 'We landed upon black, dismal-looking heaps of broken lava, forming a shore fit for pandemonium,' FitzRoy recorded. 'Innumerable crabs and hideous iguanas started in every direction as we scrambled from rock to rock.' Darwin was equally taken aback; the black cinders were difficult to walk on and burning hot. They glowed 'like a stove' in the overhead sun, their rugged inhospitability highlighted by the almost lifeless stunted trees. Every great squirl of lava looked as though it had been 'petrified in its most boisterous moments.' The air was sultry, the smell unpleasant, and the whole 'compared to what we might imagine the cultivated parts of the Infernal regions to be.'

These 'frying hot islands' were 'paradises for the whole family of Reptiles.' Turtles glided through the bay, popping their heads up to breathe, and inland giant tortoises gathered around water-holes. A thermometer in the black sand went off the scale at 137 degrees, which was perfect for the piles of 'disgusting clumsy Lizards' asleep on the shore rocks. The 'imps of darkness' someone christened them, and they were certainly strange sea-weed-eating creatures. But because marine iguanas in the museums had been mislabelled as mainland South American, Darwin did not realize that they were unique to the Galapagos.

The birds knew not man, nor any predator, and seemed 'tame.' Darwin approached a hawk and actually poked it with his gun-barrel. Where was the sport here? The slaughter was disgustingly easy, and eighteen giant tortoises, some weighing eighty pounds, were dragged aboard as fresh meat. The mockingbirds looked like the Chilean species; they 'are lively, inquisitive, active, run fast, [and] frequent houses to pick the meat' left to dry, but their song seemed different.[11] The flowers were ugly, like everything else. If the birds had a South American aspect, perhaps these blooms did too.

Volcanoes he had expected, and he was not disappointed. Inert cones, often sixty at a time rising fifty feet into the air, gave it the look of an industrial wasteland or 'the Iron furnaces near Wolverhampton.' Some of the more 'ancient chimneys' were covered in vegetation, others just 'naked, bare' lava streams, rough and uncolonized. The whole primordial scene was capped by the plodding tortoises, seven feet in circumference, chomping on prickly pears. He had anticipated some sedimentary strata, like those in Europe, but no. This was a new world, reflecting only its molten subterranean origins, and so alien that he might have been standing on 'some other planet.'

The strangeness was completed by the lack of insect swarms. His first thought was that the islands, so far out in the ocean, 'are effectively excluded from receiving any migratory colonists.' As a consequence the majority of birds were seed-eating finches, fitted to the lowland scrub and with short heavy-duty bills – like a bullfinch's – to peck seeds from the 'iron-like lava.'[12]

The Galapagos was a gulag, and on crossing to Charles Island on the 23rd the crew entered a settlement of over 200 exiles deported from Ecuador, run by an English acting-governor. They had chosen the best spot. Here, four miles inland and at 1000 feet, the southerly trade winds were cooling and the plantain groves as 'green as England in the Spring time.' But it was still a dicey 'Robinson Crusoe life,' cursed by lack of fresh water and cut off, except for passing whalers. Tortoise was the staple meat, huge reptiles that six men could not carry. But these were no longer so plentiful. Once a frigate's company could drag 200 to the shore, now only a fraction could be caught. Stocks were depleting fast, and the governor calculated that they would last barely twenty more years.

The prisoners believed that each island had its peculiar tortoise, varying fractionally in shell-shape from the next. Even the Vice-Governor boasted that he could tell the island by looking at the tortoise. It would have been easy for Darwin to collect representative samples: even on Charles Island empty saddleback carapaces were lying around, ignominiously used as flower pots. But he paid no heed and collected no tortoises, thinking the reptiles to be foreign imports. He assumed that the buccaneers had brought them from their real island homes in the Indian Ocean as a food source. By contrast, he *did* notice that the mockingbirds here differed from those on

Chatham. And from this time on he carefully kept his mockingbirds separate and tagged them by island.[13]

On the 28th they put in at Albemarle, the largest island of the archipelago. Here he was greeted by an even more charred smoke-stack landscape, with jets of steam hissing from laval cones. Darwin trekked off into the desolation, searching for fresh water. In this 'arid & sterile' scrub huge ragged lizards, land iguanas weighing up to fifteen pounds, scurried to their burrows with a 'quick & clumsy gait.' He thought these yellow and red iguanas 'hideous,' fit only for the pot, and on one day 'forty were collected' ('not bad eating,' was FitzRoy's most favourable comment on these unique lizards).[14] Water was rationed now, and in the baking sun Darwin could find only small pits in the rocks holding a gallon or so. These water-holes attracted all the finches, making it easy to compare them together. But he did not bother to catch any in the baking heat, assuming that – unlike the anomalous mockingbirds – they were similar on all the islands.

They sailed north to James Island, where Darwin's party bivouacked in Buccaneers' Cove and, like the old pirates, lived on tortoises fried in their own fat. He spent two days collecting, shooting mockingbirds (which looked different again), and trekking high up the fern-covered sides of the craters. Yard-long tortoises could be seen plodding along, using well-beaten paths to the permanent rain-water pools higher up the slopes. Darwin rode on one, which drank regardless of its rider. Unfortunately, his mounts here were like the tortoises on Chatham, the only others he had seen, which convinced him that their differences really had been exaggerated.

Water was at a premium on these lava outcrops. Sweltering, thirsty days were spent collecting; it was often 93° in the shade, and Darwin was parched. Were it not for a passing American whaler giving the party three casks of water, 'we should have been distressed.'[15] This American kindliness was typical of the voyage, the Yankees' 'hearty manner' a contrast to English reserve on the high seas.

On all the islands finches predominated in the lowland thickets, but Darwin had trouble telling them apart. The plumage was almost identical: the 'old cock birds' seemed to be black in his samples, and the females brown. FitzRoy, Covington, and others were making their own collections, and some caught black females, confusing him more. Nor were the birds' habits distinguishable, for 'they feed together . . . in large irregular flocks.' At the end of his stay he threw his hands up, admitting an 'inexplicable confusion.'

In all he shot six types of finch from three islands, and his samples from two of those were mixed together. Still, his difficulties left him feeling that these birds were 'very curious.' During his final days he had been told that many trees too, like the tortoises, were unique to each island. But by then his collecting was finished – he had tagged his specimens in a desultory manner and had rarely bothered to label by island. It had not seemed important. The mockingbirds were the exception; he had kept his specimens from four islands separate.

He had also caught a wren, several 'Icterus' (members of the oriole/blackbird family), and some heavy-billed 'Gross-beaks.' He had picked every plant in flower for Henslow, and he continued to wonder whether, like the mockingbirds, the 'Flora belongs to America' – whether, to use Lyell's phrase, its 'district or "centre of creation"' lay on the mainland.[16]

FitzRoy stocked up with pigs, vegetables, and thirty more tortoises from Chatham Island, enough to see them across the Pacific. Darwin and his servant Covington each came away with a baby giant tortoise, not for the pot though, but as pets.

On 20 October, after five weeks on the Galapagos, they put out to sea, thankful to be off. Darwin found it hard to imagine tropical islands 'so entirely useless to man or the larger animals.'[17] They were too hostile, too recently emerged from the sea. The birds, reptiles, and plants had seemed curious, but not riveting.

But at sea he began to examine his corpses more closely – or at least the mockingbirds. The Chatham and Albemarle birds looked similar, but the other two were different. So he had '2 or 3 varieties,' he noted as the *Beagle* sailed to Tahiti. 'Each variety is constant in its own Island. - This is a parallel fact to the one mentioned about the Tortoises.' But he still assumed that these were insignificant anomalies, and across the Pacific he ate his way through the tortoises and watched the cook dump their tell-tale carapaces overboard.[18]

Once outside the gloomy South American region, the long voyage to Tahiti was sunny and swift. 'Boundless ocean' could be boring, but to Darwin it verged on the 'sublime,' and the trade winds blew the *Beagle* the 3200 miles to Polynesia in just over three weeks. On 9 November the terns and gulls heralded the first of the Low Islands, although Darwin was not impressed. 'Uninteresting,' he called it, just 'a long brilliantly white beach' overhung by coconut palms. The monsoons and heat only aggravated his homesick mood. Even Tahiti, the jewel of the South Seas, which they saw on the 15th, looked uninviting from a distance. But he bucked up on spotting the tropical luxuriance, and the 'laughing merry faces' of the milling Tahitians in their canoes.

They were met by a missionary, and almost immediately Darwin sallied off on foot, delighting in the luxuriance. The island was 'a most beautiful orchard of Tropical plants' – bananas, coconuts, spreading breadfruit trees, and cultivated yams and pineapples. Even the delicious guavas were growing like weeds. The people welcomed him into their homes, with friendly expressions and 'an intelligence which shows they are advancing in civilization.' Their dress was advancing too, shirts and coloured cotton loin cloths. The men were still tattooed, but it was 'an elegant & pleasing effect.' The women wore camellias behind their ears and had taken to shaving their crowns, leaving just a ring of hair; quite why, Darwin laconically noted, no one knew: 'it is the fashion & that is answer enough at Tahiti as well as Paris.'

He went with a guide for a two-day climb into the craggy volcanic peaks, where he was emotionally lost among the ravines and precipices. He collected ferns for Henslow, weaved through groves of wild bananas, and was mesmerized by the view out to sea, where breakers marked the encircling reef. His guide baked strips of banana, fish, and beef in leaves, but would eat his meal only after fervent prayer. 'He prayed as a Christian should do,' Darwin noted, 'with fitting reverence, & without fear of ridicule or ostentation.'

The missions had done their work well, but then they had had plenty of time. The islands had long been visited; there were Tahitians alive who remembered Capt. Cook, and others who told stories of the mutiny on Bligh's *Bounty*. A mission printing press had been installed for almost twenty years, and an elder had spent forty years translating the Bible.[19] Also the islands were dry, alcohol was banned and drunkenness was non-existent.

Darwin was impressed by the 'high & respectable' standing of these men, and their successes were tangible. It came as something of a surprise: books he had read painted a much bleaker picture – of downtrodden natives living under a tyrannical regime. The missionaries' characters had been impugned so often that he felt bound to speak in their favour. Even their daughters had been subject to scurrilous attacks, yet their 'appearance & manners showed that they had been properly educated.' And so 'many merry, happy faces' among the Tahitians gave the lie to the slander that they were a crushed and demoralized race under the churches' heel. Given that twenty years previously, bloody wars, licentiousness, infanticide, 'human sacrifices & the power of an idolatrous priesthood' were reputed to be the norm, the present 'state of morality & religion is highly creditable' to the missioners. Even if the 'virtue of the [Tahitian] women' were still open to question, Christianity had achieved much. Would that such missions extended to wilder shores, making them safe for shipwrecked sailors.

Thinking of shipwrecks, Darwin canoed out to the reef, to collect 'the pretty branching Corals,' amazed that these 'tiny architects' could build such mountainous rings around the island. FitzRoy's work completed (he was policing the seas, collecting $3000 compensation for a ship plundered two years previously in the Low Islands), Queen Pomare of Tahiti was entertained aboard on 25 November. The *Beagle*, 'dressed with flags,' was lit up by sky rockets launched in her honour. She 'is an awkquard [sic] large woman, without any beauty, gracefulness or dignity of manners,' Darwin observed. Her Majesty had 'only one royal attribute, viz a perfect immoveability of expression.' The next evening, money collected, the *Beagle* pulled out in a gentle breeze and steered for New Zealand.

The crossing took three weeks, with nothing but deep blue sea, an immensity of it; but 'every league . . . which we travel onwards, is one league nearer to England.'[20] The time was lost in writing. He drew up his coral theory in full, balancing the rise of South America with the fall of the Pacific, making the atolls mark the disappearing peaks of a drowning oceanic basin.

They sighted the northern tip of New Zealand on 19 December, and two days later were sailing in to the Bay of Islands. Darwin looked out at the verdant hills dotted with tidy whitewashed houses, interspersed by 'diminutive & paltry' native huts. The cottages were part of a twenty-year-old missionary settlement; each one, with roses around the door, a reminder of England.

The hills were a different matter: fern-covered and impenetrable, and dotted with stockades once defended by Maoris during their wars. The natives struck Darwin as a fearsome people: 'a more warlike race of inhabitants could be found in no part of the world.' But Englishmen were now safe, thanks to the missions – and to the fact that their meat was too salty, or at least 'not so sweet as Maori flesh.' Cannibalism had been stamped out in this region and, as Covington reported, heads could no longer be bought, 'though much sought after.' Still Darwin was contemptuous. These people were barely above the Fuegians in his yardstick of 'civilization.' Peering down from his privileged perch, he dismissed one chief for his 'horrid & ferocious expression,' and another as 'a notorious murderer & to boot an arrant coward.' Shifty looks betrayed a fierce cunning, and tattooed faces revealed a base nature. Was there 'in the whole of New Zealand a person with the face & mien of the old Tahitian chief'?

But that said, the English miscreants were even worse. The missionaries took him to Kororarika, a settlement dominated by escaped convicts from New South Wales and dedicated 'to drunkenness & all kinds of vice.' The missionaries had built a chapel in this den of iniquity, but such were the threats that 'the only protection which they need . . . is from the native Chiefs against Englishmen!'[21]

These 'worthy men' had done their best, and the weeks in Tahiti and New Zealand convinced FitzRoy and Darwin that the missions were a success. For both, Christianity came as a civilizing package, and most of all they applauded the noblemindedness of the missionaries. In these outposts of empire, a genteel class of white man was making shores safe for Britannia's sailors, preaching good manners and promoting good government. Their 'political agency' was needed wherever ships put in and lands were being settled.

FitzRoy and Darwin looked through Christian spectacles at the heathen hordes. Both used an inflexible 'scale' of civilization, with progress measured against the European ideal. But this was not the only way that indigenous tribes could be viewed. Some travellers, no less than the 'licentious' socialists at home, looked more sympathetically on foreign cultures, and damned the missions for foisting Christianity on peoples for whom it was ill adapted. Part of Darwin and FitzRoy's target was Augustus Earle, the artist who had shipped out in 1833, leaving a copy of his *Narrative of a Nine Months' Residence in New Zealand* on board. Written before the voyage, its attack on the local missions had Darwin and FitzRoy indignant. Darwin now knew 'without doubt' that the 'very missionaries, who are accused of coldness . . . always treated [Earle] with far more civility, than his open licentiousness could have given reason to expect.'[22]

After passing the native hovels on his walks, Darwin was always pleased to see 'an English farm house & its well dressed fields, placed there as if by an enchanter's wand.' These mission houses were surrounded by well-kept gardens of flowers, fruit and vegetables, threshing barns, forges, and 'in the middle was that happy mixture of pigs & poultry which may be seen so comfortably lying together in every English farm yard.' The Maori servant girls were 'clean tidy & healthy [in] appearance, like that of dairy maids in England.' Darwin moved between the farms, sipping tea, reminded of home. 'I never saw a nicer or more merry group: – & to think that this was in the centre of the land of cannibalism, murder & all atrocious crimes!' Thanks to the missionaries, Darwin told his devout sister Caroline, white men can now 'walk with as much safety as in England,' surrounded by tribes who 'were the most ferocious savages probably on the face of the earth.'

Where the Tahiti missions sought to improve the mind, the New Zealand ones taught farming practice, although the 'moral effect' on the Maoris was the same. It was clear that the very example 'of the Missionary is the enchanter's wand.' How could the savage radicals at home damn such enterprises and demand that the natives be left to their own devices? More missions were needed, more colonization. He was mulling this over on Christmas Day, convinced that the conversion of the 'Heathen' alone brings its reward: 'so excellent is the Christian faith, that the outward conduct of the believers is said most decidedly to have been improved by its doctrines.'

A Christmas collection was taken up. Grateful for the week's hospitality and eager to enlarge this outpost, FitzRoy, Darwin, and the officers chipped in £15 towards the building of more churches. Then they bade farewell to the missionaries on 30 December and set sail for Australia.[23]

The crossing took thirteen days and after all the hovels and filth of native New Zealand, Sydney Cove was a sight for sore eyes: large trading ships, harbour warehouses, well-stocked shops – and 'Wool, Wool ... the cry from one end of the country to the other.' The broad streets were a mad crush, 'gigs, phaetons & carriages with livery servants' clattered everywhere. After South America, so singularly devoid of gentlemen, Darwin could only marvel at Sydney's wealth and ostentation. Fortunes were for the making in this 'paradise to the Worshippers of Mammon.'

'Ancient Rome, in her Imperial grandeur, would not have been ashamed of such' a colony. Fine houses were built on shipping or construction fortunes. Land was rocketing in value to £8000 an acre – the best double that. A convict once thrashed on a cartwheel now had 'an income from 12 to 15000 pounds per annum.' Another – the 'Rothschild of Botany Bay' – was worth half a million. It left everything 'villainously dear,' Charles wrote home, punning furiously, explaining why he had drawn another 'bill for 100£.' The population of 23,000 was rising astronomically; 'not even near London or Birmingham is there an aspect of such rapid growth.' Nothing, in short, had prepared him for Sydney. It was high among the '100 Wonders of the world,' and he put it down to the 'Giant force of the parent country.' 'It is a most magnificent testimony to the power of the British nation: here . . . scores of years have effected many times more than centuries in South America. – My first feeling was to congratulate myself that I was born an Englishman.'[24]

On a sunny Saturday, 16 January 1836, he set off with a guide, heading a hundred miles into the interior. They walked on macadamized roads, one of the benefits of forced labour; and he passed convict 'Iron gangs' in their yellow and grey prison garb, hard at work in the heat. Then he noticed the ale houses, seventeen in the first fifteen miles. No wonder half of the government revenues came from duty on alcohol. (Or that the gaols were full, and stocks were appearing on Sydney streets, for confining 'ladies and gentlemen who cannot pay the usual fee for indulging too freely at the shrine of Bacchus.') Even thirty-five miles away, he still saw 'substantial houses' and fenced off pastures. The scanty-leaved gum trees left the 'woods light & shadowless.' It was high summer and everywhere was dry and parched. The crops looked precarious and he could see why they periodically failed.

He stopped a 'good-humoured' group of 'Aboriginal Blacks' who gave him a display of spear-throwing for a shilling. It was their cheeriness that left him doubting that they were 'such utterly degraded beings as usually represented.'[25] What was their fate in a civilizing world? He knew that they were being destroyed by the white man's scourges, measles and liquor, and that their children's lives depended far more on immediate food availability than in Europe. It was a question he pondered as he trekked on into the Blue Mountains, passing wool-carts and scrubby eucalyptus woods. The bay view was magnificent, and even at 3400 feet he found fifteen-bed inns, much like those he had stopped at in North Wales with Sedgwick.

He visited one of the huge, spartan, sheep stations, run by a foreman with convict labour. Here 'forty profligate men' worked like slaves, yet without the same 'claim for compassion.' He launched out one morning, hunting kangaroos with the station's greyhounds. But he managed to catch only a potoroo (a rat kangaroo), although this did give him his first good look at a marsupial. Lack of big kangaroos was a sign of how destructive these settlements were to the wildlife. And to the aborigines. His mind kept turning back to the cheery blacks. It was a sad refrain, the thought that 'the White Man . . . seems predestined to inherit the country,' dispossessing the aboriginal 'children.'

Lying on a sunny bank, he reflected on the stark divide between the marsupials here and normal placental mammals. They were so anatomically different. 'An unbeliever . . . might exclaim "Surely two distinct Creators must have been [at] work",' each producing a perfect – but unique – creation. What he saw on the riverbank that evening might have required a third Creator in the pantheon. The station manager took him 'Platypi' shooting. They glimpsed several of these 'extraordinary' web-footed, duck-billed beasts snuffling along the water's edge. The manager 'actually killed one,' Darwin exclaimed. 'I consider it a great feat, to be in at the death of so wonderful an animal.' He picked up the limp corpse, examining its bill, surprised to find it soft and sensitive, rather than hard as in the stuffed specimens. Even odder, many colonists believed that the platypus laid leathery eggs like a reptile and incubated them in a nest, although the debate was still raging in London and Paris (with his old teacher Robert Grant and the Parisian Geoffroy St Hilaire taking the colonists' side).

Of course the notion of many Creators was preposterous, fit only for the primitive Maori or Aborigine. And Nature quickly proved it. He watched an ant-lion, a huge-jawed larval insect, which lived buried at the bottom of a conical pit of sand. To catch its prey, it flicked up jets of sand, causing a sand-slide which brought unwary ants to its gaping jaws. European ant-lions did exactly the same. Now what would a 'Disbeliever say to this? Would any two workmen ever hit on so beautiful, so simple & yet so artificial a contrivance'?[26] No, it was the most telling proof of a single Creative hand at work over the globe. Darwin had argued Paley's classic case, from one perfect design to one perfect Designer.

On 20 January – after suffering 120° temperatures and oven-blast winds – he arrived at Bathhurst, a troop station on the Macquarie River. This too was sheep country, with good pastures in the river valley, although in high summer he found the land parched and the river little more than drying ponds. All around bush fires were raging, and the next day 'we passed through large tracts of country in flames.'

On the return he visited Capt. King, the *Beagle*'s former commander, having last seen him at Plymouth the day the ship sailed. King's father had been governor of the colony, and the Captain had been born here. Darwin found him on his 4000-acre farm, thirty miles from Sydney, writing an account of his own South American voyage. Young Midshipman King was here too, having left the *Beagle* to join his father and mother (who had not seen her son for ten years). The Captain's collections were extensive; Darwin had seen them at the Zoological Society in London when he picked up

King's preserving tips. They shared an interest in barnacles and molluscs, and they spent a pleasant day walking around the farm, talking over 'the Natural History of T[ierra]. del Fuego.'[27]

By the end, Darwin was beginning to pall of Sydney society. The wealth had initially blinded him to its faults. The community was split, the rich emancipists vying with the free settlers, whom they considered interlopers. Who would want to walk on streets 'where every other man is sure to be somewhere between a petty rogue & bloodthirsty villain'? The climate was splendid, but intellectual stimulation was nil. Grandfather Erasmus, celebrating the growth of Sydney forty-five years earlier, had waxed poetic:

> Here future Newtons shall explore the skies.
> Here future Priestleys, future Wedgwoods rise.

Quite how Darwin could not see, considering the tiny bookshops with empty shelves. The prospect of being waited on by convicts was abhorrent. The female servants were worst, with the 'vilest expressions' hiding 'equally vile ideas.' No attempt was made to reform the criminals' morality, and, as a young offender told him, 'they know no pleasure beyond sensuality, and in this they are not gratified.' The convicts did not know any better. What really shocked him was to see so many of the higher ranks living in the same 'open profligacy.' It was an immoral slave-run economy, generating huge profits. Nothing but 'severe necessity,' he concluded, would 'compel me to emigrate.'

Society was pleasanter in Hobart, in the newly-renamed Tasmania. This was more than could be said for weather. The *Beagle* docked in the eponymous Storm Bay on 5 February. The town itself did not live up to the 'Panorama' pictures that Darwin had viewed in London. There were few large houses, although some of the farms were appealing. Polite English society was always a relief, and here at least it was not contaminated with 'wealthy Convicts.'

The finest houses as usual opened their doors. The Attorney-General provided Italian music, beautiful décor, 'dinner most elegant with *respectable*! (although of course all Convicts) Servants.' The Surveyor-General, George Frankland, offered something even better, a tour of the ancient limestone quarries. Darwin obtained more lamp-shells to compare with those from the Falklands and Wales. He spent his twenty-seventh birthday catching skinks and snakes. He took many flatworms, and over 119 species of insects. (Among them were dung beetles that he fished out of cow pats. This itself was odd, for the dairy herds had been introduced for only thirty years. How

179

had the beetles adapted so quickly?) Dinner at the Frankland household was the 'most agreeable evening since leaving home.'[28] Frankland was in his ninth year charting land for the immigrants, who were now flooding in. But there was a sinister underside to this colonial expansion. The land had been forcibly cleared, and Darwin saw no Tasmanian aborigines. Their genocide was almost complete, and the last 210 had been herded on to an island. It was the most graphic evidence that white immigration was the death-knell for indigenous races.

Still, if he ever emigrated anywhere, this would be the place. But now his heart was set on home. Every merchant ship starting for England left him with 'a dangerous inclination to bolt.' The voyage was 'reduced simply to Chronometrical Measurements,' and he saw these months as 'so much existence obliterated from the page of life.' Only the thought of the atolls in the Indian Ocean kept him going. 'There never was a Ship, so full of home-sick heroes.' 'I will take good care,' he moaned to Fox, never again 'to volunteer as Philosopher (my accustomed title) even to a line of Battle Ship.'[29]

He might 'hate every wave of the ocean' but the sea was still supplying him with exotic specimens. The intrigues of colonial life ashore were as nothing to the intriguing colonial life on the shoreline. He was fascinated by the coral animals, and walked along the Hobart coast collecting marine plants. In tidal pools he turned up broken tufts of encrusting algae, budding like Chiloé apple trees. So, plants high and low could propagate by cutting. And the same was true for the branching corals, the stony reef-forming animals – they too could grow from broken stems. As the *Beagle* dropped anchor on 6 March in King George's Sound, on Australia's south-western coast, Darwin was lost in his notes on the encrusting plants and corals. He was tying these primitive life-forms ever tighter; placing them close to the zero point, where the plants and animals meet.

As for the landfall, he had never spent a 'more dull, uninteresting time' than the eight days here. King George's Sound was a neglected outpost, not ten years old, a potential penal colony that had gone to pot, eclipsed by the new Swan River settlement (now Perth). FitzRoy had even been inclined to 'put the helm up' and move on at the sight of the 'cheerless' straggling houses, but duty prevailed. Darwin did attend an aboriginal dance, performed by the white-painted 'Cockatoo men.' To an outsider it seemed like so much marching and stamping. A 'most rude barbarous scene' it might have been, with them 'all moving in hideous harmony,' but he could not help liking these 'good humoured' aborigines, so perfectly at ease and 'in such high spirits.'

In his last few days on the continent he diligently collected shells and fish, caught a native Australian bush rat, and took notes on the grass-trees and granite outcrops. But there was no disguising the disappointment. The soil was sandy and poor, the vegetation coarse, the views uninteresting, the kangaroos scarce: he had nothing good to say, except that he never wished 'to walk again in so uninviting a country.'

The *Beagle* departed in a storm and ran aground. It was a fitting end. As the ship finally refloated Darwin waved goodbye to the colony with a grand lament. 'Farewell Australia, you are a rising infant & doubtless some day will reign a great princess in the South; but you are too great & ambitious for affection, yet not great enough for respect; I leave your shores without sorrow or regret.'[30]

13

Temples of Nature

By 1 APRIL 1836 the ship had made the Keeling or Cocos Islands in the Indian Ocean – coral paradises below the equator, 700 miles from Java. These were real atolls, Darwin's first. The mountain top had submerged, leaving the reef encircling an emerald lagoon, shallow enough for the sun's rays to sparkle on the sea floor.

From the ship, nothing but 'glittering' sandy beaches fringed by coconut trees could be seen. But on shore, Darwin discovered a complete coconut economy. The islands had been colonized by British traders and freed Malay slaves, who lived off a sole export, coconut oil. In fact, everything lived off coconuts. The pigs and poultry were fattened on them, and even 'a huge land crab' specialized on a coconut diet, which was 'as curious a piece of adaptation and instinct as I ever heard of.'

The reef itself he ranked 'amongst the wonderful objects of this world.' He spent days up to his waist, making notes on brain corals and branching corals, and the fishes darting in and out. He was lost in admiration for the hues and tints, and the brilliant flashes of colour. Under the microscope these living corals posed more of a problem: however hard he looked, he could not see any discrete polyp animals. They seemed to consist of a mass of 'fleshy matter' spread 'over the whole surface.'[1] Moreover, the stony framework of the coral appeared to grow as it did in the encrusting algae. He was now convinced that the lowest animals and plants practically touched at this primitive level. He had come round to the position of his Lamarckian teacher Robert Grant ten years earlier: the plant and animal kingdoms had a common starting point.

Evenings were spent stretched out under the palms, pondering these taxonomic profundities, watching the hermit crabs. No one knows 'how delicious it is to be seated in such a shade & there drink the cool pleasant fruit of the Cocoa nut.' He was convinced about something else. Having examined an atoll, he was certain of his reef theory.

The Sea Lords had instructed FitzRoy to use any means 'that ingenuity can devise of discovering at what depth the coral formation begins.' He too was looking for clues to the reef's origin. A mile out he took soundings, but even here the sea floor had dropped away. The line was fed out 7000 feet, and still it did not touch bottom. The reef was clearly built on an oceanic mountain top. The 'circular wall' of coral had risen as the mountain had submerged, leaving only a vivid green lagoon, as Darwin's theory predicted.[2]

The *Beagle* stocked up with provisions – fresh water from the island well, coconuts, fish, and turtles to top up the diminishing Galapagos tortoise stocks – ready for its journey to Mauritius. The homesick heroes set sail once more, knowing that barely six months of the voyage remained. Darwin, keen to cover the port calls quickly, logged wearily, 'There is no country which has now any attractions for us, without it is seen right astern.'[1]

On the high seas again, he spent three weeks 'totally rewriting' his geological notes, trying for fluency and not exactly succeeding. Even mooting the problem to his sisters left him in a syntactic mess. 'I am just now beginning to discover the difficulty of expressing one's ideas on paper. As long as it consists solely of description it is pretty easy; but where reasoning comes into play, to make a proper connection, a clearness & a moderate fluency, is to me, as I have said, a difficulty of which I had no idea.' Never mind, 'I am in high spirits about my geology.' He was feeling cut off by this point and wanting familial reassurance. No mail had reached him in New Zealand or Australia. In fact he had not received a letter in thirteen months, and he wondered how his latest geological news was being digested. 'I look forward with no little anxiety to the time when Henslow, putting on a grave face, shall decide on the merits of my notes. If he shakes his head in a disapproving manner: I shall then know that I had better at once give up science, for science will have given me up.'

He remained 'a martyr to sea-sickness.' It never let up entirely, although FitzRoy noted that 'he recovers at the sight of land.' This time the mountains of Mauritius appearing over the horizon did the trick. From far off the island had an 'air of perfect elegance,' and close up its 'beautiful scenery' and cloud-topped peaks reinforced the welcoming feeling.

Darwin toured the French-speaking town of Port Louis on 30

April, delighting in its opera and its well-stocked bookshops. After more than four years of travelling, it was wonderful to spend 'so idle & dissipated a time.' The island was exotic, full of 'glowing bewitching scenes,' the perfect place for romance. What an 'opportunity for writing love letters,' he mused; 'Oh that I had a sweet Virginia to send an inspired Epistle to.' He paced its multi-racial streets, a mélange of Europeans, 'noble looking' Indians, and Madagascar blacks. Massive sugar exports had paid for tarmac roads and Darwin was able to travel easily round the picturesque island. Not that he actually needed roads; part of his tour was by elephant, owned by a surveyor who put his house and pachyderm at Darwin's disposal.[3]

The long haul across the Indian Ocean continued, and on 31 May a gale blew them into Simon's Bay at the Cape of Good Hope, on the tip of Africa. The next day Darwin hired a gig and headed the twenty-two miles to Cape Town, past desert, past lumbering bullock-wagons pulled by a dozen oxen, and then past fine houses and plantations, set off against Table Mountain. Cape Town was a 'great inn' on the 'highway to the east,' its boarding houses packed with merchants and sailors of every nationality. The town was becoming anglicised, and everybody spoke English, to the consternation of the Dutch. By now Darwin was getting a sense of empire: of the endless colonies seeded around the globe in which 'little embryo Englands are hatching.' Here, as elsewhere, the indigenous peoples were retreating. He saw few Negroes and even fewer Hottentots, 'the ill-treated aboriginals of the country.' Some were in service. He actually had an impeccably dressed and mannered Hottentot groom to guide him – white gloves and all – to the outlying villages.

During his second week he met with scientific society. Army surgeons took him on geological rambles, and astronomers conducted him across the southern skies. One astronomer he wanted to meet above all others: his hero, Sir John Herschel, whose book he had devoured at Cambridge. Herschel had been here for two years, mapping the constellations, and had bought a 'comfortable country house,' situated amid firs and oak trees, six miles outside Cape Town. 'I have heard so much about his eccentric but very amiable manners,' Darwin said, 'that I have a high curiosity to see the great Man.'

He did not have to wait long. With FitzRoy he called on Herschel on 3 June. Sir John was 'exceedingly good natured,' inviting them to dinner, which enabled Darwin to confirm that his manners were 'rather awful.' The guests were given a tour of the 'pretty garden full of Cape bulbs.' They wandered the grounds, flanked by fir trees, the imposing Table Mountain looming up in the distance. All the while they talked volcanic eruptions and heaving continents, and Darwin discovered that these crustal convolutions were just as dear to Herschel's heart. Sir John was intrigued by the mechanics of subterranean movement. He had already written to Lyell explaining them, his interest too fired by the *Principles of Geology*. Perhaps Herschel and Darwin said more about Lyell's gradually evolving landscapes. In his letter, Herschel had criticized Lyell for not grasping the nettle on that 'mystery of mysteries,' the successive appearance of new species on the earth. If landscapes change gradually, shaped by forces no different from those of today, shouldn't life be understood the same way? Weren't the births of species just as natural? Sir John thought so. Whether or not they touched on this ticklish subject, the meeting struck Darwin as 'the most memorable event which, for a long period, I have had the good fortune to enjoy.'[4]

The news from home fortified his scientific resolve. At the Cape a letter from Catherine finally caught up with him, bringing the word that his name was on the tip of naturalists' tongues in England. Unknown to Charles, Henslow had edited ten of his technical letters on South American geology and *printed* them as a booklet for private distribution. Everyone had been revelling in them for six months. The Doctor was so pleased that he had given away half a dozen copies, allowing the Foxes, Owens, Wedgwoods and local gentry to read of his son's discoveries. Henslow had sung Charles's praises to the family, leaving them all enormously proud. Charles was delighted to hear it, but horrified to contemplate his dashed-off prose in print. He had 'written to Henslow in the same careless manner' as he had written home; what on earth did it read like set in type? 'But, as the Spaniard says, "No hay remedio"' – nothing can be done.

FitzRoy had more evangelical concerns. Attacks on missionaries were as common in Cape Town as elsewhere. Having seen the Pacific missions' successes, he was all for their defence; after all, Christianizing the Tierra savages had been his starting point for the voyage. In Cape Town he was asked to pen a piece for the *South African Christian Recorder*. At sea on 18 June, heading northward into the southern Atlantic, he wrote an open letter on the 'Moral State of Tahiti' for the paper. Extracts from Darwin's diary were patched in, on the manners of the missionaries, and the temperance and morality of the natives. A highlight was Darwin's description of his guide in the mountains, cooking bananas and falling to his knees before eating, praying 'as a christian should,' with reverence. As Darwin had written at the time: 'Those travellers, who hint that a Tahitian prays only when the eyes of the missionary are fixed on him, might have profited by similar evidence.'[5] The piece was finished at sea, and posted back on a passing ship for publication.

He was only four months from home, and it was time for assessments and reflections. In the Atlantic he drew up catalogues of his collections – listing specimen numbers, locations, and descriptions. He put together twelve catalogues over a few weeks, one for each class – 'Fish in Spirits of Wine,' 'Animals [that is, mammals],' 'Reptiles in Spirits of Wine,' 'Ornithology,' 'Insects in Spirits of Wine,' and so on. He was determined that his precious skins and pickled specimens would be properly named and described, each by an expert. Without names, his insect authority William Kirby had warned, the 'zoological treasures' shipped home on surveying vessels were worthless. They might as well be 'left to perish in their native deserts or forests' as grow 'mouldy in our drawers or repositories.'[6] That fate would not befall Darwin's cargo. The catalogues were to aid the specialists who took over his haul in England.

Listing his Galapagos mockingbirds, three of them different, each to its island, he began mulling over the implications.

> When I recollect, the fact that . . . the Spaniards can at once pronounce, from which Island any Tortoise may have been brought. When I see these Islands in sight of each other, & possessed of but a scanty stock of animals, tenanted by these birds, but slightly differing in structure & filling the same place in Nature, I must suspect they are only varieties . . . If there is the slightest foundation for these remarks the zoology of Archipelagoes – will be well worth examining; for such facts would undermine the stability of Species.[7]

If the buccaneers' imported tortoises varied by island, perhaps the original mockingbird colonists, blown in from Chile, had also dispersed among the islands and become adapted to each. But these were only 'varieties,' and naturalists accepted that variants of a single species could occur naturally. A slight pliancy was even necessary, to allow a species to spread out from its 'centre of creation.' Such suppleness stopped far short of transmutation, but it made Darwin wonder how far a species could be pushed. Herschel's 'mystery of mysteries' might not be arcane.

Home was on everybody's mind. They crossed the Tropic of Capricorn on 29 June – 'for the sixth & last time,' Darwin logged. Nine days later that forbidding rock, St Helena, appeared 'like a huge castle from the ocean.' Or perhaps prison was a more apt comparison, for the island's lava-stream walls seemed to augment the fort's defences and gun emplacements.

The whole island was sombre, with overcast skies and sheets of rain. Here the exiled Napoleon had died in 1821, and Darwin lodged for the five nights a stone's throw from his tomb. If old Boney's ghost haunted this dreary place, Darwin laughed to Henslow on 9 July, as rain lashed his windows, it was a perfect night for his 'wandering.' There was something quite incongruous about 'so great a spirit' – the conqueror of Europe – resting next to cottages by a roadside on this desolate rock.[8]

Even more incongruous were the English plants that surrounded him. The whole island was covered with imported species, Darwin noted: gorse and Scotch firs and blackberry brambles were running rampant over the rock fortress, wiping out indigenous species. He wandered the whole island on foot, glad to be off the ship, noting these British invaders. Nor did he miss the fossil shells at 2000 feet. Standard geology texts used these as proof that the island had risen recently. But Darwin was now enough of an expert to diagnose them as *land* shells, and of a now-extinct species.

Onward they voyaged, nearer to home. Five days' sailing brought them to Ascension Island in the middle of the South Atlantic. The only settlement here was a Marine barracks. The navy kept the island like a tightly run ship, with milestones on all roads, and water pumps, tapping natural wells. The water was needed. This was less a rock – or so an old joke went – more a 'cinder' in the ocean, and Darwin was eager to examine the butt of the joke: the red volcanic cones. He paced over the rugged island, staring at nature in all her 'naked hideousness.' Here were signs of primal violence: solidified lava streams, layers of pumice and ash, with 'volcanic bombs' strewn over the surface, white-hot missiles blown out of the exploding craters.

When they put to sea on 23 July, the *Beagle* should have been heading north. It was not. The ship's compass read WSW. FitzRoy, the infuriating perfectionist, had plotted a course back to Bahia in Brazil to check his longitude measurements. Darwin logged, with mild understatement, the crew's 'discomfiture & surprise,' and carried on cataloguing his shells. His sisters were already wondering 'whether you will have had sufficient travelling to serve you for life: & I think the Yes's Yes's generally carry it.' Certainly his frustration was apparent by this point, and he told them so. 'This zig-zag manner of proceeding is very grievous; it has put the finishing stroke to my feelings. I loathe, I abhor the sea.'[9]

187

Sailing time was only a week to Bahia, but it was seven days of gritted teeth. 'The novelty & surprise' were gone, Darwin lamented as he took in Brazil's 'wild luxuriance' once more. For five days in early August he twiddled his thumbs, filled his diary, and forayed into the forest, eating mangos and bananas, listening to the whining cicadas, watching the haphazard flight of tropical butterflies for the last time. The impression of the jungle, like 'one great wild, untidy, luxuriant hot house,' would remain with him for ever. He took a final walk, trying to fix the picture in his mind. Each of the 'thousand beauties' composing it would fade, yet – 'like a tale heard in childhood' – they would leave a feeling of 'the glories of another world.'

On 6 August they started for home again, and Darwin settled in to catalogue his hundreds of insects. But the weather closed in and forced them into Pernambuco further up the coast. He again whiled away his time, examining the mangrove swamps and the reef, anxious to be off. The anchor was weighed on the 17th, and the ship pitched furiously into a tropical storm. He was finally 'on the road to England' and no 'tedious misery' could dampen his spirits at the prospect. He swung in his hammock, once more planning the carriages he would take to Shropshire, and imagining the look on his sisters' faces.

They crossed the Equator on 21 August, and took on stores at St Jago early in September, mooring alongside slavers plying their evil trade. On 9 September the ship crossed the Tropic of Cancer into the temperate north. The quartermasters picked up more provisions on the island of Terceira in the Azores. While the barrels were rolling aboard, Darwin borrowed a horse from the Consul and galloped off – past Welsh scenery, country yokels, and English blackbirds – to look at an active crater. He was back on more familiar northern territory, although no fume holes at home had steam whistling from them, unless they be 'cracks in the boiler of a steam engine.' The *Beagle* sailed to the larger island of St Michael's, docking with hundreds of ships laden with oranges, many destined for England. There was still no mail, and they sailed on 25 September, plotting, 'thanks to God, a direct course' for home.

A week would see them off Land's End. In that time one thought kept flitting through his mind: 'How beautiful Shropshire will look.' He became exuberant, carried away, forgetting the lush tropics. The 'scenery of England is ten times more beautiful,' he finally exclaimed. And 'as for your boundless plains & impenetrable forests, who

would compare them with the green fields & oak woods of England?'
The smiling tropics, what 'precious nonsense.' 'Who admires a lady's
face who is always smiling? England is not one of your insipid
beauties; she can cry, & frown, & smile, all by turns.'

After five years at sea, emotions were high among the Homeric
heroes. They had survived – even sailor Davis's coati mundi. At
such times everybody wants to 'commit some act of uncommon folly
& extravagance.' 'Man of Wars men' have the right idea, Darwin
said, 'when they throw guineas into the sea or light their tobacco
pipes with Pound notes, to testify their joy.'[10]

It was a choppy last week, with the blue sea-devils chasing him.
Lying down, he reflected on 'the pain & pleasure of our five years'
wandering.' Would he advise others to make such a hazardous
journey? Yes, but only if they had a particular bent – zoology or
geology – otherwise the pleasures are outweighed by the pains, the
niggling irritations that assume gigantic proportions – 'the want of
room, of seclusion, of rest – the jading feeling of constant hurry –
the privation of small luxuries, the comforts of civilization,' and
worst by far the incessant seasickness. Even then travellers must have
no mere dilettante interest. They must gather and use the harvest of
observations: 'some fruit,' he concluded, must 'be reaped.'

Darwin was thinking of his own. The years of sowing and tending
were over for him. He had a full record, his diary, 770 pages long,
written with one eye to publication and posted home in pieces.
Erasmus had revelled in it, and Hensleigh, and both agreed that 'it
will make a most interesting book of travels when you publish it.'
His sisters had read 'it aloud, and Papa enjoys it extremely except
when the dangers you run makes [sic] him shudder.' As Susan said,
'When I have corrected your spelling it will be perfect.'[11]

He had much more: notebooks on esoteric geology (1383 large
pages) and zoology (368 pages), new species under his belt – not
least the half-eaten carcass of his small rhea – a baby Galapagos
tortoise in his cabin, still alive and two inches longer, and crates of
bones and birds, rocks and corals, awaiting him at home. The haul
had been enormous. His master catalogues listed 1529 species in
spirits and 3907 labelled skins, bones, and other dried specimens.[12]

Would these bear fruit? He certainly expected the real labour to
start now, and he looked ahead 'with a comical mixture of dread &
satisfaction to the amount of work, which remains for me in England.'
He knew he would have to live in London to see his specimens
farmed out, so he started making plans. He wrote ahead to ask
Henslow, 'my first Lord of the Admiralty,' to put him up for a

fellowship of the Geological Society, and to Eras to arrange membership of some gentleman's club.[13] Friends already had his name down
for the Entomological Society, where he could be lionized for his
tropical insects.

He knew that skins and bones and 'isolated facts soon become
uninteresting.' Something more had to be done with them. For Kirby,
one of the older generation, naming was the be-all and end-all. But
Darwin wanted more. He had questions, a million questions – what
did the old megatheriums' world look like? Why did they die out?
How do animals and birds colonize offshore islands? He already had
his grand geological theories, of continental risings and coral-reef
formation. He was already 'pushing ideas to their limits,' stretching
his views from South America to the globe. And he prophesied that,
given his views, the 'geology of [the] whole world will turn out
simple.'[14] He had started a lifelong trend, extrapolating from small
origins to big outcomes, from microscopic corals to huge reefs, from
crustal twitches to the Andes. The world – through Darwin's
Lyellian spectacles – was an accumulation of tiny changes:
everything natural, gradual, and slow.

No longer the 'lions provider,' he would devour the material itself.
Sedgwick had given a résumé of Darwin's conclusions at the Geological Society the previous November. Little was known of South
American geology and his view that the pampas 'elevation must have
been gradual, or by successive hitches,' caused a great stir. The
report in the Saturday *Athenaeum* left the Doctor overjoyed at
Charles's 'laurels.' Lyell himself was ecstatic: 'How I long for the
return of Darwin!' he regaled Sedgwick; 'I hope you do not mean to
monopolise him at Cambridge.' Sedgwick himself realized that 'it
was the best thing in the world for him that he went out on the
Voyage of Discovery – There was some risk of his turning out an
idle man: but his character will now be fixed, & if God spare his life,
he will have a great name among the Naturalists of Europe.'[15]
Darwin had to justify Sedgwick's faith and live up to Lyell's expectations. He was coming home with more pertinent questions than
pickled specimens, and it was up to him to answer them.

The biggest query of all concerned mankind. He could conceive of
no more disconcerting sight than 'a real barbarian,' a 'man in his
lowest and most savage state.' Idling in his hammock, Darwin
mused, 'One's mind hurries back over past centuries, & then asks
could our progenitors be such as these?' He had seen every grade in
his human 'scale,' from the rude Fuegian – whose 'very signs &
expressions are less intelligible to us than those of the domesticated

animals' – through the Maoris, Tahitians, and pampas Indians, to the gauchos exterminating them. And all were being eclipsed by the British colonists marching under the Union Jack.

It was a 'scale' calibrated in Eurocentric units; those at the top judged those at the bottom. Darwin ranked people by their willingness to work, to better themselves, to befriend settlers, and to adopt Christian morality. Between the high and low races was a yawning gulf. 'I do not believe it is possible to describe or paint the difference of savage and civilized man. It is the difference between a wild and tame animal.' And, as Jemmy showed, the savage instincts were strong. Fuegians were well adapted to their miserable existence, as Darwin was to a sherry-sipping society. But how could this be? How could the same Creator have made man both so primitive and so sophisticated?

The questions remained, and his spiritual sentiment. He had climbed the Andes, stood on volcanic rims, seen glaciers crashing into the sea, waded along coral reefs, but, with all said and done, none of these exceeded 'in sublimity the primeval forests.' He had sat enraptured in lush creeper-strewn jungles, 'temples filled with the varied productions of the God of Nature.' He had been filled with religious awe: 'No one can stand unmoved in these solitudes, without feeling that there is more in man than the mere breath of his body.' And this is what he now looked forward to, adoration in a new temple.

The parsonage was being crowded out by Nature – overtaken, overgrown. His sisters had guessed as much. 'Papa & we often cogitate over the fire what you will do when you return, as I fear there are but small hopes of your still going into the Church.'[16] Indeed, Charles was already worshipping elsewhere. He had felt the awesome power beneath the fragile crust, in Concepción where the cathedral collapsed, and in the elemental forces that raise and lower continents – forces that reduce man's puny efforts to 'insignificance.' Here indeed was something venerable, even numinous: the very grounds of life itself. His Cambridge professors had placed devotion to Nature's God among the highest. He would go beyond them – study Nature for its own sake, explain its powers, understand its wisdom, justify its ways.

As Falmouth hove in sight on the stormy night of 2 October he had questions enough for a career.

191

1836–1842

14

A Peacock Admiring His Tail

CHARLES RACED FROM Falmouth to Shrewsbury, dying to
see everyone, bursting, his head 'quite confused with so much delight.'
At full speed the journey took two days, the sweaty horses galloping
past West Country woods and orchards, more 'beautiful & cheerful'
than he ever remembered. 'The stupid people on the coach did not
seem to think the fields one bit greener than usual,' he mused, but –
having seen the tropical forests, the scrubby pampas, the mighty
Cordilleras – he knew 'that the wide world does not contain so
happy a prospect as the rich cultivated land of England.' He finally
reached The Mount late on Tuesday night, 4 October 1836. So late,
in fact, that the family had gone to bed. Even though he had been
away for five years and two days, he slipped quietly into his room
exhausted, without waking them.

The first they knew was when he walked in for breakfast. Surprise
led to ecstasy, with 'poor Charles so full of affection & delight' at
the sight of his father and sisters after so many years. They hugged
and kissed, and the servants got drunk to celebrate Master Charles's
return. The girls worried that he was thin, eighteen pounds
underweight, but no matter, he was home. The endless journey had
ended. Caroline was quietly pleased that the awful swell in the Bay of
Biscay had left his 'hatred of the sea . . . as intense' as ever. But even
she allowed that the trip had served its purpose, for 'he has gained
happiness & interest for the rest of his life.'

In his delirious 'dead and half alive state,' he fired a salvo of letters
to relatives, the smiles practically rising from the page. 'I am so very
happy I hardly know what I am writing,' he burbled to Uncle Jos.
Before he had even found his landlegs Squire Owen had invited him
over with his gun, to see 'whether you are *improved by your travels*'

– and perhaps a spot of shooting was the best way to become a landlubber again.[1]

But was it the same Master Charles? Five years and a world separated him from his old flustered, directionless, insecure self. There was a new confidence, a new earnestness; he had survived on his wits in inhospitable climes, encountered wars and savages, and trekked across the Andes. He was pleased just to be alive. He had become his own man, thinking for himself, confident enough to challenge authority. He had made his mark, proved his worth, and he was proud of what he had achieved. It made him the centre of family attention and he loved it. For the first time he had the unqualified approval of his loved ones. He was scarcely the same person; he had undergone his own reform.

And what had he returned to? What of the country? He was the first to admit that 'all England appears changed.' The reforms had been extensive, entrenching the power of the new urban and industrial centres. So much had the Whigs altered, one wag said, that they obviously 'mean not only to change everything on the earth, but to alter the tides, to suspend the principle of gravitation, and to tear down the solar system.'[2]

Little had been left untouched. The Reform Bill was already four years in place. Only the previous year the Tory town councils had been democratized and invaded by the Whig Dissenters, who were even now electing Unitarian mayors in some cities. Things certainly had changed. Power was tilting, as the iron Duke of Wellington complained, from decent Tory Anglicans to Whig manufacturers, shopkeepers, and atheists.

Also in place was the New Poor Law, so abominated by the swelling army of paupers. Darwin was returning to a re-energized Malthusian world – Malthus's words had finally been acted on: the old outdoor charity had been scrapped, and the poor made to compete or face the workhouse. The workhouses were going up, despite firebrands railing against them as the sign of a vicious law that 'punishes [unfortunates] for being poor.' The New Poor Law was slated as 'a Malthusian bill designed to force the poor to emigrate, to work for lower wages, to live on a coarser sort of food.' The first riots had broken out in the southern counties in May 1835, with poor-law commissioners pelted and magistrates reading the Riot Act. Resistance was ferocious that winter; workhouses were razed and running battles fought with the police.[3]

This Whig restructuring was an assertion of middle-class Malthusian values. Darwin found that Malthus had acquired a new meaning. His name was on everybody's lips, as either Satan or Saviour. His doctrine of population, progress, and pauperism was no longer academic. It was the very kernel of poor-law policy: the stuff of inflammatory oratory, popular defiance, and government propaganda.

Darwin actually encountered a deceptive calm, the eye in the hurricane. The situation was simmering, cooled by the bonanza harvest and railway boom during the summer. Even so, the government had not yet dared to introduce the New Poor Law into London or the industrial north. And a recession was already setting in, with massive unemployment in prospect.

Off the *Beagle*, he was back in his Whig element. Having humoured the staunch Tory FitzRoy aboard, he now informed him just as good-naturedly that 'by the time we meet, my politics will be as firmly fixed and as wisely founded as ever they were.' With his own party commanding the ship of state, it was now his turn to be cool and inflexible. FitzRoy, for his part, did anything but behave predictably. He astonished Darwin by promptly getting married. For five years he had kept his lady a secret, even from his daily dining companion.

Darwin could barely contain himself at home. The person he longed to see was Henslow, and he rushed off a note, still 'giddy with joy & confusion': 'I want your advice on many points, indeed I am in the clouds.' He had no idea what to do with the *Beagle* specimens, many still aboard, carefully numbered and listed, ready for the experts. He wanted them described, but which specialists should he approach? Ten days on land, 15 October, and he was back among the spires of Cambridge, picking Henslow's brains. Here at least was someone to take the plants. Professor Sedgwick also got in touch, and they breakfasted together, talking over geology and catching up on Cambridge politics. Darwin received introductions to the best London naturalists – and warnings that they were overwhelmed with work. He could but see.[4]

From the quiet of Cambridge he plunged into bustling London on the 20th, staying with Erasmus in Great Marlborough Street, off the new Regent Street. London: the 'modern Babylon,' daunting in size, so large that 'a pedestrian could not encompass [it] in a day's time.' The enormous population of two million overawed visitors, who found themselves engulfed in great 'waves of people silently surging through the gloom.' He found a city in transition. Euston Station was being built, London Bridge was finished, but nighttime revealed the sight of sights, when the town was 'magically lit by its millions of gas lights.' Lights on every street, so bright that from the high point of Hampstead Heath the city transmogrified into a shimmering constellation. Road works were a constant complaint: sewers going in, gas mains being laid. Some of the gutting had been unintended, the charred shell of the House of Commons was a sorry sight, but most of the works signified expensive renovation.[5] This was true of the wealthiest scientific institutions, the British Museum and the Royal College of Surgeons, sporting an impressive new portico behind a shield of scaffolding.

He spent days traipsing from institution to institution – the Zoological and Geological Societies, the Linnean and British Museum – all a short walk from his brother's house. He introduced himself, and dined out on his South American stories, trying to tempt the experts with his collections. He was strutting, a celebrity; the geologists had read his printed letters, and many had seen his megatherium fossils. Everyone wanted to meet the tropical traveller and hear his tales of savages and rain forests and giant ground sloths. Charles Bunbury, a fellow Cambridge-educated squire-naturalist, was typical in trying to corner him. Darwin 'seems to be a universal collector,' Bunbury reported enthusiastically, discovering new species 'to the surprise of all the big wigs.' Here Darwin was, a month after landing, moving 'in most exciting dissipation amongst the Dons in science.' At first he had mixed results in placing his specimens. The geologists seized on his South American rocks, but, as Henslow had predicted, 'the Zoologists seem to think a number of undescribed creatures rather a nuisance.'[6]

Not surprisingly, for they were inundated by shells and skins from the four corners. The Zoological Society, having solicited exotic species from émigrés and military surveyors, was now drowning under the torrent. Despite its new West End museum, it could hardly keep pace. So many colonials contributed that, Darwin realized, collections outnumbered competent naturalists to describe them.

The old museum had long been a bone of contention with the zoologists. Zoo officials had just taken over the great surgeon John Hunter's museum in Leicester Square to mitigate the problem. It was extensive, twice the size of their old building, with 'well arranged rooms and galleries, lighted from the top.' When Darwin arrived, £1200 had just been spent on fittings, giving it 460 feet of exhibition space. But it was already crammed. The walls were lined with endless glazed cases, a cornucopia of colonial mammals, birds, reptiles, and fish – 6720 as he walked round, the largest exhibition 'open to public view in this kingdom.' So many species, in fact, that half had yet to be named or labelled. Assistants could still be seen taking pickled fish and reptiles out of temporary storage jars. What hope did he have when the museum was 'nearly full & upward of a thousand specimens remain unmounted'?[7] He could see why they were loath to take still more.

Something else was obvious: the electric atmosphere. The society had been buffeted by the political winds, with rowdy democrats – led by Darwin's old tutor Robert Grant (now at University College) – trying to usher in a new zoological era. Not for them the aristocrats' interest in raising game for the rich man's table (one of the zoo's original aims). They wanted the society run by paid experts. They were out of sympathy with the old zoology, presided over by rich amateur dabblers – the parsons, dilettantes, and noblemen. The new museum was one result of their campaign, a monument to serious, imperially useful zoology. Reformers had fought to have it sited in the West End, away from the aristocrats' promenading Zoological Gardens in Regent's Park. These battles for reform left bitter feelings, as Darwin noticed. 'I am out of patience with the Zoologists,' he snorted, 'not because they are overworked, but for their mean quarrelsome spirit. I went the other evening to the Zoological Soc[iety]. where the speakers were snarling at each other, in a manner anything but like that of gentlemen.'

Darwin was beginning to get Grant's measure: his old teacher's politics had become fiercer since the Edinburgh days. Grant, like so many radicals in the turbulent, reforming 30s, was a democrat, a Church-critic, a Cambridge-hater, always attacking privilege. A comrade said that 'whenever a good, honourable, generous, and liberal cause was in agitation,' there you 'would find the name of Professor Grant.' But these honourable causes were not necessarily Darwin's. His friends were Cambridge clerics. As a Whig gentleman on a private fortune, he relished his freedom to follow his own pursuits, to make his home a lab, as the rich had done for centuries. He was not one for salaried science, or making the zoo's aristocratic grandees accountable to members. He *was* concerned with standards of behaviour, however, and he shared his family's abhorrence of the 'fierce & licentious' radicals.[8]

Not only zoologists suffered. Other institutions faced challenges to their traditional leadership. Even the British Museum was in turmoil. It was the subject of a bruising Parliamentary inquiry in 1836, instigated by radicals who wanted to oust the titled Trustees and turn it into a research institution along French lines. There again was

Grant, slamming the museum's incompetent aristocratic governors under the Archbishop of Canterbury. All this made Darwin wary of depositing his collection there. 'I cannot feel, from all I hear, any great respect even for the present state of that establishment.' It also began to make him chary of Dr Grant. More and more the prickly secularist, Grant was slated by Tories for backing the 'reptile press,' well known for its 'blasphemous derision of the sacred truths of Christianity.'[9] To the gentlemen of science, pillars of the Establishment, his gutter-press flailings were anathema.

All this rushing around, trying to place specimens, listening to weary political harangues, left Charles exhausted. 'I am quite tired,' he sighed to Caroline, '& long to be living quietly with dear old Henslow.' Cambridge was a sanctuary, away from the bickering as much as the smog and soot. Better to break the collection in Cambridge, he thought, and parcel bits out. His father's support and promise of continued backing meant he could do just that, put Church and career out of mind and do the job. The Doctor duly gave him an allowance plus stocks, bringing in about £400 a year. Comfortably off, he could pursue an independent lifestyle, unburdened by guinea-grabbing academic needs. Four hundred pounds was enough to sustain a single gentleman, pay for his servant – Covington was kept on – and more. He could actually afford to buy the help he needed. 'About the fossil shells. Is Sowerby a good man?' he asked Henslow. 'I understand his assistance can be purchased.'[10] Darwin was to bankroll a number of such specialists over the years, the illustrator and shell-trader George Sowerby among them. He could settle down as a self-financed naturalist, subcontracting his work.

But where? He squared up to the choice of life options: amid the dissipations of London with the 'Dons in science' or quietly at Cambridge with the clerical naturalists. Should he emulate Lyell and Eras in the city with its intellectually bracing atmosphere, moving in their circles of advanced intellectuals – freethinking, political, exciting? Here were the freshest fish and the freshest news, the latest shows, and the largest pool of scientific talent in the country. Eras was still enjoying his life of literary leisure, his week revolving around intellectual dinner parties. Lyell was a perfect role model, a self-financed specialist making his mark famously. Or should he retire to the pastoral fields like Henslow, giving him the quiet to think? He was torn, but it was clear that he would have to settle in the smoke eventually, to see his precious specimens farmed out, however much he blanched at the prospect.

*

In London he did have Eras for company. Or at least some of the time, for his brother was taken with that literary lioness Harriet Martineau. In these weeks he would drift back in the evening, tired 'from driving out Miss Martineau.' Martineau herself was London's prime literary apologist for the whole gamut of Whig reforms. She had even been introduced to the old Revd Malthus.[11] It might have been a meeting of minds, but neither had expected much more. With her ear trumpet and his cleft palate, it was a surprise anything transpired, but they transcended their impediments and made perfect contact. She heard every word without her trumpet, and gratifying words they were: he praised her poor-law tales as the very epitome of his views.

But she met virulent opposition. She was slammed by Tory paternalists as a Malthusian 'who deprecates charity and provision for the poor!!!' On the other side, more radical doctors than Eras were unionizing to protest at the pestilential workhouses. Yet again, here were Grant and his fanatical friends in 1836, founding the militant pressure group, the London-based British Medical Association, to hamper the poor-law commissioners and refute Malthus's statistics.[12]

But Martineau was ensconced in Whig high society, Darwin's society, where she was fêted for her Malthusian sense. She was practically one of the family. Eras was smitten, but Charles wondered about such a threateningly assertive lady. 'Our only protection from so admirable a sister-in-law is in her working [Eras] too hard. He begins to perceive . . . he shall be not much better than her "nigger". – Imagine poor Erasmus a nigger to so philosophical & energetic a lady . . . She already takes him to task about his idleness.' Martineau had just returned from a whirlwind tour of America, and was full of married women's property rights, as Charles heard. 'She is going some day to explain to him her notions about marriage – Perfect equality of rights is part of her doctrine. I much doubt whether it will be equality in practice. We must pray for our poor "nigger".'

The 'nigger' wasn't enslaved, and Martineau didn't become a Darwin. But there were other connections tying the family to Malthus. Hensleigh Wedgwood's father-in-law, the economist Sir James Mackintosh, had been Malthus's fast friend (and fellow lecturer at the East India College at Haileybury), and Malthus's daughter Emily had been a bridesmaid at Fanny and Hensleigh's wedding.[13] Darwin was becoming enmeshed in a close and personal Malthusian circle.

Lyell, fired by Darwin's reports from South America, was eager to meet his disciple. Darwin too was expectant. On Saturday 29 October they finally met, when Darwin came to dinner. He found Lyell boiling with enthusiasm beneath his hushed tones, and watched bemused as Lyell sank into his chair, almost ending on the floor as he listened to Darwin's earthquake stories. Lyell was the most adventurous geologist in town, and the most famous after the *Principles of Geology*. He had a barrister's way with words and a beautiful command of foreign languages; he was courtly, and at ease in high circles. He was also politically aware, a friend of the Whig Lords, with his finger on the pulse of reform. Then there was Mrs Lyell, Leonard Horner's daughter: pretty as a picture and a model of patience. Darwin was overawed by their kindness, praising the 'heart & soul' way they were ready to help. Lyell bent over backwards with advice about specialists, and all in the '*most* goodnatured manner.' Darwin gravitated to him, heeding his advice to stay in London and get his projects off the ground. Nor should he waste his energy running societies (Lyell, losing time as President of the prestigious Geological, told him to 'tell no one I gave you this advice').[14]

That October evening Lyell invited others to meet the globe-trotter. He introduced Darwin to a tall, striking figure with glittering eyes, Richard Owen. Owen was man of the hour, the new Hunterian Professor at the Royal College of Surgeons in Lincoln's Inn Fields. He seemed a bit diffident, even awkward, but he came supported by his best friend from the other end of Lincoln's Inn, the magistrate William Broderip. These two, Tories to the core, had just voted the 'malcontent' Grant out of a post at the Zoological Society, and doubtless over dinner Darwin heard all about the rumbles.[15] Owen now stood triumphant at the zoo, its reigning anatomist, dissecting whatever died in the Gardens without hitch or hindrance. No one was more versatile or prolific, and he already had a string of papers on the zoo's corpses under his belt. For his part, Broderip kept an impressive cabinet of shells in his Lincoln's Inn chambers. During dinner he must have salivated at Darwin's description of his exotic haul, and he offered to look them over.

Lyell had made the right choice of dining companions. Owen shared Darwin's interest in fossils and invertebrates. He lived on the top floor of the College of Surgeons, looking out over the rooftops. When Darwin later visited, he found the new library and ninety-foot museum almost finished, with workmen rushing around putting on the final licks of paint. Partly this rebuilding had been forced by the political attacks on the college, which had led to probing Parliamentary questions about its role as a repository of national treasures. In the van as always was Grant, denouncing college corruption from his soapbox.[16] The grave, moralistic Owen was more than a little suspicious of his jaundiced rival.

Owen was on the up-and-up, and ready to topple the 'great Grant' as the city's leading comparative anatomist.[17] At the college Darwin found Owen charming, vehemently opposed to Grant's evolution, and well versed in the latest German science. (Owen was busy synthesizing German ideas on the forces regulating life and growth, preparing his first lectures – ideas which were to stimulate Darwin in his own search for the laws of life.[18]) But for the moment Darwin was concerned to place his precious pampas relics. Owen took some of the animals preserved in spirits. And Darwin persuaded him to look over his fossil bones.

At this time Grant volunteered his help. He was one of the few who actively offered to examine the haul, and presumably one of the few actively turned down. Ten years earlier in Edinburgh, he had introduced the teenage Darwin to Lamarck's views and the study of corals. Now he offered to sift through the seafarer's tropical spoils. But Darwin had become a competent and competing coral expert, and he had his own plans. He was interested in the polyps' reproduction, and of course reef formation. He roped in Erasmus instead, putting him to work translating German papers on coral banks. So, at the end of the day, ironically, the corals were not monographed.[19] Nor, it seems, did Darwin and Grant have anything more to do with one another.

Darwin might have wanted his specimens described quickly, but not by a disreputable dissident, one spitting venom at Henslow's Cambridge for its 'monastic ignorance.' A compelling need for quiet respectability dominated Darwin's life. His inclination to 'take offence at rudeness of manners & any thing bordering upon ungentlemanlike behavior' had made even Henslow chide him years ago. He hated loudmouthed radicalism, and Grant was now beyond the pale.

Others were too tardy. If anyone looked like laying a 'dead hand' on his specimen Darwin manoeuvred them out of sight. When he spoke to the shy Robert Brown, botany keeper at the British Museum, the pitfalls became apparent. He 'asked me in rather an ominous manner, what I meant to do with my plants. – In the course of conversation, Mr Broderip who was present remarked to him, "you forget how long it is since Capt: King's expedition." He answered, "Indeed I have something, in the shape of Capt: Kings undescribed plants to make me recollect it".'[20] Brown had been sitting on a hoard of Galapagos plants for six years. It was no inducement for Darwin to hand his over.

By the end of October FitzRoy had brought the *Beagle* around to Woolwich and berthed her alongside the other ten-gun brigs. Here, on the Thames near London, he took his last chronometric reading, and the ship was paid off. The docks were bristling with sailors, redcoats, quartermasters, and suppliers when Darwin came down to fetch his crates. It deflated him rather, seeing all the specimens packed by Covington. He was 'at an utter loss to know how to begin.' He sent a box of Galapagos plants to Henslow by coach, followed by four crates of rocks, bird skins, insects, and spirit bottles. Everything was already arranged into groups, but he foresaw an uphill struggle. 'All I know is, that I must work far harder, than [these] poor shoulders have ever been accustomed to do.'[21]

All this time, he had practically ignored the Wedgwoods, still waiting patiently to see him. He finally got to Maer on 12 November and suffered an endless round of visiting relatives. The girls thought him better for being thinner and were not above a bit of back-handed flattery: 'it has improved his looks, and his countenance is so pleasant that his plainness does not signify.' Round the fire he regaled them with stories of his giant fossils and the wild, women-eating Fuegians.

He was still thinking of publishing a book of his travels. The whole family rallied to the idea. Fanny and Hensleigh had read his five-year diary and loved it, especially the sections on Tahiti and New Zealand. In their view it bettered '99.100[ths] of the travels that are published.' Dr Henry Holland, a distant cousin and self-important society physician, disagreed, but that only left Hensleigh taking a dim view of the doctor's faculties. Nor did Emma Wedgwood believe that cousin Henry was 'any judge as to what is amusing or interesting.' She thought it would make a wonderful book, and she was ploughing through unfamiliar fare – rival accounts of pampas crossings – ready to engage Charles. FitzRoy wanted a three-volume narrative of his and King's expeditions, with King, himself, and the 'Philosopher' contributing one each, and he drew up a contract with Colburn the publisher to that effect. Everyone at home entered into the spirit, and Charles – back at The Mount on the 16th – found his sisters deep in travelogues, picking up tips.[22]

On 2 December Darwin returned to London, and began to find takers for his prized specimens. The new zoology professor at King's College in the Strand, Thomas Bell, came forward, intrigued by the reptiles. The seaweed-eating Galapagos iguanas fascinated the Oxford geologist the Revd William Buckland. The zoologists also were turning up trumps, and experts were looking over 'whole tribes of animals, of which I know nothing.' Most required the specialist touch, beyond his competence. So much so that he was left red-faced by a botanist in the Linnean library:

> I felt very foolish, when [he] remarked on the beautiful appearance of some plant with an astoundingly long name, & asked me about its habitation. Some one else seem[ed] quite surprised that I knew nothing about a carex from [I] do not know where. I w[as] at last forced to plead most intire [sic] innocence, & that I knew no more about the plants, which I had collected, than the Man in the Moon.

Being unsure of his botany, he worried again about how the experts would react to his haul. 'Tell me whether you are disappointed with the Galapagos plants,' he pressed Henslow; 'I have some fears.'[23]

His real trophies, though, were the fossil mammals, which he had unpacked at Owen's College of Surgeons. The museum still had decorators in, and when Hensleigh dropped by he was horrified to find the huge skull that Darwin had picked up for eighteen pence near Mr Keen's ranch 'in a room with workmen.' This was the first fossil Owen diagnosed, and his conclusion was surprising. It belonged to a huge rodent, a hippo-sized capybara relative, which Owen called *Toxodon*. And the Punta Alta skeleton with an enormous pelvis and pointed snout came from a horse-sized anteater. The fossils 'are turning out great treasures,' Charles boasted to Caroline.[24] Rhino-sized rodents! 'What famous cats they ought to have had in those days!'

These spectacular fossils were his *entrée* into the world of high science. The College sent casts to the Geological Society and the British Museum; Cambridge received some, as did Oxford, where Buckland – Sir Ammon Knight himself – wanted to figure them in a new edition of his *Geology and Mineralogy*. At the end of the day no savant was ignorant of Darwin's pampas giants.

The social whirl continued. He felt duty bound to call in on Erasmus's belle, Harriet Martineau. 'She was very agreeable,' he admitted, 'and managed to talk on a most wonderful number of subjects, considering the limited time.' Martineau was writing *Society in America*, on her trip to the United States, where she too had seen new social and natural worlds in the making. She was full of American democracy, women's rights, and the horrors of slavery. At Niagara Falls she had marvelled at the 'process of world-making,' where nature sculpted scenery with an awesome 'blind and dumb' force. She too had witnessed the 'grandeur and beauty' of the earth's own 'workshop,' and it gave them a perfect talking point.[25]

'I was astonished to find how ugly she is,' Charles conceded, noting that 'she is overwhelmed with her own projects, her own thoughts and abilities.' Her literary threat was met by male hauteur: 'Erasmus palliated all this, by maintaining one ought not to look at her as a woman.' Martineau captured her beau's brother far more succinctly: 'simple, childlike, painstaking, effective,' she called Charles Darwin.

Charles thought back on his own loves. He sent Fanny Biddulph – four years unhappily married and cooped up in a Welsh castle expecting her third baby – a present of flowers, which left her lost for words.[26]

Two months home and he was already cursing 'dirty odious London.' He could not face winter in the city. It might have been 'the real capital of the world' for the fashionable set bored with Paris. But Charles was choked by the fog and smoke. Dark clouds descended from chimney-stacks like 'a soft black drizzle, with flakes of soot in it as big as full-grown snow-flakes – gone into mourning, one might imagine, for the death of the sun.' Coal smouldered in every grate. Coal, 'hell's own fuel, torn from the bowels of the earth.' It left the streets enveloped in freezing smog. It 'admits only a wan daylight and casts a funereal pall over all things. In London one draws gloom with every breath; it is in the air; it enters every pore . . . one's head is heavy and aching, one's stomach has trouble functioning, breathing becomes difficult for lack of pure air.' Mud-splattered pavements, freezing pea-soupers rising from the infernally smelly Thames: he hated it. On the cobbled roads the clatter of hoofs and iron-rimmed cartwheels was deafening. He knew he would have to settle here for a time, especially if he had to continue hawking his skins and bones around, as Lyell advised.[27] But he yearned for a few months first at Cambridge, breathing fresh air – living with the Henslows, or so he hoped.

So back he went to Cambridge on 13 December. He did manage three days with a house full of Henslows before finding 'solitary lodgings' in Fitzwilliam Street. Cambridge was a quiet, clean contrast with London. Nothing much had changed. Not even the reforms had penetrated its Anglican exterior (the bill to admit Dissenters without subscribing to the Thirty-nine Articles had failed). He could reflect on the teachers he had not seen for so long. There was kindly Henslow, growing fatter, with five children now. While still on the *Beagle* Darwin had been asked to stand godfather to the latest, and he felt for Henslow the way he did for a close relative. Sedgwick was another matter. Darwin gave a talk to the Cambridge Philosophical Society on the glassy tubes in the Maldonado sand dunes, caused by lightning fusing the sand into black shiny funnels. He discussed these over tea with Whewell and Sedgwick, the 'talking giants,' and something happened to cause an odd reflection on Sedgwick's temperament. 'I really sometimes think he will go mad,' Charles told Caroline, without explanation; the old bachelor was 'so very absent & odd,' although a 'more high-minded man does not anywhere exist.'[28]

Cambridge might not have changed, but Darwin had. There was no chance of his sinking back into old ways, even if he did spend the odd merry evening reminiscing with Herbert, and lose the occasional bet in Christ's College common room. Now he was committed to his haul, and to gilding his scientific reputation in the eyes of the Lyells and Henslows. His cold winter days were cut out, sniffling with flu as he sorted his specimens. Each evening he retired to write his first paper, proving that the Chilean coast – indeed the whole South American landmass – was rising slowly. Those inland sea shells, found at increasing heights above sea level, clinched his case.

Lyell loved the paper, but then it was he who had made mountain elevation compensate for drowning continents. Darwin was taking a partnership in Lyell's geological business, throwing himself into its operation with gusto. From the first his geology was creative, speculative, and written in ponderous English (causing Sedgwick to plead for sharper prose). Darwin had a Lyellian sense of balance, his rising Andes offset by a sinking Pacific. He extended Lyell's earthquake-cause of mountain uplift, and – on the down side – he pointed to coral reefs as the last relics of disappearing mountains. This 'knocked' Lyell's own reef explanation 'on the head.' But still Lyell was ecstatic: 'Coral islands are the last efforts of drowning continents to lift their heads above water,' he crooned, giving way gracefully. He egged Darwin on to report his South American findings, revelling in the 'idea of the Pampas going up, at the rate of an inch in a century.' 'What a splendid field you have to write upon!'[29]

Owen was struck too, and Darwin gladly sent a further crate of fossil bones from Cambridge. He followed these down in the new year, and another hectic round commenced: dining with Lyell, discussing his paper, unpacking the fossils at the College of Surgeons.

The real red-letter day was 4 January 1837. In the evening he read his paper to the Geological Society, on Chile's coast as uplifted sea floor. It was his début, and friends and family rallied round. Hensleigh was present, and of course Lyell. Many of the geologists were brilliant orators who could enliven the dullest subject. But

Darwin was a novice, and nervous. Standing in front of Lyell, the President, with rows of expert geologists on benches either side, huge maps and diagrams of mountain sections behind them on the walls, he read his paper, heart in hand, pounding furiously. On the table were his oyster fossils and other pampas samples, collected a world away. Lyell lapped up the talk, but, he cautioned, 'do not flatter yourself that you will be believed, till you are growing bald, like me.' Darwin did not have to lose his hair first. In fact, his Cordilleras and coral reefs were so well received that he felt 'like a peacock admiring his tail.'

Darwin was ambitious and the Geological was to be his forum. Elected soon after the *Beagle* docked, he was at ease here among the urban gentry, more so than with the squabbling zoological salariat. (Two years would elapse before he became a Zoological Fellow.) His public persona was as a 'hammerer' gent. He still worried about falling short in his father's eyes, but here, with hard work, he would amount to something. These were boom times for the science. The recalcitrant older strata were being conquered, rocks that revealed the first created forms; and Cambrian, Silurian, and Devonian were becoming household words. Geology provided spy-holes into a dim, distant past, a view on the comings and goings of continents as much as the fortunes of fossil dynasties. Lyell's *Principles of Geology* was read by thousands: 'every ambitious young man studies geology; so members of Parliament are made, and churchmen' – and even divines were getting used to seeing 'the *coup de grâce*' given 'to the deluge.'[30] It was a growth industry, and Darwin was about to join the captains.

Darwin's rising and falling lands had other – more covert – consequences. They raised tantalizing questions about the inhabitants; about annihilation and repopulation, about Creation itself. On this key question he was still moving away from Lyell. The Galapagos finches, all feeding in flocks together (or so he thought), suggested that Lyell was wrong – that conditions did not strictly determine what was created where.[31] So what could explain these variants? There had to be another solution.

He had one other engagement on 4 January. At the zoo's headquarters in Leicester Square, he presented 80 mammals and 450 birds to the Society. Knowing the zoologists' museum, he wisely added the proviso that all were to be mounted and described. Actually, the men in the museum were proving their worth. He popped down Regent Street from Eras's house to meet them on many days. He became friendly with George Waterhouse, an old beetle enthusiast and former architect, who – as the new curator – had finally achieved his goal of a paid post in zoology. Waterhouse was already cataloguing the museum's 870 mammals when he agreed to take on Darwin's.

It was the birds that intrigued others, if not Darwin. He remained confused by the Galapagos finches, believing that they fed indiscriminately together, unaware of the importance of their different beaks. Come to that, he still had trouble identifying the species, or their locations; and he still thought that his collection contained finches, wrens, 'Gross-beaks', and 'Icteruses' (blackbird-relatives). He had no sense of a single, closely related group becoming specialized and adapted to different environmental niches. The birds did not even seem that important when he donated them to the Zoological Society, rather badly labelled, on the 4th.[32]

The expert he turned them over to was the ornithologist, artist, and taxidermist John Gould, already making a name for himself through his lavish bird books. Gould was a prolific describer of the skinned specimens shipped to the Society. He had studied wrens, toucans, and Australian, Himalayan, African, and European birds. Unlike Darwin, he was not a leisured gentleman; a gardener's son, he had graduated to the poorly paid post of 'Animal Preserver' at the Society in 1828. Five years later he earned the grand title 'Superintendant' of the stuffed birds, but the pay was still only £100 a year. As a result he was having to print and sell a string of illustrated books to make up the shortfall. His output was prodigious, as Darwin realized that January: the fifth and last volume of his *Birds of Europe* was just appearing, and the first of his *Birds of Australia* about to be published. (In fact, these were so lucrative that he had just gone on half-pay at the zoo to concentrate on his prints.) As Darwin deposited his corpses, Gould was continuing to describe the exotic parrots shot in the New South Wales settlements.[33] If anyone could disentangle Darwin's wrens and finches and blackbirds, Gould could.

Interrupting his paying work, he quickly realized that Darwin's Galapagos birds were not so diverse at all. The reverse, in fact: the beaks were deceptive and the birds, astonishingly, were closely related. 'Gross-beaks,' 'blackbirds' – they were all in truth finches. By the next meeting, on the 10th – only six days later – Gould had linked them as 'a series of ground Finches which are so peculiar' as to form 'an entirely new group, containing 12 species.'[34] They were close-knit, despite their range of bills – although the significance would only become apparent later to Darwin. Darwin's birds and mammals were set out for display, and reporters from the dailies heard Gould's news. The papers ran the story, so that even Catherine could read about Charles's finches in the *Morning Herald*.

Meanwhile, revelations were startling the geologists. Owen, working through the fossils, had made out a gigantic ground sloth and an ox-sized armoured *Glyptodon* in Darwin's new batch. There was more: the leg and neck bones taken at Port St Julian in January 1834 turned out, judging by the arteries in the spine, to be 'fragments of a Gigantic Llama!' So Darwin could at last picture the scene – on the waterless, windswept plains dominated by the llama-like guanaco today, enormous llamas had once roamed. Lyell realized the implications. Just as the wombats and kangaroos of Australia had giant precursors, on the ancient plains of Patagonia llamas, capybaras, sloths, and armadillos had their own gigantic forebears. Lyell saw a 'law of succession' in play here: mammals are replaced by their own kind on each continent.[35]

Lyell paraded Darwin's skeletal 'Menagerie' across the stage in his presidential address to the Geological Society on 17 February. He drew out the conclusions from Owen's findings: that fossil faunas are closely related to their living replacements. At Lyell's request, Darwin came down to hear the talk. He knew of Owen's results, but the speech brought home the real importance of his fossils for the first time. He sensed the close relationship between extinct megatheriums and glyptodons and the modern sloths and armadillos.[36] Darwin had never expected this; on the voyage he assumed that he had found European and African mastodons and rhinos, not exclusive South American species. It pulled him up sharp, causing him to ask the key question: why is present and past life on any one spot so closely related?

His stock was rising, and at the same meeting he was elected to the Council of the Geological Society. Fossils were not the only things of importance to Lyell; he valued an ally, and he considered Darwin 'a glorious addition to my society of geologists.' His society was a crack corps. All were gentleman specialists, most wealthy or with Oxbridge chairs. Together they constituted a self-referential (and self-reverential) élite. These were the last of the virtuoso scholars in an age before the salaried class moved in. They were rich careerists, with no professional paymaster to pull the strings, and duty only to scientific integrity, social stability, and responsible religion. The Geological Society was the most stimulating and envied in town. The science touched the age of the earth and the Days of Creation; it was fashionable, difficult and dangerous, and as such under close 'public surveillance.' Here Darwin lived up to Lyell's expectations. He showed that he could hold his own: 'I really never saw that bore Dr. Mitchell so successfully silenced or such a bucket of cold water so dexterously poured down his back as when Darwin answered some impertinent & irrelevant questions about S[outh]. America,' Lyell grinned after one spat.[37] Darwin was now the resident expert on the subject.

All this encouraged Darwin to begin working 'tooth and nail' at a book on South American geology. His French rival Alcide d'Orbigny, back two years earlier, had already started a multi-volume account of the continent, but Darwin and Lyell had withering words for D'Orbigny's cataclysmic explanation of mountain formation. It was time for a rival account, a Lyellian one. Darwin's public career was being mapped out. A country curacy, a 'parsonage in the desert,' was fading from view. His was to be the horrid desert of cobbles and concrete, the clatter of cartwheels and choking smog. He was steeling himself for London. 'The only evil I found at Cambridge,' he said, 'was its being too pleasant.' He could never say the same for the capital. But 'I am pretty well resigned to my fate.'[38]

15

Reforming Nature

IT WAS AN IRONY that nowhere was so good for natural history as 'this odious smokey town,' because no one could see any real nature here at all. But he had to be on the spot to supervise his collections.

Lyell told him to arrive in time for one of Charles Babbage's Saturday soirées in the West End, where he would meet 'the best in the way of literary people in London,' and, more to the point, plenty 'of pretty women.'[1] The season was in full swing, so, on Friday 6 March 1837, Darwin came down from Cambridge and moved in with Eras.

At Babbage's parties you could 'see the *World*.' You could also sense the way science was going: pick up the tittle-tattle, hear remarks off the cuff. They were glittering affairs, 'brilliantly attended by fashionable ladies, as well as literary and scientific gents.' Bankers, politicians, and industrialists mixed with well-heeled savants – Lyell, Owen, Broderip, the 'King of Siluria' Roderick Murchison, and now Darwin himself. The polymathic Babbage was a mathematician, apologist for industry, advocate of the division of labour, and builder of the costly 'Difference Engine,' or calculating machine. He was a reformer (and a failed Whig Parliamentary candidate), so there was plenty of political banter. The turbulent times demanded it. The town halls were currently being democratized and the Church reformed. Even as Darwin arrived the Church looked like losing its tithes, and the clergy had lost their monopoly on the rites at birth, marriage, and death. No longer would Dissenters have to be married by Anglican parsons (or Unitarians have to perjure themselves by affirming the doctrine of the Trinity). Staunch Tories called these the worst reforms since the English Civil War of the 1640s, when Parliament tried to abolish bishops. Of course, this became the butt of the best jokes. Babbage, omnipotent himself, was once taunted, 'What do you mean to be when the revolution comes?' and replied, 'Lay Archbishop of Winchester.'[2]

In keeping with the period, Babbage had written his cheekily named *Ninth Bridgewater Treatise*, already in proof. The title gave away his target. It was a snub to the eight officially sanctioned 'Bridgewater' books. This lavish series had been financed by the late Earl of Bridgewater, in atonement for an impious life, and overseen by the Archbishop of Canterbury. The *Bridgewater Treatises* played endlessly on the theme of God's wisdom and goodness deduced from nature. Hardly a stone was left unturned in the search for divine design, even though the enterprise was positively passé to the cynics and secularists. By now the run of books had appeared and world-weary Londoners – like freethinking Erasmus – were 'somewhat *saturated*' with the subject. Critics doubted that even the buffoonish Buckland in his Bridgewater – *Geology and Mineralogy* – could add to 'so threadbare and exhausted a topic.' Babbage by contrast could. In his unofficial *Ninth*, he laughed to Lyell, 'the Devil is to have his due.'[3]

Of course, he wasn't. The book presented God as a divine programmer, and Babbage used his hand-cranked calculator to prove the point. He set out to undermine the conservative view of God as a tinkering miracle-monger. He was a divine legislator, far-seeing, not a feudal monarch acting on whim. Out went the notion of 'Creative Interference,' as Buckland called it; no more *ad hoc* miracles each time a minor mollusc or fossil feline was needed. Such nonsense undermined rational science and sound religion, denying God 'the highest attribute of omnipotence,' foresight. On Babbage's smart machine any sequence of numbers could be programmed to cut in, however long another series had been running. By analogy, God at Creation had appointed new sets of animals and plants to appear like clockwork throughout history – he had created the laws which produced them, rather than creating them direct. Babbage's God displayed 'a degree of power and of knowledge of a far higher order.'[4]

A host of geologists had been poring over Babbage's proofs. Lyell had only put down his copy in January when Darwin's South America paper arrived. Babbage's position was well known to the cognoscenti. Lyell thought that his 'philosophical speculations' were majestic. They reinforced his own views.

> No doubt some people would not like any reasoning which
> makes miracles more reconcilable with possibilities in the
> ordinary course of the Universe & its laws; but you do not
> write to please them . . . I think your estimate of the Creator's
> attributes much higher than theirs.

So did Darwin's medical cousin, Henry Holland, who was struck by Babbage's 'originality & ingenuity.' When the book came out in late spring, Babbage presented a copy to Princess Victoria, summing it up as a 'work written in defence of Science and for the support of Religion.'[5]

The *Ninth Bridgewater* had people talking. Even before it appeared, Darwin would have known all about the book, perhaps even from Babbage (whom he called a rather cold 'calculating machine' himself). He realized that a 'lawful' approach was carrying the day. Reformed nature was the product of careful legislated change, a rational plan. The prophets were proved right: the radical Whigs really were intent on changing heaven and earth.

Darwin's other heroes were making a similar point, including John Herschel, whom Darwin had met at the Cape. Herschel openly alluded to the problem, the 'mystery of mysteries,' as he called it: what caused new species to appear in place of the extinct ones? Was it miraculous? He doubted it. In his view, the same natural causes that have sculpted the earth over the aeons must explain the coming and going of life on its surface. God does not intervene personally, by supernatural meddling. He set up laws at the creation of the universe, and these have operated throughout geological history, producing species. Awesome as the birth of a species must be, it was no more miraculous than the birth of a child.[6]

Herschel was not thinking of one animal actually *transmuting* into another, nor did he envisage man as an ape descendant, which was abhorrent. In fact he could visualize no actual process. But he guessed that a good naturalist would sooner or later clear up the mystery.

Though still resident at the Cape, Herschel was influential, the de facto head of science in Britain. (Babbage had put him up as a presidential candidate at the Royal Society in 1830, although the post went to the King's son.) His letter to Lyell on the 'mystery of mysteries' was well thumbed, Lyell having passed it around. Darwin could see its impact on Babbage, who extracted it in his *Ninth Bridgewater*. It was an injunction to seek the explanation of the ultimate mystery. The searcher had to be bold. Herschel prefaced his remarks with the couplet:

Reforming Nature

He that on such quest would go must
know nor fear nor failing
To coward soul or faithless heart the
search were unavailing.

To some it looked like the holy grail's quest. But it taught Darwin that nature too needed 'reforming' and reappraising – that it had to be brought under the rule of law.[7]

Darwin also knew that any search for the cause of species would lead into deep and difficult waters. It would be a far more dangerous voyage of discovery than the *Beagle*'s had been, and anyone undertaking it would stir up 'a host of prejudices.'

Herschel's epistle was huge, and it showed how much a new historical sensitivity was spreading through the sciences. The origin of language or the origin of rocks, both had to be seen as a gradual development.

> Words are to the Anthropologist what rolled pebbles are to
> the Geologist – Battered relics of past ages often containing
> within them indelible records capable of intelligible
> interpretation – and when we see what amount of change
> 2000 years has been able to produce in the languages of Greece
> & Italy or 1000 in those of Germany France & Spain we
> naturally begin to ask how long a period must have lapsed
> since the Chinese, the Hebrew, the Delaware & the Malesass
> [from Madagascar] had a point in common with the German
> & Italian & each other. – Time! Time! Time! – we must not
> impugn the Scripture Chronology, but we *must* interpret it in
> accordance with *whatever* shall appear on fair enquiry to be
> the *truth* for there cannot be two truths. And really there is
> scope enough: for the lives of the Patriarchs may as reasonably
> be extended to 5000 or 50000 years apiece as the days of
> Creation to as many thousand millions of years.

Darwin knew this passage well. He cited it to Caroline, explaining Herschel's view of the ages 'since the first man made his wonderful appearance on this world.' It was nowhere near 6000 years: 'Sir J. thinks that a far greater number must have passed' to account for the divergence of languages 'from one stock.'[8]

But what if animals, like Lyell's pebbles and Herschel's words, were also 'relics of past ages,' a living record 'capable of intelligible interpretation'? What if they were just as natural and had slowly diverged 'from one stock'? This was the up-and-coming approach,

215

and Darwin must have realized it: the present held the genealogical key to the past. It was the high road to historical truth.

Charles was in and out of his brother's house this spring. He never strayed far from Eras. When he did move in mid-March into lodgings of his own, they were only a few doors down, at 36 Great Marlborough Street. Eras's was a hive of intellectual activity. After five lonely years at sea, Charles embraced his brother's ready-made circle of friends, revelling in his intimate dinners with Eras and Harriet Martineau. Here the buzz was radical and Dissenting and 'heterodoxy was the norm.'⁹ He gained reassurance from this home circle.

Hensleigh also joined them. He was himself a philologist, looking for the 'laws' by which alphabets slowly change. He praised the Germans for understanding the 'organic' development of language and for tracing 'every descendant' of their own Gothic tongue. Languages had to be anatomized, their underlying unity exposed, ancestral sounds teased out. The analogy with Charles's zoology was overt. Just as he uncovered fossil sloths, Hensleigh was listening for 'fossil remains' in speech. Hensleigh's job was even harder; the sloths had lain undisturbed in their tombs, but sounds, because of their 'everyday use . . . have been worn, until, like pebbles on the beach, they have lost every corner and distinctive mark, and hardly a vestige remains to indicate their original form. Yet even here we are not left entirely without traces' of parentage.¹⁰

Through Hensleigh and Herschel, Charles grasped the historical analogy. These modern developmental ideas could be stretched to do more heretical work, to explain new life, new species. The issues were probably thrashed out during Eras's literary dinners. Here the sardonic Eras counterbalanced the serious Hensleigh, with the Unitarian, necessitarian Martineau listening in on her ear trumpet. Eras and Harriet were now so close that Fanny Wedgwood, feeling left out, thought they already seemed entirely married. (The Doctor did not approve. The liaison was sparking gossip, and Emma Wedgwood wondered how Susan and Catherine were weathering it.) All were interested in German biblical criticism and language studies, and devoted to Whig Malthusian ideals. All were better read than Charles, and he relished their conversation. As at Lyell's or Babbage's, politics, science, and literature were all of a piece here.

Not that the coteries were distinct; Lyell would call on Harriet and Erasmus, and Martineau loved Babbage's 'glorious soirees.' But, given their intimacy, Charles preferred Eras's affairs. They were 'worth all other, & more brilliant kinds, many times over,' even when Thomas Carlyle was sounding off 'in high force,' as he usually was. Charles recalled one 'funny dinner at my brother's, where among a few others, were Babbage and Lyell, both of whom liked to talk. Carlyle, however, silenced every one by haranguing during the whole dinner on the advantages of silence. After dinner, Babbage, in his grimmest manner, thanked Carlyle for his very interesting Lecture on Silence.'

Back home the Doctor worried about Martineau's radicalism and its influence on the boys. As a potential daughter-in-law she was bad enough, but her politics were too extreme. Reading a piece in the *Westminster Review* on the need for the radicals to break with the Whigs and give working men the vote, he got thoroughly steamed up 'before he knew it was not hers, and wasted a great deal of good indignation, and even now can hardly believe it is not hers.' She was polluting the others. 'Poor Martineau seems going down the hill with Hensleigh and Erasmus,' Emma laughed to Fanny Wedgwood, 'so I hope you will stick by her.'[11]

Martineau's scientific attitude was typical of radical Unitarians. She saw nature as predictable, predetermined, invariant. It was subject to law and order, not the province of miracle. Among Unitarians such 'determinism' encouraged views on life's self-development. Take Dr Southwood Smith, who had studied at the same Unitarian school as Martineau and worked for the poor-law commission. His *Divine Government* pictured nature as upward-striving, with needs driving organisms higher and higher. Animals and people were all of a piece, subject to the same everlasting ascent, 'continually advancing from one degree of knowledge, perfection and happiness to another.' Self-help in society – and here Malthusians were thinking of paupers pulling themselves up by their bootstraps – was part of a larger self-developing nature: 'all reasonable beings, however inferior the condition in which they commence their existence, are destined to rise higher and higher in endless progression, and to contribute to their own advancement.'[12]

Such a view demanded that the trammels be removed, that religious and civil disabilities be lifted, to allow everyone to compete freely to realize their God-given potential – to rise as nature and God intended. The Anglican priests were keeping the people down. This, of course, was why some radical Unitarians saw reform and evolution as going hand in hand. A self-developing nature held no terrors for them. Eras's group, with Martineau at its centre, gave Charles the licence to work out his own deterministic theories.

Darwin was learning Malthusian Whig ideals: his family and friends were justifying the reforms, rationalizing middle-class values, underpinning competition, arguing for free trade, factory expansion, and the removal of religious disabilities. They saw their social world as part of nature, itself struggling and progressing in accordance with God's laws. As at Eras's, so at Lyell's, language, genealogy and development were the hot topics. Fossil bones were chewed over at dinner, with Whig grandees and suave savants gnawing on the more arcane points. After the ladies departed, the talk would turn to Herschel's letter, or the origin of 'new species, and that mystery of mysteries, the creation of man.'

These discussions took place as Darwin was pondering the divine government himself. He too came to accept that 'the Creator creates by . . . laws.' Law ruled the earth, as it did the heavens; anything else was demeaning to God. Darwin complained that 'we can allow satellites, planets, suns, universe, nay whole systems of universe[s,] to be governed by laws, but the smallest insect, we wish to be created at once by special act.'[13] It was absurd; just as the winds in the Andes obeyed regular laws, so did the comings and goings of animals on the planet's surface. Dining at Lyell's, dancing at Babbage's, he found the idea of miraculous, catastrophic interruptions increasingly deplored. The rule of law had to be upheld.

By 1837 attacks on the Anglican miracle-mongers were barbed. Up-and-coming Dissenters wanted *more* reforms, furious at being barred from jobs in the hospitals, the law courts, Oxford, and Cambridge. They fulminated against Anglican privilege, indicting the Established Church of the 'filthy crime' of adultery with the state. The 'harlot' had to be wrenched from her caress.

These fierce Dissenters saw nature as a product of self-adjusting laws, initiated by God and proclaimed to everyone through His Word and Works. All men were therefore equal before Him, and no state-endowed priests were needed to interpret life or control science. The Church should be disestablished, its privileges stripped. With the four million Dissenters making political headway under the Whigs, their lawful explanation of nature was beginning to challenge the Anglicans' supernatural one.

Conservative Anglicans saw the whole world as ruled directly by God's will, immediately upheld 'by the word of His power,' and the Church as the divine agency on earth. If it were overthrown, everything would collapse. As someone joked: 'Many of our clergy suppose that if there was no Church of England, cucumbers and celery would not grow; that mustard and cress could not be raised. If Establishments are connected so much with the great laws of nature, this makes all the difference.' Reduced to the comical, it did seem unlikely to those outside the vicarage gate.

Others weren't laughing. They considered a manikin nature dancing to the tune of Creative whim risible. The sight of the Revd William Kirby's Universe moved by angelic demigods caused one commentator to snap: 'No no. – The Almighty laid down general laws at the beginning, for man, for animals, for the elements, and even the Universe around them. The laws, being founded in infinite wisdom, require neither revision nor supervision. They are eternal and immutable.' Darwin had read Kirby's Bridgewater book on animal instincts aboard ship, and now he found it causing wry amusement ashore. The sight of Kirby's puppet creation had everyone hopping: the 'silly and superstitious nonsense' to which men 'of Mr. Kirby's class' descend![14]

Darwin – with his Unitarian family and friends – stood at the crossroads. As he pondered life's progression on the earth he continued to hear a chorus of complaints about the old miraculous explanations.

The onslaught on the corrupt Church was accompanied by new questions. Could God's goodness be deduced from the perfect adaptation of animals? Darwin had loved Paley's logic at Cambridge – which moved from the wise design of animals to the existence of a wise Designer. But it was beginning to look suspect. Some spurned the superstitious divines who encircled animal structures 'with a spiritual halo; as if truth could be more sacred when thus surrounded.' Reforming zoologists saw animals not as contingently created by God to fit their niches, but related through a unity of plan: the bat wing and whale flipper had the same bones as a human arm.

Darwin found the old design arguments in tatters in London. The medical schools were brimming with dissident ideas. The Bridgewater books were written off as 'Bilgewater.' Demagogues warned clergymen not to meddle in mental and moral speculation. These were bullish times. Things had reached such a head that most medical men were now talking of nature as a legislated '*process* of change.'[15]

Some medical men actually toyed with 'transmutation' (the mutation or change of one species into another). Grant lectured on the 'metamorphoses' of fossil species yearly at University College. And James Gully, another Edinburgh graduate and editor of a radical London newspaper, translated the Heidelberg embryologist Friedrich Tiedemann's evolutionary treatise on *Comparative Physiology*. Gully

– who in later years became Darwin's physician – endorsed what one incensed critic called 'that most extravagant of all suppositions, that most grovelling of all religions – the self-created, self-endowed, and self-creating powers of Nature.'[16]

So in Darwin's London, there was a new fuelling of excitement. Natural theology was in crisis, and many expected a new life science to arise like a phoenix from its ashes. Here Darwin could make his mark. He could see the need to solve the great 'mystery of mysteries.' Lyell was bold; he would be bolder. He would provide the sort of reforming, developmental science so admired in his brother's circle.

Almost imperceptibly, he glided towards transmutation himself. It was easy because he had been habituated to it, in his grandfather's writings and Grant's talks; because London provided a conducive environment; and because he had the time and patience and love for intractable theoretical problems. He had been wondering about the stability of species since the last leg of his voyage. Now the experts were to supply the zoological rivets to hold his ideas together. And the first of these was hammered home by the bird painter John Gould.

A few days after arriving from Cambridge, he met Gould again in the zoo's museum and learned more of his finch revelations. Gould now realized that even Darwin's Galapagos 'wren' was a finch, giving him thirteen species in all. Darwin's mixed bag of birds was in fact a unique flock of finches.

It was a surprise, but because Darwin had neglected to label most of them by island he missed the import. Gould's conclusions about the other birds were what really rocked the boat. Darwin *had* labelled the four mockingbirds by island, and he had idly speculated that if they turned out to be true varieties it 'would undermine the stability of Species.' It would suggest that castaways, cut off from their mainland stock, could start to change. They turned out to be more than varieties; Gould told him that three were distinct *species*.[17] Moreover they had relatives on the American mainland; close relatives, but not identical species.

Darwin had his intractable problem: how to explain a crop of new related species, each to its island. The evidence of separate island species was mounting. Thomas Bell confirmed that the giant tortoises *were* native to the Galapagos, not food brought in by the buccaneers. This, with the finch and mockingbird findings, made it likely that the Vice-Governor had been right – that each island did have its own indigenous tortoise. But it was too late to prove the point: Darwin had missed the opportunity, or rather eaten his way through it. Only his baby tortoise had survived, and that lacked the distinguishing features of the adult.[18]

By mid-March he realized that the original immigrants had become altered somehow, and that the alteration had actually produced an array of new species. He had joined the '*infidel* naturalists,' as Sedgwick castigated them, those adopting 'false theories' of Creation. For Anglicans such transmutation (or evolution as we call it today) threatened Christian Britain at its core. If life was self-made, what became of God's delegated power holding together a precarious paternalist society? Even for Lyell the prospect was appalling, because he feared that an ape ancestry would brutalize mankind and destroy his 'high estate.' Darwin was staring heresy in the face.

So why did he opt for transmutation? True, the zoologists' findings surprised him; the mockingbirds and tortoises *could* be seen as immigrants that had settled in differently on each island. The living llamas *could* be seen as diminutive descendants of the Patagonian giants Darwin had disinterred. But they need not have been. No one else saw them this way, not Gould nor Lyell – who were reverently reticent on such matters. Nor would Darwin's Anglican mentors like the Revds Henslow and Sedgwick have baulked at using such discoveries to applaud the providential distribution of beautifully-designed island and mainland species.

He was sailing close to the edge of his intellectual world. What drove him to live so dangerously? Why did he opt for a physical transformation of animals, so horribly bestializing in Lyell's view? His colleagues denied it pointedly, and the exception – Robert Grant – was being cold-shouldered for his reckless abandon. It required intellectual courage, and a sort of bull-headed character, pushing on determinedly to make his mark, proving he had no 'coward soul or faithless heart.' It took a certain type of person to be receptive; to see nothing heretical, nothing incompatible with his moral or social values. A person for whom there could even be something gained.[19]

Darwin had seen savage man in the flesh, in all his naked, revolting crudeness, and Lyell had not. This made much of the difference between them. For Lyell, transmutation and an ape ancestry threatened to bestialize man, drag him down to gutter-level, raze his 'high estate.' But Darwin had come face to face with men reduced to the lowest meanest level, wild, stupid, murderous, amoral – men barely above the beasts. Here was the real threat; here was man *already* brutalized and degraded. The point for Darwin was not to protect civilized gentlemen, but to explain how they and the

Fuegian could be 'essentially the same creature,' from the hand of the same Creator.

He remembered Jemmy Button and his friends. Two years after being presented at Court they had reverted to a naked, filthy existence and were apparently happy. Jemmy had shown how difficult savage habits were to break. Fuegian savages seemed as well adapted to their waterless wastes as sophisticates were to European cities. But how could this be? Again it was as if two Creators were at work. How had *one* God produced this cultural spread? Had he personally locked the Fuegian into his miserable environment? Surely he could not intend that man remain a savage? How much better to see the one God using evolution to spread the human races naturally. And how much more reassuring; evolution for Darwin posed none of Lyell's bestializing threat – the gentlemen were at the top in their rightful place. They were the evolutionary successes.

To everyone's surprise, the first fossil monkeys were announced this spring. Two had turned up simultaneously, one from the foothills of the Himalayas, the other from the south of France. Both were immensely old, contemporaries of long-extinct mammals, and this, Lyell admitted uncomfortably, bought Lamarck the time he needed. (Lamarck had mooted the slow evolution of a stooping chimpanzee into an erect human.) Lyell gritted his teeth and conceded that from 'Lamarck's view, there may have been a great many thousand centuries for their tails to wear off, and the transformation to men to take place.'[20]

The Indian monkey was baboon-like, but larger than anything living today. A 'nearly perfect head' had been found, to everyone's astonishment, and it was announced at the Geological Society on 3 May. This was the meeting at which Darwin read his next paper, on the pampas. Both he and Lyell were aware of the ancient monkey's potential. Lyell dashed off a letter to his sister that night, laughing about tails wearing off, but Darwin did what petrified his mentor most: within months he was viewing the 'wonderful' monkeys in an evolutionary light.[21] Human ancestry was on the cards from the first moment that Darwin expressed a belief in transmutation.

Richard Owen was pushing Darwin hard, making him rethink the laws governing living matter.

In the museum of the College of Surgeons Owen and Darwin talked over fossil skulls and the meaning of life. It was the perfect place: the renovations at the college were complete, and the builders were out. It had been officially reopened in February in a typically lavish way with the Duke of Wellington, Sir Robert Peel, and 500 guests. Visitors flocked to the magnificent new museum, with its three-storey galleries packed with exhibits and supported on Doric pillars. Everything was on show, from an eight-foot Irish giant to chimpanzee skeletons, platypuses to fossil armadillos. It was as though 'the whole earth has been ransacked to enrich its stores.'

Here Owen and Darwin got down to fundamentals. On a major point Owen differed from Darwin's old teacher Henslow. Owen followed the Berlin physiologist Johannes Müller, believing that there was no *outside* creative force animating 'inert' matter. On the contrary, the simplest living matter, like the embryonic germ, had a unique, intrinsic 'organizing energy.' This directed growth, enabling tissues to be built according to plan. The force was concentrated in the germ, but waned as it diffused into the developing tissues, thus slowing growth with age. There was a reciprocal relationship between degree of organization and strength of the force. Darwin accepted this 'organizing energy' but began to modify it in his speculations on species.[22]

When Darwin came to tea with Owen one day they discussed the basics of life over a microscope in the drawing-room. Darwin undoubtedly kept quiet about his real leanings; after all, his goal was anathema. *He* now wanted a way of turning one species into the next. But Owen abominated talk of chimpanzee-ancestry or life's self-development. With the life-force limited, no individual can stretch beyond the organization marking out its species. A mollusc cannot spontaneously increase its vital force to 'develope new organs' or mutate into a mackerel.[23] Darwin was stymied.

Others were more pliant than Owen. The shy botanist Robert Brown thought that even the granular matter *inside* the germs was 'self-moving.' Break open minuscule polyp eggs and the atoms gush out, rushing around like 'bees swarming.' An acceptance of 'living atoms' was almost universal among the flaming democrats. It gave a scientific basis to their belief in free men controlling their own destinies, so important in an age of democratic demands. It provided the perfect political analogy – power from below, 'mandating' upwards, rising from the 'social atoms' – the people – rather than reigning down from a godhead or monarch. The notion of self-organizing atoms was spreading like wildfire through the democratic press. Looking at Brown's swarming atoms Darwin too became convinced. He ventured beyond Owen's position, accepting that the atoms themselves were alive. He was switching a Cambridge tradition of inert matter powered by God for a more secular one.[24] Living atoms were an essential step towards his understanding of nature's self-development.

Owen was a conservative Anglican. He denounced transmutation as subversive and anti-Christian: it would submerge man in a brutal quagmire, destroy his responsibility – and the atheist agitators showed where it would all end. (Owen met this street threat in a more immediate way. He drilled with the Honourable Artillery Company, the urban gentry's own volunteer regiment, which backed up the police during riots.) Bestializing man was reprehensible; people were not super-apes. To destroy mankind's unique status by stretching the life-force was like throwing muskets to the rabble. But Darwin, with his reforming Unitarian circle, treated nature's self-development quite casually. Apes failed to frighten him; the brutalization threat passed harmlessly overhead. What angered him was quite the reverse, the arrogance of those who put mankind on a pedestal.

He was still tussling with extinction. Unlike Owen, Darwin suspected that individuals were analogous to species. He thought that they both had fixed life spans, limited by the vital force. At sea he had compared the individuals of a species to the cuttings of a rampant Chiloé apple tree. They all perish together. How else to explain the deaths of the giant sloths?

From changing conditions perhaps? Darwin spewed out counter-facts in his miscellaneous 'Red Notebook,' which he had begun on the *Beagle*. Domestic animals can live under any conditions, he noted: 'Dogs. Cats. Horses. Cattle. Goat. Asses. have all run wild & bred. no doubt with perfect success.'[25] Where is the adaptation to local conditions here? And his fossil llamas showed that species can die without the climate changing. Again, it pointed to the conclusion that their time had just run out.

He drew out other life-and-death implications. Mammals, being complex and with a more diffused life-force, must have shorter lives as species than simple microscopic creatures. These are almost immortal; they continue today as they must have in the hot primeval seas. By contrast mammals have gone extinct one after the other, hence the succession of fossils in the rocks. Darwin told the Geological Society that his own pampas mammals had much shorter lives than their molluscan contemporaries. He mooted it too in his *Journal of Researches*, the book he was writing based on his *Beagle* diary. In his account of Patagonia he threw down a cryptic teaser to his readers. His former giants were not extinguished by climatic change, he said. So maybe, 'as with the individual, so with the species, the hour of life has run its course, and is spent.'[26]

What, then, of repopulation, the birth of new species to fill the gaps? If the 'organizing energy' is limited in each species, how could more complex forms be generated?

His deeper speculations were probably kept secret from everybody, except perhaps Eras and his dining circle. Darwin listened to Owen and Lyell, but let on little.

In his Great Marlborough Street study he continued to puzzle over the Galapagos. He became impatient to know what else besides mockingbirds, finches, and tortoises were derived from South American colonists. He asked Henslow to look at the Galapagos plants first, hoping he would pinpoint equivalent but different species on each island ('representative species,' as they are called – the descendants of the same immigrant). He pressed his dour friend the Revd Jenyns, who had received the *Beagle* fish by default, when no one else wanted them. But he was too slow, having to work up the subject from scratch. Darwin was eager, and prodded him to get on with the Galapagos fish first.

He continued collaborating with Gould, speaking with him at the Zoological Society on the South American rheas. Gould confirmed that the remnants of Darwin's Christmas dinner at Port Desire was a new species, smaller and fluffier. And to 'commemorate' Darwin's gifts to the Society, he christened it *Rhea Darwinii*.[27] It set Darwin thinking about these Patagonian birds. The Galapagos islands illustrated the importance of isolation for forming new species. But how to explain the two rheas, whose ranges overlapped near the Rio Negro? No barrier separated them, so how had they evolved?

Soon the first tantalizing transmutatory notes began appearing in his Red Notebook. Cryptic notes: 'Speculate on neutral [i.e. overlapping] ground of 2. ostriches [rheas],' he scribbled. Why were there no intermediates between the big and small species at the Rio Negro? He speculated that 'change not progressif: produced at one blow.' Meaning that perhaps one sprang fully formed from the other. One was born a mutant from the other's egg. Such fetal sports – 'monsters' or 'freaks' they were called – were well known to medical men; there were bottles of them in the Hunterian Museum. Owen himself was writing on these mutants from the womb, deformed by an unknown process. Whatever the cause, Darwin jotted, these deformed babies 'present an analogy to production of species.'[28]

Was it the same with the llamas? Did the extinct giants give birth to freaks – to today's small guanacos and llamas, which remain on the same arid plains? Whatever happened, Darwin looked on the mutations as dramatic.

225

On other points the evidence was contradictory. Galapagos life had diversified because of its island isolation, and the finches showed a 'perfect gradation' in their bills. But no isolation was necessary for the rheas – they roamed free on the mainland. It showed how much more thought was needed.

Time was the problem, or the lack of it; he had to finish the *Journal* first. He began shunning parties to get on with the travelogue, grumbling about overwork and groaning with a bad stomach. He ploughed on, augmenting his diary account with bits and bobs from his *Beagle* geological and zoological notebooks, lacing it with the latest from his bevy of specialists. Everything, he told his cousin Fox, was going in: the habits of animals, the geology and the natives, and the scenery 'will make the hodge-podge complete.'

Not quite everything; the finches were barely mentioned. He simply noted his suspicions that they were probably 'confined to different islands.' He continued to believe that these birds had similar habits. This and the similar terrain on the islands left him baffled as to how they could have evolved so differently – perhaps they too had appeared at a 'blow.'[29]

He tore on, trying to meet the deadline for his book. As if the *Journal* were not enough, he began toying with a new project: to collect the experts' reports on his *Beagle* animals and edit a multi-volume *Zoology*, a spotter's guide for future travellers. He relished the idea of seeing 'the gleanings of my hands, after having passed through the brains of abler naturalists collected together in one work.' The *Zoology* looked impossibly ambitious, unless the government stepped in with a grant (at least to cover the cost of the 150 engravings, estimated at £1000). All the zoologists – Bell, Waterhouse, Owen, Gould – came out in favour; but as museum staff, they cut little weight when it came to funding.

Here great patrons were needed. Darwin arranged an interview with the Earl of Derby, President of the Zoological Society – an aristocrat who was more interested in his menagerie than debating in the Lords (where he had been placed to stack the House in the Whigs' favour). The antiquarian Duke of Somerset, President of the Linnean, was also approached, and of course the Revd Whewell at the Geological was ready to canvass government help. Darwin wondered how others had obtained sponsorship. He asked John Richardson, the naturalist who published an account of Captain Franklin's search for the Northwest Passage, and whose specimens were also stowed in the zoo's museum.[30]

Darwin might not have had an inside track to the Chancellor of the Exchequer, but he knew someone who did. Henslow could tap the old-boy network. The Chancellor was Thomas Spring Rice, the Whig MP for Cambridge, and Henslow had campaigned for him. Both men had also helped in 1836 to get a charter for that great Whig initiative, the University of London. Henslow's friends in the Cabinet had just engineered him a 'Crown Living' at Hitcham, in Suffolk, worth £1000 a year. So he was well known, and he put out feelers. Spring Rice summoned Darwin for an interview and, instead of grilling him, coolly told him to make the most of the Treasury money! Henslow had done his work. 'You have been the making of me,' Darwin acknowledged. 'If it had not been for you *alone* I should never have got the 1000£.'[31] The cash spoke eloquently for Darwin's status, contacts, and potential, even though his scientific credentials were negligible. Social inferiors had inordinate difficulty prying grants out of a retrenching government, but Darwin's came easily. It enabled him to dispense his own patronage, to act as taskmaster and paymaster, chivvying a Gradgrind work force of white-collar museum men. The *Zoology* was secured.

It meant an inordinate amount of work, cooped up in this 'vile smokey place.' He was still apportioning his precious relics. Edible fungi from Tierra del Fuego and fossil wood from the Andes went to the shy Robert Brown, causing him to open up. 'I think my silicified wood, has unflintified Mr Brown's heart,' Darwin jibed. Beetles went off to the Revd Hope, in memory of those far-off insect-hunting days, and Chonos potatoes to Henslow, now so preoccupied with his parish that he hardly seemed to notice. A rural parish: the mere thought reminded Darwin of how much he missed the countryside. He felt trapped in his Marlborough Street 'prison,' staring at the dingy walls of the house opposite. He gave a quiet inner scream, 'I do hate the streets of London.'[32]

He was becoming obsessed by transmutation. Everything kept resolving into tantalizing questions. How did plants reach the Galapagos, let alone mid-oceanic outposts like Keeling Island? What species were in his Keeling samples, he asked Henslow, and could their seeds 'endure floating in salt water'?

Continuing to collaborate with Gould, Darwin became more embarrassed by his lack of proper labels. He belatedly set out to prove that each finch had its island home. He examined FitzRoy's scrupulously documented skins, deposited in the British Museum, and contacted crewmen who had made their own collections. Even his servant,

Syms Covington, had three Galapagos finches, each with its island noted. The replies helped him to rack his memory and reconstruct his own finches' localities, although the by-guess-or-by-God approach led to errors. At the end of the day he was convinced that the finches, like the mockingbirds and tortoises, were island-specific. That allowed him to see them as the diversified descendants of mainland stock.

On 20 June the country went into mourning as William IV died. With the flags at half-mast Darwin finally finished the *Journal*. His account of the voyage had been written in record time, seven months from start to finish. Given his uncommon trouble expressing himself in 'common English,' he declared that he would 'always feel respect for every one who has written a book, let it be what it may.' As he left for ten days with the family at Shrewsbury on the 26th he looked forward to the future as an author. And as a geologist, judging by the way his third paper, on coral reefs, had been received. The applause of the 'great guns,' he conceded, 'gives me much confidence.' It encouraged him to put his 'shoulder to the wheel' and plan a book on South American geology.[33]

He also put his shoulder to another, more massive, wheel. He threw himself into a study of transmutation.

16

Tearing Down the Barriers

IN MID-JULY 1837 Darwin took the plunge and opened a clandestine transmutation notebook (called his 'B' Notebook). He was entering an intense and lonely new world of monologues and musings. The brown-covered pad was small, and on the title page he inscribed in bold letters the word *Zoonomia*, to signal that he was treading the same path as his grandfather. He then burst into a continuous series of notes covering twenty-seven or so pages, a breathless machine-gun-like effusion of telegraphic jottings, representing hurried and excited trains of thought on the laws of life. Transmutation was a fact, and these scribblings set the framework for his exploration of the ways animals and plants changed.

Odd and obvious questions litter the text. 'Why is life short' and sexual reproduction so important? Because sexual mixing produces variants and a fast turnover spreads them through the population. Sex causes variety, which is necessary to enable species to meet new conditions. If climates alter, species can respond quickly, generating new adaptations automatically.[1]

But Owen had denied that simpler species could grow more complex. They were unable to stretch up with new vitality, summon up new stocks of 'organizing energy' or life-force. Frustrated, Darwin kicked against Owen's life-force limiting each species. Darwin knew that something must 'alter the race to [fit a] *changing* world.' As he kept saying, species *must* 'become permanently changed.' They *must* pass on and build on their modifications.

One problem could be circumvented. Clearly, any varieties generated were normally blended back into the population as a result of 'intermarriages,' or crossings. This normally contained the changes, keeping a species looking uniform. It explained why classifiers had always assumed that species were fixed and immutable. Isolation of varieties was the way round this. In-breeding finches or mockingbird castaways facing a brave new world on some 'fresh isl[an]^d.' would accentuate their new traits.[2] A slightly thicker beak on one Galapagos island could not be lost by being blended back into the mainland American stock. The bill could continue growing thicker as the finches in-bred. Islands allowed the possibility of rapid, permanent deviation. The longer a country was separated – like Australia with its peculiar platypuses – the more different its mammals would be.

He then flirted with some of Lamarck's basic tenets. If the simplest monads – the building blocks of life – are spontaneously emerging from inorganic matter, they would *push* the escalator upwards. They would provide the pressure from below, forcing life onward – or, as Darwin doodled, 'the simplest cannot help . . . – becoming more complicated.' Like individuals maturing, perhaps the species stand on an escalator and are carried effortlessly upwards. As they move on, the creatures below rise to fill their old shoes. He joked about it: 'If all men were dead then monkeys make men. – Men make angels.'[3] It was a joke with terrifying consequences for the old élite, playing on a bestial image of monkey origins. It showed that this ancestry held no horrors for him.

Owen was pushing on with the *Beagle* haul. He now recognized five giant, archaic armadillos and sloths and was describing them in *Fossil Mammalia*, his contribution to Darwin's *Zoology* series. These huge herbivores must have lived on the pampas plains as African game does today. 'What an extraordin[ar]^y. mystery it is,' Darwin puzzled to Lyell, 'the cause of the death of these numerous animals, so recently, & with so little physical [i.e. environmental] change.'

The blitz of thoughts continued as he squared up to extinction in his notebook. He kept recycling Owen's idea that the complexity of a species was inversely related to its life span. He sketched an '*irregularly branched*' tree to convey the genealogical history of animals and plants. If life was like a huge old oak, growing through the ages, the fossil mammals were the 'terminal buds dying,' their life-force decayed. The trunk symbolized the ancient common ancestor, the stock from which all animals sprang. And the single trunk must have had a single origin. Darwin realized that life's initial spontaneous appearance from inorganic matter on the earth must have been a one-off affair, buried in the dim, distant past. Living molecules cannot be emerging constantly, everywhere, or millions of unrelated trees of life would be springing up, making the whole image 'excessively complicated.'[4] The origin of life was a once-only event, lost somewhere in pre-Silurian times.

The scrawling continued furiously as he worked through the implications. If everything came from one set of living atoms or 'monads' in the primeval past, then these particles could not have lifespans related to complexity; otherwise *everything* on each branch would die simultaneously, whole classes would collapse – mammals, birds, reptiles, or whatever. It didn't happen. Suddenly he saw the light. 'Monad has not definite existence.' There was *no* limited life-force holding species back. He had broken through Owen's barrier.

Life had originated only once, then ramified through history, an endless growth, terminal buds dying as others appeared. No revitalizing was necessary, no creative re-energizing. He dashed off pages exploring the family-tree image. The deaths of terminal twigs produced the gaps, between birds and mammals, or between families of beetles. The more distant two groups, the further down the stem their common ancestor, and the more dead wood must have fallen off in between.[5] With extinction no longer from old age, he became convinced (contrary to his former view of the giant llamas' demise) that it resulted from conditions changing too fast. Adaptation – the fit of an organism to its niche – was back on the agenda. If the environment changed gradually, animals adapted, transmuting to keep themselves synchronized; if they failed to keep pace, extinction was inevitable.

Adaptation was not alone in explaining an animal's make-up. There was also a 'heredetary [sic] taint.' The 'taint' was the general plan bequeathed by the first common forebear. All fishes, reptiles, birds, and mammals share a vertebrate plan. All snails, slugs, and cuttlefish conform to a molluscan blueprint. Adaptation was simply stamped on top of this structural plan.

But how do adaptive changes match the climatic rhythms? Does the climate modify the reproductive process, causing offspring to emerge ready-adapted? He assumed that all variants emerge perfect, but then he was still living in Paley's perfect world. Even so, it was not a use of Paley that his Cambridge mentors would have condoned. The idea of an organism continually adjusting itself was anathema, perfection or no. This was dynamic self-sufficiency.

His reflections became startling. Because life followed the vagaries of climate, there was no yardstick to measure progress. For Grant, the cooling planet drove life upwards towards higher, hotter-blooded forms. But Darwin forswore any unidirectional change; life adapted to the quirks of habitat. It sprawled everywhere; animals were not climbing a mythical ladder, stretching up to the highest human rung. Even races of people were spreading laterally into their peculiar

231

niches: Jemmy Button's Fuegians into a desolate, windswept wilderness, civilized Englishmen into their factory cities. Darwin was left with a shockingly relative outlook. 'It is absurd to talk of one animal being higher than another,' he mused. '*We* consider those, where the intellectual faculties most developed, as highest. – A bee doubtless would [use] . . . instincts' as a criterion.[6] In his bee's-eye view man was no longer the crown of creation. Even the radical Lamarckians kept a human-topped chain, and allowed an imperious man to look down on life. Darwin's non-human orientation was a total departure from radical wisdom, let alone religious convention.

Through a hot August he continued 'stewing in this great den of a place,' jotting down heretical notes. In September he was still teasing at the problem, while continuing to correct the *Journal* proofs, complaining that he was 'tied by the leg, hard at work as any galley slave.'

He switched to transport problems, devising ways of shipping creatures out to islands to start the process of speciation. He knew it was a serendipitous affair from the fact that there were mice on some Chonos islands and not others. Ingenuity was the key: 'Owls. transport mice alive?' he queried. Well, that might explain rodents. Seeds were easier; they could have been blown or washed ashore. Or thrushes and coots might fly out to islands and 'bring [them] in stomach.' He left a memo to look into it. What else would survive a sea crossing? He started devising tests to find out. 'Experimentise on land shells in salt water & lizards d[itt]o.,' he scrawled, hoping to try it in the future. Perhaps the extreme conditions of the crossing would themselves alter the floating seeds. 'It would be [a] curious experiment to know whether soaking seeds in salt water' changes them.[7] Perhaps the owls, and coots, and seeds did not have to travel as far as supposed. They could have hopped across island arcs that subsequently sank beneath the waves. His theory of subsidence allowed him to summon up island chains as migratory stepping-stones.

Thinking about blue seas took him back to the voyage. During those years island-hopping himself, he would have given his right arm to be home. Now he was dreaming himself back to sea again. He had missed his family so much afloat, yet here he was, trapped in his London prison, far from the Shrewsbury countryside. All that longing, all the planning, and what had come of it? He had seen his father and sisters for only nine days since his return!

He was stuck indoors, wrapped up in his covert notebook. 'What a waste of life to stop all summer in this ugly Marlborough Street &

see nothing but the same odious house on the opposite side.' He turned down Elizabeth Wedgwood's invitation to a concert in order to finish the *Journal* proofs. They were dragging on, cumbersome prose and recalcitrant commas only increasing his misery, leading to the groan: 'What a very difficult thing it is to write correctly.' His *Zoology* volumes also needed planning and Darwin lost more time liaising with authors and editors. The Treasury grant was to keep the cover price down and make the books useful to the public. Given it, the publishers calculated that they could bring out the whole 800-page edition, including 250 plates, for £9.

His cackhanded language in the *Journal*'s preface immediately landed him in trouble. FitzRoy, a stickler for etiquette, was 'astonished at the total omission of any notice of the officers' for their help, let alone the offhand way he himself was mentioned. It was tactless of Darwin, but prickly of FitzRoy. 'I esteem *you* far too highly to break off from you willingly,' FitzRoy announced in his hoity-toity way.[8] The connection of Darwin's volume with his own was 'one of feeling and fidelity – not of *expediency*.' Darwin made immediate amends, giving fulsome thanks, and honour was restored, but it showed that he still had to step lively with the Captain.

The work and worry were compounding. He had performed prodigious mental and manual feats during the voyage with no obvious ill effects. But now, deep into his clandestine work, compiling notes that would shock his geological compatriots, his health was breaking. He was living a double life with double standards, unable to broach his species work with anyone except Eras, for fear he be branded irresponsible, irreligious, or worse. It began to tell in the pit of his stomach. On 20 September he suffered an 'uncomfortable palpitation of the heart,' and his doctors urged him '*strongly* to knock off all work' and leave for the country.[9] Two days later he finished the *Journal* proofs and headed to Shrewsbury for a rest.

He did not get much of one. He returned via Maer, where Emma and the family wore him out with questions about gaucho life. Emma, at twenty-eight, was a year older than Charles and talented. She knew French and Italian, and more than a bit of German (which was a bit more than Charles). She played the piano fluently (after lessons from Chopin) and was keen on outdoor sports, being a 'dragonness' at archery. While Charles was at sea, she had parried four or five marriage proposals. Then her mother had suffered a seizure and become bedridden, requiring her constant presence at home. Her courting days seemed to have ended – despite the precedent of her brother Jos's marriage in August to Charles's sister Caroline, herself thirty-seven.

233

But Emma kept up hope while serving the family as nurse, caretaker, and aunt. For diversion she read the latest novels and worked in the garden. Here Charles now strolled, and Uncle Jos showed him some disused ground where lime and cinders, spread years before, had disappeared into the soil, leaving a layer of loam. Jos assumed that worms had done the work, although he thought such gardening trivia of little consequence to a young man working on a continental scale.[10] Charles disagreed, and from this unprepossessing beginning sprang a lifelong interest in the humble earthworm – a tiny unsung creature which, in its untold millions, transformed the land as the coral polyps did the tropical sea.

Darwin returned to London on 21 October but his palpitating heart remained in the Shropshire countryside. His talk on worms and their castings to the Geological Society on 1 November only highlighted his growing idiosyncrasies. This august body expected something grander than *worms*. Darwin knew it; he now steeled himself and began planning a technical book on South American geology. Separate papers on Chile's coastline, the fossil-tombs, and coral reefs were not enough. He had to bring them together in a rounded volume. The thought suffocated him more than the November fog. He hankered after a rural retreat of his own. He viewed his Cambridge friends, Henslow, Fox, and Jenyns in their country rectories with envy. In November he finally took a few days out from the tropical lagoons to visit Fox in his Isle of Wight parish. The contrast with his palm-fringed beaches was stark – these were bitter wintery days and the Channel was choppy and more black than blue. But he was just happy to be out of the 'abominable murky atmosphere of London.'[11]

He had a rather idealistic image of vicarage life. Jenyns was 'bitterly complaining of his solitude' at Swaffham Bulbeck. It wasn't only the isolation. 'Henslow tells me he hears a groan occasionally escape from you, when you mention my fishes,' Darwin consoled Jenyns. This was an understatement. His friend was staggering under the weight of pickled fish. Even though half the catch had deteriorated during the voyage, he was left with 137 species to describe, 75 of them new. The *Fish* volume in the *Zoology* series was coming out in parts, and Darwin hoped that he could squash sixteen fish into each number. But Jenyns was having trouble meeting the quota. Darwin was learning to cajole in his beguiling way: 'for the credit of English zoologists, do not despair and give up,' he pleaded, even if 'you have undertaken [the job] chiefly out of kindness . . . for me. – I am sure I am very much obliged to you.' Then he about-faced and floored his friend with an alternative strike: 'you must not for a moment *hesitate* about throwing it up, if your health or want of time prevents your taking any satisfaction in the employment.'[12] Darwin got what he wanted, and what he expected; Jenyns struggled on to confirm that all the Galapagos fishes were new.

Things were moving faster on the fossil front. Owen had christened the 'llama' *Macrauchenia* and worked steadily on it through Christmas and New Year 1838. His reputation for speed was deserved, and his instalment was the first of any of the *Zoology* volumes. This opening eight-shilling part of *Fossil Mammalia*, with its full-size, pull-out illustration of the two-foot skull of the rodent *Toxodon*, appeared in February. It came at an opportune moment. At the anniversary meeting of the Geological Society on the 16th Owen was 'wonderfully pleased' to receive the Society's Wollaston Medal for diagnosing Darwin's hippo-sized fossils.

Darwin himself basked in the reflected glory. But it did not pay to look too closely at Owen's conclusions, which were straying from expectation. Less a llama, *Macrauchenia* was turning out to be more a tapir 'with a soupçon of camel' thrown in.[13] This was a mite inconvenient; Darwin actually wanted a llama ancestor for his pampas guanacos. No matter, he ignored Owen's fine print. He persisted in looking at the bones through a naturalist's eyes. Because the spot where he found the fossils betrayed a harsh, arid environment, he continued to visualize them as camel-like llamas.

Darwin took Lyell's advice and turned down Geological jobs to get on with his projects. The President William Whewell had asked him to become a Secretary in 1837, and Henslow thought it his duty 'as a follower of science.' But Darwin declined, ostensibly on account of his ignorance of English geology. More embarrassing still, 'it would be disgraceful to the Society' to have a Secretary who could not pronounce a word of French. Imagine the *faux pas* as he fumbled with foreign papers! And written English was barely less mysterious to him, so the prospect of abstracting manuscripts was hardly appealing. If these weren't excuses enough, he topped them off by adding that 'anything which flurries me completely knocks me up afterwards and brings on a bad palpitation of the heart.'

By 1838 his resolve was crumbling. He was having trouble avoiding official posts, time-wasters or no. On 5 February he accepted the Vice-Presidency of the Entomological Society (founded by fellow beetle aficionados Waterhouse and Hope in 1833). Whewell's pressure was now relentless. He was still trying to recruit Darwin to the geologists' *sanctum sanctorum*. In his presidential address, he praised Owen's results and extolled Darwin's circumnavigation 'as one of the most important events for geology which has occurred for many years.' With such flattery from the podium Darwin had to succumb. He was coerced into becoming a Secretary. 'I could not refuse with fairness,' he lamented to Henslow, 'although it is an office which I do not relish.'[14]

One excuse he could never mention. He was joining the star chamber of Britain's best geologists, urban gentry and Anglican clergy mostly, upright men who execrated evolution as morally filthy and politically foul. This was no exaggeration: Sedgwick, a past President, damned Lamarck, Geoffroy, and the revolutionary French for their 'gross (and I dare say, filthy) views of physiology.' How could Darwin rub shoulders with the excitable old Proctor if he found out? Sedgwick saw science provide moral uplift in a turbulent age. It should raise men's eyes heavenward, while reminding them of their station on earth. The geological élite had to provide spiritual leadership, not spread depraved 'doctrines of spontaneous generation and transmutation of species, with all their train of monstrous consequences.'[15]

On 7 March, before Whewell, Sedgwick and the rest, Darwin read his longest paper, on the devastating Concepción earthquake. He explained how the same crustal movements were responsible for thousands of miles of volcanic and earthquake activity along the length of the Andes, which were rising slowly as a consequence. Lyell was delighted at this support for his gradualist tenets, and Darwin saw his 'geological salvation' in Lyell's principles. The new Secretary was not only reading his own papers, but other people's. Yet he remained edgy, despite hours of practice, whispering the lines to himself in private. 'I was so nervous at first, I somehow could see nothing all around me,' he recalled, '& I felt as if my body was gone, & only my head left.'[16]

This was the red public face of an ambitious young geologist, wending his way into the corridors of geological power. But his identity was split; privately he had unmitigated contempt for the arrogance of the dons. Secretly, at home, he lurched into undisguised sneers at them for bending the universe to fit man and then pronouncing a panegyric on God's design. He scorned anyone who found Whewell 'profound, because he says length of days adapted to duration of sleep of man.!!! whole universe so adapted!!! & not man to Planets. – instance of arrogance!!' This was Darwin, Whewell's right-hand man, schizoid, scorning in private, smiling in public.

His notetaking became more secretive as his public position strengthened. The deterministic talk at Eras's dinner table was a world removed from the Revd Whewell's miraculous human-centred science. Darwin pressed on, stomach notwithstanding, cleansing a corrupt science, convinced he was right, dying to make his mark – his moral sanction coming from the huge shift to Dissenting values in the country. He was leading a crusading reform, breaking Whewell's old Tory Anglican dynasty, stripping the privileges it accorded man in the cosmos, as the Whigs were stripping the clergy's privileges on earth. Darwin became more and more frustrated by an arrogant theology. 'People often talk of the wonderful event of intellectual Man appearing,' he sniffed, smashing another idol, yet 'the appearance of insects with other senses is more wonderful.' Human chauvinism now outraged him.

Yet he was desperate to earn the respect of his scientific elders. His double life became more nerve-racking as the months passed, setting off an inner turmoil. What if they saw through his false face? He took so much pleasure in unravelling the enigmas of natural history, but his thoughts were becoming dangerous, his brooding masochistic. The pandemonium in his mind made a subtle and complex counterpoint to the public turmoil in urban Britain. (The country was now deep in an economic depression, and ahead lay the grimmest five years in the nineteenth century, with massive unemployment, starvation, and riot.) What he was mooting was disreputable in Anglican eyes, and socially subversive. His vision was no longer of a world personally sustained by a patrician God, but self-generated. From echinoderms to Englishmen, all had arisen through a lawful redistribution of living matter in response to an orderly changing geological environment.

He dashed off cryptic notes with increasing confidence. Everywhere he left the prominent stamp – 'my theory' – and he was in no two minds about its importance. He exuberantly claimed that 'my' theory 'would give zest to recent & Fossil Comparative Anatomy.' It would revolutionize the 'study of instincts, heredetary. [sic] & mind,' and transform the 'whole [of] metaphysics.'[17] It would – but not yet. The *ancien régime* had to give way first, the reactionary Church-and-corporation men, the sort now being swept out of the town halls countrywide as the radical Dissenters infused a new improving, secular, industrial spirit into society.

Darwin's secret notes left him looking like a radical Unitarian. They expressed the ethical feelings of a wider Dissenting community, sick

237

of slavery, demanding equality, against privilege. His abhorrence of slavery in this emotive period coloured his evolutionary fervour. He scribbled:

> Animals – whom we have made our slaves we do not like to consider our equals. – Do not slave holders wish to make the black man other kind? Animals with affections, imitation, fear. pain. sorrow for the dead.

Pain and suffering united enslaved man and the miserable beasts. As he wrote in 1838 abolitionist passions were being fired by the Whigs' former Lord Chancellor Henry Brougham, who was fighting for the immediate release of the Jamaican slaves. Martineau too was writing more moral tales after her American trip, of the beating and murder of slaves, and the heroism of the abolitionists – tales that Emma Wedgwood found stirring, despite the 'little Harrietisms' littering the text. Darwin was reflecting what fellow anti-slavers felt, and he was not alone in extending the ethical net from oppressed men to the forlorn brutes. The Quaker doctor John Epps – a London phrenologist, homoeopathist, and disestablishment campaigner – had come 'to consider all creatures as being equally important in the scale of creation as myself; to regard the poor Indian slave as my brother.'[18]

This Dissenting mood gave Darwin his sanction as he filled his heretical pages. Radical Dissenters were openly discussing mind and pain in nature. Many were adamant that all creation was conscious and suffering. Theirs was no 'happy world' admired through Paley's rose-tinted spectacles, teeming with 'delighted existence.' It was John Wesley's bleaker image, in which 'the whole creation travaileth and groaneth.' This was Epps's reading of St Paul. He was adamant that '*animals enjoy* MIND' – and with it personality, desires, and pain.[19]

But this mental egalitarianism absorbed by Darwin had disreputable doctrinal associations. Even though some Anglicans – like old William Kirby – accepted that animals showed a modicum of reason, demagogues like Epps mixed their views so promiscuously with anti-Anglican polemics that they acquired a dangerously heretical mystique. And however much reason Kirby granted to the worms, Darwin gave them something infinitely more abominable, a place in the dirt among the roots of man's family tree. Here he was, scratching breathlessly:

> if we choose to let conjecture run wild then animals our fellow brethren in pain, disease death & suffering & famine; our slaves in the most laborious work, our companion in our

amusements. they may partake, from our origin in one
common ancestor we may all be netted together.

The dangerous point was that man's mind had emerged from the
worm's in the first place. This was the crux.[20] By subjecting mind
and morality to self-evolving forces, he threatened the ideals so
cherished by the geological gentry: human dignity and accountability.
If man was only a better sort of brute, where was his spiritual
dignity, and if he had self-evolved, what of his moral accountability
to God, no more his Creator? Since moral accountability, with
eternal punishment and rewards, was part of the fabric binding
society, that too would crash.

Had Lyell or Owen or Sedgwick or Whewell known his beliefs,
they would have found them utterly demoralizing. Darwin could
expect a furore among his geological friends if they discovered his
secret. No more 'hail fellow, well met.' He could be labelled as a
traitor. His respectability would be compromised. Not only would
his science be impugned. He himself would be accused of reckless
abandon.

17

Mental Rioting

THE NEW SECRETARY continued brainstorming, 'mental rioting' he called it. By February 1838 he was ploughing through a
second pocketbook (the maroon 'C' Notebook).[1]

He was mulling over fancy and farmyard breeds. He traipsed
down Regent Street on crisp spring mornings to talk pedigree dogs
and pigeon-fancying at the zoo museum. The subject seemed
mundane, set against the platypuses and pythons, bottled snakes and
spirit-dripping bats. But the landed gents had more esoteric lore
about dogs than about all the zoo animals put together. William
Yarrell's were the best brains for picking. Yarrell was a gun-and-dog
man himself – or rather a newspaper wholesaler, but in a town with
fourteen dailies he could afford to indulge his country passions. He
was a mine of facts on domestic varieties, crosses, hybrids, and
foreign escapees, and his tips littered Darwin's notes. He taught
Darwin about crossing farmyard stock, and how older, established
breeds always dominate the hybrid offspring. Darwin fidgeted in his
Marlborough Street study that spring, jotting anecdotes of blood
hounds, gun dogs, and horse crosses, while dreaming of galloping
over Shropshire fields.

All along, he had assumed that wild variants appeared ready-
adapted, but the breeders were leaving him uneasy. What if 'in
course of ages ten thousand varieties' are produced '& those alone
preserved which are well adapted'? It was a discordant but interesting
idea. Not *all* offspring need be a good fit; think of the grotesque, the
runts. He now conceded that two types were possible, 'adaptations'
and 'Monsters,' the good and the bad, with the latter leading to the
ugly. To produce the fanciers' whimsies, the top-knotted pigeons,
hairless dogs, tailless cats, and deformed pigs, breeders were picking

the 'monsters.' They were cutting across nature's grain. He asked Yarrell outright: weren't breeders going *against* nature? Their way of 'picking varieties' was surely 'unnatural.'[2]

Humans not only selected animals, they were self-selectors. People picked and chose mates, favouring certain traits; they were in the mêlée, part of nature's process. Darwin was convinced that *Homo sapiens* was a single species split into climatically adapted clusters. He damned slave-owners for setting themselves up as a superior species, and he whittled away at their arguments, looking at the subject from every odd angle. Since the day on Chiloé in 1834 when a whaler's surgeon mentioned that the Sandwich Islanders' lice died on Englishmen, he was fascinated, and collected parasites from the various races to try to prove the 'origin of man one.'[3]

He came up with a new word for the process of development by transmutation at this time. 'Descent' he called it, and the descent of man was as legitimate a subject as the descent of cats and cows.

As the weather warmed, he began to reassess nature's perfection in his picture of descent. The whole theology of 'perfection' had been lambasted by the secularist fanatics as a sort of justification for the status quo – the notion that everything is as it should be. It had reigned supreme in Cambridge circles, and Darwin had never doubted it. But he began to see that perfect adaptations were not the whole story. Nature herself was eliminating the 'monsters' that breeders fancied. How did her scythe work, how were the freaks killed? In one instance he actually mooted a struggle to decide the fittest. He imagined a 'chance offspring' that had 'a little more vigour' – a head start – by virtue of some peculiarity. Then he cut to talk of strutting male combat, 'warlike' cocks, and females preferring the 'victorious' males.[4] It was a flash whose light dimmed for the moment.

He was pulling away from Cambridge theology: his example suggested that perfection *might* be the serendipitous product of chance. In fact, fitness had to be chancy given the quirks of climate. A gargoyle in one environment might be a godsend in another. His doodlings became fascinating at this point. 'If puppy born with thick coat then [in warm climates it would be a] monstrosity, [but] if brought into cold country . . . [it would be a good] adaptation.' Even good and bad, adaptation and deformity, were not the absolutes they once seemed. Their value fluctuated with the environment. Again it was another brilliant flash that faded.

He overturned it all by considering a better – and more goal-directed – way to produce adaptations. How did flippers appear on land animals whose homes were frequently flooded? He followed

Lamarck in suggesting they met the challenge by altering their habits. The ancestors of ducks and otters had begun by paddling, fishing, and exploiting the new resources. These habits, repeated incessantly, became ingrained; the animals now instinctively swam, stretched the skin between the toes, strengthened the muscles, and ultimately ended up with webbed feet. This was the pure, unadulterated Lamarckism that Lyell lampooned, Sedgwick execrated, and the geologists damned as rubbish. Darwin was now deep in his Lamarckian phase. Quietly, to himself, he praised the Frenchman's 'prophetic spirit in science –. the highest endowment of lofty genius' – words he would never repeat in public.[5]

He started firing questions at breeders, not singly of course, but whole *lists*, querying the way babies take after one parent and whether females 'prefer certain males.' Being interested in the 'Effects of habit' on the body he also wanted to know about 'trades affecting form of man' – whether blacksmiths' biceps are passed on to their boys.[6] Be it Mr Wynne, his father's gardener and an oracle on farmyard breeds, or the back-room zoologists, everyone suffered his strange quizzing. He tried any and every tack to get a handle on the inheritance of peculiarities in animals and man.

He was now in and out of the zoologists' museum continually, tapping Gould's brains on birds and Yarrell's on the barnyard. He heard a French visitor announce that the Galapagos tortoises were so many distinct species, finally confirming what he suspected. Gould and Waterhouse were in the midst of describing the *Beagle* specimens, with Darwin managing the whole operation. But the Treasury money remained tight. He restricted Gould to fifty illustrations of birds, to keep within budget, and even then he could only afford five pence each to have them coloured. He turned down a naturalists' dinner with Henslow, apologizing that he was 'tied firmly by the leg' as a result of co-ordinating the *Zoology*.[7]

FitzRoy was making his own apologies. Darwin's *Journal* was printed and awaiting the Captain's volume before it could be published. But FitzRoy's was late: 'I am rather old fashioned in habits as well as ideas – Ergo – a slow coach,' he explained. Darwin was frustrated, and also a bit wary after FitzRoy's splenetic outburst about the preface. Still, he was a landlubber now. He no longer shared the Captain's table. He did not have to smile sweetly and stay silent. The FitzRoys invited him over to tea at the end of March, and Darwin told his sister: 'The Captain is going on very well, – that is for a man, who has the most consummate skill in looking at everything & every body in a perverted manner.' He began to wonder about the quality of FitzRoy's work. The third volume – Capt. King's – was frankly impenetrable; 'no pudding for little shool [sic] boys [was] ever so heavy. It abounds with Natural History of a very trashy nature. – I trust the Captain's own volume will be better.' The Secretary of the best scientific society in town was imposing his own high standards.

Darwin's geology book was taking shape by now. He raced on through the spring, mentally splashing around in blue lagoons as he wrote up coral reefs. He was 'covering so much paper' that it would be impossible to contain his ideas in a single volume. At first he thought he could keep coral atolls and volcanic islands together and follow up with another volume later, but even these two topics took on lives of their own and had to be divorced. He marched on resolutely, describing the Atlantic Islands and the Cape of Good Hope, talking on earthquakes at the Geological, managing the *Zoology*, scribbling on descent.[8]

On the question of descent, mankind was now his focus. He had reached the walls of the citadel. Evolution, he believed, explained every mental tic, every bodily posture: not only the spine and spleen, but people's habits, instincts, thoughts, feelings, conscience, and morality. 'Man – wonderful Man' must collapse into nature's cauldron. Man, 'with divine face, turned towards heaven,' – 'he is not a deity, his end under present form will come . . . he is no exception. – he possesses some of the same general instincts, & feelings as animals.' Plumbing the radical depths Darwin saw the cataclysmic consequences. 'Once grant that species . . . may pass into each other . . . & whole fabric totters & falls.'[9] The Creationist 'fabric' and all it entailed was his target. He peered into the future and saw the old miraculous edifice collapsing, even as Sedgwick saw Anglican society crumbling as a consequence.

The refrain was reinforced by his first sight of an ape. It was an unseasonably warm day, 28 March, when he rode to the zoo, and 'by the greatest piece of good fortune' it was hot enough for the rhino to be turned out. 'Such a sight has seldom been seen, as to behold the rhinoceros kicking & rearing' in high spirits, he told his sister. But what really enthralled him was Jenny, the first orang-utan ever to go on display at the Gardens. Jenny caused a sensation, with the savants as much as the socialites, and she had just been presented – in appropriate feminine apparel – to the Duchess of Cambridge. The entrepreneurial Council had bought the three-year-old in November 1837 for £105 and installed her in the specially heated giraffe house.

Here Broderip described the youngster's 'grave' though 'sage deport-ment' (he had obviously caught her in a sullen mood).[10] Darwin too saw her full range of passions, and he regaled Susan with her antics:

the keeper showed her an apple, but would not give it her, whereupon she threw herself on her back, kicked & cried, precisely like a naughty child. – She then looked very sulky & after two or three fits of pashion [sic], the keeper said, 'Jenny if you will stop bawling & be a good girl, I will give you the apple.['] – She certainly understood every word of his, &, though like a child, she had great work to stop whining, she at last succeeded, & then got the apple, with which she jumped into an arm chair & began eating it, with the most contented countenance imaginable.

His first ape made a profound impression, but this anecdote belied the deeper importance of Jenny's human-like emotions. He was struck by her comprehension; it became another missile in that cockshy he had made of human arrogance: another hard-hitting fact to knock mankind off its pedestal. He exclaimed in his notes:

Let man visit Ourang-outang in domestication, hear expressive whine, see its intelligence when spoken [to]; as if it understands every word said – see its affection. – to those it knew. – see its passion & rage, sulkiness, & very actions of despair; let him look at savage, roasting his parent, naked, artless, not improving yet improvable & let him dare to boast of his proud preeminence.

Of course he had never seen a cannibal feast, but, compared to Fuegians and Maoris, Jenny Orang came off well in her civilized cell.[11]

'So much for Monkeys, & now for Miss Martineau,' he wrote home. They were all ears for the gossip, and things between Erasmus and Harriet were shameless. Charles reported that she had been 'as frisky lately as the Rhinoceros. – Erasmus has been with her noon, morning, and night: – if her character was not as secure, as a mountain in the polar regions she certainly would lose it.' They were clearly living in each other's pockets (presumably to the Doctor's disgust), and she admitted as much without blushing. 'Lyell called there the other day & there was a beautiful rose on the table, & she coolly showed it to him & said "Erasmus Darwin" gave me that. – How fortunate it is, she is so very plain; otherwise I should be frightened.'

It pushed Charles into thinking about marriage himself, and the future. He was twenty-nine, his heart was troubling, and he faced life alone. 'We poor bachelors are only half men, – creeping like caterpillars through the world, without fulfilling our destination,' he joked as his Cambridge crony Charles Whitley was married.

> Of the future I know nothing I never look further ahead than
> two or three Chapters – for my life is now measured by
> volume, chapters & sheets & has little to do with the sun. As
> for a wife, that most interesting specimen in the whole series
> of vertebrate animals, Providence only know[s] whether I shall
> ever capture one or be able to feed her if caught.[12]

The *Journal* would soon be published, the *Zoology* was under way, the specimens farmed out. In the foreseeable future he would finish the task that had brought him to London. What then? He began a cool deliberation, counting his life options again, applying his telegraphic technique to the prospects of marriage and money. Like everything else, they had to be analysed and abstracted in an obsessively orderly fashion. He listed the pros and cons on the back of an old letter.

The advantages of staying single were manifold: 'Travel. Europe, yes? America????' He circled Europe in pencil; it was a nice idea. He had been round the world but knew almost nothing of the Continent. What he would give to make an 'exclusively geological' tour of the 'United States'! Or else 'If I dont travel. – Work at transmission of Species' and get back to the 'simplest forms of life.' That was it, days of scientific leisure with Eras pointing the way. 'Live in London for where else possible in small house, near Regents Park – keep horse – take Summer tours.'

Marriage was the down side of the equation. All this would go by the board, and the options were stark. He might have to 'work for money.' Could he continue his science 'with children & [being] poor?' 'No,' he answered poignantly. And without his zoological avocation to keep him sane, 'could I live in London like a prisoner?' Obviously not; so he would have to look out of town. What better way of earning a living than in a 'Cambridge Professorship, either Geolog[y]. or Zoolog[y].' A chair like Henslow's would suit nicely, providing an income and an agreeable lifestyle. The incongruity of a transmutationist holding a chair at an unreformed Anglican seminary did not strike him. 'Then Cambridge Professorship, – & make the best of it,' he added with a flourish.

But suppose he married and didn't get a chair? This alternative was the bleakest scenario. He would again end up in 'poverty;' and without a scientific sideline he would be a 'fish out of water' in Cambridge, an idle down-at-heel gent with a nagging wife. No, this wouldn't do either. To keep up his science he would require both independent means and a place out of town. Lyell twitted him often enough that the country dulled the intellect, no doubt believing that the shire 'mists' would extinguish his 'volcanic speculations.' But Lyell's lifestyle was losing its attractions in the wretched, dirty metropolis. At last he reached a conclusion.

> I have so much more pleasure in direct observation, that I could not go on as Lyell does, correcting & adding up new information to old train & I do not see what line can be followed by man tied down to London.
> In country, experiment & observation on lower animals, - more space.[13]

He had his line to follow, a threatening new theory to pursue, not a book like Lyell's *Principles* to go on safely revising. Accordingly, if his father would indulge him, he would marry and follow the Revds Henslow, Jenyns, and Fox into the country and continue his research.

Money was the operative, but the Doctor had considerable investments and income. His £20,000 in government bonds was dwarfed by the capital loaned as mortgages to Shropshire's first families. This brought a handsome return: by the 1830s some £7000 a year, showing that the Doctor was 'as financially agile as he was physically ponderous.' Charles was reminded of it in April, when he was invited to dinner by the 'awesomely polite Robert Clive' (a Shropshire Tory MP, son of the Earl of Powis, and grandson of the empire builder, Robert Clive of India). He had no illusions about the offer. 'It really is very civil of him, as it is of course all meant to show his friendship to my Father.' The Doctor – having no scruples about subsidizing local Tories – had lent the Earl £50,000, and even now kept the mortgage deeds under his bed.[14] If wealth could buy Charles aristocratic friends, it could certainly buy him a leisurely future. He could live life to the full, one of the last generation of self-financed scientific gents, whose home was his laboratory.

But Cambridge still appealed. On 10 May he took four days out to visit Henslow. He was lionized at Henslow's party the first night, and rode over to talk fish with Jenyns the next morning. Then back to talk plants with Henslow, to ask why oceanic islands should have so many unique species (although knowing by now that these were the descendants of mainland immigrants). After this he threw himself

246

into the serious business of parties and bowls on a college green. Having been driven mad for months by the cart-wheel clatter of cobbled London, he was pleasantly 'deafened with nightingales singing.' He dined in Trinity and gloried in Haydn's *Creation* in the chapel – 'the last chorus seemed to shake the very walls' – before moving on to Sedgwick's party.[15] This was the life: more and more he saw himself set up in Cambridge, his heresies on the creation tucked away in a private drawer. It was a tonic that put a new spring in his step.

Coming back down, he continued to mull over domestic breeds. He looked at the way show pigeons were pinched and pulled, bustled and bonneted, like the ephemeral female fashions. At this stage he believed these had nothing to do with 'real' nature, but the process of producing fancy animals was oddly instructive.

This move into the farmyard was natural given his interest in gundogs and game birds. He had grown up in the agricultural heart of England, where horticulture and husbandry magazines lay around every manor house. His mother had kept pigeons; Uncle Jos was a leading sheep breeder who had introduced short-haired Spanish merinos into his flock. Uncle John Wedgwood cultivated dahlias and advised him on plant crosses. Landowners had a wealth of knowledge about producing domestic breeds to order; they were the people to quiz, not the closet taxonomists. Look at the way Lord Orford increased his greyhounds' stamina, by 'picking out finest of each litter & crossing them.' Breeders were *selecting* their traits.

He located a pamphlet that made the point exactly. It was by that most liberal of squires, Sir John Sebright: a retrenching, free-trading Whig who had ushered the Reform Bill through Parliament. The seventy-year-old Sebright knew Yarrell. He owned land in three counties and was a brilliant bird breeder, who boasted he could 'produce any feather in [three] years & any form in [six].'[16] His pamphlet provided the key to picking and choosing. But it also went further to distinguish Nature's scythe:

> A severe winter, or a scarcity of food, by destroying the weak and the unhealthy, has had all the good effects of the most skilful selection. In cold and barren countries no animals can live to the age of maturity, but those who have strong constitutions; the weak and the unhealthy do not live to propagate their infirmities.

Darwin scored this passage with its 'excellent observations of sickly offspring being cut off' before they could breed. He was beginning to appreciate the darker side of nature. Experienced breeders like Sebright also laid emphasis on the sexual struggle. He talked of the females falling to 'the most vigorous males' and claimed that 'the strongest individuals of both sexes, by driving away the weakest, will enjoy the best food, and the most favourable situations, for themselves and for their offspring.'[17] Here was evidence of the natural wastage that Darwin had begun mooting.

The way farmers mated select animals exposed the 'whole art of making [domestic] varieties.' But Darwin did not see the breeders mimicking Nature. For him the farmyard remained an unnatural laboratory, and sheep and dogs had unnatural histories. Nature was expunging runts and thrusting the fit forward; fanciers were rescuing the freaks to breed from. The laws of the jungle were not those of a gentleman's game park. Transmuting nature and producing an ornamental duck were asymmetrical acts. The latter was a 'mere monstrosity propagated by art.'[18]

He fired questions at his cousin Fox about crossing domestic breeds. 'It is my prime hobby & I really think some day, I shall be able to do something on that most intricate subject species & varieties.' This was his first admission that he was working on more ticklish aspects.

Dogs and ducks, if nothing else, gave him strategic ammunition, and he was always trawling for facts to floor the expected opposition. He devised ripostes using these farmyard and fireside examples. There must have been 'a thousand intermediate forms' between the otter and its land ancestor, he ruminated. 'Opponents will say, show me them. I will answer yes, if you will show me every step between bull Dog & Greyhound.'[19]

The *Journal* was left sitting, waiting for FitzRoy's volume, but there was action on other fronts. He had something to show for the London sojourn, both in his *Zoology* (the first number of Waterhouse's *Mammalia* was now out), and his geology of the voyage, already up to New Zealand. The transmutation still told in the pit of his stomach, but he had learned to take long rides as a restorative, and was 'astonished to find there is in truth pretty country within three miles of London.'

In town, he restricted his party-going to Erasmus's 'brilliant' dinners ('as all his invariably are'). Eras's life of 'literary leisure' was still sustained by salmon suppers with the Hensleighs, Martineau, and Carlyle. A penny-pinching Charles reeled at their expense. After one he reported home that 'I should . . . be sorry to pay for it.' 'NB. tell the Governor [the Doctor] the desert alone cost 8^s : $6^{d.}$' At the time Martineau was starting her three-volume novel of common folk, *Deerbrook*, with its surgeon-hero. Charles waylaid her at table, flabbergasted that such fluent prose should trip off her tongue, or at least her pen, when he was stumbling and grumbling, befogged by grammar and confused by commas. He was disgusted that she 'never has occasion to correct a single word she writes.' He only salvaged something of his self-respect on discovering that she was 'not a complete Amazonian, & knows the feeling of exhaustion from thinking too much.' 'I forgot to say,' he reported to Susan, deliberately putting the cat among the pigeons (knowing the Doctor would get to hear of it), 'Miss Martineau is going to pay me a visit some day, to look at me as author in my den, so we had quite a flirtation together.'[20]

In his den life was degenerating. He continued mutating species, but each conceptual leap turned the screw on his stomach. Just down from Cambridge, he was feeling jumpy about the hysteria his views would unleash among his clerical friends. He had gone far beyond Lamarck — Lamarck, so despised by Sedgwick and Whewell, who were blowing the revolutionary storm clouds back across the Channel. He switched to a disarming tactic: 'Mention persecution of early Astronomers,' he scribbled. 'If I want some good passages against, opposition of divines to progress of knowledge. see Lyell.' His friend had written on Galileo's fate during the Inquisition, and on astronomy dealing a death blow to religious obscurantism to 'set posterity free.'[21] Darwin saw himself in the torture chair, suffering to set the future free, waving Lyell's words at the Whewells of the world.

That spring Darwin was in his deepest radical phase, playing with inflammatory issues as the country slid further into depression. His notes were acquiring a compulsive quality. He had reduced life to its starkest, to its living elements — self-organizing atoms. This sort of flaming science was favoured by street agitators, the people trying to overthrow the undemocratic state. It petrified clerical society; self-sufficiency was tantamount to atheism. With Christianity part of the law of the land, and used to keep the lower orders in check, anything that undermined it was seditious. If living atoms had the power of self-development, the divine influence of Sedgwick's God was lost. And since that influence worked through the Church, the chain of command from God down through the priesthood into nature would be snapped. And with that, Sedgwick believed, came the end of civilization.[22]

Darwin had boxed himself into a corner. He was not chaffing at Anglican thraldom, or champing at clerical iniquities, whatever the secular talk around Eras's table. Personally he envied his mentors' privileged lifestyle. But he was repeating radical talk: mind a product of matter, living atoms organizing themselves. And it did provide a ready-made solution to one problem: the evolution and inheritance of instincts. How do a father's instincts pass to a son, or a hen blackbird's to her chicks? How do mental traits pass from one generation to another? He needed some sort of physical code for thoughts and feelings, something material that can be handed on. If instincts are products of neural organization, they will be inherited as part of the brain. And if altered instincts modify the brain's physiology, these changed behaviours will be transmitted.[23] It was a solution, but it required the kind of mind-matter identity favoured by freethinkers and the most extreme Dissenters.

His notebooks were now alive with the shocking metaphors wielded by the medical hellions. He equated all mental activity with brain states. 'Thought' was inherited; 'it is difficult to imagine it anything but structure of brain,' he declared. Habits and beliefs had evolved, inextricably linked to the mental machinery. Every instinct, every desire could be located here, each an evolutionary inheritance – even the adoration of God: 'love of the deity [is the] effect of organization. oh you Materialist!' he whispered.[24] Such crudities were the stock-in-trade of the swelling ranks of secularists, slapping the faces of tithe-rich priests. He had heard this kind of challenge from the censured Plinian phrenologists ten years earlier; he could still hear it on any street corner.

He approached the inflammatory subject with a mixture of dread and exhilaration. 'Materialism' itself was a pejorative label. Technically it meant nothing but matter existing (and certainly no spirits), or thought being a function of the brain, but it was indiscriminately used to damn anyone looking for the laws of mind or the mutability of species.

It terrorized the Anglican anatomists, who saw it slooshing through the medical underworld like sewage, especially in disease-ridden London. London was sin city, the 'modern Tyre.' It was taught in the fiercer medical schools, and the artisan atheists championed a soulless self-sustaining universe.

The materialist man of the moment was the flamboyant professor of medicine at University College, John Elliotson. A self-proclaimed 'cockney,' Elliotson displayed astonishing bravura. He championed the London University over the 'barbarous' Oxford and Cambridge, and colleagues considered him the 'strongest materialist' of his day. His stock provocation was that the brain exudes thought as the liver does bile. It was Darwin's *bon mot* exactly: 'thought, however unintelligible it may be, seems as much function of organ, as bile of liver.' But Darwin's goading had a sting that even Elliotson's lacked. Everyone accepted that gravity was an intrinsic 'property of matter;' no one made it a spiritual adjunct. So 'Why is thought' not seen as 'a secretion of [the] brain' in the same way? 'It is [because of] our arrogance, it is our admiration of ourselves.'[25]

Charles tried this out on Hensleigh, the safest of sparring partners, when his cousin arrived back in town. Hensleigh had been away at Maer after resigning his magistrates' post over the swearing of unnecessary oaths, which he considered unChristian. He had made a huge financial sacrifice for his principles, and in debating the dualism of mind and body he showed similar scruples. Charles's theory of the brain was, he declared, 'nonsense.'

The talk was frank. 'Hensleigh says the love of the deity & thought of him or eternity, only difference between the mind of man & animals,' he recorded. How could this be? Savages were a living disproof – 'how faint [is this idea of God] in a Fuegian or Australian!' If God had planted the knowledge of his existence in humans, all would possess it.[26] There was no need for the Fuegian-European gradation in religious belief – unless, of course, it had evolved.

Darwin's words were private, but Elliotson's showed what could happen if he went public. The professor's lectures in the later 1830s were greeted with howls by the medical Tories. They trashed his cynical 'Spinozaism,' which denied free will and a soul and took from the 'thousands of the despised and the miserable' their 'consoling' Christian hopes in a future recompense.[27]

Darwin's materialism was no less rank and reviled, and he knew it. His geological confrères saw the social fabric being torn apart by such provocative babble. It was all that Lyell hated in Lamarck, all that upright Tories deprecated in street atheists. There were blasphemy laws and sedition acts to curb it, and courts to prosecute it. Darwin had seen harassment. He could recall the Plinian fracas, and Taylor and Carlile being hounded out of Cambridge. The clampdown was continuing, with disgraced materialists falling like London flies. No wonder he was brooding about persecution. At this point he might have begun his morbid interest in any 'curious trial' reported in the dailies, when he began to find court cases 'the most interesting part of the paper.'[28]

Medical loudmouths, Dissenting extremists, and artisan activists

251

were not the sort of company he wanted to keep. They were up on their soapboxes to contest medical or clerical privileges. All had run-ins with the authorities, and for some prison was a short step away. The cocky Elliotson hit the headlines again this June. He was carpeted by University College when his female patients ran amuck in mesmeric trances. His resignation was now inevitable. (It came at the end of December.) Whatever the cause, many heaved a mighty sigh of relief when he came crashing down.[29] *This* was where material-ism was located – on a sliding scale between disgraced doctors and loutish low-life. And it wasn't a slippery slope that Darwin wanted to be caught on.

In June his illness intensified as he sank deeper into the quagmire. Bad stomachs and headaches accompanied a fluttering heart, and all the while he transformed animals and materialized thought. He was now overworked, worried, and laid up for days on end. He faced three years' grind to finish the *Beagle* geology before he could escape the rat-race, and it would be an uphill struggle. 'I hope I may be able to work on right hard during the next three years . . . but I find the noddle & the stomach are antagonistic powers, and that it is a great deal more easy to think too much in a day, than to think too little – What thought has to do with digesting roast beef, – I cannot say.'[30]

His developing science had social implications that were just as radical. Because thoughts and actions are inherited, it was essential to educate working men *and* women – which would double the benefits passed on to the children. 'Educate all classes,' he scribbled amid the evolutionary notes, 'improve the women. (double influence) & mankind must improve.' On paper it looked similar to the demands of the red Lamarckians (who wanted women properly schooled because both parents passed acquired traits to the children). But in fact the whole Wedgwood-Darwin family was committed to limited female education, and Martineau even more so.[31] Still, it was the strongest stand on environmental conditioning that Darwin would take.

He was now sounding like a dissident. 'Man in his arrogance thinks himself a great work. worthy the interposition of a deity, more humble & I believe true to consider him created from animals.' No stone was left unturned to understand how this could have come about. He made his first forays into the origin of facial expressions at this time. Charles Bell, so mauled by Darwin's classmates in Edinburgh, had seen grinning as originally designed to expose the canines. Darwin twisted the stiletto in: 'no doubt a habit gained by formerly being a baboon with giant canine teeth,' he scoffed, taking the mauling to an unprecedented degree. It was an intriguing way of tackling human ancestry, and he saw its potential. 'Laughing modified barking., smiling modified laughing. Barking to tell [troop] . . . good news. discovery of prey. – arising no doubt from want of assistance. – crying is a puzzler.'[32]

Such a slap at human pride would leave his theories – if they became known – ripe for exploitation by the extremists. The pauper presses were adept at pirating. Any grist to their mill could be churned out cheaply and find its way to every street corner. And there was a real danger of it with the militants using materialism to underwrite their anti-clerical propaganda.

Censored works were routinely pirated, none more so than the surgeon William Lawrence's. Lawrence was a republican whose scientific rhetoric achieved a pyrotechnical brilliance. He had been forced to resign his post at the College of Surgeons and recant his views after a vicious attack in the Tory *Quarterly Review*. The *Quarterly* execrated his materialist explanations of man and mind. The Court of Chancery ruled his *Lectures on Man* blasphemous, which destroyed its copyright. This was a ringing endorsement to atheist ears. Six pauper presses pirated the offending book, keeping it continuously in print for decades. The latest disreputable edition had only just hit the streets, advertised by flyposters 'sneering at the clergy.'[33] As a result, although officially withdrawn, Lawrence's *magnum opus* could be found on every dissident's bookshelf.

Darwin had his own rough-edged edition of the *Lectures*, sandwiched in cheap boards, the sort that could be picked up for a song in any working-class bookshop. His copy had been pirated by the notorious shoemaker-turned-publisher William Benbow, who financed his flaming politics by selling pornographic prints.[34] Darwin only had to stare at this shabby tome (which he was currently using) to see the fate awaiting him. He was no atheist, nor would he countenance being highjacked by sleazy fanatics. Lawrence was a reminder of how one's good name could be dragged through the mud.

Darwin's schizoid existence intensified as he moved towards the centre of literary society. With Lyell's help, he was elected to the Athenaeum Club on 21 June (along with Charles Dickens) and found it very agreeable. He dined here daily, confessing that it made him feel 'like a gentleman, or rather like a Lord.' 'I enjoy it the more, because I fully expected to detest it,' he conceded, rather alienating Eras; 'one meets so many people there, that one likes to see.' An inveterate society watcher, he relished spying the Good and Great. A

253

gentleman had certain obligations, his science underpinned certain values. It was an age, one teacher said, when 'not *knowledge* alone, but *character* is power; when knowledge without character can procure no more than temporary and very transient pre-eminence.'[35] Of all the clubs, the Athenaeum stood for knowledge and character, and Darwin was not about to sacrifice one on an altar to the other.

Midsummer in Marlborough Street was a time for celebration. The Hensleigh Wedgwoods had moved in next door to Erasmus, and Catherine Darwin and cousin Emma were staying a week with them. Charles popped over from time to time, and they were 'a very pleasant merry party.' One evening Thomas and Jane Carlyle came for dinner. Emma missed most of what the sonorous Scot said, although she found him 'remarkably pleasant and ... straightforward.' For his part, Charles was noticing Emma's own remarkably pleasant manners.[36]

Still, London was full of 'smoke, ill health & hard work,' and when the party at the 'Darwin & Wedgwood Arms' broke up, he resolved to recuperate. He needed a tonic and travel promised it. Illness finally drove him out of town, and out of England. He took his first hammering holiday since the voyage, travelling to the Scottish Highlands.

On 23 June he set off in a steam boat for Edinburgh, and the old sea-dog 'enjoyed the spectacle, wretch that I am, of two ladies & some small children quite sea sick, I being well.' He spent a day in Edinburgh, his first since dropping out of medical school in 1827, and took 'a solitary walk on Salisbury crags' to 'call up old thoughts of former times.'[37] That was another age, separated by a gulf. He was changing, Britain was changing: here he was, on 28 June 1838, the day a slip of a girl, a month past her eighteenth birthday, was crowned Queen Victoria.

He pushed on into the remote Highlands, past Loch Leven and north through Fort William to the mouth of Glen Roy, arriving a week after leaving London. Here he enjoyed 'the most beautiful weather, with gorgeous sunsets, & all nature looking as happy' as he felt. He wandered up a dirt track, through a wide green valley, and into the rolling hills. The Glen stretched on for miles, but well before he reached the half-way point he could see the famous 'parallel roads,' three of them, running along its sides. These were among the great geological riddles, and what he had come to see. They were not actually roads. Standing on the middle one, he realized that it was not flat. It was a slanted shelf, 60 feet wide with a twenty-degree tilt. The same for the other terraces, 200 feet below and 100 feet above him. These 'parallel roads' went right around Glen Roy as far as the eye could see, while behind him, twelve miles away, Ben Nevis, Britain's tallest peak, completed the panorama, a snow-clad sentinel guarding the enigmatic formation.

None of his geological sightings – 'not even the first volcanic island, the first elevated beach, or the passage of the Cordillera' – had been so intriguing. He knew that the 'roads' had lured geologists to this remote spot for years. Were they traces of an ancient lake, which had dropped on three occasions, each time leaving a shore-line cut into the mountain side? Some thought so and assumed that the valley had once been dammed to hold the lake water.

Darwin approached the Glen armed with his theory of an oscillating earth's crust. He had seen terracing in Chile; there the 'roads' were littered in shells – they were obviously old beaches. If the mountains around Glen Roy had also risen stepwise out of the sea, old shores would be a tell-tale sign. Proving the parallel roads to be sea margins would in turn confirm his global geological theory. He was convinced that they must be old sea beaches, even if he could find no tell-tale barnacles or sea-shells. They had been formed at sea-level, after which the land had risen in three stages.

Satisfied, he started for home, his notebook bulging. 'Eight good days in Glen Roy' had done the trick. 'My Scotch expedition answered brilliantly.'[38] He was feeling on top of the world.

18

Marriage & Malthusian Respectability

FORTIFIED AND full of optimism, Charles came back via Shrewsbury in July 1838. So much had been boiling up in his mind as he thought on the religious implications of his theories that he decided to discuss everything with a sage old freethinker, his father. Marriage was also on the cards, more than ever. Three weeks after Emma Wedgwood caught his eye in Great Marlborough Street he was weighing up his options, looking for advice.

The Doctor foresaw the problems ahead. Charles could be walking into a trap. The Darwins and the Wedgwoods were united by marriage and divided by religion. Ever since old Erasmus scorned grandfather Josiah's Unitarianism as 'a featherbed to catch a falling Christian,' religion had been a sore point, so if Charles was serious about cousin Emma, he had better watch his step. The Doctor advised him to conceal his religious doubts lest they cause 'extreme misery.' His father spoke from experience. 'Things went on pretty well until the wife or husband became out of health,' he said, 'and then some women suffered miserably by doubting about the salvation of their husbands, thus making them likewise to suffer.'[1] The Wedgwood women in particular feared for their menfolk's eternal destiny.

In a way the Doctor's counsel seemed prophetic, with Charles now doubting many sacred truths and beset by debilitating illness.

Money was another desideratum, equally affecting wedded bliss. Here too the Doctor had to be consulted and Charles refined his cost/benefit analysis of marriage while at home. He plunged once more into the pros and cons of having children, balancing outgoings against obligations, future security against lost leisure. His calculations were typical of the wealthy classes, if rather blunt. Having jotted daily on animal breeding, it seemed natural that he should approach his own domestic crossing in the same fastidious way – and with the same utilitarian detachment.

On a blue scrap of paper, he filled up 'for' and 'against' columns, rambling in a self-centred way:

Marry	*Not Marry*
Children – (if it Please God) – Constant companion, (& friend in old age) who will feel interested in one, – object to be beloved & played with. – better than a dog anyhow. – Home, & someone to take care of house – Charms of music & female chit-chat. – These things good for one's health. – *but terrible loss of time.* –	Freedom to go where one liked – choice of Society & *little of it.* – Conversation of clever men at clubs – Not forced to visit relatives, & to bend in every trifle. – to have the expense & anxiety of children – perhaps quarelling – **Loss of time.** – cannot read in the Evenings – fatness & idleness – Anxiety & responsibility – less
My God, it is intolerable to think of spending ones whole life, like a neuter bee, working, working, & nothing after all. – No, no won't do. – Imagine living all one's day solitarily in smoky dirty London House. – Only picture to yourself a nice soft wife on a sofa with good fire, & books & music perhaps – Compare this vision with the dingy reality of Grt. Marlbro' St.	money for books &c – if many children forced to gain one's bread. – (But then it is very bad for ones health to work too much) Perhaps my wife wont like London; then the sentence is banishment & degradation into indolent, idle fool.

Marry – Mary – Marry Q.E.D.

The balance had shifted in marriage's favour – decisively. What the frustrated 'neuter bee' needed was a soft unsociable wife with a dowry, to allow him to work undisturbed. Without a wife there was no living on through children, 'no second life,' as he called it. The bee decided to change his caste, even though it meant 'I never should know French, – or see the Continent – or go to America, or go up in a Balloon.' 'Never mind my boy – Cheer up – One cannot live this solitary life, with groggy old age, friendless & cold, &

257

childless staring one in ones face, already beginning to wrinkle. – Never mind, trust to chance – keep a sharp look out.' It could not be that bad, after all, 'There is many a happy slave.'[2]

Better if his wife was 'an angel & had money' – like Emma. She was Josiah Wedgwood's granddaughter, Hensleigh's sister (and Eras's old companion), and about the only eligible daughter left in his small circle of acceptable family acquaintances. More importantly, her money would come as a dowry, making her more attractive than an independent breadwinner such as Martineau. Emma was safer, she offered security, and being his cousin he could accurately count the cost. Uncle Jos had given his son Josiah III a bond for £5000 and an allowance of £400 a year when he married Charles's sister Caroline the year before. With so many first-cousin marriages, Charles would not so much be tying the knot as adding another lucrative loop to the cord binding the Darwin-Wedgwoods together.

Marriage it was – a wife rather than a dog. To the obvious question, 'When?' his father advised 'soon,' and he agreed. Emma was perfect, already a model of domesticity. She could be a nursemaid, a matron, a protector, providing the comfort and seclusion he craved within four walls. Thinking himself so 'repellently plain' he actually doubted that she would accept, but, he said, 'I determined . . . to try my chance.'[3]

He recorded that he was 'very idle at Shrewsbury,' which meant working furiously to no avail. The time passed without any bombshell solutions to his problems of descent. But work he did; secure at home he opened two new leather-bound notebooks, one in the transmutation sequence ('D') and the other ('M') on its wider consequences. He was squaring up to the materialist conundrums, and setting out to explore the evolutionary basis of moral and social behaviour. Sixty pages of the 'M' notebook were filled in the 'idle' fortnight, with the opening words 'My father says . . .' setting the tone.

His shorthand scribblings became frenetic. He was still trying to explain how instincts pass from generation to generation, coded somehow in the brain. He taxed the Doctor over his demented patients, the effect of strokes, senility, the manifestations of madness, and the quirks of memory. He listened to anecdotes about old folks who could not remember anything, yet who could sing childhood songs almost instinctively, in a way that might almost 'be compared to birds singing.' A memory lying dormant throughout life, with the person unaware of it, made the idea of 'memories' passing across the generations as instincts seem less 'wonderful.'[4] Perhaps that was all instinct is: an unconscious memory physically written into the brain.

Fresh from his talks with the Doctor, and ready to take the plunge after his costing of matrimony, he rode over to Maer on 29 July in 'high spirits.' Emma too hoped that, if Charles saw more of her, 'he would really like me.' They whispered long and grew closer, later chewing a 'sentimental fat goose . . . over the Library fire' (a 'goose' being a comfy intimate chat). Nothing was said about marriage – it was too soon, or perhaps Charles lost his nerve – but they both looked forward to 'another goose.'

Unfortunately, at the sight of Emma, Charles threw his father's advice out of the window. The cousins had known each other for too long to keep secrets. He was still mulling over his heterodox brain science. At The Mount he had confessed that free will had no place in his determined world-system, and he carried his materialism with him to Maer. Neural matter acted under the iron rule of law, so how could thought have any freedom? He seemed to be sinking deeper, and it scared him. Writing notes on the psychology of panic, he turned inwards. 'I have awakened in the night. being slightly unwell & felt so much afraid.' 'The sensation of fear is accompanied by troubled beating of heart, sweat, trembling of muscles.' He must have opened his heart in more ways than one during their talks, unable to resist letting Emma in on his secret. His scribblings at Maer, in a new ink and in a new vein, suggest that he was taken aback by her response. He began devising ways of camouflaging his materialism. Don't mention it, he admonished himself, talk only of inherited mental behaviour: 'To avoid stating how far, I believe, in Materialism,' he scrawled in a rush, 'say only the emotions[,] instincts[,] degrees of talent, which are heredetary [sic] are so because brain of child resemble[s], parent stock.'[5] He was learning to guard his words.

He should have listened to his father. The Doctor said conceal, Emma made him reveal. But that was probably easy, for he had the one quality Emma prized above all others: 'he is the most open, transparent man I ever saw, and every word expresses his real thoughts.' And so, it seems, he mooted evolution too, but again she must have startled him by asking awkward questions about ultimate origins. Whatever was said, he realized the difficulty of carrying conviction and returned to his notebook chastened, warning himself to limit his remit. He must steer clear of first origins and explain only how organs or animals *change*; otherwise 'it will become necessary to show how the first eye is formed.'[6] And that he could not do.

He trained back to town on 1 August. He stood on the threshold, ready to shroud himself in family life as he up-ended conventional Anglican wisdom. He was convinced that his science was not only right, but as shattering as Galileo's. 'Mine is a bold theory,' he admitted – a profound view of human ancestry that would revolutionize philosophy and ethics. Or, as his words blared: 'Origin of man now proved. – Metaphysic must flourish. – He who understands baboon would do more towards metaphysics than Locke.' These intimations of immortality had more mundane repercussions. A rising self-importance led him to start dating his notes and to open a journal to record the key events in his life. He also penned a 1700-word recollection of his childhood, from the age of four to eleven, recording odd memories and incidents. It added up to a change, a new confidence that his pioneering research would not go unrecognized.[7]

After a few days in London he was enthralled by a review of the French mathematician Auguste Comte's *Positive Philosophy*, which convinced him that his view of the world was the right one. He sat absorbed in it at the Athenaeum, revelling in the covert swipes at Whewell, praising its tone as 'capital.' Mature science for Comte was characterized by belief in the rule of law, as Darwin himself held. All other approaches were mere relics – from the 'theological or fictitious' stage of human development (Comte was an atheist), relying on the hand of God, or the medieval 'metaphysical' stage, which had a world ruled by subtle emanations and mystic influences. This historical progression to modern science had a universal ring to it; Darwin even wondered whether children pass through similar stages, mentally recapitulating the cultural progress.

Comte believed that only 'positive' facts should make up true knowledge (hence his followers were called 'Positivists'). His notion of a 'theological state of science' was a 'grand *idea*,' Darwin jotted. And eminently exploitable; it provided a new pejorative tag for the Cambridge science to be superseded. 'Zoology itself is now purely theological,' Darwin declared. Savages like York Minster, who 'consider the thunder & lightning the direct will of the God,' were scarcely less primitive than the miracle-mongering 'philosopher who says the innate knowledge of creator has been implanted in us ... by a separate act of God,' rather than evolving according to 'his most magnificent laws.'

Divine anthropomorphisms and animisms were out; Comte was content in 'tracing facts to laws.' The review that Darwin sat reading in the Athenaeum baulked at following Comte *too* far, lest his rampant positivism end up 'poisoning the springs' of morality and religion. But Darwin was already one jump ahead, doing what the reviewer dreaded. Even 'our will may arise' from the 'laws of organization,' he declared; 'it is what my views tend to.' A few days later he reread the review so intently that he developed a headache from the stress. Dipping into Dickens cured it. But his migraines were getting worse, and he later visited Woolwich dockyards, 'trying to unbend my mind.'[8]

Others were taken by Comte's Positivism. Martineau went on to translate his book and wrote ecstatically: 'We find ourselves suddenly living and moving in the midst of the universe . . . not under capricious and arbitrary conditions . . . but under great, general, invariable laws, which operate on us as part of a whole.' Darwin had already indulged in similar flights, and Positivism simply intensified them. 'What a magnificent view one can take of the world,' he exclaimed. The vast sweep of law controlled the climate, the landscape, the changes in animals and plants, with everything synchronized 'by certain laws of harmony.'[9]

It was 'far grander' than the perverse idea of God individually crafting every slug and snail. The Almighty – personally creating 'a long succession of vile Molluscous animals – How beneath the dignity of him'! Darwin was working out a persuasive strategy, like Babbage giving God back his omnipotence, like the Dissenters giving the Creator some consistency: after all, what were miracles, but God interrupting himself? His laws stood supreme, no subsequent tinkering was necessary. Unitarians knew this, and so did Darwin. Only a 'cramped imagination' would have God 'warring against those very laws he established in all organic nature.'[10] Privately, Darwin was plugging into the larger Unitarian movement, summoning up Dissenting support, preparing to fire a wider audience with familiar clarion calls.

Darwin's denial of free will edged him closer to the metaphysical abyss. He now routinely reduced thought and behaviour to cerebral structure, boiling it down to bits of the brain. If wishes are a consequence of neural organization – evolving under the constraints of 'circumstance & education' – then anti-social behaviour can be inherited. 'Verily the faults of the fathers, corporeal & bodily are visited upon the children.' *That* was frightening. Acknowledging that patterns of behaviour and thought were inherited 'would make a man a predestinarian of a new kind, because he would tend to be an atheist.' But Darwin was no atheist. He accepted that all this resulted from God's natural laws, and if it looked like leading to a godless conclusion, a 'Man . . . would more earnestly pray "deliver us from temptation".' On the other hand, accepting this evolutionary determinism could transform human conduct, for a father would 'strive to improve his organization for his children's sake.' Men 'would only marry good women & pay detail[ed] attention to education & so put their children in way of being happy.'[11]

As he wrote this he was reading a predestinarian of the old kind,

Harriet Martineau. She was arguing against any 'universal moral sense,' claiming that among humans 'right' and 'wrong' are culturally conditioned, not spiritual endowments. Such moral relativism was common among radical Dissenters, and Darwin was primed to appreciate it after the *Beagle*'s visits to Tierra del Fuego and New Zealand. He accepted Harriet's axiom that moral norms are formed by external influences, that all vices and virtues depend on their social context.[12] Virtue could lie in slaughtering men in tribal war, or in altruistically saving life; it manifested in bizarre and unpredictable ways across the globe.

What if Polynesian mothers drown their children out of duty, or Eastern potentates laugh at English kings for lacking a hundred wives? This moral spectrum was no odder than dog breeds exhibiting different instincts. And the fact that all humans have some sort of morality (however expressed) was because 'man, like deer,' was a 'social animal.' Moral acts were as instinctive as a deer's warning bark. They had evolved from the social instincts to aid the cohesion of the human ancestral troop. They were socially useful, helping to cement relations. Even the Christian precepts, 'do unto others as yourself,' and 'love thy neighbour as thyself,' had evolved naturally out of our ancestors' 'sexual, parental & social instincts.'

He saw that his evolutionary prescriptions and the New Testament's morality 'come very near each other.' Both led to similar behaviour. Both demanded that people act morally out of 'dread of misery of future' – in this life for the evolutionist worried about his children, and in the next for the Christian. For both, duty before God meant providing for future happiness.[13] By the autumn of 1838 he had thrashed out all the social and moral issues with Hensleigh, Harriet, and Erasmus, and worked them into his evolutionary formula, enormously expanding its scope.

He had so much on the front burner that things were beginning to boil over. His geology book, now restricted to *Coral Reefs*, was grinding on slowly; he was trying to prove Glen Roy a former arm of the sea; and the *Zoology* numbers 'murder much of my time.' The notebooks were draining his energy and the *Journal* still was not out. Lyell had cannibalized the proofs for the '*juicy*' new edition of his textbook *Elements of Geology*, and Darwin was gratified that he had 'made such infinitely more use of my journal than I could have anticipated.' But there was no sign of FitzRoy's volume or a publication date. Lyell complained of the hold-up in his own preface, and Darwin recorded that FitzRoy 'looked rather black' and 'made a kind of growl' as he read it. 'I never cease wondering at his character,' he reported back to Lyell, 'so full of good & generous traits but spoiled by such an unlucky temper.' 'Some part of the organization of his brain wants mending,' he concluded, covertly introducing a topic dear to his heart.

Other ugly expressions intrigued him. He spent long hours peering at the zoo's baboons, trying to decipher their eyebrow movements. He teased monkeys by withholding nuts to induce 'peevish' expressions. Similarly tormented, the new orang-utan 'threw itself down on its back & kicked & cryed like [a] naughty child.' He climbed into the orang's cage to study her bashful, scheming, quizzical countenance close up. She would pout at her reflection, use straw as a tool, play the harmonica, and hide after disobeying her keeper.[14] The pouting and shame-face were eminently human, reflecting similar mental states, which left her cell-mate to conclude once again that there was no great gulf between a Fuegian savage and a civilized ape.

Even the human tantrum had evolved. We have emotions like 'revenge & anger,' however sublimated, because they have benefited our ape ancestors. 'Our descent, then,' is the root 'of our evil passions!!' he jotted. Good and evil were not moral absolutes so much as monkey attributes. Or, to put it more graphically: 'The Devil under form of Baboon is our grandfather!' Evolution explained the passions in a way nothing else could. Erasmus joked that Plato thought 'our "*necessary ideas* [of good and evil]" arise from the preexistence of the soul' – and that they 'are not derivable from experience' – which Darwin capped by adding 'read monkeys for preexistence [of the soul].'[15]

On 6 September he finished the important Glen Roy paper, destined for the Royal Society. He started reading voraciously, singling out books on human statistics that emphasized the law-like moral and social behaviour of populations. Religion, morality, and descent now dominated his thoughts. He still ploughed a lonely furrow, bottling up his feelings and fears. Mid-month he did timidly tell Lyell that he was ruminating 'on the classification & affinities & instincts of animals – bearing on the question of species – note book, after note book has been filled, with facts, which begin to group themselves *clearly* under sub-laws.'[16] Lyell could not have known the direction of his research, but it was a pointer.

Darwin was isolated. He needed an ally of Lyell's stature. He was also vulnerable, and a week later, on 21 September, his fear of persecution translated into a strange dream of execution. No sombre nightmare, this; it was almost flippant as he recalled it. Yet the execution was vivid enough to be remembered the next day. He dreamed 'that a person was hung & came to life, & then made many

263

jokes. about not having run away &c having faced death like a hero.'
Here was Darwin, standing his ground scientifically, still languishing
in his Marlborough Street 'prison,' waiting to plead that his views
were not actionable, perhaps recalling the poor devil hanged while he
was at Cambridge. Then he remembered from his anatomy days that
a person could not recover from hanging. So he switched mid-dream
to decapitation, the victim taking delight in 'showing [the] scar
behind [his neck]' where his head had been cut off, proving that 'he
had honourable wounds.'[17] The transmutationist was in the highway-
man's place, pleading honourable motives, but paying the price for
his treachery.

The condemned man continued reading, still interested in human
statistics. Late in the month he picked up the sixth edition of
Malthus's *Essay on the Principle of Population* – the polemical
account of humanity outstripping its food supply, and the weak and
improvident succumbing in the struggle for the available resources.

Malthus had rarely been more topical. In the depth of the depression, with unprecedented distress, the poor law and pauper riots
were on everybody's lips. Workhouses were still being attacked,
commissioners still being pelted. Malthus had denounced charity,
and the rioters abominated anything Malthusian that propped up the
New Poor Law. By now the dissident groups had come together
under an umbrella organization known as Chartism: they supported
the People's Charter, a list of demands for universal suffrage, annual
elections, and salaried MPs. This was a countrywide mass movement,
and the New Poor Law was one of its prime targets. Christian
Chartists denounced a system that would deny 'the distressed poor
their God-given right to a dignified support on their native soil.'
They were marching under banners in September that proclaimed
with the Psalmist, 'Dwell in the land, and verily thou shalt be fed.'
Chartist speeches, lambasting the 'cruel and detestable doctrines of
the Malthusians,' were heard by tens of thousands in the manufacturing towns, and reported in *The Times*.[18] Love him or loathe him,
Malthus could not be ignored.

Darwin knew the theory. With Martineau his dinner guest, how
could he not? Getting the poor off welfare increased competition among
working men and reduced taxes. Competition was paramount, making
Malthus a Whig free trader's godsend in the 1830s. But it was Malthus's
statistics that struck Darwin with a vengeance in his primed state.
Malthus calculated that, with the brakes off, humanity could double in
a mere twenty-five years. But it did not double; if it did the planet would

be overrun. A struggle for resources slowed growth, and a horrifying catalogue of death, disease, wars, and famine checked the population. Darwin saw that an identical struggle took place throughout nature, and he realized that it could be turned into a truly creative force.

He *had* thought that only enough individuals were born to keep a species stable. Now he accepted that wild populations, too, bred beyond their means. Like the architects of the poor law, nature showed no charity; individuals had to scrimp and struggle, like the growing gangs of scavengers on London's refuse heaps, with starvation staring them in the face. Darwin gained a unique understanding from Malthus. Others such as the botanist Augustin de Candolle wrote of plants being 'at war one with another.' But nobody, Darwin said, conveys 'the warring of the species' so strongly as Malthus.[19] Even then De Candolle meant only one species fighting another for space – no one had suggested that this was a civil war fought among members of the *same* species. In society and nature, paupers and brutes were both struggling, the best alone surviving. The face of nature was no longer smiling; it scowled at a gladiatorial arena, strewn with the corpses of the losers.

This population pressure became 'a force like a hundred thousand wedges' rammed between the members of a species, forcing 'gaps by thrusting out weaker ones.'[20] The best adapted varieties survive to breed, expanding at the expense of the rest, changing the whole species slowly. The same 'grand crush of population' that shook men from their indolence kept life at its peak of perfection.

In Darwin's nature, the many fall that the few might progress. Death acquired a new meaning, and there was enough of it around: with rising joblessness and homelessness, medical statisticians were compiling their 'ledgers of death' (mortality statistics) among the slum dwellers.[21] Nature's ledgers were always open; the Reaper sat, draped in black, with scratch pen permanently in hand. Progress was not so much a hymn to divine beneficence as a dirge accompanying the savage struggle. Both Darwinian science and poor law society were now reformed along competitive Malthusian lines. Ruthless competition was the norm; it guaranteed the progress of life and a low-wage, high-profit capitalist society.

Emigration surged in 1838 as the factories closed and lay-offs grew. The 'surplus' workers shipped to the colonies rose exponentially. Malthus sanctioned such an escape in his sixth edition, which differed strikingly from the unrelentingly bleak first edition. That had been a frontal assault on William Godwin's visions of utopian progress. (It was also an attack on the nonsense of the 'noble savage,' and Darwin knew from experience how ignoble the Fuegian really was.) Malthus had used the population crush to prove that co-operative progress was pie-in-the-sky. But Godwin's threat and the egalitarian evils of the French Revolution had long passed, and in the sixth edition Malthus allowed that the population explosion might be mitigated by education, celibacy, and emigration. That said, the price of 'progressive improvement in . . . society' was still a terrible struggle for existence.[22]

Malthus's followers in the 1830s circumvented death by deportation and shuffled the poor out of the country. Another free-trading evolutionist, Patrick Matthew, was showing the way. His *Emigration Fields*, being written at this moment, directed the paupers who lost out to the colonies. Huge numbers were leaving as the Depression deepened, 400,000 annually – to America, Australia, the Cape – and radical MPs planned to side-step government bureaucracy and open up New Zealand as well. Indeed, 'the whole of the unpeopled regions of the earth may now be said to be British ground.' Shipping out the surplus would reduce poverty at home, raise wages, and the Malthusian 'curse, will become . . . a blessing.' The emigrants would create new markets abroad, so that '*our paupers would be transformed into rich customers.*' The race itself would be invigorated, because

> change of place . . . seems to have a tendency to improve the species equally in animals as in plants, and agricultural and trading occupations are far more congenial to health and increase, than manufacturing occupations. It cannot therefore be doubted that the increase of the British race . . . and their extension over the world, and even the vigour of the race itself, will be more promoted by this colonizing system.

Like Darwin's, Matthew's social and organic evolution were all of a piece, dominated by Malthusian competition and selection.[23]

Emigration might solve the pauper problem at home, but others saw these boatloads of rejects wreaking havoc abroad. Dire predictions accompanied this tidal wave of flotsam. European settlers had always been 'harbingers of extermination to the native tribes,' and it was prophesied that all the 'aboriginal nations' would be wiped out within a century. At every outpost the *Beagle* crew had witnessed the destruction: the Tasmanians were all but exterminated, the aborigines were dying from European diseases, General Rosas's policy was deliberate genocide. But Darwin believed that colonial warfare was necessary 'to make the destroyers vary' and adapt to the new terrain.

Destruction was becoming integral to his Malthusian view of humanity:

> When two races of men meet, they act precisely like two species of animals. – they fight, eat each other, bring diseases to each other &c, but then comes the more deadly struggle, namely which have the best fitted organization, or instincts (ie intellect in man) to gain the day.

The 'stronger [are] always extirpating the weaker,' and the British were beating the lot. This imperial expansion ended the isolation of the indigenous races, and thwarted their development in other ways. As whites spread out from the Cape, the black tribes were pushed together in the interior, blending races and ending their species-making isolation. Had this not happened, Darwin speculated, 'in 10,000 years [the] Negro [would] probably [have become] a distinct species.'[24]

With emigration in the headlines, Lyell was convinced that animals too are driven by overpopulation to migrate. He agreed with Darwin that burgeoning species become colonizers, invading new terrain and defeating the natives. But Darwin's population pressure was pushing species to the limit in other ways. The crush was a creative force. The overcrowding that sent boatloads to the colonies meant that only animals with a competitive edge survived.

Darwin's biological initiative matched advanced Whig social thinking. This is what made it compelling. At last he had a mechanism that was compatible with the competitive, free-trading ideals of the ultra-Whigs. The transmutation at the base of his theory would still be loathed by many. But the Malthusian superstructure struck an emotionally satisfying chord; an open struggle with no hand-outs to the losers was the Whig way, and no poor-law commissioner could have bettered Darwin's view. He had broken with the radical hooligans who loathed Malthus. Like the Whig grandees – safe, immune, their own world characterized by *noblesse oblige* – Darwin was living on a family fortune, and thrusting a bitter competition on a starving world for its own good. From now on he could appeal to a better class of audience – to the rising industrialists, free-traders, and Dissenting professionals.

Paley's 'happy nature' was losing its Arcadian benignity. Life wasn't a vicarage garden on a summer's afternoon, but a battle among the down-and-outs on London's mean streets. From this conflict came continual adaptation. Progress from perpetual strife: it seemed like a paradox, but it was the conundrum of the age, 'an age of beauty, yet deformity, – an age of darkness, and yet of brightness.

Steam, iron, smoke, egoism, doubt, and distrust, are all alike in colour.' Darwin was asking momentous questions and was confident of the answers, even if they threw up still more doubt. His brazen speculations seemed characteristic of an entrepreneurial society pushing to extremes. 'The charm is broken – chivalry, charity, the church, lie cold,' someone summed up the spirit of the age; 'we interrogate a new godhead – we interpret it in our own way – it may be for good, it may be for evil – it may be a deity, it may be a demon.' As much could be said for the Malthusian strife at the core of Darwin's new evolutionary theory.

Eyes were turning to the citadel. 'Man has been called a microcosm,' a reviewer wrote, yet 'we have as yet no great key to unlock those secret chambers where the great laws of his nature are revealed; we are still fumbling at the door.'[25] Darwin, his stomach shouting 'no,' his head countering 'yes,' was quietly turning the key.

Darwin was approaching the Victorian dilemma, becoming 'destitute of faith, yet terrified at scepticism.' His new Malthusian evolution might have been implicitly secular, but it was not atheistic. How could it be, he asked, when God's laws have produced so 'high a mind' as ours? This pointed to a purpose behind the whole messy process. To deny it was to deny that descent was geared to the 'production of higher animals' or that 'we are [a] step towards some final end.'[26]

None of this was incompatible with Unitarianism, not even his denial of a 'superadded' soul. (Unitarians like Harriet Martineau also held that matter was spiritually endowed, obviating the need for a separate spirit world.) So much underlying Darwin's transmutation smacked of this creedless rational faith in a law-giving God – from the cultural conditioning of morality to the mental continuum between humans and brutes. Even so, it is debatable how many Unitarians would actually have accepted a monkey ancestry or have found hope in a higher life form rather than a material heaven. Indeed, as Darwin shifted on these grounds his own religious beliefs were shaking. All he knew was that children are visited with rewards and punishments in this life for the actions of their parents. What happens 'when we turn into angels' was immaterial, he shrugged.[27]

October saw him start two new notebooks, 'E' in the transmutation series and 'N' on metaphysics. It was a time for polishing his views and practising his rhetorical skill. He started grandly:

To study Metaphysics . . . appears to me to be like puzzling at Astronomy without Mechanics. – Experience shows [that]

the problem of the mind cannot be solved by attacking the
citadel itself. – the mind is function of body. – we must
bring some *stable* foundation to argue from.

'Descent' was that foundation; it offered a rational key to the mind.
Human conscience was perhaps the hardest nut to crack, and he
looked for its origin in the pack behaviour of dogs and baboons. He
argued in a typically anthropomorphic way that a deviant dog, going
against its 'social & sexual instinct' and harming the pack, would
feel remorse *if* it could reflect on its act. Such a reasoning dog would
have acquired a conscience. But this hypothetical 'dogs conscience
would not have been same with mans because original instincts different.' He was now fully convinced that, from troop instincts alone, he
could derive 'all that is most beautiful in the moral sentiments.'[28]

Thus were character and conscience formed, not from reading the
Bible, but from an ancestral ape's family feelings. Conscience lay
outside a person's control. 'A man ... may be congratulated [for
doing good],' but the act is conditioned and 'deserves no credit.' By
the same token 'wickedness is no more a man's fault than bodily
disease!!' This cultural determinism extended even to our knowledge
of God, and here Darwin leaped beyond most Dissenters. Our 'innate
knowledge of [the] creator' had evolved as a consequence of 'his
most magnificent laws.'[29] It was a grand instinct, developed because
of its social utility.

Worries about his heresies made him repeatedly ill, and on 25
October, pondering the origins of shame and beauty, he visited the
salubrious castle town of Windsor for two days' rest, making the
most of the 'glorious weather.'

Shame and beauty were recurrent thoughts as he prepared to ask
for Emma's hand. After an excruciating early November, he was well
enough to set off for Maer. The 11th was 'The day of days!,' he
noted in his new journal. He did the deed and proposed. It took
Emma by surprise. She had 'thought we might go on in the sort of
friendship we were in for years.' Her acceptance left Uncle Jos in
tears of joy. Fanny, Hensleigh's wife, twigged at once what had
happened, and the women sat up all night giggling and talking.
Others had a more direct insight; Aunt Jessie, being a palm-reader,
had known it all along. Emma now carried out her own calculus,
praising Charles's openness and honesty. He is so 'perfectly sweet
tempered, and possesses some minor qualities ... such as not being
fastidious, and being humane to animals.'[30]

Charles galloped to The Mount the next day, where Caroline congratulated him on having 'secured the very sweetest . . . of wives.' The engagement was kept private, Lyell being one of the few outsiders to hear. Emma was Hensleigh's and Josiah's sister, Darwin told him, 'so we are connected by manifold ties, besides on my part, by the most sincere love & hearty gratitude to her, for accepting such a one, as myself.' Letters went off to all the relatives, although one became confused, thinking that Emma was marrying Dr Darwin, and panicked about their 'disparity of age.'

For his part the Doctor was mightily pleased, the more so because Emma's mother continually teased him that Charles would end up with Harriet Martineau, and the thought gave him apoplexy.[31] Not that Charles had the chance, with Erasmus monopolizing her day and night. Eras himself heard the news as he was about to escort Harriet out, and they turned their jaunt into a house-hunting foray for the happy couple.

These idyllic days at Maer had a down side, for Emma was still privately troubled. Unable to conceal his doubts, Charles had again broached the prickliest subject of all with her, religion. Now she could not contain her anxiety:

> When I am with you . . . all melancholy thoughts keep out of
> my head but since you are gone sad ones have forced
> themselves in, of fear that our opinions on the most important
> subject should differ widely. My reason tells me that honest
> & conscientious doubts cannot be a sin, but I feel it would be
> a painful void between us. I thank you from my heart for
> your openness with me & I should dread the feeling that you
> were concealing your opinions from the fear of giving me
> pain. It is perhaps foolish of me to say this much but my own
> dear Charley we now do belong to each other & I cannot
> help being open with you. Will you do me a favour? yes I am
> sure you will, it is to read our Saviours farewell discourse to
> his disciples which begins at the end of the 13th Chap[ter] of
> John. It is so full of love to them & devotion & every
> beautiful feeling. It is the part of the New Testament I love
> best. This is a whim of mine[,] it would give me great pleasure,
> though I can hardly tell why.[32]

Unwittingly, Emma had pointed him to the Gospel that Caroline suggested he read a decade earlier at Edinburgh. It was Jesus's emotive farewell before his crucifixion, with its 'new commandment' to 'love one another.'

In the discourse Jesus assures his disciples that after his death he will 'prepare a place' in heaven for them and then return 'to receive you unto myself.' But doubting Thomas asks the way to the place being prepared: Jesus replies, 'I am the way, the truth, and the life.' Emma wanted Charles to remember the way lest she lose him for ever, and recalled Jesus's words:

I am the vine, ye are the branches . . . If a man abide not in me, he is cast forth as a branch and is withered; and men gather them, and cast them into the fire, and they are burned.

The farewell discourse might have been full of love but this was the fiery underside, and Charles could hardly have missed the warning. He doubted the existence of hell, he doubted the existence of a soul, and in fact this Gospel would always stand between them. But he sent Emma a warm reply, and she took comfort that at least he had entered into her heart's concern 'a little more.'[33]

Charley wanted to rush the ceremony and he repeated his opening notebook gambit to Emma, 'remember life is short.' But she was used to caring for invalid parents and worried about leaving her tiny hunchback sister Elizabeth to cope. She hoped he would 'take things leisurely.' Elizabeth did too, sad at the prospect of losing her sister. She wrote to Catherine, 'Do dear Catty clog the wheels a little,' let Emma glory in being a fiancée. Get Charles to 'wait till Spring & fine weather!'

Back at Maer on the 17th, Charley had more sentimental 'gooses' by the fire, discussing practical matters, the 'question of houses, – suburbs versus central London,' and such. 'My chief fear is, that you will find . . . our quiet evenings dull,' he alerted Emma. 'You must bear in mind, as some young lady said, "all men are brutes", and that I take the line of being a solitary brute.' Solitary and wealthy now, for Emma's father promised a dowry of £5000 plus £400 a year, to which the Doctor added £10,000 for Charles, the sum to be invested, with Eras and Josiah III as executors. The family fortune would be secure.[34]

The couple took the Doctor's advice and opted for a London house until, Charles said, 'I have wearied the geological public with my newly acquired cacoethes scribendi [itch to write].' Then they would 'decide, whether the pleasures of retirement & country . . . are preferable to society.' Charles scouted out houses, traipsing the misty November streets. The West End was out, the traffic noise was deafening (so much so that trials with wood block road surfaces were about to start in Oxford Street). Bloomsbury, near the British

271

Museum, was quieter and its leafy squares preferable. Emma gave Charley his marching orders: to investigate 'the back lanes about the Regents Park' or nearer to Covent Garden 'if it is not too dear.' But the astronomic rents came as a shock. The 'landlords are all gone mad. they ask such prices,' £150 a year was nothing. (And Charley remained canny, even with £15,000 in prospect.) He and Eras decided that the Bloomsbury squares were the most affordable.

Meanwhile Emma's 'old curmudgeon' was doing the social rounds and getting in as much snuff as possible before his bachelor days ended. He dined with the Lyells and Henry Holland, and Eras took him to tea with Thomas Carlyle (whose wife Jane he considered not 'quite natural or lady-like,' with her 'hysterical sort of giggle'). The invitations were already coming in for the married couple. Sedgwick invited them to his house, suitably impressing Emma. 'What an honour for the great Sedgwick to invite me to his house. *Me* only think of it! I feel a greater person already for it & how my head will stand it when I am really Mrs D.'[35]

At night, after house-hunting, the cogitations on Malthus continued. Darwin was pulling the implications out like stretched wire. By this point he had every tissue, every organ, 'capable of innumerable variations,' with nature selecting the best. More and more he realized the irony of perfection arising from cut-throat competition. The perfect adaptive nuance was 'the surviving one of ten, thousand trials. each step being perfect or nearly so . . . to the then existing conditions.'[36] Out of the millions that perish comes the one perfect being.

Or as perfect as inheritance allowed, for nipples on the male were hardly functional adaptations. Selection could only sculpt the existing model, the basic groundplan, and even then animals retained useless vestiges, like the human coccyx (the tail). Darwin scorned the common idea that God had created these rudimentary bits and pieces to round out the vertebrate plan, following his 'original thought, or design . . . to its utmost exhaustion.' '**What bosch!!**' he exploded – 'the designs of an omnipotent creator, exhausted . . . Such is Man's philosophy. when he argues about his Creator!' These were inherited holdovers, ancestral remnants, diminishing and disappearing slowly. The traces of limbs in whales reveal their land ancestry, and on the coccyx hung an interesting tale.

In the absence of human fossils, rudimentary organs provided the pointers to 'the parent of man.' The tail stump indicated a monkey. Nor need one stop there. He followed this reasoning to its rather slimy conclusion. The clue to our lowly ancestry lay in the skull, which London medical men considered a modification of the spine: 'The head being six metamorphosed [expanded and welded] vertebrae, the parent of all vertebrate animals,' Darwin concluded, 'must have been like some molluscous bisexual animal with a vertebra only & no head-!!'[37] We had come from a squid-like animal with a cuttlefish backbone.

Nothing was sacrosanct in his notebooks, and analysing his own feelings set off new trains of thought. Courting Emma, he began considering sexual arousal, slobbering and kissing, tracing them to our animal ancestors. As he jotted, breathing heavily:

> November 27th.- Sexual desire makes saliva to flow[,] yes
> *certainly* – curious association: I have seen Nina [the dog]
> licking her chops. – someone has described slovering
> teethless-jaws. as picture of disgusting lewd old man. ones
> tendency to kiss, & almost bite, that which one sexually loves
> is probably connected with flow of saliva, & hence the action
> of *mouth* & jaws. – Lascivious women. are described as biting:
> so do stallions always.

Blushing too must be sexual, because it intensifies when men and women interact. Perhaps thinking of 'one's appearance' drives 'blood to surface exposed, face of man ... bosom in woman: like erection.'[38]

Still Malthus was being digested, and it was a slow bovine process. Even now, two months after reading the book, Darwin was breaking new ground. He had assumed that habitual behaviour becomes instinctive and causes the necessary changes in mind and body: that is how variations occur. Now he introduced a strikingly different image, suggesting that odd variants might be thrown up by *chance*.[39] Perhaps even instincts appear randomly, with selection keeping only the useful ones.

There was a bonus. If nature was sifting the fit from the random variants, then she mimicked the breeders more than he had imagined. Fanciers built their pigeons and pigs by discarding all but the desired traits. Nature was evidently doing the same. She was a supreme selector, a superior Sir John Sebright, more vigilant, ruthless, and efficient. Think of her as 'a being infinitely more sagacious than man,' he suggested, though 'not an omniscient creator.' The gentry selected greyhounds the way Nature sifted jackals – except that, while the breeders looked to one or two points, Nature juggled a million variations, making sure that 'every part of [every] newly acquired structure is fully practised & perfected.' By December he

273

admitted that this similarity between natural and artificial selection was the most 'beautiful part of my theory.'[40] He had his theory, and a fancy animal analogy; but in these riot-torn years they were safely tucked away in his secret notebooks, and only in the very distant future would he even think of publishing.

His thoughts were now swinging between Malthus, marriage, and house prices. The *Zoology* was still a burden. Owen's mother had just died, causing him to halt work on *Fossil Mammalia*, and Darwin was lumbered with the half-finished *Birds* after Gould sailed for Tasmania: 'What can a man have to say, who works all morning in describing hawks & owls; & then rushes out, & walks in a bewildered manner up one street & down another, looking out for the word "To let".' Emma could see how stressed he was:

> I want to persuade you dear Charley to leave town at once
> & get some rest. You have looked so unwell for some time
> that I am afraid you will be laid up . . . I want you to cast
> out of your mind all anxiety about me on that point & to feel
> sure that nothing *could* make me so happy as to feel that I
> could be of any use or comfort to my own dear Charles when
> he is not well . . . So don't be ill any more my dear Charley
> till I can be with you to nurse you.

It was the beginning of the pact, with Emma willingly exchanging an invalid mother for a dyspeptic husband. She did not want a 'holiday husband' putting on a brave face. She expected to continue nursing and he was happy to oblige.

Emma came to town on 6 December to help with the house-hunting. She stayed with the Hensleighs and spent her days 'galivant-ing' with Charley 'in the flies [one-horse cabs] & omnibusses,' checking Bloomsbury's squares, buying pots and pans, and theatre-going. At the end she felt quite 'cockneyfied.'[41]

At the Geological Society this month Darwin was reminded of his predicament. The geologists' seething hatred of evolution erupted into the open on the 19th, when his old teacher Robert Grant's views were finally given the 'coup de grace.'[42]

Darwin found himself trapped between the devil and the deep blue sea. Grant had been lined up for summary justice because he insisted that the world's oldest mammal, an 'opossum' known only from four inch-long jaws found in Oxford's rocks, was in fact a reptile. This fitted better with Grant's Lamarckian image of an upward-sweeping evolution from lower to higher forms. These Oxford rocks were laid down as sediments during the age of reptiles. They were too old; mammals should not have existed that far back. The first real marsupials only appeared much later, Grant believed, during the age of mammals. By contrast the clerics, with their contingently active Creator, could accommodate mammals anywhere, anytime. They opted for an ancient opossum and put Grant's view down to his deviant Lamarckism.

They set Grant up. Conspiratorial letters flew between Buckland and Owen about how he was to be nailed. Egged on, Owen – now London's marsupial expert – postponed the second number of Darwin's *Fossil Mammalia* to do the deed. There was even back-room talk about how to publicize the coup, and Buckland cannily invited the omniscient Lord Brougham along 'to witness our Skirmish.'

The irony was complete. Darwin – from his Secretary's chair – watched the polite company convene to bury Grant's fossil heresy. Here he sat, a silent witness, before Sedgwick, Buckland, and the rest, most of them Oxbridge-educated, many Anglican divines, all loathing Lamarckism. Yet even as he watched the spectacle unfold, he was hatching his own evolutionary scheme. True, he had outgrown Grant's nonsense. Owen had convinced him that this *was* a true opossum. And yet Darwin did not doubt that its ancestors lay among the extinct reptiles. As Owen and Buckland lashed Grant, Darwin in his notebook was secretly calling their primitive opossum 'the father of all Mammalia in ages long gone past,' a blast to send tremors under the Creationist edifice.[43] What was he thinking as Grant was trounced? Did his heart bleed on hearing Grant's spirited defence? Probably not, for he was out of sympathy with the ultra-radical, and he went off to dine with the 'élite' at the Crown and Anchor tavern that night, as they gloated over their victory.

He could salvage something from the episode. It pushed him further from the Lamarckian minefield. He had already dumped the idea of an inexorable, upward-sweeping nature: 'in my theory,' he scribbled, 'there is no absolute tendency to progression.' Environments change only 'slowly & insensibly,' and life follows suit. Conditions might remain stable, in which case species would not alter at all. Not even man was exempt; he had shown no improvement since ancient Greek times. Some animals – parasites, for example – had even simplified, and if these died out, others would 'degenerate' to fill their niche.[44] So inexorable ascent and guaranteed progress was a radical myth.

Darwin's new way of viewing nature was defiantly at odds with

Grant's utopian notions. It kept faith with the competitive, capitalist, Malthusian dynamics of a poor-law society, Brougham's society. At the time Darwin was actually reading Brougham's lordly *Dissertation on Subjects of Science*. The former Lord Chancellor was renowned for his encyclopaedic knowledge; some called it 'encyclopaedic ignorance,' but the book further undermined Darwin's old ideas. Brougham convinced him that many instincts could not have originated from conscious purposeful habits. What about a parasitic wasp paralysing a caterpillar and placing it with its own eggs? Darwin had seen these wasps in Brazil doing exactly that. The caterpillar might have been food for the grubs, but the wasp could not have known it. The grubs hatch only after the wasp's death. No adult lived to see its young. So how could this instinct have originated as a knowingly purposeful act?[45] It must have appeared at random and been found useful.

This had crucial ramifications. If conscious habits had ceased to drive his evolutionary machine, then it was irrelevant whether or not they were coded in the brain. He could drop the argument about the conscious mind being synonymous with the brain. He could ditch the mental materialism that was associated with ultra-radicalism, and which – if he ever published – would cost him votes. He was back hunting with the urban gentry, rather than running with the radical hounds.

As chance crept into the picture the idea that man was a divine forethought became less tenable (did God plan chance events?). Babbage's programmed nature took a battering as Darwin resorted to haphazard variations. Contingency and unpredictability became the norm. But Darwin remained muzzy on the subject and never really let go of his harmonious law-based system. Sometimes he viewed 'chance' as the unintentional intersection of causal chains, an idea woolly enough to allow any number of accommodations. At others he spoke as deterministically as Martineau, calling it an event with an unknown cause, or meaning that the variations were not ready-directed.[46] It was the making of future confusion.

Confusion was exchanged for chaos as Emma left town on 21 December. With the wedding a month away, Charles shut his 'E' notebook to sort out somewhere to live. They had their heart set on a terraced house in Upper Gower Street. The estate was ideally quiet, with no pubs or shops, and almost no mews. University College was down the road, but here the street turned into a private track and was closed off by a gate. The house was gaudily furnished and ugly, but it had the advantage of being cheap. 'Gower St is ours, yellow curtains & all,' he rejoiced to Emma on the 29th.[47] The rent was 'extraordinarily low' and the furniture and crockery a snip at £550, even if there was an unseemly dead dog in the back garden.

Sunday, New Year's Eve, Darwin and Covington spent packing books and rocks, and New Year's Day 1839 two vanloads were taken over to Gower Street. He reported to Emma:

> I was astounded, & so was Erasmus at the bulk of my luggage
> & the Porters were even more so at the weight of those
> containing my Geological Specimens. – The dining room,
> hall, & my own room are crammed & piled with goods –
> One servants room up stairs, & my own charming room
> below will hold all most admirably. There never was so good
> a house for *me*, & I devoutly trust you will approve of it
> equally . . . My room is so quiet, that the contrast to
> Marlborough is as remarkable, as it is delightful.

By six in the evening the house was looking suitably like a museum.

Out of the blue Charles suddenly recalled having been in the house before. Leonard Horner – the erstwhile Warden at the university – had lived here, and Charles had dropped in before the voyage. But since Horner's day the décor had degenerated atrociously. 'Macaw Cottage' they dubbed it, and the reason for the gaudiness soon became apparent. The 84-year-old owner Colonel Irvine had lived here with his beautiful 30-year-old second wife. The azure walls and garish yellow curtains said something about her taste, 'which, like her character,' Charles chuckled, 'I presume, is none at all.' The horrified Hensleighs ordered them to send the curtains 'to the dyers at once.'

Still it was perfect after the West End noise. Uncle Jos thought it 'the quietest place he had ever been.' The dog removed, Darwin took to pacing the ninety-foot narrow garden daily, starting a trend that lasted for life. And he planned to plant laburnums to shelter them from the neighbours.[48]

Macaw Cottage was a stone's throw from Grant's college classroom, but by now the threads were irrevocably broken. Darwin wanted nothing more to do with this soapbox Lamarckian, nor his guinea-grabbing zoology. More to the point Gower Street was only a few hundred yards from Regent's Park, where Charles could parade with Emma in her best bonnet.

Days were now spent piling up crates in the front attic, 'hence forward to be called the Museum.' So much hefty work left him feeling 'stupid & comfortable, so dull in the noddle & weary in the legs.' In that state he cabbed to the Athenaeum for his evening meal, or Eras made him break to dine with the Hensleighs and Carlyles, although the talk inevitably turned to the difficulty with domestics. Likewise discussions with Lyell were now less about the origin of coal, than the best coal merchant in the neighbourhood.

He eased off and grew grumpy on hearing that the Wedgwoods had put the wedding day back from 24 to 29 January. He squeezed in a few notebook jottings, analysing love in an outrageously unromantic way. Only a clinical naturalist could ask, 'What passes in a man's mind, when he says he loves a person'! Then it was off for a final round at Shrewsbury and Maer on 11 January, and back to London on the 18th, making last-minute preparations. It only remained for him and Eras to scour the Baker Street bazaar for cheap furniture for the servants to make Macaw Cottage complete.[49]

He recognized that five years of solitude had left him inward-looking, as he candidly apologized to Emma.

> I was thinking this morning how on earth it came, that I . . . should so entirely rest my notions of happiness on quietness & a good deal of solitude; but I believe the explanation is very simple, & I mention it, because it will give you hopes, that I shall gradually grow less of a *brute*, – it is that during the five years of my voyage (& indeed I may add these two last) . . . the whole of my pleasure was derived, from what passed in my mind . . . I think you will humanize me, & soon teach me there is greater happiness, than building theories, & accumulating facts in silence & solitude.

He had found his 'nice soft wife on a sofa,' or rather a soft nursemaid while he lay on the sofa. Already he was giving her full-blooded accounts of his 'stomachic disasters' and relishing her coming to 'take final charge of me.' 'Thank Providence,' he sang out, 'I shall not be a free agent much longer.'

Emma was to humanize the brute, care for him, take charge of the sofa. Her role from the first was narrowly circumscribed – the solitary beast did not want an intellectual soul-mate. She tried to dip into Lyell's *Elements of Geology* only to be told not to bother. Lyell's treatment of his long-suffering wife was a paradigm. Charles sent an account of the couple's visit: 'we talked for half an hour, un-sophisticated geology, with poor M[rs] Lyell sitting by, a monument of patience. – I want *practice* in illtreating the female sex.' Another joke of course, but women were spectators in the male preserve of science, as unwanted here as at the Athenaeum. They had to tolerate this masculine preoccupation, and Emma would prove his equal in forbearance.

Charles was itching to get the ceremony over with. On 24 January 1839, the original date, he took consolation in being elected a Fellow of the Royal Society – still largely a privilege of the wealthy, well-connected, scientific élite. The next morning he trained to Shrewsbury, where he heard from Emma, dreaming of the big day:

> I shall always look upon the event of the 29th as a most happy one on my part . . . There is only one subject in the world that ever gives me a moments uneasiness & I believe I think about that very little when I am with you & I do hope that though our opinions may not agree upon all points of religion we may sympathize a good deal in our *feelings* on the subject.

He arrived at Maer on the 28th and the following day they were married at St Peter's Church by the vicar, their cousin John Allen Wedgwood.

The service, although Anglican, was by special arrangement, so as not to offend Unitarian sensibilities. Emma wore a 'greenish-grey rich silk [dress] . . . and a white chip bonnet trimmed with blonde and flowers.' Charles was nervous and escaped the relatives' clutches by whisking Emma off to the railway station afterwards with undignified haste. She barely had time to change her bonnet, and their precipitous departure raised eyebrows and upset sister Elizabeth. The couple ate their 'sandwiches with grateful hearts' on the train and toasted the future from a 'bottle of water.' Emma took comfort from knowing that her bedridden mother had slept through the service, sparing them both 'the pain of parting.'

Never mind. They were back at Macaw Cottage. Darwin jotted in his journal: 'Married at Maer & returned to London 30 years old.' But his real obsession did show on this, his wedding day. He re-opened his secret 'E' notebook specially to record Uncle John Wedgwood's views on turnips.[50]

19

The Dreadful War

A SHADOW FELL over the couple from the start. Forty-eight hours after the ceremony, on 31 January 1839, Charles's sister Caroline lost her first baby, six-week-old Sophie. There could have been no sadder end to a happy month, and it clouded their first weeks together. Emma longed for 'news of poor Caroline,' knowing that few infant deaths 'have caused more bitter grief than hers.' Caroline was thirty-eight, her husband Josiah (Emma's brother) forty-three. The child was weakly from birth, 'a poor puny little delicate thing,' the first-born of a first-cousin marriage, like Charles and Emma's.[1] It did not bode well.

Emma found solace in her snug urban 'cottage' and new life. They lived at the back overlooking the garden. It was much quieter here, and the month was spent settling in, with her shopping for morning gowns, plates, and a mahogany pianoforte.

But her fears about Charles's future life kept returning. On finding herself pregnant a few months later she set down her anxieties. She found it easier to express herself in a letter to Charles, for 'when I talk to you . . . I cannot say exactly what I wish to say.' Of course he was 'acting conscientiously' in 'trying to learn the truth' about nature, but equally she knew it could not be the whole truth. His scientific pursuits excluded 'other sort of thoughts,' religious thoughts. And always there was the wretched example set by Eras, who had 'gone before you,' removing 'some of that dread & fear' that accompanies doubt.

Charles had lost any qualms about scepticism, dismissing them in his notes as 'an unreasonable or superstitious feeling.' Emma realized that his private work was leading him into perilous waters. The habit of 'believing nothing till it is proved' had prevented him from considering 'other things which cannot be proved in the same way, & which if true are likely to be above our comprehension.' She was tortured by the thought of him giving up Christ's revelation of eternal life and sacrificing his salvation. Ever since losing her beloved sister Fanny she had lived in hope of 'being with her again, never to part.' She hoped to spend eternity with her precious husband too, but his doubts threatened to separate them at death. It would be a nightmare, she finished, 'if I thought we did not belong to each other forever.'[2]

Emma's Christianity was a simple evangelical prescription to gain everlasting life by believing in Jesus. Eternal life 'cannot be proved;' it might not even be comprehensible but, with so momentous an issue, she implored her Charley to be 'careful, perhaps even fearful' of 'casting off' what Jesus had 'done for your benefit as well as for that of all the world.' The letter reduced him to tears, and he was never to forget it.

As they grew closer, she would take him on Sundays to King's College church on the Strand. (There was, needless to say, no church attached to the godless college of Gower Street.) At the same time his illness increased, and her anxieties only exacerbated his own. 'The question' that divided them, as Emma called it, was not whether the Bible was an unimpeachable divine revelation. He already doubted that, understandably, given his integration into Erasmus's circle. It was whether he would spend eternity in heaven or hell.[3]

Still, the present life went on happily enough. The home was run, like all upper-middle-class households, by a retinue of domestics. They carried on a back-breaking daily grind, trudging up and down stairs with coal and water, laying out clothes, serving meals, cleaning hearths – ministering, as Darwin might have said, to the king and queen termite for little succour. The faithful Syms Covington, with Darwin since the voyage, stayed a while after the nuptial flight to London, and then left in February with a £2 golden handshake. A few months later he emigrated with the hordes to Australia, working his passage as a cook, and carrying Darwin's letter of introduction to Capt. King. The new manservant was the redoubtable Joseph Parslow, who carried Aunt Jessie's accolade as 'the most amiable, obliging, active, serviceable servant that ever breathed.'

The vetting of domestics was obviously fraught. Charles depended on friends and family for recommendations, with little success: 'The Cook from Shrewsbury is a failure as she cannot cook, & has a drunken husband. I am fearful of getting a converted Jewess from Miss Farrer.' Emma was just as pernickety about her attendants. The new cook was 'too cute' and had to go, the maid 'vulgar and plain,' although some better excuse was needed to sack her.

It was a very proper house, with the proprieties observed to the last detail. Charles was even more of a stickler for etiquette than Emma. Permitting her maid to forgo a bonnet led to a terrible tiff. He was horror-struck, as was everyone at Shrewsbury: she was a *lady*'s maid not a grocer's girl, inviting men to take liberties. Nor was Parslow's long hair tolerated, and the Doctor gave him a public and sarcastic dressing-down about his judicial locks, unbecoming in one so lowly.[4]

Darwin was freed for the pleasures of untrammelled thought. His paper on Glen Roy at the Royal Society in January 'crowned the series' on global elevation. But there was no sign of the published *Journal* and Whewell at the Geological Society had to be dissuaded from protesting publicly, so as not to rile FitzRoy. The Captain ploughed on, and to be fair his own volume would top Darwin's at a thousand pages, when it eventually appeared in print.

In private Darwin was now watching the way horticulturalists worked. They certainly capitalized on chance peculiarities. He noted growers talking of the '*accidental production of seedling*[s] *with hardier constitution*[s],' and himself saw the 'vigorous battle between strong & weak' leading to 'the preservation of *accidental* hardy seedlings.'[5] His whole habit-driven mechanism was irrelevant to plants anyway; he was now adamant that hardier seeds could only be produced by chance.

In smoky London he remained a country gent at heart, writing to farmers on their methods of selection, and moving far from the concerns of the closet zoologists and academic botanists. He opened a 'Questions & Experiments' notebook, cramming it with queries and plans for rearing daisies in rich soils, sowing seeds under coloured glass, hybridizing cabbages, crossing dogs, skeletonizing ducks, and comparing blood corpuscles, all ingenious approaches to the enigma of variation. Indeed, they were bizarre by contemporary standards. No Cambridge don expected peach-nectarine crosses to hold the key to Creation.

He printed queries, a sheaf for each specialist, framing his *Questions about the Breeding of Animals* in such a way as to elicit the required responses. They went out to gentlemen farmers, for their nurserymen and gamekeepers, quizzing them on the way they crossed varieties or picked offspring to achieve the 'requisite qualities.' This blitz of queries plainly proved too much. Only three replied, and one

of these was overwhelmed, despairing that 'Mr Darwin's questions
. . . require a longer course of experience than the life of one man . . .
can furnish.'[6]

Darwin's Malthusian specs were beginning to fit comfortably, and
peering through them revealed 'the dreadful but quiet war of organic
beings. going on the peaceful woods. & smiling fields.' Or rather, on
the capital's dirty, disease-ridden streets, because he was hardly
seeing nature at all any more. His increasingly bleak image of nature
was a counterpoint to a society in the grip of depression, with the
war in London's slums forcing the starving poor to emigrate or
march in protest.

He entertained the visiting Swiss botanist De Candolle to dinner
and was able to talk over nature's 'war' face to face with the man
who had first mooted the idea. The contest was paramount, with
nature a charnel house, strewn with losers. For each tiny gain, many
must die. Consider the ages it would take for small advantages to
carry through to an entire population of dogs: suppose 'that one out
of every hundred litters is born with long legs & in the Malthusian
rush for life, only two of them live to breed.' If the terrain is hard
and the prey swift, 'the long legged one shall rather oftener . . .
survive' and 'in ten thousand years the long legged race will get the
upper hand.' But look at how many had to perish to achieve that
end!

It seemed so obvious that he tried it out on Hensleigh. Knowing
his cousin's developmental approach to language he surely would see
the subtlety of it. But no, Hensleigh 'seemed to think it absurd . . .
that [a] tiger springing an inch further would determine his preservation.' Even transmutation itself was baffling.[7] Java and Sumatra were
similar islands, he protested, yet each had a unique rhino. Why? Of
course, this was the nut Darwin had already cracked with the
Galapagos, but it was clear that others would need persuading.

It wasn't only his cousin he went beyond, but Hensleigh's late
father-in-law Sir James Mackintosh. As a tyro Charles had first met
Sir James at the Wedgwood mansion, but a world had passed since
then. Now, in May, he looked again at Mackintosh's *Ethical
Philosophy* while visiting Maer with Emma. Mackintosh thought the
moral faculties inborn, and the knowledge of right and wrong instinctive. This fitted Darwin's scheme wonderfully, but he wanted to
know how these moral instincts appeared.[8] Miraculously was no
answer. They must have emerged from herding and bonding instincts
that were useful in cementing relations in the ancestral troop.

Hensleigh was a regular at the dinner parties, and Emma endured the scientific ones stoically. On 28 March Sedgwick called, and even she recognized that 'there is something remarkably fresh and odd about him.' By April her bemused feelings were making themselves known. Keeping the conversation flowing on Easter Monday with the likes of Lyell and Robert Brown taxed her to the limit. Lyell's whispers were 'enough to flatten a party' and Brown was so shy that he looked as if 'he longed to shrink into himself and disappear entirely; however, notwithstanding those two dead weights, viz., the greatest botanist and the greatest geologist in Europe, we did very well and had no pauses.'[9] But then Emma struck everybody as reserved and grave – it was Charles who disgraced himself by cracking all the jokes.

Late May 1839 – two and a half years after the *Beagle*'s return – was a time for jubilation. His first book, the *Journal* of the voyage, finally went on sale. For the new author these were nail-biting days as the reviews appeared. Capt. Basil Hall's in the *Edinburgh Review* was complimentary and applauded FitzRoy for spending 'considerable sums from his private funds to complete the survey of the Peruvian coast.' Even so, FitzRoy found the piece 'very shilly shally and self-contradictory.' What struck everybody about Darwin's volume was its 'spirit of bold generalization.' For the Saturday *Athenaeum* this was meant as a rebuke in an age recruiting facts. Why, exclaimed the hack, on Mr Darwin's slow elevation theory, 'at least one million of years must have elapsed since . . . the sea washed the feet of the Cordillera of the Andes!'[10] *This* was the shilly-shally review, which criticized the publishers for lumping the three volumes together and causing endless repetitions. (It was taken to heart, and on 15 August, after the three-volume set had been given a ten-week run, Darwin's *Journal* was issued separately.)

His colleagues were much more gracious, particularly Owen: 'It is as full of good original wholesome food as an egg, & if what I have enjoyed has not been duly digested it is because it has been too hastily devoured.' What another liked (digging at the French) was 'the tone of kind & generous feeling that is visible in every part.' He meant that 'it is the work of a plain English gentleman – travelling for information, and not for Effect. – & viewing all things *kindly*.' Even the thin-skinned FitzRoy, combing through the luxuriant forests for lapses of etiquette, doubted that he would find 'an expression in it – referring to me personally – which I could wish were not in it' and he expected to 'be thoroughly at ease in that respect.'

By contrast, FitzRoy's tailpiece had Lyell and Darwin in fits. FitzRoy, at home now and with a religious wife, had turned into a scriptural literalist and closed his tome with an exegesis of Genesis. He regretted doubting the existence of the Deluge in Darwin's presence. Now he could plainly see how wrong the geologists were: all Darwin's high-and-dry shells, all his fossil trees in the Andes, all the gravelly pampas plateaux, all the fossil bones attested one thing only – a great catastrophic flood. It was a direct hit at Darwin's science and Lyell's *Elements of Geology*. Lyell thought it 'beats all the other nonsense he has ever read on the subject.' 'Although I owe very much to FitzR[oy],' Darwin admitted, 'I . . . am anxious to avoid seeing much of him.' He was too peppery, his wife too patronizing, 'but then this cannot be wondered at from so very beautiful & religious a lady.'[11]

Darwin's hero Alexander von Humboldt wrote a paean of praise. He called the *Journal* one of the most remarkable travelogues published. Even 'a young author cannot gorge such a mouthful of flattery,' Darwin replied. Humboldt repeated the praise later in London, fulsomely; Darwin listened to him talk for three hours nonstop, coming away more wearied than worshipping. Always first off the mark, the Germans wanted a translation, and Carl Hartmann, the Brunswick commissioner of mines who had translated Lyell's *Elements*, offered to do the job. But it eventually fell to Ernst Dieffenbach. He was surgeon to the New Zealand Colonization Company (founded this year by radical MPs to ship surplus labourers to the new country), and he got to work after arriving back in Berlin.

The praise was opportune. In June Darwin closed his last major notebook and continued *Coral Reefs* with the thought: 'it is very pleasant easy work putting together the frame of a geological theory, but it is just as tough a job collecting & comparing the hard unbending facts.'[12] As the reviewers recognized, Darwin was a theorist in an age concerned with detail. Hypothesizing was tainted. Understanding God's handiwork in nature was time-consuming and Truth could only emerge from a collation of dry facts, according to the Revd Sedgwick. Any attempt to circumvent this toilsome process with a quick hypothesis or a priori guess was sinful.

The criticism would strike even harder at Darwin's evolutionary theory. The frame for this was also in place, the facts stretched across it in a Malthusian manner. Was it true? Truth for the Cambridge dons led from nature to God, and was moral, conservative, and guarded by the élite. Darwin's speculation served quite different masters, the up-and-coming industrial and professional middle classes. And what was to stop out-and-out dissidents from appropriating his theory for real revolutionary ends?

*

By summer the disorder on the streets was impossible to avoid. The arming of Chartist mobs was discussed in the House of Commons. At the first Chartist Convention in London, the moderate Perth delegate Patrick Matthew, the Malthusian evolutionist, was ousted as a 'middle-class traitor.' The radical workers, having lost out in the Reform Bill, were taking matters into their own hands. A national petition demanding universal manhood suffrage containing 1.3 million signatures had been rejected by Parliament in July. In August, when Darwin attended the week-long jamboree of the British Association in Birmingham, he found a city almost under martial law. The Chartist Convention had switched to the town. Socialists had joined them – some of them red Lamarckians – distributing half a million pamphlets, denouncing marriage, property, and the unco-operative state. Rioting had broken out the month before, and the scientific gentlemen had been ready to call off the event. Darwin arrived in a city that was 'feverish quiet' with peace preserved by 'men in green and men in red, police staves and cavalry sabres.'[13]

Darwin was sick with worry. Yet he felt compelled to confess to the priests vilified by the mob – or at least to the orthodox Henslow – that he was 'steadily collecting every sort of fact, which may throw light on the origin & variation of species.' It would have been music to the ears of street atheists, but not of course to Henslow. Darwin desperately hoped that his old mentor would understand. In Shrewsbury for ten days in September he was 'so languid & uncomfortable' that he laid low and saw no one. Emma was six months pregnant and ill herself many days, and they cocooned themselves more and more, retreating into the home.

Entertaining grew uncomfortable: 'we are living a life of extreme quietness . . . We have given up all parties, for they agree with neither of us; & if one is quiet in London, there is nothing like its quietness – there is a grandeur about its smoky fogs, & the dull distant sounds of cabs & coaches.' Gower Street was now a sanctuary: 'we see nothing, do nothing & hear nothing.' The old circle had lost its charm, and members were drifting away. Harriet, fearing she had a tumour, had moved to Newcastle, to be near her medical brother, although she and Eras still wrote. Eras, left in his own hazy world, 'sticks to his opium with many groans.' Hensleigh had become trying, and Carlyle was even more of a bore: Darwin had 'become quite nauseated with his mysticism, his intentional obscurity & affectation.'[14]

The days became alike 'as two peas:' up at seven leaving Emma asleep, tinker with *Coral Reefs* until ten, 'eat our breakfast, sit in our arm-chairs – and I watch the clock as the hand travels sadly too fast to half past eleven – Then to my study & work till 2 o'clock luncheon time.' Off to town after lunch, back in time for dinner at six. 'Sit in an apoplectic state, with slight snatches of reading till half past seven – tea, lesson of German, occasionally a little music & a little reading & then bed-time makes a charming close to the day.' It was monotonous but, he comforted himself, 'how much worse it would have been if I had been in any business.'

As Emma's confinement approached his sickness increased, and he suffered from migraines daily. On Christmas Eve he 'became unwell, & with the exception of two or three days remained so' for a couple of months.[15] As his sickness grew worse and the country careered towards ruin (the Welsh Chartist uprising had just been crushed and its leaders sentenced to death), he began thinking again of escaping London. A morbid air settled over the family; Emma was even more sickly, although he was getting the attention. His theorizing portended grave consequences; he was frightened for his respectability, and he would soon have the added worry of a family.

After Christmas, Emma's sister Elizabeth arrived to assist with the delivery. The grisly business upset a peaky Charles. 'What an awful affair a confinement is: it knocked me up, almost as much as it did Emma herself.' A baby boy, Charles's 'little Prince,' was born at 9.30 a.m. on 27 December – 'a prodigy of beauty & intellect.' William Erasmus he called the boy, after a great grandfather who had unearthed an ichthyosaurus before such a thing was dreamed of, 'so that *we* have a right of hereditary descent to be naturalists & especially geologists.'[16] He was baptized but without godparents, Charles and Emma objecting to religious proxies. Immediately the baby with his scrunched face and instinctive movements became the object of obsessive notetaking, his doting father peering over the cot at this convenient source of facial contortions. Willy Darwin's response to a looking-glass was compared with Jenny Orang's, and his first signs of anger, fear, pleasure, and reason were recorded.

Other work in 1840 ground to a spluttering halt. He missed deadlines for his *Birds* numbers and put *Coral Reefs* aside. Sickness finally sent him to Dr Holland, to no avail. 'Is it not mortifying [that] it is now nine weeks, since I have done a whole day's work,' he wailed to Lyell in February. 'But I wont grumble, any more.' The slightest excitement laid him up, so he shunned it, opting for quiet isolation. His 'little animalcule of a son' learnt to smile half-way through February, but his father saw less and less to smile about. He skipped four Geological Society meetings in a row and tried to resign his Secretary's job on 24 March, only to be talked out of it. It was soul-destroying for Emma. He was 'constantly in a state of languor that is very distressing.' At least he was 'not like the rest of the Darwins, who will not say how they really are; but he always tells me how he feels and never wants to be alone . . . so that I feel I am a comfort to him.'[17]

Emma nursed him, and Willy, while reading Carlyle's pamphlet on Chartism – this 'bitter discontent grown fierce and mad,' seethed the Scottish prophet. Botany Bay and heavy-handed policing were no solution; nor the workhouse a way of ridding society of its problems. Parliament, Church, and Aristocracy must cease abdicating their responsibilities, cease their obsession with game laws, cease their high-flown, dreary Malthusian apologetics, and start facing the grievances. Emma thought it 'full of compassion and good feeling but utterly unreasonable.' On his sick bed Charles too kept on 'reading and abusing him.'

Fanny and Hensleigh had moved to Gower Street, four doors down, making visiting and helping easier, yet life remained grim in Macaw Cottage. Willy was vaccinated, protecting him against smallpox, but nothing could protect his father, who had lost eight pounds in as many months. When he went home to Shrewsbury in April, the Doctor was unable to diagnose the problem.[18]

Charles began to pick up in May, and he was evidently strong enough to accept a seat on the Council of the Royal Geographical Society, even if he did then decamp to Maer and Shrewsbury to recuperate for five months. Although he thought furiously about evolution he managed only a couple of desultory notes on bees, and in August he suffered a relapse, forcing him back to bed. It was a long, idle, lost summer, the summer of '40.

He returned to London on 14 November and was in the Zoological Society the next day, examining snake skulls. Looking at the pickled exotica, he faced up to some seemingly insuperable problems. How on earth had bats evolved? Envisaging a half-way house was nonsensical, a *half*-winged bat! 'It is not possible to imagine what *habits* an animal could have had with such structure.' But he perked up as he thought of the mangrove-climbing mud skippers, with a fan-like fin on their back: 'Could anyone. have foreseen, sailing, climbing & mud-walking fish?'

His other problem was the fossil evidence for evolution. There was hardly any to speak of. But he was optimistic; the fossil scraps that we possess are 'a mere vestige' of what once existed, and more will turn up to plug the gaps. Even now, 'wonderful discoveries' were being made, none more so than a fossil ape, larger than a chimpanzee, found in Brazil. Just let detractors try to rubbish an ancestral 'monkey-man' now, he whooped defiantly.[19]

Darwin's outstanding problem was his audience. Ironically, he was dying to tell his old Anglican friends. But more unsympathetic ears could not be imagined, especially in this era of mounting class hostility. The clergy was under siege; the barbarians were at the gate. Talk of 'monkey-men' recalled the filth spouted by gutter atheists. None of the zoologists would have been appreciative, so what chance of finding allies in vicarage drawing-rooms? Yet the obsessions he shared with his cousin Fox – for Abyssinian cats and bizarre birds – overrode his caution. He told Fox that he was hammering away at 'Varieties & Species,' and begged crumbs of information on dog crosses and 'domestic birds.' Skeletons were his latest thing, so if Fox wanted to ship him a 'little hamper,' his dead 'half-bred African Cat' or any cross-bred fowl carcass would be 'more acceptable than the finest haunch of Venison or the finest turtle.'[20]

His own 'poor carcase' was improving in 1841. He could work for an hour or two a couple of days a week, and he devoted the time to a paper on the transport of boulders by ice-floes in South America. 'I am forced to live, however, very quietly and am able to see scarcely anybody & cannot even talk long with my nearest relations. I was at one time in despair & expected to pass my whole life as a miserable useless valetudinarian but I have now better hopes of myself.' He was still skipping the Geological Society (and he finally resigned his post in February), but it was easy to have Hensleigh read his iceberg paper and relay the comments.[21] He had begun delegating in a way that was to become characteristic. Proxies were quite acceptable here.

Emma was happy to be 'debarred from all London's gaieties' herself while attending to her ailing husband. Indeed, her second pregnancy made this exclusion easier. It was again a worrying time, but Anne Elizabeth was born safely on 2 March, a fair sunny-hearted rival to 'Doddy,' as Willy was now called. Charles doted on his first daughter from the start. She was a normal restless baby but a touch could soothe her as nothing else, and he delighted in cuddling and kissing her. One day, he knew, all his love would be returned, and more. Annie would be their 'solace in old age,' his nurse to the end.[22]

Even now her father was becoming delicate, 'bad & shivery,' as he put it, with headaches and sickness. Alarmed that he was sinking back into 'my old beggarly self,' he sojourned alone at Maer and Shrewsbury for June and July. Here he was 'scandalously indolent,' ignoring letters and dabbling with vegetable experiments. He had the Doctor's gardener try pea crosses, to obtain new varieties, but without much joy. 'I have gather the seed Peas,' the grower drawled in his Shropshire accent, 'but i dount see heney new kinds at all in them as the came up true to the sorts.'[23] At Maer during his strolls he was more successful in understanding the relationship between bees and flowers.

It was all he could do these summer days, drained of 'mental energy.' The doctors thought that 'it will be some years, before my constitution will recover itself.' He was miserable and wanted mollycoddling. His *cri de coeur* went out to nursing Emma: 'I was very very desolate & forlorn without my own Titty's sympathy & missed you cruelly.' And fate had another trick in store. His fears about first-cousin marriages were realized when the Doctor diagnosed Willy 'a very delicate child,' needing a special diet. A melancholy air now settled over the whole family; father and son were both afflicted. In the 'Malthusian rush' they were losing, the unhealthy results of inbreeding. The Doctor doubts 'that I shall become strong for some years – it has been a bitter mortification for me, to digest the conclusion, that the "race is for the strong" – & that I shall probably do little more, but must be content to admire the strides others make in Science.'

Comfort and quiet were what he needed, a rural retreat away from the urban tumult and calls on his time. Others had already gone. FitzRoy had moved fifteen miles out of town. Herschel, back from the Cape, had taken a country seat in the hop-picking county of Kent. This summer Charles persuaded his father to buy him a house, something about twenty miles away near a railway line, he fancied.[24]

In July he returned to the smoke and picked up the coral atoll book after a thirteen-month interval. He managed to spend a couple of hours each morning on the volume, and that, plus a short walk or ride, was his day.

He started to house-hunt in August, scouring the south-east along the chalk Downs. His Cambridge friends – Fox, Henslow, and Jenyns – had parishes, which seemed to suit them. Henslow was 'happy & flourishing – giving lectures, displays of fireworks, initiating agricultural prizes, & I do not know what besides, for his Parishioners.' It was the life; just switch the public lectures for private science, which Henslow had all but given up. Still, Henslow was turning up fossil footprints of extinct amphibians, which had Darwin green with envy.

In the depression London's streets were running sores, and he

longed 'to be settled in pure air, out of all the dirt, noise vice &
misery of this great Wen, as old Cobbett called it.' He read William
Cobbett's sprightly *Rural Rides*, the demagogue's diary of a
horseback trip through southern England. Bloody old Cobbett hated
London too, but his book offered little comfort. It was culled from
his 'twopenny trash' newspaper, the *Political Register*, and mixed
serene sights and political diatribe. Between images of Kent's pretty
villages he sniped at the clergy, Sir James Mackintosh, 'PARSON
MALTHUS,' and the corn laws.[25] There was no escaping the spirit of
the age.

Charles was unfit and unwilling to go out or receive visitors. By
his own admission he had 'grown a dull old spiritless dog.' Owen
was one of the few scientific friends who still came to tea, and when
he turned up on 10 November, he found Darwin handicapped more
than usual, with his arm in a sling. The two got on well; they mixed
in the Geological star chamber, and could snooze after confabs at the
Athenaeum. Both moved behind the scenes at the zoo, but Owen was
more interested in the apes' anatomy than in their expressions, and
he carved his way through the rare carcasses. He was petted and
patronized by the Anglican élite, who were scheming to obtain him a
Crown pension even now, at the age of thirty-seven. In August he
had been fêted at the British Association for his talk on fossil reptiles,
in which he created the concept of the 'dinosaur.' But in the same
speech he received even bigger cheers for castigating Lamarck's
fancies. He damned the notion of life's 'self-developing energies,' and
would have been horrified at Darwin's closet beliefs.[26]

Friendships had foundered on less. Owen execrated talk of an ape
ancestry. He denied it emphatically when describing the first adult
chimpanzee skeleton, which was unlike the appealing, wide-eyed
baby ape, and more of a beetle-browed, dog-jawed beast. Strip away
man's soul, make him a hairless ape, and he will sink degraded. But
Owen had done the *Zoology* proud, and his College of Surgeons was
always welcoming. It was filling with South American relics, many of
them Darwin's. The library had an enormous shell of an extinct
armadillo at one end, and workmen were about to set up a giant
ground sloth. The Owens had Darwin to breakfast in their rooms
here, unaware that he was a transmutationist. For Darwin this
double life was the stuff of inner confict, as his sickness confirmed.
Any moment his confidants could turn on him as they had on Grant.
He tried to re-join Owen and the others at the Geological Society, but
he finally gave up the attempt 'as I must remain quiet in the evenings,
or be utterly knocked up next day.'[27] Self-preservation came first.

Yet he was always on the verge of spilling his secret from sheer excitement. He knew his theory's sophistication and power; he knew that it was the way of the future. To cover up and disguise his three-year struggle had not been easy, nor had living a lie. Just as he had blurted out his doubts to Emma against good advice, he could not resist telling Lyell. The temptation was too much. Lyell could be trusted to keep a secret, however much he loathed Lamarck. In January 1842, Darwin let the cat out of the bag, probably cautiously, cryptically, and with some trepidation.

Lyell was on his American tour at the time, escaping the Boston winter by travelling south to geologize. Before sailing for the New World, he had heard that Darwin was leaving London. He doubted that 'a congenial soul so occupied with precisely the same pursuits & with an independance enabling him to pursue them will [ever again] fall so nearly in my way.' In America Darwin's letter must have stunned him. His geological twin a transmutationist! He was surely disappointed, but he merely noted on a fly-leaf that Darwin 'denies seeing a beginning to each crop of species.'[28] They did not have such parallel interests after all; on the most fundamental point of all they disagreed. Transmutation destroyed the biological base of Lyell's *Principles of Geology*, built to resist the Lamarckian onslaught. Perhaps it was better that the Darwins were moving away.

Charles was still panicky. After finishing the *Coral* proofs, Emma convinced him to go to Shrewsbury 'to see if a change would shake me right again.' But even as he arrived at The Mount on 7 March he was vomiting and shivery, and that night Susan nursed him to sleep. He was no better.

Throughout the spring he searched for a house, wanting one no more than five miles from a station, which, he laughed, was 'the length of my tether.' His work was finally finishing. In May *Coral Reefs* came out. He had lived with it, on and off, for three years and seven months, but it was a technical book that no 'human being will ever read.' (Not that it made any financial difference. His *Journal* had sold 1337 copies, but he had not seen a penny.) The huge *Fish* volume was finished too. The grant for the rest of the *Zoology* was petering out, and he wondered how to get the remaining bits of the *Beagle* haul into print without dipping into his own pocket.[29]

On 18 May they left town for two months, visiting the folks at Maer, where Charles continued bee-watching, before moving to Shrewsbury on 15 June. Taking advantage of the seclusion, he finally fleshed-out a thirty-five-page sketch of his evolutionary theory in pencil. He drained it of all references to the origin of conscience and morality, but the remaining body of work was far from anaemic. It looked good on paper, pieced together for the first time.

He described how farmers selectively bred race or dray horses, beef or tallow cows, according to need, before describing Nature as an analogous super-selectionist. By now he had it down pat: overpopulation and competition led to a '*Natural Selection*,' as the victors emerged triumphant from the 'war of nature.' This was the mechanism of descent. Everything at the present day was related. But animals were not steadily advancing up a Lamarckian ladder, one behind the other, with each grading into the next. Life had a tree-like pedigree; we could relate mammals – say the 'horse, mouse, tapir, elephant' – by searching back through the genealogy for the 'common parent.'

Then he piled on the arguments for 'descent' in general. The old fossils became common ancestors of diverse modern groups. He explained island colonization and diversification. Classification became as simple and natural as a gentleman's genealogy. So much was explicable: the rudimentary organs – remnants of once-functioning parts; and the unity of plan, where wings, hands, and flippers reflected a common inheritance.

He now had his sub-headings, and the format would remain constant. He also had his strategy: 'We no longer look on [an] animal as a savage does a ship,' he wrote, 'as a thing wholly beyond comprehension.' Wild animals are not a product of God's whim any more than planets are held up by his will. Everything results from grand laws – laws that 'should exalt our notion of the power of the omniscient Creator.' This was a modified Unitarian view of the divine government. And like a Unitarian Darwin (with a certain amount of double-think) argued that it got God off the hook for evil and suffering, bundling the blame on to 'natural law.' He finished with a flourish:

> It is derogatory that the Creator of countless systems of worlds
> should have created each of the myriads of creeping parasites
> and [slimy] worms which have swarmed each day of life on
> land and water on [this] one globe. We cease being astonished,
> however much we may deplore, that a group of animals should
> have been directly created to lay their eggs in bowels and
> flesh of other [parasitic wasps] – that some organisms should
> delight in cruelty . . . that annually there should be an
> incalculable waste of eggs and pollen. From death, famine,

rapine, and the concealed war of nature we can see that the highest good, which we can conceive, the creation of the higher animals has directly come.

Here was realism and reverence combined, a theological advance on Paley's rose-tinted Creationism. 'There is a simple grandeur in [this] view of life with its powers . . . being breathed into matter under one or a few forms.'[30]

But grandeur to him was heresy to the geologists and blasphemy to the parsons. Were this not so, he could have planned to publish. The *Journal* was acclaimed, *Coral Reefs* in the shops, and the *Zoology* on its way, so why not follow these up with a book on evolution? He had enough material, but absolutely no intention of going ahead – at least not in this hysterical climate.

Consider, who would read the book? There was a genteel audience for his geology, but not for his species theory.

At most his science might tempt the odd breeder. But the best of them believed that domestic races had already been stretched to the limit. And anyway the salts of the earth wanted farming manuals, not arcane treatises. There *was* an audience in the wider sense. Some medical men and Dissenting industrialists might have applauded. More and more these oligarchs of new wealth were occupying the back benches of the learned societies: mining engineers, empire builders, improving doctors, and London professors.[31] Darwin's Nature sanctioned no privilege; everything was thrown into competition, and talent was rewarded. The new meritocrats wanted nothing more.

Further, law and order in science and society was the Dissenters' creed. A legislative harness guaranteed John Bull's freedoms and prevented social upheaval. For Darwin, too, law kept populations in their place and a capricious Deity out of earthly matters. Revolutionary upheavals were as illegitimate in civil as in geological history. Evolution was the key. The 'regular laws [of development],' he noted, 'baffles idea of revolution.'[32] And with Chartists massing, it was time for middle-class Malthusians to stand up and show that nature was on the side of the bosses.

On the religious side, the book would have sat beside Southwood Smith's *Divine Government*, which promised natural progress, civil liberties, and freedom to compete, everything Unitarian reformers wanted. But these social improvers were envious of Anglican power and trying to oust the privileged élite. Darwin thought like a Unitarian but felt for the Cambridge clerics. Henslow, Sedgwick, and Jenyns had all helped to make his career and reputation; he coveted their lifestyle and respectability. His theory – with its improving nature and cut-throat competition – would have armed their urban enemies. And ultimately – the crux of course – at its core stood a damnable transmutation that would make man a beast and throw their world into confusion. How could he unleash such a work?

Nor was this the worst scenario. Imagine if it fell into the hands of the gutter snipes. The pauper presses might have execrated his weak-to-the-wall ethic. They might have hated Malthus, loathed the poor laws, and damned Darwin's 'base, brutal and bloody Whigs.' For these socialist tykes, nature could never condemn the co-operatives or condone the workhouses. Competition and exploitation were anathema.[33] But they *could* have cut up and cannibalized his book for their own ends. There was a real risk of this.

The atheists had already founded an illegal penny paper, the uncompromising *Oracle of Reason*, a year old and still selling in its thousands. It vilified the rich priests and armed infidel missionaries with geological tidbits to use against them. One of the cadre, the working-class printer William Chilton, fashioned a revolutionary Lamarckism, driven from below, pushing nature and society towards a higher, brighter, co-operative future (a meaningless concept to the port-swilling nobility). The hard-bitten editors were fitting evolution into their militant credo. Materialism was given revolutionary class overtones. Man was just a collection of organized atoms. 'Life is nothing and nothing life' was Chilton's slogan, tailored to the poor and downtrodden.[34]

The *Oracle* cynics denigrated Paley's 'happy' nature. It was a 'pernicious' way to justify the status quo. Chilton's nature had a satanic air that would have shocked even Darwin. Where was the design? Had God existed, he would have planned 'less suffering and more enjoyment, less hypocrisy and more sincerity, fewer rapes, frauds, pious and impious butcheries.'[35] It was raw, rough, and calculated to insult. Accordingly, a succession of *Oracle* editors were jailed for blasphemy after well-publicized trials.

Their evolution was a world removed from Darwin's. His suited the rising industrial professional classes. Theirs was for socialist workers. His was stabilizing, theirs revolutionary. And yet, they would have relished seeing simians substituted for souls. Nothing could have stopped them from pirating his book and playing up a monkey ancestry. No one escaped their democratic depredations. Lyell, Southwood Smith, Elliotson, Lawrence – all were grist to their mills, all plagiarized. Darwin's lawful chains would be even better to truss up the Anglicans' meddling God.

Of course Darwin could not publish. Materialism petrified him, and one can see why, with it condemned by the forces of Church-and-State as a blasphemous derision of the Christian law of the land. He was too worldly-wise not to sense the danger, the damning class implications. He had no illusions about how he would be treated. Carlile and Taylor had been hounded, Lawrence's trial was notorious, Elliotson was being trashed in the Tory press, and Grant had been humiliated before his very eyes. By netting man and ape together he risked being identified with atheistic low-life, or with extreme Dissenters cursing the 'fornicating' Church. The 'whole fabric' was ready to be ripped apart without his help. As the old world 'totters & falls,' he could not be seen aiding the demolition.

Ultimately he was frightened for his respectability. For a gentleman among the Oxbridge set, priming itself to guard man's soul against the socialist levellers, publishing would have been tantamount to treachery – a betrayal of the old order. It was a terrifying predicament. His crisis might have been precipitated by an industrializing society, but it was the stuff of nightmares. He might have been formulating a science for the expanding market economy. But for the moment it threatened the existing élite – the Church leaders, who were resisting change, suspicious of a greedy capitalism destroying the old order.[36]

On 18 July Darwin returned to London and started copying his evolutionary sketch, revising and over-writing until it was barely legible. He found the city a cauldron. The ledgers of death were filling up, Malthusian hatreds were festering, the northern diehards were resisting a second onslaught by London poor-law commissioners, wage-cuts and unemployment were swelling the Chartist ranks. Society was teetering.

The Darwins' house-hunting acquired a new urgency, and within days they found a place, a former parsonage, in the rural hamlet of Down, near Farnborough in Kent, 'a quiet most rustic spot on the chalk.' They spent 22 July exploring the village and outlying district with its thatched barns, spending the night in the local public house. Emma – pregnant again – was 'a good-deal disappointed' with the North Downs, thinking how 'desolate' they would look on a bleak wintery day. The house was 'square and unpretending, built of shabby bricks,' but it came with a smallholding. And the village was 'extraordinarily rural & quiet,' away from trouble spots, with an old-world charm where the locals still tipped their hats as the great folks passed.[37] Moreover it was cheap: Charles talked the price down to £2000.

In mid-August the country was paralysed by a general strike called by the Chartists. Half a million workers were out, fighting wage cuts and demanding the vote – what the Attorney General damned as the 'most formidable conspiracy ever.' Leaders declared it permanent, until the People's Charter was accepted. The Cabinet went into emergency session and put the troops on alert. The Riot Act was read in many cotton towns, and in some the troops shot and killed demonstrators.

For three days, from 14 – 16 August, battalions of Guards and Royal Horse Artillery marched up through central London to the new Euston Station to put down the riots in Manchester. The troops were trailed by jeering crowds. The commotion was terrible as they passed Darwin's road, with screams of 'Remember, you are brothers,' and 'Don't go and slaughter your starving fellow countrymen.' By the time the battalions reached Gower Street the demonstrators were hemming them in and the soldiers had fixed bayonets. The Darwins were also hemmed in, with gangs everywhere. The streets were frightening, even with a huge police presence. Each day the situation worsened. On the 16th the station (only a few hundred yards from the house) was actually blocked and the troops repeatedly charged the crowds to clear a way in.[38]

The geological squires damned the Chartists for 'trying to extort concessions by the terror of civil war,' and were thankful that 'the insurgents do not seem to have any good leaders.' Those they had were being rounded up. Following *The Times*'s law reports, Darwin might have caught the unfolding drama as the *Oracle* editor George Holyoake was tried on 17 and 18 August. Holyoake's blasphemy was to deny God's existence and to consider the people too poor to support parsons during the depression. Trial provided a public platform, and Holyoake defended himself in style, rhapsodizing on atheism, socialism, and other 'wretched sophistries and absurdities' continuously for eight hours. These agitators sought respectability in martyrdom, and he was duly convicted of the 'heinous offence' and given a six-month term. During this, *The Times* added, 'he will have ample opportunity of reflecting upon the enormity of his guilt, and of discovering the futility of the impious doctrines which he has the effrontery to avow.'[39] What he did discover was bitterness, when his elder daughter died of malnutrition while he was inside. It left him with an abiding hatred of Christianity.

A week later the Duke of Wellington so feared an uprising in London that he called for the Guards to return and special units of police were put on stand-by. The gentlemen of science also stood their ground. Darwin's *Zoology* collaborator Richard Owen drilled with the Honourable Artillery Company, and it was called out to back the police. For days on end, up to ten thousand demonstrators massed on the commons all over the capital. Working men and women milled about the streets, shouting and cheering. Even scientific institutions were preparing to resist attack. The worst was expected. In the north troops were refusing to fire on the people. In London the Home Secretary kept an enormous police and military presence on the streets.

Emma, her confinement almost due, was overseeing the packing. It was now the fourth week of the general strike, and the transportation of the ringleaders had begun. The Darwins were thankful to be getting out. Willy, Annie, and Emma left on 14 September and two days later the last trunk was ready for removal. 'I long for tomorrow,' Charles wrote excitedly. 'I feel sure I shall become deeply attached to Down.'[40]

1842–1851

26. The Zoological Gardens in Regent's Park. Darwin spent endless hours watching the animals as a landlubber back in England.

27. Seeing Jenny in 1838, the first orang to go on display, led to a burst of notes: 'Let man visit Ourang . . . see its intelligence . . . let him look at savage, roasting his parent, naked, artless, not improving . . . & let him dare to boast of his proud preeminence.'

28. Emma Wedgwood at the time of her marriage to Charles in 1839.

29. (*Opposite, above*) Charles and Emma's first home, 'Macaw Cottage,' 12 Upper Gower Street. Darwin finished devising his theory of evolution here in 1839.

30. (*Opposite, below*) Troops marching through hostile crowds to Euston Station, on their way to suppress the Manchester riots in August 1842. For three days the battalions passed close by Darwin's house.

31. Charles and his eldest son William in an 1842 daguerreotype: the only known photograph of Darwin with a member of his family.

32. (*Below*) Down House as Charles and Emma first saw it.

33. (*Above*) Darwin's old
study: to the right his tiers of
working files, to the left a
curtained privy. His book-
lined back wall is reflected in
the mirror on the mantelpiece.

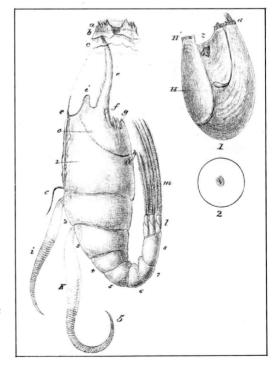

34. Here Darwin dissected the
world's smallest barnacle, 'Mr
Arthrobalanus' (seen actual
size within the circle).

35. At the 1847 British Association for the Advancement of Science meeting at Oxford University the geologists (seen here) carpeted Robert Chambers, author of the evolutionary *Vestiges*. Darwin was present, but unknown to anyone he was carrying his own evolutionary essay.

36. (*Opposite, above*) Darwin at forty.

37. (*Opposite, below*) Great Malvern, dominated by Dr Gully's water-cure hotel and the Priory Church. In 1851 Charles and Annie stayed at Montreal House, the larger residence on the hillside, level with the church tower.

Great Malvern

38. (*Above*) The photo Charles wept over for life, his beloved Annie (b. 1841), at the time of her first trip to Malvern. Her tragic death at Easter 1851 destroyed the final shreds of Darwin's Christianity.

39. The headstone still stands beneath a cedar of Lebanon in the Priory Churchyard. Darwin was too distraught to attend the funeral and avoided Malvern for the next twelve years.

40. Queen Victoria re-opening the Crystal Palace in 1854. When Clara
Novello backed by the mighty choir sang 'God Save the Queen' Emma
burst into tears.

41. (*Inset*) Herbert Spencer, railway surveyor turned evolutionary
ideologue.

42. (*Above*) The George Inn,
Down's main public house and
grocer's shop, where Charles and
Emma stayed on their first visit in
1842. The Down Friendly Society,
with Darwin as Honorary
Treasurer, held its meetings in the
pub from 1850 until 1882.

43. Charles's freethinking elder
brother Erasmus, after a decade of
'literary leisure' and opium-eating.

44. (*Above left*) William (b. 1839), bookish and well-mannered, on his way to Rugby School.   45. (*Above right*) Henrietta (b. 1843), aged six, wearing a dress to match Annie's.   46. (*Below left*) George (b. 1845), schoolboy soldier. Darwin thought that he might become a naturalist.   47. (*Below right*) Francis (b. 1848), private to Georgy's lieutenant, and his father's scientific aide-de-camp.

48. The Royal Society. Darwin received its Royal Medal in 1853.

49. The man who summoned up lost supercontinents to explain the distribution of species, Edward Forbes.

50. Revd John Brodie Innes, Tory High Churchman, Darwin's vicar and confidant: 'one of those rare mortals' from whom 'one can differ & yet feel no shade of animosity'.

51. Darwin in 1854, finished with barnacles at last. The strain had begun to show.

52. His sounding board, the botanist Joseph Hooker, photographed at the same time.

53. Fancy pigeons. Top (left to right): baldheads, pouters, jacobins (with head ruff), magpie and swallow. Bottom: two fantails with a carrier in-between, brunswick, nun, and turbit. Darwin kept them all and thought the 'diversity of the breeds . . . astonishing'.

54. The gentlemen's annual pigeon show at the Freemasons' Tavern in 1853. Darwin visited all the feather clubs, high and low.

20

The Extreme Verge of the World

THE DAY ARRIVED, 17 September 1842. Charles dressed, collected his valuables, and slammed the door on 12 Upper Gower Street for the last time. The traffic was worse than when he moved in four years ago – students streaming back to University College, barristers bustling up to Euston Station to catch trains to the north, where 1500 strikers awaited prosecution. It was no place for a growing family, or for a couple who loved the country. Certainly it was no place for an ambitious young naturalist with a secret. Fond memories, yes – Macaw Cottage had been his and Emma's first home. But he was leaving none too soon.

In the street his new 100-guinea horse and carriage stood at the ready. The quickest way out of town lay due south, over Waterloo Bridge, past the gin shops and brothels to the Elephant and Castle. On the right in the distance, the Palace of Westminster. On the left, the Rotunda and Horsemonger-lane gaol, with prisoners' relatives outside, a reminder that this was radical territory. Still further and the great landmarks vanished. At New Cross Gate they left the smoke behind and breathed country air. The traffic thinned out past Bromley as they made for Keston. The horse was working harder now, plodding up the chalky North Downs. Flinty fields surrounded them on either side. Countless millions of years ago these vast chalk slopes had been eroded to form flat-bottomed valleys – 'bottoms,' the locals called them – separated by strips of woodland that provided fringes of autumn colour. Near Keston the road became a narrow stony lane.[1] Slower now, rising 200 feet in the last two miles, the lane led through beech woods into the village of Down.

Two hours out of London, sixteen miles from St Paul's, this was the perfect rural retreat: a parish like Henslow's at Hitcham, or Fox's

301

new one in Cheshire – a parish like the one Charles himself had dreamt of aboard the *Beagle*, the one in which the Doctor would have installed him all those years ago. The scene struck a responsive chord. He breathed an enormous sigh of relief. Here he was at a safe distance from society. No more worrying about what people might say; the rustics would respect him for the gentleman he was, not judge him by what he thought or wrote. He would see everyone on his own terms, when and as he pleased. The nearest train station, Sydenham, was eight miles away, and the hilly drive cut Down off, secured its inhabitants, preserved their past. A parish set in aspic – the ideal habitat for a gentleman evolutionist. 'Down, near Bromley, Kent,' was the address he sent his old servant Covington in Australia. 'N.B.,' he added, 'this will be my direction for the rest of my life.'²

The lane went straight to the centre of the village. There, against the churchyard wall, stocks had stood until recent years. The great yew at the lychgate was centuries old. The flint-walled parish church of St Mary dated from the fourteenth century. A 29-year-old curate, the Revd John Willott, had charge of Down's 444 souls, but it was a meagre living, his income from rents and tithes barely topping £100 a year. The Baptist chapel lay a stone's throw away, and for thirty years its little band of members had lived patiently under the Anglican regime.³

The parishioners were agricultural labourers and tenant farmers mostly. Scattered over two and a half square miles, they worked with their hands and walked everywhere. Their life centred on the village. In that cluster of forty houses lay all their essential services: a butcher, a baker, a carpenter, as well as the grocer's shop, a post office, and a pub. The George and Dragon Inn stood conveniently opposite the church. What could not be obtained here the 'carrier' would fetch on his weekly run to London. It was a stable, closely knit community, like ten thousand hamlets in Victoria's England.

Down had its great folks too. Some twenty men owned property enough to qualify as voters, but few were really wealthy. The better-off lived in houses that bore the names of old village families, such as Petleys and Trowmers. The occupants of Down Court, a 'most beautiful old farm-house with great thatched barns' and traces of a moat, were successors to the lords of the manor.⁴

On the outskirts was a 3000-acre estate with a mansion being built. This was High Elms farm, with Sir John Lubbock, his wife and four children in residence. A third-generation City banker – of Sir John William Lubbock, Forster & Co. – he was less interested in money than science. For his work in astronomy and mathematics he had been elected a Fellow of the Royal Society. The folk at Down knew nothing of this. To them the money was what counted, and Sir John obliged them by spending it. The mansion building and estate gave jobs to dozens of local craftsmen, staff, and tenants. Sir John was the chief landowner and employer in the area. Naturally, the squire's friends would be great folks too. Sir John had already announced the good news to his eldest son John, aged seven: 'Mr. Darwin is coming to live at Down.'[5]

With villagers peering quizzically, touching their hats as he passed, Charles drove his carriage to the right at the church, down Luxted Road, past the village pond and gently up into open country. On the right, a few hundred yards along, was a plain brick building hugging the road – Down House.[6] This would be home.

For a parsonage it was modest enough – 'oldish & ugly' but 'largish & . . . cheap.' Built as a farmhouse and extended some sixty years before, it comprised kitchen, scullery, and stores in the oldest part; drawing-room, dining-room, and study on the main ground floor; and bedrooms enough for half the Darwin–Wedgwood clan on the two floors above. Down's previous incumbent had lived there for three years and made various improvements. Not that these were obvious now. Two years standing empty had taken their toll, and the faded musty rooms were due for refurbishment. But with all his furniture '& chattel' in place, the fires lit, and Willy 'in ectasies,' tearing around 'country ouse,' Charles thought it good enough to be going on with.[7] Alterations could wait.

Besides, with Emma at full-term, the first priority was to make life comfortable for her and the baby. No sooner done than the confinement began, six days after Charles arrived. The village surgeon rushed over from 'two fields off' and delivered a girl, Mary Eleanor. The baby, though small and feeble, helped relieve Emma's anxiety about her father, who she now heard was dying. And her recovery was quicker than ever, owing to the 'country air,' Darwin assumed. At nine days old, on a Sunday, Mary was baptized in the parish church. Erasmus came down for the event. Afterwards the baby went on 'fairly well,' but she lived only another fortnight. On 19 October Charles, Emma, and the Revd Willott gathered in the churchyard to inter the body. Charles soldiered through the funeral, which he had dreaded. Emma's grief was worse. She had hoped that the baby's 'likeness to Mamma,' now an elderly invalid, 'might run through her mind as well as face.'[8] Both of them took comfort from the fact that the child had not lived longer and suffered more.

It was a grim start to their new life. They threw themselves into the house, and Willy and Annie distracted them. Charles rejoiced to Fox that 'our two little souls are better & happier' than in London. He omitted to explain why there were not three. Fox still had not come to terms with his wife's death in childbirth the previous spring; not even a trip abroad had healed his heart. 'Strong affections,' Charles consoled him, 'have always appeared to me, the most noble part of a man's nature . . . Your grief is the necessary price for having been born with . . . such feelings.' 'But,' he added, 'I am writing away without really being able to put myself in your position – you have my sincerest sympathy & respect in your sorrow.'⁹ Losing Mary was the closest that death had touched his adult life.

Other children, too, distracted Charles and Emma, though not without bringing their own heartaches. That autumn Emma's brother Hensleigh had a long illness. To relieve the strain on Fanny, they agreed to take in the older cousins, Snow aged nine, Bro eight, and Erny five. With their own, aged three and two, it was quite a houseful. One day in early November Emma sent them out for a hike with the nursery maid Bessy, herself only a teenager. They had permission to explore Cudham Wood, but Bessy took them in the wrong direction, across a sprawling bottom into the 'Big Woods,' full of giant oaks with a tangle of hazel coppices cut by footpaths. It was wintery, with frosty fields. Snow and Willy got separated and turned up at home, their feet caked in clay. Fighting back the tears, Snow told Uncle Charles that the others were lost. He set off urgently with Parslow, and after asking at a farmhouse, tracked them down, huddled together, cold and frightened, Erny and Bro and Bessy, who had been carrying Annie for three hours. The men scooped up the little ones and took them all to the farmhouse for a reviving snack, then, with the neighbour's help, brought the babes back home safely.¹⁰

Charles and Emma were learning about Kentish country ways. Down was nothing like London, more like Maer. The rural economy was as different from the urban cash nexus as the Big Woods were from Gower Street. People here were closely interdependent. They bartered and bargained as familiars if not equals. Relationships were all-important, and these began at home. As the Darwin home itself began to take shape, with Parslow as their most trusted servant, other household staff would have to be found locally, and hiring could be difficult unless the family observed the proprieties and kept on good terms with the neighbours. A cook was vital for Emma, as a coachman was for Charles. A footman would assist Parslow at door and table. In the spring a gardener would have to be found; and, soon afterwards, another nurse.

Emma was pregnant again, a few months after Mary's death. With the prospect of three children under the age of four, young Bessy required expert help. Enter Brodie, a staunch Scottish lass with 'carrotty hair, china-blue eyes,' and a face made memorable by smallpox. She had proved her worth by spurning a suitor to tend the deranged wife and children of the impoverished writer William Makepeace Thackeray. Down House was like a holiday compared to the Thackerays' ménage in Paris. True, there was a problem of Bessy's 'pertness' towards her, but Emma – a stickler for tranquillity – used a 'sledge-hammer' to keep the peace.

While Emma ran the household, Charles passed the winter surveying his new estate. He did make a start on the 'second very thin part' of the *Beagle* geology, on volcanic islands. And he intended to spend a night or two in London every month 'to keep up my communication with scientific men,' so as not to 'turn into [a] complete Kentish Hog.' Even so, the thought of it turned his stomach. Going there 'so generally knocks me up, that I am able to do scarcely anything.'[11] But the country got the better of him. Like Henslow in Hitcham, criticized for neglecting his botany, Charles took to pottering around the parsonage.

Down House sat high and exposed, with a 'desolate air.' The old clump of stunted trees beside it – yew, fir, mulberry, chestnut – accentuated the bleakness rather than giving any shelter. To the rear lay the rest of the property – fifteen acres of hayfield – with only a hedge separating the house from a 'rather ugly distant horizon.' The public footpaths were too close. Charles's only real protection was the primeval terrain: a great chalk escarpment to the south, cutting off the estate from the low country of Kent; a deep valley to the north between the village and the road to London; and to the east and west 'impassible' valley bottoms. 'We are absolutely at [the] extreme verge of [the] world,' he boasted to Fox – but even this was not safe enough for him.

The wind was vicious. In the south-westerly gales the children could taste the salt on the drawing-room window-panes, although the sea was forty miles away. And that winter the exposed north face of the house took a brutal beating. He craved solitude, a 'quiet routine.' Nothing must happen out of the ordinary, nothing unexpected. 'I cannot dine out or receive visitors, except relations with whom I can pass some time after dinner in silence.'[12] For such a man, artifice had to help nature; fortifications had to be built.

Charles was full of home-improvement schemes. The Doctor put up the money – 'a cool 300£' to start – against his future inheritance. Upstairs the bedrooms needed a rethink. Emma would have a 'truly magnificent' one of her own, and there had to be some for relations. A schoolroom was also imperative – soon there would be a governess to give the children lessons. Downstairs the kitchen and pantry were not quite right. The drawing-room, and master bedroom above, were large but undistinguished spaces. They overlooked the garden in the direction of the Big Woods, towards the setting sun. What each needed was a handsome bow, with three windows to catch the light and warmth.[13] And after all the structural work was done, complete redecoration.

Bricklayers and carpenters moved in as spring arrived. 'A most deceptious property to buy Sir,' one said, meaning a compliment. His architect was right on how much cheaper labour was here than in London. Outside, security arrangements were being stepped up. The kitchen garden would be re-designed, with a high wall running 100 yards along it to form the northern boundary of the property. Other 'great earthworks' would be undertaken to embellish the grounds and raise a large mound outside the front door, to 'make the place much snugger.' Beyond the mound an orchard would be planted. And further still lay a slip of land beside Luxted Road, which Charles would have to buy.[14]

That road was a problem. Though only a cart track, it permitted easy access from north and south, skirting the frontage just yards from his study window. As things stood passers-by could peer right inside. 'The publicity of the place is at present intolerable,' he declared, and in April 1843 he sought leave from the parish vestry to lower the road and build a perimeter wall. The officials were 'as civil, as civil could be,' and work began immediately. He hired 'a sort of jack of all knowledge' named Vinson to help him. 'I suspect he is an old rogue, but he is a useful one.' The 'effects of a 1£ present & the hopes of another' set him calculating the volume of earth to be moved – some 200 cubic yards. Then the heavy spadework began. It was a mammoth undertaking: from 18 to 24 inches of flinty clay were laboriously dug from the road along a 500-foot stretch, the flints being used to build a wall over six feet high, running from the far end of the house to the northernmost point on the property. But the whole job cost only £110.

These projects dragged on for many months, although the worst of the disruption – everyone hoped – would be over in time for the new baby. When eventually the walls were up and Charles felt secure, he added the finishing touch: a mirror outside his study window, so that callers could be spied approaching the front door.[15]

The 'capital study 18 x 18,' as Charles called it, was the focal point. Two great shuttered windows lit the corniced room with clear, white northern light, ideal for writing, dissecting, and microscopy. The fireplace, surrounded by milky marble, made up for the absent sun, with a chimney-breast separating ample alcoves for books and files. An arm-chair sat in one corner, between hearth and window, and tables were placed within easy reach. In the corner opposite, the door opened on to a long hallway leading from the front entrance to the kitchen. Life went on far above, in the children's rooms, and in the servants' quarters at the other end of the house.[16] In his insular laboratory, cut off from the world, he could think clear thoughts and contain the contradiction that was tearing him apart. It was an Archimedean point from which, given time, he would move the world.

Not that much earth-moving was going on at present, except outdoors. He tried dabbling with his species sketch in the spring, but the commotion made it impossible. Indeed, he spent a desultory first year at Down, only occasionally getting to grips with the greater upheavals in the past. He worried that his explanation of the strange parallel roads of Glen Roy – as prehistoric sea beaches – was already crumbling. The Swiss naturalist Louis Agassiz, promoting his novel idea of a former Ice Age, was suggesting that a glacier had once blocked Glen Roy, damming it to form a lake – making these 'roads' old lake margins. Agassiz's icy catastrophism made Darwin shiver; gentle rising and subsidence of the land was the key.[17]

For years his manuscript on volcanoes had kicked around; now, as he picked up the subject again, he was mortified to discover just how much remained to be done. He rummaged through his old *Beagle* notes and called in the specialist reports on his 'beastly rocks.' He even made a couple of flying visits to the Geological Society, imploring the curator to have books, maps, and nodules of glassy obsidian '*ready* for my inspection, as my time is short.' The whole process took him back to those seasick days of discovery, when he set foot on the Galapagos, St Helena, and St Jago; and his first sight of the obsidian beds and lava 'bombs' strewn over Ascension. How much more those romantic places had meant to him than his turgid 150-page *Volcanic Islands* would mean to the geological community. 'I hope you will read my volume,' he despaired to his preceptor Lyell, 'for if you don't, I cannot think of anyone else who will!'[18]

He craved recognition from his fellow geologists – approval shored up his respectability – and it drove him to finish the *Beagle* reports. Other writings that year hinted at more heretical concerns. Reproduction, such a fact of life in Down House, was still fascinating for the light it shed on descent. He penned a short paper on the spawning arrowworms he had trawled from Brazilian seas ten years before. His interest in their eggs was never-failing, and the granular matter they released when disrupted. In another note, on peculiar double-flowered gentians, posted off to the *Gardeners' Chronicle*, he showed that the flowers on a single plant can be arranged in 'a series ... by which the stamens are seen to become deformed, and gradually to pass into small petals and scales.' Perhaps some alteration of the environment determined this 'metamorphic change ... early in the plant's life.' 'Is there any shadow of truth in this theory?'[19]

Coy but provocative, he concealed much more than readers realized. 'Metamorphic changes,' environmental causes, these terms had double meanings. They referred to individual development, but evolutionists gave them wider connotations – tadpoles metamorphosed into frogs, but evolutionists also talked of fish 'metamorphosing' into reptiles, and apes into men. Language was a screen; metamorphosing plants could be mooted safely, but they pointed up Charles's contradiction. He had unselfconsciously assumed the guise of an orthodox clerical-naturalist, a pottering, parsonage-living harmless soul, and it was making his quandary worse. And he wasn't just *living* in a clergyman's house; he was actually beginning to emulate the most eminent of parish naturalists, the Revd Gilbert White.

For almost fifty years White's *Natural History and Antiquities of Selborne* had inspired clergymen and country folk to observe the rhythm of the seasons. It taught them to record nature's trifling phenomena, even – as White did so famously – to compile a country diary. Charles had pored over the *Natural History* as a teenager; in February 1843 he had read it again in the edition just published by his friend, the Revd Jenyns. Then in May he reacquainted himself with two of the best known books to have come from rectories, Paley's *Natural Theology* and *An Introduction to Entomology* by the Revd William Kirby and William Spence. And that month he started a country diary of his own.[20] He called it 'The General Aspect.'

His observations were largely geological, made during extensive rambles. Flints, footpaths, farmhouses, each was discussed. The 'slippery red clay' from October to April, the brilliant flowers of early spring, the 'quite extraordinary' humming of hive bees in the summer were also mentioned, showing that in his first cycle of seasons he made the parish his own, took charge of its natural-history aspect, became nature's 'parson' (as rustics liked to say) to Lubbock's new-model squire. With the gentlest condescension, so like a man of the cloth, he noted the prevalence of error among the yokels concerning the overhead humming heard on hot days. 'The labourers here say it is made by "air-bees," and one man, seeing a wild bee in a flower different from the hive kind, remarked: "That, no doubt, is an air-bee".'[21]

With renovations going on all around and workmen to keep an eye on, Charles filled up the idle moments by bestowing favours and good advice. 'Get up your steam ... & have a ramble in Wales,' he jollied Fox, still down in the dumps; 'its glorious scenery must do every one's heart & body good.' Covington in Australia was going deaf, and Darwin sent him an ear trumpet. Like a true country curate, he was dispensing patronage everywhere. He interceded with FitzRoy, recently appointed Governor of New Zealand, on behalf of the émigré son of his successor as Secretary of the Geological Society. He gave a glowing reference to the sacked Assistant Curator of the Zoological Society George Waterhouse – the man who had described the *Beagle*'s mammals – to help him obtain a post at the British Museum. He even stood godfather, with Richard Owen, to Waterhouse's son (who was christened Charles Owen Waterhouse). Most portentous of all (though he did not know it), he heard news of a young ship's surgeon and botanist named Joseph Hooker. Hooker, sailing with Capt. Ross's Antarctic expedition, was the son of the Director of the Royal Botanic Gardens at Kew, Sir William Hooker. Darwin told Sir William that, when Joseph returned, his own plants from 'T[ierra]. del. Fuego & of Southern Patagonia will be joyfully laid at his disposal.'[22] Such generosity would be rewarded.

In the first week of July 1843 word came that Emma's father was dying. Charles and Emma, seven months pregnant, set off immediately on the long, sad, anxious farewell journey to Maer, arriving with just days to spare. At seventy-four, Josiah was the ghost of his former self. Once the commanding industrialist and Whig statesman, he had become a hallucinating bedridden wreck, clutching at the last threads of life with quivering, senile hands. This was the revered uncle – 'so high, so pure, so true and so engaging by his exquisite modesty' – whose intervention had smoothed Charles's path aboard the *Beagle*. His wife Bessy, too, was now a total invalid, and scarcely able to grieve for her pathetic husk of a husband. Her life seemed 'sadder than death;' Maer was melancholy as never before. Only Elizabeth was left, Emma's hunchbacked eldest sister, who cared unstintingly for their parents. The old days of autumn shoots and parties were gone for ever. Josiah died on the 12th, peacefully. The women sought religious consolation, the more earnestly because they all worried about their father's indifference to God. Charles lingered, then made his usual summer pilgrimage to Shrewsbury before heading home.[23]

He returned to find letters from Waterhouse waiting. Waterhouse wanted advice on that be-all and end-all of British natural history, classification. Conventional classification meant ordering nature, all living things in their place, each given its due rank, slotted into a fixed hierarchy. Classifiers, legions of them, were taming a chaotic world, providing a rock on which an immutably Creative biology could be built. They were revealing God's Plan. Darwin had struggled with the problem of a 'natural classification' ever since he opened his species notebooks. It was obvious to him that few were taking the right approach, and Waterhouse least of all. 'It has long appeared to me, that the root of the difficulty in settling such questions as yours,' Darwin told him, 'lies in our ignorance of what we are searching after.' Why construct a classification? What was it designed to show?

Waterhouse was poor and powerless, a minor salaried official. When Darwin praised him in his testimonial as 'so infinitely my superior' he meant in his stock of zoological facts. Waterhouse was above all a describer. Beyond this, Darwin saw him wandering in circles. Waterhouse's nature consisted of clusters of wheels. All groups – species, genera, families – sat on circles. The circular classification kept nature safely and aimlessly revolving. There was no 'chain of life,' no linear piling of creature upon creature; thus it was safe from the Lamarckian evolutionists, who might turn the chain into an escalator, and set it gliding upwards towards man.

Darwin had Waterhouse's confidence. Now was the moment to try to turn him. Indeed, a week back from seeing his sage old freethinking father, a fortnight since his beloved uncle died, he was feeling bloody-minded. 'Most authors,' Charles snapped, referring to classification,

> say it is an endeavour to discover the laws according to which the Creator has willed to produce organized beings – But what empty high-sounding sentences these are – it does not mean order in time of creation, nor propinquity to any

one type, as man. – in fact it means just nothing. According to my opinion, (which I give every one leave to hoot at . . .) classification consists in grouping beings according to their actual *relationship*, ie their consanguinity, or descent from common stocks.

He had tipped his hand to a colleague; he was out in the open now, a new brusqueness masking his fear. He believed in a real genealogy, a pedigree, a bloodline.[24] He was proposing a system far less aesthetic, and much messier and more contingent, with a proper historical aspect supplied by fossils. He had exploded with a force that surprised even himself.

Nor was that the last word. A few days later he skewered Waterhouse with another well-honed letter. He rammed the same point home. '*All rules for a natural classification are futile until you can clearly explain, what you are aiming at.*' He protested that anything less than an actual genealogical relationship is useless as a criterion. Then he chanted his credo:

> I believe (though why I should trouble you with my belief, which must & ought to appear the merest trash and hypothesis?) that if every organism, which ever had lived or does live, were collected together . . . a perfect series would be presented, linking all, say the Mammals, into one great, quite indivisible group – and I believe all the orders, families & genera amongst the Mammals are merely artificial terms highly useful to show the relationship of those members of the series, *which have not become extinct.*

Charles had broached the heretical subject, but then trembled. Why, indeed, tease Waterhouse on the genealogy of mammals and man when he knew it would appear 'the merest trash' to an anti-evolutionist?[25] He was exposing himself and felt torn.

'But it is no use my going on this way,' he quickly added, and he turned the spotlight back on to Waterhouse, challenging him: 'I beg you to think clearly . . .' 'What do you exactly mean . . .' 'I shall be curious to hear . . .' Then, farewell, and a P.S.: 'Will you . . . keep this *one* letter of mine to be returned; as at some future year, I shall be curious to see, what I think now.' Security was of the essence, and Waterhouse complied. But he did not like the ungodly way his son's godfather had treated him. He felt browbeaten – no, downright crucified. 'You nail me to the stake and grumble because I wriggle a bit. . . . Well, I *will* explain what I am aiming at.' He carried on,

311

discussing how nature can be 'symbolically represented,' and how spiritual man was the 'standard of perfection.'[26]

The summer wore on, with workmen gravelling walks – 'Ave Maria how the money does go' – and Emma grieving the loss of her father with sister Elizabeth, who had come for the confinement. September was sunny; the great wall was up and, a year since leaving London, Charles's health had improved. On the 25th, almost on poor Mary's birthday, Henrietta was safely delivered, much to his relief. Then October saw delivery of the fifth and final part of the *Zoology*, at long last. Charles celebrated with a trip to Shrewsbury, where he rambled leisurely around old haunts and felt 'very much in love with my own dear three chickens' and their nursing mother, 'My dear old Titty.' He saw something of his own mother too, finding two of her 'very old letters . . . such kind & considerate ones,' written in a hand 'very like that of the Wedgwood family.'

Waterhouse got the job, but his ensuing article showed that he had gone his own way. Worse, in fact. In print Waterhouse, cued by Richard Owen, attacked the heretics who believe that all groups of animals 'blend perceptibly into each other.' Darwin assumed that he was being fingered as 'one of the very guilty ones' who accept *living* 'links' between the groups, whereas he only acknowledged ancestral intermediates. Anyway, Waterhouse's own mammals sat on circles, with no links between them, and this explained nothing about their real relationships.

'*Vicious* circles,' Darwin spat back; they had done 'infinite harm.' Of course the descriptive approach was important, and Waterhouse had 'done good service in pointing out how rare half-way-links are, if indeed they [now] exist.' This was grist to Darwin's mill in a way, because for him the 'half-way-links' were *extinct*: they were the common ancestors, sitting at the forks in a family tree, not half-way houses among living animals. Classification was a genealogical task, not a geometrical one, and it could only be explained by evolution. Darwin had to get rid of those symbolic circles, which stood in his way. 'I admire my own impudence in criticising you,' he strutted at the end; 'as for your wicked circles, I wish they were all d – – d to-gether.'[27]

21

Murder

A 'MURDER,' Darwin compared it to. He was writing to his new friend, the botanist Joseph Dalton Hooker, just back from four years at sea. It was 11 January 1844, and he was talking about the transmutation of life. *Volcanic Islands* had just gone off to the printers and Darwin was mulling over his 1842 pencil sketch again. Hooker – young, buoyant, fresh from abroad – had promise. Darwin waylaid him. From behind his great wall at Down he plucked up courage and confessed his awful secret, his belief that all animals were descended from common stocks.

Hooker was unprepared for the revelation. As a boy 'croaky Joe' had been brought up in Puritan strictness, taught to despise the 'scoffer and the sceptic' and accept 'the hand of an overruling Providence in every turn of events.' Glasgow medical studies were perhaps liberating – even Charles's brother Erasmus had been horrified to see Glasgow students playing football inside college. And Hooker's stint as an assistant surgeon in the navy must have broadened his outlook still further.[1] But his was still a pretty disciplined evangelical background, with none of the male Darwins' history of freethought.

Why, then, did Darwin confide in Hooker? He hardly knew the man, addressing him as 'My Dear Sir.' (It would be another six weeks before he threw aside 'old-world formality' and adopted the bluntly familiar 'Dear Hooker.') Maybe it was because Hooker, too, was 'well salted.' He had returned in September 1843 from his 'long & glorious' Antarctic voyage aboard HMS *Erebus* under Capt. Ross. Maybe it was because he was a prolific worker, familiar with island flora, and delighted to accept Darwin's offer of plants from the *Beagle*.[2]

313

Darwin had met Hooker a couple of times fleetingly, long before, in 1839. Hooker, then twenty-one and getting ready to sail, was walking in Charing Cross with Robert McCormick, the *Erebus*'s surgeon (and the *Beagle*'s as far as Rio). They bumped into Darwin, who impressed Hooker with 'his animated expression, heavy beetle brow, mellow voice, and delightfully frank and cordial greeting to his former shipmate.'[3] He was eight years Hooker's senior, with his own expedition behind him. Of course there was an obvious difference in their circumnavigations: Darwin travelled as a self-financed companion to the captain, Hooker as a salaried assistant surgeon, a menial grade in young Victoria's navy. Darwin had a magnificent *Journal* to show for his trip. Unknown to him, Hooker had actually read the proofs of the *Journal*. Lyell's copy passed to Hooker's father as Joseph prepared for his voyage; he had slept with them under his pillow so that, at first light each day, he might 'devour their contents.' The proofs made him despair of ever following in Darwin's footsteps, 'at however great a distance.' But they also increased his 'desire to travel and observe.' 'A copy of the complete work was a parting gift from Mr Lyell on the eve of my leaving England,' Hooker remembered, 'and no more instructive and inspiring work occupied the bookshelf of my narrow quarters throughout the voyage.'[4] This too – youthful adoration – played its part in winning Darwin's confidence.

These two young salts, having seen the world and its ways, gravitated towards one another in late 1843. It was really Darwin's doing. In a long letter welcoming Hooker home, Darwin urged him to think on the broader implication of the South American flora, and compare it to the European. He made the request seem like a 'trust,' and Hooker hoped that he would not be 'unworthy' of it. He drafted a paper immediately showing the striking similarities in the plants across the whole of the Southern Hemisphere, from Tasmania to Tierra del Fuego.[5] Hooker exuded confidence and had total command of the data. Darwin was impressed; and in reply he blurted out his confession, wrapped in his usual disarming prose.

For seven years he had been 'engaged in a very presumptuous work,' perhaps 'a very foolish one.' Having been struck by Galapagos life and the South American fossils, he said, he had 'blindly' collected everything bearing on species, including 'heaps of agricultural & horticultural books.' Slowly, reluctantly, he had been forced to a conclusion. 'I am almost convinced (quite contrary to the opinion I started with) that species are not (it is like confessing a murder) immutable.' Murder it might have been, but in his plea nature was to blame. He had *blindly* collected; there was no intention to commit a crime – to *deliberately* come up with something so gross as evolution. Puritanical young Hooker, placed in a judicial seat, was asked to weigh up the mitigating circumstances. Not murder, his correspondent was pleading, but helpless manslaughter. Darwin was angst-ridden. 'You will groan, & think to yourself "on what a man have I been wasting my time in writing to".'[6]

Why a 'murder,' the ultimate affront to society? Transmutation in January 1844 was still associated with riot and revolution – in other words, the gutter press. Even as Darwin incriminated himself, extremists were touting their penny papers around London's streets. That week's *Movement*, a scurrilous atheistic rag printed by George Holyoake – now out of gaol – and the *Oracle* evolutionists, ran attacks on Christianity and Paley's natural theology. True, theirs was a different evolution, one in which life strove for its own betterment. No Malthusian weak-to-the-wall mechanism here. Still, transmutation was being touted by street atheists intent on smashing the Anglican state. Darwin's clerical friends – the Foxes, Jenynses, and Henslows – stood to be stripped of their tithes by the red Lamarckians. The fat clergy, the revolutionaries screamed, would have to prove that they had something worth bartering for the products of labour.[7] So these were the subversives who were associated with evolution in January 1844. This is why Lamarckism had murderous overtones.

Darwin distanced himself more and more from Lamarck. 'Heaven forfend me from Lamarck['s] nonsense of a "tendency to progression" "adaptations from the slow willing of animals" &c.' Darwin's own Malthusian 'means of change' was unlike anything coming from the revolutionary French. In short, he told Hooker, 'I think I have found out (here's presumption!) the simple way by which species become exquisitely adapted to various ends.'

He posted the confession, hoping his faith in Hooker was not misplaced, and waited and waited. Two weeks passed with no word; Hooker was busy, collating his pressed flowers and looking for his land legs. Then at the end of the month a long unruffled response arrived. Hooker sent screeds as usual on South American plants. He seemed flattered and a bit chary of Darwin's attentions; aware that Darwin was hanging on to his every word, and worried that he would not come up to snuff. 'You take so much notice of me, that I am almost afraid of saying too much, & of destroying the illusory character you give of my little notes.' He did not say too much on species, but what he did was encouraging. He went as far as he would for the next decade, bending over backwards to preserve their budding friendship. There may have been 'a gradual change of species. I shall be delighted to hear how you think that this change may have taken place, as no presently conceived opinions satisfy me on the subject.'[8]

Darwin could not have asked for more; his faith had been vindicated. From this time on transmutation became a ghostly presence in his letters, always there but never quite seen. Hooker knew full well why his brains were being picked. Given the all-clear, Darwin started setting his young friend tasks, pushing him to look at island faunas through Darwinian eyes. The Galapagos birds and shells were all distinct species, he said, but related to South American stock – was the same true of Galapagos plants? Hooker became a sounding board for a thousand such queries, a co-opted assistant in Darwin's quest for the laws of life.

After this effectual absolution, Darwin looked over his two-year-old species sketch again, relieved. He had been tinkering with it continually. Now he decided to flesh it out properly, make it more fluid, less telegraphic, less crabbed. He followed the same format: the first part spelled out his mechanism – variation and selection – based on what breeders had done with domestic animals, and the second covered the proofs of descent in general. As he reworked it, he still saw natural selection operate only intermittently. Normally, he believed, animals and plants do not vary much in the wild. They remain well adapted so long as conditions are steady; only as the environment changes does the reproductive system become affected. This has a destabilizing effect: 'the organization of the beings' becomes 'plastic,' as it does 'under domestication.'[9] New variants are thrown up, competition occurs, and selection picks out the best. In 1844 he understood it as a sort of automatic feedback loop, which restored the balance.

Through the spring the sketch expanded into a full 189-page essay. Darwin sensed its power and he saw its truth.[10] He also knew, grinding away month after month, that he could not publish – he would be accused of social delinquency, or worse.

Transmutation was still a weapon wielded by militants, angrily eyeing the islands of gentrified opulence. The first week in July, when Darwin entrusted the finished manuscript to the local schoolmaster to be copied, the feminist Emma Martin published her inflammatory pamphlet *Conversation on the Being of God*, arguing that evolution needed no Creator. She then toured the country, lecturing in markets and socialist Halls of Science, and was summoned for causing disturbances at churches. The old infidel order might have been passing, indeed the 'Devil's Chaplain,' the Revd Taylor, had died in exile only the month before. But others were emerging to carry on the crusade, shocking prim Victorians by their behaviour. Mrs Martin was held up as an example. She had left her Baptist husband for the socialist cause; she was hard up, living on hand-outs, and carting her children around with her. She was hounded from town to town, harassed by rectors and magistrates. This was no way for a mother to behave. But like her friend Holyoake, she was a mesmerizing orator, who criss-crossed the country smashing the *'thraldom* of religion,' drawing crowds of 3000 whenever she challenged the clergy.[11]

No, publishing would be suicidal. Clergy-baiting was on the increase, and country parsons were among Darwin's friends and family. He risked being accused of betraying his privileged class.

On 5 July, with the evolution essay gone, he wrote his wife a difficult letter, one he would hide away, to be opened in the event of his 'sudden death.' Maybe his constitution would break, or cholera could carry him off. (Epidemics still raged periodically. He later copied out an opium-based prescription to ease the symptoms of cholera.) The letter contained his 'most solemn & last request' – that she should publish the essay posthumously. Maybe he half-hoped that he would die first. He reposed a terrible trust, for they differed grievously on religion. But he was so sure of the essay. 'If, as I believe that my theory is true & if it be accepted even by one competent judge, it will be a considerable step in science.'[12] She was to give a good editor £400 plus his books and clippings, to enlarge and publish the work, and he hoped that she or her brother Hensleigh would promote it.

He ran through possible editors, scrubbing some, adding others. Lyell should be approached first. Or perhaps Edward Forbes, a good all-rounder – a biogeographer and botanist, a pioneer of deep-sea dredging with a book on starfishes behind him. No, probably Henslow was 'best in many respects,' but then again Hooker was a '**very** good' choice. Owen's name went on, then came off as Darwin thought of his abomination of transmutation. This was the trouble. He would be placing each man in a moral quandary: Lyell had devoted his *Principles of Geology* to refuting Lamarck, Forbes was a High Anglican who hated materialism, Henslow a clergyman, Owen a Tory who was combating radical propaganda on nature's 'self-development.'[13] One studied comparative anatomy, Owen proclaimed, to eradicate such pernicious theories; no amount of bribe would have persuaded him to *publish* one. Darwin was expecting his nominees to be impossibly impartial, to ignore their social duty and do something deeply repugnant.

And why should they? How far did friendship extend? Forbes believed that an 'ill book well written is like poisoning a fountain that runs for ever.' How could any of them contemplate polishing Darwin's prose to make a poisonous philosophy attractive? – to make it what Sedgwick called one book on evolution a few months later, a 'rank pill of asafoetida and arsenic, covered with gold leaf.'[14] Darwin's was a terrible trust. He wondered if anyone would accept.

He did not tell Hooker of the essay, but he was dying to discuss its contents. At times, he tended to forget Hooker's youth and lack of fortune, which gilded a gentleman's path. He kept urging him to put his name down for the Athenaeum Club, where they might discuss the world's plants in plush surroundings, only to learn that Hooker had done so long ago, and could not get in. Nor could they meet at the Geological Society, whose six-guinea admission fee and three-guinea annual dues deterred the young botanist. With the essay finished Charles got up his 'steam & courage' and went with Emma one fine July day to visit Hooker at Kew Gardens. At last they met properly. Hooker really was 'a most engaging young man,' Lyell heard.[15] Soon Emma was exchanging recipes with Hooker, still a bachelor, trying his apple preserve and cakes.

A week later Darwin started his third geological book based on the *Beagle* voyage. *Geological Observations on South America* would describe the pampas, the plateaux, the Andes, showing how they had been pushed up with Lyellian slowness. Not for him D'Orbigny's nonsense about catastrophic upheaval. Darwin knew that the pampas had been built up gently in fresh water, not cataclysmically as the sea invaded the land, sweeping animal carcasses before it. He had written sixty pages by September 'on the elevation & great gravel terraces & plains of Patagonia & Chile & Peru,' and they were 'pretty good.'[16]

In his weekly epistles to Hooker, he was releasing equally tantalizing matter from his essay. Why for instance were species numerous in some spots and not in others? The production of species on islands was the key, as the Galapagos had shown. Here the bird and reptile colonists had diversified into varied niches created on the newly emerged volcanic outcrops. Each had its peculiar fauna. Elsewhere submerging continents were breaking up into islands, isolating species, encouraging new adaptations as habitats changed. He could not go into details, but

with respect to original creation or production of new forms
. . . isolation appears the chief element: Hence . . . a tract of
country, which has oftenest within the later geological periods
subsided & been converted into isl[an]^{ds}, & reunited, I sh[oul]^d
expect to contain many forms.

Hooker mooted the exceptions: the Falklands and Iceland, which had
hardly anything indigenous. *Their* plants were identical to South
America's or Europe's. And even granting the point, how does a
species reaching the outlying islands radiate into the diverse forms?
Are we to believe 'Lamarck's twaddle' or the other 'mad' theories
doing the rounds? Species may be mutable 'but I should not think
they set about it themselves so systematically as he says.' Darwin
agreed that Lamarck was 'veritable rubbish' and the others no better,
but then none of them had 'approached the subject on the side of
variation under domestication.'[17] Another tantalizing clue, did
Hooker but know it.

By late September the evolution essay was back in Down House.
Charles broke off from *South America* to correct the fair copy, which
had grown to 231 pages in the schoolmaster's hands. It was a month
of recuperation after a summer that had played havoc with his
stomach. Emma made him comfortable with a holiday at home. She
now had the house in perfect order – 'pretty, brilliantly clean, quiet,'
her Aunt Jessie observed on a visit, with Emma 'the dearest little
hostess in the world.' The furnishings were plain and dignified. In the
'charming drawing room,' which she made specially her own, were
some gifts from Shrewsbury – an arm-chair, an ottoman, a sideboard
– and her prized wedding present, the Broadwood grand pianoforte.[18]
She liked to sit there in the afternoon while Charles worked, watching
Willy and Annie play with the nurses in the garden. One day he came
in, carrying the essay. With trepidation, he asked her to read it.

He could never hope to convert her. And the last thing he intended
was to rub salt into old wounds. But since Emma would be entrusted
with the manuscript if he died, why not ensure that it would not
offend her? Her opinion was conventional and safe, the gentlest
foretaste of what the world would say one day. She sat with the pile
of papers, pointing out unclear passages, leaving tell-tale notes in the
margin, showing where she disagreed. 'A great assumption/E.D.' she
scribbled against his claim that the human eye 'may *possibly* have
been acquired by gradual selection of slight but in each case useful
deviations.' He softened the passage still more; but, from then on, the
piecemeal evolution of a complex, integrated organ like the eye left

him in a cold sweat.[19] On the other hand, he never doubted the viability of his theory, even if Emma withheld her blessing.

By the mid-forties transmutation was moving off the streets, out of the shabby dissecting theatres, and into the drawing-rooms. No longer was it to be the province of socialist revolutionaries and republican physicians. One book was responsible for this sea-change more than any other. In October 1844 the Edinburgh publisher of popular periodicals, Robert Chambers, galvanized the intelligentsia with his anonymous *Vestiges of the Natural History of Creation.*

A golf-playing, overworked, man of the people, Chambers knew of the advanced anatomy and evolution floating around the medical schools and he determined to make this 'alternative scientific vision of progress' more accessible. The book was brilliantly written and marketed; it was also highly impressionistic. Nature's self-development was treated journalistically in a way never tried before. He surveyed the whole of cosmic evolution, from the coalescence of planets, through the chemico-electrical generation of first life, to the fossil series – the 'vestiges' of the title – and the emergence of man. He made this progression not just exciting, but titillating in an earnest, evangelical society. This was reforming science, not ornamental knowledge for an old élite. He deplored the scientists' specialist approach and static nature, which consecrated a paternalist set of values. He wanted to reach 'ordinary readers.'[20] He provided what many clamoured for in an age of progress and aspiration, the reassurance of an upwardly mobile nature.

By contrast the élite remained Darwin's target: the rulers of the learned societies, the shepherds of parish folk. Those 'dogs of clergy,' as Chambers vilified them, were Darwin's warmest friends. He would never dream of alienating vicar-naturalists like Fox, Henslow, and Jenyns with a rabble-rousing production. His would be 'responsible' knowledge. It would respond to the needs of a new scientific aristocracy, the aristocracy of talent. Darwin's would be a 'palace coup.'[21]

Vestiges caused a sensation when it hit the high streets. It was a massive seller and passed into a new edition immediately. Even Hooker thought it good value for a hack-work, despite its egregious blunders. But what a 'funny fellow' the author must be! Darwin was less amused. The prose was perfect, but the 'geology strikes me as bad, & his zoology far worse.' Hooker labelled it a '9 day wonder,' but the nine days dragged on, and it was already heading for a third edition as he spoke. Each edition was patched and polished, cutting out more mistakes, leading one Tory naturalist to fume that his 'deformities no longer appear so disgusting.' Critics thanked God that the author began in 'ignorance and presump .ion.' Had he begun with the revised versions 'he would have been more dangerous.'[22]

In an unsettled Chartist age, when science had a moral dimension, it *could* be dangerous in the wrong hands. As a result the clergy, benefactors of the old paternalism, met the work head-on. A few responses were cranky; as Hooker laughed to Darwin – 'a funny thing. Some Liverpool Parson, after reading "Vestiges," had written to all Geologists for proofs on the contrary, & rather coolly, printed all the answers.' But that was not the most telling part. All the geologists, bar one, 'referred said parson to their own works!' It showed how widespread anti-transmutatory sentiments were among the wealthy specialists. Anglican dons believed that God actively sustained the natural and social hierarchies from on high. Destroy this overruling Providence, deny this supernatural sanction for the status quo, introduce a levelling evolution, and civilization would collapse. And, more to the point, Church privileges. The Revd Adam Sedgwick, an honest Dalesman used to calling a spade a spade, apocalyptically predicted 'ruin and confusion in such a creed.'[23] Picked up by the querulous working classes, 'it will undermine the whole moral and social fabric,' and will bring 'discord and deadly mischief in its train.'

Those querulous classes disagreed. Sedgwick told the British Association that new species appeared 'not by the transmutation of those before existing – but by the repeated operation of creative power.' What was he, 'God's reporter,' one atheist shouted. How did he *know* this? Where was his evidence? The gutter presses were fizzing with anger. Embittered artisans fighting for a secular state ignored *Vestiges*' providential veneer and saw its science represent 'the transition state at which the religious world will presently arrive,' after which 'men will glide into atheism.'[24]

Even Darwin thought that Sedgwick's over-the-top review of *Vestiges* smacked of the 'dogmatism of the pulpit,' and he knew it was 'far from popular with non-scientific readers.' Radical Quakers and Unitarians demurred too. But they eyed the opulent Anglican Church financed by feudal tithes with disdain, and denounced the corrupt privileges brought by Establishment. They favoured more emancipating forms of knowledge. Many liked *Vestiges*; it might have been badly marred, but it was 'a very beautiful and a very interesting book,' Darwin's physiologist friend William Carpenter said, and he went on to help Chambers patch it up. Some were

321

pleased to see it choke the 'bigoted saints,' others thought the idea of Creation by natural law more ennobling. Unitarians like Carpenter doubted that 'the great-grandfather of our common progenitor [was] a chimpanzee or an orang-utan,' but on the rule of law he was adamant – God with his 'perfect knowledge of the future' had unleashed one law at the Creation and the universe has gone on unfolding ever since.[25]

Radical Quakers and Baptist doctors argued that nature had to be naturalized – spiritually unfrocked. Evolution for many of them was a better way for God to operate. The Almighty had instituted moral and physical laws at the Creation and made them known to everyone through nature and the Bible. No hierarchy of priests was necessary, no Established Church. Like Tom Paine, they lambasted the Church's 'adulterous connection' with the State; 'fornication' with aristocratic government one called it, and they tried to tear her from this 'illicit embrace.' Sedgwick responded in kind, equal to this sexual rhetoric. In *Vestiges*, he growled, evolution and spontaneous generation coupled in an 'unlawful marriage' and spawned a hideous monster; it would be merciful to crush 'the head of the filthy abortion, and put an end to its crawlings.'[26]

Sedgwick's review was his first ever, and it showed. 'Unmitigated contempt, scorn, and ridicule are the weapons to be used,' he seethed, but this sledge-hammer approach partly defeated the object. Darwin read his outburst with 'fear & trembling.' This was Sedgwick the Cambridge Proctor who had once slept at The Mount and taken Darwin on a geological tour of Wales. The whole sordid affair made it impossible to view *Vestiges* dispassionately. Sedgwick's histrionics only harmed his cause. When 'Mr. Vestiges' replied in the temperate *Explanations: A Sequel to the 'Vestiges'* (another bestseller), Darwin thought his 'spirit,' though not his 'facts, ought to shame Sedgwick.' All in all he had mixed feelings. He alternately decried *Vestiges* for muddying the waters and welcomed it for drawing the poison; if it stole his thunder, it also habituated people to nature's development. It did teach him one lesson, which was to avoid detailing specific genealogies – of pigs, or horses, or men: they simply presented a barn-door target.[27]

The author's anonymity increased the *frisson* of excitement. Wild rumours abounded. Sedgwick initially ascribed it to the frail intellect of a woman – privately he pinned it on to wicked Byron's daughter, Ada Lovelace. But fingers were pointing in all directions, and with Darwin's predilections known, at least by a few, some began pointing at him. 'Have you read that strange unphilosophical, but capitally-written book, the Vestiges,' he asked Fox; 'it has made more talk than any work of late, & has been by some attributed to me. – at which I ought to be much flattered & unflattered.' London geologists quickly had Chambers pegged as the author; letters flew thick and fast comparing *Vestiges'* errors with those in his other works. The case was actually clinched for Darwin a couple of years later.[28] He dropped in for an hour's chat with Chambers one day when he was in London – to talk over Glen Roy, which Chambers was working on. Lo and behold, a complimentary copy of the sixth edition of *Vestiges* arrived through the post shortly afterwards, convincing Darwin that Chambers was the man.

A future son-in-law once asked Chambers why he never owned up to his 'greatest work.' Chambers 'pointed to his house, in which he had eleven children, and then slowly added, "I have eleven reasons".' By 1845 Darwin had three reasons of his own, with another on the way. He also had public esteem to forfeit. The *Journal* had made him well known. It had given him an *entrée* into scientific society worldwide, and a reputation among travellers. His success was tangible. Animals and plants were routinely named after him, anything from the giant sloth *Mylodon Darwinii* to the imponderably tiny *Asteromphalus Darwinii*. Global travellers could fish in Galapagos waters for *Cossyphus Darwini* or pick a shelly *Pecten Darwinianus* from Patagonian rocks.[29] Among London's savants, too, he rated high. He was a Vice-President in the Geological Society in 1844, and was targeted by aspiring geologists wanting to get their papers into print. An ill-spoken word and all this could be jeopardized.

Then there was the company he kept, which made his quandary worse. His parish friends were as eager as Sedgwick to keep science on the straight and narrow. Darwin understood this conservative moral attitude – he knew what gave offence. Hence his self-condemning talk of the 'sin of speculation.' It was a sin denounced by many: Hooker censured naturalists for taking speculation as the easy route, and his shaft struck hard.[30] So while Darwin was dying to divulge his secret to Fox and Jenyns, he was reticent. He moved forward tactfully.

The month *Vestiges* came out, he was quizzing Jenyns on mortality rates among song birds, the Malthusian 'checks' that prevented populations from exploding. He had the right person. Jenyns was the compleat parson-naturalist, an antiquarian fact-gatherer. But Darwin was always supportive. Jenyns's 'trifling facts' – whether on bird territories or beak sizes – provided spy holes into Nature's innermost workings. Darwin delighted in snuffling through such trifles, collecting clues, the oddball, the unnoticed, the incongruous – becoming, he laughed, 'a complete millionaire in odd and curious little facts.' Jenyns's tidbits, the sort disdained by deskbound taxonomists, were the stuff of a new science. And this, Darwin intimated, was what he was engaged on – studies that would explain Jenyns's 'trifling points.'

He broached the inflammable subject gently. Jenyns's observations on bird mortality were part of a 'grand body of facts' from which he could draw morally unimpeachable conclusions. Honesty of intent was the key:

> The general conclusion at which I have slowly been driven
> from a directly opposite conviction is that species are mutable
> & that allied species are co-descendants of common stocks. I
> know how much I open myself, to reproach, for such a
> conclusion, but I have at least honestly & deliberately come
> to it.

Jenyns found the Malthusian 'checks' quite explicable. The surviving young were driven out of parental territories into those where the death-rate had been high. He viewed the process as a static system of curbs and balances, not competition and progress. Like any parson supporting the Creative stasis of nature, he damned talk of life's self-development. He saw through all Darwin's cagey talk and accused him of implying that his 'conclusions were inevitable.'[31]

Darwin flinched: 'In my wildest day-dream, I never expect more than to be able to show that there are two sides to the question of the immutability of species, ie whether species are *directly* created, or by intermediate laws, (as with the life & death of individuals.)' Darwin was polarizing the issue: either supernaturalism or natural laws, which he, at least, equated with the mutation of organic forms (although many others didn't). He repeated that the results had been forced on him, and that he was sensitive to stepping on hallowed ground: it must all look 'absurdly presumptuous,' he admitted. 'I am a bold man to lay myself open to being thought a complete fool, & a most deliberate one.'[32] His motives were pure. His image as an objective, neutral 'scientist' – a neologism that still seemed faintly foreign – was in the making. If 'the fabric falls,' it was Nature's doing, not his. If this spiritual unfrocking, this secularizing of nature, seemed uncomfortable, Nature was to blame. Darwin offered Jenyns his newly copied essay, which explained his theory in full. The offer was never accepted.

He did not give up on his clergymen friends, but he could at least keep the dialogue going with the younger career-naturalists. Hooker was eager to help, showering Darwin with books, rooting out obscure ones. Darwin put in his orders:

> When you tell me not to buy Kingdons trans[lation]. of Decand[olle's]: veg[etable]: organ[ography]: do you mean you can *sometime* lend it me. I will order Jussieu: I hope you will not forget the French pamphlet on variation. & I sh^d like to see the iceberg-paper in Boston Journal. I have got Couthouy's paper on Coral-Reefs.

Hooker spilled out information on plant distribution, wanting nothing for himself and resting 'content to be a gatherer of facts for you.' Darwin thought 'a little vanity' would not go amiss; after all, 'say just what you please, I am sure no one could put them to better use than yourself.' But it did not stop him firing questions, in order 'to screw knowledge' out of his compliant friend. Hooker's assistance, he claimed, was more 'than I have received from anyone else, & is beyond valueing [sic] in my eyes.'[33]

He came to rely on this help, constantly inviting Hooker to Down, almost to the point of pestering him. Eventually Hooker did plan to 'run down and look at your habitat.' On his first visit, the weekend of 7 December, Darwin picked his brains on island floras, milking him mercilessly – 'pumping' he called it – and it became a regular feature of their get-togethers. After breakfast he would take Hooker into the study for twenty minutes and bring out a list of questions. Some Hooker answered on the spot, a few required consideration, and others protracted research in Kew Gardens. The answers came on slips of paper, which Darwin deposited in pockets that hung against the study wall near his chair, each one devoted to a special topic.[34] From then on, secure on home ground, he plagued his young assistant with requests to come down, refusing Hooker's return invitations on health grounds.

The obsessive questioning continued in letters. Hooker, himself neutral, had become so inured to talk of evolution that he routinely laughed at the ways *Vestiges*, Lamarck, and others would describe an ugly fact – like the same plants turning up in Tasmania and across the globe in Tierra del Fuego. But it was such anomalies that Darwin had to explain; he refused to sweep them under the carpet. If the élite were to be turned, it would be on *these* grounds, not by sinful speculation or a piece of racy journalism. Anything on distribution and variation was ruthlessly hunted down. He followed up reports, fired off letters, set a thousand hares running, intoning all the time 'every variation must have some cause.'

But what? Was it external, the environment? He was no longer so sure, and beginning to gravitate to some internal cause of the change. He needed more case studies. He sniffed out the unusual, collecting factual knick-knacks until it became a kind of kleptomania. Hooker said he had 'the power of turning to account the waste observations ... of his predecessors,' and he had.[35] Whether it was the Earl of Enniskillen's odd yew tree, Dorking fowl in the farmyard, Galapagos snakes' tails, or variegated plants, every variation was fastidiously followed up.

Other naturalists were taxed, especially those setting off on exploratory voyages. With the distribution of animals and plants the 'keystone of the laws of creation,' he needed precise geographical information. Biogeography was a very British concern, which is why Darwin's was a very British science. It reflected the nation's maritime ambitions, at a time when the Royal Navy was busily mapping the world. Every year a batch of raw assistant surgeons sailed on Her Majesty's surveying ships, doubling as naturalists and filling up journals, becoming 'well salted,' like so many of the Hooker-Darwin circle. The Admiralty's Capt. Beaufort actually told Darwin to list any facts he wanted checking anywhere in the world and he would see to it; sooner or later a brig would be passing by.[36] Indeed, this year – 1845 – young Harry Goodsir, working away on crustaceans, set off with Capt. Franklin in Hooker's old ships *Erebus* and *Terror* to search for a Canadian north-west passage to the Pacific, carrying Darwin's list of requirements in his trunk.

In six short months Hooker had become a mainstay. He worried that Darwin was too attached, that his expectations were too high, his sentiments 'too flattering.' The fall came in February 1845, when Hooker was invited to teach botany at Edinburgh, standing in for old Professor Graham, then 'on his last legs' (he had been there since Darwin's day). It was a blow; Hooker might be furthering his career, but Darwin could only 'most heartily deplore it.' 'There is something so chilling in a separation of so many hundred miles ... You will hardly believe how deeply I regret for *myself* your present prospects – I had looked forward to seeing much of each other during our lives. It is a heavy disappointment.' He worked himself up into such a state that he even talked of visiting his friend that summer in Scotland. Darwin was 'awe-struck' by the idea of lecturing, but then Hooker too thought that his heart might not take the strain. Darwin's fatherly advice was to take care, and go for 'walks, like a good boy.' 'I dread the thought of your breaking down.'[37]

*

The previous autumn a long 'parchment talk' with his father left Darwin convinced that he should invest in land. Sir John Lubbock, Down's chief landowner, agreed that it was a wise buy, providing insurance against a stock-market crash. Properties around the village were 'absurdly dear,' he learned from Sir John, so Charles followed the example of his father and sister Susan; he planned to plough his inheritance into the fertile farmland of Lincolnshire. 'How very grand we shall be,' he wrote Susan in anticipation, 'when we go arm & arm & astonish our tenants.'

Lincolnshire was a county of few squires, lax parsons, and absentee landlords. (The advice from the future Bishop of Oxford, Samuel Wilberforce, to the local squires was to take the yokels' education in hand, lest they learn a 'smattering of science' and forget their God-given duties.) Charles's own agent found him an estate of 324 acres near the village of Beesby, a few miles from the coast. It had out-buildings and a modest farmhouse occupied by an 'industrious good Tenant.' The annual tithes due to the incumbent were about £70, the parochial charges 'very moderate'; the church had just been rebuilt and 'the money borrowed . . . paid off.' Local obligations would thus be minimal, and it promised a better return than government bonds: a 'steady clear Rental of 3¼ Prcent, free from deductions,' on an outlay of £12,500.

In March 1845 Charles snapped it up. Or rather the Doctor did and passed it to Charles, for father took charge in such matters. The farm would have been a sound investment, producing about £400 a year – but for a national calamity. Still, that was months away and unforeseeable; for the moment Charles gloated to Fox, 'I am turned into a Lincolnshire squire!' He was thinking of the future. The family was growing. Emma was pregnant and 'as bad as she always is,' and a 'Boy-Baby' was born on 9 July. George, Darwin christened him, recalling the 'pleasant associations' of Henslow's son George. Maybe, he said wistfully, he will 'turn out to be a Naturalist' like his father.[38]

His father, meanwhile, was working furiously. Darwin interrupted *South America* to revise his *Journal*, after John Murray suggested a cheaper edition for his Colonial Library. The offer was welcome – Darwin had 'never received one penny' from the old publisher, despite selling 1400 copies.[39] Murray knew how to treat an author; he gave Darwin £100 for the copyright, and upped it £50 on request.

All summer Darwin revamped the book, incorporating the latest on the *Beagle* specimens. It was ten years since he had visited the Galapagos, and he was still reconceptualizing the islands. By now he had had ample time to reinterpret the fauna in the light of John

Gould's work on the birds and his own theory. 'The archipelago is a little world within itself, or rather a satellite attached to America, whence it has derived a few stray colonists,' he explained. It was a new lava-strewn Eden of 'aboriginal creations.' Here 'we seem to be brought somewhat near to that great fact – that mystery of mysteries – the first appearance of new beings on this earth.'

But finches were still a minor part of his evolutionary proof. Admittedly he now illustrated the various types, showing their range of beaks. 'Seeing this gradation and diversity of structure in one small, intimately related group of birds,' he hinted, 'one might really fancy that from an original paucity of birds in this archipelago, one species had been taken and modified for different ends.' It was a broad clue, and as much as he would ever say on finch evolution. He also now nailed down the evidence for the differing island tortoises. Or rather, he disinterred it from an older book. Capt. Porter, recounting his voyage in the United States ship *Essex* in 1815, had reported saddleback tortoises from Charles and Hood Islands, and 'rounder, blacker' and better-tasting ones from James Island. There were further vindications. Hooker, who had slept on the proofs of the first edition, now found himself botanical adviser for the second. He confirmed that the flowering plants, too, were mostly 'aboriginal productions.' Why, Darwin teased as he rewrote the Galapagos chapter, all these 'new birds, new reptiles, new shells, new insects, new plants'? Why, on these tiny islands so recently emerged from the sea, were so many beings created slightly different from their South American counterparts?[40] It was rhetorical; he already had the answer.

He took the opportunity to repay another debt while revamping. *Coral Reefs* and *Volcanic Islands* had both come 'half out of Lyell's brains.' Swearing everyone to secrecy, Darwin dedicated the new edition of the *Journal* to Lyell, as a sign, he said, of 'how much I geologically owe to you.' But the compliment came with a nasty sting.

Lyell dropped by early in June, accompanied by Mrs Lyell. ('You ought to have a wife,' Darwin advised Hooker, 'to stop you working too much, as Mrs Lyell peremptorily stops Lyell.') Lyell's *Travels in North America* was just coming out, and he was planning a new trip to the United States. Perhaps the mention of America swung the discussion to slavery. Certainly when Darwin glimpsed the *Travels* he was horrified. Unlike Martineau, who supported the 'martyr' abolitionists, Lyell saw them doing no good. Darwin might have owed the world 'geologically' to Lyell, but on this subject he stood back, aghast. After a sleepless night in August, pent-up with rage, he exploded on this 'odious deadly subject.' How could Lyell relate 'atrocious' tales of slave children being taken from their parents and then 'speak of being distressed at the Whites not having prospered'?

Darwin distilled his feelings, pushing a slamming indictment of slavery into the last pages of his *Journal*, just as they were leaving his hands:

> I thank God, I shall never again visit a slave country. To this day, if I hear a distant scream, it recalls with painful vividness my feelings, when passing a house near Pernambuco [Brazil], I heard the most pitiable moans, and could not suspect that some poor slave was being tortured . . . Near Rio de Janeiro I lived opposite to an old lady, who kept screws to crush the fingers of her female slaves. I have stayed in a house where a young household mulatto, daily and hourly, was reviled, beaten, and persecuted enough to break the spirit of the lowest animal. I have seen a little boy, six or seven years old, struck thrice with a horse-whip (before I could interfere) on his naked head, for having handed me a glass of water not quite clean.

His catalogue of 'heart-sickening atrocities' continued – deeds 'done and palliated by men, who profess to love their neighbours as themselves, who believe in God, and pray that his Will be done on earth!' 'It makes one's blood boil,' he stormed. He cursed those who, seeing only the well-fed slaves of the 'upper classes,' call it a 'tolerable evil.'[41] He claimed that these last-minute additions were not in answer to Lyell, just an 'explosion of feeling,' but it sounded hollow.

Murray was delighted with the new edition, and did well with it. He continued courting his new author, softening him up with twelve complimentary copies. One went to Lyell, just leaving in September for America; another to Hooker in Edinburgh. By now Hooker was standing for the botany chair – Graham having died – and finding canvassing 'detestable work.' Darwin wrote him a reference, half-grudgingly, wondering who would now show him 'a daisy from a Dandelion.'[42] He was quite relieved when Hooker did not land the job.

Hooker's letters continued full of recommended reading. Hewett Watson was the author he particularly pushed – Edinburgh-trained, a phrenologist, and Graham's gold medallist in 1831. Hooker rated him 'at the very head of English botanists,' with an unrivalled knowledge of plant distribution. In 1845 Watson was still publishing the results of his trip to the Azores three years earlier. More controversially, he was in the midst of a series of articles on 'Progressive Development,' prompted by *Vestiges*. Hooker said Watson had a 'philosophical' cast of mind, meaning he was that rare breed, a plant geographer with a statistical bent. The 'demography' of species was his forte; he treated plants like a Public Records officer carrying out a census, trying to understand plant population trends. As a radical, he sympathized with the great Victorian demographic surveys. More than a radical, he was an atheist, touchy, and a transmutationist to boot – in short, a 'renegade,' said Hooker, intriguing Darwin no end.

What did that make Darwin then? 'You will be ten times hereafter more horrified at me,' he replied; his own renegade 'views of descent' were just as heretical. Hooker was unimpressed; the more he looked at island floras, the less he accepted mutation. It might be an 'active agent,' but only in 'perturbating' species, causing them to wobble slightly. But then he still had no inkling of Darwin's 'sublimely grand' mechanism for magnifying the wobble, natural selection. Only two months later would Darwin finally offer him his 'rough sketch (well copied) on this subject' for comments. Even then he thought it 'too impudent a request.'[43] Perhaps it was.

Over and over Darwin invited Hooker to Down. Eventually in December, a year after his first visit, he came for a weekend with an up-and-coming bunch of naturalists. An all-round group they were: Hooker covered botany, Waterhouse zoology; Edward Forbes astonished all with his biogeography, and the agreeable Hugh Falconer – currently working on Indian fossils in the British Museum – spoke for palaeontology. Darwin revelled in this kind of occasion, on home ground, where he was able to 'pump' the young bloods. 'I shall have the four most rising naturalists in England around my table,' he chortled.[44]

It was the first time for Forbes. Breezy and likeable, he was six years Darwin's junior and another Edinburgh product (he had even lodged in Darwin's old digs, with Mrs Mackay).[45] He had sailed with an expedition in Mediterranean waters, where he dredged for deep-sea creatures, and now, back in London after his father's bankruptcy, he was attached to the Geological Survey. He could be breathtakingly speculative, and Darwin wanted to hear of his lost continent – a sunken supercontinent supposedly stretching from Ireland to Portugal and out into the Atlantic past the Azores.

Forbes had conjured it up to explain the distribution of related plants, and even the fickle Hooker, to Darwin's chagrin, seemed to be leaning Forbes's way. Actually he was swinging to and fro, 'as unstable as water,' but currently arguing that Darwin's means of plant dispersal – sea-transport, wind, and so on – 'has been ridden to death.' Hooker accepted that each species migrates from one 'centre of creation,' rather than being created in many centres. But how did animals and plants, seeds and eggs, spread and ultimately colonize islands? Did dry land – continental extensions – once stretch out to embrace them, as Forbes suggested? If so, where has this land gone? The notion of a lost Atlantis staggered Darwin. It was an appallingly 'bold step . . . to sink into the depths of *ocean, within the period of existing species,* so large a tract of surface.' He was flabbergasted. Island-making, oceanic subsidence, and marooned species were the stuff of Darwin's evolutionary theory all right, but he envisaged a much slower process. Sinking supercontinents in one species' lifetime was rash to the point of reckless, when dispersal by sea currents and birds would do. Forbes 'will injure his reputation' with this wild speculation.[46] Getting him to Down, Darwin could confront the issue head-on.

The weekend went off brilliantly, with 'raging discussions' on all the hot topics. Falconer and Darwin presumably tried to scupper the supercontinent, with the good-natured Forbes giving as good as he got. Species were probably skirted; all the guests were anti-transmutationists, Forbes not least. He refused to see the fossil succession prove the *'real or bodily change'* of one animal into another.[47] Fish and reptiles and apes could not transmute themselves; they had no power of self-development. He was an extreme idealist: species were divine ideas incarnate, and only in God's mind did any real change occur.

Like many materially minded Unitarians Darwin hated this other-worldly Platonism, where species change only in the Creator's mind, where genera are 'God-born thoughts that become manifest in living shapes.' It stopped all attempts at finding a physical mechanism. Nor could he extract anything more positive from the others. Hooker held 'aloof from all speculation on the origin of species.' He plumped for 'the old assumption that each species has one origin [and] is immutable,' and stuck with it. Darwin bridled a bit at this unyielding fudge and wondered 'whether we shall ever be public combatants.'[48] The lack of allies was beginning to frustrate him.

Not that he was unappreciative of Hooker's help. Far from it. He said over and over that he had extracted more from him 'than from any other person.' As a result in the new year, 1846, he even contemplated the 'bold step' of staying at Kew with his friend – bold because he *'literally'* had 'not slept out of *near* relations house or inn for five years!!' (What he confided to Fox was even stronger: that he had not slept out of a safe house since he married.) It was a sign of his growing dependence, even if he did not eventually go.

He kept up the pressure on his friend. He rejoiced on hearing of Hooker's appointment in February as botanist to the Geological Survey, where he was to join Forbes and that 'loose set of dogs' gathered loyally round the Director Henry de la Beche. It meant he would be based in Charing Cross, two hours from Down. So when, Darwin asked, would he be down to look at the Kent Chalk? – a horse and a bed were waiting. And with the British Association meeting coming up, he wanted to know 'why cannot you come here afterwards & work.'[49] These lures, and refusals to make a return journey, showed that he was less a recluse, more a man who needed to control the situation; he needed to be at home with his problems, or in familiar surroundings.

Darwin was still Henslow's student in parish matters, learning how to look after his villagers by example. He saw Henslow 'doing wonders' for his Suffolk labourers, organizing horticultural shows, lectures to the farmers, fireworks on the rectory lawn, as well as setting up a savings club, a benefit society, a library, and a school. 'How you are astonishing all the clod-hoppers,' Charles enthused. And to think that none of this had 'aroused the envy of all the good surrounding sleeping parsons.'[50]

Most clergymen lacked Henslow's enterprise and tact. Young 'Mr. Willott' – the Darwins always avoided 'Reverend' – had Charles's confidence, and he subscribed £5 towards redecorating the parish church. But the feeble man had trouble handling village disputes. One day Willott came out to Down House seeking advice, only to be silenced by his companion, the Rector of Hayes. The Rector gossiped 'grand nonsense' about the schoolmaster being religiously 'unsound,' then looking around in an awesome voice declared, 'and we all know what that will come to.' Immorality, of course; but Charles demurred at his conclusion that 'unsound religion was worse than none at all.'[51]

The Revd Willott died suddenly in March, leaving his two innovations, a Sunday School and a Coal and Clothing Club, to another callow curate, the Revd John Innes, who came from neighbouring Farnborough. Innes, a product of High Church Oxford in its heyday, was Hooker's age; Darwin had actually met him years previously, soon after moving to Down. Now, thanks to his own 'dear patron' Henslow, Darwin could help Innes educate the clodhoppers and insure them against the need for winter coal and clothing.[52]

As an improving Lincolnshire landlord, there was a thing or two he might try himself. Beesby farm, like Down, gave new scope for proving his social worth. In the previous September, when Darwin went to see his father, he had looked over his estate and authorized contractors to demolish the old buildings and put up a new farm house. This cost the Doctor another £1000, but modernizing was necessary, his agent insisted, to keep 'a Tenant of respectability.' When he heard how Henslow was trying to assist his parishioners by letting them small allotments, Darwin did the same. Self-sufficiency had to be encouraged, as much in Lincolnshire as Tierra del Fuego, where he had helped to plant gardens for the savages. (And it would reduce the rates that he paid to maintain the local poor.) While Beesby was being rebuilt, he instructed his agent to arrange a cottage garden for every labourer on his land. And he started supporting Beesby school, contributing £10 a year to its upkeep from his rent.[53]

By now, though, something more than allotments was needed. In 1845 the country's potato crop had failed, killed by a virulent fungus disease. It was the first of many failures and, with the poor subsisting largely on bread and potatoes, famine and devastation followed. Ireland was worst hit; here 700,000 were to die and one million emigrate over the next five years in the greatest natural disaster of the nineteenth century. Shielded at first, Darwin, like Henslow – an expert on crop diseases – saw the blight as a 'painfully interesting subject.'[54] An intriguing problem, or so it appeared to a squire-naturalist who could do without potatoes for a while. But the parish poor were starving.

Famine and death crept closer to Down House. Charles's own workmen, with only a few weeks' supply of potatoes laid in, and those diseased, were alarmed. Matters were made worse by the price of flour, forced up by the corn import duty. His handyman was having to spend over a shilling more a week from his twelve shillings wages on it. 'This would be nearly as bad,' Darwin calculated, as if 'we had to pay an additional 50 or 100£ for our bread: how soon in that case, would those infamous corn-laws be swept away.' His squire's fortune sustained him. Having tightened his belt, he was managing to live on £1000 a year, and the saving made the family feel 'as rich as Jews.' But he remained worried as the rural economy collapsed, and he tried to play his part. He agreed with Henslow 'about gentlefolk not buying potatoes,' and Emma probably told the cook to stop. She even started giving away penny bread tickets at the door, which could be exchanged with the village baker. Charles put his naturalist's mind on the problem, suggesting that his potato seeds from Chile might be used to replenish affected stocks – but he found that these too were infected.[55]

The disaster confirmed his free-trade principles. Protectionism had to be abolished, whatever Disraeli and diehard farmers thought. The duties on imported corn which kept bread prices high were iniquitous. As a free-trading Malthusian he also hated primogeniture, that is, inheritance by the eldest male; this had to be destroyed 'to lessen the difference in land wealth & make more small freeholders.' It would create more competition and sift out the clever, ingenious, 'fittest' sons. The stamp duty also had to go. It was so 'atrociously unjust,' rendering it difficult 'for the poor man to buy his ¼ of an acre, it makes one's blood burn with indignation.'[56] Darwin remained a competitive free-trader, in science and out.

No fortune could shield him from the human cost of the tragedy. During the unseasonably stormy June, while Emma took Willy and Annie to her aunts' in Tenby, more alterations were carried out to the house. At last there would be a schoolroom and two more bedrooms upstairs. And a new back door would help keep traffic out of the kitchen; after all, it seemed 'selfish making the house so luxurious for ourselves and not comfortable for our servants.' Charles, taking opium pills, feeling sick, watched the domestic dramas unfold as walls came down and workmen fell out. John Lewis, the Down builder and foreman, eventually became fed up with the bickering and fired the lot. With the famine biting and no pay, one labourer broke down in the half-renovated rooms. Charles, gripped by the trauma, gave a blow-by-blow account to Emma: his 'wife had come from a distance with a Baby & is taken very ill – The poor man was crying with misery.' It was too much for an emotional household and the Darwins 'persuaded Lewis to take him back again.'[57]

That month Parliament finally acted. The famine had intensified calls for the repeal of the Corn Laws. After the disaster in Ireland, the Tory Prime Minister Sir Robert Peel was converted to free trade and the corn duty was slashed. Ironically it hit Darwin in the pocket, for as corn prices fell, so did farm incomes and therefore the rent his Beesby tenant could afford to pay. He agreed a fifteen-per-cent rent reduction, grumbling to his agent that it seemed 'unusually large.' How much had the 'great landowners' in the district – Lord Yarborough, Robert Christopher, MP – cut their rents? he wanted to know. Suddenly he realized that he was comparing himself with Tory protectionists, and he backpedalled at once: 'Although I am on principle a free-trader, of course I am not willing to make a larger reduction than necessary to retain a good tenant.' He reconciled himself to the drop. While hardline Tories and hard-up farmers wanted a return to the old protectionism, he 'saw no cause whatever to despair.' He rallied his tenant, telling him to 'hope for better times.'[58]

He was vomiting again; the old sickness was as virulent as ever. His stomach had not really been right for a single night since his move to Down and left him fit for only a few hours' work a day. Friends thought him a hypochondriac, because he routinely trotted it out as an excuse. He dreaded going anywhere, especially 'horrid' London, that 'old Babylon,' whose choking smogs rose straight from the 'subterranean kingdom of his Infernal Majesty.' Trips left him 'knocked up' and good for nothing. He had avoided the British Association at Cambridge the previous year because he 'expected more mortification than pleasure.' When he went to visit his father he kept quietly out of the way if the house was full.

But he was no malingerer. The sickness was real and distressing, although no one knew what caused it. He experimented with all manner of remedies. His father put him on a non-sugar diet, and he tried bitter 'Indian Ale.' He sacrificed snuff for a month, only to be told by an unsympathetic Hooker to 'knock it off altogether.' He even resorted to quackery. He laughed at the dupes taken in by mesmerism, and at Harriet Martineau for mesmerizing young girls, muttering about the 'diseased tendency to deception in disordered females.' Yet he was galvanizing his own insides using plate batteries for an hour a day, which he knew was an equal 'piece of quackery.' These crazes sweeping the country – mesmerism, galvanization – were the 'Devil's laws,' in Carlyle's view, as disreputable as any that made men the sons of monkeys.[59] They all oozed from the same quagmire on the lunatic fringe. Darwin tried them, but he had little faith in alternative medicine and doubted that he would ever be cured.

Self-absorbed, some thought self-centred, Charles demanded constant attention. In the midst of everything else that spring – neighbours starving, builders hammering – Emma's elderly mother gently slipped away. The Wedgwood household would be broken up, Maer sold. Elizabeth would move to a new place of her own. Forty years of family life, their golden age, was at an end. But Emma never went back to her childhood home, staying to pamper and protect Charles. When she did finally get away with the children in June, going to see her favourite Aunt Jessie (a 'most unusual' thing for her to do), Charles felt bereft. He longed to have her back, urged her to cut her visit short, complained day after day of feeling sick. Then one afternoon, sitting alone in the summer-house watching the thunderstorms, he half-came to his senses and counted his blessings. 'I am an ungracious old dog to howl, for I have been . . . thinking what a fortunate man I am, so well off in worldly circumstances, with such dear little children & . . . more than all with such a wife.' A selfless wife; as her sister Elizabeth said, she had never heard a complaint pass Emma's lips. More and more Charles felt that 'I can . . . say so & shall say so on my death-bed, – bless you my dear wife.'⁶⁰

Down was more than ever a sanctuary. Its rurality was invaluable. Hooker wondered why he plumped for such 'an impracticable part of the country,' but Darwin purposely chose it. Down provided his retreat, and it was continually made more secure. He rented a one-and-a-half-acre strip of land at the back from Lubbock early in 1846, which he fenced and replanted with bushes and trees to shelter the house. In this plot he marked out his quarter-mile thinking path, the 'Sandwalk,' on which he would plod henceforth on his midday constitutional. He was still a creature of habit. Life was now totally 'Clockwork,' a tick-tock routine of breakfast – work – mail – work – walk – lunch – letters – nap – work – rest – tea – books – bed. He liked life humdrum, and the pace of Down provided it. He told everyone that 'I am fixed in the spot where I shall end it.' Emma too liked the solitude, and bore the dull life with her 'poor old sickly complaining husband' with great forbearance.⁶¹

He pushed on with *South America* all year. The Treasury grant had by now run out, so the book had to be subsidized by Darwin and his publishers. Both forked out, even if it did not promise much of a return. By August two-thirds had passed through the press and he expected to 'be a comparatively free man' again soon.⁶² In September, finally, he penned the Preface, then ventured out with Emma to the British Association at Southampton.

As usual he found the sessions dreary. Not surprisingly so in this case; the proceedings were dominated by Owen's numbingly technical paper comparing the homologous bones in fish, reptiles, and mammals. Owen was the anatomical 'master mind' who awed Hooker, and even Darwin confessed himself an 'ignoramus' on the technicalities. There was the odd interesting item. Later Owen described some new fossil mammals, including llama-sized toxodons, shipped to the College of Surgeons by Capt. Sulivan (formerly of the *Beagle*) at Darwin's suggestion. Darwin was just one of the milling delegates, an élite geologist and gentleman, but hardly perceived in Owen's category. He never cared much for conferences, but it was a chance to meet friends and glimpse the up-and-coming men. He thought Jenyns looked thin, and cursed missing that 'renegade' Hewett Watson, who had been there in person to face down Forbes with accusations of plagiarism. Best of all were the convivial tours that went with the occasion. He took a Sunday jaunt to Winchester Cathedral with a party that included the Dean of Armagh and 'never enjoyed a day more in my life.'[63]

The next month Sulivan and his family came to stay – 'a real good rattling fellow,' whooped Darwin, trying to tempt Hooker into joining their 'reunion of naturalists.' They nattered about old times, meaning the Falklands, fossils, and FitzRoy. Sulivan had done sterling work in South America, returning home with six crates of fossils from Patagonia. Coincidentally, a letter from FitzRoy arrived while he was at Down. FitzRoy, too, was home, dismissed as the Governor of New Zealand. Sulivan put FitzRoy's fall down to his 'old *Aristocratic*' hauteur. It was the 'Beagle all over again, *temper violent* saying *any thing* to any body, doing most hasty and extraordinary things.' Once he was 'so violent as even to cause a *deputation* to take up their hats and walk out of his room in the middle of his *attack* on them, leaving him storming.' He was 'in fact, being the Capt[n]. of a ship over again.'[64]

Darwin got FitzRoy's address from the Admiralty and dropped him a line. But he realized that it was the end of an era even as he wrote. The *Beagle* work was all but finished. Nothing had been wasted; not even the dust from the decks, or the soil stuck to roots – it had been posted to Christian Ehrenberg in Berlin, on the look-out for micro-organisms. Darwin was finishing his last book of the journey, on the pampas and land elevation, and it would be, he warned FitzRoy, 'geological & dull.' Nor was he sanguine about sales. Look at *Volcanic Islands*, he moaned to Lyell, 'it cost me *18 months!!!*,' yet few had bought it. It left him feeling that geologists did not actually read each other's books and that the only reason to write one was to show 'proof of earnestness.' Darwin had convincingly proved his. He was now a fully accredited geologist, no longer the tyro scrambling alongside the Captain. There were other changes, too, he told FitzRoy: 'I am a different man in strength and energy to what I was in old days, when I was your "Fly-catcher", on board the Beagle.'

On 1 October he returned the final proofs of *South America*. That was almost it. The binders did have one last '*stupid* trick' to play –

they bound the only coloured plate of geological sections back to front, and it had to be cut and repasted in the entire stock.[65] But then that was an author's lot.

22

Illformed Little Monsters

OF THE *BEAGLE* SPECIMENS, only a single barnacle species was left to describe. 'You cannot think how delighted I feel at having finished,' he told Henslow on 5 October 1846. But the time it had taken – ten years. Henslow's prediction had not been so far off the mark: 'Your words, which I thought preposterous, are come true, that it w^d take twice the number of years to describe, that it took to collect & observe.'

The barnacle beckoned. He anticipated a short descriptive paper. It would not take long; the house was tranquil now, the refurbishment complete, his study freshly painted. And he had only one species to describe, after all, even if it was bizarre: 'some months,' he optimistically reckoned, 'a year' at most. Then, finally, he would begin sifting his 'accumulation of notes on species.' Writing them up 'will take me five years, & then when published, I daresay I shall stand infinitely low in the opinion of all sound naturalists – so this is the prospect for the future.'[1]

The barnacle was that 'illformed little monster' he had collected from the shores of southern Chile in 1835. Hooker heard that it was 'quite new & curious' and was intrigued. Aberrant was the word: it was the world's smallest barnacle and lived as a parasite, boring inside the conch-shell of the mollusc *Concholepas*. Darwin could not imagine how to classify the unique creature. Even christening it foxed him, loathing Latin as he did: 'how to invent a name completely puzzles me,' he said, dragooning Hooker. It seemed to be articulated when they looked under the microscope, so they opted for *Arthrobalanus* ('Jointed Balanus' – *Balanus* being a common conical-shelled barnacle on sea shores), although Darwin was not entirely happy with it.

339

He began dissecting 'M^r. Arthrobalanus' and Hooker helped, despite the crush of his Kew work (he was still describing the Galapagos plants). Darwin's microscope left something to be desired, so Hooker also contacted a good optician, and a new 3s. 6d. lens worked wonders. Darwin perfected his technique: he cut down the strain of dissecting for long periods by putting woodblocks under his wrists. It was not only technical advice that Hooker fed his friend; jars of his homemade relish also arrived at Down. 'The porcupine quills better than the glass tube; the Chutney Sauce capital,' Darwin replied after one parcel. Hooker's willingness to drop everything and assist had Darwin crowing with delight: 'You really are the most goodnatured man I ever knew.' They grew still closer. It had been only three years since Hooker's return, but Darwin felt as if they had been friends for 'fifty years.'[2]

Progress reports went out to interested parties. He told FitzRoy that he had spent two weeks 'dissecting a little animal about the size of a pin's head' from Chile '& I could spend another month on it, & daily see some more beautiful structure!' After so many years devoted to grand geological projects – coral reefs, parallel roads, volcanoes, and icebergs – he relished the idea of using his 'eyes & fingers' again in filigree anatomical work.

Arthrobalanus was odd, but only a comparison with normal species could show to what extent. So Darwin began borrowing other barnacles. He sent Owen his notes and asked for the loan of comparable specimens from the College of Surgeons. Not only other species; he began looking at other growth stages, especially the barnacles' larvae. What started as a trickle of specimens soon became a torrent. Conchologists – who specialized in every conceivable type of seashell, from exotic conches to boring barnacles – offered to lend him entire collections. Many explorers traded commercially in shells. These were big business in mid-century. The bizarre and unusual fetched high prices at auction as the gentry and collectors outbid one another to augment their showy cabinets. Shells even attracted *hoi polloi* now that the new trains could whisk them to the seaside.[3] As a result sellers were eager to see their specimens classified expertly, to increase their value. Darwin was sucked in deeper; the whole enterprise snowballed uncontrollably.

He began to contemplate other barnacle groups. Not that this worried him, for a comprehensive study would boost his reputation. An up-to-date reference work on barnacles was cried out for; Louis Agassiz, the new professor of natural history at Harvard in 1847, told the British Association that it was 'a pressing desideratum.' As things stood, the whole subject was in a 'state of chaos.' Until recently barnacles had been totally misunderstood; indeed, they had just been transferred lock, stock, and barrel from one division of the animal kingdom to another. Originally barnacles – being shell-covered – had been thought molluscs, relatives of mussels and snails. But in 1830 an army surgeon, John Thompson, had penetrated their 'disguise' by studying, not the immobile adults, but their free-swimming larvae.[4] They turned out to be crustaceans – relatives of crayfish and crabs. It was an astonishing revelation. No one had imagined that the barnacle cemented to its seaside rock was cousin to the crabs that scuttled beside it, or that those feathery filaments wafting through the water were modified feet. A barnacle was like a shrimp lying on its back waving its legs in the water. Moving the barnacles in with the crabs and shrimps necessitated a complete reappraisal of their anatomy. The field was wide open.

There was another reason, closer to home, why he was happy to embark on a larger study. Hooker, grumbling about the French botanist Frédéric Gérard's book *On Species*, told Darwin that no one had the right to 'examine the question of species who has not minutely described many.' This stung. Darwin took it personally, as an attack on his right to speak on the origin of species. What did it matter, he answered, if he had not described his 'due share of species.' It did 'not alter one iota my long self-acknowledged presumption in accumulating facts & speculating on the subject of variation.' The work had at least given him 'the greatest amusement' for 'nine years.' It was a sad refrain; Darwin had not expected this sort of criticism. Actually Hooker was not thinking of Darwin at all, and he was embarrassed when he realized the misunderstanding. And yet, privately, he *did* believe that Darwin was 'too prone to theoretical considerations about species.' If anything could dampen his speculative ardour, Hooker reasoned, it would be an exhaustive study of one group.

It made Darwin more determined than ever. If only museum curators who handle hundreds of specimens and produce ponderous monographs could speak on the great questions, he would earn that right. Barnacles would establish his credentials. And like Gérard, he would be on the look-out for variations.[5] A thorough examination of all the barnacle varieties could put him in a commanding position when discussing natural selection.

So barnacles were not totally irrelevant to his evolutionary work. In fact, as he proceeded, he began to uncover the most extraordinary proofs of his notebook speculations.

He pushed deeper into the subject, only to be limited by his equipment. His simple lens just could not resolve the detail in his pin's-head dissections. He took advice from Carpenter, an adept microscopist, and ordered a good compound microscope. Even then, he found it wearisome work, and tiring on the wrists and eyes. 'I have been nearly 3 months,' he complained to Hooker, '& have done only 3 genera!!!'[6] Four months later he had finished only two more. It really was taking an age, and he wondered whether it was worth it.

By late 1847 the conchologists were pushing him hard. The most flamboyant, Hugh Cuming, agreed that he should study the entire barnacle group. Cuming was laid up quietly, partly paralysed after a heart attack; but from 1827 until the early 1840s he had been a sort of conchological privateer. Immensely wealthy, he had built himself a schooner, the *Discoverer*, fitted out to hold the world's natural treasures. He had roamed the seven seas plundering islands of their pearls, exotic birds, tropical plants, and prized shells. Sometimes he took the last of their kind – at least one species went extinct after he passed through. From Polynesia, South America, and the Philippines he had shipped back tens of thousands of shells. He traded in this booty, and one can imagine 'what a bull market in conchology set in when Cuming's molluscs reached the auction room.'[7] He was an acute financial operator. His mercenary tactics looked to many like plain '*meanness*,' leaving Hooker, at least, with a low opinion of the man. Darwin had always found him fair. He had known Cuming since 1845, and had examined his Galapagos seashells (so complete a series, of course, that Cuming had advised him to ignore all previous books on the subject). Forced to rest up now, Cuming put his 'whole magnificent collection' – a treasure trove of barnacles – at Darwin's disposal and urged him on.

More scholarly systematists, particularly J. E. Gray at the British Museum, also thought a monograph was needed, and Gray pledged his public collection. Darwin was convinced. He made a formal – and highly irregular – request to the Trustees of the British Museum. Specialists were expected to work inside the museum, but he asked that the barnacles be sent to his home. He was not prepared to travel to Bloomsbury; he wanted them at Down, and in stages, for it took at least two days to soak, clean, dissect and describe each one. As a sweetener he promised the Trustees his own prepared specimens after finishing, and they accepted.

He called in specimens from far and wide. Even Sir James Ross – Hooker's old Captain – setting off to search for the missing Franklin expedition, was cajoled into gathering Arctic barnacles on his melancholy voyage. (The *Erebus* and *Terror* had been caught in the Canadian pack ice and were lost with all hands.) With the empire expanding – the quest for the Northwest Passage was a reminder of how much Britain needed this route to the Pacific – the flow of new animal species to the imperial capital was unabated; the natural world lay at John Bull's feet. Darwin, well connected through the Zoological and Geological Societies and with time to spare, was perfectly placed to carry out the definitive study: to name and describe every species of one sub-class.

Even this had its imperial ramifications. Naming is possessing, said the old insect specialist William Kirby. Science was a sort of metaphoric appropriation: when an animal 'is named and described, it becomes . . . a possession for ever, and the value of every individual specimen of it, even in a mercantile view, is enhanced.' Hence the glory seeking, as describers rushed into print. Here Darwin drew the line. Where was the scientific 'disinterest'? he asked Hugh Strickland, looking into new procedures for naming animals. Darwin thought it pure vanity that a naturalist should suffix his name to every species he describes, as though he owned it personally. The practice led to too many hasty 'baptisms' in the race for priority.[8] Darwin's own study would be conducted at a more dignified pace.

To be definitive a monograph would have to embrace fossil barnacles as well. Darwin had originally turned down a collection from the Bristol Institution. Now he wrote accepting it, and he notified the Geological Society of his needs. It was dogged, grinding work. The modern species had to be dissected, the fossils disarticulated or sectioned. He was inundated with so many species that the labour became exhausting and the smell of spirits nauseating. 'I hope to Heaven I am right in spending so much time over one subject,' he exclaimed to Hooker.[9]

From that day in 1844 when Darwin bared his soul, Hooker had come to play an increasingly important role. He was Charles's confessor, his confidant, a sounding board on the 'criminal' subject of species, an endless source of geographical lore. Their friendship blossomed. Darwin revelled in Hooker's weekend visits, and even more his longer working stays.

By now Hooker was spending 'a week at a stretch' at Down. He brought his work, which he set out on the dining-room table, and Emma made him feel at home. Walking through the room to her store cupboard, 'she would take a pear or some good thing, and lay it by my side with a charming smile as she passed out. Then in the evening she always played [the piano] with me and sometimes asked me to whistle to her accompaniment of some simple airs!'[10] Clearly, he was becoming one of the family.

Hooker spent the third week of January 1847 at Down. Here he polished off papers and polished up fossils, finishing his account of the coal plants and their living relatives for the Geological Survey. The subject gave the two men plenty to argue over as they paced briskly through the grounds. But the deterioration in Darwin's health was evident. Even pumping Hooker took its toll: the half-hour sessions forced Darwin to take 'a complete rest, for they always exhausted him, often producing a buzzing noise in the head, and sometimes what he called "stars in the eyes," the latter too often the prelude of an attack of violent eczema in the head, during which he was hardly recognisable.'[11]

On this occasion Hooker – finally – came away with a copy of the evolution essay. Goodness knows Darwin had dropped enough hints over fourteen months. Now the moment had arrived. Hooker's would be the first expert opinion. Darwin was apprehensive; he would finally be able to talk it over with his friend, tease out his views. If, that is, he could get to town: he made date after date, only to cancel, sick, debilitated, and infuriated. Eventually Hooker scribbled a page of telegraphic notes and posted it to Down.

And what did he make of this 231-page manuscript? London's freethinkers all accepted that some natural law or other explained the appearance of new species of fossil animals in the rock strata. But what this law was, few could say. Some, like the 'renegade' Watson or reprobate Robert Grant (Darwin's old tutor), were radical transmutationists. Others professed ignorance and simply spoke of 'Creation' out of convention. Or in Hooker's case, default: he had long agreed that it was a 'fair & profitable subject,' but that, having 'no formed opinion' of his own, he opted 'for immutability, till I see cause to take a fixed post.' Darwin was now giving him cause, and wondering which mast he would nail his colours to. Hooker would not say. But he did argue that Darwin's tirade against the continual Creation of life was 'uncalled for:'

> All allusions to superintending providence unnecessary – The Creator [who is] able to make first [organisms is] able also to go on directing & [it is a] matter of moonshine to [the] argument whether he does or no.

All he wanted to know was the mechanism of 'Creation.' He rather mistook Darwin's intent. If Darwin really wanted to show Creative foresight, he should point out the reason for 'retaining [those] *useless* organs' which in later species might be turned into something useful.[12] *This* would illustrate God's intentions. This would demonstrate nature's design aspect. It would also scupper Darwin's strategy entirely.

At last Darwin was getting feedback. Calm feedback, with no sign of Sedgwick's histrionics, or the savagery meted out to the hapless *Vestiges*. But Darwin was not dealing with an unreconstructed Anglican cleric. Hooker lived up to his expectations by providing the 'highly suggestive,' geographically precise criticisms he needed. And more: Hooker annotated the copy before giving it back – 'very good,' he thought the arguments against multiple centres of creation for the same species. 'Goodish,' he scribbled alongside the summary on artificial selection bending species into 'infinitely numerous races.' But the way domestic races were derived from one or more wild species was 'not clear' at all.[13]

Darwin had groomed young Hooker for just this: a series of detailed discussions on nature's way of making species. Hooker might have been unimpressed by the overarching argument – much later, with a modicum of hindsight, he admitted that he 'failed to grasp its full significance' – but this did not stop him feeding Darwin a stream of geographical tidbits.[14]

Hooker's next move was totally unexpected. The very day he took away the essay he dropped a bombshell: he was planning another voyage. After his 'Antarctic herborizations' in 1839-43, he had always wanted to see the Tropics. But no one had expected him to be off so soon, and even he thought he might crack 'like a glass tumbler' on bouncing from the polar ice to the palm beaches. He had only been home for four years; it hardly seemed possible. Darwin had come to know him so well, he had grown so close, so reliant. Suddenly all talk of the essay was overshadowed. It left Darwin confused, casting a pall over their relationship. He was deflated and groaned on being told the news. Without Hooker's help he would be 'lost.' He kept trying to come up to town, to tax Hooker over the essay, fearing that he would 'forget all about' it, anxious lest he leave England suddenly. But he was now retching non-stop. For weeks through March and April he was almost continuously ill, tormented by 'boils & swellings,' and signing off his apologetic notes 'Ever yours rather wretchedly C. Darwin.'[15]

Their first tiff, in May, only aggravated the situation. Considering the ideological issues at stake – murders, confessions, creations – it is ironic that the flare-up was ignited by coal. For months they had disagreed over the origin of coal, which Hooker was analysing for the Survey. (With Britain the 'workshop of the world,' mining over half the world's output of coal to fuel its growing industries, the publicly funded Survey paid particular attention to mapping the coalfields.) Darwin imagined the ancient coal-plants growing in warm shallow seas like mangroves. He twitted Hooker that coal was a sort of 'submarine peat,' betting him '5 to 1 that in 20 years this will be generally admitted'; 'sneer away,' he said, misjudging the mood, goading him with his mangrove theory. Hooker's temper snapped. Darwin was 'mad' for thinking the ferns of the coal seams marine; these were terrestrial, unequivocally so. He could speculate on species as wildly as he wanted, but on fossil plants Hooker was the expert. The 'savage onslaught' left Darwin reeling. Hooker's short fuse had shown itself. He was quick to snap, soon to make up. Not that Darwin didn't deserve it. A few days later he tried his long-shot on Falconer, the expert on Indian fossils, who thought 'such infernal nonsense ought to be thrashed out' of him. But it gave Darwin an inkling of Hooker's darker side. There was no 'man more lovable,' and none more 'peppery,' he later said, even if 'the clouds pass away almost immediately.'[16]

Another pet theory was taking a pounding at the time – his ancient sea beaches running along the Glen Roy valley. Louis Agassiz had already convinced almost everybody that a glacier had dammed the valley, forming a meltwater lake. Now the Scottish geologist David Milne added new evidence. He had gone to Glen Roy convinced that Darwin was right, and come away a sceptic: these were ancient lake margins. But Darwin clung to his seashores, holding tight because of his *idée fixe* with bobbing landmasses. Dry sea beaches on the mountain sides testified to a risen land. Lose this evidence of rising and subsiding continents and his whole geological edifice was at risk – including his island-making mechanism. Continents must sink to make isolated islands, cutting off species which start to adapt differentially. 'M^r. Milne will think me as obstinate as a Pig, when I say, that I think' his Glen Roy theory 'more utterly impossible than words can express.' Privately he was sensitive to the criticism. He wobbled precariously over Agassiz's glacial lake. Anxiously, he fired off a succession of letters supporting his side. 'I have been bad enough for these last few days,' he grumbled to Hooker, 'having had to think & write too much about Glen Roy (an audacious son of dog (Mr Milne,) having attacked my theory) which made me horribly sick.'[17]

His condition worsened. Every trip was 'stomacho volente,' and invariably deferred. But illness had its consolations. It provided psychological security, allowing him to cry off visits, escape jury service, turn down dinners. And dining clubs; in April he refused a nomination for the Royal Society's élite Philosophical Club. Not that society do's were unappealing. He was half-tempted by Lord Northampton's soirées, where the literati danced and élite geologists plumed themselves. Here Roderick Murchison would strut, discussing the military precision of his Silurian campaigns, and the haughty Owen would boast of moas and megatheriums; here William Broderip, who had sorted the *Beagle* shells, would show the ladies his sponge the size of Cardinal Wolsey's hat.[18] At these fashionable galas, rich patrons could meet their young protégés. Hooker even offered to escort Darwin, as one would an invalid. But no, he was too 'stomachy.' The undiagnosed sickness and swellings were his release. And yet, however useful an excuse, they were no less real, no less debilitating, and he dosed himself with bismuth or opium. He retreated further into the family fold, revelling in Emma's care, refusing to believe that his own protégé was really leaving.

Hooker had finished his *Flora Antarctica*, and the coal plants for the Geological Survey. He was making his mark; even Darwin had heard the Survey's head, De la Beche, heap praise on Hooker's 'coal-doings.'[19] He was also publishing voluminously and elected a Fellow of the Royal Society that April as a consequence. He turned thirty in June and should have been settling down. The more so because of his attachment to Henslow's eldest daughter, Frances, which became obvious to all during the British Association meeting at Oxford the following month.

Darwin planned to attend Oxford, with his evolution essay, determined to probe Hooker more deeply on his reaction to it, even though Emma – about to give birth again – would be left at home alone. It was the supreme sacrifice, not so much on Emma's count, but because he had not slept in a stranger's house for five years. He was breaking his own most solemn rule. He felt awful, but here he was, asking to lodge with Hooker's relations. He still stipulated rooms which would guarantee peace and privacy. Only a 'secure solitary retreat' would do, he said, aware that he was making a 'ridiculous fuss' about his 'precious self.' Following some juggling, he boarded with Hooker's uncle, the Vice-Principal of Magdalen Hall, but again, only after reassurances that 'I can have my meals to myself & a room to be by myself in.'[20] And that is what he did: dined in and refused evening invitations, even from Capt. Ross, who had already proved himself by turning over his Antarctic barnacles.

Darwin attended the geological section, only to be made painfully aware of how anathema evolutionary speculation was to the gentlemen present. For the moment, though, they had easier prey in their sights. Robert Chambers was down from Edinburgh to give a talk on ancient beaches. This was Darwin's subject, so he must have sat in and have seen Chambers mugged by his friends. According to an observer, Chambers

> pushed his conclusions to a most unwarrantable length, and got roughly handled on account of it by Buckland, De la Beche, Sedgwick, Murchison, and Lyell. The last told me afterwards that he did so purposely that C[hambers]. might see that reasonings in the style of the author of the *Vestiges* would not be tolerated among scientific men.[21]

And not only scientific men. On Sunday Samuel Wilberforce, the new Bishop of Oxford, delivered a cautionary sermon in St Mary's Church on the wrong way of doing science. It was a brilliantly aimed blow at the 'half-learned,' at those seduced by the 'foul temptation' of speculation. In other words, at Chambers, with his drawing-room notion of development. The scholars loved it. The church 'was crowded to suffocation' with geologists, astronomers, and zoologists, all feeling that Wilberforce had hit his mark. Science was the province of quiet, cloistered, respectable thinkers. The demagogues, Wilberforce said, looked for a self-sustaining universe, one they could praise in a 'mocking spirit of unbelief.' Such deluded souls do not understand the 'modes of the Creator's acting,' nor the grave responsibilities of a gentleman. This warning about humility before the facts was another slap in the face. Chambers, fuming in his pew, denounced it as an attempt to stifle progressive opinion. He must have gone home, the geologist Andrew Ramsay guessed, 'with the feeling of a martyr.'[22]

Darwin missed this; Sunday was probably the 'Heavenly day' he spent with Henslow's party looking over the great house and grounds of Dropmore. But for the rest of the week, there he was at Oxford, essay in hand, chasing up Hooker for his opinions, watching his colleagues come crashing down on Chambers. There was an irony to the situation. But no surprise: the Association was a coalition of clergy and gentlemen, whose geological science provided the bedrock for the established order. It wasn't that they were slating an outsider. Lyell himself could invite the Archbishop of Canterbury to Geological Society dinners. They objected to sloppy science with evil consequences coming from a magazine publisher. The sloppiness also allowed Darwin to abuse *Vestiges* in Lyell's presence, in order to distance himself from it. He deplored the author's 'poverty of intellect,' and dismissed the book as a 'literary curiosity.'[23]

Still, for all that, here he was, surreptitiously touting an essay that would bruise many a gentleman's virtuous view of nature. Darwin achieved his aim in coming. He met up with Hooker and dragged him off to hear the organ at New College Chapel, where the celestial music sent a tingle 'up and down' his spine.[24] He led Hooker point by point through key parts of the essay. He heard at first hand Hooker's objection to the natural colonization of islands: to the wind-and-waves dispersal of seeds and plants. Hooker responded with his identical mountain plants in Tasmania and Tierra del Fuego, at opposite ends of the globe. How could migration account for this astonishing distribution? How indeed; Darwin determined to work on it, but for the moment he feared that Hooker's objection would reinforce Forbes's sunken supercontinent nonsense.

More than one knot was being tied at this meeting. Hooker broke the news that he was to become a Henslow-in-law: he and Frances were engaged. This bound him ever tighter to Charles, who saw a trusted scientific circle closing round himself. Everyone noticed how happy Hooker was in these weeks. But not even Frances could cure his wanderlust. Charles did not know 'whether to be glad or sorry,' balancing the betrothal against Hooker's determination to travel – glad 'for your sake,' or sorry 'for mine.'[25]

Hooker was unsettled because the government had not given him a post at Kew, under his father, and he was loath to canvass aristocratic patronage. (Kew was still a promenading park for noblemen and their ladies.) Sir William wanted him to kick his heels, perhaps write up his diary of the Ross expedition – indeed, John Murray even offered to publish it as a companion to Darwin's *Journal*. But Hooker said no. He was itching to travel again. Any voyage would do, he told Capt. Ross in desperation. He applied for an Admiralty expedition to Borneo, and an East India Company trip to Goa. But each time money proved the obstacle. 'I wish I had a private fortune,' he wailed, knowing how Darwin's had put him at the Captain's table. By now he was 'ready to make any sacrifice to get to the tropics.'[26] Before he knew it he was on a team planning to trek through the Sikkim valley and Tibet, the exotic land of 'Lama worship' and soaring peaks that he had dreamed of as a boy. Just as precipitously he obtained a Treasury grant to collect Himalayan plants for Kew. It was all so sudden; he was rushed off his feet. The needs of Down were now forgotten.

What his fiancée thought we do not know. Darwin was dejected, even despite Emma's safe delivery of Elizabeth in July. He had

349

repeatedly tried to get to Kew through the summer and autumn, treating his own twenty-mile trek with grim determination – 'I *must* go over the remainder of my species sketch' – but each occasion found him face down on a sofa, with 'fiercely reinflamed' boils or debilitating sickness. In the event, he saw Hooker only once more, on 20 August, when he was finally strong enough to make the carriage drive to Kew. Darwin wished him well. The terms were touching, but there was no disguising his remorse: 'It will be a noble voyage & journey but I wish it was over, I shall miss you selfishly & all ways to a dreadful extent.' His only consolation was that Frances, that 'beautiful magnet,' would bring him back.[27]

With that, Charles went off to Shrewsbury, where his father's condition was giving cause for concern. Here for days he lay writhing on a sofa, 'groaning & grumbling,' plagued by bursting boils, immersed in Bulwer-Lytton's epic of tragedy and disaster, *The Last Days of Pompeii*. Hooker tried to get to Down in early November. The attempt was seen by Charles 'as the greatest proof of friendship I ever received from mortal man' – hyperbole which reflected his emotional state.[28] A few days later Hooker was aboard ship, HMS *Sidon*, sharing a suite with Lord Dalhousie, on his way to India as the new Governor-General. Darwin never did clasp him in a fond farewell.

23

Al Diabolo

CHARLES WAS ON his own now. Yet he was not lonely – the patter of little feet up and down the corridor outside the study made sure of that. Seven-year-old Annie often popped in, her face aglow. She would give him a naughty pinch of snuff from the jar that had been moved upstairs to break his habit. He loved her the more for it. And Emma was expecting again, her seventh. With an influenza epidemic gripping London, Charles – ever careful of disease – had another reason to avoid town, and went up for little more than the obligatory meetings of the Geological Society. Anyway, with Emma and babies and barnacles, as well as the genial new incumbent of the parish, the Revd John Innes, who was fast becoming a friend, he had all the company he wanted at Down. But he missed Hooker. Their months apart were dragging and it would be years before they met again – if indeed Hooker survived his perilous Himalayan expedition. Charles would have to bottle up his feelings about the origin of species until then.

Not that he could get back to species with the barnacles snowballing out of control. He had expected to be finished now and back to natural selection. Instead, he was bracing himself for another two years of smelly dissections. Each one took longer than planned, leaving him little time for anything else. But some calls had a royal ring about them and could not be refused. In February 1848, he was contacted by the leader of British Science, Sir John Herschel. Writing at the behest of the First Sea Lord, he invited Darwin to join an élite team drawing up instructions on scientific field work for sailors. When Sir John crooked a finger, scientists jumped. Just let him finish a dissection, Darwin replied; it would take a week or so, then he would oblige. As he put it to Richard Owen, 'When men like

351

Herschel & yourself give up your time to the task, I could not of course refuse.'[1]

In the Admiralty manual, Darwin explained that any gentleman could geologize abroad. It required slight preparation and little apparatus, in fact only the sort of curiosity and systematic habits that the officers of a man-of-war were expected to possess. Aboard ship they were ideally placed to observe those slow 'still active causes' that had shaped the geological past: sedimentary deposition, erosion of cliffs, icebergs, coral reefs – just the things Darwin himself was interested in. They should collect dust that settled on the deck, and, ashore, concentrate on fossils, volcanoes, and coal samples. The writing cost him five weeks, to his dismay, but it was worth it to train future Sea Lords to be good Lyellians – indeed good Darwinians.

At home the tensions were mounting, along with the barnacles. He fretted about the family, and his perennially wretched stomach. The condition of his 81-year-old father was grave; Charles was horrified to see how much he had 'changed bodily during the last six months.' And Emma's condition was always uncertain. These were matters of life and death, and the thought of them made a grim counterpoint to the fetid corpses he was dismembering. Outwardly, all seemed well on the weekend of 12 February, when the Lyells and Owen, along with those young Turks of the Geological Survey, Edward Forbes and Andrew Ramsay, stayed at Down to celebrate Darwin's thirty-ninth birthday. Ramsay had never enjoyed himself more. Darwin struck him as an 'enviable man,' with 'a pleasant place, a nice wife, a nice family, station neither too high nor too low, a good moderate fortune, and the command of his own time.'[2] Little did he realize his host's inner turmoil. But then Darwin gave little away, merely begging off a post-prandial promenade around the Lubbock estate on Sunday.

Darwin's was a privileged life, as Ramsay recognized, and it stood on a precipice in the dark days of 1848. That weekend the insurrection sweeping Italy was threatening to explode nearer home. France – in Alexis de Tocqueville's phrase – was 'sleeping on a volcano.' Sure enough, the barricades went up in Paris on the 22nd; protesters were shot, the troops mutinied, and an interim ministry was installed under the moderate reformer Adolphe Thiers. The French King abdicated on the 24th and headed for exile in England. In London the rumours flew. At the Tory leader Sir Robert Peel's party on Saturday the 26th, Darwin's colleagues – Lyell, Owen, Buckland, and De la Beche – were given a graphic account of the Paris uprising by the

Prussian ambassador, a member of whose staff had escaped through the revolutionaries' lines. They heard of the '30,000 communists in Paris who are for property in common and no m..riage, and who are much to be feared by those who have aught to lose.'³ After the ladies retired, there was hectic talk of the revolution, and how, with a few sensible reforms, the throne could have been saved. Peel told Lyell he feared a financial crisis in Britain as the measures of the new Republican government – to be proclaimed the next day – frightened capitalists on both sides of the Channel.

Peel's guests were the gentlemen and clergy who rubbed shoulders with Darwin at his clubs, the Geological and the Athenaeum. Some had shared his hospitality at Down the fortnight before. All were concerned to see stabilizing reforms put into place and to police the radical masses, now demanding total suffrage at home. Darwin's friends were fearful. Lyell had long deplored 'mob-rule.' Forbes, the son of a banker, was himself shortly to take up his baton against rioters. And Owen's Honourable Artillery Company had seen service during the working-class demonstrations.⁴

After the initial bloodletting in Paris, when the populace took the city, Emma's aunt sighed with some relief that the revolution had become 'more a social than a political one.' She still wondered whether the new leaders would be 'able to realise their promises to the working classes,' and dreaded the 'vengeance of the monster they have unchained' if they could not. But while French workers had gained concessions, British unions were frustrated over the government's intransigence. There was nothing like the French 'Right to Work,' and unemployment remained high during the 40s. Worse, no promise was held out of an extended franchise. The British monster began seeking its own vengeance. The 'Marseillaise' was sung and the Parisians praised in radical London. The uprising across the Channel gave a new impetus to the Chartist leaders, spurring them to plan a huge demonstration.

Panic spread among the wealthy. With 150,000 Chartists expected to converge on Kennington Common on 10 April, there was feverish activity in the capital. No one knew what would happen as they tried to take their petition demanding suffrage to Parliament. The Queen left the Palace for her own safety, and plans were drawn up to 'quell the insurrection by force.' Eighty-five thousand special constables were sworn in over some weeks – mostly gentlemen and their employees and servants – and 7000 troops were mobilized. The Bank, Downing Street, the Foreign Office, and all public buildings were sandbagged, and their officials sworn in as specials. Those at the

General Post Office were issued with hand grenades; some at the British Museum had muskets.[5] Everything was done to ensure that demonstrators did not occupy any buildings, as they had in Paris.

The jitters were as pronounced among Darwin's colleagues, who mounted guard in the scientific institutions. At Charing Cross, Ramsay, sworn in as a special, patrolled with Forbes at the Geological Survey, shouldering his truncheon in defence of his trilobites. The Director, De la Beche, brought in an armful of cutlasses and prepared for a siege. Owen took his watch at the College of Surgeons; big and burly, he was ready for the rioters, and afterwards he set off for Peel's house to make sure the Tory leader was safe. The Revd Buckland, Dean of Westminster, waited at the Abbey, armed with a crowbar. Darwin might have thought him an amusing 'fool' for flapping like a pterodactyl during his geological lectures, but the tomfoolery stopped now, and Buckland threatened to bludgeon any rioters who broke in through Poet's Corner. His protégé, William Broderip (Darwin's shell identifier), sentenced Chartists in the Thames Police Court, where he was a magistrate.[6]

The air of frantic preparation left everybody panicky, Darwin not least. His reading took on a new aspect. In March, as fears of the Chartist demonstration turned to hysteria, he read Thiers's *History of the French Revolution*, only to throw it down as 'dull & poor.' Later he tackled Mary Wollstonecraft's inflammatory *Vindication of the Rights of Women* and the libertarian William Godwin's *Memoirs of Wollstonecraft*, although he was far happier with De Tocqueville's *Democracy in America*. During this unsettled period his nausea increased, which prevented him from attending the March Council meeting of the Geological Society.[7] London was now up in arms, anyway. The agitators' demands – for land taxes, property taxes, wealth taxes – would have hit him hard. Here he was, a member of the despised gentry, a leisured gentleman, living, as the extremists would say, off the backbroken poor. His father was ill, he had a growing family to fend for, and, if events took a nasty turn, his investments could be wiped out.

He was a closet evolutionist besides. This was the heart of the matter. His Anglican friends were quelling the rioters, some of whom were armed with transmutation and godless sciences. Owen and Forbes were holding the line and protecting his privileges. But wouldn't they condemn him as a fifth-columnist if they uncovered his secret? When he had cried 'the fabric falls!' ten years before, he did not have this sort of insurrection in mind. Anyhow, he had been a tyro then, speculating privately. Now he was a squire, a family man, a member of the geological élite. For all his theory's middle-class Malthusian core, and its capitalistic roots, he could still be branded a traitor by the Tory diehards.

Ensconced at Down, with the world around him threatening to tear itself apart, Darwin kept up the tedious dissections. 'It's dogged as does it,' he would mutter to himself. In late March, as his Creationist colleagues made plans to resist the radicals, he made a crucial breakthrough. Many of his specimens appeared to be infested with tiny parasites. He had always picked these off and thrown them away, but now he looked closer. Barnacles are usually hermaphrodite (each animal has both male and female sexual organs), but among Cuming's Philippine species was an exception. It was undescribed and Darwin christened it *Ibla cumingii*. Not only did it have separate sexes, but the males and females were so different as to appear almost unrelated.

Henslow was the first to hear the news:

> the female has the ordinary appearance, whereas the male has no one part of its body like the female & is microscopically minute; but here comes the odd fact, the male or sometimes two males, at the instant they cease being locomotive larvae become parasitic within the sack of the female, & thus fixed & half embedded in the flesh of their wives they pass their whole lives & can never move again.

Here was a reproductive set-up almost unparalleled in the animal kingdom. And how had Darwin uncovered it? He told Henslow that he felt an 'instinct for truth,' akin to 'the instinct of virtue;' and this had helped him.[8]

It seemed like a veiled challenge. What virtue could an Anglican Creationist be expected to find in parasitic polyandry among barnacles? If true, there was little in it to praise God for. Nature could hardly have moved further from 'Time's Noblest Offspring,' Man. A dominant female, tolerating a clutch of dependent, degenerate males clinging to her skirt-tails! 'Is it not strange,' Darwin prodded his old friend, 'that nature should have made this one genus unisexual, & yet have fixed the mates on the outside of the females.' Later he taunted Lyell with similar evidence: an *Ibla* female with a pocket in each valve of her shell in which 'she kept a little husband.' These half-inch-long females were apparently 'parasitized' by their own tiny mates. The males were a tenth of the size and remained almost embryo-like. In their 'flattened, purplish, worm-like' bodies most of the thoracic segments were vestigial and, in fact, useless. 'Truly,' he jibed, 'the schemes and wonders of nature are illimitable.'[9]

All this revived Darwin's flagging interest; he announced he had found the most interesting barnacle 'in the world.' And the surprises continued. In a second species of *Ibla* – this time a hermaphrodite – he also detected parasitic males, 'supplemental' males he called these hermaphrodite-companions. They were tiny larva-like sacs, sixteen hundredths of an inch long. This was even more unexpected: a *hermaphrodite*, in which the male organs were dwindling, accompanied by a tiny, embryonic mate, rudimentary in all but its sex organs. Suddenly he became suspicious of all those parasites he had thrown away. He looked closer. Some, it turned out, were true, unrelated parasites. But those on a similar genus, *Scalpellum*, were yet more minuscule males.

He went on to identify six species of *Scalpellum*, all showing different degrees of sexual differentiation. This came as a splendid vindication of his earlier evolutionary hypotheses. In an 1838 notebook he had speculated on the way the 'sexes separate in some of the lowest tribes:' from ancestral hermaphrodites had evolved the molluscs, in which the males and females retained 'abortive traces' of one another's sexual organs.[10] But he needed a fuller series to illustrate this divergence of the sexes. Now he had it. Barnacles suggested the sequence of events: from hermaphrodites proper, to those with reduced male organs and minute 'supplemental' males, to females that had obliterated their male organs entirely and acquired 'simple' male companions.

Curiouser and curiouser, he wrote in reply to Hooker's welcome first letter from India. He told Hooker of his *Ibla* males in order 'to boast of my species theory, for the nearest & closely allied genus to . . . these parasites, I can now show, are supplemental males,' living on hermaphrodites, whose own male organs are tiny.

> I never sh[d]. have made this out, had not my species theory convinced me, that an hermaphrodite species must pass into a bisexual species by insensibly small stages, & here we have it, for the male organs in the hermaphrodite are beginning to fail, & independent males ready formed. But I can hardly explain what I mean, & you will perhaps wish my Barnacles & Species theory al Diabolo together. But I don't care what you say, my species theory is all gospel.[11]

Hooker did not rise to this outburst. Nor did he wish him to the devil; in fact he thought the evidence staggering. Darwin was convincing them both of the value of his taxonomic work. They could now see what needed to be done: sex and ancestry took top place on the hidden agenda being drawn up as work proceeded. A new 'gospel' was in the making.

Darwin remained enthralled. His minute males were 'truly wonderful.' They were 'rudimentary to a degree, which I believe can hardly be equalled in the whole animal kingdom.' Breathlessly he told Hooker the latest: 'they have no mouth or stomach' and the larva 'fixes itself on the hermaphrodite, [and] develops itself into a great testis!' They grew up as 'mere bags of spermatozoa.' Nor was there necessarily a one-to-one relationship; he found up to ten supplemental males embedded in some hermaphrodites. These tiny mouthless hangers-on never ate, but died off quickly to be replaced by others. So there was a swift turnover in mates. Hooker, taking it all in his stride, replied from Darjeeling that ten mates were commonplace. 'The supplemental males of Barnacles are really wonderful,' he conceded, 'though the supplemental males in the Bhothea families' – the 'uncouth' Himalayan tribe which provided his coolies and where 'a wife may have 10 husbands by Law' – 'have rather distracted my attention of late.'[12] He had caught the Darwinian drift. Primitives of all sorts lacked the virtues innate to gentlemen of the highest Victorian class.

While Darwin marvelled at his barnacle bonanza, the Chartist demonstration on 10 April passed off peacefully. In May, as he told Hooker about the barnacles, fully expecting to be sent 'al Diabolo' for his efforts, he suddenly cut away to the hoary subject of coal. Coal, that old bugbear, the one thing they disagreed on most. Hooker had been seeking evidence for its origin in India, hoping to solve the problem once and for all. Good, replied Darwin: 'I shall never rest easy in Down church-yard' if it is not solved 'before I die.' This sounded glib, but mortality was now a sombre undercurrent in his thought. 'Talking of death,' he went on, 'my confounded stomach . . . has been rather worse.' His sickness increased alarmingly as he watched his father sink.

The corpulent Doctor was now breathing with difficulty and suffered a sort of 'dyeing sensation.' Charles travelled to Shrewsbury with a heavy heart a week later, fearing the worst. Emma stayed at home, pregnant, but she received daily health reports on both Charles and his father. The Doctor's prognosis of his own condition was good and bad: he would live a little longer, he said, but then die suddenly. Charles was only slightly sick during his first few days at

The Mount. He took comfort in Emma's letters, egging her on to write 'all I like to hear.' She posted him newspapers, although he only relished the 'damnable' *Globe*, with its vitriolic reports on the new Frankfurt Parliament and the French National Assembly. But his health slowly deteriorated and within a few days he could not forget his 'stomach for 5 minutes.' The mollycoddling continued, with a simpering Charles caressed from a distance.[13]

The Doctor began to have trouble talking and his legs became weak; his health, Charles realized, was finally failing. Two weeks passed in this way, two weeks of anxiety. As he kept vigil, he too began cracking under the strain. He came over faint and had shivering and vomiting fits, after which he was listless and drained. 'My attack was very sudden,' he wrote home; 'it came on with fiery spokes & dark clouds before my eyes; then sharpish shivery and rather bad . . . sickness.' Feeling vulnerable, he longed to be home. The 'sounds of the town & blackguards talking & want of privacy' left him crying for his rural retreat. 'I did yearn for you,' he wailed to Emma, and continued plaintively: 'Without you, when I feel sick I feel most desolate.' Away from her – even in his birthplace – he lacked security, he missed the caring hands. Oh to be the centre of attention again: 'Oh Mammy I do long to be with you & under your protection for then I feel safe.'

He stayed to celebrate the Doctor's eighty-second birthday, on 30 May. Then, with some relief, he returned to Emma's care. Life at Down ticked on, although his heart was not in the barnacle work. Nor can it have been pleasant, gutting tiny corpses while constantly retching himself. With Emma now seven months pregnant, he began to worry about his own scientific gestation. 'Never will a mountain in labour have brought forth such a mouse as my book . . . It is ridiculous the time each species takes me.' Emma's time grew closer. Charles, extraordinarily sensitive to the slightest pain, planned to have the new anaesthetic, chloroform, administered during the delivery. Ever since his sickening surgical experience as a teenager, he had hated the sight of suffering. Chloroform was a godsend, and he never ceased extolling it. No sooner had the Edinburgh professor James Simpson knocked himself out by inhaling it in 1847 – in the very hospital that Charles had fled from in such terror twenty-one years earlier – than Charles was trying it out for himself. He doctored the Revd Innes, telling him to put a drop of it on his gums for toothache, and he took advice from a London physician on its use in childbirth.[14] His third son, Francis, was born on 16 August, presumably painlessly.

The summer passed, with Darwin hardly seeing a soul. His condition worsened almost daily. As his work slowed to a spluttering, vomiting snail's pace, he saw his friends getting on famously: Lyell was knighted by Queen Victoria at her new Scottish castle, Balmoral, in September. Hooker was making great gains in the Himalayas, discovering new roses, magnolias, and rhododendrons. He was engaged, and Forbes now married. So 'no more of the old *bachelor* parties,' Darwin joked.[15] He remained at Down, a captive to his stomach, attending only the Geological Society Council meetings as required, although they wearied him. More and more, he cried off dinner invitations. Trapped in his self-imposed exile at Down, he lived vicariously through books, trawling them for facts, escaping to exotic locations. With death hounding him, he turned to religious literature again.

Charles and Emma read together almost every day. Novels, travels, histories, biographies – the turnover was immense. Many came by post from the London Library; some were borrowed from Erasmus. As Charles toppled headlong into depression, fearing for his father, Emma must have swayed his reading. For her *The Evidences of the Genuineness of the Gospels*, two fat volumes of cold erudition by Andrews Norton, the late Harvard professor of sacred history, provided hope. Norton, dubbed the 'Unitarian Pope' by Thomas Carlyle, insisted that the Gospels were genuine, untouched, and 'ascribed to their true authors.'[16] If Emma wanted to give Charles reasons for believing in Jesus's promise of eternal life, these were they.

But with the onset of 'swimming head, depression, trembling, [and] many bad attacks of sickness,' he plunged back into heterodoxy. He became absorbed in the life of John Sterling, a young clergyman who had succumbed to chronic illness. Perhaps he saw a reflection of himself: Cambridge, a curacy in rural Sussex, illness, doubt and disillusion. Sterling had moved in the same Carlyle circle in London, and, as with Darwin, this period saw his 'greatest moral and intellectual energy.' By 1840 Sterling was as hopeful as Darwin would ever be of resting his 'faith in the possibility of deep and systematic knowledge on the laws and first principles of our existence.' Darwin's deeper fears too were reflected in Sterling's life. Sterling saw his wife die in childbirth, and died himself prematurely in September 1844, assuring his friends that 'we shall meet again ... Christianity is a great comfort and blessing to me, although I am quite unable to believe all its original documents.'

Darwin, desperately ill himself, was absorbed in this account of a fallen curate, critical only of Sterling's continued emotional attachment to Christianity. 'I simply feel, that I *cannot* believe,' he confessed to his clergyman-cousin Fox, 'in the same spirit . . . that ladies do believe on all & every subject.'[17] Maybe he could no longer believe at all.

He was following the religious journeys of others, dreading his father's death. He read Coleridge too this summer. Emma's father had been taken with Coleridge. He was another Cambridge drop-out who had flirted briefly with religious and political radicalism until the Wedgwoods became his literary patrons. He then made his way back to Anglican conservatism of a sort, and documented his journey in *The Friend* and *Aids to Reflection*, which Darwin read. Christianity for Coleridge was not a theory to be proved but 'a life and a living process.' It required a leap of faith that Darwin could not make. For Coleridge religious feeling was innate to the soul and had nothing to do with inherited instinct, but Darwin's heretical notebooks belied this. Coleridge was wrong.

And what of unbelievers? Darwin thought of his dying father, himself even. Coleridge ascribed their lack of feeling for Christianity to an 'enslaved will.' Leave these *'enfans de Diable,'* he said, to suffer divine retribution. Will 'any of you,' he asked doubters, 'be cured of that common disease, the fear of death?'[18] He answered with a paraphrase of the Gospel of John, Emma's favourite.

Darwin was unmoved, even as he watched his father subside. There was no cure in Coleridge's books. He had learned his Christianity too well from the likes of Paley and Norton – Christianity based on evidence – to think that its doctrines could survive based on vague emotion. He had long abandoned Coleridge's distinction between soul and body, reason and instinct. For all his protestations, Coleridge ended up sounding like an evangelical. Hellfire still put the steam in his religious appeal. The Doctor – Erasmus too, perhaps Charles himself – stood to be eternally burnt. This was a monstrous doctrine.

Death was close for the Doctor. Charles travelled to Shrewsbury on 10 October. He stayed a fortnight, ill himself. As he turned to leave, he saw his father 'serene & cheerful,' a memory he would cherish ever after. On Monday, 13 November, while Emma was away visiting relatives, Charles heard from Catherine that the Doctor was sinking fast. After a number of bad nights, he seemed to be past pain – the suffering had stopped, and his face, she said, was not 'so distressed,' even though he could barely speak and gasped for breath. He was now resigned to death. To see him, enormous and immobile, sitting in the greenhouse was 'one of the most beautiful and pathetic sights that can be imagined.' The next day the inevitable note arrived. The Doctor had died at 8.30 in the morning, propped up in his chair, with Susan 'close to him the whole time.'[19] After so much suffering, it was a peaceful end.

Five-year-old Henrietta – Etty – too young to comprehend death, was 'awe-struck' by the effect the news had on her father and cried 'bitterly out of sympathy.' Charles was devastated and Emma rushed home. Her 'sympathy & affection' was beyond all value. He was now so miserable that he could not even attend the funeral on Saturday. He did set off for Shrewsbury, worrying that he had exhausted Emma with his emotions. But he arrived after it had started, and stayed at The Mount with his sister Marianne who was so distraught that she too could not attend. It was 'only a ceremony,' he admitted, yet he grieved at missing it. Nor was he well enough to act as an executor a few weeks later.[20] For the rest of the year and well into the next, he hid from the world at Down.

He felt unable to see anybody, except perhaps Sir John Lubbock's teenage son John. The boy's fascination for his microscope helped rescue Charles from total despair. He escaped with the lad into an unimaginable microscopic world, teeming with life. He became John's scientific father, in a way, obtaining for him an identical instrument.[21] He was carrying on the Doctor's practice – giving the wise guidance that his father had given him.

Nine months of nagging fears and obsessive work had taken their toll, leaving Charles chronically depressed. Waves of dizziness and despondency swept over him. Through the winter he suffered dreadful vomiting fits every week. His hands started trembling and he was 'not able to do anything one day out of three.' There were disquieting new symptoms: involuntary twitching, fainting feelings, and black spots before his eyes. For the first time he became convinced that he himself was 'rapidly going the way of all flesh.' When his melancholy maiden sisters, Susan and Catherine, came to stay, he avoided them and never talked about their mutual loss. He could not bear to tell them of his numbing fear: that he was the next to go.

Emma alone was left to comfort him. Ever since her sister Fanny's tragic death at the age of twenty-six, she had found deep consolation in the Scriptures. She now drew from her inner source of strength, binding Charles to herself with cords of love, ministering to his daily needs and praying for him. They failed to see eye-to-eye on the question of eternal life – the Gospel of John still stood between them. In fact, Charles was entertaining many more religious doubts than

Emma knew about. But she could bear Christian witness in this stressful time and help him rest.

Three miserable months after the Doctor's death, in February 1849, a maudlin Darwin immersed himself in Harriet Martineau's new book. He and Eras had grown impatient with her scientific credulity. It was her 'Mania' over mesmerism that prompted Darwin to decry the way ladies believe everything. Now Martineau redeemed herself. Her *Eastern Life, Present and Past* contained an unholy guide to the Holy Land. Unholy enough for John Murray to throw it out, objecting to its 'infidel tendency.'[22] So far had Martineau departed from the manner in which, conventionally, ladies believed.

The travelogue was a thinly disguised critical history of religion, and more to Darwin's taste. The dominant note is death; the text is littered with tombs. The 'black pall of oblivion' followed her from Egypt across the Sinai desert to Palestine. There, at Easter, she visited the grave of Lazarus, the Dead Sea, the tombs of the prophets on Mount Olivet, the Potter's Field necropolis where Judas Iscariot hanged himself, and the Valley of Gihon 'where the worm died not, and the fire was not quenched.' All are set against the paschal 'puppet-show' in the Church of the Holy Sepulchre. Darwin was intrigued by Martineau's message, that Christian beliefs about reward and punishment were based on heathen superstitions. And how little the world had moved on. Martineau marvelled at the untouched tomb of a rich Egyptian, painted with scenes of his family, his deeds, his expected hereafter. 'How like ours were his life and death!' 'Compare him with a retired naval officer made country gentleman in our day, and in how much less do they differ than agree!'[23]

But some country gentlemen had moved on. Darwin had done with superstition, and he enjoyed Martineau's excursus. Even so thoughts of death still filled him with foreboding, and his fortieth birthday, a week away, augured no lessening of the gloom. Having shunned society for so long, he could barely answer letters or do anything that required effort. 'Incessant vomiting,' he told Owen, explained why the barnacles were taking so long. 'I have,' he added, 'lost for the last 4 or 5 months at least 4/5 of my time.' Clearly, enough was enough.[24] Something had to be done.

24

My Water Doctor

FRIENDS WORRIED about him. His old *Beagle* companion Capt. Sulivan, on three-year's leave and about to sail with his family to the Falklands, had dropped in to say goodbye and found Charles in a dreadful state: frail and hardly able to walk. He recommended that the 'Philosopher' try Dr James Gully's Water Cure Establishment, which had worked for others.

Charles toyed with the idea. Fox had heard good reports about Gully's fashionable hydropathic home in the beautiful Malvern hills. It had been open seven years, and was already the top watering hole for the gout-ridden rich. During the summer months the charming, erudite Gully would take in a hundred or more dyspeptic patients. Literary figures and loungers alike paid their two guineas a week for the tonic: Tennyson had tried it; Carlyle, Macaulay and Dickens would follow. Charles could see that Gully was making a fortune, which did not exactly instil faith. He was also sceptical about the treatment itself and inclined to dismiss it as so much quackery. Nor would his London consultant, Dr Henry Holland, vouch for it. In fact, Holland was baffled by Darwin's case. He had never seen one like it and diagnosed it as a sort of 'suppressed gout.'[1] Unlike his father's gout, Charles's acted internally, on the stomach. It was, Holland thought, caused by poisons in the blood activating a hereditary disposition. But there was still nothing he could do for it.

If his condition baffled the specialists, then, as his father had said before he died, nothing was to be lost. Charles read Gully's book *The Water Cure in Chronic Disease* to learn about it for himself. Cold water over the body was used to stimulate the circulation and draw the blood supply away from the inflamed nerves of the stomach. But Gully warned that dyspepsia took time to cure and recommended a two-month stay, with no miracles guaranteed. Emma thought that

363

he sounded like a sensible man. With some trepidation, Charles decided to take the plunge. Only experiencing it would prove whether 'there is any truth in Gully & the water cure,' he concluded, as experimental as ever. 'It will cause a sad delay in my Barnacle work, but if once half-well I c^d do more in 6 months than I now do in two years.'[2] Little did he realize just how long a delay it would be.

The whole household would have to move, and Emma quailed at the prospect of transplanting six children, 'bag and baggage,' all the way to Malvern. 'It is a great trouble . . . but we think he could not give Dr Gully's treatment a fair trial under 6 weeks or 2 months & that would be too long to leave the children even with their Aunts.' Everyone decamped to foggy Worcestershire on 8 March 1849, the older children in the care of their new governess, Miss Thorley, and the servants, Charles and Emma separately with baby Francis. The 150-mile journey took two days and Francis screamed all the way. Great Malvern lay in an undeveloped no man's land, fought over by railway companies competing to extend their lines into south Wales. From London they took the Cheltenham and Great Western line to Gloucester, where a special coach set off over turnpikes on a nerve-rattling three-hour trip to the spa. By the time they arrived, the whole family was in need of recuperation. The village had several thousand inhabitants, but its white stone buildings, clustered on the steep slope beneath the Worcester Beacon, had a clean genteel appearance, and the atmosphere was one of 'peaceful solitude.'[3] The Darwins rented a house, The Lodge, a quarter of a mile out on the Worcester Road. There the children could romp on the wooded slopes of the North Hill. And Charles could maintain his accustomed privacy while being in touch with Dr Gully. His spirits began to rise.

Charles and Dr Gully were an interesting mix. They were almost direct contemporaries. Both had matriculated at Edinburgh in 1825. Gully, though, had gone on to Paris and had graduated in 1829. Like so many medical radicals coming out of Edinburgh at this time, he was devoted to heterodox science, and had evolutionary sympathies himself. He had a radical's faith in all manner of unorthodox practices – homoeopathy, hydropathy, mesmerism – none of which Charles shared. Charles never overcame his distrust of homoeopathy, nor did he have much to say for the rest. It was a 'sad flaw' in Gully's character that 'he believes in everything.'[4] But for all that, Gully was cautious in his diagnoses. He was also caring, and Charles, his father gone, his nerves shattered, appreciated this more than anything.

So he began the cold water cure. He sent his sister Susan a splash-by-splash account of the regime.

¼ before 7. get up, & am scrubbed with rough towel in cold
water for 2 or 3 minutes, which after the first few days, made
& makes me very like a lobster – I have a washerman, a very
nice person, & he scrubs behind, whilst I scrub in front. –
drink a tumbler of water & get my clothes on as quickly as
possible & walk for 20 minutes . . . At same time I put on a
compress, which is a broad wet folded linen covered by
mackintosh & which is 'refreshed' – ie dipt in cold water
every 2 hours & I wear it all day.

He was kept off sugar, salt, bacon and stimulants, in fact 'anything
good,' although, against the rules, he was allowed the odd pinch of
snuff. Gully dosed him with homoeopathic medicines, which Charles
took 'without an atom of faith.' The family liked Gully, and Charles
thought he sounded a lot like the Doctor, authoritative but benign.
The bond grew very quickly and he even referred to him later as 'my
beloved Dʳ Gully.' 'He is very kind & attentive,' Charles noted from
the start, and even if he had been 'puzzled with my case,' Charles
was responding well to treatment.[5]

So was everyone else. Paralytic gentlemen, female invalids, and
emaciated children could be seen all over the village. They had come
– at great trouble and expense – expecting a cure, and most believed
it was occurring. 'Malvern is always merry,' noted a contemporary.
'The patients . . . are generally given to intoxication – sure to be tipsy
with water.' This had a beneficial effect on their families, the Darwins
not excepted. With spring in bloom, it was turning out to be a
glorious holiday. They always remembered it as a happy time.
Charles took four-year-old Georgy to a toy bazaar and bought him a
musical instrument. Emma went shopping for gifts and hiked on the
hill with Annie and Willy. Annie in her large leghorn hat and black
polka jacket took dancing lessons and learned to do quadrille duets.
Francis was christened in the Priory Church. The festive atmosphere
further buoyed Charles's spirits. He began to calm down and feel idly
content. He went beetle hunting 'for auld langsyn,' and reminisced to
Henslow about their fenland botanical outings. He even bought a
horse and relived those 'delightful days.'[6] His sickness subsided, the
tremors vanished, his strength returned, and he put on weight. Soon
Emma was expecting again.

His stomach trouble was diagnosed as nervous in origin – the
result of excessive mental exertion – and the resulting bad circulation
was remedied by the compress. He told Hooker, sweating away in
India, how 'I am heated by Spirit lamp till I *stream* with perspiration,

& am then suddenly rubbed violently with towels dripping with cold water: have two cold feet-baths, & wear a wet compress all day on my stomach.' By mid-April he had been free of sickness for a month and was walking seven miles a day. By early May Gully believed that a full recovery would be made. Feeling good, Charles had to admit that the water cure was no quackery after all. Whatever else it achieved, the regime stopped him from working and deflected his overcharged mind from anxieties about persecution and death. This was no mean feat, quackery or not, although the months of enforced idleness were beginning to tell in other ways. Soon he complained that his mind was stagnating.[7] Down and his 'beloved Barnacles' beckoned; he was dying to get home.

The retinue finally arrived back on 30 June. Charles had been away longer than he intended – longer, indeed, than he would ever be away from Down again. We 'staid *16* instead of *6* weeks', he told Fox. But it was worth it; the nausea had passed, his head was clear, his hands steady – he was ready to pick up the dissecting needles again.

He continued the cure at home, 'though in a somewhat relaxed degree, so as to avoid bringing on a crisis.' In the garden, near his spectacular well – 100 yards deep – he had the village carpenter build a miniature church-shaped hut to contain a tub with a platform in it and a huge cistern above holding 640 gallons of water. The carpenter's son, John Lewis, remembered,

> I had to pump it full every day . . . Mr. Darwin came out and
> had a little dressing place, and he'd get on the stage and . . .
> pull the string, and all the water fell on him through a two-
> inch pipe. A douche they called it.

Young Lewis, fifteen, also helped with Darwin's other regime, the morning plunge.

> He used to get up . . . at seven, and I had to have the big
> bath outside the study on the lawn . . . and Mr. Darwin would
> come down [into his hut] and sit in a chair with a spirit lamp
> and all rolled round with blankets till the sweat poured off
> him in showers when he shook his head . . . I've heard him
> cry to . . . Parslow, 'I'll be melted away if you don't hurry!'
> Then he'd get into the ice-cold bath in the open air.

Parslow the butler served as bathman, scrubbing Darwin until he was red and raw. He already considered himself 'absolutely cured,' but it was better to play safe, and he now opened a health diary to keep a check of his day-to-day progress. Hydropathy certainly was 'a grand discovery' – if only he had tried it 'five or six years' earlier.[8]

First on the agenda after settling in were the barnacles. He continued sending out requests for specimens. Even at Malvern he had written to ask his old *Beagle* servant Syms Covington, now in New South Wales, to collect in the colony – which he did expertly. But processing them all was slow work so long as he remained a 'slave to treatment.' Gully permitted at most two or three hours of intellectual activity a day, and then only with a minimum of 'mental excitement.' He understood his patient well.

Still, some engagements were pressing, such as the Birmingham meeting of the British Association in September. He could hardly avoid this, having been elected one of the Vice-Presidents, and anyway he wanted to comment on a paper by Albany Hancock on burrowing barnacles. Emma went along too, to keep an eye on him. But the meeting was not 'brilliant.' He grew weary 'of all the spouting,' and got irritated by 'Sir H. Delabeche's harsh loud voice & empty noisy speeches.' The whole place was 'so large & nasty,' and to cap it all his retching returned with the excitement. In desperation, he made a flying visit to Dr Gully at Malvern. Then he returned home, where he spent a day in bed feeling dreadful. Obviously the treatment was only going to work so long as he lived the 'life of a hermit.' Two weeks afterwards his stomach still had not recovered. He had learned his lesson: even though he was elected a Council-member of the Royal Society a few weeks later, he shamefully attended only once the next year.[9] Such absenteeism was not condoned by the Society's young reformers, and he was not re-elected.

Through all, Darwin continued to be fascinated by 'Mr. Arthrobalanus.' This 'ill-formed little monster' had started him on his onerous dissections and even after three years it still held surprises. In fact, the 'Mr.' was a misnomer, for his specimens turned out to be females with minute males clinging to their shells – as in *Ibla* and *Scalpellum*. Here the reduction was just as drastic: the male was a 'mere bag, lined by a few muscles, enclosing an eye,' antennae, and a gigantic sexual organ. To Darwin, it seemed, the member came first and the male followed. 'Mr. Arthrobalanus' himself was little more than a rudimentary head atop an 'enormous coiled penis' – with no vestige of the other fourteen segments of a normal barnacle body.[10]

Having worked out this segmentation, he knew how barnacles had diverged from their crab-like relatives. With other comparative anatomists in the 1840s, he accepted that all animals were constructed according to a few basic patterns. These were the 'archetypes' of life. By studying these blueprints, zoologists could work out homologies among different creatures. In mammals and birds, for instance, arms, wings, and flippers are homologous: they are derived from the same part of the blueprint. Richard Owen championed this approach. Darwin himself had been dealing with homologies since studying under Grant at Edinburgh, but he interpreted them very differently from Owen.

Although Darwin praised Owen's work, and coyly told him that he too had deciphered homologies 'on a very **small** scale,' he never let on about his own private interpretation. This he scribbled in Owen's new book *On the Nature of Limbs*:

> I look at Owen's Archetypes as more than ideal, as a real
> representation as far as the most consummate skill & loftiest
> generalization can represent the parent form of the Vertebrata
> – I follow him that there is a created archetype, the parent of
> its class.

Darwin believed in a Creator, as Owen did. But Owen was a Coleridgean idealist; his 'archetype' existed only in the divine Mind. Darwin was heir to a rival Unitarian tradition that rooted itself in material events. He was thinking of real, historical parents.[11] Homologies for him indicated blood ties, and he used them to work out how barnacles were actually related to crabs and lobsters.

In Paris Henri Milne-Edwards had shown that the archetypal crustacean had twenty-one segments. This primitive shrimp-like creature, Darwin believed, gave us an idea of the common ancestor of the various crabs, lobsters, and barnacles. Using Milne-Edwards's model, Darwin could show how they diverged. He deduced that everything visible externally in barnacles was equivalent to the first three segments of a crab's head, but 'wonderfully modified,' and 'so enlarged as to receive the whole rest of the body' inside them.[12] Fourteen body segments – the last four had vanished altogether – were tucked up inside this shell, and only the animal's feathery feet protruded occasionally to strain the water for food. In the miniscule males, even these body segments were reduced to a remnant.

Darwin was 'cock-a-hoop' at having cracked this relationship. It also helped him to work out the barnacles' life-cycle. Their metamorphosis, he told Louis Agassiz, was odd to say the least. In the free-swimming larva a part of the reproductive system, the ovarian tube, becomes 'modified & glandular & secretes a cement.' Even stranger, these ducts open, of all places, at the tip of the antennae. The larva pours cement from its head and glues itself to the rock and thus begins its sedentary adult life upside down. It all sounded 'extremely improbable,' Darwin was the first to admit, but barnacles were improbable beasts.[13] From a crab's oviduct to a cement gland: this was far more surprising than feet turning into feeding nets. It provided Darwin with his most dramatic evidence of the way an organ could change function as an animal exploited new conditions.

Darwin was now internationally known through his *Journal* of travels, and he traded off his name. He fired off letters far and wide. The American response was munificent. Agassiz shipped a crate of barnacles. His co-author, Dr Augustus Gould, the real expert, currently describing the shells collected by the United States Exploring Expedition, also sent one. In return both received up-to-the-minute reports of supplemental males and cement glands. By the autumn, too, major European collections were arriving at Down. Milne-Edwards arranged for Darwin to have specimens from the Paris Muséum, and the physiologist Johannes Müller sent some from Berlin. He already had Sir James Ross's polar specimens. Others came from the Continent. Or didn't in one case: Professor Johan Forchhammer's, sent from Copenhagen University, vanished coming across the Channel. Darwin was now drooping, weighed down by the 'odiously tedious job' of compiling descriptions. It rubbed off on Hooker. Letter after letter he endured, crammed with barnacle news, and he was beginning to wilt. On reflection, he said, he really did prefer to hear the evolutionary speculations after all. The irony was not lost on Darwin. Now 'this is too bad,' he snorted, for it was 'your decided approval of my plain Barnacle work' that led 'me to ... defer my species-paper' in the first place.[14]

The test of his new-found stamina came with approaching winter. All his morbid symptoms had gone – the muscle spasms, fainting feelings, spots before the eyes – as well as the vomiting. Indeed, after Etty's and Willy's brief fevers in the summer, the whole family was 'flourishing.' But Charles had to keep up the water torture. 'Lamp 5 times per week & shallow bath for 5 minutes afterwards; douche daily for 5 minutes & dripping sheet' was the rigmarole. The water got colder with the onset of winter. 'Sharp work my Baths have been for 5 minutes under 40°.' But it was wonderfully invigorating and had other advantages. It provided an excuse, and not only to cut down work. He had already given up 'all reading, except the newspapers.' Now he had the medical authority for avoiding personal contacts. 'I have never been so much cut off from all scientific friends,' he consoled Hooker in his mountain bivouac.[15]

Cut off was not the word. But at least Darwin had his freedom. Hooker by this time was a prisoner. One day Darwin was 'indolently skimming through the Paper' when he read, to his horror, that his friend had been kidnapped. On 7 November, Hooker and the government agent to Sikkim were returning from Tibet through a Himalayan pass, when they were seized by a local anti-British ruler. It was a common tactic to express grievances and wring concessions, and Hooker was not badly treated. Still Darwin, who knew his priorities, 'feared that his collection' would go 'to rack & ruin.' In fact, the reverse was true, comically so: Hooker was allowed to collect rhododendron seeds even as he was marched south. The group was held for six weeks, and released just before Christmas after threats from Lord Dalhousie, who moved a regiment up to Darjeeling. To stop such banditry and show – in Hooker's words – that the rajahs 'could not play fast and loose with a British subject,' southern Sikkim was promptly annexed for the Crown, with Hooker advising the expeditionary force. In future, botanizing would be a safer business in the Himalayas. For Darwin, the adventure was a little too close for comfort. He feared losing his confidant. 'Heaven grant that poor Joseph Hooker may be spared,' Lyell prayed – after hearing that four of Hooker's colleagues had died on the trip – to which Darwin would have added 'Amen.' Darwin hoped that at least some good would come of this skulduggery, namely, he said, that 'Sir William and Lady Hooker will insist on your coming home.'[16]

Nor was Hooker's captivity the end of Darwin's concern. At the close of 1849 the causes for disquiet were mounting ominously. In November, first Annie, then Etty and two-year-old Elizabeth – Lizzy – came down with scarlet fever. Forchhammer's fossils had still not turned up, and he waited on tenterhooks. They did eventually arrive, but only after some nail-biting weeks. He was also keen to obtain some rare fossil barnacles from Robert Fitch, a Norwich pharmacist and amateur geologist. But when Fitch's parcel came early in the new year, one of his specimens was shattered into thirteen fragments. Darwin painstakingly gummed it back together, petrified that the accident would reflect ill. on him and kill Fitch's co-operation. Meanwhile, as Darwin worried about the fossils and fever, his theory of coral reefs was under scrutiny in the United States, by a geologist 'as "d – – d cocked sure" as Macaulay.' Darwin regained his composure on discovering that James Dwight Dana at Yale differed only a little from him. But for one who confessed himself 'as tender of his

370

theories as of his child[ren],' reading Dana's *Geology* was an emotional ordeal. It left him in a lather, the sort that came over him whenever he thought his work slighted.

To cap it all, Emma was about to deliver again – her eighth. On 15 January Charles was just patching up Fitch's fossil when her contractions started. He sent for the doctor, but he was delayed, and 'her pains came on so rapidly & severe,' he told Fox, 'that I c$^{d.}$ not withstand her entreaties for Chloroform.' He had to administer it himself, which was 'nervous work not knowing from eye-sight anything about it or of midwifery.' He placed a soaked pad over Emma's nose, and the effect was instantaneous. Unfamiliar with the procedure, he kept her unconscious for a dangerously long time – one and a half hours. The doctor arrived with ten minutes to spare and she woke knowing nothing of the ordeal to be told that it was a boy. They called him Leonard, after Henslow's firstborn and the Revd Jenyns. Chloroform was 'the grandest & most blessed of discoveries,' Darwin informed Henslow.[17] It had worked for Emma as the water cure was working for him. Together, thanks to medical science, they had got through the winter's worst perils almost painlessly. He now felt better than he had for months.

A few days after Leonard's birth Darwin started to describe the fossils. So often fossil barnacles consisted of nothing more than disarticulated shells, which had separated soon after the animal's death. But a few, a very few, held out the promise of something more. Fitch had built up his 'unrivalled collection' over a period of twenty years, and in all that time he had managed to find only two that were whole (and not broken into pieces before they were fossilized). Darwin now crowed with delight at the sight of Fitch's rare fossil *Pollicipes* from the Norfolk Chalk, which still had its shells complete, suggesting that a cast of the animal might exist inside. It left him drooling: Fitch had '*incomparably* the best specimens' he had ever seen 'from any Secondary rock.'[18]

He also removed the surface valve from one of James Bowerbank's intact fossils to expose the interior, which made it 'a **hundred**-fold more instructive.' Bowerbank was a distiller by trade, a sponge expert by avocation. He owned a brewery, Bowerbank & Co., but devoted much of his time to natural history, and his *Fossil Fruits of the London Clay* was definitive. He had an excellent collection of barnacles, now in Darwin's hands. More to the point, he ran a new specialist society – the Palaeontographical – dedicated to publishing monographs on British fossils. In February he recruited Darwin and the Society paid his illustrator, James de Carle Sowerby, to engrave the plates. Darwin, always cost-conscious, was grateful to be saved the expense. (He already had Sowerby's brother George on the payroll, drawing his dissections and translating his descriptions into Latin.)

With two publishers in hand – the Ray Society had agreed at the outset to publish his monograph on the living species – he still had a way to go. Boxes of fossils were coming in by the week, and he continued to open them with trepidation. Two more specimens, he reported to Fitch in 'grief & shame,' were 'broken slightly but can be **perfectly** repaired: a third is rather more injured.' Then began the hard work of describing each species in the minutest detail. He finally settled into a routine: a spartan douse for five minutes in freezing water, later two hours of barnacles. But two hours – the doctor's limit – meant that the work dragged on. Fitch became anxious as time passed. In letter after letter Darwin wriggled and apologized for his snail's pace. 'I **cannot** work quicker,' he finally exploded, promising to return his fossils just as soon as he could.[19]

Four years into the barnacles, and it seemed like an eternity. Some days he had to force himself to go on, working his way through the sub-class, species by species. 'I groan under my task,' he sighed to Lyell. 'Heaven only knows' when he would finish. The work was never-ending. He had started the year with forty or fifty fossils, now he had two hundred. Down House was beginning to look like a museum. It dawned on him, with some horror, that a one-volume monograph was no longer feasible. Each of the books on fossil and living barnacles would have to be a two-volume affair. The first, to be published straightaway, would concentrate on the stalked barnacles – those which attach themselves by a leathery stem to driftwood or the hulls of ships. Such types were geologically the oldest; the earliest known, *Pollicipes*, lived in Jurassic and Cretaceous seas, a contemporary of the dinosaurs.[20] In June 1850 Darwin had almost finished his descriptions for this volume, although James Sowerby was dragging his feet over the engravings.

That month Charles went back to Malvern. With Emma dividing her time between him and the baby, the pressure of barnacles had been his undoing. He had begun to lose whole working days, to complain again of 'excitement & fatigue,' to cancel trips to London. Varying his treatment had made some difference – alternating heat lamp and douche – and he never vomited now. His weight indeed was up to nearly 170 pounds. But still something was amiss. A week together with Emma, cheered by Dr Gully's optimism, would clear it up. 'My Water Doctor continues to give me hopes,' Charles beamed, and everybody at Malvern told him that he looked 'blooming &

beautiful.'[21] The refresher week at the spa also gave him time to reflect, to stand back and assess his taxonomic odyssey. What was his major conclusion after scrutinizing so many specimens? Hooker – now safely delivered from his captors – asked this. Darwin's answer, as he slapped himself with wet towels, was that barnacles were infinitely variable.

At the time Hooker was actually trying to test Darwin's ideas in the Himalayas. He was looking for terraces and parallel roads, guided by Darwin's geological books; and, knowing Darwin's fascination with domestic breeds, he sent back a flood of details on dogs, elephants, and cattle. In return he received a string of new marching orders: bring home silkworms, and don't forget a local beehive. But there was a more subtle influence too. Hooker now admitted that Darwin's evolutionary ideas 'have possessed me, without however converting me.' In fact, the Indian evidence was not encouraging. He was looking for a graded sequence of floras on passing from the tropics up the temperate hills to the snowy Himalayan heights.[22] But without success, so he asked whether the barnacle work had caused Darwin to modify his theories. He had expected it to make Darwin more cautious.

But no. Rather than undermining his theory, it had proved to Darwin that variation was ubiquitous. Ten years earlier he had thought variation the exception in nature, but barnacles had changed that. Wide-ranging barnacle species were '*eminently* variable.' Every part 'of every species' was prone to change; the closer he looked, the more stability seemed an illusion. While many curators accepted that varieties were natural productions, he went further to see them as incipient species. Yet however reassuring in one respect, all this variation made a mockery of his attempt to define each species precisely. Where did the varieties end and new species begin? Half the time he found it impossible to tell. This 'confounded variation' was a mixed blessing, he told Hooker, rubbing his nose in it rather. It 'is pleasant to me as a speculist though odious to me as a systematist.'[23]

Indeed he was hopping. So often he had described specimens as separate species, had second thoughts and made them all variants of one species, changed his mind, torn up his paper, and started all over again. And each time 'I have gnashed my teeth, cursed species, & asked what sin I had committed to be so punished.'[24] Since today's species were yesterday's varieties, he ended up cutting the Gordian knot by simply lumping the variants into recognized species. None of it mattered. There were no absolute, unvarying forms, so a precise classification was, in any case, impossible.

Still, he remained coy about it. Years earlier he had lectured Waterhouse on classification, telling him it was 'a logical process,' or rather genealogical: it 'consists in grouping beings according to their actual *relationship*, ie their consanguinity, or descent from common stocks.' But this was easier to preach than practise, and anyway the *Vestiges* had warned him off presenting a tree-like target. When it came to the crunch in the monograph, he conventionally listed the genera of each barnacle family. He did moot relationships in the text, but he made no effort to picture a genealogical tree.[25] That would have been a give-away.

The second stay at Malvern had perked Charles up. He admitted that he had grown quite fond of his aquatic habits, 'except the dressing & undressing.' His stomach was still never 'right for 24 hours,' and he went back to his garden privy for 'douching &c &c' in a spirit of patient resignation. 'I have given up all hopes of ever being a strong man again,' he rather plaintively wrote to Covington, acknowledging his rich crop of pickled specimens. But now at least the Grim Reaper was held at bay. The 'wondrous Water Cure' seemed cheap at any price. Even partial health 'is, compared to my state two years ago, of inestimable value.'[26]

25

Our Bitter & Cruel Loss

AFTER CHARLES ARRIVED HOME from Malvern, a cold shadow crept over the household once again. He was petrified that his ailment was a heritable defect. Now, he thought he could detect a glimmer of it in the children.

At the end of June 1850, as he sat scratching his fossils, a clutch of Wedgwood cousins came for a visit – there were now fourteen of them under the age of twelve, besides Charles's and Emma's seven. They romped together and enjoyed an outing in Knole Park at nearby Sevenoaks. But Annie, the Darwins' eldest daughter, complained of feeling sick. She was not just a clever nine-year-old seeking attention. When the others left she was miserable for weeks on end. Her lessons became an endurance test, for her and the governess Miss Thorley. She sometimes burst into tears for no apparent reason and often woke at night crying pitifully. Charles began to fear that the problem was 'wretched digestion' again.[1] Clearly, the child was no longer herself.

In the last two years she had won her father's heart in a special way. The Doctor had had a favourite daughter, Susan, who lavished attention on him until the end. Charles, fearing he would soon die, naturally grew attached to his eldest girl for the same reason. And Annie reminded him of Emma. Tall for her age, with long brown hair and greyish eyes, she had a sunny, affectionate disposition. She delighted in straightening his clothes, combing his hair and 'making it beautiful,' before joining him on the Sandwalk. She loved being kissed, and showed a wonderful sensitivity to others' feelings, which made her the apple of her father's eye. At Malvern the year before, she gave Miss Thorley a little lesson on the rigours of the water cure. 'And it makes Papa so angry,' she added with a pout, at which Papa, who was present, had to admit that it did sometimes make him feel rather cross.[2]

Now all that had changed. Annie's bright spirit was beginning to break. She picked bilberries at Leith Hill near Dorking with Jos and Caroline Wedgwood's girls, but these few pleasant days in August failed to restore her. In October Miss Thorley took her to the seaside – Ramsgate – with the other children for three weeks. Charles and Emma joined them briefly at the end, but Annie became so feverish and headachy that Emma had to stay on with her when the others left. In November and again in December Emma took her to London to see Dr Holland, who believed that Charles's stomach troubles were inherited. He could do little for the child, who clung more and more to her parents. Her nights became worse; she cried and complained, and it upset her to go any distance from home.[3] Dr Holland had been Charles's last port of call before taking the water cure. If Annie's condition persisted, he would take her to Malvern too.

By this time Emma was pregnant yet again. Charles was 'working like a wretched slave,' mindlessly describing barnacles, without the 'heart to begin work of interest.' He remained as well as could be expected, though Annie worried him a good deal. Emma, once over her usual morning sickness, enjoyed the intimacy of a visit with him to her sisters at Hartfield in East Sussex.[4] At home their life together went on like clockwork, eased by the loyal domestic staff. When Charles was not shut up in the study, hunched over his brittle beasts, he and Emma had ample time to read. He continued to dip into religious books. His health had improved dramatically since his last such reading; his mortal fears had subsided. Still, he would not countenance anything remotely orthodox now. He had begun to look beyond Christianity.

He turned to Francis Newman, the Latin professor at University College. Among Unitarians and freethinkers he was the man of the hour: an evolutionist – following *Vestiges* – calling for a new post-Christian synthesis. Charles had already read *The Soul*. Its later chapters came 'with the shock of a shower-bath,' complained a pious aunt of Emma's; but Charles must have found them as invigorating as his daily douche. In the book Newman gave up trying to prove human immortality from the Bible. Such proof was inaccessible 'to the great mass of mankind' whose salvation is supposed to depend on it. And he rejected 'the dreadful doctrine of the Eternal Hell.' Real assurance of a blessed hereafter, he maintained, came only through 'a full sympathy of our spirit with God's Spirit.'

That was how Emma felt, but Newman's intuitive spirituality made Charles uneasy. When he opened Newman's *History of the Hebrew Monarchy* after returning from Leith Hill, his misgivings were confirmed. For all its criticism of Old Testament history based on advanced German scholarship, the book left 'the relations between the divine and the human mind . . . the same as ever.' But how could that be? How could faith in 'the Holiness of God' have arisen amid the death, famine, and wars of Semitic tribes? No, Charles insisted, the religious instinct had evolved with society. The primitive Jewish God, whose atrocities had 'lit up hell-fires in Christendom,' could be nothing but a barbaric tyrant.

Newman was consolidating Charles's doubts. With the restoration of England's Catholic dioceses in 1850 many saw religious barbarism making a come-back. It was an opportune moment for Charles to reflect – with Newman's help – on what he actually believed. He could admit the religious thrust of his old notebook speculations on morality and the afterlife, at least to himself, in the privacy of Down. Certainly, two years after his father's death, he was not tortured by anxiety as he contemplated the fate of unbelievers. His reading and the water cure had calmed him, and Newman's freethinking example helped to restore his sense of security.[5]

Annie, though, was still not out of danger. Christmas came and went with little respite from her vague stomach complaint. Charles, his spirits lifted by the tidings that Hooker was heading home, felt confident enough to experiment with medications. In the new year, 1851, he began rubbing tartar emetic ointment on his stomach and perhaps on Annie's too. By March she was well enough to play outdoors and ride on horseback for the first time. Charles meanwhile began returning borrowed barnacles. He sent Fitch's back at last and saw his first fossil volume through the press. Then, shortly after Annie's tenth birthday, influenza struck the household. Both of them were laid low. Annie stayed beside Emma in bed, weak and miserable. Charles lay propped up on his sofa dosing himself with tonics and reading Newman's powerful, agonizing, spiritual autobiography *Phases of Faith*.[6]

Here were shades of Charles again: Newman's odyssey saw him destined for the Church, suffering qualms about the Thirty-nine Articles, rejecting hell, and passing through Unitarianism (knowing it 'could never afford . . . a half-hour's resting-place') to end up on the fringes of free religion. Its potent, emotional tone struck Charles at this moment. If a person deserves infinite punishment for offending an Infinite Being, Newman reasoned, 'the fretfulness of a child is an infinite evil!' Charles looked at poor Annie.

Religiously he had moved on, and, as with Newman, the Bible had disintegrated in his hands – the Old Testament with its Creation legends and moral monstrosities, the New Testament bristling with inconsistencies and myths. The Gospel of John, Newman's 'impregnable fortress of Christianity,' collapsed with the evidence that Jesus may never have uttered the words attributed to him there, and the simple Jewish Rabbi 'melted into dimness' and vanished from Newman's faith, even as he had from Charles's. 'I felt no convulsion of mind, no emptiness of soul, no inward practical change,' Newman recalled.[7] The glide to a purely theistic religion, combining Christian virtue with the rigour of modern science, was as anodyne as it was complete.

Charles finished *Phases of Faith* and snapped the covers shut. It was 'excellent,' he jotted in a notebook – fit reading for a Sunday while Emma was at church. The story of a gentleman with the courage to pursue an enquiry to its end. Emotional attachment to Christianity was not enough; faith had to comply with reason, morality, and historical evidence. There was no stopping short at Unitarianism, that 'feather bed to catch a falling Christian,' as Charles's grandfather said. Christianity had to be rejected once and for all. The moral logic that condemned eternal punishment could not condone the New Testament where the monstrous doctrine was taught. Evolution – the new 'gospel' – explained mind, morality, and religious beliefs as part of the social development of the human species.

Lying on his back, recovering from the flu, Charles had several days to ponder such thoughts. But although he began to feel stronger, Annie remained downcast. Nothing Emma did seemed to help, so they decided to take her to Dr Gully. On Monday, 24 March, Annie sat crying on the sofa beside Emma. Her bags were packed, the carriage was ready, and it was time to set off. Etty was going along to keep her company, with Brodie the nurse. But Annie clung to her mother, sobbing. It would be so lonely in Malvern without her – a whole month away.[8] Mama would soon be having a baby, yes, and Papa would leave her in good hands. But as Charles bundled Annie into the carriage for Sydenham station, it felt as if she was going away for ever.

As the Great Western coach clattered up the Severn valley, through the toll gates, and into the Malvern Hills, Charles could feel relieved. Annie, nestling beside him and Etty, would soon be safe in the care of his trusted physician, the man who all but saved his own life.

Spring dappled the fields and hedgerows, reminding Charles of the first trip to Malvern just two years before. How precarious human existence again seemed.

Safely in Malvern, Charles settled his charges in lodgings with Eliza Partington at Montreal House, overlooking the village and the vale of Worcester. Once Annie got better, she and Etty could play together on the hillside where Emma used to take them hiking. On examining Annie, Dr Gully recommended that she be seen by a clairvoyant. Charles was highly sceptical but tolerated the expense. Hydropathy, after all, had originally seemed like quackery too; and once when Gully's own daughter was gravely ill, he had employed a far-sighted female to report on her internal state and – somehow – the girl recovered. But Charles first put Annie's clairvoyant to the test. He offered her a banknote sealed in an envelope if she could reel off its number. The woman scorned the trick as beneath her professional dignity, dismissing it as something her 'maid-servant at home' could do. Whereupon she turned, peered long and hard, and described in lurid detail the horrors she saw in Annie's innards. Charles assumed that she was following 'some unconscious hints' from Gully.[9]

Still, there was no doubt that Annie's stomach was the root of the problem, and that Gully would cure it if anyone could. Charles stayed on until he saw all was well. On Friday the 28th he kissed the girls goodbye for a month, promising that Miss Thorley would come soon, and set off for London. The next morning he called on Lyell in Harley Street. Word had it that Hooker was back in town. On Sunday the Darwin brothers dined in palatial splendour at Hensleigh and Fanny Wedgwood's, overlooking Regent's Park. It became an impromptu reunion – Carlyle dropped in, joining Emma's seventy-year-old maiden aunt, Fanny Allen, and a clerical friend. Only Harriet Martineau was missing from the old circle. And just as well, for Aunt Fanny would have roasted her for dinner. Martineau's correspondence with a garrulous, self-styled scientist named Henry Atkinson had just been published. Already these *Letters on the Laws of Man's Nature and Development* were outraging literary London. Martineau now preened herself as a mesmeric evolutionary atheist. Aunt Fanny blanched at the boldness of 'these two criminals' with their 'miserable' book. Charles was intrigued. He made sure to borrow it from Erasmus.[10]

Back at Down on Monday, things were looking up, and his health was back to normal. Annie had the best medical supervision he could buy. The precious barnacle collections were being returned, intact, to their long-suffering owners. And the first fruits of five years' work, volume one of his monograph on fossil barnacles, printed by the Palaeontographical Society, arrived in the post. More auspicious still, Hooker was indeed back, safe and well, loaded with specimens and full of facts about Indian species.[11] Of course he would soon be married – Fanny Henslow now took pride of place in his life. Still, it was a relief to know he was home at Kew, and able to visit Down. Charles settled in and expected to be on hand for weeks.

It was not to be. Late on Tuesday 15 April came an urgent message: Annie had relapsed, seriously. She was feverish and vomiting. Brodie was beside herself. Miss Thorley was distraught. Someone was needed from home, and Dr Gully called for Charles. The news sent Down House into a whirl. Emma, now eight months pregnant, dared not think of going, and Charles would not hear of it anyway. She prepared for the worst, providing everyone with emotional support. She asked sister-in-law Fanny Wedgwood to meet Charles at Malvern. What about Fanny's six children, and Etty? She arranged for cousins Jos and Caroline to take them all at Leith Hill. And the baby? An early confinement was unlikely, but already Emma felt overwhelmed. Just in case, ask Aunt Fanny to come down from London, and send for sister Elizabeth to take the 'first good steamer' from Jersey – and fetch chloroform.[12]

Charles collected his belongings, some books for diversion, and a mass of painful thoughts. The next day he set off. Once before he had rushed this way to the Severn valley, too late for a funeral. Afterwards he had fled to the Malvern hills fearing he was going to die. Those hills loomed up before him again as the carriage sped along the turnpike, the rocks laced with extinct shells and trilobites. It was Maundy Thursday when he arrived.

Montreal House was in an emotional spin. Annie seemed a trifle better but Brodie and Miss Thorley were wringing their hands. Dr Gully, with eighty-eight patients, had little time to spare. Etty had to be jollied constantly to prevent her fretting about her sister. Everyone was anxious and exhausted. Keeping up hopes all round meant that no one really knew what was happening. Charles stepped into the vortex at Annie's bedside. It was a scene where his ragged medical knowledge, his ability to become like Doctor Darwin, would be tested to destruction. When he first saw Annie he completely broke down, flinging himself on a sofa, agonized and desolate. The pinched face and withered body, the smell of camphor and ammonia – he had been there once before.[13] At Edinburgh he had run in terror from the scene of a tortured child. This time the child was his own. He must compose himself, maintain everyone's spirits, serve as orderly, nurse, and locum. Emma, soon due, was to be kept informed, but with calm discretion; more than one life was at stake. Much as Charles longed for her protective presence, as he had in Shrewsbury at his father's bedside, he had to prop her hopes up. She would hear what was necessary about their poor child, but never know how much he was suffering.

That night the crisis deepened. Wishing for the best, Charles had fallen for Gully's early optimism. Now he was violently cast down. Annie's pulse became irregular and she sank into semi-consciousness. Gully rushed to her side, watching anxiously for the restlessness and chill that precedes death. He thought it would probably be all over before the morning and agreed to stay the night. At 6 a.m. Annie vomited, showing she still had strength. Charles was in a wretched state. Choking back what remained of his tears, he described to Emma the hourly 'struggle between life & death.' 'Oh my own it is very bitter indeed,' he let on, then added anxiously, 'God preserve & cherish you.' Throughout the day Annie failed to keep down the brandy and gruel they gave her. Once she alarmed them by vomiting the 'bright green' contents of her gall bladder. By early evening the child was 'dreadfully exhausted' – but no worse, said Gully. 'He yet has hopes – *positively he has Hopes*,' Charles rejoiced to Emma as the sun set on Good Friday. 'Oh my dear be thankful.'[14]

As Emma pored anxiously over Charles's letter the next morning, taking what comfort she could, Fanny arrived in Malvern, with a servant to escort Etty to her cousins. The sisters kissed farewell, never dreaming it might be their last. Annie had rallied overnight – 'turning the corner,' Gully said – and Charles dared to picture 'my own former Annie with her dear affectionate radiant face.' He sent word by telegraph to Emma. The message came mid-afternoon, while she was outside looking for a blossom in Annie's flower patch. 'What happiness! How I do thank God!' she replied in haste. Now she could 'wait very well' until Monday for his next report.

Even as she wrote, Annie was improving. Charles and Fanny had been watching hopefully all day. Her fever was gone and her pulse was quickening; her food was staying down. She lay tranquilly – perhaps too tranquilly – and looked more comfortable by the hour. Fanny told Emma that Charles himself appeared 'sadly overcome & shaken,' but not ill. He was loath to leave his child, though twice that day he did go out to wander alone on the hillside, confident of Fanny's care. The wind, the view, the freshness everywhere felt like life made new. Tomorrow Emma would be thanking God in church.

When he got back Dr Gully came. Annie had vomited a little, but there was 'decided improvement in the tongue,' he announced, 'a most important point.'[15]

All night Fanny and Charles kept watch by the bedside. 'Poor dear devoted Miss Thorley' had her first unbroken sleep. Annie vomited slightly a second time and took less of the gruel. As Brodie sponged her face and hands, she put her arms round the nurse's neck and kissed her. Then she slept peacefully. In the small hours Charles sat circled in candle-light and poured out his heart to Emma. 'Whilst writing to you, I can cry; tranquilly,' he confessed. Otherwise 'I . . . am constantly up & down: I *cannot* sit still.' First thing in the morning, Dr Gully came. Annie had brought up another mouthful, but he hastened to assure them that she really was no worse. If only she could last two more days, there would be every chance of recovery. But as the Priory Church bells rang out that Easter Sunday, Annie began vomiting again. Her bladder was now paralysed, and a catheter had to be used, though she put up a pathetic struggle. Afterwards, exhausted, she took a little brandy and water. 'I quite thank you,' she breathed. Gully examined her and reported that her pulse was 'rather better, certainly not worse.' In the evening he pronounced her 'decisively better.' Charles no longer knew what to think. 'These alternations of no hope & hope sicken one's soul,' he groaned to Emma.

Monday brought little relief. Early in the morning Annie's bladder and bowels acted spontaneously, which Charles thought an excellent sign. He was 'foolish with delight' and pictured her whirling merrily about the garden at Down – 'making custards,' she used to say. He told her that he thought she would get better. 'Thank you,' she replied meekly. But Gully came at 8 a.m. and dashed his hopes. The diarrhoea was ominous, he declared, and Annie's pulse was faltering. Then the mail arrived and suddenly Charles felt overwhelmed. On reading how Emma had gone to Annie's garden for a flower, he burst into tears. 'I wish you could see her now,' he sobbed to his wife, 'the perfection of gentleness, patience & gratitude, – thankful till it is truly painful to hear her. – poor dear little soul.' In the afternoon Annie weakened, rambling incoherently, and then fell asleep. On waking she called out, 'Where is poor Etty?' Later at dinner she thanked Fanny for a spoonful of tea, exclaiming in a strong voice, 'It is beautifully good.' One more day on this form, as the doctor said, and Annie would be in the clear. Charles assured Emma that she was 'going on very well.'

At Down Emma was helpless except to save the life within her. She hung on to the words of the telegraph message, and prayed. By post time on Monday morning she felt desperate. She tore open the reports from Charles and Fanny but hardly knew what to make of them. Annie's ups and downs pointed nowhere. She tried to feel hopeful and told Charles that she and baby remained well. 'I . . . have considered every thing in case I should be taken short, but I don't the least expect it.' On Tuesday came better news. Now she detected a note of 'progressive improvement' in Charles's letters and became more hopeful. Just before post time on Wednesday morning she let herself go, revelling in 'the pleasure of fancying I have something to do for her.' She sent Charles some simple recipes for Annie 'when she can take a little food.' And then came a letter from Fanny which plunged Emma into despair. 'Alas my own how shall we bear it,' she added to her recipes. 'It is very bitter.'[16]

Tuesday had been the turning point, as Gully predicted. But Annie did not improve. Violent diarrhoea set in, and with each bout she lost strength. Charles was fatigued, Fanny told Emma, sparing her the awful truth. As Annie lay writhing helplessly, his own stomach gave way, and he ran from the room, convulsed and retching. The attack lasted all day. By evening father and daughter were both prostrate. He could not bring himself now to write a single line to Emma. Annie was sinking. Even Dr Gully admitted it.[17]

While Emma wept at home over the news, her hopes crushed, the struggle in Malvern was ending. Annie continued to sink throughout the night, only now and then regaining consciousness. Twice amid her wanderings she made pathetic attempts to sing. Southerly winds blew storm clouds across the hills and it was unseasonably warm. By the morning, Wednesday 23 April, she lay tranquilly, her breathing soft and gentle, her wasted body a jagged outline beneath the sheets. The wind played at the curtains beside an open window. Charles sat motionless, drained, quietly waiting and weeping. He stared out past the bed into the grey immensity beneath the Worcester Beacon. His thoughts were racked and torn, like the Poet Laureate's in Emma's favourite, *In Memoriam*.

> Are God and Nature then at strife,
> That Nature lends such evil dreams?
> So careful of the type she seems,
> So careless of the single life.

Annie's breathing became shallower. Fanny came in with Brodie and Miss Thorley. The wind picked up. Charles and Fanny moved closer to the bed. Annie lay still, unconscious. It was just twelve o'clock midday. Thunder began to sound, great peals far above them, the mighty knell of Nature. They edged nearer and heard the breathing stop. She was dead.[18]

Brodie went to pieces. Miss Thorley had an attack and collapsed. Fanny rushed to help them, quite overcome herself, while Charles kissed the shrunken little face one last time and hid himself by the window. It was raining now, pouring. The sodden landscape, a graveyard of extinct life, made a mockery of his bitter tears.

> 'So careful of the type?' but no.
> From scarpèd cliff and quarried stone
> She cries, 'A thousand types are gone:
> I care for nothing, all shall go.'

This was the end of the road, the crucifixion of his hopes. He could not believe the way Emma believed – nor *what* she believed. There was no straw to clutch, no promised resurrection. Christian faith was futile.

Dragging himself to his room, he lay agonized in bed for hours, his stomach churning. He stopped crying long enough to see Dr Gully, who gave the cause of death as a 'Bilious Fever with typhoid character.' But when writing to Emma, he broke down again. Annie had gone 'to her final sleep . . . without a sigh.' How desolating to think of her 'frank cordial manners.' It was impossible to recall 'ever seeing the dear child naughty.' 'God bless her,' he sobbed at last. 'We must be more & more to each other my dear wife.' Towards six o'clock Fanny went in and found Charles still crying bitterly. It kept the nausea at bay, he said. But there was something else tormenting him now. He longed to be with Emma, yet how could he go until his beloved child was buried? The rites, the graveside, would break him completely. Fanny urged him to go – to take the first coach in the morning.[19] She would attend to the funeral.

This was what Charles wanted to hear. He rose early on Thursday, still ill, and left instructions: Brodie was to pick up the washing, Miss Thorley to bring the books, Fanny to return to Erasmus one by the atheistic 'Miss Martineau.' And 'once again my dearest Fanny God Bless you & thank you.' Then he turned his back on Malvern with all its memories, picturing to himself once more Annie's precious ruined face, and fled. He travelled directly to Down with hardly a delay, arriving in the early evening.[20]

When no word had come on Wednesday, Emma knew that the struggle was over and felt 'as if it had all happened long ago.' She bore the blow 'gently & sweetly,' crying 'without violence.' Her 'only hope of consolation' was to have Charles back, but her power of hoping seemed to be gone. She knew he would be ill, perhaps gravely ill. To her horror, she began to think the unthinkable – that he might actually die. But these were unreasonable fears, she chided herself; and when he appeared unexpectedly at the door, some of the light returned. They clung to each other and wept.[21]

The next morning at nine o'clock Annie was buried in the Priory Churchyard. Fanny herself had chosen the final resting-place, beneath a cedar of Lebanon, not far from the magnificent north transept window depicting the joys of Mary. The vicar performed the last offices; Fanny was joined at the graveside by Hensleigh, who helped support Brodie and Miss Thorley. 'There never could have been a child laid in the ground with truer sorrow round her than your sweet & happy Annie,' Fanny told Charles and Emma. And Dr Gully had come afterwards to enquire kindly how the two of them were.[22]

Once the family was reunited, the older children realized the severity of their loss. Willy, eleven, had been grief-stricken for days. Seven-year-old Etty had a special burden to bear, the last of the playmates to see their sister. She had been told the tragic news already, at Leith Hill, but when she returned and heard how Annie had called for her just two days before the end, she sobbed as if her heart would break. The whole experience marked the child for life, much in the way Emma herself was affected by her elder sister's death. Not long afterwards Etty began to be distressed about seeing Annie again. 'But Mamma,' she once cried while Miss Thorley was singing at the piano, 'where do the women go to, for all the angels are men?' Emma, seeing that she was upset, asked her whether she had been thinking about Annie. Etty let go with floods of tears. She knew about Annie's reputation as a 'good' child, never needing punishment; now she wanted to be as good herself. Emma wondered why she was so concerned. Etty answered one night at bedtime, 'I am afraid of going to hell.' Emma reassured her that she 'thought Annie was safe in heaven.' The next night Etty asked, 'Do you think you shall come to Heaven with me?' 'Yes,' Emma sighed, 'I hope so & we shall have Annie.'[23]

The truth was that both Emma and Charles had been severely shaken. It was easier to give religious reassurance to a child than to take it for oneself. 'Poor Emma is well and bodily firm,' Charles wrote to Eras in London, asking him to insert obituary notices in *The Times* and 'any other one or two Papers of largest circulation.' But, he added, she 'feels bitterly, & God knows we can neither see on any side a gleam of comfort.' For Emma the wound never healed. She hoped 'to attain some feeling of submission to the will of Heaven,' but it is doubtful whether she ever managed it.[24] The small keepsakes she put away and cherished through the years – the childish notes, the half-finished woolwork, the locks of hair – were a constant reminder of her favourite daughter, wrenched away at Easter.

Charles's reaction was more decided. He had borne the brunt of their 'bitter & cruel loss,' as he told Fox on 29 April. He had watched helplessly as a 'low & dreadful fever' took its toll. He had stood by in that awful passion scene, high on the Malvern hillside, and witnessed Annie expire 'as tranquilly as a little angel.' For him the death marked an impasse and a new beginning. It put an end to three years' deliberations about the Christian meaning of mortality; it opened up a fresh vision of the tragic contingency of nature. The day after writing to Fox, exactly a week after Annie was gone, he struck the new note in a brief memoir of the child, written solely for himself and Emma 'in after years, if we live.' Free of all taint of bitterness, it was the most beautiful – and certainly the most intensely emotional – piece he would ever write.

He portrayed Annie as an example of all the highest and best in human nature. Physically, intellectually, and morally she was all but perfect: her movements 'elastic & full of life & vigour;' her mind 'pure & transparent;' her conduct 'generous, handsome & unsuspicious; . . . free from envy & jealousy; good tempered & never passionate.' He repeated that 'she hardly ever required to be found fault with, & was never punished in any way whatever.' 'A single glance of my eye, not of displeasure (for I thank God I hardly ever cast one on her,) but of want of sympathy would for some minutes alter her whole countenance.' It was this fine sensitivity that left her 'crying bitterly . . . on parting with Emma even for the shortest interval' and that made her exclaim when very young, 'Oh Mamma, what should we do, if you were to die.' The perfection of Annie's character was shown by her physically affectionate ways. From infancy she would fondle her parents, much to their delight. And 'she liked being kissed.' Indeed, 'every expression in her countenance beamed with affection & kindness, & all her habits were influenced by her loving disposition.' Charles remembered Annie's face above all, her tears and kisses, her 'sparkling eyes & brindled smiles,' her 'dear lips.' Again and again he summoned the innocent features before his mind, comparing them with the daguerreotype taken two years before. 'Oh that she could now know how deeply, how tenderly we do still & shall ever love her dear joyous face,' he ended. 'Blessings on her.'[25]

Annie had not deserved to die; she had not even deserved to be punished – in this world, let alone the next. 'Formed to live a life of happiness,' as Charles put it, she had stumbled on ill health and nature's check fell upon her, crushing her remorselessly. The struggle was 'bitter & cruel' enough without the prospect of retribution. Yet, against the odds, he still longed that she might survive. He was haunted by her face, her loving kisses, and her tears when leaving Emma. Eventually he must part from Emma too.

That very day Emma's contractions started. Childbirth, even aided by chloroform, was a risky business, especially for a mother two days short of her forty-third birthday. It was a false alarm. Emma, who had endured so much, still had a fortnight to wait. She was so looking forward to the event. Taking care of an infant, she said, would be a 'very soothing occupation.' When Horace arrived safely on 13 May, however, she found her sorrow did not diminish. New life had come to Down House but she missed a pair of helping hands. And the baby would have to be her last.

Annie's cruel death destroyed Charles's tatters of belief in a moral, just universe. Later he would say that this period chimed the final death-knell for his Christianity, even if it had been a long, drawn-out process of decay. He was also freer to hold his beliefs in the home. Through nine pregnancies, always difficult and dangerous, Emma had needed the security of thinking that they belonged to each other for ever.[26] With no more babies, the threat of separation lifted. They would certainly be together for many years to come. Charles now took his stand as an unbeliever.

1851–1860

26

A Gentleman with Capital

THE SUMMER SUN of 1851 beamed reassuringly on Victoria's England, a pledge of peace and progress for the richest empire in the world. Gold had been discovered in Australia, Livingstone had just reached the Zambesi, and the first successful cross-Channel cable was being laid. A new era was dawning, bright with imperial promise, and the signs were no less auspicious nearer home. Free trade and *laissez-faire* had brought unparalleled prosperity to the few, with rising expectations for the rest. Old political allegiances were crumbling and from the old Whigs a new 'liberal party' had emerged. The storms that swept away half the governments of Europe had passed harmlessly over the British Isles, and the last lingering fears of domestic conflict now vanished like morning dew. There was 'just as much chance of a revolution in England as of the falling of the moon.'[1]

The Great Exhibition was Britain gloating in its success. It was the first international showcase of arts and manufactures, held in London's Hyde Park. It opened on 1 May, housed in a vast new glass-and-iron edifice, the Crystal Palace. Strong but brittle, capacious but combustible (it burned in 1936), Joseph Paxton's masterpiece was the architectural symbol of English economic supremacy. Its towering nave and transept promoted a sense of reverential awe. Inside, like a gargantuan hot-house, it displayed the first fruits of thriving free enterprise, the enormous engines and myriad manufactured goods that had been forced from native soil. Here the industrial dreams of the Lunar Society – of Boulton and Wedgwood, Priestley and Erasmus Darwin – came abundantly true. Half of all the exhibits came from British factories. Albert, the Prince Consort, presented them to his Queen on opening day as a tribute, the outcome of social harmony 'aided by . . . modern science.'[2]

391

Victoria's nation flocked as one to the dazzling spectacle. Three weeks after the opening, the weekday admission price was reduced to a shilling. The railways issued concessionary fares and day-tripping became the rage. More people made their first rail journey in 1851 than had ever travelled by train before. Landowners, shareholders, businessmen, and the masses met on common ground. They all seemed 'ruled and subdued by some invisible influence . . . Not one loud noise was to be heard, not one irregular movement seen; the living tide rolls on quietly.'[3] New deference and respectability were springing from a science-based industry.

While religious pundits praised God for the Exhibition, the literary freethinkers were otherwise inspired. Many had been lured to London by the more mundane need for a job. They were poets and professors, doctors and lawyers, novelists and naturalists, journalists and politicians. Some of them had independent means, but many struggled to survive. Most were in their thirties or early forties and on the make. All believed that the new age of the Crystal Palace demanded liberal, progressive reforms; that nature's interpreters had a fair claim to the status and rewards enjoyed by the Anglican Establishment. They formed an uneasy coalition whose creeds ran the gamut of Positivism, Republicanism, Secularism, Materialism, and even the more extreme '-isms' of unbelief. This intellectual élite began recasting nature as a competitive market-place. They were the new constituency for evolution, committed to progress, technology, and the naturalizing of morals and man. As the champions of change, they were making the world safe for Darwin.

The focus of their alliance was the house of John Chapman at 142 the Strand. Chapman was a medical man by training – once Dr Gully's homoeopathist in fact – and a publisher by vocation. Not yet thirty, he had built an impressive list of the latest dissolvent literature, including titles by Newman, the Atkinson-Martineau *Letters*, and brash first books by Darwin's student friend, the retired millowner W. R. Greg, and by a budding journalist named Herbert Spencer. The catalogue was put together by the brilliant but unknown Marian Evans – later George Eliot – with whom Chapman and his wife shared an awkward *ménage*. Chapman had acquired the ailing *Westminster Review* and was refurbishing it as a platform for his authors. They came to his Friday soirées that summer, full of support for the new flagship of freethought and reform. Other dissidents joined them, 'the world's vanguard,' as Evans called them: there was the philosopher John Stuart Mill and the Unitarian physiologist William Carpenter, the author of *Vestiges*, Robert Chambers, and even the mellowing atheist Holyoake, just preparing to launch 'Secularism' as a moderate movement.[4] Soon an angry young ship's surgeon would join them, Thomas Henry Huxley.

As the warm weeks passed Evans laboured over a prospectus for the new journal. Chapman needed a document that would do justice to the common beliefs of his circle – beliefs in progress, melioration of ills, and rewards for talent. The four-page flyer went out to the intelligentsia at the end of August. This was a vital moment. For the first time, progressive evolution had collective middle-class support. What artisan agitators had risked gaol to proclaim now became 'the fundamental principle' of one of the nation's leading literary reviews. Chapman and Evans called it the 'Law of Progress.' The editors declared that 'the institutions of man, no less than the products of nature, are strong and durable in proportion as they are the results of gradual development.'[5]

But what sort of 'development' were the *Westminster* reviewers plumping for? There was no unanimity beyond the belief that evolution consisted of a perfectly natural, unbroken process. *Vestiges* conformed to this view, and Newman and Carpenter had thrown their weight behind the book. But it was still a hack-work, and flawed. None of the Chapman circle found it adequate now, certainly not Chambers himself, who was engaged in a major revision for the tenth edition. A smart, sophisticated, and scientifically reputable notion of evolution was an urgent need, and the dissidents were casting around for one. Chapman asked Richard Owen, but got nowhere. Anyhow Owen's idea of development was a Platonic ideal, something that existed in the divine Mind. The 'Law' of evolution would have to explain human life rather more materially. It would have to account for the magnificent sights of the Crystal Palace – industrial achievement, English supremacy, and above all progress.[6] Only one of Chapman's friends was grasping the nettle.

Herbert Spencer had been living on the cheap in the offices of *The Economist* where he worked. This was opposite Chapman's house, amid the 'eternal rattle' of the Strand, and Evans consulted him about the prospectus during the summer. He came from Derby, from Methodist and Unitarian stock; his *Social Statics*, published by Chapman the year before, was an attempt to recast the Dissenters' moral universe as a beneficent natural process. Spencer had long accepted evolution, seeing it as an accumulation of changes acquired and passed on by each individual. Progress was a necessity. It was a 'law underlying the whole organic creation;' civilization was 'a part of nature; all a piece with the development of the embryo or the unfolding of a flower.' It was a guarantee that evil will ultimately disappear and man 'become perfect.'[7]

By the summer of the Great Exhibition he realized that progress meant something more. George Lewes, another of Chapman's circle, introduced him to the French zoologist Henri Milne-Edwards's concept of the 'physiological division of labour.' And Carpenter convinced him that evolution was a continuous change from the 'general' to the 'special;' it honed organisms to their environments, adapted each to its task, as in Milne-Edwards's industrial analogy. Spencer now believed that what was true for animals held for society: progress came through specialization. Was it not Prince Albert who said that the 'great principle of the division of labour' was the 'moving power of civilization,' and that the Great Exhibition was a 'living picture of the point of development at which the whole of mankind has arrived'?[8]

However, a great stumbling block still had to be overcome, one that had damped down belief in human perfectibility for half a century. There were always too many mouths to feed, with never enough food to go round; a painful struggle for existence was inevitable. This was the Malthusian 'principle of population' and for most liberals its status was sacrosanct. Humanity's only hope lay in abstinence from sex until each couple had the means to support children. But such 'moral restraint,' as the Revd Malthus called it, had never been practised by the great mass of humanity.[9] If past experience counted for anything, Spencer's visionary faith was doomed.

In fact, the *Westminster* reviewers were deeply divided over Malthus. To those, like Holyoake, with working-class sympathies, Malthus's principle was an evil invention. It was the ideology of the workhouse, blaming poverty on the poor and blessing the rich. But to those who sided with the cotton kings and their apologists – like Greg and Martineau – the Malthusian principle was a beneficent law of nature, encouraging responsibility and self-improvement. Chapman was so concerned about the lack of unanimity that, on acquiring the *Review*, he asked Spencer to write about population in the first issue.

Spencer's 'Theory of Population deduced from the General Law of Animal Fertility' actually appeared in the second number. It had something for everyone – but the lion's share was for the comfortably well-off. In his view the painful Malthusian principle is both true and self-correcting. People who multiply beyond their means take 'the high road to extinction;' they die off in droves, as 'we have recently seen exemplified in Ireland.' Those who remain are 'the select of their generation.' Having exercised moral restraint and foresight, they bequeath their powers of 'self-preservation.' Progress is ensured, and eventually human wants and needs will be perfectly balanced: there will be no more mouths to feed than food.[10]

The Darwin family waited two months before going up to the Exhibition. Charles wanted to finish his volume on the stalked barnacles and deliver it to the publishers by hand. Emma also needed ample time to recover from Horace's birth. They all arrived mid-week, on 30 July, at Erasmus's Park Street town house in fashionable Mayfair. The Crystal Palace was only a short cab ride away, and just as well. Several trips were needed to take in all the exhibits. Etty and Georgy, aged eight and six, got bored; Uncle Ras plied them with sweets, and they stayed at home after that. But Charles and Emma had never seen anything like it. Only nature itself – an earthquake, a rain forest, a Fuegian savage – provoked greater awe. Vast whirling pumps and presses, loud clattering looms, stately boilers and hissing engines; glass-covered velvet stands decked with gold and silver finery; closely guarded caskets bearing a queen's ransom in gems – all this came from other worlds. But Charles tired easily. It was hot, the great glasshouse was packed, and he returned with headaches. Then his stomach erupted and pestered him for days.[11]

He missed Hooker. Hooker, like Lyell, was an Exhibition 'juror' – a scientific judge asked to draw up reports on the exhibits – and he took the job for the £100 as much as the kudos. By the time Charles came up, he was off in Paris with his bride, wining and dining with the other jurors at Louis Napoleon's expense. In London Charles had a servant deliver his only copy of the huge barnacle manuscript to the Ray Society. It was five years' work and he was 'very unwilling to trust it to the tender mercies of a public conveyance.' Nor could he leave for Downe‡ until he made sure others handled it with the same care. Send it to the printer by some 'trustworthy messenger,' he urged the Society, and confirm the fact at once. '*Forgive* my silly particularity,' he added, understandably concerned.[12]

Back in Downe life went on, one day like the next. An early breakfast, then barnacles until the post arrived; afterwards more barnacles, a brisk walk, and lunch; the afternoon for recovery, with

‡ The village changed its spelling to Downe in mid-century, to avoid confusion with County Down in Ireland. Down House retained the old spelling.

reading, letter-writing, and a nap; then another bout of barnacles until tea-time, followed by backgammon and bed. Nights for Charles were '*always* bad.' He could never clear his mind. Thoughts, or things he had seen, haunted him: an awkward dissection, a social indiscretion, a troublesome letter. Safe at home, the Exhibition still made him feel unwell.[13] The future troubled him too. A gentleman had to plan ahead. Prudent foresight had brought him the security he craved, including moderate wealth. But with seven small mouths to feed, his responsibilities were greater than ever. The family was now complete – 'send only condolences' if another child comes, he told Fox. It was the long-term he had to plan for.

The girls would take care of themselves under suitable governesses and Emma's example. The boys were the main concern – the five of them. They required solid, upstanding professions to enable them to live in the manner to which they were accustomed. Charles was in more than a pother about this 'bug-bear.' In their future hands lay the family fortune – if indeed there would be a fortune to pass on.[14]

Money was the root of the matter. On paper Charles and Emma were doing nicely. Their joint annual income had just passed £3000, putting them in the top few per cent of *rentiers* nationwide. It came from shrewd investment of their inherited capital. Besides the Beesby farm in Lincolnshire, valued at some £14,000, Charles had acquired assets worth about £40,000 on his father's death. The Doctor left him another Lincolnshire farm at Sutterton Fen, a £13,000 mortgage to the Earl of Powis, and sufficient other funds to enable him to invest massively in British and American industry. Emma, too, had profited handsomely from her father's will. Her assets were held in trust by brother Josiah and Erasmus Darwin, a contemporary caution to shield a wife from her husband's creditors. This Wedgwood wealth came to something over £25,000, including an interest in the family firm, canal and railway shares, and a big mortgage to the son of a Shropshire squire.[15] In all she and Charles had more than £80,000 in investments.

A large and growing proportion was in securities, mostly railway stock. Charles was financing the new age of iron and steam. Britain in 1851 had 6800 miles of track, seven times the length of all the rail networks of the five countries of western Europe put together. This achievement, like the building of the pyramids or the Great Wall of China, had cost dear. The railway boom had been a free-for-all, fuelled by mad speculation and condoned by laissez-faire. Fortunes were made overnight, then lost – and so were lives. Savants might travel in sixty-mile-per-hour expresses to British Association meetings, but the carnage was awful with all the unregulated companies competing to get there faster. Crashes became so common that the papers reported only the major disasters. Carelessness was sometimes to blame. Charles's friend Hugh Strickland was killed near Retford station on his way home from the Hull meeting of the British Association in 1853.[16] Geologizing his way through the railway cuttings, he stood watching a coal train pass in one direction when an express hit him from the other.

Charles himself was too cautious to make a killing on the railways. He and Emma came into their money as the boom was subsiding, but he still bided his time, bought when the market was sluggish, and went in for low-risk loans. In 1847, after the spring panic and the rise in interest rates, he began pouring thousands into the Leeds and Bradford Railway. A few years later he got out of London and North Western shares too late and lost about £800, but in 1854 he put £20,000 into the Great Northern Railway and lived on the proceeds for years. He had become an astute financier. 'The present low prices of Guaranteed Railway shares,' he reasoned with his Lincolnshire land agent, who was then scouting another farm for him,

> has put it into my head, that I should act wiser in investing
> . . . in such shares; for supposing I could get nearly 5 per cent,
> the extra interest beyond what I shd. get from land, would
> during the rest of my life (as I do not spend my whole income)
> make up a depreciation fund at compound interest, to
> compensate for any fall in Gold.

That year his income went up to £4600 in all, half of which was reinvested.[17]

But Charles did not come by this financial know-how easily. For years he had read the news, watched the markets, taken expert advice. Often he felt jittery too. On paper he and Emma were set up for life, but in practice their future – and the boys' – could be jeopardized at a stroke. Most of their income was vulnerable to stock-market fluctuations. When shares fell, companies – the railways notoriously – went to the wall, taking their investors with them. One panic could lead to another and the railway bubble burst. He began to consider land a safer bet. 'With my *large* & growing family,' Charles explained to his land agent, asking him to look out a property worth £5000, 'it behoves me to do my best in making safe & wise investments.'[18]

The Darwins weren't the only big family needing security in Downe. The villagers with their thriving broods far outnumbered the 'great folks,' and Charles – his 'patron' Henslow's example before him – was also giving them a stake in the economy. He now served as treasurer of the local Coal and Clothing Club, which the Revd Innes had asked him to take over. The kindly curate was a regular visitor to Down House, and one day as they exchanged pinches of snuff Charles had proposed starting a benefit society. It would teach 'our Clodhoppers' thrift, encourage them to lay up against sickness, old age, and death. A small monthly premium would bring them a few shillings weekly to live on and £5 to be buried with. Innes welcomed the plan, and in 1850 the Down Friendly Society was duly founded, with its 'clubroom' at the George and Dragon Inn, across from the parish church. Henslow helped them draw up the rules and regulations – a 2s. 6d. fine for swearing in the clubroom, 5s. for drunkenness or fighting, and expulsion from the Society for drinking, gambling, or working while receiving benefits. Darwin became guardian and treasurer, investing the men's pennies in the Bank of England.[19] His paternal responsibilities now extended far beyond the home.

He kept scrupulous accounts. It was his own insurance against public disgrace and private penury in uncertain times. Indeed, the signs were ominous in the early 1850s. Another 'bug-bear' was haunting him, gold. It caused mass migrations. In 1849 the glittering stuff was discovered in California; two years later came Australia's turn. People rushed to seek their fortunes – over 80,000 were lured from England to Australia in 1852 alone – and the fear was that capital would follow. With the price of gold rising, a surge of share-selling would follow. Once the rush started it would be too late. His and Emma's portfolios would be wiped out, the family ruined. The boys would have to move and he would 'certainly emigrate' with them. For without a comfortable inheritance, their prospects in England were nil. They could all 'slave for years in any profession and not make a penny.'

'Though I am a rich man,' he wrote to his old ship's servant Covington, long since relocated down-under, 'when I think of the future I very often ardently wish I was settled in one of our Colonies . . . Tell me how far you think a gentleman with capital would get on in New South Wales . . . What interest can you get for money in a safe investment? How dear is food . . . How much land have you?' Actually, the place Charles said 'I fancy most' was 'the middle States of N. America.' The Empire also held out promise, a bolthole if the economy plunged. 'The English certainly are a noble race,' he added, 'and a grand thing it is that we have got securely hold of Australia and New Zealand.' Covington's reply egged him on, and soon they were back in regular correspondence. Charles wanted to hear about the gold. He was amazed to learn that 'all great and novel schemes' for working the mines were 'planned & executed' by American immigrants. The colony was 'getting decidedly republican,' Covington said. This struck Charles as the best of both worlds, and before long he was reading every book he could on Australia.[20]

There was another reason to emigrate. On 2 December 1851 Louis Napoleon seized power in a *coup d'état*. The spectre of a new Napoleonic empire sent the patriotic British into a spin. 'The fall of France seems decreed by Heaven,' Emma's Aunt Jessie mused. 'Now I think everything may be possible, even an invasion.' Over dinner at Downe Capt. Sulivan frightened everybody with his scenario for a French landing and occupation of the home counties. It left Charles with a recurrent nightmare of the French army sweeping up 'the Westerham & Sevenoaks roads' in a pincer movement and surrounding Downe. Seeing the village cut off by Napoleon – the 'Beast' as Jessie called him (from personal acquaintance) – was not total paranoia. Charles's friends were equally vehement. The anti-Catholic Lyell cursed the dictator 'and his pretorian guards and Jesuits.' There was enough of a threat to set England cleaning 'old rusty cannons' and Prince Albert begging his brother for 'a Prussian needle-gun.' The government actually fell in the new year after Lord Palmerston forced a debate on whether a local or national militia should be revived.[21]

Of course the French did not invade, and the Darwins remained safe at Downe. The family fortune grew by leaps and bounds while the sons prepared to take it over. The boys' education as much as anything ensured that Darwin stayed put, and his moans about 'bugbears' rapidly became a ritual. 'Oh the professions, oh the gold, & oh the French,' he stuttered to Fox. Really there was only one nagging uncertainty.[22] 'The worst of my bugbears,' he complained, 'is heredetary [sic] weakness.'

Twelve-year-old Willy, the future head of the family, was 'backward for his age.' Darwin agonized over the boy's education. He toyed with the Bruce Castle School in Tottenham, north of London. Founded by Rowland Hill, inventor of the penny post, it reinforced class distinctions, emphasized rigid discipline, and gave scope to modern languages and science. This might be good for Willy, who already showed the 'hereditary principle' in his passion for collecting butterflies. Charles paid the school a visit. It looked good, and it was 'cheap *with extras* about 80£' per annum. But it seemed an 'awful experiment' to make on one's eldest son. Charles was already paying the Vicar of Mitcham in Surrey, Henry Wharton, £75 a term to drill Willy in nothing 'but the Latin grammar.' Willy was getting on swimmingly. If a boy who can conquer Latin can conquer anything, as Charles believed, why disrupt the process? There was 'so much novelty' at Bruce Castle – who could predict the result?

Better to play safe and follow the example of his eminent neighbour Sir John Lubbock. He had sent his eldest to Eton, one of the 'great schools,' and already the seventeen-year-old could be seen setting out each morning from High Elms with his father to catch the train for the City, where they were banking partners. Worse fates could befall a firstborn. And young John was turning into an excellent naturalist. Charles helped him with dissections and found him 'a remarkably amiable pleasant young man.' No, one of the public schools it was. It was an agonizing decision. Charles hated the 'old stereotyped stupid classical education,' which he remembered all too well from Shrewsbury.[23] Such was his aversion that he even dispensed with the wretched Latin descriptions in the second volume of his Ray Society monograph, on the acorn-shell barnacles. But it was better to be safe than sorry: Willy would follow his Wedgwood uncles to Rugby. At £120 per annum all-in, it was still cheaper than his tutor. Willy started in February 1852.

He fitted in perfectly. At the Revd Wharton's he had learned to overcome his adolescent awkwardness, to put away 'grave & gruff manners' and strive to 'please *everybody*' he met. Charles never regretted sending him to the genteel old school. Rugby remained Anglican through and through: the headmaster's predecessor and successor both became Archbishops of Canterbury. But the reforms of Thomas Arnold a generation earlier had paid off, and the school was now grooming future bankers, industrialists, and politicians – an oligarchy for the Empire. Formation of character, development of moral muscle, and a sense of duty were all implicit within the curriculum, and Charles heartily approved. If anything, he wished Rugby did more to develop character. Altogether he felt sure that the risk of exposing a boy to 'the temptations of the world' would be reduced once he had 'undergone the milder ordeal of a great school.' His only regret was in tearing Willy from 'the affections of the family' at so tender an age. He missed his son. And it was not long before he noted that Willy's 'steady attention to classics' was having a 'contracting effect' on his mind, 'checking interest in anything in which reasoning & observation come into play.' He vowed to send his other boys to a 'smaller school, with more diversified studies,' and nearer home.[24]

Willy came home for the summer, and everybody had a splendid time. The main attraction was gangly Uncle Ras, who stayed for weeks. The children had never seen him for more than a few days at a time, when they visited London. Now they had him all to themselves, to drag around their garden haunts, to pommel into submission. Such excitement – Eras was totally unused to it. He lived on his own except for servants, at forty-seven a confirmed bachelor. His demeanour was languid, his disposition melancholic, as if he had resigned himself to some unmentionable fate. But he shone at dinner parties, where his playful wit made him the 'universal solvent,' and he delighted his nieces and nephews. He loved them dearly – especially Hensleigh and Fanny Wedgwood's six – as only a man could who longed for a family of his own. And the children adored him. Romping with them, he escaped his world-weariness. He got down on his hands and knees and became a playmate.[25] The little Darwins never forgot the fun.

Three of them had birthdays in those months – Georgy and Lizzy on successive days in July – and celebrations were held. But no school chums joined them, no village friends dropped in. The children's life was self-contained, with only Uncle Ras and the household staff on hand. Charles did take at least one of them round the Sandwalk each day, but for hours on end he was secreted away with his barnacles. The boys began to look on the study as a 'sacred place,' not to be entered 'without some really urgent cause.' One of them finally resorted to bribery – Emma's ploy for getting their co-operation – by offering him sixpence if he would come out and play.[26] Of course Charles could not resist. But still, after Uncle Ras left the children felt bored; their usual inventiveness had to be rediscovered.

Horace hurled toys in the playroom watched by the new nurse – Brodie never recovered after Annie's death – and Lenny, now two, tottered menacingly, throwing his considerable weight around. The older boys stuck together. Willy took the lead, when his nose was not in a book. Georgy and four-year-old Franky struggled to keep up. They leapt from the banisters over the top-floor stairwell, swinging precariously on a trapeze suspended from the ceiling, with much 'crashing and banging and shouting.' In the garden a swing was suspended between the twin yew trees, suitable for the girls. Stilts came in two styles, short ones on which 'even girls had been known to walk,' and the pair that made a boy as big as Uncle Ras. These were for outdoor use, for scaling the humpy landscape like Papa's friend Mr Hooker in the Himalayas.[27]

Etty and Lizzy usually stayed near the house. They were born four years apart, and Emma did little to bridge the gap. She had Charles to look after, and the babies to attend at intervals; so the girls attached themselves in turn to the cook, governess, or nurse, with Etty helping Mama as allowed. Sometimes they traipsed over to great-aunt Sarah Wedgwood's in the village. Her huge house, Petleys, lay just opposite the pond, only a quarter-mile across the fields. She had come there in 1847, a spinster in her seventies, waiting to die. Encounters with her were 'rather awful but rare events.' But her servants were the real attraction. Ringing the back door always brought a cheerful welcome. Martha Hemmings taught them catchy tunes and Mrs Morrey served heavenly gingerbread. The girls could wander about the garden, where the flowers had a 'mysterious charm,' picking the plums in autumn.[28]

But none of this made up for the girls' lack of stimulus at home. With busy grown-ups on the one hand, babies on the other, and a gang of brothers in between, they had to fend for themselves – separately too often. Rare trips to Jos and Caroline's at Leith Hill in Surrey, where there were three female cousins, helped a bit. The family went for a week in September. Etty renewed old friendships but Lizzy, the youngest, behaved like a stranger. Now that she was five, her isolation was beginning to tell. She easily became tongue-tied, using words in the oddest way, and she seemed increasingly self-absorbed. When concentrating on something, Lizzy had begun by 'twiddling her fingers as Charles used to do,' but now she had grown into the habit of 'talking to herself for an hour.' And 'she does not like to be interrupted,' her worried mother noted. The little monkey 'shivers & makes ... extraordinary grimaces,' Charles observed. 'Poor little dear.'[29]

One thing they did do together was attend the parish church. Lizzy, Lenny, and Horace had been christened there; Emma regularly took the sacrament. On Sunday the boys put on their best jackets, Etty and Lizzy their frocks, and they all trooped up the Luxted Road, past Aunt Sarah's, to the centre of the village. Charles sometimes went along, but nowadays he left them at the lychgate and set off on a stroll. The Revd Innes understood perfectly. He enjoyed Charles's backing in parish business, but only Mrs Darwin and the children were to be expected. Emma led her brood into the large family pew at the front, just beneath the lectern. Its green baize covering, the whitewashed walls, the organ now sounding better than ever – all owed something to Charles's largesse. When the Creed came to be recited, however, Emma kept faith with her heritage. The congregation turned to face the altar but she faced forward, refusing any truck with Trinitarianism.

Outside was the one sure chance each week to see new faces. The children gawked, but scarcely mixed. There were labourers in smocks – some the worse for Saturday night – with wives and babes in arms and the children scrubbed clean; tradesmen with their families exchanging friendly gossip; the awesome Sir John Lubbock, High Sheriff of Kent, followed out of church by eight sons.[30] The Darwins observed the differences and stood apart, on Sundays not least.

For an upwardly-mobile ex-Methodist such as Spencer, large, well-fed families like the Darwins represented the cutting-edge of progress – 'the select of their generation.' This is what his theory predicted – a theory of human ascent that was moving closer towards Darwin's own. Ideas on progress, population, and evolution were catching on among the literary freethinkers in London. A social network was forming, and one day it would serve Darwin well.

Spencer went fishing for proofs of evolution in Owen's lectures at the College of Surgeons. But Owen abhorred transmutation, the more vehemently because High Church 'reptiles' had accused him of pantheism and of promoting the infidel doctrine himself, which he adamantly denied. Spencer tried Owen again with his new theory of human population. Or rather Chapman did. Would the great comparative anatomist lend his weight to the dissenters' cause? Owen had read Spencer's *Westminster* article, he told Chapman; but no, he would not pronounce on its merits. Given Owen's 'known caution as to new views,' Spencer took consolation and he continued to canvass support.[31]

Copies of Spencer's article went out to 'leading men,' who acknowledged them politely. One went to an astute, dark-eyed young naturalist, making his name with a series of technical studies on sea-squirts. This was Thomas Huxley. Twenty-seven years old and fiercely ambitious, he had returned from a four-year stint on the surveying ship HMS *Rattlesnake* just in time for the Great Exhibition. Angry, down on his luck, out of money, he had been eking out an existence, searching in vain for a job. Universities turned him down; the Admiralty refused to pay him to write up his shipboard research and the Royal Society wouldn't either. He was on the point of badgering Owen (yet again) for a testimonial, this time to send to the Secretary of State himself.

Huxley was livid: in science England wanted all the credit without paying the cost. One had to be an independent gentleman to make a vocation of it. Here he was, a newly elected Fellow of the Royal Society, living in tawdry St John's Wood. He could not even afford decent lodgings, let alone bring his fiancée from Australia where they had parted three years before. Talk about Malthusian 'moral restraint' – this was ridiculous; it drove him 'wild.' Months of lecture-grubbing and other profitless pursuits left him in despair. How he had envied Hooker at the British Association a year ago, destined to succeed his father as the Director at Kew, and engaged to Professor Henslow's daughter, who was sitting by his side. Huxley's mother had just died, leaving his own father a dependent mental wreck.[32] When Spencer's article arrived in September, Huxley was close to a break-down.

Something sparked between them. Maybe it was Spencer's sanguine theory, maybe his ingenuous accompanying note. Huxley called on him straightaway and they rapidly became friends. Spencer, five years older, was a schoolmaster's son like himself and had already tasted success. At least he lived adequately by his pen. They both were bachelors with lady problems, although Spencer's were quite different: he could not get away from Marian Evans, who was infatuated with him. Huxley and Spencer spent afternoons at the zoo, evenings at Covent Garden – and Spencer moved to St John's Wood to make their meetings easier. They became sparring partners too. Huxley was a freethinker like the *Westminster* set but his approach to natural history was idiosyncratic. He would have none of Owen's etherial 'archetype' – that mythical ideal of vertebrate structure – still less of evolution. He dismissed the author of *Vestiges* as a crackpot and thought that Spencer, the evolutionist he knew best, needed a dose of expert advice. It was bad science, Huxley warned him, and harmful to one's career. There was no inexorable ascent in nature. Those who toyed with a '*chain* of beings' always ended up in shackles. Spencer, riding back with him from Lewes's house in Kensington, past the Crystal Palace, retorted that he no more accepted that symbol than Huxley did. The 'true symbol' was a tree.[33]

27

Ugly Facts

DARWIN'S HEALTH was holding up – just. He was still keeping a running record. Every day, morning and night, he scratched cryptic notes in a foolscap diary. Using minuscule handwriting, he made one cramped page cover a whole month. He had code-words for the water cure, special terms for how he felt, and left spaces in between for the nasty symptoms. It was obsessive work. 'Very well,' with double underlining, meant he was comfortable enough for a three-hour stint of barnacles. 'Poorly' meant he was incapacitated by some ache or pain, or plagued by his stomach. Towards the end of 1852 the number of hale 'double dash' days was on the increase. He totted them up each month, a rough index of his well-being. For over a year the index had hovered in the teens – half the time he had been under the weather – but by December there were twenty-four double dashes, his second best month. Nights were still bad, 'wakeful' was how he described them.[1] Yet the days had become pleasantly productive. He was in the pink and decided to take a risk.

He stopped the water cure. The aquatic ritual had been performed religiously until Annie died. Morning baptisms in the garden hut were his salvation, and even when away from home he had begun his day in a shivery shower or dripping sheet. But the trauma of his last trip to Malvern had tainted everything connected with the ritual, right down to the snuff allowed by Gully, which Annie used to fetch. And Gully himself, having failed to save the girl, was no longer his patron saint. Charles went on dowsing himself intermittently, his faith faltering. He experimented with other remedies, including 'electric chains' made of brass and zinc wires. He looped them around his neck and waist, then drenched his skin with vinegar. They did nothing for him but tingle and leave unsightly marks. Finally he

405

decided that his health index was more or less water-resistant, and at the end of November he turned off the tap. Hydropathy only helped to ease his mind; when he felt really agitated, it was useless.

And what really agitated him was still London. A day trip to the city brought on violent vomiting. Even the prospect of going made him unwell. Painful or intense thoughts had similar effects, regardless of where he was, or with whom. When Hooker came to Downe for a week, Charles was ill half the time. They tangled over species and the stress left him on the sofa. On 18 November they were due to meet to attend the Duke of Wellington's funeral at St Paul's Cathedral. It was the fourth anniversary of his own father's funeral, which he had missed through illness, and the memory left him doubled up the night before. Alone with his thoughts, he was miserable for the first time in weeks.[2] But the next day the state spectacle monopolized their attention, and Charles – who revelled in pomp – felt fine again.

Tens of thousands braved the damp and cold to pay their last respects to the 'Iron Duke,' among them young Huxley. Arriving early at the cathedral, he got a 'capital seat' at the front, and remained there frozen from eight until three. Darwin would not have recognized him – they had never met – but Huxley had sent him a scientific paper or two, and they were now in correspondence. A testimonial from Darwin failed to get Huxley a post at the University of Toronto, and he was still doing odd jobs, cataloguing the sea-squirts in the British Museum and so on. He was also taking an interest in other marine invertebrates. Darwin had sent him the first barnacle volume. (The price – a subscription to the Ray Society – was beyond Huxley's means.) Technical quibbles aside, Huxley thought the monograph was one of the 'most beautiful and complete' of its kind, and 'the more remarkable' coming from a distinguished geologist, 'not an anatomist *ex professo*.'[3] When he and Darwin finally came face to face, at the Geological Society in April 1853, he mooted reviewing it.

Darwin was pretty shrewd. Years of cajoling correspondents for barnacles – a bit like extracting money from his father – had taught him how to get what he wanted, and what he wanted now was a good press. So he baited Huxley.[4] On the shelf were some splendid sea-squirts in spirits – 'it would give me *real pleasure* should you wish to have and examine them.' And how about a copy of Johannes Müller's German book on echinoderms, 'which is really wasted on me, and would be at the service of *anyone* who would value it'? By the way, 'it would give me *great* pleasure to see my work reviewed by any one so capable as you.' 'Upon my honour I never did such a thing before as suggest . . . a review to any human being. But . . .' – and, having done so, he went on to specify those 'most curious points' he wanted mentioned: the cement glands, the homologies, the 'sexual peculiarities.' 'I daresay I *greatly* exaggerate their curiosity,' he half-apologized, 'for I have become a man of one idea,' barnacles 'morning & night.'

Huxley did not bite, but the contact was good for future reference. Here was an established gentleman-naturalist who wanted his support. Patronage had stranger guises. There could be something in it for them both.

Darwin was pleased to see his first volume in print, announcing 'my little friends, the complemental males.' 'I greatly feared that no one w^d believe in them,' he told Albany Hancock, '& now I know that Owen, Dana & yourself are believers, I am most heartily content.' Besides, there were further curious discoveries to report in volume two, on the acorn-shell barnacles. Darwin was bedevilled by the sheer unpredictability of these beasts, just as he had been by their stalked cousins. Every time he hit an abnormal type, like Hancock's *Alcippe*, he was 'almost driven mad.' To his surprise, he found this parasitic barnacle nothing like *Arthrobalanus*, despite the presence of tiny males. It was 'one of the most difficult creatures' he had ever attempted to make out. Females had the most uncongenial life – and presumably felt like Darwin on a bad day: 'after a good meal,' he said, they have 'to vomit forth the residuum, for there is no other exit!' The males, of course, were even odder, he prodded Lyell, and 'the most negative creatures in the world; they have no mouth, no stomach, no thorax, no limbs, no abdomen, they consist wholly of the male reproductive organs in an envelope.' He had found twelve of these living negations '*permanently* attached by cement to one female!'[5]

Yet, for all their sex appeal, the barnacles remained a chore. Darwin had come to hate them 'as no man ever did before, not even a Sailor in a slow-sailing ship.' He was 'working like a slave,' chained to his desk, seeing almost no one except Sowerby the engraver, going up to London once a month or less, and only when forced. He kept missing deadlines – his health index dropped – and the seventh year of his odyssey was speeding by. The younger children saw it as his life's work; they had never known Papa do anything else. Indeed, they began to think all adults must be similarly employed, leading one to ask of a neighbour, 'Where does he do *his* barnacles?' The end, though, was now in sight. In the autumn the 'everlasting barnacles' were all but through.[6] Darwin felt quietly proud, but nothing prepared him for the news in November as he was finishing off.

He was summoned to London. The Royal Society wished to bestow on him that 'Philosophic Order of Knighthood,' the Royal Medal. Traditionally awarded to a naturalist who had published in the Society's journal, the Royal Medal that year – for the first time – was thrown open to all comers. It was initially intended to honour Darwin's three volumes on the geology of the *Beagle* voyage plus his invertebrate research; but at the final meeting of the Council, Hooker reported ecstatically, there was 'such a shout of paeans for the Barnacles that you would have [sunk] to hear.' The news brought tears to Darwin's eyes. And hearing it from 'one that is loved . . . made me glow with pleasure till my very heart throbbed.' Of course, self-effacing as ever, he thought it '*ridiculous*' that his rival for the award, the botanist John Lindley, had not got the medal 'long before me' (and he was careful to nominate Lindley himself in subsequent years). But it suddenly made his whole prodigious project worthwhile. 'When work goes badly & one ruminates that all is vanity,' he beamed to Hooker, 'it is pleasant to have some tangible proof, that others have thought something of one's labours.'[7]

Darwin received the medal in person at the anniversary meeting of the Royal Society on 30 November 1853. It was traumatic as always, going to the podium to express a few words of thanks, faced by the serried rows of savants. He stood flanked by the two Secretaries, with the President sitting behind; above him was a huge chandelier, hanging from the ornate ceiling, and on the walls all around two centuries of British scientific gentlemen captured in oils, staring at him. The medal was a great 'nugget,' he boasted to Covington, out in the Australian gold fields, having to dig the hard way for his; 'it weighs 40 sovereigns.' But the command performance sent him back to the bath for a spell, after a year's break. The water did the trick, his health index shot back up and the *matins* ceased. Then, with an enormous, protracted sigh of relief, he put his second, 900-page barnacle manuscript to bed.

What had started as a few months' work in 1846 on one strange, boring barnacle ended almost eight years later in two technical treatises overhauling the entire sub-class. It was the longest piece of sustained research he would ever undertake; and it was punctuated by the worst illness, tragedy, and despair he would ever endure. Had he gone 'the way of all flesh' at this point, he would have been remembered as a tropical traveller and gentleman geologist who had withdrawn into his lonely shell to conquer the least archetypal of crustaceans. (Indeed, the novelist Bulwer-Lytton would immortalize him as the blinkered boffin 'Professor Long' who had written 'two huge volumes on Limpets.') He had persevered, Job-like, to become the world's authority on barnacles. His was a monumental, definitive work, with a hundred printed pages on the fossil forms and over a thousand on the living ones. It established him as a zoological specialist, and no longer just the geological expert. More important, it was his licence to speak on species.[8] He had taken Hooker at his word all those years ago and earned this right. No one deserved it more.

After so much wrist-aching, eye-straining work, Darwin some days yearned for the old romance of geology. He liked a humdrum life, but he still experienced a twinge of envy as friends came and went. Lyell, back from America, turned him green with his talk of exhuming '3 skeletons of Reptiles out of the *Carboniferous* strata.' He was setting sail again for Madeira in December. Darwin was left at Downe, building air-castles: 'It really makes me quite envious to think of you clambering up & down those steep valleys . . . I often think of the delight which I felt when examining volcanic islands; & I can remember even particular rocks which I struck – & the smell of the hot, black, scoriaceous cliffs.' He daydreamed of more exotic places: 'Tasmania has been my head quarters of late,' he said after hearing that the colonial government was financing Hooker's *Flora Tasmania*; 'I feel very proud of my adopted country.'

There was vicarious pleasure in Hooker's *Himalayan Journals*, with their vivid descriptions of the perilous mountain terrain: 'one can feel that one has seen it,' Darwin reported after devouring the book, '& desperately uncomfortable I felt in going over some of the Bridges.' His complimentary copy arrived in February 1854, and with it another shock – it was dedicated to him. Since the Antarctic voyage Hooker had wanted to honour his friend in a book, 'out of love for your own "Journal".' And he had gone about testing the waters in a devilish way: he had asked Darwin how *Lyell* would like it dedicated to him. 'You *bad* man,' Darwin laughed when he twigged, 'who ever would have dreamed of you being so *crafty*?'[9]

His voyages complete, the wanderlust over, Hooker was now happy to stay at home and 'jog-trot at Botany till the end of my days.' He was at last settling down: 'the craving of 30 years is satisfied.' He was mellowing into a family man, with a son, born in 1853, and a thumping daughter – eleven pounds at birth – in June 1854. 'Did you administer the Chloroform?' inquired Darwin, an old hand; it is 'very composing to oneself as well as to the patient.' Hooker's star was rising and becoming brighter all the time. Darwin mentioned him to an acquaintance, saying 'we shall see him some day the first Botanist in Europe,' only to be pulled up sharp: 'Sir, he is decidedly *now* the first Botanist in Europe.' The first botanist was a fast friend, everything Darwin had hoped for. He dug out the secret letter to Emma, concerning the £400 to edit his ten-year-old essay, and scribbled on the cover definitively: 'Hooker by far best man to edit my Species volume.'[10]

Another potential editor was rising fast. In London that year Darwin again met the jovial Edward Forbes and found him looking well. Forbes was hoping to take the natural history chair at Edinburgh. Jameson, now old and creaky, had hung on to it too long – fifty years – and not without some unkind cuts. Darwin, who never forgave his dull lectures, described him as an 'old brown, dry stick;' others called him 'a baked mummy.'[11] Forbes had long wanted the chair, and when Jameson died in April, he got it.

By now Darwin was relatively hearty. As an insurance he sucked lemons, whole ones twice a day, which were supposed to be good for the stomach, and he felt safe enough to come out into society. In the spring of 1854 he finally accepted an invitation to join the Royal Society's élite Philosophical Club. In years to come it would be the powerhouse of evolutionary science, but for the moment Darwin was to rub shoulders with the young guard: a whole cadre – Huxley, his good friends George Busk and the pugnacious Irish physicist John Tyndall among them – were elected the following year. The Club suited Darwin perfectly. 'Only two or three days ago,' he told Hooker in March, 'I was regretting to my wife, how I was letting drop & being dropped by nearly all my acquaintances, & that I would endeavour to go oftener to London.' Now he could see fresh faces, be lionized, catch the gossip among the new men – the ones, he hoped, who would swing behind his species work. To his surprise, he rather enjoyed his trips to town. They 'suit my stomach admirably,' he admitted in May. 'I begin to think, that dissipation, high-living, with lots of claret is what I want, & what I had during the last visit. – We are going to act on this same principle & in a very profligate manner have just taken a pair of Season-tickets to see the Queen open the Crystal Palace.'[12]

Paxton's huge iron-frame, glass-curtain building had been dismantled and re-erected at Sydenham in south London, where it occupied a spacious site, laid out with beautiful gardens, artificial lakes, and even Owen's life-size concrete dinosaurs. The Hookers could visit Downe and take in the Crystal Palace grounds on the way home: 'paradisaical,' they called it after one weekend – 'We both of us said we had never spent 5 happier days since our marriage.' The

Ugly Facts

Queen visited time and again, once even escorting Louis Napoleon when Charles and party attended, although on this outing 'Aunt Elizabeth fainted dead away' which was rather 'frightening & disagreeable.'[13]

Generally Charles loved these social occasions. He preferred strolling around the Palace to attending Royal Society meetings, and given the choice – 'pray conceal the scandalous fact,' he ordered Huxley – he did just that. Huxley, intent on stamping out the Society's old amateur ethos, was the last person he should have confessed to. But Charles remained a country gentleman at heart, so different from the rising generation, who clamoured for professional reforms. In many ways he kept both feet in the old school. When Huxley talked of his 'scientific young England,' he envisioned new standards, new status, new rewards: a science seized from the old clergy's hands and revamped – naturalized – and made serviceable to new mercantile masters. The spider-stuffers, the 'old buffers,' the country parsons – all had to go.[14] But the professionals still needed a new legitimating philosophy, a new competitive, capitalist sanction in place of Anglican Oxbridge paternalism; a dynamic biological science to replace the old static, creative hierarchy. And Huxley at this stage had no idea who would provide it.

The societies were transforming rapidly, with great stirs inside the Royal and even the soporific Linnean, which Darwin joined in 1854 in the hope of new times. The Royal Society was now awash with fresh blood, and it showed in the way the medals were falling. Huxley took the Royal Medal in 1852; Tyndall was named with Darwin in 1853, and Hooker in 1854, for his work on 'the origin and distribution' of plants. The pushing and prodding on Darwin's part had paid off for Hooker too. These young bloods were all destined to be 'scientific giants,' Darwin prophesied; and he thought it only right that the young men should get the accolades, to spur them on.[15]

In fact, the fast non-Oxbridge set were already sliding into positions of power. Huxley got his break in November 1854 and started regular teaching at the Royal School of Mines in Jermyn Street, Piccadilly. Then, 'sick of the dilettante middle class,' he began his famous working men's lectures a year later. Tyndall had taken the chair of natural philosophy at the Royal Institution in 1853, and was soon helping Huxley run the science section of the *Westminster Review.* Hooker, following in his father's footsteps, was shortly to become ensconced at Kew Gardens. All of them swore by London, 'the centre of the world.'[16] Here they would stay and make their mark.

*

411

Biology was liberalizing, along with society. Looked at from inside or out, there was real change. Even one man of the cloth, the Revd Baden Powell, Savilian Professor of Geometry at Oxford (and father of the Chief Scout), was sympathetic to evolution. Admittedly, he was an extreme liberal and his argument theological: God is a lawgiver – miracles break the lawful edicts issued at Creation, therefore belief in miracles is atheistic. QED. A clever riposte to miracle-mongering Creationists. He was an idiosyncratic Anglican apologist. 'These parsons,' Hooker complained, 'are so in the habit of dealing with the abstraction of doctrines as if there was no difficulty about them whatever . . . that they gallop over the [science] course . . . as if we were in the pews and they in the pulpit. Witness the self confident style of . . . Baden Powell.'[17]

Hooker was coming around. He had not embraced Darwin's new gospel but, 'Oh dear, oh dear,' he sighed to the botanist Asa Gray at the Harvard Herbarium, 'my mind is not fully, faithfully, implicitly given to species as created entities *ab origine.*' In fact, he could see that 'Creation' was empty verbiage. 'It is very easy to talk of the creation of a species,' he agreed with Darwin, 'but the *idea* is no more tangible than that of the Trinity & . . . is neither more nor less than a superstition – a believing in what the human mind cannot grasp.'

The problem Hooker still faced was a common one: the origin of life itself. He could follow Darwin 'back to the vital spark' – and then what? Surely *this* involved 'a vis creatrix or whatever you may call it; which is a fact as inscrutable as a full blown species.' But unlike the atheists, seeking an alternative to Anglican Creationism in a chemical soup, Darwin kept ultimate origins out of the picture. Life's initial appearance on the earth was inscrutable, he implied to Hooker. All that should concern the naturalist was its subsequent change. The origin of the first living globule was as irrelevant as the origin of matter was to the 'laws of chemical attraction.' At its starkest, he insisted, the only question was 'whether species of a genus have had a common ancestor.'[18]

This narrow focus left his project looking more professional, less ideological. It had to, if he was to bring about a *coup d'état* in science. It distanced his study from the shabbier cosmological works, the sort that left his Church mentors foaming. Rival evolutionists all betrayed their reforming, anti-Anglican intent. Herbert Spencer's 'law' of progress in *Social Statics* had been generalized in 1852 as 'the development hypothesis' in a disreputable rag, *The Leader.* Robert Chambers's *Vestiges* had been relaunched a year later in a slick tenth edition. Robert Grant, now a melancholy sixty-year-old, laughed at by Huxley and Forbes, was still insisting on the 'direct generation' of one species from another. Then again, stop on a street corner in 1854, or drop into a newsagent around Fleet Street, and pick up the scurrilous *London Investigator* for a penny and read its shocking revelations on the 'origin of man.'[19] Here, in a crusading atheistic paper, the emphasis was on co-operation rather than the fit and rich killing the weak and wan. Each of these offered a cosmic alternative to 'Creation' – an upward-sweeping progression, powered from below, underwritten by strict laws. And all promoted, as part of a naturalistic package, the atomic origin of life. They were levelling, progressive, democratic works.

And that is what petrified Lyell. Man would lose his 'high estate,' his special status in creation. He would be reduced to gutter level. Lyell was still shoring up human dignity, protecting it from radical degradation. He was still denying any progress (or therefore transmutation) in the history of life. No species had a genealogy, least of all the noblest one, on whom God had conferred immortality. As late as 1851 he had reaffirmed to the Geological Society that there had been *no* 'gradual advance towards a more perfect organization . . . resembling that of man.'[20]

Sir Charles Lyell was an urbane Whig, Unitarian by conviction, wealthy by inheritance. He called Harley Street his home when not travelling on the Continent or occupying his Scottish family seat. Politics to him was all of a piece with religion, and religion with science. The 'high estate' of man was his own, and he guarded it jealously. Back from Madeira, he and Lady Lyell spent several days at Downe with Hooker and his wife. Species were on the agenda, and the party cost Darwin two nights' sleep. Lyell boggled at Darwin's 'ugly facts.' It was these anomalous facts, he warned his brother-in-law afterwards, 'which will figure in C. Darwin's book on "Species".'[21] Lyell saw the writing on the wall and began mulling over mutability again, worrying once more about mankind's place in nature.

Darwin's strategy, as old as his own notebooks, was to stick to species and let Creation collapse by itself. And his Malthusian, capitalist, competitive mechanism was quite unlike any rival evolutionary theory. He pooh-poohed the attacks of libertarians and socialists on Malthus's 'most logical writings.' Many doubted that more food led to more animals, which were therefore doomed to struggle. Some claimed the reverse: that potting plants in rich soil actually *lessened* their fertility. Darwin thought this absurd and experimented with seed-beds and compost to prove it.²² Not for him old William Godwin's optimism of a naturally progressive meliorating society. Darwin's version of evolution promised no inevitably rosy progress based on utopian co-operation. On the other hand it did underwrite many reformers' demands: for free trade and unfettered competition, for a breaking of the old 'unnatural' monopolies and privileges. It made Nature an ally of the middle-classes.

But could he convert a tyro such as Huxley, who was contemptuous of the rabble-rousing, evolutionary pot-boilers? Huxley scorned the 'cynics who delight in degrading man.' He thought that Grant had missed his vocation and that Spencer misunderstood science. While his fellow writers on the *Westminster Review* were sympathetic to a meliorating evolution, Huxley was not. He savaged the *Vestiges* so badly as to cause him qualms later. Progressive transmutation was 'pretentious nonsense,' he pronounced in his brash way. The rancour stemmed partly from his own predicament; he was disgusted to see an author making a mint from his 'charlatanerie.' Huxley hated the book because it explained nothing. To his mind *Vestiges*'s theme – 'creation by law' – was gibberish. Natural law, conceived as a divine edict causing the development of life, had no 'intelligible meaning at all.' It offered no '*explanation* of creation,' short of saying that it was an 'orderly miracle.'²³

'How capitally you analyse his notion about law,' Darwin cooed, knowing that such shafts could not be aimed at him. But for the rest he had mixed feelings, and ultimately thought Huxley too hard on the hapless book. 'I am perhaps no fair judge,' he teased, 'for I am almost as unorthodox about species as the Vestiges itself, though I hope not *quite* so unphilosophical.' Huxley's review was clever, he agreed with Hooker; nay, the best review 'I have seen, on poor Vestiges, but I think he is too severe, – you may say "birds of a feather flock together," & therefore I sympathise with the author.'²⁴ Maybe he did; maybe he saw himself, a few years on, in the same boat. Huxley would have to be won over.

By September 1854, when Darwin read Huxley's review, the second volume of his monograph on living barnacles, huge at 684 pages, was out, and he was busy dispatching copies to friends. Huxley, *au fait* with French and German zoology – dissecting barnacles himself in the light of Darwin's work – supplied the addresses of authorities who should receive a copy, garnished with spare pickled specimens. On the 7th Darwin told Hooker that he had 'been frittering away my time for the last several weeks in a wearisome manner, partly idleness, & odds & ends, & sending ten-thousand Barnacles out of the house all over the world. – But I shall now in a day or two begin to look over my old notes on species.'

At last the way was clear to carry on with natural selection. The time was ripe to begin; with the young reformers on the rise, the *Westminster* evolutionists already in place, the social basis of science was visibly changing. And Darwin now had his licence. Two days later he jotted in his pocket diary, 'began sorting notes for Species Theory.'[25]

The next month Lyell and Hooker came down to find out how Darwin was getting on with his 'ugly facts.' Lyell was shaken, Hooker teetered, and Darwin took heed. Caution was still imperative – the question was too momentous for anything else. Though fifteen years had passed since he closed his notebooks, the supernatural fabric of creation in shreds around him, he was still telling Hooker that he would 'give the arguments on *both* sides.' He would not plump for 'the mutability side alone.' Unsure on so touchy a subject, even of intimates, he tied himself in knots of self-abnegation. To his clerical cousin Fox he disclosed his plan to

> view all facts that I can master (eheu, eheu, how ignorant I find I am) in Nat[ural]. History, (as on geograph. distribution, palaeontology, classification Hybridism, domestic animals & plants &c &c &c) to see how far they favour or are opposed to the notion that wild species are mutable or immutable: I mean with my utmost power to give all arguments & facts on both sides. I have a *number* of people helping me in every way, & giving me most valuable assistance; but I often doubt whether the subject will not quite overpower me.[26]

Balance and doubt were a public mask. Despite appearances, he knew exactly what he was doing. For fifteen years he had committed himself unequivocally to one side.

In-coming books were routinely tested, to see how his theory explained their data. He was characteristically modest about it. The exercise left him, as he growled to Hooker on reading his essays, having to 'gnash my teeth & abuse you for having put so many hostile facts so confoundedly well.' There was no 'for and against' here; he was singling out hostility to his own view. Hooker still had botanical doubts about the '*Elastic* theory,' as he dubbed it. Darwin took it all on the chin: 'what a villain you are to heap gratuitous insults on my *elastic* theory; you might as well call the virtue of a lady *elastic*, as the virtue of a theory accommodating in its favours.'

But then, regretting it, he begged off as usual: 'I feel deadly sick, & decidedly an animal of low development.' That week, with a houseful of guests, his special plague was boils. Your 'cautions on the species-question ought to overwhelm me in confusion & shame,' he reproached himself to Hooker another time; 'it does make me feel deuced uncomfortable.'[27]

Confusion and shame: the old thoughts were there, but the words rang hollow. Uncomfortable he may have been – sick in fact – but Darwin felt more assured with the barnacles and the Royal Medal under his belt. He was internationally known from the *Journal*, the geology books, and the barnacles, enough for Professor Asa Gray – sending information on American plants – to invite him to Harvard, all expenses paid. (Of course he turned it down on health grounds.) He was emboldened by each step Hooker took in his direction. And Hooker was quickening his pace, informing Gray that he now had 'an utter disbelief in the stability of my own genera and species.' Or, as he admitted to Darwin, he no longer cared a hoot whether species 'are all pups of one generic type or not.'[28]

28

Gunships & Grog Shops

BARELY HAD DARWIN put his barnacles away than the great Crimean struggle began. War preparations had been going on steadily throughout 1853. In November, as he received his medal, Russia – wanting a toehold in the Ottoman Empire – was blasting Turkish ships in the Black Sea port of Sinop. At stake was not merely the protectorate of the Christian holy places, which had been ceded to France, but control of the Mediterranean and the trade routes to India and the Near East. The British could not afford to lose these. Her Majesty's fleet had lain at anchor outside the Dardanelles during the summer. In autumn it had moved opposite Constantinople, awaiting orders.

The country was on a war footing, not least the great folks at Downe. Young John Lubbock, now a published naturalist (thanks to Charles), marched off to Dover to train with the Kent Artillery Militia. The Darwin family went with the Harry Wedgwoods to the Chobham army base to see the manoeuvres. There were twelve small cousins in the party, eight of them boys; and who should be on hand to show them around but Capt. Sulivan, recently returned from the Falklands. Battle had already commenced, with the bloodcurdling shouts and thundering mounts of over 10,000 men: the grandest war games yet staged by a peacetime British army. For a moment, in fact, it became all too real. The Darwin-Wedgwood contingent found themselves being charged by the 13th Light Dragoons and had to flee for their lives. It was part of the thrill that made three happy days unforgettable. And the one who enjoyed them most was Charles.[1]

Back at home the mood changed as the flotilla put to sea again. 'We are all much afraid of war with Russia, which, pray God, may be prevented,' wrote Charles to Covington. It could not. With the papers howling for revenge against the Tsar, the fleet passed through the Bosporus under orders to clear the Black Sea of Russian warships. The French joined in, and on 28 March 1854 the allies declared war. Charles kept in touch with Sulivan, who was returning to active service in the Baltic in command of HMS *Lightning*.[2] The slaughter was dreadful – 15,000 allied dead alone – and still the Russian naval base at Sebastopol lay intact.

The young Darwins were bitten by the warfare bug, and Emma abetted them with 'galloping tunes' on the piano. With William away at school, Georgy was now in charge. He had dismissed the Duke of Wellington with a seven-year-old's sang-froid – or was it Papa's gloss on immortality that he captured when he jotted in his funny, cryptic way, 'The Duke is dead. Dodos are out of the world'? But, now, after the Chobham manoeuvres he too became a hot-headed little soldier. With himself as sergeant, to Franky's private, they mastered the childhood arts of war.

They took on men's names and measurements. Georgy constructed a short foot-rule so that, on the cloakroom wall under the stairs, he could conscientiously record his height as six feet, and Franky's as something less, in accordance with his age and rank. They learned the parts of guns, practised drills, and then, donning knapsacks, hoisted toy rifles and trooped down the Sandwalk to pitch camp. Georgy built a touch-wood fire for warming the gingerbread and milk; Franky stood guard until released by his brother's bugle. No one dared interfere. When Papa came out for his daily stroll and went to kiss the guard, Franky bristled and presented his homemade bayonet. Indoors the fantasies continued. There was much playing with tin soldiers – ferocious troopers with swords raised and a regiment of French dragoons whose coats Emma laboriously reddened with sealing wax to make them thoroughly British. Upstairs in the long hallway the boys attacked each other with lead-weighted darts, which crashed harmlessly against their wooden shields. Their sisters were dumbfounded, even shy Lizzy. 'Georgy is such a soldiery boy,' she pouted. 'He never speaks to a single girl.'[3]

At Sebastopol the siege had started. Then came Balaclava, Inkerman – news of the carnage was being flashed by telegraph from war correspondents in the field for the first time. As the nation faced up to reports of 3000 British dead, news came of another loss: on 18 November 1854 Forbes, the genial soul who had shown Hooker how to summon up a supercontinent, died of kidney failure. In a time of heightened emotions, Darwin and his friends were stunned. Huxley had 'never felt so crushed by anything before.' Ramsay could 'scarce realise it. My grief breaks out in short fits, and then I struggle to suppress its signs.' It was a cruel and ironic twist; Forbes had fulfilled his lifelong ambition to take the Edinburgh chair, only to die seven months later. For Lyell it was 'the greatest loss of an active scientific friend I have ever sustained, and he was but thirty-nine.' It was 'dreadful,' Darwin lamented, recalling his own mortal fears at the same age.[4] 'What a loss to his singularly numerous friends & to Natural Science!' 'As for his poor wife I pity her from my soul; I have lost a child, & I can, therefore, in some degree realise what death in its worst form is.'[5]

Darwin was thinking about the parallel warfare of nature, and how sea-borne invaders, seeds and fruit, frogs and snails, could establish a beachhead on alien terrain and oust the occupiers. More and more he concentrated on the idea of struggle; how it took place, and with what result.

The last major rethink of the theory was underway. Faced with grim reports from the Crimea and the tragic news of Forbes's death, he sat uncomfortably at Downe in November – only fifteen 'double dashes' that month, with a week of 'wakeful' nights – pondering the diversity and extinction of animals. He looked at aberrant species, those out on a limb, like the peculiar egg-laying platypus, far removed from the rest of creation. Were they ill adapted and dying out? Had intermediates, connecting them with normal animals, already become extinct?[6] This brought a flood of new questions. How did animals radiate into every conceivable form – even into broody, duck-billed mammals? What caused a species to split into two? How could *selection* generate this branching 'tree' of life – the one he had first sketched in his 1837 notebook? And if animals are diverging along lateral branches, away from one another, what of the old notions of 'high' and 'low' in nature?

The tree was the key. By the 1850s it was the accepted metaphor among naturalists: gnarled branches, forking, spreading. Even from Calcutta, the curator of the Asiatic Society's museum, Edward Blythe – 'a very clever, odd, wild fellow,' who sent Darwin reams on Indian domestic animals – compared life to a tree that 'branches off, & still divides & subdivides & resubdivides.' It was Darwin's image exactly: he had long visualized nature as *'irregularly branched.'* But why should offspring depart from their parents and go a different way? How to explain this forking?

'I can remember the very spot in the road, whilst in my carriage, when to my joy the solution occurred to me,' he later recalled – the cause of the forking. A eureka moment maybe, but he was now to spend three years refining and applying his solution.[7]

Just as his Malthusian insight had come from population theory, so his mechanism for creating diversity looked like a blueprint for industrial progress. Darwin was a heavy investor in industry. His Wedgwood cousins were among the pioneers of factory organization. They created a production-line mentality with a marked division of labour among the work force, pushing up productivity by giving each operative a single, specialized function.[8] This mechanisation of the labour force, and its effect on output, was totally familiar to Darwin. Endless trips to Uncle Jos's house as a young man had ensured that, and the Darwin library was stocked with books on economy and manufacture.

Every gentleman living off his industrial shares understood 'division of labour.' It was synonymous with specialization and speed in a steam-powered society. It promised wealth and booming markets, and the industrial metaphor seemed to stretch to nature herself. It was the catch-phrase of the age; Prince Albert called it the engine of civilization, thundering through every aspect 'of science, industry and art.'[9] Herbert Spencer, that erstwhile railway surveyor, thundering down his own branch line, was not alone in importing it into science.

Darwin recognized that, just as industry expanded when the workers specialized, so did life. But Nature had the 'more efficient workshops.' He argued that natural selection would automatically increase the 'physiological division of labour' among animals caught in competitive situations. Stressful competition in overcrowded areas – what he called Nature's 'manufactory of species' – favoured variants that could exploit free niches. These individuals would seize on new opportunities, exploit the available openings on that spot.[10] Isolation on islands was clearly not so crucial as he had thought. Competition pried apart dense local populations, fanning them out and forcing a greater number to escape the rat-race by finding their own unpressured nook. New varieties were actively pushed away from the parental stock, thus mitigating the blending effects of cross-breeding. Just as a crowded metropolis like London could accommodate all manner of skilled trades, each working next to one another, yet without any direct competition, so species escaped the pressure by finding unoccupied niches in Nature's market place. The greater the functional diversity of animals, the more an area can support.

The metaphoric extension was complete. Nature was a self-improving 'workshop,' evolution the dynamic economy of life. The creation of wealth and the production of species obeyed similar laws. Division

420

of labour was nature's way as well as man's. But economic doctrine was promiscuously mixed with partisan politics in Britain, and Darwin introduced the subject by citing the zoologist Milne-Edwards's use of the term 'division of labour' rather than an economist's.[11] A political taint would have made natural selection too much of a target. To be successful, evolution had to be seen standing on the solid rock of science.

With progress guaranteed in Nature's workshop, as much as it was in Uncle Jos's, Darwin's self-evolving Nature was like the expanding, diversifying empires of the Dissenting cotton kings and pottery patriarchs. And indeed, the 50s were a decade of accelerating production; the boom years when economic laws seemed as iron-clad as Nature's own. But the masters' views were very unlike those from the shop-floor. Darwin was siding with the factory bosses and his fellow investors, and he would have no truck with any other.

He dismissed critics who saw mechanization beggar the workforce, and those included Emma's uncle, the economist Jean Sismondi. Brutal competition, a dehumanizing division of labour, the 'unjust' distribution of profits: Sismondi had slated them all as 'scourges.'[12] So Darwin *did* have alternative models available. But he rejected them. He accepted that Nature's struggle, like the nation's in the Crimea, took a terrible toll. This was the price of progress and diversification, and there was no bucking it. This rift with Sismondi ran deep, right down to the ownership of land. Sismondi thought that those who worked it should own it. Hardly surprising that Darwin rejected his theories, when he was himself an absentee landlord in Lincolnshire.

Evolution and utilitarian economics were perfectly attuned, and to many Dissenting industrialists this seemed natural. But few were investing so heavily in both areas as Darwin. Economists had called for a specialized work force, free markets, and a rail network to reduce transport costs. Their utilitarian ethos had led to the railway mania as much as a *laissez-faire* Nature. Darwin put his mouth where his money was. He spent tens of thousands of pounds on railway companies, and twenty years of his life revealing the competitive, specialized, and labour-intensive aspect of Nature's 'workshops.' He was placing Nature on industry's side.

Christmas that year was gloomy. Franky and Lenny had fevers and on the 22nd Franky threw a fit. To buck them all up, Charles decided to ring in the changes and spend a month in town. They took a house off Baker Street on 18 January 1855, only to have the weather close in behind them. It was that 'terrible Crimean winter,' with bitter, below-zero temperatures, when even the Thames froze over. Charles, like Emma, felt the cold acutely and regretted ever setting foot in 'dirty and snowy' London.[13]

While they were there Lord Aberdeen's government fell, censured for mismanaging the war, and Palmerston, who had helped instigate the fiasco, became Prime Minister. A dirge was playing in society. Britain lost 30,000 men in all, half of them to disease and the cold. The Wedgwood women collected clothes for the troops, and then threw themselves into the 'playful gaiety' of Sydney Smith's *Memoirs* to shake the 'stern reality of life' staring at them from every newspaper. But it was no good; nor did London society seem pleasanter knowing what 'the noble Flo Nightingale' was enduring. There were parties at the Horners and Lyells but the talk was of a half-million dead on all sides.[14] The family returned to Downe on 15 February, relieved to be snowed in at home.

While the fleet were besieging Sebastopol, Darwin kept worrying at the sea-borne dispersal of species: how they migrated, whether they could compete successfully with occupying plants when they beached. He was still looking for a way to scupper Hooker's supercontinents. According to Hooker, Tierra del Fuego had plants in common with Tasmania and Kerguelen Land, a remote island midway between Australia and South Africa. These similarities were 'far more than can be accounted for by any known laws of migration – I am becoming slowly more convinced of the probability of the southern flora being a fragmentary one – all that remains of a great Southern Continent.' Darwin hated hypothetical continents almost as much as another alternative, that God had created identical life in different places, or 'multiple centres of creation.' Plants could cross the oceans to conquer new lands and he would prove it.

Islands and castaways were important to Darwin for another reason – how else to explain species like the Galapagos finches and tortoises, each peculiar to its own island?[15] If islands and continents were where they had always been, at least for untold millions of years, the only question was how animals and plants had colonized them.

Darwin was in no two minds: plants, seeds, eggs, and animals made the journey by accident, carried by wind, water, and rafts. But he needed evidence. So off went letters, as usual to the oddest places. He tracked down a sailor who had been shipwrecked on Kerguelen, to see if he recalled driftwood on the beach, which might give a clue to colonization. He tried other tacks, asking if naturalists had found seeds in ducks' stomachs; or if, as a Hudson's Bay man told him, seeds were carried out to sea on ice-floes. But still, he grumbled, Hooker's facts were 'the greatest anomaly known in the distribution of beings over the whole world.'[16] The trouble was, everybody – Hooker included – assumed that seeds were killed by sea-water. But were they?

Late in March 1855 Darwin resolved to find out. Like a country vicar, with the time and patience and a love of pottering, he set up a series of experiments brilliant in their mundanity. He bought sea-salt from a chemist. Seeds from the kitchen garden – cress, radish, cabbages, lettuces, carrots and celery – were placed in small bottles of brine. Some he left in the garden, others in a tank of snow in the cellar, to check whether the cold would make any difference. He took a few from each bottle at intervals and planted them in glass dishes on the study mantelpiece, where he could watch for signs of life. It worked. Almost everything came up after a week in sea-water, a fact he delighted in telling Hooker. He twitted the poor man, telling him to send the seeds that he expected 'to be *most easily killed*,' and to guess at their survival times.[17] Two weeks later and the vegetables still sprouted.

Hooker took it 'like a good Christian,' as befitted the new Assistant Director-elect of Kew Gardens. He suggested that Darwin experiment on a massive scale, plying him with exotic seeds for the purpose. But Down House lacked Kew's facilities. Darwin was already coping with forty or fifty bottles. He could not manage any more; as it was, the chimneypiece was covered and the water had to be changed every other day, or it 'gets to smell horribly.' And he was having to cancel engagements if they fell on days when his salted seeds 'come due.'[18]

The whole thing became a vicarage industry. He had the Revd Henslow paying schoolgirls sixpence a time to collect seeds, and Miles Berkeley, the Northamptonshire curate who had described the *Beagle* fungi, sending bags of seeds to Ramsgate to sit in Channel water. Meanwhile the stalwart Revd Fox was posting reward notices to encourage boys to find lizard and snake eggs – there was nothing Darwin would not try, however ludicrous. What other objects he was testing he would not say. 'If you knew,' he told Hooker, 'you would have a good right to sneer for they are so *absurd* even in *my* opinion that I dare not tell you.'[19]

In the *Gardeners' Chronicle*, he announced that cress, lettuce, carrot, and celery had germinated well after forty-two days' immersion, radishes less well, and cabbages hardly at all. He also explained *why* he was experimenting; he did not mind audaciously dismissing

Forbes's Atlantis 'in a temporary publication like a newspaper.' A quick calculation followed. His atlas gave the average current in the Atlantic as thirty-three nautical miles a day – so in forty-two days a seed might cover 1400 miles. This was highly convenient, for it just happened to be the distance to the mid-Atlantic islands, the Azores. No Atlantis need have risen from the sea floor. To suggest that it had was reckless; 'it cuts the knot instead of untying it.' He was untying the knot slowly and deliberately. Seeds of European plants could have drifted out to conquer the Azores. At least, the distance was no problem. He went one stage further. 'The real interesting thing would be to get a list of the Azores plants, & try & get the seeds of as many as I could, & test them; & by Jove I will!'[20] And he did. He wrote to the British consul asking what seeds came ashore on the Azores and had Henslow's schoolgirls collect the British equivalents.

That pods could travel these distances was also proved by tropical seeds washed up by the Gulf Stream in Norway. The British consul forwarded two types to Darwin. Hooker identified them as coming from Caribbean plants; he sowed them at Kew and to his 'unutterable mortification' they germinated. And still the records fell. Some celery and onion seeds actually sprouted after eighty-five days. Even odder, the celery came up faster than seeds spared the trial. But the prize went, surprisingly, to the sensitive pepper plant, which germinated after almost five months in cold salt-water. Once again, Darwin's experiments, so simple, seemed so obvious. Gray at Harvard, reprinting Darwin's newspaper article in the *American Journal of Science*, kicked himself, wondering why no one had thought of them before.

But the real problem as Darwin presented it was not dispersal. He finished his *Gardeners' Chronicle* tally of survival times on a deliberate teaser. When the seed reaches its 'new home then,' he said, 'comes the ordeal.' Will it be able to establish a beachhead? Will 'the old occupants in the great struggle for life allow the new and solitary immigrant room and sustenance?'[21] With the British fleet still battling at Sebastopol it must have seemed curiously topical: as though warfare ran through nature and society, and colonialism was all of a kind. But Darwin was actually smuggling in one of the major themes of his theory, and the subject would vex more than gardeners and arm-chair admirals in the years to come.

The war dragged on. The nation wanted dramatic victories, not a drawn-out struggle; and to Charles it did seem as if the whole conflict was being conducted 'very badly.' But Capt. Sulivan came home, full of valiant tales, and was preparing to set off again for the Baltic with a new command. Charles saluted him. 'The men and officers have behaved most nobly, and have made the name of Englishmen a prouder thing than ever,' he rejoiced to Covington. Out in his 'clay fort,' Georgy felt much the same. When Sebastopol fell at last, in September 1855, the guns of thanksgiving boomed out across the country. He would never forget the sound.[22]

Struggle and selection – these were the guiding themes of Darwin's system. But examples were still needed to underpin this ramifying view of nature, and his picture of specialization continued to raise new questions. For example, however diverse mammals, reptiles and fishes, their embryos, if traced back, quite clearly converged in appearance. Foetal mammals and fishes were much more alike than the adults. It was wonderful proof of 'community of descent,' he believed, but how to *explain* it by natural selection?[23]

From the first he had wanted to bring such embryological evidence into the fold and make it work for him. But he had long departed from conventional wisdom. Medical men had always assumed that freaks were formed in the womb, and that this is where all variations originated. But was it? What if in some cases only dispositions to vary were inherited, and the actual variations manifested later, in the youngster or adult? Selection could only act later, when they appeared, sustaining or quashing them. After all, people had hereditary dispositions towards illness that only manifested at a certain age. The embryos in this case, being left unaltered by selection, would look more alike than the adults: the changes – the divergence – would remain hidden until the individual began to grow. In the wake of Annie's death, Darwin became more and more convinced that his own affliction was inheritable, and even now lay dormant in the children. 'My dread is hereditary ill-health,' he told Fox. 'Even death is better for them.'[24] It was morbid confirmation that he was on the right track.

He needed a graphic demonstration of this embryonic similarity and selection of emerging variants. He turned to domestic animals. Fanciers copied nature by breeding from the best of their stocks and drawing out new strains. How did they operate? There was one way to find out: he had been reading up on domestication since his notebook days. Now he would knuckle under and study fancy animals first-hand. 'Get young pigeons,' he had scribbled on his evolution essay a year or so before.[25] Expose the similarities among the hatchlings of the breeds cropped and coiffed by man – breeds that were derived from a single ancestral stock – and the model of nature would be complete.

In March 1855, just as the seed experiments were beginning, he started asking around. He cornered Fox: 'As you have a noah's ark, I do not doubt that you have pigeons; (how I wish by any chance they were fantails!) Now what I want to know is, at what age nestling pigeons have their tail feathers sufficiently developed to be counted. I do not think I ever even saw a young pigeon.' At first he just wanted information, not to get too closely involved. He needed fledglings 'to see how young, & to what degree, the differences appear.' He could either breed them himself, which would be 'a horrid bore,' or buy the young, and – this being a pleb's hobby – he wanted to be genned up before he put his money down so as 'not to expose my excessive ignorance, & therefore be excessively liable to be cheated & gulled.'[26]

Domestication had always fascinated transmutationists. In Paris and Edinburgh they had seen its potential, and even detractors believed that it was the best evidence of a 'plastic' nature. But few deskbound scientists had ever got their hands dirty, leaving it to tree cultivators like the curmudgeonly Patrick Matthew to prove the point. Darwin on the other hand had never ceased collecting scraps and facts. He followed up hearsay stories of exceptional hounds, silkworms, hybrid geese, feral and farm animals in the colonies – anything in fact on selection, inheritance, and breeding. For fifteen years he had ploughed through manual after manual on pigs and poultry, and the more he studied the bizarre types, the odder it seemed 'that no zoologist sh^d. ever have thought it worth while to look to the real structure of varieties.'[27]

It was hard to realize the novelty of his move. Most naturalists disdained pigeons and poultry. Science was not done in the farmyard. The gentry might have kept ornamental ducks on shooting estates. They might have founded zoological gardens to celebrate Britain's colonial control over nature. But such gamekeeping was a world removed from contemplative philosophy. It was this elevated pursuit – of wild species and their order and meaning in God's Creation – that commanded the philosopher's attention. Hence the scientist's disdain: no one expected pigs and pigeons to hold the key to the mystery of mysteries.[28]

But unconventional science required unconventional support, and Darwin strayed far beyond the normal bounds. He looked anew at the gamekeepers' familiar fare; agricultural shows, animal husbandry, farmhouse lore, and the *Poultry Chronicle*. And he began quizzing those who knew most about breeding and inheritance: fanciers and nurserymen.

Even before Christmas 1854 he had begun boiling up wild and domestic ducks to compare their skeletons, although sometimes with a lingering gastronomic interest: 'oh the smell of well-boiled, high Duck!!' But it was pigeons, to his surprise, that became his passion in the summer of '55. Like barnacles, seeds, and so much else, the enterprise took on a life of its own. All talk of cheating tradesmen ceased. Once inside the 'fancy' he was drinking with breeders, joining their clubs, picking up the lore and the gossip. And what a change: he built a pigeon house in the garden, bought choice fantails and pouters for £1 a pair, and declared them an 'amusement to me, & a delight to Etty.' He ordered almond tumblers and runts and soon had quite an aviary. Come, he told Lyell, see the pigeons, 'which are the greatest treat . . . which can be offered to [any] human being.'[29] He stocked up with books on the 'Art': how to judge proportion, carriage, and the beak, and how to select and breed from those offspring that show the desired combination.

His enthusiasm soon got the better of him. Boiling and measuring were now daily routines, and he became adept at judging the breeds and their young. His letters acquired a ghoulish air: I 'am watching them outside,' he said, eyeing his birds, '& then shall skeletonise them & watch their insides.' It was not only pigeons. Fox showered him with dead ducklings and chicks, and volunteered mastiffs and turkeys. 'Very many thanks for your offer,' Darwin responded. 'I have puppies of Bull-dogs & Greyhound in salt. – & I have had Carthorse & Race Horse young colts carefully measured.' Horses, dogs, ducklings – 'I am getting out of my depth.' He tried all means of killing his pigeons: chloroform took too long and he squirmed at the sight. Better was potassium cyanide in a bottle; the prussic acid gas it gave off was quick and painless. But however swift, the death of his pigeons affected him; 'I love them to that extent that I cannot bear to kill & skeletonise them,' he wailed to Hooker. Seeing his funny gawky chicks lose consciousness was always sad. 'I have done the black deed & murdered an angelic little Fan-tail & Pouter at 10 days old.' The corpses mounted, skeletons, measured and unmeasured, lay everywhere; cadavers were arriving by post, boxes crushed and intestines hanging out. Even he admitted it was becoming 'a chamber of horrors.'[30]

Etty might have been entranced by the birds, but what Emma thought of the stench as their remains rotted in a witches' brew of potash and silver oxide no one knows. At first Charles was overcome, the putrid flesh 'made my servant and myself (we not having had much experience in such work) retch so violently, that we were

Darwin

compelled to desist.' 'It really is most dreadful work,' he admitted, taking expert advice, and the following year he sent the birds out to be skeletonized professionally.[31]

Fox – the 'kindest of Murderers' – dispatched all the duckling varieties he had and began purloining farmyard animals from neighbouring estates. The fossil-collecting Sir Philip Egerton, whose Cheshire manor adjoined Fox's parish, was ever ready to help. But Egerton became intrigued. Running into Darwin at the Glasgow meeting of the British Association in September 1855, he inquired – Darwin related to Fox – 'why on earth I instigated you to rob his Poultry yard?'[32] As a shire Tory MP, patron of Richard Owen, and spokesman for respectable Anglican science, Egerton might not have appreciated the true answer.

Darwin wanted to show nature composed of myriad tiny variations, invisible to all but experienced fanciers. These enthusiasts could judge to one-sixteenth of an inch. And the differences that only they could spot formed the raw material to be accentuated through generations of selective breeding. From such minute aberrations, enormous sculpted changes had been wrought by fanciers, leading to today's pouters, fantails, runts, and tumblers. So enormous, in fact, that had these birds been wild, zoologists would have classified them as different species, perhaps different genera: 'Darwin finds, among his fifteen varieties of the common pigeon,' Lyell reported, astounded, the equivalent of 'three good genera and about fifteen good species.' Even their red blood corpuscles were differently shaped, as Darwin discovered when he had an expert examine samples. The same diversity was apparent in other domestic breeds. He pointed out the variations in domestic rabbit skeletons to Waterhouse at the British Museum, and asked whether 'they were not as great as between species.' More so, was Waterhouse's reply.[33] Here, then, were single species, so modified as to fox even the best zoologists. From infinitesimal variations, common rabbits and pigeons had been stretched to the extent of emulating whole new genera.

Darwin believed that similar imperceptible variations held the key to Nature's own Malthusian selection. Weak, ill-adapted variants were discarded by Nature, as they were by the fancier. The good ones thrived and over the generations particular trends were encouraged. Adaptive features were drawn out, as if by an invisible breeder. 'Artificial selection' showed the craftsman sculpting nature; Nature's own 'selecting' hand was infinitely superior.

He had seen the 'selecting hand' – but it was rather a grubby one. The feathers he admired were largely the handiwork of artisans.

428

Working men had always taken pride in their pigeons and sought solace in the loft after the drudgery of the day. 'I am hand & glove with all sorts of Fanciers, Spital-field weavers & all sorts of odd specimens of the Human species,' he said.[34] Of course, not really hand-in-glove; there was always a certain detachment. Even educated fanciers and poultry journalists who plied him with information were reimbursed their expenses. They were treated as paid technicians, offered cash to check his facts and read his manuscripts. These fanciers, appalled at the indifference of the scientific nobs, welcomed his interest in their prize breeds. His kindly paternalism gave their backyard hobby a certain cachet. But to the end he remained imperturbably a gent among working fanciers.

This also showed in his favoured club. He was easiest in the exclusive Philoperisteron, which met up in town at the Freemason's Tavern. It had all the snobbish appeal of a Piccadilly club, and its shows attracted hundreds of exhibitors, despite a lack of prizes. The 'Philo' was an attempt to escape the grimy associations of the fancy. This ruffled a few feathers, and the vulgar thought it fit only to 'bird-lime the House of Lords.'[35] The velvet waistcoats cut no ice with ordinary breeders. They preferred the cheap feather clubs of the City and Borough, in south London. Darwin joined the Borough club himself. In fact, the 'Squire,' as he became known here, visited them all, high and low, with a sense of anthropological mission: from the rowdy beer-halls of Spitalfields to the posh venues of the West End, he was attempting to see nature through the eyes of the natives.

Grog shops were not his normal haunt, yet here he was, eaves-dropping:

> I sat one evening in a gin palace in the Borough amongst a set
> of pigeon fanciers, when it was hinted that Mr. Bult had
> crossed his Pouters with [larger] Runts to gain size; and if you
> had seen the solemn, the mysterious, and awful shakes of the
> head which all the fanciers gave at this scandalous proceeding,
> you would have recognized how little crossing has had to do
> with improving breeds.[36]

Darwin could see no substitute for hob-nobbing with fanciers. It was the only way to pick up the lore.

And with the lore came the initiation. The Borough club, he told William, a world away at Rugby, was populated by a 'strange set of odd men.' After dinner one handed me a clay pipe, saying 'Here is your pipe' as if it was a matter of course that I sh^d. smoke. – Another odd little man (N.B. all Pigeon Fanciers are little men, I begin to think) . . . showed me a wretched little Polish Hen, which he said he would not sell for £50 & hoped to make £200 by her, as she had a black top-knot.[37]

But these odd little weavers and costermongers were skilled at finishing pigeons to exacting standards. They could pinch, bustle, and crown birds, creating forms scarcely less marvellous than the changing female fashions. It was they who gave the squire his first sight of artificial selection at work.

On the other hand, it was Darwin's own dedication to the fancy – visiting the beer-halls, buying the *Poultry Chronicle*, breeding his own pigeons – that gave such authority to his comparison of Art and Nature. He had found analogies of selective transmutation in the grubbiest, most unsuspecting quarter.

29

Horrid Wretches Like Me

BY 1856 THE YOUNG GUARD was organizing. Huxley, Hooker, Tyndall and their fellow travellers were discussing strategy and marking out enemies. First on their list of priorities was to claw more power for London's science lecturers and gain a greater 'command over the public' – and the public purse.[1] They saw themselves as grossly underpaid compared to the clerical naturalists of Cambridge and they bitterly resented it.

Huxley was rising fast: a specialist on molluscs, medusae, and other marine creatures, teacher at the School of Mines, and now – in 1856 – Fullerian Professor at the Royal Institution (which he accepted for the £100 pay). This year, too, with Darwin's and Sir John Lubbock's help, he followed Carpenter as an examiner at the University of London. He was accumulating posts as a clergyman collected livings, and the pay rose with the overwork. He was razor-sharp; a 'very clever man,' Darwin recognized, the sort he was counting on to convert quickly. Fearsomely clever, in Hooker's view. He found Huxley's lectures 'overwhelming,' his facts 'revolutionary,' to the extent that he could not master the half of them. Darwin did not attend the lectures, but he was just as daunted, claiming to know no more about Huxley's molluscs 'than a man does, who has only eat[en] oyster patties.'[2]

Huxley's London teachers were scientific outsiders who sneered at the cloistered Cambridge mentality and the privileged, old-boy network. Yet incongruously, here Darwin was, playing Huxley's 'Father confessor.' Little did the group know that the Downe recluse, once educated to the cloth, was to supply the iconoclastic science to match their ambitions.

For the moment they had their own strategy, which involved

431

creating a new tightly knit, highly regulated 'profession.' It meant selling themselves to the public as 'scientists,' a respectable white-collar body who should be decently paid for providing a public utility – however novel 'knowledge' was as a commodity. The profession had to be self-validating. Science could owe no allegiance to theology, and Huxley rushed around, baiting bishops, making a public show of dissociation. Proper pay, too, would bring in talent and push out the dilettantes. The science section of the *Westminster* was proving too cramped; soon the coterie was agitating for a house journal and a club of its own – an 'intellectual resort' where these traders in science could sup and scheme without being bothered by the 'pitiful botchers.'[3]

Ties were strengthening all the time. Huxley, now in regular employment, had brought his fiancée Henrietta from Australia in 1855. After six years apart, they were married, with Hooker, Tyndall, and the Carpenters in attendance. Darwin sent his blessing, although warning that 'happiness, I fear is not good for work.' Holidays were spent together, with mountain climbing the manly rage. The dreaming spires they admired were not Oxford's, but the Tyrol's. Huxley would join Tyndall in the Alps, or spend Christmas with Hooker and George Busk, a naval surgeon friend, on Snowdon, glorying in the scenery. Huxley, bellicose, brash, a good hater and a fast friend, knew the value of men like Hooker, Tyndall, and Darwin, and admonished them all to 'pitch into me when necessary.'[4]

Already the young bloods were mugging old hands like Owen, the newly appointed Superintendent of the Natural History collections at the British Museum in 1856. Owen, the darling of Oxbridge divines and politicians, symbolized all that they despised. New standards were needed, not deference to old vanities; a new accountability to one's peers. The clique cringed at Owen's deferential mysticism, never mind his personal quirks. Huxley, that 'Roundhead who had lost his faith,' with his flashing eyes and lacerating wit, smeared Owen physically and mentally. A 'queer fish,' he called the vertebrate specialist, and 'not referable to any [known] "Archetype" of the human mind.' Cronies sniped continuously at the 'Autocrat of Zoology.' Almost literally at times – when Owen hit back at Huxley's 'blindness,' Carpenter told Huxley 'to put a bullet into some fleshy part' of his enemy to prove his eyesight. What the tyros lacked in respect they certainly made up for in bravado. Owen might have published more than all of them put together, but they wanted the Superintendent superintended. Make him answerable, Carpenter urged, 'to a body of scientific men, who are competent to estimate and criticize his proceedings.'⁵ A body, of course, that would be Huxley-led, and responsible to no man. The chill winds of professionalism were blowing across the old order.

All this was brewing in April 1856, when Darwin called a meeting at Downe. 'I am very glad that we shall meet at Darwins,' Hooker wrote to Huxley. 'I wish that we could there discuss some plan that would bring about more unity in our efforts to advance Science.'⁶

Darwin desperately wanted to get Huxley to Downe for other reasons. His anatomy was brilliant, but he seemed to be drifting in the wrong direction. He hated evolution and damned talk of a progressive fossil record. Like everyone else he dismissed *Vestiges*'s uninterrupted ascent of life. But he went on to repudiate Owen's vision of progress as well, which baffled Darwin. Owen imagined fossil animals as less specialized than today's. Trace each lineage back and the more general the animals become. Eventually we must arrive at the original archetype – the ideal mould from which they were all forged. Owen gave an example that became a classic. Today's thoroughbred horse stands on tip-toe – a single toe – but it was preceded by the smaller, extinct *Hipparion* with two small extra toes in each foot, while further back the tapir-like *Palaeotherium* had a full three-toed foot. He believed that this kind of specialization typified the ascent of life.⁷ So did Darwin.

Huxley did not. He hated Owen, hated his 'metaphorical mystifications,' and denied the whole progressionist kit-and-caboodle. Worse, the horses made their début during Owen's onslaught on Lyell's non-progressionist geology. Owen was so vicious that it made Hooker sick. It further angered Huxley, who greatly respected Lyell and his science. Darwin too had done with Owen's mysticism and 'detested' his murky Platonic thinking.⁸ But he appreciated the great man's fossil framework. He realized that Owen, for all his wishy-washy rationalizations, had simply traced the bloodline of the horse. His whole scheme could be translated into evolutionary terms; the genealogy was perfect. Darwin was happy for it to be left intact, ready for his own new explanation. Huxley's gleeful demolition was not appreciated.

Huxley's own views were disquieting, inscrutable even. He thought of species in a strange way. He saw them clustered as if on the surface of a sphere, each the same distance from the archetypal centre. There was no place for intermediates, and no possibility of higher and lower forms. Darwin was baffled – it was all geometry again, not genealogy. 'I am,' he said, 'surprised at what you say.' He was dumbfounded at Huxley's denial of any progression – and

433

nonplussed by his archetype, the central abstraction. This appeared Ptolemaic in its crudity, in its unyielding, unchanging form. It bore no relationship to the ancestor Darwin had in mind when he continued: 'I sh^d. have thought that the archetype in imagination was ... capable & *generally undergoing* further development.'[9] But if Darwin was disbelieving, Huxley must have found an *evolving* archetype positively absurd.

Darwin annotated Huxley's reviews, trying to gauge the strength of his anti-evolutionary argument.[10] He needed to probe further. This was why he invited Huxley to his Downe gathering, to get his objections first-hand.

Hooker and his wife were to arrive on Tuesday 22 April. Also invited was the punctilious T. Vernon Wollaston, a quiet, cultured Cambridge man, an insect-specialist '& very nice & pleasant into the bargain.' Here, surely, was someone after Darwin's own heart. At the time Wollaston was arranging his beetles in the British Museum. His new book *On the Variation of Species* was dedicated to Darwin and made the strongest case yet for 'a legitimate power of self-adaptation' in insects – for their tendency to vary *'within fixed specific bounds.'*[11] He shared Darwin's interests, and his ill health. His own work on Madeira (where he had gone to recuperate) had shown that island isolation and climatic change were major causes of variation in beetles, and he repeatedly cited Darwin's *Journal* to prove the point. He seemed to be leaning the right way.

To complete the party Darwin invited the renegade, Hewett Watson. He had met the fiery atheist and phrenologist the previous August, and found him 'a bit sarcastic.' This at first made him suspicious, as he always was of radicals. But the more Watson plied him with plant statistics, the more Darwin came to value his 'clearness of mind & acuteness,' and he soon had the *'highest* opinion' of the man. Watson too opened up, confiding his own evolutionary views.

As it turned out, Watson could not come that weekend. There was also doubt about Huxley. He was exhausted, and his wife ill with morning sickness – she could hardly have wanted to go anywhere. Tuesday was also his day for lecturing. Darwin was not sanguine, although he suggested that a 'little change' might do them both good. Emma promised that Henrietta 'could be as quiet as she liked, & sh^d. have a comfortable arm-chair in her bedroom, so as to live upstairs' if she preferred.[12] The Huxleys eventually came on the Saturday – their first trip to Downe – probably taking the train to Sydenham, where Darwin's carriage met them.

It was one of those occasions relished by Hooker, with 'long walks, romps with the children on hands and knees,' and strolls through the garden. They ambled out to the Sandwalk, Hooker and Huxley planning the reformation of science, Wollaston full of beetles. Darwin, with his 'hearty manner,' led the way in his grey shooting coat, staff in hand, pointing out his pigeons. John Lubbock, just married, joined them for dinner on the 26th, the night the Huxleys arrived. In the morning, after breakfast, came the 'interviews' one by one in the study, like a doctor's surgery, when Darwin brought out a pile of slips with questions needing answering. The slips were now ready for Huxley.

Lyell was astonished to hear of the events that weekend. 'When Huxley, Hooker, and Wollaston were at Darwin's last week,' he informed his wife's botanical brother-in-law Charles Bunbury, 'they (all four of them) ran a tilt against [immutable] species farther I believe than they are deliberately prepared to go. Wollaston least unorthodox. I cannot easily see how they can go so far, and not embrace the whole Lamarckian doctrine.'[13] In truth the tilting was Darwin's and Hooker's. Wollaston had been expected to join in. From his talk of 'legitimate variation,' Darwin had thought that he was a potential convert. But no. 'Least unorthodox' was an understatement. His views were as fixed as his species: he made exceptions only for minor variations.

Darwin reckoned that his exceptions would eventually get the better of him. He twitted Wollaston mercilessly and threw grandfather Erasmus's adage at him:

> I have heard Unitarianism called a feather-bed to catch a falling Christian; & I think you are now on just such a feather bed, but I believe you will fall much lower & lower. Do you not feel that 'your little exceptions' are getting pretty numerous? It is a funny argument of yours that I (& other horrid wretches like me) may be right, because we are in a very poor minority! anyhow it is a comfort to believe that *some others* will soon be with me.

Wollaston's 'funny argument' – the minority might be right after all – was meant as a mock concession. It was drawn from the Gospel of Matthew: 'strait is the gate, and narrow is the way, which leadeth unto life, and few there be that find it.' But twisting a text like this played straight into Darwin's post-Christian hands. If he and 'other horrid wretches' who believed in evolution were such a minority, perhaps they had found the way of life; the damned were those like Wollaston who equivocated.[14] Maybe Darwin could even be credited with saving *'some others'* – Hooker and Huxley, he hoped.

But as a wealthy rector's son Wollaston was shocked at these implications. While he allowed insects to vary 'to a much greater extent' than most, he still insisted that their power of change was 'positively circumscribed.' Each species had 'only certain *limits* to vary between,' he told Darwin, 'beyond which . . . it cannot pass.' This posed no 'danger,' he boasted, because 'it does not touch the question of development in its *larger* sense.' To him the idea of transmutation was 'monstrous.' Darwin was thwarted. It is pretty 'rich,' he groused, 'considering how very far he goes,' that he denounces 'those who go further, "most mischievious" "absurd", "unsound". Theology is at the bottom of some of this. I told him he was like Calvin burning a heretick.'[15]

Theology was never behind Huxley's opposition. Hadn't he slammed *Vestiges* for making nature an 'orderly miracle'? And yet he was even more adamant that progressive transmutation was pernicious nonsense. Later he recalled his 'first interview' with Darwin, and how he argued for the 'sharpness' of species and 'the absence of traditional forms, with all the confidence of youth,' and then puzzled over Darwin's smiling response 'that such was not altogether his view.' Darwin of course knew Huxley's position; he had annotated and 'grieved' at his reviews and speeches. He was frankly dismayed at the brilliant tearaway.[16] Darwin now fired a series of questions at him – although without tipping his hand on natural selection.

In the study, Huxley ran through his objections. He pointed out that even ancient fossil animals have little-changed living relatives, that crustaceans could not pass into fishes, that intermediate forms were missing, and that fossil history did not mirror an individual's embryonic growth. As soon as Huxley had gone Darwin scribbled a series of notes, picking at Huxley's quibbles, unravelling his fallacious reasoning, reconceptualizing his static spherical nature as a dynamic, ramifying tree: in short, knocking his objections down, one by one.[17]

More strategic differences were also emerging. While Darwin was looking for a bloodless coup in science, Huxley had other ideas. He was pugnacious to a degree. And iconoclastic, rushing into scientific citadels, slaying emperors – Cuvier, Owen, and Agassiz – and challenging their minions. Hooker wanted to get Huxley elected to the Athenaeum, as he himself had been five years before; but Darwin worried about Huxley's brazenness. Whatever the strengths of his science, his tone was 'too vehement.' Two weeks after the meeting, Darwin decided against putting Huxley's name up, guessing that Owen would only blackball him anyway: 'Cannot you fancy him, with a red face, dreadful smile & slow & gentle voice, asking, "Will

[you] tell me what M^r. Huxley has done, deserving this honour; I only know that he differs from, & disputes the authority of Cuvier, Ehrenberg & Agassiz".' We 'had better pause,' Darwin cautioned Hooker; 'to try in earnest to get a great Naturalist into [the] Athenaeum & fail, is far worse than doing nothing.'[18] He would mellow out, they guessed, given a couple of years.

The new men were closing ranks, like any cadre: identifying outside 'aggressors,' forcing cohesion, a common policy, common enemies. All were sympathetic to Darwin, with his technically excellent science, uncontaminated by theology. Owen was alienated and excluded, for his hauteur as much as his idealist heresies. Morality came into it too, as it always did with Huxley. Owen delivered guest lectures in Huxley's School of Mines in 1856-57. They were, by all accounts, a roaring success and attended by a smattering of lords and ladies, who were shown 'the power of God in His Creation.' The Duke of Argyll (the Postmaster General) scarcely missed one, nor Dr Livingstone, back from Africa. The lionizing alone must have galled Huxley, who was forced to watch the socialites parade through his institution to applaud his enemy. But Owen also craftily advertised himself as the 'Professor,' usurping Huxley's position in the school. At this Huxley hit the roof. 'Of course I have now done with him, personally. I would as soon acknowledge a man who had attempted to obtain my money on false pretences.'[19]

But Owen gave as good as he got. Better sometimes, and even Hooker realized that Huxley's hotheadedness could catch him out. He reported the latest to Darwin breathlessly:

> Owen I hear committed a cutting telling & flaying alive assault on Huxleys adaptation views at the Geolog[ical]. Soc[iety]. & read it with the cool deliberation & emphasis & pointed tone & look of an implacable foe. – & H. I fear did not defend himself well (though with temper) & perhaps had not a popular champion in Carpenter who barbed him – These embroglios are very bad indeed & must insensibly have a bad effect upon Huxley.

Darwin, who also derived a jot of guilty pleasure from Huxley's antics, nonetheless warned him again, 'for Heaven sake do not come the mild Hindoo to Owen (whatever he may be): your Father confessor trembles for you.'[20]

Shortly after the Downe gathering Darwin began working out a strategy for presenting his theory. Lyell, intrigued by Darwin's speculations (though not realizing their extent), egged him on to write and publish, fearing that he would be scooped.

What had alerted Lyell was a cryptic, guarded paper on the 'introduction' of species, published in the workaday *Annals and Magazine of Natural History*. He had tipped Darwin off, as had the ebullient Edward Blythe, raving about it, 'Good! Upon the whole!' A self-financed globetrotter – a specimen-hunter selling bird skins, beetles, and exotic butterflies for a living – Alfred Russel Wallace, had composed it in Borneo, idling away his time trapped indoors by a tropical monsoon. In Blythe's words, 'friend Wallace' had 'put the matter well' – and in a way which suggested that 'the various domestic races of animals have been fairly developed into *species.*'

This ought to have shaken Darwin out of his complacency. But Wallace's guarded language threw him: his statement that '*Every species has come into existence*' coincident in space and time with an earlier allied one could have been Owen's 'ordained continuous becoming,' or a cryptic gloss on Creative continuity. Darwin missed its import, as did others. It is 'nothing very new,' he scribbled on his copy of the *Annals*. 'Uses my simile of tree,' but 'it seems all creation with him.'[21] Darwin misread Wallace's coded talk, putting him down as just another alert young Creationist.

Lyell did not. He was considerably shaken, enough to open a notebook on species, where he mulled over the consequences for humanity, frightened that the world was again tumbling towards transmutation. Lyell churned the subject over and over, peering at it from every angle. How had the 'Author of Nature' introduced species on to the earth? Did a new species look like its predecessor because 'Omnipotence' was fitting it to similar conditions?[22] Lyell was now grappling with the issues directly.

At Downe Darwin, knowing he could trust Lyell implicitly, watching him waver, finally spelt out the full details of natural selection. Lyell toured Darwin's pigeon house, admiring the runts and tumblers and, by now, almost every other breed known in England. He did not really agree in his heart of hearts, but he urged Darwin to publish, for priority's sake.

Lyell went away staggered. As always, he saw the starkest implications. At home, pondering the selectively bred pigeons, he extrapolated to man's selected origin 'from an Ourang.' He cut to the heart of the problem; animals did not really matter – but was *man* only a better sort of brute? Was he 'improved out of' some Old World ape? It seemed unthinkable; humans differed in kind. And yet, if Darwin was right, 'the whole geological history of the globe is the history of Man.' It was a sublime and sobering thought. Lyell, the mentor who had refuted Lamarck a quarter of a century earlier, was playing with fire, hesitant yet hypnotized, tantalized by Darwin's 'species-making' mechanism. His quandary increased when he raised the issue at the Philosophical Club. Talking to the young bloods, it was obvious that fixity was a thing of the past, even if they had 'no very clear creed to substitute.' Natural selection was ripe. It would fall into their hands, Lyell realized; 'whether Darwin persuades you and me to renounce our faith in species,' he prophesied to Hooker, 'I foresee that many will go over to the indefinite modifiability doctrine.'[23]

Pushed by Lyell, Darwin began collating his notes. Other gentrified naturalists spurred him on, not realizing the consequences. Bunbury, Lyell's in-law, was intrigued by his 'speculations on species' and delighted that he intended to press on with publication. He knew Darwin went further than most, but even Darwin, he insisted, 'would not assert an *unlimited* range of variation: he would hardly . . . maintain that a Moss may be modified into a Magnolia, or an oyster into an alderman.' Many an alderman, too, eating his oyster patty, would have been startled at the prospect. Bunbury advised Darwin to show 'caution & candour,' to avoid the dogmatism which so easily creeps into discussions 'of *multiple* creation, & of transmutation.' Give 'every fact & argument on any side,' he advised.[24] This, of course, is what Darwin planned.

But when nip came to tuck, it was a tall order. For the first time Darwin began to face up to the logistical problem, and his own partiality. 'To give a fair sketch would be absolutely impossible' because of the welter of facts. Perhaps he should 'only refer to the main agency of change, selection.' But a skimpy paper would hardly spark a *coup d'état* in the scientific citadel, among the people he really wanted to convince. Only a commanding tome – sizeable, abstruse, and referenced – stood any chance of converting them. But if he did not seize priority, it could be twenty years wasted. And with so much transmutationist talk about – in *Vestiges*, all over the gutter press, among the *Westminster* crowd – time was running short. He was flurried: 'I do not know what to think: I rather hate the idea of writing for priority, yet I certainly sh^d. be vexed if any one were to publish my doctrines before me.'

And then, where to publish? 'I positively will *not* expose myself to an Editor or Council,' so an academic journal was out. Maybe a modest monograph was best after all. 'If I publish anything it must be a *very thin* & little volume, giving a sketch of my views &

difficulties,' he told Hooker, imploring his advice; 'but it is really dreadfully unphilosophical to give a résumé, without exact references, of an unpublished work.'[25] And, anyway, how could he? He would 'sneer at any one else doing this.'

In the end proprietorial fears won out, and on 14 May 1856 he started a sketch, putting off the decision whether to publish until later. Hooker could see the advantage of getting out a 'Preliminary Essay,' but wondered if it would not destroy the impact of his full tome. Fox too evidently counselled against a slight work. No, no, said Watson, go ahead, publish now and perfect it later. 'This I have begun to do,' Darwin announced, 'but my work will be horridly imperfect.' His self-doubt set in again: the traumatizing feeling, the 'wibber-gibbers,' as he called it. 'I begin *most heartily* to wish that Lyell had never put this idea of an Essay into my head.'[26]

It was an auspicious time to start. The Crimean War was over at last, and two weeks later, on the night of 29 May, when Charles was in town for a Royal Society meeting, he saw 10,000 coloured rockets launched simultaneously to celebrate the peace-treaty. Russia had been defeated, the eastern trade routes secured. The future for Britain was looking bright, the age of sterling imperialism and Pax Britannica. And the young bloods were determined to make a new 'science, pure and free, untrammelled by religious dogma' part of her success story.[27]

30

A Low & Lewd Nature

AT FIRST HIS MIND was not totally on the book. Emma, now forty-eight, had had nine children, and they confidently expected no more. Then in 1856, as he began writing, she found herself pregnant again. It came as a complete surprise. Horace's birth, her last, had been five years earlier. Now Emma was once more 'as wretched as ever.' Through May and June she was sick, and by July 'general oppression' had replaced the nausea.[1]

He also became het up again about supercontinents as more naturalists jumped on the bandwagon. Wollaston was connecting Madeira to the mainland, others were conjuring up a lost Pacific land, and the old Atlantis was still below the waves. Darwin 'fairly exploded' on the subject: 'my blood gets hot with passion & runs cold alternately.' It was so absurd. Add up all the lost continents and 'half the present ocean was land within the period of living organisms.' And did the extensions help? Why the absence of Australian Banksia plants in New Zealand if they were formerly connected? And couldn't ice-sheets pushing animals and plants down from the Arctic explain the common American and European forms? And why were old continental strata never found on mid-oceanic islands? He was now 'fairly *rabid*' on the subject, admonishing himself to become more 'humble,' and allow the miscreants 'to make continents, as easily as a Cook does pan Cakes.'[2]

By mid-July he had drafted forty pages on the migration of Arctic species. On paper his ideas looked good, 'but Lord knows it may be all hallucination.' He had finally stopped vacillating on the book's size. No skimpy précis would do; it had to be a full-blooded work, although little did he realize how full that would make it. He asked Lyell to be allowed to dedicate the volume to him. Sir Charles –

considering his old loathing of Lamarck – was squaring up well; 'he is coming round at a Railway pace on the mutability of species,' Darwin told Hooker, and allows 'me to put some sentences on this head in my preface.'[3]

That was in public; the private Lyell was still tormented. What really racked him was an issue that never bothered Darwin, the threat of human degradation. By 1856 Lyell was desperately assuring himself that a brute ancestry was only ignoble or 'lowering' to people who denied an after-life. He kept trying to persuade himself that the future was important, not the past. Where was man's dignity anyway, given 'the hundreds of millions of savage or semi-barbarous races' and 'the millions of idiots & of the insane' born barely a step above the brute level? 'If a race of savages of the lowest capacity exist for 1000 years without progress, why not a race intermediate between them & the Chimpanzee.'

Lyell turned the issues over and over in his notebook, agonizing about the moral consequences. For all his twisting and turning, he still feared that humanity would lose its noble 'rank' and submerge in brutal nature. Could nature 'evolve the rational out of the irrational'? This was the crux. Fighting off feelings of 'moral repugnance,' he sought to rationalize man's ape ancestry. Think of a 'sensible Man . . . born of two idiotic parents.' Surely this was no different from a savage born of brutes? Think of Shakespeare's birth from ordinary mortals. He kept reworking it into his own terms – the emergence of genius, of greatness. And what heralded the birth of this exalted being – Man – on the earth? No one believed that the 'front of heav'n was full of fiery shapes.' But the more he tried to see man stealing quietly into the world, the more he wanted a miraculous moral moment when 'a responsible soul' first appeared.[4]

The rise from savagery to Shakespearean nobility was a comforting crumb to the Victorian gentry. But it was a short step to the racist slurs that Darwin was already hearing. Given the dinner-table wisdom that genteel Anglo-Saxons towered above their black butlers, evolution cast a shadow over ancestral purity. Lyell himself was irresistibly drawn to the theme: go back umpteen generations and would blacks and whites find a common ancestor? Itself the descendant of an ape? The very idea 'w^d. give a shock to . . . nearly all men.' No university would sanction it; even teaching it 'w^d. ensure the expulsion of a Prof. already installed.' Race was blowing up as an emotive issue in the 1850s. The hardbitten Robert Knox (he of the Burke and Hare scandal) achieved a new notoriety by his doom-mongering about coming racial wars. He made the races separate species. Others like

Louis Agassiz made them separate Creations; and one of Darwin's contacts thought it 'fortunate for those of us who respect our ancestors & repudiate even the contamination of Negro blood – that Agassiz remains, to do battle with the transmutationists.' Darwin instantly confessed his evolutionary 'heresy' as a rebuke, declaring himself 'as bad as the worst.' But this deep-rooted racism left no doubt that evolution threatened more than one cultural taboo. He knew that Agassiz 'will throw a boulder at me, & many others will pelt me.'[5]

It wasn't only Lyell who was moving. Others were cautiously coming round. Darwin was struck by 'the change in Hookers & Huxley's opinions on species during the last few years.' Like Lyell, Hooker still put up objections, wondering why duplicate species did not evolve under similar conditions, but Darwin swept them aside, repeating that he attributed 'very little to the direct action of climate.' By now he had no truck whatever with the radicals' environmentalism; life neither lifted itself nor was moulded by its surroundings. His brand of competitive evolution would not have appealed to the Hookers and Huxleys if he had. But he was still edgy, his nerves jagged; it was a terrifying feeling, knowing that he was about to break ranks with the Anglican élite and go public. He could not stop thanking Hooker for all his help: 'my Book may be wretched,' but 'you have done your best to make it less wretched. Sometimes I am in very good spirits & sometimes very low about it. My own mind is decided on the question of origin of species but good Heavens how little that is worth.'[6]

He was focusing again on his original target audience: it was not to be a flimsy paper, nor a racy, unreferenced pot-boiler like *Vestiges*. Only a technical treatise would do, one that piled on cumulative layers of evidence. Nothing less would convert the reforming tyros making their way up the Royal Society ladder.

All the while he kept his teeth in the continent-makers, especially in an impenitent Hooker. He fretted and fumed, unable to 'get the subject out of my head.' While continents rise and sink, willy-nilly, 'scarcely anything is known of means of distribution.' As he worked up the section on dispersal he ploughed on with his counter-experiments. He was not past salting frog spawn, or floating snails' eggs, however unsuccessfully. Eventually he noticed that hatchling snails will crawl on to a dead duck's foot, where they can live for a day or so out of water. It set off another train of experiments. Snails were not floating, he guessed; birds were flying them to their island destinations. As for plants, he was still trying to show how Hooker's

Edwardsia and other species could end up in New Zealand and South America but nowhere else. Hooker plied him with exotic seeds, goaded on occasions: 'I believe you are afraid to send me a ripe *Edwardsia* pod,' Darwin chivied him, 'for fear I sh^d float it from N[ew]. Zealand to Chile!!!'[7]

But difficulties were piling up all around. The salting had already hit a serious snag. Although many seeds survived, almost all of them had sunk. Without being able to stay afloat, they could not drift to distant shores. It seemed insuperable, and he cursed the 'horrid seeds.' 'I have been taking all this trouble in salting the ungrateful rascals for nothing.' He adopted a fall-back position; branches buoyed up by fruit and pods, he assumed, were washed down the rivers and out to the islands. Even this hypothesis was soon in tatters. He kept fruit-laden plants in sea-water 'with sorrowful result.'[8] Within a month they were rotting at the bottom of his tank. He was becoming disconsolate.

He began casting around for other mechanisms; perhaps ice-floes. Or ducks' feet again – it sounded laughable, but from a 'table-spoon-full of mud' out of a pond he raised twenty-nine plants. Once word got around, the strangest things started arriving by post. 'I have just had a parcel of partridges feet well caked with mud!!!,' he reported, triumphant. Eight-year-old Franky suggested ghoulishly that he try floating a dead well-fed bird. 'No sooner said, than done: a pigeon has floated for 30 days in salt water with seeds in crop & they have grown splendidly.' Of course, he admitted, scavengers would eat the corpse '999 [times] out of a thousand' but 'one might escape: I have seen dead land birds in sea-drift.' Nature was not looking quite so recalcitrant.

Seed-eating birds suggested another line of off-beat experiments. He began collecting birds' droppings. He poked through them microscopically, tweezered out the undigested seeds and germinated them. And there were still more tortuous methods of transport to be investigated. He fed oats to fish, and imagined herons flying off with their catches to some distant island. While many tests went well, others were a wash-out. Everything 'has been going wrong,' he exclaimed on one occasion: 'the fan-tails have picked the feathers out of the Pouters in their Journey home – the fish at the Zoological Gardens after eating seeds would spit them all out again – Seeds will sink in salt-water – all nature is perverse & will not do as I wish it.'[9]

The first chapter – on stock breeding and artificial selection – was left unfinished as he carried on measuring and experimenting. He kept buying pigeons – scanderoons, and polands, and laughers (who wouldn't laugh) – and now had ninety or so. Skins were arriving from every continent, and sometimes birds too: 'I have just had Pigeons & Fowls *alive* from the Gambia!' he informed an astonished Fox. The 'blessed Pigeons' were invaluable, providing him with a wonderful analogy of descent. He waded through innumerable old records to 'trace the gradual changes in the Breeds,' searching, in effect, the fancy's own 'fossil' record, tracking the races back to a wild ancestor.

The next chapter stayed with domestication and was complete by 13 October. The fragment on distribution was ready, too, and he warned Hooker, 'you unfortunate wretch,' that it was about to land in his lap. Three days later he handed it over during a Royal Society meeting, wanting to know, in his disarming fashion, 'how *atrociously* bad it is,' for it was certainly 'too long, & dull, & hypothetical.'[10] He would finally learn whether his pottering had paid off, and if his ideas could satisfy the 'King of Sceptics.'

While in town he took the opportunity to test another of his grisly dispersal ideas at the zoo. He had brought up some dead sparrows, their crops stuffed with oats, and fed them to a bateleur eagle and snowy owl, whose regurgitated pellets he then took home. 'The Hawks have behaved like gentlemen,' he reported to Hooker, and a few seeds survived the eagle's gastric juices. 'Hurrah!,' he shouted after planting a whole owl's pellet, 'a seed has just germinated after $21\frac{1}{2}$ hours' in its stomach. This, he announced, with a mite less than his usual precision, 'w^d carry it, God knows how many miles.' Here, then, was 'an effective means of distribution of any seed eaten by any Birds.' Seeds did not have to blow across a mythical land mass; they could hitch a macabre lift.

Hooker wobbled and wavered as he read the manuscript, 'delighted & instructed,' suddenly getting Darwin's drift, and a clearer picture 'of *change*.' 'I never felt so shaky about species before,' he finally confided. He pencilled comments, and found bits 'rather stiff reading,' but he did not, as Darwin feared, suggest the lot be burnt. Ice-age migrations he was not sure about, but iceberg transport he accepted. The verdict was '*incomparably* more favourable' than Darwin had anticipated. He came up to town one lunchtime – not for long, Emma was soon due – to talk more. He continued pressing points that Hooker had still not grasped. The critical one was that 'external conditions do *extremely* little.' It was the selection of '*chance*' variations that resulted in a new species. Selection in dense-population struggles depended more on competition among 'associates' than the environment.[11]

The book was progressing, but it exacted a mental toll. Having gone for a huge tome, he now groaned at the prospect. 'I find to my sorrow it will run to quite a big Book.' He was palling, complaining that the labour 'tries me a good deal & sets my heart palpitating.' As he staggered under its weight, the old symptoms began to return. 'Charles's health,' as Emma had long recognized, was 'always affected by his mind,' and his mind was in turmoil.[12] He feared he would break down, swamped with work. He was on a knife's edge and in need of the water cure.

But Emma, who now found even writing a letter 'a considerable exertion,' came first, at least until the baby was born. Other duties were also pressing. Her octogenarian aunt Sarah (the last of the elder Josiah Wedgwood's children), who still lived shut away in the village, had become crippled on fracturing her thigh in September. She died suddenly on 6 November, leaving Charles to arrange the funeral and cope with a house full of uncles. At the graveside, he reported sadly, the Revd Innes 'did not read [the] very impressive service well' and the old servants cried a lot. Then everyone went back to Petleys for the reading of the will. Aunt Sarah's property was to be sold, with Charles seeing to the auction. On the 22nd all the children but William, who was still at Rugby, traipsed down to the grand old house one last time for a farewell tea party. How they would miss the place, with Mrs Morrey's gingerbread and Martha Hemmings's songs. Etty felt specially bereaved; it was her first big emotional loss since Annie. Now thirteen, she had a cold that weekend, and it got worse. The doctor said it was a 'low fever' and recommended that she should have breakfast in bed for a spell.[13]

Two weeks later, just before the sale, Emma had her sixth son, Charles Waring. Her sister Elizabeth was again in attendance, and it was, as always, a tense time. With all the talk now of chloroform's dangers, Charles gave Emma less than usual – nothing like the hour-and-a-half's worth he had used at first. In fact, 'I never gave it till she shri[e]ked out for it,' he confided, comparing notes after Hooker's fourth child was born some months later. Wollaston congratulated Darwin on 'the addition of another ♂ to your vivarium.' As it sank in that the child was 'born without its full share of intelligence,' Darwin must indeed have felt trapped in capricious Nature's cage, one of her monstrous experiments in fertility and futility.[14]

The auction of Aunt Sarah's property took place on 9-10 December, admission by ticket only. He watched her carriage go for £11, her 'American clock' for twice its purchase price, then vases, an arm-chair . . . a lifetime's prized possessions. She had lived in 'Spartan simplicity,' dispensing her fortune to the needy, and thus she died. No tablet was to be erected; her *largesse* would perpetuate her memory. The remnant of Josiah Wedgwood's wealth, the last legacy from England's first great industrialist, was to be passed on to numerous charities, with a bit for the servants. Such was the time-honoured obligation of the rich: to sustain life's casualties, without regard for the necessity of Nature's wastage.[15]

Through the births and deaths and illness Darwin ploughed on with chapter three. By now any 'satisfaction in writing' was destroyed by the 'tiresome' length of the manuscript. However brutally he chopped and condensed, it grew hopelessly. This latest chapter on 'fertility & sterility,' he grumbled to Hooker, had 'run out to 100 pages M.S., & yet I do not think I have put in anything superfluous.' He had. He threw in everything, from Huxley's hermaphrodite jellyfish to bees and cross pollination – example after example, the whole designed to wear down resistance by attrition, to prove that outbred offspring fare better in the 'severe struggle for existence.'[16] But then it was a subject close to his heart.

Family inbreeding had long worried him. There were now four first-cousin marriages between the Darwins and Wedgwoods, with his and Emma's own. Of the ten Darwin children, two had died young from natural causes and the signs were ominous for the rest: George was sick and home from school, Etty languished in bed every morning, Lizzy still behaved strangely, and the baby was not normal. Charles believed that the main problem was hereditary: that his own constitutional weakness had been passed on, accentuated by Emma's Wedgwood blood. The struggle for existence had already set in, and he expected the children's health to fail at any time. Nine or so was the critical age; that was when Annie became so ill. Since her death the thought had put him through agonies, and he waited for nature to exploit the fatal flaw. All of them except William, who was nearly seventeen, were potential victims.

In the book he belaboured the 'evil' effects of inbreeding and the good effects of crossing. As always, he was looking for moral meaning: birth, death, and chronic illness needed some rationale, and Nature provided it. 'When relations unite,' there is a 'decrease in . . . general vigour' and an increased likelihood of 'infirmity' among the offspring. The struggle for existence then inevitably takes its toll, and the Darwin children were not immune. It was often hard to see the good, but Nature was working for a better world. 'The survivors' were the more 'vigorous & healthy, & can most enjoy life.' He finished chapter three the week after the auction, rounding off by debunking the radicals' benign population studies and vindicating Malthus's pessimistic work.[17] There was no escaping Nature's ruthless scythe, and no virtue in the attempt.

He knew he was overworking. His nerves were stretched, his heart still palpitating. Fox had tried Gully's water cure for his lumbago a few months earlier and had checked Annie's headstone while he was there. Charles had never even seen 'our poor dear child's grave,' and the thought of Malvern brought back such bitter memories that he went off the water cure. He tried alternative remedies, sipping concoctions of acids on the chance that his gastric juices needed strengthening. But still he was overwhelmed. The book was growing out of all proportion; pigeon skins were 'flocking in from all parts of the world,' and snails, too.[18] He wondered how long he could hold out.

Just before Christmas he cannibalized his twenty-year-old transmutation notebooks, sorting the pages into thirty or forty large portfolios, ready to be reworked. It was indeed a season for reflection, and a quiet one too. Lady Lubbock had offered to take the noisy younger boys after the baby was born, but the staff managed to subdue them, allowing Emma to recover peacefully. Etty, too, remained in her bed each morning; Lizzy was as silent as a mouse. William and George spent Christmas in London with Fanny's and Hensleigh's boys, returning on the 27th for William's birthday. George was full of first-term talk from Clapham Grammar School, where he had been sent in August to get a grounding in maths and science under the Revd Charles Pritchard (his father's Cambridge contemporary). As 1856 waned, they all said goodbye to their governess Miss Thorley. After ten years, it was her last holiday with them.[19]

Darwin pushed on into 1857, analysing the plant data supplied by Hooker, Watson, and Gray. He filled 300 foolscap sheets with tabulations to prove that wide-ranging 'large genera,' those containing many species, were expanding and the 'manufacturing' sites of varieties. The chapter on variation, finished at the end of January, was another case of bludgeoning by bountiful instances. But then, 'I am like Croesus overwhelmed with my riches in facts,' and the overwhelming was intended to carry over.[20]

A week on and he was well into 'The Struggle for Existence.' Here he would show how the variants were weeded, how endless numbers fell in the 'War of Nature.' His new theory of divergence created a chilling image. Nature became a seething slum, with everyone scrambling to get out, rushing to break from the rat-pack. Only the few survived, bettering themselves by creating new dynasties. Most remained trapped on the breadline, destined to struggle futilely, neighbours elbowing one another aside to get ahead, the weak trampled underfoot. Sacrifice and waste were endemic, indeed necessary. Nature was abortive, squandering, profligate. Her failures were discarded like the breeder's runts to rot on some domestic dump. In Victorian poor-law society, the image did not seem unduly sombre.

There was a baseness about it all. At one point, he was trying to prove that hermaphrodite jellyfish cross-fertilize (rather than impregnate themselves). It had to happen, he believed, to keep the species vigorous – just as cross-breeding was good for human beings. He taxed Huxley, suggesting that the water washing into the mouths of jellies contained the sperm. This was a soft lob from a straight man. 'The indecency of the process is to a certain extent in favour of its probability,' Huxley shot back in his ribald way, 'nature becoming very *low* in all senses amongst these creatures.' Darwin shared the lewd remark with Hooker. Nature's depravity cried out against a noble Providence; good grief, Darwin spurted in the next breath, 'What a book a Devil's Chaplain might write on the clumsy, wasteful, blundering low & horridly cruel works of nature!'[21]

But he was the one in the mocking surplice now, perched in his Down House pulpit; and the protracted sermon he was writing would read like a grim indictment: progress through pain, life from death. He had seen it all at first-hand. So had others, if they were honest. It should not be hard to convince a Church Establishment of the savagery beneath Nature's surface, any more than of the brutishness of London's slum dwellers. (Everyone had been reading Henry Mayhew's monumental dossier, *London Labour and the London Poor*, even Darwin.) Look at the carnage in the Crimea – it was finally sinking in, vividly brought home by the gaslight photographs being exhibited in London. Who could doubt old Erasmus Darwin's line 'One great slaughter-house the warring world!' Even Tennyson's 'Nature, red in tooth and claw,' was shrieking against a complacent creed.[22]

How different from Archdeacon Paley's 'happy' nature in his *Natural Theology*. The world had been turned upside down in fifty years. Seen through Paley's rose-tinted spectacles, it was a continual summer's afternoon, with the rectory garden buzzing with contented life. But no longer. An expanding industrial society meant that more and more people were herded, hungry and angry, into factory towns.

Those on the sharp end had been hammering away at Paley's image for ages. Working-class agitators had denounced Paley's pernicious justification of the status quo. George Holyoake had long ago written *Paley Refuted in His Own Words*, after his two-year-old daughter died of malnutrition.[23] At Downe Darwin peered hard into nature's 'horridly cruel' face; the time had come for him too to challenge Paley, whose words he had once embraced.

Seen through Malthusian spectacles, the parsonage garden became a battlefield. 'One may well doubt this,' he allowed, when viewing 'the contented face of a bright landscape or a tropical forest glowing with life;'

> ... & at such periods most of the inhabitants are probably living with no great danger hanging over them & often with a superabundance of food. Nevertheless the doctrine that all nature is at war is most true. The struggle very often falls on the egg & seed, or on the seedling, larva & young; but fall it must sometime in the life of each individual, or more commonly at intervals on successive generations & then with extreme severity.[24]

It had to if reproductive rates were totted up. When one sea-slug could lay 600,000 eggs (he had calculated the figure on the Falklands), only wholesale destruction could stop the South Atlantic being over-run.

He was writing up his Malthusian case on 23 February when Capt. FitzRoy and his new wife came to lunch. FitzRoy had known enough grief – his first wife had died, and recently his only daughter – but believing in a beneficent Providence who ordains nature's economy, he could hardly have sympathized with this harsh view. Others fully shared if not sympathized with Darwin's secret now. Fox remained a mainstay, warning him against overworking and recommending holidays, fearing that nature's scythe would cut down his cousin. Of course Darwin could not leave his salted snails and frogs, his pigeons and seeds. The book, Fox heard, was huge, and even Darwin wondered if he would survive to see it in print.

He was in a dilemma: desperate for recognition, yet fearing it; dreading death, yet looking for a form of release. 'I wish I could set less value on the bauble fame, either present or posthumous,' he maundered, 'yet, if I know myself, I would work just as hard, though with less gusto, if I knew that my Book w^d be published for ever anonymously.'[25] In short, he felt a sense of mission; he believed implicitly in his self-imposed task.

31

What Would A Chimpanzee Say?

His FEARS WERE hardly assuaged by the mandarins of science manoeuvring around him. Before getting a word into print, obstacles were appearing in his path. Lyell might have reconciled himself to humans stealing into the world, born – somehow – of ape parents, but Owen had not.

Richard Owen had probably dissected more apes than any man, and he had always used his results to crush treacherous theories of human origins. He met the threat again in 1849, shortly after the missionary Thomas Savage announced that West Africa housed another, still unknown ape, huge and 'indescribably fierce' – the gorilla. By now Owen was being pestered by a new class of dissidents, the Chapmans and Spencers, and the author of the *Vestiges*. Evidently some stronger antidote was needed, and he reassured audiences that the 'villainous low' ape-features, as Lyell called them – the overhanging brows and stabbing canines – were not modifiable. Man was not an ape descendant.

Owen had acquired four gorilla skulls, covered in sacred tribal marks, from an old sea captain. The taints of barbarism were easily washed off, but not the feeling that this was a 'peculiarly forbidding' creature, with a 'scowling physiognomy' that mocked humanity in sinister caricature. The gorilla became a crucial pawn. Owen's whole speech before the British Association in 1854 centred on the impossibility of apes standing erect and being counted men. The brute could not transmute; man was safe, his dignity assured. But the pressure continued. Even Darwin had sounded Owen out on transmutation (and found him 'vehemently opposed'), and by 1857 Owen must have known that he was writing a book on the subject.[1]

'Gorilla' suddenly became a household word in the late 1850s.

There was a flurry of interest in this new black-skinned ape, whipped up by salacious stories, macabre tales of ferocity and woman-snatching. To glimpse any ape in captivity was a thrill. Because of the East India Company trade, baby chimps and orangs had arrived intermittently at Bristol docks, to be snapped up by zoos. But never a gorilla; in fact nobody in Europe had seen one alive. Only in 1855 could crowds finally gawk at this grotesque beast. Wombwell's travelling menagerie, which paid the top prices at the docksides to ensure star attractions, managed to obtain a young female.[2] The show trooped hundreds of miles that year, from the West Country through Oxford up to Yorkshire. At the head marched a brass band, with trumpeting elephants, and the noisy parade attracted huge crowds.

But the gorilla's début, among the milling, unwashed masses, could only heighten fears about the bestialization of man. Respectable savants disdained the razzmatazz and worried about the consequences. As well they might, judging by the gutter press. Already working-class militants, latching on to anything to back their cry that 'man is nothing' in an impersonal universe, were heralding his monkey origin.[3]

This kind of provocation needed a firm rebuff. Like Lyell, Owen feared that man would lose his high-born status in creation. And the scholars who dabbled in transmutation only inflamed the situation, arming the militants. This was treachery. Such faulty science had to be stamped on with an iron heel, and Owen was the one to do it. By now he had a European reputation; he had just taken the Royal Society's Copley Medal, Oxford University had awarded him an honorary Doctorate, and the French government the Légion d'Honneur. He was well connected, attending ex-Chancellor Gladstone's breakfasts, and hob-nobbing with bishops and earls to an extent that infuriated the young Turks. (He was already living in a 'royal house' in Richmond Park, granted him by the Queen.)[4] In 1857 he was President-elect of the British Association. Naturally it was to Owen – the trusted authority on apes – that the squires of science turned. They wanted reassurance about the gorilla.

Owen was no reactionary. He now announced that Creation was constantly sustained, an ongoing event. Clumsily, he called it a process of 'ordained continuous becoming,' without going into particulars. This looked like a sort of providential evolution. Yet he was loath to let a gorilla transmute into a human. He envisaged more of a Creative leap, but he needed proof. Others wondered where he was going to find it. Worried divines would question him about the gorilla's similarity to humans. What 'places man so far above brutes?'

one asked. Do the nerves and muscles make the human hand and tongue unique, 'or is the mind working on almost the same anatomy?'[5] It was a morally loaded question, and he had to handle it carefully.

Owen needed some factor that would allow him to classify man apart, and he found it in the brain. He had been studying ape brains for a generation, and being 'so great an authority,' Darwin scoffed, he 'ought to be right.' In 1857 he announced that humans possess a unique lobe, the hippocampus minor, and cerebral hemispheres that are larger than any other mammal's, completely covering the cerebellum. Because of this, man should stand in a special sub-class, one reserved for him alone. He was as different from a chimp as the ape was from a platypus. Darwin was incredulous and threw up his hands: 'I cannot swallow Man' being *that* 'distinct from a Chimpanzee.' Then he asked, in his blithely brilliant way, 'I wonder what a Chimpanzee w^d. say to this?'[6]

Darwin's pace was now visibly slackening. Illness cut his working day 'ridiculously short,' and he despaired of finishing. He plodded on with chapter six, 'Natural Selection.' This looked at which of the competing variants 'shall live & which die.' At the font of life – in the expanding, huge genera moving out across the world – Nature was ruthless, sifting and selecting, picking the most 'profitable.' She was the paramount pigeon-fancier, a supra-mundane snail selector. Infinitely superior to the little Spitalfields weavers, 'she cares not for mere external appearance; she may be said to scrutinise with a severe eye, every nerve, vessel & muscle; every habit, instinct, shade of constitution ... The good will be preserved & the bad rigidly destroyed.' Her 'productions bear the stamp of a far higher perfection.' 'By nature,' he put in as an afterthought, 'I mean the laws ordained by God to govern the Universe.'[7]

He was on to the causes of variation when the crunch came. Croesus was suffocating under his riches, with no one to rescue him. In March Etty's complaints worsened; Emma took her to Hastings for a month to breathe the sea air, leaving him alone. Finally, after a few days, the 'everlasting species-Book' just overwhelmed him. 'It is beyond my powers,' he cried to Lyell. A year before, Fanny Allen had seen him as 'fresh and sparkling as the purest water.' Now he was washed out, a wreck, in need of a tonic, slapping towels and slooshing baths to invigorate the system. He needed to top up with mineral water (being bottled commercially at Malvern by this time). He could not think of going to Malvern, though; the thought of Annie stabbed his heart.[8]

He settled on a 'fortnight of hydropathy & rest' at Dr Edward Lane's establishment closer by. It was on the rolling Farnham heathland, about forty miles away across the patchwork-quilt landscape of the south of England. At the luxurious Moor Park estate, once home to Jonathan Swift, patients could rest up, relax, and wander the warm sandy heaths. Lane was another Edinburgh medical man, like Gully, but still in his early thirties, and an MD of barely three years: 'too young,' Darwin reckoned, but 'that is his only fault.' More to the point, 'he is a Gentleman & very well read.' Nor did he 'believe in all the rubbish which D^r. G. does,' the clairvoyance and clap-trap, even if Darwin had to endure his dottier patients' crotchets. Darwin became attached very quickly. The doctor had made a good marriage, to Lady Drysdale's daughter, and Darwin thought them 'some of the nicest people, I have ever met.'

Lane found Darwin much as Gully had, and was as surprised at his condition. 'I cannot recall any [case] where the pain was so truly poignant as his. When the worst attacks were on he seemed almost crushed with agony.' But they were so stoically borne, and Darwin's 'sweetness and gentleness' showed in the 'gratitude with which he received the most ordinary services.'[9] Lane made him give up snuff but, despite that, away from the pressures of home and the crippling workload, Darwin rather enjoyed himself. The walks were wonderful among the secluded pines and silver birches bordering the heath. He dismissed the patients as a dull lot, but Lane remembered him roaring at jokes around the dinner table, and taking to a garrulous Irish lady and her ghost stories, because she also put salt on the tablecloth to pinch with her bread.

A week into the treatment and he was effervescing. What 'an amount of good,' he burbled to Hooker. It is 'quite unaccountable. – I can walk & eat like a hearty Christian; & even my nights are good. – I cannot in the least understand how hydropathy can act as it certainly does on me. It dulls one's brain splendidly, I have not thought about a single species of any kind, since leaving home.' Then followed a screed on hairy Alpine plants that rather belied the point. Still, he was now sure of his science: 'I sometimes despise myself as a poor compiler,' he mused, 'though I do *not* despise my whole work, as I think there is enough known to lay a foundation for the discussion on origin of species.'[10]

Others did too. Alfred Russel Wallace had been in touch from the opposite side of the world and was now working for Darwin, sending him the skins of domestic fowl. 'The carriage is costing me a fortune!' Darwin moaned, but that was the price of having a first-rate collector in the Far East. He wrote a cheery letter to Wallace from Moor Park, thanking him for his encouragement. 'I can plainly see that we have thought much alike & to a certain extent have come to similar conclusions.' This was to reassure Wallace, feeling rather cut off and fearing that his paper on the introduction of species (which Darwin was partly going on) had been ignored. But the pleasantry had a deeper motive too. He continued:

> This summer will make the 20th year (!) since I opened my first-note-book, on the question how & in what way do species & varieties differ from each other . . . I am now preparing my work for publication, but I find the subject so very large, that . . . I do not suppose I shall go to press for two years . . . It is really *impossible* to explain my views in the compass of a letter . . . but I have slowly adopted a distinct & tangible idea, – whether true or false others must judge.[11]

Wallace – Creationist or not – was receiving the nicest kind of trespass notice. Shrewdly, Darwin staked his claim without giving his case away.

Like the blessed chloroform, the hot heathlands anaesthetized Darwin's brain. And yet, he began to see them as no other patient did. The sanatorium had been deliberately sited on the heath for its serenity. But what was serene to most was a battle zone to him. He began to notice that fenced areas had tall sapling firs, whereas those on the open heath were stunted, browsed by the cattle. He was ruminating again on the checks and balances, the turbulence beneath the tranquillity. One gnarled fir, grazed for twenty-six years (he counted the growth rings), was still only three inches high. 'What a wondrous problem it is, – what a play of forces, determining the kinds & proportions of each plant in a square yard of turf!' Not even a sanatorium could provide an escape from the killing fields. There was no safe haven; his obsession was transforming the world around him.

He came home with a cold in early May ready for a fresh assault. He pushed on into his huge chapter on variations, trying to find some reason for their appearance. Even when he mooted one in animals – noting that it was the abnormally developed organs in barnacles that tended to be most variable – he had to run Hooker's gauntlet to prove it in plants.[12] He also looked with fresh eyes on his own meadow, experimentally seeded with sixteen kinds of competing plants. They were smothering one another on such a scale that he doubted whether more than one would survive to flower.

A few days later Emma arrived back from Hastings with Etty, clearly 'not one bit better.' They were just in time to celebrate Horace's sixth birthday and begin receiving a house full of guests. A troop of Wedgwood cousins were due, and Charles's sisters Susan and Catherine. A week afterwards Down House was groaning. There were ten children and six adults, not counting the staff and extra servants who catered for the crowd. 'A good lot too many,' Charles lamented, 'now poor dear Etty is so indifferent.' They had all come for the christening of his namesake, the defective baby Charles, which took place on the 21st in the parish church. Darwin's cold 'suddenly turned into my old vomiting,' and he was back to square one. It was all 'very disheartening.' The work, the worry, the crush – it destroyed in a fortnight all 'the wonderful good which Moor Park did me.' His health had vanished 'like a flash of lightning.'[13]

There was only one thing to be done. Both invalids had to go back to Dr Lane's: first Etty with Emma on the 29th, and when Emma returned two weeks later, Charles would 'relieve guard' and join Etty, who was staying there all summer. Still he pressed on, piecing together one after another of 'my *many* horrid puzzles,' declaring that 'I would sooner be the wretched contemptible invalid, which I am, than live the life of an idle squire.' He dropped a letter to the *Gardeners' Chronicle* about dun-coloured ponies, trying to fathom the origin of the domestic horse, and then readmitted himself to the sanatorium.

Here he continued his half-begging, self-mocking letters, eliciting information while converting the donor – softening up breeders to obtain gulliver runts (pigeons) and softening up old presbyterians like Asa Gray at the Harvard herbarium: 'It is extremely kind of you to say that my letters have not bored you very much, & it is almost *incredible* to me, for I am quite conscious that my speculations run beyond the bounds of true science.' Or, at least, true science as then was. He played backgammon with Etty every day, watching her tenderly for fear that he would have to relive the Malvern tragedy all over again. But no, she seemed to be getting her strength back, and Charles returned to Downe on 30 June much happier.[14] Back to the grindstone; back to the old problem – the laws of variation.

It was turning into a long, hot summer – the time of the Indian Mutiny: an 'Indian Summer' when he should have been in his meadow, watching his pigeons, salting his snails, not sitting indoors. He finally finished 'variation' in July and posted pages to Huxley for checking. He was still trying to relate foetal divergence and the distinctness of species – trying to put some embryological muscle behind his theory. Huxley agreed that the more distinct the adults, the earlier their embryos begin to differ. But Darwin had also cited French opinion that the specialized organs appear first in the foetus. Huxley would have none of this. The body is like a house, he laughed; the builder starts with the walls and rafters, not 'the cornices, cupboards, & grand-piano.' The point was taken. With a sigh Darwin expunged the passages, 'which I rather grieve about, as I wished it to be true; but alas a scientific man ought to have no wishes, no affections, – a mere heart of stone.'[15]

Clearly, it was a case of two steps forward, and one back. He was still tabulating the ratio of varieties in plants a week later when young Lubbock spotted 'the grossest blunder' in one of his assumptions, which cost him '2 or 3 weeks lost work.' He had to borrow the plant catalogues and start all over again. 'I am the most miserable, bemuddled, stupid Dog in all England,' he howled. From then on he paid Downe's 'laboriously careful Schoolmaster,' Ebenezer Norman, to do the tabulating in his free time.[16] And Hooker too went to pains to help.

Others offered aid. Gray supplied details on American plants. He was not only a 'cautious . . . reasoner,' but clearly a 'loveable man;' and Darwin, at the risk of seeming 'horribly egotistical,' now told him what he was up to. He ran through his twenty-year labour, ending up: 'As an honest man I must tell you that I have come to the heterodox conclusion that there are no such things as independently created species – that species are only strongly defined varieties. I know that this will make you despise me.' How species changed from their ancestral stock, he had come to understand from the 'agriculturists & horticulturists.' 'I believe I see my way pretty clearly on the means used by nature to change her species and *adapt* them.' Hooker, he said, had already read his section on geographical distribution and 'had never been so much staggered about the permanence of species.'[17]

Gray was fascinated, admitting his long-held belief 'that there is some law, some power inherent in plants,' causing variants to appear. 'I suppose this is your starting point,' he ventured – and then asked 'can you get at the *law* of variation'? This was Darwin's cue. He knew that Gray had not cottoned on; they had similar interests but were working on separate lines. On 5 September he did what he told Wallace was impossible in a letter. He sent Gray a detailed account of his views, explaining the difficulties he faced, the 'frightful' problems of embryology, facts which had kept him orthodox the longest, and the impossibility of 'climate or Lamarckian habit' explaining them. He included an abstract of *Natural Selection*, as he had decided to call the book, copied out legibly by the schoolmaster. Gray digested it and warned him against personifiying 'Natural Selection,' making it a causal agent – Nature's Guiding Hand – when it simply described ways of winning life's race.[18]

Darwin swore Gray to secrecy, for fear that someone 'like the Author of the Vestiges' hear of his views and 'work them in.' Transmutation might no longer be rogue's terrain, but he was still afraid of a hack queering his pitch. Natural selection could be discredited for good. Darwin had to present it properly. He had to address the leaders of science with an original, authoritative tome. This was now more important than ever, because the 'mode of creation' was on their own agenda for the first time: teasers were appearing, questions being asked. The subject was even turning up in addresses to the Geological Society; quietly, perhaps, but it was there. Liberal Presidents were calling for unbiased attitudes towards the origin of new life: 'it is a speculation worthy of the exercise of the highest intelligence,' one had said earlier in 1857 – but 'let us avoid the fatal error of connecting the results of scientific enquiry with the articles of religious belief.' He admitted that the 'mode of creation' had once been 'proscribed from inquiry.'[19] But perhaps no longer. If the Geological, once a bastion of Oxbridge orthodoxy, was hearing rumbles, then things were really changing.

Darwin knew that he had to address this august body. He had to convince his peers that 'natural selection' was the evolutionary mode. He had the scientific standing to do it, and his words carried weight. Indeed, his status was increasing – the German Academy of Naturalists this autumn was the first European society to elect him a member. It made his job easier and harder: his words would command attention from the élite. They could not write him off as a crank, as they had his teacher Grant; or point out blunders, as they had in *Vestiges*. But that actually made him more dangerous in some eyes. His big book was aimed at the new specialists. He was recruiting treacherously, like a mole with impeccable old-boy credentials. This is how others judged it: 'my dear old friend Falconer,' he complained, 'attacked me most vigorously, but quite kindly, & told me "you will do more harm than any ten naturalists will do good" – "I can see that you have already *corrupted* & half-spoiled Hooker"(!!).' As he told Gray, 'when I see such strong feeling in my oldest friends, you need not wonder that I always expect my views to be received with contempt.'[20]

On the other hand the young guard – those who would support him – were becoming a force in their own right. Fired by Hooker, they were re-energizing the Linnean Society. This had just moved to Burlington House, Piccadilly, in the same prestigious block as the Royal Society. Huxley, Tyndall, and Hooker were still planning their own journal, and Huxley was busy arranging them a column in the *Saturday Review*. Darwin was held in high regard by the whole group. Huxley's praise for the barnacle books was unbounded: some of the most 'admirable' monographs ever published, he announced in his lectures in 1857. Here was the best sort of support; 'you will turn my head,' Darwin cooed.[21]

Huxley did not know the details of natural selection, but Darwin never missed a chance to push his pedigree approach. While Huxley retained strange views of nature's symmetry, embedding circles within circles, like a taxonomic Chinese puzzle, Darwin told him that the natural system of classification was 'simply genealogical.' And, he added, 'whenever heterodoxy becomes orthodoxy,' the realization 'will clear away an immense amount of rubbish about the value of characters . . . The time will come I believe, though I shall not live to see it, when we shall have very fairly true genealogical trees of each great kingdom of nature.' But a pugilistic Huxley was looking another way. He was still squaring up to Owen, looking for a fight. He doubted that a sound zoology was possible until the 'servile' Owen's science was scotched. Only then could a new phoenix rise from the ashes 'of the old Comparative Anatomy.' As for classifying, he missed the point entirely. The 'pedigree business' might be a matter of 'profound interest,' he granted, 'but to my mind it has no more to do with pure Zoology – than human pedigree has with the Census.'[22] Classification was a count of the living, not a family tree of the dead.

During the Indian summer carcasses continued to arrive (rabbits were now his passion) and the skeletonizing went on as usual. But Darwin was finishing up with pigeons. He even thought he might give his birds away the following year. Seeds were his new passion. He was trying 'to break their constitutions,' rearing them under coloured glass, trying to create 'monsters.' Minor monsters – mere varieties – nothing as grand as the deformed creatures aimed at by Geoffroy and his son Isidore in France. He asked Hooker if his botanical friends had ever tried '*inducing varieties* by playing tricks with plants? as by high manuring wild species; plucking all their flowers off for several years; pruning; &c.' After raising a plant with green flowers, Darwin reckoned he 'could make any flower in some degree monstrous in 4 or 5 generations.'[23]

459

The younger generation became involved. In Papa's spare time the boys helped him keep track of the flowers' friends, the humble bees, and to play tricks on them too. On Sandwalk strolls Charles had noticed that the bees interrupted their journeys and buzzed momentarily at the same places among the shrubs. He wondered what flight paths they took and why they stopped to buzz. This was the fourth summer he made observations with the children. Warm days around lunchtime were best. The boys crawled on their tummies like trainee cadets, tracking the bees under hedges and brambles. They mapped out the buzzing places, stationed themselves along the flight paths, and yelled 'Here is a bee!' as one passed. The calls carried down the line until the bee reached Charles. He found that the flight paths were the same year by year, and the buzzing places 'fixed within an inch.' Pulling up the undergrowth, or sprinkling white flour on a spot, made no difference.[24] The bees stayed on track. He never did fathom why they adopted fixed flight paths.

The boys were coming on. Franky was his father's shadow, good for all kinds of odd jobs in a house full of skinned animals and experimental plants. George, back from Clapham, would certainly be an engineer if homesickness did not get the better of him. And William was headed for Cambridge after another stint of tuition with a clergyman. Charles saw him as a barrister, the 'future Lord Chancellor of all England.' His annual allowance of £40 – 'nearly as much as Parslow's wages' – was only for basic expenses. Artistic outings, desk supplies, and his latest indoor hobby brought extra calls on the exchequer. The craze this summer was photography, and it was not cheap. Charles forked out for the equipment when William returned from Rugby in July. A room upstairs was set aside, and soon the boy was 'rushing up & down the House' grasping glass plates with 'dirty hands,' or poring over containers of chemicals.[25] In the autumn he would take up painting again.

Emma had her hands full too, even in Etty's absence. Horace was learning to read, using the story book that Emma had written for her Sunday school at Maer. All the children had heard about Jane doing Sally a good turn; about Mary and her mother going to market; about the lying child who was to ask God's forgiveness. Emma had sat patiently with each of them, instilling duty and literacy. But Horace it seemed would be the last, for baby Charles was backward and showed no sign of walking or talking. Though 'remarkably sweet' and affectionate, with a 'wicked little smile,' he was totally passive, and 'made strange grimaces & shivered, when excited.' He had a 'passion for Parslow,' and a special claim on his mother.[26]

55. Emma aged about fifty, after bearing her tenth child.

56. (*Below left*) Henrietta in her early teens, already an invalid. Over-whelmed by Annie's death she lived in morbid fear of illness. 57. (*Below right*) Elizabeth (b. 1847), the youngest daughter, quiet, nervous and dependent.

58. Richard Owen had been Darwin's friend, but the relationship turned sour.

59. (*Above*) Owen lecturing at Huxley's School of Mines in 1857. The deed caused a breach of diplomatic relations.

60. A gorilla skull, pictured by Owen in 1849, when he first described the beast. The ape's novelty ensured its emotive role in the Darwinian debate.

61. Alfred Russel Wallace, the young animal collector from the Malay Archipelago. His letter prompted Darwin to start writing the *Origin of Species*.

62. (*Below*) Ilkley Wells hydropathic hotel on the North Yorkshire moors, where Darwin was 'living in Hell' as he sent out advance copies of the *Origin*.

63. T. H. Huxley, lecturing on the gorilla. He made evolution serve his secular interests.

64. (*Inset*) Irishmen slurred as apes: 'Mr G-O'rilla,' a ranting national-ist editor. *Punch* asks, 'Shouldn't he be extinguished at once?'

DRESSING FOR AN OXFORD BAL MASQUÉ.

"THE QUESTION IS, IS MAN AN APE OR AN ANGEL? (*A Laugh.*) NOW, I AM ON THE SIDE OF THE ANGELS. (*Cheers.*)"—MR. DISRAELI'S *Oxford Speech, Friday, November 25.*

65. Disraeli as an angel, after the Tory Chancellor sided with Bishop Wilberforce at the Oxford Diocesan Society in 1864.

66. Down House from the rear in the 1860s. (The earliest known photograph.)

67. The family at home about 1863: from left to right, Leonard, Henrietta, Horace, Emma, Elizabeth, Francis, and a visitor.

68. The haggard paterfamilias in the 1860s, contemplating the *Descent of Man*.

69. (*Below*) The Down House staff in the late 1870s: included are Jackson the butler and his wife, John the coachman, Fred the groom, Tommy Price the under-gardener, Mrs Evans the cook, Jane the head housemaid with Harriet her assistant, and Mary Anne the nurse. The boy on the pony may be Charles's grandson, Bernard, who lived at Down.

70. The Sandwalk forty years after Darwin planted it.

71. Darwin, an excellent rider when young, posing on old Tommy in the late 1870s. He thought he looked like the postman and, inundated with mail, inscribed the photo, 'Hurrah – no letters today!'

72. The Darwin children, on holiday with their parents at Barmouth in 1869: left to right, Henrietta, Francis, Leonard (standing), Horace and Elizabeth.

A LOGICAL REFUTATION OF MR. DARWIN'S THEORY.

Jack (who has been reading passages from the "Descent of Man" to the Wife whom he adores, but loves to tease). "So YOU SEE, MARY, BABY IS DESCENDED FROM A HAIRY QUADRUPED, WITH POINTED EARS AND A TAIL. WE ALL ARE!"

Mary. "SPEAK FOR YOURSELF, JACK! I'M NOT DESCENDED FROM ANYTHING OF THE KIND, I BEG TO SAY; AND BABY TAKES AFTER ME. SO, THERE!"

IN THE HANDS OF THE SANSCULOTTES.

FAIN we would turn our eyes; spare easy blame;
　Nor take her plight for text wise saws to spin.
Has she passed through the famine, and the flame,
　By her endurance half redeemed her name
From its foul taint of wantonness and sin,
To sink to this extremity of shame!

If willing captive of this ruffian-swarm,
　How fallen—fair, frail Paris—from the pride
With which the harlot-houri plied her charm
Of beauty, weird and witch-like, and the harm
　Of those Circean spells that none defied,
But her sweet smile was potent to disarm.

Or if unwilling victim, blacker still
　Her infamy, and deeper yet her fall,
Whose nerveless arm and palsy-stricken will,
For fear of less enduring greater ill,
　Leave her of shameful fear the shameless thrall,
And, changeful in all else, a coward still.

Beneath the canopy of lurid smoke,
　Brooding above the blood that stains her stones,
Pale phantoms of old terror, new awoke,
The Furies of red Ninety-three invoke,
　All but the fiery hearts and trumpet tones
Of the wild zealots that the invader broke.

Out of the gathering woes—wherewith close bound,
　Like the scathed scorpion in its ring of fire,
Mad tail on helpless head writhes rancorous round,

Slaying and slain with suicidal wound,—
　Comes "*Vive la République!*" from those whose ire
Lays the Republic death-struck on the ground.

Till none can say if other hope remain,
　Than to seek shameful safety from the foe!
So dyeing deeper her disgrace's stain,
And turning all men's pity to disdain,
　Making us own her due in her worst woe,
And bidding those that smote her smite again.

WELL SAID, SIRE!

" I am impelled above all things to give expression to my humble thanks for the Historic Successes which have blessed the armies of Germany."
Emperor to the Reichstag, March 21.

A BRACE of approximate words well expresses
　The difference 'twixt Gallic idea and Teutonic:
The German aspires to Historic successes,
　The Frenchman's are nothing unless Histrionic.

A Case for the Police.

LAST Thursday night, as the family were retiring to rest about half-past ten o'clock, great consternation was caused in the household of two highly-respected maiden ladies residing in a genteel villa on the banks of the Thames, not five minutes walk from a railway station and omnibuses both to the City and West End, within a convenient distance of two packs of hounds, and in the centre of a good shooting country, by the alarming discovery of a thief in the—

A GREAT "MESS."—Our Army.

73. (*Above and opposite*) *Punch*'s political poke at the *Descent of Man*.
Bearded Jack teases Mary about her ancestry (left) while the rape of

LIBERTÉ
EGALITÉ
FRATERNITÉ

NATIONAL (BLACK) GUARDS.

Paris. "MURDER! THIEVES! HELP!!"

Paris during the commune in 1871 by hairy blackguards with pointed ears (right) suggests where such evolutionary nonsense must lead.

74. (*Above*) Ernst Haeckel (left) in 1867, the bombastic young biologist and leading advocate of Darwinism in Germany, who dubbed the Deity a 'gaseous Vertebrate'.

75. Pope Darwin, a lightning sketch on a letter from Huxley in 1868. He sought an audience for a visiting German naturalist, who wished to pay 'his devotions at the shrine of Mr. Darwin'.

THAT TROUBLES OUR MONKEY AGAIN.

Female descendant of Marine Ascidian:—"REALLY, MR. DARWIN, SAY WHAT YOU LIKE ABOUT MAN; BUT I WISH YOU WOULD LEAVE MY EMOTIONS ALONE!"

76. Darwin with his finger on the pulse of femininity. In *The Expression of the Emotions in Man and Animals* he wrote that 'a pretty girl blushes when a young man gazes intently at her' because she immediately thinks about the 'outer and visible parts' of her body, and this alters their 'capillary circulation'.

77. Uncle Ras, shortly before his death, with Darwin's sons: left to right, Horace, Leonard, Francis and William.

78. The new drawing-room, added to Down House in 1858. At the end of his life Darwin would enter wearily to see whether the clock went any faster than the one in his study.

79. Darwin's new study after 1881, hat and cape at the ready. Darwin wrote his last book on earthworms here, beneath portraits of Joseph Hooker, Charles Lyell and Josiah Wedgwood I.

80. (*Right*) Bernard (b. 1876), Charles and Emma's first grandchild, whose mother died in childbirth. He lived at Down House with Francis, his father, until after Darwin's death.

81. Darwin about 1874, photographed by his son Leonard.

Emma's kindness was known throughout the neighbourhood, however much her rectitude set her apart. The parish folk felt they could depend on her. Like a parson's wife, she ministered to them, giving bread tokens to the hungry, and 'small pensions for the old, dainties for the ailing, and medical comforts and simple medicines.' Having lost her sister Fanny and nursed her crippled mother, having married a broken-down gent and been almost permanently pregnant into her forties, she understood human suffering. Indeed, since Annie's death, sickness had been a way of life – illness was normal. She lived to make others comfortable, to soothe their pains. Down House was like a hospital for the occupants, and a dispensary for the parish, with Emma the staff nurse. She used Dr Darwin's old prescription book, translated with Charles's help, and offered her own remedies for croup, 'pain of cancer,' and 'weakly girls of 15 or 16.' The servants delivered the medicines, which the children would help make up; and all who received Emma's house-calls found her 'like a rock to lean on.'[27]

Charles, too, had acquired a reputation locally and was taking on new duties. While Emma prescribed opium and gin cordial, he was preparing to dispense justice. He had been approached by the Kent Commission of the Peace to join the ranks of squires and parsons on the bench. He accepted, even though it would cost time and energy he could ill afford. (Ironically, he had evaded jury service, 'incapable of the fatigue' of a single trial.) Becoming a Justice of the Peace consolidated his sense of worth; it spoke eloquently for his responsibility. It did for his social standing what the Royal Medal had done for his science. With testimonials from the Revd Innes and the former High Sheriff, Sir John Lubbock, he became a magistrate. On 3 July he swore on the Bible to 'Keep the Peace of one said Lady Queen in the said County, and to hear and determine divers felonies and also trespasses and other misdemeanours in the same County perpetrated.'[28] Who could 'despise' an evolutionist who pledged himself thus?

As if this were not enough for an overstressed man with an overstretched family, September found him extending the house. The crush of children, never mind the squash when the cousins came, made expansion imperative. Workmen began building a huge new dining-room with a bedroom above, essentially creating a north wing, and making them all 'jolly & big.' 'I often feel dreadfully ashamed of my extravagance,' he told everyone, but it was mock modesty. The £500 costs were easily absorbed by his £4200 investment income that year. The labourers had to keep the noise down outside the study as he pushed on with the book. 'I have been writing an audacious little discussion,' he said, alerting Hooker to a major point, 'to show that organic beings are not perfect, only perfect enough to struggle with their competitors.'[29] The fog over 'perfect adaptation' had long cleared and he explicitly rejected the idea. New adaptations could not be perfect, as the old theologians had taught, or there would be no competition, no selection, and no progress. Imperfection was Nature's rule – it seemed so obvious now.

And, lest he forget, Nature gave him a poignant jolt. A few days later, in the 'midst of brick & rubbish,' with labourers everywhere, seven-year-old Lenny collapsed. Emma rushed him upstairs to bed. Charles took his pulse and found it 'extremely irregular & feeble.' It was the wretched inheritance again, what Papa experienced as 'palpitations.' The 'darling little fellow' was failing '*exactly* as three of our children have before,' Hooker heard. Hoping it was 'something temporary,' but knowing how ruthlessly Nature targeted imperfections, Charles felt 'bitter' for weeks.[30]

What with the sanatorium, the children's health, the tabulations, seeds, and skeletonizing, two chapters had taken him six months: 'Pleasant prospect!' he said of the future. Nor was it getting any easier, with the house in a shambles. The plasterers left and the scaffolding came down half-way through a chapter on hybrids. Etty returned, better but still weak, and Lenny now had only occasional 'attacks,' so Charles indulged in a bit of luxury. He took himself off again to Moor Park in November for a week's recuperation. 'I only wanted rest,' he admitted to Hooker, and that he got in plenty. He 'took quite long walks & enjoyed the scenery like a gentleman at large.'[31] He tramped the countryside, enjoying the solitude, away from the children, the work, and the worry.

By Christmas Day 1857 the *Natural Selection* manuscript was piling up. 'I have just finished a tremendous job, my chapter on Hybridism,' he wrote to Hooker; 'it has taken me 3 months to write, after all facts collected together!' But he suffered from one chill feeling, which Lyell understood well. Wallace did too, even at the other end of the empire. He wrote from the Malay archipelago to ask whether *Natural Selection* would delve into human origins. For Darwin, discretion was imperative. He was sensitive to Lyell's fears about bestialization. He could see Owen tinkering with the brain, making man an impregnable fortress, a fit repository for an immortal soul. 'I think I shall avoid the whole subject, as so surrounded with prejudices,' Darwin replied, 'though I fully admit that it is the highest & most interesting problem for the naturalist.' Others knew that the subject could not be shirked. Lyell was asking crucial questions in his notebook: 'Mind & the Soul of Man will be found to be a development of the instinct of Animals?' Even Darwin found it difficult to keep man out. In his 'Instinct' chapter just starting, humans were thrown in pell-mell among the puppies, bees, and parasitic wasps. Infant habits, sneezing, old ladies dropping stitches, instinctive piano playing, all crept in almost unintentionally.[32] And yet the chapter continued the theme: instincts were inherited and modified by selection. If these examples stood, the implications for people would be obvious.

Darwin praised Wallace's collecting in the Far East. And he encouraged his theorizing, for 'without speculation there is no good & original observation.' But he did not really catch Wallace's drift and continued to assume that 'I go much further than you.' His proprietary attitude was also still clear. For twenty years he had been working on species; his book, 'about half written,' would contain 'a large collection of facts with one definite end,' but it remained 'too long a subject to enter on my speculative notions.' Secure in his non-competitive niche, Darwin added in leisurely fashion, 'I do not suppose I shall publish under a couple of years,' and he closed with the warm sentiment, 'May all your theories succeed.'[33] Not surprisingly, Wallace had now targeted him as a sympathizer, eager to hear speculations on the subject.

Expansive, bold books were cried out for in the age of empire and progress. Darwin, like the rest of Britain at the beginning of 1858, revelled in Henry Buckle's breathtaking *History of Civilisation in England*. The first volume, with 500 fancy-footnoted pages, caused a sensation. It 'is *wonderfully* clever and original,' Darwin thought. Buckle, the son of a wealthy merchant, was as devoted to London as Darwin was to Downe. He hitched history to the capital's mid-century mood. Barbarism, priestcraft, superstition were on the way out – 'the signs of the time are all around,' he announced. True religion was to believe in the 'one glorious principle of universal and undeviating regularity' taught by physical science.[34] All this made him a man after the *Westminster's* heart. Social improvement and morality were statistically and scientifically explicable without recourse to divine caprice. It was a song secularists had been singing for a long time, and now – as with *Vestiges* – Buckle's *History* was attracting huge high street sales.

Erasmus thought it wonderful: 'a clear, flowing, easy style,' the sort to aim for in *Natural Selection*. Charles eventually read the

History through twice, and once met 'the great Buckle' at Hensleigh Wedgwood's. But he was not too taken with the man, who was glib and garrulous and dominated the conversation. They were discussing the 'astonishing number of references' in the book when Charles miffed him by jumping up to hear pretty young Effie Wedgwood sing. 'Well Mr Darwin's books are much better than his conversation,' Buckle whispered, which Darwin topped by adding, 'What he really meant was that I did not properly appreciate his conversation.'[35]

All the scientific parvenus had heard Buckle, or knew him. He joined Spencer and Huxley on their Sunday afternoon strolls, and debated the emergence of morality with Tyndall. For Spencer the evolution of life and civilization was all of a piece. His second book, *Principles of Psychology*, already dealt with 'the genesis of mind in all its forms, sub-human and human.' Now he planned a ten-volume treatise that would take in everything else – all knowledge was to be systematized from 'the evolution point of view.'[36]

And yet Buckle's lionizing was not without its backlash. There was an unsettling cost for 'setting people thinking,' as Lyell recognized. Old fogies were 'up in arms,' frightened of the new secularism. Hooker had only just got Huxley into the Athenaeum in January, and now the two of them planned to introduce the rest, Tyndall, Busk, and Buckle. But the old gents blanched at the thought of Buckle and threatened to blackball him.[37]

If Darwin was comforted by the changing ethos, he sensed the greater uproar that would greet his own bold book. Buckle's unfinished epic was as massive, but nowhere near so controversial. It was the work of a dusty dilettante who had broken ranks with no one. *Natural Selection* would bear the name of a Royal Medallist, a county magistrate, a squire who had once trained for the Church. And in March it was nearing completion. After twenty-three months, Darwin had done with chapter ten. That put him two-thirds of the way through, with a quarter of a million words.[38] The finished book would out-weigh Spencer's leaden works and out-class Buckle's sprightly ones; it would find a fitting rival only in Lyell's multi-volume *Principles of Geology*.

Elsewhere, too, the social lines were becoming sharper. The future protagonists over apes and ancestry were striking up their positions. In March Huxley attacked Owen's human sub-class. Owen could be crucified on the question; Huxley knew it, and he relished a propaganda victory.

Owen had already delivered his stock talk on man and apes at the

Royal Institution. Spencer had heard the lecture here in 1855 and called it 'anything but logical.' Now Huxley took a diametrically opposing line on the very same platform. In his own Royal Institution lecture in March 1858 on 'The Special Peculiarities of Man,' he compared the baboon, gorilla, and man, and emphasized their complete continuity. Man was no further from the gorilla, structurally speaking, than the gorilla was from a baboon. 'It is true that we are in possession of the links between the [baboon] & the Gorilla which we have not between the latter & man – but that does not affect the question. No one will pretend that, of two roads, one is shorter than the other because it has milestones along it.' Huxley was prepared to go even further, wondering just how much he could get away with: 'Nay more I believe that the mental & moral faculties are essentially & fundamentally the same in kind in animals & ourselves.' 'I can,' he continued, 'draw no line of demarcation between an instinctive and a reasonable action.' It left only one conclusion: 'to the very root & foundation of his nature man is one with the rest of the organic world.'

Of course, in another sense, there was an 'infinite' gap. Man had speech, and thus tradition, which made him the 'only organic being in whose very nature is implanted the necessary condition for unlimited progress.' But while Huxley admitted this, there was no disguising his iconoclastic intent; he was rushing towards a collision with Owen. Man was finding his own polemical way into the picture of progress and evolution.

This tit-for-tat antagonism did not augur well for *Natural Selection* being considered dispassionately. But it did ensure the gorilla's central role in the coming debate. With Huxley and Owen at one another's throats, apes and morality were to become explosively intertwined. And Huxley's heterodoxy, fired by hatred for Owen, was easing him towards evolution. Indeed, in his next Royal Institution lecture he tackled the species problem in a more open way than ever before. He still believed that 'the question is at present insoluble.' But if a solution *is* possible, it 'must come from the side of indefinite modifiability.'[39] He had never admitted that much before.

Huxley knew virtually nothing of natural selection, but he did know that Darwin was well into his big book. And he was beginning to realize that he had been wrong-footed. The more he argued that 'Theology & Parsondom' are the 'irreconcilable enemies of Science,' the more he sensed that a certain type of evolution could serve his purpose well.[40] Indeed, having squared up to Owen and seen him slip on a pickled brain, he sensed the pay-off in adopting an antagonistic theory of mind and morals. His gladiatorial attitude was at last pushing him Darwin's way.

As Huxley spoke, Darwin was still cranking out calculations on 'large genera,' not without some tribulations. The work was 'turning out badly,' he groused to Hooker, 'and I am sick at heart.' It was getting on top of him again, and in April, with his stomach in 'a horrid state,' he returned to Moor Park. Here he rested and relaxed, and wrote to reassure Emma:

> The weather is quite delicious. Yesterday . . . I strolled a little beyond the glade for an hour and a half . . . At last I fell fast asleep on the grass, and awoke with a chorus of birds singing around me, and squirrels running up the trees, and some woodpeckers laughing, and it was as pleasant and rural a scene as ever I saw, and I did not care one penny how any of the beasts or birds had been formed.

Indoors he perfected his billiards, read novels, and devoured *The Times*'s reports on the attempt on Napoleon's life. He also dispensed advice to William, now occupying his old rooms at Christ's College, warning him against the 'temptations there are at Cambridge to idleness' – ones that Charles remembered well. He visited the barracks near by at Aldershot, loving military manoeuvres, and watched Victoria review the troops. It gave him another lease of life, and by the time he came home in early May he was fit for anything. The cure 'made a man of me for a short time,' and he was determined to take advantage of it.[41]

He threw himself into work once more. Chunks of *Natural Selection* went off to Hooker, with the warning that it was 'tough and obscure.' As usual he expected Hooker to call it 'bosh,' which of course he did not.[42] Day in, day out, he continued, cursing species, tightening up the prose. Then on the 18 June, as the postman arrived, the bottom dropped out of his world.

All those years, the terrifying ordeal, the mental destruction he had endured worrying about the reaction, let alone his respectability. All the sickening delays, the soul-searching as he touched the untouchable, and finally, after twenty years, getting so close to publishing. Now, on a quiet Friday morning, a packet arrived from half-way around the world. Inside were a score of pages from Wallace, responding – ironically – to Darwin's encouragement.

Darwin saw his life's work 'smashed,' in pieces. 'Your words have come true with a vengeance,' he cried to Lyell. He had been 'forestalled.'[43]

32

Breaking Cover

DARWIN'S CAREFULLY ORDERED world started to crumble. Etty was seriously ill with diphtheria. *The Times* was running daily more lurid reports of Dr Lane's trial for adultery. His health deteriorating yet again, Darwin stood to lose his favourite hydropathist, destroyed by the notoriety. (Like the doctors testifying, he supported the defendant, convinced that the lady patient's sensational testimony of their affair was a morbid case of erotic delusion.) Baby Charles Waring, severely retarded, was a constant worry; on the night of 23 June 1858, he came down with the scarlet fever raging through the village. Darwin had to fight his way through an emotional tangle just to think about Wallace's letter.

True, his evolutionary mechanism seemed identical. Dolefully, almost disbelievingly, Darwin wrote to Lyell, 'If Wallace had my MS. sketch written out in 1842, he could not have made a better short abstract!'[1] Unknown to him, there were significant differences, if not on the pages.

Alfred Russel Wallace came from another world, betrayed by his specimen-haggling, socialist origins. He was no independently wealthy squire-naturalist, nor one of Huxley's career teachers, but an impoverished lawyer's son, born on the Welsh borders, and apprenticed to a builder in London at fourteen. His nights were spent in the socialists' 'Hall of Science' just off the Tottenham Court Road. The coffee was free and the 'social missionaries' stirring in their tirades against private property and religion. Here he picked up the political values that stayed with him on and off for life. Many were reinforced by his work. As a trainee land-surveyor back in Wales in the early 1840s, he had been paid to redraw property boundaries after the commons were fenced and divided among the squires following the Enclosure Act. It was, he later said, 'a legalized robbery of the poor.'

As a self-taught socialist Wallace saw humanity as part of a progressive world governed by natural law; and in his Hall of Science he had learned to see morality as a cultural product, equally valid in any race. Like so many with his background, he was instantly drawn by the 'ingenious' *Vestiges*, delighting in its vision of an upward-sweeping nature. It set him pondering the problem of species. The 21-year-old was left with 'an intense appreciation of the beauty, harmony and variety in nature . . . and an equally strong passion for justice as between man and man.'[2]

Fired by Humboldt's *Narrative* and Darwin's *Journal*, he scrimped and saved the money to pay his passage to the tropics to collect specimens and test *Vestiges*: to the Amazon in 1848, and (after a two-year spell in London in 1852-54) to the Malay archipelago, a vast group of equatorial islands, including Borneo, the land of orang-utans, where he hoped to gain clues to man's ancestry. His shipments of beetles, butterflies, and bird skins to a London dealer paid his way. He had to pack a thousand labelled beetles per box, but it was a living. From here he had sent Darwin long screeds and consignments. His latest letter, dated February, had been posted from the volcanic island of Ternate. Wallace had reached the Moluccan Group, the Spice Islands, *en route* to New Guinea.

Here, in a feverish fit, he had conceived his evolutionary theory. Malaria was not the only sign of derangement; the world was turning upside down for socialists. Malthus had been their bogey man, but by the late 1850s his population *Essay* was less taboo. A new generation was changing tactics to make his evidence for overpopulation underline the need for birth control (another socialist hobby-horse).[3] Wallace had read Malthus's sixth edition, and in the Spice Islands, bed-ridden by hot and cold flushes one afternoon, he too switched its logic on overpopulation from man to the animals.

Still, the ensuing theory differed from Darwin's. Wallace's idea of selection was the environment eliminating the unfit, rather than a cut-throat competition among individuals. Moreover, he viewed his Dyaks, not as Darwin had his bestial Fuegians, but in an egalitarian socialist light. And Wallace was to pose the question dismissed by Darwin – what was the *purpose* of natural selection? Evolutionary forces worked towards a just society, this was the point – 'to realize the ideal of perfect man.'[4]

Darwin accepted nothing so utopian. But for the moment, in 1858, all he had in front of him was Wallace's stark twenty-odd page letter

– and it did look very much like an abstract of *Natural Selection*. It mooted 'variations' being pushed 'further and further' from parent species by a 'struggle for existence.' Here was talk of overpopulation: how a pair of birds would increase ten-millionfold in fifteen years if not checked, how the weak succumb, leaving 'the most perfect in health and vigour.' The system works, Wallace said, like 'the centrifugal governor of the steam engine, which checks and corrects any irregularities almost before they become evident.'[5] But nature was a self-chugging steam engine; the variations build up, pushing the superior varieties past their parents.

Darwin 'never saw a more striking coincidence,' partly because he read his own thought into it. Wallace asked him to send the paper to Lyell, which he did, with a wailing note. Wallace did not mention publication, but Darwin would 'of course, at once write and offer to send [the paper] to any journal' of Wallace's choice. Yet 'all my originality, whatever it may amount to, will be smashed.' Lyell mulled over the problem and came up with the solution; they should announce their discoveries jointly. Darwin concurred, trying to suppress the niggling fear that this might look suspicious, as though he were stealing Wallace's credit. Hooker had seen his 1844 essay, Asa Gray at Harvard had a long abstract of it,

> so that I could most truly say and prove that I take nothing from Wallace. I should be *extremely* glad **now** to publish a sketch of my general views in about a dozen pages or so. But I cannot persuade myself that I can do so honourably . . . I would far rather burn my whole book than that he or any man should think that I had behaved in a paltry spirit.

No more sickening piece of scientific misfortune could have befallen him, even if Lyell had prophesied it.

With three children dead from scarlet fever in the village, he was preoccupied with baby Charles. He wanted Lyell to ask Hooker for a second opinion, fearing it unethical to put out a preemptive paper, given his insider's knowledge. But he was in a state beyond caring. Baby Charles died two days later. On the 29th Hooker wrote, but Darwin responded, 'I cannot think now . . .' Later that night he tried again: 'I am quite prostrated, and can do nothing, but I send Wallace, and the abstract of my letter to Asa Gray . . . I hardly care about it . . . I will do anything. God bless you.' And he threw the whole affair into Hooker's and Lyell's hands.[6]

They agreed on a joint paper. The venue was quickly settled – the Geological Society was inappropriate and anti-theoretical, Owen held court at the Zoological, and that only left the Linnean, fresh in its premises in Piccadilly. Hooker was still trying to revive the venerable old lady, and a controversial communiqué by Darwin and Wallace would be a shot in the arm. Under its new President, Thomas Bell (describer of the *Beagle* reptiles), meetings were livelier. There was a *Journal* now, and papers were discussed at meetings rather than simply read to a stony-faced audience.

How to slip it in with the summer recess looming? An ill wind finally blew some good these gloomy June days. To make up for a meeting postponed when Darwin's shy old friend Robert Brown died, the Council fitted in an extra one before the break, on Thursday 1 July. At the eleventh hour – on 30 June – Hooker and Lyell inserted the Darwin-Wallace papers on to the agenda. The next evening the Secretary read them to thirty-odd nonplussed fellows: extracts from Darwin's 1844 essay, part of his 1857 letter to Gray, and Wallace's paper – followed by six scheduled papers from the postponed meeting, ending on the vegetation of Angola. ('New facts' rather than novel theories were still the society's *raison d'être*.)[7] Darwin stayed at home, grief-stricken and ill, but also continuing a trend of absenteeism that would see him through the next stormy decade.

He had finally gone public. After twenty years of fret and frustration, he had exposed himself. But no fireworks exploded, only a damp squib. The meeting was overlong, the talks rushed, and the whole was greeted in silence, although listeners left muttering 'with bated breath.' Bell was hostile, but the fellows were evidently flummoxed by Hooker's and Lyell's tacit approval.

For Darwin's peace of mind such a lack of response was probably best. But it was cold comfort. The President had walked out of the meeting lamenting, as he later put it, that the year had not 'been marked by any of those striking discoveries which at once revolutionize, so to speak, [our] department of science.'[8] (Although, tellingly, the Vice-President promptly struck out all talk of immutability from his own pending paper.)

Not that Charles cared. While the Linnean meeting went on he and Emma were burying their son in the parish churchyard, comforted by the Revd Innes. And by now their fears about an epidemic had 'almost driven away grief.' The next morning Charles evacuated all the children except Etty to his sister-in-law's in Sussex. Four days later he collected his thoughts and informed Hooker that the family was less panic-struck, now that we have sent out of the house every child, and shall remove H[enrietta]., as soon as she can move. The first nurse became ill with ulcerated throat and quinsy, and the second is now ill with the scarlet fever, but, thank God, is recovering. You may imagine how frightened we have been [six children were eventually to die in the village of the fever]. It has been a most miserable fortnight.

And not only a fortnight. His eldest sister Marianne died on 18 July, aged sixty, her five grown-up children being adopted by Catherine and going to live at The Mount. Charles remembered Marianne as an 'admirable woman,' but they had not been close. After her 'long continued & latterly severe suffering,' he could 'thank God' that she was at rest.[9]

Still, he was '*more* than satisfied' with the Linnean proceedings. The stunned silence augured well for a fuller statement of his theory, which would have to be rushed into print before the book was finished. He took his ailing children and stomach off to the Isle of Wight for sea air, and here, at the King's Head Hotel in Sandown on 20 July, he began an 'abstract' of *Natural Selection*. At first he simply anticipated a paper, condensed 'to the utmost,' intended for the Society's *Journal*. But it was the same old story: the condensation expanded out of all proportion. By August he had forty-four folio pages on domestic animals alone, and this while he was still at the seaside. By October the manuscript was an 'inordinate length,' and inevitably it turned back into a book. Indigestion plagued him constantly. He was aiming to finish by the spring and anxiety played havoc with his stomach. At last he returned to Moor Park and the water cure. His wails resumed their eerie familiarity: 'It is an accursed evil to a man to become so absorbed in any subject as I am in mine.'[10]

Wallace's approval for the whole proceedings arrived in January 1859. Not only was he gracious; he was gratified to have galvanized Darwin. He told Hooker that he would have suffered 'much pain & regret' if they had published his paper alone. Darwin, still sheepish, reassured him that 'I had absolutely nothing whatever to do in leading Lyell and Hooker to what they thought a fair course of action.' Wallace was curious about Lyell's views on evolution. 'I think he is somewhat staggered,' Darwin replied, 'but does not give in, and speaks with horror ... [of] what a job it would be for the next edition of "The Principles," if he were "perverted." But he is most candid and honest, and I think will end up by being perverted.'

Darwin never grasped the depths of Lyell's difficulty. His mentor, tormented by transmutation, was still struggling to rationalize immortal man's origin from the beast. Was kinship limited to 'the animal nature of man,' with his 'Moral & Intellectual & Progressive part' created unique? Lyell mooted it to Huxley and Tyndall, only to find them opting for transmutation, body and mind. He came away wanting a 'moral' flash at the birth of the species; a sacred instant when the gift of immortality was bestowed. It was hard for a knighted geologist from the older generation. Still Darwin was pleased. 'Considering his age, his former views and position in society, I think his conduct has been heroic on this subject.'[11]

The young bloods were manoeuvring fast. Fresh from hammering Owen, Huxley now seized on transmutation as a solid wedge to split science from theology. It fitted his campaign for a decently salaried scientific civil service, a new professional authority at the call of an imperial nation. Authority came with a single voice, and any clerical dilution of the message was abhorred.

His parson-hating was at its height. The 'origin of man' question allowed him to skewer 'whatever dares to stand in the way' of a secular biology, and whoever doubts that 'it is as respectable to be modified monkey as modified dirt.' This militance moved him further into Darwin's camp. He did not *want* reconciliation with the clergy. It defeated his object: hence his desire to push the debate in more inflammatory directions. If the orthodox were allowed to prove that Genesis was compatible with geology, then 'I for my part,' he announced that January, 'will undulate to prove that rape, murder & arson are positively enjoined in Exodus ... Depend upon it there is no safety in trying to put new wine into old bottles.' He wanted to make the old curates uncomfortable and vacate their chairs for his new specialists. A 'new Reformation' was dawning, a fresh revolt against ecclesiastical privilege. 'If I have a wish to live thirty years, it is that I may see the foot of Science on the necks of her enemies.'[12] There spoke a man who had scrimped and struggled, trying to make ends meet, only to see the Cambridge clergy on a thousand pounds a year.

Huxley was swinging into line with Spencer, Chapman, and the *Westminster* crew, most of whom believed in evolution. On other points they were aligning too. Spencer was castigating Richard Owen's rival science of ideal archetypes, of divine thoughts made incarnate, words made flesh in the stately procession of animal life through the ages. 'Terrible bosh,' Spencer called this, a sop to the priests, and he set out to make a 'tremendous smash of it.' Simpler, material explanations were called for. Animals had developed gradually, by the piling '*of adaptations upon adaptations.*'

For years Huxley had been lampooning Owen's philosophy, using comparative anatomy. The previous June (1858), at the prestigious Royal Society, he had pulled off a coup, smashing Owen's majestic etherial archetype while Owen himself was in the chair. On the morning Darwin received Wallace's paper, Huxley was regaling Hooker: 'I wonder how Richardus, "Rex anatomicorum" feels this morning. I am deuced seedy but that is just punishment' for us 'democrats.'[13] Owen was being alienated, squeezed out – the future Darwinian generals were making any accommodation with Darwin's old friend impossible. Hatreds were already festering, a public fight over evolution was assured. It made Darwin's predicament worse as he agonized over his book.

He was back to his 'old severe vomiting' and swimming head. Towel-slapping during another Moor Park stay in February perked him up for his fiftieth birthday, but by March he had sunk again. Hooker checked the chapters of his 'abstract' one by one. 'You have not attacked it nearly so much as I feared,' Darwin rejoiced, receiving one back on 15 March. 'You do not seem to have detected *many* errors. It was nearly all written from memory, and hence I was particularly fearful.' 'P.S. I shall to-morrow finish my last chapter (except a recapitulation) . . .' The labour was not eased by Hooker's children, as a disconsolate Hooker relayed to Huxley:

> I proposed ending the week by finishing Darwin's MS when to my consternation I find that the children have made away with upwards of ¼ of the MS., By some screaming accident., the whole bundle, which weighed over 1 lb when it came (Darwin sent stamps for 2 lbs) got transferred to a drawer where my wife keeps paper for the children to draw upon – & they have of course had a drawing fit ever since. – I feel brutified if not brutalized for poor D. is so bad that he could hardly get steam up to finish what he did. – How I wish he could stamp & fume at me – instead of taking it so good naturedly as he will.

The family tried every trick to keep Charles's spirits high during this period. He even sold his father's gold watch and Wedgwood pottery to buy a billiard table, which was installed next door to the study. He resorted to it daily to drive 'the horrid species out of my head.'[14]

He struggled on through April, stripping off the references, smoothing the text, and removing the umpteen illustrations of every esoteric point. Finally he had boiled down *Natural Selection* to its core theory in 155,000 words. It was a most atypical science book for the age, turgid but saleable.

Lyell agented it, selling the idea to John Murray. Murray had one of the best back lists in London, with the *Principles of Geology*, Hooker's *Himalayan Journals*, Darwin's *Journal*, Layard's *Nineveh*, Grote's *Greece*, and even a *Muck Manual* for farmers, and he was already planning his autumn leads – an account of the search for Sir John Franklin's lost expedition, Wellington's dispatches, and Samuel Smiles's *Self-Help*. 'Does he know at all the subject of the book'? Darwin asked. There was some worry; after all, Murray had rejected Martineau's *Eastern Life* for its 'infidel tendency.' Darwin added a PS to Lyell. 'Would you advise me to tell Murray that my book is not more *un*-orthodox than the subject makes inevitable'? – by which he meant that 'I do not discuss the origin of man. That I do not bring in any discussion about Genesis, &c. &c.' Murray was reassured by Lyell, and indeed broke his cardinal rule and agreed to publish the manuscript sight unseen, offering Darwin two-thirds of the net proceeds.

Being a practical man, Murray was more concerned with the title. Darwin was set to call it *An Abstract of an Essay on the Origin of Species and Varieties through Natural Selection*, and even with the Victorians' propensity for top-heavy titles Murray saw the profits draining away. Sample chapters went off to him, including the 'dry and dull' one on distribution that Hooker's children had enjoyed, accompanied by the squeal, 'God help him if he tries to read it.' Darwin thought it 'will be popular to a certain extent . . . amongst scientific and semi-scientific men,' but not with the literary set; and it was too 'intolerably dry and perplexing' to sweep *Vestiges*-like through the novel-grubbing middle class.[15] Murray must have agreed because he anticipated printing only 500 copies.

In late May Darwin's health failed again, but a week's hydropathy fortified him for the proofs. He needed it; the prose appalled him in print, and he made drastic revisions, blackening pages and pinning notes to the smudged mess, offering to defray the cost. Through late June he continued chopping and changing; 'my corrections are terrifically heavy,' he told Lyell. He bemoaned the 'miserable' mire to Hooker; but the man was 'deep in the mud' of his own proofs, writing up the flora of Darwin's favourite colony, Tasmania. Here Hooker publicly signalled support for Darwin. Not that he would compare his effort with the *Origin of Species*. That, Hooker beamed, would be like putting 'a ragged handkerchief beside a Royal Standard.'

Huxley too was generous. He had only one cavil: that domestic races originating from a single stock (say bulldogs and greyhounds, descendants of the same wild dog) do not produce sterile offspring when crossed, as distinct wild species do. Until breeders achieved this degree of separation – actually made new species from a single stock – the analogy with natural selection remained incomplete. 'You speak of finding a flaw in my hypothesis,' Darwin rallied him, '& this shows you do not understand its nature. It is a mere rag of an hypothesis with as many flaw & holes as sound parts.' But 'I can carry in it my fruit to market for a short distance over a gentle road; not I fear that you will give the poor rag such a devil of a shake that it will fall all to atoms; & a poor rag is better than nothing to carry one's fruit to market in.'[16]

Darwin was 'as weak as a child' by September and barely able to carry anything, however delicately. He planned a long sojourn at a spa when it was all over, perhaps the new one beside the bleak Yorkshire moors, at Ilkley, suitably remote from anywhere. Through fits of sickness and gloom he trudged on, scrawling on the revised sheets, driven by 'an insanely strong wish to finish my accursed book' and 'banish the whole subject from my mind!' Murray absorbed the enormous £72 bill for corrections and upped his estimate of the *Origin*'s saleability, fixing to print 1250 copies and setting the publication date for November. The title continued to evolve under Murray's selective pressure. It had slimmed down to *On the Origin of Species and Varieties by Means of Natural Selection*, when Darwin improved matters more by docking '*and Varieties*.'[17]

Clean sheets of the 'abominable volume' went off to Lyell. Darwin remained 'foolishly anxious' about his verdict, keen for him 'to come round,' more so than for 'any other dozen men.' Lyell did indeed give Darwin 'very great *kudos*,' and others noted 'how eager Charles Lyell is ... about Darwin's forthcoming book on Species.' But then, as Lyell's relative Bunbury admitted, it is 'sure to be very curious and important ... however mortifying it may be to think that our remote ancestors were jelly fishes.' Lyell was still grappling with imponderables, still sensing that 'the dignity of man is at stake.' How to accept a soulless ape ancestor while saving human face? Darwin had little sympathy. 'I am sorry to say that I have no "consolatory view" on the dignity of man. I am content that man will probably advance, and care not much whether we are looked at as mere savages in a remotely distant future.'[18]

A ghastly fifteen months was capped on 1 October, when Charles finished the proofs amid fits of vomiting. During that whole time he had rarely been able to write free of stomach pains for more than twenty minutes at a stretch. The next day, in torrential rain, he took himself off to Ilkley, there to sit out in his bath the calm before the storm. Not wanting to be alone in his new hydropathic home, he cajoled amusing Miss Butler to accompany him (the old Irish lady full of ghost stories at Moor Park). With her there, he confided, it would 'feel safe & home-like.'

Ilkley Wells House was a grand palazzo set in ornamental grounds on the edge of Rumbold's Moor, commanding sweeping views over the village and wooded Wharfedale. Opened only three years before, it offered the ultimate in civilized seclusion, with bowling alleys, billiard tables, and teams of consultants to meet every genteel whim. The baths were at the spring, in a stubby brick terrace on a nearby hill dappled with deciduous trees. Donkeys bore the invalids there from the mansion, a twenty-minute ride. As Charles jolted up the narrow dirt track, the gorse and heather rattled in the north-west wind, chilling him even before he took the awful plunge. Winter came early that year, and when the family joined him on the 17th they were unprepared. Everyone remembered it as a time of 'frozen misery.'[19]

His two months' stay at Ilkley was one of relapses and recoveries, occasionally crashing to awful depths. With only ten days to go before the proofs were bound, he moaned to Hooker: 'I have been very bad lately; having had an awful "crisis" one leg swelled like elephantiasis – eyes almost closed up – covered with a rash & fiery Boils: but they tell me it will surely do me much good. – it was like living in Hell.' Job-like in his torture, he sought reassurances from friends. Convince Hooker, Lyell, and Huxley about natural selection, he believed, and the 'subject is safe.' Beyond these intimates he expected a rough ride; ridicule at least, being 'execrated as an atheist' at worst, with its damning implication of social irresponsibility.

On 2 November Murray sent a specimen copy, in royal green cloth, the text printed on heavy cream paper, price fifteen shillings, tickling Darwin with 'the appearance of my child.' On the 11th and 12th, two weeks before the launch, he faced the moment he had dreaded for twenty years: he wrote notes from the spa to accompany the complimentary copies. All were laced with disarming self-deprecations: two went to Harvard, to Louis Agassiz (it was not sent in 'a spirit of defiance or bravado') and Gray ('there are very many difficulties'); others to Henslow ('I fear you will not approve of your pupil'), to Jenyns ('I may . . . be egregiously wrong'), to De Candolle ('you will entirely disagree'), to the Oxford geologist John Phillips (you will 'fulminate anathemas'), Falconer ('Lord, how savage you will be . . . how you will long to crucify me alive'), and Owen (it will seem 'an abomination').

Bracing himself against the elements, Darwin felt a 'cold shudder' surge through him once more. The howling wind was as nothing to the storm of self-doubt, his nagging, gnawing fear that 'I . . . have devoted my life to a phantasy' – and a dangerous one. At night he thought of Hooker's enthusiasm and Lyell's openness, and so managed to 'rest in peace.' But still, as he wrote to Wallace in the Far East, sending him a copy of the *Origin of Species*, 'God knows what the public will think.'[20]

The first surprises were agreeable. Safe in his spa, he heard that the stock of 1250 copies was oversubscribed when the book went on sale to the trade, 22 November. The Franklin blockbuster might have sold 7600, and *Self-Help* 3200, but Darwin was staggered at orders for 1500 *Origins*. Such was the success that he immediately started corrections for a second edition in Ilkley. A letter from a romantic country rector came just in time. Charles Kingsley, renowned as a novelist, reviled as a Christian socialist, was full of praise for the book. It '*awes* me,' he enthused; 'if you be right I must give up much that I have believed.' And he was willing to, it seemed. He found it 'just as noble a conception of Deity, to believe that He created primal forms capable of self development . . . as to believe that He required a fresh act of intervention to supply the *lacunas* which He Himself had made.' Darwin was ecstatic, and slipped these lines into the last chapter, attributing them to 'a celebrated author and divine.'[21]

The reviews were another matter. The day after Kingsley's letter the *Athenaeum* – required reading for London's literati – set the tone, leaving no doubt that the book had touched a raw nerve. Though 'Man' was scarcely mentioned in the book, he was rarely avoided in the press. The *Athenaeum* had histrionics about men from monkeys and snubs to theologians. It knew the jury to be summoned. Darwin should be tried in 'the Divinity Hall, the College, the Lecture Room, and the Museum.' Too late, the *Saturday Review* noted; the book had already broken its academic bounds and found its way 'into the drawing-room and the public street.' Conservatives saw it falling into the wrong hands, and even Darwin was flabbergasted to hear of it being snapped up by commuters outside Waterloo Station. The *Athenaeum* summed up his 'creed' rather crudely: man 'was born yesterday – he will perish tomorrow.' No longer immortal, he was incidental. It struck Emma's weak spot and infuriated Charles. 'The manner in which [the reviewer] drags in immortality, and sets the priests at me, and leaves me to their mercies, is base,' he growled. 'He would, on no account, burn me, but he will get the wood ready, and tell the black beasts [priests] how to catch me.'[22]

But no mind. Even before coming home from Ilkley on 9 December, he heard that Murray was gearing up for a second-edition print run of 3000 copies, and that Professor Heinrich Bronn of Freiburg was planning a German translation (expurgated, as it turned out). And those he most hoped to 'convert' were coming round. Hooker was aboard, Lyell was 'absolutely gloating' over the book, and Huxley wrote 'with such tremendous praise' that Darwin was embarrassed. Huxley, like Carlyle's hero, the prophet Mohammed through whom the forces of Nature spoke, was sharpening his 'beak and claws,' ready to disembowel 'the curs which will bark and yelp.'[23] Clerical curs, of course, barking Owen's abuse. Huxley was spoiling for a fight, and the *Origin* provided the excuse. Darwin would not participate directly in these public controversies (he was always 'too ill,' not that he would have taken part in any public debate). But he inspired and occasionally goaded his disciples from the safety of Downe.

The big question-mark hung over Owen's head. London's leading comparative anatomist had an arrogance that masked an inner sensitivity, though he had been courteous to Darwin. The first to reply to the complimentary copies, he was charm itself, claiming he had long believed that 'existing influences' were responsible for the 'ordained' birth of species. He could never regard the *Origin* as 'heterodox.' This was extraordinarily encouraging. Early in December Darwin had long talks with Owen, who confirmed that it offered the best explanation 'ever published of the manner of formation of species.' Even so, he retained the gravest doubts; he still saw transmutation bestialize man. His was a providential non-transmutatory approach. As President of the British Association in 1858 he had talked of the 'continuous operation of Creative power' through geological time. Since the President gave 'a sort of Queen's Speech of Science,' this was clearly the rising orthodoxy. Animal species had appeared on the planet in a 'successive and continuous' fashion. Not, however, by one slowly transmuting into the next, but by species appearing in a jump, each from the womb of its antecedent, according to some Creative law.

If Owen loathed transmutation, why the generosity? Possibly

Darwin told him that he was 'inclined to look at everything as resulting from designed laws' (as he told Asa Gray a few months later). By this he meant that God had appointed natural laws to evolve life rather than intervene himself; but Owen, seizing on 'designed laws,' presumed that they shared common ideological ground, both believing in an immediate 'Creative Power.' Hence his politeness, and Darwin's impression that 'he goes at the bottom of his hidden soul as far as I do!'[24]

But Darwin's 'design' was a far cry from Owen's 'ordained' nature. Like Carpenter, Southwood Smith, and other Unitarians, Darwin made nature an immutable chain of material causes and effects. There was no providentialism; natural causes did not express the 'continuous operation' of God's will. There was none of Sedgwick's Anglican view that the Creator designs and updates each dragonfly personally. Darwin told Lyell that if each step in evolution was providentially planned, the whole procedure would be a miracle and natural selection superfluous. To Gray, Darwin mooted 'designed laws,' but he had 'the details, whether good or bad, left to the working out of what we may call chance.' Like a good Unitarian, Darwin saw a rational, lawful nature offer a solution to the problem of evil. Why the 'misery' if everything is ordained? he asked Gray. 'I cannot persuade myself that a beneficent and omnipotent God would have designedly created the Ichneumonidae [parasitic wasps] with the express intention of their feeding within the living bodies of Caterpillars.' Such adaptive accidents merely happened in a world governed by laws; they were not God's responsibility.[25]

Here spoke an old Unitarian who had fallen off the feather-bed. He was holding to a semi-respectable theism and packaging it under a designer label for the Owens and Grays. But his God was an absentee landlord, and nature self-sufficient.

Not unexpectedly, Carpenter came over, convinced that only a world of 'order, continuity, and progress' befitted an omnipotent Deity. He was writing on the *Origin* for the Unitarian *National Review* in December. 'Any theological objection' to the derivation of one breed of dog or one species of slug from another was 'simply absurd,' he announced, and he ridiculed the '"most straitest" sectarian organs' for their dogma on such matters. Human evolution was no obstacle, though he shelved the issue. It was enough that the struggle for existence tended 'inevitably . . . towards the progressive exaltation of the races engaged in it.'[26]

At this point Darwin's carefully built bridge with Owen was dynamited, and of course it was Huxley's doing. Darwin revelled in

The Times's anonymous review on Boxing Day. The staff reviewer, 'as innocent of any knowledge of science as a babe,' had turned the book over to Huxley. How 'did you influence Jupiter Olympus and make him give three and a half columns to pure science? The old fogies will think the world will come to an end.' Darwin cherished the piece more than 'a dozen reviews in common periodicals.' But it contained the usual 'naughty' snipe at Owen, which Huxley was constitutionally incapable of avoiding:

> Upon my life I am sorry for Owen [Darwin piped up]; he will be so d – – d savage; for credit given to any other man, I strongly suspect, is in his eyes so much credit robbed from him. Science is so narrow a field, it is clear there ought to be only one cock of the walk![27]

Damned savage or no, Owen was an arbiter of London science and received a string of complaints about the book. Sedgwick in Cambridge, Livingstone in the Sudan, the Duke of Argyll in government, and Jeffries Wyman at Harvard, all contacted him. Livingstone could see no struggle for existence on African plains, Sedgwick could not see the point in a world without providence; Argyll thought Darwin might have caught 'a few *bits* of the truth,' but Wyman knew that these certainly did not include chance variations.[28]

Five days after Huxley's, Hooker's review appeared in the *Gardeners' Chronicle*. Darwin was well known to its readers, and the piece was carefully tailored to the sons of the soil. Hooker treated the *Origin* as an extension of horticultural lore. Like strawberry varieties, created by the 'gardener's skill,' prize species have been picked by nature – and he added the chauvinistic thought that the book would 'fructify' first in the agriculturalist's mind.

Hooker made it sound like easy meat. But even he had to chew on it for weeks. He praised Darwin for publishing the *Origin* first, 'for the three volumes [of *Natural Selection*], unprefaced by this, would have choked any Naturalist of the nineteenth century.'[29] In fact the book's very toughness made it seem more respectably scientific, a hand's remove from the flighty *Vestiges* pandering to the lowest taste.

But the real enthusiasts were the radical atheists, like Hewett Watson and old Robert Grant; transmutationists of course, and more concerned with the scale and power of Darwin's opus than his mechanism. Watson hailed Darwin as 'the greatest revolutionist in natural history of this century' (and it was the first time anybody had said that). Grant, sixty-eight and still teaching evolution weekly at

University College, put out a slim book on classification and dedicated it euphorically to his former companion: 'With one fell-sweep of the wand of truth, you have now scattered to the winds the pestilential vapours accumulated by "species-mongers".'[30]

1860–1871

33

More Kicks Than Halfpence

TWENTY YEARS after its inception, Darwin's theory was in print. To some it looked like a belated piece of Reform Age business. Its bleak, uncharitable survivalism seemed more suited to the poor-law 1830s than the optimistic 1860s. Ironically Malthus was passing out of vogue. So even where evolution was accepted, natural selection – the 'law of higgledy-piggledy,' in Herschel's words – usually was not.

A 'bitter satire' on man and nature, Marx and Engels called the *Origin of Species*, detesting Malthus. Darwin's secular, struggling nature might have served Marx 'as a basis in natural science for the class struggle in history,' but he laughed at the way 'Darwin recognizes among beasts and plants his English society.' This was nature in the technology age, with divisions of labour, manufactories, and workhouse losers. Worst of all it was 'Hobbes' *bellum omnium contra omnes.*' Others were appalled at the implicit message of this 'war of all against all.' *Laissez-faire* run amok, throat-slitting competition: one press squib had Darwin proving that '"might is right," and therefore that Napoleon is right, and every cheating tradesman is also right.' Another knew that the *Origin* would gratify the free-market fanatics 'who reduce all the laws of action and human thought habitually to the lowest and most sordid motives.'[1]

But closer to home the old 30s Malthusian circle was ecstatic. Erasmus thought it 'the most interesting book I ever read,' and he posted a copy to his old flame Harriet Martineau, now fifty-eight and living in the Lake District, still reviewing and sprightly enough to be receiving champagne from anonymous admirers. There was plenty of time to read the *Origin* that January 1860. Cold north-easterlies brought blizzards from Siberia, keeping the nation huddled around the fireside. Martineau sat in her 'snow landscape' revelling in the book, unable to thank Eras enough: 'one might say "thank you" all one's life without giving any idea of one's sense of obligation.' She had often praised

> the quality & conduct of your brother's mind, but it is an unspeakable satisfaction to see here the full manifestation of its earnestness & simplicity, its sagacity, its industry, & the patient power by w^h. it has collected such a mass of facts, to transmute them by such sagacious treatment into such portentious knowledge. I sh^d. much like to know how large a proportion of our scientific men believe that he has found a sound road . . . It does not very much matter; for it is the next generation that effectively profits by such books.

Who wrote *The Times*'s review? she asked, and what did Owen think of the *Origin*? – not that anybody 'trusts Owen's manners or speech on such occasions: but there is some wonder about what he thinks.'[2]

Harriet read it as an atheist and simplistically summed it up to fellow campaigner George Holyoake: 'What a book it is! – overthrowing (if true) revealed Religion on the one hand, & Natural (as far as Final Causes & Design are concerned) on the other. The range & mass of knowledge take away one's breath.' Other rationalists were equally taken. The 'great Buckle highly approves,' Darwin chortled. And John Chapman spoke for many when he called it 'one of the most important books of this century,' which was 'likely to effect an immense mental revolution. The sagacity, knowledge and candour displayed in the work are unusually great and wonderful.'[3]

Martineau demurred at only one point. Darwin had traced all animals and plants back to an ancient 'progenitor.' To avoid stirring up a secondary storm with spontaneous generation to start the process, he talked of this having been 'created,' of life having been 'first breathed' into it. 'I think it is a pity that 2 or 3 expressions' seemed theological, Harriet complained. She assumed that they were used colloquially, 'without reference to their primitive meaning. If so, they ought not to have been used: but the theory does not require the notion of a creation; & my conviction is that Charles D. does not hold it.'[4]

She dropped a note to Fanny Wedgwood to make the same point.

> I rather regret that C.D. went out of his way two or three times . . . to speak of "the Creator" in the popular sense of

the First Cause . . . It is curious to see how those who w^d. otherwise agree with him turn away because his view is "derived from" or "based on" "Theology" . . . It seems to me that having carried us up to the earliest group of forms, or to the single primitive one, he & his have nothing to do with how those few forms, or that one, come there. His subject is the "Origin of Species," & not the origin of Organisation; & it seems a needless mischief to have opened the latter speculation at all. – There now! I have delivered my mind.[5]

The Unitarian approval, secular glee, and young Turks' optimism was a world removed from the distress felt by Darwin's Cambridge mentors. Old patrician Anglicans still feared that a nature not actively upheld by God's Word boded ill, threatening the command structure of a paternalist society, just as a vicious free-for-all capitalism destroyed its harmony. Sedgwick spoke bluntly. Old and lined, he was now marginal to the world of London science, but his anguish was real. He had received his copy

> with more pain than pleasure. Parts of it I admired greatly, parts I laughed at till my sides were almost sore; other parts I read with absolute sorrow, because I think them utterly false and grievously mischievous. You have *deserted* . . . the true method of induction, and started in machinery as wild, I think, as Bishop Wilkins's locomotive that was to sail with us to the moon.

The old proctorial hackles rose: he accused Darwin of trying to sever the link between material nature and its moral meaning. Only this indication of divine love can keep the social fabric secure. 'Were it possible . . . to break [the link], humanity, in my mind, would suffer a damage that might brutalize it, and sink the human race' into a cesspit. He called himself 'a son of a monkey and an old friend of yours' but then signed off with a sentiment that stung Emma. 'If you and I' accept God's revelation in nature and the Bible, he told Charles, 'we shall meet in heaven.' This questioning of Charles's future life upset her and she refused to show the letter to Henrietta.[6]

Henslow was more magnanimous. He told his brother-in-law, the Revd Jenyns, that 'the Book is a marvellous assemblage of facts & observations – & no doubt contains much legitimate inference – but it pushes *hypothesis* (for it is not real *theory*) too far. It reminds me of the age of astronomy when much was explained by Epicycles – & for every fresh difficulty a fresh epicycle was invented.' He showed better grace than Sedgwick, but in the end he too dissented: 'Darwin attempts more than is granted to Man, just as people used to account for the origin of Evil – a question past our finding out.'⁷ Publicly he admitted that the *Origin* was 'a stumble in the right direction,' but when his name was linked with Darwin's supporters he protested to the papers.

This Anglican censure had more personal repercussions. Darwin may even have lost a knighthood. Lord Palmerston, the incoming Liberal Prime Minister in June 1859, had apparently mooted Darwin's name to Queen Victoria as a candidate for the Honours List. Prince Albert concurred; he was a friend of science, a friend of Owen's, President of the British Association in September 1859, where Lyell had spoken of Darwin's forthcoming work, and he had seen Sir Charles similarly honoured. Darwin would have been delighted and astonished. But then came the *Origin*. The Queen's ecclesiastical advisers, including the Bishop of Oxford Samuel Wilberforce, scotched it. The honour would imply approval, and Palmerston's request was turned down.⁸

Not that all Anglicans stood in opposition. Charles Kingsley, as eager to side with the evolution *avant garde* as he had been with the Chartists, struck up a dialogue with Huxley, who admitted in February 1860 that Kingsley

> is a very real, manly, right minded parson but I am inclined to think on the whole that it is more my intention to convert him than his to convert me. He is an excellent Darwinian to begin with, and told me a capital story of his reply to Lady Aylesbury who expressed her astonishment at his favouring such a heresy – "What can be more delightful to me Lady Aylesbury, than to know that your Ladyship & myself sprang from the same toad stool." Whereby the frivolous old woman shut up, in doubt whether she was being chaffed or adored for her remark.⁹

But generally the young guard had no time for priests; their strategy called for confrontation, for edging out the men with dual callings.

Huxley's gladiatorial attitude was being noticed. In February he lectured at the Royal Institution on Darwin's theory of 'Species and Races, and their Origin.' He arrived at the theatre armed with Darwin's drawings, skulls of pouters and tumblers, and sheaves of the *Natural Selection* manuscript. He left in an 'ocean of hot water,' having 'disappointed & displeased' everybody by trying to be even-handed. Or so he said. In fact some of the disappointing was deliberate. 'I had a Bishop & a Dean among my auditors, and, to please *them* I wound up with the most' confrontationist appraisal 'of Science *versus* Parsonism that is likely to have reached their ears.'[10]

He was openly goading the prelates, exploiting the *Origin* to wrench science from ecclesiastical control, leaving those in the audience like Owen seething. Huxley perfected his stock-in-trade metaphors – about clerical oppositions being 'crushed and maimed in every battle' since Galileo's day, about 'Canutes of the hour enthroned in solemn state, bidding the great wave to stay,' about the *Origin* heralding a 'new reformation.' He damned the pious 'meddlers' and ended on a question. Would England play a noble role in this 'revolution' of thought?

> That depends upon how you, the public, deal with science.
> Cherish her, venerate her, follow her methods faithfully and
> implicitly in their application to all branches of human
> thought, and the future of this people will be greater than the
> past. Listen to those who would silence and crush her, and I
> fear our children will see the glory of England vanishing like
> Arthur in the mist.

Secular expertise was being wedded to Britain's technological and imperial salvation. The nation's health was linked to the professional scientist's own. It was a self-serving plea on behalf of the new white-collar specialist, standing at arm's remove from the dog-collared dogmatist. In his first public lecture on the *Origin* Huxley had prepared the future ground. Not that Darwin, the Downe squire and anything but white-collar, really appreciated it. He thought the flashy rhetoric so much 'time wasted.'[11] The talk should have been on the *Origin*'s arcana, not Canute and Arthur.

Yet by March Darwin was typically drawing up lists of supporters. He too had a polarized view of events: everybody was for or against him, on 'our side' or with 'the outsiders.' Huxley became his 'good and kind agent for the propagation of the Gospel – *i.e.* the devil's gospel.' The camaraderie between Huxley, Hooker, and Darwin strengthened, fired by a sectarian spirit which manifested in mock religious metaphors – despite some doubt as to whose side Satan was on: 'the alternative, for men constructed on the high pressure tubular boiler principle, like ourselves,' Huxley told Hooker, 'is to lie down and let the devil have his own way. And I will be torn to pieces before I am forty sooner than see that.'[12]

Owen was the unknown quantity. His public verdict on the *Origin* was anxiously awaited, and indeed the Superintendent of the natural history collections at the British Museum was being forced to grapple with the book. Owen told a Parliamentary Committee, inquiring into the feasibility of erecting a purpose-built Natural History Museum, that 'in the present phase of natural history philosophy' expansion was more necessary than ever:

> The whole intellectual world this year has been excited by a book on the origin of species; and what is the consequence? Visitors come to the British Museum, and they say, "Let us see all these varieties of pigeons: where is the tumbler, where is the pouter?" and I am obliged with shame to say, "I can show you none of them" . . . As to showing you the varieties of those species, or any of those phenomena that would aid one in getting at that mystery of mysteries, the origin of species, our space does not permit; but surely there ought to be space somewhere, and, if not in the British Museum, where is it to be obtained?

But however useful the *Origin* might have been as a lever to pry open government coffers, Owen viewed it as a dangerous weapon in the wrong hands. Huxley's religious provocations and goading on apes were hitting the mark. When Owen's *Edinburgh* review of the *Origin* appeared in April Darwin, hypersensitive, was so shocked that he lost a night's sleep. 'Spiteful,' he called it: 'extremely malignant, clever, and . . . damaging.'[13]

Owen himself was now furious, alienated by Huxley's pugnacious posturing. His review boiled at the *Origin*'s crude caricature of 'creationists,' fumed at Darwin's asking whether they really believed that animals appeared out of thin air, as 'elemental atoms suddenly flashed into living tissues.' ('Preposterous and unworthy' he was to call this, especially with Darwin *himself* writing of the first 'progenitor' having been 'created'! How were they created? Owen snapped – from 'elemental atoms'?) Left prickly by Huxley, Owen took Darwin's talk of 'the blindness of preconceived opinion' to heart. He accused Darwin of setting up straw men. Was Owen's own ugly 'axiom of *the continuous operation of the ordained becoming of living things*' to be ignored? Didn't most modern geologists believe that the 'mystery of mysteries' had a natural explanation? That none accepted transmutation was beside the point. Darwin had fallen into the error of assuming that selection was the only possible natural Creative law.[14] There was a more godly, less chancy, alternative: new species appeared at a stroke, by natural birth.

Others joined the fray, nailing their colours to Owen's mast. Angered by Huxley, many gentlemen of substance believed it their duty to steer science in a respectable direction. The Duke of Argyll, the Lord Privy Seal in Palmerston's government, currently defending the Budget with its repeal of the newspaper tax, saw Owen's distinction as crucial. Creation by natural selection was inconceivable – bloody, wasteful, and chaotic – whereas 'Creation by Birth' harmonized with experience; the reproductive process was 'the only "Law" which we know of as capable of "Creating".'[15] Of course Huxley and Hooker, with their secular professional needs, treated this distinction as pernicious. It threatened to fragment their scientists' coalition and let the priests and princes back in.

Owen's bitterness was exacerbated by Huxley's conclusion that 'man might be a transmuted ape.' In his review he slated Darwin's 'disciples' for their 'short-sighted' adherence. He mauled Hooker. Then he turned to Huxley's Royal Institution lecture, having sat through it in utter disgust. England owed its 'greatness' to books like the Origin of Species! Owen thought that it more accurately symbolized an 'abuse of science,' the sort 'to which a neighbouring nation, some seventy years since, owed its temporary degradation.' This would not be the last time that revolutionary France was thrown in Darwin's teeth.

The cadre of disciples bunched up for protection. 'He is atrociously severe on Huxley's lecture,' Darwin lamented on reading the review, 'and very bitter against Hooker. So we three enjoyed it together.' Huxley had calculated well. Owen stood ostracized and caricatured, and it was too much for his overweening pride. Everyone knew why he retaliated. An admirer put it to Huxley, 'You had some forecast of what was to happen I suppose as you have given him as good.' Darwin had a different, rather glib, explanation. 'The Londoners say he is mad with envy because my book has been talked about,' he told Henslow. 'It is painful to be hated in the intense degree with which Owen hates me.'[16]

The disciples continued to stake claims. Huxley, reviewing for the Westminster in April, first uttered the rallying cry 'Darwinism.' He gave them a flag to march under; no longer would they be a stateless nation, they were set to conquer scientific Britain. Huxley slated Owen, hailed the Origin as a 'Whitworth gun in the armoury of liberalism,' and projected 'the domination of Science' over 'regions of thought into which she has, as yet, hardly penetrated.' It was clear by April that Darwin's and Huxley's fates were now irrevocably entwined. Huxley's was 'a brilliant review,' Darwin admitted, 'with

491

capital hits.' It no longer mattered that he hardly 'advances the subject.'[17]

Darwin took the knocks very personally. Most reviewers wrote with great respect, however dumbfounded that a squire of science should have turned to heresy. But his older friends were often negative. Wollaston insisted with Coleridge that Nature is a 'pestilent abstraction' and can select nothing. The pannings depressed Darwin. The attacks were raining down 'hot and heavy.' Few were grasping natural selection, which left him cursing that 'I must be a very bad explainer.' Selection for most implied a Selector, and they wondered why Darwin did not see it. 'I suppose "natural selection" was a bad term,' he admitted. 'Natural Preservation' might have been less anthropomorphic. He tried it out on Lyell. But Lyell could not read his abysmal handwriting and read it as 'Natural Persecution,' which, considering the fraught circumstances, raised a laugh at Downe.[18]

Love it or loathe it, at least nobody was ignoring the *Origin*. Three publishing houses in America tried to pirate it (there was no international copyright protection), but Gray at Harvard twisted arms, made two withdraw, and closed with a five per cent royalty from Appleton's in New York, on the adage that 'all got is clear gain.' Darwin had hoped that Gray's review in the *American Journal of Science* could be bound in at the head, making it a joint publication (and mollifying the opposition). He was happy to have the botanist 'baptize' the *Origin* 'nolens volens, which will be its salvation.' It was not to be. The US *Origin* stood alone on its publication in May, in a print run of 2500 copies. But he was mightily pleased. 'I never dreamed of my book being so successful' with Yankee readers, he chortled, offering Gray a cut of the £22 revenue. Once 'I should have laughed at the idea of sending the sheets to America.'[19]

Every potential triumph was now talked up by the evangelical Darwinians. Feeling themselves beleaguered, they needed visible gains. Thus it was that a witty bit of repartee on Saturday 30 June 1860, at a section meeting of the British Association for the Advancement of Science, was destined to be blown out of all proportion to become the best known 'victory' of the nineteenth century, save Waterloo.

Oxford was the venue in 1860, the home of High Anglicanism, Bishop Samuel Wilberforce's diocese. There was no set-piece debate on Darwinism, but Professor John William Draper of New York University was slated to talk on Darwin and social progress, so no one doubted that the bishop would eloquently vent his spleen, if called upon. But much had changed since the last Oxford meeting in

1847, when Soapy Sam floored Chambers for his *Vestiges*: dissident scientific Londoners were seizing the reins of power and Wilberforce was no longer guaranteed unanimous support. To start with he was in a brand new museum, not St Mary's Church; even in Oxford, science now had its own house. On the other hand, this *was* still Oxford, and the gothic revival museum was a shrine to nature's God. An angel stood over the entrance. The dons, on passing through, were transported into the light glass-roofed atrium. Here they imagined themselves in a 'temple of science,' glorying in all the designs of nature, 'by which the Author of the universe manifests himself to His creatures.'[20]

That Saturday was a routine 'Botany and Zoology' meeting, but Draper and the bishop drew a large crowd, seven hundred at least. The clergy gathered in the middle, undergraduates at the back; Oxford dons, science teachers, and gentlewomen clustered around. The make-up might have ensured an anti-Darwin consensus, but these were uncertain times. Some of the same Londoners were here as in 1847, but thirteen years had taken their toll. Many felt out of place among the spires and out of sorts with the dons.

Consider the Geological Survey corps. These were young middle-class salaried professionals, jealously guarding their autonomy. Andrew Ramsay was a Survey careerist. In 1847 he had applauded Sam's slap at those succumbing to the 'foul temptation' of speculation. But he had been lecturing alongside Huxley and Hooker for years. In their School of Mines lines of ancient shells were glued to boards around the walls to indicate pedigrees. Ramsay told Darwin that he had long done with a 'succession of small miracles' and come over to transmutation.[21] This wasn't the Ramsay of 1847. In 1860 he was working specifically to plug the embarrassing gaps in Darwin's geological evidence.

The London audience might have changed, but it was the same loquacious, plum-in-mouth Wilberforce. He was no supple Kingsley, prepared to follow Darwin's 'villainous shifty fox of an argument, into whatsoever unexpected bogs and brakes he may lead us.' The liberal *Daily Telegraph* abused the bishop as one of the 'old style Tories,' men who 'have not advanced one iota beyond their ancient notions.'[22] Owen, lodging with Wilberforce the night before, was suspected of priming him. He probably did; during the port the talk undoubtedly turned to Darwin's book. But Owen believed in the 'continuous creation' of life, so he was probably pushing Sam beyond Genesis miracles to a more enlightened view; not Darwinian, but not traditional.

Huxley had been spoiling for a fight. He was razor-sharp; but his shaking temper could still reduce his effectiveness, and Owen had bettered him on occasions. Hooker was cooler and clearer, if less cutting. Later legends depicted a bloody clash, with Wilberforce scotched if not slain. But the first play-by-play account received by Darwin painted a very different picture.

Darwin had settled into Dr Lane's new hydropathic home, in Sudbrook Park, Richmond. (Lane had been acquitted of adultery and moved premises.) Here he sat, 'utterly weary of life,' reading Hooker's long letter. Hooker remembered when they were together at the last Oxford meeting of the Association, but he too noticed the changes. Clerical Oxford no longer held its attractions: 'without you & my wife I was as dull as ditch water & crept about the once familiar streets feeling like a fish out of water. I swore I would not go near a Section,' and indeed he did not enter a meeting room for two days, lazing about the colleges instead, admiring the gardens.

Clearly nothing had been premeditated that Saturday. Huxley was not even going to wait for the meeting, until Robert Chambers – of all people – ran into him in the street the day before and remonstrated about his 'deserting them.'[23] Of course Chambers, once ritually humiliated, was hoping for vicarious revenge. Hooker too was lackadaisical. He wandered to the meeting door, he told Darwin, not in the best mood, '& swore as usual I would not go in; but getting equally bored of doing nothing I did.' He described the scene in his letter:

> A paper of a Yankee donkey called Draper on "civilization according to the Darwinian hypothesis" or some such title was being read, & it did not mend my temper; for of all the flatulent stuff & all the self-sufficient stuffers – these were the greatest, it was all a pie of Herb[ert]ᶜ Spenser [sic] & Buckle without the reasoning of either.

In fact Draper was English-born and London University-educated, even if he had lived in America for twenty-eight years. He was the star attraction, because he was applying Darwin's theory to society. But his numbing speech droned on for an hour, although he 'was listened to with the profoundest attention, no one went out indeed no one stirred.'[24] Hooker continued to Darwin:

> however hearing that Soapy Sam was to answer I waited to hear the end. The meeting was so large that they had

adjourned to the Library which was crammed with between 700 & 1000 people, for all the world was there to hear Sam Oxon. Well Sam Oxen got up & spouted for half an hour with inimitable spirit[,] uglyness & emptyness & unfairness. I saw he was coached up by Owen & knew nothing & he said not a syllable but what was in the Review [Wilberforce's *Quarterly Review* diatribe on the *Origin*, just out] – he ridiculed you badly & Huxley savagely.

What Hooker did not say was that the bishop, after two hours of boring speeches in a stuffy room, tried to lighten the proceedings with a joke that palpably missed its mark. He turned to Huxley and asked whether it was on his grandfather's or grandmother's side that he was descended from an ape.[25] Whereupon Huxley retorted to the 'savaging'

> & turned the tables, but he could not throw his voice over so large an assembly, nor command the audience; & he did not allude to *Sam*'s weak points nor put the matter in a form or way that carried the audience. The battle waxed hot. Lady Brewster fainted, the excitement increased as others spoke.

Hooker mentioned no names, but 'a grey haired Roman nosed elderly gentleman' then stood in the centre of the audience to protest at 'Mr Darwin's book' and 'Prof. Huxley's statement.' It was FitzRoy, now head of the Government's Meteorological Department and at Oxford to read a paper on storms. With military bearing the Admiral, 'lifting an immense Bible first with both and afterwards with one hand over his head, solemnly implored the audience to believe God rather than man.'[26] He admitted that the *Origin of Species* had given him 'acutest pain.' It was a sad sight as the crowd shouted him down. Hooker continued:

> my blood boiled, I felt myself a dastard; now I saw my advantage – I swore to myself I would smite that Amalekite Sam hip & thigh if my heart jumped out of my mouth & I handed my name up to the President (Henslow) as ready to throw down the gauntlet. I must tell you that Henslow as president would have none speak but those who had *arguments* to use, & 4 persons had been burked [silenced] by the audience & President for mere declamation: it moreover became necessary for each speaker to mount the platform & so there I was cocked up with Sam at my right elbow, &

there & then I smacked him amid rounds of applause – I hit
him in the wind at the first shot in 10 words taken from his
own ugly mouth – & then proceeded to demonstrate in as
few more 1 that he could never have read your book & 2 that
he was absolutely ignorant of the rudiments of Bot[anical]
Science. I said a few more on the subject of my own
experience, & conversion, & wound up with a very few
observations on the relative positions of the old & new
hypotheses, & with some words of caution to the audience.
Sam was shut up – had not one word to say in reply & the
meeting *was dissolved forthwith* leaving you master of the
field after 4 hours battle. Huxley who had borne all the
previous brunt of the battle & who had never before (thank
God) praised me to my face, told me it was splendid, & that
he did not know before what stuff I was made of. I have been
congratulated & thanked by the blackest coats & whitest
stocks in Oxford.[27]

This was certainly not the old Hooker of 1847. He had acquitted
himself splendidly, faced down a bishop in his own diocese. Darwin
trembled reading this, secure at Sudbrook Park, hearing about his
absent body being tugged this way and that. The body itself was
falling apart. 'I have been very poorly,' he replied, 'with almost
continuous bad headache for forty-eight hours, and I was low enough,
and thinking what a useless burthen I was to myself and all others,
when your letter came.' 'It is something unintelligible to me how any
one can argue in public like orators do . . . I am glad I was not in
Oxford, for I should have been overwhelmed.'

It looked as if Hooker had carried the day, not Huxley. Darwin
asked for *his* account of the 'awful battles.' 'I often think that my
friends (and you far beyond others) have good cause to hate me, for
having stirred up so much mud . . . I honour your pluck; I would as
soon have died as tried to answer the Bishop in such an assembly.'[28]

Huxley's version, however, was substantially different. On being
asked about his ancestry, 'I had said that I could not see what
difference it would make to any moral responsibility if I *had* had an
ape for a grandfather.' This was flat, as Hooker said; 'saponaceous
Samuel thought it was a fine opportunity for chaffing a savan' and he
pitched into Huxley.

However he performed the operation vulgarly & I determined
to punish him, partly on that account & partly because he

talked pretentious nonsense. So when I got up I spoke pretty much to this effect – that I had listened with great attention to the Lord Bishops speech but had been unable to discern either a new fact or a new argument in it – except indeed the question raised as to my personal predilection in the matter of ancestry – That it would not have occurred to me to bring forward such a topic as that for discussion myself, but that I was quite ready to meet the Right Rev. prelate even on that ground. If then, said I, the question is put to me would I rather have a miserable ape for a grandfather or a man highly endowed by nature and possessed of great means & influence & yet who employs these faculties & that influence for the mere purpose of introducing ridicule into a grave scientific discussion I unhesitatingly affirm my preference for the ape.

Whereupon there was inextinguishable laughter among the people, and they listened to the rest of my argument with the greatest attention. Lubbock & Hooker spoke after me with great force & among us we shut up the bishop & his laity.

Huxley insisted that he 'said my say with perfect good temper,' but eye-witnesses reported that he was 'white with anger,' too wrought up to 'speak effectively.' His hot-head had stymied him again.

Soapy Sam, a Tory bishop who 'presumed on his position' to pronounce on science, was everything the new men despised. Huxley had the 'most unmitigated contempt' for 'the round-mouthed, oily, special pleading of the man.' Anyway, like Hooker, Huxley came away believing that he was himself 'the most popular man in Oxford for full four & twenty hours afterwards.' Faced by the conflicting propagandist claims, Darwin did not know who had triumphed exactly, except that it must have been 'our side.' (On the other, Wilberforce went away happy that he had given Huxley a bloody nose, while many in the crowd adjudicated it an entertaining draw.)[29]

Mooting an ape for a grandmother was a risky gambit, playing on Victorian sensibilities about the sanctity of the female sex. Had it not been so clever, it would have been in shocking taste. Sedgwick had tried a parallel tack against the *Vestiges*, saving 'our glorious maidens' from such depravity. Maidens stood for the Church and the chaste against the sordid evolutionists. Wilberforce might have succeeded in his ploy, but for Huxley's righteous riposte. He reformulated the issue as one of rectitude. He co-opted Darwin's clean unsullied 'truth' for the New Model Army of scientists. He brought an earnestness to the rhetoric that the bishop lacked, but then, of course, 'no man ever manifested more of the moral presuppositions of a Puritan evangelicalism.'[30]

Huxley's strategy was to portray a morally regenerative science combating a corrupt Church. He was taking over an old radical ploy and using it to advance the career scientists. No one with a double calling was henceforth to be granted a hearing. Clerical geologists like Sedgwick, Hooker said, 'are like asses between bundles of hay.'[31] Wilberforce was something worse. The asses had to choose their trough, science or theology. Scientific power was being closely circumscribed by the new professionals.

Darwin at Sudbrook Park pored over Hooker's account 'with infinite pleasure.' He re-read Huxley's letter, sent it home to Emma, and 'when I get home shall read it again.' Having had 'more "kicks than halfpence",' he was thankful for champions, and voluble ones; but he would still have preferred a calm discussion about pouters and poultry. From his Richmond rest home he twitted Huxley: 'how durst you attack a live bishop in that fashion? I am quite ashamed of you! Have you no reverence for fine lawn sleeves?'[32] But for all the mock heroics, he knew the die was cast, and that his old mentors were not to be reconciled now.

More colourful stories began to circulate, sealing the legend. William Darwin – following his father at Christ's College – heard from one of the tutors that after the meeting blind Henry Fawcett (a Darwin sympathizer, shortly to become professor of political economy at Cambridge) and another Cambridge man 'happened to be near the B[ishop]. of Oxford; and the one asked Fawcett whether he thought the Bishop had ever read the Origin' and the blind man shouted out in a loud voice '"Oh no, I would swear he has never read a word of it." The Bishop bounced round with an awful scowl and was just going to pitch into him, when he saw that he was blind, and said nothing.'[33]

One hopes Sam read the *Origin*, because he was paid £60 to write it up for the Tory *Quarterly*. This completed the trinity of heavy-weight reviews (with Owen in the *Edinburgh* and Huxley in the *Westminster*), and in late July Darwin caught up with Wilberforce's article. It was slick. The bishop had even disinterred a sixty-year-old parody of grandfather Erasmus's evolutionary prose, to show that a Darwin never changed his spots. (The political message was obvious – the parody came from the reactionary government-sponsored *Anti-Jacobin*, cracking down in the aftermath of the French Revolution.) But the day of arbitrating Tory bishops was over. Darwin took his pencil to the piece, out of all sympathy. If 'transmutations were actually occurring,' Wilberforce argued, we should see them today in the rapidly reproducing invertebrates; since we don't, why believe that 'the favourable varieties of turnips are tending to become men.' Darwin slashed 'rubbish' in the column. This was truth sacrificed for a slippery style, like Soapy Sam's jibe at Huxley. The bishop's explanation of animal classification left Darwin in even higher dudgeon: 'all creation is the transcript in matter of ideas eternally existing in the mind of the Most High'!! 'Mere words' Darwin scribbled, the sort spouted by Owen, and anathema to lapsed Unitarians with their feet on the ground.[34]

34

From the Womb of the Ape

WHATEVER THE FURORE over Darwin, liberal theologians were generating even fiercer passions in their own world. Seven – 'seven against Christ' – responded to the likes of Wilberforce by issuing a manifesto with the deceptively innocuous title *Essays and Reviews* only three months after the *Origin* appeared. They were a miscellaneous lot, Oxford professors, country clergymen, the headmaster of Rugby School, and even a layman. But Anglican divines declaring miracles irrational whipped up unprecedented anger in a country still hardly touched by German biblical criticism. *Essays* sold 22,000 copies in two years (as many as the *Origin* in two decades) and provoked a ferocious paper war. Four hundred books and pamphlets contested and defended the issues over five years, hardening attitudes on both sides.[1]

With *Essays and Reviews* deflecting the clerical mind, the *Origin* escaped behind the smokescreen. Some related the two books. The most scientific of the seven, Baden Powell, slipped a sentence into his *Essays* proofs commending 'Mr. Darwin's masterly volume,' while restating his argument that belief in miracles was atheistic. An unbroken causal nexus was proof of Creative intent, and the *Origin* therefore a boon to faith: it 'must soon bring about an entire revolution in opinion in favour of the grand principle of the self-evolving powers of nature.' Darwin's detractors turned on Powell. Sedgwick scowled at his 'greedily' adopting such nonsense. Tory reviews charged him with joining 'the infidel party.' (Time ran out before he had the chance; he died of a heart attack two weeks before the British Association debate, in June 1860, otherwise he would have been on the platform at Oxford facing the bishop.) After slating Darwin, Wilberforce retrained the *Quarterly*'s sights on to *Essays*.

His iron fist came down again in a letter to *The Times*, signed by the Archbishop of Canterbury and twenty-five bishops, which threatened the heretics with the ecclesiastical courts.[2]

This many prelates were never to be trusted. Darwin rattled out his favourite proverb, 'A bench of bishops is the devils flower garden' – then, a bottle of anaesthetic in hand, went about the latest Satanic experiments in his own beds, chloroforming carnivorous sundew plants. With Lubbock, Busk, Lyell, Carpenter, and others (including the mathematician and Queen's printer William Spottiswoode), he signed a counter-letter supporting the *Essays* for trying to 'establish religious teachings on a firmer and broader foundation.' Hooker declined (as did Huxley), arguing that if the signatories were 'chiefly men of one way of thinking, in such matters as "Origin of Species",' it would give the impression that science had dictated 'our religious views.'[3] But there was no disguising the fact that pro-*Origin* scientists – with a strong flank of Unitarians – were aligning with liberal churchmen. Not that it was to any avail. Two of the *Essays*' authors were indicted for heresy and out of a job by 1862.

In science the lines were also sharpening as Huxley indicted Owen again. Perjury was the charge, ape brains the issue, and the brawl was every bit as rancorous as the *Essays* débâcle. At the British Association Owen had repeated his view that human and ape brains differed on two points. Humans had a peculiar lobe, the hippocampus minor, and their enormous cerebral hemispheres were unique in covering the underlying cerebellum. Huxley denied both distinctions, and promised to prove it. The outcome might have had nothing to do with evolution but, with these two involved, nobody doubted that the squabble was over Darwin's 'absent body.'[4]

The bloodletting began in Huxley's new *Natural History Review*, which made Owen its *bête noire*. This was the first Darwinian house organ, bought and refurbished by Huxley, Lubbock, Busk, and other 'plastically minded young men' (a code for Darwin's men). The tone 'will be mildly episcophagous,' Huxley gloated to Hooker, 'and you and Darwin and Lyell will have a fine opportunity if you wish it of slaying your adversaries.' The first issue in January 1861 set the scene with Huxley's paper on man's relationship to the apes (which he duly posted to Wilberforce out of bravado). 'What a complete and awful smasher (and done like a "buttered angel") it is for Owen!' Darwin cooed. How 'Owen is shown up' by the whole issue, '"this great and sound reasoner"!'[5]

Through the excitement Darwin continued quietly at home, cutting the early chapters out of his unfinished 'big book,' *Natural Selection.* Nothing was wasted, everything recycled at Downe; just as the carpets were well worn, so old manuscripts were continually re-read, and every trifling fact re-deployed somewhere. It was back to pigeons and poultry, the pages to be worked up into a separate volume on the way breeders made domestic animals. This was more necessary than ever. Lyell and Gray still believed that variations were providentially planned – that nature's course was steered. The pigeons alone should scotch this. Their ruffs and frills were not supernaturally selected, so why was a wild bird? As he explained to Gray:

> you believe 'that variation has been led along certain beneficial lines.' I cannot believe this; and I think you would have to believe, that the tail of the Fantail was led to vary in the number and direction of its feathers in order to gratify the caprice of a few men. Yet if the Fantail had been a wild bird, and had used its abnormal tail for some special end, as to sail before the wind . . . everyone would have said, 'What a beautiful and designed adaptation.'

He asked Lyell if 'the shape of my nose was designed.' If it was, 'I have nothing more to say. If not, seeing what Fanciers have done by selecting individual differences in the nasal bones of pigeons . . . it is illogical' to suppose that variations in nature have been planned. Noses were no less natural than fancy beaks. The new book would hammer the point home: it would illustrate 'what an enormous field of undesigned variability there is ready' in the farmyard and the forest.[6]

Not that he was above exploiting Gray's providential defence of 'my deity "Natural Selection".' Over the winter he let go the pigeons to organize a third edition of the *Origin.* He added a perfunctory historical sketch, a cursory list of 'precursors,' and prefaced it with a clever piece of self-promotion. Asa Gray had published three supportive articles in the *Atlantic Monthly.* Darwin persuaded him to reprint them as a pamphlet, and even to have its title reflect their providential tone. When Gray came up with 'Natural Selection Not Inconsistent with Natural Theology,' Darwin was delighted, paid half the cost, and imported 250 copies into England. He was rubbing balm on to the theological rash. He advertised the pamphlet in the periodicals, and posted a hundred copies to scientists, reviewers, and theologians, not forgetting Wilberforce. In the new edition, before the 'Historical Sketch,' he recommended it to the theologically squeamish, to be purchased for 1*s.* 6*d.* from Trübner's in Paternoster

Row. Yet, happy as he was to run this religious endorsement, afterwards he went 'crawling on' with his fancy animal book, trying to convince the Grays of the world that natural selection was actually self-sufficient.[7]

The Huxleys and Darwins grew closer in these years. The Down House doors were always open, Emma ever ready to help. The Huxleys lost their first son Noel from scarlet fever three months after the British Association meeting. He was almost four, and his sudden death prostrated Henrietta, six months pregnant, and brought her husband to the edge of a breakdown. Huxley tried to rationalize the 'holy leave-taking' as he stood over the body, with its staring blue eyes and tangled golden hair, but the tragedy left a deep scar. At the funeral, 'with my mind bent on anything but disputation,'

> the officiating minister read, as a part of his duty, the words, "If the dead rise not again, let us eat and drink, for to-morrow we die." I cannot tell you how inexpressibly they shocked me. [The parson] had neither wife nor child, or he must have known that his alternative involved a blasphemy against all that was best and noblest in human nature. I could have laughed with scorn. What! because I am face to face with irreparable loss . . . I am to renounce my manhood, and, howling, grovel in bestiality? Why, the very apes know better, and if you shoot their young, the poor brutes grieve their grief out and do not immediately seek distraction in a gorge.

A desolate Henrietta Huxley brought her three infants to Down for a fortnight in March 1861, where Emma lavished consolation. Huxley remained in town to start his working-men's lectures at the School of Mines. But he sent reports on his men-and-apes talks, and the cloth-cap crowd which lapped them up. 'My working men stick by me wonderfully, the house fuller than ever,' he regaled his recuperating wife. 'By next Friday evening they will all be convinced that they are monkeys.'[8]

A few days later his slanging match with Owen spilled over into the *Athenaeum*. The 'slaying of the slain' continued week in, week out in this emotionally charged period, Huxley's refutations becoming more acrimonious with each resuscitation of the corpse. He was joined by the entire Darwinian camp, which turned out ritually to refute Owen. Some put his ape-brain blunder down to his use of brains deformed in their preserving spirits, others to his poor dissectors. The Christians who sided with Huxley maintained that cerebral differences bore no relation to psychology, or the debate to human ancestry. But Owen tried to whip up sympathy by tarring Huxley as an 'advocate of man's origin from a transmuted ape.' Eventually the *Athenaeum* even printed one of Owen's ripostes under the head 'Ape-Origin of Man as Tested by the Brain.' The ruse backfired. In private Huxley had already talked provocatively of 'pithecoid man' – ape-like man – delighting Darwin, who called the term 'a whole paper & theory in itself.' (But then he had been mooting 'monkey-men' in secret for twenty years.) Now Huxley could go public on the issue, accepting Owen's terms of debate.[9] By turning a question of brain structure into one of human ancestry, Owen had ensured that Huxley would proclaim his defeat as a vindication of Darwinism in its most sensitive aspect.

Darwin sat down to each Saturday's *Athenaeum*, crowing with delight at Huxley's ridiculing responses; 'well done, but almost too civil,' he gleefully replied after one. 'It is a good joke, that since Owen attacked me, I do not feel at all a good monitor, & feel more inclined to clap anyone on the back, than to cry hold forth! I wonder whether he will answer you. Oh Lord what a thorn you must be in the poor dear man's side.'[10] Mock concern, of course; he now evinced no shred of sympathy for the poor dismembered man. Darwin's 'demoniacal' hatred of Owen grew like a boil and burst into the open as he egged Huxley on.

In this hysterical atmosphere Huxley's anatomical compatriots forlornly tried to disentangle the issues. One of his Oxford protégés declared that 'our higher and diviner life is not a mere result of the abundance of our convolutions.'[11] But this wasn't the point for Huxley. Owen was being indicted for perjury, and it was made to seem symptomatic. His whole toadying ideology was in the dock. Huxley intended to create a spectacle, promising, 'Before I have done with that mendacious humbug I will nail him out, like a kite to a barn door, an example to all evil doers.' As prosecuting attorney, he was exposing the incriminating evidence: religious contaminants had led to Owen's blindness and evil doing. He was another, like the priests, who 'prostitute Science.' Darwin's new professionals were the more faithful followers of Nature.

It was a powerful call: a denunciation of Owen and Wilberforce designed to appeal to the up-and-coming meritocrats who despised the Anglican *ancien régime*. In the eyes of older chivalrous souls Huxley had stepped well beyond the bounds of good taste, and they loathed his 'offensive manner.' But he deliberately trumpeted his efforts to 'get a lie recognised as such.' Moralizing served his group well. Sucking up to 'the "peace & make-things-pleasant party"' promised no return. He would dump these reconcilers in a 'hot locus in the lower regions' if he 'were Commander in Chief in their universe.'[12]

The campaign was devastingly effective, with each 'slaying' followed by a recruiting drive by the Darwinians. The sniping lasted two years and left a festering cancer for life. When Huxley joined the Zoological Society Council in 1861, Owen left. A year later Huxley moved to stop Owen being elected to the Royal Society Council, on the grounds that no 'body of gentlemen' should admit a member 'guilty of wilful & deliberate falsehood.'

Huxley's belligerence worried Lyell. He was equally troubled by what Huxley was advocating, an ape ancestry. For years he had denied such bad blood in the family; now he was forced to confront the problem head on. He decided to face it in a book, to reconcile himself – somehow – to the artefacts and fossils that proved man's ancient pedigree. Darwin had little sympathy for the loss of human 'dignity,' teasing his old friend: '*Our* ancestor was an animal which breathed water, had a swim bladder, a great swimming tail, an imperfect skull, and undoubtedly was an hermaphrodite! Here is a pleasant genealogy for mankind.' Even pleasanter, 'mankind will progress to such a pitch' that nineteenth-century gents will probably be looked back on 'as mere Barbarians.'[13]

Huxley was even less help on dignity or design. He was too happy to pit the 'anthropomorphism' of Providence against 'the passionless impersonality of the unknown and unknowable,' itself becoming the commanding orthodoxy of the secular Darwinians. Nor would he disentangle men and apes. He told Lyell that there was more difference in size between the brains of people than between small-brained men and gorillas. 'Under these circumstances it would certainly be well to let go the head [as a way of distinguishing the species] though I am afraid it does not mend matters much to lay hold of the foot.'[14]

By April 1861 Lyell had toured the archaeological sites in England and France to confirm that stone tools occurred alongside extinct hyaenas. He had denied such human antiquity for thirty years, but the evidence was now overwhelming. Falconer had found pre-glacial scrapers in 1858 in a cave in Brixham, a fishing village on the Devon coast; and in 1859, after touring the Abbeville flint site in France, Lyell had signalled his conversion. Examining flints in a Bedford gravel pit he had a clearer picture of the pre-Ice Age dating for ancient man. Darwin was ecstatic. 'It is great. What a fine long pedigree you have given the human race.' Others were stretching it further. A new fossil human had opportunely made his début, a Neanderthal skull from a cave near Düsseldorf, described by the anatomist Hermann Schaaffhausen in 1858. It had a swept-back forehead, overhanging brow ridges, and brutal looks. Lyell questioned Huxley about it, intriguing him too. Busk translated Schaaffhausen's paper for the *Natural History Review* in April, and Huxley set to, examining the cast of the 'degraded' cranium at the College of Surgeons.[15] Now he had a new line of lectures in mind, on fossil man.

That spring Henslow lay dying of heart disease. Hooker stood vigil at his father-in-law's bedside, watching him bid 'farewell to his friends, parishioners and little botanical school children, one by one.' For two months Hooker sent harrowing reports of Henslow's decline. They threw Darwin into agonies of indecision, and he finally apologized about not visiting, on 23 April. It was a melancholy moment. Ten years to that day Annie had closed her eyes for the last time. Darwin had everything to thank Henslow for: his *Beagle* trip, his grants, his support, his parish advice – Annie, George, and Leonard even bore his own children's names. But he declined a last call: 'I sh[d]. not like to be in the House (even if you could hold me) as my retching is apt to be extremely loud.' His own health was precarious, and a few minutes speaking at the Linnean Society that month had brought on '24 hours vomiting.' The decision racked him with guilt: 'I never felt my weakness [a] greater evil.'[16] He did not see Henslow again. After his death on 18 May, Darwin penned a short, clinical note for the family *Memoir*, but it could not assuage his feelings.

He went his sick way, worrying about the children. His youngest, Horace, was Annie's age when she died, and Charles waited for the hereditary weakness to show. Lenny, eleven, was being tutored by a local vicar and seemed 'slow & backward' in his lessons. His deficiency, Charles feared, was only 'in part owing to loss of time from ill-health.' Sixteen-year-old George came home from Clapham School for surgery on his decaying teeth. As he passed out under the chloroform, so death-like in its effect, Charles relived old memories and was overcome with nausea.

Henrietta's condition upset him most. She remained weak and wan, an invalid at eighteen. A typhoid infection the previous year had left her dangerously close to death; for months she had required three attendants around the clock. Her fevery spells and indigestion caused Charles such 'incessant anxiety' that sometimes his 'tender sympathy and emotion' were too 'agitating' for her, and she could 'hardly bear to have him in the room.' The lack of recovery left Emma at her wits' end. 'I have succeeded pretty well in teaching myself not to give way to despondency,' she sighed, but she could only 'live from day to day.'[17]

Amid this backdrop of painful thoughts, lost children, lost friends, Emma poured her heart out in another touching letter to Charles, reminiscent of the one she had written after their marriage. The strength of her pleading reflected her own painful experience: the 'only relief' was to take affliction 'as from God's hand' and 'try to believe that all suffering & illness is meant to help us to exalt our minds & to look forward with hope to a future state.'

> When I see your patience, deep compassion for others[,] self command & above all gratitude for the smallest thing done to help you I cannot help longing that these precious feelings should be offered to Heaven for the sake of your daily happiness . . . I often think of the words 'Thou shalt keep him in perfect peace whose mind is stayed on thee.' It is feeling & not reasoning that drives one to prayer.

Charles had done with Christianity, damned hell's torments, but Emma was now urging prayer for his present happiness, not as insurance against future suffering. She wished him to find the meaning of his pain in an after-life, where their love would go on for ever. But the hope of heaven was dim. He only scrawled 'God Bless you' on the bottom of the note. In the end all that stood between his grief and thoughts of oblivion was Emma's unshakeable faith. He became twitchy whenever she left him alone.[18]

Huxley's spring lectures on men and apes to the labourers and shopkeepers were a roaring success. Lyell, boning up for his book, sat among the cloth-caps and was 'astonished at the magnitude and attentiveness of the audience.' The scene might have been his worst fears realized, teaching a gorilla-ancestry to the great unwashed, yet the carters and cabbies were polite, and they would, he conceded, 'devour any amount of your anthropoid ape questions.'

The lecture was rapturously received because human origins had been trailed in the radical press for decades. (Even as Huxley was talking, the secularist *Reasoner* was running an evolutionary series combating 'Theological Theories of the Origin of Man,' arming infidel missionaries with human fossils and Darwin's book.) Radical workers were evolutionists long before the neophyte addressing them. Inflammatory tracts had sought to undermine priestly power with materialist explanations of man's ancestry. The *Origin* was grist to their mill, like *Vestiges* and French Revolutionary science before it. One tailor offered Darwin services in exchange for an inscribed copy; a baker plagued him with a whole manuscript assessing the *Origin*. This audience was prepared for any anatomist who would stand on their ground and relate man to the 'under-world of life.' Gutter-press hacks gleefully turned up pad in hand to report Huxley's 'exciting and even solemn' words.[19]

Huxley was capturing a new constituency for Darwin. Each talk was carefully tailored. He started off iconoclastically, like one of their own infidel missionaries, praising those 'cursed with the spirit of mere scepticism' and casting off tired traditions. As on so many radical broadsheets, he intimated that man was made in the image of an ape. 'Brought face to face' with chimpanzees, 'these blurred copies of himself, the least thoughtful of men is conscious of a certain shock.' The clinical anatomy was dressed with a bit of artisan cynicism. 'It is as if nature herself had foreseen the arrogance of man,' he said, speaking of the mirror held up by the gorilla, 'and with Roman severity had provided that his intellect by its very triumphs, should call into prominence the slaves, admonishing the conqueror that he is but dust.'

Yet he distanced himself from the gutter cynics bent on degrading mankind. Man might have come from the brutes, but 'he is assuredly not *of* them.' A common origin implies no 'brutalization' – man is not 'degraded from his high estate' by his descent from a 'bestial savage,' Huxley pleaded, mindful of Lyell sitting incongruously among the carters.

Rather, he promoted evolution as a form of self-betterment, urging that the downtrodden masses, 'once escaped from the blinding influences of traditional prejudice, will find in the lowly stock whence Man has sprung, the best evidence of the splendour of his capacities; and will discern in his long progress through the Past, a reasonable ground of faith in his attainment of a nobler Future.' This 'lowly-origin, noble-future' picture would have fallen flat among the port-swilling aristocracy, but the idea of promotion through the ranks was devoured by the aspiring sweeps and enterprising shopmen. Others caught Huxley's drift. One correspondent fleshed the pedigree out. 'Man's descent reads very much like a Law Lords pedigree in the Peerage, a remote ancestor temp. Will. 1 [in William the Conqueror's time]. Seventy fourth in descent a Wig-maker – and then the full-blown Chancellor or Chief Justice.'[20] Exactly; evolution bestowed scientific dignity on lowly parentage and promised better things.

It might not have been Darwin's image; Huxley mentioned no callous competition, no going to the wall. But the lecture served a purpose, blowing aside the smoke on the burning human question. Where once it was taboo, the subject now seemed obligatory, and the question was carved and apportioned in every way. Lyell was plotting human antiquity, Lubbock publishing on Danish shell mounds, and Falconer finding more Brixham tools, including an extinct bear's arm bone carved as a stave. There was no doubt among Darwin's group that humans could be pushed into the fossil past, or that man lived alongside extinct hippos, even if Huxley's dinosaur-spearing *Homo ooliticus* was a bit strong.[21]

Given the excitement, Darwin's continuing obsession with stewed rabbit bones verged on the mundane. He was now deep in his domestication book, borrowing collections of fowls' skulls, and posting pleas for more carcasses: 'get me, if you can, another specimen of an old white Angora rabbit,' he asked one breeder. 'I want it dead for the skeleton; and not knocked on the head.'

He stopped for July and August to take Henrietta to the fishing village of Torquay, opposite Brixham on the Devon coast. Here in the warm sun Charles spent hours on his hands and knees, watching insects visit wild orchids. Bizarre petals guided the bees to the nectaries, enticing them into position. Pollen sacs were then glued to their probosces, precisely where they could be removed by a stigma of another flower. Since the late 30s, in the gardens at Maer and The Mount, he had speculated on the ways bees cross-pollinate, convinced by his theory that crossed plants give stronger offspring. Orchids offered the most exquisite devices for achieving that end. Coming home from Torquay, he searched for little orchids on the hillocks around Downe. In the idyllic sun it seemed infinitely preferable to stewing pigeons. The lure was too strong; he put 'the confounded cocks, hens and ducks' down and switched.[22] He was side-tracked again.

There was a flourishing orchid fancy in Victorian Britain. But no back-street, grog-shop hobby this; it was an élite fancy. Wealthy enthusiasts gave over hot-houses to the fantastic flowers and dispatched orchid hunters to the tropics. Darwin shot out feelers and was showered with rare specimens. Orchids proved the ultimate test case. What more glorious example of floral whimsy could exist? 'Who has ever dreamed of finding an utilitarian purpose in the forms and colours of flowers'? Huxley had once asked incredulously. Darwin of course. He took the hardest case and cracked it. Orchid petals were exquisite devices for guiding bees and moths to particular spots for dobbing or docking pollen. Every ridge and horn served this end. Natural selection could not explain useless or frivolous or pretty flowers; it *could* explain functional ones.

He became lost in the floral intricacies, delighting in the outrageous. The orchid *Catasetum*, peculiar enough for having three flowers – male, female and hermaphrodite (themselves thought to have been three species until his study) – was actually sensitive to insects and fired arrows with a sticky pollen head as they brushed past. He described the preposterous mechanism to Huxley, to be greeted by, 'Do you really think that I can believe all that!'[23]

The subject was genteel and a perfect foil. He worked out the homologous parts of every flower, making them 'modifications of one and the same ancestral organ.' As in barnacles, each homologous organ twisted and turned to a different role, switching tactics as needs arose, adopting any contingency to deposit the packet of pollen. He talked Murray into taking a book, selling it as a fashionable subject seen through evolutionary eyes. And if that wasn't enticement enough, it would be a new 'Bridgewater Treatise' for the old fogies. But a Bridgewater with a kick: a glorious lampoon on design, pointing not to God, but a series of accidents. It was 'a "flank movement" on the enemy,' he twitted Gray. Darwin was following his grandfather yet again. But this was to be no *Loves of the Plants*, nothing as salacious; 'any woman could read it,' and Murray was wise enough to see that many would. With German and Dutch translations of the *Origin*, and a French one in press, Darwin was rising up the list.

He still wondered whether the whole venture wasn't the 'most ridiculous thing.' And no sooner had he sold the idea in September than he fell ill again; the work piled up, the prose proved intractable, his stomach erupted, and he seethed through gritted teeth 'I ought to be exterminated.'[24]

Friends proved a mixed blessing, and bulldogs infuriating. Huxley continued to cavil about sterility: breeders had not produced infertile hybrids by crossing fancy breeds. Until they did, Huxley argued – until they produced, in effect, separate species – the analogy between artificial and natural selection was incomplete, and the *Origin*'s theory unproved. So Darwin ended up experimenting, losing hundreds of hours pollinating plants and sifting seeds. He was collating his results on primroses in January 1862, and trying to persuade Huxley to mute his criticisms. He showed that primroses and cowslips, nearly identical in structure and long thought to have been varieties, produced sterile hybrids.[25] Sterility, he suggested, evolved to allow close species like these to diverge. It was a mechanism to stop them both being blended back to some unadapted middle line. Huxley was half-convinced.

While Darwin sifted seeds, his letters chased Huxley to Edinburgh, where the evangelist was 'preaching Darwinism pure & simple as applied to man to the Scotch presbyterians. Whats more I made 'em listen . . .'

He 'found sinners enough in "Saintly Edinburgh",' as in London. But then the tabloid talk was all of salacious apes, thanks to the French-American traveller Paul du Chaillu, whose chilling gorilla hunts were sensationalized in his *Explorations and Adventures in Equatorial Africa*. Du Chaillu was in England lecturing and talking, visiting Owen and exhibiting skins and skeletons. The tall stories of women-snatching gorilla males and screaming females clinging to their babies amid a hail of bullets dominated the gutter press; everybody was talking gorillas, every Irishman in a *Punch* cartoon was a 'Mr. G. O'Rilla' or 'Mr. O'Rangoutang.' More and more, audiences flocked to Huxley's serious talks, lapping them up, not realizing, the Free Church *Witness* said, the 'foul outrage' being committed upon them. When 'their kindred to the brute creation was most strongly asserted, the applause was the most vigorous,' it reported, appalled. Given the anti-slavery furore during the American Civil War, the *Witness* expected the hood-winked workers to form a 'Gorilla Emancipation Society.' The 'vilest and beastliest paradox ever vented in ancient or modern times amongst Pagans or Christians,' was the kindest cut.[26]

This was what Huxley had planned. He gloried in the provocation, sending press cuttings to Hooker and Darwin. 'I told them in so many words that I entertained no doubt of the origin of man from the same stock as the apes.' He was revelling in the Darwinian jingoism: 'Everybody prophesied I should be stoned and cast out of the city gate,' he reported to Darwin, but 'I met with unmitigated applause!!' The gung-ho mood was infectious. 'By Jove,' Darwin responded, 'you have attacked Bigotry in its strong-hold. I thought you would have been mobbed.'[27]

Still he pottered on with orchids, refusing to enter another side-show. The flanking-movement became obvious on 15 May when his book appeared under the unpromising title, *On the Various Contrivances by which British and Foreign Orchids are fertilised by Insects*. This was the first of his books on beauty and the bizarre, the evolution of the inexplicable. It also proved the benefit of crossing; orchids were engineered to receive pollen-bearing insects. Only the odd one held out; the bee orchid, which seemed to be a self-fertilizer, and predictably doomed to extinction. Darwin must have been the only man on the planet who wanted to live a thousand years just to see the bee orchid's demise.

Orchids was published just in time to give the newly returned Wallace a complimentary copy. Wallace announced his arrival in England with a present of a wild honeycomb from Timor. He was home finally after eight years in the East, and lodging on the fringe of London's West End, where he could get 'doctored,' read the backlog of reviews, and recover from exhaustion. Through the summer he sifted and organized his six-year tally of 125,660 specimens, as Darwin had done in more salubrious surroundings so long ago.[28]

Huxley gathered his lectures on apes, origins, and Neanderthals into a slim book on *Man's Place in Nature*. No fat, two-volume tome for him, but the effect was just as devastating. Although reading the proofs was a 'great treat' for Lyell in August 1862, he worried about parts and warned that they were 'not in good taste & will do no good.' But advising Huxley 'to write as if you were not running counter to . . . old ideas' was like dragging a bull backwards out of a china shop. He was too intent on smashing Owen's providential pots and humiliating him at every turn. And anyway Lyell's tall order was countermanded by the militant strategy of the younger naturalists.

Huxley and Darwin had forced the agenda on apes and origins, unsettling more orthodox Anglicans who looked to Owen for a response. Even the *Athenaeum* goaded Owen. The Darwinians on their side had said enough 'to freeze us.' Darwin had spoken and 'found a bold and able advocate in Prof. Huxley. Is Prof. Owen, then, to be reserved?'[29]

Owen was taking a very different approach. He believed that jellyfish and liver flukes and the like, which pass through complex life cycles involving different forms, each one 'giving birth to another,' held the key. He was pressing for sudden jumps, for the analogous birth of one species direct from another. What did this mean for man? The Revd Gilbert Rorison, a Scottish Episcopalian minister, writing his orthodox article on the Genesis 'Creative Week' for the *Replies to 'Essays and Reviews'*, wondered just this. Did Owen believe that man was 'produced by *Creative Law* (& in so far supernaturally) *through* the lower: e.g. the womb of the Ape'? Did the 'special Creative Energy' work on the gorilla's reproductive system to create the first human?

Owen would only admit some pre-ordained natural cause of man's birth; he intimated that it did not matter religiously if the ape's womb were the mediating organ, or, astonishingly, if '"original sin" should prove to be only the remnant of the untransmuted ape still lingering in our constitution.' If 'God's ministers' *were* natural causes it would not diminish our duties and responsibilities. Rorison published Owen's letter in the *Replies*, failing to see it as a chide to literalists.[30] But, of course, ending up in the reactionary *Replies* – edited by Bishop Wilberforce – and contributing to Rorison's 'theological hash' only damned Owen further in Darwin's and Huxley's eyes.

Owen did not deny that man might change, even hinting that *Homo sapiens* might be replaced by higher species 'at an inconceivably remote date,' only that transmutation was the mechanism. Nevertheless he was ostracized, dumped by the Darwinians *en masse*, who were making sure he was by-passed by history. Darwin thought Owen 'so dishonest that I really now care little what he says,' eventually confessing to Huxley, 'I believe I hate him more than you do.'[31]

At Downe the grind continued, and the summer saw Darwin 'slaving on bones of ducks and pigeons.' Unable to let Huxley's cavil go, he delegated as his health deteriorated, offering breeders £5 to cross Spanish cocks with white Silk hens to check the chicks' fertility. He was going against the fancy grain, coercing breeders to undo their varieties by producing sterile hybrids. No mind, he reassured them, they will always 'do for the pot.' By now he had gardeners experimenting at Kew and Edinburgh Botanic Gardens, apiarists and fanciers shipping hives and corpses, and breeders examining every cross, from melons to mastiffs.

When Sulivan and Wickham visited on 21 October for a *Beagle* reunion, they found the philosopher inundated in orchids, sundews, and interminable trays of seeds, with farmyard bones everywhere, and dead ornamentals brewing in foul-smelling spirits. The old dyspeptic himself had aged badly. They caught him at a low moment, after Emma's and Lenny's scarlet fever attack in the summer, and typically sipping the latest quack remedy, 'Condy's Ozonized Water Cure.'

He was so wrapped up in orchids now that he had Sir John Lubbock's gardener build him a hot-house over winter, and he sent a tax-cart to Kew for plants to stock it. It was the pigeons over again: 'You cannot imagine what pleasure your plants give me,' he thanked Hooker. Henrietta 'and I go and gloat over them.' It was his only consolation in another uncomfortable winter. His skin inflammation left him sloughing like a reptile. He gruesomely related to his friend

Falconer how eczema had 'taken the epidermis a dozen times clean off.'[32]

Falconer, the only fossil expert in London to rival Owen, cheered him with a tip-off in January 1863 about a 'sort of mis-begotten-bird-creature,' a part-reptilian feathered fossil from Solenhofen in Germany, and by all accounts a prize ready to drop into his lap. Owen had bought the exquisitely preserved bird for the British Museum. Darwin's old friend George Waterhouse had been dispatched to Pappenheim in Bavaria, to pay the unheard-of sum of £450 (increasing the fossil's notoriety). Darwin had predicted that a proto-bird would one day turn up with unfused wing fingers, but this exceeded all expectations. He pressed Falconer for more 'about the wondrous bird.'[33] As the news dribbled in he pieced together an astonishing picture. It was as old as the dinosaurs, with a long, lizard-like tail, and Owen had detected four free fingers in each wing, clawed.

'The fossil bird,' he agreed, 'is a grand case for me.' Others feared as much and were trying to forestall him. At the Munich Natural History Museum the ageing Andreas Wagner guessed that Darwin, lost in his 'fantastic dreams,' would hail it as an ancestral bird. He dismissed it on hearsay as an aberrant reptile to ward off 'Darwinian misinterpretations.' Owen was also worried. He officially described the fossil, christening it *Archaeopteryx* in a paper read to the Royal Society. He called it unequivocally a bird, but primitive, its fingers and tail placing it closer to the primal vertebrate archetype.[34]

Darwinians rushed to regain the initiative. The beak was detected on the slab, and most controversial of all, four, perhaps five, teeth, the lustre of the enamel still visible. Announced in the *Natural History Review*, the discovery of teeth left no doubt about the archaic bird's relevance to 'the great question of the Origin of Species.' Hooker saw another great lesson. He caught part of Owen's paper and realized that the fossil, suddenly turning up in a lithographic quarry, proved Darwin's point about the bittiness of the fossil record. Darwin, at home sipping his 'Ozonized Water' and sifting strawberry varieties, revelled in the splendid 'bird-creature with its long tail and fingers.' A note was filed away for the next edition of the *Origin*.[35]

Huxley's lectures to the labourers this winter popularized Darwinism. His ensuing little book, sewn together from six fourpenny pamphlets (published by an enterprising hack taking notes in the audience), appeared in December. Darwin was full of praise; it was 'capitally written,' 'simply perfect.' So good, in fact, that 'I may as well shut up shop altogether.' As for the substance, the talks flew high and low. Huxley might have vindicated Mr Darwin's science, which was no 'modern black art;' he might have scotched the humbug about the *Origin*'s speculative method.[36] But he *still* overcalled the sterility objection. The ferocity of newshounds Darwin expected, but not the continual nipping of a friendly bulldog.

None of his friends moved far or fast enough for him. He coveted their public praise, and craved their emotional support to dispel his perennial fears. On 4 February 1863 Lyell's *Antiquity of Man* arrived. Darwin cheered 'the great book,' then took it to Eras's for ten days to read. Sir Charles's endorsement would be the most important to date; he expected his old mentor to give 'the whole subject of change of species' an enormous boost. But apes and immortality gnawed at the sexagenarian, and Hooker knew that he would 'have a pretty job to reconcile all his old Geology and Biology to the new state of things.' Even so 'the sale of his work will be *prodigious*.' 'What a sale!' Darwin exclaimed; 4000 went into the shops on publication day. Hooker was right, 'he has the ear of the public.'[37]

The *Antiquity of Man* was tame, and Darwin despaired at Lyell's timidity, even if the book as a whole produced a striking effect. Much was said, but so much more was missing. Part was a stale hash, a 'compilation' from archaeologists far ahead of him in the game, although Lyell covered his tracks by implying that 'nothing is to be trusted until he has observed it.' Part – a small part – was a feeble summary of the evidence for transmutation. He attacked Owen's brain work (cued by Huxley) but nowhere said 'openly that he believed in change of species, and as a consequence that man was derived' from an ape-like ancestor. Lyell was visibly straining, but unable to move. He made man old but refused to degrade him, reverting to 'new and powerful causes' to explain the spiritual part of human nature.[38]

Back at Downe, Darwin's patience ran out. The Lyells were coming to stay for a few days and he braced himself for a confrontation: 'I dread it,' Hooker heard, 'but I must say how much disappointed I am that he has not spoken out on species, still less on man. And the best of the joke is that he thinks he has acted with the courage of a martyr of old.' But Lyell *had* struggled, and no martyr moved so far from accepting man as an 'archangel ruined' to seeing him as an elevated animal. As he explained to Darwin, 'I have spoken out to the full extent of my present convictions, and even beyond my state of *feeling* as to man's unbroken descent from the brutes.' It had been unrealistic to expect Lyell to 'go the whole orang,' one who had devoted thirty years and nine editions of the *Principles of Geology* to refuting bestial transmutation. 'Your judgment would have been an epoch in the subject,' Darwin groaned; now 'all that is over with me.'[39] He felt so sick that he cancelled the Lyells' visit.

No wonder he shouted 'Hurrah the Monkey Book has come' as Huxley's *Man's Place in Nature* arrived later in February. It was more to his taste, and to Hooker's – 'amazingly clever' he called it. The frontispiece spoke more loudly than the text. It showed a line of skeletons, as though they were standing at a tram stop, with a gibbon at the rear, stooping apes in the middle, and a man at the head. 'It is a grim and grotesque procession,' the Duke of Argyll squirmed, thankful that their brains could not be similarly queued. This line of 'gibbering, grovelling apes' set the *Athenaeum*'s teeth chattering. It lumped Lyell and Huxley as cynical degraders; the one making man 'a hundred thousand years' old, the other giving him 'a hundred thousand apes for his ancestors.'[40]

Man's Place mined the last ounce of gold from the Owen debate. Owen was his own worst enemy; his tongue-twisting expressions invited parody. His 'continuous operation of the ordained becoming of living things' simply meant that God was an *'anticipating* Intelligence' constantly re-fitting species to the world by means of natural law (itself a sort of divine edict). Huxley, however, treated it as a piece of semantic pandemonium. Such providential platitudes galled the swelling ranks of rationalist Darwinians. Owen's words even sounded evasive, and it was Huxley who extracted the capital in *Man's Place*:

> though I have heard of the announcement of a formula
> touching 'the ordained continuous becoming of organic forms,'
> it is obvious that it is the first duty of a hypothesis to be
> intelligible, and [this] . . . may be read backwards, or forwards,
> or sideways, with exactly the same amount of signification.

Darwin relished the 'delicious sneer.' The theatrics used in nailing Owen boosted sales, and the 1000 copies of *Man's Place* sold quickly, requiring a reprint within weeks.[41]

But nothing made up for his disappointment over Lyell. While reading the *Antiquity of Man* Charles was vomiting so badly again that Emma resorted to drastic measures. 'It breaks my heart,' he sighed to Hooker, 'but Emma says . . . that we must all go for two months to Malvern.' He had avoided the spa for twelve years, the memories cut too deep. Even now he thought 'a good severe fit of Eczema . . . might save me' from the trauma. But no, a mild one simply delayed his departure and left him languid. In desperation he tried visiting the family, hoping that the change would cure him. He only grew worse, and by June was confined to his couch, fit only to watch his new tendril-bearing plants. Gray had started him off with a packet of wild cucumber seeds, which had sprouted and rather hooked the patient. Day and night, from his sickbed, he observed the long lasso-like tendrils sweeping around in a circle, first one way then the other. 'I am getting very much amused by my tendrils,' he told Hooker, requesting more exotic ones to watch, 'it is just the sort of niggling work which suits me.'[42]

The eczema cleared up, but then word came that Dr Gully was ill, and the Malvern trip was postponed once more. Charles lived a 'hermit's life' all summer, more so 'than ever.' 'Devilish headaches' set in and by August he was retching again every morning. He posted off vials of vomit for analysis, but to no avail. As the partridge season opened in September, Emma finally had her way. She took him off to the sounds of shooting, reminding them of the 'old times.' In Malvern they avoided their former lodgings, but there was no escaping the sad associations of the town. Charles and Emma had never seen Annie's grave. It was hard enough for Emma to venture into the churchyard, but soul-destroying not to find the headstone. Charles jumped to the conclusion that it had been stolen in a despicable act of vandalism. Fox, who had seen it once, was contacted and he directed Emma to the overgrown spot.[43]

By the most crushing coincidence, within days – on Tuesday 29 September – they received a note from Hooker, sobbing 'My darling little 2^d girl died here an hour ago.' Hooker's six-year-old Minnie was carried off 'after a few hours *alarming* illness.' He was given three minutes' warning by the doctor, and spent the precious moments by her bedside. 'I have just buried my darling little girl,' he wrote a few days later. She was

> the flower of my flock in everyone's eyes, the companion of my walks, the first of my children who has shown any love for music and flowers, & the sweetest tempered affectionate little thing that ever I knew. It will be long before I cease to hear her voice in my ears – or feel her little hand stealing into mine, by the fire side & in the Garden – wherever I go she is there.

The memories came flooding back at Malvern. 'I understand well your words: "wherever I go she is there",' Charles answered mournfully. 'God bless you my best of friends.' Re-reading the letter, he cried again 'over our poor darling.' But time heals, and the tears had 'lost that unutterable bitterness of former days.'[44]

35

A Living Grave

GULLY ORDERED SIX MONTHS' rest, but all Charles managed was six months' sickness. He became too weak even to raise a
pen, and Emma took dictation. The good news, an Italian translation
of the *Origin*, was not enough to rally him. Nor the family news
enough to shock him – even though widower Charles Langton's
marriage to Darwin's poorly, 53-year-old sister Catherine struck
everybody else as an act of futility. Darwin was spreadeagled every
day on a sofa, 'steadily going downhill,' wishing he were dead on
one, wanting 'to live to do a little more work' the next. Visitors were
banned, friends and pilgrim freethinkers put off. Harley Street doctors
came and went with vials of urine. Nothing worked; nobody could
find anything wrong with his 'brain or heart.' He sank lower, unable
to walk 100 yards to the hot-house, unable even to cope with *The
Times*, and Emma had to move on to 'trashy' novels. He vomited
after every meal, and several times nightly – at one point for twenty-
seven days in a row. Washed out and wiped out, he hoped he could
'crawl a little uphill again' or, if not, that 'my life may be very short.'[1]
 The debilitating sickness lasted until spring 1864. April was merciful and found him on the mend, sitting in the greenhouse. For years,
on and off, he had been breeding purple loosestrifes (*Lythrum*),
struck as always by the oddities of nature, and there was nothing
odder than their triple sexuality.[2] He loved sexual enigmas because
they bore so closely on sterility and evolution – and provided the
ultimate excuse to potter. He had induced all manner of 'illegitimate
marriages' among loosestrifes, attempting to determine the reason for
their peculiar flowers. As his strength returned, he tweezered seeds
and planted a new generation.
 Lythrum has three kinds of flower. The female (pollen-receiving)

519

stigma can be either tall, medium, or short-styled; and whatever its size, two sets of male (pollen-producing) stamens occupy the remaining two slots – so if the female stigma is tall, the male stamens will be medium and short-sized. Nobody had asked why nature had resorted to such a peculiar arrangement, and nobody had thought in functional terms. Darwin revelled in inducing the eighteen possible sexual combinations, brushing pollen from every sized stamens on to every sized stigma, counting the seeds and growing them in dozens of pots to test their fertility.

He sorted hundreds of seeds this April, tabulating the results and writing them up for the Linnean Society. Only six 'marriages' proved 'legitimate,' and in each case the stamens and styles proved to be the same height. His tables clearly revealed that the greater the disparity in height, the greater the 'illegitimacy' and frequency of sterility. Tall styles and short stigmas (which occurred in the same plant) produced sterile seeds: it was another of nature's ad hoc mechanisms to ensure cross-pollination.

Talk of illegitimacy might have shocked the ladies' guilds, at least coming from Erasmus Darwin's grandson. (Grandfather's own bastardizing experiments were still supplying tittle-tattle. At this moment Darwin suspected the widow of a botanical friend, Francis Boott, to be an illegitimate granddaughter of old Erasmus.) But Darwin was stolid and methodical, reducing the loves of the plants to cold, clinical calculation. Sterile seed counts somehow fitted an unromantic, data-crunching age. Not for him Erasmus's flowery personifications, as styles and stamens bent to embrace in a kiss:

> Two knights before thy fragrant altar bend,
> Adored Melissa! and two squires attend.

Still he could tease. Solicited by a Mrs Becker for something edifying for her ladies' literary society, he posted 'On the Sexual Relations of the Three Forms of *Lythrum salicaria*.' Goodness knows how many red faces left after hearing that 'nature has ordained a most complex marriage-arrangement, namely a triple union between three hermaphrodites, – each hermaphrodite being in its female organ quite distinct from the other two hermaphrodites and partially distinct in its male organs, and each furnished with two sets of males.'[3]

By the time Darwin had finished with *Lythrum* the bedroom, study, and greenhouses were choking with climbers and coiling tendrils. Everywhere was covered with Hooker's exotics and commercial creepers: Queensland wax flowers, *Cerepegia*s from Ceylon, passion flowers and bryony. And never of course just one, but seven species of clematis, eight species of Indian cress . . . As he sat down to pen a short paper on the sweeping tendrils in May, others were tending rather more warily to the varieties of man.

Lyell's *Antiquity* and Spencer's *Social Statics* had spurred Wallace to speak out on human evolution. That month Darwin pored over Wallace's first paper, delivered to the unpleasantly ultra-racist, pro-slavery Anthropological Society.

The Society itself was an abomination, and the American Civil War only heightened Darwin's detestation. Despite Gray's dispatches on the 'dreadful carnage' during the Battle of the Wilderness, he remained adamant 'that the destruction of Slavery would be well worth a dozen years war.' There was no scientific justification for slavery, and the entire rival Ethnological Society agreed. London partisans were now busy shoring up positions on the race question with the inalienable truths of biology. The white supremacist Anthropologicals were at the throats of the abolitionist Ethnologicals (led by Huxley, Busk, Lubbock, Galton, and Wallace, with Darwin an honorary fellow and Eras on the Council), and the reviews provided cover for literary assassination.[4] Wallace, the co-operative peace-broker, was trying to engineer a truce based on a daring evolutionary compromise. He proposed that the races had long been separate (pleasing the Anthropologicals), yet had emerged from a single stock just after the ape stage (pleasing the Ethnological Darwinians).

As a good – or at this time rather wobbly – socialist Wallace started on the social differences of men and animals. Even primitive societies had a 'division of labour:' members of a tribe hunt or fish, others gather or plant. 'Mutual assistance' is all-important: the sick are cared for, food is shared, internal competition is reduced for the good of the group. As social organization strengthens, these shared 'moral' qualities will be honed to perfection by natural selection.

Competition was not between individuals, but the groups themselves. The hardiest races with the greatest ingenuity and co-operation would prevail, while the struggle 'leads to the inevitable extinction of all those low and mentally undeveloped populations with which the Europeans come into contact.' This Darwin could agree with; he marked the passage heavily. Imperial expansion from the north was wiping out the indigenous tribes. The *Beagle* voyage had shown him as much. He scribbled at the top of the page: 'natural selection is now acting on the inferior races when put into competition with the New Zealanders – high New Zelander[s] [sic] say the [Maori] race dying out like their own native rat.'[5] The hordes of

European colonists, rats and rural farmers, were wreaking havoc in the colonial bywaters.

So far a co-operative ethic was compatible with Darwinism in Wallace's political vision – indeed, mutual care was the product of natural selection. But then he changed tack: the advent of building, fire, clothing, and agriculture had made man master of his environment. The human physique, with its basic racial differences, was no longer subject to natural forces; the intellect prevailed over selection. Man's body had stopped evolving, except for aspects of skin colour or hair, while over hundreds of centuries intellectual progress had continued unabated, leaving humans with the body of an upright ape but the mind that could fashion a utopia.

Wallace's naturally selected group morality was leading society in a very unDarwinian direction. The old socialist peered optimistically at the millennium under this moral regime: everybody will 'work out his own happiness;' policing will be unnecessary, freedom will be the order of the day, 'since the well balanced moral faculties will never permit any one to transgress on the equal freedom of others;' coercive governments will wither ('every man will know how to govern himself'), the lot to be 'replaced by voluntary associations for all beneficial public purposes.'[6] On that upbeat, oddly anarchist note – intelligent selection leading to an egalitarian society – Wallace closed.

Darwin was presumably nonplussed to find the path to utopia paved by his science. He told Wallace that the brain/body dichotomy was 'grand and most eloquently done,' but he demurred on the abating of selection and played dumb on the politics. As he reasoned, the Australian savage is subject to selection, given his 'constant battles.' And English society will stay vital and progressive only through unimpeded competition. The sickly and degenerate deserve to be scythed down, he believed, even as he sent subscriptions to the Downe charities to maintain his own paternal order and worried about his sons' in-bred ailments. He decried 'primogeniture for destroying Natural Selection' even as he had Lubbock set up his eldest William in the banking business.

Wallace shook his head. Wars did not pick the fit, for the 'strongest and bravest' die first. Nor could he see much to 'sexual selection,' with each race choosing mates according to its own standards of beauty – nor, come to that, Darwin's claim that the European aristocracy is handsomer than the middle classes. Mere '*manner*' and refinement among the leisured classes were being 'confused' with beauty.[7] Politics was coming between the two men.

*

Wallace was brimming with ideas. He convinced Lyell that the caves of Borneo might reveal 'our progenitors.' Erasmus tipped off his brother that Lyell was for sending an expedition, and trying to whip up support among the Brixham Cave excavators. Lyell even set up a meeting with Sir James Brooke, the government-appointed Rajah of Sarawak, spurring him on with the thought that they might get 'extinct ourangs, if not the missing link itself.'[8] But no money was forthcoming and the British consul agreed to scout out the giant caverns himself.

What cave fossils there were seemed to confuse the issues. Neanderthal man was tugged this way and that. He was a 'poor idiot' to some, a primal human with brutish 'thoughts and desires' to others – *Homo neanderthalensis*, the first non-sapient man. Fossil skull-caps coming on top of antediluvian tools pushed the religious press to new exegetical lengths. Even granting a 'pre-Adamite' man, the Quaker *Friend* reasoned, there was no telling that he 'had any closer connection with the descendants of Adam than have the possible inhabitants of the Moon.' The Low Church *Morning Advertiser* wondered if this was 'the "man" who is without the "living soul," spoken of in Genesis.' Probably he was a brute-man, a 'mere animal, and of no more account than the bats and lizards of those long-past times.' The speculations and Huxley's attempt to turn the moral tables led Cardinal Wiseman to issue a Pastoral, appalled that 'a solitary cranium' or 'an antiquated fishbone' could be 'put in the scale against the doctrines of Scripture.' He condemned professors who teach that man has 'the matured intelligence,' and woman the 'ripened graces,' of a baboon. Shall we, he asked in *The Times*'s paraphrase, 'submit our belief in moral and spiritual truth to the judgment of those who claim to hold the key of scientific truth?'[9]

Through all of this the *Essays and Reviews* debate dragged on, its liberal Anglicanism a national scandal. Prelates fumed at the authors' dynamic, non-miraculous Christianity. Tolerate it and the Thirty-nine Articles mean nothing; the very Establishment would be imperilled. The two clerical essayists convicted of heresy for loose views on the Bible and eternal punishment had appealed to the Judicial Committee of the Privy Council, which now overturned the judgment, 'dismissing hell with costs.' Wilberforce was furious, as no doubt were the 137,000 laity who signed a letter of thanks to the Archbishops of Canterbury and York for voting against the Committee. With legal channels exhausted, churchmen united in public protest; evangelicals and High Church prelates buried their feuds and clasped hands. A declaration in favour of biblical inspiration and eternal torments was drawn up at Oxford and circulated to the 24,800 clergy. Wilberforce, armed by the 11,000 signatories, went to the Convocation of Canterbury and in June secured a 'synodical condemnation' of *Essays and Reviews*.[10] A backlash was brewing, and it boded ill for evolution.

Not that Darwin himself took much notice. While society grappled with imponderables, he hacked through creepers, trying to figure out how they evolved. Tables and sills were an entangled mass of twiners and tendrils; pots perched on every ledge as he timed sweeps and tested the effect of light. Warm summer days were spent in the hop fields watching the plants snake up their poles. He brought hops indoors, and sat ill in bed, tying weights to their tips in an attempt to slow their ascent. Around the house the vines took on a surreal appearance, covered in paint markers as he timed their twisting movements.

Clematis also clamped tight using its hooks, and since Darwin's studies were nothing if not inclusive, he started examining these leaf-climbers as well. He guessed that they were evolutionary links between the stem-twiners and tendril-waving plants. They served his purpose: he showed that hooks were modified leaf stems, and that tendrils were leaves or flower stalks drawn out drastically to form lassoes. The alterations aided a plant in its grappling, gyrating struggle for existence. Like the orchids' reproductive apparatus, they ensured the species' survival. His *divertissement*, as always, had grown into a major project. For four summer months he had been sidetracked as a result of Gray's wild cucumber seeds, and his paper, finished on 13 September, had grown so large that the Linnean Society published it as a 118-page monograph, 'The Movements and Habits of Climbing Plants.'

The next day he crept back to his domestic ducks and geese. He was not totally well; the slightest flurry could floor him. In October ten minutes with the Lyells gave him an 'awful day of vomiting' and he felt 'confined to a living grave,' showing how much he still resented Lyell's failure to support transmutation. From his mausoleum he continued cajoling fanciers and dispensing his largesse. He supported distressed breeders, helped a horticulturalist buy his ticket for India, and sent admirers his autograph.[11] He needed this humdrum existence – he preferred dealing with the world by post.

He lived vicariously through letters, especially his sons'. George, a Cambridge fresher, kept him up on collegiate life, and Frank at Clapham School recalled the agony of maths, bemoaning the tedious 'logrithmic calculations' set by the Revd Wrigley, the headmaster. Lenny and Horace, slow and frail, were still at home, being tutored by local clergymen. Everyone coddled them, dreading a breakdown. Charles also feared for their future, even despite the sound advice on suitable schools from Downe's old vicar, the Revd Innes.

Innes was now a correspondent, with a new name, Brodie Innes. He had changed it on inheriting property in the Scottish Highlands and had retired there with his wife and sickly son, putting the parish in the dubious hands of his curate, the Revd Thomas Stephens. Without a vicarage it proved impossible to attract a priest of calibre to Downe. Brodie Innes, still the patron, relied on Darwin as his deputy and informant. For years they had been pillars of the Coal and Clothing Club and the Friendly Society; and, on leaving, the vicar had made Darwin treasurer of the village school. The Revd Henslow's old protégé took on the job gladly, despite his own work. Tending the temporal needs of poor neighbours was as much a duty as meeting their spiritual ones, and he plied Brodie Innes with the parish politics even as Stephens reported on religious matters. They were a good combination. Liberal and Tory they might have been, but Darwin and Brodie Innes, as landowners, saw their interests coinciding. From the wilds of Elgin, Innes regaled Darwin with hunting stories while deploring his crofters' morals. 'They are certainly far from honest, but ... all as full of pious talk as an English Dissenter. What can I say more?'[12]

As Huxley's ring encircled defensively around Darwin, he began to feel easier. It tightened dramatically in 1864, but by then a militant upsurge was evident on all sides. At the Anglican Convocation evangelical scientists presented a declaration reaffirming their faith in the harmony of God's Word and his Works, which they tried to make a 'Fortieth Article' of the Church of England. They carried it to the British Association, where Huxley's 'dangerous clique' was spreading its heresies 'as a prop to the scepticism which has of late years met with disciples even in the ranks of duly authorised Christian ministers.'[13] Schisms and splits appeared as they evangelized the delegates and destroyed the Association's decades-old veneer of religious neutrality.

The Darwinians and radical Dissenters strained on the other side. Outraged at a blinkered Toryism that would crush the 'new reformation,' they united in defence of evolutionary naturalism. On 3 November, at St George's Hotel in Albemarle Street, Huxley, Hooker, Tyndall, Busk, Spencer, Lubbock and two others constituted themselves into a sort of masonic Darwinian lodge, invisible to outsiders: a dining club devoted to science 'untrammelled' by any theology. Spottiswoode joined them, making nine, but they never recruited a tenth for what came to be called the 'X Club.' They would free nature from a reactionary theology, free science from aristocratic patronage, and place an intellectual priesthood at the head of English culture. Manoeuvring inside the Royal Society, they altered the election procedures to get their allies elected and were soon pulling the Presidential strings.[14]

The X's first act was to bestow 'the ancient olive crown of the Royal Society' on Darwin – the Copley Medal. Busk and Falconer nominated him, and despite furious politicking, with the Cambridge men putting up old Sedgwick in opposition, the votes ran 10 to 8 in Darwin's favour. It shocked some old members, who dreaded 'crowning anything so unorthodox as the "Origin",' Lyell reported back. As an indication, the President slipped a debilitating disclaimer into his address on 30 November, announcing that the Council 'expressly omitted' the *Origin* 'from the grounds of our award.' This caused fury; Lubbock, Hooker, Huxley, and Busk complained (and it miffed Darwin too, when he heard). Huxley called for the minutes, to prove that the Council had agreed no such thing, and he tried to have the offending statement struck from the record. The snub was mitigated somewhat by Lyell, who declared in his speech that he had been 'forced to give up' his 'old faith' in fixed species, even if he could not see his 'way to a new one.' The medal exhilarated Darwin, fortified the X, and incensed the evangelical Anglicans; no wonder Huxley told Darwin of the 'satisfaction the award has given to your troops of friends.'

Darwin stayed away, his stomach erupting at the mere thought of the pomp and ceremony. Busk accepted the medal and dropped it off at Eras's. Darwin feigned surprise that 'so old a worn-out dog as I am is not quite forgotten,' although 'such things,' he said, 'make little difference.' Huxley's and Hooker's congratulations 'are the real medal to me, and not the round bit of gold.' His coyness was topped by Eras, who had the last word on his younger brother's accolade. He reported the medal's arrival, but 'it is rather ugly to look at, & too light to turn into candlesticks.'[15]

The *Natural History Review* had failed to 'appeal to the masses,' as Huxley had hoped, so the X Clubbers ploughed their energies and money – £100 from each shareholder – into a new weekly review, *The Reader*. Darwin gave his blessing, but Spencer wanted more, the odd publishable letter at least to give the journal a boost. The *Reader* supported Darwin in turn, printing the Copley presidential address (minus the offensive disclaimer). The *Reader* was probably the last attempt in Victorian England to keep together liberal scientists, theologians, and men of letters. Galton acted as editor, as did Huxley, who penned a crushing leader on 'Science and Church Policy' in the last number for 1864. Here he made his famous claim that a deep sense of religion was compatible with the total absence of theology. Religion was important, and he advised secularists against 'burning your ship to get rid of the cockroaches.' But still the ecclesiastical pests had to be eradicated. In a blistering provocation he warned that science had no 'intention of signing a treaty of peace with her old opponent, nor of being content with anything short of absolute victory and uncontrolled domination' over theology.[16]

A sarcastic Tory opposition outdid even Huxley in polarizing the issues. Benjamin Disraeli, the Jewish defender of the Church, the witty littérateur who had satirized *Vestiges* in his novel *Tancred*, stood at the Oxford Diocesan Society in an outlandish black-velvet shooting coat and wideawake hat to tell Wilberforce: 'The question is this – Is man an ape or an angel? My Lord, I am on the side of the Angels.' With that, thoughtless Toryism made its stand. Darwin had no love of literary Tories, even less of Jewish jokes, and he looked back in scorn on *Tancred*. He was pleased to see its parvenu author – that 'blank page between the Old Testament and the New' – deliver himself to Mr *Punch*, who rendered him a suitably Jewish angel.[17]

Three weeks later opposition took a more serious turn. Pope Pius IX issued an encyclical with an appended Syllabus of Errors announcing the Catholic Church's hostility to everything that the new Englishman held dear – 'progress . . . liberalism, and . . . modern civilization.' It was the first step towards the proclamation of papal infallibility. Huxley answered with a rival 'encyclical' in the *Reader*, a 'slashing' rejoinder which effectively scuppered the paper's broad church.[18] This militance coupled with editorial incompetence brought the publishing venture to an end, and the proselytizing Darwinians went their own way, looking for a partisan periodical.

With X Clubbers answering the Pope, Darwin had all the troops he needed. He could afford to drop his older conciliationist allies. He had reached an impasse with Gray over design and stopped advertising his pamphlet in the *Origin*. Lyell continued to disappoint. It was infuriating to hear him agree with the Duke of Argyll that selection was not the real 'creational law.' It was even more irritating to hear His Grace maintain in a well-dressed speech that life is led from above, and that the shimmering iridescence of hummingbirds demolished Darwin's crude view of nature's utility. Glorious beauty defied such a base explanation. Owen agreed; through Darwin's pessimistic Malthusianism he could perceive the pure light of Nature's goal – 'One true soul, like one seed of corn that grows and one egg of spawn that develops,' he told Argyll, might be 'a rare exception – for "narrow is the gate."' But if 'it pleases the Great First Cause' to usher in a moral order by this roundabout route, so be it. All concurred – selection was directed; nature was not a blind, accident-prone cripple.

Darwin was dismayed. His Grace's talk of beauty for beauty's sake showed that, like any politician, he was all mouth and no ears. 'The Duke, who knows my Orchid book so well,' he complained to Lyell, 'might have learned a lesson of caution from it.' As for minute variations in the beak and wings making no practical difference, that was preposterous. He demurred at Argyll's belief in the dramatic appearance of species or his calling them 'new births.' 'That may be a very good theory, but it is not mine, unless indeed he calls a bird born with a beak 1/100th of an inch longer than usual "a new birth".'[19] Darwin's variants crept forward, and sideways, by infinitesimal stages, but it took a pigeon-fancier rather than a politician to see it.

Behind all the cavils lurked the human question. Neanderthals, apes, black ancestors – it was emotionally fraught and for many frightening. The old certainties were threatened, the rules that had governed conduct for centuries. This is why Huxley in his lay lectures substituted Nature's laws for religious dictates, and saw obedience to science lead to the same end, social order and right morality. But there was no escaping the traumatic upheaval – or the surge of messianic materialism. From the gutter to the Palace, man's standing in nature was the issue. Back from a three-week trip to Berlin in January 1865, Lyell recounted how he had engaged the Princess Royal of Prussia in 'an animated conversation on Darwinism,' and found her 'very much *au fait* at the "Origin" and Huxley's book, the "Antiquity," &c. &c.' Darwin, with his 'instinctive reverence for rank,' lapped it up.[20]

By February Darwin was so weak that even the weight of Lyell's new *Elements of Geology* was intolerable in bed. He broke it in half and ripped off the covers. There he lay, amid a chaos of shredded pages, lost in morbid thoughts brought on by Falconer's agonized death from rheumatic fever. Years earlier Hugh Falconer had been one of the privileged few at the Downe gatherings. Only weeks before he had helped engineer the Copley Medal. Darwin was stunned by a spate of existential nightmares, Hooker adding to them by maundering on about 'meeting in a better world.' 'Personal annihilation,' Darwin answered wryly, paled into insignificance alongside his own 'pet horror,' the ice-death of the whole planet. Listen to the physicist Sir William Thomson on the cooling of the sun, and the inescapable refrigeration of earth at some determinable date! What solace for men with no faith in the divine society? The slow evolution of mankind hardly mattered, Darwin added, with 'the sun some day cooling and we all freezing. To think of the progress of millions of years with every continent swarming with good & enlightened men all ending in this . . . Sic transit gloria mundi with a vengeance'![21]

By April he was horribly ill again. He dropped the ducks and geese, doubting if he would ever finish the domestication book. He sacked his Harley Street consultant and cast around for a better one. Busk recommended a specialist on 'gouty complaints,' but none really seemed able to do anything about his 'suppressed gout.' At best his faith in the medical profession was shaky, and Hooker did not help. 'What the devil is this "suppressed gout" upon which doctors fasten every ill they cannot name?' he inquired. 'If it is *suppressed* how do they know it is gout? If it is apparent, why the devil do they call it *suppressed*.'[22] It was hardly reassuring coming from an Edinburgh MD.

Nor was it a laughing matter. Darwin now slumped into an appalling period of sickness, lasting the best part of eight months. 'What a life of suffering his is,' Emma's aunt sympathized. 'Oh! that a pure sunshine would rise for them.' But the summer sun did not shine; it was a penumbral shadow, where death again seemed a release. He lay in bed for weeks on end, with Emma reading aloud to him: novels from the London Library, so long as they had happy endings, and more esoteric matter if the postbag provided it. She gave a running translation of Fritz Müller's powerful apologia *Für Darwin*, and Friedrich Rolle's *Der Mensch*, which traced the roots of the human race to South African bushmen. Charles's ideas, dubbed *Darwinismus*, were racing ahead in Germany, with its long liberal traditions of biblical criticism and unabashed materialism.

He sank again on hearing that Lubbock was throwing himself away on politics, standing for the Liberals in the West Kent constituency – 'oh, dear! oh, dear! oh, dear!' he moaned at the prodigious mental waste. Only in *The Times*'s 'poor short-sighted view' was politics more interesting than science. Emma tried to stir him with Lubbock's book, *Prehistoric Times*, and he did perk up at the talk of savages. He rallied even more on hearing that Lubbock was trounced by the sitting Tory member, saving a great brain for science. But then science had been his undoing. *Prehistoric Times* had appeared midway through the campaign and unnerved the floating Kent voters, who considered expertise on stone-age savages inappropriate for solving Maidstone's traffic problems.[23]

Wanting release himself, he was unprepared for FitzRoy's escape. In the first days of May news came of the Admiral's end. FitzRoy, pressured at the Meteorological Department, his weather forecasting ridiculed, had fallen into one of his black moods. Darwin had seen them on the *Beagle*, the rages, the mental collapse. Everything conspired: FitzRoy had been passed over, Sulivan, his subordinate, taking the post he craved as Chief Naval Officer in the Marine Department. He brooded over the *Origin*, suffered fits of depression, and overworked; his health failing, his hearing going, he became caught up in one of his own tempestuous storms. On Sunday 30 April he walked into his bathroom in a melancholy fit and slit his throat.

The news pulled Darwin up sharp. 'I never knew in my life so mixed a character. Always much to love & I once loved him sincerely; but so bad a temper & so given to take offence, that I gradually quite lost my love & wished only to keep out of contact with him. Twice he quarreled bitterly with me, without any just provocation on my part. But certainly there was much noble & exalted in his character.'[24]

A few days later Darwin contacted John Chapman – the *Westminster* and book publisher – now a qualified specialist in dyspepsia, sickness, and psychological medicine. Chapman was Spencer's and Huxley's intimate, and the nub of a neurosis-ridden circle of dissidents. He had seen them all 'knocked up' one time or another as they pressed their rationalist claims in a hostile society. He specialized in the highly strung, those 'whose minds are highly cultivated and developed, and often complicated, modified, and dominated by subtle psychical influences, whose intensity and bearing on the physical malady it is difficult to apprehend.' Darwin the heroic evolutionist was the ultimate challenge. Chapman sent his book *Sea-Sickness* ahead, giving Darwin a foretaste. His treatment – ice-bags in the small of the back – assumed that nervous complaints could be affected by freezing and anaesthetizing the spine.

Darwin invited Chapman to Downe, listing his symptoms in gory detail:

A *Living Grave*

Age 56-57. – For 25 years extreme spasmodic daily & nightly flatulence: occasional vomiting, on two occasions prolonged during months. Vomiting preceded by shivering, hysterical crying[,] dying sensations or half-faint. & copious very palid urine. Now vomiting & every passage of flatulence preceded by ringing of ears, treading on air & vision. focus & black dots[,] Air fatigues, specially risky, brings on the Head symptoms[,] nervousness when E[mma]. leaves me . . .

The list went on. Dr Chapman must have been as astonished as his predecessors: the patient was not highly strung but stretched taut. He fitted Darwin with a spinal bag, freezing him three times a day for ninety minutes a time.[25] Darwin felt sprightlier to start with and, given the ray of hope that Emma's aunt had prayed for, he wrote the most controversial chapter of his domestic animal book.

Frozen-backed, he finished forty pages on his novel hypothesis about heredity. He ended them in a flutter. Even christening his theory ruffled domestic feathers: trying to convey his idea that every bodily cell buds off a representative part of itself, he called it 'pangenesis.' The 'pan' was supposed to convey the idea that these bits – or gemmules – came from the whole body and congregated in the reproductive organs, but 'my wife says it sounds wicked, like pantheism.' The ice seemed to work, and he posted 'pangenesis' to Huxley as proof. Only Huxley was shown and then Darwin cringed, calling it 'rash and crude.' It was a rough-hewn hat-stand on which to hang all his favourite hats. Pangenesis could explain buds on a plant, or a newt regenerating a severed foot, or the strengthening and shrivelling of organs from use or disuse, or sexual generation – it was an all-purpose descendant of those ancestral unifying ideas of his London days. Not least he needed it to explain how tissues altered by selection can be transmitted. Why do pouters – pigeons coiffed and coutured by backyard breeders – hatch little pouters?

The gist was 'that each cell throws off an atom of its content or a gemmule, and that these aggregated form the true ovule or bud.' Every region of the body is democratically represented in the egg. In fact he compared the whole body to a colony (like his colonial polyps of old), where each individual buds off a representative bit of 'generative protoplasm.'[26] Forty years on, his student fascination with the granules composing pollen and eggs was still there.

After a month spent carrying ice-packs four hours a day, he was wearying in every sense. With pangenesis off his hands, he was lying prostrate, hoping Huxley would be tender with his baby Pan. Huxley donned his 'sharpest spectacles and best thinking cap' and weighed his words. He was dubious; but, having been wrong-footed by the *Origin*, he was cautious about throttling Darwin's embryonic god. 'Somebody rummaging among your papers half a century hence will find *Pangenesis* and say, "See this wonderful anticipation of our modern theories, and that stupid ass Huxley prevented his publishing them".'[27] But the message was clear enough. Don't.

Darwin was as sick as a dog again, and Huxley's deicide did not help. Despondent, he dropped Chapman and the ice-packs in July, realizing that nothing worked, and he returned to bed for the rest of the year.

Here he watched the world revolve and old friends fall out. Lyell was embroiled in a furious row. In the *Antiquity of Man* he had lifted whole paragraphs from Lubbock's paper on Danish archaeology. This sort of 'compiling' was despicable even in Darwin's eyes. 'Lyell took and forgot whole sentences from Lubbock,' he admitted. 'It is horrid.' Hooker explained what really lay behind the rancour. 'And now my dear D. shall I tell you what is at the bottom of it all? Perhaps you won't believe it, it is just this – that Lady Lyell will not call on Mrs Busk nor invite the Busks to her parties. This the Lubbocks and Huxleys resent.' Busk was routinely 'pumped dry of his knowledge' by Lyell (who lived in the same street), even while his lower-class wife was snubbed. It was a sign that not all members of the X (or at least their YVs, as the joke went) fitted the old social bill.

But times were changing, and with them the control of official science. The Xs continued to penetrate the British Association, manipulating its byzantine political machinery. They themselves were climbing into positions of power. Following his father's death, Hooker had been appointed Director of Kew Gardens, and Lubbock's Parliamentary career looked set.[28]

Huxley's power came from his ability to draw huge crowds. Two thousand were turned away in January 1866 as St Martin's Hall overflowed with Londoners wanting to hear him inaugurate the 'Sunday Evenings for the People.' Jenny Marx (Karl's daughter) squeezed in and found it 'packed to suffocation.' She had waltzed in the hall on the anniversary of the First International, but to hear a 'genuinely progressive' scientific lecture here was something new, especially at a 'moment when the flock are supposed to be grazing in the house of the Lord.' Huxley's was a hymn to material salvation. He had humanity escaping the 'fine-spun ecclesiastical cobwebs' to a bright new world of Tyndall's deterministic physics, Buckle's progressive history, and Darwin's evolving life. It was a world no longer static; a world in Heraclitan flux, like Turner's *Rain, Steam, and Speed*, a blur of movement, 'a world thrown out of focus by the driving motion of the steam engine.'[29]

The rhetoric was brilliant, and to outsiders bellicose. Owen was livid at Huxley's 'extremist views,' peddled in the hall to the 'youth of both sexes.' Having hoodwinked workers that they were the sons of gorillas, he was now inflaming them by 'attacks on the common basis of beliefs.' Lyell was just as appalled at Carpenter's subsequent Sunday speech, which 'rudely assailed' Calvinistic doctrines. The scandal of lay sermons on the Sabbath was too shocking and the Lord's Day Observance Society shut the hall. Huxley tediously fended off accusations of atheism, complaining that such a position was absurd where the 'possibilities of nature are infinite.' But with every year he felt the need for some new label, some new '-ism,' which would legalize doubt in the absence of evidence and leave faith in the realm of the 'immoral.'[30]

It was all Darwin could do to marvel from a distance. He was now 'half starved to death' on a crash diet (scanty amounts of 'toast & meat') under a new doctor. The slightest reading left his head beginning 'to sing violently.' So his 'good womenkind' did their duty, stroking his vanity by reading him 'advanced' books. Emma's self-sacrifice was tested as she read aloud Lecky's *Rise of Rationalism* and Tylor's evolutionary account of culture and religion in *The Early History of Mankind*. Left to his own devices for fifteen minutes, Charles's idea of entertainment was to skim back numbers of the middle-brow *Annals and Magazine of Natural History*. The diet seemed to work; he lost fifteen pounds and the doctor had him up and walking. Hopping in fact; he put on his magistrate's hat and threatened a neighbouring landowner with action over the mangy state of his horses.[31]

But the ravaging months had done their damage; Darwin's new photograph revealed a haggard figure, glazed and drawn. A year earlier he had been rugged and venerable, with a passing likeness to Moses in the fresco at the House of Lords, according to Hooker. Burn it and try again, was Eras's unhelpful suggestion on the latest effort. 'Cartes' (photographic calling cards) were *de rigueur* and Darwin had a wretched yearly record of his facial deterioration. He collected cartes enthusiastically, and posted his own wan physiognomy to English and German scientists. They might not have done much for his profile, but in Germany, they put a craggy face to the terrible *Darwinismus*.[32] This was fast becoming the face of evolution – and well-enough known for his calling card to be seen on sale in a shop window.

There was a stony sadness also in his reflection. Sister Susan, still at The Mount caring for Marianne's orphans, was suffering from fainting fits. In January 1866 Catherine wrote her farewells, knowing she was dying. Death came easily a few weeks later. Hers was the 'great soul,' as the Doctor long ago called it; but her life was one of unfulfilled ambitions and discomfort. Her passing was 'a blessing, for there was much fear of prolonged and greater suffering.' 'Sad, sad Shrewsbury! which used to look so bright and sunny,' Emma's aunt lamented, and Charles and Eras felt it as they met to arrange Catherine's estate and modify their wills.[33]

The doctor's walking and dieting regime at least had Charles on his toes, and he re-emerged into society protected by a bushy beard. His patriarchal face disappeared behind the hirsute mask. Fashion was the excuse; even Huxley sported a black beard (only to realize his error). But now the author of the *Origin* could travel incognito – no more alarms as strangers recognized him among the Crystal Palace crowds. Unfortunately his friends were equally stymied. He was sprightly enough to put in an appearance at a Royal Society soirée on 27 April, appearing like Moses down from the mountain. Hooker was staggered. So was everyone else, once they realized. The bearded gent with the drawn features was forced to introduce himself to friends and strangers alike, including the Prince of Wales. The young Prince said something *sotto voce*; Darwin failed to pick it up. Flustered, he 'made the profoundest bow he could' and fled.[34]

He might be crumbling bodily but it was galling to be attacked for scientific blindness. The Grays, Lyells, Owens, and Argylls all marvelled at his failure to see that nature's selection required as much thought and direction as the farmer's. Darwin's Nature 'preferred' and 'favoured,' his writings proclaimed it. The selecting hand was intelligent and could only evince God's long reach. Darwin was being painfully hoisted on his own petard.

Spencer offered an easy escape, and Wallace alerted Darwin to it. The socialist was now swept up by Spencer's cosmic optimism, indicating as much by calling his son Herbert Spencer Wallace. 'I hope he will copy his father's style and not his namesake's,' Darwin politely replied, taken aback. In his *Principles of Biology* Spencer had coined 'survival of the fittest' as a replacement for 'natural selection.' It avoided the anthropomorphism of 'selecting' and 'favouring' – and

Wallace went through his copy of the *Origin* striking out 'selection' and substituting 'survival,' arguing the advantages.

Darwin had struggled through the turgid tome – deterred by its 'detestable style,' thinking that Spencer must be 'very clever' and himself very dense, for he was no wiser at the end. If only Spencer observed a little more and thought a little less he might have something to say. 'Noisy vacuity' was Hooker's description of Spencer's numbing *Synthetic Philosophy*. Darwin subscribed to the endless volumes, but he had to agree. 'Survival of the Fittest,' he told Wallace, lost the analogy between nature's selection and the fanciers'.[35] Still, the phrase might stop the churlish criticisms and get him off the anthropomorphic hook, and he planned to use it judiciously in his *Variation under Domestication*.

36

Emerald Beauty

IN 1866, FOR THE first time, Darwinism – or descent at any rate
– dominated the British Association meeting at Nottingham. The
newspapers were full of it. The Anglican *Guardian* reported that
Darwin's theory 'was everywhere in the ascendant.' It was 'impossible
to pass from Section to Section without seeing how deeply those
views have leavened the scientific mind of the day.' The President,
physicist and barrister W. R. Grove, took a judicious view of nature's
continuous constitutional change. Soon to sit on the judge's bench,
he practised summing up in robes and wig, advising the scientific jury
that evolution did on balance serve the Crown's interest. Continuity
was the key, from the swarming specks on a microscope slide to the
greatest galaxies, and we should be prepared 'to see it in the history
of our own race:'

> the revolutionary ideas of the so-called natural rights of man
> . . . are far more unsound . . . than the study of the gradual
> progressive changes arising from changed circumstances,
> changed wants, changed habits. Our language, our social
> institutions, our laws, the constitution of which we are proud,
> are the growth of time, the product of slow adaptations,
> resulting from continuous struggles. Happily in this country
> practical experience has taught us to improve rather than
> remodel; we follow the law of nature and avoid cataclysms.[1]

England had found that Nature did things her way. The Wilberforces
and Sedgwicks were stood on their heads: evolution threatened no
bloodcurdling cries at the enthronement of the Goddess of Reason,
only the security and peace of a progressive reform.

Darwin felt gypped because the speech about natural progress and social order 'dealt in such generalities.' But Grove had avoided the *Origin* by arrangement. He had called Hooker to the bench in advance and counselled him to 'carry Darwinism through the ranks of the enemy.' With Huxley President of the biology section, Hooker talking on island colonization and 'blessing Nat[ural]. Selection,' and Wallace President of the new anthropology sub-section, the best addresses went Darwin's way.

Hooker's ended on a savage allegory, satirizing the anti-evolution savants at the 1860 Oxford British Association as an uncivilized tribe who regarded 'every month's moon as a new creation of their gods.' They devoured 'the missionaries of the most enlightened nation' for explaining its real motion. 'The priests first attacked the new doctrine, and with fury, their temples were ornamented with symbols of the old creed, and their religious chants and rites were worded and arranged in accordance.' 'The medicine men, however . . . sided with the missionaries – many from spite to the priests, but a few, I could see, from conviction.' Now six years were as six centuries, and the elders were duly baptized in the faith, and applauded their 'presiding Sachem' (Grove) for leading them out of the wilderness. Two thousand listened agog to all this, and were 'sent into fits by the conclusion,' Hooker boasted to Darwin. Darwin had heard as much; Fanny Wedgwood had been there, and she graphically described the stunned silence at the start of the lecture, followed by 'roars of laughter.'[2]

No guffaws greeted it in the religious press. The *Methodist Recorder* was 'surprised and grieved' by Grove's address. So was Owen, but then it left him out of the picture. He complained that scoffing was 'in fashion at that meeting,' and ranting and ridicule were the Darwinians' stock 'weapons.' They showed a 'contemptuous relegation' of design arguments and deliberately trampled on higher feelings. It reflected ill on the Downe naturalist: 'Darwin is just as good a soul as his grandfather,' Owen conceded, 'and just as great a goose.'[3]

Ironically, as Huxley's and Tyndall's parson-bashing appeals to the labourers reached a materialist pitch, the radical audience itself was splintering, with factions drifting off in totally different directions. After the collapse of Chartism many middle-aged agitators were swept along by the tide of spiritualism. The American fad of table-turning and spirit-rapping had taken hold by the 1860s; rooms were darkened, hands held as the dead signalled. No 'science,' not even phrenology, was more popular – or more directly accessible. Robert Chambers was won over and started revamping *Vestiges* in a more spiritual light. For old radicals, if not old ladies, it was a democratic outlet, a new dissident healing religion – the human spirit had progressive tendencies, driving society to its co-operative conclusion.[4] Unseen forces were undermining capitalism and ushering in the millennium. The doyen of socialists Robert Owen was won over, and even the reprieved leader of the 1839 Welsh Chartist uprising John Frost saw the light.

Séances also started in the capital's genteel drawing-rooms, to the annoyance of the hard-nosed scientists striking out on their own priest-free path to the New Jerusalem. Huxley's evolutionary prob-abilities now had to vie with spiritual certainties in the Mechanics' Institutes. *The Reader* in 1864 ran a slashing piece, 'Science and Spirit Rapping,' intriguing Darwin as to the author (Hooker confirmed that it was Tyndall's response to a séance). Huxley had already exposed a medium at his brother George's house, although he admitted that spiritualism could be advantageous in cutting the suicide rate: 'Better live a crossing-sweeper,' he laughed, 'than die and be made to talk twaddle by a "medium" hired at a guinea a *séance*.'[5]

But Wallace – the best sort of scientific crossing-sweeper – stood apart. Phrenologist, mesmerist, and old socialist, he had a self-help mentality shaped by millennial ideals. He attended his first séances with Mrs Marshall, England's most famous medium, in 1865. Darwin's cousin Hensleigh knew of this, and within a few years so did everyone else when Wallace acknowledged a higher spiritual reality. At home his own table tilted, and fresh flowers appeared from the other side to adorn it (he typically analysed them, '15 chrysanthemums, 6 variegated anemones, 4 tulips . . .' to trace their provenance). He printed a pamphlet, *The Scientific Aspect of the Supernatural*, and began importuning. Huxley declined to attend his séances, not wishing to be bored by the 'disembodied gossip.'[6] Having seized power from the priests, he was loath to see it devolved on dotty ladies. This spiritual legerdemain diluted the serious message that sober scientists were the new moral authority. But the worst of it was to come. Wallace was revamping evolution to take account of these unseen spirits.

In October the Darwins met Charles's most bombastic, prolific German admirer, the zoologist ultimately to be designated the 'German Darwin,' Ernst Haeckel. It was a meeting of opposites. Haeckel, thirty-two, was the son of Prussian civil servants. His evangelical upbringing and admiration for Goethe's pantheistic philosophy had led him to a mystical Nature-worship at the University of Würzburg. He was a superb field naturalist with a string of publications, but he and Darwin came from different worlds.

For years Haeckel had sent long flattering accounts of the progress of Darwinism in Germany – *Darwinismus* – listing converts. Huxley had vouched safe the new Extraordinary Professor of Zoology at Jena, confirming that he was 'one of the ablest of the younger zoologists of Germany.' Haeckel was turning liberal Jena, Goethe's university, into a 'citadel of Darwinism.' Here, Darwin heard, he had built up huge classes of 150 students for his lectures on *Darwinismus*. His pupils were taught to venerate the Downe naturalist. One, Anton Dohrn, immersed in barnacle larvae, considered a letter from Darwin like being granted a 'scientific knighthood.' These students looked back on 1859 as a year of crowning significance in the century; the war with Lombardy or the end of the Papal States paled beside the publication of the *Origin*. No wonder that Darwin told William Preyer, an English physiologist teaching at Bonn (and soon to take a chair at Jena) that the German response was the 'chief ground for hoping that our views will ultimately prevail.'[7]

The *Origin* had 'profoundly moved' Haeckel as well. He rushed in where Darwin feared to tread. It was Haeckel who started the debate in Germany by extending selection and struggle to society, seeing it 'drive the peoples irresistibly onward . . . to higher cultural stages.' Progress was a natural law that 'neither the weapons of the tyrant nor the anathemas of the priest' could rescind. To Haeckel the *Origin* was a political document affecting everyone's 'personal, scientific and social views' – and he was proving it. As a way of drowning his sorrows after the tragic death of his young wife in 1864 (whose photo he touchingly sent Darwin) he had thrown himself heroically into a systematic rearrangement of all biological knowledge along Darwinian lines.[8] The *Generelle Morphologie* was a monumental work astonishingly written in a year, and Darwin had the first proof sheet in hand by August 1866.

Their meeting at Down House was a religious experience for Haeckel. From the moment Darwin's hand gripped his, he felt his heart being taken 'by storm.' Darwin to him was

> tall and venerable . . . with the broad shoulders of an Atlas
> that bore a world of thought: a Jove-like forehead, as we see
> in Goethe, with a lofty and broad vault, deeply furrowed by
> the plough of intellectual work. The tender and friendly eyes
> were overshadowed by the great roof of the prominent brows.
> The gentle mouth was framed in a long, silvery white beard.

Overawed, Haeckel began jabbering in broken English. Darwin said something and found that Haeckel did not understand him either. They stared at each other for a moment and then burst into laughter. Speaking slowly worked wonders, and over lunch communication was finally established – until Haeckel became excited again. Waving his arms, he railed against 'the stubborn and bewigged professors who still held out against the luminous truth of the theory of evolution.' No one could make out what he was saying and Emma looked impatient. Darwin just put his hand on Haeckel's broad shoulder, nodded and smiled. To Haeckel it was a benediction.

Darwin had 'seldom seen a more pleasant, cordial, and frank man.' Links were quickly cemented with the whole group: Lubbock came over from High Elms to meet Haeckel, and Darwin introduced him to Hooker. There was much mutual back-slapping; Haeckel praised Huxley as 'the most eminent English zoologist' and was in turn hailed as a Coryphaeus among German naturalists.[9]

Within a few weeks Darwin, still pounding away at *Variation under Domestication*, had knocked the chapter on pangenesis into shape. The theory left him in jitters – it would be 'classed as a mad dream,' or worse. 'Wildly abominably speculative,' he called it to a head-scratching Hooker, staggered by all the hypothetical gemmules, which were 'worthy even of Herbert Spencer.'

Not that Spencer's speculations weren't useful. He was generalizing evolution to explain the universe in his *Synthetic Philosophy*, projecting the social ambitions of his X Club friends on a cosmic scale. And politically he was a brick. In November he roped Darwin into the Governor Eyre debate, then racking the English intelligentsia. A year earlier the Jamaican Governor's troops had brutally crushed a local peasant revolt – over 400 blacks executed, 600 flogged, 1000 suspect houses razed. Anti-slavery radicals and liberal politicians formed the Jamaica Committee to bring Eyre to justice; Wallace, Lyell, Huxley, and Spencer had joined, and now Darwin added his name with a £10 donation towards the prosecution. An Eyre Defence and Aid Committee also had a fund, enlisting scores of clergymen, peers, and members of the armed forces. Tyndall chipped in, the Revd Kingsley jumped on the bandwagon, and even Hooker seemed sympathetic. The principles of Governor Eyre's prosecutors, Hooker told Darwin, were 'fiddlesticks.'[10]

Darwinian emotions flared, fanned by the *Pall Mall Gazette*'s nasty jibe that Huxley's and Lyell's views on the 'development of species' had 'influenced them in bestowing on the negro that sympathetic recognition which they are willing to extend even to the ape as "a man and a brother".' Huxley lashed back, boiling everything down to the constitutional proposition that 'English law does not permit good persons, as such, to strangle bad persons, as such.' If it did, he would 'take the first opportunity of migrating to Texas or some other quiet place.' For Darwin's part, the issue ran deeper. He detested all forms of cruelty; the Eyre defenders' attitudes to blacks reminded him of FitzRoy's defence of slavery. He burned at their arrogance and wondered that some of his friends could agree. Once his feelings even overpowered him when an Eyre lobby turned up at home.

William, twenty-six, was now a banking partner in Southampton; his sympathies had been under suspicion since August, when his name was published 'by accident' as having attended a banquet in Eyre's honour in the town. So incensed was Charles that he actually wrote to the Lord Chancellor to rectify the error. But now the truth came out. At Ras's in November, William made a disparaging remark about the Jamaica Committee raiding the prosecution fund for its own dinners. Charles turned on him with a blistering fury and bellowed that if he felt that way, then he 'had better go back to Southampton.' William stayed another night, and at seven the next morning his father came in and sat on his bed. He hadn't slept one wink, he said; his anger had been cruel, and he was sorry.[11]

This was Charles's first visit to Ras since Susan's terrible lingering death at the beginning of October. They had lost two sisters this year, and it was an emotional time. Susan's effects were being distributed, and Charles had first refusal on her Indian chessmen. Ras had just returned from The Mount, which was being sold. Charles heard about the auction from Hooker, who had also been there. Hooker was a fanatical collector of Wedgwood ware, and could be seen poking around London's dingy bric-à-brac shops searching for pieces. He had visited The Mount hoping to buy a few medallions, knowing that the Darwins were – as Charles laughed – 'the degenerate descendants of old Josiah W.' He came home empty-handed.[12] The Mount was bare, the last ties with Shrewsbury severed, and Hooker had been there at its break-up.

At Downe the two 500-page volumes of Haeckel's *Generelle Morphologie* thumped in Darwin's letterbox. They were designed to daunt, and Darwin was duly humbled. He struggled through the thicket, losing his way in the profusion of genealogical trees, sagging under the weight of neologisms. 'The number of new words, to a man like myself, weak in his Greek, is something dreadful:' 'ontogeny' for the course of foetal growth, 'phylogeny' for the evolutionary history of the race, and 'ecology.' Nor was his German much better. Word after word was extracted with the pain of pulled teeth, using a dictionary. He knew 'no grammar whatever' and so read each sentence over and over until at last the meaning dawned. (The constructions infuriated him – he was convinced that Germans 'could write simply if they chose.')

By this dogged means, he snatched painful glimpses of Haeckel's ambition, pushing evolution beyond its legitimate bounds. For Haeckel selection was only a fragment of a 'universal Theory of Development, which embraces in its vast range the whole domain of human knowledge.' Darwin's quintessentially English light – an incandescence of Paley's design, Malthus's pessimism, pigeon lore, and maritime life – was being passed through a distorting lens. Here was *Darwinismus* shaped to suit Bismarck's unifying Germany. Priest-baiting patriotism formed a backdrop to anatomy and embryology, and the whole was blended into a unitary evolutionary cosmology. It was pushy and provocative, unnecessarily so in Darwin's view.[13]

But then Haeckel's books had a political punch. His liberal *Darwinismus* was associated with calls for a national state that would guarantee free speech and free trade. At its crudest, an ape ancestry could level the privileged aristocracy – noblemen and dogs were all of a kind in the womb, he once commented. On another level, the laws of biological and national evolution offered hope for a new Teutonic superiority in a unified Germany. Haeckel had an almost Messianic idea of the German *Volk*, the spirit binding all to the fatherland, and he was busy underwriting it. Welcoming Bismarck to Jena, he declared: 'While the booming of guns at the Battle of Königgrätz in 1866 announced the demise of the old Federal German Diet and the beginning of a splendid period in the history of the German Reich, here in Jena the history of the phylum was born.'[14] The *phylum*, a higher group whose racial integrity was explained by evolution, had developed through the same struggle and selection as the new Prussian state.

The polemical *Morphologie* was impressive and galling. Darwin grappled with it for weeks. 'I see he often quotes both of us with praise,' he told Huxley. 'I am sure I should like the book much, if I could read it straight off instead of groaning and swearing at each sentence.' By Christmas he had conquered 'a page or two here and there.' His only hope was a translation, but however much Huxley revelled in Haeckel's attempt 'to systematise biology' along Darwinian lines, he thought it hopeless 'without too great an outlay.'

The real problem was that Haeckel's *Darwinismus* came wrapped in an anti-clerical package, and the wrappers would have to be stripped off. The immutability of species was 'a colossal dogma . . . empowered by blind belief in authority' – Christian authority, a crude backward religion whose Creator-God was a 'gaseous vertebrate.' Nothing was more guaranteed to raise hackles. Huxley took vicarious satisfaction in its 'polemic *excursus*,' sympathizing that 'it is a good thing for a man' once in a while 'to perform a public war-dance against all sorts of humbug and imposture.'[15] But he knew that English propriety too easily took fright.

True, Haeckel was less scurrilous than Darwin's other admirer, the socialist Carl Vogt. Vogt, a German exiled after the revolution of 1848 to Geneva (where he translated *Vestiges*), was now bidding to translate *Variation*; but Darwin knew enough to opt for Huxley's man Victor Carus, the Leipzig professor who had translated *Man's Place in Nature*. Carus himself warned Darwin against letting a church-baiting revolutionary like Vogt do the job. Indeed, there was a real worry about Vogt's language. No one outside the gutter press in England would have dared call certain 'simious' skulls from the Dark Ages 'Apostle skulls' on the assumption that they belonged to degraded Christian missionaries.

Not that Carus was totally happy with Haeckel either – a man who could point to the 'pious inquisition' as proof that the cosmos lacked moral order. Only Darwin could put a stop to such mischief, Carus said; Haeckel would heed no one else. Darwin did try pulling in Haeckel's horns, advising that to lance the theological boil 'will excite anger, and that anger so completely blinds every one.' Do not 'unnecessarily make enemies,' for 'there is pain and vexation enough in the world.'[16] But Haeckel was uncompromising, replying that only a vigorous assault could overcome prejudice and usher in a radical reform.

Just before Christmas Darwin sent *Variation* to the printers – all except the last chapter. He was popping in a special present for Gray, a knock-down argument against his notion of divinely guided variation. So many had seized on Gray's leading idea (thanks partly to the advertisement for his pamphlet in the *Origin*) that it seemed 'shabby to evade' it any longer.

He presented an analogy that he had been perfecting for years. Consider the stones at the base of a cliff, each having broken off naturally; suppose that an architect uses these to build a house. 'Can it be reasonably maintained that the Creator intentionally ordered

... that certain fragments of rock should assume certain shapes so that the builder might erect his edifice?' Obviously not. So, Darwin asked, 'can it be maintained with any greater probability that He specially ordained' the minuscule variations that breeders work on to make their fancy races? No. Well, nor were they ordained in nature. Variations arise by 'general laws' and some *happen* to be useful. Natural selection – the architect – picks them to improve plants and animals, 'man included.'[17]

'Man included' was a hint that no heavens opened to herald mankind's birth. He was just as natural, just as accidental. Darwin had wanted to add a chapter on the subject to *Variation*, but the book was now so 'horridly, disgustingly big' that Murray was already making two volumes of it, each over 400 pages. The referee found the tome indigestible, and Murray planned only 750 copies. In March 1867, after the compositors had come up with a better title, *The Variation of Animals and Plants under Domestication*, Murray did double the print run, but by then Darwin had decided to turn his man chapter into a separate 'short essay,' concentrating on ape ancestry, sexual selection, and human expression. He would finally speak out, tired of being 'taunted that I concealed my views' on human origins.[18]

Translations were sewn up quickly. Carus would do the German and Vladimir Kovalevsky the Russian. Considering how much Darwin had suffered from polemically packaged foreign editions of the *Origin*, he reposed some faith in Kovalevsky. Bronn's translation, the first in Germany, came with critical notes and appendix; Clémence Royer prefaced hers in France with an anticlerical harangue, and added insult to injury by changing the title. Kovalevsky, fiery and only twenty-five, was translating Huxley and Lyell in style, so he should have been all right. On the other hand he was using evolution in his Nihilist crusade against Russia's Orthodox autocracy. Darwin had proofs hot off the press sent to St Petersburg – and Kovalevsky, translation notwithstanding, pulled out all the stops and beat Murray's publication date. The earliest edition of *Variation* was Russian.[19]

Darwin struggled with sexual selection this spring, explaining the causes of variation in that 'eminently *domesticated* animal,' man. Why do the races differ in their physical and emotional features and yet all belong to one species? Why do males and females have different hair and habits? He could see no evolutionary advantage in beards, big lips, or large buttocks – nothing for natural selection to work on – so he put it down to the mating game. Nature does not select, individuals do; their racial and sexual differences show what is successful in winning wives and attracting husbands. Aesthetic preferences are translated into anatomy.

He called in evidence from molluscs to monkeys, but concentrated on the glorious plumage and mating rituals of birds. He had the bower birds in London zoo given a choice of worsted to test their colour preference; he had breeders trimming and daubing game cocks to see whether the mutilation would make them less 'successful in getting wives;' he had male pigeons dyed magenta to see how far 'it excited in the other pigeons, especially the females, admiration or contempt.' By analogy, Darwin believed that insect colours had also been sexually selected, and he once even had a dragonfly 'painted with gorgeous colours,' though the experiment never got off the ground.[20]

The Duke of Argyll's *Reign of Law* rammed home the need for a book on sexual selection. The Duke, or 'Dukelet' as Huxley demoted him ('how can you speak so of a living real Duke?' Darwin wondered), rounded up the providential criticisms of the *Origin* and rehashed them in a pot-boiler. Darwin was rather annoyed. 'The Duke's book strikes me as very well written, very interesting, honest, & clever & very arrogant,' he told Kingsley. He whittled away at it, wrote to Lyell about it, and complained to William.[21] Clearly his own book would have to crush this dilettante nonsense, and provide a thousand counter illustrations for every clever flick of Argyll's pen.

Argyll's intellectual heritage showed. He had attended Owen's lectures and learned the lesson well. Natural selection explains the 'success and establishment and spread of new Forms when they have arisen,' but gives no clue to their origin. The *Origin* was a misnomer; the book should have been called *The Selection of Species*. So what causes the variations? Argyll captured the new consensus on design, in which species were preordained, and natural laws the outcome of God's legislative will. Judicial rule still held, Argyll announced in the *Reign of Law*, chaos and anarchy had not descended on nature; the back-street slum hordes had not overrun the citadel.

The Duke had put his chapters together while trying to juggle Gladstone's new Reform Bill through the Commons in 1866. He envisioned nature controlled by a similar guided meliorative reform, ordered from above. Like Owen, he could never accept that random variations were the font of progress. He talked of some unknown cause steering the 'variations in a definite direction.' Lyell agreed, so did Gray. So did Owen; in fact it could have been Owen speaking through Argyll's mouth in the *Reign of Law*, talking of a force guiding life, 'working to order, subject to direction, and having that direction determined by foresight.'[22]

But the real sting in the book came with Argyll's discussions of hummingbirds. He asked the crunch question, the one that made Darwin flinch. Why should a topaz crest be selected in shimmering hummingbirds in preference to sapphire? Or a frill end in emerald spangles rather than ruby? This was beauty for God's sake – there was no earthly reason for it, no struggle could explain it.

Argyll accused Darwin of giving mindless natural selection the credit. But for Darwin selection *was* creative. His Grace

> depreciates the importance of natural selection, but I presume he w^d not deny that [husbandry experts] had in one sense made our improved breeds of cattle, yet of course the initial variations have naturally arisen; but until selected, they remained unimportant, & in this same sense natural selection seems to me all-important.

He protested in vain. Argyll's sort of Creative evolution was immensely appealing to non-Darwinians. With Owen, they hailed the Duke's 'healthy' intervention as 'a timely & wholesome antidote' to Darwin's 'mischievous fallacies.' No one was better placed to refute Darwin's and Huxley's belief that everything is 'governed by invariable Laws with which no volitions, natural or supernatural, interfere.'[23]

Huxley did not even bother to read the *Reign of Law*. Hooker skimmed it 'with utter disgust and uncontrollable indignation.' Imagine, he fumed, 'God being compelled to dab on rudimentary organs *to keep up appearances*,' the divine architect adding useless bits to conform with Owen's blueprints. Darwin agreed, scorning Argyll's picture of God as 'a man, rather cleverer than us.' But then it was a Duke writing, 'no common mortal.' Perhaps he was 'not to be judged by common rules.'[24]

Wallace countered Argyll chapter-and-verse in a razor-sharp review, delving into hummingbird splendour. There was a pitfall in putting it down to God's beauty – how to explain stink bugs and snakes? He pulled up His Grace on the gaudy orchids too, which functioned in attracting bees, reminding him that continual interference implies a lack of Creative foresight. Petty tinkering might do for Reform Bills, but nature got it right from the start.

How nature got things right was another matter. Wallace and Darwin were differing more and more. Darwin had sexual selection replacing God the artist, just as natural selection ousted God the architect. Brutes were their own breeders, forming fancy varieties; humans sculpted themselves by selecting mates. But for every brilliant bird that Darwin ascribed to sexual selection, Wallace described another that was due to natural selection. Dull-coloured female birds are camouflaged to survive sitting in an open nest. Gaudy moths, distasteful to their predators, wear warning colours; still others mimic them.

Wallace rejected sexual selection as the 'main agent' forming the human races. Natural selection was quite equal to the task. To Darwin this came as 'the heaviest blow possible.' No amount of evidence on birds and insects would turn Wallace. Darwin now played the apostate devil, arguing against the very theory that he had spent his life supporting. Wallace for his part was turning out the more single-minded adherent of natural selection, more Darwinian than Darwin.[25]

For each Wallace reply to Argyll came a clutch of new criticisms, and worse was in store. Darwin's most prestigious opponents were physicists with close ties to the Glasgow professor Sir William Thomson (later Lord Kelvin). Thomson was recalculating the earth's age, putting crippling limits on the time a clumsy, wasteful natural selection had to work in. In June his partner in the submarine cable business, the engineer Fleeming Jenkin, applied an even crueller logic. He showed that no single variation could survive being blended back into an ocean of normal peers. Blood always mixes; a white sailor with a black wife has 'mulatto' children. No old salt marooned on African shores, however resourceful and superior, was going to 'blanch a nation of negroes.' Boat-loads of whites were needed. As Jenkin said, only if many simultaneous 'sports' or mutations appeared and bred true could a species change.

But that was tantamount to a 'theory of successive creations' – or at least a divinely directed evolution. Jenkin had turned the tables. He convinced Darwin that 'freak' variations could not survive, only a wave of them appearing simultaneously.[26] Others cut the knot and sought refuge in Argyll's 'creation by birth,' with each sport preplanned and fixed. It was a retreat on all fronts.

In July Lyell was in despair, working on a tenth edition of the *Principles of Geology*, trying in vain to turn what was an anti-Lamarckian opus into a pro-Darwinian fudge. Darwin, ever hopeful, rejoiced that he was going to 'speak out plainly about species' for the first time, even if his proof chapter on man, 'who thinks too much of his fine self,' was a flop. It was 'too long . . . and too orthodox, except for the beneficed clergy,' a remark not guaranteed to put the seventy-year-old Lyell at ease.

Lyell for his part loved Darwin's proofs of *Variation*, on the exotic pigeons and rabbits and the ways the breeds have fanned out from their wild ancestors. All this would be 'most persuasive to real naturalists,' he replied magnanimously, pushing them further towards the *Origin of Species*.[27]

Darwin needed this reassurance. *Variation* was his biggest book and the proofs were killing him, with every page 'greatly altered.' Twice that summer he downed pen and went to Eras's for a week, but it was no use. Back at Downe he worked overtime to make up for the breaks. There were endless letters from Carus and Kovalevsky, regular queries about the index, fresh batches of revised proofs, and always the obsessive fact-finding and fact-filing on sexual selection and man.

For all Darwin's fears and phobias, and Lyell's procrastination, and Argyll's aggravation, the world was turning. Kingsley symbolized its comically elliptical orbit. Here was a parson who preached that God created beauty for its own sake, but who crowed that 'the best and strongest men' in Cambridge were 'coming over' to 'what the world calls Darwinism, and you and I and some others, fact and science.'

> The younger M.A.'s are not only willing, but greedy, to hear what you have to say; and . . . the elder (who have, of course, more old notions to overcome) are facing the whole question in quite a different tone from that they did three years ago. I won't mention names, for fear of 'compromising' men who are in an honest but 'funky,' stage of conversion: but I have been surprised . . . at the change since last winter.

Fancy evolution all the go at Cambridge! Kingsley knew that Darwin made man's ancestors 'hairy beasts' – did no one else? Or was the idea now as debatable at Oxbridge as it was desirable among the secularists? Once Darwin's worst nightmare might have been to turn up in a rogues' gallery like Holyoake's secularist tract *Half-Hours with Freethinkers*. Now his potted biography was included there, cheek-by-jowl with those of Emma Martin, Robert Owen, and Lucretius, even while the Revd Kingsley, the Cambridge professor of modern history, sang his praises.[28]

He pushed on with *Variation*. After seven months of scratching and correcting, the proofs were finished on 15 November. Emma wished that he would relax and 'smoke a pipe or ruminate like a cow,' but 'enjoying leisure' was hard work. He worried whether anyone would read his mammoth volume. Still, he breathed a sigh and exhaled his relief to Hooker, telling him how to get through the two volumes: 'Skip the *whole* of Vol. 1., except the last chapter (and that only to be skimmed) and skip largely the 2nd volume; and then you will say it is a very good book.'[29]

37

Sex, Politics, & The X

THIRTEEN YEARS AFTER breeding and brewing up his first pouters the book was in the high-street shops – the book that rammed home the real plasticity of species: *The Variation of Animals and Plants under Domestication*. Of course now it also had multiple other functions: it pointed up the 'evil from interbreeding,' introduced Darwin's latest deity, the 'great god Pan,' and put paid to Gray's divine designer as the cause of variation.

On publication day, 30 January 1868, Darwin advised Fritz Müller, 'The great part, as you will see, is not meant to be read; but I should very much like to hear what you think of "Pangenesis".' Every recipient was so cajoled and Darwin was deflated by the response. Hooker thought the 'gemmules' and what not were better left mysterious. 'This power of packing into a cell the potentiality of an infinite number of the indefinite properties of its ancestors, is as much beyond our comprehension as atoms, or ethics, or time, or gravity, or God.' Darwin began to agree. And still he was expecting a 'blowing up' from Huxley, who put pangenesis in the same category as Genesis. Suddenly the sight of the book sickened him; his old insecurities resurfaced, his fear of rejection and loss of status: 'if I try to read a few pages I feel fairly nauseated.' He was protective about Pan, but for the rest, 'The devil take the whole book.'[1]

The public thought better, and even Murray underestimated demand. The 1500 copies vanished in a week. Demand was so high that eleven days found the presses reprinting. That afternoon George Lewes in the *Pall Mall Gazette* gave it a wonderful send off, praising the 'noble calmness' of its exposition. To read of himself 'undisturbed by the heats of polemical agitation' made Darwin laugh, and all in all the review left him 'cock-a-hoop.' As usual the *Athenaeum* jumped in with a panning; but that was par for the course and Darwin was inured to its Saturday morning sneers, if not quite hardened. 'The writer despises and hates me,' he flinched, half-suspecting his identity.[2] Only one man could 'cut me up so severely' – Owen.

Still, he worried about pangenesis. He doted on it like a 'beloved child,' believed in it like a god. It was the offspring of his fertile imagination, a *deus ex machina* to explain the phenomena of inheritance. Fearing that it would 'expire unblessed and uncursed by the world,' he was determined to 'stick up' for the theory; but like God and his children's health, its status was constantly in doubt. He blew hot and cold. Hooker's and Huxley's reactions made him want to give up 'the great god Pan as a still-born deity.' Then Wallace's enthusiasm made him sanguine again. Later, when Gray treated the theory sympathetically Darwin fancied that the 'infant . . . will live a long life. There is parental presumption for you!'[3]

Parental presumption was on the rise. For years he had never been sure whether his sickly sons would succeed in life's struggle. William, the fittest, was succeeding in managing his bank, a safe sedentary occupation. But what prospects for the rest? Would they follow their father and take to science or would the family weakness hold them back? Leonard, eighteen and minding Horace at Clapham School, had just been placed high on the Sandhurst list and was headed for the Royal Military Academy at Woolwich, where he came second in the entrance exam. 'Who would have ever have thought that poor dear old Lenny would have got so magnificent a place,' Charles exclaimed, doubting its significance. 'I shall be curious to hear how many tried.' Lenny would have a solid engineering education but limited scope for attainment. It suited him actually, the son in whom 'the collecting mania' had taken 'the poor form of collecting Postage stamps.'

Horace, a year behind Lenny, remained an enigma. He had a mechanical bent; if his health held, he might follow Frank to Cambridge and read natural science. George was proving what a feeble Darwin could achieve there, and now his father's eyes were on him. At twenty-three he was only just finishing a maths degree. He stood at the crossroads. Just as pangenesis reached the reviewers a telegram came: he had done magnificently, runner-up in his class. Charles's hand trembled as he penned congratulations. He had 'never expected such brilliant success as this.' At Clapham, where the Revd Wrigley had prepared the new Second Wrangler, there was a 'regular saturnalia.' Everyone was given a half holiday and packed off to the nearby Crystal Palace. George was offered a science mastership at Eton but turned it down to read for the bar. He could hardly refuse a fellowship of Trinity College, which Uncle Ras thought 'the most enviable position on earth.'[4]

Darwin too was collecting accolades. The *Origin* had been translated half-a-dozen times. Everywhere naturalists grappled with its arguments, intellectuals debated their implications. Love it or loathe it, the book was a work of genius. A few days after George's telegram, and while congratulations were flooding in, he heard that the King of Prussia had conferred the Order *Pour le Mérite* on him. Only weeks later the Imperial Academy of Sciences at St Petersburg elected him a Corresponding Member. He rushed a note to the revolutionary Vladimir Kovalevsky, hoping to lard the title-page of the Russian *Variation*. There was plenty of time, with Kovalevsky temporarily dropping his translations and travelling 1000 miles a week on a relief committee for Russian agricultural distress.[5]

The day after hearing from the Prussian Embassy he picked up sexual selection again. On a normal day he fired off eight or ten letters, garnering information, becoming a billionaire in bizarre facts: the manes of macaque monkeys, the antlers of deer, the breeding plumage of scarlet ibises or the hue of a toucan's beak – no frill or eyespot was lost that might have been favoured by a mate. He even plucked up courage to contact Louis Agassiz at Harvard. Agassiz was back from the Amazon, where he had travelled searching for evidence of former glaciers to prove that his Ice Age had been global, thus cutting off the old Creation from the new. Everyone knew that his apocalyptic ice-shroud was intended to stifle 'Darwinian views' and was so much 'wild nonsense.' Darwin considered him 'glacier mad.' But that did not preclude his pumping Agassiz on spawning Amazonian fishes – turning the poor man's anti-Darwinian gains into serviceable spoil, pickpocketing him so gently that he was none the wiser.

Darwin's sexual selection, like the fish, was transmuting and taking on a life of its own. It had grown to a 'gigantic subject.' He dropped on to his knees to scrutinize the Kingdom's lowliest inhabitants. Old helpers from the barnacle days were reactivated: Albany Hancock sent reams on gaudy sea-slugs, others on breeding crabs, the courtship of blind beetles, sadistic spiders, and brilliant butterflies. Come to that, 'how low in the scale [do] sexual differences occur which require some degree of self-consciousness in the males'? There were questions that only he could ask; were cricket chirps sexually selected? Could 'dumb' *Cicada*s breed?[6]

He started cornering commercial breeders, and he soon had them daubing, damaging, and docking prize specimens – pigeons were painted, game cocks had their tail feathers plucked, and he looked for a fancier to buff a bullfinch's rose-pink breast and spy on its sexual prowess. And still he cast around for a wealthy gent, willing to snip the eyes out of a peacock's tail – 'but who would sacrifice the beauty of their bird for a whole season to please a mere naturalist?'

Worrying and working obsessively, he left scant room for anything else. Hearing Hooker one day in ecstasies after taking in Handel's 'Messiah,' Darwin declared his soul 'too dried up to appreciate it as in the old days.' Orchids moved him more than pipe organs, corals more than the Hallelujah Chorus. 'I am a withered leaf for every subject except Science.'[7] But he had enough paper science for an entire civil service. His one-man collation agency was as usual out of control. By March he was inundated by daily bundles of letters from fanciers, farmers, fisheries experts, census statisticians, collectors, and colonists.

Partly he was being pushed by Argyll to explain jewelled hummingbirds, goaded by His Grace's claim that 'mere ornament or beauty is in itself a purpose, an object, and an end,' a Creative whim to please man. Wallace too was looking at scales and plumage, and the way leaf-like moths or camouflaged brooding birds were selected, and how the rest, the brilliant snakes or iridescent insects, were announcing their venom – or mimicking those that did. But this left the topaz and emerald nectar-sippers, and that was Darwin's terrain. The eye spots on a caterpillar might mimic a snake's face, but the eyes on a peacock's tail enamoured the hen. They had to be the result of conscious choice.

Did minuscule variations make any difference to star-crossed admirers? Wallace was dubious. Would 'an inch in the tail of the peacock, or ¼-inch in that of the Bird of Paradise . . . be noticed and preferred by the female'? Darwin was convinced of it.

> A girl sees a handsome man, and without observing whether his nose or whiskers are the tenth of an inch longer or shorter than in some other man, admires his appearance and says she will marry him. So, I suppose, with the pea-hen.

An extra fleck added to the effect, but what was appreciated was the 'gorgeous appearance.' Mates were selecting, with beauty in the eye of the beholding peahen. 'It is an awful stretcher to believe that a peacock's tail was thus formed; but, believing it, I believe in the same principle somewhat modified applied to man.'[8]

He brought his work along when Emma and the girls took him to London in March for four weeks' rest. His gardener sympathized: a month away was certainly a 'terrible thing' for his experiments. Still, after a week with Eras they took over Elizabeth Wedgwood's Regent's Park house, ten minutes' stroll from the zoo. Here, apart from entertaining luncheons and popping 'over the way' to Hensleigh's to discuss mankind's descent with the freethinking feminist Frances Power Cobbe, his time was spent in the zoo, carousing with keepers, making the elephants trumpet (to see if tears formed), and watching the pheasants display. Even more, he was retracing the steps of his old metaphysical notebooks, investigating the social instincts of monkeys – or at least putting snakes into their cages to test the communal reaction.

The unnaturally hectic trip was a sign of improving health. He thanked Grove at the Royal Institution in Piccadilly for helping George enter Lincoln's Inn to study law, talked pigs at the British Museum, sat in on an X Club meeting, and almost made it to Kew Gardens.[9]

Perhaps he also had a confab with John Murray about a new promotional scheme. Darwin was an adept self-publicist, but importing the Gray pamphlet was small fry compared to the plan he now had in mind. Whatever the rash of Germanic *Darwinismus*, no single, satisfactory book had appeared in England to support the side. He was greeted by a thundering silence. Lyell's *Antiquity of Man* was namby-pamby and off-beam; Huxley's working-men's pamphlets had a tiny sale, and surrounded Darwinism with caveats; his *Man's Place in Nature* was splendid on apes but silent on natural selection. With Argyll's wretched *Reign of Law* garnering the laurels, drastic measures were demanded.

Darwin had to cast his net wide – all the way to the Amazon – for a real chapter-and-verse disciple. He tried to interest Murray in translating Fritz Müller's *Für Darwin*. Müller was another radical exiled after the abortive 1848 revolution, but to Brazil, where he studied prawns and barnacles and scraped by as a schoolteacher. Murray feared the financial risk, so Darwin commissioned the book, subsidizing it to the tune of £100. He arranged the translator, oversaw the operation, picked up the advertising tabs, and organized the review and presentation copies. What to title it? The translator impertinently suggested *A Lift for Darwin*, a joke too near the knuckle. Lyell came up with *Facts and Arguments for Darwin*, which won the day – and the compositors took it upon themselves to set '*Darwin*' in larger type than '*Müller*' on the title-page. Murray printed 1000 copies at six shillings apiece, and both publisher and patron did quite well by it.[10]

*

Through the spring one of Huxley's protégés plied Darwin with esoteric notes on breeding newts. St George Mivart was a zoological sophisticate and a convert of twenty-five years to Catholicism. He was a suave Old Harrovian, stately in manner, brought up among the swells who flocked to his father's 'Mivart Hotel' in Grosvenor Square (later Claridge's). He had qualified as a barrister at Lincoln's Inn, only to throw over a law career after hearing Owen lecture next door at the College of Surgeons. But the turning point came when he met Huxley in 1859. Compared to the ponderous, taciturn Owen, Huxley was frank, exciting, and zoologically nimble. Mivart was mesmerized by the 'deep-set dark eyes,' the quick wit, and awed by his relentless debunking. He found himself between David and Goliath; and a reference each from Owen and Huxley had been enough to gain him the lectureship in zoology at St Mary's Hospital in Paddington in 1862. He continued to sit Huxley's lectures at the School of Mines and to visit the family.[11] And under Huxley's tutelage, he gained Darwin's ear.

Darwin fired strings of questions at him, tapping his brains on the colour, crests, and courtship of spawning newts. Mivart bent over backwards to help. He was a brilliant technical anatomist and could talk on the muscles of newts or the limbs of apes. But on grander issues, of man and morality, his position was becoming ambiguous. He had been a 'hearty' Darwinian, or so he said. In the wake of Huxley's *Man's Place* he had studied monkeys and lemurs and debated life and mind. 'As to "natural selection" I accepted it completely,' he told Darwin. But anyone who could add that, whatever the similarity of man's 'dead body' to a gorilla's, our 'intellectual, moral & religious nature' set us farther 'from an Anthropoid Ape than such an Ape differs from a lump of granite' was not going to sit docilely in Huxley's class for long.

Mivart's conversion and lapse were probably not blindingly Pauline. He had hedged his bets, kept faith with his Church. Deep down a love of Owen's science persisted, along with fears for a degraded humanity, and in fact he confessed to Darwin that his 'doubts & difficulties were first excited by attending Prof. Huxley's lectures.'[12] In 1868 Mivart hovered equivocally on the Darwinian fringes.

By now Darwin had reached Argyll's bottom line as he wrote his book: bedazzling birds. Enthusiasts were still buffing bullfinches and dyeing white doves for him, testing female ardour to its limit. The situation had a new urgency with Argyll's criticisms snowballing through the press. What of Darwin's vaunted selection if it could not produce 'the japanned peacock and Bohemian pheasant'? wondered the *Edinburgh Review*, musing on the *Variation*. Selection required utility, but there was none in gaudiness. Darwin had to prove that birds could choose their mates' fine feathers to prevent a holy Haberdasher from being invoked.

Hooker was sizing up Argyll's *Reign of Law*, ready to pounce on it as President of the British Association this year. The Duke's cockiness left him in 'utter disgust.' 'I like a man to sneer at me out of malice and envy, but cannot stand a man's sneering at me from atop of a high horse.' It all smacked of Owen, right up to Argyll's lofty remarks on rudimentary parts, which were 'very droll.' Owen's belief that rudiments related an animal to a Plan, rather than an ancestor, was squashed by the Darwinians with a vengeance. As a critic laughed, when Darwin pointed out our monkey bits, like 'the persistent tips in our ears, he did more to discomfort' his enemies than with a million other facts. Rudiments were easy; the real problem was to prove that iridescence and showy eyes are not similar pieces of Creative whimsy.

Talking to Hooker, watching the reviews, reading the likes of Lubbock and Tylor, it was clear that the new book – which he had decided to call *The Descent of Man* – would have to range widely, from sexual selection and ape ancestors to the evolution of morality and religion. His old notebooks had covered the ground. Indeed, Hooker thought that 'morals and politics would be very interesting if discussed like any branch of natural history.' Nor were he and Darwin the only ones to view these fields in the light of natural selection. Darwinizing about society was now a booming intellectual business.[13]

The quality magazines bulged with offerings. Darwin read them all, pencil in hand, culling ideas for his book. Wallace, the old socialist, had been the first to argue that co-operation made groups compact and fitted them to survive life's struggle. This was questionable meat and drink to Darwin – but evidence at least of inherited moral qualities. His cousin Francis Galton served up richer puddings. Of Quaker stock, heir of an arms manufacturer and a Birmingham banker, he had profited by Darwin's example and abandoned medicine to take a Cambridge maths degree before settling for a life of travel and scientific leisure. 'Hereditary Talent and Character' were his forte, and his *Macmillan's Magazine* article galvanized Darwin. It stressed the inheritance of every moral and mental trait, from drunkenness and stupidity to sobriety and genius. Races and classes assume the character of their individual members, and Galton called for better breeding, as with 'horses and cattle,' to ensure that the 'nobler varieties of mankind' prevail over the feebler. Above all, advancing civilization was to be saved from 'intellectual anarchy' by the rise of scientific 'master minds' to power.[14]

Galton's line was shared by Darwin's old Plinian Society friend, now a retired Lancashire millowner, W. R. Greg. His article in *Fraser's Magazine* on natural selection in society raised sinister fears about the 'unfit.' Darwin read it assiduously, pondering the problem of the upper middle classes – those who delayed marriage until they had the means to support a family – being swamped. The idle rich outbred them because they could afford to, the idle poor because they lacked Malthus's 'moral restraint.'

> The careless, squalid, unaspiring Irishman multiplies like rabbits: the frugal, foreseeing, self-respecting, ambitious Scot, stern in his morality, spiritual in his faith, sagacious and disciplined in his intelligence, passes his best years in struggle and in celibacy, marries late, and leaves few behind him. Given a land originally peopled by a thousand Saxons and a thousand Celts – and in a dozen generations five-sixths of the population would be Celts, but five-sixths of the property, of the power, of the intellect, would belong to the one-sixth of Saxons that remained. In the eternal 'struggle for existence,' it would be the inferior and *less* favoured race that had prevailed – and prevailed by virtue not of its good qualities but of its faults.

Whither progress, when society was being genetically drained? The dynamic, competing, improving part of the population was strangled by its own success. Natural selection failed them. Darwin was brought up sharp on the ultimate Malthusian dilemma.

Military help arrived with Walter Bagehot's essays on 'Physics and Politics' in the *Fortnightly Review*. Darwin had his pencil out again. To Bagehot, a comfortable banker and editor of *The Economist*, progress depended on a society's command structure. Civilization began with obedience, a respect for law, and a 'military bond.' The greater a tribe's disciplined coherence, the better its chances of triumphing in battle and carrying on its success. Through imperial blood-contests, new human racial and national types emerge, honed and heightened by selection, and this is a moral boon. 'The characters which do win in war are the characters which we should wish to win in war.' Darwin was fascinated. Thinking of the colonial English no doubt, he jotted the proviso, 'nations which *wander* & cross would be most likely to vary' – because they would face unceasing competition. But he agreed with Bagehot's analysis of 'prehistoric politics' and commended it to Hooker.[15]

Hooker was the first Darwinian to take the British Association Presidency. It was a sure sign that, in the 'Parliament of Science' at least, Darwin's statesmen were moving across to the government benches. Hooker moaned at the prospect of his 'Queen's Speech.' The address was crucial, with the hacks reporting it as if it were 'a budget speech by Mr. Gladstone' (which caused only marginally more of a furore). Darwin was even more appalled. 'I pity you from the bottom of my soul about the address: it makes my flesh creep.' Hooker's own flesh was wobbling. 'I would give 100 guineas that it were over, even with a failure, a fiasco, or worse.' At first he thought he would talk on the 'non-acceptance of Natural Selection.' Darwin cued him, reminding him that Newton's theory of gravitation was rejected by the 'extraordinarily able' Leibniz. Word crept out that the speech would be a party pronouncement, and Wallace hoped that it would 'promulgate "Darwinianism"' pure and simple.[16] The X Clubbers seized the opportunity, and it was arranged at party headquarters that Huxley would move the vote of thanks and Tyndall second it.

With the party preparing and Hooker rehearsing, the Darwins trooped off on holiday. They took the train and ferry to the Isle of Wight, with Eras in tow and even old Tommy, Charles's huge horse. Charles himself was a wreck, but the sea air braced him. It was wretched away from home, divorced from his experiments, and he grumbled at having to 'live the life of a drone.' They leased a cottage at Freshwater for six weeks from the photographer Julia Cameron. The haggard evolutionist provided a perfect subject for a portrait in her elemental and manic sepia shades (the Darwins pronounced the shot 'excellent'). Her more poetic subjects appeared on Darwin's doorstep; Tennyson visited several times, as well as the Americans Longfellow and Thomas Appleton. And the Irish poet William Allingham wrote:

> . . . to the Darwins. Dr. Hooker in lower room writing away at his Address; going to put 'Peter Bell's' primrose into it and wants the exact words. Upstairs Mrs. Darwin, Miss D. [Henrietta] and Mr. Charles Darwin himself –, yellow, sickly, very quiet. He has his meals at his own times, sees people or not as he chooses, has invalid's privileges in full, a great help to a studious man.[17]

Hooker had joined them, composing his speech to the greater glory of the yellow sickly soul upstairs.

The Darwinians minus Darwin assembled at Norwich for the Association jamboree. From far and wide they came, a rallying of evolutionary pilgrims of every persuasion. The fiery materialist Carl Vogt travelled from Geneva, telling fellow socialist Wallace that the 'Germans are all becoming converted' by the *Variation*. Victor Carus arrived from Leipzig, hoping to pay homage at Downe afterwards. With so many sects gathered, each holding aloft the *Origin*, friction was inevitable. Mivart came with his confessor Father Roberts, currently leading an austere life in a Drury Lane slum and weaning St George off a Darwinian explanation of ethics. What hope of Huxley's 'new reformation' if the old had yet to take effect? Huxley stumbled upon the two in the nave of Norwich cathedral and expostulated with a wink: 'Oh! for the time when the king shall have his own again.'

Hooker's address was a wild success for the Xs, a stew of hot topics cooked in a Darwinian pot: orchids, tendrils, origins, and 'Tom Tiddler's Ground,' a prehistoric diorama on which he observed the rise of ancient man and demise of archaic theology. He praised Lyell's heroism, and Darwin's more, and damned 'that most dangerous of all two-edged weapons, Natural Theology.' The *Variation* was applauded, the *Athenaeum* abused, and natural selection made out to be part of the mental equipment of every 'philosophical naturalist.'[18] No President could have said more.

Darwin arrived home from holiday on 21 August carrying that day's *Times*, *Telegraph*, *Spectator*, and *Athenaeum*, all running the address. And having devoured them he ordered another bundle of newspapers. The Tory press kicked up a fuss about the theology. *John Bull* bridled at Hooker's 'puffing Mr. Darwin's latest hallucinations,' slating the speech as 'a melancholy exhibition of verbose mediocrity in excelsis,' which increased Hooker's stock no end. He told Darwin that he felt like 'the Turk in Hogarth's picture, calmly smoking his pipe as he gazes in through the window of a Church where the congregation are in a state of religious excitement.'

But who was inside and who out? Party spirit was high as the Darwinians invaded the church scientific with Hooker. Wallace gloated to Darwin that 'Darwinianism' was 'in the ascendant.' The 'worst of it is that there are no opponents left who know anything of natural history, so that there are none of the good discussions we used to have.' The liberal *Telegraph* backed Hooker to the hilt, the Anglican *Guardian* acknowledged that Darwinism's 'reign was triumphant,' and even the grumpy *English Churchman* conceded that 'rank infidelity' was now the scientific norm.[19]

Everywhere the press noted that Darwin's disciples were ready to 'push their consequences more fearlessly than the master himself.' Huxley rubbed the point in, dropping Darwin a note:

> The only fault was the terrible 'Darwinismus' which spread over the [biology] section and crept out when you least expected it, even in Fergusson's lecture on 'Buddhist Temples.' You will have the rare happiness to see your ideas triumphant during your lifetime.

Even in the physics section Tyndall held out hope that eventually science would resolve the 'mystery' of the relation between mind and brain, making them identical. He was too sanguine for Huxley, who genially summed up Tyndall's question for a future physics: 'Given the molecular forces in a mutton chop, deduce Hamlet or Faust therefrom.'[20]

But Darwin revelled in Tyndall's speech. Tyndall and Huxley led the new breed of star performers, their lectures enrapturing audiences and leaving the religious press in a lather. (True to form, Huxley 'offended the clergy twice without cause or warrant,' Hooker tittered to Darwin.) They were persuasive and visionary, hell-bent on dominion, sweeping aside the remnants of privilege and dilettantism. Science was losing its strictures; the old Oxbridge restraints were being shaken off. The X Clubbers with an evolutionary axe to grind deplored 'the stream of cold water which has steadily flowed over geological speculations.' Tyndall despised the 'Tories . . . in science who regard imagination as a faculty to be feared.' Their protest was aimed at lifting sanctions against Darwin's new naturalism, enabling Tyndall to issue a hands-off demand, warning scientists 'to be cautious in limiting [Darwin's] intellectual horizon.'

Tyndall's appeal was universal, which made him dangerous. In these combative years he initiated the Association's working-class talks, and outrageously. Faces were agog with teasing talk of babies built from chemicals, and the thinking capacity of robots. His gloriously deterministic cosmological system left every priest and pauper a soul of fire and child of the sun. All bowed to the same unyielding necessity. He captured its beauty and inescapability, exulting that 'at the present moment, all our poetry, all our science, all our art – Plato, Shakespeare, Newton, and Raphael – are potential in the fires of the sun.'

Darwin's New Model Army had inherited the ethical rigour of the evangelicals. They were positivists in part, Darwinians at heart, and X Clubbers to a man, but they weren't atheists, or materialists, and in fact they lacked any identifying label. They wielded biblical metaphors but were anti-theological. They embedded morality in acquiescence to positive facts, and crucified their enemies for the 'sin of faith.' They retained 'a scientific hell, to which the finally impenitent, those who persist in rejecting the new physical gospel, might be condemned,' and portrayed the Darwinian scientist as the real heir to the Reformation – all of which made Mivart doubly contemptuous of Tyndall's 'new creed – "I believe in One Force".' The 'terrible "Darwinismus"' was being hitched to a pantheistic superstructure and underwritten by its aggressive middle-class exponents.[21] Darwin could only watch in wonder.

In Haeckel's work, *Darwinismus* became even more terribly encompassing, taking in life, mind, society, politics, and knowledge itself. Darwin was still agitating for an expurgated translation of his *Generelle Morphologie*. He offered to defray some of the cost, and at Norwich the Ray Society agreed to publish it with the 'aggressive heterodoxy' toned down. Savage cuts were needed, Huxley insisted; the God-as-gas jibe had to go and the book be 'condensed to the uttermost.' 'We don't much mind heterodoxy here if it does not openly proclaim itself as such,' he warned incongruously, meaning that in England unbelief had to be polite. Haeckel actually prepared a shorn version, ready for translation. But still they met insuperable problems and the scheme eventually fell through. The book was just 'too profound and too long.'[22]

It was also eclipsed by Haeckel's *History of Creation*. Darwin was astonished at another thumping tome arriving on his doorstep, wondering at the 'indomitable worker' who could gestate books at Herbert Spencer's speed. Haeckel rushed in once more with a ream of ancestral pedigrees, precisely where Darwin feared to tread. There was a breathlessness to it, and so much scintillating speculation. 'Whether one agrees or disagrees with him,' Huxley conceded, it was 'more profitable to go wrong than to stand still.' Huxley finally bowed to the inevitable and adopted Haeckel's approach. At the Zoological Society he drew up a heraldic tree for the partridges and pigeons, doing what he once told Darwin was impossible and wrong. He produced 'a *genetic classification*,' signifying the route by which 'all living beings have been evolved one from the other.' He carried on, pushing birds back, past their ostrich-like ancestors to the dinosaurs themselves.[23] After a decade of cavils and caveats, he had finally come round to Darwin's position.

No doubt it was Haeckel's doing, and Huxley paid his debt. He named a primal slime creature *Bathybius Haeckelii*, an enucleate organism dredged from the deep by a sounding ship preparing for the transatlantic cable. Unfortunately it proved less a creature than a creation of the preserving fluid; but the homage was indicative, a tacit admission that the Germans were stealing a march. Huxley also sought audiences for German pilgrims who wanted to pay their 'devotions at the shrine of Mr Darwin' – or 'Pope Darwin,' as he appeared in one accompanying sketch, complete with thurible-swinging acolyte. At Downe Parslow ushered the professors into the study, where they glowed and gloated about the impact of *Darwinismus* in German universities. Jena, where Haeckel taught, was rapidly becoming the centre of the subject. At Bonn Wilhelm Preyer was outdoing even Haeckel, attracting up to 500 students for his lectures. Days after being elevated by Huxley to the papal throne, Darwin received a greater honour: an honorary doctorate from Preyer's university.[24]

The autumn was memorable for the garlands, the touching dedications from one side of the world to the other. French fossil tomes with lavish family trees; an account of the Smithsonian Institution's expedition to the Amazon; Wallace's *Malay Archipelago* – all were dedicated to Darwin.[25] With *Orchids* about to be translated into French, Hooker reckoned that even the French Académie would eventually cave in and elect him a member.

These were the most sociable months the children could remember. Asa Gray, overburdened at the Harvard herbarium and 'half dead with drudgery,' arrived in England with his wife for a long rest in mid-September, after a fast steamship crossing of two weeks. He spent his time in the Kew greenhouses with Hooker, who took the Grays to visit Downe, with Darwin roping in Tyndall on one occasion. On these weekend trips the Grays observed the Darwins at home – the casual untidiness, the worn furniture, the unvarying routine. Emma's and Charles's evening backgammon battles became a spectator sport, with Mrs Gray cheering Emma's gains and her husband consoling the loser. ('Bang your bones'! Charles would explode in mock anger at his wife.) Darwin struck Mrs Gray as 'entirely fascinating,' tall, craggy, with 'a full grey beard cut square across the upper lip.' But not even 'the sweetest smile, the sweetest voice, the merriest laugh' could disguise the ravages. His 'face shows the marks of suffering and disease ... He never stayed long with us at a time, but as soon as he had talked much, said he must go & rest, especially if he had had a good laugh.'

It was like the old gatherings. Gray's friend Charles Eliot Norton, editor of the *North American Review*, was staying at nearby Keston rectory and dropping into Downe for lunches with his wife and her nineteen-year-old sister Sara Sedgwick (who caught William's eye). On another occasion Wallace and Edward Blythe visited, both tropical travellers to be pumped on hummingbirds and brilliant butterflies. Down House had not seen so many comings and goings for a decade. 'I shall enjoy it immensely,' Darwin chortled before one dinner, 'if it does not kill me.'

Gray, among the natives, found himself rather swamped by Hooker, Huxley, and Tyndall. He was theologically stalemated by the *Variation*, and realized that the *Origin* was irretrievably in the X Club's court. He could hardly condone Hooker's address, or Tyndall's fantasies, and while he took one English fashion back to Harvard (a 'venerable white beard'), he left behind any remaining desire to indulge in '*Darwinian* discussions,' not wishing 'to be at all "mixed up" with the Huxley set.'[26]

A million first-time voters helped rout the Tories in the November General Election and sweep the new Liberal leader, William Gladstone, into 10 Downing Street. The X Club also came within a hair's breadth of getting its own Parliamentary representative. Lubbock fought West Kent again, with Darwin giving moral support (as well as the loan of his carriage), and almost turned out the sitting Tory. It was a crumb of comfort for Downe's old vicar Brodie Innes, who had twitted Darwin for trying to get the Birmingham MP and working-class hero John Bright 'made Dictator.' Innes, however, now had rather more urgent local politics to contend with. From his family estate in Scotland he was making common cause with Darwin to sort out Downe's sitting curate.

It was a sad saga of an 'impoverished benefice' ill served. The lax curate Brodie Innes had left in charge, the Revd Stephens, had departed the previous year, and Innes had been keen to rid himself of responsibility for the living. He even offered to sell the 'advowson' – the right to appoint Downe's priest – to Darwin (who replied that 'it w^d not be in my way'). Stephens's replacements were worse, and Brodie Innes plied Darwin with anxious letters about their conduct. The Revd Samuel Horsman had lasted only three months. He ran up a string of debts and made off with the school's cash after Darwin mistakenly shared the treasurer's duties with him. Horsman was 'more an utter fool than knave,' Darwin pronounced, and Innes could only 'think he is mad.' But no sooner had he been forced out, vapouring threats of litigation, than his successor, the Revd John Robinson, proceeded to disgrace himself by 'walking with girls at night.'[27]

Or so it was rumoured that autumn, according to Brodie Innes's eyes and ears in Down House. Darwin wrote:

> My wife found Mrs. Allen very indignant about Mr. R.s conduct with one of her maids. I do not believe that there is any evidence of actual criminality. As I repeat only second hand my name must not be mentioned. – Our maids tell my wife that they do not believe that hardly anyone will go to church now . . .

Brodie Innes replied with a written 'challenge' to be circulated in the parish, urging Robinson's accusers to come forward. This put Darwin in a pother – passing on the challenge might expose him to 'an action for defamation of character.' But still, something had to be done.

Rumours were now 'rife against Mr R.' Darwin dug deeper, acting like a sleuth around the village. Brodie Innes heard the magistrate's verdict just before Christmas.

> Mr Allen knows nothing from his own observations. The name of the girl is Esther West. Mr Allen's cook saw Mr R. talking to her in the road near the house. He had heard from Mrs Allen that the mother of the girl (who has left M$^{r.}$ Allen) had written to Mr R. forbidding him to call at her cottage; also that Mr R. had been seen to go into some house in the village where some girl supposed to have a bad character lives. Mr Allen said that he believed this 2nd story came from Mrs Engleheart, & about the girls mother thro' Mrs Buckle the wife of the bailiff.

All hearsay evidence. So Darwin cross-examined Mrs Allen, who had started the story, observing her emotions with a practised eye.

> Judging by her manner, [she] knew a good deal, but said she was nervous & w^d not commit herself – accordingly she said she c^d not remember who had told her any one single thing; or the name of the girl in the village; & further that her cook did not want to commit herself & declined to say whether it was in the daylight or after dark that Mr R. talked with the girl.

The 'only evidence worth any thing c^d be obtained from the girl's mother' but 'perhaps she w^d refuse to commit herself,' Darwin summed up, and so returned the circular, 'sincerely sorry for all this vexation & trouble.' Brodie Innes thanked him profusely for helping 'an old friend out of a most distressing dilemma.' Robinson's days were numbered. 'I hope there may very soon be a resident vicar.'[28]

At home sexual sleuthing of a different kind was gathering pace. Down House had become the hub of a correspondence network across the Empire, its tentacles touching every little England. The sack of mail brought gems daily to aid his sexual selection. Botanists from Ceylon to Calcutta sent reports on monkey manes and bearded Indians; mining engineers from Malacca to Nicaragua told of indigenous customs; tile manufacturers in Gibraltar attended to merino lambs; wine exporters in Portugal followed the local tailless dogs; Laplanders measured reindeer horns; New Zealanders heroically tackled the Maori's sense of beauty; and missionaries and magistrates from Queensland to Victoria ceased converting and incarcerating to observe aboriginal ways – with even an old *Beagle* shipmate Philip King helping out.[29] This is what Darwin excelled at: collecting and collating, tracking down facts, verifying, extending his old notebook speculations to embrace the globe.

38

Disintegrating Speculations

WHATEVER THE GROWING appreciation of evolution, friends and foes alike opposed Darwin's blind, stumbling, accident-prone mechanism: Lyell and Gray stood on the same ground as Owen and Argyll; not one could reconcile himself to it. Where was the time for man to have evolved by Darwin's 'higgledy-piggledy' process – where one accidental variation in ten thousand was usable – with Scots physicists crimping millions from the earth's age? Waiting for chance variants was time-consuming, and time was running out. Lyell had once called up almost infinite reserves; Darwin in 1859 had mooted 300 million years alone since the dinosaurs' reign. But William Thomson's latest calculations, based on the earth as a cooling globe, suggested 100 million years since crustal condensation, which was 'preposterously inadequate' for Darwin's slow, hit-or-miss method.[1] Not for providentialists of course; they were happy to speed up the process, using 'guided' rather than random variations, keeping the flow under Creative control. The physicists' monkey was now on Darwin's back.

Thomson loomed 'like an odious spectre' from one of Wallace's séances. Darwin was appalled at this curtailing of the time available for the evolution of life. His own mathematical geology being wobbly, he asked George, fresh from Cambridge with his maths degree, to check Thomson's figures, incredulous at the 'brevity of the world.' Endless ages *must* have preceded the earliest Silurian sea creatures 'else my views w^d be wrong, which is impossible – Q.E.D.' How could the thousands of feet of sediments have been laid in such short time? Or the old strata have been weathered away? It was absurd.

Nonetheless he met the criticisms with cosmetic surgery to a new (fifth) edition of the *Origin* through the winter of 1868-69. Sometimes the cutting went a little deeper. He had the environment cause a greater number of useful variations to appear. This sped up the process and cut down the risk of new varieties being blended back into a population by intercrossing. And he reactivated the old notion that excessive use of an organ causes its growth (as in the case of a blacksmith's biceps), and that this change can be passed on ('use-inheritance').[2] All this gave a more focused direction to the variations, accelerating evolution, allowing the wonderful richness of life to be a product of a mere 100 million years. He finished on 10 February 1869, two days before his sixtieth birthday.

A week later Huxley turned 'attorney-general' and advised the Geological Society as its President on the time question. His brief was to lift spirits, Darwin's not least: 'Biology takes her time from geology,' he announced, speaking for the evolutionary lobby. 'If the geological clock is wrong, all the naturalist will have to do is to modify his notions of the rapidity of change accordingly.' And it appeared a big 'if' after he had finished with the vagaries of solar heating and terrestrial cooling.

Darwin thought the talk wonderfully 'brilliant,' but shafts rained down on Huxley for compromising the queen of sciences, physics. He was like his execrable 'Trades-Unionists,' another of Thomson's co-workers wrote, smashing the sophisticated machinery supplied by the physicists which would make the biological drudges redundant. 'That educated scientific men should thus fall into the wretched fallacies of handloom-weavers . . . is surely a very singular psychological phenomenon, worthy the attention of sensational writers on obscure diseases of the mind and brain.' If anything, Thomson had been too generous to these biological yahoos, *'ten* or *fifteen* millions' was the *real* age of the earth. This figure, were it true, would have scotched any evolutionary accommodation.

Reading this, Darwin 'felt very small,' and his earth shrank even smaller. Frankly, he did not believe the figure for a moment. He took comfort in the review's 'severe fling' at Hooker and fatuous remarks about Huxley, knowing that he was not alone. 'This review shows me – not that I required being shown – how devilish a clever fellow Huxley is, for the reviewer cannot help admiring his abilities.' George guessed that this latest estimate was by a Thomson co-worker, P. G. Tait, a Bible-toting Edinburgh professor of natural philosophy. He also impressed on his father the gravity of Thomson's case. 'Tell George from me not to sit upon you with his mathematics,' Hooker rallied him. 'Take another dose of Huxley's . . . Address, and send George back to college.'[3]

Darwin's discomfort was more than scientific this spring. In April he was riding Tommy on Keston Common when his favourite old horse tripped, threw him on to the ground and rolled over him. The bruising was extensive, and the doctors advised him to rest for a few months. He mended within weeks and resumed work under Emma's watchful eye, but they agreed that Tommy was unreliable.[4] At sixty, Charles needed a sure mount, but he never found one and his riding days came to an end.

Huxley, who had instructed Haeckel on metaphysical rectitude, found himself charged with heresy after preaching a Sunday 'lay sermon' in Edinburgh 'on the physical basis of life.' It *sounded* like materialism – life and mind a glorified chemical process – although he insisted that materialism was as absurd ultimately as spiritualism. To no avail. His lecture, published in the *Fortnightly Review*, caused a sensation and the issue ran to an unheard-of seven editions. The religious hacks foamed. Was he not Darwinism personified, the high priest of the new secular faith, conducting 'Sunday Evenings for the People,' canvassing for 'scientific Sunday schools,' and chairing London's 'Sunday Lecture Society'?[5] They portrayed him as a man of matter without a soul, an atheist and immoral.

He was none of these, even if there was some dispute as to what he was. He came clean in April, when a group of liberal churchmen made a last attempt to reach a religious consensus among the nation's feuding intelligentsia. Their monthly discussion group, the 'Metaphysical Society,' was a menagerie of faiths and heresies; bishops and archbishops mingled with Positivists, deists, and Unitarians, and for spice there was even the odd atheist. Huxley joined with Tyndall and Lubbock, representing the Darwinian faction, but before anyone could pin him down he came up with a new identifying label – he coined the name 'agnostic.' An agnostic did not deny or affirm God's existence; he did not pretend to know whether the world is made of matter, spirit, or whatever. Like 'lunar politics,' the subject was endlessly and pointlessly debateable. Darwin's science stood above such squabbles, dealing with the knowable world. To Huxley Darwinism was 'not only "unsectarian" but . . . altogether "secular".'[6]

Huxley loved military issues and he needed a reactionary enemy. Catholicism provided it. He constantly vilified the Roman Church as 'our great antagonist,' the supreme foil. He pictured it as a Jesuitical militia, whose priests, trained to combat scientific change, were, next to the Dad's army of Dissenters, like 'the trained veterans of Napoleon's Old Guard.' These strategic attacks racked his Catholic admirer St George Mivart to breaking point. To hear of 'Pithecoid Man' was distressing; to be told that the Catholic Church 'must, as a matter of life and death, resist the progress of science and modern civilization' was too much – even if recent papal condemnations seemed to imply it. (Mivart was too liberal to take Pius IX's 'Syllabus of Errors' seriously.) Nor had crusading Continental works like Vogt's inflammatory *Lectures on Man* and Haeckel's *Generelle Morphologie* helped. Mivart was torn; his letters to Darwin became a desperation of pleasantries.

> For my part I shall never feel anything but gratitude & sincere
> esteem for the author of 'natural selection' but I heartily
> execrate some who made use of that theory simply as a
> weapon of offence against higher interests and as a means of
> impeding Man's advance towards his 'end' whatever may have
> been his 'origin.'

He had Huxley in mind. In his 'wandering about Italy' he had been 'amazed and saddened' to see Huxley's *Man's Place in Nature* on sale at 'most of the railway stations amongst a crowd of *obscenities*.'[7] Huxley's aggressive posturing was losing Darwin followers.

Darwin also knew that trouble was brewing with Wallace, and he awaited his review of Lyell's tenth-edition *Principles* with trepidation. The High Church *Guardian* had already smiled on Lyell's mild Darwinism. 'Really,' Wallace wrote, 'what with the Tories passing Radical Reform Bills and the Church periodicals advocating Darwinianism, the millennium must be at hand.' But it was Wallace's spirit-driven evolution that worried Darwin. 'I shall be intensely curious to read' the review. 'I hope you have not murdered too completely your own and my child.' Poignant, anxious words. The review appeared in April and Darwin identified the child's corpse, horrified at the disfiguring torture. He stabbed exclamation marks at Wallace's text, and triple underlined 'No.'[8]

Wallace had plucked mankind's expansive consciousness from the realm of selection altogether. Savages have a mental capacity far beyond their needs. Little more than a gorilla's brain would suffice; as it is they possess the egg-head of an Englishman, and as such an intellectual over-capacity. Selection, which deals in the immediately useful, could not have given it to them, but the spiritual forces could. Having gone native while collecting in the Amazon and Far East, the socialist held savages in high esteem. He did not share Darwin's defamatory view, based on the crafty, cannibalistic Fuegians. 'The more I see of uncivilized people,' Wallace had said while living with the Dyaks in Borneo, 'the better I think of human nature.' The brain was an over-endowment, but some tribes had used it to develop a higher morality than the colonists trying to exterminate them.

The big brain was an essential prerequisite for the development of civilization. But selection had no foresight – it provided for day-to-day existence, not future needs. And judging by the 'social barbarism' of Victoria's England, morally crippled by a cut-throat capitalism, selection had no power to enhance civilization. No, for Wallace higher spiritual powers guided human destiny. They were responsible for the brain, and they would be man's salvation, putting him on the path to the millennium.

'I differ grievously from you,' Darwin wrote, 'and I am very sorry for it.' It was sad, the stoutest defender unaccountably calling in other-worldly intelligences. It was also 'incredibly strange.' Not knowing better, Darwin 'would have sworn' the brain passages 'had been inserted by some other hand.' An invisible spiritual hand, as Wallace explained by return; his opinions had been modified, he confessed, after studying 'the existence of forces and influences not yet recognized by science.'[9]

The spring of defections was turning into a summer of despair. On 3 June, with Huxley's help, Mivart gained his Fellowship of the Royal Society. It was a crowning testimony to his studies of monkeys, and gave no indication of the cruel blow to come. Twelve days later, he turned traitor. He told Huxley face to face that he was going to publish his objections to Darwinian views of human nature and morality. 'As soon as I had made my meaning clear, his countenance became transformed as I had never seen it before,' Mivart recalled. 'Yet he looked more sad and surprised than anything else. He was kind and gentle as he said regretfully, but most firmly, that nothing so united or severed men as questions such as those.' Mivart had been groomed, ready for the charmed inner circle. His desertion was viewed as treachery, and the Darwinians closed ranks as a period of bitterness and recrimination set in.

The breach had already opened, with Mivart placing anonymous articles in the Catholic *Month* criticizing natural selection. He raised a host of difficulties: how could selection explain a placental dog and marsupial wolf converging so miraculously? And can it explain an incipient wing? What use is half a wing, yet selection is supposed to keep the animal functional at every stage? These were puzzlers. 'How incipient organs can be useful is a real difficulty,' Wallace admitted to Darwin after reading the *Month*, 'so is the independent origin of similar complex organs.' Darwin heavily annotated the anonymous reprint. He could not accept Mivart's inner force working to a definite end. Nor could he see life swept forward on a wave front according to God's will, any more than he could agree with Lyell, Gray, and Argyll.[10]

While Mivart and Wallace muddied the waters, Argyll stirred the sediment. The result was more best-selling froth. The new Secretary of State for India found time to push Gladstone's Irish policies, organize the Indian railways, and, like everyone else, publish on man. *Primeval Man* was no more than one might expect from a Liberal duke charged with running India from a desk in Whitehall, but the public loved such things.

Argyll took on Lubbock, admitted a long prehistory, but saw no signs of original bestiality. Mankind could not rise unaided from 'utter barbarism.' But he could have sunk from some higher state. Modern savages were not Stone Age relics but degenerates, forced into the worst regions by fitter races. Nor were our ancestors morally barbarous. And how could selection produce all this? Look at man's pink skin and puny frame – how could selection evolve greater weakness without the counter-balancing gift of reason being bestowed first? Where would such a helpless savage stand in the struggle for existence? One newspaper knew exactly: 'Place a naked high-ranking elder of the British Association in [the] presence of one of M. de Chaillu's gorillas, and behold how short and sharp will be the struggle.'[11]

Argyll was adamant: 'Man must have had the human proportions of mind before he could afford to lose bestial proportions of body.' And just because Sir John's savage had no knowledge of metal did not mean 'he was also ignorant of duty or ignorant of God.' Darwin found it all immensely clever and rather tedious. He ploughed on with the real *Descent of Man*, pointing out that, in the absence of ancestors, no one can assume that we are 'smaller and weaker.' Anyway, he added, standing Argyll on his head, man's vulnerability encouraged social cohesion and with it the moral sense. Lubbock prepared to restate the case at the British Association, that savage customs are stone-age hold-overs, which 'tell a tale of former barbarism.'[12] And – armed by Darwin on the Fuegians – he hammered the point home in his second edition of *Prehistoric Times*.

While Lubbock prepared for the bustling Association, Darwin was spirited away by 'his ladies' on holiday, grumbling and grousing as he got over his riding accident. They started on 10 June for Caerdeon in the Barmouth valley, sleeping at Shrewsbury on the way. He revisited The Mount, but the new owners dutifully followed him around. 'If I could have been left alone in that green-house for five minutes,' he whispered with a melancholy sigh, 'I know I should have been able to see my father in his wheel-chair as vividly as if he had been there before me.' The purple-heathered hills of North Wales, full of old memories, depressed him. He longed to pound up to the peaks as he used to as a student, but he could barely walk half a mile from the house. 'It is enough to make one wish oneself quiet in a comfortable tomb,' he mumbled, and he joined George on a sick-bed while the other children larked and posed for a group photograph.

The resort drew other notables. Plodding up a gentle rise one afternoon, he was stopped by a shout. He peered through the 'impenetrable brambles' to see, on the road sixty feet away, the redoubtable Miss Cobbe, the women's and animals' rights campaigner, bursting to tell him about Mr Mill's emancipationist book *On the Subjection of Women*. It was perfect for his study of human descent, she yelled, especially the chapters on sexual selection. Darwin bellowed back that Mill 'could learn some things' from biology. Men's superiority was the product of the 'struggle for existence;' their special 'vigour and courage' came from battling 'for the possession of women.' Hearing that, Cobbe offered her copy of Kant on the 'moral sense' to sort out his obvious ethical problems. He politely refused.[13]

The X Club gained their permanent press outlet in November when *Nature* was founded. While Hooker used it to review, and Huxley to extol Goethe, Darwin was reading another *Nature* supporter, Francis Galton's *Hereditary Genius*. He wrote in praise to his cousin: 'you have made a convert of an opponent in one sense, for I have always maintained that, excepting fools, men did not differ much in intellect, only in zeal and hard work; and I still think [this] is an eminently important difference.'[14]

Darwin ended the year as he came in, at the grindstone, 'putting ugly sentences rather straighter' and struggling to finish sexual selection, 'weary of everlasting males and females, cocks and hens.' It left him as 'dull as a duck.' And still the colonists and empire builders showered scraps on him: sons off to China acted as his eyes; from the Colonial Office in Cape Town came information on African moths; and natives were scrutinized from India to Sierra Leone in response to his printed 'Queries about Expression.' If nothing, the *Descent of Man* would carry the mark of empire.

All eyes were turning to Darwin. Everybody had spoken on the rise or fall of man but him. He was expected to clear the mud with a definitive pronouncement. Murray's new literary monthly, *The Acad-*

emy, trailed the work in the opening issue. As always the Germans were quick off the mark and competing to translate the *Descent of Man*. Darwin felt secure with Carus, but the fiery Vogt was bidding for the rights, to Darwin's horror. At Eras's he told Frances Cobbe that Vogt in London 'gave a lecture, in which he treated the Mass as the last relic of that *Cannibalism* which gradually took to eating only the heart, or eyes of a man to acquire his courage.' Darwin's only comment was 'how much more *decency* there was in speaking on such subjects in England.' He could never let the *Descent* go to such a sneering cynic.

The prospect of speaking out on this contentious issue filled Darwin with dread. This time his critics were lying in wait, forearmed. 'Whenever I publish my book,' he told Mivart half-accusingly, 'I can see that I shall meet with universal disapprobation, if not execution.'[15]

Charles kept the study fire stoked and wrote through the long hard winter, wrapping up the chapters on man's 'mental powers' and 'moral sense.' He posted them to Cannes, where Henrietta, twenty-seven and rather eligible, had swanned off for a reconnoitre. A stylist and petty moralist, she touched up his prose and guarded the proprieties. Parts were too evangelical, he feared; they read like a sermon. 'Who w^d ever have thought I sh^d turn parson'!

An infidel parson at that, given his argument's atheistic overtones. As he saw it, the 'feeling of religious devotion' was not basically different from a monkey's affection for its keeper, or Henrietta's dog Polly's 'deep love' for her. Nor was the 'ennobling belief in God' innate and universal, merely the highest sanction for keeping society in order. All beliefs and mores had originated in animal instincts and savage superstitions. These were old views, from Charles's notebook days. But even now, ten years after the *Origin* furore, publication might injure the family; Henrietta had to ensure that the wrong inferences would not be drawn. As she preened the text, her own guardian angel – Emma – jogged her. The treatment of morals and religion might be 'very interesting,' Emma wrote, but she would still 'dislike it very much as again putting God further off.'[16]

Soon he was exhausted and Emma carried out her threat to 'force him off somewhere' for a break. He went willingly this time, to Cambridge. Frank was graduating with a good maths degree and Horace had joined him at Trinity. It was mid-May and the backs of the colleges were 'paradaisical.' When better to visit the ancient town after more than thirty years? Henrietta came along with her sister Bessy to check on Horace's health, and they all stayed at the Bull

Hotel. Besides the bustling market and teeming shops, there was a new chapel at St John's, refurbishments in Great St Mary's, and museums and lecture rooms where the old Botanic Garden once stood. Charles, recalling his student strolls, was haunted by 'dear Henslow.' Cambridge was just 'not itself' without him.

The day before leaving they ran into Professor Sedgwick. Elderly and 'living in cheerless solitude,' he was 'overflowing with joy' to see Charles in 'a dear family party' and sat him down for a long chat. He carried on as if the *Origin of Species* had never been published – in politeness perhaps, but Charles thought his brain 'enfeebled.' He then proposed to show off his pride and joy, the Woodwardian Museum, full of fossils and rocks. It was late but a refusal unthinkable, and the old Proctor, hobbling on his stick in flowing robes, frogmarched him through the streets for the geological tour. By the end Charles was 'utterly prostrated;' the next morning he could barely drag himself to the train. 'Is it not humiliating,' he sighed, 'to be thus killed by a man of eighty-six, who evidently never dreamed that he was killing me?'[17]

Safely home, he carried on nailing down the coffin of Sedgwick's divinely created man. Some did not realize what he was up to. The new Tory Chancellor of Oxford, Lord Salisbury, invited him to the June commencement to receive an honorary Doctorate of Civil Laws. Darwin, fit enough for Cambridge, invoked poor health and refused. An honour from the High Church stronghold was dubious at best, and anyway, as Huxley squealed, he had been a compromise candidate. When the venerable Revd Edward Pusey, Regius Professor of Hebrew, got wind of the nominations there had been a 'tremendous shindy.' He agreed to 'your being doctored' only 'to keep out seven devils worse than the first.' But 'I wish you could have gone,' Huxley grinned wryly, 'not for your sake, but for theirs . . . oh Coryphaeus diabolicus.'[18]

Other titles suited better. Moscow's Imperial Society of Naturalists elected him an honorary member, and the South American Missionary Society offered to do the same. His last sight of bedraggled Jemmy Button left him swearing that wild Fuegians were untameable; FitzRoy's failure proved the impossibility of breaking their habits. But Sulivan, believing that no humans were 'too low to comprehend the simple message of the Gospel,' and reeling off the Society's record, had made Darwin repent. An Anglican outpost had been established in Tierra del Fuego, the natives converted and clothed, and the strategic Cape Horn region secured for English shipping. As proof, Sulivan had sent a photo of Jemmy's upright-looking son. Darwin, keen to spread the blessings of civilization, had made small donations to the mission for several years. Yes, he would be proud to be an honorary member. Only, he warned Sulivan, 'I shall ... publish another book partly on man, which I dare say many will decry as very wicked.'[19]

The election that most pleased him was Lubbock's. In February 1870 his neighbour had been returned for Maidstone, squeaking into the Commons by 100 votes, and Darwin wasted no time in putting him to work. The telegraph service to Downe was paltry; 'all the inhabitants' wanted their new MP to lean on the Post Office to make improvements. Also there was a census coming up. With his old protégé's help, it could turn into an anthropological questionnaire. Darwin had sent out scores of printed queries over the years, pestering farmers, surgeons, missionaries, and colonial travellers for first-hand reports. Here was his chance to turn the nation into a network of informants on the vexed question of in-breeding.

Darwin had crossed pigeons *ad infinitum*; even now he was running growth trials on crossed and self-fertilized plants. But on humans he drew a blank – the *Descent of Man* lacked evidence. The country was experimenting daily, the population booming, yet no one had investigated the fertility of inbred families. With four first-cousin marriages in his generation of Darwin-Wedgwoods, the question was personal. If his own frail children were victims, then surely the nation's stock suffered likewise. Would it not pay to find out whether defects like 'deafness, and dumbness, blindness, &c.' were associated with close intermarriage?[20]

The question was this: did married cousins have as many surviving children as unrelated parents? Bigger families were fitter, he reasoned; size would tell. Lubbock asked the House of Commons on 22 July during the second reading of the Census Bill: since naturalists held that 'consanguineous marriages were injurious throughout the whole vegetable and animal kingdoms,' would it not be 'desirable to ascertain whether that was ... the case with the whole human race'? In the bill's committee stage Lubbock moved an amendment 'to insert the words, "whether married to a first cousin",' in the relevant census question. A furious debate erupted. It was 'inquisitorial,' howled the opposition, and 'the grossest cruelty ever thought of.' If 'the philosophers' had their way, it would naturally lead to 'further inquiries as to the number, health, and mental condition of ... children.' Parliament might even be called on to decide whether first cousins could marry, causing 'mental torture' to couples.[21] The amendment was defeated by a margin of two to one.

*

Charles gnashed his teeth and pressed on to finish the manuscript, by which time Parliament was forgotten and the talk was all of France's war with Prussia. Tens of thousands were dying daily, and in August the family thought about nothing else. Leonard at Woolwich declared himself a staunch Prussian, even though his fellow soldiers, itching for a fight, supported the French, knowing that war with England would be more likely if they triumphed. Emma stoked her pro-Prussian ardour by reading up on the intrigues of Napoleon I. In France she saw 'no national value for truth.' 'What an enormous collapse it is,' a nation self-deceived, 'tumbling headlong into . . . war, without a notion of what the enemy was capable of'! Charles joined in the chorus of condemnation, but worried about his allies, Haeckel, Preyer, and Carus. The war would 'stop all science . . . for a long time.'[22]

War games started at Downe, like those during the Crimea, but with a new battalion of troops. The seven little Huxleys came for a fortnight so that the 'General' – as Huxley senior was known – could attend the British Association at Liverpool. The people's scientist had taken the Presidency, after a lot of politicking, although it outraged *The Times*. The popular press hooted at the 'thunderer': 'Mr. Huxley is so indiscreet,' they roared in imitation. 'If only we had an "indiscreet" Archbishop!' Failing that the tabloids hoped for an 'indiscreet President' and some fun. But a sobered-up Huxley reassured everyone that the agnostic was no hell-raiser and gave a guarded address on the origin of life, which was hissed at by the tabloids as 'not naughty enough.' Darwin, agonizing over his 'accursed proofs,' suddenly missed his old hellion. Tyndall was still performing though, justifying the use of hypothesis and metaphor in science, much to Darwin's pleasure.[23]

Darwin was rattled by the war. By now, late September, Napoleon had surrendered at Sedan. Paris, besieged, was in pandemonium and Strasbourg had fallen. The carnage was awful, the country overrun, and yet the French spurned Prussian peace terms and fought on for *la gloire*. 'I have not yet met a soul in England who does not rejoice in the splendid triumph of Germany over France,' Darwin boasted to Fritz Müller in Brazil. 'It is a most just retribution against that vainglorious, war-liking nation.' In Leipzig Carus astonished him by his readiness to translate the *Descent of Man* while the conflict raged. It would not hurt sales, he reported, though he wished the struggle between the 'Romanic' and 'Teutonic' races could be conducted less primitively. Darwin, sharing the sentiment, promised to rush him the corrected proofs. Kovalevsky had earlier written from Berlin bemoaning England's Prussian sympathies; now, his proofs not having arrived, he feared that he had committed some political infelicity in speaking out. He had to finish the translation quickly, he told Darwin, because he wanted to go to his sister-in-law's in besieged Paris.[24]

Darwin worked on at his 'frightful' corrections, sensitive to the offence his book would give. It 'half kills me by fatigue,' he told Wallace in November as he came to the last page of proofs, and 'I much fear will quite kill me in your good estimation.' Family and friends would feel worse. For all Henrietta's pruning, he knew the *Descent* would offend them. Already Fox had heard 'sad tales' circulating about the book and denied the existence of illegitimate apes in his family tree. And Sulivan; he and the mission would be up in arms. 'Ailing and grumbling,' Darwin warned him again at Christmas that the *Descent of Man* would 'disgust you & many others.'[25] He was battening down for the storm.

The proofs went off on 15 January 1871. He doubted that the book was 'worth publishing' and launched straight into his next one, using the left-over materials on emotional expressions. Others doubted it too. Within a week Mivart's clever critique *On the Genesis of Species* arrived, the most devastating all-round attack on natural selection in Darwin's lifetime. It was also a pre-emptive strike on the *Descent of Man* and, coming from a man close to the inner circle, it left Darwin badly 'shaken.' He was so angry he could barely speak.

Like an Old Bailey barrister, Mivart – trained at Lincoln's Inn – shrewdly caricatured Darwinism as natural selection 'pure and simple.' He put it in the dock and produced such a welter of counter-evidence as to overwhelm the jury. Much of it was unimpeachable at the time, and it was certainly persuasive, judging by book sales. He piled on refutation after refutation, aiming for a cumulative effect: he conjured up Thomson's time spectre, laid waste to pangenesis, lampooned the notion of a half-evolved wing, raised the problem of convergent species, exploited the differences between Darwin, Huxley, and Wallace, and ended by slating Darwinians for meddling in metaphysics. This was his real object, to show that selection was not only false, but dangerous applied to morals and religion – and he knew that Darwin was about to apply it.

Privately Mivart professed nothing but 'sympathy and esteem' for Darwin himself. He wrote earnestly, looking forward to a chat. He blamed the reckless extension of Darwinism on its overzealous supporters, though he regretted that 'you do not more protest against [their] unnecessary irreligious deductions:'

the acceptance of your views means with many the
abandonment of belief in God and in the immortality of the
soul together with future rewards & punishments . . . I think
that the destruction of such beliefs is most important viewed
from the . . . standpoint of the temporal happiness of mankind
. . . God grant we in England may not be approaching a
religious decay at all similar to that of the middle of the 18th
century in France which Frenchmen are now paying for in
blood & tears!

Atheism, anarchy, and national ruin – as Darwin winced at the old
equation, Paris was under siege. Dogs and cats were being eaten, and
rats brought a franc each in the starving streets. Some in Mivart's
circle were affected more directly. Owen, an investor in the *Jardin
d'Acclimatation* (which was modelled on London zoo), saw his
holdings wiped out as the exotic mammals, even the beloved
elephants, were slaughtered to feed the citizens. Darwin's old
nightmares began to return. In the hysterical climate he expected a
backlash. Not only would 'the pendulum swing against' natural
selection; the author of the *Descent of Man* would be depicted as a
black-caped anarchist.[26]
    Advance copies went out, to Mivart, Wallace, Cobbe, and a host
of other critics. While Darwin awaited the reviews, he faced further
ignominy. The parish was now in the good hands of the Revd Henry
Powell, but his predecessor Robinson, despatched to a nearby curacy,
had teamed up with the previous curate Horsman, who was on the
point of suing Darwin for defamatory remarks about absconding
with the school's cash. Robinson, it seemed, was the informant. 'I
really think being examined in court could half-kill me,' Darwin
moaned to Brodie Innes, now valuing his vicar's friendship more
than ever. The case would 'never come to trial,' Innes assured
Darwin. The incongruity of their soothing alliance struck Innes: 'dear
me! if some of your naturalists, and my ritualist friends were to hear
us two saying civil things to each other, they would say the weather
was going to change, or Paris to be relieved, both [of] which I wish
might happen.'
    But *belle* Paris did fall and was thronged by Prussian troops.
Charles and Emma, with old memories of the city, felt for the people.
Emma even had words with a German guest, who resented it: 'we
each spit our spite,' she told Aunt Fanny, 'and then made peace.'
Letters with Continental franks were opened with bated breath.
Carus was getting on with the German edition, delayed only by a

bout of illness. Haeckel reported the birth of a daughter, named Emma. Kovalevsky and his wife had actually carried the proofs of the *Descent of Man* twenty-five miles through the Prussian lines into Paris, losing only a few sheets on the way. He kept on translating, even though knowing that the Russian interior minister had banned the 'materialistic' book and threatened to impound copies. A 'fearful piece of tyranny,' Darwin fumed.[27]

The *Descent of Man* went on sale at such a time, two portly 450-page volumes retailing for twenty-four shillings. A second edition was called for within three weeks; by the end of March 4500 copies were in print and Darwin was almost £1500 better off, a 'fine big sum,' he boasted to Henrietta, offering her a £30 memento for her labours. The early response was astonishing. 'Everybody is talking about it without being shocked.' Few howls of abuse, few anti-Darwinian rants; it was so perplexing that he asked Murray to note reviews in 'out-of-the-way papers, especially the religious,' to confirm his worst fears. Nothing turned up. Most reviewers let out a low moan, and that was it. Like the *Edinburgh* critic, they conceded that the book was 'raising a storm of mingled wrath, wonder, and admiration' among the populace. They grudgingly admitted some sort of evolution but denied that man's 'spiritual powers' were selected from brute instincts, otherwise 'earnest-minded men will be compelled to give up those motives by which they have attempted to live noble and virtuous lives.'

Inured to monkey-men and materialism by Huxley and Tyndall, informed by Galton, Greg, and Bagehot about the struggle for civilization, people seemed to be snapping up the *Descent* simply because it carried the name 'Darwin.' The subject was less bad news than old news. To Darwin, immensely relieved, it was 'proof of the increasing liberality of England.'[28]

It was, and more. In many ways the book *was* the man – pudgy and comfortable, sedate in its seniority, full of anecdote and rather old-fashioned. There was little fire and flair about it, nothing of Huxley, Haeckel, or Vogt. Like a doting uncle, it did not tax one's tolerance so much as entertain. It told an arm-chair adventure of the English evolving, clambering up from the apes, struggling to conquer savagery, multiplying and dispersing around the globe. In Darwin's early anxious jottings such a story seemed dangerously implausible; his secret assault on man's ancestry had been a brazen act of faith, fit only for radicals and their ilk. But now, habituated to material progress, social mobility, and imperial adventure, the *arriviste* reading classes lapped it up. A romantic pedigree suited them, an epic genealogy. Disregarding the apes, as many did, they found the *Descent* a tremendous family saga.

All Victorian life was there, from the Fuegian savage York Minster up to 'our great philosopher, Herbert Spencer.' Each race moves along the ladder of civilization, propelled by natural selection, aided by use-inheritance, with selfish instinct giving way to reason, morality, and English customs. Fidelity and courage are on the rise, chastity in women, temperance in men; slavery, superstition, and senseless conflict are passing away, so that 'virtue will be triumphant.' Yet it is an undeniable tale of Malthusian struggle. Always there are heroes and the hapless, victorious civilizations and vanquished 'barbarians,' expanding nations and exterminated ones, large families and small. The 'intellectually superior' out-breed the inferior, the better classes out-distance the 'intemperate, profligate, and criminal classes,' and even the rich tend to leave more offspring than the swelling poor, who are cut down in infancy. And yet through it all a lofty humanitarianism prevails. The 'noblest part' of human nature dictates sympathy for the 'inferior members of society.' The 'bad effects of the weak surviving and propagating their kind' are to be borne 'without complaining.'[29]

The Darwins fitted the picture perfectly. The *Descent* was essentially their story. Natural and sexual selection had made and maimed them. Charles had strutted like 'a peacock admiring his tail' courting Emma. Coy and impressionable, she had selected him, admiring his 'courage, perseverance, and determined energy' after a voyage around the world. Her 'maternal instincts' and feminine intuitions had been the mainstay of their marriage (even if partly a hold-over from 'a past and lower state of civilization'). Endowed with wealth, they had a head-start in the struggle – and an 'accumulation of capital' was essential if civilized Westerners were to spread and subdue the lower races. The wealthy 'who have not to labour for their daily bread' were vital to society. 'All high intellectual work is carried on by them, and on such work material progress of all kinds mainly depends.' Their sons, however, must be exposed to competition, kept up to nature's mark, and 'the most able should not be prevented by laws or customs from succeeding best and rearing the largest number of offspring.'

Darwin ended the book on a personal note, still telling tales, still praising the real heroes, the animals. He told of the 'heroic little monkey, who braved his dreaded enemy in order to save the life of his keeper,' and the old baboon who saved 'his young comrade from a crowd of astonished dogs.' 'For my own part,' he confessed, 'I would as soon be descended' from them as from a naked, degraded savage.'[30]

In Paris peace had come and the Prussian troops were gone. But an insurrection had broken out, with angry citizens attacking the army. Led by socialists and republicans, they drove the troops from the city, repudiated the national government, and on 26 March elected their own, the Commune. A week later came the second siege of Paris, this time by French forces, and the butchery began once more. The English papers railed against the Communards, and *The Times* against Darwin. He was undermining authority. If his views of moral development were accepted, the eternal principles of right and wrong would lose their force. Conscience would fail to check 'the most murderous revolutions.' In France 'loose philosophy' had rotted moral principles with dreadful results. A 'man incurs a grave responsibility when, with the authority of a well-earned reputation, he advances at such a time the disintegrating speculations of this book.'[31]

Darwin dismissed the hack as a 'windbag full of metaphysics and classics,' even while worrying about its impact on sales. From the 'thunderer' to the Welshman who called him 'an old Ape with a hairy face,' the cranks could no longer hurt him. Nor could Brodie Innes: 'Man was made a man,' the old Tory taunted, and he split 'into niggers who must be made to work' and into 'better men able to make them,' or such was God's scheme before being thwarted by the interfering 'radicals.' Darwin replied, 'I consider myself a good way ahead of you, as far as this goes.' Not even the 200,000-circulation, down-market *Family Herald*, shrieking 'society must fall to pieces if Darwinism be true,' could touch him. There were simply too many plaudits, too much weighty discussion for such silly jibes to matter. The serious magazines were now chocked with essays 'on Darwinism and Religion, Darwinism and Morals, Philosophy and Darwinism,' and he devoured them all.[32]

He shrugged off Cobbe's kind but untutored defence of the supernatural conscience. He praised the brilliant editor of the *Fortnightly Review*, John Morley, for agreeing that 'the foundations of morality, the distinctions of right and wrong, are deeply laid in the very conditions of social existence.' Wallace's review in the *Academy* had little impact; its objections seemed 'almost stereotyped' by now. But, in Eras's words, it was a 'perfectly beautiful' piece of controversy, generous and polite. 'In future histories of science,' he predicted, 'the

Wallace-Darwin episode will form one of the few bright points,' a shining example of how gents managed their disputes.³³

By contrast, the Mivart fracas was an ignoble tale, which Darwin took too personally and Mivart too casually. Darwin was watching himself shudder in a mirror, wrestling with his manuscript on facial expressions, when Mivart's letter arrived. He was being stalked. Mivart laid down the terms of engagement, while wishing 'with all my heart we did *not* differ so widely.' The debate was to be on metaphysics, on the basic assumptions of science. And he repeated that, 'while combatting (as duty compels me to do) positions you adopt, I am not so much combatting *you*, as others to whose views your scientific labours give additional currency.'

Darwin felt irritatingly targeted, and by a turncoat. Mivart could not be written off as a windbag, though theology made him moralize. A few days later Darwin threw down his expressions manuscript, the rough draft done, and began planning a new edition of the *Origin*. A cheap one, he told Murray: working men in Lancashire were clubbing together to buy the fifth at fifteen shillings.³⁴ He wanted them all to have copies. The sixth would take on Mivart. It would challenge his assumption that a half-evolved wing was an absurdity, and that selection cannot explain the similarity of marsupial and placental wolves. It would destroy his claim that some unplumbed inner force drives evolution to its goal.

May and June shot by, and he raced into the summer, plundering old notes, building defences, shoring up his reputation. Paris was ravaged and the Communards crushed. And while they were making themselves 'everlastingly infamous,' as Darwin wrote to Kovalevsky, Mivart's wretched *Genesis of Species* was 'producing a great effect against Natural Selection, and more especially against me.' He was determined to defend himself, hold his ground, and wait for philosophical reinforcements. Mivart's *ancien régime* would not be revived.

A week at Eras's in June brought news from the United States. Ras's dinner guest, Edward Youmans, was America's top scientific salesman. He was over from New York to recruit big names – Huxley, Tyndall, Spencer, Lubbock – to write for his new popular library, the 'International Scientific Series.' Darwin insisted that Youmans's plans be canvassed at a fringe meeting of the British Association at Edinburgh in August. He was 'all curiosity' about the progress of science in the States, where he was sending George and Frank on holiday this summer. Youmans told him about lecturing on the descent of man to a 'clerical club' in Brooklyn. The topic seemed less surprising than the audience. 'What!' Darwin burst out. 'Clergymen of different denominations all together? How they would fight if you should get them together here!'[35]

At Downe another American cheered him. One of Gray's students, Chauncey Wright, a shy young philosopher ekeing out a living compiling the Nautical Almanack, sent a damning analysis of Mivart's *Genesis of Species*. It was due out in the *North American Review* and Darwin realized that it could prove useful to neutralize his keenest critic at home. He was a dab hand at pulling in support from abroad. He asked Wallace, 'an incomparably better critic than I am,' whether he should import the article, only to be told that it was heavy and obscure. He mooted the idea to Henrietta, who thought the piece merely 'interesting.'[36] He dithered.

Then Mivart's review of the *Descent of Man* arrived. It was a long, deadly dissection, laced with accusations of 'dogmatism,' question-begging, and spurious metaphysics. It was also anonymous, but Darwin knew the 'wonderfully clever' anatomist's hand behind it, scissoring him into shreds. Work on the new *Origin* made him 'sick of everything;' this left him in despair.

Here was the Catholic convert in the *Quarterly Review*, exposing 'the entire and naked truth as to the logical consequences of Darwinism.' Mivart roused the slumbering Tories against his former mentor. The *Descent of Man* was calculated to disturb time-honoured convictions held by 'the majority of cultivated minds.' It would unsettle 'our half-educated classes.' Morality was no 'development of brutal instincts;' if it were, who would know whether society 'is right or wrong,' or even 'why we should obey society at all.' People would do as they please, breaking laws and customs as they liked. No, man is a 'free moral agent,' created with a supernatural soul. He has 'a consciousness of an absolute and immutable [divine] rule *legitimately* claiming obedience.'[37]

Darwin saw himself an offender, a villain. 'I shall soon be viewed as the most despicable of men,' he burst out, 'the most arrogant, odious beast that ever lived.' Mivart's 'bigotry arrogance illiberality & many other nice qualities' made him furious, and the bile built inside, eating at his intestines. Wright's review of Mivart suddenly seemed perfect. It turned the tables, took natural selection as a model of good science and Mivart as a case of bad metaphysics. His inner driving force would take evolution nowhere.[38] With Wright's help, Darwin would see to it.

He dashed off a letter asking Wright for permission to reprint his article as a pamphlet. Then Emma took him away for a month to recuperate. He was in a mess, so 'giddy and bad' at Croydon Station that she could not leave him for a moment. They rested in the North Downs hamlet of Albury (where Malthus had once been curate), looking out on the sandy fern-covered hills and pine forests. It was a sunny August, with nothing to do but sit or stroll. But Charles's head remained 'rocky and wretched.' He read a little – Lubbock's latest work on insects, Thomson's snubbing of natural selection in his British Association address – but his mind kept drifting back to Mivart. Wright's permission came and Darwin wrote to Murray about running off 750 copies of the pamphlet. His damage-limitation exercise began. 'Some 200' would see every scientific journal and society supplied, together with 'clubs & . . . all private individuals' he could think of.³⁹ That would leave plenty for the public.

They returned for Henrietta's wedding on the 31st. The courtship had been a brief whirlwind. Her fiancé Richard Litchfield was a stout, shortsighted barrister who worked for the Ecclesiastical Commission, managing Church property, and in off hours he taught music, maths, and science at the Working Men's College in London. Singing was his passion, conducting his *forte*, and Henrietta had fallen for the artist in him, not to mention his 'sweet' smile and 'long thick brown beard.' The ceremony was simple and without festivity afterwards. Nor were friends or relations invited, for Charles had to be kept calm. However, on arriving with his old butler Parslow he found strangers in the pews. Parslow, ever protective, was thunderstruck; he thought that he knew 'every face' in the village. A handful of Litchfield's working men had discovered the time of the service, trained out from London, and walked four miles from Orpington Station to surprise him.

Henrietta, taking her trousseau to London, left her fox terrier Polly behind. From now on Polly would trot dutifully behind Charles.⁴⁰

Murray posted copies of the pamphlet in September. *Darwinism*, it was called, a 'somewhat sensational title' that Wright thought would sell. The word had Darwin's blessing; it would set his seal of approval on a safe notion of science, above the metaphysics and religious mumbo-jumbo. Huxley received his copy in Scotland, where he was on holiday. He thought it would 'do good,' but by chance he had already done better, having just taken a few days off from golfing to castigate Mivart's *Genesis of Species* and *Quarterly* article in a review. Mivart, though not a 'bad fellow,' was 'poisoned with . . . accursed Popery and fear for his soul' and had sinned unpardonably by being 'insolent to Darwin.' Worse, his arguments were actually swaying people. Punishment was called for, Huxley snarled, and 'the devil has tempted me' to administer it.[41]

Darwin, disconsolate and sick, slaving away at the *Origin*, sprang to life when Huxley's news came. 'The pendulum is swinging against our side, but I feel positive it will soon swing the other way; & no mortal man will do half as much as you in giving it a start in the right direction.' Huxley's proofs arrived a week later, further fortifying him.

Huxley indulged in what he loved most, religious exegetics. He effectively side-stepped science and came crashing down on the Catholic Church – showing that Mivart's position was as pernicious theologically as it was disastrous scientifically. Mivart had suggested that evolution could be reconciled with the Catholic fathers – Augustine, Aquinas, and the last great scholastic, Suarez. Huxley denied it and upstaged him with pages of painstaking Latin exegesis, proving that his wayward pupil did not understand scholastic philosophy any more than Darwin's.

> If Suarez has rightly stated Catholic doctrine, then is evolution utter heresy. And such I believe it to be . . . Indeed, one of its greatest merits in my eyes, is the fact that it occupies a position of complete and irreconcilable antagonism to that vigorous and consistent enemy of the highest intellectual, moral, and social life of mankind – the Catholic Church.

Huxley revelled in these military matters, pitting Church against Evolution, and the *Genesis* had simply offered another unbridled opportunity. Mivart, the lapsed protégé, was told that he could not be 'both a true son of the Church and a loyal soldier of Science.'[42] Face to face, the cut was unkinder; he was ordered to stop running with the hare and hunting with the hounds.

Huxley spoke *ex cathedra*, the way Owen used to. Such had the world changed. 'How you do smash Mivart's theology,' Darwin crowed, 'Nothing will vex him so much as this part of your review . . . He may write his worst & he will never mortify me again.' To Hooker, laid low by his mother's health, the essay was a 'god-send,' and Huxley the 'defender of the faithful.' Surely though, he wrote his friend at Downe, you are 'not the happier' for Mivart's humiliation. 'I am not so good a Christian as you think me,' Darwin fired back, 'for I did enjoy my revenge.'[43]

He was not out of his misery. Science had gone by the board; the defence of natural selection was ignored. Huxley had simply chipped at the bedrock of Mivart's metaphysics, smiting Amalekites with his usual dexterity. Natural selection had to be shored up somehow, given the 'impression Mivart's book has made.' And the omens were worrying. Wright's pamphlets had not shifted – only fourteen had sold by the end of October.[44] The way ahead looked daunting.

1871–1882

82. Charles Lyell just before his death in 1875, a blind widower obsessed with the problem of an afterlife. Darwin admitted that, similarly
placed, the same fears would strike him 'in the dead of the night with
painful force'.

GREAT INTERNATIONAL QUADRUMANOUS CONGRESS.

(From our Special Correspondent.)

83. Cambridge students, who lowered a monkey marionette from the gallery when Darwin received his honorary doctorate in 1877, gave the *Punch* cartoonist this idea about the 'missing link' between men and apes.

84. Darwin on the verandah at Down House, about 1880, dressed for his daily constitutional on the Sandwalk.

85. George Romanes, who gave up Christianity under Darwin's influence and continued his research on mental evolution.

86. John Lubbock, Darwin's neighbour and childhood protégé, in his study at High Elms near Downe. As a Liberal MP and scientific polymath he helped to engineer Darwin's burial in Westminster Abbey.

87. Darwin immortalized among the nation's heroes: the graveside scene in the Abbey, with the leaders of science, state, and Church in attendance.

88. Ticket for the better seats at the funeral.

FUNERAL OF MR. DARWIN.

WESTMINSTER ABBEY,

Wednesday, April 26th, 1882.

AT 12 O'OLOCK PRECISELY.

Admit the Bearer at Eleven o'clock to the **CHOIR** (Entrance by West Cloister Door, Dean's Yard)

G. G. BRADLEY, D.D.
Dean.

N.B.—No Person will be admitted except in mourning.

89. Darwin as the secular 'sun of the nineteenth century', spreading enlightenment by ridding the world of bishops, the Bible and priestly hobgoblins.

90. Huxley (right), presenting Darwin's statue to the Prince of Wales in the Natural History Museum, South Kensington, in 1885.

yours sincerely
Charles Darwin

91. A saintly Darwin icon, based on a photo from the early 1870s: the kind of serene and untroubling image that the family sought to substitute for the anxious 'Devil's Chaplain'.

39

Pause, Pause, Pause

HE STILL PACED the Sandwalk. A quarter-century had seen it worn smooth, his private turnpike beneath the full-grown trees – this thinking path leading his mind to untold destinations. In 1871, as the autumn days closed in and the beeches shed their leaves, he plodded on, reflecting and recuperating.

The year had aged him. Stooped and grisled, he felt older than sixty-two. The children were grown, leaving him and Emma alone with Bessy. William, a banking partner in Southampton, George reading for the bar, Frank studying medicine in London, Leo training for the Royal Engineers, Horace taking the Little Go at Cambridge, all destined for great things. If, that is, their health held, for they still came home often enough for nursing. Not Henrietta, though. Losing her to the solemn fop Richard Litchfield was 'awful and astonishing,' and life would never be the same. Only Emma was left to pamper Charles. 'Keep her as an example,' he advised his daughter, 'and then Litchfield will in future years worship and not only love you, as I worship our dear old mother.'[1]

His stomach had aged him most. Even now, each turn around the Sandwalk made his insides spin. Emma might distract him but she failed to stay his thoughts, and ruminating had led to retching as Mivart's challenge unfolded. He knew that he was vulnerable. Evolution had triumphed, but only time would tell about natural selection. And what about 'the citadel itself,' human mind and morality? In the *Descent of Man* he had stormed this last religious redoubt and explained the most sacred human traits. Yet the citadel had not fallen; man, guarded by Mivart, stood proud and impregnable. It was Darwin's crowning frustration. Would defeat be added to his notoriety for making men out of monkeys? Perhaps he should have kept his worst heresy to himself. Perhaps publishing the *Descent* had been a mistake.[2]

But the vicious secret was out and he had to stand by it. One lap to go. He strode back to his study to finish revising the *Origin*. In December, after months of fitful progress, he was finishing the herculean task. Over two thousand sentences had been added or rewritten, including a new chapter against Mivart. The word 'evolution' appeared for the first time. A helpful glossary was added. Most encouraging of all, Murray planned a new sales drive based on a popular half-price edition.[3] This would be Darwin's last chance to answer Mivart, and he knew it.

It was a virtuoso thrust. He slashed at the strongest thread running through Mivart's *Genesis of Species*, cutting the knot that the Argylls and Owens thought secure, and whose strength worried even Wallace. Were partially evolved structures – half a wing, an incipient eye – functional absurdities? Could the whole structures have appeared only in a single Creative leap? Darwin piled fact upon fact with effortless effrontery. He showed some organs switching function, obviating the problem: swim bladders becoming amphibian lungs, and breathing tubes extending into lacey insect wings. Mivart had missed the point: incipient lungs and eyes and wings need not have breathed or seen or flapped. As always Darwin paraded nature's oddities – whale baleen, the migrating eyes of flatfish, prehensile tails, and the pinching forceps on starfish – showing how each had gradually developed. He buried Mivart under a plethora of details, while hedging and wriggling himself, downgrading natural selection in some cases, backpedalling to admit 'spontaneous variations in the right direction' or a growth from increased use in others. What he could never admit was Mivart's emasculating inner force, or his monstrous jumps to ready-made wings and lungs.

The stakes were high, and Mivart was enlisting the same starfishes and whales to guard the sacred citadel: the 'intellectual powers' and moral disposition of man. Darwin's sword was also aimed at his opponent's metaphysical heart. A million odd facts were showered not simply to vindicate natural selection, but to discredit Mivart's allegiance to theology. Mivart's benign relationship with his master had turned poisonously sour, with Darwin convinced that Catholic fanatacism was at root. Mivart never understood why: his 'natural laws' were divine edicts, as were Owen's, Argyll's, and Gray's – expressions of Will Power, guiding and directing. They kept a proper scientific order in the universe, pushing life forward on a co-ordinated wavefront. But for Darwin, Mivart's directed, guided jumps from one beautifully co-ordinated fish or frog to another were unnatural and intolerable: science was entering 'the realms of miracle.'⁴

The debate nudged Darwin further into once taboo areas. As he ploughed through the *Origin* proofs, he posted a ringing endorsement to a leading freethinker, himself safely distanced in the United States.

Francis Abbot was editor of *The Index*, weekly voice of the radical wing of the Free Religious Association, a ginger-group of disaffected Unitarians and philosophical unbelievers. They were on the look-out for contributors who would foster 'the spirit of reform' without 'deference to the authority of the Bible, the Church, or the Christ.' Charles Eliot Norton, who had lunched at Downe, was a founder of the Association, and Abbot had sent Darwin his manifesto *Truths for the Times* and asked for a paper. 'I do not feel that I have thought deeply enough [about religion] to justify any publicity,' came the lame reply. Yet Darwin did subscribe to *The Index*, pore over the issues, and approve of Abbot's tract. Brazenly, in fifty pungent propositions, it augured 'the extinction of faith in the Christian Confession' and the development of a humanistic 'Free Religion' in which 'lies the only hope of the spiritual perfection of the individual and the spiritual unity of the race.' These were evolutionary 'truths' and Darwin responded warmly, 'I admire them from my inmost heart, & I agree to almost every word.'

'Almost' was an insertion, an afterthought. Just as he had casually subscribed to the Thirty-nine Articles on graduating from Cambridge, so now, as he angrily penned his last words on evolution, he held by the fifty propositions of a post-Christian creed. Uncharacteristically, he allowed Abbot to print his endorsement in *The Index*. It appeared in the Christmas issue, an ocean away from English eyes. Nor did he let up in his support: a few years later, when *The Index* fell on hard times, Charles and William sent a generous gift by courtesy of William's bank, a token of deep sympathy 'in your noble & determined struggle' for free religion.⁵

Charles cheered another infidel supporter abroad, Ernst Haeckel, whose anti-clerical bombast had once unnerved him. That was long ago, and the situation had changed. Most of what Haeckel stood for had been presentably packaged in the *Descent of Man*. And Darwin was retiring slowly, handing on freedom's flame. 'I doubt whether my strength will last for much more serious work,' he confided to the zoologist. 'I shall continue to work as long as I can, but it does not much signify when I stop, as there are so many good men fully as capable, perhaps more capable than myself, of carrying on our work; and of these you rank as the first.'⁶

Darwin had reached an impasse. Religious controversy had deflated him and he hated it. Ten years and he was running out of answers, tired of repeating himself. After the last revisions to the *Origin*, what more was there to say? The world knew all that was worth knowing about his views. Speaking out further would incur yet more abuse and might injure Emma, who still differed grievously from him on religion. In future he would keep his counsel.

With the changes to the *Origin* in hand, Murray put his plan into practice. He reset in tiny type. This left the edition riddled with errors, but it did cut 142 pages, saving sixpence a copy on paper alone. He sold the plates to Appleton in New York for £50, and as a result projected a six shillings cover price, putting it within reach of working people.[7]

Controversy ended, natural selection defended, Darwin turned to unfinished business in January 1872. Nothing would deflect him. Mivart did try to prod him once more. Breezily 'wishing you very sincerely a happy new year,' he wanted a disclaimer of the 'fundamental intellectual errors' in the *Descent of Man*. Their letters were now fraught, the pleasantries more desperate than ever, laced with denials of ill intent yet exuding mistrust. Darwin had had enough. He cut him dead. Further communication would be futile; life was too short. They went their own ways. While Mivart worried over the highest member of creation, Darwin worked at the lowest, the worm. With 'the little strength left to me,' he was turning to uncontentious subjects.[8]

Correspondents obliged, and earthworm anecdotes began surfacing in his mountain of mail. Everyone answered his queries – not just colleagues on three continents, but Wedgwoods, Darwins, and even Frank's Welsh girlfriend Amy Ruck. Darwin had kept a soft spot for the recyclers of the soil since his first fishing days at The Mount and flirting days at Maer. Now he was stuffing an old folder with notes, the prelude to another book. Having started his geological career by speculating on continents, he would end it digging in the garden. The evolutionist was working his way down to worms.

Worm-like himself, he moved slowly; writing up took endless time. Even now there was an another unfinished book, hived off from the *Descent of Man*, and nine months delayed by the Mivart crisis. After a break, completing *The Expression of the Emotions in Man and Animals* would be his first priority. He spent five weeks in London, visiting Erasmus and arranging for the new *Origin of Species* to be reviewed favourably with Mivart's *Genesis*. Publication day was 19 February, and even though the torrent of revisions had pushed the cover price to 7s. 6d., sales still soared from 60 to 250 a month. He went back to the *Emotions* manuscript, knowing that he was reaching a wider audience.[9]

The book was the amputated head of the *Descent* that had assumed a life of its own. And just as well, for it would prove popular. Responses to his questionnaires asking how the races expressed joy and grief, pleasure and pain, had flooded in from missionaries, entrepreneurs, and government colonials. He collated his bundles on Bombay beards and gaucho gestures, Aboriginal habits and Sinhalese signs. Like a phrenologist of old, he showed evidence for human descent on the face of everyday life. And like the Plinian phrenologists in particular, forty-five years before at Edinburgh, he made Sir Charles Bell's pious *Anatomy and Physiology of Expression* his prime target. Man's facial muscles had not been divinely created to express his exquisite feelings. They had evolved – look at nature, at monkey's faces, look at savages, idiots, and the insane to appreciate their social origins. Any sympathetic observer could see that man and animals shared not only feelings, but the means of expressing them.

Long ago Jenny Orang had shown her human side, behaving 'precisely like a naughty child.' His studies on the terror, rage, and noiseless laugh of chimps led to a fatherly fascination with his own infants. He had peered over numerous cots noting every squint and squall, as a succession of smiling, scowling, down-turned mouths witnessed their own ape ancestry. Latterly, he used the latest technology to capture these images. Hundreds of photographs had poured in to Down House, of actors cringing and babies wingeing and 'dreadful . . . imbeciles' in a Yorkshire asylum, their 'degraded' features evoking an ape-like primevalism.[10]

The manuscript swelled with the evidence. And as he cursed his convoluted prose, cancelled and recast his paragraphs, he also wrote helplessly of himself. He remembered his feeling of horror when a child had been 'exposed to . . . instant and crushing danger;' his 'frantic grief' and 'despair' following a family death; and his subsequent tearful thought that 'long-past happy days' will 'never return.' Englishmen, he owned, 'rarely cry, except under pressure of the acutest grief.' Yet he had known this feeling, watched himself weep, and had learned to read strangers' faces.

> An old lady with a comfortable but absorbed expression sat nearby opposite me in a railway carriage. Whilst I was looking at her, I saw that her *depressores anguli oris* [muscles at the corners of the mouth] became very slightly, yet decidedly,

contracted; but as her countenance remained as placid as ever, I reflected how meaningless was this contraction, and how easily one might be deceived. The thought had hardly occurred to me when I saw that her eyes suddenly became suffused with tears almost to overflowing, and her whole countenance fell. There could now be no doubt that some painful recollection, perhaps that of a long-lost child, was passing through her mind.[11]

No detached observer, Darwin. He perceived with pathos, and the thought of his own long-lost child still moved him to tears. In death as in life, Annie opened his heart.

All spring he wrestled with the book, braced by the news of his election to national academies in the Netherlands and Hungary. The proofs were no less a nightmare, and farmed out to Leo and Henrietta, with instructions to make cosmetic changes. As usual this proved impossible. His intractable style called for major surgery. He groaned at the humiliation and delay, 'sick of the subject, and myself, and the world.' The *Expression* had seven heliotype plates, making it one of the first books with photographs. But the production problems were horrendous – and the cost. At £75 per 1000 sets, and with a print run of 7000 copies, the plates would poke 'a terrible hole in the profits,' Murray warned.[12] Worrying, that was all he was good for. It clouded his week's holiday in August at Leith Hill with sister Caroline and Emma's brother Jos, but at least he finished the proofs there.

Back home a letter from Wallace awaited; it emphasized the gulf that had grown up between the joint inventors of natural selection. Wallace had moved twenty miles east of London, using his surveying skills to help build a new family house. Still surviving on royalties and reviews, he had failed to gain full-time work as a museum director, even with Darwin's backing. Their differences over spiritual forces and sexual selection had become irreconcilable. Each was dogged, but Wallace remained an enthusiast, irrepressible, always lapping up the latest.

And the latest was H. Charlton Bastian's *The Beginnings of Life*. The Victorians liked their shocking science in two laboured volumes, and the professor of pathology at University College provided it. Germs and their origin was the unlikely subject. These must have first appeared in a chemical soup on the archaic earth, starting evolution off, and Bastian proved that the process continues today. (He was one of eighty-year-old Robert Grant's students, and there was no stopping them, still marching defiantly along their own evolutionary path.) 'Nothing more important has appeared since your "Origin",' Wallace announced, hoping to spark Darwin's interest, and he declared himself a 'thorough convert.'

Not Darwin. Spontaneous generation, he admitted tactfully, would be 'a discovery of transcendent importance' if it really were proved. Huxley was less polite, scoffing at Bastian's alchemical brew of boiled phosphates and escaping bugs: 'Transubstantiation will be nothing to this if it turns out to be true.' Once, on the earth, yes, in primeval soups, but not today. Too many facts told against Bastian. And Darwin had spent too many decades examining minutiae to be taken in. Anyway he was swearing off controversial science, preferring to sit instead with his sun-dews. He had waited twenty years to tease these insect-eaters properly and was in no mood to be diverted. 'I have taken up old botanical work,' he informed Wallace in a peremptory PS, 'and have given up all theories.'[13]

By the end of September he was nearing collapse again. He never felt comfortable except at work or in bed, and sleep was not restoring him. Emma blamed it on the 'fatiguing and unwholesome' microscope and called George, Frank, and Horace to the rescue. She sent the boys scouting for lodgings, hoping that she could get him away from his wretched work. Horace located a house on Sevenoaks Common, only a few miles away, and between them they managed to pry Charles out of the study. He had to admit that three weeks away worked wonders. A spell like this every couple of months would keep him sane, slow his slide into oblivion. He was no longer sick, only 'growing old and weak,' and dreading the day when his intellectual powers began to fail.[14]

Friends awaited his convenience. Kovalevsky, translating the *Expression* into Russian, delayed a trip to Downe while Darwin recuperated. Even Hooker was put off, though he had his own preoccupations as Director of Kew Gardens.

For over a year Hooker had been 'in the most detestable position that a scientific man, or an officer, or a gentleman can be with my Lord and Master.' His Lord and Master was the Commissioner of Works in Gladstone's government, Acton Smee Ayrton, an acid-tongued, thick-skinned, heavy-handed cost-cutter. He was a no-nonsense populist, known for his 'reckless toughness,' elected on a platform of keeping down the proliferating 'architects, sculptors, and gardeners,' and intent on pruning Kew. The gardens were publicly funded, and Hooker believed that Ayrton's secret aim was to close down Britain's premier plant collection – built by the Hookers with sweat and tears over thirty years – discard the scientific research, ignore the imperial need, and turn it into a cheap public park.

Hooker had appealed to the Prime Minister and denounced Ayrton to the First Lord of the Treasury, to no avail. So the X Club swung into action, determined to raise Kew's political profile. A petition was drawn up, signed by Darwin and other scientific sympathizers, and handed to Gladstone. Lubbock raised the matter in the Commons. However, among the papers tabled in Parliament was an official report on Kew that Hooker himself had never seen. The author's name gave the game away, Richard Owen – it had been drawn up at Ayrton's request by the X's *bête noire*. The old autocrat, loathing Hooker and his henchmen, was angling to bring the plant collections under his own control at the British Museum. Darwin seethed, 'I used to be ashamed of hating him so much, but now I will carefully cherish my hatred & contempt to the last day of my life.'[15]

Ultimately Hooker's post was secured, although in October he still squirmed under Ayrton's heel as he sent Darwin sun-dews and Venus's fly-traps for experiment. He was deflated enough, but he then suffered a blow which poisoned any desire to fight on. His aged and bedridden mother died, leaving him 'a man of 55,' feeling 'as if orphaned.' At Sevenoaks Darwin was touched by the news and tried to empathize. Unable to recall his emotions at his own mother's death, he thought on other losses: 'with the exception of ones wife, it is the greatest that a man can suffer; – though God knows the loss of a child is bitter enough & overwhelming.' Between them, Hooker and Darwin had watched five young ones die. They had shared their deepest feelings for years and would do so more and more. Age was no barrier to their intimacy. As Darwin weakened he needed Hooker's strong 'affections' to keep him going, to breathe life into his work.[16]

In November Darwin put his insect-eaters through their paces, looking for nervous and digestive similarities between plants and animals. What strange chemistry made the sticky tentacles of the sundew contract and hold their prey? He dabbed on all manner of household substances: milk, urine, saliva, alcohol, even strong tea. And what could the tentacles digest? He served them roast beef, vegetables, hard-boiled egg – there was nothing an old dyspeptic on odd diets would not try. Amazingly, the plants flourished. They took their food like animals, secreting similar digestive juices, itself 'a new and wonderful fact.' So he poisoned them. Strychnine, quinine, and nicotine were all more or less fatal, but morphine had little effect and cobra's venom acted as a stimulant. Proof, he laughed at last, that the sun-dew was not a 'disguised animal' with a nervous system.

Even so, it was extraordinarily sensitive, more than 'the most delicate part of the human body.' He marvelled that 'so inconceivably minute a quantity as the one-twenty-millionth of a grain of phosphate of ammonia' made a tentacle bend through 180 degrees.[17]

Fly-traps, bladderworts, and butterworts were similarly wined, dined, and poisoned. They arrived from around the world to be held on remand in the garden hot-house. They presented a rogues' gallery in their pots, displaying every devious means of gluing, trapping, and drowning their prey. Darwin's torture and trickery was fitting for them. As the experiments proceeded he began writing *Insectivorous Plants*. Inevitably, the strain proved too much. The news that the *Expression of the Emotions* had sold over 5000 copies – tickling a shocked, blushing, eyebrow-raising Victorian generation – failed to spur him on. (Even the *Athenaeum*, giving a deep swallow, thought the notion of 'forcing Expression into the service of the Evolution Theory . . . a brilliant one, worthy of the acumen and ingenuity of its author.') He was exhausted and more than ever a 'confirmed invalid.' Decamping to Eras's for a week before Christmas did nothing for him. He sat engulfed in fog, downhearted, drawing up his will. One sixth of his estate for each of the boys, Ras suggested; one sixth between the girls – that would be 'as much as is good for them.'[18]

Seeing Huxley in town did not help. The old bulldog was himself feeling mangy, crushed by overwork and in the throes of moving the family to a new house. Incessant dyspeptic nausea signalled that he was juggling too many jobs – Secretary of the Royal Society, lecturer in biology at the new Normal School in South Kensington, Hooker's second in the Ayrton affair – while countering criticism for opposing the medical education of women. The doctors warned him that 'all sorts of wonderful things will happen if I do not take some more efficient rest,' he told Haeckel's student Anton Dohrn, himself in a more congenial climate on the Mediterranean. On top of it, Huxley had just been elected Lord Rector of Aberdeen University (after Darwin declined), but when the two met no toasts were raised. Huxley was struggling to survive on 'strictly ascetic principles,' drinking water only. Not that he was in a mood to celebrate anyway, with a neighbour taking out a lawsuit over his damp basement, threatening to ruin him with legal costs.[19]

Charles had his own troubles. George and Horace were ill and home for nursing. To spare his own health Charles stopped writing on insect-eaters and began a more leisurely update of his old monograph on climbing plants. The family seemed cursed, blighted by biology. Only when Galton sent his latest deliverance on 'hereditary improvement' did Charles perk up. Society, cousin Galton proposed, should breed out feebleness in body and mind by creating 'a sentiment of caste among those who are naturally gifted.' Register their families, have their children intermarry, and offer them incentives to reproduce – the genetic drain would be plugged and the nation's stock must improve. Charles wondered about the practicality of creating such racial supermen. Only the odd child in each 'large superior family' would be the breeders' pick, like the choicest pigeon – William alone of the Darwins enjoyed good health. These would naturally refuse to be listed and 'stick to their own families,' scotching the whole enterprise. The alternative, compulsory registration, gave Charles the political jitters. It was an illiberal 'utopian' nostrum, even if the 'sole feasible' one for 'improving the human race.' Better simply to publicize 'the all-important principle of inheritance' and let people pursue the 'grand' objective for themselves.

Galton's scheme came too late for the Darwins. What they needed was short-term relief. By March 1873 Charles was unwell again. He would 'much rather stay at home, but knows his place and submits,' Emma bustled, dragging him to a West End town house for a break. The city held no terrors, provided that he was cosseted and secure. The Litchfields and the Hensleigh Wedgwoods were safe company, always solicitous of his health. Now reports of Huxley's deterioration were rife. The court action was breaking him in every way. The X men's YVs suggested taking up a collection, and Emma floated the idea to Charles. He primed the pump with £300 of his thousand-guinea royalties for the *Expression of the Emotions*. He called on the Xs – Hooker, Tyndall, Spencer, and Spottiswoode – who passed the hat, and an attractive stove-pipe it turned out. Over £2000 was raised from eighteen colleagues. Darwin put the money directly into Huxley's account through Lubbock's bank. It was to enable 'an honoured and much loved brother' to take a 'complete rest,' he informed Huxley on 23 April. 'We are convinced that we act for the public interest.'[20]

Fate mocked the fraternity, bereaving them the very next day. Lyell's wife succumbed to typhoid fever. She was twelve years younger than her husband, who at seventy-five had not expected to survive her. Erasmus broke the news to Emma, leaving her to tell Charles gently. Hooker increased his anguish by tenderly describing 'that most lovable face shrouded in flowers in the coffin – looking so calm and beautiful.' Darwin could picture her perfectly, a model of patience, listening to the men talk geology over thirty years before. His feelings welled up, but words failed him. He drafted and redrafted a condolence, settling at last to assure his old friend that 'you are now suffering . . . the greatest calamity, which a man can endure in the world. God grant that you may have strength to bear your misery.'[21]

At the end of May, Fanny's and Hensleigh's daughter Effie married her persistent suitor Thomas ('Theta') Farrer at Little Portland Street Unitarian Chapel in London, where the Lyells had attended. He was twenty years her senior, a powerful Secretary to the Board of Trade, and a botanical barrister, one of Charles's informants and a contributor to the Huxley fund. The couple settled at Abinger Hall, not far from the Wedgwoods of Leith Hill, offering the Darwins yet another convenient retreat.

In June Charles resumed work on his sun-dews, not without distraction. Huxley brought his entire brood to Downe in advance of his expenses-paid holiday. Emma served the 'public interest' and took the seven children to give his wife a break. No sooner had Huxley left with Hooker for the Continent than the young ones were poking into every greenhouse, investigating every experiment.

It was like summers in the fifties, children clambering everywhere. Old toys came out, old games were played, and Emma basked in memories. The Huxley children joined in greater festivities on Sunday 6 July, when Down House played host to Litchfield's singing class from the Working Men's College. It was a 'brilliant day with the roses full out, hay in the fields,' and Charles and Emma in rare form. Some seventy came, many young labourers walking from Orpington station, others arriving with Henrietta and her husband in horse-drawn carts. All were received in the drawing-room and directed out to the new verandah – Charles's pride and joy – and the garden. 'There were long tables . . . for tea and strawberries, singing under the lime trees, dancing on the lawn, and games in the field.' Everyone joined in, heartened by their host's 'cordiality and warmth.'[22]

The Huxleys were dutifully indulged, with Mr Darwin rumpling curly heads at breakfast and bidding them to 'take large mouthfuls.' Then out to the Sandwalk, where they played at 'Red Indians . . . armed with javelins of hazel from the gardener's store of bavins behind the pigeon-house.' Just before lunch Mr Darwin would join them, his 'blue eyes beaming' as he took his turns with Polly trotting at his heels. Tea-time might find the Huxleys 'roasting potatoes in the embers of a real gipsy fire' when the same tall figure would return, clad in a wide black cloak and soft felt hat, always with a 'cheery word.' Evenings were serene. Portly Parslow, 'white-haired and apple-faced,' saw to the children's needs, while Mr and Mrs Darwin played their ritual backgammon matches beside a bright lamp in the parlour.[23]

Down House was heaven, but the parish was purgatory. A staunch new vicar had taken charge in November 1871, the Revd George Sketchley Ffinden. He was a reforming High Churchman, not an emollient type like Brodie Innes. He believed in architectural improvements, liturgical finesse, and the renewal of priestly authority. His theology made the parish his command, rather as the *Beagle* had been FitzRoy's; and it had set him at odds with the Darwins even before they met. In truth, they belonged to different worlds. Ffinden had been ordained in 1861 by Bishop Wilberforce and served as domestic chaplain to Lord Carington. He ran with top Tories and ecclesiastical toffs, and was tapping them to pay for a new vicarage and church restorations.[24]

Downe's great families went along with Ffinden as far as possible. The Darwins had given the church £50 the previous year and donated £35 towards the vicarage. In the winter Charles took time off to advise on Ffinden's purchase of a meadow from Emma's sister Elizabeth, now living in Trowmer Lodge. But the vicar was manoeuvring. First his restoration plans upset the vestry, and Brodie Innes – the hapless patron – had to ask Darwin why. Then Ffinden usurped control of the village school. For years it had been run for the parish poor by an informal committee consisting of Darwin, Lubbock, and the incumbent. Even after the Education Act of 1870, which brought in rates support and government inspectors, the committee maintained much of its independence. It still insisted on a 'conscience clause,' which protected the children from Anglican indoctrination. Ffinden ended that. He was now chairman and treasurer of the committee and had designs on the curriculum. In future Downe's eighty urchins would have lessons on the Thirty-nine Articles from the vicar.

Ffinden was acting within his rights but he trod on too many toes, and Anglican indoctrination really was the last straw. Darwin dropped off the school committee and slashed his annual donation to the church. Except for the Friendly Society, his parish responsibilities were winding up, like his public controversies, and he was 'half killing' himself instead with *Insectivorous Plants*.[25]

On 5 August the Darwins drove to Abinger to join the newly-wed Farrers for a few days. This itself was a milestone, the first time in twenty-five years that Charles had been anyone's house guest outside the immediate family. The last thing they expected was a morgue, or

Effie's and Theta's grisly greeting. Two weeks before, it transpired, the servants had been called to an accident. They found the leader of the Lords, Earl Granville, distraught, doubled over a dead body, slumped on the ground. His riding companion had been bragging about his horsemanship when his mount stumbled, hurling him over its head. The corpse was laid out in the drawing-room, where they now sat. It was Samuel Wilberforce. Here the bishop had remained, flat on the floor, vested in his robes of office, his Garter ribbon, and a cross of roses in place of his jewelled crucifix. For two days he lay in state, while an inquest was held and dignitaries paid their respects. Gladstone knelt beside his friend's cold smiling face, sobbing audibly. Then as village church bells tolled, the bishop was borne away.

Wilberforce had always thought Darwin a 'capital fellow,' whatever his dismay at evolution, and there was no satisfaction in such an end. Huxley of course cried crocodile tears and wise-cracked to Tyndall, 'For once, reality and his brain came into contact and the result was fatal.'[26] But others knew more of equestrian accidents. Charles recalled his own fall in '69, when Tommy rolled over him. He and Emma expressed dismay at the bishop's fate, and left for ten days with William in Southampton.

At home Hooker dropped in, burbling about Huxley's recuperation and expecting to be cross-examined on Darwin's latest hobby-horse, the waxy 'bloom' on certain plant leaves. Darwin was sure that this protected them from burning when watered in direct sunlight and wanted the authority of Kew's Director – and now President of the Royal Society – on his side. They hammered at the subject too hard, for it left Darwin prostrate. He agonized in bed with a 'severe shock continually passing through my brain,' his memory gone, unable to recall anything Hooker had said. Nothing like it had ever happened and Emma feared an epileptic fit. They called Huxley's doctor, Andrew Clark, who put him on an 'abominable diet' and pronounced that 'the brain was affected only secondarily.' By mid-September Charles was back at his insect-eaters. 'Thank God,' he sighed to Hooker; 'I would far sooner die than lose my mind.'[27]

His mind was indeed still nimble and working overtime. Between trips to the greenhouse he wrote to *Nature* about barnacles, posted £75 to help found Anton Dohrn's marine biological station at Naples, and acknowledged countless gifts. Karl Marx sent the new edition of *Das Kapital*, inscribed from a 'sincere admirer.' It was a 'great work,' Darwin realized, as he cut open the first few dozen pages. But the German language befuddled him and the tenor of the book seemed 'so different' from his own. He wished that he was 'more worthy to receive it, by understanding more of the deep & important subject of political economy,' he wrote to Marx darkly. But no doubt their respective efforts towards 'the extension of knowledge' would 'in the long run . . . add to the happiness of mankind.'[28]

Haeckel's *History of Creation* was different. Charles had ploughed through rather more of it in the German and praised the new edition fulsomely, knowing it would 'do a wonderful amount of good in spreading the doctrine of Evolution.' But then 'young and rising naturalists,' the ones appealed to in the *Origin*, needed every encouragement.

And Darwin was adept at giving it, experienced at pushing and prodding his own sons. Even now Frank's medical studies were flagging. He had been living with Uncle Ras, whose dilettante culture was contagious (not that Charles had set a better example in medicine). They agreed that Frank should finish his thesis on animal tissues and then assist at Downe with botanical ones. The old first-floor nursery was duly fitted out as a lab in anticipation.[29]

George was also floundering. Tense, his stomach in knots, he had spent the best part of two years travelling to spas, scuppering his legal career. Back in Cambridge at the begining of October, he was desperate to make his mark and began writing topical essays. One had appeared in the *Contemporary Review*, backing Galton's eugenic proposals for a family register, and advocating legal changes that would permit divorce on the grounds of insanity, criminality, or vice – all hereditary defects. His father applauded it, but George's latest offering was another matter.

It pooh-poohed prayer, divine morals, and 'future rewards & punishments,' all issues his father had carefully skirted in public. The problem was strategy.

> I w[d]. urge you not to publish it for some months, *at the soonest*, & then consider whether you think it new & important enough to counterbalance the evils; remembering the cart-loads which have been published on the subject. – The evils on giving pain to others, & injuring your own power & usefulness.

Hadn't Voltaire found that 'direct attacks on Christianity . . . produce little permanent effects,' that 'good seems only to follow from slow & silent side attacks'? Or take Lyell: he had 'shaken the faith in the Deluge &c far more efficiently by never having said a word against the Bible.' Even John Stuart Mill, England's greatest philosophical unbeliever, had seen his writings become 'text-books at Oxford' by keeping his 'religious criticisms' quiet. The author of the *Origin of Species* had been circumspect too.

> It is an old doctrine of mine that it is of foremost importance for a young author to publish (if with his name) only what is very good & new; so that the public may have faith in him, & read what he writes . . . I have marked one or two passages in which you give your own conviction: remember that an enemy might ask who is this man, & what is his age & what have been his special studies, that he sh^d. give to the world his opinions on the deepest subjects? This sneer might easily be avoided . . . but my advice is to pause, pause, pause.

Charles, with one eye on the 'enemy,' had delayed for decades. Nor should George act impulsively, go public with damaging views that might reflect ill on the family. 'I wish that you were tied to some study on which you could not hope to publish anything for some years.'[30]

The 'moral problem' of speaking out on religion was 'frightfully difficult,' and Darwin had 'never been able to make up my mind' about it. Although he had used theological language freely in the *Origin* and discussed the evolution of religion in the *Descent of Man*, he only mooted his personal beliefs with the utmost discretion. Even now the most he would say, to a student admirer in Holland, was that the question of God's existence is 'beyond the scope of man's intellect.'[31]

Many of his admirers had come to the same conclusion. This November he received a whirlwind visit from the corpulent cosmic theist John Fiske, the genial Harvard philosopher-turned-popularizer, touring Europe to glimpse his heroes. Fiske, having rebelled against the New England Congregationalism of his youth and finished his *Outlines of Cosmic Philosophy*, was kneeling at Spencer's shrine to the Unknowable and Unthinkable. He ingratiated himself with the X set through his infectious humour, keeping even Tyndall in stitches. 'There is nothing so pleasant as *seeing* these men, after one has known them in a shadowy way so long,' Fiske wrote home. 'Reading their books doesn't give you the flesh-and-blood idea of them.'

And flesh and blood was what the earthy New Englander was after. He had been warned about Huxley by an expatriate cockney in New York. 'What, that 'orrid hold hinfidel 'Uxley?' Fiske related to roars of laughter, trying to bend his tongue around the London accent. 'Why, we don't think *hanythink* of 'im in Hingland! We think 'e's 'orrid!' While the big and little 'Uxleys were used to hearing of the headman as a 'cannibal,' Fiske was happy to report the ogre among the most 'charming and lovely' of men and as 'tender as a woman.'

> I am quite wild over Huxley. He is as handsome as an Apollo
> . . . I never saw such magnificent eyes in my life. His eyes are
> black, and his face expresses an eager burning intensity . . .
> He seems earnest, – immensely earnest, – and thoroughly frank
> and cordial and modest. And, by Jove, what a pleasure it is
> to meet such a clean-cut mind! It is like Saladin's sword which
> cut through the cushion.

The pilgrimage to Downe was his highlight. The ebullient Fiske reported that

> old Darwin is the dearest, sweetest, loveliest old grandpa
> that ever was. And on the whole he impresses me with his
> strength more than any man I have seen yet. There is a
> charming kind of quiet strength about him and about
> everything he does. He isn't burning and eager like Huxley.
> He has a mild blue eye, and is the gentlest of gentle old
> fellows.

Fiske pictured him in the Galilean mould, his 'long white hair and enormous white beard' making him 'very picturesque.' Overriding everything was the 'guileless simplicity' of this savant shut away from society. 'I am afraid I shall never see him again, for his health is very bad . . . Of all my days in England I prize today the most.'[32] However Darwin and Emma took this whirlwind sweeping through Downe – it must have nonplussed Emma and knocked up Charles – jovial John Fiske, a Spencerian so typical of America's Gilded Age, certainly went away happy.

Darwin recovered to tackle a new edition of the stolid *Descent of Man*. With two or three books on the boil, he hated another interruption, and without help he saw the changes taking him for ever. He thought of Wallace, struggling as a self-financed writer and in need of work.

Darwin approached him rather sheepishly in November, hating to see colleagues turn ignominiously into hired hands (although familiar with buying dissectors and draughtsmen since his London days). Seven shillings an hour, Wallace quoted; he had helped Lyell edit his

Principles for five, but that was low pay for 'the class of work.' A good deal of revision might be needed and Darwin's abominable handwriting doubled the labour involved. He would keep a record of the hours put in and not even 'think of offering criticisms' of substance. Labour was money for the socialist, and he hired it out in any good cause. You 'have perhaps seen that I am dipping into politics'? he asked Darwin. In fact he was submerged in it, arguing in the *Daily News* that the country's coal reserves should be made a national trust, or the mines be taken out of private hands altogether.

Emma put a stop to Charles's deal. She had him give George the job; he lacked nothing but literary direction and would do it free. Charles agreed – never mind that the subject was technical and outside his scope. An even more sheepish Darwin told Wallace that if 'my son could not do the work, I will write again and *gratefully* accept your proposal.' But meanwhile 'I hope to Heaven that politics will not replace natural science.'[33]

Not that the Darwins could keep out of parish politics themselves. While Charles rose in the middle of the night to watch his twitching Indian telegraph plant – 'it was dead asleep, all but its little ears, which were having most lively games' – Emma lay awake planning a winter reading room for local labourers. Previous ones had proved a great success. They were a model of quiet parish paternalism, the sort practised in a thousand sleepy hamlets. 'Respectable newspapers & a few books were provided & a respectable householder was there every evening to maintain decorum.' The men subscribed a penny a week and came to smoke and play games, 'without the necessity of resorting to the public house.' The schoolroom had been an ideal venue and Lubbock was prepared to loan it again. Emma hoped the vicar would join them in petitioning the school committee.[34]

Ffinden had tolerated the reading room for two winters, but no longer. 'Coffee drinking, bagatelle & other games' had been allowed, and 'the effects of tobacco smoke & spitting' were evident when the children returned in the morning. This was a 'perversion of the building' and he opposed it. Not to be outdone by an unfeeling Tory, Emma had Charles contact the education inspectorate in London. He received a favourable reply, with the proviso that the room be tidied before the next day. The Darwins and the Lubbocks – Elizabeth Wedgwood too – laid this before the committee, offering to pay for any repairs.

The confrontation came just before Christmas. Emma drafted a final plea to the committee, which Charles signed. It was essential, they believed, 'to afford every possible opportunity to the working class for self-improvement & amusement.' Indeed, 'the working men of this country have so few amusements, beyond the brutish one of drinking, that even if the Reading Room be looked at merely as a place of amusement, it is *desireable* [sic] to grant them' the facility. The committee ruled in Emma's favour, as Ffinden was obliged to report in the curtest of notes. He was furious that Darwin had contacted the education department behind his back. 'As I am the only recognized correspondent of the School according to rule 15. Code 1871, I deem such a proceeding quite out of order, especially as I myself had undertaken to communicate with the Office.'[35]

Pulling rank came easily for a gentleman of Darwin's position. And it was a trifle after petitioning the Prime Minister in the Ayrton affair. Still, the parish was a fragile political world and damage had been done. If the clergy and great folks did not stand shoulder to shoulder, how would the rural order hold? Given the kerfuffle, it was as well that moving plants still mesmerized him, diverting his mind from Ffinden's pettiness.

40

A Wretched Bigot

FEELING 'OLD & HELPLESS,' Charles trained to London with Emma on 10 January 1874 to consult Dr Andrew Clark. He toured the publishers, talking to Murray about the *Descent of Man* and Smith Elder about a new edition of *Coral Reefs*, wearing himself out. The afternoons with Erasmus should have offered a respite. But no, Ras too had become fascinated by séances.

London's polite parlours had reverberated to rapping spirits for ten years or more. Noble ladies hosted the 'manifestations' and the cream of society came, keen for the latest *divertissement*. True to form, Huxley had stonewalled a high-level inquiry into the possibility of spirit-produced phenomena. But Wallace still saw nature manifest a progressive spirit, and William Crookes, a prominent chemist (who discovered the element thallium), had conducted experimental séances to prove the power of 'psychic force.' Francis Galton attended one and the goings-on 'confounded him.' No 'vulgar legerdemain,' he told Charles, something queer was happening.[1]

Darwin could dismiss Wallace's low-brow credulity with a twist of the wrist, but not Galton. And now his own brother was about to be swayed by the spirits and duped in front of friends. They all gathered around Eras's dining table one afternoon: Galton and the Litchfields, Hensleigh and Fanny Wedgwood with their eldest daughter Snow, George Lewes and Marian Evans (George Eliot) – Snow's literary mentors – Charles and Emma, who had been eager to meet the author of *Middlemarch*, and son George, who had hired the medium, Charles Williams. One more held hands in the chain, Huxley, 'incognito, so far as the medium was concerned,' at Darwin's urgent request. George and Hensleigh sat on either side of Williams, securing his hands and feet. The curtains were drawn and doors shut. Everyone sat silently in the dark – except Lewes who cracked jokes – waiting for the spirits to move.

With two dozen eyes and ears straining, the room grew stuffy. Charles found it 'so hot and tiring' that he broke the spell, made his excuses, and dragged himself upstairs to lie down. The show began without him. It 'took away all their breaths' – a bell ringing, a candlestick jumping, the sound of wind rushing, sparks flashing, and then the table moving. When he returned he heard that it had risen above everyone's heads, with the chairs ending up on top, as he could see. Understanding how Williams performed these 'astounding miracles, or jugglery,' was beyond him. Galton called it a 'good séance' but Charles had no sympathy. 'The Lord have mercy on us all, if we have to believe in such rubbish,' he moaned to Hooker from the safety of Downe.[2]

While Erasmus dabbled in 'spirit photographs,' Huxley rushed to prop up Darwin's wobbling faith. He joined George in arranging another séance with Williams. They sat beside him and detected subtle movements, proving that he was nothing but 'a cheat,' much to Darwin's relief. He had already told Emma that the events at Ras's were 'all imposture.' It would take 'an enormous weight of evidence' to convince him otherwise. Emma detected the creak of a closing mind. Neutral herself about a psychic explanation, she told Snow that 'he *won't* believe it, he dislikes the thought of it so very much.' A disillusioned Snow recalled that Uncle Charles 'used to look upon it as a great weakness if one allowed wish to influence belief.' 'Yes,' Emma nodded, 'but he does not act up to his principles.' 'Well,' Snow retorted, 'that seems to me what one means by bigotry.' 'Oh, yes,' Emma smiled; 'he is a regular bigot.'[3]

The winter wore on with little to show for it. Darwin did talk Lubbock into selling him the Sandwalk, rented all these years, but Lubbock charged top price and chilled their friendship. Otherwise Darwin trudged about a humdrum existence, moving between plant experiments and book revisions. Henrietta helped with *Coral Reefs*, but the later chapters had to be substantially rewritten. He seemed to be getting nowhere in his race against time. The botany books were languishing and so was he. Dr Clark's regime could not be kept up. The diet proved impossible and his 'strychnine' preparation 'did me harm.' Little wonder that it had killed his sun-dews.[4]

The *Descent* was being doctored too, not as extensively as the *Origin of Species* but with equal pains. While George pieced together the manuscript and made a new index, Charles scribbled scores of insertions – suicide among savages, courtship among butterflies, and the effects of castration on sheep. Anecdotes from correspondents vied for place with snippets from magazines, and his hoarded references tricked out the already copious notes. Sexual selection remained powerful but natural selection was somewhat curbed. 'With highly civilised nations continued progress depends in a subordinate degree on natural selection,' he jotted optimistically; 'for such nations do not supplant and exterminate one another as do savage tribes.' Yet the winnowing still went on, less violently perhaps but no less effectively. Galton's work on mental inheritance had convinced him. 'The more intelligent members within the same community will succeed better in the long run than the inferior, and leave a more numerous progeny, and this is a form of natural selection.' Progress now depended on 'a good education during youth whilst the brain is impressible' combined with 'a high standard of excellence, inculcated by the ablest and best men.'[5]

His own brain was good for settling old scores. 'What a demon on earth Owen is. I do hate him,' Darwin ranted to Hooker after hearing of the latest shenanigans. A conspiracy to oust the superannuated Darwinian President of the Linnean Society, the botanist George Bentham, was supposedly masterminded by the botany keeper at the British Museum, spurred on by Owen. Since Bentham had Hooker's backing, it looked like spite for Owen's failure to control the Kew collections. The old wounds, left festering after Huxley's slashes, had not healed in a decade. Tyndall did once try to mediate, only to be pulled up short by Owen, who demanded that the 'base and mischievous' Huxley first retract his charge of perjury.

Given this new duplicity Darwin was not above aggravating the sore. He resurrected the ape-brain debate for one final reslaying of the slain. An update in the *Descent*'s final edition would enshrine Owen's defeat and put paid to recent critics. Huxley obliged on spec with a stringent reassertion of his old views. It 'pounds the enemy into a jelly,' he strutted, although 'none but anatomists' would know it.[6]

Darwin dropped the *Descent* manuscript off in April. Fired by the success of the cheap *Origin*, Murray planned a half-price edition, at twelve shillings. That was it; Charles had finally washed his hands of evolution – he could not even face the proofs, which went to George. No more books on the subject, he told Fox, now retired to the Isle of Wight. His remaining strength was to be devoted to the genteel savagery of his insectivorous plants.

609

He roped in all hands: Hooker and his assistant William Thistelton-Dyer at Kew; the physiologist John Burdon Sanderson at University College, who ran lab tests on their digestive juices; Asa Gray at the Harvard herbarium, still defending him against the theologians; even old John Price from Shrewsbury, who offered a rare bladderwort. Through the spring specimens arrived, cluttering up the greenhouses, to be fed scraps from the family's table. He never lost his knack of winkling out information. He only had to drop a note to *Nature* on greenfinches severing his primrose nectaries to receive a fresh crop of mail. [7] At least Frank was now helping, which made the load lighter.

The other sons were away, making successes of themselves. Horace had his degree and an engineering apprenticeship, and Leo had been posted to New Zealand with the Royal Engineers to observe the transit of Venus. Frank was the mainstay, and had settled in to Brodie Innes's old house in the village, preparing for his marriage to Amy Ruck. The wedding took place on 23 July just as another 'scientific son' was joining the family, like Lubbock long ago. This was George Romanes, one of Burdon Sanderson's students, who had been with Frank at Cambridge. Wealthy, twenty-six, and once destined for the Church, he had a penchant for marine invertebrates and an inquisitive mind – it was all agreeably familiar.[8]

George, still sickly, kept his nose in the proofs and carried out statistical analyses of first-cousin marriages. (He found them to be three times more frequent in 'our rank' than the lower.) He took up Galton's human-breeding scheme and had already published an article on 'beneficial restrictions to marriage.' Mivart read it with alarm. Having broken with Darwin, he saw George's essay as a perfect pretext to renew the attack on the *Descent of Man*. What better proof of Darwinian social tendencies, Mivart sniped anonymously in the July issue of the *Quarterly Review*, than George's proposals to loosen the bonds of marriage – widen the grounds of divorce – for the sake of better breeding? This was moral anarchy. Mivart had composed the piece in Dresden from hasty notes and misconstrued thoughts. George advocated divorce in cases of criminality or vice, but Mivart garbled this to accuse him unaccountably of standing for 'the most oppressive laws, and the encouragement of vice in order to check population.' Shades of national degeneracy, of revolutionary France and pagan Rome. Indeed, 'there is no hideous sexual criminality of Pagan days that might not be defended on the principles advocated by the school to which this writer belongs.'

'Vice,' 'sexual criminality,' 'oppressive laws,' this was slanderous. It slurred George's father, impugned the family's respectability, and cast the whole Darwinian 'school' into a moral cesspit. Charles was seething – even without knowing who wrote the piece. He told George to seek legal advice while he tackled the *Quarterly*'s publisher, John Murray. It would be a 'dreadful evil' if they 'came to a quarrel,' but either the *Quarterly* printed George's reply in the next number or he would take his business elsewhere.[9]

The affair overshadowed his August holiday at Southampton, even though William was a brick. Charles drafted a reply for George and tried to divert himself with the proofs of the Orangeman John Tyndall's address to the British Association, due in Belfast that month. It was to be an X Club jamboree, with Huxley, Hooker, Lubbock, and Tyndall – half the *Quarterly*'s damned 'school' – making speeches. Tyndall's clarion call only served to emphasize how much militancy was on the upsurge on every side: 'We claim,' he announced in his Irish brogue, 'and we shall wrest from theology the entire domain of cosmological theory,' which led to calls for his prosecution for blasphemy. Set against these evangelical demands by the new 'sect of the Darwinian evolutionists,' Mivart's postures seemed less threatening than defensive. Reviewers were already castigating the religious dogmatism, 'missionary zeal,' and Puritan fervour of the Darwinians, in which enthusiasm 'has a tendency to outrun discretion' and a 'spirit of latent intolerance' is 'tinged with sectarian bitterness.' In sectarian Belfast Darwin was appointed the head of a reformed biology. 'He moves over the subject with the passionless strength of a glacier,' Charles read of himself; 'and the grinding of the rocks is not always without a counterpart in the logical pulverization of the objector.'[10]

Quite so, as the Catholic Mivart was about to find out. Murray, anxious not to lose a bread-and-butter author, leaned on the *Quarterly*'s editor, and in the October issue George's flat contradiction appeared beside an 'apology' from his traducer. It bore all the hallmarks of Mivart's ingenuous backstabbing. Without implying that the younger Darwin had 'approved of anything which he wishes to disclaim,' it ended, 'we must still maintain that the doctrines which he advocates are most dangerous and pernicious.' This was sophistical nonsense – damning the sin but not the sinner. Darwin was livid and took it personally. 'He has gained his object in giving me pain, and, good God, to think of the flattering, almost fawning speeches which he has made to me!' To what depths Mivart had stooped in the name of Christianity.

Even as he seethed, his antipathy to religion was tempered by thoughts of Lyell. Now almost blind and in parlous health, Lyell had generously applauded Tyndall's fillip to 'you and your theory of evolution,' whatever his qualms about the 'fearless out-speaking.' More than ever he was absorbed in the question of a future life, and he let it show. Darwin could offer little comfort. Many accepted it by intuition, '& I suppose that I must differ from such persons' – Emma included – 'for I do not feel any innate conviction.' Still, to be 'circumstanced as you are' was a ghastly thought. Darwin knew that if he were blind, without Emma, and facing the end, the problem of the hereafter would 'recur in the dead of the night with painful force.'

Back at the microscope by day, he thrust it out of mind. He lost himself in his plants and plotted Mivart's downfall. Huxley and Hooker would know best what punitive action to take. Meanwhile he let off steam at the Revd Ffinden and formally resigned from the school committee on health grounds.[11]

On 13 November the new *Descent of Man* was hot off the press, priced down to nine shillings, though Murray conceded that it would cut the profits to the bone.

That day Hooker's wife Fanny died suddenly. Hooker was at the pinnacle of his career and already severely strained: he sat on fifteen committees at the Royal Society and was struggling with the new Disraeli government to increase Kew's funding. At home he had six children, three young. Fanny had held the household together, helped him write and proof-read, and escorted dignitaries around Kew, being a botanical Henslow herself. She had been the perfect partner for twenty-three years, since his return from the East. Now he felt as though he were wandering again in the Himalayas, cut off, desperately alone. He entered 'a sort of trance,' scarcely able to fathom the calamity. The prospect of returning home after the funeral stunned him, and he begged refuge at Downe. The house as so often turned into a hospice, with Hooker staying for a few days and leaving the children to Emma's care. Returning home he was unable to function. 'Utter desolation' overcame him as he stepped into his house at Kew, and his first impulse was to return to the Darwins. Charles passed on his own remedy, encouraging him to banish harrowing thoughts 'by hard work.'[12]

But Hooker kept 'stumbling into pitfalls of recollections.' Darwin waited a couple of weeks and then raised Mivart's iniquity. Hooker agreed that the so-called apology was abominable and proposed forcing him to admit to the anonymous piece and to recant. A joint letter from X Club members should twist his arm. For Huxley it was another excuse to pitch into his old pupil's split loyalties, to evolution and the Church, and he took the opportunity in a book review. 'Unless I err,' he bristled, the *'Quarterly Reviewer'* is 'good enough to include me among the members of that school whose speculations are to bring back . . . the gross profligacy of Imperial Rome.' With his usual sensual pleasure in smiting Amalekites – now sitting oddly against Darwin's unsmiling earnestness – Huxley rehearsed his sectarian theme: that 'misrepresentation and falsification are the favourite weapons of Jesuitical Rome' and that 'anonymous slander' culminates not in 'the profligacy of a Nero or of a Commodus, but the secret poisonings of the Papal Borgias.'

The X Club were closing ranks, forming a protective circle. 'You ought to be like one of the blessed gods of Elysium,' Huxley counselled Darwin before Christmas, 'and let the inferior deities do battle with the infernal powers.' He himself passed word to Mivart via a Catholic priest that scurrility of this sort was unacceptable. Mivart was being pinned out, like Owen before him, and he knew it. He erupted with pleas and protestations, and in confidence asked Huxley how to go about making amends.

Huxley plotted Mivart's excommunication from the church scientific with Darwin: 'the severest and most effectual punishment for this sort of moral assassination is quietly to ignore the offender and give him the cold shoulder.' Darwin, not brimming with seasonal spirit, drummed his fingers. Emma, his X friends, and even George backed Huxley's advice, but he was itching to do the 'manly thing' and speak his mind. Malicious twisting of the truth and stabbing at the family was unforgivable. On 12 January 1875, when no further apology had come, Darwin acted. He sent a note with icy formality, vowing never to communicate with him again.[13] Mivart's worm twisted on the Darwinian hook and died of its improprieties. There was never any spirit of forgiveness; years later Huxley and Hooker were still blackballing Mivart's application to join the Athenaeum Club.

Darwin sprinted on with *Insectivorous Plants*, plagued by the interminable manuscript. The prose was muddy, and by February he was bogged down and gasping. He hardly helped George's low spirits by commiserating, 'I know well the feeling of life being objectless & all being vanity of vanities.' He was even 'ready to commit suicide,' a startled Hooker heard, and the death of an old, sad Lyell on the 22nd left him feeling 'as if we were all soon to go.'

After Lyell's failure to back the *Origin*, their camaraderie had cooled. It was a grim end to a once famous friendship. Hooker arranged for Lyell's place in Westminster Abbey but Darwin declined to be a pall-bearer. 'I should so likely fail in the midst of the ceremony, and have my head whirling off my shoulders.'

In March he clambered out of the mud, throwing his finished book down, sick of his insect-eating companions. He gazed at his oil portrait by Walter Ouless, a birthday present. It showed 'a very venerable, acute, melancholy old dog,' he decided, which fairly reflected his mood. But the old dog had a bone or two to bury yet. He carried the manuscript to Murray and spent a fortnight with Eras and Henrietta in town. With Lyell departed, an April Fools' day séance at the Hensleigh Wedgwoods' seemed ill judged, a tragic joke if it were not so tasteless, so much 'rubbish' to please the dreary dictates of fashion.[14]

Life was wearying on so many fronts. The parish added to his woes with the Ffinden fiasco chuntering on. For a year the vicar had cut every member of the family, making Darwin the parish Mivart. He felt 'so grossly insulted' that any word now had to go through an intermediary. Lubbock had asked on Darwin's behalf for the loan of the schoolroom to hold two evening lectures for the village. The committee consented, but Ffinden demurred. He refused to co-operate with an infidel who impugned his authority, adopting a sugar-of-lead smile:

> I had been long aware of the harmful tendencies to the cause
> of revealed religion of Mr. Darwin's views, but on coming
> into this parish I had fully determined, as far as lay within my
> power, not to let my difference of opinion interfere with a
> friendly feeling as neighbours, trusting that God's Grace might
> in time bring one so highly gifted intellectually & morally to
> a better mind.

This Sir John diplomatically side-stepped as he tried to patch up the schoolroom quarrel. With Henrietta beside him, Charles drafted a tortuous self-vindication, designed to elicit another clerical climb-down. 'If M^r F bows to Mrs D. and myself, we will return it,' he condescended, showing that High Church Tories had no monopoly on hauteur. With no parish X Club to extort an apology, restoring peace was going to be a 'herculean task.'

The asperity was evident. Having forsworn public controversy, he found his private hostility to Christianity increasing. Ffinden and Mivart had stretched his tolerance to breaking point.[15] Dogmatism of their sort needed a dose of liberal humanitarianism; closed minds needed to be opened by the rush of a reforming science.

Scientific progress was his other preoccupation during his spring break in London. He was master-minding a rear-guard action against the rising anti-vivisectionist movement. Henrietta, a confirmed hypochondriac, had jumped on the bandwagon. Like so many closeted Victorian matriarchs, she identified with suffering life. Victoria's maidens formed the anti-vivisectionist core and 'read their own misery into the vivisector's victims.' Henrietta supported a petition drawn up by the women's campaigner Frances Power Cobbe. Cobbe was marshalling lay support for a crackdown on live animal experiments. Her petition – signed by archbishops, poets, and politicians – even threatened legislation that would take the moral decisions out of the hands of the experimenters. Darwin was atypically British, an animal lover who loved his colleagues' autonomy more. 'Physiology,' he warned Henrietta, 'can progress only by experiments on living animals.' These must be conducted freely, 'in the search for abstract truth.' Any abuses should be corrected by 'the improvement of humanitarian feelings.' In other words, legislation would be fatal. If the hare-coursing, hypocritical House of Commons passed Cobbe's 'puerile' law, physiology in England would 'languish or quite cease.'[16]

The more he thought, the more he worried. Cobbe's meddling had to be trumped. He toyed with a counter-petition, but it was Huxley who recognized that the fox-hunting Commons would have to save science, fearing for their own skins. 'If physiological experimentation is put down by law, hunting, fishing and shooting, against which a much better case can be made out, will soon follow.' To preserve liberty all around, let the physiologists propose their own legislation. In London Darwin frantically mustered support for a pre-emptive law. There was 'not a day to lose' if his 'Vivisector's Bill' – as opponents dubbed it – was to be introduced in the current session.

Neither he nor Huxley had conducted experiments on live animals, but friends who had, like Burdon Sanderson, were easily won over. Darwin even swayed Henrietta, and her lawyer-husband helped draft a bill. Regulation, not restriction, was its aim. Licensing experimenters would ensure their freedom and minimize animal suffering. Darwin sent it to Hooker for the rubber stamp, so that he could 'say that it meets with your approval as President of the Royal Society.' Then he offered it to Lord Derby, the Foreign Secretary, urging him to have a word with select members of the Tory cabinet in order to head off 'hasty legislation versus science.'[17]

It was a splendid piece of lobbying. His name opened doors and, Derby told him, placed the scientists' bill on the Home Secretary's desk. At Downe Ffinden was still buzzing about 'uncalled for interference,' like a gnat on a rhino's back; now Darwin, surrounded by insect-eaters, had shown what interference could do. When Huxley and Romanes, Darwin's new protégé, came out on 17 April there was only the bill's mechanics to arrange – who would sponsor it and when. At home the topic remained a male preserve. The bumptious Romanes, on his first visit, was told by Darwin not to 'talk about experiments on animals' in the 'presence of my ladies.'

One lady got the better of them. On 4 May Cobbe's bill was presented in the Lords. The scientists' alternative, with its 'more humanitarian aspect,' as Darwin put it, reached the Commons eight days later. The Home Secretary reacted by announcing a Royal Commission of inquiry into 'the practice of subjecting live animals to experiments for scientific purposes.' In the event it was opportune, with the physiologists falling out over their bill's intent. Darwin pinned his hopes on Huxley, co-opted on to the Commission, and they 'let the present madness subside.'[18]

Darwin was a man trapped on a literary treadmill, walking faster and faster towards the grave. One book led to another, and there were always a couple on back burners should he feel bored. *Insectivorous Plants* sold out quickly, and in July a 1000-copy reprint vanished within a fortnight. The name 'Darwin' was a draw now, however odd the subject. Who could imagine a 450-page catalogue of plant experiments selling faster than the original *Origin of Species?*[19] A new edition of *Variation of Animals and Plants* followed, its additions culled from the hundreds of letters and scores of monographs that had swamped Downe over seven years. Even more idiosyncratic, this piece of science; he changed his mind about the hairy throats of goats, added bits on the selection of goldfish during the Sung Dynasty, and discarded Robert Chambers's hexadactyl daughter, whose amputated extra finger had appeared to be regrowing ('we are manifesting a tendency to return to the reptilian type,' the six-fingered Chambers had once joked, and in the first edition Darwin had taken him literally).[20]

Then he re-throned his 'great god Pan,' altering his appearance but leaving his powers intact. The deity had not acquired many worshippers, though Romanes presented himself at the altar. Overawed by Darwin's father-figure, Romanes had set aside his jellyfish and started grafting vegetable plants, miscegenously mixing the 'gemmules' (or so he hoped) to produce a hybrid with the characters of both the scion and stock. Darwin knew that 'the world will be much more influenced by experiments on animals,' but success with plants would be a start.

He also knew that Galton had tried and failed. Galton's house had been overrun with rabbits as he experimented on blood transfusions, intrigued by 'pangenesis.' But pure-bred silver-grey bucks and does given the blood of common rabbits still bred true – eighty-eight offspring in thirteen litters showed no adulteration. Darwin protested that he had never mentioned 'gemmules' in the blood, but his brave face was getting a little stiff. Galton suspected that heredity was not a democratic process: gemmules do not convene from all over the body in the egg and sperm. Instead, those in the reproductive cells are sovereign, governing all. Offspring are determined by the genetic make-up of these cells, not by changes in their parents' bodies.[21]

But Darwin was loath to let go of the notion that a well-used and strengthened organ could be inherited. For decades he had amassed evidence that tradesmen's physiques were passed on – that blacksmiths' children are born with hammering biceps, or that parental scars reappear on a baby. More and more he fell back on this, making pangenesis essential. In the *Descent* such inheritance was presented as a powerful factor in human evolution. Nothing would induce him to emulate Huxley and strangle his baby god. So he left Pan essentially intact, allowing organisms literally to grow from their inherited gemmules. Bitter experience had taught him that the children shared his weakness. It was pleasanter to think that they shared his mental strengths, and that the modified gemmules of his young over-worked brain had passed on his peculiar psychological gifts.[22]

For proof there was Frank. His love of natural history was like Charles's at the same age. Frank came down from the village most days and was always pottering in the greenhouse, experimenting on plant fertilization, or tinkering upstairs in the lab. Charles, proud of his new assistant, put him up for a Fellowship of the Linnean Society.

Fame left Darwin pestered by every fool with a thought. He was plagued by sermon-senders and soul-savers, by foreigners wanting papers published, or just wishing for his *imprimatur*, by lecturers wanting chairs and scientists their fellowships. Most were treated graciously, a few received grudging treatment. Some refused to give up. The brash Birmingham surgeon Robert Lawson Tait currently had his foot in Darwin's door. Just thirty, Tait specialized in removing ovaries and wombs, with a side-line in plant physiology. His reputation was on the rise and he wanted a Fellowship of the Royal Society to garnish his gynaecology practice. After months of shameless sycophancy, he forced Darwin in October to send his paper on pitcher plants to the Royal Society for publication. It seemed to be an 'important contribution to science,' not that Darwin read it carefully.[23]

His own publications took every waking hour. There were endless negotiations with Murray about prices, print runs, and rights. His translators Victor Carus in Leipzig and Giovanni Canestrini in Padua were straining to catch up with him, working on several of his books simultaneously. And they were losing. The *Variation of Animals* was at the printer's; an old botanical essay was due out in November – *The Movements and Habits of Climbing Plants* – with 'illustrations ... drawn by my son, George.' And Charles was already scribbling 'vile' screeds for *The Effects of Cross and Self Fertilisation in the Vegetable Kingdom*. Only a noble invitation from London stayed his hand. Lord Cardwell asked him to testify before the Royal Commission on vivisection.[24]

Huxley demanded he attend. A young Austrian physician, Edward Klein, had outraged the panel, muttering in broken English about his 'entire indifference to animal suffering.' 'He only gave anaesthetics to keep animals quiet!' Huxley spat. Klein tarred everyone with the same brush, sickening the committee by his deliberate probings and torturings. 'He has done more mischief than all the fanatics put together' – but 'don't mention' it 'outside the circle of discreet Darwindom.' High authority was needed to counter Klein's testimony, and an 'astonished and disgusted' Darwin agreed to testify. He made a flying visit on 3 November. Cardwell met him at the door, sat him in a special oversized chair, and treated him 'like a Duke.' They wanted his 'confession of faith' about the importance of physiology and 'the duty of humanity' towards animals, that was all. Ten minutes from him was worth two hours of risky vivisectionist apologias. It was a painless episode, but the cab left him at Ras's that night 'unwell.'[25]

This was the first Christmas at Downe without Parslow. Darwin had set him up in the village with a £50 pension and the rent of Home Cottage in Back Lane, his reward for thirty-six years' unfaltering service. Jackson, a comic little man 'with red cheeks [and] ... loose curly wisps of side whiskers' took over, but no one could really replace the redoubtable old butler. Other servants came and went; there was always a coachman and a footman, a pair of housemaids and at least two gardeners. Mrs Evans, the cook, was second in seniority to Parslow, though her cuisine in Charles's view left something to be desired. But she was cheap, less than £8 a quarter. Actually no one bar Jackson received more, and this year the total servants' wage bill came to only £86.

This was a fraction of their outgoings. At Christmas Emma balanced the books. Charles was full of 'dismal forecasts' as usual, predicting penury and ruin. He worried about his fortune, even as it swelled, and begrudged every penny of household expenditure. With the children away, expenses hit a five-year low, with meat – the biggest item – down to £221. The total was just £900, or ten per cent of their earnings and interest. Rates and income tax were negligible, less than the servants' pay, but even after deductions for beer and brandy, sweets and champagne, and the boys' allowances, they had the second-best surplus ever of £4658 to reinvest.[26]

Typically, everything was listed and accounted for in the house, from fat drippings, £3, to the village Friendly Society. Their clockwork lives ran by calculations; balances were continually totted. Even games were recorded religiously. Charles kept the account in a notebook tucked away in the parlour. Each evening, after precisely two games of backgammon, he and Emma entered their scores, a practice that amazed and amused their guests. It had tickled Mrs Asa Gray on her husband's visit years before and on 28 January 1876 Charles posted the current tally, as 'she likes to hear men boasting, it refreshes them so much.' Emma, 'poor creature, has won only 2490 games, whilst I have won, hurrah, hurrah, 2795 games!'[27]

But then notebooks were nothing new. Since his shooting days at Maer every aspect of life was entered on a list. He had counted and classified, sifted and sorted – beetles at Cambridge, birds on the *Beagle*, books to be read, and 'double dash' days in his health diary. All was to some end. Since 1866 he had kept records on thousands of plants hand-reared from seed, and his pollination experiments now reached a climax in *Cross and Self Fertilisation*.

From his first jottings on evolution, he had guessed that the offspring of self-fertilized plants would be weaker. In the *Origin* he made the point, but then it was personal to him. For plants or marriages, outbreeding was best. Self-pollinators and first-cousin offspring suffered in life's struggle. *Orchids* had illustrated the bizarre adaptations ensuring that bees could only cross pollinate, and for a decade he had been crossing plants under controlled conditions, trying to prove statistically that it was beneficial.[28]

This was his most prodigious, painstaking series of experiments.

The plants had to be protected from insects by sheets of gauze. He cross-fertilized some batches and selfed others. Seeds were carefully collected, labelled, and grown to maturity under identical conditions. These were themselves bred to test for sterility: crossed plants had to be crossed again, the others self-pollinated. For up to ten generations this went on, with records kept at every stage of the lengths of plants, times of flowering, the number and weight of seed pods, and the quantity of seeds in each. Nor was just the odd species involved; morning glories, foxgloves, violas, poached-egg plants, petunias, and dozens of others were all tested simultaneously, the greenhouse bursting and space so restricted that many were crammed into the same pot. Then Chinese primroses, French poppies, and hothouse exotics were tried . . .

Thousands of paintbrush pollinations took place, tens of thousands of seeds were counted. It was obsessive work: each seed became 'a small demon trying to elude him by getting into the wrong heap or jumping' from under the microscope. Now, peering over his pince-nez spectacles, ledgers of data lay before him as he tabulated the results. Galton checked his statistics, and the figures quantified the 'selective force' at work in modifying flowers. Crossed plants came out markedly superior to self-fertilized ones in height, weight, vigour, and fertility. And why, Darwin asked at the end? Because nature blesses 'legitimate marriages' – among those from different backgrounds.

People or plants, it was all the same, and the personal dimension was too evident. After the fruitless effort to get a census question on cousin-marriages, George had followed up with an analysis of data culled from lunatic asylums and wedding announcements in the *Pall Mall Gazette*. According to his statistics, which Darwin cited, the evils produced by first-cousin marriages might be 'small' but they could be condoned 'amongst the upper classes,' among gentlefolk brought up in richly different environments.[29] And Charles and Emma? Theirs was a fertile union with sickly seedlings. Evidently the beds at Maer Hall and The Mount had been too alike. The couple had not been well crossed.

Cross and Self Fertilisation was turning out to be his biggest plant book and the writing dragged on into the summer. Charles paced himself with short breaks – or rather Emma did – and made the most of the time, revelling in 'my sole pleasure in life,' work.

Not even the setbacks destroyed that pleasure. Haeckel came out against pangenesis. Tait's paper was ignominiously rejected by the

Royal Society. Romanes started secret inquiries into spiritualism, though Darwin confessed himself 'a wretched bigot on the subject.' And a 'cruelty to animals' bill was introduced in Parliament that went far beyond the Commission's recommendations and fell into Cobbe's lap. Darwin vented his spleen in *The Times*, the old patrician targeting those women who 'from the tenderness of their hearts and ... their profound ignorance' oppose all animal experiments.

He let none of it get him down. By May the first draft of the fertilization book was finished and, unable to relax for a moment, he promptly threw himself into a new edition of *Orchids*.[30]

Emma dragged him away almost before he started. Hensleigh and Fanny had built a house in the Surrey countryside, and Charles and Emma accepted an invitation to visit, dying to tell them the good news.

41

Never an Atheist

THEY WERE TO BE grandparents! Frank's wife Amy was five months pregnant. Charles and Emma had been expecting the announcement – the marriage was after all two years old – and Hensleigh and Fanny celebrated with them. In their seventies, the Hensleighs longed for their own grandchild, and they spent the weeks with the Darwins thinking on the future.

For Charles time was running out, with so much left to do. He had *Orchids* to revise and two more plant books in prospect. Earthworms still intrigued him and he hoped to write on their habits before joining them. He would have a grandchild to see him buried. And what then? He imagined himself 'a dead man in another world' looking back. He pictured the baby growing up, haunted by his name, wondering about the author of the *Origin of Species*. Hadn't he often wished to know more about his own grandfather Erasmus?

Basking in the sun with new life swarming about him, he decided to compose a posthumous message to the family. He started on Sunday, 28 May 1876, scrawling 'Recollections of the Development of my mind and character' across a fresh foolscap sheet. The paragraphs poured out quickly, racing through his naughty childhood and wasted schooldays, his Edinburgh apprenticeship under Dr Grant, his extramural interests at Cambridge and walks with Professor Henslow, his tangles with FitzRoy on the *Beagle* and growing love for science. None of this was for publication: there were too many casual comments about old friends, not to mention the intimacy and mild self-criticism. This was for the family's eyes.

Off to a flying start, he wrote for an hour most afternoons at Downe. It was easy going, unlike the hair-tearing revisions to *Cross and Self Fertilisation*, which he laboured over after breakfast. The story reached London – geology, his *Journal*, and Lyell – when he broke off to start a section headed 'Religious Belief.' Chronologically, it stood on the threshold of his marriage, but Charles ranged far beyond. Just weeks before Amy's confinement, he was tackling his long dispute with Emma.

Nothing curbed his candour; these were private pages. At first he had been unwilling to give up the faith, and had even tried to 'invent evidence' to bolster the Gospels, which had prolonged his indecision. But, just as his clerical career had died a slow 'natural death,' so his belief in 'Christianity as a divine revelation' had withered gradually. There had been no turning back once the death-blow fell. His dithering had crystallized into a moral conviction so strict that he could not 'see how anyone ought to wish Christianity to be true.' If it were, 'the plain language' of the New Testament 'seems to show that the men who do not believe, and this would include my Father, Brother and almost all my best friends, will be everlastingly punished. And this is a damnable doctrine.'[1]

Hard heartfelt words, they recalled the bitter months and years after the Doctor's death. But what about the wider issues? How could belief in God and immortality be justified, given the conflicting evidence? 'Inward convictions and feelings' were unreliable because the human mind had evolved. Blind nature had given them a survival value, like other instincts. So while he sometimes felt himself a theist, at others he distrusted his own feelings, let alone anyone else's.

Altogether it was a grim indictment of Emma's sentimental, Bible-based faith. The enormity of what he had written shook him. It exposed their intimate conflict, laid it bare before the family. As he wrote on, his affection turned to tears. 'You all know well your mother,' he added, 'so infinitely my superior in every moral quality . . . my wise adviser and cheerful comforter.' He recalled her 'beautiful letter' after their marriage, with its fear for his eternal destiny. Here was her side of the story, and he wanted the family to know it. Then his melancholy thoughts turned to Annie, and how she would now 'have grown into a delightful woman . . . Tears still sometimes come into my eyes, when I think of her sweet ways.'

Anxious memories flooded back. Twice he had tended dying loved ones while awaiting a confinement: his father a few months before Frank was born, and Annie just before Horace. Now he looked back on his own life like a 'dead man' as Amy prepared to give birth.

Through July he continued the autobiography. He piled on anecdotes from the Gower Street years and relived writing the *Origin of Species* and his other books. After *Cross and Self Fertilisation* was published 'my strength will ... probably be exhausted,' he closed. Like the devout old priest Simeon, on seeing the infant Jesus, 'I shall be ready to exclaim "Nunc dimittis".'[2]

He finished the manuscript on 3 August, ready for his grandchild, and returned to his perennial *Orchids* and parish responsibilities. He pumped £25 into the Revd Ffinden's 'vicarage endowment fund,' matching Lubbock's subscription.[3] Nothing but solid respectability for the second squire of Downe, building for the future. The baby – Bernard – arrived on 7 September, born at the house. He was fine but his mother contracted a fever, which turned into convulsions. She fell unconscious, and on the third day the prognosis was bleak. Frank stayed the night at her bedside, stroking her raven hair and slender face. On the 11th, at seven in the morning, Charles came in, and they watched her die. Amy was just twenty-six.

Frank went into shock. Bessy collapsed and Emma herself was almost overcome. For Charles it was 'the most dreadful thing' that had ever happened – worse for Frank than 'poor Annie's death' for him. Comfort came in the knowledge that Amy 'never knew she was leaving her beloved husband for ever,' but that was a 'miserable consolation.' His son was enduring what he himself most feared. Surviving Emma was unthinkable.[4]

Months passed before anything like normal life resumed. Frank, distracted by grief, moved into Down House with the baby. He did mechanical chores for his father, making a fair copy of his autobiography and correcting the proofs of *Orchids*. Charles extended the house for him, which meant more upheaval. It had been twenty years since contractors vied with a crying child to disrupt the daily routine. A two-storey extension was added on the north side of the house, with a purpose-built billiard room downstairs and a bedroom-cum-dressing-room for Frank above. The old billiard room became Frank's study, next to his father's, and down the hall the workmen made a new front door.[5]

In October Charles and Emma braced themselves for another of Haeckel's whirlwind visits, which Emma dreaded. Again he stormed the house, bellowing enough 'bad English' to leave them 'nearly deafened,' but for all that she found him 'hearty and affectionate.' Charles regaled him with the quirky news. Huxley's protégé, the stormy Ray Lankester, a good fossil fish man and now Grant's successor at University College, had exposed a marauding American medium in *The Times*. As a result Henry Slade had been sentenced to three months' imprisonment with hard labour – despite the defence calling Wallace as a witness! Emma was scandalized, believing that the credulous deserved the rogues. But not Charles; the affair was a 'public benefit,' and he had secretly sent £10 towards the prosecution's costs.[6]

Parish politics still bedevilled them, even if they scored some successes. A reading room was opened before Christmas, cheering Emma because Ffinden had tried everything to oppose it. Charles, on to his next book on flowers, saw *Orchids* and *Cross and Self Fertilisation* published, and in February 1877 won a small victory of his own. During the farm slump, with wages down and jobs in jeopardy, the village labourers wanted to disband the Friendly Society and share out the proceeds. Only Mr Darwin as treasurer stood in their way. A deputation duly called at Down House and an extraordinary general meeting was convened, at which Mr Darwin would speak.

Donning his black overcoat and soft felt hat, Charles trudged to the George and Dragon one frigid Saturday night and sat surrounded by his tipsy cottagers in the reeking smoke-room. He harangued them about their losses if the society were dissolved, about thrift, about exchanging long-term security for a few pounds in hand. What if the distress got worse? Without the society, who would provide for their families? The room erupted into quarrels and Charles left in a haze of blue smoke, his 'bombshell' demolishing the spendthrifts.[7] The men compromised, agreeing to distribute their surplus funds while keeping the books open.

A parish paternalist, he was promoting the self-help values of his fellow Murray author Samuel Smiles. Darwin had been impressed by *Self-Help* and later gloried in Smiles's biographies of self-made men – stories of heroic prudence, industry, and enterprise, not unlike Martineau's mythic poor-law tales. Smilesian values had made England and evolution great. The unfettered individual, pursuing his self-interest in a freely competitive society, had been the political ideal for half a century, since the days of the radical Whigs and free-traders. It was Darwin's manifesto in the *Descent of Man*, and he himself remained a 'thorough Liberal.'[8]

That meant a thorough Gladstonian. Darwin followed the Grand Old Man even in his opposition foreign policy. In December he had signed up as one of the convenors of the great St James's Hall demonstration against the bloody 'Bulgarian horrors,' the massacre of 15,000 Bulgarian rebels by Turkish troops. He also contributed to the relief effort – £50 all told – and backed Gladstone's call for the Russians to secure Christian Bulgaria against the Muslim Turks. This slavish support did not pass unnoticed. Freethinkers branded Gladstone an opportunist for rousing the religious rabble against the pro-Turkish Tories. To Marx he was just a hypocrite, a High Anglican putting his Christianity before his Liberalism, who preferred an Orthodox Tsarist oppressor for a Turkish one. Marx expected more of Darwin and lashed his support for the 'piggish demonstration.'

But political loyalty paid off, and the Olympian deities of Victorian Liberalism shortly descended on the sleepy village of Downe. Gladstone was making the rounds of his backbenchers, spending the weekend with Lubbock at High Elms. With them were Lyon Playfair MP, with a brief for science and a supporter of the vivisection bill; the *Fortnightly*'s John Morley, who had puffed the *Descent of Man* so helpfully; and even Huxley, his black eyes flashing scorn at Gladstone's biblical bombast. On Saturday 10 March the deities turned up on Darwin's doorstep and settled into his drawing-room. The Grand Old Man took for granted his host's interest in Turkish terrorism and like Zeus himself 'launched forth his thunderbolts with unexhausted zest,' reading from the proof of his latest pamphlet. Darwin was stunned into a bemused silence for almost two hours. Before sweeping out, Gladstone asked what evolution held in store. Did the future belong to America as the Eastern civilizations decayed? A better question perhaps for Disraeli, but after mulling it over Darwin ventured, Yes. As he watched Gladstone's 'erect alert figure' walking back towards the village, he murmured to Morley, 'What an honour that such a great man should come to visit me!' That night in his diary Gladstone noted merely his host's 'pleasing & remarkable' appearance.[9]

Even Tories were not above paying Darwinians tribute, though not, understandably, for their Darwinism. While the Duke of Argyll had failed to honour Hooker as the head of Kew Gardens because 'he don't like my Darwinism,' the new Secretary for India in Disraeli's cabinet, the staunch Anglican Lord Salisbury, put his name up for a knighthood, a very specific, complimentary honour, the Star of India, acknowledging Hooker's monumental, decades-long work on the Himalayan flora. Hooker told Darwin he 'would rather go down to posterity as one of the "Star of India" than as of any other dignity whatever that the Crown can offer,' and he accepted the investiture.[10] Sir Joseph, President of the Royal Society, showed that Darwinism was no longer a social hindrance.

As the disciples tended to exalted circles, Darwin was even more loath to become mixed up with disreputable radicals. They appealed in vain for his support. Charles Bradlaugh, a big boisterous solicitor's clerk from London's East End, was the dominant Secularist of the day. A militant atheist, he had stood as an unofficial Liberal candidate for Northampton in every election since 1868 – unsuccessfully, but with the best political machine of any radical outside the trade unions. His hard-hitting demands for electoral reform were matched by a commitment to contraception: birth control would rescue working people from the Malthusian poverty trap, free them from domestic slavery. Two weeks after Gladstone's visit, Bradlaugh outraged the genteel nation by publishing do-it-yourself contraceptive advice from an American doctor, James Knowlton. The sixpenny pamphlet, *Fruits of Philosophy*, was branded a vicious obscenity. Bradlaugh and his co-publisher Annie Besant (a latter-day Emma Martin – an atheist mother-of-two who had left her parson-husband) were committed for trial at London's Central Criminal Court, the Old Bailey, on 18 June – the day Darwin heard of Hooker's honour.

The case was splashed all over the press. Nothing so notorious had hit the headlines since Holyoake's trial thirty years earlier. It split the radicals themselves – even old, cigar-smoking, respectable Holyoake fumed that it compromised them before a Christian public, who damned such 'neo-Malthusian' nonsense as immoral and subversive. Contraception was 'vice' and execrated by Malthus as a way of checking population. Who in their right minds would divorce sex from babies and invite women to become wanton, to corrupt men and to destroy the family? The defendants fought back by calling medical and scientific authorities to testify that 'the doctrine of the limitation of the family' was freely discussed in other publications.[11]

Darwin was appalled to be subpoenaed two weeks before the trial. Bradlaugh and Besant, defending themselves, had made a gigantic miscalculation, assuming that the author of the *Descent of Man* would back them. Had not he liberated mankind from superstition? Darwin replied instantly, protesting his years of illness, his forced withdrawal from 'all society or public meetings,' and the 'great suffering' that a court appearance would entail. Underneath he was a flurry of old fears, for his family, his reputation, his status as a justice of the peace. If compelled to testify, he finished, he would have to denounce the defendants, for he had 'long held an opposite opinion' on birth control.

As proof, he sent an extract from the *Descent of Man*: 'our natural rate of increase, though leading to many and obvious evils, must not be greatly diminished by any means.' Plain speaking, that meant any 'artificial means of preventing conception.' Otherwise he spelt out the nightmarish consequences – such practices would 'spread to unmarried women & w^d destroy chastity on which the family bond depends; & the weakening of this bond would be the greatest of all possible evils to mankind.' No compromise could be struck; 'my judgment would be in the strongest opposition to yours.' He passed on addresses at Leith Hill and Southampton where he was holidaying that month, should the subpoena be renewed. But he hoped not, and he wanted to know immediately, 'as apprehension of the coming exertion would prevent the rest which I require doing me much good.'

'Rest' of course meant working furiously away from home. Mercifully, the atheists withdrew their subpoena and left him in peace with his worms.

He was back on the ground, exalting the humble in his own peculiar way. As with all his work, he moved from minuscule, unnoticeable changes to their global consequences. Worms burying castles, earthquakes throwing up the Andes, flecks and specks adding up to an eye or wing: he looked for tiny effects that were cumulative and creative. From William's he made a day-trip to Stonehenge – his first – to see how worm castings had buried the ancient monoliths. Emma thought that the two-hour rail trip and twenty-four-mile drive would 'half kill' him, but even after digging in the blazing sun he was in wonderful form.[12]

Fifteen years tampering with the sex-life of plants culminated in *The Different Forms of Flowers on Plants of the Same Species* in mid-July – with a fetching and rare dedication, to Asa Gray. This book continued another old theme, strategies for safe sex and fertile reproduction. No 'little discovery' ever gave him 'so much pleasure' as cracking the *raison d'être* of double- and triple-sexed flowers – it was like the *frisson* of finding the barnacles' 'complemental males:' each female in heterostyled plants was most fertile with the same-sized males, which always occurred on another flower.

Forms of Flowers capped his work on nature's complex 'marriage arrangements.' It was a botanical voyeur's diary. He had contrived all sorts of liaisons among the blossoms, spying on them through his eyeglass. After endless manual pollinations, myriad microscopic seed-counts; and he described the results with due delicacy, showing how 'legitimacy' was conferred in cross-fertilizations.[13] Even before the first reviews appeared, he was wrapped up in his next book on plant movement. No time could be lost, nor could he 'endure being idle.'

Not that idleness was on the cards. He continued collecting seeds and specimens, scrounging all he could from Hooker and Thistelton-Dyer at Kew. He kept up a massive correspondence, on everything from worm lore and butterflies to drunken monkeys. In October he even found time to dodge Gladstone's thunderbolts and dared to criticize him on the colour-sense in Homeric Greece. Politically, though, he was steadfast. A young Russian botanist, Kliment Timiriazev, dropped by one afternoon and heard Darwin declare unqualified support for the Tsarist war against Turkey. But months later, when Russia threatened to overstep her bounds and trench on English interests, Darwin toed Gladstone's neutral line: he endorsed a public 'Declaration against War' and put his name forward to collect signatures.[14]

Every month or two Emma still winkled him out of the study for a break, although it was getting harder. They missed their usual visit to Southampton this autumn – William, just engaged, received a gift of £300 – but a week at rustic Abinger on the North Downs made up for it. Wallace was living at Dorking, a few miles away, having had to sell his idyllic new house. Darwin avoided him. They were out of tune after the spiritual Slade trial, and hopelessly discordant over sexual selection. Wallace seemed as incorrigible as Mivart, though infinitely more pleasant. It was futile arguing with him on any 'difficult subject.' A reunion would have ruined the holiday, though Darwin phrased it more politely. 'I . . . wished to come over to see you, but driving tires me so much that my courage failed.'[15]

In November Darwin did trek to Cambridge, to be honoured. By now even his Alma Mater had come round. Here robed Darwinians taught, organized the new labs, and placed their protégés in posts, while Hooker and his fellow examiners taxed students on natural selection. Nothing was left but to capitulate and award Darwin an honorary Doctorate of Laws. On the day of the ceremony, Saturday the 17th, the Senate House was packed, everyone wanting to catch sight of the bearded sage. Undergraduates spilled out of the galleries, perched on statues, and stood in the windows. They strung a cord across the chamber and sent a monkey-marionette dangling above the waiting crowd. A Proctor climbed up and snatched it to antiphonal cheers and groans. Then a real 'missing link' appeared, a fat ring garnished with gaudy ribbons, which remained suspended in mid-air throughout the ceremony. Darwin was ushered in, robed in red, and a mighty roar went up from the students. He beamed back. The Vice-Chancellor followed in his scarlet and ermine gown and with two mace-bearers marched him up to the front, where he had taken his oath of matriculation fifty years before.

The Public Orator came forward and uttered his panegyric to occasional 'shouts and jeers.' 'Most unmannerly,' Emma hissed, sitting in the audience with Bessy and the boys, even if it was a 'tedious harangue.' Coral reefs, pigeons, fly-traps, barnacles, climbing plants, and volcanoes – all things Darwinian were decked in the purplest Latin prose. When the Orator paused for breath, a breezy voice in the crowd rang out, 'Thank you kindly,' which brought the house down. This was Cambridge still, rowdy but respectable; and the Orator, like the zealous Proctor, kept up the dialectic, distancing the dignitaries from 'the unlovely tribe of apes.' 'We may yet have the consolation of saying with the Roman orator, who was a great philosopher too, "Mores in utroques dispares"' – the moral nature of the two races is different.[16]

The ritual conferment followed, and afterwards feasts and celebrations. Emma had a headache, so Charles backed out of dinner with the Cambridge Philosophical Society, even though he was the guest of honour. Hooker could not attend, but laughably his new wife sent a bunch of bananas from Kew. Romanes and all the Darwin boys except William stood in to hear Huxley take the toast with a dulcet attack on the university for failing to honour Darwin twenty years earlier. On Sunday there was a 'brilliant luncheon' with George at Trinity College and guided tours of the new university buildings. Emma felt 'very grand walking about with my LL.D. in his silk gown.' She watched with amusement as wide-eyed dons met the renowned recluse. 'A strong ... looking man with iron grey hair,' marvelled the engineering professor James Stuart, who took Darwin around his workshop. He seemed to have been 'rough hewn from a rock with a heavy ... hammer.' He had an aura about him, like an ancient megalith, which cast Huxley and all the other celebrities 'into the shade.' 'A man of genius' this, 'indeed one of "the few".'[17]

Amy's death still haunted him. 'Life would be a most weary blank without a dear wife to love with all one's soul,' he told William's fiancée, Sara Sedgwick. The wedding at the end of November helped him to bury the past. Sara bashfully proclaimed herself 'so American,' but the Darwins loved her anyway, and they had already taken to her Boston brother-in-law, Charles Eliot Norton. She had an openness that Charles always admired about Americans, and a 'readiness to trust and confide' that made her presence like a balm.

The family settled in for a quiet winter, with Frank's baby Bernard – 'Abbadubba' – everyone's favourite. So possessive were the family that Charles complained of not seeing enough of him. The grown-up children appeared from time to time: George, studying mathematical astronomy beyond his father's ken, Leo, now teaching chemistry for the Royal Engineers at Chatham, and Henrietta, who stayed on beyond Christmas while her husband recuperated from appendicitis. In the drawing-room Litchfield catalogued all Emma's piano music, a grateful 'labour of love,' while across the corridor Charles and Frank toiled from morning to night on moving plants.[18]

This too was a labour of love. Spring turned the study into a pungent jungle, with seeds sprouting in biscuit tins on the chimneypiece, cabbages and runner beans in floor pots, and nasturtiums, cyclamens, cacti, and telegraph plants scattered on tables. Charles was in his element, infatuated with every rootlet and blossom. All these were his companions; he had a feeling for their 'aliveness.' He talked to them unselfconsciously, praising their ingenuity or twitting the 'little beggars' for 'doing just what I don't want them to.' Sometimes a flower caught his eye, and he would stroke it gently, childlike in his 'love for its delicate form & colour.' The plants moved him, like the romances Emma read aloud in the afternoons, and when the plants moved themselves they stirred him most of all.[19]

How did they do it? Alone in the Brazilian forest, he had felt the seething life, vines twisting, palms aquiver, snagging barbs dangling. In his study too the plants lassoed and grappled, but here he and Frank could catch them at it. They devised ways for mapping the movements and even making the plants perform. They grew seeds upside down and watched their root-tips hour-by-hour tracing minute zig-zags as they turned back to the ground. Faced by obstacles, the roots twisted to and fro, searching for the way. They tied up, tampered with, and tormented sprouts and found that the upward spiralling persisted, even in total darkness. Darwin at first thought that the zig-zags might be a response to vibration. But Frank's bumping the table, slamming doors, and serenading them on his bassoon proved that wrong. Every part of every plant was constantly and spontaneously on the move, in a continuous rhythmic rotation, or 'circumnutation,' as they called it.

At night they followed the sleeping movements, catching plants drooping or folding their leaves. And they proved that these were necessary for survival. By March 1878 he and Frank had killed dozens of plants by tying their leaves to prevent them from hanging or closing at night. They observed house plants, which slept only if left outside during the day, and tropical ones that did not need to sleep at all. A whole series of intricate experiments had led them to conclude that exposure was the critical factor. In every case the leaves adjusted spontaneously, protecting their upper surfaces.[20]

The work went on non-stop. 'I shan't be easy till I've tried it,' Charles would announce on dreaming up another 'fool's experiment.' To Frank it seemed 'as if an outside force were compelling him.' Needless to say, the strain proved too much – the old sickness set in. In March he saw Dr Clark in London about the attacks of dizziness, which were an 'intolerable bother.' The doctor's 'dry diet' left him panting for a 'wine-glass of water,' but it seemed to do good. Clark refused to charge his famous patient, so Darwin, flush as ever, sent £100 towards the development of a fungus-proof Irish potato – making sure first that the Belfast breeder in question was 'highly respectable.'

His old shipmate Sulivan, now Admiral of the Fleet, was less concerned with respectability, and more with savages. He wanted help in supporting an orphan, and all the *Beagle* officers were chipping in. Darwin obliged as always, struck with the civilizing successes of the South American mission. The boy was the grandson of Jemmy Button.[21]

Romanes was now Darwin's leading protégé. A dyed-in-the-wool Darwinian, he had worked with Hooker at Kew, backed Huxley on vivisection, and even impressed crusty Spencer with his work on the nervous reactions of jellyfish. Huxley, Hooker, and Darwin had him elected to the Linnean and Royal Societies. More than a high-flier, Romanes was a kowtowing convert, and little wonder. At Cambridge he had been an out-and-out evangelical. All the zeal of his prize-winning undergraduate essay *Christian Prayer and General Laws* was now laid on the altar of evolution. Darwin was his new deity.

Romanes shadowed his master, writing long letters and currying favour. His 'respect and affection' were genuine enough, and Darwin could not help but like him, for all his 'superficial faults.' He admired Romanes's brashness, his determination to test hopeless hypotheses, and he egged him on with his motto, 'It is dogged as does it!' The pangenesis experiments were flopping, but Darwin still offered his kitchen garden for onion graft trials. Spiritualism was another dead-end, Romanes having failed to settle 'between Ghost *versus* Goose.' Darwin welcomed his negative results with mediums, including the 'clever rogue' Williams, believing their deceptions to be 'wicked and scandalous.'[22]

But in private Romanes's new faith too was faltering. With his sister delirious on her deathbed that spring, he yearned for some assurance that they would meet again. He sought out an eminent spiritualist, one of the defence counsel in the Slade trial. It was a pathetic meeting. Romanes, looking 'terribly ill and cut up,' poured out his awful doubts. He wanted conviction, pleaded for facts, but went away empty-handed. Days later his sister died.[23] When Darwin heard the news he invited Romanes to Downe.

The situation was emotionally fraught. Four years since joining the Darwinian set, Romanes had reasoned himself into an unrealistic scepticism. His head belonged to evolution but his heart would not co-operate. He was a perambulating paradox, the embodiment of Charles's and Emma's dilemma. Darwin talked of his own moral outrage at the doctrine of eternal damnation. Christianity was no longer an option for either of them, but try as he would, Romanes simply could not believe in God and immortality either. To make matters worse he was courting, and soon to acquire a devout wife of his own. He asked Darwin's help.

It was the old 'frightfully difficult' problem of 'speaking out on religion.' In his first flush of evolutionary enthusiasm a couple of years earlier Romanes had penned a strident refutation of theism, but then followed Darwin's advice to pause. Now he felt driven to publish, certain of his convictions, sad perhaps, but eager for an audience. There was no stopping him, any more than the Doctor could once keep Charles from opening his heart to Emma. Darwin counselled him to publish anonymously, leaving the argument to be judged on its merit. It also helped, as Darwin knew, to think on the way religious reasoning had evolved. He turned over his notes and unused chapter on instinct from *Natural Selection*, launching Romanes on the study of comparative psychology.[24]

Darwin's prodding paid off, and Romanes was given a standing ovation for his talk on mental evolution at the British Association in August. In the absence of actual ancestors, *The Times* reported, he lined up an ugly ersatz collection of 'savages, young children, idiots, and uneducated deaf-mutes.' These dubious stand-ins seemed to show that 'man and brute have much more in common intellectually, and perhaps, even morally, than is dreamt of.' Each was 'arrested' at some lowly stage. Darwin savoured it all, especially the eulogium in the 'grand *finale*.' Try 'keeping a young monkey, so as to observe its mind,' he advised. Frank added a less than practical suggestion. 'Frank says you ought to keep an idiot, a deaf mute, a monkey, and a baby in your house!'

Idiots were unnecessary with the family offering its own throwbacks. Hensleigh daftly clung to spiritualism even though his favourite medium Williams was exposed as a charlatan in September. Even sillier, he now called Williams a charlatan *with* supernatural powers, and he claimed to have seen a ghost, dirty clothes and all, at one of Williams's séances. Is this not a 'psychological curiosity!' Darwin marvelled. He tried to expose Williams in the press in the hope that the story would snowball. He detested mediums, triflers with the transcendent. Imagine manipulating people's fear and grief for a handful of loose change![25]

In November Romanes, new book in hand, drove to the Litchfields, where Charles and Emma were staying. He introduced his fiancée, and presented them *A Candid Examination of Theism* by 'Physicus.' Darwin was not sanguine. One might as well try to 'illuminate the midnight sky with a candle' as throw the light of reason on metaphysics. But he agreed to browse it, and back home found that he could not put it down. Romanes was a tragic spirit. He had embraced the 'lonely mystery of existence' with the 'utmost sorrow,' more a convert to unbelief than Darwin ever was. The universe without God had 'lost its soul of loveliness,' and the biblical precept to 'work while it is day' took on a frightful force from its closing words, 'the night cometh when no man can work.' Philosophy had become 'a meditation, not merely of death, but of annihilation.'

Darwin rushed a note to Romanes. His tolerance for religious literature was low, but he had read *Candid Examination* with 'very great interest.' Not that it convinced him. Romanes's arguments did not rule out God creating matter and energy at the beginning of the universe with a propensity to organize and evolve. Nor was it necessarily 'more *human*' to doubt God's existence, just because this seemed more 'rational.' If theism is true, 'reason may not be the only instrument for ascertaining its truth.' Our instinctive feelings might point to heaven – though who could say? But Romanes, just engaged, was in an '"idiotic" state of mind,' unfit to ponder imponderables. 'You will wish me at the Devil for bothering you,' Darwin apologized, tucking a photo of himself in the letter for 'the future Mrs Romanes.'[26]

The world wanted to know Darwin's religious views. With public honours showering on him, he had entered his Delphic Oracle phase. The audacity of the sermon-senders, the evangelists, and the spiritual Peeping Toms was excruciating. 'Half the fools throughout Europe write to ask me the stupidest questions,' he groaned. He sometimes managed a terse retort – 'I am sorry to have to inform you that I do not believe in the Bible as a divine revelation, & therefore not in

Jesus Christ as the Son of God' – or infrequently a guarded response, especially if his interlocutor was eminent.[27]

No, he answered a young count studying with Haeckel, he did not 'believe that there ever has been any Revelation. As for a future life, every man must judge for himself between conflicting vague probabilities.' No, he responded to the prelate E. B. Pusey's sermon, the *Origin* had no 'relation whatever to Theology,' although when he wrote it his own 'belief in what is called a personal God was as firm as that of Dr. Pusey himself.' No, he stonewalled the Archbishop of Canterbury, he would not attend a 'Private Conference' of devout scientists at Lambeth Palace to harmonize science and religion, for he could 'see no prospect of any benefit arising' from it.

Dodges and denials were safer than declarations. He was unwilling to be drawn or exposed. Huxley might bait bishops, Tyndall might indulge in pantheistic pyrotechnics, and he would cheer them for it. But he intended to keep the peace – to his vicar's applause. Brodie Innes (who had sent Pusey's sermon) deplored the 'unwise and violent' theological attacks on the amiable sickly squire. They were opposed on most things except the parish, and Innes had some inkling of his friend's contempt for Christianity. And yet, he smiled, 'How nicely things would go on if other folk were like Darwin and Brodie Innes.'[28]

What Charles actually believed was of 'no consequence to any one but myself.' Outside Down House, only Eras and a few intimates knew. Only *The Index* in America carried his endorsement of a creed. But in early 1879 he did open up a little more as he turned his hand to family history.

It began with a glowing essay on his grandfather Erasmus. This appeared in the German scientific periodical *Kosmos* as a seventieth-birthday tribute to Charles. In March he arranged with the author, Ernst Krause, for it to be translated in book form, enabling him to add a biographical preface. Setting his grandfather's record straight was urgent now, with the appearance of Samuel Butler's wretched *Evolution Old and New* – which elevated old Erasmus to the head of the Darwinian pantheon and threw out the *Origin* as an 'intellectual sleight-of-hand.' Charles sent Butler's book to Krause, urging him not to 'expend much powder and shot' on it, as Butler knew no science.

He set into the biography with gusto. Rummaging through dusty letters and manuscripts, he was almost 'having communion with the dead.' By May old Erasmus had materialized on his side. Not that his science was much use, too wildly theoretical. But they shared a larger social and evolutionary world view. Erasmus was a humanitarian liberal, devoted to educational reform and technological advance. His intellectual and moral qualities were outstanding, and he too was traduced as a radical atheist. It was reassuring.[29]

Fortified, Charles returned to his own biography, which had lain fallow for three years. He scribbled fond notes about his father: his prodigious powers of observation and memory, and his marvellous business sense. He 'formed a theory for almost everything,' though his mind was not strictly scientific; and his sympathy and sagacity made him a moral beacon for his sons. Charles recalled especially his father's ways with women, how he handled their emotions, and his premarital advice about concealing religious doubts – good advice as it turned out. Too often wives agonized over the salvation of their freethinking husbands, causing them to suffer in turn.

Charles saw no salvation and suffered for it. Now he absolved himself on paper. As one with 'no assured and ever present belief in the existence of a personal God or of a future existence with retribution and reward,' he had not lived in fear of divine wrath. Instead he had followed his inherited 'social instincts' with a clear conscience. A freethinking Darwin ancestry had left him with neither moral obliquity nor guilt. 'I feel no remorse from having committed any great sin,' he assured Emma and the family. 'I believe that I have acted rightly in steadily following and devoting my life to science.'

As he wrote, another prying letter came. Did he believe in God? Were theism and evolution compatible? He replied that a man undoubtedly can be 'an ardent Theist & an evolutionist,' look at Charles Kingsley and Asa Gray. For himself, he had 'never been an atheist in the sense of denying the existence of a God,' but he still felt profoundly uncertain. If he had to wear a label, Huxley's suited better. 'I think that generally (& more & more as I grow older), but not always, that an agnostic would be the most correct description of my state of mind.'[30] Even if, in his clear-headed confusion, he was agnostic about his agnosticism on occasions, in ten years it had become the respectable thing.

Biography was not his *forte*. The sketch of his grandfather was hard enough. It was terminally boring, and he mutilated proofs all summer. It was worse than that, Henrietta said, too long and too frank. While Krause tinkered with the German text, she snipped at her father's, removing the religiously *risqué*. John Murray was the only one satisfied with the end-product, and he offered to issue 1000 copies of

Erasmus Darwin on spec and split the profits. Charles, feeling a 'perfect fool' for taking on the job, swore 'never again' to be 'tempted out of my proper work.'[31]

42

Down Among the Worms

HE WAS TIRING faster now and resigned to it, though still working hard at shoots and roots for several hours a day. 'I have nothing else to do,' he sighed to his old *Beagle* shipmate Admiral Sulivan, 'and whether one is worn out a year or two sooner or later signifies but little.' Emma, spry as ever, kept an eye on him. Without her supervision he would work himself to death.

She dragged him to Dorking for a weekend in June 1879 and in August joined forces with the Litchfields to haul him to the Lake District for a month.[1] Having recovered his 'horrid sinking feeling' at leaving home, Charles enjoyed himself. They made their headquarters at the Waterhead Hotel on Coniston Water, and took trips to Furness Abbey and Grasmere. Several times they crossed the lake to meet Litchfield's friend from the Working Men's College, John Ruskin.

Ruskin had just retired from the Slade Professorship at Oxford and settled into Brantwood Cottage, to concentrate on his art. Darwinism was nonsense to him, so much gratuitous conflict, but he greeted 'Sir Charles' with politeness and gave him a tour of the Turners in his bedroom. Darwin did his best to screw up interest. He could make 'absolutely nothing of what Ruskin saw' in the paintings, although he disliked a Titian, for which his host was 'very glad.' Then the bedroom conversation turned delicately to sexual selection, with talk of peacocks, primates, and courtship. When the party left Ruskin chased them with some fine studies of peacock's feathers, hardly appreciating how sick the furore about such objects made his guest. The prickliness cut both ways. Ruskin's sexual difficulties – his failure to consummate his marriage after the appalling discovery that his young bride had pubic hair – rather flavour his observation that

638

Darwin had a 'deep & tender interest' in the 'brightly coloured hinder half of certain monkeys.' He was right, Darwin laughed on hearing it.[2]

Haeckel came to Downe when they returned and wore Darwin out by *'roaring'* for an hour about the freedom of science. Even if foppish Litchfield found 'something pleasant in his . . . exuberant muscularity,' Emma was not so sure. Charles retreated to his blessedly silent plants. He hired another gardener, and fretted over the Belfast potato trials, on which he had lavished £100 the previous year. The breeder was now in 'much distress,' with all his work in jeopardy. Maybe the Board of Trade would come up with money to help feed the Irish? He approached the Permanent Secretary, 'Theta' Farrer – Effie Wedgwood's husband – but to no avail. It was 'very difficult for Ministers to decide what to do in such cases,' Theta prevaricated; they were always meeting 'cavillers in the H[ouse]. of Commons.' Charles fumed at the way 'politicians waste their time squabbling and neglect doing any good.'[3]

In truth, Farrer's thoughts were elsewhere. With only one daughter (from his first marriage) he was determined to see her well matched. Ida had fallen for Horace, the youngest and feeblest of the Darwin boys. He had a mechanical bent but no career, and was still kicking around machine shops, living on an allowance. His prospects looked dismal, or so Theta had whispered loudly from the time Horace and Ida first mooted an engagement. Ida was too good for him. Her father, a worldly man – Eton, Balliol, Lincoln's Inn – had hoped for a banker or barrister. A sickly, unsuccessful Darwin would not do.

Emma and Charles felt 'terrible,' the Hensleighs were embarrassed, and the besotted couple adamant. But they had their way and before Christmas the marriage settlement was reached. Darwin assured Farrer that his son would inherit enough to retire on comfortably, and he gave Horace £5000 of railway stock as proof. The wedding took place on 3 January 1880 at St Mary's, Bryanston Square, in London, next door to the Litchfields. But the relations remained frosty, and at the reception the families were still not speaking to one another.[4]

More petty tempests were in store. Frank, now serving on the Downe school committee, was embroiled in a bid to oust Ffinden as chairman. The vicar did not go quietly. As the *'legally* constituted head' of the parish, Frank heard, he would not deign to serve under another's authority. Nor was it 'a becoming part of a Priest's Office "to serve tables," if you can understand what I mean as a High Churchman.' Democracy was too much for Ffinden, and he tendered his resignation from the committee. For spite, he sent the note to Frank's father.[5] This grated, but Emma and Bessy had long worshipped at the neighbouring parish of Keston.

Priests might lie like strangled snakes beside the cradle of Hercules, but new enemies were rising as if sown from dragon's teeth. Apostates worried Darwin most, those disciples-turned-enemies: Mivart, and now Samuel Butler. And it did not help to imagine these ostracized evolutionists hobnobbing together. 'Have you read Butler's *"Evolution Old & New"*?' Mivart asked Owen. 'There is method in his madness & it will I think help to burst the inflated bubble of "Natural Selection".'[6] Owen, Mivart, and Butler now constituted the demonic Trinity.

Samuel Butler was the grandson of Darwin's old Shrewsbury headmaster. His father had been at Cambridge with Darwin, preparing for holy orders, and had joined his beetling expeditions. Destined himself for the Church, Butler had read the *Origin* and become a devout Darwinian and an unbeliever. His anonymous novels, *Erewhon*, an anti-Christian satire, and *The Fair Haven*, a sly attack on the Resurrection, had won Darwin's praise. He had visited Downe twice, dined with Charles and Eras in London, and even helped with illustrations for the *Expression* book. But Mivart's dissenting *Genesis of Species* left him disillusioned with natural selection, and the materialists' exploitation alienated him further: 'It is not the bishops and archbishops I am afraid of,' Butler admitted. 'Men like Huxley and Tyndall are my natural enemies.' He re-read the *Origin* and moved rapidly away, convinced that Darwin had humbugged the world by slighting his evolutionary predecessors, whose cause he espoused in *Evolution Old and New*. It was to set the record straight, to place Dr Erasmus Darwin over his degenerate grandson, to propose that mind is the moving force in nature, not matter. Life evolves consciously through changing habits, he insisted, not mechanically through natural selection.[7]

Butler was primed to take *Erasmus Darwin* personally. And not surprisingly; in his preface Darwin vouched for the accuracy of the translation of Krause's article. He indicated that it had come out in German *before* publication of *Evolution Old and New*. But Butler pointed to passages in translation that could only have been written *after* his book – including a dismissal of attempts to rehabilitate Erasmus as showing 'a weakness of thought and a mental anachronism which no one can envy.' Darwin admitted that Krause had revised his German text before translation, 'so common a practice' that it had not seemed worth mentioning. Butler took this to mean that the affront had been deliberate. He protested to the *Athenaeum* (once the home of vitriolic anti-Darwinism) that Darwin had disguised a condemnation of *Evolution Old and New*, putting the words into the mouth of an 'unbiassed' third party.[8]

Emma fulminated at Butler's 'odious spiteful letter.' Charles hated it. Ignorant theological attacks he could bear, but to be accused of 'duplicity and falsehood' before the literary world was too much. He would as soon be known as an atheist or neo-Malthusian. It sent him into a tailspin of tortured self-acquittal. For a week in February he drafted replies, posting them to the family for advice. Nobody liked the first, opinion was divided on the second, and Litchfield's legal advice was to forget Butler altogether. It would bring about '*exactly* the result he most wants . . . a "Butler-Darwin affaire" as the French w[oul]d say.' Huxley agreed, suspecting that Mivart had 'bitten him and given him Darwinophobia.' 'Its a horrid disease and I would kill any son of a [bitch] I found running loose with it.'

Suffocation by silence was the answer. Darwin took Huxley's advice, thankful to be spared the agony of self-defence. 'I feel like a man condemned to be hung who has just got a reprieve,' he exhaled wearily. Butler naturally felt like one of his pre-Darwinian evolutionists, deliberately ignored. To him Darwin's silence was a tacit admission of guilt.[9]

Spring 1880 brought a sad reminder that a generation was passing. Word came of Josiah's death. Emma's brother was eighty-five. No man with a 'sweeter disposition' ever lived, Charles consoled Hensleigh. Emma missed her brother's funeral because Charles was feeling under the weather. He was not well enough to see Fox buried either. They had drifted apart over the decades, but were sustained by vivid memories. Charles looked up from his *Movement in Plants* manuscript, closed his eyes, and travelled back fifty years. He pictured Fox's 'bright face, so full of intelligence,' at their breakfasts in Christ's – he could even make out his cousin's voice 'as clearly as if he were present' in the study.[10]

Time had to be passing for Huxley to title his Royal Institution talk 'The Coming of Age of the Origin of Species.' Had twenty-one years passed since the *Origin*'s publication? Charles thought that the title referred to 'the maturity of the subject' until Emma tipped him off. Of course Huxley was presenting the key of science's door to Darwin. It was propaganda, and as such a fair piece of distortion, which argued that 'great and sudden physical revolutions, wholesale creations and extinctions' had been the order of the day in 1859

641

before the *Origin*. (They had not; Owen had advanced the world dramatically by the 1850s with his uniform continuous creation.) It was the bulldog at his best. Charles read the reports on holiday at Abinger with the Farrers. With the families speaking to one another again, he chortled to Theta about the press coverage. Then he read the text. It was a distortion in more insidious ways. His great leading idea – natural selection – the theory that he had given half his life to, was not even mentioned.

Huxley had always been non-committal about selection. Now Mivart and other critics were winning. It was ignominiously jettisoned, an impediment to a belief in the actual 'fact of evolution.' The bulldog's tail should have been between his legs. Darwin admitted that he sometimes saw natural selection 'of quite subordinate importance.' At others, when he discovered the survival-value of some 'useless' part of a plant, he knew that it was all-pervasive. But never for a moment had he doubted that his 'deity "Natural Selection"' existed at all. He was sad that true believers were so few. He had turned the world to evolution, and practically no one to natural selection, not even his champions.[11]

Much the best news in April was the Tories' crushing defeat after Gladstone's brilliant campaign. At seventy Gladstone launched his second ministry as a moral crusade; the Union Jack flew for all humanity, in Egypt and the Transvaal, in Ireland and the Middle East. 'Mercy and profits had met together, economy and peace had kissed.' Emma and Charles were ecstatic, despite the boys' waywardness. Frank 'hardly cares,' Emma shrugged. 'George cares a little the wrong way,' and the Litchfields' opinions were 'diametrically opposite.' But she and Charles had the country behind them and Aunt Elizabeth in the village shared their 'mental champagne.' Charles, buoyed by the Liberal tide, sent a large subscription to Abbot's 'excellent Journal' *The Index*, 'most heartily' wishing him success in his 'admirable endeavours in the good cause of truth.'[12] 'Free religion' was still the Darwin creed.

But Liberalism had limits. On the extreme edge of the party Bradlaugh was finally elected MP for Northampton. After losing the Knowlton trial, his mastery of legal procedure kept him and Besant out of prison, but it had done nothing to redeem his reputation. The Christian nation now faced the prospect of an avowed atheist and convicted purveyor of obscenity swearing on the Bible in order to take his seat in the House of Commons. MPs erupted at the outrage. Every trick of parliamentary procedure was used to exclude Bradlaugh. He was forbidden to take the oath of allegiance, which referred to God, and prevented from 'affirming' like Quakers. Atheists were by nature immoral; their word meant nothing, the Commons could not accommodate them. Northampton would have to vote again – responsibly.

By the end of May atheism was a burning political issue. Select committees were smouldering, the press fanned the flames, and 'Bradlaugh' was a household word. Secularists pitched into the fray. Edward Aveling, a young anatomy lecturer and popularizer of evolution, had joined up with Besant (in more ways than one, though both were married) and they stumped the country, haranguing crowds about Christian hypocrisy and the curtailment of civil liberties. Aveling wrote for Bradlaugh's paper, the *National Reformer*. In fact he was running a series on 'Darwin and His Works' when the parliamentary struggle began, a continuation of articles he had published in a student magazine two years before. Darwin had written to thank Aveling for these first offerings and asked to see future instalments.[13]

That was two years earlier. Now Darwin was worried that his letter to the newly-prominent Aveling would return to haunt him – scruffy infidels of dubious morality were not above printing private correspondence. For a gentleman of the parish, public association with these reprobates was intolerable. He was taking no risks. He packed *Movement in Plants* off to Murray and went to William and Sara's in Southampton at the beginning of June. He talked with William about the freethought *Index*, supposedly safe from prying English eyes in America. They both read it avidly but agreed that after nine years – with the English papers now kicking up a pother about atheism – Charles's weekly endorsement of Abbot's *Truths for the Times* should be scrubbed. It could be appropriated by these English headline-grabbers and republished in Britain. Charles, having just sent Abbot a generous subscription, found it a bit embarrassing, so William took on the task. He posted a letter, larded with cordiality, but he blundered in stating that 'My Father . . . had no intention that his words should be used for this purpose.' The words had of course been sent expressly as advertising copy – Abbot held the proof.[14] But Abbot complied anyway.

At Downe work was piling up, but Charles liked it that way. Worms were his chief occupation again, and he co-opted the family, even having Theta send soil samples from Abinger's Roman ruins to make up for his mud-slinging. He was inundated in requests for advice, and loans, and audiences. It was nothing to donate £25 to a Birmingham committee as a prize to encourage local research, or welcome the Lewisham and Blackheath Scientific Association to Down House. But his work came first, Emma made sure of it. After forty years his priorities had become her own, and 'if it was a condition of his living, that he sh[oul]d do no work, she was willing for him to die.'[15]

By August he needed a break, and Horace and Ida, settled in Cambridge, invited them. For the old man the trip was daunting. With no command performance to galvanize him, no silk gown in store, he started niggling about the seventy-mile ride. A panic started at the prospect of negotiating London's tumultuous train stations. So Emma planned a piece of unadulterated luxury. She and the boys booked a special railway carriage for him to travel in style. Here he could remain with his entourage, without changing, like the Queen on her sweeps through the country. On the day, he royally got on at Bromley, six miles away, and at London's Victoria Station his carriage was shunted across town to the Cambridge line out of King's Cross. They sat in plush first-class comfort, watching the slums and gasometers pass by. So unfamiliar now was Emma with the city that she even mistook 'some small church' for St Paul's Cathedral.

The trip was set off by a leisurely week in Cambridge, being shown the latest sights by Horace and his 'charming wife.' Emma heard the organ at Trinity Chapel and had a private demonstration of the stops. Charles took her arm-in-arm through the courts of St John's to admire the gothic 'grandeur' of King's College Chapel, which reminded him disgracefully of old Herbert and the Gluttons. Cambridge still played hard, drank long, and dodged the Proctors – the new women's colleges notwithstanding. Everywhere Charles gazed wistfully on 'scenes of my early life,' half-suspecting that this would be his last view.

At home in September he polished off the proofs of *Movement in Plants*, a gargantuan job. With 600 pages and 196 wood-cuts, it was his largest botany book and, he suspected, as dull as ditchwater. 'I am turned into a sort of machine for observing facts & grinding out conclusions,' he was heard to sigh. Never mind, he arranged for a German translation and set into the next book, on the homely earthworm. Meanwhile the correspondence mounted – facts to file, honours to acknowledge, invitations to refuse – and he dashed off a half-dozen replies most afternoons, seated in a huge horse-hair chair by the fire.[16]

On 13 October the letter he feared arrived, Aveling's. He had not forgotten Darwin's encouragement. Aveling was collecting his evolution articles from the *National Reformer* into a book and asked permission to dedicate it to Darwin. It was to appear in the 'International Library of Science and Freethought' under the editorship of 'my friends Mrs. Annie Besant and Charles Bradlaugh, M.P.' Enclosed was Besant's translation of a pamphlet by the German physician Ludwig Büchner (whose fierce materialist literature was already on Darwin's shelves), with an advert explaining that the aim of the Library was to 'spread heresy' among the English 'reading masses.'

Heresy was nothing new. The *Origin* and *Descent* had spread it politely for years. What set off a tremor was the company he would be keeping. He replied by return, a four-page letter marked conspicuously 'Private.' No, he would not permit the dedication, 'though I thank you for the intended honour.' It would imply 'to a certain extent my approval of the general publication,' the International Library – 'about which I know nothing,' Darwin dissembled, knowing the editors full well.

> Moreover though I am a strong advocate for free thought on all subjects, yet it appears to me (whether rightly or wrongly) that direct arguments against christianity & theism produce hardly any effect on the public; & freedom of thought is best promoted by the gradual illumination of men's minds, which follow[s] from the advance of science. It has, therefore, been always my object to avoid writing on religion, & I have confined myself to science. I may, however, have been unduly biassed by the pain which it would give some members of my family, if I aided in any way direct attacks on religion.

Here spoke one who had been hand in glove with Christians all his life, one whose entire well-being depended on his devout wife and daughters. 'Gradual illumination' had always been his luxury, religious reticence his practice. Now even Aveling's proofs were too hot to handle. 'I am old & have very little strength, & looking over proof-sheets (as I know by present experience) fatigues me much.' He was still his own man.[17]

That autumn life began closing in as he saw his relatives failing. Sister Caroline at Leith Hill was plagued by heart trouble and crippled with arthritis. She welcomed him and Emma for a visit but found it difficult to cope. Fanny Wedgwood too had a heart condition, although when they visited Ras she still came trundling down Queen Anne Street in a bath chair to hold his hand at tea. Ras himself was poorly. His effete existence had gone on too long. Time and opium had ravaged him and he was in constant pain, scarcely able to leave home. Emma's last sister, the tiny hunchback Elizabeth, also kept indoors, blind and mostly bedridden. Her bent figure, tottering around on a stick, had been a fixture in Downe for a dozen years, but now she lay in Trowmer Lodge, wizened and forlorn, her servants driving off the 'beggars and imposters' who sought to tap her Wedgwood wealth. She died on Sunday, 7 November, aged eighty-five. A small family circle gathered in the churchyard to hear the Revd Ffinden read the burial service. Emma took it calmly, feeling 'nothing but joy' at Elizabeth's release.

Natural selection continued under a barrage of criticism, and Mivart's ghost hovered about the zoological report of the government's latest scientific circumnavigation, conducted by Sir Wyville Thomson. Thomson, knighted for his efforts aboard HMS *Challenger* (an honour that Darwin would have loved), made a point of slighting 'the theory which refers the evolution of species to extreme variation guided only by natural selection.' Darwin was wounded, and let it show. 'Can Sir Wyville Thomson name any one who has said that the evolution of species depends only on natural selection?' he seethed in a letter to *Nature*. No one had paraded such a plethora of additional causes as himself in the *Variation of Animals*, including 'the effects of the use and disuse of parts' and of the 'direct action of external conditions.' Evolution was a multi-causal affair; he had admitted it. These crude caricatures would not do. Thomson's was 'a standard of criticism not uncommonly reached by theologians and metaphysicians, when they write on scientific subjects.' Darwin was tempted to use 'irreverent language,' and only Huxley stopped him swearing.[18]

Through the carping and cavilling Darwin continued to shower patronage. Wallace was still out of a job, his meagre investments drying up in the depression, and he had moved to Croydon to find a day school for his two children. On a fixed income of about £60 a year with tiny supplements from his writing, he had barely enough to support his family 'in the most economical way.' It was a source of 'ever-increasing anxiety,' and some embarrassment to a naturalist in his fifties. A year earlier, when the superintendency of Epping Forest eluded him, despite support from Darwin, Hooker, and Lubbock, he had become so depressed that his friend Arabella Buckley, Lyell's old secretary, pleaded for him. She asked Darwin whether some 'modest work' might not be found.

Darwin thought of a Crown pension, in recognition of Wallace's services to natural history. Hooker pooh-poohed it. Wallace had 'lost

caste terribly,' both for his spiritualism and for dishonourably pocket-
ing a bet won from a rich flat-earth fanatic for proving that the
planet was a globe. (Litigation over the case had dragged on for a
decade, costing Wallace the entire £500 and more.) Anyway, Hooker
jabbed, 'a man not in absolute poverty has little chance,' and 'Wallace's claim is not that he is in need, so much as that he can't find
employment.' Darwin caved in – Wallace's misdemeanours had 'never
once' crossed his mind – and he informed Buckley it was hopeless.[19]

He may have cringed at Wallace's credulity and 'quite doubted' his
scientific sanity – indeed, Romanes had returned from his first visit
to Wallace laughing that he was 'rather queer on . . . astrology' – but
Darwin never forgot Wallace's magnanimity over natural selection.
Now, in November, there was a further reason to reopen the pension
file. Wallace's 'best book' to date, *Island Life*, was acclaimed by the
critics. The incongruity struck Hooker: 'that such a man should be a
Spiritualist is more wonderful than all the movements of all the
plants.' Hooker thought the book 'splendid,' as well he might, for it
was dedicated to him. Darwin seized the moment. He knew that
Lubbock was on his side, another admirer of Wallace's 'characteristic
unselfishness;' he won Huxley over and they twisted Hooker's arm.
Huxley took the case to fellow X Clubber, William Spottiswoode,
President of the Royal Society, who drafted a request to Gladstone.
Having entertained Gladstone at Downe, Darwin even anticipated
returning the honour. He had 'seldom wished for anything so much'
as the pension to be granted and would 'gladly come to London' and
present the petition in person at 10 Downing Street.[20]

He composed his own moving testimonial, pointing up Wallace's
'love of natural history,' his jobless situation, failed investments,
pitiful return on his publications, and his weak health caused by
'tropical exposure.' (And there, but for the grace of God and a family
fortune, went Charles.) The final draft was ready before Christmas,
and he collected signatures feverishly. Emma saw him 'so full of
Wallace's affair [that] he has no time for his own,' referring to his
worm book. The memorial had to reach Gladstone before Parliament
reopened in the new year. While Emma did the annual accounts over
the holidays, Charles enlisted his old sparring partner on the 'beauty'
question, the Duke of Argyll, ex-Secretary of State for India. His
Grace urged the Prime Minister to assent, and the memorial reached
the Grand Old Man in the first week of January 1881. Twelve
Darwinians good and true had signed.

Before the Queen's Speech on the 6th, Gladstone wrote to Darwin
that he would recommend Wallace for a modest civil list pension of

£200 a year, backdated six months. An overjoyed Darwin relayed the news to Wallace on his fifty-eighth birthday, and tutored him in the proprieties of returning thanks.

As Wallace received his £200, Emma finished the family accounts, allowing Charles to distribute the surplus from the year's £8000 investment income to the children.[21]

Still old controversies returned to haunt him. Butler had been busy rewriting history, like Huxley, only portraying himself and other evolutionists as the victims of a Darwinian conspiracy. His *Unconscious Memory* repeated the charges against Darwin – 'duplicity and falsehood' – and compounded the injury by printing their private correspondence about old Erasmus's biography.

Darwin writhed while the family wrangled. The boys wanted an explanatory slip inserted in the unsold copies of *Erasmus Darwin* stating that the German text had been altered in translation. (They now realized that Krause had actually borrowed whole passages from Butler.) But the Litchfields cautioned silence. Their friend Leslie Stephen, editor of the *Cornhill Magazine*, an uncassocked clergyman who had lost his faith as a result of the *Origin* and now 'admired Darwin as a god,' arbitrated and settled the matter: silence was the very 'slap in the face' that Butler deserved. But one 'scientific son' was not bound by the family's compunctions. Romanes, knowing Darwin's feelings, administered a loud slap in public. Now living with a monkey in his nursery, he was an authority on lesser intelligences. Butler was a 'psychological curiosity' to Darwin, but to Romanes he was a 'lunatic beneath all contempt – an object of pity were it not for his vein of malice.' 'Punishment' was due, and he dished it out in *Nature*, arraigning Butler as a character assassin.[22]

Charles returned to more dignified subjects, worms and pigs, which were easier to deal with. Swine disease was rife around the village and a strict quarantine in force. Snowed in at Downe, he had to issue a magistrate's order daily just to allow farmers to move their animals across the road. He felt the burden of public responsiblity more than ever as the days ticked by. 'My life is as regular & monotonous as a clock,' he droned to Kovalevsky, thanking him for a huge box of Russian tea. 'I make sure, but wofully [sic] slow progress, with my new book.'[23]

The twilight years brought back strange memories. Late in February Charles went to town with Emma, staying with the Litchfields. Charles had heard from Sarah, one of the Owens of his Woodhouse youth, that her sister Fanny was living in town, now seventy and a widow. He hoped for a short reunion, maybe their last. More august first-time visits were arranged on this trip. He called on the Duke of Argyll, a critic for so many years. The butler ushered him into Argyll House where the Duke welcomed him warmly and accepted his heartfelt thanks for assisting Wallace. There were political talking-points aplenty – the conflict in the Transvaal, land reform in Ireland, Gladstone's health after a fall in Downing Street – and they had a long and 'awfully friendly' discussion. The Duke was 'not at all cocky,' as Darwin had feared, but inevitably the talk swung to religion.

Sitting before Argyll was the man who had convulsed English science, who had made beasts of men and taken Mind out of nature. Argyll, like everyone, wanted to know what the sage of Downe really believed. He harked back a dozen years, picking up the threads of tattered debates. Orchids and their wonderful design: did Darwin really suppose them a chance evolution? Surely now, Argyll insinu-ated, it was 'impossible to look at these without seeing that they were the effect and the expression of Mind'? Darwin looked at him 'very hard' before replying. Yes, he could see how this view might have 'overwhelming force.'[24] But, he shook his head gravely, he could no longer accept it.

Back at Downe Darwin did see a million individual minds at work – or, to be precise, 53,767 per acre. Worms were clever creatures, how so he was beginning to find out. He experimented indoors, in the new billiard room, now turned into his study to make more space. Worms littered it, triturating through earth in glass-covered pots. Darwin stumbled around at night and flashed lights at them – candles, paraffin lamps, and even lanterns with red and blue slides. Only an intense beam brought a reflex response, when they bolted – 'like a rabbit' lisped Bernard – into their burrows. Heat made little difference, even a red-hot poker held near by. Nor were they sensitive to sound. Bernard blew a whistle, Frank played his bassoon, Emma performed on the piano, and Bessy shouted, but no worms were roused. Touch was different – a puff of breath sent them into headlong retreat. Charles tested for their sense of smell by exhaling gently into the pots while chewing tobacco or sucking on scented cotton wool. Their culinary sense was assessed and their preferences determined – green to red cabbage, celery to both of these, and raw carrots above all.

What struck him most was their mentality. They seemed to 'enjoy the pleasure of eating,' judging from their 'eagerness for certain kinds of food,' and their sexual passion was 'strong enough to overcome

... their dread of light.' He even found 'a trace of social feeling,' for they tolerated 'crawling over each other's bodies' and touching. He observed how they dragged leaves into their burrows. The habit was instinctive, but what of the technique? All sorts of leaves were tried, and finally triangular slips of stiff paper. Digging the objects out of the burrows, he discovered that the great majority had been pulled in the easiest way, by their narrower end or apex. It was clearly not a trial-and-error learning process. Worms somehow acquired a 'notion, however rude, of the shape of an object,' probably by 'touching it in many places' with their bodies. This heightened sense was like that of 'a man ... born blind and deaf.' It enabled them to solve geometrical problems. Intelligence was there.[25]

Not quite Argyll's notion of supramundane intelligence, but then more earthy matters had preoccupied Darwin for fifty years. He retired to write the last chapters of *The Formation of Vegetable Mould through the Action of Worms.* It would be 'a small book of little moment,' he told Victor Carus in mid-March, and certainly his last. 'I have little strength & feel very old.'

As he finished, the vivisection debate boiled up again and he fired off letters to *The Times.* Cobbe was in the thick of it, as he knew women always were. They committed a 'crime against mankind' by retarding the 'progress of physiology.' They were too soft on suffering, too squeamish about death. Death now entered his thoughts as he stared into his pots of dirt. The old worm was turning as he contemplated the endless sculpting of the earth's surface by myriad slimy, semi-intelligent beings. Worms buried and preserved our past, like Theta's ruins at Abinger. They ploughed farmers' fields, as Uncle Jos first mooted at Maer. We 'ought to be grateful' to them. And they bore into the earth 'five or six feet,' even 'here at Down,' at which depth he expected to be consumed soon.[26]

Darwin packed the manuscript up on the weekend before Easter and found himself at a loose end. He had no 'heart or strength ... to begin any investigation lasting for years,' which was all he really enjoyed. 'Never happy except when at work,' he was facing his first fortnight in a quarter-century without a manuscript to complete.

Then he remembered his autobiography. With Ida and Horace expecting a baby there was another reason to leave a good record. After Easter he picked up the pieces, inserting his notes about his father and reworking the passages on religion. He thought of Emma and their religious differences. Her anxiety lest they should not 'belong to each other forever' had made him suffer, just as the

Doctor had predicted, and now he was sorry. At the end he slipped in a coded reminder to Emma – a date. Beside the paragraph with his father's advice about concealing doubts he jotted, 'copied out Ap[ri]l 22, 1881.'[27]

It was the Friday of Easter week, thirty years to the day since Annie was laid in the Priory Churchyard at Malvern. Whenever he pictured her beaming face, 'her sparkling eyes & brindled smiles,' her 'dear lips' and kisses, her 'crying bitterly . . . on parting with Emma,' his emotions would overflow.[28] Now, looking over his autobiography for the last time, he had her daguerreotype beside him. He read on – of Emma, his 'wise adviser and cheerful comforter,' of her 'beautiful letter' to him after their marriage, of their grief, and Annie's 'sweet ways.' He had written these words as if he were 'a dead man . . . looking back.' Emma would be left behind, still longing for a reunion. He was helpless to reassure her, to ease her pain.

Tears were flowing again – tears at the thought of their parting, the tears that Annie had shed, kissing her mother goodbye before going to die. He reached for Emma's beautiful old letter, preserved with the other mementos beside his manuscript. He read again of her fears for him, and her undying love. Dwelling a moment on Annie's face, he scratched miserably at the bottom, 'When I am dead, know that many times, I have kissed & cryed over this.'[29] It was the only comfort that he could give.

43

The Final Experiment

HIS REASON FOR LIVING was gone. Without a fresh mountain of facts to conquer, without a new experimental odyssey to embark on, nothing seemed worthwhile. One look at the proofs of *Worms* and he passed the pile to Frank, unable to face the revisions. He turned down Gladstone's invitation to become a Trustee of the British Museum. He listened to Hans Richter at Emma's piano, but even the visiting conductor of the Vienna Opera, who had taken London by storm, only roused him for an hour. Charles gritted his teeth and pulled up plants to look at the cell-structure of their roots. It was paltry work compared to barnacles, species, and flowers but it helped fend off despondency.

At the start of June Emma and the Litchfields took him to the Lake District. With Bernard and William along, it should have been a happy family time, cosy in a big house on Ullswater. But Charles brought his troubles. Bernard's cavorting and the lakeside strolls with Emma did little good, nor the stunning scenery. The weather was bitter, the sky 'like lead,' and the lake 'as black as ink.' An attempt to climb left spots before his eyes; almost fainting, he stumbled back down and they called a doctor. He diagnosed angina, called his heart condition 'precarious,' and ordered relaxation, not mountain climbing. 'Idleness is downright misery to me,' Darwin groaned to Hooker. 'I cannot forget my discomfort for an hour' and 'must look forward to Down graveyard as the sweetest place on earth.'[1]

The unlikeliest 400-page tome perked him up, *The Creed of Science*, by the Irish philosopher William Graham. Housebound, he read it from cover to cover and puffed it to Romanes. Graham was reassuring, adamant that many traditional beliefs – in God, free will, morals, and immortality – could survive the fad for materialism. Darwin doubted many of Graham's conclusions, though he was swayed by one, telling him, 'You have expressed my inward conviction . . . that the Universe is not the result of chance.' But even on this a 'horrid doubt' crept back in, as it always did. What value any such belief if the mind has evolved? 'Would any one trust in the convictions of a monkey's mind, if there are any convictions' in it? The issue was insoluble, and there he took his stand.

Less welcome was Graham's down-playing of natural selection as the engine of social progress. Darwin still fought on this score. What a struggle had gone on between Spaniards and South American Indians, between English settlers and Australian Aborigines, between colonists and the colonized everywhere. 'Remember what risk the nations of Europe ran, not so many centuries ago of being overwhelmed by the Turks, and how ridiculous such an idea now is! The more civilized so-called Caucasian races have beaten the Turkish hollow in the struggle for existence.' Packing for home, he assured Graham that the elimination of 'lower races' by 'higher civilized races' was inevitable as the Malthusian struggle pushed mankind onward.[2]

At Downe a letter from Wallace showed that he too would remain a social missionary to the end, although a world separated them now. He was promoting the American Henry George's socialist tract *Progress and Poverty*. 'It is the most startling novel and original book of the last twenty years,' he enthused to Darwin; its impact would probably be 'equal to that made by Adam Smith a century ago.' Wallace, President of the Land Nationalization Society, was prepared for George's remedy for chronic poverty and unequal wealth – 'make land common property.' The 'ultimate defence' of private land, the notion of inevitable struggle, was wrong, and the belief that 'some have a better right to existence than others' immoral. Malthus might apply to animals, but not to people. Wallace remained at a political distance. An abyss stood between him and Darwin, as it really had that fateful day in 1858 when his Ternate letter arrived.

Squire Darwin, the Lincolnshire landlord, parried him politely, but refused to be censured and complained that such books had 'a disastrous effect' on his mind. Of course 'something ought to be done' about land and poverty, but he hoped that Wallace would not 'turn renegade to natural history.' The two men, seemingly so close, had spent a lifetime missing one another's point. Darwin was past caring, an absent-minded old naturalist who thoughtlessly admitted to the astute-minded old socialist, 'I have everything to make me happy and contented.'[3]

It was a time of tranquil recollection, abetted by a stable stomach. 'Pleasant memories of long past days,' he told Hooker, when they had 'many a discussion and . . . a good fight.' Hooker was pushing on with the world's plants, still not too proud to lean on his oldest colleague, craving his criticism 'as your pupil.' Darwin remained a sounding board, able to reel off facts, pick holes, and 'pour out my idle thoughts.' They had mellowed, but neither had lost his edge. 'As iron sharpeneth iron,' they had forged the toughest friendship. Hooker, longing to 'throw off the trammels of official life' and retire from Kew, felt for Darwin's misery at having no projects to 'fall back upon.' In his sixties now, Hooker too was facing the end of his useful days and found it 'difficult to resist the pessimist view of creation.' But 'when I look back . . . to the days I have spent in intercourse with you and yours,' he consoled his 'beloved friend,' 'that view takes wings to itself and flies away.'[4]

Darwin's was a twilight contentment, spent not only with his plant roots. With the Litchfields he sat under the limes at Downe and whiled away the summer afternoons. He was in his 'happiest spirits' and chatted 'deliciously' for hours. In the evenings, reclining on the sofa, he asked for Bach and Handel to be played over and over. Romanes would stop by with his wife and new baby, and left the old man as 'grand and good and bright as ever.' But in the small hours, with Emma breathing softly beside him, he felt the rot inside.

Time was running out and of course he worried about his *Worms*. He urged Murray to bring publication forward, even if it meant a loss.[5] The book, forty years in the making, hung over him like a pall.

Honours crowned his dotage. An oil portrait was commissioned by the Linnean Society. He went to London to sit for Huxley's son-in-law John Collier in the first week of August, and by common consent the painting was his 'best likeness.' He stayed with Eras, melancholy and wasted, dwelling on the death of his old companion Thomas Carlyle. On the 3rd Charles dined by special invitation with the Prince of Wales, the Crown Prince of Germany, and eminent physicians at the start of the Seventh International Medical Congress.

As he sipped port with the regal heads that day, the real atheists – those who plagued him, those he had always feared being associated with – were out on the streets, literally. Bradlaugh, re-elected MP for Northampton after his seat was declared vacant, had arrived at the Commons with Aveling and Besant, only to be dragged down the lobby stairs and flung into Palace Yard by a mob of messengers, policemen, and Tory MPs. Darwin walked on eggshells with such people, aware of the prejudices they stirred. A week later Aveling sent his collected articles, *The Student's Darwin*, minus a dedication, with a note apologizing for his atheistic extrapolations. Darwin replied with a cool thanks, admitting that he could hardly stop writers from taking his views 'to a greater length than seems to me safe.'[6]

Erasmus became gravely ill within days. The Litchfields rushed over. So did Fanny Wedgwood, 'the true love of his life,' and she stayed at his bedside until the end. He died quietly on the 26th. A telegram came for Emma, who broke the news to Charles. He had seen Ras dying slowly 'for many years.' He was not 'a happy man,' but always kindhearted, clearheaded, and affectionate. There was no consolation. Indeed, Hooker thought it worse to lose such a lifetime's companion than a brother when young, as he had. No, Darwin replied, missing the point. The death of a child, 'where there is a bright future ahead, causes grief never to be wholly obliterated.' Always he thought of Annie.

The funeral took place in Downe churchyard on 1 September with the whole family present. Ffinden stood aside for Charles and Emma's 85-year-old cousin John Allen Wedgwood, who had married them. It was wretchedly cold; frost dusted the graveside as he performed the last offices in the pale morning light. Charles, looking 'old and ill,' huddled in a long black funeral cloak, a picture of 'sad reverie' as the coffin was lowered. On the marble slab were to be Carlyle's words, 'one of the sincerest, truest, and most modest of men.'[7]

London would never be the same. The house in Queen Anne Street was sold within a week and the contents dispersed quickly. Jolted by the 'heavy loss,' Charles looked to his own death. With half of Ras's estate and his own investments, he was worth over a quarter of a million pounds, an astonished William announced, and this '*without* mother's' fortune. Charles redrafted his will. He planned to bequeath £34,000 to each of the girls and £53,000 to the boys. This would leave them 'beyond want' should their health give way. And he thought of others, colleagues who had seen him through the hard times, old friends who had protected him when the *Origin* was published: Hooker and Huxley were to receive £1000 each, 'as a slight memorial of my life long affection and respect.' The will was signed on the 7th, with Jackson the butler as witness. Afterwards there was a subdued party. It was Bernard's fifth birthday.

Charles sent a sad note to Caroline about her half of Eras's estate. Only the two of them remained to recall the childhood days. He enclosed a miniature of their mother. It showed a 'most sweet expression' – if only he could remember her face as vividly as his father's. He did recall her 'black velvet gown' and the 'death scene,' and how they cried together, but little more. Maybe he had forgotten that precious face because no one had been 'able to endure speaking about so dreadful a loss.'[8]

His reverie was interrupted by a cryptic telegram:

> Doctor Ludwig Büchner Germany is in London could he have Honour of interview Wednesday or Thursday at hour most convenient to you leaves Friday Pardon abruptness and Boldness of request.

It threw the family into commotion. The wire was from Aveling, attending the Congress of the International Federation of Freethinkers in the capital. Büchner, President of the Congress, was fifty-seven and renowned; Aveling, thirty and notorious. As a land nationalizer and leader of the workers' movement, Büchner might have descended on Wallace; as a zealous materialist he might have singled out Tyndall. But no, Darwin for German physicians had assumed heroic status, elevated by a crusading *Darwinismus*. Büchner thought that he was greeting a noble ally. The gentle squire of Downe had always feared such a grotesque misunderstanding.

Charles asked Emma: how could he refuse the distinguished Büchner, atheist or no? And Aveling had always treated him civilly. They could come for lunch, stay an hour or so, and that would be that. An appalled Emma, expected to play hostess to notorious atheists, bargained for something better. Since Brodie Innes was near by, shouldn't he be invited too? And she trusted that Herr Büchner 'talks English & will refrain from airing his very strong religious opinions.'[9]

The next afternoon, Thursday the 28th, Jackson ushered everyone to the dining-room table at one o'clock. (A nervous Bessy stayed upstairs.) At the head sat Emma, her serene face haloed in sunlight from an Indian summer day. Opposite her, near the door where the servants passed with steaming platters, was Frank, and beside him Bernard and some friends. Across from the children, in a single imposing row, sat Charles and the atheists. Between Aveling and Emma, as if to shield her, was the white-haired Revd Brodie Innes, amiable and upright. The table became an embodiment of Darwin's life-long dilemma. It was less a lunch, more a last supper; everybody he had loved, everything he had feared, every paradox of his career had come together in a penultimate act. Here, his disapproving evangelical wife, his kindly Tory vicar, his genetically weak children, and his atheistic disciples, Büchner to his right and Aveling on the left, gloating in his physical repulsion, a malevolence emanating from his presence 'as from a diabolical source of being.' In the middle sat the parish naturalist, the failed ordinand, the Devil's Chaplain, damning and defying all expectations.

Some explanation of the parson's presence was evidently required. Mindful of the mixed company, Charles put it masterfully: 'B[rodie] I[nnes] & I have been fast friends for 30 years. We never thoroughly agreed on any subject but once and then we looked hard at each other and thought one of us must be very ill."[10] Nerves were jangled, the situation fraught. It would have been a nightmare, but for the funny turn.

Worms came up during the first course. Aveling expressed pious horror that the author of the *Origin* had stooped to a 'subject so insignificant.' The freethinking missionaries had the great Victorian social problems in mind. Neither expected to find their hero obsessed by the sods rather than sons of the soil. Turning gravely, Charles stated, 'I have been studying their habits for forty years.' For him the humble explained the great, but not in a way that Aveling – soon Marx's 'son-in-law' – could appreciate. After the sweet, which he was forbidden but ate anyway, Charles adjourned with Frank and the guests to the smoking room, his old study, where he had written the *Origin*.

They lit cigarettes and Darwin, completely out of character, pitched in. 'Why do you call yourselves atheists?' In his dotage, forty years since his covert notebook days, he finally dragged the issue into the open. He preferred the word agnostic, he said. '"Agnostic" was but "Atheist" writ respectable,' Aveling replied, searching for common ground, 'and "Atheist" was only "Agnostic" writ aggressive.' But, Darwin retorted, 'Why should you be so aggressive?' Is anything to be gained by forcing new ideas on people? Freethought is 'all very well' for the educated, but are ordinary people 'ripe for it?' Here spoke the comfortable squire, seeking not to disturb the social equilibrium.

The atheists realized this, and Aveling rounded on him. What if 'the revolutionary truths of Natural and Sexual Selection' had been addressed only to 'the judicious few'? What if he had delayed publishing the *Origin* until the time was 'ripe'? Had he 'kept silence,' where would the world be in 1881? Surely 'his own illustrious example' was encouragement to every freethinker to proclaim truth 'abroad from the house-tops'! Still they missed the real Darwin. He *had* buried evolution for twenty years, petrified for his respectability, upholding the paternalist order for a generation before being forced into the open.

Only one subject could they agree on, Christianity. Darwin admitted that it was not 'supported by evidence.' But – he dug at his guests – he had reached this conclusion only slowly. He did not force new ideas even on himself but waited until the time was ripe. In fact, he told them openly, 'I never gave up Christianity until I was forty years of age.'[11] It had taken his father's and Annie's deaths to make him shake off the last shreds. And even then he had refused to speak out, or violently to assail people's faith. He never was a comrade at arms.

Worms appeared in October and sold phenomenally, thousands within weeks. But the 'laughable' number of letters, especially the 'idiotic' ones! Everyone had a query, a theory, a petty observation. Worms were, after all, the commonest of beasts. 'Worn out,' he escaped to Cambridge with Emma, trying to follow orders and relax. They spent a 'happy week' with Horace and Ida, who was shortly to give birth to a boy, baby Erasmus. The trip 'quite set up' Darwin, and he went home ready to section his roots.

He had them standing in an ammonia solution. Did a struggle for existence take place among the cells in this environment? Had the cells clogged with 'effete matter' become 'unfitted,' or was collecting it their job – evidence of a root's 'physiological division of labour'? He was working 'all the harder now,' extending natural selection to the tiniest living entities, rounding out his life's work. Not a second was wasted; his head bobbed from microscope to notes. He fumbled for his spectacles, tugging at his waistcoat with 'violent confoundings.'[12] He lost himself for hours in the ammonia vapour. He even forgot his heart.

Charles and Emma stayed with Henrietta in London before Christmas, their first trip to town since Ras's death. It should have been a time of shopping and presents. Strangely the West End seemed empty, subdued, despite the holiday crush. On the 15th Charles called unannounced at Romanes's house in Cornwall Terrace, opposite Regent's Park. Romanes was not at home. The butler realized that the old gent at the door was having trouble. His face was pale and contorted, he was gripping his chest. Darwin declined an invitation to rest inside and stumbled away to take a cab back to Emma. He crossed over and tottered towards Baker Street, the butler watching apprehensively. As he neared the corner, a few hundred yards off, he staggered and clutched the park railings. He turned and started back as the butler ran towards him, then stopped, turned again, and hailed a cab.

Dr Clark came at Emma's call the next morning, but Charles seemed better and the doctor pronounced him fine. Emma took no chances, keeping him indoors under a watchful eye. Invitations were sent out instead, and a galaxy of scientific stars turned up to pay court – Romanes, Hooker, Huxley, Galton, Burdon Sanderson, and the geologist John Judd. Darwin seemed bright and animated, if 'perhaps a little forced.' Nonetheless, he told Judd, he had 'received his warning.'[13]

It was too easily ignored by a man absorbed in cells. At home he drove himself relentlessly into 1882. He rose early, breakfasted with Bernard, and paced the day with turns around the Sandwalk – fewer now and slower, his iron-tipped walking stick ticking against the flints. In the mornings he wrote technical papers about the effect of ammonium carbonate on roots and leaves. At lunch there were sometimes guests, including Graham, whose religious book he still touted. Afterwards came endless letters – arguing with an American feminist that women are 'inferior intellectually,' sponsoring a translation of August Weismann's *Studies in the Theory of Descent*, promising Hooker £250 a year towards a catalogue of all known plants, the great *Index Kewensis*. Then a cigarette at three while Emma read aloud, another at six before tea, two games of backgammon with perhaps a pinch of snuff and he was ready to retire. The new study was his dressing room. At 10.30 p.m. sharp he blew his nose loudly and mounted the stairs with a 'slow tired step.'[14]

A cough left him 'miserable to a strange degree' in February. Emma prescribed quinine, which helped, but a week after he turned seventy-three he vomited badly and the chest pain returned. It stopped him walking for a while. Through the torment his fascination with nature's revealing oddities never wavered. Someone sent him a water beetle with a bivalve stuck to it. He planned to take it to the British Museum for identification when he was well, welcoming this example of hitch-hiking to his pond-hopping methods of dispersal. For Darwin, old hobby-horses were ridden to death.

On 7 March, hobbling around the Sandwalk, he had another seizure. He was alone and terrified, 400 yards from the house. Somehow he picked his way back, lurching from tree to tree, and collapsed in Emma's arms. Dr Clark confirmed angina and prescribed morphia pills for the pain. Charles froze. He felt condemned, a prisoner of his body, an innocent about to be hanged. He gave in to despair. For days he lay on the drawing-room sofa staring blankly at a display of old family china, 'Henrietta's shrine.' He was terminally ill. His mind reeled, his stomach churned. When he rose the pain came on with 'half-fainting feelings' and Emma rushed to his side. She suggested sitting on the verandah, but he refused. Nor would he dine with the family, preferring to eat in his bedroom alone. Prostrate, he could hardly sleep.[15]

Dr Norman Moore, a young and rising physician, assured him that his heart was only weak. Within days Charles rejoined the evening meals, played backgammon, and caught up with correspondence. The London trip was abandoned; instead he posted the shell-encrusted beetle. And he wrote a note to *Nature* on how beetles disperse their hitch-hikers, flying from pond to pond with bivalves hanging on tight. It rekindled old memories, of Cambridge collecting and his seed-floating experiments. Maybe he had more time. The thought put a spring in his step. One day he forgot himself and walked quickly upstairs, without pain.

Company heartened him too. Leo stopped by with his fiancée on 23 March and seeing how '*very* happy' she was, he chaffed her with gentle jokes. Henrietta arrived, accompanied by her friend Laura Forster (aunt of the young E. M. Forster), herself convalescing after an illness. Laura's rapid recovery made him hopeful. Day after day he described his symptoms to her, pouring out his feelings. It eased Emma's lot, which 'made her more cheerful & bright for him.' The exquisite spring weather helped. Emma and Henrietta coaxed Laura out past the pigeon house to the kitchen garden, then through the gate in the great wall to the orchard. As they sat under the trees in the still sunshine, a blaze of crocuses about them, Charles emerged and eased himself on to the grass. He put his arm around Emma's shoulders and pulled her to him, murmuring, 'Oh Laura, what a miserable man I should be without this dear woman.'[16] An eternal moment, it seemed to augur a return to health.

Charles knew better and could feel the changes, almost hourly. He observed his body with morbid interest, uncertain yet calm. He shuffled from the study one afternoon to lie on the drawing-room sofa, and found Laura seated by the fire. 'The clocks go so dreadfully slowly,' he groaned. 'I have come in here to see if this one gets over the hours any quicker than the study one does.'

Laura and Henrietta left on Tuesday 4 April because Emma wanted a quiet Easter together. That day and the next Charles had dreadful attacks. With habitual cold-blooded precision, he began making notes. 'Much pain,' he jotted clinically. Emma sent for Dr

Moore and a local physician, Dr Allfrey, who urged her to get a special chair for carrying him upstairs. On the 6th Charles was very tired, with pain in the evening, and he took two amyl nitrite capsules, an antispasmodic. The weekend brought a reprieve. On Monday the 10th George arrived and helped Frank and Jackson move him to and from the bedroom. He was glad for the extra company but had no breath to talk long. The next two nights were excruciating. 'Stomach excessively bad – went to bed at 2° but no pain & no dose,' he scrawled on Thursday. And on Friday, '1 attack slight pain 1 dose.' He was running his final experiment.[17]

The Litchfields came for dinner on Saturday the 15th. Everyone sat at table, with Bernard in his high chair. After the meat was served Charles felt a violent stab in his head. 'I am so giddy I must lie down,' he croaked, and staggered into the drawing-room. He braced himself for a moment against the mantelpiece, then fell face down on the sofa. He was unconscious for only a minute. George gave him a tot of brandy and helped him to the study, while Emma shooed the servants away. 'Dropped down,' he recorded before retiring, as if he were some night-drooping plant.

Emma, 'calm & self possessed,' refused to summon the doctors, who flustered him. He survived Sunday with 'very slight pain several times' and no drugs. 'It's almost worth while to be sick to be nursed by you,' he petted Emma. Monday saw further improvement. He even walked as far as the orchard, supported on both sides. He seemed 'fully up to his average,' so the next day the Litchfields left and George set off for Cambridge. Charles continued to eat well and in the evening stayed in the drawing-room later than usual, chatting with Bessy.[18]

The pain came on just before midnight. It was brutal, gripping him like a vice, tightening by the minute. He woke Emma and begged her to fetch the amyl from the study. She darted from the bedroom and became confused, finally calling Bessy. They took minutes to find the capsules. Charles, in agony, felt that he was dying but unable to cry out. As he slumped unconscious across the bed, Emma and Bessy returned. They rang for a servant and, propping him up, gave the brandy. It trickled through his beard and down his nightdress on to the quilt. Struggling, they forced his head back and poured it into him. Emma was distraught, thinking it was the end.

Seconds later he spluttered and retched; his eyes flickered open. She pressed close to him, searching his face for some sign of recognition. 'My love, my precious love,' he whispered, barely audible. 'Tell all my children to remember how good they have always been to me.'

He choked and grimaced. Emma clasped his hand tightly – it was so awful, words failed her. He started again, fully conscious now, looking into her eyes, 'I am not the least afraid to die.' He became calm.

She sent for Dr Allfrey, who arrived at two o'clock. He applied mustard plasters to Charles's chest, which gave some relief. Just after seven the servants brought breakfast up and he managed to take a few mouthfuls before falling asleep. Allfrey, finding his pulse stronger, wondered that he had ever regained consciousness. The doctor left at eight.

Immediately Charles started vomiting. It was violent and prolonged. When there was nothing left the nausea kept on in waves, overpowering him. His body heaved and shuddered, as if possessed by an outside force. An hour passed, then two. Still he gagged and retched. 'If I could but die,' he gasped repeatedly, 'if I could but die.' Emma clung to him, trembling, as another spasm started. He was cold, clammy, his skin grey and ghostlike. Blood spewed out, running down his beard. She had never seen such suffering.

Frank returned from London before ten. Bessy sent Jackson for Henrietta, who arrived by one. She ran upstairs to find her father sleeping and Emma about to break down, trying to comfort Frank. Henrietta insisted that she take an opium pill and rest, which she did without a murmur. She had slept less than two hours in twenty-four.

Charles awoke in a daze, and asked to be propped up. He recognized the children and embraced them with tears. Frank spooned soup and brandy for him while Henrietta lightly rubbed his chest. Then the nausea struck and convulsed him again. 'Oh God,' he cried helplessly, 'oh Lord God,' and began to faint. Henrietta gave him smelling salts, which he sniffed eagerly, falling back exhausted. 'Where is Mammy?' he called in a thin, hollow voice. They said that she was resting. 'I am *glad* of it,' he sighed. 'You two dears are the best of nurses.' He grew drowsy. It confused him; he thought that he was sinking, and with a 'feeble quivering motion' held out his hands to be lifted. But as Frank raised him, the pain came on. He begged for a little whisky, remembering that Dr Allfrey had suggested it.

Time stood still for Henrietta. Frank, taking his father's pulse at intervals, knew that the hour was near. At twenty-five minutes past three, while sitting up, Charles groaned 'I feel as if I sh^d faint.' They called Emma, who came immediately and held him. His face dropped, but after a few teaspoons of whisky he revived, and she helped him to lie down. But the pain was excruciating in any position. Rising, he began to faint again. The doorbell rang – the doctors. Henrietta raced downstairs to meet them as Charles clutched at Emma. Frank shouted for them to come instantly, and Bessy.

He lost consciousness. They saw it was hopeless. There was only the deep stertorous breathing that precedes death. Emma cradled his head on her breast, swaying gently, her eyes closed. His life ended at four o'clock in the afternoon, Wednesday 19 April, 1882.[19]

Frank, choked with grief, fetched Bernard from the nursery. They walked into the garden, slowly, hand-in-hand, past the drawing-room window, where Bernard saw his aunts together. 'Why are Bessy and Etty crying?' he asked; 'because Grandpa is so ill?' They were by the kitchen garden before Frank could speak. 'Grandpa has been so ill that he won't be ill any more.' When they reached the Sandwalk, Bernard gathered a bouquet of wild lilies.[20]

44

An Agnostic in the Abbey

THE NEXT DAY the papers announced that Darwin would be buried in St Mary's churchyard at Downe. Interment would take place in the 'family vault,' on the following Monday or Tuesday. He would lie under the great yew that had stood sentinel for six centuries at the lychgate – next to his infant children and beside Erasmus. Darwin had expected to be placed here, glimpsing his death the previous summer, and it was clearly the wish of the family and village folk.

Brodie Innes offered to perform the burial rites. William and George, Leo and Horace, hurried home to join the others. John Lewis, the village carpenter, who as a lad had helped with Darwin's cold garden baths, was already at work on the coffin, and the body was placed in the inner shell, 'composed and almost lifelike.' The family gathered round. Emma found her sons' grief 'so violent and affecting' that she finally broke down and wept.[1]

Letters, so difficult at this time, had to be penned. They were a duty and provided their own sort of catharsis. Emma and Henrietta wrote touchingly to female friends and relatives, relating intimate details and last words. Frank and George contacted their father's scientific colleagues, breaking the news of the heart attack in a more clinical manner.

Galton and Huxley had received their black-edged notes by Thursday afternoon. Both were consummate publicists. They acted immediately out of love and loyalty for their old friend. Huxley spent hours anguishing over a short memorial notice for *Nature* before taking the sombre news to the Athenaeum. Galton set off for the Royal Society, which met that day.

Both were part of that influential group within the Society that had struggled to usurp the clergy's role. A new 'scientific priesthood,' Galton called these new professionals, whose duties affected 'the health and well-being of the nation,' and whose growing social prestige reflected it. One of the priesthood's functions, Galton believed, was to emphasize 'the religious significance of the doctrine of evolution,' and what grander way of doing so than a fitting commemoration of Darwin's death? The scientific priesthood had lost a great fellow naturalist, and Galton his first cousin and spiritual father. 'There was no man who I reverenced or to whom I owed more, *spiritually*, than to him,' Galton consoled George Darwin. 'His *Origin of Species* first put me so to speak in harmony with Nature.'[2] For such a man, a 'royal character,' the ultimate remembrance was necessary.

Galton tackled William Spottiswoode, the President of the Royal Society, and arranged for him to telegraph the Darwins asking if they would consent to burial in Westminster Abbey. The request was more official coming from the scientific 'Woolsack,' and more proper from a scientist unrelated to the family. Spottiswoode was influential, by virtue of his office and as printer to Her Majesty. A fellow member of the Athenaeum and an X Clubber, he was one of the Huxley-Galton group and perfectly placed to expedite the plan. Everything was to be done properly, with no risk of upsetting public proprieties. A careful word in the right quarters would have the required effect. Could the Revd Charles Pritchard, a Fellow of the Royal Society who had prepared George and Frank Darwin for Cambridge, write urging the family's assent? Perhaps someone might arrange for a leading conservative newspaper like *The Standard* to call independently for an Abbey burial?[3]

Word was passed to Huxley, Hooker, and Lubbock, tipping off the scientific curia and members of the X. Hooker, forty years Darwin's friend, was grief-stricken and depressed. For days he had been suffering angina pains himself and was now 'utterly unhinged and unfit' for any sort of work. He at first demurred, having 'no fancy for the bitter taste of these ceremonials.' But Huxley and Lubbock were enthusiastic. They knew how much Darwin had rejoiced at Lyell's interment in the Abbey in 1875.

The next day, Friday, Huxley and Spottiswoode discussed Galton's plan at the Athenaeum. They were joined by the Revd Frederic Farrar, Canon of Westminster, and the former headmaster of Marlborough School. In the sixties Farrar had chaired – and Huxley had served on – the British Association's committee on public-school education. Spottiswoode and Huxley respected Farrar as a friend of the new sciences and a critic of the classical curriculum. Darwin, no lover of classics, had also warmed to Canon Farrar, praising his work on the origin of language and supporting his successful candidacy for the Royal Society. Farrar asked why the scientists had not approached the Dean of Westminster, Revd George Granville Bradley, with a request that Darwin be buried in the Abbey.

Getting a freethinker into the Abbey was not easy. A couple of years earlier Huxley had actually refused to ask Bradley's liberal predecessor to allow George Eliot's burial there, thinking it unfair to press him to do 'something for which he is pretty sure to be violently assailed.' But Darwin had not lived openly in sin as Eliot had. This time he reckoned that the Dean could be persuaded, and he knew the way to go about it. He goaded Farrar, intimating that there was little point in making a request, for it would surely be turned down. This was devilishly disingenuous. After all, Huxley knew Bradley well. He had even been offered his post of Master of University College, Oxford, the previous November, when Bradley became Dean. And he was aware of Bradley's strong interest in science, having discussed Oxford science fellowships with him. It was actually because of this interest that Galton, Huxley, and Spottiswoode had supported Bradley's election to the Athenaeum in 1873. He felt sure that, with the right overtures, the Dean would acquiesce.[4]

The ruse worked. Farrar informed them that if a petition were sent, the Dean would no doubt look kindly on it, and he went off to make sure. Meanwhile Spottiswoode sent a note on Athenaeum stationery to William Darwin, now the head of the family:

> I consulted with Huxley, one Bishop, 2 canons (one of whom has a very extensive acquaintance with clergy metropolitan & other), one public school master. All heartily encouraged the proposal being carried out. I saw the L[or]d. Chancellor who was naturally rather more cautious. Lord Aberdare, on his own part, & on that of the Geograph[ical]. Society, was most urgent that the thing should be done, & expressed his sincere hope that your family would consent. –
>
> There is a place beside Lyell where your father could be laid; arrangements could, so far as would be done in & from London, be easily completed for Wednesday next.

That Friday evening Huxley jumped the gun, telling Hooker, 'I think the Westminster Abbey business is all settled though it is unfortunate the Dean is out of town.'[5]

While Spottiswoode approached the family, and Farrar the Dean of Westminster, Lubbock summoned support in the corridors of power. He was President of the Linnean Society, and when word of Darwin's demise reached him on the Thursday, he adjourned the Society out of respect. His own wish had been for a local burial, among their friends and neighbours. But duty came first. He bowed to 'the will of the intelligence of the nation,' as Huxley called it in his *Nature* eulogy – and as a City banker and Liberal MP he had long since deferred to professional middle-class opinion.[6] On Friday, hearing that a petition would be needed, he went to the Houses of Parliament.

In the Commons, Ireland had been dominating the debates. The Liberal Party was divided as Fenian atrocities continued, and Gladstone was deeply involved in his Irish Land Act. That Friday, with 150 members on the benches, Lubbock moved among his colleagues collecting signatures, and Ireland was pushed aside for a moment in favour of Darwin and English pride. Lubbock left the House with a petition stating that 'it would be acceptable to a very large number of our countrymen of all classes and opinions that our illustrious countryman Mr. Darwin should be buried in Westminster Abbey.'[7]

'It was very influentially signed,' he told Frank Darwin after sending the petition to the Dean the next morning. Leading the twenty-eight signatories in this essentially Liberal document were four Fellows of the Royal Society, including the education minister, and Lyon Playfair, now the Deputy Speaker. Also down were the Under Secretary of State for Foreign Affairs, and Sir G. O. Trevelyan, Secretary of the Admiralty. There followed the Solicitor General, the Postmaster General, a Sea Lord, and the Speaker of the House. Arthur Russell, a silent member of the Commons, was the cousin of a schoolboy named Bertrand Russell. Another signatory, Henry Campbell-Bannerman, would one day be Prime Minister. As Lubbock confirmed, 'If there had been time many other signatures would have been added.' He now told William Darwin that the Abbey interment was 'very right.'[8]

Following Spottiswoode's telegram and letter, the family was showered with letters urging them to consent. On Saturday, *The Standard* made an emotive plea – a request, as it were, from ordinary people to Emma and the children.

> Darwin died, as he had lived, in the quiet retirement of the country home which he loved; and the sylvan scenes amidst which he found the simple plants and animals that enabled

him to solve the great enigma of the Origin of Species may
seem, perhaps, to many of his friends the fittest surroundings
for his last resting place. But one who has brought such
honour to the English name, and whose death is lamented
throughout the civilized world, to the temporary neglect of
the many burning political and social questions of the day,
should not be laid in a comparatively obscure grave. His
proper place is amongst those other worthies whose
reputations are landmarks in the people's history, and if it
should not clash with his own expressed wishes, or the pious
feelings of the family, we owe it to posterity to place his
remains in Westminster Abbey, among the illustrious dead
who make that noble fane unrivalled in the world.[9]

Other papers also latched on to the crusade. Patriotism was the
paramount theme. Who was the Abbey's hallowed ground for, if not
those who had made Britain great, extended her Empire, civilized
new worlds at home and abroad? David Livingstone and the heroes
of the Indian Mutiny lay there beside the engineers, Stephenson and
Telford, whose feats had paved the way for the iron-clad Victorian
age. And near by were memorials to others who had harnessed
nature's forces – Watt, Trevithick, and Brunel. Towering above them
all stood Sir Isaac Newton, still the man against whom all others
were measured; and by his standard Darwin was not found wanting.
Was he not 'the greatest Englishman since Newton'? Had he not
given 'exactly the same stir, the same direction, to all that is most
characteristic in the intellectual energy of the nineteenth century, as
did Locke and Newton in the eighteenth?'[10]

The obituarists alone almost ensured an Abbey interment by their
comparisons with Newton. The demand became even more pointed
as the foreign tributes poured in. The Prussian, French, and American
newspapers gushed praise, highlighting Britain's neglect of her own
native genius. The Prussian king – the *Telegraph* pointed out – had
honoured Darwin with a knighthood of the Order 'Pour le Mérite' a
full fifteen years earlier, yet England had shabbily ignored her first
son. She had failed to 'honour herself' by conferring a title. Unlike
the Lyells, Herschels, and Newtons, Darwin had gone to his grave,
like the muddy engineers, a plain 'Mr.' Amends had to be made,
before it was too late. Britain must not be outdone by her foreign
rivals. Comparison with the immortal Newton would ring hollow
unless it was acted upon; Newton's honour had to be Darwin's.[11]
The State must take and enshrine the body.

Canon Farrar had done his work well. Even before receiving the Parliamentary petition, the Dean, then in France, telegraphed his cordial acquiescence. The family was told. By Saturday afternoon, they had all but relented, accepting that Charles was destined to lie beside his old mentor Lyell at Westminster. Still, they made it clear that they would not consent if there were 'any opposition or discussion.'[12] And they felt anxious lest the proposal be thought to have come from them. Their fears were allayed, even if, as X Clubbers knew, the instigator had indeed been a relative, Galton.

The sudden switch in arrangements left little time for mourning. Pall-bearers had to be selected, guests invited, and the former funeral arrangements cancelled. New undertakers were engaged, Messrs T. and W. Banting of 27 St James's Street, who had organized the Duke of Wellington's funeral. They were to collect the body and lay it out for burial on Wednesday. William and George lined up the pall-bearers. Lord Derby and the Dukes of Devonshire and Argyll represented the State, and Devonshire was Chancellor of Darwin's Alma Mater, Cambridge University. They were to be joined by the American ambassador, James Russell Lowell, in 'grateful recognition of the interest taken by Americans in Mr. Darwin's works.' And from English science, the X Club stalwarts Spottiswoode, Lubbock, Huxley, and Hooker would help bear the coffin. Canon Farrar, who had done so much to ease the way, was to accompany them. Stupidly, Huxley forgot to ask Wallace. Wallace, that perennial afterthought in the Darwinian story, was hastily contacted and it was agreed that he would bring up the rear. The undertakers dispensed tickets of admission. Mrs Huxley and the boys received theirs – Leonard, now in his twenties, was Darwin's godson after all. There was a problem with pernickety Herbert Spencer, who wanted to sit with friends rather than scientific dignitaries. But even he was allotted his chosen seat – in the choir – after Huxley hinted that his Dissenting views might otherwise stop him from attending.[13]

Through all the hurry and bustle, Emma stayed outwardly calm, Henrietta and Bessy beside her. But she thought on the future, and how she would cope in a world now 'so empty and desolate.' She poured out her feelings to Fanny and Hensleigh.

> You will hear about West[minster]. Abbey wh[ich]. I look
> upon as nearly settled. It gave us all a pang not to have him
> rest quietly by Eras –; but William felt strongly, and on
> reflection I did also, that his gracious & grateful nature w^d
> have wished to accept the acknowledgement of what he had

done . . . I am sure dearest Fanny that you w^d have wished to attend if you had been in London; but it will be long & agitating & prob[ably]. cold & considerable risk & I am sure this applies to Hensleigh too.

In the event, 79-year-old Hensleigh braved the cold and emotion on Wednesday and walked down the aisle with the rest.[14] Emma stayed at Down House alone. She felt closer to Charles there.

Apparently no villagers journeyed to Westminster either. Old Parslow did go. But he was practically a part of the family he had served so faithfully since the days in Gower Street. As a downstairs-man close to the 'great folks,' he blended the sentiments of locals and family alike. Not long afterwards, he recalled the 'great disappointment' among the people of Downe that Darwin had not been buried in the village. 'He loved the place, and we think he would have rested there had he been consulted.'

The tradesmen were peeved. The publican at the George and Dragon accused the chiselling politicians of undermining local business. 'All the people wished to have Mr. Darwin buried in Downe, but the Government would not let him. It would have helped the place so much, for it would have brought hosts of people down to see his grave.' St Mary's churchyard could have become a shrine, providing a steady stream of customers for his pub across the road. The joiner John Lewis was equally put out. His reward would have been more than financial; it would have been the knowledge that his coffin held the mortal remains of his illustrious neighbour, Mr Darwin. But after the rough oak box had been made and the body had reposed in it for a day, a smart Piccadilly undertaker had turned up with a resplendent and expensive coffin. Nothing less, he said, would suffice for a state funeral. 'I made his coffin just the way he wanted it,' Lewis lamented, 'all rough, just as it left the bench, no polish, no nothin.' But when they agreed to send him to Westminster . . . my coffin wasn't wanted, and they sent it back.' The replacement one 'you could see to shave in.' Lewis thought it was an outrage. 'They buried him in Westminster Abbey, but he always wanted to lie here, and I don't think he'd have liked it.'[15]

None of the papers saw any religious obstacle to an Abbey burial. *The Standard*, in proposing the honour, maintained that 'true Christians can accept the main scientific facts of Evolution just as they do of Astronomy and Geology, without any prejudice to more ancient and cherished beliefs.' *The Times* on Friday had declared the clash between Huxley and Bishop Wilberforce in 1860 a piece of 'ancient history'; and the Liberal *Daily News* added that Darwin's doctrine was quite consistent 'with strong religious faith and hope.'[16] On Sunday the preachers outbid one another to prove the hacks right.

Morning, noon and night, the pulpits resounded with praise for Darwin. At the Abbey, Canon George Prothero, the Queen's chief Chaplain-in-Ordinary, toed his usual Broad Church line and inveighed against extremism and superstition. However one viewed the new science, it was certainly born of Mr Darwin's moderation, impartiality, and patient industry in pursuing truth. In scholars like him lived 'that charity which is the essence of the true spirit of Christ.' That evening at the Abbey, Canon Alfred Barry echoed the weighty sermons on politics and business that he had delivered the previous autumn. These had sanctioned the time-honoured assumptions implicit in Darwinism. He had dismissed equality as unnatural, an 'impossible figment,' and assigned each person his station – professional, merchant, trader, or worker – to help England work with God for the progress of 'all mankind.' Every man was still in his place, and Darwin's death provided the excuse for a more particular appreciation. Natural selection was 'by no means alien to the Christian religion' – not if it was rightly understood, with selection acting 'under the Divine intelligence' and governed by 'the spiritual fitness of each man for life hereafter.'[17]

The star attraction that Sunday afternoon was Canon H. P. Liddon at St Paul's, lauding Darwin for 'the patience and care with which he observed and registered minute single facts.' In this way he had brought about a 'revolution' in modern thought and shed 'high distinction upon English science.' It did not show, but Liddon's sermon masked a deep anxiety. Privately he felt queasy and confided that the occasion had caused him some 'discomfort and misgiving.' Nevertheless even an awkward emphasis on Darwin's facts could only swell the chorus of demands for his burial in the Abbey. The *Guardian*, voice of Liddon's High Church party, acquiesced in his authority and discarded 'any misgivings lest the sacred pavement of the Abbey should cover a secret enemy of the Faith.' The Abbey service was to be a visible sign 'of the reconciliation between Faith and Science.' On this point, the Anglo-Catholics at St Paul's and the latitudinarians at Westminster were as one. The 'new truths' of biology were 'harmless,' their discoverer a secular saint.[18]

With Darwin's canonization assured, the newspapers played up their role in the affair. *The Standard* congratulated itself that 'the suggestion which we threw out on Saturday has been acted upon.' Evidently tolerance was 'the latest evolved and not the least satisfactory mode of clerical thought.' The thinking public would be able to honour the memory of a man who had 'set the stamp of his individual intellect on the age.' Professional gentlemen and their families would find it easy to obtain admission cards to the funeral. These, the papers said, could be collected from Banting's in St James's Street during office hours on Tuesday.[19]

So many applied that the undertakers did not complete the preparations for the burial until early the next morning. All day Tuesday the hearse, drawn by four horses, had progressed slowly, sombrely, the sixteen miles from Downe to Westminster. The weather was awful, drizzling rain, with temperatures in the forties. Frank, Leo, and Horace, who had followed the hearse, were chilled, spiritually and bodily. William and George had been in town all day making final arrangements. They hastened to the Abbey, just in time to meet their brothers. It was late, eight o'clock at night, before they bore the coffin through the cloisters. The cortège was led into the Chapel of St Faith, a bare, formal chamber dimly lit by two old lamps. In this cold, sepulchral room, the feeling of death was overwhelming. Guards took up their posts to protect the body overnight.[20]

On Wednesday 26 April Queen Victoria was at Windsor Castle, preparing for Prince Leopold's wedding the next day. Gladstone remained in Downing Street, wrapped up in Irish politics. Neither would attend the funeral; neither had been an avid reader of the *Origin of Species*. But elsewhere that grey day committees adjourned, judges put on mourning dress, and Parliament emptied as members trooped across the road. From embassies, scientific societies, and countless ordinary homes they came. Under leaden skies they converged on the Abbey, anticipating the awe and spectacle of a state occasion. The Darwins and Wedgwoods queued in the Jerusalem Chamber, thirty-three in all, including Galton. William, the principal mourner, stood at their head, Parslow and Jackson behind the family. In the Chapter House, where Parliament had once met, the elders of science, State, and Church, the nobility of birth and talent, stood waiting to file through the cloisters, behind the coffin. They were 'the greatest gathering of intellect that was ever brought together in our country,' said one. The transepts were filled with friends and guests; the south side of the nave with the bearers of black-edged admission cards. The Lord Mayor of London took his place in the sacrarium, before the altar, with still more family members. In the choir, Spencer sat forlornly among the distinguished ladies, now regretting that he was simply 'one of the spectators.' Finally, the doors opened to the multitudes without tickets.[21] They flooded into the dank, gaslit building, filling the less desirable seats on the north-west side of the nave.

Then, at midday, the moment arrived. As the Abbey bell tolled, Canon Prothero entered from the West Cloister door, leading the procession, with the choristers singing 'I am the resurrection.' The train of family and dignitaries shuffled past the tombs of the famous and made their way slowly through the candle-lit choir to the centre of the transept. There the coffin, draped in black velvet and covered in a spray of white blossoms, was placed beneath a lantern. A specially commissioned hymn was sung after the lesson. Composed by the Abbey's deputy organist, it was sensitive to the occasion. The lyrics were taken from the Book of Proverbs. The opening line, 'Happy is the man that findeth wisdom, and getteth understanding,' paid tribute to Darwin's lifework. The closing refrain, sung by the cassocked choirboys, left a sacrilegiously unDarwinian image of nature: 'Her ways are ways of pleasantness, and all her paths are peace.' William, seated at the front, felt a draught cross his bald pate. Worrying, as all Darwins did, about ill health, he perched his black gloves on top of his head and sat there incongruously, with the nation's eyes upon him, until the service ended. Then the family, with the pall-bearers carrying the coffin, made its way to the north-east corner of the nave, to the accompaniment of Schubert and Beethoven.[22]

In the end – fitting though it would have been – Darwin was not laid beside Lyell, but beneath the monument to Newton at the north end of the choir screen, and next to another mentor, Sir John Herschel. The floor was draped with black cloth, which dropped away into the dry, sandy grave. Henrietta, Bessy, and the ladies sat down, while the others crowded around. American freethinkers rubbed shoulders with orthodox churchmen; Romanes and agnostic X men stood next to devout old Fellows of the Royal Society; and Liberal lords closed ranks with the Tory leaders Sir Stafford Northcote and Lord Salisbury. The coffin was lowered, and the choristers sang 'His body is buried in peace, but his name liveth evermore.' Then, to the 'Dead March' from *Saul*, the mourners filed past, sombre, sable-suited figures, lit by coloured beams from the overlooking stained-glass panes commemorating the railway pioneers, George and Robert Stephenson.[23] The sky outside was clearing.

Galton was satisfied at this reverence for the new scientific priest-hood. The country's rulers were seen honouring a ruler of nature, and the ritual served as a visible reminder of evolution's 'religious

673

significance.' But work was still to be done. The next day, in the *Pall Mall Gazette*, Galton suggested that at church services the following Sunday the 'Benedicite' should replace the regular 'Te Deum.' Its invocation of praise – 'O all ye Works of the Lord: bless ye the Lord: praise him and magnify him for ever' – underscored what clergymen 'would probably wish to say afterwards from the pulpit' regarding Darwin. Galton perhaps raised the point directly when he coached Canon Farrar for his Sunday evening sermon at the Abbey. Nor was this the end of his commemorative scheme. He suggested a bust be erected, and also the incorporation of a new stained-glass window in the Abbey. Its panels would symbolize the works of nature praised in the Benedicite – the rocks, plants, fish, birds, and beasts – each to be contributed in Darwin's memory by a different country.[24]

The dignitaries of science and State liked the idea of worldwide homage to an English naturalist. One told the Bishop of Carlisle that the whole splendid pageant made him 'thankful for his native land.' The bishop assured his congregation at the Abbey that Sunday that the great scientist had been placed there 'in accordance with the judgment of the wisest of his countrymen.' He went on to strike the same patriotic note: 'Had this death occurred in France, no priest would have taken part in the funeral, or, if he had, no scientific man would have been present.' It was Galton's view entirely. He was the first to grasp the cultural significance of Darwin's burial in such hallowed ground. He talked of the higher 'feeling promoted by the ceremony,' the thrill of 'national honour and glory.' It proved that the scientists' moral duty in furthering human evolution was best exercised in harmony with the old religious ideals 'upon which the social fabric depends.'[25]

Nothing came of the evolution pane. But the idea of a bust had taken root and, at a meeting of scientists at Burlington House on Saturday, it was decided to start a fund. At the Royal Society two weeks later, a provisional committee was appointed, with Spottiswoode as chairman.[26] It decided on a bronze plaque in the Abbey. But the committee also commissioned a statue to stand on the central sweeping staircase in that great new Romanesque cathedral of science, the Natural History Museum at South Kensington.

Huxley took over the presidency of the Memorial Committee after Spottiswoode's own death and Abbey burial in 1883. He was aided by Galton, Lubbock, and Hooker, a cluster of sixty-one FRSs, the Lord Chief Justice, five MPs, and a phalanx of prelates led by the Archbishop of Canterbury. The High Church cried off – Canon Liddon declined to serve out of deference to his anti-Darwinian superior, the aged E. B. Pusey. Another conspicuous by his absence was Wallace. Nor did he contribute to the fund. The money began to pour in, and the scientists chivied their colleagues overseas, who started similar committees, making this a truly imperial endeavour. At home the largest individual contributions, £100 each, came from the instigators of the Abbey affair, Galton, Spottiswoode, and Lubbock. Emma and the family gave £200, and the X Club subscribed to a person – even Spencer, perennially penny-pinching, chipped in £2.

In all £4500 was raised, half of which went on the statue for the Natural History Museum. This 'Temple of Nature,' as *The Times* called it, had been completed only in 1880. The figure of Adam stood high over the entrance (he fell during World War Two) and an unapproving Richard Owen was still the towering presence. The unveiling of the Darwin statue had to wait until 1885, after Owen's retirement. Again the occasion was one of pomp and ceremony. The Prince of Wales was present, as were the family – except Emma – and Charles's close friends, Hooker, Galton, Romanes, Theta Farrer, and Admiral Sulivan. But it was the scientists, in the person of 'Pope' Huxley, who now occupied the pulpit.[27] And standing at the back among the congregation, scarcely noticed, was an old man, Parslow.

The Abbey interment gave tangible expression to the public feeling that Darwin, in his life and work, symbolized English success in conquering nature and civilizing the globe during Victoria's long reign.

Religious writers of all persuasions now testified to his 'noble character and his ardent pursuit of truth.' The *Church Times* was lost for epithets – patience, ingenuity, calmness, industry, moderation. Others added the Pauline graces perseverance and faith, and depicted him as a 'true Christian gentleman.' Even the evangelical *Record*, cagey about the burial itself, noticed his defence of missionaries as harbingers of civilization. And it reported the Bishop of Derry's speech at the annual meeting of the South American Missionary Society, in which he revealed, to some hear-hears, that Darwin had subscribed on a regular basis. The *Nonconformist and Independent* rang the changes on the 'moral influence' of his example.

But the most tireless supporters were the Unitarians and free religionists, proud that Darwin had been brought up in their rational Dissenting tradition and always appreciative of his naturalistic views. His trusted friend William Carpenter carried the entire British and Foreign Unitarian Association with his resolution applauding Darwin for unravelling 'the immutable laws of the Divine Government,' and for shedding light on 'the progress of humanity.' He sent the resolution to Emma, trusting that a Wedgwood would approve. Others too welcomed 'the most emphatic lesson' of Darwinism, 'the gospel of infinite progress.' They gloried in the 'universal applicability' of Darwin's teaching, which had brought 'order . . . and peace into life and thought.' From New York city, a Unitarian preacher, John Chadwick, described the momentous day at the Abbey in profanely Messianic language: 'The nation's grandest temple of religion opened its gates and lifted up its everlasting doors and bade the king of science come in.'[28]

The elegies stressed Darwin's exemplary character, his simple 'everyday virtues,' and his wealthy respectability. Mr Darwin's was 'an ideal life,' according to the *Saturday Review* – a private fortune, a great opportunity capitalized on the *Beagle*, 'immense labours, wisely planned and steadily executed,' amid scenes of 'quiet domestic happiness,' and all crowned by a 'sweet and gentle nature blossomed into perfection.' Many found Darwin's homeliness especially attractive. It was 'difficult to imagine a more beautiful picture of human happiness than that which he presented in his Kentish home, working at those great books which are acknowledged to have been a priceless gift to humanity, surrounded by a devoted family.'

Some even inverted the honour of official burial. Westminster did not bestow dignity on the naturalist from Downe – his body was hallowed already. 'The Abbey needed it more than it needed the Abbey,' thundered *The Times*. This saintly man, who had 'borne the flag of science,' extended the boundaries of knowledge, and 'established new centres whence annexations of fresh and fruitful truths are continually to be made,' gave the Abbey 'an increased sanctity, a new cause for reverence' on being laid beneath its stones. 'The Abbey has its orators and Ministers who have convinced reluctant senates and swayed nations. Not one of them all has wielded a power over men and their intelligences more complete than that which for the last twenty-three years has emanated from a simple country house in Kent.'[29]

Above all, the national and imperial theme was trumpeted in the press coverage. The *Pall Mall Gazette*, staunchly Liberal under John Morley's editorship, and staple fare for London's professionals, proclaimed that Great Britain had 'lost a man whose name is a glory to his country.' It noted Darwin's support for Gladstone and pictured him an equal world statesman. This emphasis on Darwin's global status – particularly by Liberals – came in final recognition of his politically comforting science. His image of biological and social progress, resting on individual competition, free trade and fair selection, had risen to dominance alongside the party that gave it political expression in mid-Victorian Britain.

'The Darwinian creed . . . runs through almost all the best thought of our time,' boasted Morley's Liberal rag on the day of the ceremony.

> It tinges our unformed public notions; it reappears under a
> hundred disguises in works on law and history, in political
> speeches and religious discourses, in artistic theories and vague
> social speculations. Our very novels and poems are full of
> latent Darwinian gems. If we try to think ourselves away
> from it we must think ourselves entirely away from our
> age.[30]

So Darwin's body had to be appropriated and buried with ecclesiastical pomp. The Abbey interment celebrated the vast, unfinished social transformation that England was undergoing. There were new colonies, new industries, new men to run them – not least a 'new Nature,' as Huxley called it, speaking through new priests, promising progress to all who obeyed.[31] Darwin's body was enshrined to the greater glory of the new professionals who had snatched it. The burial was their apotheosis, the last rite of a rising secularity. It marked the accession to power of the traders in nature's marketplace, the scientists and their minions in politics and religion. Such men, on the up-and-up, were paying their dues, for Darwin had naturalized Creation and delivered human nature and human destiny into their hands.

Society would never be the same. The 'Devil's Chaplain' had done his work.

Abbreviations

Annotated Calendar	Carroll, *Annotated Calendar of the Letters of Charles Darwin*, 1976.
APS	American Philosophical Society Library, Philadelphia.
ARW	Marchant, *Alfred Russel Wallace*, 2 vols., 1916.
Autobiography	Barlow, *Autobiography of Charles Darwin*, 1958.
BL	British Library, Department of Manuscripts.
BM(NH), OCorr./OColl.	British Museum (Natural History), Owen Correspondence / Owen Collection.
Calendar	Burkhardt and Smith, *Calendar of the Correspondence of Charles Darwin, 1821-1882*, 1985.
CCD	Burkhardt and Smith, *Correspondence of Charles Darwin*, 7 vols., 1985-91.
Charles Darwin	Barlow, *Charles Darwin and the Voyage of the 'Beagle'*, 1945.
Companion	Freeman, *Charles Darwin: A Companion*, 1978.
CP	Barrett, *Collected Papers of Charles Darwin*, 2 vols., 1977.
CUL	Cambridge University Library.
DAR	Darwin Archive, Cambridge University Library.
Darwin's Journal	De Beer, 'Darwin's Journal,' *Bulletin of the British Museum (Natural History), Historical Series*, 2 (1959), 1-21.
Descent	Darwin, *The Descent of Man*, 2 vols., 1871; rev. ed., 1 vol., 1874.
Diary	R. Keynes, *Charles Darwin's 'Beagle' Diary*, 1988.

679

Darwin

DON	Barlow, 'Darwin's Ornithological Notes,' *Bulletin of the British Museum (Natural History), Historical Series,* 2 (1963), 201-78.
Down House	Charles Darwin Museum, Down House, Downe, Kent.
ED	Litchfield, *Emma Darwin,* 2 vols., 1915 (otherwise 1904 private edition).
EUL	Edinburgh University Library.
Foundations	F. Darwin, *Foundations of the 'Origin of Species',* 1909.
Journal	Darwin, *Journal of Researches,* 1839; rev. ed., 1845/60.
KAO	Kent County Archives Office, Maidstone, Kent (collection transferred to Central Library, Bromley, Kent).
LJT	Eve and Creasey, *Life and Work of John Tyndall,* 1945.
LLAS	Clark and Hughes, *Life and Letters of the Reverend Adam Sedgwick,* 2 vols., 1890.
LLD	F. Darwin, *Life and Letters of Charles Darwin,* 3 vols., 1887.
LLJH	L. Huxley, *Life and Letters of Sir Joseph Dalton Hooker,* 2 vols., 1918.
LLL	K. Lyell, *Life, Letters, and Journals of Sir Charles Lyell,* 2 vols., 1881.
LLR	E. Romanes, *Life and Letters of George John Romanes,* 1896.
LLTH	L. Huxley, *Life and Letters of Thomas Henry Huxley,* 2 vols., 1900.
LRO	R. S. Owen, *Life of Richard Owen,* 2 vols., 1894.
MLD	F. Darwin and Seward, *More Letters of Charles Darwin,* 2 vols., 1903.
Narrative	Stanbury, *Narrative of the Voyage of H.M.S. 'Beagle',* 1977.
Natural Selection	Stauffer, *Charles Darwin's Natural Selection,* 1975.
Notebooks	Barrett *et al., Charles Darwin's Notebooks, 1836-1844,* 1987.
Origin	Darwin, *On the Origin of Species by means of Natural Selection,* 1859.
Pedigrees	Freeman, *Darwin Pedigrees,* 1984.
PRO	Public Record Office, Kew, and Quality Court, London.
RBL	Litchfield, *Richard Buckley Litchfield,* 1910.
RFD	Recollections of Francis Darwin, Darwin Archive 140.3, Cambridge University Library.
TBI	Colp, *To Be an Invalid,* 1977.

Abbrevations

THP	Thomas Huxley Papers, Imperial College of Science and Technology, London.
UCL	University College London.
W/M	Wedgwood-Mosley Collection, Keele University Library.
Wedgwood	B. and H. Wedgwood, *The Wedgwood Circle*, 1980.

NOTES

A DEVIL'S CHAPLAIN?

1. For a survey of previous studies: Colp, 'Charles Darwin's Past and Future Biographies.'
2. Greene, 'Reflections;' Churchill, 'Darwin.'
3. J. Moore, 'Darwin's Genesis.' The Darwin Industry is analysed in Ruse, 'Darwin Industry,' and J. Moore, 'On Revolutionizing.'
4. Oldroyd, 'How did Darwin arrive at His Theory?' 334ff; La Vergata, 'Images,' 953-58; R. Young, *Darwin's Metaphor*, 23ff.
5. Churchill, 'Darwin,' 62; Kohn, *Darwinian Heritage*, 4; Lenoir, 'Darwin Industry,' 115-16; Desmond, 'Kentish Hog' and 'Darwin;' R. Young, 'Darwinism;' Schweber, 'Correspondence.'
6. J. Moore, 'Freethought,' 293; Desmond, *Politics*, 373-414; R. Young, 'Darwin,' 71; Lenoir, 'Darwin Industry,' 117; Rudwick, 'Charles Darwin,' 186 n. 2.
7. Colp, 'Charles Darwin's Past and Future Biographies,' 167; *ED*, 2:203.

1 CATCHING A FALLING CHRISTIAN

1. Krause, *Erasmus Darwin*, 45; also *LLD*, 2:158.
2. The words of grandson Charles, referring to those like himself who had gone beyond Unitarianism: Darwin to T. Wollaston, 6 June [1856], EUL, Gen. 1999/1/30.
3. King-Hele, *Doctor*, 289 and *Letters*, 127.
4. Darwin to Reginald Darwin, 4 April 1879, in Colp, 'Relationship,' 11; J. Moore, 'Of Love,' 204–205.
5. *Pedigrees*, 35; King-Hele, *Doctor*; McNeil, *Under the Banner*; R. Porter, 'Erasmus Darwin;' J. Browne, 'Botany.'
6. Corrected proof sheets of Darwin's 'Preliminary Notice' to Krause, *Erasmus Darwin*, DAR 210.20; *Wedgwood*, 239; *Autobiography*, 93.
7. King-Hele, *Doctor*, 73, 77, 89, 100–101, 106, 130 and *Letters*, 35–37, 54, 65, 130; McNeil, *Under the Banner*, 9–15; McKendrick, 'Josiah Wedgwood;' *Wedgwood*, 36, ch. 6.
8. Holt, *Unitarian Contribution*, ch. 2; Seed, 'Theologies,' 108–14; King-Hele, *Letters*, 38.
9. McNeil, *Under the Banner*, 83; King-Hele, *Doctor*, 93-94, 135, 142-43 and *Letters*, 284, 286; *Wedgwood*, 8, 11, 16; *Memorable Unitarians*, 166–67; McKendrick, 'Role,' 297–302; Brooke, 'Joseph Priestley,' 12.
10. King-Hele, *Letters*, 8-9, 43; Rowell, *Hell*, 33–38; Willey, *Eighteenth Century*

Background, ch. 10; Brooke, 'Sower,' 439–48; Webb, 'Unitarian Background,' 10–13.

11. R. Porter, 'I Live too Chaste. 'Tis Not a Common Fault,' *Independent* (London), 28 July 1990, p. 27; King-Hele, *Letters*, 91, 297 and *Doctor*, 121–22, 131, 134, 136, 138–40, 172; *Wedgwood*, 74; Woodall, 'Charles Darwin,' 9; *Pedigrees*, 35; *Autobiography*, 30.

12. King-Hele, *Doctor*, 123–24, 176–78 and *Letters*, 164–65; Woodall, 'Charles Darwin,' 11; *LLD*, 1:8–9.

13. H. Gruber, *Darwin*, 46–47; King-Hele, *Doctor*, 204, 211–13, 217, 230, 232–33 and *Letters*, 166, 204–205, 215–16, 225–26; McNeil, *Under the Banner*, 79–85; *Wedgwood*, 98, 101–104.

14. *Wedgwood*, 102–103, 108; Keith, *Darwin*, 4; *Autobiography*, 29–30; *LLD*, 1:9; King-Hele, *Doctor*, 258.

15. D, 'Death;' *LLD*, 1:9; *Companion*, 209; King-Hele, *Doctor*, 273–74, 284–85; *Pedigrees*, 10.

16. *Wedgwood*, 132–38; *ED*, 1:26.

17. Colp, 'Mrs. Susannah Darwin,' 4–6; Woodall, 'Charles Darwin,' 1; *Autobiography*, 28, 40; *Pedigrees*, 34; *Wedgwood*, 116–17.

18. Woodall, 'Charles Darwin,' 12; E. Thompson, *Making*, 529–42; King-Hele, *Doctor*, 264–65, 297.

19. Broadbent, *Story*, 5, 9, 12; Woodall, 'Charles Darwin,' 11–12; *Autobiography*, 22; recollections of W. Leighton, DAR 112. In 1798, when a minister was being sought, Samuel Taylor Coleridge had stood as a candidate, but then Susannah's father granted him a fat £150 annuity to pursue his literary interests, and the post fell to Case.

20. *Autobiography*, 22–24, 26–27; CCD, 1:537, 2:438; Woodall, 'Charles Darwin,' 14; *Wedgwood*, 117.

21. Mansergh, 'Charles Darwin;' Bowlby, *Charles Darwin*, 56; recollections of W. Leighton, DAR 112; *Autobiography*, 23, 27; CCD, 2:439–40.

22. CCD, 2:439–40; *Autobiography*, 22, 24; Colp, 'Mrs. Susannah Darwin,' 7–11; Colp, 'Notes on Charles Darwin's *Autobiography*,' 364; *Wedgwood*, 181.

23. *Autobiography*, 30, 32, 39; *ED*, 1:60; *Charles Darwin*, 8–9.

24. CCD, 1:537; *Wedgwood*, 165; *ED*, 1:139–40; E. Richards, 'Darwin,' 82.

25. CCD, 2:440; Bowen, *Idea*, 213.

26. Recollections of W. Leighton, DAR 112; *Autobiography*, 27–28, 43.

27. E. Craddock to F. Darwin, 10 July 1882, DAR 112:16–17; *Autobiography*, 25, 42, 44; Colp, 'Notes on Charles Darwin's *Autobiography*,' 363–64.

28. CCD, 1:538; 2:440–41; *Autobiography*, 44–45; Bowlby, *Charles Darwin*, 64; recollections of W. Leighton and of J. Price, DAR 112.

29. CCD, 1:1–15; *Wedgwood*, 112; Chaldecott, 'Josiah Wedgwood.'

30. Green, *Address*, 36, 41–42.

31. *Autobiography*, 45–46; CCD, 1:1–15.

32. *Autobiography*, 44, 46; *Wedgwood*, 138, 195–96.

33. *ED*, 1:56, 61, 141–42, 160–61; *Wedgwood*, 195, 198; E. Wedgwood, *My First Reading Book*; Thackray, 'Natural Knowledge,' 679–80.

34. *Autobiography*, 28, 36, 39; CCD, 1:14–15.

2 THE NORTHERN ATHENS

1. *Autobiography*, 47-48; *TBI*, 3-4.

2. *CCD*, 1:15–16; Shepperson, 'Intellectual Background,' 17–20; Audubon, *Audubon*, 1:210.
3. *Report from the Select Committee on Medical Education* . . . (Parliamentary Papers, 13 Aug. 1834), pt 1, 93; Chitnis, 'Medical Education;' Parry and Parry, *Rise*, 105–107.
4. *CCD*, 1:15, 18–19; Mudie, *Modern Athens*, 23.
5. Mudie, *Modern Athens*, 252–53; *CCD*, 1:19, 28.
6. *Pedigrees*, 10, 31; King-Hele, *Doctor*, 123.
7. *CCD*, 1:25, 28–29, 41; *Autobiography*, 52; Audubon, *Audubon*, 1:206.
8. Mudie, *Modern Athens*, 185; *CCD*, 1:38–40, 44.
9. McMenemey, 'Education,' 138–39; Desmond, *Politics*, 166; *CCD*, 1:34.
10. *CCD*, 1:16, 39, 45; Shepperson, 'Intellectual Background,' 27.
11. *CCD*, 1:25; *Medico-Chirurgical Review*, 20 (1833–34), 315–19; Morrell, 'Science;' Mudie, *Modern Athens*, 220; A. Grant, *Story*, 2:389–90.
12. In 1826–27 Knox taught 207 anatomy students, compared to Lizars's 104 (the next highest) and Monro's 78: Struthers, *Historical Sketch*, 92. On Robert Knox: E. Richards, 'Moral Anatomy.'
13. *CCD*, 1:25; *Autobiography*, 47; Audubon, *Audubon*, 1:146, 174. Knox lectured at 10 Surgeons' Square, Lizars at No. 1: Cathcart, 'Some of the Older Schools,' 775–78.
14. *CCD*, 1:iv, 25, 36; A. Grant, *Story*, 2:424–5; *Evidence*, 1:220–22.
15. *Autobiography*, 39–40, 47–48; recollections of G. Darwin, DAR 112; Richardson, *Death*, 41.
16. Morrell, 'Science,' 54–55; Ashworth, 'Charles Darwin,' 98; *CCD*, 1:25, 29; *Autobiography*, 47.
17. *CCD*, 1:29; Freeman, 'Darwin's Negro Bird-Stuffer;' *Autobiography*, 51. Waterton had a flair for notoriety. He had just launched his sensational hoax, the 'Nondescript' – a Red Howler Monkey with a face recast in grotesque caricature of the Secretary to the Treasury: Aldington, *Strange Life*, 112–14.
18. *CCD*, 1:22, 36–39, 41.
19. Diary for 1826, DAR 129; *Autobiography*, 45. Darwin's copy of White's *Natural History of Selborne* (2 vols., 1825) is in the Darwin Library, CUL.
20. R. Porter, 'Erasmus Darwin,' 58; *Autobiography*, 49.

3 SEA-MATS & SEDITIOUS SCIENCE

1. *Autobiography*, 46; Peterson, 'Gentlemen,' 462.
2. *Evidence*, 1:146.
3. W. Browne, 'Observations.'
4. Plinian Minutes MSS, 1:ff. 34–36, EUL, Dc.2.53; G. Bell, *Letters*, 251; Kirsop, 'W. R. Greg,' 377–83; Desmond, *Politics*, 210, on the deterministic science and theology taught at Lant Carpenter's Unitarian school in Bristol, which Greg attended.
5. *Phrenological Journal*, 5 (1829), 141; Kirsop, 'W. R. Greg,' 378–83; Shapin, 'Phrenological Knowledge,' and Cooter, *Cultural Meaning*, on phrenology's social appeal.
6. Ainsworth, 'Mr. Darwin.' William F. Ainsworth, later to become famous as an Oriental scholar, was a Plinian President who sometimes accompanied Darwin on his coastal walks.
7. *Autobiography*, 48; Balfour, *Biography*.

8. Desmond, 'Making,' 163, 167; Corsi, *Age*, chs. 3–4.
9. Audubon, *Audubon*, 1:149, 223; R. Grant, 'Notice of a New Zoophyte.' The details of Grant's life are from 'Biographical Sketch of Robert Edmond Grant,' *Lancet*, 2 (1850), 686–95; Poore, 'Robert Edmond Grant,' 190; Desmond, 'Robert E. Grant' and *Politics*. For his zoology: Sloan, 'Darwin's Invertebrate Program,' 73–87.
10. Beddoe, *Memories*, 32; Godlee, 'Thomas Wharton Jones,' 102; Poore, 'Robert Edmond Grant,' 190; *Autobiography*, 49.
11. Wernerian Society Minutes, 1:f. 272, EUL, Dc.2.55; 'Edinburgh Zoology Notebook,' DAR 118, in *CP*, 2:283–91.
12. R. Grant, 'Notice regarding the Ova.' Darwin exhibited the leech's eggs at the 3 April Plinian meeting: Ainsworth, 'Mr. Darwin'. On the Wernerian Society: *Evidence*, 1:146; *Autobiography*, 51; Audubon, *Audubon*, 1:186. Despite Grant's patronage, his seniority remained paramount, judging by the fact that he once warned Darwin against seizing priority and publishing on *his* subject: Jesperson, 'Charles Darwin,' 164–65. Grant, like so many naturalists before professional standards were introduced into science, was bedevilled by 'plagiarists:' Desmond, *Politics*, 401–402.
13. 'Edinburgh Zoology Notebook,' DAR 118, f. 6, in *CP*, 2:288. His transcription of Lamarck can be found in DAR 5. See also Egerton, 'Darwin's Early Reading,' 454–55; *CCD*, 1:22.
14. Plinian Minutes, 1:ff. 56–57, EUL, Dc.2.53; H. Gruber, *Darwin*, 479; Desmond, *Politics*, 67–69, 402. Greg, Browne, Grant, and Ainsworth joined in the *mêlée* at the end of the talk.
15. McMenemey, 'Education,' 145; Desmond, *Politics*, 120, 264–67.
16. Wernerian Society Minutes, 1:ff. 241–43, EUL, Dc.2.55; Desmond, *Politics*, ch. 2 and Desmond, 'Lamarckism' for Grant's friendship with Geoffroy and the radical basis of his philosophical anatomy. Grant was in the Geoffroyan mainstream. Appel, *Cuvier-Geoffroy Debate*, ch. 5, describes the excitement in Paris at this time as Geoffroy's disciples announced all manner of homologies between insects, crustaceans, molluscs, and vertebrates.
17. Jameson, 'Observations.' Jameson's authorship was ascertained by Secord, 'Edinburgh Lamarckians.' See also: R. Grant, 'Structure,' 283–84; Desmond, 'Robert E. Grant's Later Views,' 405–406; Desmond, *Politics*, 59–81, 398–403; *Autobiography*, 49; and Corsi, *Age*, ch. 8 on French science in this period.
18. R. Porter, 'Erasmus Darwin,' 39; R. Grant, *Dissertatio Physiologica*, 8; R. Grant, *Tabular View*, v; Shepperson, 'Intellectual Background,' 27.
19. Sloan, 'Darwin's Invertebrate Program,' 78–84; Jameson, 'Observations,' 295.
20. Matthew, *On Naval Timber*, 364–69; Dempster, *Patrick Matthew*, 98–99. Wells, 'Historical Context,' discusses Matthew's *laissez-faire* radicalism and evolutionary views.
21. Hugh Miller, in Hodge, 'England,' 11; Corsi, *Science*, 273; Balfour, *Biography*, 7–12, 39.
22. *Evidence*, 1:145; Secord, 'Discovery;' Mudie, *Modern Athens*, 221 on Jameson as one of the immortals.
23. *Evidence*, 1:141–42, App., 115–18; Secord, 'Discovery.'
24. Jameson's testimony, *Evidence*, 1:141–42. The course included 'Instructions and Demonstrations as to the mode of collecting, preserving, transporting, and arranging objects of Natural History' (App., 118), something that was to

prove immensely important to Darwin during his *Beagle* voyage. See also Sweet, 'Robert Jameson.'

25. Ainsworth, 'Present State,' 271, 276; 'Phrenology and Professor Jameson,' *Phrenological Journal*, 1 (1824), 56; *Evidence*, 1:142, 144–45; Chitnis, 'University of Edinburgh's Natural History Museum,' 86–88, 90–93.

26. *Evidence*, 1:223; *Autobiography*, 52. Duncan opposed the botany professor Robert Graham's rival – and rather antiquated – Linnean system. On De Candolle's botany: J. Browne, *Secular Ark*, 52–57.

27. Kirsop, 'W. R. Greg,' 377–78; Coldstream, *Sketch*, 10–11; Balfour, *Biography*, 38; Desmond, *Politics*, 81; *ED*, 1:194.

4 ANGLICAN ORDERS

1. *CCD*, 1:58, 539; *ED*, 1:198.

2. Brent, *Charles Darwin*, 56; *ED*, 1:183, 200-202, 208.

3. *ED*, 1:139–40, 227; *CCD*, 1:22, 24, 28, 40–41, 44.

4. *ED*, 1:206–10, 227; *Autobiography*, 55; *Wedgwood*, 200.

5. Such a place of last resort was also in Squire Owen's mind when, years later, he asked Darwin about a tutor for his third son, 'a very honorable, & well disposed Boy,' but immature and rather slow, 'who if nothing better offers I intend for the Church:' *CCD*, 1:528–29; *Autobiography*, 56-57.

6. Trollope, *Clergymen*, ch. 5; Addison, *English Country Parson*; Hart, *Country Priest* and *Curate's Lot*; Colloms, *Victorian Country Parsons*; Evans, 'Some Reasons,' 85-101; Halévy, *History*, 342-52; J. Moore, 'Darwin of Down,' 441–42.

7. *Companion*, 116, 296; cf. *Wedgwood*, 198.

8. *Autobiography*, 56–57; Darwin's notes on Sumner's *Evidences of Christianity*, DAR 91:114–18. Cf. H. Gruber, *Darwin*, 125–26 and Dell, 'Social and Economic Theories.' Darwin's notes are undated, but they appear for the most part on the same kind of paper he used for his 'Early notes on guns and shooting' (DAR 91:1–3), datable between 1825 and 1827 (*Autobiography*, 44, 54). A later dating is also possible: J. Moore, 'Darwin of Down,' 478 n.3.

9. *Autobiography*, 58; *CCD*, 1:48, 51, 70–71.

10. *Cambridge Guide*; E. Evans, 'Some Reasons;' E. Thompson, *Making*, 246ff; Hobsbawm and Rudé, *Captain Swing*, ch. 4.

11. *Cambridge Guide*, 9-10; Brace of Cantabs, *Gradus*, 83–84; Winstanley, *Unreformed Cambridge*, 22–24; Parker, *Town and Gown*, ch. 15.

12. *Cambridge Guide*, 29–35; Brace of Cantabs, *Gradus*, 90; Winstanley, *Unreformed Cambridge*, 197–203.

13. *Cambridge Guide*, 18; Winstanley, *Unreformed Cambridge*, 16–33.

14. Parker, *Town and Gown*, 142–43; Stokes, *Cambridge Parish Workhouses*, 27; Winstanley, *Later Victorian Cambridge*, 92–93.

15. *LLD*, 1:163; *CCD*, 1:1–18.

16. Brace of Cantabs, *Gradus*, 14, 121–31; cf. Winstanley, *Unreformed Cambridge*, 203ff.

17. Peacock, *Observations*, 76.

18. *CCD*, 1:3; *LLAS*, 1:317; Speakman, *Adam Sedgwick*, ch. 5; Secord, *Controversy*, ch. 2.

19. Spinning House committals, 1823–1836, CUL, University Archives, T.VIII.1, esp. 149-96. Cf. Marcus, *Other Victorians*, esp. 100–103.

20. *CCD*, 1:48–49, 53–55.

21. Reid, *Life, Letters,* 1:75; Pope–Hennessy, *Monckton Milnes,* 10ff; Preyer, 'Romantic Tide,' 43-46; P. Allen, *Cambridge Apostles,* ch. 1; CCD, 1:112.
22. Gascoigne, *Cambridge,* 252–62; Reid, *Life, Letters,* 1:51; W. Carus, *Memoirs,* 641, 648ff; Smyth, *Simeon,* 98ff, 202ff, 296–98; Barclay, *Whatever Happened,* ch. 1; O. Chadwick, *Victorian Church,* 1:110, 442, 449.
23. J. Cameron to F. Darwin, 15 Sept. [1882], DAR 112:14; *Autobiography,* 61–62; J. Herbert to F. Darwin, 26 May and 12 June 1882, DAR 112:50–51, 58–59; CCD, 1:58.
24. CCD, 1:539; D. Allen, *Naturalist,* 101–103; Barber, *Heyday,* chs. 1-2.
25. *Pedigrees,* 15, 28; LLD, 1:322; *Autobiography,* 63; RFD, 110; CCD, 1:74, 82.
26. CCD, 1:57, 91; Blomefield, *Chapters,* 54; *Autobiography,* 62–63.
27. CCD, 1:58–59 and cf. *Autobiography,* 62; Samouelle, *Entomologist's Useful Compendium,* 160; K. Smith, 'Darwin's Insects,' 7ff.
28. CUL, University Archives, C.U.R. 39.16.6–7 and O.XIV.109; [Blomefield], *Memoir,* 29-30, 49–51; Todhunter, *William Whewell,* 1:36–37.
29. CCD, 1:7; *Autobiography,* 64, 66–67; CP, 2:72.

5 PARADISE & PUNISHMENT

1. CCD, 1:56, 59, 61, 72, 325, 430; J. Heaviside to F. Darwin, 15 Sept. 1882, DAR 112:56–57.
2. CCD, 1:59, 61; recollections of J. Herbert, DAR 112; *Autobiography,* 58.
3. CCD, 1:62, 64–65.
4. CCD, 1:62–67, 70.
5. CCD, 1:51, 54, 66, 69, 71–72.
6. *Cambridge Guide,* 145–49; LLD, 1:165; *Companion,* 55; CCD, 1:70.
7. *Cambridge Guide,* 29; CCD, 1:68, 70–77, 98; TBI, 7–8.
8. CCD, 1:73–76, 78, 80, 539; [Blomefield], *Memoir,* 8; recollections of J. Price, DAR 112; *Cambridge Guide,* 304. On entomological society in London: D. Allen, *Naturalist,* 103–106; Desmond, 'Making,' 157ff.
9. Recollections of J. Herbert, DAR 112; LLD, 1:171; CCD, 1:64, 67.
10. Recollections of J. Price, DAR 112; CCD, 1:76, 79.
11. CCD, 1:79, 81–82.
12. CCD, 1:79–82; *Autobiography,* 60.
13. Acta Curiae, 1822–1835, CUL, University Archives, V.C.Ct.I.19:146–51; Cooper, *Annals,* 561–62; CCD, 1:82–83.
14. CUL, University Archives, UP 7.234; Cooper, *Annals,* 560–63; CCD, 1:8. On Castle Hill: *Cambridge Guide,* 232, 235–36; Parker, *Town and Gown,* 143.
15. CCD, 1:79, 82, 84–85.
16. *Cambridge and Hertford Independent Press,* 9 May 1829, p. [2], col. 1, and 16 May 1829, p. [2], col. 1; Joseph Romilly diary, 1829, CUL, Add. 6810; Cooper, *Annals,* 563; Reid, *Life, Letters,* 1:65–67; CCD, 1:85.
17. Royle, *Victorian Infidels,* 34–39; J. Wiener, *Radicalism,* esp. 130ff, 463; Desmond, 'Artisan Resistance,' 82; Royle, 'Taylor, Robert;' W. Carus, *Memoirs,* 308; Hole, *Pulpits, Politics,* 190–93, ch. 14.
18. *Lion,* 3 (24 April 1829), 519 and (29 May 1829), 673–74, 678, 682, 684. On Darwin's print purchases: CCD, 1:70–71; *Autobiography,* 61; RFD, 95–96; recollections of W. Darwin and of J. Herbert, DAR 112.

19. *Lion,* 3 (29 May 1829), 674–75; J. Moore, 'Freethought,' 290–93.
20. *Lion,* 3 (29 May 1829), 673, 675, 678, 682, 686.
21. *Lion,* 3 (29 May 1829), 682–83; CUL, University Archives, UP 7.244 and C.U.R. 124 for the regulations, and Rose Crescent lodging houses as late as 1854; Winstanley, *Early Victorian Cambridge,* 59–60.
22. *Lion,* 3 (29 May 1829), 678, 685, and (5 June 1829), 705–707; Joseph Romilly diary, 1829, CUL, Add. 6810; CUL, University Archives, UP 7.245; R. Taylor, *Devil's Pulpit* (1881 ed.), 2:vi.

6 THE MAN WHO WALKS WITH HENSLOW

1. Briggs, *Age,* 227ff; Hole, *Pulpits, Politics,* ch. 16; Cooper, *Annals,* 559–60, 563–64; Gascoigne, *Cambridge,* 236; C. Wordsworth to J. Brogden, 28 Mar. 1829, CUL, University Archives, UP.5; *LLAS,* 1:341–49; Brilioth, *Anglican Revival,* 93–96; CCD, 1:85–86.
2. CCD, 1:88–90.
3. CCD, 1:90–93; *Pedigrees,* 11.
4. CCD, 1:90, 93–94, 96; *Autobiography,* 63; K. Smith, 'Darwin's Insects,' 7–9.
5. CCD, 1:93–94; recollections of J. Price, DAR 112.
6. CCD, 1:95–96; 'Names of Men who attended the Botanical Lectures . . .,' CUL, University Archives, O.XIV.261; Blomefield, *Chapters,* 10, 12, 23; Blomefield, *Naturalist's Calendar;* Leonard Jenyns, '[ta peri emauta]' MS diary, commonplace books, and notes in possession of R. G. Jenyns, Bottisham Hall, Bottisham, Cambridgeshire; *Autobiography,* 66–67.
7. CCD, 1:96–97.
8. CCD, 1:98; CUL, University Archives, C.U.R. 28.11 (2 July 1829), 8; Examination Papers, 1830, CUL, L952.b.1.7.
9. Clarke, *Paley,* ch. 4; LeMahieu, *Mind,* ch. 1; Gascoigne, *Cambridge,* 241–44; Cole, 'Doctrine, Dissent.'
10. *Autobiography,* 59; Paley, *View,* 2:24–25, 395, 410. On Paley and revelation: Clarke, *Paley,* ch. 8; LeMahieu, *Mind,* ch. 4.
11. Paley, *View,* 2:395; CCD, 1:101; Previous Examination, 1824–1843, CUL, University Archives, Exam.L.67.
12. CCD, 1:99–102.
13. CCD, 1:102; recollections of J. Rodwell and of W. Leighton, DAR 112
14. [Blomefield], *Memoir,* 4–7, 13, 16–21, 30–39, 46–47; *Cambridge Guide,* 13; Walters, *Shaping,* 47–58.
15. CP, 2:72–73; Spinning House committals, 1823–1836, CUL, University Archives, T.VIII.1, esp. 209–97; *Autobiography,* 64–65; CCD, 1:104.
16. CP, 2:72–73; [Blomefield], *Memoir,* 41; recollections of J. Rodwell, DAR 112; CCD, 1:80; 'Plants gathered in five herborizing expeditions . . .,' CUL, University Archives, UP.5.
17. Sloan, 'Darwin, Vital Matter,' 373; 'Names of Men who attended the Botanical Lectures . . .,' CUL, University Archives, O.XIV.261; [Blomefield], *Memoir,* 39; recollections of J. Rodwell and of W. Leighton, DAR 112.
18. 'Edinburgh Zoology Notebook,' DAR 118 f. 13; *Autobiography,* 66; Sloan, 'Darwin, Vital Matter,' 373–87, 395 and 'Darwin's Invertebrate Program,' 86–87.
19. CCD, 1:95, 103–106, 272. The Bembidiidae beetles (Stephens, *Systematic Catalogue,* 1:36–41) are now the Family Bembidiini.

20. CCD, 1:50, 100, 105–109, 115, 192–93, 208, 255, 634. What Fanny enclosed was 'some scrawl of mine . . . out of my Book.' Her offer to 'do you another' was contingent on Charles's next visit. For her portrait: *Calendar*, 8917, 8926.

7 EVERY MAN FOR HIMSELF

1. R. Taylor, *Devil's Pulpit* (1881 ed.), 2:79; E. Thompson, *Making*, 843–44; J. Wiener, *Radicalism*, 164–70; Royle, *Victorian Infidels*, 39–40.
2. CCD, 1:109–11, 123, 180; *Autobiography*, 59, 64; [Blomefield], *Memoir*, 48, 57–58.
3. CCD, 1:110; Sedgwick, *Discourse*, 95–102; Todhunter, *William Whewell*, 2:174–78.
4. Gascoigne, *Cambridge*, 241–44; Paley, *Principles*, 1:217, 2:138–39, 302; Francis, 'Naturalism;' Clarke, *Paley*. chs. 5–6.
5. [Blomefield], *Memoir*, 60–61; *Autobiography*, 65.
6. E. Thompson, *Making*, ch. 7; E. Evans, 'Some Reasons;' Hobsbawm and Rudé, *Captain Swing*, 165–67; *Cambridge Chronicle and Journal*, 3 Dec. 1830, p. [3], col. 4; 10 Dec. 1830, pp. [1], col. 4 and [2], col. 5.
7. Recollections of J. Herbert, DAR 112.
8. CCD, 1:111–12; Examination Papers, 1831, CUL, L952.b.1.8; *Autobiography*, 59.
9. Recollections of J. Herbert, DAR 112; F. Watkins to F. Darwin, 18 July [1882?], DAR 112:111–14; LLD, 1:169–70; CCD, 2:125–26.
10. J. Heaviside to F. Darwin, 15 Sept. 1882, DAR 112:56–57; Monsarrat, *Thackeray*, 42; CCD, 1:113–19.
11. CCD, 1:112, 124; Blomefield, *Chapters*, 54; L. Jenyns to J. Hooker, 1 May 1882 (copy), DAR 112:67–68.
12. 'Names of Men who attended the Botanical Lectures . . .,' CUL, University Archives, O.XIV.261; CCD, 1:123.
13. Paley, *Natural Theology*, vii, 465, 490; Francis, 'Naturalism,' 212–16; Gillespie, 'Divine Design;' Clarke, *Paley*, ch. 7; LeMahieu, *Mind*, ch. 3.
14. Paley, *Natural Theology*, 465; Herschel, *Preliminary Discourse*, 350, 353 in Darwin Library, CUL; CCD, 1:118; *Autobiography*, 68; Ruse, 'Darwin's Debt,' 160ff; Schweber, 'John Herschel.'
15. [Blomefield], *Memoir*, 11, 13–15; Cannon, *Science*, 86ff; CCD, 1:539. Henslow later presented Darwin with Humboldt's book: CCD, 1:120.
16. *Autobiography*, 67–68; CCD, 1:120, 122–23, 125, 539.
17. J. Wiener, *Radicalism*, 174–79; Royle, 'Taylor, Robert,' 469; *The Times*, 31 May 1831, p. 4, cols. 1–2; ED, 1:234.
18. CCD, 1:121–22, 147; *Autobiography*, 68; Halévy, *Triumph*, 32–33.
19. Cooper, *Annals*, 570; CCD, 1:122–24; LLAS, 1:374–76; Todhunter, *William Whewell*, 2:118; Gascoigne, *Cambridge*, 236.
20. LLAS, 1:204, 376; [Blomefield], *Memoir*, 13–14; Secord, *Controversy*, 45–47; recollections of J. Rodwell, DAR 112; CCD, 1:25, 125.
21. CCD, 1:125–27.
22. Secord, *Controversy*, 47–53; LLAS, 1:378–80; *Autobiography*, 69; CCD, 1:540.
23. Secord, 'Discovery;' LLAS, 1:381; Barrett, 'Sedgwick–Darwin Geologic Tour,' 147–48, 157–58.
24. *Autobiography*, 69–71; LLAS, 1:381; recollections of G. Darwin, DAR 112; CCD, 1:127–31; Barrett, 'Sedgwick-Darwin Geologic Tour,' 149, 161–62.

8 MY FINAL EXIT

1. CCD, 1:127–30; Diary, 3.
2. CCD, 1:132–35, 151, 165, 382; Diary, 3; Graber and Miles, 'In Defence,' 99; cf. Autobiography, 71–72.
3. CCD, 1:135–16, 139–41, 145; L. Jenyns to J. Hooker, 1 May 1882 (copy), DAR 112:67–68; Diary, 3.
4. CCD, 1:140–41, 144, 146; Mellersh, FitzRoy; Burstyn, 'If Darwin wasn't;' Stanbury, 'H.M.S. Beagle,' 82; S. Gould, 'Darwin.'
5. CCD, 1:140, 144, 148–50, 156; Barlow, 'Robert FitzRoy,' 496; F. Darwin, 'FitzRoy,' 547.
6. CCD, 1:144, 146, 149; Autobiography, 72; Hyman, 'Darwin Sidelight.'
7. CCD, 1:154; F. Darwin, 'FitzRoy,' 547; Basalla, 'Voyage;' Nicholas and Nicholas, Darwin, 3–5.
8. CCD, 1:154; Narrative, 27–33; Barlow, 'FitzRoy,' 501–502; Stanbury, 'H.M.S. Beagle,' 76–78.
9. CCD, 1:154–56, 177, 553–54; B. Sulivan to [F.] Darwin, 12 Dec. 1884, DAR 112; K. Thomson, 'H.M.S. Beagle,' 665–66, 670–71; Stanbury, 'H.M.S. Beagle,' 86–92; R. Keynes, Beagle Record, 21, 39.
10. CCD, 1:155–57, 161, 167; Autobiography, 110. Henslow's gift, inscribed 21 September 1831, is in the Darwin Library, CUL.
11. CCD, 1:163, 165, 168–69, 171, 192–93, 540; Wedgwood, 215.
12. J. Wiener, Radicalism, 176–80; 'Trial of the Rev. Robert Taylor,' The Times, 5 July 1831, p. 4, col. 3; 9 July, p. 3, col. 1; 21 July, p. 5, col. 3; 23 July, p. 3, col. 5; Halévy, Triumph, 40; Briggs, Age, 251–53; CCD, 1:172, 174–76, 393; E. Thompson, Making, 888ff.
13. Notes on preserving specimens, DAR 29.3:78ff; Reports of the Council and Auditors of the Accounts of the Zoological Society of London, read at the Anniversary Meeting, April 30th 1832 (London: Taylor, 1832), 9–10; Desmond, 'Making,' 232; CCD, 1:146–48, 171, 173; Autobiography, 103.
14. CCD, 1:143–44, 148–50, 172, 175.
15. CCD, 1:172, 176–77, 180, 182; J. Gruber, 'Who,' 271ff; Diary, 4–7. So wretched was the navy surgeon's lot that passions were flaring. A riot actually broke out in the London College of Surgeons over the snubbing of ships' surgeons in 1831: London Medical Gazette, 7 (1830–31), 765.
16. CCD, 1:175, 177–80; Diary, 6–7, 133; Narrative, 35.
17. CCD, 1:163, 179–80, 183, 186; Diary, 8–9; Autobiography, 79–80; Colp, 'Pre-Beagle Misery.'
18. CCD, 1:127, 145, 168–69, 173–74, 181–84, 186; Diary, 9.
19. CCD, 1:177, 182; Diary, 7–8, 10–11.
20. CCD, 1:187; Diary, 11–12, 13–15.
21. CCD, 1:180, 190; Diary, 15–17; F. Darwin, 'FitzRoy,' 547.

9 A CHAOS OF DELIGHT

1. Narrative, 40–41; Diary, 17–18; CCD, 1:201.
2. Diary, 19–20; CCD, 1:201–202; Narrative, 44–45.
3. Diary, 21–25; CCD, 1:202; Narrative, 46.
4. Secord, 'Discovery;' Diary, 24–26, 30, 33; Charles Darwin, 156–57.
5. Autobiography, 81; Diary, 27, 34.

6. Diary, 36–37; Narrative, 49–52; CCD, 1:203, 240.
7. Diary, 37–41, 48; CCD, 1:206; Charles Darwin, 158.
8. Diary, 41–44; CCD, 1:205; Cannon, Science, 87; Paradis, 'Darwin,' 95ff.
9. Diary, 43–46; Narrative, 56; Autobiography, 73–74.
10. CCD, 1:192–93, 197–98, 219–20; Diary, 46–51.
11. Diary, 52–60, 74; Journal (1839), 21–28, 605; CCD, 1:247, 252; Charles Darwin, 164–65.
12. Diary, 61–78; CCD, 1:226.
13. Diary, 64–77; CCD, 1:227, 230, 232, 237–38, 241, 247; CP, 1:182–85; Journal (1839), 35, 38.
14. Diary, 71–72, 77–80; CCD, 1:225, 231–32; J. Gruber, 'Who,' 275–76; Burstyn, 'If Darwin wasn't,' 67–68.
15. Diary, 81–83; CCD, 1:247, 248, 251–52; Autobiography, 85; Schweber, 'John Herschel,' 52–55.
16. CCD, 1:222–23, 248–50, 261, 277; Diary, 78, 84, 87–91, Narrative, 74–78; Parodiz, Darwin, 76–78.
17. Sloan, 'Darwin, Vital Matter,' 388–91; CP, 1:181. These were arrowworms, the chaetognaths.
18. Journal (1839), 117–18; Sloan, 'Darwin's Invertebrate Program,' 87–91; Thomson and Rachootin, 'Turning Points,' 26–27.
19. Diary, 92–94, 99–101, 104–105, 121; CCD, 1:276; Narrative, 83; Parodiz, Darwin, 99–102.
20. CCD, 1:276, 280–81; Narrative, 82; Diary, 106–110; Charles Darwin, 166; Journal, 204; Gruber and Gruber, 'Eye,' 195; H. Gruber, 'Going,' 18. The Punta Alta fossils were identified by Richard Owen after Darwin had returned to London: Owen, Fossil Mammalia, 7–9, 29 (the huge rodent Toxodon), 68–69 (the ground sloth Mylodon), 107–108 (a cow-sized armadillo or glyptodont).
21. Diary, 111; Schweber, 'John Herschel,' 55–56; Narrative, 95–96; cf. Bush, Milton, i:180–88.
22. CCD, 1:222–23, 235, 245, 255–59; Diary, 111–12, 117.
23. Diary, 113, 115; CCD, 1:222, 245, 257, 277–78, 281, 286.
24. R. Hamond to F. Darwin, 19 Sept. 1882, DAR 112:54–55; Charles Darwin, 167–69; Diary, 114, 116–18.
25. C. Lyell, Principles, 2:2, 10; Bartholomew, 'Lyell;' Desmond, Politics, 327–30.
26. Diary, 117–18; CCD, 1:281–82, 308.

10 TROUBLED SPIRITS FROM ANOTHER WORLD

1. Diary, 120–25; CCD, 1:306, 397.
2. Diary, 122, 124–29, 444; CCD, 1:303, 307, 316; Narrative, 102–103.
3. Diary, 130–32; Narrative, 105–106; CCD, 1:303; Stanbury, 'H.M.S. Beagle,' 84.
4. Diary, 133, 138–40; Narrative, 115, 124–25; CCD, 1:304.
5. Diary, 135, 139, 141, 143, 224; CCD, 1:303, 305; Narrative, 127–28.
6. Diary, 144–45; CCD, 1:304, 307; Narrative, 134–36; Parodiz, Darwin, 85, 106–108.
7. Diary, 145–47; Narrative, 139–40; CCD, 1:307; Charles Darwin, 178–79.
8. Sloan, 'Darwin, Vital Matter,' 391–92 and 'Darwin's Invertebrate Program,' 98–100; Diary, 149; CCD, 1:307, 399–400.

9. CCD, 1:247–48; Diary, 148–54; Narrative, 158–59.
10. Diary, 154–60; CCD, 1:321; Charles Darwin, 182–83; Journal (1839), 55, 69–70, 105–107.
11. Diary, 160–61; DON, 214–24; Journal (1839), 54ff; CCD, 1:311–12, 315, 321.
12. CCD, 1:288, 290–91, 299, 309, 311, 313, 320; F. Darwin, 'FitzRoy,' 548; A. Mellersh to F. Darwin, 10 June 1882, DAR 112:83; Diary, 167; Wedgwood, 219.
13. CCD, 1:266, 269, 271–72, 274–75, 291, 299, 309; ED, 1:61; Wedgwood, 155.
14. CCD, 1:311–12, 314, 316, 320–22, 398; Diary, 162.
15. DON, 273; Journal (1839), 108; Charles Darwin, 199; Diary, 99–100, 163–71; Parodiz, Darwin, 103ff; CCD, 1:330–31.
16. CCD, 1:330–31, 343; Diary, 172, 175, 178–81; Charles Darwin, 194–98; Gruber and Gruber, 'Eye,' 195–96. The long-snouted skull was identified by Richard Owen later in London as a giant anteater-like Scelidotherium: Owen, Fossil Mammalia, 73–74.
17. Diary, 182–98; Charles Darwin, 199, 206–13; CCD, 1:336, 342–43, 352; Parodiz, Darwin, 108–10, 116–17.
18. Diary, 198–99; Narrative, 173; CCD, 1:230, 318, 323–25, 328–30, 344–45, 351–53.
19. Diary, 203–204; CCD, 1:344, 378–79; Journal (1839), 180–81; LRO, 1:119–20; Owen, Fossil Mammalia, 16ff. Later in London Owen identified it as a hippo-sized rodent Toxodon, an antecedent of the South American capybara.
20. Diary, 205–209; CCD, 1:335, 354, 359. The asthmatic Earle died in London in December 1838.
21. Diary, 208–12, 215; DON, 229, 271; Journal (1839), 108–109, 208–209; CCD, 1:369–70, 2:373; Owen, Fossil Mammalia, 35–36. Later in London Owen called this camel-sized llama-forerunner Macrauchenia: Rachootin, 'Owen and Darwin.'
22. Diary, 213–22; Narrative, 177; CCD, 1:358, 370; Journal (1839), 109–10; DON, 272, 273.
23. Diary, 222–24; C. Lyell, Principles, 2:21.
24. Diary, 222–24; C. Lyell, Principles, 2:60–62; Herbert, 'Place of Man, Pt 1,' 227–29.
25. Diary, 226–27; Narrative, 182–83, 185; CCD, 1:378, 380.

11 SHAKEN FOUNDATIONS

1. Diary, 228; Narrative, 185–87; CCD, 1:378, 380.
2. CCD, 1:316, 327–28, 333–34, 359, 363; Morrell and Thackray, Gentlemen, 165–75 on the Cambridge BAAS meeting in June 1833, under Sedgwick's Presidency.
3. CCD, 1:368–71, 398; DON, 246; Charles Darwin, 218–19; Diary, 229–31; Herbert, 'Darwin,' 492–93; Sulloway, 'Darwin's Early Intellectual Development,' 132–44.
4. Narrative, 188; CCD, 1:370, 381; Diary, 232.
5. R. Keynes, Beagle Record, 199, 203; Diary, 231–33; Narrative, 193–96.
6. R. Keynes, Beagle Record, 202, 210; Diary, 232–37; Charles Darwin, 221–22; Narrative, 196ff, 369.
7. Diary, 236–40; Narrative, 198–200; Charles Darwin, 222.
8. CCD, 1:336–42, 345–47, 356–58, 392–93.
9. LLL, 2:33; CCD, 1:345–46, 392; Erskine, 'Darwin,' 261–63; H. Martineau, Autobiography, 1:218–19, 260–63, 327; Diary, 240–41; Wheatley, Life, 95–97.

10. Austin, *Memoir*, 2:383; Harrison, *Early Victorian Britain*, 23, 73, 107–12; H. Martineau, *Autobiography*, 1:211–12, 219; Hilton, *Age*, ch. 3 on religious Malthusianism.
11. CCD, 1:338, 389; *Diary*, 243; *Charles Darwin*, 223.
12. *Diary*, 244–49; *Narrative*, 205–207; CCD, 1:392, 3:38; DON, 250–53; Gruber and Gruber, 'Eye,' 193.
13. *Diary*, 249–50, 253–55; CCD, 1:393, 405–406, 419.
14. *Diary*, 257–63; *Charles Darwin*, 226; CCD, 1:396–97, 410; Parodiz, *Darwin*, 123–25.
15. CCD, 1:312, 397–402, 410–11, 418–20; *Narrative*, 210–11; *Diary*, 263.
16. *Diary*, 264–71, 274–76; *Charles Darwin*, 229; *Narrative*, 216–18.
17. *Diary*, 275–80; *Narrative*, 221–23; *Journal* (1839), 351; CCD, 4:258, 389, 436.
18. *Diary*, 247, 269, 280–86; CCD, 1:432, 434, 437; Parodiz, *Darwin*, 126–27.
19. Hodge, 'Darwin and the Laws,' 18–22; Kohn, 'Theories,' 70–71; H. Gruber, 'Going,' 16–18.
20. Sloan, 'Darwin, Vital Matter,' 393–95; Hodge, 'Darwin and the Laws,' 22–27; *Diary*, 287; *Journal* (1839), 363–64.
21. CCD, 1:419, 434; *Diary*, 286–93. Cf. *Autobiography*, 75.
22. *Diary*, 293–302; *Narrative*, 229–30; CCD, 1:434, 436; Parodiz, *Darwin*, 127–28; Rudwick, 'Strategy,' 4, 16. Cf. Darwin's copy of Humboldt's *Personal Narrative*, 2:207 in Darwin Library, CUL.

12 COLONIAL LIFE

1. *Narrative*, 235; CCD, 1:432–37.
2. *Diary*, 304–13; CCD, 1:440, 445–46.
3. *Diary*, 314–18; *Charles Darwin*, 236; CCD, 1:442; *Journal* (1839), 354–55. The Vinchuca insect hosts a trypanosome parasite that causes Chagas's disease in humans. But Darwin did not mention coming down with the fever that accompanies the initial infection, and it is now doubted that the Vinchuca bite was the cause of his later recurrent sickness: *Diary*, 315; TBI, 126ff. Leonard Darwin, recalling his father's opinion, did not attribute the illness to anything that happened on the voyage: L. Darwin, 'Memories,' 121.
4. CCD, 1:440, 445; *Diary*, 321; *Charles Darwin*, 232–33.
5. CCD, 1:419, 435, 440, 443, 445–48; *Diary*, 318–19, 322–23; *Charles Darwin*, 237; Parodiz, *Darwin*, 119–21.
6. *Diary*, 324–43; *Charles Darwin*, 238–43; CCD, 1:449, 457–58.
7. *Diary*, 343–50; CCD, 1:458, 462, 466; *Charles Darwin*, 244.
8. Stoddart, 'Darwin, Lyell,' 200–204; C. Lyell, *Principles*, 2:290; R. Keynes, *Beagle Record*, 350–51; *Charles Darwin*, 243–44; *Autobiography*, 98–99; CCD, 1:460, 567–68.
9. CCD, 1:416, 460, 462, 465–66; *Diary*, 350.
10. Davis presented it to the zoo after arriving back in England. See the entry for 4 November 1836, 'Occurrences at the Gardens,' Zoological Society of London: 'Rec^d. A brown Coati Mundi Pres. by J. E. Davis Esq RN H.M. Sloop Beagle, off Woolwich.' J. Davis is one of the forecastle men listed in CCD, 1:549.
11. DON, 262; *Diary*, 354, 362–63; *Charles Darwin*, 247; *Narrative*, 270, 272; CCD, 1:489; Sulloway, 'Darwin's Conversion,' 339 n. 23 on the museum mislabelling of the marine iguana.

12. *Narrative*, 286; *Diary*, 351–54; *Charles Darwin*, 247–48; *CCD*, 1:485.
13. Sulloway, 'Darwin's Conversion,' 338–44; *Journal* (1839), 465; DON, 262.
14. *Narrative*, 279; *Diary*, 357–59; Sulloway, 'Darwin,' 19.
15. *Diary* 360–63.
16. *Diary*, 355–57; DON, 261–62; Sulloway, 'Darwin,' 6–19; *CCD*, 1:485.
17. *Diary*, 360; *Narrative*, 277, 283, 286. Much later he admitted that 'it never occurred to me, that the production of islands only a few miles apart, and placed under the same physical conditions, would be dissimilar. I therefore did not attempt to make a series of specimens from the separate islands:' *Journal* (1839), 474–75.
18. Sulloway, 'Darwin,' 12, 19; DON, 262.
19. *CCD*, 1:471; Pennington, 'Darwin,' 4; *Narrative*, 295–98, 302; *Diary*, 365–73.
20. *Diary*, 376–79; *CCD*, 1:569; Stoddart, 'Darwin, Lyell,' 205.
21. *Diary*, 380–87; Pennington, 'Darwin,' 5-8; *Narrative*, 322.
22. *CP*, 2:20–21, 34–37; *CCD*, 1:472, 485, 560; *Diary*, 384–85.
23. *Diary*, 389–93; *CCD*, 1:472. We are grateful to David Stanbury for information about the collection, including a copy of FitzRoy's letter that accompanied it.
24. *Diary*, 395–96; Nicholas and Nicholas, *Charles Darwin*, 20–21; *CCD*, 1:482, 484–85, 492.
25. *Diary*, 396–400; Marshall, *Darwin*, 11; Nicholas and Nicholas, *Charles Darwin*, 22–44.
26. *Diary*, 401–403; *CCD*, 1:481; Nicholas and Nicholas, *Charles Darwin*, 45–54. Desmond, *Politics*, 279–87.
27. *Diary*, 403–405, 408; Desmond, 'Making,' 247 n. 169; *CCD*, 1:483; Nicholas and Nicholas, *Charles Darwin*, 18, 63–64.
28. *Diary*, 406–10; *CCD*, 1:485, 490; King-Hele, *Letters*, 190; Nicholas and Nicholas, *Charles Darwin*, 83–104; Darwin, *Volcanic Islands*, 138, 158; *Journal* (1839), 583n.
29. *CCD*, 1:490–91; Nicholas and Nicholas, *Charles Darwin*, 86–87.
30. *Diary*, 410–13; *Narrative*, 339; Nicholas and Nicholas, *Charles Darwin*, 105–17; P. Armstrong, *Charles Darwin*, 17–19, ch. 4; Sloan, 'Darwin's Invertebrate Program,' 104–108.

13 TEMPLES OF NATURE

1. Sloan, 'Darwin's Invertebrate Program,' 108–109; P. Armstrong, *Charles Darwin*, 31; *Diary*, 413–16.
2. *Diary*, 416–18; *CCD*, 1:495, 570; R. Keynes, *Beagle Record*, 350–51; *Narrative*, 344.
3. *CCD*, 1:492–93, 495–96; *Diary*, 419–22; F. Darwin, 'FitzRoy,' 548.
4. *Autobiography* 107; *CCD*, 1:497–98, 500; Kohn, 'Darwin's Ambiguity,' 222; *Notebooks* RN32; Cannon, 'Impact,' 304–11.
5. *CP*, 1:3–16, 19, 24–25; *CCD*, 1:473–74, 487, 498–99; *Diary*, 422–27.
6. Kirby, 'Introductory Address,' 5; Desmond, 'Making,' 168. Sulloway, 'Darwin's Conversion,' 332–37, argues from Darwin's spelling pattern that the ornithology catalogue (published as DON) was drawn up between the Cape and Ascension Island, that is between 18 June and 19 July 1836.
7. DON, 262. Unlike Sulloway, Hodge thinks that Darwin was already looking favourably on transmutation by this time: Hodge, 'Darwin, Species,' 236.
8. *CCD*, 1:500, 502; *Diary*, 424–30.

9. Darwin had known at least since Mauritius that FitzRoy intended to put in at Bahia, but that did not soften the blow: *CCD*, 1:488, 495, 503; *Diary*, 431–32.
10. *CCD*, 1:492, 501; *Diary*, 432–42.
11. *CCD*, 1:469; *Diary*, 441–42.
12. Sulloway, 'Darwin's Conversion,' 333 n. 17; D. Porter, *'Beagle* Collector,' 979–88; Gruber and Gruber, 'Eye,' 189; *Narrative*, 286.
13. *CCD*, 1:492, 495, 499–500.
14. *Notebooks* RN18, 72; H. Gruber, 'Going,' 25; *Diary*, 446.
15. *CCD*, 1:469, 474–75, 503; *LLL*, 1:460–61; *CP*, 1:18.
16. *CCD*, 1:488; *Diary*, 443–47.

14 A PEACOCK ADMIRING HIS TAIL

1. *CCD*, 1:504–507.
2. Austin, *Memoir*, 2:352; *CCD*, 1:506; Halévy, *Triumph*, 56; Holt, *Unitarian Contribution*, 23, 132, 217–41.
3. Edsall, *Anti-Poor Law Movement*, 21, 59; Harrison, *Early Victorian Britain*, 28; Berman, *Social Change*, 109–10; E. Thompson, *Making*, 904.
4. *CCD*, 1:507–509, 512.
5. Tristan, *London Journal*, 1–2; Harrison, *Early Victorian Britain*, 26. For a graphic illustration of the metropolitan works under way on Darwin's return: Jackson, *George Scharf's London*, 70–71, 100, 112–13, 131–36. Darwin was told of the gutting of Parliament while on the *Beagle*: *CCD*, 1:413.
6. *CCD*, 1:509, 514, 516; Bunbury, *Life*, 1:147.
7. *Reports of the Council and Auditors of the Zoological Society of London, Read at the Annual General Meeting, April 29, 1836* (London: Taylor, 1836), 20; (1837), 15; (1838), 10; Zoological Society, Minutes of Council, 4:396–7; Desmond, 'Making,' 233; *CCD*, 1:512. The Society had moved from its old museum, Lord Berkeley's former town house at 33 Bruton Street, to Hunter's museum on 11 July 1836: cf. *CCD*, 1:514 n. 2.
8. *CCD*, 1:299, 513–14; Desmond, 'Making,' 224–25, 232–41; *Lancet*, 1 (1840–41), 117.
9. *London Medical Gazette*, 13 (1833–34), 293, 676; Desmond, 'Robert E. Grant,' 217; Desmond, *Politics*, 122, 149; *Report from the Select Committee on British Museum* (Parliamentary Papers, 14 July 1836), 133; Gunther, *Founders*, ch. 8; *CCD*, 1:512.
10. *CCD*, 1:510, 534; Keith, *Darwin*, 221–22.
11. *LLL*, 2:33; *CCD*, 1:345–46, 2:518; Erskine, 'Darwin,' 261–63; H. Martineau, *Autobiography*, 1:218–19, 260–63, 327.
12. Quoted in Erskine, 'Darwin,' 109; Martineau, *Autobiography*, 1:204–209; Desmond, *Politics*, 126–27 on the BMA.
13. *CCD*, 1:518–19; Erskine, 'Darwin,' 260–61.
14. *CCD*, 1:514, 532; *LLL*, 1:474–75.
15. Broderip, 'Zoological Gardens,' 321; *LRO*, 1:96, 102, 169; Desmond, 'Making,' 238, 240–41; *CCD*, 1:515; Bunbury, *Life*, 1:187.
16. R. Grant, *Study*, 17–19; Desmond, *Politics*, 126–33, 385, 402–403.
17. As the radicals hailed him: *Lancet*, 2 (1841–42), 246; *LRO*, 1:102.
18. Sloan, 'Darwin, Vital Matter,' 399ff.
19. *CCD*, 1:512, 520; D. Porter, *'Beagle* Collector,' 1006–1007. Particular polyps are mentioned in *Journal* (1839), 552–53 and Darwin's *Coral Reefs*, esp. ch. 1.

20. *CCD*, 1:14, 183; Herbert, 'Place of Man, Pt 1,' 241, and 'Place of Man, Pt 2,' 174–75; Desmond, *Politics*, 122.
21. *CCD*, 1:511–12, 514–15; D. Porter, '*Beagle* Collector.'
22. *ED*, 1:272–74; *CCD*, 1:513, 519, 524, 526, 530, 533, 535; 2:2.
23. *CCD*, 1:515–16, 2:14, 23.
24. *CCD*, 1:518, 527–28, 531, 534. Darwin left Owen fifty-odd preserved mammals and birds in addition to the fossil bones.
25. Quoted in David, *Intellectual Women*, 36–37; *CCD*, 1:524.
26. H. Martineau, *Autobiography*, 1:355; *CCD*, 1:524, 2:1, 5; *LLL*, 2:34.
27. Tristan, *London Journal*, 7; Dickens, *Bleak House*, 1; Raumer, *England*, 1:7; Jackson, *George Scharf's London*, 75; *CCD*, 1:511–13.
28. *CCD*, 1:395, 421, 525; 2:8; *Journal* (1839), 69.
29. *LLL*, 2:12; Stoddart, 'Darwin, Lyell,' 206–207; Herbert, 'Darwin,' 490–94; Rudwick, 'Charles Darwin,' 195ff; Babbage, *Ninth Bridgewater Treatise*, 209–20; Cannon, 'Impact;' *CCD*, 1:532, 2:1; *LLD*, 1:278–79, 2:12; *CP*, 1:41–43.
30. Gillispie, *Genesis*, 140; Dean, 'Through Science,' 121; Herbert, 'Darwin,' 485.
31. *CCD*, 2:4, 29; Sulloway, 'Darwin,' 6ff; Hodge, 'Darwin and the Laws,' 47.
32. *DON*, 261; Sulloway, 'Darwin,' 6, 8–9, 13–19 and 'Darwin's Conversion,' 356–57; *CCD*, 2:2; Zoological Society, *Reports* (1837), 15.
33. *Proceedings of the Zoological Society*, 4 (1836), 142; 5 (1837), 7; on wrens, vol. 4 (1836) 88–89; J. Gould, *Birds of Europe* and *Birds of Australia*. On Gould's position in the museum: Desmond, 'Making,' 231, 246 n. 164.
34. Zoological Society, Minutes of Scientific Meetings. Oct. 1835 – Aug. 1840, f. 120. The final draft of Gould's 10 January paper was not submitted for publication until 3 October that year (as explained in *Proceedings of the Zoological Society*, 107 [1937], 79), by which time he had designated fourteen species, and this figure appears in the printed version: J. Gould, 'Mr. Darwin's Collection,' 4. Sulloway brilliantly disentangles Gould's maturing views in 'Darwin,' 21 n. 32 and 'Darwin's Conversion,' 358–61. Ultimately Darwin's 'Icterus' turned out to be a cactus finch, his 'wren' a warbler finch, and his 'Gross-beaks' heavy-billed finches.
35. Wilson, *Charles Lyell*, 437–38; C. Lyell, 'Address,' 510–11; Rachootin, 'Owen,' 156–59. Owen called this llama-forebear *Macrauchenia*.
36. *CCD*, 2:4, 8; C. Lyell, 'Address,' 511; Sulloway, 'Darwin's Conversion,' 252–55.
37. Wilson, *Charles Lyell*, 441; R. Porter, 'Gentlemen,' 810, 821–24.
38. *CCD*, 1:259, 516, 2:11, 13; Rudwick, 'Charles Darwin.'

15 REFORMING NATURE

1. *CCD*, 2:8, 11.
2. *LLL*, 1:466, 472; *Hansard*, 3rd ser., 32 (1836), 162; 34 (1836), 491; *CCD*, 2:175. In March 1837 the Parliamentary debates over Church tithes were furious (Bunbury, *Life*, 1:149). Darwin already knew these soiréeing guests; he was attending the geologist Roderick Murchison's lavish dinners with Babbage and Owen as early as 5 Nov. 1836: *LRO*, 1:103.
3. *LLL*, 1:467; 'Geology and Mineralogy,' *Athenaeum* (1837), 79.
4. Babbage, *Ninth Bridgewater Treatise*, 25, 45–47, 92; Desmond, *Archetypes*, 214–15.
5. C. Babbage to Victoria, 24 May 1837, BL, Add. MSS 37,190, f. 147; H.

Holland to C. Babbage, 26 May 1837, f. 153; C. Lyell to C. Babbage, 6 Jan., 17 Feb., May 1837, ff. 8, 37, 185.

6. *CCD*, 2:106; Schweber, 'John Herschel,' 33; Cannon, 'Impact,' 305.

7. Cannon, 'Impact,' 305, 312; Wilson, *Charles Lyell*, 438–39. Because it contained some controversial geological points, the letter was finally read aloud to the Geological Society on 17 May 1837: *LLL*, 2:5, 11; Babbage, *Ninth Bridgewater Treatise*, 226–27. On the Royal Society: MacLeod, 'Whigs,' 64–65; Desmond, *Politics*, 225–26. And on the Herschelian high road: Kohn, 'Darwin's Ambiguity,' 222–23.

8. *LLL*, 1:467, 2:5; Bartholomew, 'Lyell;' Cannon, 'Impact,' 308; *CCD*, 2:7, 8–9.

9. Erskine, 'Darwin,' 34; *CCD*, 2:13.

10. Wedgwood, 'Grimm,' 170, 175; *Notebooks*, N31, 39 for Charles's discussion with Hensleigh on the parallel evolution of sounds.

11. *CCD*, 2:155; H. Martineau, *Autobiography*, 1:355; *ED*, 1:277, 284; *Autobiography*, 112–13; Erskine, 'Darwin,' 106.

12. Southwood Smith, *Divine Government*, 109, 111. By the depression year of 1837, though, even Smith was losing his rosy view of inevitable progress. He alerted the Poor Law Commissioners to the epidemics in London's East End and he showed Dickens the squalor, shaking him to an extent that he based episodes from *Oliver Twist* and *Bleak House* on Smith's report.

13. *LLL*, 2:8; *Notebooks* N36, B98; Brooke, 'Relations,' 46–47; Ospovat, *Development*, 30–33; Cornell, 'God's Magnificent Law,' 387–89.

14. Epps, *Church of England's Apostasy*, 3; *CCD*, 1:259; Austin, *Memoir*, 2:384; *Medico-Chirurgical Review*, 23 (1835), 413; Jacyna, 'Immanence,' 325–26.

15. *British and Foreign Medical Review*, 5 (1838), 86–100; Rehbock, *Philosophical Naturalists*, 56; Epps, 'Elements,' 100; Desmond, *Politics*, 110–17, 199.

16. *Medico-Chirurgical Review*, 30 (1839), 450. Gully, like so many Edinburgh graduates, had studied at the republican Hôtel Dieu in Paris (in 1828). He helped run the Dissenting *London Medical and Surgical Journal* in the mid-1830s (Mann, *Collections*, 5–6, 10), which supported many of the heterodox sciences: Desmond, *Politics*, ch. 4, esp. 175.

17. Sulloway, 'Darwin,' 12, 21–22 and 'Darwin's Conversion,' 359–62; Kottler, 'Charles Darwin's Biological Species Concept,' 281; Herbert, 'Place of Man, Pt 1,' 236–37; J. Gould, 'Three Species.'

18. What happened to Darwin's tortoise is not known. There is no record in the 'Occurrences at the Gardens' ledger, held at the Zoological Society of London, of it being presented alive to the Zoological Gardens in 1836 or early 1837; nor is it mentioned in Flower, *List*, 3:33.

19. *LLL*, 2:36; C. Lyell, *Principles*, 2:20–21; Bartholomew, 'Lyell;' Desmond, *Politics*, 328–29; Schweber, 'Origin,' 265; H. Gruber, 'Going,' 10.

20. *LLL*, 2:10–11; *CP*, 1:44–45; *Notebooks* B94, 126, 133. The Indian monkey, from the Siwalik Hills, was found in Pliocene to Lower Pleistocene strata (in today's terminology). It was found in the same deposits as the tapir-like *Anoplotherium* and huge *Sivatherium*, with their four foliated antler-like horns. The monkey's discoverers, Hugh Falconer of the Bengal Medical Service and Capt. Proby Cautley of the Bengal Artillery, had only ten weeks earlier received the society's Wollaston medal for their Himalayan work: D. Moore, 'Geological Collectors,' 404; Cautley and Falconer, 'On the Remains,' 569.

21. *Notebooks* B126; Cautley, 'Extract,' 544.

22. Knight, *London*, 3:200–203; Bunbury, *Life*, 1:186; Sloan, 'Darwin, Vital Matter,' 405ff; Desmond, *Politics*, 346ff. Owen was borrowing from Müller's *Handbuch der Physiologie*.
23. Sloan, 'Darwin, Vital Matter,' 418–19, 425–30; CCD, 2:32; LRO, 1:108; Desmond, *Politics*, 291–93, 347.
24. Sloan, 'Darwin, Vital Matter,' 424, 434; *Notebooks* RN inside front cover; Jacyna, 'Immanence,' 314–327; Desmond, 'Artisan Resistance,' 95–104 and *Politics*, 265–66.
25. *Notebooks* RN 129–30, 133; Hodge, 'Darwin on the Laws,' 19–28; Kohn, 'Theories,' 75, 77–78; cf. C. Lyell, *Principles*, 3:85; Sloan, 'Darwin, Vital Matter,' 433ff; *Journal* (1839), 212.
26. *Journal* (1839), 212; CP, 1:45; Sloan, 'Darwin, Vital Matter,' 434; *Notebooks* RN inside front cover.
27. *Notebooks* RN 127; CCD, 3:14; Blomefield, *Chapters*, 29 on Jenyns's fish; J. Gould, 'New Species;' CCD, 2:11.
28. *Notebooks* B161, RN 127, 130, 153; Herbert, *Red Notebook*, 6–12; E. Richards,'Question,' 148; Kohn, 'Theories,' 73–76; Sulloway, 'Darwin's Conversion,' 371ff; Hodge, 'Darwin and the Laws,' 44–45, 48–49.
29. CCD, 2:11, 14; *Journal* (1839), 462, 475; Sulloway, 'Darwin,' 33.
30. CCD, 2:15–17, 20–21, 24, 38; Zoological Society, *Reports* (1832), 9–10 on Richardson's Arctic species.
31. CCD, 2:26, 31 n. 4, 37, 59; Desmond, *Politics*, 384.
32. CCD, 2:16–18, 27.
33. CCD, 1:14, 31, 2:29; CP, 1:40, 46–49; Sulloway, 'Darwin,' 23–29; LLL, 2:12.

16 TEARING DOWN THE BARRIERS

1. *Notebooks* B2–3; Kohn, 'Theories,' 81–87; Ospovat, *Development*, 40ff. Hodge, 'Darwin and the Laws,' 38–39, 80 calls these early pages a discrete 'Zoonomical Sketch.'
2. *Notebooks* B3–6, 15; Sloan, 'Darwin, Vital Matter,' 436–39; Kohn, 'Theories,' 88–92.
3. *Notebooks* B18, 169; Hodge, 'Lamarck's Science,' 343–45, on Lamarck's escalator of life. Herbert, 'Place of Man, Pt 2,' 196 on man's animal ancestry holding no terrors for Darwin (but then neither did it for many Unitarians and secular radicals in London in the late 1830s).
4. *Notebooks* B21, 23, 25–26; CCD, 2:32, 41, 48; Kohn, 'Theories,' 109–13; Hodge, 'Darwin and the Laws,' 78–79; H. Gruber, *Darwin*, ch. 7.
5. *Notebooks* B29, 35, 38, 39, 42; Sloan, 'Darwin, Vital Matter,' 442–43; Kohn, 'Darwin's Ambiguity,' 223–24.
6. Ospovat, *Development*, 33–37; Kohn, 'Darwin's Ambiguity,' 224; Kohn, 'Theories,' 86, 98–99, 104–105; *Notebooks* B46, 74.
7. CCD, 2:39; *Notebooks*, B82, 92, 125, 224, 248; Grinnell, 'Rise,' 264–71.
8. CCD, 2:39–40, 44–45, 49, 58.
9. CCD, 2:47–48, 52; TBI, 14–16.
10. ED, 1:216, 220, 255, 266, 273, 278–79; *Companion*, 293; E. Richards, 'Darwin,' 82–83, 87; *Pedigrees*, 11; *Wedgwood*, 221; CP, 1:49–52.
11. CCD, 2:55 n. 1, 70; CP, 1:49–53.
12. CCD, 2:61–63, 86; Jenyns, *Fish*, v–vi; he was to produce the fattest of the books in the *Zoology* series.

13. *LLL*, 2:37, 39; *LRO*, 1:121; Owen, *Fossil Mammalia*, 16, 55; Freeman, *Works*, 28; Rachootin, 'Owen,' 166; *CCD*, 2:66.
14. *CCD*, 2:10, 13, 50–52, 69–70; Whewell, 'Address,' 643; D. Porter, *'Beagle* Collector,' 994.
15. Sedgwick, 'Address,' 206, 305; Napier, *Selections*, 491.
16. *CCD*, 2:104–105, 6:344; *LLL*, 2:39–40, 43–44; *CP*, 1:53–86.
17. *Notebooks* B207, 215, 224, D49.
18. Epps, *Diary*, 61; H. Martineau, 'Right and Wrong,' 2, 58; *CCD*, 2:148; Halévy, *Triumph*, 239; *Notebooks* B231, C154.
19. Epps, 'Elements,' 118; Paley, *Natural Theology*, 490; Desmond, *Politics*, 184–85, 407–408.
20. *Notebooks* B232; Desmond, *Politics*, 184; *Notebooks* N62 n. 1; R. Richards, 'Instinct,' 213–16, 227 and *Darwin*, 130–42; H. Gruber, *Darwin*, 202.

17 MENTAL RIOTING

1. *CCD*, 4:40; *Notebooks* C1–2; Ospovat, *Development*, 46–47.
2. *Notebooks* B90, C4, 52, 120.
3. *Notebooks* B142, C60, 233–234; *CCD*, 3:38, 53.
4. *Notebooks* C61; Kohn, 'Theories,' 124–25.
5. *Notebooks* C65–66, 119; Kohn, 'Theories,' 131–2; R. Richards, 'Instinct,' 196ff and *Darwin*, 91ff. But, as Richards shows, Darwin was still distancing himself from the maligned Lamarck. Where Lamarck, Darwin mistakenly thought, attributed changing habits to will-power, Darwin made unconscious instincts the cause of new structures.
6. *Notebooks* C inside front cover; *CCD*, 2:70–71; H. Gruber, *Darwin*, 424–25; Wynne is identified as The Mount's gardener in *Calendar*, 5583.
7. *CCD*, 2:72, 79; *Journal* (1839), 628; *Notebooks* C54; Sulloway, 'Darwin's Conversion,' 345.
8. *CCD*, 2:69, 75, 80, 85.
9. *Notebooks* C76.
10. Scherren, *Zoological Society*, 65, 85; Flower, *List*, 1:4; *CCD*, 2:80. The zoo had purchased other orangs, but none had lived long enough to be exhibited. Because of the new heated giraffe house, Jenny was the first to survive a winter.
   An orang named 'Jenny,' seen sipping tea by the Owens in 1842, and presented to Queen Victoria that year, was a different ape, purchased on 13 Dec. 1839. Darwin's 'Jenny' died after an illness on 28 May 1839: 'Occurrences at the Gardens, 1839,' MS, Zoological Society of London; *LRO*, 1:193–94, 206.
11. *CCD*, 2:80; *Notebooks* C79, also M138.
12. *CCD*, 1:510, 2:80, 7:Supplement.
13. *CCD*, 2:105, 443.
14. *CCD*, 2:83; Brent, *Charles Darwin*, 17–18.
15. *CCD*, 2:86; *Notebooks* C100.
16. *Natural Selection*, 36; *Notebooks* C120, E13; Secord, 'Darwin,' 525; Ruse, *Darwinian Revolution*, 178.
17. Sebright, in *Notebooks* C133; Ruse, 'Charles Darwin,' 344–49.
18. *Notebooks* C133, D107; Kohn, 'Theories,' 137–39; Herbert, 'Darwin, Malthus,' 212–13; Cornell, 'Analogy,' 316–18.
19. *CCD*, 2:92; *Notebooks* B216–217.

20. CCD, 2:84, 86, 431; H. Martineau, *Autobiography*, 2:115–18.
21. *Notebooks* C123, N19; H. Gruber, *Darwin*, 38.
22. Jacyna, 'Immanence;' Desmond, *Politics* and 'Artisan Resistance.'
23. R. Richards, 'Instinct,' 198–99 and *Darwin*, 94–98.
24. *Notebooks* C166; Kohn, 'Darwin's Ambiguity,' 224–25; Manier, *Young Darwin*, 56, 129–30; H. Gruber, *Darwin*, ch. 10; cf. Ospovat, *Development*, 67.
25. De Morgan, *Memoir*, 325; Elliotson, 'Address,' 33; *London Medical Gazette*, 11 (1832–33), 213–21; *Lancet*, 2 (1832–33), 341; *Notebooks* C166, OUN 37.
26. *Notebooks* C244, M61, OUN 39–41; Manier, *Young Darwin*, 129–31, 220–23; Erskine, 'Darwin,' 216ff.
27. Robertson, 'Dr. Elliotson,' 205, 256–57; Elliotson, *Human Physiology*, 39; Elliotson, 'Reply,' 289–90. Darwin read Elliotson's *Physiology*: *Notebooks* OUN 10v.
28. RFD, 23; also recollections of William Darwin, DAR 112.2 and *LLD*, 2:114.
29. *Lancet*, 1 (1838–39), 561–62. Elliotson was not alone. Martineau's Unitarian schoolfellows had all run into similar trouble. W. B. Carpenter was declared 'unfit for the duties of a Public Instructor' after suggesting that 'one simple law' impressed on matter at the Creation controlled the emergence and peopling of the planets. Southwood Smith was upbraided for saying that 'Life is nothing but organization in action.' C. Bell to T. Coates, 2 Sept. 1829, UCL, SDUK Correspondence; Carpenter, *Remarks*, 1–3.
30. CCD, 2:85, 431; *TBI*, 16–17.
31. H. Martineau, *Autobiography*, 1:401; *Notebooks* C220; E. Richards, 'Darwin,' 91. Erasmus and Hensleigh went on to become Chairman and Trustees of Bedford College for Women (founded in 1849 by Elizabeth Reid, Martineau's friend): Erskine, 'Darwin,' 166. On the socialist Lamarckians' education policy: W. Thompson, 'Physical Argument,' 250–54.
32. *Notebooks* C196, 243.
33. *London Medical Gazette*, 17 (1835–36), 783; Desmond, 'Artisan Resistance.'
34. Darwin's copy of Lawrence's *Lectures on Man* (London: Benbow, 1822) is in Darwin Library, CUL; CCD 2:142, 4:535; McCalman, 'Unrespectable Radicalism,' on Benbow's pornographic sideline; Desmond, *Politics*, 120 on Lawrence's pirates.
35. *Lancet*, 1 (1828–29), 50–52; *Notebooks* E52; CCD, 2:94, 97.
36. CCD, 2:91; ED, 2:287; *Wedgwood*, 232.
37. CCD, 2:95–96, 432.
38. CCD, 2:96, 432; Rudwick, 'Darwin,' 114–17, 153–57, 161–65; *Notebooks* GR29ff.

18 MARRIAGE & MALTHUSIAN RESPECTABILITY

1. *Autobiography*, 95.
2. CCD, 2:444–45; Macfarlane, *Marriage*, 8–9 for Malthus's description of these sorts of upper–class calculations.
3. CCD, 2:114, 445; ED, 2:1; H. Martineau, *Autobiography*, 2:175–77.
4. *Notebooks* M7–8; R. Richards, *Darwin*, 96–97; CCD, 2:432.
5. CCD, 2:95; ED, 1:5; *Notebooks* M54, 57; Kohn, 'Darwin's Ambiguity,' 225, reveals that these notes were written at Maer.
6. *Notebooks* D21; ED, 2:6.

7. *Notebooks* D26, M84; Herbert, 'Place of Man, Pt 2,' 208; Colp, '"I was born",' 20; *CCD*, 2:438–41.
8. Brewster, 'M. Comte's Course,' 274, 278, 280; *Notebooks* M69–70, 81, 89, 135–136, N12; *CCD*, 2:104; Manier, *Young Darwin*, 41; Schweber, 'Origin,' 245.
9. *Notebooks* D36–37; Ospovat, 'Darwin,' 215; Schweber, 'Origin,' 255; Martineau, in Burrow, *Evolution*, 106.
10. *Notebooks* D37. For a Unitarian who held similar views: Carpenter, 'On the Differences' and *Remarks*, 3.
11. *Notebooks* M73–74, OUN 25 n. 1.
12. *Notebooks* M75–76, 142, 151; R. Richards, *Darwin*, 112; Manier, *Young Darwin*, 140; Desmond, *Politics*, 182, and 'Artisan Resistance,' 91ff, for this moral relativism in radical circles.
13. *Notebooks* M76, 120–21, 132, 150, N3–4.
14. *CCD*, 2:92, 95, 98; *Notebooks* M107, 129, 138–40, 151, 153, N13.
15. *Notebooks* M122–23, 128.
16. *CCD*, 2:107, 432; Schweber, 'Origin,' 283ff.
17. *Notebooks* M143–44; Colp, 'Charles Darwin's Dream,' 287–88.
18. Erskine, 'Darwin,' 271; E. Yeo, 'Christianity,' 111.
19. *Notebooks* D134; C. Lyell, *Principles*, 2:131; J. Browne, *Secular Ark*, 52ff; Herbert, 'Darwin, Malthus,' 214–17; Bowler, 'Malthus,' 632–36.
20. *Notebooks* D135, E9; Hodge and Kohn, 'Immediate Origins,' 195.
21. E.g., the activist William Farr at the General Register Office used the mortality statistics in 1839 to attack the Malthusian basis of the Poor Law and embarrass the government about urban squalor and slum disease: Farr, 'Medical Reform;' Desmond, *Politics*, 130, 132; Kohn, 'Theories,' 144.
22. H. Martineau, *Autobiography*, 1:399; Malthus, *Essay*, 2:440–41; R. Young, *Darwin's Metaphor*, 26; Bowler, 'Malthus,' 637–38, 642; Erskine, 'Darwin,' 251–55.
23. H. Martineau, *Autobiography*, 1:210; Malthus, *Essay*, 1:94–95; Matthew, *Emigration Fields*, vii, 3, 6, 9; Wells, 'Historical Context,' 242ff. The proposed new steam passage to New Zealand and the west coast of America would cut the journey time to a month.
24. Prichard, 'On the Extinction,' 169; *Notebooks*, TAN81, D38, E64–65; *Journal* (1839), 520.
25. Herbert, 'Darwin, Malthus,' 214; Hodge and Kohn, 'Immediate Origins,' 195; *Notebooks* D135; Gallenga, 'Age,' 3, 4, 7; Gale, 'Darwin,' 327–31; Kohn, 'Darwin's Ambiguity,' 229; Keegan and Gruber, 'Love, Death,' 17–20.
26. Carlyle, in Harrison, 'Early English Radicals,' 206; *Notebooks* OUN30, 37.
27. *Notebooks* OUN32, 36. On the Unitarian tradition: Willey, *Eighteenth Century*, ch. 10; Rowell, *Hell*, 33–57; O. Chadwick, *Victorian Church*, 1:396–98; Brooke, 'Sower,' 446ff. See also Murphy, 'Ethical Revolt' and J. Moore, '1859.'
28. *Notebooks* E49, N2–3, 5; R. Richards, *Darwin*, 118–19.
29. *Notebooks* M136, OUN 25 n. 1; H. Gruber, *Darwin*, 409 n. 50.
30. *ED*, 2:5, 6, 9; *CCD*, 2:432; *Notebooks* N25–27.
31. *CCD*, 2:114–16, 123.
32. *CCD*, 2:123; Brooke, 'Relations,' 68.
33. John 14:2–3, 5–6; 15:5–6 (AV); *CCD*, 2:126. Three weeks later Henslow sent Darwin some kindly pre–nuptial advice, asking him 'to remember daily that

our greatest earthly blessings may be taken from us in a moment:' *CCD*, 2:141.

34. *CCD*, 2:116–19; *ED*, 2:12; Davidoff and Hall, *Family Fortunes*, 209.
35. *CCD*, 2:120, 123, 125–26, 128–29; Jackson, *George Scharf's London*, 74–75.
36. *Notebooks* Mac58v, E57; Ospovat, 'Darwin,' 221; Kohn, 'Darwin's Ambiguity,' 229–32.
37. *Notebooks* Mac54v, E66–68, 89; Brooke, 'Relations,' 58.
38. *Notebooks* N41, 51–52.
39. *Notebooks* N42; Hodge and Kohn, 'Immediate Origins,' 197–200; R. Richards, *Darwin*, 102.
40. *Notebooks* D104 n. 5, E63, 71, 75, 136; *Foundations*, 6; Hodge and Kohn, 'Immediate Origins,' 199; Cornell, 'Analogy,' 320.
41. *CCD*, 2:131, 133, 144, 150, 432; *LRO*, 1:140–41; E. Richards, 'Darwin,' 80.
42. W. Buckland to Henry Lord Brougham, 14 Dec. 1838, UCL, Brougham Papers 1957. These events are reconstructed in detail in Desmond, *Politics*, 308–18.
43. *Notebooks* B88, D62; *CCD*, 2:106.
44. *Notebooks* N47, E4, 95–96, TAN19. In 1839 Edouard Lartet (who had found the French fossil monkey) unearthed a fossil musk shrew identical to the living Pyrenean one. This evidence of a mammal undergoing no alteration over untold aeons was, Darwin said, 'valuable because it shows [that species have] no *innate* power of change:' *Notebooks* TAN41, Frag 4ʳ·
45. *Notebooks* N62; R. Richards, *Darwin*, 135–39; Kohn, 'Darwin's Ambiguity,' 228; Stewart, *Brougham*, 198.
46. Ospovat, *Development*, 220; Brooke, 'Relations,' 59–60; Schweber, 'Origin,' 266ff; Manier, *Young Darwin*, 121.
47. *ED*, 2:16, 18; *CCD*, 2:147–49; Freeman, *Darwin and Gower Street*, 5.
48. *ED*, 2:30, 33, 50; *CCD*, 2:148–49, 151, 155, 159–60.
49. *Notebooks* N59; *CCD*, 2:151, 155–57, 159, 161, 165.
50. *CCD*, 2:169, 171, 433; *ED*, 2:17, 26, 28; *Notebooks* E98 for Darwin's wedding–day notes on propagation.

19 THE DREADFUL WAR

1. *CCD*, 2:157, 169, 235; *ED*, 2:31.
2. *Notebooks* C244; *CCD*, 2:171–72; *ED*, 1:251, 2:29.
3. *ED*, 2:38. Emma's Christianity, in which Jesus's revelation of a future life is not to be proved from Scripture but simply to be believed through the transforming power of the Gospels on the individual heart, was being defended at the time by the Unitarian theologian James Martineau, Harriet's brother: J. Martineau, *Bible*, 8–9, 39–44.
4. *ED*, 2:39, 55; Freeman, *Darwin and Gower Street*, 5; *CCD*, 2:147, 194, 296. Nicholas and Nicholas, *Charles Darwin*, 119 on Covington, who took a clerk's job with King's powerful Australian Agricultural Company.
5. Rudwick, 'Charles Darwin,' 197; *CCD*, 2: 174, 178; *Notebooks* E111–12; Hodge and Kohn, 'Immediate Origins,' 200–201; Cornell, 'Analogy,' 323–25.
6. *CCD*, 2:179, 182, 187–89, 446–49; Vorzimmer, 'Darwin's *Questions*;' Freeman and Gautrey, 'Darwin's *Questions*.'
7. *Notebooks* E114, 144, TAN51, Mac28v; *CCD*, 2:237–38; Hodge and Kohn, 'Immediate Origins,' 201–202.

8. *Autobiography*, 55; *ED*, 2:42; *Notebooks* OUN42–55; R. Richards, *Darwin*, 114–18.
9. *ED*, 2:40–41, 45.
10. 'Narrative of the Surveying Voyages,' *Athenaeum*, no. 607 (15 June 1839), 446–49; B. Hall, 'Voyages,' 485–86, 489; *CCD*, 2:178.
11. *CCD*, 2:197, 199, 236, 255; *Narrative*, 372–74.
12. *CCD*, 2:207, 214, 218–22, 230 n. 4, 372; *ED*, 2:67; Halévy, *Triumph*, 232. In July 1839 he did begin what has subsequently been characterized as the *Torn Apart Notebook* on transmutation.
13. Morrell and Thackray, *Gentlemen*, 252; Desmond, *Politics*, 331; Wells, 'Historical Context,' 241; *Hansard*, 3d ser., 48 (1839), 33.
14. *CCD*, 2:233, 234, 236–38; H. Martineau, *Autobiography*, 2:145ff.
15. *CCD*, 2:236, 249.
16. He was mistaken. It was actually unearthed by Robert Darwin of Elston Hall (1682–1754), his great-grandfather, who thought it a 'human Sceleton.' This Robert was the *son* of William Darwin of Elston (1655–1682): *CCD*, 2:235 n. 6, 250, 269–70, 303; *Pedigrees*, 26–27; *ED*, 2:44; H. Gruber, *Darwin*, 465–74.
17. *ED*, 2:51; *CCD*, 2:253, 255, 260–61; *TBI*, 21.
18. *ED*, 2:52; *CCD*, 2:262; *Wedgwood*, 236; Carlyle, *Chartism*, 4, 12, 32. Darwin was a stickler for vaccinations, and kept up with the medical breakthroughs. Willy was vaccinated against smallpox twice in 1840, chicken pox in 1845, measles in 1855, and scarlet fever thrice (1853–55), according to the inside cover of the family Bible, Down House.
19. *CCD*, 2:268, 269, 434; *Notebooks* TAN55–57, 63, 79, 177, D60.
20. *CCD*, 2:279; Herbert, 'Place of Man, Pt 2,' 189; Rudwick, 'Charles Darwin,' 203. The gutter presses did indeed pick up on the fossil monkeys and throw them in the face of the priests: Desmond, 'Artisan Resistance,' 100.
21. *CCD*, 2:279, 289; *CP*, 1:145–63 for the paper on erratic boulders read by Hensleigh.
22. *ED*, 2:56; *CCD*, 2:294, 315–16, 319, 399; 5:540, 542.
23. *CCD*, 2:292–93, 306; *Notebooks* TAN91–135, 151. On 22 June he finally finished taking notes on species, closing the *Torn Apart Notebook*.
24. *CCD*, 2:292–94, 296, 298, 300 nn. 2–3, 303.
25. Cobbett, *Rural Rides*, 170–225; *CCD*, 2:304–305, 4:459.
26. Owen, 'Report on British Fossil Reptiles,' 196–99, 201–202; *LRO*, 1:168, 184, 188–89; Desmond, 'Making,' 230–41 and *Politics*, 325–26, 333, 351–58; *CCD*, 2:303, 305.
27. Owen, 'On the Osteology,' 343; Knight, *London*, 3:198; Bunbury, *Life*, 1:186; *CCD*, 2:307.
28. Annotation, 26 Jan. 1842, on Lyell's copy of his *Elements of Geology*, 2d ed., Down House; *CCD*, 2:299; *LLL*, 2:59.
29. *CCD*, 2:312–13, 318–19; *ED*, 2:70.
30. Herbert, 'Place of Man, Pt 2,' 191; *CCD*, 2:435; *Notebooks* Summer 1842; *Foundations*, 51–52; also 3, 6–8, 17, 23–24, 27, 35–36, 38, 45–47.
31. On Darwin's utilitarian audience: Desmond, *Politics*, 408–11. The utilitarian grip on London science is discussed in Berman, *Social Change*, ch. 4. One receptive breeder was the tree grower Patrick Matthew. He openly brought his Malthusian evolution to the aid of capitalist society.
32. *Notebooks* E6.
33. E. Yeo, 'Christianity,' 113. While the militants were abominating Malthus,

Hensleigh was entertaining the Darwins and Malthuses to dinner: *CCD*, 2:312. Obviously, Darwin read Adam Smith and the classical economists, not William Thompson and their socialist rivals. Hence his framework was always one of individuals in competition, not communities in co-operation: Schweber, 'Origin' and 'Darwin.'

34. Chilton, 'Regular Gradation,' *Oracle*, 19 Feb. 1842, 27 Nov. 1841, and *Oracle of Reason*, 12 Feb. 1842; Desmond, 'Artisan Resistance,' 85ff.

35. Southwell, 'Is There a God,' and Chilton, 'Regular Gradation,' *Oracle*, 11 Nov. 1843.

36. *Notebooks* C76; H. Gruber, *Darwin*, 202; S. Gould, 'Darwin's Delay;' J. Moore, 'Crisis,' 66.

37. Kohn *et al.*, 'New Light,' 424–26; *CCD*, 2:324, 326, 328, 332, 435; *ED*, 2:75.

38. Jenkins, *General Strike*, 19, 95–104, 165–71; *Illustrated London News*, 20 Aug. 1842; Goodway, *London Chartism*, 106.

39. *The Times*, 11 June 1842, p. 9; 17 Aug., p. 7; 18 Aug. 1842, p. 7; Royle, *Victorian Infidels*, 80–81; Desmond, 'Artisan Resistance,' 85; Bunbury, *Life*, 1:220–21. Holyoake's fellow editor, the rough–edged Charles Southwell, was already serving a two-year stretch at Bristol.

40. *LRO*, 1:167, 198, 321; Desmond, *Politics*, 332; *CCD*, 2:332.

20 THE EXTREME VERGE OF THE WORLD

1. Jenkins, *General Strike*, ch. 10; *CCD*, 2:324, 332; Tristan, *London Journal*, 74–75; Howarth and Howarth, *History*, 82; B. Darwin, 'Kent,' 83; Atkins, *Down*, 7–8, 22.

2. *CCD*, 2:324, 350, 395.

3. Howarth and Howarth, *History*, 10–11, 34; J. Moore, 'Darwin of Down,' 477; 1851 religious census, Parish Church of Down, PRO HO.129/49.

4. Howarth and Howarth, *History*, 48, ch. 7; *CCD*, 2:324.

5. Howarth and Howarth, *History*, ch. 8; Hutchinson, *Life*, 1:2–4, 15.

6. *CCD*, 2:324; *ED*, 2:75.

7. *CCD*, 2:326, 332, 335–36, 345; Atkins, *Down*, ch. 2; Howarth and Howarth, *History*, 76–77.

8. *CCD*, 2:332, 334–36, 338; 'Register of baptisms . . .,' KAO P123/1/10; Death Certificate, Mary Eleanor Darwin, General Register Office, London; 'Register of burials . . .,' KAO P123/1/14; *ED*, 1:255, 2:78.

9. *CCD*, 2:315–16, 352.

10. *CCD*, 2:345; *ED*, 2:80–81; B. Darwin, *World*, 19, 21.

11. *Companion*, 126; Freeman, 'Darwin Family,' 15; *CCD*, 2:345, 348, 350, 355; Monsarrat, *Thackeray*, 113–19; *ED*, 2:85–86.

12. *CCD*, 2:324, 336, 345, 348, 352–53; *ED*, 2:76; J. Moore, 'Darwin of Down,' 460–61.

13. *CCD*, 2:326, 332, 352, 360–61, 414; 3:248; Atkins, *Down*, 25; Freeman, 'Darwin Family,' 13–15.

14. *CCD*, 2:352, 360, 409, 418; 3:134, 248; Atkins, *Down*, 34.

15. *CCD*, 2:360, 387; *Historical and Descriptive Catalogue*, 21; Gay, *Bourgeois Experience*, 403–62 on 'fortifications for the self.'

16. *CCD*, 2:325; Glastonbury, 'Holding,' 31.

17. *CCD*, 2:285–86, 321–22, 338, 387, 435; *CP*, 1:163; Wilson, *Charles Lyell*, 496–502.

18. CCD, 2:105, 339, 341, 389–90; Darwin, Volcanic Islands, 36, 61–65.
19. CP, 1:175–82.
20. CCD, 3:67; 4:466; Darwin's 1826 diary, DAR 129; J. Moore, 'Darwin of Down,' 460.
21. Atkins, Down, 24; Trollope, Clergymen, 54; MLD, 1:33–36.
22. CCD, 1:97, 2:330–31, 351, 354, 359–60, 371, 373, 387, 395; Stearn, Natural History Museum, 210.
23. ED, 2:82–83; CCD, 2:333–34, 345, 374, 435; Freeman, 'Darwin Family,' 13; E. Darwin to H. Wedgwood, April 1837, in Kohn, 'Darwin's Ambiguity,' 226.
24. CCD, 2:373, 375–77; Waterhouse, 'Observations,' 399 for the circles; Desmond, 'Making,' 161ff on the circular classification as a buffer against Lamarckism.
25. CCD, 2:378; Colp, 'Confessing,' 12–13.
26. CCD, 2:377–79, 381–82.
27. CCD, 2:387, 389, 397–99, 405, 415–16; Waterhouse, 'Observations,' 403, 406.

21 MURDER

1. CCD, 1:34, 3:394; LLJH, 1:20.
2. CCD, 2:408, 3:10; LLJH, 1:161; D. Porter, 'Darwin's Plant Collections,' 520.
3. Hooker, 'Reminiscences,' 187; LLJH, 1:41–45; LLD, 2:19; D. Porter, 'Darwin's Plant Collections,' 519. Hooker does not mention McCormick by name, only that it was one of Darwin's crewmates who 'had accompanied him in the Beagle to Rio.' McCormick befriended Hooker in 1839 and took him in tow before the Erebus trip, which leaves little doubt that it was he who introduced him to Darwin.
4. Hooker, 'Reminiscences,' 187; LLJH, 1:41; LLD, 2:19.
5. CCD, 2:408, 410–11, 419.
6. CCD, 3:2; Colp, 'Confessing.'
7. Desmond, 'Artisan Resistance,' 90 n. 47.
8. CCD, 3:2, 5, 7, 11.
9. Foundations, 85, 91; Ospovat, Development, 82–3; Kohn et al., 'New Light,' 427. According to Ospovat, Darwin believed that species were 'perfectly' adapted in these stable periods, and that he had still to shake off the old theological framework. Kohn ('Darwin's Ambiguity,' 230) disagrees, maintaining that 'relative' adaptation had been Darwin's working concept since writing his 'E' Notebook. The 'imperfection' of nature's contrivances in Paley's own natural theology has also recently been emphasized: Francis, 'Naturalism,' 214.
10. Foundations, xix.
11. B. Taylor, Eve, 131; Martin, First Conversation, 5–6; Movement, 6 July 1844, p. 239 and 31 Aug., p. 315; Royle, Victorian Infidels, 88.
12. CCD, 3:43–44; TBI, 158.
13. Desmond, Politics, chs 6–8, p. 376; CCD, 3:43–44; Colp, 'Confessing,' 16–19.
14. Napier, Selections, 492; Forbes, Literary Papers, 120.
15. CCD, 3:28, 42, 47–49, 57, 79, 83, 310. John Thackray of the Geological Society supplied the figures for GS membership.

16. Darwin, *South America*, chs 1–4; D'Orbigny, 'General Considerations,' 367; CCD, 3:56, 59, 162, 193, 391.
17. CCD, 3:61, 70–72, 79; *Foundations*, 183–94.
18. CCD, 2:413–14, 3:56, 67; ED, 2:88; Raverat, *Period Piece*, 142.
19. CCD, 3:396; Colp, 'Confessing,' 19–20; Kohn, 'Darwin's Ambiguity,' 226; *Foundations*, xvii; LLD, 2:12, 296; Eng, 'Confrontation.'
20. Secord, 'Behind the Veil,' 166, 168; R. Yeo, 'Science,' 25–27; Desmond, *Politics*, 175–80.
21. Secord, 'Behind the Veil,' 166, 173. The vast conceptual differences between Darwin's science and *Vestiges* are explored in Hodge, 'Universal Gestation.' Chambers rejected *common* ancestry, picturing life as a series of parallel – but unrelated – lineages, each originating in a spontaneously generated base.
22. Words of the dour Episcopalian professor at Edinburgh, James D. Forbes. Forbes was an expert on glacial movement; Darwin thought him clever, civil, and 'as frigid as one of his glaciers:' Shairp *et al.*, *Life*, 178; CCD, 3:103, 108, 166.
23. Gillispie, *Genesis*, 169–70; CCD, 3:184.
24. Chilton, 'Vestiges,' 9; Chilton, 'Regular Gradation,' *Movement*, Nov. 1844, 413; Desmond, 'Artisan Resistance,' 102.
25. Carpenter, 'Vestiges,' 155, 160, 180; Desmond, *Politics*, 195; CCD, 3:258.
26. Napier, *Selection*, 492; Epps, *Church of England's Apostacy*, 3; Desmond, *Politics*, 178–79 for the deeper context.
27. CCD, 3:253, 258, 289; Egerton, 'Conjecture'; Napier, *Selections*, 494.
28. CCD, 3:181, 289, 4:19, 36, 152; A. Sedgwick to M. Napier, 17 April 1845, BL, Add. MSS 34,625, ff. 113–19; Napier, *Selections*, 491–93; Desmond, *Archetypes*, 210.
29. Chambers, in Secord, 'Behind the Veil,' 186. For the species named after Darwin: CCD, 3:46, 196, 232, 276; Darwin, *South America*, 92, 253; *Companion*, 82–86.
30. CCD, 3:65, 168.
31. CCD, 3:67–68, 332, 354; LLD, 3:27.
32. CCD, 3:85; Ospovat, 'Perfect Adaptation,' 39ff; Gillespie, *Charles Darwin*, ch. 5.
33. CCD, 3:164, 166, 177.
34. Hooker, 'Reminiscences,' 187–88; CCD, 3:88–90, 399–403.
35. Hooker, 'Reminiscences,' 188; CCD, 3:34–35, 62, 149, 167, 181–82, 288.
36. CCD, 3:140, 149, 167–68, 177, 207.
37. CCD, 3:139, 147, 166, 186; LLJH, 1:191, 194.
38. Hill, 'Squire,' 337, 342, 344–45; Ashwell and Wilberforce, *Life*, 1:130; CCD, 3:68, 86, 157, 181, 214, 216, 229, 256, 260; Beesby estate papers, DAR 210.25.
39. CCD, 3:169, 176.
40. *Journal* (1845), 360–61, 363, 375, 376; Sulloway, 'Darwin' and 'Darwin's Conversion,' 345; Hooker, 'Reminiscences,' 187.
41. CCD, 3:55, 203, 213, 233, 242; *Journal* (1845), 469–70.
42. CCD, 3:208, 240, 339; LLJH, 1:204.
43. CCD, 3:211, 217, 264, 336–37; J. Browne, *Secular Ark*, 65–68, 77–80; Egerton, 'Hewett C. Watson,' 89, 92.
44. CCD, 3:274, 289.
45. Mills, 'View,' 372.
46. CCD, 3:71, 149, 163, 245, 250, 253, 291, 294–95, 300, 304–305; *Foundations*,

168–71; Sulloway, 'Geographic Isolation,' 30–49. For Forbes's science: Rehbock, *Philosophical Naturalists*, 157–75, 186–87; J. Browne, *Secular Ark*, 114ff.
47. E. Forbes to R. Owen, 2 Nov. 1846, BM(NH), OCorr.; Desmond, *Politics*, 365; CCD, 3:274.
48. CCD, 3:282–83, 287; Mills, 'View,' 377; Rehbock, *Philosophical Naturalists*, 72–73.
49. CCD, 3:141, 285, 287, 339.
50. CCD, 2:346, 353, 306; Russell–Gebbett, *Henslow*, ch. 3; J. Moore, 'Darwin of Down,' 466–67.
51. CCD, 3:248; 'Subscription towards embellishments of the Church . . .' and copy notebooks, KAO P123/6/1–3.
52. KAO P123/2/1, 5 and P123/5/26; Stecher, 'Darwin–Innes Letters,' 255; CCD, 2:406; J. Moore, 'Darwin of Down,' 477.
53. CCD, 2:406, 3:49, 192, 228, 256, 260, 321, 377; 4:256–57, 304; Barnett, 'Allotments.'
54. CCD, 3:260; Harrison, *Early Victorian Britain*, 27.
55. CCD, 3:248, 259–60, 347–48; ED, 2:309.
56. CCD, 3:228.
57. CCD, 3:325.
58. CCD, 4:290, 337; 5:94; Crouzet, *Victorian Economy*, 165. In fact, Darwin had started paying for the first free-trade reforms in 1842, when Peel introduced his income tax to make up the lost revenues. Darwin's tax bill was about £30 in 1842.
59. CCD, 3:68, 84, 86, 95–96, 141–42, 166, 181, 215, 264, 311–12, 327; ED, 1:250.
60. CCD, 3:312, 326; ED, 2:98–99, 102–103.
61. CCD, 3:68, 141, 246, 277, 331, 345; Atkins, *Down*, 28 and RFD.
62. CCD, 3: 307, 332, 390.
63. CCD, 3:111–12, 164, 346, 4:127; Owen, 'Notices,' 66; Rehbock, *Philosophical Naturalists*, 176–84.
64. CCD, 3:124, 323, 345–46, 359. Ministers were riled by FitzRoy's maverick action; he adopted 'free trade in *every* thing,' dropped customs duties, gave up the Crown rights to the land and allowed settlers to buy direct from the Maoris, slashing the government fee from ten shillings to a penny an acre. The colonial office might have baulked, but even Sulivan agreed that his decisive action had saved New Zealand.
65. CCD, 3:331, 338, 345, 356.

22 ILLFORMED LITTLE MONSTERS

1. CCD, 3:346, 350.
2. CCD, 3:356–58, 365–66.
3. CCD, 3:359, 363; D. Allen, *Naturalist*, 124–31; LLL, 2:129.
4. J. Thompson, *Zoological Researches*, 71–73, 79; Winsor, 'Barnacle Larvae,' 295–98; Huxley, 'Lectures,' 238; CCD, 4:100, 178; Ghiselin, *Triumph*, ch. 5. For the best analysis of Darwin's work on barnacles, containing many fresh insights, [M. Richmond], 'Darwin's Study of Cirripedia,' CCD, 4:388–409.
5. LLJH, 1:190; CCD, 3:251, 253, 256, 4:327. Hooker and Darwin tellingly disagreed over Gérard's worth. Hooker thought Gérard's listing of hundreds

of variations of species wretched. Hooker was a 'lumper,' determined to 'cut down ... all the intermediate forms' and parcel them out to 'everyday' species. But Darwin, concerned with change rather than taxonomy, sympathized with Gérard's enterprise. It gave the information he needed: the variations on which selection acted.

6. *CCD,* 3:375, 4:38.
7. Quoted in Dance, 'Hugh Cuming,' 477; Darwin, *Monograph on the Sub-Class,* 1:v–vi; *CCD,* 3:137, 231, 297, 4:98–100; *Journal* (1845), 372–73.
8. Jardine, *Memoirs,* clxxiv–v; Kirby, 'Introductory Address,' 5; Desmond, 'Making,' 168; Gillespie, 'Preparing,' 102; *CCD,* 4:187, 189, 192. In 1842 Darwin had served with Strickland on the British Association committee on Zoological nomenclature: *CCD,* 2:311.
9. *CCD,* 4:11.
10. J. Hooker to [a Darwin son], 19 Feb. 1905, BL, Add. MSS 58,373 (unbound).
11. Hooker, 'Reminiscences,' 188; *LLJH,* 1:213–14; *CCD,* 4:10–11, 25, 382.
12. *CCD,* 3:254, 4:21.
13. *Foundations,* 71–74, 80, 170–71; Colp, 'Confessing,' 30–31; *CCD,* 4:25.
14. Hooker, 'Reminiscences,' 187.
15. *CCD,* 4:11, 29–30; *LLJH,* 1:167.
16. *Autobiography,* 105; *CCD,* 4:37, 40, 44, 5:300; Secord, 'Geological Survey,' 233–34.
17. *CCD,* 4:71, 74; Rudwick, 'Darwin,' 131–45, 153–65; Barrett, 'Darwin's "Gigantic Blunder",' 25–27.
18. Desmond, *Politics,* 296–97; Secord, *Controversy,* 123; Morrell, 'London Institutions,' 137; *CCD,* 4:25. The opium and bismuth are mentioned in *CCD,* 3:247, 325.
19. *CCD,* 4:48; Secord, 'Geological Survey,' 253; *LLJH,* 1:210, 221.
20. *CCD,* 4:44–45, 47, 51, 53; *LLL,* 2:130.
21. Geikie, *Memoir,* 103.
22. Andrew Ramsay, diary for 1847, f. 59, Imperial College Archives, London, KGA Ramsay/1/8 (we thank Jim Secord for giving us this reference); Wilberforce, *Pride,* 15–20; *Illustrated London News,* 3 July 1847, p. 10. Ramsay approved the sermon; the Owens also thought it 'very fine': *LRO,* 1:299.
23. *CCD,* 4:152, 269; *LLL,* 2:154; Morrell and Thackray, *Gentlemen,* on the BAAS's social ethos.
24. Hooker, 'Reminiscences,' 188; *CCD,* 4:49–50.
25. *CCD,* 4:55, 61; *LLJH,* 1:219.
26. *LLJH,* 1:216, 219.
27. *CCD,* 4:56, 61, 87.
28. *CCD,* 4:92–93.

23 AL DIABOLO

1. *CCD,* 4:107, 109.
2. *CP* 1:227; *CCD,* 4:24, 383; Geikie, *Memoir,* 130.
3. *LLL,* 2:139, 141. Buckland and Owen had acted as Peel's scientific advisers while he was Prime Minister (1841–46), and they were personally close to the Tory leader. Sir Robert had given Owen a huge Civil List Pension in 1842, and he appointed Buckland Dean of Westminster and offered Owen a

knighthood in 1845, shortly before leaving office: Gordon, *Life*, 220; Desmond, *Politics*, 354–58.

4. Desmond, *Politics*, 328, 331–32; LRO, 1:167; LLL, 1:291; CCD, 4:108–109.
5. ED, 2:115; Goodway, *London Chartism*, 68–96; Wilson and Geikie, *Memoir*, 432.
6. CCD 4:151, 157; Geikie, *Memoir*, 129; Wilson and Geikie, *Memoir*, 433; LRO, 1:320; W. Broderip to R. Owen, 13 Mar. 1848, BM(NH), OCorr.
7. CCD, 4:128, 476–78.
8. CCD, 4:128; MLD, 1:370–71; Darwin, *Monograph on the Sub-Class*, 1:186, 189, 198, 202. The barnacles' hermaphroditism made them even odder crustaceans; crabs are single sexed: J. Thompson, *Zoological Researches*, 80–81.
9. CCD, 4:252–53.
10. CCD, 4:249; Darwin, *Monograph on the Sub-Class*, 1:205–208, 231–32; *Notebooks* D157, 162.
11. CCD, 4:140, 159.
12. Darwin, *Monograph on the Sub-Class*, 1:232, 291; 2:23; CCD, 4:169, 180, 204 (Darwin in his *Monograph* eventually reported seeing 'as many as fourteen adhering on one female!'); Hooker, *Himalayan Journals*, 2:206; LLJH, 1:270, 312.
13. CCD, 4:139, 142, 144–46.
14. CCD, 4:102, 145, 147, 154; TBI, 38.
15. CCD, 4:169–70, 269; LLL, 2:146.
16. Norton, *Evidences*, 1:11; CCD, 4:476; Stevens, 'Darwin's Humane Reading.'
17. CCD, 3:141, 4:384, 477; Hare, *Essays*, 1:lxxxii, cvi, cl, ccxiv.
18. Coleridge, *Aids*, 1:89–90, 133, 144–45, 152, 157, 194–96, 245, 281, 333 (cf. Barth, *Coleridge*, 137, 191–93); ED, 2:284; CCD, 4:477.
19. CCD, 4:178, 181–82, 209.
20. ED, 2:119; CCD, 4:183; 5:9; *Autobiography*, 117; *Wedgwood*, 249–50; Will of Robert Waring Darwin, PRO 11/2084.
21. Hutchinson, *Life*, 1:22–25.
22. CCD, 3:96, 4:223, 225–27; Wheatley, *Life*, 264.
23. H. Martineau, *Eastern Life*, 1:67, 277, 2:9, 3:158, 162, 167.
24. CCD, 4:209, 219, 228, 478.

24 MY WATER DOCTOR

1. CCD, 4:209, 234; Mann, *Collections*, 12–21; TBI, 39.
2. CCD, 4:219; TBI, 39–40.
3. Billing, *M. Billing's Directory*, 412; B. Smith, *History*, 194; RFD, 85; CCD, 4:209, 223.
4. CCD, 4:354; Mann, *Collections*, 5–6, 12ff; Desmond, *Politics*, 175 n. 81.
5. CCD, 4:224, 354.
6. 'Malvern Water,' *Household Words*, 11 Oct. 1851, pp. 67–71; E. Darwin's recollections of Annie, DAR 210.13; recollections of G. Darwin, DAR 112; Baptismal Register, Parish of Great Malvern, 5 June 1849, County of Hereford and Worcester Record Office, Worcester; CCD, 4:234, 236, 239–40.
7. CCD, 4:227; TBI, 40.
8. CCD, 4:246, 5:78; TBI, 43; RFD, 84; 'A Visit to Darwin's Village: Reminiscences of Some of His Humble Friends,' *Evening News* (London), 12 Feb. 1909, p. 4.
9. CCD, 4:247, 256–57, 269, 311, 314; CP, 1:250–51; TBI, 49; Morus, 'Politics of

Power,' on the reform of the Royal Society (cf. MacLeod, 'Whigs').

10. Darwin, *Monograph on the Sub-Class*, 2:26.

11. *CCD*, 4:127, 219; Ospovat, *Development*, 146, 150 and Owen, *On the Nature of Limbs* in Darwin Library, CUL; Desmond, *Archetypes*, 50 and *Politics*, ch. 6, esp. 216, 267–68 on specific antagonisms between the Unitarian materialists and Coleridgean idealists; Di Gregorio, 'In Search,' 249.

12. *CCD*, 4:179, also 156, 169; Darwin, *Monograph on the Sub-Class*, 1:2, 25–28 (cf. T. Huxley, 'Lectures,' 238, 241 for a rejigging of Darwin's barnacle homologies); Desmond, *Politics*, ch. 8, on the prevalence of archetypal thinking in London in the 1840s.

13. *CCD*, 4:179, 314; Darwin, *Monograph of the Sub-Class*, 1:34–7.

14. *CCD*, 4:270, 273.

15. *CCD*, 4:269, 272, 303, 311.

16. *LLJH*, 1:312–20; Hooker, *Himalayan Journals*, 2:206–14, 233, 247; *CCD*, 4:294, 310, 478; *LLL*, 2:153.

17. *CCD*, 4:282–83, 289, 293, 300–303; Trenn, 'Charles Darwin.'

18. Darwin, *Monograph on the Fossil Lepadidae*, v, 1; Trenn, 'Charles Darwin,' 471, 479; *CCD*, 4:300, 305; *CP*, 1:251–2.

19. *CCD*, 4:304–305, 310–11; Trenn, 'Charles Darwin,' 481–82.

20. *CCD*, 4:319, 323, 349, 361; Darwin, *Monograph on the Fossil Lepadidae*, 3.

21. *CCD*, 4:312, 315, 319, 321, 335, 344; *TBI*, 44.

22. *CCD*, 4:114–15, 139, 268–69, 327–28.

23. *CCD*, 4:344; Darwin, *Monograph on the Sub-Class*, 2:155; Gillespie, 'Preparing,' 107–108.

24. *CCD*, 5:155–56.

25. *CCD*, 3:376; T. Huxley, 'Lectures,' 240 on Darwin's classification. Ghiselin and Jaffe, 'Phylogenetic Classification,' 137, have subsequently constructed a dendrogram of barnacle relationships according to Darwin's known views. Such diagrams were common in Darwin's day (Ospovat, *Development*, 161), but it was telling that Darwin did not draw one.

26. *CCD*, 4:344, 353, 369.

25 OUR BITTER & CRUEL LOSS

1. E. Darwin's recollections of Annie, DAR 210.13; *CCD*, 4:369, 5:9.

2. *CCD*, 4:225, 5:540–41; *ED*, 2:184; *TBI*, 149.

3. E. Darwin's recollections of Annie, DAR 210.13; *CCD* 4:385–87.

4. *CCD*, 4:379–80, 386–87.

5. Corsi, *Science*, 262–65; Robbins, *Newman Brothers*, 107–16; *CCD*, 4:479; *ED* 2:125; Newman, *Soul*, 227, 230, 233, 258; Newman, *History*, iv, 210, 370; O. Chadwick, *Victorian Church*, 1:291–301.

6. *TBI*, 45; E. Darwin's recollections of Annie, DAR 210.13; *CCD* 4:479, 5:69.

7. Newman, *Phases*, 78, 81, 101, 141, 172, 188, 200, 233.

8. *CCD*, 4:479, 5:519; *LLD* 2:158; E. Darwin's recollections of Annie, DAR 210.13.

9. Billing, M. *Billing's Directory*, 415; *CCD*, 4:354; *RFD*, 85; Colp, *TBI*, 44–45. Francis and George Darwin recalled that Gully wanted the clairvoyant to report on their father. If true, this family tradition can be only part of the story. Charles was feeling fairly well in March 1851; Gully had already successfully diagnosed his ailment. Annie was now their prime concern. Since

Gully's own daughter had been helped by a clairvoyant, it stood to reason that Annie should also be seen. Clairvoyant females were supposed to have special insight into female patients.

10. M. Lyell to F. Wedgwood, 28 April [1851], W/M 310; *LLJH*, 1:332; Froude, *Carlyle*, 2:67–77; Fielding, 'Froude's Second Revenge;' *ED*, 2:128–29; *CCD*, 5:25. Charles did not indicate reading the book until August 1852 (*CCD*, 4:488). But Erasmus and Fanny were close friends of Martineau and held decided views on the 'priestess' and her outrageous book (Calder, 'Erasmus Darwin,' 38; Arbuckle, *Harriet Martineau's Letters*, 113). It is inconceivable that the first time Charles was in Eras's and Fanny's company after the book's publication (in early February), they did not discuss it and arouse his reading interests.

11. *CCD*, 5:10, 13.

12. C. Thorley to E. Darwin, [14 April and 15 April 1851], DAR 210.13; *CCD*, 5:13, 16–17, 22; *ED*, 2:132–33.

13. *ED*, 2:132; *CCD*, 5:13, 16.

14. *CCD*, 5:13–15, 21.

15. *CCD*, 5:16–17; F. Wedgwood to E. Darwin, [19 April 1851], DAR 210.13.

16. *CCD*, 5:18–23.

17. *CCD*, 5:23–24. F. Wedgwood to H. Wedgwood, [23 April 1851], W/M 310.

18. F. Wedgwood to H. Wedgwood, [23 April 1851], and to K. E. Wedgwood, 25 April 1851, W/M 310; 'Thunderstorms,' *Barron's Worcester Journal*, 1 May 1851, p. [3]; *ED*, 2:286; H. Montgomery, 'Emma Darwin;' Ricks, *Poems*, 910 (lv:5–8).

19. F. Wedgwood to H. Wedgwood, [23 April 1851], W/M 310; F. Wedgwood to E. Darwin, [23 April 1851], DAR 210.13; Ricks, *Poems*, 911 (lvi:1–4); Death Certificate, Anne Elizabeth Darwin, General Register Office, London.

20. *CCD*, 5:25; E. Darwin to F. Wedgwood, [25 April 1851], W/M 310.

21. *CCD*, 5:24–26; F. Allen to F. Wedgwood, 23 Ap[ril 1851], and E. Darwin to F. Wedgwood, [25 April 1851], W/M 310.

22. *CCD*, 5:28–29; F. Wedgwood to K. E. Wedgwood, 25 April 1851, W/M 310; Burial Register, Parish of Great Malvern, 25 April 1851, County of Hereford and Worcester Record Office, Worcester.

23. *CCD*, 5:25, 542–43; S. E. Wedgwood to F. Wedgwood, [27 April 1851], W/M 310.

24. *CCD*, 5:26–27; *ED*, 2:137, 139; E. Darwin to F. Wedgwood, [24 April 1851], W/M 310; Annie's keepsakes, DAR 210.13.

25. *CCD*, 5:32, 540–42; Colp, 'Charles Darwin's "insufferable grief";' J. Moore, 'Of Love.'

26. *CCD*, 5:33; *ED*, 2:140; Darwin to J. Hooker, 6 June [1868], DAR 94:69–70.

26 A GENTLEMAN WITH CAPITAL

1. Best, *Mid-Victorian Britain*, 252; T. Macaulay, in Golby, *Culture*, 3.

2. McNeil, *Under the Banner*; Prince Albert, in Harvie *et al.*, *Industrialization*, 234-38.

3. Charlotte Brontë, in Jennings, *Pandaemonium*, 262.

4. *CCD* 4:354; Haight, *George Eliot*, 20ff, 60; Rosenberg, 'Financing,' 169-72; Van Arsdel, 'Westminster Review,' 544-49; Heyck, *Transformation*, 17; Corsi, *Science*, 204; Holyoake, *Sixty Years*, 1:239.

5. Rosenberg, 'Financing,' 175; J. Moore, *Religion*, 432.
6. Corsi, *Science*, 273-76; Desmond, *Archetypes*, 29-32.
7. Spencer, *Autobiography*, 1:348, 394ff; Rosenberg,'Financing,' 174; Spencer, *Social Statics*, 80; J. Moore *et al.*, *Science*, 6ff.
8. Spencer, *Autobiography*, 1:377, 384; Prince Albert, in Golby, *Culture*, 1-2.
9. R. Young, *Darwin's Metaphor*, 23-55.
10. Spencer, *Autobiography*, 1:372, 388; J. Moore, *Religion*, 406, 408; R. Young, *Darwin's Metaphor*, 51-52.
11. CCD, 5:49-52, 55, 538; ED, 2:142; TBI, 49.
12. CCD, 5:54, 57.
13. CCD, 5:55, 81, 83; RFD, 17, 38; TBI, 48.
14. CCD, 5:83; Davidoff and Hall, *Family Fortunes*, 205-207, 360-65.
15. Hobsbawm, *Industry*, 156; Keith, *Darwin*, 222, 225; CCD, 3:375-77, 4:xx, 52, 62-63, 154-55, 185, 375-77; 5:119, 183-84.
16. Austin, *Memoir*, 2:472; Jardine, *Memoirs*, cclix; Crouzet, *Victorian Economy*, 285-87; LLL, 2:129; CCD, 3:303-304; Burn, *Age*, 30; Schivelbusch, *Railway Journey*, chs 8-9.
17. CCD, 4:62-63, 375; 5:99, 101, 190-91; Atkins, *Down*, 97.
18. CCD, 4:377, 378; 5:40, 94, 143, 191.
19. CCD, 4:138, 264-65; 5:222-23; 'Down Coal Club: Honorary Subscriptions, 1841-1876 Inclusive,' Down House; recollections of J. Brodie Innes, DAR 112; registration document, 'N° 3043 Down Friendly Society . . .,' PRO FS1/232/643, pp. 12-13, 18, 32; cf. J. Moore, 'Darwin of Down,' 466-69.
20. Briggs, *Age*, 388; CCD, 4:362, 369; 5:85-6, 163, 174.
21. CCD, 5:83-84; ED, 1:144; LLL, 2:172; H. Bell, *Lord Palmerston*, 2:58.
22. CCD, 5:83, 100, 104, 111.
23. CCD, 4:353-54, 362; 5:51, 52, 55, 63, 83, 147-48; TBI, 49; Hutchinson, *Life*, 22-24, 29-30.
24. CCD, 5:63, 97, 100, 112, 147-48, 536; Duman, 'Creation,' 120-23; F. Darwin, *Rustic Sounds*, 157.
25. CCD, 5:96; ED, 2:146-50.
26. L. Huxley, 'Home Life,' 6; recollections of G. Darwin, DAR 112; ED, 2:81.
27. CCD, 5:81; F. Darwin, *Springtime*, 60-62 and *Rustic Sounds*, 154.
28. ED, 2:105-106, 154.
29. CCD, 4:425; 5:81, 141-42, 536.
30. ED, 2:173; Foote, *Darwin*, 20; F. Darwin, *Springtime*, 51-53; 'Register of baptisms . . .,' KAO P123/1/10; Hutchinson, *Life*, 1:32.
31. Duncan, *Life*, 64, 541; E. Richards,'Question;' Desmond, *Archetypes* 30ff.
32. Duncan, *Life*, 62-63; Spencer, *Autobiography*, 1:402; LLTH, 1:81, 83, 90; Desmond, *Archetypes*, 25-29.
33. Duncan, *Life*, 65, 543; Spencer, *Autobiography*, 1:350; Schoenwald, 'G. Eliot's "Love" Letters;' LLD, 2:188; Desmond, *Archetypes*, 37ff, 99.

27 UGLY FACTS

1. Health diary, Down House; TBI, 43–53.
2. TBI, 45–46; Freeman, 'Darwin Family,' 17; Health diary, Down House, April, Aug.–Nov. 1852; CCD, 5:96, 98, 100, 194.
3. LLTH, 1:89, 102, 107; CCD, 5:49, 64, 75, 131. T. Huxley, 'Lectures,' 238–39 adopted the terminology of Darwin's 'very admirable' monograph, accepted

his views on the tiny males, but had reservations about the cement glands and thought that Darwin had mistaken the site of the 'true ovaria.'

4. CCD, 5:130.
5. CCD, 5:103, 105, 108, 110, 113–15, 117–18.
6. CCD, 5:82, 100, 123, 147, 212; MLD, 1:38.
7. CCD, 5:165–66, 225, 307; 6:406. The Royal Medal is likened to a scientific knighthood in 'The Royal Society,' Lancet, 1 (1846), 635. On the reforms: MacLeod, 'Of Medals,' 92; Morus, 'Politics of Power.'
8. Health diary, Down House; CCD, 3:253, 5:157, 163, 172, 536, 539; 6:55; Autobiography, 117. Bulwer–Lytton parodied Darwin as the crusty 'Professor Long' in What Will He Do With It?, 1:284–96.
9. CCD, 5:113, 174–75, 177, 179–81.
10. CCD, 3:45, 5:113, 178, 196–97, 215.
11. CCD, 5:174, 195; Geikie, Memoirs, 165.
12. CCD, 5:186, 194, 331.
13. CCD, 5:224, 321; LRO, 2:5–6.
14. CCD, 5:351; LLTH, 1:133; MacLeod, 'Whigs,' 79–80; Morus, 'Politics of Power.'
15. CCD, 5:224–25, 278, 6:408; LJT, 45–48; LLTH, 1:101ff; Gage and Stearn, Bicentenary History, 53.
16. CCD, 5:424; LLTH, 1:85, 114–15, 119, 137–38; LJT, ch. 4.
17. LLJH, 1:477–78; Corsi, Science, ch. 17.
18. CCD, 5:345, 350; LLJH, 1:474.
19. 'Origin of Man: Science versus Theology,' London Investigator, 1 (1854–55), 8ff; Desmond, 'Robert Grant's Later Views,' 402, 404; Beddoe, Memories, 32–33; E. Forbes to T. Huxley, 16 Nov. 1852, THP 16.170; LLTH, 1:94.
20. C. Lyell, 'Anniversary Address,' xxxiii, xxxix; Corsi, 'Importance,' 224, 241; Bartholomew, 'Lyell' and 'Singularity.'
21. CCD, 5:537; LLL, 2:199; Desmond, Politics, 327–30.
22. CCD, 5:416; Natural Selection, 89.
23. T. Huxley, 'Vestiges,' 425–27, 429; Huxley's notes on Vestiges, THP 41.57–63; Bartholomew, 'Huxley's Defence,' 526–28; Desmond, Archetypes, 49; LLD, 2:188–89; LLTH, 1:224.
24. CCD, 5:213–14; Pearson, Life, 2:204.
25. CCD, 5:212–13, 215, 537.
26. CCD, 5:155, 294, 379.
27. CCD, 5:159, 186, 201; Health diary, Down House.
28. CCD, 5:322, 334, 348, 372; 6:196, 209; LLJH, 1:374.

28 GUNSHIPS & GROG SHOPS

1. Hutchinson, Life, 30, 36; CCD, 5:105; ED, 2:154; TBI, 49–50; recollections of G. Darwin, DAR 112; Health diary, Down House.
2. CCD, 5;164, 182, 187, 265.
3. F. Darwin, Rustic Sounds, 154–55 and Springtime, 59–60; G. Darwin's 'manual exercise' and diary, 1852–54, DAR 210.7; CCD, 4:427.
4. LLTH, 1:116; Geikie, Memoir, 224; LLL, 2:201; CCD, 5:241.
5. LLL, 2:202.
6. CCD, 5:196–97, 199, 201, 230, 247–49; Ospovat, Development, 177–78; Kohn, 'Darwin's Principle,' 251; J. Browne, Secular Ark, 205–16.

7. *Autobiography*, 120–21; *Natural Selection*, 249; *Notebooks*, B21; *CCD*, 4:139, 5:475; Ospovat, *Development*, 171; Kohn, 'Darwin's Principle,' 250.
8. McKendrick, 'Josiah Wedgwood,' 30–34.
9. Prince Albert, in Golby, *Culture*, 1–2; Schweber, 'Wider British Context,' 64–65; Schweber, 'Darwin,' 258–59, 265; *Autobiography*, 55.
10. *Origin*, 56, 380; *Natural Selection*, 228ff. Schweber, 'Darwin,' 212; Ospovat, *Development*, 181–83; Kohn, 'Darwin's Principle,' 250; *CCD*, 5:197; J. Browne, *Secular Ark*, 210–16. In today's language, Darwin was developing a theory of sympatric speciation, where the parents and (different) offspring inhabit the same area, rather than being isolated by geography.
11. Even though Milne–Edwards acknowledged his debt to the economists openly: Schweber, 'Darwin,' 197, 213, 255–56, 285; *Natural Selection*, 233; cf. Conry, *Introduction*, 387.
12. Seed, 'Unitarianism', 1–3; Schweber, 'Darwin and the Political Economists,' 269–70; *CCD*, 4:473.
13. *CCD*, 5:253, 265; *ED*, 2:156.
14. *ED*, 2:155–56; *CCD*, 5:537–38; Ereira, *People's England*, 78–85.
15. *CCD*, 5:68; *LLJH*, 1:445; *CP*, 1:255; Sulloway, 'Geographic Isolation,' 41–47.
16. *CCD*, 5:237, 241, 263.
17. *CCD*, 5:299, 305, 308; *CP*, 1:256–57; J. Browne, *Secular Ark*, 198. Although these experiments came as a response to the supercontinent threat, they had actually been on the cards for fifteen years: *Journal* (1839), 541–42; *Notebooks*, Q10, where he jotted, 'Soak all kinds of seeds for week in Salt. artificial water.'
18. *CCD*, 5:305, 308, 321, 328; *LLJH*, 1:352.
19. *CCD*, 2:282, 5:320, 331, 364; *CP*, 1:265; D. Porter, '*Beagle* Collector,' 1015.
20. *CCD*, 5:338–39, 364–67, 374–75; *CP*, 1:257.
21. *CCD*, 5:363, 370, 440–41, 477, 483, 500; 6:122; *LLJH*, 1:494; *CP*, 1:257–58, 261–62.
22. *CCD*, 5:265; F. Darwin, *Springtime*, 53.
23. Ospovat, *Development*, 153–57.
24. *CCD*, 5:84, 100, 147, 194; Ospovat, *Development*, 153ff. He first gave hint of this embryological view in *Notebooks* Summer 1842, 7, where he jotted: 'You can select cattle & sheep for horns & yet no difference in calves – how is this in young pigeons – dogs – cattle? . . . as in trades there is no reason, why the peculiarities sh^d be born, – may come in corresponding time of life of offspring . . . may just as well be born a tendency to alter or assume some form late in youth, – only facts can decide.'
25. *Foundations*, 221; Ospovat, *Development*, 156.
26. *CCD*, 5:288.
27. *CCD*, 6:217, also 3:9, 4:18, 30, 63–64, 89–90, 231 and Colp, 'Darwin and Mrs. Whitby;' Wells, 'Historical Context,' 228–29; Desmond, *Politics*, 310; Secord, 'Darwin.'
28. Secord, 'Darwin;' Desmond, 'Making,' 224–29.
29. Secord, 'Nature's Fancy,' 166; *CCD*, 5:250, 321, 337, 359; *Notebooks*, Q3, p. 493.
30. *CCD*, 5:326, 352, 386, 492, 497.
31. Darwin, *Expression*, 259; *CCD*, 5:508.
32. *CCD*, 5:415, 482.
33. *CCD*, 5:528, 6:24, 217; *LLL*, 2:213; Secord, 'Nature's Fancy,' 164, 170.

34. *CCD*, 6:236; Secord, 'Nature's Fancy,' 165, 175, 178 and 'Darwin,' 537.
35. Secord, 'Nature's Fancy,' 173.
36. Secord, 'Nature's Fancy,' 177; *LLD*, 2:281–82.
37. *CCD*, 5:509; *ED*, 2:157.

29 HORRID WRETCHES LIKE ME

1. *LLJH*, 1:368-69.
2. *CCD*, 5:282, 425, 6:114; *LLJH*, 1:375; *LLTH*, 1:138-39, 148.
3. J. Hooker to T. Huxley, 4 April 1856, THP 3.23; *LLJH*, 1:369-70, 412.
4. *LLTH*, 1:128-29, 144, 157; *CCD*, 5:442.
5. T. Huxley to E. Forbes, 27 Nov. 1852, THP 16.72; W. Carpenter to T. Huxley, 16 July 1855 and 22 Oct. 1858, THP 12.78, 94; *LLTH*, 1:95; Baynes, 'Darwin,' 505-506; Desmond, *Archetypes*, 22, 123. Macaulay engineered Owen's job at the British Museum, and the £800 pay that went with it: *LRO*, 2:13-15.
6. J. Hooker to T. Huxley, 4 April 1856, THP 3.23.
7. Owen, 'Lyell,' 448-50; Ospovat, *Development*, 129-40; Desmond, *Archetypes*, 42-46; Bowler, *Fossils*, 101-106; E. Richards, 'Question,' 145-46.
8. *CCD*, 5:68, 133; Desmond, *Archetypes*, 42; Bartholomew, 'Huxley's Defence,' 527-29.
9. *CCD*, 5:133; T. Huxley, 'Contemporary Literature,' 243; Ospovat, 'Darwin on Huxley;' Winsor, *Starfish*, 90-97.
10. Darwin made notes on Huxley's attack on W. B. Carpenter's enunciation of the principle (T. Huxley, 'Comparative Literature,' 243-46): Ospovat, 'Darwin on Huxley,' for the transcription from DAR B.C.40f.
11. Wollaston, *Variation*, 186, 189; *CCD*, 5:268-70, 6:100.
12. *CCD*, 5:403, 498-99; 6:66, 74, 361.
13. *LLD*, 2:26-27; *CCD*, 6:87, 89; *LLL*, 2:212. Like Lyell, Bunbury had married one of Leonard Horner's daughters, Frances, whom Darwin knew well from his London days.
14. Darwin to T. Wollaston, 6 June [1856], EUL, Gen. 1999/1/30 (cf. *CCD*, 6:134); Matthew 7:13-14 (AV); J. Moore, 'Of Love,' 220-23.
15. *CCD*, 5:270; 6:147; Wollaston, *Variation*, 186, 188; Darwin's notes on Wollaston, DAR 197.2
16. *LLD*, 2:196 (Huxley was undoubtedly referring to this April 1856 meeting; he confused the dates in his reminiscences); *CCD*, 5:351. Darwin's dismay was caused by Huxley's Royal Institution talk in April 1855 denouncing progressive development, an abstract of which Huxley posted to him: T. Huxley, 'On Certain Zoological Arguments.'
17. Ospovat, 'Darwin on Huxley,' 11-16, transcribing DAR B.C. 40e.
18. *CCD*, 3:83, 6:103, 106, 111-12; *LLTH*, 1:150.
19. *CCD*, 6:147, 175-76; *LLJH*, 1:427; T. Huxley to F. Dyster, Dec. 1856, THP 15.80; *LRO*, 2:60.
20. *CCD*, 6:260, 484.
21. *CCD*, 5:519, 522; Wallace, 'On the Law;' Brooks, *Just Before*, ch. 5.
22. Wilson, *Sir Charles Lyell's Scientific Journals*, 6-7.
23. *LLL*, 2:213-14; *CCD*, 6:58, 90, 152, 236; Wilson, *Sir Charles Lyell's Scientific Journals*, 54-57, 60: Lyell talked species with Busk, Carpenter, Hooker, Huxley, and John Stuart Mill at the 28 April meeting of the Philosophical Club.

24. CCD, 6:78; Bunbury, Life, 2:90, 99-100.
25. CCD, 6:100, 106.
26. CCD, 6:109, 130-31, 135, 142, 238.
27. Jensen, 'X Club,' 63; CCD, 6:122-23.

30 A LOW & LEWD NATURE

1. CCD, 5:83, 6:87, 151–52, 191.
2. CCD, 6:140, 143–44, 147, 153, 155, 193; Natural Selection, 534–44.
3. CCD, 6:169, 179, 193.
4. Wilson, Sir Charles Lyell's Scientific Journals, 86–87, 102, 119–20, 153, 233, 259, 279; LLL, 2:215; CCD, 6:194; Bartholomew, 'Lyell.'
5. CCD, 6:184, 189, 236; Wilson, Sir Charles Lyell's Scientific Journals, 57–58, 94–95, 97–98; E. Richards, 'Moral Anatomy,' 391–96, 406–10; Lurie, Louis Agassiz, ch. 7; Lorimer, Colour, ch. 5; Bolt, Victorian Attitudes, ch. 1.
6. CCD, 6:100, 199, 201.
7. CCD, 6:198, 200–201, 239, 385, 408.
8. CP, 1:258, 262, 268; CCD, 5:329–30, 500, 6:244.
9. CCD, 5:326, 6:100, 174, 248, 305.
10. CCD, 6:152, 218, 234, 238, 247, 409.
11. CCD, 6:248, 250, 259, 266–67, 274, 282; LLJH, 1:449.
12. ED, 2:132; CCD, 6:238, 267.
13. CCD, 6:238, 264, 268–69, 303, 285, 301, 385; ED, 2:105, 161; Raverat, Period Piece, 122; Wedgwood, 260.
14. CCD, 6:305, 438; ED, 2:162.
15. ED, 2:105, 162; CCD, 6:268–69, 274–75, 286, 303; Roberts, Paternalism, 115–16, 151–52.
16. CCD, 6:304; Natural Selection, 73, 89.
17. CCD, 5:84, 100; Natural Selection, 35–36, 89, 208.
18. CCD, 6:335, 237–38, 249; TBI, 57.
19. Natural Selection, 6; CCD, 5:112, 6:218, 301, 303–304; J. Moore, 'On the Education,' 53–54.
20. CCD, 6:335; Origin, 57; Autobiography, 137; Natural Selection, 92–94; J. Browne, Secular Ark, 204–205.
21. Natural Selection, 172–75, 569; Darwin to J. Hooker, 13 July [1856], DAR 114.3:169 (cf. CCD, 6:178); Colp, 'Charles Darwin's Reprobation.'
22. CCD, 4:479; LRO, 2:12; Natural Selection, 172; Ricks, Poems, 912 (lvi:15–16).
23. Desmond, 'Artisan Resistance;' Holyoake, Sixty Years, 1:166–70; McCabe, Life, 1:85–87, 95–96; Royle, Victorian Infidels, 80–81.
24. Natural Selection, 175–76.
25. CCD, 6:345–46.

31 WHAT WOULD A CHIMPANZEE SAY?

1. CCD, 3:253; Owen, 'On the Anthropoid Apes' and 'Osteological Contributions,' 414–17; Desmond, Politics, 288–94 on the 1830s debates. Thomas Savage discussed the gorilla's discovery in a long letter to Owen, 24 April 1847, BM(NH), OCorr. 23.103.
2. Flower, List, 1:2; Middlemiss, Zoo, 10–11, 23; Barnaby, Log Book, 36–37.

The German comparative anatomist Carl Gustav Carus saw his first living orang–utan in London: C. Carus, *King of Saxony's Journey*, 62.

3. Chilton, 'Geological Revelations;' 'Origin of Man: Science *versus* Theology,' *London Investigator*, 1 (1854–55), 8–122 *passim*; Desmond, 'Artisan Resistance,' 100.
4. *LRO*, 1:377, 2:73, 385; Argyll, *George Douglas*, 1:408–11; Desmond, *Archetypes*, 62–64.
5. W. Whewell to R. Owen, 3 April 1859, BM(NH), OCorr. 26.285; Owen, 'Presidential Address,' xlix–li and *Classification*, 62–63.
6. Owen, 'On the Characters,' 19–20; *CCD* 6:367, 419; Desmond, *Archetypes*, 74–76. Owen had first begun casting alcohol–hardened ape brains in 1830, so he was extremely experienced in the matter: R. Owen, Notebook 1 (Oct.– Dec. 1830), BM(NH), OColl.
7. *Natural Selection*, 214, 223–24; *CCD*, 6:366.
8. *CCD*, 6:368–69, 372–73, 377, 385–86, 394; *ED* 2:159.
9. *CCD*, 6:377, 385, 395, 416; *TBI*, 59–60.
10. *CCD*, 6:384, 389.
11. *CCD*, 6:290, 387–88, 457.
12. *CCD*, 6:395–96, 407; *Natural Selection*, 307–12, 570–71.
13. *CCD*, 6:394–95, 404, 407; 'Register of baptisms . . .,' KAO P123/1/10.
14. *CCD*, 6:412, 416; *CP*, 1:274; *ED*, 2:163; *LLD*, 1:137; *CCD*, 6:524 and Emma Darwin's diary, 9 April 1857 *et seq.*, on deposit in DAR, for the travel movements that spring. (We thank Anne Secord for alerting us to the diary.)
15. *CCD*, 6:420–21, 424–28; *Natural Selection*, 275–79, 303–304; *ED*, 2:163.
16. *CCD*, 6:429, 443; *Natural Selection*, 94; *LLJH*, 1:496.
17. *CCD*, 6:325, 412, 432–33.
18. *CCD*, 6:437, 445–50, 492. He was writing chapter eight, 'Difficulties on the Theory of Natural Selection,' at this time. Although not mentioned in the letter to Gray, the instincts of bees were among Darwin's more pressing problems. So pressing, Robert Richards believes, that they were the stumbling block holding up publication of his entire theory through the 1840s and 1850s (R. Richards, 'Why' and *Darwin*, 144–52; also Prete, 'Conundrum'). The problem was the sterile worker bees: not breeding, they had no offspring to select from. So how did their instincts evolve?

Whether this technical teaser prevented Darwin from publishing is another matter. To start with, he only recognized the conundrum on reading Kirby and Spence's *Introduction to Entomology* in 1843, so it could not have spiked his 'Sketch' of 1842. Moreover, no sooner had he spotted the problem than he had an answer. He guessed that ancestral bees had all been working queens, and through the generations the majority had turned into sterile workers, retaining their instincts. In 1848 he still accepted this for wasps and humble bees, but in addition he toyed with the novel notion of 'family' selection (today called kin selection) for sterile soldier ants, whose body and behaviour are quite unlike the queen's. He thought that the whole colony stood to be selected if new armaments or protective instincts appeared by chance among the soldiers.

He did not doubt that the neuter castes offered 'the greatest *special* difficulty' (quoted in R. Richards, *Darwin*, 146). But it was not so overpowering as to stop him writing *Natural Selection* in the meliorative 1850s. This is the crux: he had no new solution in 1856, and yet he began his 'big book.' Neuter insects did not delay him, nor need they have in the 1840s. His strategy in 1856 was, as in 1848, to pose the problem and suggest plausible mechanisms. Only in 1857, well into the big book, did he finally plump for kin selection as *the* mechanism.

Strategic presentation was Darwin's forte. He singled out sterile insects as potentially 'fatal' to his theory in the *Origin* (236) in order to disarm critics before confronting them with his 'family' selection mechanism. But all along he had had one theory or another in mind, and he could have published at any point. Had insect sterility truly been lethal he would never have laid himself on the line by beginning *Natural Selection* in 1856.

19. Portlock, 'Address,' 1858, clvii–iii; 1857, cxliv–v; *CCD*, 6:445–50. In Portlock's words: if Creation was 'an act imposing laws upon nature, and calling into existence organisms subject to the controlling and modifying action of physical circumstances, why should not an alteration in these circumstances produce the same change in a created being'?
20. *CCD*, 6:445–46.
21. *CCD*, 6:108, 454; *LLTH*, 1:139; Gage and Stearn, *Bicentenary History*, 53. T. Huxley, 'Lectures,' 238.
22. *CCD*, 6:456, 461–62.
23. *CCD*, 5:376, 6:459, 467, 489; *LLJH*, 1:452; Appel, *Cuvier–Geoffroy Debate*, 125–36 on the Geoffroys' attempts to create 'monsters' in Paris.
24. Freeman, 'Charles Darwin;' cf. *CCD*, 2:300–303.
25. *CCD*, 5:253, 537, 6:345–46, 394, 451, 475–76, 478.
26. *ED* (1904), 1:183–84; E. Wedgwood, *My First Reading Book*; Darwin's memoir of Charles Waring Darwin, DAR 210.13.
27. *ED*, 2:45–48, 164–65; *TBI*, 161–64; Healey, *Wives*, 148–68.
28. *CCD*, 4:103; Marsh, 'Charles Darwin;' Zangerl, 'Social Composition.'
29. *CCD*, 6:451–52, 460, 477; Atkins, *Down*, 28, 97; *Natural Selection*, 380; Ospovat, 'Perfect Adaptation;' Ospovat, *Development*, ch. 9; Kohn, 'Darwin's Ambiguity.'
30. *CCD*, 6:460–61; *TBI*, 120–21; *Darwin's Journal*, 14.
31. *CCD*, 6:461, 475, 487; *Natural Selection*, 339.
32. *CCD*, 6:515–16; *Natural Selection*, 387, 467–68, 477, 481; Wilson, *Sir Charles Lyell's Scientific Journals*, 85; R. Richards, *Darwin*, ch. 3. It was well known that habits, and 'even the trifling peculiarities of an individual, have a tendency to become transmitted' (Lewes, 'Hereditary Influence,' 162). Darwin's innovation was to see the best adapted selected, so that change would take place over time.
33. *CCD*, 6:514–15.
34. *LLD*, 2:110; G. Allen, *Miscellaneous and Posthumous Works*, 1:3ff; Buckle, *History*, 1:174–77; 3:481–82; Ruse, *Darwinian Revolution*, 146; Irvine, *Apes*, 166.
35. *Autobiography*, 110; *LLD*, 2:110; Bunbury, *Life*, 2:138–39.
36. Spencer, *Autobiography*, 2:4, 10, 15–16; *LJT*, 76l; Duncan, *Life*, 85, 97, 550.
37. J. Hooker to T. Huxley, 26 Jan. 1858, THP 3.28; *LLL*, 2:279–80.
38. *Natural Selection*, 10, 463. The nine extant chapters of *Natural Selection* were finally published in 1975.
39. T. Huxley, Royal Institution Lecture 10, 'On the Special Peculiarities of Man,' 16 Mar. 1858: Lecture 11, 'Modifiability of Vital Phenomena,' 22 Mar. 1858, THP 36.98–100, 114; Spencer, *Autobiography*, 1:462.

40. T. Huxley to F. Dyster, 30 Jan. 1859, THP 15.106.
41. *LLD*, 2:103, 112–14; *TBI*, 61–63; *ED*, 2:166.
42. *MLD*, 1:109; *LLJH*, 1:458; *LLD*, 2:107.
43. *LLD*, 2:116. On the dating of the letter's arrival: Brooks, *Just Before*, 251–57; Brackman, *Delicate Arrangement*, ch. 3; and especially the response by Kohn, 'On the Origin.'

32 BREAKING COVER

1. Darwin to J. Hooker, 23 [June 1858], DAR 114:238; Colp, 'Charles Darwin, Dr. Edward Lane,' 205, 210; *LLD*, 2:116.
2. Wallace, *My Life*, 1:87, 224; Durant, 'Scientific Naturalism,' 35ff; Hughes, 'Wallace;' Brooks, *Just Before*, ch. 1; Desmond, 'Artisan Resistance,' on the Halls of Science.
3. Durant, 'Scientific Naturalism,' 39; Brooks, *Just Before*, ch. 4.
4. R. Smith, 'Alfred Russel Wallace,' 178, 182, 184ff; Kottler, 'Charles Darwin,' 374. Kohn, 'Origin,' 1106, discusses Darwin's and Wallace's differences on divergence in 1858.
5. Wallace, *Natural Selection*, 27–36, 42.
6. *LLD*, 2:115–20; *MLD*, 1:119; Darwin's memoir of Charles Waring Darwin, DAR 210.13; *Calendar*, 2295; Brooks, *Just Before*, 264.
7. *LLD*, 2:126; Gage and Stearn, *Bicentenary History*, 53–57.
8. *LLJH*, 2:301; Moody, 'Reading;' Gage and Stearn, *Bicentenary History*, 57; *LLD*, 2:294.
9. 'Register of burials . . . ,' KAO P123/1/14; Darwin to W. Fox, 2 July [1858], 21 [July 1858], and 30 [July 1858], Christ's College Library, Cambridge; *LLD*, 2:126, 132; *TBI*, 63ff; *Companion*, 116.
10. *LLD*, 2:128, 131–32, 137–39, 143; *TBI*, 64.
11. Wilson, *Sir Charles Lyell's Scientific Journals*, 195, 198–99, 202; *LLD*, 2:146, 326; *ARW*, 1:134–35; *Calendar*, 2337.
12. T. Huxley to F. Dyster, 30 Jan. 1859, THP 15.106; Desmond, *Archetypes*, 81; Turner, 'Victorian Conflict,' 359ff.
13. T. Huxley to J. Hooker, 18 June 1858, THP 2.153; *LLTH*, 1:161; Duncan, *Life*, 87; Spencer, 'Owen,' 415; Spencer, *Autobiography*, 1:368, 462; 2:24; Desmond, *Archetypes*, 97–98. On the way the Positivist in the Chapman group, George Eliot's lover G. H. Lewes, dumped the 'Archetype,' see S. Bell, 'Lewes,' 288–90.
14. J. Hooker to T. Huxley, [Mar. 1859], THP 3.47; *LLD*, 2:149–50; *RFD*, 75; *TBI*, 64ff.
15. Peckham, *Origin*, 13–16; *LLD*, 2:151–54, 160; Paston, *At John Murray's*, 169–70.
16. *LLJH*, 1:510; *LLD*, 2:159, 160, 163; Darwin to T. Huxley, 2 June [1859], THP 5.65; *MLD*, 1:137.
17. *Calendar*, 2488; *LLD*, 2:163–65, 171, 178.
18. *LLD*, 2:166–68, 262; Wilson, *Sir Charles Lyell's Scientific Journals*, 330–32, 335–36; Bunbury, *Life*, 2:185.
19. *Calendar* 2489; *TBI*, 66–67; Judd, *Coming*, 117; Peckham, *Origin*, 16; *ED*, 1:172; *LLD*, 2:170; *RFD*, 86; *Denton's Ilkley Directory*, 46; *Shuttleworth's Popular Guide*, 50–51.
20. Darwin to J. Hooker, [27 Oct. or 3 Nov. 1859], DAR 115:25; *Calendar*, 2515, 2521; *LLD*, 2:166, 175, 215–20, 230; Peckham, *Origin*, 16–17

21. Peckham, *Origin*, 17, 748; *LLD*, 2:287–88; *MLD*, 1:174.
22. *LLD*, 2:229, 266; *Calendar*, 2542; *Athenaeum*, 19 Nov. 1859, pp. 659–60; Ellegard, *Darwin*, 41, 43, 294.
23. *LLTH*, 1:176; Carlyle, *On Heroes*, 96; *LLD*, 2:228–29, 232; *LLL*, 2:325; *LLJH*, 1:510; Himmelfarb, *Darwin*, ch. 12.
24. *MLD*, 1:149; *Calendar*, 2526, 2575; *LLD*, 2:240, 312; Owen, 'Presidential Address,' li; Wilson, *Sir Charles Lyell's Scientific Journals*, 227 on humans as the 'offspring of anthropoid species,' but somehow created at conception; Desmond, *Archetypes*, 60–62 for Owen's philosophy of Creation; Ellegard, *Darwin*, 65 on the status of Presidential Addresses to the BAAS.
25. *LLD*, 2:303–304, 312; cf. Southwood Smith, *Divine Government*; Gillespie, *Charles Darwin*, chs 5–6.
26. *LLD*, 2:239, 262; Hull, *Darwin*, 93–94, 114; Ellegard, *Darwin*, 35–38, 362–67 on the Unitarian response.
27. Darwin to T. Huxley, 28 Dec. 1859, THP 5.92; *LLD*, 2:235; *MLD*, 1:135; *LLTH*, 1:176.
28. D. Livingstone to R. Owen, 29 Dec. 1860, BM(NH), OCorr. 17.415; A. Sedgwick to R. Owen, 1860, vol. 23.268, 308; J. Wyman to R. Owen, June 1863, vol. 27.254; Argyll to R. Owen, 2 Dec. 1859 and 27 Feb. 1863, vol. 1.230.
29. *LLD*, 2:242; Hull, *Darwin*, 81–84.
30. R. Grant, *Tabular View*, vi; Desmond, 'Robert E. Grant's Later Views;' *LLD*, 2:226.

33 MORE KICKS THAN HALFPENCE

1. Ellegard, *Darwin*, 56; *LLD*, 2:241, 262; Marx and Engels, *Selected Correspondence*, 9:125-26; Engels, *Dialectics*, 19; R. Young, *Darwin's Metaphor*, 52; Durant, 'Scientific Naturalism,' 45 n. 75.
2. H. Martineau to E. A. Darwin, 2 Feb. 1860, W/M 32974-57. We thank Fiona Erskine for showing us transcriptions of this and the Harriet-Fanny letter; cf. Erskine, 'Darwin,' 92, 108 and *LLD*, 2:234.
3. Poynter, 'John Chapman,' 7; *LLD*, 2:315; H. Martineau to G. Holyoake, Friday [1859], BL, Add. MSS 42,726, f.26.
4. H. Martineau to G. Holyoake, Friday [1859], BL, Add. MSS 42,726, f.26; *Origin*, 484, 488. Darwin did indeed regret having 'truckled to public opinion' in resorting to the word 'creation,' 'by which I really meant "appeared" by some wholly unknown process:' *LLD*, 3:18.
5. H. Martineau to F. Wedgwood, 13 Mar. 1860, W/M 32975-57.
6. A. Sedgwick to Darwin, 24 Nov. 1859, DAR 98.2:17-18; *LLD*, 2:250; *ED*, 2:172, 196. Sedgwick, 'Objections,' 335 gave a blow-by-blow refutation in the Mar. 1860 *Spectator*, using 'Dame Nature's old book' to damn talk of 'the bestial origin of man.'
7. J. Henslow to L. Jenyns, 26 Jan. 1860, Bath Reference Library, Letters from Naturalists, &c to Rev. L. Jenyns, 1826-1878, vol. 1, 1 (9); Ellegard, *Darwin*, 45.
8. Bunting, *Charles Darwin*, 88-89, based on evidence apparently found while researching Parliamentary history. The sources have not been located and the author is deceased.
9. Huxley to F. Dyster, 29 Feb. 1860, THP 15.110.

10. Huxley to F. Dyster, 29 Feb. 1860, THP 15.110; Huxley's draft notes of the Royal Institution lecture, THP 41.9-56; LLD, 2:251, 281; MLD, 1:130-31.
11. LLD, 2:282-4; MLD, 1:139-40; Desmond, Archetypes, 110.
12. LLTH, 1:222-23; LLD, 2:293, 331.
13. LRO, 2:39; LLD, 2:300.
14. Owen, Palaeontology, 403 and Anatomy, 3:796, Hull, Darwin, 176, 181, 191.
15. Argyll to R. Owen, 27 Feb. 1863, BM(NH), OCorr. 1.230; Argyll, George Douglas, 2:ch. 23.
16. Hull, Darwin, 177, 182, 201, 202; G. Rolleston to T. Huxley, 13 April 1860, THP 25.142; LLD, 2:300; MLD, 1:149.
17. T. Huxley, Darwiniana, 23, 78, 79; LLD, 2:300; Barton, 'Evolution.'
18. MLD, 1:171-72; LLD, 2:316-18; Calendar, 2809; Hull, Darwin, 134; R. Young, Darwin's Metaphor, ch. 4.
19. Darwin's Journal, 15; Dupree, Asa Gray, 271; Loewenberg, Calendar, 17-25; LLD, 2:269-70; J. Moore, Post-Darwinian Controversies, 270-71.
20. Morrell and Thackray, Gentlemen, 395-96.
21. Wilson, Sir Charles Lyell's Scientific Journals, 355; Geikie, Memoir, 276-77; LLD, 2:291, 293, 366-67; Calendar, 2711, 2787; Secord, 'Geological Survey,' 260.
22. Daily Telegraph, 10 April 1863, p. 4; LLD, 2:287; Desmond, Archetypes, ch. 2; E. Richards,'Question,' 145-48.
23. LLTH, 1:187; LLD, 3:270.
24. 'Recent Acquisitions of the Manuscript Division,' Quarterly Journal of the Library of Congress, 31 (1974), 257.
25. Jensen, 'Return,' 166-67 and LLL, 2:335, on this equivocal point. One London weekly, The Press, did report this specific jibe.
26. G. Stoney to F. Darwin, 17 May 1895, DAR 106/7:36-39; Athenaeum, 14 July 1860, p. 65; Burton, 'Robert FitzRoy,' 151-61.
27. J. Hooker to Darwin, 2 July 1860, DAR 100:141-42 and LLJH, 1:525-27. Lucas, 'Wilberforce,' emphasizes how these on-the-spot accounts differ from the later legend of Huxley's triumph.
28. LLD, 2:323-24.
29. Huxley to F. Dyster, 9 Sept. 1860, THP 15.115; Tuckwell, Reminiscences, 54-55; Poulton, Charles Darwin, 155; Jensen, 'Return,' for an assessment of Huxley's rejoinder. Huxley's actual letter to Darwin is lost, but this to Dyster undoubtedly reflects its content.
30. Brown, Metaphysical Society, 139; Lucas, 'Wilberforce,' 327; Jensen, 'Return,' 166-67; cf. Gilley, 'Huxley-Wilberforce,' 333; J. Browne, 'Charles Darwin – Joseph Hooker Correspondence,' 361-62.
31. LLJH, 1:520.
32. MLD, 1:152, 158; Calendar, 2856.
33. Darwin to T. Huxley, [Aug. 1860?], DAR 145 and Calendar, 2887.
34. Wilberforce, 'Darwin's Origin,' 239, 255, 259, Darwin Reprint Collection, R.34, CUL; MLD, 1:156; ARW, 1:144.

34 FROM THE WOMB OF THE APE

1. Ellis, Seven; Crowther, Church Embattled.
2. Church, Life, 188; Corsi, Science, 283-84; Powell, in Essays, 139; Ellis, Seven, 62; MLD, 1:174-75; LLJH, 1:514.

3. RFD, 69; *LLJH*, 2:55; J. Moore, *Religion*, 425, 437; *MLD*, 2:266-67. For the political significance of this 'whig-liberal' alliance: Parry, *Democracy*, ch. 1.
4. J. Hooker to Darwin, 2 July 1860, DAR 100:141-42; *Athenaeum*, 7 July 1860, p. 26.
5. *MLD*, 1:177-78; T. Huxley to S. Wilberforce, 3 Jan. 1861, THP 227.101; *LLTH*, 1:210.
6. *LLD*, 2:353-54, 373, 378; Dupree, *Asa Gray*, 296-97; *MLD*, 1:191.
7. Dupree, *Asa Gray*, 298ff; Loewenberg, *Calendar*, 100, 103, 134; Peckham, *Origin*, 57; *LLD*, 2:351, 355-56, 361, 370-71, 373; *MLD*, 1:166, 169-70; *Darwin's Journal*, 15; J. Moore, *Post-Darwinian Controversies*, 270ff, 389 n. 48.
8. *LLTH*, 1:152, 190, 220, 225; *Calendar*, 3066, 3085; *ED*, 2:177.
9. Darwin to T. Huxley, 1 Nov. [1860], THP 5.141; *MLD*, 1:460; Owen, 'Gorilla,' 395-96; Owen, 'Ape-Origin,' 262; T. Huxley, 'Man,' 498; Desmond, *Archetypes*, 75. Huxley's Christian compatriots included the Oxford anatomist George Rolleston and William Henry Flower at the Royal College of Surgeons.
10. Darwin to T. Huxley, 1 April 1861, THP 5.162; *MLD*, 1:185; Huxley, 'Man,' 433.
11. G. Rolleston to ?, 1 Oct. 1861, Wellcome Institute, London, AL 325619. Rolleston, who pitched into Owen on anatomical grounds, was promoted at Oxford with Huxley's help, but he was too cautious for Hooker, who saw him living 'in fear and trembling "of God, man, and monkeys":' *MLD*, 1:185.
12. Huxley to F. Dyster, 11 Oct. 1862, THP 15.123; *LLTH*, 1:192; 'Professor Huxley on Man's Place in Nature,' *Edinburgh Review*, 117 (1863), 563.
13. T. Huxley to W. Sharpey, 13 and 16 Nov. 1862, UCL, Sharpey Correspondence MSS Add. 227 (no. 122, 124); *MLD*, 2:30; *LLD*, 2:264, 266.
14. T. Huxley to C. Lyell, 26 June 1861, THP 30.35; *LLTH*, 1:239.
15. *LLD*, 2:364; *LLL*, 2:341, 344; *LLTH*, 1:197; C. Lyell to T. Huxley, 26 Nov. 1860, THP 6.40; T. Huxley, *Man's Place*, 168, 178; Bynum, 'Charles Lyell's Antiquity,' 161ff; Grayson, *Establishment*, 212 etc.
16. Darwin to J. Hooker, 23 [April 1861], DAR 115:98; *LLJH*, 2:60; *Calendar*, 3101 et seq.; *CP*, 2:72-74; *TBI*, 71.
17. J. Moore, 'On the Education,' 57; *TBI*, 69; *LLD*, 1:136; *ED*, 2:176-77; *MLD*, 1:460.
18. E. Darwin to C. Darwin, [June 1861], DAR 210.10; *ED*, 2:174; *TBI*, 83; Healey, *Wives*, 173-74.
19. C. Lyell to T. Huxley, 5 July 1860 [sic, 1861], THP 6.36; *LLTH*, 1:190; T. Huxley, *Man's Place*, 81; 'Professor Huxley at the Royal Institution,' *Reasoner*, 25 (1860), 125; Watts, 'Theological Theories,' 119, 134; *Calendar*, 3466, 4464, 4468.
20. R. Godwin-Austen to T. Huxley, 30 Mar. 1863, THP 10.183; T. Huxley, *Man's Place*, 81, 144, 146, 152-55; *LLTH*, 1:224.
21. Bynum, 'Charles Lyell's Antiquity,' 161, 170-71; *LLTH*, 1:174; Desmond, *Archetypes*, 83-86.
22. *MLD*, 1:181, 2:270, 278; *Calendar*, 3070; Darwin, *Orchids*, 113; Allan, *Darwin*, 195ff; *LLD*, 3:262-63
23. Basalla, 'Darwin's Orchid Book,' 972; *LLD*, 3:255; *MLD*, 2:280, 373; Darwin, *Orchids*, 178-79; *CP*, 2:63.
24. *Calendar*, 3662; *MLD*, 1:195, 202; Ghiselin, *Triumph*, 136; *LLD*, 2:267, 383; 3:254, 266; Darwin, *Orchids*, 233.

25. *LLTH*, 1:194-95; *Calendar*, 3386; *MLD*, 1:252; *CP*, 2:60-61. *LLD*, 2:384.
26. T. Huxley to F. Dyster, [Jan. 1862], THP 15.113; Ellegard, *Darwin*, 295; LRO, 2:115-23 (Du Chaillu set off for West Africa again, intending to capture Owen a live specimen: P. du Chaillu to R. Owen, 19 Aug. 1864, BM(NH), OCorr. 10.173); *LLJH*, 2:25; *LLTH*, 1:192-95; *Witness*, 11 and 14 Jan. 1862.
27. Darwin to T. Huxley, 14 Jan. 1862, THP 5.167; *LLD*, 2:384; *LLTH*, 1:194-95; Huxley to J. Hooker, 16 Jan. 1862, THP 2.112.
28. *LLD*, 3:276; *ARW*, 1:143-44, 146; Brooks, *Just Before*, 69.
29. C. Lyell to T. Huxley, 9 Aug. 1862, THP 6.66 (reply *LLTH*, 1:200); 'Palaeontology,' *Athenaeum*, 7 April 1860, pp. 478-79.
30. G. Rorison to R. Owen, 25 April 1860, BM(NH), OCorr. 22.379; Rorison, 'Creative Week,' 322, 517; Hull, *Darwin*, 182-83; Desmond, *Archetypes*, 78; E. Richards, 'Question,' 147; *MLD*, 2:341.
31. Darwin to T. Huxley, 14 Jan. and 10 Dec. 1862, THP 5.167, 183; Ellis, *Seven*, 121-22; Owen, *Monograph on the Aye-Aye*, 62.
32. *Calendar*, 3728, 3741, 3763, 3775, 3809, 3972; *TBI*, 72; *MLD*, 1:200, 223-26; *LLD*, 3:269; Atkins, *Down*, 29-30.
33. *MLD*,1:228-29; *Calendar*, 3899, 3909; Owen, 'On the Archaeopteryx.'
34. Owen, 'On the Archaeopteryx,' 46; Wagner, 'On a New Fossil Reptile,' 266-67; *Calendar*, 3905, 3928.
35. Peckham, *Origin*, 509; *MLD*, 1:234, 472; *LLD*, 3:6; *LLJH*, 2:32; *Calendar*, 3926; J. Evans, 'On Portions,' 418, 421. On the initial interpretations of *Archaeopteryx*: Desmond, *Archetypes*, 124-31.
36. T. Huxley, *On Our Knowledge*, 56; *MLD*, 1:216-17, 229-30; *LLTH*, 1:206.
37. *Calendar*, 3905, 3967; *MLD*, 1:472; *LLJH*, 2:32.
38. Bynum, 'Charles Lyell's *Antiquity*'; *MLD*, 1:472; *LLD*, 3:8-9; C. Lyell, *Geological Evidences*, 405ff, 429.
39. *LLD*, 3:9, 12; *LLL*, 2:361-65, 376; *TBI*, 74.
40. 'Evidence as to Man's Place in Nature,' *Athenaeum*, 28 Feb. 1863, p. 287; *LLTH*, 1:201; *LLD*, 3:14; Argyll, *Reign of Law*, 265; T. Huxley, *Man's Place*, 76; *LLJH*, 2:32; Darwin to T. Huxley, 18 Feb. 1863, THP 5.173.
41. T. Huxley, *Man's Place*, 147; *MLD*, 1:237; Owen, 'Summary,' 115; Desmond, *Archetypes*, 64; Huxley to F. Dyster, 12 Mar. 1863, THP 15.125; *LLTH*, 1:201.
42. Darwin to J. Hooker, 5 Mar. [1863], DAR 115:184; *Darwin's Journal*, 16; *TBI*, 74-75; *LLD*, 3:312-13; Allan, *Darwin*, ch. 12.
43. Darwin to J. Brodie Innes, 1 Sept. [1863], APS, Getz Collection B/D25.m; Darwin to W. Fox, 4 Sept [1863], and E. Darwin to W. Fox, [29 Sept. 1863], both Christ's College Libary, Cambridge; W. Fox to E. Darwin, 7 Sept [1863], DAR 164; *TBI*, 74-75.
44. *LLJH*, 2:62; Darwin to J. Hooker, [4 Oct.] and [22-23 Nov. 1863], DAR 115:206, 211; J. Hooker to Darwin, [28 Sept.] and [1 Oct. 1863], DAR 101:159, 160-62.

35 A LIVING GRAVE

1. *Calendar*, 4334, 4338, 4347, 4367, 4368; *ED*, 2:180–81; *LLD*, 3:3; *MLD*, 1:247, 2:338; *TBI*, 76–77.
2. *CP*, 2:106; Allan, *Darwin*, 271–72.
3. *Calendar*, 4389, 4667, 5316, 5391; *CP*, 2:106; J. Browne, 'Erasmus Darwin,' 602.

4. Loewenberg, *Calendar*, 55; Colp, 'Charles Darwin: Slavery,' 487; E. Richards, 'Moral Anatomy,' 415–24 and 'Huxley,' 261ff.

5. Greene, *Science*, 103.

6. Wallace, *Natural Selection*, 303–31; Schwartz, 'Darwin, Wallace,' 283–84; R. Smith, 'Alfred Russel Wallace,' 179–80; Durant, 'Scientific Naturalism,' 40–45; Kottler, 'Charles Darwin,' 388; Vorzimmer, *Charles Darwin*, 190; *ARW*, 1:150.

7. *MLD*, 2:31–37; *LLD*, 3:89–91; *Calendar*, 3158 *et seq.*; *ARW*,1:152–59.

8. *Calendar*, 4458; *LLL*, 2:382–83; *ARW*, 1:152.

9. *The Times*, 25 May 1864, pp. 8–9; King, 'Reputed Fossil Man,' 92, 96; Ellegard, *Darwin*, 165; Bowler, *Theories*, 33–34.

10. Ellis, *Seven*, 109–11, ch. 4.

11. Allan, *Darwin*, ch. 12; *MLD*, 1:251; *Calendar*, 4527, 4582, 4607, 4619; *TBI* 80.

12. J. Moore, 'On the Education,' 59–60 and 'Darwin of Down,' 468–69; F. Darwin, *Springtime*, 63; Stecher, 'Darwin–Innes Letters,' 215–17.

13. Brock and MacLeod, 'Scientists' Declaration,' 41, 48.

14. Barton, 'Influential Set,' 61ff; Jensen, 'X Club,' 63; MacLeod, 'X Club.'

15. *Calendar*, 4671, 4686, 4689, 4690, 4696, 4700–712, 4719; *MLD*, 1:252–56, 258; *LLD*, 3:28, 29; *LLTH*, 1:255; *LLJH*, 2:75–76; *LLL*, 2:384; MacLeod, 'Of Medals,' 83; Bartholomew, 'Award.'

16. Huxley, in Barton, 'Evolution,' 263–64; Roos, 'Aims,' 164; *Calendar*, 4817; *LLL*, 3:28; X Club Notebook, Tyndall Papers, Royal Institution; T. Huxley to J. Hooker, 21 July 1863, THP 2.120.

17. *Calendar*, 4712; Ashwell and Wilberforce, *Life*, 3:154–55; Ellis, *Seven*, 136.

18. T. Huxley to F. Dyster, 26 Jan. 1865, THP 15.129; J. Hooker to Darwin, 1 Jan. 1865, DAR 102:1–3; Barton, 'X Club,' 225; J. Moore, *Post-Darwinian Controversies*, 25; Huxley–Rolleston correspondence, THP 25.171–74, 180–84, for the divisive effect of the leader.

19. Argyll, *George Douglas*, 2:167; *LLL*, 2:384–85; *LLD*, 3:32.

20. *LLL*, 2:385; *LLD*, 3:32; Desmond, *Archetypes*, 159; Paradis, *T. H. Huxley*, chs 2, 3.

21. *LLD*, 2:35; J. Hooker to Darwin, 3 Feb. [1865], DAR 102:8–9; Darwin to J. Hooker, 9 Feb. [1865], DAR 115:260; W. Thomson, *Popular Lectures*, 1:349ff.

22. *LLJH*, 2:72; *Calendar*, 4820.

23. Hutchinson, *Life*, 1:74; *LLD*, 3:36–38, 40–41; *ED*, 2:183; *Calendar*, 4829, 4986.

24. J. Hooker to Darwin, 2 May 1865, DAR 102:20–21; Darwin to J. Hooker, 4 May [1865], DAR 115:268; B. Sulivan to Darwin, 8 May 1865, DAR 177; *TBI*, 82; Burton, 'Robert FitzRoy,' 164ff; *Narrative*, 26.

25. *TBI*, 82–84; Poynter, 'John Chapman,' 15–17; *Calendar*, 4834, 4837, 4846; *ED*, 2:182.

26. Hodge, 'Darwin as a Lifelong Generation Theorist,' 227–36; Olby, 'Charles Darwin's Manuscript;' *MLD*, 1:281; *LLD*, 3:43–44; *Calendar*, 4837.

27. *LLTH*, 1:267–8; *Calendar*, 4841.

28. Bynum, 'Charles Lyell's *Antiquity*,' 178, 182; *LLD*, 3:39; *Calendar*, 4858, 4860, 4883, 4892.

29. Paradis, *T. H. Huxley*, 75; *English Leader*, 13 Jan. 1866; T. Huxley, *Method*, 38. We thank Simon Schaffer for providing a translation of the Jenny Marx letter from Lefebvre, *Marx–Engels*.

30. Owen, 'The Reign of Law,' Autograph Manuscripts of Sir R. Owen, BM(NH), OColl. 59.1–2; C. Lyell to T. Huxley, 22 Jan. 1866, THP 6.120; *English Leader*, 3 and 24 Feb. 1866.
31. LLD, 3:39; *TBI* 86; Irvine, *Apes*, 166; Bowler, *Theories*, 52; *Calendar*, 4963.
32. *Calendar*, 4529, 4942, 4971, 4973, 4985, 4990. Haeckel distributed them in Germany.
33. ED, 2:184; E. C. Langton (*née* Darwin) to Charles and Emma Darwin, [Jan. 1866], W/M 444; Darwin to J. Hooker, 21 [Jan. 1866], DAR 115:280; *Calendar*, 5009–10; MLD, 1:477.
34. *Calendar*, 5089; RFD, 70; ED, 2:184–85;
35. Paul, 'Selection,' 413–16; *Calendar*, 4794; Spencer, *Autobiography*, 2:102, 484; LLD, 3:46, 56; *Calendar*, 4645, 4650; ARW, 1:170, 188, 191; MLD, 1:267–69.

36 EMERALD BEAUTY

1. Grove, *Correlation*, 346; Morus, 'Politics of Power;' Ellegard, *Darwin*, 78-79.
2. LLJH, 2:98-99, 100-106; *Calendar*, 5165, 5167, 5201-202, 5229; LLD, 3:47-48; 'British Association for the Advancement of Science,' *Journal of Botany*, 5 (1867), 29-30.
3. Hutchinson, *Life*, 1:92; Owen, 'The Reign of Law,' Autograph Manuscripts of Sir R. Owen, BM(NH), OColl. 59.7, 18, 24; Ellegard, *Darwin*, 79.
4. Barrow, *Independent Spirits*, chs. 2, 6; Oppenheim, *Other World*, 276; Harrison, 'Early Victorian Radicals,' 198-99, 212 n. 3.
5. LLTH, 1:419-20; LJT, 115; *Calendar*, 4742-43; Kottler, 'Alfred Russel Wallace,' 170, 171-72; T. Huxley, in *Report*, 230.
6. Kottler, 'Alfred Russel Wallace,' 164-65, 167-72; Wallace, *My Life*, 2:277-81; ARW, 2:187-88.
7. *Calendar*, 4646, 4555, 4934, 6540, 6676; LLTH, 1:266; Weindling 'Ernst Haeckel,' 314, 317; Groeben, *Charles Darwin – Anton Dohrn Correspondence*, 10, 22; LLD, 3:88.
8. *Calendar*, 4555, 4586, 4646, 4934, 4973, 5193; Bölsche, *Haeckel*, 133ff, 150; Corsi and Weindling, 'Darwinism,' 694; Bayertz, 'Darwinism,' 297-98.
9. Bölsche, *Haeckel*, 242; RFD, 36; RBL, 159; MLD, 2:350; *Calendar*, 5252, 5257, 5262; T. Huxley, 'Natural History,' 13-14; Haeckel, *History*, 2:248.
10. LLD, 3:53, 73; *Calendar*, 5051, 5265-66, 5281; Spencer, *Autobiography*, 2:143; LLTH, 1:278; Lorimer, *Colour*, ch. 9; Bolt, *Victorian Attitudes*, ch. 3; Semmel, *Governor Eyre*, chs 4-5.
11. LLTH, 1:279-82; recollections of W. Darwin, DAR 112.2 (cf. LLD, 3:53).
12. *Darwin's Journal*, 17; Darwin to J. Hooker, 25 Sept. 1866 and [4 Oct. 1866], DAR 115:300, 302; LLJH, 2:77-79; *Calendar*, 5230, 5238, 5283-84, 5487.
13. MLD, 1:274; RFD, 37-39; Haeckel, *History*, 1:1-2; Haeckel, *Generelle Morphologie*, 2:451. On Haeckel and Darwin: Altner, *Charles Darwin*; Schwarz, 'Darwinism;' Kelly, *Descent*; Roger, 'Darwin.'
14. Gasman, *Scientific Origins*, 17-18; Corsi and Weindling, 'Darwinism,' 689; Weindling 'Ernst Haeckel,' 311; Haeckel, *History*, 1:295; S. Gould, *Ontogeny*, 78.
15. MLD, 1:274, 277; LLTH, 1:288; Haeckel, *Generelle Morphologie*, 1:90, 173-74n; LLTH, 1:288.

16. Vogt, *Lectures*, 378; Gregory, *Scientific Materialism*, ch. 3; *Calendar*, 5256, 5269, 5489, 5495, 5499-500, 5503, 5506, 5533; W. Montgomery, 'Germany,' 82-83; *LLD*, 3:69.
17. *LLD*, 3:62; Darwin, *Variation*, 2:426-28; Loewenberg, *Calendar*, 53 and De Beer, 'Some Unpublished Letters,' 40-41 for early formulations.
18. *MLD*, 1:277, 2:40; *LLD*, 3:59-60, 72, 98; *Calendar*, 5380, 5382, 5448, 5450.
19. *Calendar*, 5443, 5446, 5464; *LLD*, 2:279, 3:72-73; Vucinich, *Darwin*, 62ff; Vucinich, 'Russia,' 249; Freeman, *Works*, 123. On Royer: Miles, 'Clémence Royer;' Stebbins, 'France,' 125-27; Conry, *Introduction, passim*.
20. *ARW*, 1:179, 181; *MLD*, 2:57-58, 65.
21. Darwin to C. Kingsley, 10 June [1867], APS, Getz Collection B/D25.165; *MLD*, 1:277, 282-83; *LLD*, 3:65; *Calendar*, 5466.
22. Argyll, *Reign*, 219, 259-60; Mozley, 'Argument of Design,' 162; *LLL*, 2:431-2; Gillespie, *Charles Darwin*, 93-104. Bowler has emphasized the prevalence of this non-Darwinian view: Bowler, *Charles Darwin*, ch. 9 and *Non-Darwinian Revolution*, 90ff.
23. Darwin to C. Kingsley, 10 June [1867], APS, Getz Collection B/D25.165; Owen, 'The Reign of Law,' Autograph Manuscripts of Sir R. Owen, BM (NH), OColl. 59.1-2, 26.
24. *LLJH*, 2:114; *LLD*, 3:62; *MLD*, 1:302.
25. Wallace, *Natural Selection*, 34-90, 280, 282-85; Durant, 'Ascent,' 298; *ARW*, 1:178-80, 183, 185, 189; *Calendar*, 5522; Kottler, 'Charles Darwin,' 417ff.
26. Russell, 'Conflict Metaphor;' Burchfield, *Lord Kelvin*, 27ff, 70ff; Jenkin, 'Origin,' 289, 291-94; *LLD*, 3:107-108; *MLD*, 2:379; Vorzimmer, *Charles Darwin*, 27-30, 44-45.
27. *LLD*, 3:71-72; *MLD*, 1:272; *LLL*, 2:415-16.
28. *MLD*, 1:300; *Darwin's Journal*, 17; Kingsley, *Charles Kingsley*, 2:248-49; *Calendar*, 3427, 3439; Watts and [Holyoake], 'Charles R. Darwin.'
29. *Darwin's Journal*, 17; *ED*, 2:187; *Calendar*, 5781; *LLD*, 3:74-75.

37 SEX, POLITICS, AND THE X

1. *LLD*, 3:75, 84; *MLD*, 1:287; *LLJH*, 2:113; *Calendar*, 6036.
2. *Calendar*, 5844, 5874, 5885, 5915, 5918, 5972; *LLD*, 3:76-77; *ARW*, 1:199. The *Athenaeum* reviewer was evidently Berthold Seemann: *Calendar*, 5931, 5951.
3. *LLD*, 3:78, 80, 84; *Calendar*, 5914.
4. *Calendar*, 5773, 5843, 6047, 6127, 6219, 6289, 6294; *ED*, 2:187-88, 190-91; Loewenberg, *Calendar*, 42; J. Moore, 'On the Education,' 63-64.
5. *Calendar*, 5836, 5938, 5976, 5979; Vucinich, *Darwin*, 62ff.
6. *Calendar*, 5198, 5217, 5852, 5864, 5870-71, 6009, 6082, 6382; *LLD*, 3:77, 97, 99-100, 103, 111-12; *MLD*, 2:68, 90, 103, 159; *LLL*, 2:410; Agassiz and Agassiz, *Journey*, 15, 33, 399, 425; Lurie, *Louis Agassiz*, 353ff, 382.
7. *MLD*, 2:64-65; *LLD*, 3:92.
8. *MLD*, 2:63, 90; Wallace, *Natural Selection*, ch. 3; Ellegard, *Darwin*, 251.
9. *LLD*, 3:82; *ED*, 2:188-89; *MLD*, 2:69, 71, 99 and *Calendar*, 5885, 6042, 6052, 6062, 6067, 6070, 6127; *Descent* (1871), 1:43; X Club Notebook (5 Mar. 1868), Tyndall Papers, Royal Institution.
10. *Calendar*, 5919, 6107, 6114, 6629, 6635; *LLD* 3:86; *MLD*, 1:312, 2:92; W. Montgomery, 'Germany,' 83-85.
11. Mivart, 'Some Reminiscences,' 988-89; J. Gruber, *Conscience*, chs 1-2.

12. St G. Mivart to Darwin, 20 May 1868, 22 April 1870, and 10 Jan. 1872, all DAR 171; *Descent* (1871), 2:24-25; J. Gruber, *Conscience*, 31ff.
13. Dawkins, 'Darwin,' 436; Durant, 'Ascent,' 298-99; Ellegard, *Darwin*, 284-85; *LLJH*, 2:114; *LLD*, 3:98-99.
14. Forrest, *Francis Galton*, chs 1-2; Greene, *Science*, 102-106.
15. Greene, *Science*, 106-11; Greg, in *Descent* (1871), 1:174; Helmstadter, 'W. R. Greg;' Bagehot, *Physics*, 215.
16. *ARW*, 1:219; *MLD*, 1:297, 302, 305; *LLJH*, 2:114; Ellegard, *Darwin*, 65.
17. *TBI*, 87; *ED*, 2:190; *ARW*, 1:219; *Companion*, 276.
18. *ARW*, 2:221; *Calendar*, 6321; Mivart, 'Reminiscences,' 994; *LLJH*, 2:115-18; Hooker, 'Address.'
19. Ellegard, *Darwin*, 82-83; *LLJH*, 2:121; *LLD*, 3:100; *ARW*, 1:121.
20. 'The British Association,' *Guardian*, 23 (2 Sept. 1868), 977; *LLTH*, 1:231, 297; *MLD*, 1:297; *LLJH*, 2:119; Tyndall, 'Address,' 6.
21. *Calendar*, 6327, 6333, 6413; *LLD*, 3:100; Mivart, *Essays*, 228; Baynes, 'Darwin,' 505-506; Tyndall, *Fragments*, 92-93, 163-64, 130, 198, 441; Cockshut, *Unbelievers*, 91; Lightman, *Origins*, ch. 5; G. Young, *Portrait*, 116; Barton, 'John Tyndall;' T. Huxley, *Discourses*, 319-20; Mivart, 'Some Reminiscences,' 987.
22. Uschmann and Jahn, 'Briefwechsel,' 15, 17-19; *Calendar*, 6239; E. Haeckel to T. Huxley, 28 Feb. 1869, THP 17.198; *LLD*, 3:104; *MLD*, 1:277-78; *LLTH*, 1:305; Darwin to T. Huxley, THP 5.239.
23. T. Huxley, in *Ibis*, 4 (1868), 357-61; T. Huxley, 'Natural History,' 41; Foster and Lankester, *Scientific Memoirs*, 3:303-13, 365; E. Haeckel to T. Huxley, 27 Jan. 1868, THP 17.183; *LLTH*, 1:294-95, 303; *LLD*, 3:104-105; *Calendar*, 6450; Di Gregario, 'Dinosaur Connection,' 413-17; Desmond, *Archetypes*, 127-30, 156-58.
24. *LLTH*, 1:295-96; T. Huxley to Darwin, 20 July 1868, DAR 221; Weindling, 'Ernst Haeckel,' 317; Rehbock, 'Huxley;' Rupke, '*Bathybius Haeckelii*.'
25. *Calendar*, 6561, 6655; *ARW*, 1:232-33, 235; Wallace, *Malay Archipelago*, [v]; *Calendar*, 6542 on James Orton's *The Andes and the Amazon*; *Calendar*, 6454 and *MLD*, 2:235 on Albert Gaudry's *Animaux fossiles et géologie de l'Attique*, with its dynastic charts of horses, elephants and pigs, and praised by Darwin as 'the most striking which I have ever read on the affiliation of species;' Desmond, *Archetypes*, 165.
26. *ED*, 2:191, 221; *Calendar*, 6424; Dupree, *Asa Gray*, 337-41; Loewenberg, *Calendar*, 94; *MLD*, 1:309.
27. Stecher, 'Darwin-Innes Letters,' 219-20, 223, 226; Darwin to J. Brodie Innes, 15 June [1868], APS, Getz Collection B/D25.m. On curates as a contemporary problem for the Church: Halcombe, 'Curate Question.'
28. Darwin to J. Brodie Innes, 16 Dec. 1868, APS, Getz Collection B/D25.m; Stecher, 'Darwin-Innes Letters,' 227-29; J. Moore, 'Darwin of Down,' 470, 477.
29. India: *Calendar*, 5872, 6080, 6160, 6184, 6285, 6295, 6420, 6514, 6815, 7030; Nicaragua: 6546; Gibraltar, 6547, 6553; Portugal, 6577; Lapland, 6430, 6438, 6517; New Zealand, 6520; Australia, 5899, 5916, 6314, 6374, 6419, 6635; Nicholas and Nicholas, *Charles Darwin*, 136; for the rest, Darwin, *Expression* 19-20.

38 DISINTEGRATING SPECULATIONS

1. Jenkin, 'Origin,' 301; W. Thomson, *Popular Lectures*, 2:64; Sharlin, *Lord Kelvin*, chs 9–10; Burchfield, *Lord Kelvin*, 32ff; *Origin*, 285–87.
2. *Calendar*, 5974, 6496; *MLD*, 1:312, 2:163–64, 379; *LLD*, 3:107, 109; Vorzimmer, *Charles Darwin*.
3. Tait, 'Geological Time,' 407, 438; *Calendar*, 6688; *LLD*, 3:113; T. Huxley, *Discourses*, 306, 329; *MLD*, 1:314–16, 2:6–7.
4. *ED*, 2:195; *Calendar*, 6705, 6716, 6718; Loewenberg, *Calendar*, 63; *Annotated Calendar*, 369.
5. T. Huxley, *Method*, 155; Paradis, *T. H. Huxley*, 100ff; Block, 'T. H. Huxley's Rhetoric,' 379–81; Bibby, *T. H. Huxley*, ch. 8.
6. Hutchinson, *Life*, 1:101; A. Brown, *Metaphysical Society*, 50–56; T. Huxley, *Method*, 162; T. Huxley, 'On Descartes' "Discourse",' 79–80; Lightman, *Origins*, 10ff; R. Young, *Darwin's Metaphor*, ch. 5.
7. St G. Mivart to Darwin, 25 April 1870, DAR 171; T. Huxley, *Science*, 120.
8. Annotations on Wallace, 'Principles,' DAR 133; *MLD*, 2:39–40; *LLD*, 3:114, 117; *ARW*, 1:232–33.
9. R. Smith, 'Alfred Russel Wallace,' 181–84, 193–94; Wallace, *Natural Selection*, 335–43, 351–60; Wallace, *My Life*, 1:342; Kottler, 'Alfred Russel Wallace,' 150–56; Durant, 'Scientific Naturalism,' 46–47; *ARW*, 1:227, 243–44.
10. Mivart, 'Difficulties,' in Darwin Reprint Collection, R.145, CUL; *ARW*, 1:246–47; Mivart, *On the Genesis*, 67–73; Mivart, 'Reminiscences,' 988–93; Root, 'Catholicism,' 162–70.
11. Ellegard, *Darwin*, 308; Argyll, *Primeval Man*, 4–5, 33, 66–68, 124ff; Argyll, *George Douglas*, 2:246–47, 272–73.
12. Gillespie, 'Duke of Argyll,' 48; *Descent* (1871), 1:65–69; Argyll, *Primeval Man*, 70, 133; *Calendar*, 6433, 7024.
13. *LLD*, 1:11, 3:106; *ED*, 2:195; *RFD*, 82; F. Darwin, *Rustic Sounds*, 162; *MLD*, 1:313; Cobbe, *Life*, 488–89; *Calendar*, 7145, 7149.
14. *MLD*, 1:317, 2:41; *LLJH*, 2:146–47.
15. *MLD*, 1:316; *Calendar*, 6897, 6900, 6947, 6954, 6956, 6960, 6995, 7022, 7030, 7036; *LLD*, 3:119; *Annotated Calendar*, 375; Cobbe, *Life*, 490.
16. *Calendar*, 7107; Darwin to H. Darwin, [Mar.– June 1870], BL, Add. MSS 58373; *Descent* (1871), 1:34, 67–68, 106; *ED*, 2:196.
17. *LLD*, 3:125; F. Darwin, *Springtime*, 67; *Calendar*, 7200; *MLD*, 2:236; *LLAS*, 2:402, 464.
18. *Calendar*, 7222, 7225, 7246; *LLD*, 3:126; *LLTH*, 1:330.
19. *Calendar*, 5873, 5889, 7195; *LLD*, 3:126–28; 'Speech of His Grace the Archbishop of Canterbury . . .,' DAR 139.12.
20. *Calendar*, 7057, 7117, 7182–83, 7257; *LLD*, 3:129.
21. *Calendar*, 7277 *et seq.*; *Hansard Parliamentary Debates*, 3d ser. (22 July 1870), 817; (26 July 1870), 1006–10.
22. *ED*, 2:198–99; *MLD*, 2:92; Ensor, *England*, 6–7.
23. *ED*, 2:186; T. Huxley, *Discourses*, 257; *MLD*, 1:323; Ellegard, *Darwin*, 85.
24. *MLD*, 1:324, 2:92; *Calendar*, 7332–33, 7340, 7342, 7381, 7389, 7442, 7485.
25. T. Huxley, *Discourses*, 271; *Calendar*, 7374, 7376, 7400; *ARW*, 1:254.
26. *Darwin's Journal*, 18; Stecher, 'Darwin–Innes Letters,' 233; Mivart, *On the Genesis*, 211; St G. Mivart to Darwin, 22 Jan. and 24 Jan. 1871, both DAR 171; *ARW*, 1:258; Owen, 'Fate.'

27. Stecher, 'Darwin–Innes Letters,' 232–34; ED, 2:202; Calendar, 7485, 7488, 7510, 7583, 7735; Vucinich, Darwin, 66. Three Russian translations of the Descent of Man were published at St Petersburg in 1871–72: Freeman, Works, 140.
28. Freeman, Works, 129; ED, 2:202; LLD, 3:138–39; Ellegard, Darwin, 296; Dawkins, 'Darwin,' 195.
29. Descent (1871), 1:67, 101, 104, 167–80, 238; G. Jones, 'Social History;' Durant, 'Ascent,' 293ff; J. Moore, 'Socializing,' 46–51.
30. Descent (1871), 1:169, 2:326–27, 403–4; E. Richards, 'Darwin;' Bowler, Theories, 7ff.
31. 'Mr. Darwin on the Descent of Man,' The Times, 8 April 1871, p. 5, cols. 4–5.
32. LLD, 3:139; Calendar, 7705; ED, 2:203; Stecher, 'Darwin–Innes Letters,' 235, 237; Ellegard, Darwin, 101; Fiske, Life, 267.
33. Cobbe, Life, 489; MLD, 1:329; ARW, 1:260; ED, 2:202–203.
34. LLD, 3:142; ARW, 1:262; St G. Mivart to Darwin, 23 April 1871, DAR 171; Darwin's Journal, 18; Calendar, 7730, 7755, 7798; Peckham, Origin, 22.
35. Calendar, 7761, 7796; ARW, 1:264; Darwin's Journal, 18; Fiske, Life, 266, 276; MacLeod, 'Evolutionism,' 65–69.
36. Calendar, 7829; P. Wiener, Evolution, ch. 3 and App. A; ARW, 1:264–65, 268.
37. ARW, 1:268–69; Calendar, 7878; Mivart, 'Descent,' 47, 52, 81–90.
38. ARW, 1:269; MLD, 1:333; Calendar, 7963; Wright, Darwinism, 9, 13, 15, 37, 43.
39. LLD, 3:149; ARW, 1:265, 270; ED, 2:204; MLD, 1:329–32; H. Litchfield to F. Darwin, 18 Mar. 1887, DAR 112:79–82; Darwin to C. Wright, 13–14 July and 17 July [1871] (copies), both DAR 171; Calendar, 7907, 7916.
40. Wedgwood, 299; RBL, 121, 124–25; ED, 2:210.
41. C. Wright to Darwin, 1 Aug. 1871, DAR 181; LLTH, 1:363; T. Huxley to Darwin, 20 Sept. 1871, DAR 99:39–42; T. Huxley to J. Hooker, 11 Sept. 1871, THP 2.181.
42. Darwin's Journal, 19; LLD, 3:152; Darwin to T. Huxley, 21 Sept. [1871], THP 5.279–82; T. Huxley to Darwin, 28 Sept. 1871, DAR 99:43–46; T. Huxley, Darwiniana, 145, 147, 149.
43. Darwin to T. Huxley, 30 Sept. [1871], THP 5.283–87; LLJH, 2:130; MLD, 1:333; Desmond, Archetypes, 141.
44. LLD, 3:148; Darwin to T. Huxley, 9 Oct. 1871, THP 5.289–90; R. Cooke to Darwin, 1 Nov. [1871], DAR 171; Bartholomew, 'Huxley's Defence,' 533–34.

39 PAUSE, PAUSE, PAUSE

1. Autobiography, 163; ED, 2:204–205.
2. H. Litchfield to F. Darwin, 18 Mar. 1887, DAR 112:79–82; TBI, 87; Darwin's Journal, 19; Calendar, 7964, 8013, 8199; LLD 3:133.
3. Peckham, Origin, 22–23; Freeman, Works, 79–80; MLD 1:332.
4. Peckham, Origin, 242–67; Vorzimmer, Charles Darwin, 246–49; Origin (6th ed.), ch. 7. In the same way he controverted Mivart on the impossibility of explaining convergence. He cited example after example – from electric organs in unrelated fishes to placental and marsupial mice (chs 6, 14) – to show how selection, not some converging inner force, had caused similar structures under similar conditions.

5. *Calendar*, 7924, 8070, 8099, 8110, 8145, 9105; Darwin to F. Abbot, 6 Sept. [1871] (copy), DAR 139.12; RFD, 23; Abbot, *Truths*, 7–8; *CP*, 2:167; J. Moore, 'Freethought,' 303–304; W. Darwin to F. Abbot, 20 Dec. 1875, University Archives, Harvard University Library.

6. *Descent* (1871), 1:4; *MLD*, 1:335–36.

7. Peckham, *Origin*, 22–24; Freeman, *Works*, 79–80; *MLD* 1:332; *Calendar*, 8209.

8. St G. Mivart to Darwin, 6 Jan. 1872, DAR 171; Darwin to St G. Mivart, [6–10 Jan. 1872], DAR 96:141; *MLD*, 1:335; *Calendar*, 8186.

9. *Darwin's Journal*, 19; *Calendar*, 8168 etc., 8209, 8212; *MLD*, 1:335; *Descent* (1871), 1:5; Peckham, *Origin*, 22–24.

10. Darwin, *Expression*, 15–19; *CCD*, 4:410–30; Freeman and Gautrey, 'Charles Darwin's Queries;' *Calendar*, 7698; J. Browne, 'Darwin;' Ritvo, *Animal Estate*, 39–40.

11. Darwin, *Expression*, 80, 155, 179, 195–96, 217, 305.

12. *Calendar*, 8302, 8383, 8404, 8427, 8435, 8567, 8473–75; *LLD*, 3:171; *Darwin's Journal*, 19.

13. Wallace, *My Life*, 2:90ff; *ARW*, 1:273–78; *LLTH*, 1:333; Bastian, *Beginnings of Life*, 2:165–66, 584; R. Grant to H. Bastian, 26 June 1872, Wellcome Institute, London.

14. *Calendar*, 8533, 8585; *ED*, 2:210; *Darwin's Journal*, 19; *LLD*, 3:171.

15. *Calendar*, 8406, 8449, 8525, 8533, 8577; *LLJH*, 2:131, 159–77; MacLeod, 'Ayrton Incident.'

16. *Calendar*, 8542, 8586; J. Hooker to Darwin, 19 Oct. 1872, DAR 103:124–25; Darwin to J. Hooker, 22 Oct. [1872], DAR 94:231–32.

17. Darwin, *Insectivorous Plants*, 76–84, 92ff, 134–35, 199–209, 232–33, 272; *MLD*, 2:267; Allan, *Darwin*, 235ff; Ghiselin, *Triumph*, 198–200.

18. *Calendar*, 8616, 8620, 8675; *Annotated Calendar*, 425; *Darwin's Journal*, 19; 'The Expression of the Emotions,' *Athenaeum*, 9 Nov. 1872, p. 591.

19. *Calendar*, 8606, 8682; *LLTH*, 1:367–89; E. Richards, 'Huxley,' 277ff. We assume that a meeting could have taken place before Darwin left town.

20. *MLD*, 2:43; *Darwin's Journal*, 19; *Calendar*, 8747, 8761, 8763, 8799, 8839, 8843 *et seq.*, 8870; *ED*, 2:212; *LLJH*, 2:183–84; *LLTH*, 1:366–67.

21. *LLL*, 2:450–51; E. A. Darwin to E. Darwin, 24 April [1873], DAR 105.2:88–89; *LLJH*, 2:188; Darwin to C. Lyell, [after 27 April 1873], DAR 96:167.

22. Register of Marriages, 1854–74, Little Portland Street Unitarian Chapel, Dr Williams's Library, London; *Wedgwood*, 303; *Calendar*, 8855, 8956; *Companion*, 170; *RBL*, 139; RFD, 103.

23. L. Huxley, 'Home Life,' 3–4.

24. J. Moore, 'Darwin of Down,' 470, 478; 'Downe Parsonage House Building Fund,' KAO 123/3/5; 'Downe Vicarage Endowment Fund,' KAO 123/3/6.

25. 'Contributions Received,' KAO P123/3/7; *Calendar*, 8842, 9000; S. Wedgwood to G. Ffinden, 14 Mar. 1873, KAO P123/3/4; Stecher, 'Darwin–Innes Letters,' 238; school regulations and annual reports, KAO P123/25/5; parish of Down, PRO Ed. 2/234, no. 4431; *CCD*, 5:161–62; accounts and letters, KAO P123/5/7.

26. Ashwell, *Life*, 3:424–27; T. Huxley to J. Tyndall, 30 July 1873, THP 9.73 and in Blinderman, 'Oxford Debate,' 127; *LLD*, 2:325, 3:340; *ED*, 2:214; *ARW*, 1:243; *Darwin's Journal*, 19.

27. *LLJH*, 2:152–53; *LLD*, 3:339–40; *Calendar*, 8839, 9040, 9052; H. Litchfield to F. Darwin, 18 Mar. 1887, DAR 112:79–82; *TBI*, 88–89.

28. *Calendar*, 9061, 9148; *CP*, 2:177–82; Colp, 'Contacts,' 393; presentation copy of *Das Kapital*, Down House.
29. *LLD*, 3:180; *Calendar*, 9060, 9069; F. Darwin, *Springtime*, 67–68.
30. F. Darwin, *Rustic Sounds*, 162–63; *Calendar*, 8997, 9088; Darwin to G. Darwin, 21 Oct. 1873, DAR 210.1.1.
31. Darwin to G. Darwin, 24 Oct. 1873, DAR 210.1.1; Darwin to N. Doedes, 2 April 1873 (copy), DAR 139.12 and *LLD*, 1:306.
32. Fiske, *Personal Letters*, 121–22, 147–48.
33. *Calendar*, 9149; *ARW*, 1:281–84, 2:261; Wallace, *Studies*, 2:138–44.
34. *ED*, 2:216; E. Darwin to G. Ffinden, [Nov.–Dec. 1873], and Darwin to Downe School Board, [Nov.–Dec. 1873], KAO P123/25/3.
35. G. Ffinden to Privy Council office, 1 Dec. [1873]; Darwin to Downe School Board, [Nov.–Dec. 1873] and 19 Dec. 1873; G. Ffinden to E. Darwin, 24 Dec. 1873; G. Ffinden to J. Lubbock, 8 Feb. 1875, all KAO P123/25/3; Hart, *Parson*.

40 A WRETCHED BIGOT

1. *Calendar*, 8173, 8256, 8258, 8263, 8293, 9229, 9236; Oppenheim, *Other World*, ch. 1, 293–94; Barrow, *Independent Spirits*, 125; Crookes, *Researches*.
2. Oppenheim, *Other World*, 291–92; *Wedgwood*, 298, 305; *Calendar*, 8831, 8832; *LLTH*, 1:419; *ED*, 2:216–17; *LLD*, 3:186–88.
3. *LLTH*, 1:419–23; *LLD*, 3:187; *ED*, 2:217; J. [Snow] Wedgwood to E. Gurney, 9 July 1874, in *Wedgwood*, 305. Snow recalled a conversation with her uncle twenty years earlier when he had explained his belief in evolution as an alternative to special creation. She had expressed 'extreme repugnance to this idea & the sense of loss in giving up' the traditional doctrine. He replied, 'I cannot conceive any *wish* about the matter one way or another.' His manner and tone of voice left her with the profound impression 'that he was confronting some influence that *adulterated the evidence of fact:*' J. Wedgwood to F. Darwin, 3 Oct. 1884, DAR 139.12.
4. *RFD*, 64–65; Atkins, *Down*, 28; *Calendar*, 9310, 9318, 9325, 9327, 9333, 9373, 9386; *TBI*, 89; H. Litchfield to F. Darwin, 18 Mar. 1887, DAR 112:79–82.
5. *Descent* (1874), v–vi, 143.
6. *Calendar*, 9333, 9376, 9409 (cf. 9510); *LLJH*, 2:114; J. Hooker to Darwin, 3 Mar. [1874], DAR 103:189–92; Darwin to J. Hooker, 4 Mar. [1874], DAR 93:313–16; *LLTH*, 1:419; R. Owen to J. Tyndall, 14 June 1871, BM(NH), OCorr. 21.28; *Descent* (1874), v, 199–206; Desmond, *Archetypes*, 143.
7. *Calendar*, 9388, 9402, 9446, 9454, 9474, 9496 etc.; *CP*, 2:183–87.
8. *Calendar*, 9234, 9227, 9417 *et seq.*, 9440, 9475, 9529, 9550; *ED*, 2:217; *Pedigrees*, 12; Stecher, 'Darwin–Innes Letters,' 239; *MLD*, 1:352–54; *LLR*, 1–18.
9. *Calendar*, 9568, 9579, 9596, 9598; J. Gruber, *Conscience*, 99–100.
10. *Calendar*, 9580 *et seq.*, 9597–98; Tyndall, *Address*, 44, 61; Barton, 'John Tyndall;' *LJT*, 187; Baynes, 'Darwin,' 502–505.
11. J. Gruber, *Conscience*, 100–101; *ARW*, 1:292; *Calendar*, 9685, 9687, 9720; *LLL*, 2:455; Cobbe, *Life*, 449–50; Darwin to C. Lyell, 3 Sept. [1874], APS 448 and *MLD*, 2:237.
12. *Calendar*, 9717; *LLJH*, 2:139–40, 189–90; Turrill, *Joseph Dalton Hooker*, 191; Darwin to J. Hooker, 22 Nov. [1874], DAR 95:342; J. Hooker to

Darwin, 25 Nov. 1874, DAR 103:228–29; Darwin to J. Hooker, 26 Nov. [1874], DAR 95:345–46.

13. *LLD*, 2:186; *LLJH*, 2:191; *Darwin's Journal*, 19; J. Gruber, *Conscience*, 102–10; *LLTH*, 1:426; *Calendar*, 9757 et seq., 9785, 9807, 9809, 9812–13; *ARW*, 1:291–92.

14. *LLD*, 3:195, 197, 328; *Calendar*, 9851, 9869, 9911.

15. Grant Duff, *Life-Work*, 15; G. Ffinden to J. Lubbock, 30 Jan., 8 Feb., 29 Mar., 3 April, and 23 June 1875 (drafts); and J. Lubbock to G. Ffinden, 4 Feb., 9 Feb., 31 Mar., and 12 April 1875, all KAO P123/25/3; Darwin to J. Lubbock, 8 April [1875] (draft), DAR 97.3:15–17; J. Moore, 'Darwin of Down,' 471–72; J. Wedgwood to F. Darwin, 3 Oct. 1884, DAR 139.12.

16. Lansbury, 'Gynaecology,' 426; *RBL*, 143–45; Ritvo, *Animal Estate*, 164; Rupke, *Vivisection*.

17. *LLTH*, 1:437; *Calendar*, 9923, 9933–34, 10251; *LLD*, 3:204; *RBL*, 143, 145; French, *Antivivisection*, 62–75.

18. G. Ffinden to J. Lubbock, 23 June 1875 (draft), KAO P123/25/3; *Calendar*, 9916; *Annotated Calendar*, 465; *LLR*, 22; French, *Antivivisection*, 69, 73, 79; *LLTH*, 1:438–39.

19. *Calendar*, 10024, 10044, 10071; *TBI*, 89; *Darwin's Journal*, 19.

20. *Calendar*, 7620, 10096–97, 10106, 10114, 10119, 10124; Darwin, *Variation*, 1:106, 312, 459; R. Chambers to R. Owen, 6 Mar. 1849, BM(NH), OCorr. 17.19 on Chambers's six–fingered joke.

21. *MLD*, 1:359–62, 2:71; *LLR*, 32, 39–42; *LLD*, 3:195; Galton, *Memories*, 294–98.

22. *MLD*, 1:360; *Calendar*, 10241, 10243; Darwin, *Variation*, 1:xiv, 2:389, 398.

23. *Calendar*, 10011, 10080, 10091, 10098, 10168, 10190, 10193, 10200, 10268, 10279–80; *LLR*, 34; Shepherd, 'Lawson Tait.'

24. *Darwin's Journal*, 20; Darwin, *Movements*, v; *Autobiography*, 137; *Calendar*, 10231–32, 10234; Pancaldi, *Darwin*, ch. 3.

25. *LLTH*, 1:439–40; *Calendar*, 10231–32, 10234, 10242; *ED*, 2:221; *Darwin's Journal*, 20.

26. RFD, 71; Atkins, *Down*, 97–99.

27. Atkins, *Down*, 99; L. Huxley, 'Home Life,' 4; *ED*, 2:221.

28. *Notebooks* B96; *Origin*, 92.

29. Darwin, *Effects*, 10ff, 448–49, 465–66; RFD, 7, 125; F. Darwin, 'Botanical Work,' xv; Allan, *Darwin*, 250–62; G. Darwin, 'Marriages.'

30. *Darwin's Journal*, 20; *LLR*, 50, 61; *Calendar*, 10452, 10462, 10501, 10506, 10522, 10530, 10546; *Annotated Calendar*, 488; French, *Antivivisection*, 114; F. Darwin, *Rustic Sounds*, 164; *ED*, 2:221; *Wedgwood*, 308.

41 NEVER AN ATHEIST

1. *Darwin's Journal*, 20; *Autobiography*, 21, 57, 78, 85-87, 145; Colp, 'Notes on Charles Darwin's *Autobiography*.'

2. *Autobiography*, 91-93, 96-98, 133; J. Moore, 'Of Love,' 196-97, 206-208.

3. Darwin to G. Ffinden, 5 Sept. 1876 (draft), DAR 202; 'Downe Vicarage Endowment Fund,' KAO P123/3/6.

4. Darwin to J. Hooker, 11 Sept. [1876] and 17 Sept. [1876], DAR 95:417-20; *ED*, 2:255; E. Darwin to W. Darwin, [13 Sept. 1876], DAR 210.6; Darwin to E. Haeckel, 16 Sept. 1876, Ernst-Haeckel Haus, Friedrich-Schiller-Universität,

Jena; Darwin to W. Darwin, 11 Sept. [1876], and to L. Darwin, 11 Sept. [1876], both DAR 210.6; Darwin to W. Thistleton-Dyer, 16 Sept. 1876, Royal Botanic Gardens, Kew.
5. E. Darwin to W. Darwin, [13 Sept. 1876], DAR 210.6; *Calendar*, 10611; Atkins, *Down*, 29; *Annotated Calendar*, 499-501.
6. *Darwin's Journal*, 20; *ED*, 2:223; Milner, 'Darwin, Pt 1,' 29; Oppenheim, *Other World*, 23.
7. Stecher, 'Darwin-Innes Letters,' 242, 248; *Darwin's Journal*, 20; Freeman, *Works*, 157; Crouzet, *Victorian Economy*, 166ff; *Calendar*, 10853, 11057-58, 11064-65, 11079.
8. Vorzimmer, 'Darwin Reading Notebooks,' 153; *Calendar*, 10720; *LLD*, 3:178; recollections of W. Darwin, DAR 112.2; cf. Beer, *Darwin's Plots*, 23 on Smiles.
9. Colp, 'Notes on William Gladstone;' Royle, *Radicals*, 209-10; J. Morley, *Life*, 3:562; *Wedgwood*, 307.
10. *LLJH*, 2:147, 150.
11. Royle, *Radicals*, 12-24, 254ff; Bonner, *Charles Bradlaugh*, 2:23.
12. Darwin to C. Bradlaugh, 6 June [1877] (draft), DAR 202, transcribed with the kind help of Peter Gautrey; *Descent* (1874), 618; J. Moore, 'Freethought,' 305-307; *ED*, 2:225-27; Ghiselin, *Triumph*, 201.
13. *LLD*, 3:295-96, 306; *Autobiography*, 128, 134; Darwin, *Different Forms*, 276; F. Darwin, 'Botanical Work,' xvi; Allan, *Darwin*, 263-76.
14. *LLD*, 3:309; *Calendar*, 11134, 11148, 11163; De Beer, 'Further Unpublished Letters,' 88-89; H. Gruber, *Darwin*, 53; Colp, 'Notes on William Gladstone,' 183; *ED*, 2:234-35.
15. *Darwin's Journal*, 20; *Calendar*, 11169; Wallace, *My Life*, 2:98; *ARW*, 1:298-300.
16. *Calendar*, 10822, 10958, 10974, 10991, 11211; *ED*, 2:230-31; 'Speech delivered by the Public Orator . . .,' DAR 140.1; Ruse, *Darwinian Revolution*, 262.
17. *ED*, 2:231; *Calendar*, 11234, 11238; *LLTH*, 1:480; *MLD*, 1:371-72; J. Stuart to his mother, 18 Nov. 1877, CUL Add. 8118, box 1, letterbook (with thanks to Simon Schaffer for a transcription).
18. *ED*, 2:226, 230; *RFD*, 56; *Calendar*, 10919, 11266, 11358; *RBL*, 151-52.
19. *RFD*, 105; Jordan, *Days*, 1:273; Campbell, 'Nature;' Stevens, 'Darwin's Humane Reading.'
20. Allan, *Darwin*, 279-89; F. Darwin, 'Botanical Work,' xvii-xviii; *RFD*, 130; *LLD*, 3:330; F. Darwin, 'Darwin's Work.'
21. *RFD*, 131; *TBI*, 90; *Calendar*, 11373 et seq., 11459, 11481 (cf. 11501, 12258); *MLD*, 1:372-74.
22. *LLJH*, 2:230-31; Duncan, *Life*, 181; *Annotated Calendar*, 495, 503-504, 509, 513-14; *RFD*, 65-66; *LLR*, 46, 67-68.
23. *LLR*, 69-71; Oppenheim, *Other World*, 281; *Annotated Calendar*, 533.
24. G. Romanes, *Thoughts*, 98-99, 108, 182-83; Darwin to G. Darwin, 24 Oct. 1873, DAR 210.1.1; G. Romanes, *Candid Examination*, vii; *LLR*, 71ff (cf. 128); *Natural Selection*, 463-66; R. Richards, *Darwin*, 335-42; Turner, *Between*, ch. 6.
25. *The Times*, 22 Aug. 1878, p. 8; *LLR*, 74-76, 78; *Annotated Calendar*, 548-49.
26. *LLR*, 87-88; G. Romanes, *Candid Examination*, 113-14; Darwin to G. Romanes, 5 Dec. [1878], APS 553; Darwin to W. Greg, 31 Dec. 1878, APS

557; Darwin's annotation in his presentation copy of *Candid Examination*, 112, Darwin Library, CUL.

27. *Calendar*, 11982; J. Moore, 'Darwin's Genesis,' 577; Darwin to F. McDermott, 24 Nov. 1880, xerox copy in CUL.

28. Darwin to N. von Mengden, 5 June 1879 (copy), DAR 139.12; Darwin to [H. Ridley], 28 Nov. 1878, DAR 202 and *LLD*, 3:235-36 (cf. Pusey, *Unscience*, 43-58); W. Browne to Darwin, 16 Dec. 1880, and Darwin to [W. Browne], [16-21 Dec. 1880], both DAR 202; Stecher, 'Darwin-Innes Letters,' 244-45.

29. De Beer, 'Further Unpublished Letters,' 88; *Calendar*, 11918, 11920, 12052; *Autobiography*, 176; Colp, 'Relationship,' 11-15; Butler, *Evolution*, 346.

30. *Autobiography*, 29, 32, 40-42, 94-95; *Calendar*, 12040-41 and De Beer, 'Further Unpublished Letters,' 88 (compared with original); J. Moore, 'Of Love,' 204-206.

31. *Calendar*, 12149, 12152-54, 12156, 12163, 12217; *LLD*, 3:220.

42 DOWN AMONG THE WORMS

1. *Calendar*, 12119; *LLD*, 3:356; *Darwin's Journal*, 21.

2. *ED*, 2:238; *LLR*, 98; *RBL*, 153–55; *RFD*, 81, 97; *Calendar*, 12220; Darwin to V. Marshall, 25 Aug. and 14 Sept. 1879, APS, Getz Collection B/D25.m.

3. *RBL*, 59; *Calendar*, 12207, 12235–36, 12241–42, 12268, 12279, 12282, 12289, 12297, 12326, 12372.

4. L. Forster to F. Darwin, 15 Nov. 1885, DAR 112:46–47; *Calendar*, 12125, 12253, 12256, 12280, 12294 *et seq.*, 12378; Raverat, *Period Piece*, 203–206; *Pedigrees*, 12, 55; *Wedgwood*, 314.

5. *ED*, 2:239–40; G. Ffinden to F. Darwin, 30 Mar. 1880 (draft), and G. Ffinden to Darwin, 19 Mar. 1880 (draft), both KAO P123/25/2; J. Moore, 'Darwin of Down,' 472.

6. St G. Mivart to R. Owen, 8 June 1879, BM(NH), OCorr. 29.261.

7. J. Moore, 'Darwin of Down,' 473; H. Jones, *Samuel Butler*, 1:99–100, 125, 157, 165, 186, 258, 385; Darwin, *Expression*, 26, 54–55; Butler, *Evolution*, 58, 60, 196.

8. H. Jones, *Samuel Butler*, 1:323–27; *Autobiography*, 177–82. Copland, 'Side Light,' points out that Krause himself referred to his earlier article on page 135 of *Erasmus Darwin*. Butler knew this, and in a copy of the text deposited in the British Museum (cf. Butler, *Unconscious Memory*, xxxvii) he pencilled beside the passage, 'clearly written after the article appeared in Kosmos.' But then he erased his remark (which however is still legible in a good light). It was tantamount to an admission that Darwin had *not* deliberately concealed the revision of Krause's article.

9. *Autobiography*, 182–88, 202–11; Butler, *Evolution*, 393; Willey, *Darwin*; Pauly, 'Samuel Butler.' Huxley gave a demure lightning sketch of a bitch rather than write the word.

10. *Calendar*, 12593; *Annotated Calendar*, 573; Milner, 'Darwin, Pt 2,' 45–46; *Wedgwood*, 314; Darwin to C. Fox, 29 Mar. and 10 Mar. [*sic*, April] 1880, University of British Columbia Library.

11. *Darwin's Journal*, 21; *LLD*, 3:216–17; T. Huxley, *Darwiniana*, 227–43; *LLD*, 2:373, 3:240–41; *LLTH*, 2:12–13; *Calendar*, 12597; *MLD*, 1:387; Bowler, *Eclipse*, 26–28.

12. Shannon, *Crisis*, 140; Wingfield–Stratford, *Victorian Sunset*, 169; recollec-

tions of W. Darwin, DAR 112.2; *ED*, 2:240; Darwin to F. Abbot, 15 April 1880 (copy), DAR 139.12.

13. Royle, *Radicals*, 23–25, 171, 268–71; Bonner, *Charles Bradlaugh*, 2:203ff; J. Morley, *Life*, 3:11ff; E. Aveling to Darwin, 23 Sept. 1878, and Darwin to E. Aveling, [after 23 Sept. 1878], both DAR 202.

14. *Darwin's Journal*, 21; *Calendar*, 12618; W. Darwin to F. Abbot, 13 June [1880], University Archives, Harvard University Library (cf. *LLD*, 1:304–306 and RFD, 24); J. Moore, 'Freethought, 307–309.

15. *Calendar*, 12638 *et seq.*, 12662, 12677 *et seq.*, 12749, 12755; *Wedgwood*, 316; H. Litchfield to F. Darwin, 18 Mar. 1887, DAR 112:79–82.

16. *Darwin's Journal*, 21; *ED*, 2:240–41; De Beer, 'Darwin Letters,' 73; *Calendar*, 12697; Stecher, 'Darwin–Innes Letters,' 246; *LLD*, 1:119, 3:217.

17. E. Aveling to Darwin, 12 Oct. 1880, DAR 159; Darwin to [E. Aveling], 13 Oct. 1880, in Feuer, 'Is the "Darwin–Marx Correspondence" Authentic?,' 2–3; J. Moore, 'Freethought,' 309–11. Darwin's letter to Aveling was long thought to have been addressed to Marx: Colp, 'Case of the "Darwin–Marx" Letter' and 'Myth.'

18. *Darwin's Journal*, 21; *ED*, 2:235, 242–43; *Wedgwood*, 315–16; *CP*, 2:223; *LLTH*, 2:14; *LLD*, 3:242–43.

19. Wallace, *My Life*, 2:98, 102, 376–78; *ARW*, 1:303, 306; Colp, '"I will gladly do my best",' 1–7.

20. Colp, '"I will gladly do my best",' 7–12; *Calendar*, 11891, 12170, 12540; *LLR*, 97; Wallace, *My Life*, 2:311–15; *ARW*, 1:304, 307; *LLJH*, 2:244; De Beer, 'Further Unpublished Letters,' 89.

21. Colp, '"I will gladly do my best",' 12–24; *ED*, 2:243; J. Morley, *Life*, 3:33, 567; *ARW*, 1:314–15; *Calendar*, 12972, 13019; Atkins, *Down*, 97.

22. Butler, *Unconscious Memory*, ch. 4; *Autobiography*, 212–16; *Calendar*, 12939, 12998 *et seq.*, 13032; *LLR*, 104–105; Pauly, 'Samuel Butler,' 172–73.

23. *Annotated Calendar*, 518; *Calendar*, 13060.

24. *Darwin's Journal*, 21; *Calendar*, 12908; *ED*, 2:245; J. Morley, *Life*, 3:32–38, 51ff, 566; Argyll, 'What,' 243–44 and *LLD*, 1:316 (cf. *Autobiography*, 92–93). Huxley called the Duke an 'unmitigated cad' for his recollection of this conversation: T. Huxley to F. Darwin, 20 April 1888, DAR 107.

25. Darwin, *Worms*, 19–35, 67ff, 97–100; Ghiselin, *Triumph*, 202; cf. *Calendar*, 13077 and G. Romanes, *Animal Intelligence*, 24.

26. *Calendar*, 13096; *LLD*, 3:205–209; Darwin, *Worms*, 31, 37, 112, 313–14; Colp, 'Evolution,' 201.

27. *MLD*, 2:433; De Beer, 'Darwin Letters,' 74; *Autobiography*, 95n.

28. Darwin referred to Annie or alluded to her death at least thirteen times between 1853 and 1881 in unpublished correspondence: *Calendar*, 1527, 1547, 1967, 4292, 4318, 4345, 4547, 4901, 7194, 7718, 8569, 10593, 13304. Only two of the letters (7194, 7718) were sent outside the family and neither mentions Annie by name.

29. E. Darwin to Darwin [c. Feb. 1839], DAR 210.10 and *CCD*, 2:171–72. Darwin probably attached the annotated letter to his manuscript, just as he also 'enclosed in a separate envelope' some short notes written by his father. The letter was found among Emma's papers after her death in 1896, where it may have been removed to preserve the annotation for her own eyes. The annotation was omitted when the letter was first printed in 1904: *Autobiography*, 35, 235; *ED* (1904), 2:187–89.

43 THE FINAL EXPERIMENT

1. *Darwin's Journal*, 21; De Beer, 'Further Unpublished Letters,' 90; *LLD*, 1:124, 3:223; *Companion*, 242; *ED*, 2:246–47; *Calendar*, 13169 etc., 13184, 13194; *MLD*, 2:433; *TBI*, 92–93.
2. Darwin to G. Romanes, 27 June [1881], APS, Getz collection B/D25.m; Darwin to G. Romanes, 4 July [1881], APS 494; *LLR*, 119; *LLD*, 1:316; *MLD*, 2:395; cf. Graham, *Creed*, 343–50 and William Darwin's notes in DAR 210.28 for the passage that perhaps most struck Darwin.
3. *ARW*, 1:317–19; George, *Progress*, 233, 239; Wallace, *My Life*, 2:27, ch. 34; Durant, 'Scientific Naturalism.'
4. *MLD*, 2:26–28; *LLJH*, 2:223–26, 245, 258.
5. *MLD*, 2:394; *ARW*, 1:319; *ED*, 2:247; Symonds, *Recollections*, 215; *LLR*, 129; *Calendar*, 13255 et seq.
6. *Darwin's Journal*, 21; *LLR*, 118–20; *LLD*, 3:223; *LLTH*, 2:33; Bonner, *Charles Bradlaugh*, 2:286; Tribe, *President Charles Bradlaugh*, 209–11; *Wedgwood*, 317; E. Aveling to Darwin, 9 Aug. 1881, and Darwin to E. Aveling, 11 Aug. [1881], both DAR 202.
7. *LLD*, 1:22, 3:228; *MLD*, 1:395; *LLJH*, 2:258; Darwin to J. Hooker, 30 Aug. 1881, DAR 95:530–31; *Wedgwood*, 318; E. Darwin to G. Darwin, 23 Aug. 1881, DAR 210.3; H. Litchfield to H. Wedgwood, [2 Sept. 1881], W/M 575; RFD, 79.
8. *MLD*, 1:395; *Wedgwood*, 318; Keith, *Darwin*, 230–31; Atkins, *Down*, 100; recollections of W. Darwin, DAR 112.2; 'Last Will and Testament of . . . Charles Darwin,' Somerset House, London; Darwin to C. Darwin, 20 Sept. [1881] (copy), DAR 153. Darwin subsequently modified his will: *Calendar*, 13330, 13335, 13353, 13356.
9. E. Aveling to Darwin, [27 Sept. 1881] (telegram), DAR 159; E. Darwin to G. Darwin, 28 Sept. 1881, DAR 210.3; Gregory, *Scientific Materialism*, 204ff.
10. Aveling, *Religious Views*, 3; *LLD*, 1:139–40; Feuer, 'Marxian Tragedians,' 26; Stecher, 'Darwin–Innes Letters,' 256; cf. pp. 249–51, 253, 256 and *Calendar*, 12343, 12349 for Brodie Innes's unplanned visit. Darwin's remark was made, according to Brodie Innes, 'on my last visit . . . at dinner,' which was usually the midday meal. Clergymen were infrequent guests: M. Keynes, *Leonard Darwin*, 2.
11. RFD, 9–14; Aveling, *Religious Views*, 4–6; cf. *LLD*, 1:317n, where Francis, an eyewitness, confirms that Aveling gave 'quite fairly his impressions of my father's views.' For Büchner's meagre recollection: Büchner, *Last Words*, 147.
12. *Darwin's Journal*, 21; *ED*, 2:248–50; *Annotated Calendar*, 603; *Calendar*, 13476; *LLR*, 127; RFD, 8, 116; *CP*, 2:254–56; *LLD*, 3:244.
13. *Darwin's Journal*, 21; *Calendar*, 11633, 13458, 13560; *Annotated Calendar*, 603–604, 606; *LLD*, 3:357; H. Litchfield to F. Darwin, 18 Mar. 1887, DAR 112:79–82; Judd, *Coming*, 158.
14. *CP*, 2:236–76; *Calendar*, 13570, 13579, 13607, 13650, 13652, 13662; *MLD*, 1:397, 2:171, 447–48; *LLJH*, 2:237–39; *LLD*, 3:351–54; W. Graham to E. Darwin, 26 April 1882, DAR 215; RFD, 8, 14.
15. *MLD*, 2:28–29, 446–47; *Calendar*, 13692, 13696; E. Darwin to G. Darwin, 20 Feb., 28 Feb., and 11 Mar. 1882, all DAR 210.3; H. Litchfield MS, Down House, 1–2.
16. *TBI*, 93–94; *Calendar*, 13722, 13734, 13741; *CP*, 2:276–78; *ED*, 2: 251, 253

(1904 ed., 329); E. Darwin to G. Darwin, 14 Mar. 1882, DAR 210.3; H. Litchfield MS, Down House, 3–5; L. Forster to F. Darwin, 15 Nov. 1885, DAR 112:38–47.

17. L. Forster to F. Darwin, 15 Nov. 1885, DAR 112:38–40; H. Litchfield MS, Down House, 5; TBI, 94–95; E. Darwin to G. Darwin, 6 April 1882, DAR 210.3; ED, 2:253.

18. H. Litchfield MS, Down House, 6–7; TBI, 95; LLD, 3:358; ED, 2:251, 253.

19. H. Litchfield MS, Down House, 7–11; E. Darwin to F. and H. Wedgwood, [22 April 1882] (typescript copy), APS, Loewenberg Collection B/L 828; F. Darwin to T. Huxley, 20 April 1882, THP 13.10–11; Miller, 'Death;' H. Litchfield to F. Wedgwood, [19 April 1882], W/M 579; chronology in DAR 210.19; ED, 2:251–53; TBI, 95–96.

20. B. Darwin, World, 27.

44 AN AGNOSTIC IN THE ABBEY

1. 'Charles Darwin,' Standard, 21 April 1882, DAR 140.5; 'The Late Mr. Darwin,' Pall Mall Gazette, 21 April 1882, DAR 216; Nash, 'Some Memories,' 404; MLD, 2:433; LLD, 3:360-61; J. Brodie Innes to F. Darwin, 22 April 1882, DAR 215; E. Darwin to F. and H. Wedgwood, [22 April 1882] (typescript copy), APS, Loewenberg Collection B/L 828.

2. F. Darwin to T. Huxley, 20 April 1882, THP 13.10-11; Pearson, Life, 2:197; T. Huxley to J. Hooker, 21 April 1882, THP 2.240-41; LLTH, 2:38; Galton, English Men, 260 and Inquiries, 220; F. Galton to G. Darwin, 20 April 1882, DAR 215; F. Galton to M. Conway, 24 April 1882 (copy), APS, Misc. MSS 1975 578.f ms.

3. Pearson, Life, 2:198; F. de Chaumont to W. Darwin, 22 April 1882, and C. Pritchard to G. Darwin, 21 April 1882, both DAR 215; [Editorial], Standard, 22 April 1882, p. 5; J. Hooker to T. Huxley, 23 April 1882, THP 3.261-62.

4. J. Hooker to T. Huxley, 23 April 1882, THP 3.261-62; LLD, 3:197; F. Farrar, Men, 140-48; R. Farrar, Life, 106-109; LLTH, 2:18-19; G. Bradley to T. Huxley, 24 Mar. 1881, THP 121.19; Ward, History, facing p. 94; Rules; Cowell, Athenaeum, 52.

5. W. Spottiswoode to W. Darwin, 21 April 1882, DAR 215; T. Huxley to J. Hooker, 21 April 1882, THP 2.240-41.

6. RFD, 64-65; Atkins, Down, 28; J. Lubbock to W. Darwin, 25 April 1882, and to F. Darwin, 20 April 1882, both DAR 215; T. Huxley, 'Introductory Notice,' x; Gardeners' Chronicle, 22 April 1882, DAR 215.

7. Hammond, Gladstone, chs 14-15; Hansard Parliamentary Debates, 268 (21 April 1882), 1202-203; memorial to G. Bradley, 21 April 1882, DAR 215 (copy showing twenty signatories) and in Hutchinson, Life, 1:184 (inaccurate transcription but with eight additional names).

8. J. Lubbock to F. Darwin, 22 April 1882, and to W. Darwin, 23 April 1882, both DAR 215.

9. [Editorial], Standard, 22 April 1882, p. 5.

10. A. Hall, Abbey Scientists; Bradley, 'Introductory Chapter;' 'Mr. Charles Darwin,' St. James's Gazette, 21 April 1882, and 'The Death of Mr. Darwin,' Pall Mall Gazette, 21 April 1882, both DAR 215.

11. [Editorial], Standard, 22 April 1882, DAR 140.5; [Editorial], Daily Telegraph, 22 April 1882, DAR 215; [Editorial], The Times, 26 April 1882, DAR 140.1.

12. *LLD*, 3:360-61; E. Darwin to F. and H. Wedgwood, [22 April 1882] (typescript copy), APS, Loewenberg Collection B/L 828.
13. J. Morley, *Death*, 30, 85; *LLD*, 3:361; *Daily News*, 27 April 1882; Argyll to G. Darwin, 24 April 1882; Devonshire to W. Darwin, 25 April 1882; T. Huxley to G. Darwin, 22 April 1882; H. Spencer to G. Darwin, 24 April (twice) and 4 May 1882; family funeral scrapbook, all DAR 215; F. Galton to M. Conway, 24 April 1882 (copy), APS, Misc. MSS 1975 578.f ms.
14. E. Darwin to F. and H. Wedgwood, [22 April 1882] (typescript copy), APS, Loewenberg Collection B/L 828; list of mourners, DAR 140.5.
15. *Companion*, 228; list of mourners, DAR 140.5; Jordan, *Days*, 1:273; Colp, 'Charles Darwin's Coffin;' 'A Visit to Darwin's Village: Reminiscences of Some of His Humble Friends,' *Evening News* (London), 12 Feb. 1909, p. 4.
16. [Editorial], *Standard*, 22 April 1882; [Editorial], *The Times*, 21 April 1882; [Editorial], *Daily News*, 21 April 1882, all DAR 140.5.
17. Prothero, *Arthur Penrhyn Stanley*, 10-11 and *Armour*, 168 etc.; Barry, *Sermons*, 39-40, 54, 61-62; 'The Late Mr. Darwin,' *The Times*, 24 April 1882, DAR 140.1.
18. Liddon, *Recovery*, 26-28; Johnston, *Life*, 275; 'Charles Darwin,' *Guardian*, 26 April 1882, DAR 216.
19. [Editorial], *Standard*, 24 April 1882, DAR 140.1; [Editorial], *Daily News*, 25 April 1882, DAR 215; 'Darwin's Home,' *Daily News*, 24 April 1882, and *Morning Advertiser*, 24 April 1882, both DAR 216.
20. 'The Late Charles Darwin,' *Standard*, 26 April 1882; 'The Funeral of Mr. Darwin,' *The Times*, 26/27 April 1882, all DAR 140.1; 'Funeral of the Late Charles Darwin,' *Standard*, 27 April 1882, DAR 140.5; 'Funeral of the Late Mr. Darwin,' *Daily News*, 27 April 1882, DAR 215.
21. 'The Judges and Mr. Darwin's Funeral,' *Pall Mall Gazette*, 25 April 1882, DAR 215; Carpenter, 'Science,' 43; 'The Funeral of Mr. Darwin . . . Order of Procession,' instructions for ushers, admission card, all APS; 'The Funeral of the Late Mr. Darwin, List of Mourners . . .,' family procession, family sacrarium list, admission cards, all DAR 140.5, 215; H. Spencer to G. Darwin, 4 May 1882, DAR 215.
22. Newspaper accounts (n. 20 above); Bridge, *Westminster Pilgrim*, 67, 124; 'Words of Anthem composed by J. Frederick Bridge,' DAR 140.5; Raverat, *Period Piece*, 176.
23. 'Funeral of the Late Mr. Darwin,' *Daily News*, 27 April 1882, DAR 215; 'The Funeral of Mr. Darwin,' *The Times*, 27 April 1882, DAR 140.5; Conway, *Autobiography*, 2:328; G. Romanes, 'Work,' 82.
24. F[rancis] G[alton], 'The Late Mr. Darwin: A Suggestion,' *Pall Mall Gazette*, 27 April 1882, DAR 215; Pearson, *Life*, 2:199; F. Farrar to T. Huxley, 29 April 1882, THP 16.21.
25. Rawnsley, *Harvey Goodwin*, 222-23; Atkins, *Down*, 49-50; Goodwin, 'Funeral Sermon,' 301-302; 'The Late Mr. Darwin,' *The Times*, 1 May 1882; 'The Late Mr. Charles Darwin,' *Morning Post*, 1 May 1882; 'Mr. Darwin's Funeral,' *Guardian*, 3 May 1882, all DAR 140.5; Pearson, *Life*, 2:199; Galton, *Inquiries*, 220.
26. T. Huxley to W. and G. Darwin, 1 May 1882, DAR 215; Pearson, *Life*, 2:200; *Darwin Memorial Fund: Report of the Committee* (n.p., n.d.), in British Library, Department of Printed Books.
27. *Darwin Memorial Fund*; Johnston, *Life*, 275-76; 'The Darwin Memorial

Statue,' *The Times*, 10 June 1885, DAR 215; Stearn, *Natural History Museum*, 47, 73; *ED*, 2:270-71.

28. Woodall, 'Charles Darwin,' 47; 'Mr. Darwin,' *Church Times*, 28 April 1882, DAR 140.5; 'Charles Darwin,' *Liverpool Diocesan Gazette*, May 1882, DAR 215; 'The Late Mr. Darwin,' *Record* (supplement), n.s., 1 (28 April 1882), 152; 'South American Missionary Society,' *Record*, n.s., 1 (28 April 1882), 335; 'Charles Darwin,' *Nonconformist and Independent*, 27 April 1882; [Stopford A. Brooke], 'Charles Darwin,' *Inquirer*, 20 May 1882; W. Carpenter to E. Darwin, 30 April 1882, all DAR 215; R. Armstrong, 'Charles Darwin,' 33; J. Chadwick, 'Evolution,' 43.

29. 'Mr. Darwin,' *Saturday Review*, 22 April 1882, DAR 140.5; Miall, *Life*, 58, 62; 'Charles Darwin,' *British Medical Journal*, 29 April 1882, DAR 216; [Editorial], *The Times*, 26 April 1882, DAR 140.1.

30. 'The Death of Mr. Darwin,' *Pall Mall Gazette*, 21 April 1882, DAR 140.5; J. Morley, in Hammond, *Gladstone*, 546; J. Morley, *Life*, 2:562; 'Mr. Darwin's Influence on Modern Thought,' *Pall Mall Gazette*, 26 April 1882, DAR 140.5.

31. T. Huxley, *Method*, 51.

Bibliography

Anonymous reviews and editorials, and other press articles, are cited fully in the notes. Place of publication is London unless stated otherwise.

AMNH   *Annals and Magazine of Natural History*
AS   *Annals of Science*
BAAS   *Report of the British Association for the Advancement of Science*
BBMNH   *Bulletin of the British Museum (Natural History), Historical Series*
BJHS   *British Journal for the History of Science*
BJLS   *Biological Journal of the Linnean Society*
ENPJ   *Edinburgh New Philosophical Journal*
ER   *Edinburgh Review*
HS   *History of Science*
JHB   *Journal of the History of Biology*
JHBS   *Journal of the History of the Behavioural Sciences*
JHM   *Journal of the History of Medicine and Allied Sciences*
JSBNH   *Journal of the Society for the Bibliography of Natural History*
NQ   *Notes and Queries*
NR   *Notes and Records of the Royal Society of London*
PAPS   *Proceedings of the American Philosophical Society*
PGSL   *Proceedings of the Geological Society of London*
PZSL   *Proceedings of the Zoological Society of London*
QJGS   *Quarterly Journal of the Geological Society of London*
QR   *Quarterly Review*
SHB   *Studies in History of Biology*
SHPS   *Studies in History and Philosophy of Science*
U.P.   University Press
VS   *Victorian Studies*

Abbot, F. E. *Truths for the Times*. Ramsgate, Kent: Thomas Scott, [1872].
Addison, W. *The English Country Parson*. Dent, 1947.
Agassiz, L. 'A Period in the History of our Planet.' *ENPJ*, 35 (1843), 1–29.
— and Agassiz, [E]. *A Journey in Brazil*. Boston: Ticknor & Fields, 1868.
Ainsworth, W. F. 'On the Present State of Science in Great Britain. No. 1.

Bibliography

Edinburgh College Museum.' *Edinburgh Journal of Natural and Geographical Science*, 1 (1830), 269–77.

—. 'Mr. Darwin.' *Athenaeum*, 13 May 1882, p. 604.

Aldington, R. *The Strange Life of Charles Waterton, 1782–1865.* Evans, 1949.

Allan, M. *Darwin and His Flowers: The Key to Natural Selection.* Faber & Faber, 1977.

Allen, D. E. *The Naturalist in Britain: A Social History.* Harmondsworth, Middx: Penguin Books, 1978.

Allen, G., ed. *The Miscellaneous and Posthumous Works of Henry Thomas Buckle.* New abridged ed. 2 vols. Longmans *et al.*, 1885.

Allen, P. *The Cambridge Apostles: The Early Years.* Cambridge: Cambridge U.P., 1978.

Altner, G. *Charles Darwin und Ernst Haeckel: Ein Vergleich nach theologischen Aspekten.* Zurich: EVZ-Verlag, 1966.

Appel, T. A. *The Cuvier-Geoffroy Debate: French Biology in the Decades before Darwin.* New York: Oxford U.P., 1987.

Arbuckle, E. S., ed. *Harriet Martineau's Letters to Fanny Wedgwood.* Stanford, CA: Stanford U.P., 1983.

Argyll, The Dowager Duchess of. *George Douglas, Eighth Duke of Argyll, K.G., K.T. (1823–1900): Autobiography and Memoirs.* 2 vols. Murray, 1906.

Argyll, The Duke of. *The Reign of Law.* 5th ed. Strahan, 1868.

—. *Primeval Man.* Strahan, 1869.

—. 'What is Science?' *Good Words*, 26 (1885), 236–45.

Armstrong, P. *Charles Darwin in Western Australia: A Young Scientist's Perception of an Environment.* Nedlands, W. A.: University of Western Australia Press, 1985.

Armstrong, R. A. 'Charles Darwin: A Lecture delivered at Nottingham, on 10th December, 1882.' *Modern Sermons*, 23–35. Manchester: Johnson *et al.*, [1883].

Ashwell, A. R. and Wilberforce, R. G. *Life of the Right Reverend Samuel Wilberforce, D.D., Lord Bishop of Oxford and afterwards of Winchester, with Selections from His Diaries and Correspondence.* 3 vols. Murray, 1880.

Ashworth, J. H. 'Charles Darwin as a Student in Edinburgh, 1825–1827.' *Proceedings of the Royal Society of Edinburgh*, 55 (1935), 97–113.

Atkins, H. *Down, the Home of the Darwins: The Story of a House and the People who lived there.* Rev. ed. Phillimore, for the Royal College of Surgeons of England, 1976.

Audubon, M. R., ed. *Audubon and His Journals.* 2 vols. Nimmo, 1898.

Austin, Mrs, ed. *A Memoir of the Reverend Sydney Smith.* 2nd ed. 2 vols. Longmans, 1855.

Aveling, E. *The Religious Views of Charles Darwin.* Freethought Publishing Co., 1883.

Babbage, C. *The Ninth Bridgewater Treatise: A Fragment.* 2nd ed. Murray, 1838.

Bagehot, W. *Physics and Politics, or Thoughts on the Application of the Principles of 'Natural Selection' and 'Inheritance' to Political Society.* 6th ed. Kegan Paul, 1881.

Balfour, J. H. *Biography of the Late John Coldstream, M.D., F.R.C.P.E., Secretary of the Medical Missionary Society of Edinburgh.* Nisbet, 1865.

Barber, L. *The Heyday of Natural History, 1820–1870.* Cape, 1980.

Barclay, O. R. *Whatever Happened to the Jesus Lane Lot?* Leicester: Inter-Varsity Press, 1977.

Barlow, N. 'Robert FitzRoy and Charles Darwin.' *Cornhill Magazine*, 72 (1932), 493–510.

—, ed. *Charles Darwin and the Voyage of the 'Beagle'*. Pilot Press, 1945.

—, ed. *The Autobiography of Charles Darwin 1809–1882, with Original Omissions Restored*. Collins, 1958.

—, ed. 'Darwin's Ornithological Notes.' *BBMNH*, 2 (1963), 201–78.

Barnaby, D., ed. *The Log Book of Wombwell's Royal No. 1 Menagerie, 1848–1871*. Sale, Cheshire: ZSGM Publications, 1989.

Barnett, D. C. 'Allotments and the Problem of Rural Poverty, 1780–1840.' In E. L. Jones and G. E. Mingay, eds., *Land, Labour and Population in the Industrial Revolution: Essays presented to J. D. Chambers*, 162–83. Arnold, 1967.

Barrett, P. H. 'Darwin's "Gigantic Blunder".' *Journal of Geological Education*, 21 (1973), 19–28.

—, 'The Sedgwick-Darwin Geologic Tour of North Wales.' *PAPS*, 118 (1974), 146–64.

—, ed. *The Collected Papers of Charles Darwin*. 2 vols. Chicago: University of Chicago Press, 1977.

—, Gautrey, P. J., Herbert, S., Kohn, D., and Smith, S., eds. *Charles Darwin's Notebooks, 1836–1844*. Cambridge: British Museum (Natural History)/Cambridge U.P., 1987.

Barrow, L. *Independent Spirits: Spiritualism and English Plebeians, 1850–1910*. Routledge & Kegan Paul, 1986.

Barry, A. *Sermons Preached in Westminster Abbey*. Cassell, 1884.

Barth, J. R. *Coleridge and Christian Doctrine*. Cambridge, MA: Harvard U.P., 1969.

Bartholomew, M. J. 'Lyell and Evolution: An Account of Lyell's Response to the Prospect of an Evolutionary Ancestry for Man.' *BJHS*, 6 (1973), 261–303.

—. 'Huxley's Defence of Darwin.' *AS*, 32 (1975), 525–35.

—. 'The Award of the Copley Medal to Charles Darwin.' *NR*, 30 (1976), 209–18.

—. 'The Singularity of Lyell.' *HS*, 17 (1979), 276–93.

Barton, R. 'The X Club: Science, Religion, and Social Change in Victorian England.' Ph.D. diss., University of Pennsylvania, 1976.

—. 'Evolution: The Whitworth Gun in Huxley's War for the Liberation of Science from Theology.' In Oldroyd and Langham, *Wider Domain*, 261–86.

—. 'John Tyndall, Pantheist: A Rereading of the Belfast Address.' *Osiris*, 2nd ser., 3 (1987), 111–34.

—. '"An Influential Set of Chaps": The X-Club and Royal Society Politics, 1864–85.' *BJHS*, 23 (1990), 53–81.

Basalla, G. 'Darwin's Orchid Book.' *Actes du Xe Congrès International d'Histoire des Sciences Naturelles et de la Biologie* (1962), 2:971–74.

—. 'The Voyage of the *Beagle* without Darwin.' *Mariner's Mirror*, 59 (1963), 42–48.

Bastian, H. C. *The Beginnings of Life: Being Some Account of the Nature, Modes of Origin and Transformations of Lower Organisms*. 2 vols. Macmillan, 1872.

Bibliography

Bayertz, K. 'Darwinism and Scientific Freedom: Political Aspects of the Reception of Darwinism in Germany, 1863–1878.' *Scientia*, 118 (1983), 297–307.

[Baynes, T. S.] 'Darwin on Expression.' *ER*, 137 (1873), 492–508.

Beddoe, J. *Memories of Eighty Years*. Bristol: Arrowsmith, 1910.

Beer, G. *Darwin's Plots: Evolutionary Narrative in Darwin, George Eliot, and Nineteenth-Century Fiction*. Routledge & Kegan Paul, 1983.

Bell, G. J., ed. *Letters of Sir Charles Bell*. Murray, 1870.

Bell, H. C. F. *Lord Palmerston*. 2 vols. Longmans, 1936.

Bell, S. 'George Lewes: A Man of His Time.' *JHB*, 14 (1981), 277–98.

Berman, M. *Social Change and Scientific Organization: The Royal Institution, 1799–1844*. Heinemann, 1978.

Best, G. *Mid-Victorian Britain, 1851–75*. Fontana, 1979.

Bibby, C. T. H. *Huxley: Scientist, Humanist, Educator*. Watts, 1959.

[Billing, M.] M. *Billing's Directory and Gazetteer of the County of Worcester*. Birmingham: M. Billing, 1855.

Blinderman, C. S. 'The Oxford Debate and After.' *NQ*, 202 (1957), 126–28.

Block, E., Jr. 'T. H. Huxley's Rhetoric and the Popularization of Victorian Scientific Ideas.' *VS*, 29 (1985–86), 363–86.

[Blomefield, L.] Jenyns, L. *Fish*. Pt 4, *The Zoology of the Voyage of H.M.S. 'Beagle'*, ed. C. Darwin. Smith, Elder, 1840–42.

[—]. Jenyns, L. *Memoir of the Rev. John Stevens Henslow*. Van Voorst, 1862.

—. *Chapters in My Life, with Appendix containing Special Notices of Particular Incidents and Persons; also Thoughts on Certain Subjects*. New ed. Bath: privately printed, 1889.

—. *A Naturalist's Calendar kept at Swaffham Bulbeck, Cambridgeshire*. Ed. F. Darwin. Cambridge: printed at the U.P., 1903.

Bölsche, W. *Haeckel: His Life and Work*. Trans. J. McCabe. Unwin, 1906.

Bolt, C. *Victorian Attitudes to Race*. Routledge & Kegan Paul, 1971.

Bonner, H. B. *Charles Bradlaugh: A Record of His Life and Work*. 2 vols. Unwin, 1895.

Bowen, D. *The Idea of the Victorian Church: A Study of the Church of England, 1833–1889*. Montreal: McGill U.P., 1968.

Bowlby, J. *Charles Darwin: A Biography*. Hutchinson, 1990.

Bowler, P. J. *Fossils and Progress: Paleontology and the Idea of Progressive Evolution in the Nineteenth Century*. New York: Science History Publications, 1976.

—. 'Malthus, Darwin, and the Concept of Struggle.' *Journal of the History of Ideas*, 37 (1976), 631–50.

—. *The Eclipse of Darwinism: Anti-Darwinian Evolution Theories in the Decades around 1900*. Baltimore, MD: Johns Hopkins U.P., 1983.

—. *Theories of Human Evolution: A Century of Debate, 1844–1944*. Oxford: Blackwell, 1987.

—. *The Non-Darwinian Revolution: Reinterpreting a Historical Myth*. Baltimore, MD: Johns Hopkins U.P., 1988.

—. *Charles Darwin: The Man and His Influence*. Oxford: Blackwell, 1990.

A Brace of Cantabs. *Gradus ad Cantabrigiam; or, New University Guide to the Academical Customs, and Colloquial or Cant Terms Peculiar to The University of Cambridge; observing wherein it differs from Oxford . . . to which is affixed, A Tail-Piece; or, the Reading and Varmint Method of Proceeding to the Degree of A.B.* Printed for John Hearne, 1824.

Darwin

Brackman, A. C. *A Delicate Arrangement: The Strange Case of Charles Darwin and Alfred Russel Wallace.* Times Books, 1980.

[Bradley, G. G.] 'Introductory Chapter.' *The Popular Guide to Westminster Abbey.* 'Pall Mall Gazette' Office, 1885.

Brent, Peter. *Charles Darwin: 'A Man of Enlarged Curiosity'.* Heinemann, 1981.

[Brewster, D.] 'M. Comte's Course of Positive Philosophy.' *ER*, 67 (1838), 271–308.

Bridge, F. *A Westminster Pilgrim: Being a Record of Service in Church, Cathedral, and Abbey; College, University, and Concert Room; with a Few Notes on Sport.* Novello, [1919].

Briggs, A. *The Age of Improvement, 1783–1867.* Longmans, 1959.

Broadbent, A. *The Story of Unitarianism in Shrewsbury.* Shrewsbury: Livesey Printers, 1962.

Brock, W. H. and MacLeod, R. M. 'The Scientists' Declaration: Reflexions on Science and Belief in the Wake of *Essays and Reviews*, 1864–5.' *BJHS*, 9 (1976), 39–66.

[Broderip, W.] 'The Zoological Gardens – Regent's Park.' *QR*, 56 (1836), 309–32.

The Bromley Directory. Bromley: Strong, 1880.

Brooke, J. H. '"A Sower Went Forth": Joseph Priestley and the Ministry of Reform.' In *Oxygen and the Conversion of Future Feedstocks: Proceedings of the Third BOC Priestley Conference*, 432–60. Royal Society of Chemistry, 1984.

—. 'The Relations Between Darwin's Science and his Religion.' In Durant, *Darwinism*, 40–75.

—. 'Joseph Priestley (1733–1804) and William Whewell (1794–1866), Apologists and Historians of Science: A Tale of Two Stereotypes.' In R. Anderson and C. Lawrence, eds., *Science, Medicine and Dissent: Joseph Priestley (1733–1804)*, 11–27. Wellcome Trust/Science Museum, 1987.

Brooks, J. L. *Just Before the Origin: Alfred Russel Wallace's Theory of Evolution.* Columbia U.P., 1984.

Brown, A. W. *The Metaphysical Society: Victorian Minds in Crisis, 1869–1880.* Columbia U.P., 1947.

Browne, J. 'The Charles Darwin – Joseph Hooker Correspondence: An Analysis of Manuscript Resources and Their Use in Biography.' *JSBNH*, (1978), 351–66.

—. *The Secular Ark: Studies in the History of Biogeography.* New Haven, CT: Yale U.P., 1983.

—. 'Darwin and the Expression of the Emotions.' In Kohn, *Darwinian Heritage*, 307–26.

—. 'Botany for Gentlemen: Erasmus Darwin and *The Loves of the Plants*.' *Isis*, 80 (1989), 593–621.

Browne, W. A. F. 'Observations on Religious Fanaticism.' *Phrenological Journal*, 9 (1836), 288–302, 532–45, 577–603.

Buckle, H. T. *History of Civilization in England.* New ed. 3 vols. Longmans *et al.*, 1867.

Büchner, L. *Last Words on Materialism and Kindred Subjects.* Trans. J. McCabe. Watts, 1901.

Bunbury, F. J., ed. *Life, Letters and Journals of Sir Charles J. F. Bunbury, Bart.* 3 vols. Privately printed, 1894.

Bunting, James. *Charles Darwin: A Biography.* Folkestone, Kent: Bailey Brothers & Swinfen, 1974.

Bibliography

Burchfield, J. D. *Lord Kelvin and the Age of the Earth.* Macmillan, 1974.

Burkhardt, F. and Smith, S., eds. *A Calendar of the Correspondence of Charles Darwin, 1821–1882.* New York: Garland, 1985.

—, eds. *The Correspondence of Charles Darwin.* 7 vols. Cambridge: Cambridge U.P., 1985–91.

Burn, W. L. *The Age of Equipoise: A Study of the Mid-Victorian Generation.* New York: Norton, 1965.

Burrow, J. W. *Evolution and Society: A Study in Victorian Social Theory.* Cambridge: Cambridge U.P., 1966.

Burstyn, H. L. 'If Darwin wasn't the *Beagle*'s Naturalist, Why was he on Board?' *BJHS*, 8 (1975), 62–69.

Burton, J. 'Robert FitzRoy and the Early History of the Meteorological Office.' *BJHS*, 19 (1986), 147–76.

Bush, D., ed. *Milton: Poetical Works.* Oxford: Oxford U.P., 1966.

Butler, S. *Evolution Old and New*, 1879. New ed. Fifield, 1911.

—. *Unconscious Memory*, 1880. New ed. Fifield, 1910.

Bynum, W. F. 'Charles Lyell's *Antiquity of Man* and Its Critics.' *JHB*, 17 (1984), 153–87.

Calder, G. J. 'Erasmus A. Darwin, Friend of Thomas and Jane Carlyle.' *Modern Language Quarterly*, 20 (1959), 36–48.

The Cambridge Guide; or, a Description of the University and Town of Cambridge. Rev. ed. Cambridge: printed for Deighton *et al.*, 1830.

Campbell, J. A. 'Nature, Religion and Emotional Response: A Reconsideration of Darwin's Affective Decline.' *VS*, 18 (1974), 159–74.

Cannon, W. F. 'The Impact of Uniformitarianism: Two Letters from John Herschel to Charles Lyell, 1836–1837.' *PAPS*, 105 (1961), 301–14.

[—]. Cannon, S. F. *Science in Culture: The Early Victorian Period.* New York: Science History Publications, 1978.

Carlyle, T. *Chartism. Past and Present.* Chapman & Hall, 1858.

—. *On Heroes, Hero-Worship, and the Heroic in History.* 4th ed. Chapman & Hall, 1852.

Carpenter, W. B. 'On the Differences of the Laws Regulating Vital and Physical Phenomena.' *ENPJ*, 24 (1838), 327–53.

—. *Remarks on Some Passages in the Review of 'Principles of General and Comparative Physiology', in the 'Edinburgh Medical & Surgical Journal'.* Bristol: Philip & Evans, 1840.

—. 'Vestiges of the Natural History of Creation.' *British and Foreign Medical Review*, 19 (1845), 155–81.

—. *Nature and Man: Essays Scientific and Philosophical.* Routledge & Kegan Paul, 1888.

—. 'Science and Religion.' In J. M. Lloyd Thomas *et al.*, *Dogma or Doctrine? and Other Essays*, 17–44. British & Foreign Unitarian Association, 1906.

Carroll, P. T. *An Annotated Calendar of the Letters of Charles Darwin in the Library of the American Philosophical Society.* Wilmington, DE: Scholarly Resources, 1976.

Carus, C. G. *The King of Saxony's Journey through England in the Year 1844.* Chapman & Hall, 1846.

Carus, W., ed. *Memoirs of the Life of the Rev. Charles Simeon . . . with a Selection from His Writings and Correspondence.* 2nd ed. Hatchard, 1847.

Cathcart, C. W. 'Some of the Older Schools of Anatomy connected with the

Royal College of Surgeons, Edinburgh.' *Edinburgh Medical Journal*, 27 (1882), 769–81.

Cautley, P. 'An Extract of a Letter.' *PGSL*, 2 (1837), 544–45.

— and Falconer, H. 'On the Remains of a Fossil Monkey.' *PGSL*, 2 (1837), 568–69.

Chadwick, J. W. 'Evolution as related to Religious Thought.' *Evolution: Popular Lectures and Discussions before the Brooklyn Ethical Association*, 317–40. Boston: West, 1889.

Chadwick, O. *The Victorian Church*. 2 vols. New York: Oxford U.P., 1966–70.

Chaldecott, J. A. 'Josiah Wedgwood (1730–95) – Scientist.' *BJHS*, 8 (1975), 1–16.

Chapman, R. and Duval, C. T., eds. *Charles Darwin, 1809–1882: A Centennial Commemorative*. Wellington, NZ: Nova Pacifica, 1982.

Chilton, W. 'Theory of Regular Gradation.' *Oracle of Reason*, 27 Nov. 1841, 19 Feb. 1842, 11 Nov. 1843.

—. 'Geological Revelations.' *Oracle of Reason*, 29 July 1843.

—. 'Theory of Regular Gradation.' *Movement*, 6 Nov. 1844, pp. 413–14.

—. 'Vestiges of the Natural History of Creation.' *Movement*, 8 Jan. 1845, pp. 9–12.

Chitnis, A. C. 'The University of Edinburgh's Natural History Museum and the Huttonian-Wernerian Debate.' *AS*, 26 (1970), 85–94.

—. 'Medical Education in Edinburgh, 1790–1826, and Some Victorian Social Consequences.' *Medical History*, 17 (1973), 173–85.

Church, M. C. *Life and Letters of Dean Church*. Macmillan, 1894.

Churchill, F. B. 'Darwin and the Historian.' *BJLS*, 17 (1982), 45–68.

Clark, J. W. and Hughes, T. M. *The Life and Letters of the Reverend Adam Sedgwick*. 2 vols. Cambridge: Cambridge U.P., 1890.

Clarke, M. L. *Paley: Evidences for the Man*. SPCK, 1974.

Cobbe, F. P. *Life of Frances Power Cobbe as told by Herself, with Additions by the Author*. Sonnenschein, 1904.

Cobbett, W. *Rural Rides*, 1830. Harmondsworth, Middx: Penguin, 1987.

Cockshut, A. O. J. *The Unbelievers*. Collins, 1964.

Coldstream, J. P. *Sketch of the Life of John Coldstream, M.D., F.R.C.P.E., The Founder of the Edinburgh Medical Missionary Society*. Edinburgh: Maclaren & Macniven, 1877.

Cole, G. A. 'Doctrine, Dissent and the Decline of Paley's Reputation, 1805–1825.' *Enlightenment and Dissent*, no. 6 (1987), 19–30.

Coleridge, S. T. *Aids to Reflection*. 5th ed. 2 vols. Pickering, 1848.

Colloms, B. *Victorian Country Parsons*. Constable, 1977.

Colp, R., Jr. 'Charles Darwin and Mrs. Whitby.' *Bulletin of the New York Academy of Medicine*, 48 (1972), 870–76.

—. 'The Evolution of Charles Darwin's Thoughts about Death.' *Journal of Thanatology*, 3 (1975), 191–206.

—. 'The Contacts of Charles Darwin with Edward Aveling and Karl Marx.' *AS*, 33 (1976), 387–94.

—. 'Charles Darwin and the Galapagos.' *New York State Journal of Medicine*, 77 (1977), 262–67.

—. *To Be an Invalid: The Illness of Charles Darwin*. Chicago: University of Chicago Press, 1977.

—. 'Charles Darwin: Slavery and the American Civil War.' *Harvard Library Bulletin*, 26 (1978), 478–89.

Bibliography

—. 'Charles Darwin's Coffin, and Its Maker.' *JHM*, 35 (1980), 59–63.

—. '"I was born a naturalist": Charles Darwin's 1838 Notes about Himself.' *JHM*, 35 (1980), 8–39.

—. 'The Case of the "Darwin-Marx" Letter, Lewis Feuer, and *Encounter.*' *Monthly Review*, 32 (1981), 58–61.

—. 'Charles Darwin, Dr. Edward Lane, and the "Singular Trial" of *Robinson and Lane.*' *JHM*, 36 (1981), 205–13.

—. 'Charles Darwin's Reprobation of Nature: "Clumsy, Wasteful, Blundering Low & Horribly Cruel".' *New York State Journal of Medicine*, 81 (1981), 1116–19.

—. 'The Myth of the Darwin-Marx Letter.' *History of Political Economy*, 14 (1982), 461–82.

—. 'Notes on William Gladstone, Karl Marx, Charles Darwin, Kliment Timiriazev, and the "Eastern Question" of 1876–78.' *JHM*, 38 (1983), 178–85.

—. 'The Pre-*Beagle* Misery of Charles Darwin.' *Psychohistory Review*, 13 (1984), 4–15.

—. 'Notes on Charles Darwin's *Autobiography.*' *JHB*, 18 (1985), 357–401.

—. 'Charles Darwin's Dream of His Double Execution.' *Journal of Psychohistory*, 13 (1986), 277–92.

—. '"Confessing a Murder": Darwin's First Revelations about Transmutation.' *Isis*, 77 (1986), 9–32.

—. 'The Relationship of Charles Darwin to the Ideas of His Grandfather, Dr. Erasmus Darwin.' *Biography*, 9 (1986), 1–24.

—. 'Charles Darwin's "insufferable grief".' *Free Associations*, no. 9 (1987), 7–44.

—. 'Charles Darwin's Past and Future Biographies.' *HS*, 27 (1989), 167–97.

—. '"I will gladly do my best": Charles Darwin's Memorial for Alfred Russel Wallace.' Unpublished typescript.

—. 'Mrs. Susannah Darwin: Mother of Charles Darwin.' Unpublished typescript.

Conry, Y. *L'introduction du Darwinisme en France au XIXᵉ siècle*. Paris: Vrin, 1974.

Conway, M. D. *Autobiography, Memoirs, Experiences*. 2 vols. Cassell, 1904.

Cooper, C. H. *Annals of Cambridge*, vol. 4. Cambridge: printed by Metcalfe & Palmer, 1852.

Cooter, R. *The Cultural Meaning of Popular Science: Phrenology and the Organization of Consent in Nineteenth-Century Britain*. Cambridge: Cambridge U.P., 1984.

Copland, R. A. 'A Side Light on the Butler-Darwin Quarrel.' *NQ*, 24 (1977), 23–24.

Cornell, J. F. 'Analogy and Technology in Darwin's Vision of Nature.' *JHB*, 17 (1984), 303–44.

—. 'God's Magnificent Law: The Bad Influence of Theistic Metaphysics on Darwin's Estimation of Natural Selection.' *JHB*, 20 (1987), 381–412.

Corsi, P. 'The Importance of French Transformist Ideas for the Second Volume of Lyell's Principles of Geology.' *BJHS*, 11 (1978), 221–44.

—. *The Age of Lamarck: Evolutionary Theories in France, 1790–1834*. Berkeley: University of California Press, 1988.

—. *Science and Religion: Baden Powell and the Anglican Debate, 1800–1860*. Cambridge: Cambridge U.P., 1988.

— and Weindling, P. J. 'Darwinism in Germany, France, and Italy.' In Kohn, *Darwinian Heritage*, 683–729.

Cowell, F. R. *The Athenaeum: Club and Social Life in London, 1824–1974.* Heinemann, 1975.

Crookes, W. *Researches in the Phenomena of Spiritualism.* Burns, n.d.

Crouzet, F. *The Victorian Economy.* Trans. A. Forster. Methuen, 1982.

Crowther, M. A. *Church Embattled: Religious Controversy in Mid-Victorian England.* Newton Abbot, Devon: David & Charles, 1970.

D. 'Death of Dr. Darwin.' *NQ*, 3rd ser., 10 (1866), 343–44.

Dance, S. P. 'Hugh Cuming (1791–1865), Prince of Collectors.' *JSBNH*, 9 (1980), 477–501.

Darwin, B. 'Kent.' *Men Only*, 15 (1940), 81–86.

—. *The World That Fred Made: An Autobiography.* Chatto & Windus, 1955.

Darwin, C. *Journal of Researches into the Geology and Natural History of the Various Countries visited by H.M.S. 'Beagle'.* Henry Colburn, 1839; rev ed. (1845/60). Ward, Lock & Bowden, 1894.

—. *The Structure and Distribution of Coral Reefs.* Smith, Elder, 1842.

—. *Geological Observations on the Volcanic Islands visited during the Voyage of H.M.S. 'Beagle'.* Smith, Elder, 1844.

—. *Geological Observations on South America.* Smith, Elder, 1846.

—. *A Monograph on the Sub-Class Cirripedia.* 2 vols. Ray Society, 1851–54.

—. *A Monograph on the Fossil Lepadidae, or, Pedunculated Cirripedes of Great Britain.* Palaeontographical Society, 1851.

—. *A Monograph on the Fossil Balanidae and Verrucidae of Great Britain.* Palaeontographical Society, 1854.

—. *On the Origin of Species by Means of Natural Selection, or the Preservation of Favoured Races in the Struggle for Life.* Murray, 1859.

—. *The Descent of Man, and Selection in relation to Sex.* 2 vols. Murray, 1871; 2nd ed. rev., 1874.

—. *The Expression of the Emotions in Man and Animals.* Murray, 1872.

—. *The Movements and Habits of Climbing Plants.* Murray, 1875.

—. *The Variation of Animals and Plants under Domestication.* 2nd ed. rev. 2 vols. Murray, 1875.

—. *The Effects of Cross and Self Fertilisation in the Vegetable Kingdom.* Murray, 1876.

—. *The Various Contrivances by which Orchids are Fertilised by Insects.* 2nd ed. Murray, 1877.

—. *The Different Forms of Flowers on Plants of the Same Species.* Murray, 1877.

—. *The Formation of Vegetable Mould, through the Action of Worms, with Observations on Their Habits.* Murray, 1881.

Darwin, F., ed. *The Life and Letters of Charles Darwin, including an Autobiographical Chapter.* 3 vols. Murray, 1887.

—. 'The Botanical Work of Darwin.' *Annals of Botany*, 13 (1899), ix–xix.

—. 'Darwin's Work on the Movements of Plants.' In Seward, *Darwin and Modern Science*, 385–400.

—, ed. *The Foundations of the 'Origin of Species': Two Essays written in 1842 and 1844.* Cambridge: at the U.P., 1909.

—. 'FitzRoy and Darwin, 1831–36.' *Nature*, 88 (1912), 547–48.

Bibliography

—. *Rustic Sounds and Other Studies in Literature and Natural History.* Murray, 1917.

—. *Springtime and Other Essays.* Murray, 1920.

— and Seward, A. C., eds. *More Letters of Charles Darwin: A Record of His Work in a Series of Hitherto Unpublished Letters.* 2 vols. Murray, 1903.

Darwin, G. 'Marriages between First Cousins in England and Their Effects.' *Fortnightly Review,* new ser., 18 (1875), 22–41.

Darwin, L. 'Memories of Down House.' *Nineteenth Century,* 106 (1929), 118–23.

David, D. *Intellectual Women and Victorian Patriarchy: Harriet Martineau, Elizabeth Barrett Browning, George Eliot.* Macmillan, 1987.

Davidoff, L. and Hall, C. *Family Fortunes: Men and Women of the English Middle Class, 1780–1850.* Hutchinson, 1987.

[Dawkins, W. B.] 'Darwin on Variation of Animals and Plants.' *ER,* 128 (1868), 414–450.

[—]. 'Darwin on the Descent of Man.' *ER,* 134 (1871), 195–235.

De Beer, G. 'Further Unpublished Letters of Charles Darwin.' *AS,* 14 (1958), 83–115.

—. 'Darwin's Journal.' *BBMNH,* 2 (1959), 1–21.

—. 'Some Unpublished Letters of Charles Darwin.' *NR,* 14 (1959), 12–66.

—. *Charles Darwin: Evolution by Natural Selection.* New York: Doubleday, 1964.

—. 'The Darwin Letters at Shrewsbury School.' *NR,* 23 (1968), 68–85.

De Morgan, S. E., ed. *Memoir of Augustus de Morgan.* Longmans *et al.,* 1882.

Dean, D. R. '"Through Science to Despair": Geology and the Victorians.' In Paradis and Postlewait, *Victorian Science,* 111–36.

Dell, R. S. 'Social and Economic Theories and Pastoral Concerns of a Victorian Archbishop.' *Journal of Ecclesiastical History,* 16 (1965), 196–208.

Dempster, W. J. *Patrick Matthew and Natural Selection.* Edinburgh: Harris, 1983.

Denton's Ilkley Directory, Guide Book, and Almanac. Ilkley, Yorks.: Denton, 1871.

D'Orbigny, A. 'General Considerations regarding the Palaeontology of South America compared with that of Europe.' *ENPJ,* 35 (1843), 362–72.

Desmond, A. *Archetypes and Ancestors: Palaeontology in Victorian London, 1850–1875.* Blond & Briggs, 1982; Chicago: University of Chicago Press, 1984.

—. 'Robert E. Grant: The Social Predicament of a Pre-Darwinian Transmutationist.' *JHB,* 17 (1984), 189–223.

—. 'Robert E. Grant's Later Views on Organic Development: The Swiney Lectures on "Palaeozoology", 1853–1857.' *Archives of Natural History,* 11 (1984), 395–413.

—. 'Darwin among the Gentry.' *London Review of Books,* 23 May 1985, pp. 9–10.

—. 'The Making of Institutional Zoology in London, 1822–1836.' *HS,* 23 (1985), 153–85, 223–50.

—. 'Artisan Resistance and Evolution in Britain, 1819–1848.' *Osiris,* 3 (1987), 77–110.

—. 'The Kentish Hog.' *London Review of Books,* 15 Oct. 1987, pp. 13–14.

—. 'Lamarckism and Democracy: Corporations, Corruption and Comparative Anatomy in the 1830s.' In J. Moore, *History,* 99–130.

—. *The Politics of Evolution: Morphology, Medicine, and Reform in Radical London.* Chicago: University of Chicago Press, 1989.

Di Gregario, M. A. 'The Dinosaur Connection: A Reinterpretation of T. H. Huxley's Evolutionary View.' *JHB*, 15 (1982), 397–418.

Dickens, C. *Bleak House.* Bradbury & Evans, 1860.

Duman, D. 'The Creation and Diffusion of a Professional Ideology in Nineteenth Century England.' *Sociological Review*, new ser., 27 (1979), 113–38.

Duncan, D. *The Life and Letters of Herbert Spencer.* Williams & Norgate, 1911.

Dupree, A. H. *Asa Gray, 1810–1888.* New York: Athenaeum, 1968.

Durant, J. 'Scientific Naturalism and Social Reform in the Thought of Alfred Russel Wallace.' *BJHS*, 12 (1979), 31–58.

—. 'The Ascent of Nature in Darwin's *Descent of Man*.' In Kohn, *Darwinian Heritage*, 283–306.

—, ed. *Darwinism and Divinity: Essays on Evolution and Religious Belief.* Oxford: Blackwell, 1985.

Edsall, N. C. *The Anti-Poor Law Movement, 1834–44.* Manchester: Manchester U.P., 1971.

Egerton, F. N. 'Refutation and Conjecture: Darwin's Response to Sedgwick's Attack on Chambers.' *SHPS*, 1 (1970), 176–83.

—. 'Darwin's Early Reading of Lamarck.' *Isis*, 67 (1976), 452–56.

—. 'Hewett C. Watson, Great Britain's First Phytogeographer.' *Huntia*, 3 (1979), 87–102.

Ellegard, A. *Darwin and the General Reader: The Reception of Darwin's Theory of Evolution in the British Periodical Press, 1859–1872.* Chicago: University of Chicago Press, 1990.

Elliotson, J. 'Reply to the Attacks on Phrenology.' *Lancet* 1 (1831–32), 287–94.

—. 'Address Introductory to the Winter Medical Session.' *Lancet*, 1 (1832–33), 33–41.

—. *Human Physiology.* Longman *et al.*, 1835.

Ellis, I. *Seven against Christ: A Study of 'Essays and Reviews'.* Leiden: E. J. Brill, 1980.

Eng, E. 'The Confrontation between Reason and Imagination: The Example of Darwin.' *Diogenes*, 95 (1976), 58–67.

Engels, F. *Dialectics of Nature.* New York: International Publishers, 1963.

Ensor, R. C. K. *England, 1870–1914.* Oxford: Clarendon Press, 1936.

[Epps, J.] 'Elements of Physiology.' *Medico-Chirurgical Review*, 9 (1828), 97–120.

—. *The Church of England's Apostacy.* Dinnis, 1834.

—. *Diary of the Late John Epps.* Kent, 1875.

Ereira, A. *The People's England.* Routledge & Kegan Paul, 1981.

Erskine, F. 'Darwin in Context: The London Years, 1837–1842.' Ph.D. thesis, Open University, 1987.

Essays and Reviews. 4th ed. Longmans *et al.*, 1861.

Evans, E. J. 'Some Reasons for the Growth of English Rural Anti–clericalism, *c.* 1750 – *c.* 1830.' *Past and Present*, no. 66 (1975), 84–109.

Evans, J. 'On Portions of a Cranium and of a Jaw, in the Slab Containing the Fossil Remains of the Archaeopteryx.' *Natural History Review*, 5 (1865), 415–21.

Eve, A. S. and Creasey, C. H. *Life and Work of John Tyndall.* Macmillan, 1945.

Bibliography

Evidence, Oral and Documentary, taken and received by the Commissioners appointed by His Majesty George IV. July 23d, 1826 . . . visiting the Universities of Scotland. 4 vols. Parliamentary Papers, 1837.

Farr, W. 'Medical Reform.' *Lancet*, 1 (1839–40), 105–11.

Farrar, F. W. *Men I Have Known*. New York: Crowell, 1897.

Farrar, R. *The Life of Frederic William Farrar*. New York: Crowell, 1904.

Feuer, L. 'Marxian Tragedians: A Death in the Family.' *Encounter*, 19 (1962), 23–32.

—. 'Is the "Darwin–Marx Correspondence" Authentic?' *AS*, 32 (1975), 1–12.

Fielding, K. J. 'Froude's Second Revenge: The Carlyles and the Wedgwoods.' *Prose Studies*, 4 (1981), 301–16.

Fiske, J. *Life and Letters of Edward Livingston Youmans: Comprising Correspondence with Spencer, Huxley, Tyndall, and Others*. Chapman & Hall, 1894.

—. *The Personal Letters of John Fiske*. Cedar Rapids, IA: Torch Press, 1939.

Flower, S. S. *List of the Vertebrate Animals exhibited in the Gardens of the Zoological Society of London, 1828–1927*. 3 vols. Zoological Society, 1929.

Foote, G. W. *Darwin on God*. Progressive Publishing Co., 1889.

[Forbes, E.] 'Vestiges of the Natural History of Creation.' *Lancet*, 2 (1844), 265–66.

—. *Literary Papers of the Late Professor Edward Forbes*. Reeve, 1855.

Forrest, D. W. *Francis Galton: The Life and Work of a Victorian Genius*. Elek, 1974.

Foster, M. and Lankester, E. R., eds. *The Scientific Memoirs of Thomas Henry Huxley*. 4 vols. Macmillan, 1898.

Francis, M. 'Naturalism and William Paley.' *History of European Ideas*, 10 (1989), 203–20.

Freeman, R. B. 'Charles Darwin on the Routes of Male Humble Bees.' *BBMNH*, 3 (1968), 177–89.

—. *The Works of Charles Darwin: An Annotated Bibliographical Handlist*. 2nd ed. rev. Folkestone, Kent: Dawson, 1977.

—. *Charles Darwin: A Companion*. Folkestone, Kent: Dawson, 1978.

—. 'Darwin's Negro Bird-Stuffer.' *NR*, 33 (1978), 83–85.

—. *Darwin and Gower Street*. Printed at University College London, 1982.

—. 'The Darwin Family.' *BJLS*, 17 (1982), 9–21.

—. *Darwin Pedigrees*. Privately printed, 1984.

— and Gautrey, P. J. 'Darwin's *Questions about the Breeding of Animals*, with a Note on *Queries about Expression*.' *JSBNH*, 5 (1969), 220–25.

— and Gautrey, P. J. 'Charles Darwin's *Queries about Expression*.' *BBMNH*, 4 (1972), 205–19.

French, R. D. *Antivivisection and Medical Science in Victorian Society*. Princeton, NJ: Princeton U.P., 1975.

Froude, J. A. *Thomas Carlyle: A History of His Life in London, 1834–1881*. 2 vols. Longmans *et al.*, 1884.

Gage, A. T. and Stearn, W. T. *A Bicentenary History of the Linnean Society of London*. Academic Press, 1988.

Gale, B. G. 'Darwin and the Concept of a Struggle for Existence: A Study in the Extrascientific Origins of Scientific Ideas.' *Isis*, 63 (1972), 321–44.

[Gallenga, A.] 'The Age We Live In.' *Fraser's Magazine*, 24 (1841), 1–15.

Galton, F. *English Men of Science: Their Nature and Nurture*. Macmillan, 1874.

—. *Inquiries into Human Faculty and Its Development*, 1883. Everyman's ed. Dent, n.d.

—. *Memories of My Life*. Methuen, 1908.

Gascoigne, J. *Cambridge in the Age of the Enlightenment: Science, Religion and Politics from the Restoration to the French Revolution*. Cambridge: Cambridge U.P., 1989.

Gasman, D. *The Scientific Origins of National Socialism: Social Darwinism in Ernst Haeckel and the German Monist League*. Macdonald, 1971.

Gay, P. *The Bourgeois Experience: Victoria to Freud*, vol. 1, *The Education of the Senses*. New York: Oxford U.P., 1984.

Geikie, A. *Memoir of Sir Andrew Crombie Ramsay*. Macmillan, 1895.

Geison, G. L. 'The Protoplasmic Theory of Life and the Vitalist–Mechanist Debate.' *Isis*, 60 (1969), 273–92.

George, H. *Progress and Poverty: An Inquiry into the Cause of Industrial Depressions, and of Increase of Want with Increase of Wealth. – The Remedy*. Kegan Paul et al., 1885.

Ghiselin, M. T. *The Triumph of the Darwinian Method*. Berkeley: University of California Press, 1969.

— and Jaffe, L. 'Phylogenetic Classification in Darwin's *Monograph of the Sub-Class Cirripedia*.' *Systematic Zoology*, 22 (1973), 132–40.

Gillespie, N. C. 'The Duke of Argyll, Evolutionary Anthropology, and the Art of Scientific Controversy.' *Isis*, 68 (1977), 40–54.

—. *Charles Darwin and the Problem of Creation*. Chicago: University of Chicago Press, 1979.

—. 'Preparing for Darwin: Conchology and Natural Theology in Anglo–American Natural History.' *SHB*, 7 (1984), 93–145.

—. 'Divine Design and the Industrial Revolution: William Paley's Abortive Reform of Natural Theology.' *Isis*, 81 (1990), 214–29.

Gilley, S. 'The Huxley–Wilberforce Debate: A Reconsideration.' In K. Robbins, ed., *Religion and Humanism*, 325–40. Oxford: Blackwell, for the Ecclesiastical History Society, 1981.

Gillispie, C. C. *Genesis and Geology: A Study in the Relations of Scientific Thought, Natural Theology, and Social Opinion in Great Britain, 1790–1850*. Cambridge, MA: Harvard U.P., 1951.

Glastonbury, M. 'Holding the Pens.' In *Inspiration and Drudgery: Notes on Literature and Domestic Labour in the Nineteenth Century*, 27–48. Women's Research and Resources Centre Publications, 1978.

Glick, T. F., ed. *The Comparative Reception of Darwinism*. Austin: University of Texas Press, 1974.

Godlee, R. J. 'Thomas Wharton Jones.' *British Journal of Ophthalmology*, 93 (1921), 97–117, 145–56.

Golby, J., ed. *Culture and Society in Britain, 1850–1890*. Oxford: Oxford U.P., 1986.

Goodway, D. *London Chartism, 1838–1848*. Cambridge: Cambridge U.P., 1982.

Goodwin, H. 'Funeral Sermon for Charles Darwin.' *Walks in the Region of Science and Faith*, 297–310. Murray, 1883.

Gordon, E. O. *The Life and Correspondence of William Buckland*. Murray, 1894.

Gould, J. *The Birds of Europe*. Printed for the Author, 1837.

—. 'Mr. Darwin's collection of *Birds*, a series of *Ground Finches*.' *PZSL*, 5 (1837), 4–7.

Bibliography

—. 'Three species of the genus *Orpheus*.' *PZSL*, 5 (1837), 26–27.

—. 'A new species of *Rhea*.' *PZSL*, 5 (1837), 35–36.

—. *The Birds of Australia and the Adjacent Islands.* Printed for the Author, 1837–38.

Gould, S. J. 'Darwin and the Captain.' *Natural History*, Jan. 1976, pp. 32–34.

—. 'Darwin's Delay.' *Ever Since Darwin*, 21–27. New York: Norton, 1977.

—. *Ontogeny and Phylogeny.* Cambridge, MA: Harvard U.P., 1977.

Graber, R. B. and Miles, L. P. 'In Defence of Darwin's Father.' *HS*, 26 (1988), 97–102.

Graham, W. *The Creed of Science: Religious, Moral, and Social.* Kegan Paul, 1881.

Grant, A. *The Story of the University of Edinburgh during its first Three Hundred Years.* 2 vols. Longmans *et al.*, 1884.

Grant, R. E. *Dissertatio Physiologica Inauguralis, de Circuito Sanguinis in Foetu.* Edinburgh: Ballantyne, 1814.

—. 'Notice of a New Zoophyte (Cliona celata, Gr.) from the Firth of Forth.' *ENPJ*, 1 (1826), 78–81.

—. 'On the Structure and Nature of the Spongilla friabilis.' *Edinburgh Philosophical Journal*, 14 (1826), 270–84.

—. 'Notice regarding the Ova of the Pontobdella muricata, Lam.' *Edinburgh Journal of Science*, 7 (1827), 121–25.

?[—]. 'Of the Changes which Life has Experienced on the Globe.' *ENPJ*, 3 (1827), 298–301.

—. *On the Study of Medicine.* Taylor, 1833.

—. *Tabular View of the Primary Divisions of the Animal Kingdom.* Walton & Maberly, 1861.

Grant Duff, [U.] *The Life-Work of Lord Avebury (Sir John Lubbock), 1834–1913.* Watts, 1924.

Gray, A. *Natural Selection Not Inconsistent with Natural Theology: A Free Examination of Darwin's Treatise on the Origin of Species and of Its American Reviewers.* Trübner, 1861.

Grayson, D. K. *The Establishment of Human Antiquity.* New York: Academic Press, 1983.

Green, J. H. *An Address delivered in King's College, London, at the Commencement of the Medical Session, October 1, 1832.* Fellowes, 1832.

Greene, J. C. 'Reflections on the Progress of Darwin Studies.' *JHB*, 8 (1975), 243–73.

—. *Science, Ideology, and World View: Essays in the History of Evolutionary Ideas.* Berkeley: University of California Press, 1981.

Gregory, F. *Scientific Materialism in Nineteenth Century Germany.* Dordrecht, Holland: Reidel, 1977.

Grinnell, G. 'The Rise and Fall of Darwin's First Theory of Transmutation.' *JHB*, 7 (1974), 259–73.

Groeben, C., ed. *Charles Darwin – Anton Dohrn Correspondence.* Naples: Macchiaroli, 1982.

Grove, W. R. *The Correlation of Physical Forces . . . followed by a Discourse on Continuity.* 5th ed. Longmans *et al.*, 1867.

Gruber, H. E. *Darwin on Man: A Psychological Study of Scientific Creativity, together with Darwin's Early and Unpublished Notebooks, transcribed and annotated by Paul H. Barrett.* New York: Dutton, 1974.

—. 'Going the Limit: Toward the Construction of Darwin's Theory (1832–1839).' In Kohn, *Darwinian Heritage*, 9–34.

— and Gruber, V. 'The Eye of Reason: Darwin's Development during the *Beagle* Voyage.' *Isis*, 53 (1962), 186–200.

Gruber, J. W. *A Conscience in Conflict: The Life of St. George Jackson Mivart.* New York: Temple University Publications/Columbia U.P., 1960.

—. 'Who was the *Beagle*'s Naturalist?' *BJHS*, 4 (1969), 266–82.

Gunther, A. E. *The Founders of Science at the British Museum, 1753–1900.* Halesworth, Suffolk: Halesworth, 1980.

Haeckel, E. *Generelle Morphologie der Organismen: Allgemeine Grundzüge der organischen Formen-wissenschaft, mechanisch begründet durch die von Charles Darwin reformirte Descendenz-Theorie.* 2 vols. Berlin: Reimer, 1866.

—. *The History of Creation; or, the Development of the Earth and Its Inhabitants by the Action of Natural Causes.* 2 vols. New York: Appleton, 1876.

Haight, G. S. *George Eliot and John Chapman, with Chapman's Diaries.* 2nd ed. Hamden, CT: Archon, 1969.

Halcombe, J. J. 'The Curate Question.' In J. J. Halcombe, ed., *The Church and Her Curates: A Series of Essays on the Need for More Clergy and the Best Means of Supporting Them*, 17–36. Gardner, 1874.

Halévy, E. *The Triumph of Reform, 1830–1841.* Benn, 1950.

—. *A History of the English People in 1815.* Ark, 1987.

Hall, A. R. *The Abbey Scientists.* Nicholson, 1966.

[Hall, B.] 'Voyages of Captains King and Fitzroy.' *ER*, 69 (1839), 467–93.

Hammond, J. L. *Gladstone and the Irish Nation.* Reprint ed. Cass, 1964.

Hare, J. C., ed. *Essays and Tales by John Sterling.* 2 vols. Parker, 1848.

Harrison, J. F. C. *Early Victorian Britain, 1832–51.* Fontana, 1979.

—. 'Early English Radicals and the Medical Fringe.' In W. F. Bynum and R. Porter, eds., *Medical Fringe and Medical Orthodoxy, 1750–1850*, 198–215. Croom Helm, 1987.

Hart, A. T. *The Country Priest in English History.* Phoenix House, 1959.

—. *The Curate's Lot: The Story of the Unbeneficed English Clergy.* Newton Abbot, Devon: Country Book Club, 1971.

—. *The Parson and the Publican.* New York: Vantage Press, 1983.

Harvie, C., Martin, G., and Scharf, A., eds. *Industrialisation and Culture, 1830–1914.* Macmillan, 1970.

Healey, E. *Wives of Fame: Mary Livingstone, Jenny Marx, Emma Darwin.* Sidgwick & Jackson, 1986.

Helmstadter, R. J. 'W. R. Greg: A Manchester Creed.' In Helmstadter and Lightman, *Victorian Faith*, 187–222.

— and Lightman, B., eds. *Victorian Faith in Crisis: Essays on Continuity and Change in Nineteenth-Century Religious Belief.* Macmillan, 1990.

Herbert, S. 'Darwin, Malthus, and Selection.' *JHB*, 4 (1971), 209–17.

—. 'The Place of Man in the Development of Darwin's Theory of Transmutation. Part 1. To July 1837.' *JHB*, 7 (1974), 217–58.

—. 'The Place of Man in the Development of Darwin's Theory of Transmutation. Part 2.' *JHB*, 10 (1977), 155–227.

—, ed. *The Red Notebook of Charles Darwin.* Ithaca, NY: Cornell U.P., 1980.

—. 'Darwin the Young Geologist.' In Kohn, *Darwinian Heritage*, 483–510.

Herschel, J. F. W. *A Preliminary Discourse on the Study of Natural Philosophy.* New ed. Longman *et al.*, 1830.

Bibliography

Heyck, T. W. *The Transformation of Intellectual Life in Victorian England.* Croom Helm, 1982.

Hill, F. 'Squire and Parson in Early Victorian Lincolnshire.' *History,* 58 (1973), 337–49.

Hilton, B. *The Age of Atonement: The Influence of Evangelicalism on Social and Economic Thought, 1785–1865.* Oxford: Clarendon Press, 1988.

Himmelfarb, G. *Darwin and the Darwinian Revolution.* Chatto & Windus, 1959.

Historical and Descriptive Catalogue of the Darwin Memorial at Downe House, Downe, Kent. Edinburgh: Livingstone, 1969.

Hobsbawm, E. J. and Rudé, G. *Captain Swing.* Lawrence & Wishart, 1969.

Hodge, M. J. S. 'Lamarck's Science of Living Bodies.' *BJHS,* 5 (1971), 323–52.

—. 'The Universal Gestation of Nature: Chambers' *Vestiges* and *Explanations.*' *JHB,* 5 (1972), 127–51.

—. 'England.' In Glick, *Comparative Reception,* 1–31.

—. 'Darwin and the Laws of the Animate Part of the Terrestrial System (1835–37): On the Lyellian Origins of his Zoonomical Explanatory Program.' *SHB,* 6 (1983), 1–106.

—. 'Darwin, Species and the Theory of Natural Selection.' In S. Atran *et al., Histoire du concept d'espèce dans les sciences de la vie,* 227–52. Paris: Fondation Singer–Polignac, 1985.

—. 'Darwin as a Lifelong Generation Theorist.' In Kohn, *Darwinian Heritage,* 207–43.

— and Kohn, D. 'The Immediate Origins of Natural Selection.' In Kohn, *Darwinian Heritage,* 185–206.

Hole, R. *Pulpits, Politics and Public Order in England, 1760–1832.* Cambridge: Cambridge U.P., 1989.

Holt, R. V. *The Unitarian Contribution to Social Progress in England.* 2nd rev. ed. Lindsey Press, 1952.

Holyoake, G. J. *Sixty Years of an Agitator's Life.* 3rd ed. 2 vols. Unwin, 1906.

Hooker, J. D. *Himalayan Journals: Notes of a Naturalist in Bengal, the Sikkim and Nepal Himalayas, the Khasia Mountains, &c.* 2nd ed. 2 vols. Murray, 1855.

—. 'Address of Joseph D. Hooker . . .' *BAAS* (Norwich 1868), 1869, pp. lviii–lxxv.

—. 'Reminiscences of Darwin.' *Nature,* 60 (1899), 187–88.

Howarth, O. J. R. and Howarth, E. K. *A History of Darwin's Parish, Downe, Kent.* Southampton: Russell, [1933].

Hughes, R. E. 'Alfred Russel Wallace: Some Notes on the Welsh Connection.' *BJHS,* 22 (1989), 401–418.

Hull, D. L. *Darwin and His Critics: The Reception of Darwin's Theory of Evolution by the Scientific Community.* Chicago: University of Chicago Press, 1983.

Hutchinson, H. G. *Life of Sir John Lubbock, Lord Avebury.* 2 vols. Macmillan, 1914.

Huxley, L. *Life and Letters of Sir Joseph Dalton Hooker, O.M., G.C.S.I., based on materials collected and arranged by Lady Hooker.* 2 vols. Murray, 1918.

—. 'The Home Life of Charles Darwin.' *The R.P.A. Annual for 1921,* 3–9. Watts, 1921.

[Huxley, T. H.] 'The Vestiges of Creation.' *British and Foreign Medico-Chirurgical Review,* 13 (1854), 425–39.

—. 'Comparative Literature: Science.' *Westminster Review*, new ser., 7 (1855), 241–47.

—. 'On Certain Zoological Arguments Commonly adduced in favour of the Hypothesis of the Progressive Development of Animal Life in Time.' In Foster and Lankester, *Scientific Memoirs*, 1:300–304.

—. 'Lectures on General Natural History. Lecture XII. The *Cirripedia*.' *Medical Times and Gazette*, 15 (1857), 238–41.

—. 'Man and the Apes.' *Athenaeum*, 30 Mar. and 13 April 1861, pp. 433, 498.

—. *On Our Knowledge of the Causes of the Phenomena of Organic Nature.* Hardwicke, 1862.

—. 'Criticisms on "The Origin of Species".' *Natural History Review*, 4 (1864), 566–80.

—. 'The Natural History of Creation.' *Academy*, 1 (1869), 13–14, 40–43.

—. 'On Descartes' "Discourse Touching the Method of Using One's Reason Rightly, and of Seeking Scientific Truth".' *Macmillan's Magazine*, 22 (1870), 69–80.

—. 'Introductory Notice.' In T. H. Huxley *et al.*, *Charles Darwin: Memorial Notices reprinted from 'Nature'*, [ix]–xiii. Macmillan, 1882.

—. *Darwiniana.* Macmillan, 1893.

—. *Method and Results.* Macmillan, 1893.

—. *Science and Education.* Macmillan, 1893.

—. *Discourse Biological and Geological.* Macmillan, 1894.

—. *Man's Place in Nature and Other Anthropological Essays.* Macmillan, 1894.

Hyman, S. E. 'A Darwin Sidelight: The Shape of the Young Man's Nose.' *Atlantic Monthly*, 220 (1967), 96–104.

Irvine, W. *Apes, Angels, and Victorians: Darwin, Huxley, and Evolution.* New York: McGraw–Hill, 1955.

Jackson, P. *George Scharf's London: Sketches and Watercolours of a Changing City, 1820–50.* Murray, 1987.

Jacyna, L. S. 'Immanence or Transcendance: Theories of Life and Organization in Britain, 1790–1835.' *Isis*, 74 (1983), 311–29.

[Jameson, R.] 'Observations on the Nature and Importance of Geology.' *ENPJ*, 1 (1826), 293–302.

Jardine, W. *Memoirs of Hugh Edwin Strickland.* Van Voorst, 1858.

[Jenkin, H. C. Fleeming]. 'The Origin of Species.' *North British Review*, 46 (1867), 277–318.

Jenkins, M. *The General Strike of 1842.* Lawrence & Wishart, 1980.

Jennings, H. *Pandaemonium, 1660–1886: The Coming of the Machine as seen by Contemporary Observers.* Ed. M. Jennings and C. Madge. Deutsch, 1985.

Jensen, J. V. 'The X Club: Fraternity of Victorian Scientists.' *BJHS*, 5 (1970), 63–72.

—. 'Return to the Wilberforce–Huxley Debate.' *BJHS*, 21 (1988), 161–79.

Jenyns, Leonard. *See* Blomefield, Leonard.

Jesperson, P. H. 'Charles Darwin and Dr. Grant.' *Lychnos* (1948–49), 159–67.

Johnston, J. O. *Life and Letters of Henry Parry Liddon.* Longmans *et al.*, 1904.

Jones, G. 'The Social History of Darwin's *Descent of Man*.' *Economy and Society*, 7 (1978), 1–23.

Jones, H. F. *Samuel Butler, Author of Erewhon (1835–1902): A Memoir.* 2 vols. Macmillan, 1920.

Jordan, D. S. *The Days of a Man: Being Memories of a Naturalist, Teacher, and Minor Prophet of Democracy*. 2 vols. Yonkers–on–Hudson, NY: World Book, 1922.

Judd, J. W. *The Coming of Evolution: The Story of a Great Revolution in Science*. Cambridge: Cambridge U.P., 1910.

Keegan, R. T. and Gruber, H. E. 'Love, Death, and Continuity in Darwin's Thinking.' *JHBS*, 19 (1983), 15–30.

Keith, A. 'Neglected Darwin.' *The R.P.A. Annual for 1923*, 3–9. Watts, 1923.

—. *Darwin Revalued*. Watts, 1955.

Kelly, A. *The Descent of Darwin: The Popularization of Darwinism in Germany, 1860–1914*. Chapel Hill: University of North Carolina Press, 1981.

Keynes, M. *Leonard Darwin, 1850–1943*. Cambridge: printed at the U.P., 1943.

Keynes, R. D., ed. *The Beagle Record: Selections from the Original Pictorial Records and Written Accounts of the Voyage of H. M. S. 'Beagle'*. Cambridge: Cambridge U.P., 1979.

—, ed. *Charles Darwin's 'Beagle' Diary*. Cambridge: Cambridge U.P., 1988.

King, W. 'The Reputed Fossil Man of the Neanderthal.' *Quarterly Journal of Science*, 1 (1864), 88–97.

King–Hele, D. *Doctor of Revolution: The Life and Genius of Erasmus Darwin*. Faber & Faber, 1977.

—, ed. *The Letters of Erasmus Darwin*. Cambridge: Cambridge U.P., 1981.

[Kingsley, F.] *Charles Kingsley: His Letters and Memories of His Life*. 2 vols. King, 1877.

Kirby, W. 'Introductory Address.' *Zoological Journal*, 2 (1825), 1–8.

Kirsop, W. 'W. R. Greg and Charles Darwin in Edinburgh and After – An Antipodean Gloss.' *Transactions of the Cambridge Bibliographical Society*, 7 (1979), 376–90.

Knight, C. *London*. 6 vols. Knight, 1841–44.

Kohn, D. 'Theories to Work By: Rejected Theories, Reproduction, and Darwin's Path to Natural Selection.' *SHB*, 4 (1980), 67–170.

—. 'On the Origin of the Principle of Diversity.' *Science*, 213 (1981), 1105–108.

—, ed. *The Darwinian Heritage*. Princeton, NJ: Princeton U.P., 1985.

—. 'Darwin's Principle of Divergence as Internal Dialogue.' In Kohn, *Darwinian Heritage*, 245–57.

—. 'Darwin's Ambiguity: The Secularization of Biological Meaning.' *BJHS*, 22 (1989), 215–39.

—, Smith, S., and Stauffer, R. C. 'New Light on *The Foundations of the Origin of Species*: A Reconstruction of the Archival Record.' *JHB*, 15 (1982), 419–42.

Kottler, M. J. 'Alfred Russel Wallace, the Origin of Man, and Spiritualism.' *Isis*, 65 (1974), 145–92.

—. 'Charles Darwin's Biological Species Concept and Theory of Geographic Speciation: The Transmutation Notebooks.' *AS*, 35 (1978), 275–97.

—. 'Charles Darwin and Alfred Russel Wallace: Two Decades of Debate over Natural Selection.' In Kohn, *Darwinian Heritage*, 367–432.

Krause, E. *Erasmus Darwin . . . with a Preliminary Notice by Charles Darwin*. Trans. W. S. Dallas. Murray, 1879.

La Vergata, A. 'Images of Darwin: A Historiographic Overview.' In Kohn, *Darwinian Heritage*, 901–72.

Lansbury, C. 'Gynaecology, Pornography, and the Antivivisection Movement.' *VS*, 28 (1985), 413–37.

Darwin

Lefebvre, J. P., ed. *Marx–Engels: Lettres sur les sciences de la nature*. Paris: Editions Sociales, 1973.

LeMahieu, D. L. *The Mind of William Paley: A Philosopher and His Age*. Lincoln: University of Nebraska Press, 1976.

Lenoir, T. 'The Darwin Industry.' *JHB*, 20 (1987), 115–30.

Lewes, G. H. 'Hereditary Influence, Animal and Human.' *Westminster Review*, 66 (1856), 135–62.

Liddon, H. P. *The Recovery of St. Thomas: A Sermon preached in St. Paul's Cathedral on the Second Sunday after Easter, April 23, 1882, with a Prefatory Note on the Late Mr. Darwin*. Rivingtons, 1882.

Lightman, B. *The Origins of Agnosticism: Victorian Unbelief and the Limits of Knowledge*. Baltimore, MD: Johns Hopkins U.P., 1987.

Litchfield, H. (*née* Darwin). *Richard Buckley Litchfield: A Memoir written for His Friends*. Cambridge: printed at the U.P. 1910.

—. *Emma Darwin: A Century of Family Letters, 1792–1896*. 2 vols. Murray, 1915; private ed. Cambridge: printed at the U.P., 1904.

Loewenberg, B. J., ed. *Calendar of the Letters of Charles Robert Darwin to Asa Gray*. Wilmington, DE: Scholarly Resources, 1973.

Lorimer, D. A. *Colour, Class and the Victorians: English Attitudes to the Negro in the Mid-Nineteenth Century*. Leicester: Leicester U.P., 1978.

Lucas, J. R. 'Wilberforce and Huxley: A Legendary Encounter.' *Historical Journal*, 22 (1979), 313–30.

Lurie, E. *Louis Agassiz: A Life in Science*. Chicago: University of Chicago Press, 1960.

Lyell, Charles. *Principles of Geology*. 3 vols. Murray, 1830–33.

—. 'Address to the Geological Society.' *PGSL*, 2 (1837), 479–523.

—. 'Anniversary Address.' *QJGS*, 7 (1851), xxxii–lxxvi.

—. *The Geological Evidences of the Antiquity of Man, with Remarks on the Theories of the Origin of Species by Variation*. 2nd ed. rev. Murray, 1863.

Lyell, [K. M.] *Life, Letters, and Journals of Sir Charles Lyell, Bart.* 2 vols. Murray, 1881.

[Lytton, B.] *What Will He Do With It?* 4 vols. Edinburgh: Blackwood, 1859.

McCabe, J. *Life and Letters of George Jacob Holyoake.* 2 vols. Watts, 1908.

McCalman, I. 'Unrespectable Radicalism: Infidels and Pornography in Early Nineteenth Century London.' *Past and Present*, 104 (1984), 74–110.

McClachlan, H. *The Unitarian Movement in the Religious Life of England: I. Its Contribution to Thought and Learning, 1700–1900*. Allen & Unwin, 1934.

Macfarlane, A. *Marriage and Love in England: Modes of Reproduction, 1300–1840*. Oxford: Blackwell, 1986.

McKendrick, N. 'Josiah Wedgwood and Factory Discipline.' *Historical Journal*, 4 (1961), 30–55.

—. 'The Role of Science in the Industrial Revolution: A Study of Josiah Wedgwood as a Scientist and Industrial Chemist.' In M. Teich and R. Young, eds., *Changing Perspectives in the History of Science: Essays in Honour of Joseph Needham*, 274–319. Heinemann, 1973.

MacLeod, R. M. 'The X Club: A Social Network of Science in Late-Victorian England.' *NR*, 24 (1970), 305–22.

—. 'Of Medals and Men: A Reward System in Victorian Science, 1826–1914.' *NR*, 26 (1971), 81–105.

—. 'The Ayrton Incident: A Commentary on the Relations of Science and

Bibliography

Government in England, 1870–1873.' In A. Thackray and E. Mendelsohn, eds., *Science and Values: Patterns of Tradition and Change*, 45–78. New York: Humanities Press, 1974.

—. 'Evolutionism, Internationalism and Commercial Enterprise in Science: The International Scientific Series, 1871–1910.' In A. J. Meadows, ed., *Development of Science Publishing in Europe*, 63–93. Amsterdam: Elsevier, 1980.

—. 'Whigs and Savants.' In I. Inkster and J. Morrell, *Metropolis and Province: Science in British Culture, 1780–1850*. Hutchinson, 1983

McMenemey, W. H. 'Education and the Medical Reform Movement.' In F. N. L. Poynter, ed., *The Evolution of Medical Education in Britain*, 135–54. Pitman, 1966.

McNeil, M. *Under the Banner of Science: Erasmus Darwin and His Age*. Manchester: Manchester U.P., 1987.

Malthus, T. R. *An Essay on the Principle of Population*. 6th ed. 2 vols. Murray, 1826.

Manier, E. *The Young Darwin and His Cultural Circle: A Study of the Influences which helped shape the Language and Logic of the First Drafts of the Theory of Natural Selection*. Dordrecht, Holland: Reidel, 1978.

Mann, P. G. *Collections for a Life and Background of James Manby Gully, M.D.* [Malvern]: privately printed at Bosbury Press, 1983.

Mansergh, J. F. 'Charles Darwin.' *NQ*, 7th ser., 5 (1883), 46.

Marchant, J. *Alfred Russel Wallace: Letters and Reminiscences*. 2 vols. Cassell, 1916.

Marcus, S. *The Other Victorians: A Study of Sexuality and Pornography in Mid-Nineteenth-Century England*. New York: Basic Books, 1966.

Marsh, J. 'Charles Darwin – Justice of the Peace in Bromley, Kent.' *Justice of the Peace*, 147 (1983), 636–37.

Marshall, A. J. *Darwin and Huxley in Australia*. Sydney: Hodder & Stoughton, 1970.

Martin, E. *First Conversation on the Being of God*. Printed by Emma Martin, 1844.

Martineau, H. 'Right and Wrong in Boston.' *London and Westminster Review*, 32 (1838–39), 1–59.

—. *Eastern Life, Present and Past*. 3 vols. Moxon, 1848.

—. *Harriet Martineau's Autobiography*, 1877. 2 vols. Virago, 1983.

Martineau, J. *The Bible: What It Is, and What It Is Not; A Lecture delivered at Paradise Street Chapel, Liverpool, on Tuesday, February 19, 1839*. Liverpool: Willmer & Smith, 1839.

Marx, K. and Engels, F. *Selected Correspondence, 1846–1895*. Lawrence & Wishart, 1943.

Matthew, P. *On Naval Timber and Arboriculture*. Longman, 1831.

—. *Emigration Fields: North America, The Cape, Australia, and New Zealand, describing these Countries, and giving a Comparative View of the Advantages they present to British Settlers*. Edinburgh: Black, 1839.

Mellersh, H. E. L. *FitzRoy of the Beagle*. Hart–Davis, 1968.

Memorable Unitarians: Being a Series of Brief Biographical Sketches. British & Foreign Unitarian Association, 1906.

Miall, L. C. *The Life and Work of Charles Darwin: A Lecture delivered to the Leeds Philosophical and Literary Society, on February 6th, 1883*. Leeds: Jackson, 1883.

Middlemiss, J. L. *A Zoo on Wheels: Bostock and Wombwell's Menagerie*. Burton-on-Trent, Staffs.: Dalebrook, 1987.

Darwin

Miles, S. J. 'Clémence Royer et *De l'origine des espèces*: traductrice ou traîtresse?' *Revue de synthèse*, 4th ser. (1989), 61–83.

Miller, G. 'The Death of Charles Darwin.' *JHM*, 14 (1959), 529–30.

Mills, E. I. 'A View of Edward Forbes, Naturalist.' *Archives of Natural History*, 11 (1984), 365–93.

Milner, R. 'Darwin for the Prosecution, Wallace for the Defense: Part I, How Two Great Naturalists Put the Supernatural on Trial.' *North Country Naturalist*, 2 (1990), 19–35.

—. 'Darwin for the Prosecution, Wallace for the Defense: Part II, Spirit of a Dead Controversy.' *North Country Naturalist*, 2 (1990), 37–49.

[Mivart, St G.] 'Difficulties of the Theory of Natural Selection,' *Month*, 11 (1869), 35–53, 134–53, 274–89.

[—]. 'The Descent of Man.' *QR*, 131 (1871), 47–90.

—. *On the Genesis of Species*. 2nd ed. Macmillan, 1871.

—. *Essays and Criticisms*. 2 vols. Osgood, 1892.

—. 'Some Reminiscences of Thomas Henry Huxley.' *Nineteenth Century*, 42 (1897), 985–98.

Monsarrat, A. *Thackeray: An Uneasy Victorian*. Cassell, 1980.

Montgomery, H. E. L. 'Emma Darwin.' *The Month*, 29 (1963), 288–94.

Montgomery, W. M. 'Germany.' In Glick, *Comparative Reception*, 81–116.

Moody, J. W. T. 'The Reading of the Darwin and Wallace Papers: An Historical "Non–Event".' *JSBNH*, 5 (1971), 474–76.

Moore, D. T. 'Geological Collectors and Collections of the India Museum, London, 1801–79.' *Archives of Natural History*, 10 (1982), 399–427.

Moore, J. R. 'Could Darwinism be introduced in France?' *BJHS*, 10 (1977), 246–51.

—. 'On the Education of Darwin's Sons: The Correspondence between Charles Darwin and the Reverend G. V. Reed, 1857–1864.' *NR*, 32 (1977), 41–70.

—. *The Post-Darwinian Controversies: A Study of the Protestant Struggle to come to terms with Darwin in Great Britain and America, 1870–1900*. Cambridge: Cambridge U.P., 1979.

—. 'Creation and the Problem of Charles Darwin.' *BJHS*, 14 (1981), 189–200.

—. 'Charles Darwin Lies in Westminster Abbey.' *BJLS*, 17 (1982), 97–113.

—. '1859 and All That: Remaking the Story of Evolution-and-Religion.' In Chapman and Duval, *Charles Darwin*, 167–94.

—. 'On Revolutionizing the Darwin Industry: A Centennial Retrospect.' *Radical Philosophy*, no. 37 (1984), 13–22.

—. 'Darwin of Down: The Evolutionist as Squarson–Naturalist.' In Kohn, *Darwinian Heritage*, 435–81.

—. 'Darwin's Genesis and Revelations.' *Isis*, 76 (1985), 570–80.

—. 'Evangelicals and Evolution: Henry Drummond, Herbert Spencer, and the Naturalization of the Spiritual World.' *Scottish Journal of Theology*, 38 (1985), 383–417.

—. 'Herbert Spencer's Henchmen: The Evolution of Protestant Liberals in Late Nineteenth–Century America.' In Durant, *Darwinism*, 76–100.

—. 'Crisis without Revolution: The Ideological Watershed in Victorian England.' *Revue de synthèse*, 4th ser. (1986), 53–78.

—. 'Socializing Darwinism: Historiography and the Fortunes of a Phrase.' In L. Levidow, ed., *Science as Politics*, 38–80. Free Association, 1986.

—. 'Born-Again Social Darwinism.' *AS*, 44 (1987), 409–17.

Bibliography

—, ed. *Religion in Victorian Britain*, vol. 3, *Sources*. Manchester: Manchester U.P., 1988.

—. 'Freethought, Secularism, Agnosticism: The Case of Charles Darwin.' In G. Parsons, ed., *Religion in Victorian Britain*, vol. 1, *Traditions*, 274–319. Manchester: Manchester U.P., 1988.

—. 'Darwinizing History: Sociobiology versus Sociology.' *BJHS*, 22 (1989), 429–32.

—, ed. *History, Humanity and Evolution: Essays for John C. Greene*. New York: Cambridge U.P., 1989.

—. 'Of Love and Death: Why Darwin "gave up Christianity".' In J. Moore, *History*, 195–229.

—. 'Theodicy and Society: The Crisis of the Intelligentsia.' In Helmstadter and Lightman, *Victorian Faith*, 153–86.

—. 'Deconstructing Darwinism: The Politics of Evolution in the 1860s.' *JHB*, 24 (1991), 353–408.

— *et al. Science and Metaphysics in Victorian Britain*. Milton Keynes, Bucks.: Open U.P., 1981.

Morley, J. *The Life of William Ewart Gladstone*. 3 vols. Macmillan, 1903.

Morley, J. *Death, Heaven, and the Victorians*. Pittsburgh, PA: University of Pittsburgh Press, 1971.

Morrell, J. B. 'Science and Scottish University Reform: Edinburgh in 1826.' *BJHS*, 6 (1972), 39–56.

—. 'London Institutions and Lyell's Career, 1820–41.' *BJHS*, 9 (1976), 132–46.

— and Thackray, A. *Gentlemen of Science: Early Years of the British Association for the Advancement of Science*. Oxford: Clarendon Press, 1981.

Morus, I. R. 'The Politics of Power: Reform and Regulation in the Work of William Robert Grove.' Ph.D. thesis, University of Cambridge, 1989.

Mozley, J. B. 'The Argument of Design.' *QR*, 127 (1869), 134–76.

Mudie, R. *The Modern Athens: A Dissection and Demonstration of Men and Things in the Scotch Capital*. Knight & Lacey, 1825.

Müller, J. *Handbuch der Physiologie des Menschen für Vorlesungen*. Koblenz: Hölscher, 1833–34.

Murphy, H. R. 'The Ethical Revolt against Christian Orthodoxy in Early Victorian England.' *American Historical Review*, 60 (1955), 800–817.

Napier, M. *Selection from the Correspondence of the Late Macvey Napier*. Macmillan, 1879.

Nash, L. A. 'Some Memories of Charles Darwin.' *Overland Monthly*, 2nd ser., 16 (1890), 404–408.

[Newman, F. W.] *A History of the Hebrew Monarchy from the Administration of Samuel to the Babylonish Captivity*. Chapman, 1847.

—. *The Soul, Her Sorrows and Her Aspirations: An Essay towards the Natural History of the Soul, as the True Basis of Theology*. 2nd ed. Chapman, 1849.

—. *Phases of Faith; or, Passages from the History of My Creed*. Chapman, 1850.

Nicholas, F. W. and Nicholas, J. M. *Charles Darwin in Australia, with Illustrations and Additional Commentary from Other Members of the 'Beagle's' Company, including Conrad Martens, Augustus Earle, Captain FitzRoy, Philip Gidley King, and Syms Covington*. Cambridge: Cambridge U.P., 1989.

Norton, A. *The Evidences of the Genuineness of the Gospels*. 2nd ed. 2 vols. Chapman, 1847.

Olby, R. C. 'Charles Darwin's Manuscript of *Pangenesis*.' *BJHS*, 1 (1963), 251–63.

Oldroyd, D. R. 'How did Darwin arrive at His Theory? The Secondary Literature to 1982.' *HS*, 22 (1984), 325–74.
— and Langham, I., eds. *The Wider Domain of Evolutionary Thought.* Dordrecht, Holland: Reidel, 1983.
Oppenheim, J. *The Other World: Spiritualism and Psychical Research in England, 1850–1914.* Cambridge: Cambridge U.P., 1985.
Ospovat, D. 'Perfect Adaptation and Teleological Explanation: Approaches to the Problem of the History of Life in the Mid–nineteenth Century.' *SHB*, 2 (1978), 33–56.
—. 'Darwin after Malthus.' *JHB*, 12 (1979), 211–30.
—. *The Development of Darwin's Theory: Natural History, Natural Theology, and Natural Selection, 1838–1859.* Cambridge: Cambridge U.P., 1981.
—. 'Darwin on Huxley and Divergence: Some Darwin Notes on His Meeting with Huxley, Hooker, and Wollaston in April, 1856.' Unpublished typescript.
Owen, R. 'On the Osteology of the Chimpanzee and Orang Utan.' *Transactions of the Zoological Society* (London), 1 (1835), 343–79.
—. *Fossil Mammalia.* Pt 1, *The Zoology of the Voyage of H.M.S. 'Beagle'*, ed. C. Darwin. Smith, Elder, 1838–40.
—. 'Report on British Fossil Reptiles. Part 2.' In *BAAS* (Plymouth 1841), 1842, pp. 60–204.
—. 'Notices of Some Fossil Mammalia of South America.' In 'Notices and Abstracts.' *BAAS* (Southampton 1846), 1847, pp. 65–66.
—. 'Osteological Contributions to the Natural History of the Chimpanzee (Troglodytes, Geoffroy), including the description of the Skull of a large species (Troglodytes Gorilla, Savage) discovered by Thomas S. Savage, M.D., in the Gaboon county, West Africa.' *Transactions of the Zoological Society* (London), 3 (1849), 381–422.
[—]. 'Lyell – on Life and its Successive Development.' *QR*, 89 (1851), 412–51.
—. 'On the Anthropoid Apes.' In *BAAS* (Liverpool 1854), 1855, pt. 2, pp. 111–13.
—. 'On the Characters, Principles of Division, and Primary Groups of the Class Mammalia.' *Journal of the Proceedings of the Linnean Society* (Zoology), 2 (1858), 1–37.
—. *On the Classification and Distribution of the Mammalia.* Parker, 1859.
—. 'Presidential Address.' In *BAAS* (Leeds 1858), 1859, xlix–cx.
—. 'Summary of the Succession in Time and Geographical Distribution of Recent and Fossil Mammalia.' *Proceedings of the Royal Institution*, 3 (1859), 109–16.
—. *Palaeontology; or, A Systematic Summary of Extinct Animals and Their Geological Relations.* Edinburgh: Black, 1860.
—. 'The Gorilla and the Negro.' *Athenaeum*, 23 Mar. 1861, pp. 395–96.
—. 'Ape–Origin of Man as Tested by the Brain.' *Athenaeum*, 21 Feb. 1863, pp. 262–63.
—. *Monograph on the Aye-Aye.* Taylor & Francis, 1863.
—. 'On the Archaeopteryx of Von Meyer, with a Description of the Fossil Remains of a Long-Tailed Species, from the Lithographic Slate of Solenhofen.' *Philosophical Transactions of the Royal Society*, 153 (1863), 33–47.
—. *On the Anatomy of Vertebrates.* 3 vols. Longmans *et al.*, 1866–68.
[—]. Zoologus. 'The Fate of the "Jardin d'Acclimatation" during the Late Sieges of Paris.' *Fraser's Magazine*, new ser., 5 (1872), 17–22.
Owen, R. S., ed. *The Life of Richard Owen.* 2 vols. Murray, 1894.

Bibliography

Paley, W. *The Principles of Moral and Political Philosophy*, 1785. 17th ed. 2 vols. Printed for J. Faulder, 1810.

—. *A View of the Evidences of Christianity*. 3rd ed. 2 vols. Printed for R. Faulder, 1795.

—. *Natural Theology; or, Evidences of the Existence and Attributes of the Deity, collected from the Appearances of Nature*, 1802. 5th ed. Printed for R. Faulder, 1803.

Pancaldi, G. *Darwin in Italia: Impresa scientifica e frontiere culturali*. Bologna: Il Mulino, 1983.

Paradis, J. G. *T. H. Huxley: Man's Place in Nature*. Lincoln: University of Nebraska Press, 1978.

—. 'Darwin and Landscape.' In Paradis and Postlewait, *Victorian Science*, 85–110.

— and Postlewait, T., eds. *Victorian Science and Victorian Values: Literary Perspectives*. New Brunswick, NJ: Rutgers U.P., 1985.

Parker, R. *Town and Gown: The 700 Years' War in Cambridge*. Cambridge: Stephens, 1983.

Parodiz, J. J. *Darwin in the New World*. Leiden: Brill, 1981.

Parry, J. P. *Democracy and Religion: Gladstone and the Liberal Party, 1867–1875*. Cambridge: Cambridge U.P., 1986.

Parry, N. and Parry, J. *The Rise of the Medical Profession: A Story of Collective Social Mobility*. Croom Helm, 1976.

Paston, G. *At John Murray's: Records of a Literary Circle, 1843–1892*. Murray, 1932.

Paul, D. B. 'The Selection of the "Survival of the Fittest".' *JHB*, 21 (1988), 411–24.

Pauly, P. J. 'Samuel Butler and His Darwinian Critics.' *VS*, 25 (1982), 161–80.

Peacock, G. *Observations on the Statutes of the University of Cambridge*. Parker, 1841.

Pearson, K. *The Life, Letters, and Labours of Francis Galton*. 3 vols. in 4. Cambridge: Cambridge U.P., 1914–30.

Peckham, M., ed. *The Origin of Species by Charles Darwin: A Variorum Text*. Philadelphia: University of Pennsylvania Press, 1959.

Pennington, E. L. 'Charles Darwin and Foreign Missions.' *Georgia Review*, 1 (1947), 1–9.

Peterson, M. J. 'Gentlemen and Medical Men: The Problem of Professional Recruitment.' *Bulletin of the History of Medicine*, 58 (1984), 457–73.

Poore, G. V. 'Robert Edmond Grant.' *University College Gazette*, 2/34 (May 1901), 190–91.

Pope–Hennessy, J. *Monckton Milnes: The Years of Promise, 1809–1851*. Constable, 1949.

Porter, D. M. 'Charles Darwin's Plant Collections from the Voyage of the *Beagle*.' *JSBNH*, 9 (1980), 515–25.

—. 'The *Beagle* Collector and His Collections.' In Kohn, *Darwinian Heritage*, 973–1019.

Porter, R. 'Gentlemen and Geology: The Emergence of a Scientific Career, 1660–1920.' *Historical Journal*, 21 (1978), 809–36.

—. 'Erasmus Darwin: Doctor of Evolution?' In J. Moore, *History*, 39–69.

Portlock, J. E. 'Anniversary Address of the President.' *QJGS*, 13 (1857), xxvi–cxlv.

763

Darwin

—. 'Anniversary Address of the President.' *QJGS*, 14 (1858), xxiv–clxiii.

Poulton, E. B. *Charles Darwin and the Theory of Natural Selection.* Cassell, 1896.

Poynter, F. N. L. 'John Chapman (1821–1894): Publisher, Physician, and Medical Reformer.' *JHM*, 5 (1950), 1–22.

Prete, F. R. 'The Conundrum of the Honey Bees: One Impediment to the Publication of Darwin's Theory.' *JHB*, 23 (1990), 271–90.

Preyer, R. O. 'The Romantic Tide Reaches Trinity: Notes on the Transmission and Diffusion of New Approaches to Traditional Studies at Cambridge, 1820–1840.' In Paradis and Postlewait, *Victorian Science*, 39–68.

Prichard, J. C. 'On the Extinction of Human Races.' *ENPJ*, 28 (1840), 166–70.

Prothero, G. *The Armour of Light, and Other Sermons preached before the Queen.* Rev. and ed. Rowland E. Prothero. Rivingtons, 1888.

—. *Arthur Penrhyn Stanley: A Sermon.* Macmillan, 1881.

Pusey, E. B. *Un-science, Not Science, Adverse to Faith: A Sermon preached before the University of Oxford.* Oxford: Parker, 1878.

Rachootin, S. P. 'Owen and Darwin Reading a Fossil: *Macrauchenia* in a Boney Light.' In Kohn, *Darwinian Heritage*, 155–83.

Raumer, F. von. *England in 1835.* 3 vols. Murray, 1836.

Raverat, G. *Period Piece: A Cambridge Childhood.* Faber & Faber, 1952.

Rawnsley, H. D. *Harvey Goodwin, Bishop of Carlisle: A Biographical Memoir.* Murray, 1896.

Rehbock, P. F. 'Huxley, Haeckel, and the Oceanographers: The Case of *Bathybius Haeckelii*.' *Isis*, 66 (1975), 504–33.

—. *The Philosophical Naturalists: Themes in Early Nineteenth-Century British Biology.* Madison: University of Wisconsin Press, 1983.

Reid, T. W. *The Life, Letters, and Friendships of Richard Monckton Milnes, First Lord Houghton.* 2nd ed. 2 vols. Cassell, 1890.

Report on Spiritualism of the Committee of the London Dialectical Society, together with the Evidence, Oral and Written, and a Selection from the Correspondence. Longmans et al., 1871.

Richards, E. 'Darwin and the Descent of Woman.' In Oldroyd and Langham, *Wider Domain*, 57–111.

—. 'A Question of Property Rights: Richard Owen's Evolutionism Reassessed.' *BJHS*, 20 (1987), 129–71.

—. 'Huxley and Woman's Place in Science: The 'Woman Question' and the Control of Victorian Anthropology.' In J. Moore, *History*, 253–84.

—. 'The "Moral Anatomy" of Robert Knox: The Interplay between Biological and Social Thought in Victorian Scientific Naturalism.' *JHB*, 22 (1989), 373–436.

Richards, R. J. 'Instinct and Intelligence in British Natural Theology: Some Contributions to Darwin's Theory of the Evolution of Behavior.' *JHB*, 14 (1981), 193–230.

—. 'Darwin and the Biologizing of Moral Behavior.' In W. R. Woodward and M. G. Ash, *The Problematic Science: Psychology in Nineteenth-Century Thought*, 43–64. New York: Praeger, 1982.

—. 'Why Darwin Delayed, or Interesting Problems and Models in the History of Science.' *JHBS*, 19 (1983), 45–53.

—. *Darwin and the Emergence of Evolutionary Theories of Mind and Behavior.* Chicago: University of Chicago Press, 1987.

Bibliography

Richardson, R. *Death, Dissection and the Destitute.* Harmondsworth, Middx: Penguin, 1988.

Ricks, C., ed. *The Poems of Tennyson.* Longmans, 1969.

Ritvo, H. *The Animal Estate: The English and Other Creatures in the Victorian Age.* Harmondsworth, Middx: Penguin Books, 1990.

Robbins, W. *The Newman Brothers: An Essay in Comparative Intellectual Biography.* Cambridge, MA: Harvard U.P., 1966.

Roberts, D. *Paternalism in Early Victorian England.* New Brunswick, NJ: Rutgers U.P., 1979.

Robertson, J. 'Dr. Elliotson on Life and Mind.' *London Medical Gazette,* 17 (1835–36), 203–10, 251–57.

Roger, J. 'Darwin, Haeckel et les Français.' In Y. Conry, ed., *De Darwin au darwinisme: science et idéologie,* 149–65. Paris: J. Vrin, 1983.

[Romanes, E.] *The Life and Letters of George John Romanes.* Longmans et al., 1896.

[Romanes, G. J.] Physicus. *A Candid Examination of Theism.* Trübner, 1878.

—. 'Work in Psychology.' In T. H. Huxley et al., *Charles Darwin: Memorial Notices reprinted from 'Nature',* 65–82. Macmillan, 1882.

—. *Animal Intelligence.* 6th ed. Kegan Paul et al., 1895.

—. *Thoughts on Religion.* Ed. C. Gore. Longmans et al., 1895.

Roos, D. A. 'The "Aims and Intentions" of *Nature*.' In Paradis and Postlewait, *Victorian Science,* 159–80.

Root, J. D. 'Catholicism and Science in Victorian England.' *Clergy Review,* 66 (1981), 138–47, 162–70.

Rorison, G. 'The Creative Week.' In S. Wilberforce, ed., *Replies to 'Essays and Reviews',* 277–345. 2nd ed. Oxford: Henry & Parker, 1862.

Rosenberg, S. 'The Financing of Radical Opinion: John Chapman and the *Westminster Review*.' In J. Shattock and M. Wolff, eds., *The Victorian Periodical Press: Samplings and Soundings,* 167–92. Leicester: Leicester U.P., 1982.

Rowell, G. *Hell and the Victorians: A Study of Nineteenth-Century Theological Controversies concerning Eternal Punishment and the Future Life.* Oxford: Clarendon Press, 1974.

Royle, E. 'Taylor, Robert (1784–1844).' In J. O. Baylen and N. J. Gossman, eds., *Biographical Dictionary of Modern British Radicals,* 1 (1770–1830):467–70. Brighton, Sussex: Harvester Press, 1979.

—. *Victorian Infidels: The Origins of the British Secularist Movement, 1791–1866.* Manchester: Manchester U.P., 1974.

—. *Radicals, Secularists and Republicans: Popular Freethought in Britain, 1866–1915.* Manchester: Manchester U.P., 1980.

Rudwick, M. J. S. 'The Strategy of Lyell's *Principles of Geology*.' *Isis,* 61 (1970), 4–33.

—. 'Darwin and Glen Roy: A "Great Failure" in Scientific Method?' *SHPS,* 5 (1974), 97–185.

——. 'Charles Darwin in London: The Integration of Public and Private Science.' *Isis,* 73 (1982), 186–206.

Rules and Regulations and List of Members. Privately printed for the Athenaeum, 1884.

Rupke, N. '*Bathybius Haeckelii* and the Psychology of Scientific Discovery: Theory instead of Observed Data controlled the Late 19th Century "Discovery" of a Primitive Form of Life.' *SHPS,* 7 (1976), 53–62.

Darwin

—, ed. *Vivisection in Historical Perspective*. Croom Helm, 1987.

Ruse, M. 'The Darwin Industry: A Critical Evaluation.' *HS*, 12 (1974), 43–58.

—. 'Charles Darwin and Artificial Selection.' *Journal of the History of Ideas*, 36 (1975), 339–50.

—. 'Darwin's Debt to Philosophy: An Examination of the Influence of the Philosophical Ideas of John F. W. Herschel and William Whewell on the Development of Charles Darwin's Theory of Evolution.' *SHPS*, 6 (1975), 159–81.

—. *The Darwinian Revolution*. Chicago: University of Chicago Press, 1979.

Russell, C. A. 'The Conflict Metaphor and Its Social Origins.' *Science and Christian Belief*, 1 (1989), 3–26.

Russell–Gebbett, J. *Henslow of Hitcham: Botanist, Educationalist and Clergyman*. Lavenham, Suffolk: Dalton, 1977.

Samouelle, G. *The Entomologist's Useful Compendium*. Longman *et al.*, 1824.

Scherren, H. *The Zoological Society of London*. Cassell, 1905.

Schivelbusch, W. *The Railway Journey: The Industrialization of Time and Space in the 19th Century*. Leamington Spa, Warwicks.: Berg, 1986.

Schoenwald, R. L. 'G. Eliot's "Love" Letters: Unpublished Letters from George Eliot to Herbert Spencer.' *Bulletin of the New York Public Library*, 79 (1976), 362–71.

Schwartz, J. S. 'Darwin, Wallace, and the *Descent of Man*.' *JHB*, 17 (1984), 271–89.

Schwarz, H. 'Darwinism between Kant and Haeckel.' *Journal of the American Academy of Religion*, 48 (1980), 581–602.

Schweber, S. S. 'The Origin of the *Origin* Revisited.' *JHB*, 10 (1977), 229–316.

—. 'Darwin and the Political Economists: Divergence of Character.' *JHB*, 13 (1980), 195–289.

—. 'The Wider British Context in Darwin's Theorizing.' In Kohn, *Darwinian Heritage*, 35–69.

—. 'The Correspondence of the Young Darwin.' *JHB*, 21 (1988), 501–19.

—. 'John Herschel and Charles Darwin: A Study in Parallel Lives.' *JHB*, 22 (1989), 1–71.

Secord, J. 'Nature's Fancy: Charles Darwin and the Breeding of Pigeons.' *Isis*, 72 (1981), 163–86.

—. 'Darwin and the Breeders: A Social History.' In Kohn, *Darwinian Heritage*, 519–42.

—. *Controversy in Victorian Geology: The Cambrian–Silurian Dispute*. Princeton, NJ: Princeton U.P., 1986.

—. 'The Geological Survey of Great Britain as a Research School, 1839–1855.' *HS*, 24 (1986), 223–75.

—. 'Behind the Veil: Robert Chambers and *Vestiges*.' In J. Moore, *History*, 165–94.

—. 'The Discovery of a Vocation: Darwin's Early Geology.' *BJHS*, 24 (1991), 133–57.

—. 'Edinburgh Lamarckians: Robert Jameson and Robert E. Grant.' *JHB*, 24 (1991), 1–18.

Sedgwick, A. *A Discourse on the Studies of the University*. Cambridge: Deightons & Stevenson, 1833.

—. 'Address by the President.' *PGSL*, 1 (1834), 187–212, 281–316.

[—]. 'Objections to Mr. Darwin's Theory of the Origin of Species.' *Spectator*, 24 Mar. 1860, pp. 285–86; 7 April 1860, pp. 334–35.

Bibliography

Seed, J. 'Theologies of Power: Unitarianism and the Social Relations of Religious Discourse, 1800–1850.' In R. J. Morris, ed., *Class, Power, and Social Structure in British Nineteenth-Century Towns*, 108–56. Leicester: Leicester U.P., 1986.

Semmel, B. *The Governor Eyre Controversy*. Macgibbon & Kee, 1962.

Seward, A. C., ed. *Darwin and Modern Science: Essays in Commemoration of the Centenary of the Birth of Charles Darwin and of the Fiftieth Anniversary of the Publication of 'The Origin of Species'*. Cambridge: Cambridge U.P., 1909.

Shairp, J. C., Tait, P. G., and Adams–Reilly, A., eds. *Life and Letters of James David Forbes, F.R.S.* Macmillan, 1873.

Shannon, R. *The Crisis of Imperialism, 1865–1915*. Paladin, 1976.

Shapin, S. 'Phrenological Knowledge and the Social Structure of Early Nineteenth–Century Edinburgh.' *AS*, 32 (1975), 219–43.

Sharlin, H. I. *Lord Kelvin: The Dynamic Victorian*. University Park: Pennsylvania State U.P., 1979.

Shepherd, J. A. 'Lawson Tait – Disciple of Charles Darwin.' *British Medical Journal*, 284 (1982), 1386–87.

Shepperson, G. 'The Intellectual Background of Charles Darwin's Student Years at Edinburgh.' In M. Banton, ed., *Darwinism and the Study of Society*, 17–35. Tavistock, 1961.

Shuttleworth's Popular Guide to Ilkley and Vicinity. 8th ed. Ilkley, Yorks.: Shuttleworth, n.d.

Sloan, P. R. 'Darwin's Invertebrate Program, 1826–1836: Preconditions for Transformism.' In Kohn, *Darwinian Heritage*, 71–120.

—. 'Darwin, Vital Matter, and the Transformism of Species.' *JHB*, 19 (1986), 367–95.

Smith, B. S. *A History of Malvern*. Malvern, Worcs.: Alan Sutton & The Malvern Bookshop, 1978.

Smith, K. G. V., ed. 'Darwin's Insects: Charles Darwin's Entomological Notes.' *BBMNH*, 14 (1987), 1–143.

Smith, R. 'Alfred Russel Wallace: Philosophy of Nature and Man.' *BJHS*, 6 (1972), 177–99.

Smith, T. Southwood. *The Divine Government*. 4th ed. Baldwin *et al.*, 1826.

Smyth, C. *Simeon and Church Order: A Study of the Origins of the Evangelical Revival in Cambridge in the Eighteenth Century*. Cambridge: Cambridge U.P., 1940.

Southwell, C. 'Is There a God?' *Oracle of Reason*, 7 May 1842.

Speakman, C. *Adam Sedgwick, Geologist and Dalesman, 1785–1873: A Biography in Twelve Themes*. Heathfield, E. Sussex: Broad Oak Press *et al.*, 1982.

Spencer, H. *Social Statics; or, the Conditions Essential to Human Happiness Specified, and the First of Them Developed*, 1851. New ed. Williams & Norgate, 1868.

[—]. 'Owen on the Homologies of the Vertebrate Skeleton.' *British and Foreign Medico-Chirurgical Review*, 44 (1858), 400–16.

—. *An Autobiography*. 2 vols. Williams & Norgate, 1904.

Stanbury, D., ed. *A Narrative of the Voyage of H.M.S. 'Beagle': Being Passages from the 'Narrative' written by Captain FitzRoy, R.N., together with Extracts from His Logs, Reports and Letters; Additional Material from the Diaries and Letters of Charles Darwin, Notes from Midshipman Philip King and Letters from Second Lieutenant Bartholomew Sulivan*. Folio Society, 1977.

767

—. 'H. M. S. *Beagle* and the Peculiar Service.' In Chapman and Duval, *Charles Darwin*, 61–82.

Stauffer, R. C., ed. *Charles Darwin's Natural Selection: Being the Second Part of His Big Species Book written from 1856 to 1858.* Cambridge: Cambridge U.P., 1975.

Stearn, W. T. *The Natural History Museum at South Kensington.* Heinemann, 1981.

Stebbins, R. E. 'France.' In Glick, *Comparative Reception*, 117–67.

Stecher, R. M. 'The Darwin–Innes Letters: The Correspondence of an Evolutionist with His Vicar, 1848–1884.' *AS*, 17 (1961), 201–58.

Stephens, J. F. *A Systematic Catalogue of British Insects.* 2 pts. Printed for the author, 1829.

Stevens, L. R. 'Darwin's Humane Reading: The Anaesthetic Man Reconsidered.' *VS*, 26 (1982), 51–63.

Stewart, R. *Henry Brougham, 1778–1868: His Public Career.* Bodley Head, 1986.

Stoddart, D. R. 'Darwin, Lyell, and the Geological Significance of Coral Reefs.' *BJHS*, 9 (1976), 199–218.

Stokes, H. P. *Cambridge Parish Workhouses.* [Cambridge: printed for the Cambridge Antiquarian Society], 1911.

Struthers, J. *Historical Sketch of the Edinburgh Anatomical School.* Edinburgh: MacLachlan & Stewart, 1867.

Sulloway, F. J. 'Geographic Isolation in Darwin's Thinking: The Vicissitudes of a Crucial Idea.' *SHB*, 3 (1979), 23–65.

—. 'Darwin and His Finches: The Evolution of a Legend.' *JHB*, 15 (1982), 1–53.

—. 'Darwin's Conversion: The *Beagle* Voyage and Its Aftermath.' *JHB*, 15 (1982), 325–96.

—. 'Darwin's Early Intellectual Development: An Overview of the *Beagle* Voyage.' In Kohn, *Darwinian Heritage*, 121–54.

Sweet, J. M. 'Robert Jameson and the Explorers: The Search for the North–West Passage.' *AS*, 31 (1974), 21–47.

Symonds, Mrs. J. A., ed. *Recollections of a Happy Life: Being the Autobiography of Marianne North.* 2nd ed. 2 vols. Macmillan, 1892.

[Tait, P. G.] 'Geological Time.' *North British Review*, 11 (1869), 406–39.

Taylor, B. *Eve and the New Jerusalem: Socialism and Feminism in the Nineteenth Century.* Virago, 1984.

Taylor, R. *The Devil's Pulpit, containing Twenty-three Astronomico-Theological Discourses.* 2 vols. Reprint eds. Dugdale, 1842; Freethought Publishing Co., 1881.

Thackray, A. 'Natural Knowledge in Cultural Context: The Manchester Model.' *American Historical Review*, 79 (1974), 672–709.

Thompson, E. P. *The Making of the English Working Class.* 3rd ed. Gollancz, 1980.

Thompson, J. V. *Zoological Researches, and Illustrations; or, Natural History of Nondescript or Imperfectly Known Animals ... Memoir IV, On the Cirripedes or Barnacles.* Cork: King & Ridings, 1830.

Thompson, W. 'Physical Argument for the Equal Cultivation of all the Useful Faculties or Capabilities, of Men and Women.' *Co-Operative Magazine*, 1 (1826), 250–58.

Thomson, K. S. 'H. M. S. *Beagle*, 1820–1870.' *American Scientist*, 63 (1975), 664–72.

Bibliography

— and Rachootin, S. P. 'Turning Points in Darwin's Life.' *BJLS*, 17 (1982), 23–37.

Thomson, W. *Popular Lectures and Addresses*. 3 vols. Macmillan, 1889–94.

Todhunter, I. *William Whewell . . . An Account of His Writings, with Selections from His Literary and Scientific Correspondence*. 2 vols. Macmillan, 1876.

Trenn, T. J. 'Charles Darwin, Fossil Cirripedes, and Robert Fitch: Presenting Sixteen Hitherto unpublished Darwin Letters of 1849 to 1851.' *PAPS*, 118 (1974), 471–91.

Tribe, D. *President Charles Bradlaugh, M.P.* Elek, 1971.

Tristan, F. *Flora Tristan's London Journal: A Survey of London Life in the 1830s*. Trans. D. Palmer and G. Pincetl. Prior, 1980.

Trollope, A. *Clergymen of the Church of England*, 1866. Reprint ed. Leicester: Leicester U.P., 1974.

Tuckwell, W. *Reminiscences of Oxford*. 2nd ed. Smith, Elder, 1907.

Turner, F. M. *Between Science and Religion: The Reaction to Scientific Naturalism in Late Victorian England*. New Haven, CT: Yale U.P., 1974.

—. 'The Victorian Conflict between Science and Religion: A Professional Dimension.' *Isis*, 69 (1978), 356–76.

Turrill, W. B. *Joseph Dalton Hooker: Botanist, Explorer, and Administrator*. Nelson. 1963.

Tyndall, J. 'Address.' *BAAS* (Norwich 1868), 1869, pp. 1–6.

—. *Fragments of Science*. 2nd ed. Longmans *et al.*, 1871.

—. *Address delivered before the British Association assembled at Belfast*. Longmans *et al.*, 1874.

Uschmann, G. and Jahn, I. 'Der Briefwechsel zwischen Thomas Henry Huxley und Ernst Haeckel: Ein Beitrag zum Darwin Jahr.' *Wissenschaftliche Zeitschrift der Friedrich-Schiller-Universität Jena*, Mathematisch–Naturwissenschaftliche Reihe, Heft 1/2, 9 (1959–60), 7–33.

Van Arsdel, R. 'The Westminster Review, 1824–1900.' In W. Houghton, ed., *The Wellesley Index to Victorian Periodicals, 1824–1900*, 3:528–58. Toronto: University of Toronto Press, 1979.

Vidler, A. R. *The Church in an Age of Revolution*. Harmondsworth, Middx: Penguin Books, 1961.

Vogt, C. *Lectures on Man: His Place in Creation, and in the History of the Earth*. Longmans *et al.*, 1864.

Vorzimmer, P. J. 'Darwin's Questions about the Breeding of Animals.' *JHB*, 2 (1969), 269–81.

—. *Charles Darwin, The Years of Controversy: The 'Origin of Species' and Its Critics, 1859–82*. University of London Press, 1972.

—. 'The Darwin Reading Notebooks (1838–1860).' *JHB*, 10 (1977), 107–153.

Vucinich, A. 'Russia: Biological Sciences.' In Glick, *Comparative Reception*, 227–55.

—. *Darwin in Russian Thought*. Berkeley: University of California Press, 1988.

Wagner, A. 'On a New Fossil Reptile supposed to be Furnished with Feathers.' *AMNH*, 9 (1862), 261–67.

Wallace, A. R. 'On the Law which has regulated the Introduction of New Species.' *AMNH*, 16 (1855), 184–96.

[—]. 'Principles of Geology.' *QR*, 126 (1869), 359–94.

—. *Natural Selection*. Macmillan, 1875.

—. *Studies Scientific and Social*. 2 vols. Macmillan, 1900.

Darwin

—. *My Life: A Record of Events and Opinions.* 2 vols. Chapman & Hall, 1905.

Ward, H. *History of the Athenaeum, 1824–1925.* Printed for the Club, 1926.

Waterhouse, G. 'Observations on the Classification of the Mammalia.' *AMNH*, 12 (1843), 399–412.

Watts, J. 'Theological Theories of the Origin of Man.' *Reasoner*, 26 (1861), 102–104, 119–21, 132–34.

— and [Holyoake, G. J.] Iconoclast, eds. 'Charles R. Darwin.' *Half-Hours with Freethinkers.* Austin, 1865.

Webb, R. K. 'The Unitarian Background.' In B. Smith, ed., *Truth, Liberty, Religion: Essays celebrating Two Hundred Years of Manchester College*, 1–27. Oxford: Manchester College, 1986.

—. 'The Faith of Nineteenth–Century Unitarians: A Curious Incident.' In Helmstadter and Lightman, *Victorian Faith*, 126–49.

Wedgwood, B. and Wedgwood, H. *The Wedgwood Circle: Four Generations of a Family and Their Friends.* Westfield, NJ: Eastview, 1980.

Wedgwood, E. (later Darwin). *My First Reading Book.* Newcastle, Staffs.: [printed by J. Smith?], [c. 1823]; reprint ed. Cambridge: privately printed, 1985.

[Wedgwood, H.] 'Grimm on the Indo–European Languages.' *QR*, 50 (1833), 169–89.

Weindling, P. 'Ernst Haeckel, Darwinismus, and the Secularization of Nature.' In J. Moore, *History*, 311–27.

Wells, K. D. 'The Historical Context of Natural Selection: The Case of Patrick Matthew.' *JHB*, 6 (1973), 225–58.

Wheatley, V. *The Life and Work of Harriet Martineau.* Secker & Warburg, 1957.

Whewell, W. 'Address to the Geological Society.' *PGSL*, 2 (1833–38) [1838], 624–49.

Wiener, J. H. *Radicalism and Freethought in Nineteenth-Century Britain: The Life of Richard Carlile.* Westport, CT: Greenwood, 1983.

Wiener, P. P. *Evolution and the Founders of Pragmatism.* Philadelphia: University of Pennsylvania Press, 1972.

Wilberforce, S. *Pride a Hindrance to True Knowledge: A Sermon preached in the Church of St. Mary the Virgin, Oxford, before the University, on Sunday, June 27, 1847.* Rivington, 1847.

[—]. 'Darwin's Origin of Species.' *QR*, 102 (1860), 225–64.

Willey, B. *The Eighteenth Century Background: Studies on the Idea of Nature in the Thought of the Period.* Chatto & Windus, 1940.

—. *Darwin and Butler: Two Versions of Evolution.* Chatto & Windus, 1960.

Wilson, G. and Geikie, A. *Memoir of Edward Forbes.* Cambridge: Macmillan, 1861.

Wilson, L. G., ed. *Sir Charles Lyell's Scientific Journals on the Species Question.* New Haven, CT: Yale U.P., 1970.

—. *Charles Lyell, The Years to 1841: The Revolution in Geology.* New Haven, CT: Yale U.P., 1972.

Wingfield–Stratford, E. *The Victorian Sunset.* Routledge, 1932.

Winsor, M. P. 'Barnacle Larvae in the Nineteenth Century.' *JHM*, 24 (1969), 294–309.

—. *Starfish, Jellyfish, and the Order of Life: Issues of Nineteenth-Century Science.* New Haven, CT: Yale U.P., 1976.

Bibliography

Winstanley, D. A. *Unreformed Cambridge: A Study of Certain Aspects of the University in the Eighteenth Century.* Cambridge: Cambridge U.P., 1935.

—. *Early Victorian Cambridge.* Cambridge: Cambridge U.P., 1940.

—. *Later Victorian Cambridge.* Cambridge: Cambridge U.P., 1947.

Wollaston, T. V. *On the Variation of Species with especial reference to the Insecta; followed by an Inquiry into the Nature of Genera.* Van Voorst, 1856.

Woodall, E. 'Charles Darwin.' *Transactions of the Shropshire Archaeological and Natural History Society,* 8 (1884), 1–64.

Wright, C. *Darwinism: Being an Examination of Mr. St. George Mivart's 'Genesis of Species'.* Murray, 1871.

Yeo, E. 'Christianity in Chartist Struggle, 1838–1842.' *Past and Present,* 91 (1981), 109–39.

Yeo, R. 'Science and Intellectual Authority in Mid-Nineteenth-Century Britain: Robert Chambers and *Vestiges of the Natural History of Creation.*' *VS,* 28 (1984), 5–31.

Young, G. M. *Portrait of an Age: Victorian England.* 2nd ed. Oxford U.P., 1953.

Young, R. M. 'Darwinism *is* Social.' In Kohn, *Darwinian Heritage,* 609–38.

—. *Darwin's Metaphor: Nature's Place in Victorian Culture.* Cambridge: Cambridge U.P., 1985.

—. 'Charles Darwin: Man and Metaphor.' *Science as Culture,* 5 (1989), 71–86.

Zangerl, C. H. E. 'The Social Composition of the County Magistracy in England and Wales, 1831–1887.' *Journal of British Studies,* 11 (1971–72), 113–125.

Index

Index

206, 309, 669; reticence about, 602, 603, 635, 643, 645; South American Missionary Society, 575, 632, 675; on spiritualism, 608, 614, 621, 625, 632, 634; on theism, 603, 634, 636; as theist, 218–9, 253, 261, 268–9, 293, 479; theological language, 486, 490; Unitarianism, 12–14, 237, 261–2, 268, 293–4, 331, 368, 479, 499

Science: chemistry, 17–18, 27; anatomy at Edinburgh, 26 *et seq.*; taxidermy, 28; marine invertebrates, 28, 33, 36–8, 127, 136–7; geology lectures, 41–3, 94–7; at Cambridge, *see* Beetles; botany, *see* Henslow, J. S., Living matter; on *Beagle*, *see* Fossils, Individuality, Rheas, Galapagos Islands; geology, gradualism, 117, 145, 151, 159, 162, 165, 190, 207, 236, 255, 282, 284, 307, 318, 346; *see also* Glen Roy; coral reefs, 168, 174, 183, 207, 371; studies *Beagle* specimens in London, ch. 14; on laws of nature, 213 *et seq.*; developmental approach to nature, 215–17; becomes evolutionist, 220–5; laws governing organic life, 222 *et seq.*; early theories of evolution, 229–64; Malthusian evolution, 264 *et seq.*, *see also* Artificial selection, Pigeons, Natural selection, Sexual selection; Darwin a theoretician, 284–5, 341; scientific method, 457; strategy, 413, 437, 439; homologies, 368, *see also* Barnacles; dispersal mechanisms, 443–5; *see also* Seed experiments; climbing plants, 517, 521, 524; insectivorous plants, 596; orchids, 509–11; plant

movements, 631; fertilization, 510, 520, 575, 619, 628; pangenesis, 617; human inheritance, 598; *see also*, Evolution, Emotions, Worms, Mankind

Social role: BAAS vice-president, 367; Down Friendly Society treasurer, 625; Down School treasurer, 525; Entomological Society vice-president, 235; Geological Society Council, 210; Geological Society, secretary, 235, 289, vice-president, 323; magistrate, 461, 464, 533, 648; patronage, 575, 596, 598, 639, 643, 646, 647, 659, 675; Royal Geographical Society Council, 288; Royal Society Council, 367

Darwin, Charles Waring (Charles's son), 467, 470; birth, 446; christened, 456; characterized, 447, 460; death, 469

Darwin, Elizabeth (Charles's daughter), 370, 401, 402, 418, 447, 448, 573, 589, 624, 630, 640, 649, 656, 661–3, 669, 673; birth, 349; characterized, 402, 447

Darwin, [Emily] Catherine, later Langton (Charles's sister), 13, 14, 19, 24, 46, 69, 102, 121, 129, 139, 185, 210, 216, 254, 271, 360, 361, 456, 471, 519, 534

Darwin, Emma; *see* Wedgwood

Darwin, Erasmus, [I] (Charles's grandfather), 23, 42, 90, 104, 179, 220, 229, 256, 378, 391, 435, 449, 498, 520, 537, 622, 635, 636, 640, 648; *Loves of the Plants*, 510; *Zoonomia*, 10, 29, 40, 229

Darwin, Erasmus, [II] (Charles's uncle), 9

Darwin, Erasmus Alvey (Charles's brother), 13, 15–18, 28, 43, 49, 51, 52, 61, 64, 69, 77, 92, 93, 104, 112,

Index

Index

Index

Index

Index

Materialism, 38–9, 41, 250–3, 258–9, 261, 276, 295–6, 317, 392, 508, 528–9, 537–8, 559–60, 568, 579, 640, 645, 653, 656
Mathematics, 62, 88, 111, 302, 567
Matthew, H., 88, 112
Matthew, P., 40, 266, 286, 426; *Emigration Fields*, 266
Matthews, R., 106, 133, 135
Mauritius, 183
Mayhew, H., *London Labour and the London Poor*, 449
Medicine, Erasmus studies, 21; Charles studies, 21–44
Megatheriums, 128, 130–1, 141, 144, 150–1, 159–60, 190, 198, 210, 347
Melville, H., Revd, 68
Mendoza, 164
Mercedes, 144
Mesmerism, 252, 335, 362, 364, 379, 538
Metaphysical Society, 568
Methodists, 393, 403, 537
Methodist Recorder, 537
Microscopes, 82, 93, 110, 127, 158, 182, 223, 307, 339–40, 342, 361, 536, 595, 602, 612, 620, 658
Middle classes, 84, 92, 153, 196, 218, 281, 285–6, 294, 355, 393, 411, 414, 474, 493, 522, 557, 561, 666
Mill, J. S, 392; *On the Subjection of Women*, 572
Milne, D., 346
Milne–Edwards, H., 368–9, 394, 421
Milton, J., 63; *Paradise Lost*, 124, 129, 166
Mind, in man and animals, 32, 465, 649; relationship to matter, 38, 250, 261, 276, 560, 568; evolution of, 243, 250, 442, 462–3, 464, 522, 556–7, 569–70, 573, 580; unique, 453, 555, 579, 583
Miracles, 9, 49, 78, 213–4, 217–8, 260–61, 363, 412, 414, 436, 442, 479, 493, 500, 591, 608

Missionaries, 44, 56, 71–2, 84, 106, 111, 114, 129, 132–4, 147, 173–6, 185–6, 295, 429, 450–1, 467, 507–8, 537, 543, 565, 574–5, 577, 593, 611, 632, 653, 657, 675
Mivart, St G., 555, 559, 561, 569–71, 573, 577–8, 582–6, 589, 590, 592, 610–4, 629, 640–2, 646; *Genesis of Species*, 577, 582–4, 590, 592, 640
Mockingbirds, 138, 169–72, 186, 220, 221, 225, 228, 230
Moluccan Islands, 468
Molluscs, 37, 39, 123, 136, 179, 213, 223, 339, 341, 342, 356, 431, 545
Monads, 40, 230, 231
Monkeys, 35, 65, 123, 146–7, 222, 230, 244, 263, 268, 272, 289, 295, 335, 402, 452, 472, 477, 487, 503–4, 516, 545, 552, 554–6, 565–6, 570, 573, 579, 580, 589, 593, 629, 633, 648, 653
Monro, A., [III], 26
Monsters, 225, 240–1, 248, 459
Montevideo, 126, 129, 131, 132, 137, 138, 143, 144
Month, The, 570
Montrose Lunatic Asylum, 32
Moor Park, Surrey, 454–6, 462, 466, 471, 473, 476
Moore, N., 660
Moral relativism, 262, 268
Morality, evolution of, 258, 262, 269, 283, 293, 521–2, 556, 573, 623, 633–4
More, H., 63
Morley, J., 581, 626, 676, 677
Morning Chronicle, 25
Morning Herald, 210
Morrey, Mrs, 402, 446
Mortality statistics, 265, 323
Moths, 16, 64, 509, 547, 553, 572
Mount, The, 11–6, 18, 20, 46, 75, 82, 95, 103, 108, 195, 204, 259, 270, 292, 322, 358, 361, 471, 509, 534, 541, 571, 592, 620

Index

Index